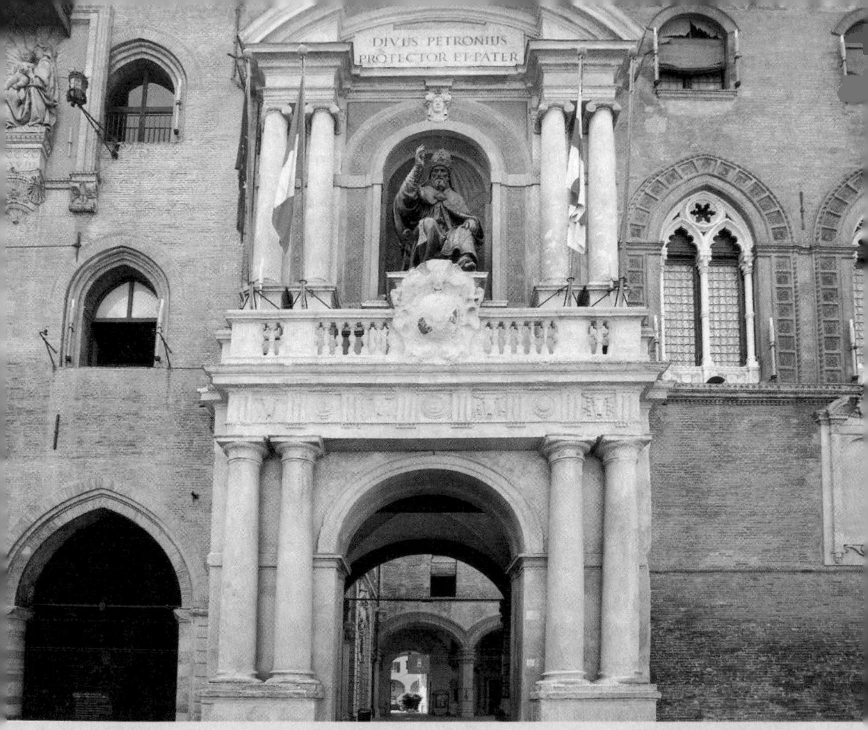

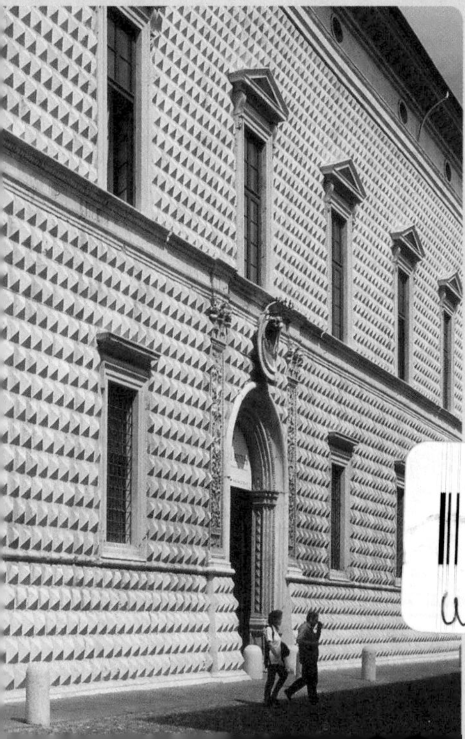

3. Palazzo della Pilotta (p431), Parma
Built between 1583 and 1622, but heavily bombed in WWII, this *palazzo* dominates Piazza della Pace.

4. Palazzo dei Diamanti (p437), Ferrara
The spiky diamond-shaped ashlar stones on its facade have given this *palazzo* its name.

5. Basilica di San Vitale (p443), Ravenna
Inside the chancel, mosaics depict Emperor Justinian amd Empress Theodora.

DOMENICO TONDINI / ALAMY ©

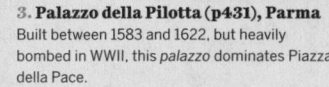

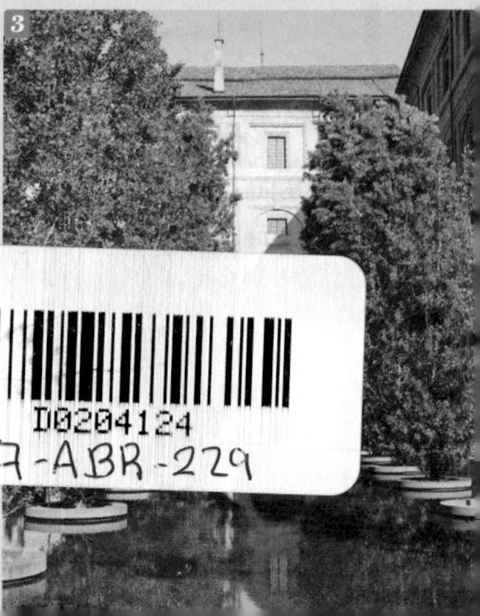

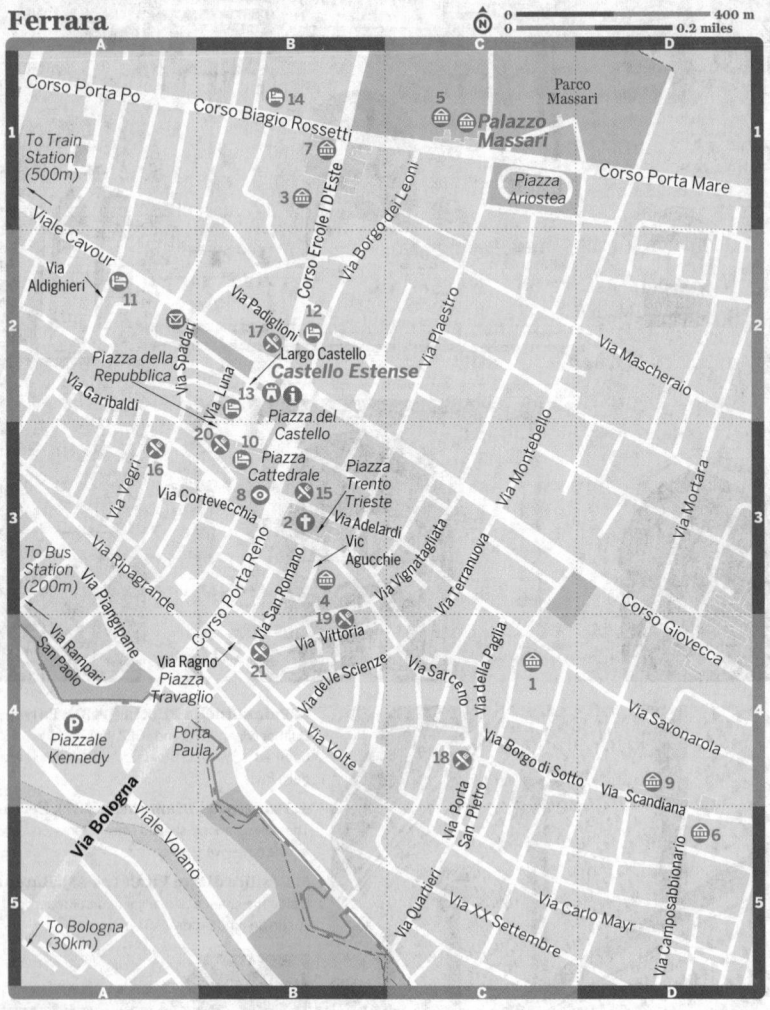

Ferrara Balloons Festival HOT-AIR BALLOONS
(www.ferraraballoonsfestival.it) Italy's largest hot-air balloon gathering, in late September.

🛏 Sleeping

TOP CHOICE **Albergo Annunziata** HOTEL €€
(☎0532 20 11 11; www.annunziata.it; Piazza della Repubblica 5; s €94-120, d €105-240; ❄@) When Casanova spent the night here, the Annunziata was little more than a simple *locanda* (inn). Today it's a refined top-end hotel with minimalist rooms and abundant creature comforts. There are also six modern apartments (€125 to €300) 150m from the main hotel. Parking costs €3.

Hotel Ferrara HOTEL €€
(☎0532 20 50 48; www.hotelferrara.com; Largo Castello 36; s/d/apt €85/125/160; ❄@🛜) Slick modern furnishings in the ancient centre a mere arrow-shot from the castle, the Ferrara is what design gurus would call 'contemporary' – ie accented colours, minimalist lines, up-to-the-minute electronics, and lots of glass and shiny surfaces. But any pretensions are cancelled out by genuine good

◎ **Top Sights**

EMILIA-ROMAGNA & SAN MARINO EAST OF BOLOGNA

service and value-for-money rates. The hotel also has 10 apartment suites from €160.

Hotel Astra   HOTEL €
(☏0532 20 60 88; www.astrahotel.info; Viale Cavour 55; s/d €65/89; ❄@) An old dame in need of a bit of Botox, Astra can still cut it with the budget-minded thanks to spacious rooms, equally ample bathrooms, voluminous (for Italy) breakfasts, and plenty of downstairs seating space where the antediluvian furniture is doing its best to look antique-like. The *centro storico* is within strolling distance and the station is close enough to drag your suitcase.

Hotel de Prati   HOTEL €€
(☏0532 24 19 05; www.hoteldeprati.com; Via Padiglioni 5; s €49-85, d €75-120, ste €110-150; ❄) Smarter than the average three-star, de Prati charms with its central location, antique furniture and friendly owner. Wrought-iron bedsteads reign upstairs while downstairs public rooms are enlivened by contemporary art.

Student's Hostel Estense   HOSTEL €
(☏0532 20 11 58; www.ostelloferrara.it; Corso Biagio Rossetti 24; dm/s/d/tr incl breakfast €16/35/40/48; ☏) Ferrara's hostel has classic hostel rooms plus extras like geothermal hot water, bar, back patio, and fantastic amenities for cyclists (bike pumps, a maintenance area and a bike storage zone).

✗ Eating

Like all Emiliano cities Ferrara has its gastronomic nuances. Don't leave town without trying *cappellacci di zucca,* a hat-shaped pasta pouch filled with pumpkin and herbs, and brushed with sage and butter. Delicious! *Salama da sugo* is a stewed pork sausage, while *pasticcio di maccheroni* is an oven-baked macaroni pie topped with Parmesan. Even Ferrarese bread is distinctive, shaped into a crunchy twisted knot.

Self-caterers can fill up at the **covered market** (Via Vegri; ☉7am-1.30pm Mon-Sat).

TOP CHOICE Osteria del Ghetto   OSTERIA €€
(☏0532 76 49 36; www.osteriadelghetto.it; Via Vittoria 26; meals €25-30; ☉Wed-Mon) Yet another understated jewel amid the winding streets of Ferrara's old Jewish ghetto, this *osteria* leads you through a nondescript downstairs bar up to a bright upstairs dining room embellished with striking modern murals. The excellent menu mixes Ferrara staples like *cappellacci di zucca* with a less predictable fish menu.

Al Brindisi   OSTERIA €€
(www.albrindisi.net; Via Adelardi 11; meals €25-30) The oldest *osteria* in the world (according to Guinness), this scruffy-meets-stylish wine bar was already an established drinking den in 1435. Titian drank here, while the soon-to-be Pope John Paul II dropped by 550 years later. Succinct pasta dishes are well supplemented by a wine drawn from

PO DELTA

Italy's greatest river dissolves into the Adriatic Sea in the Po Delta (Foci del Po), an area of dense pine forests and extensive wetlands often doused in an eerie fog, especially in winter.

The wetlands, protected in the Parco del Delta del Po (www.parcodeltapo.it), are one of Europe's largest and are notable for their birdlife – 300 species have been registered here.

The delta's main centre, Comacchio, a picturesque fishing village of canals and brick bridges, harbours a good tourist office (www.turismocomacchio.it; Corso Mazzini 4; ⊙9.30am-12.30pm & 3.30-6.30pm) offering reams of information about hiking, cycling, birdwatching, horse riding and boat excursions.

Due to the flat terrain, cycling is particularly popular here and a network of paths, many of them on raised dykes, offer day and long-distance excursions. Of note is the 46km route linking the freshwater lagoons of Argenta to their saltwater equivalents in Comacchio. You can lengthen this excursion at both ends heading west from Argenta to Ferrara (41km), or north from Comacchio aside the Adriatic and the bird-filled Valle Bertazzi to Mesola. The *Panoramic Wheels* booklet in Ferrara's tourist office has more details.

From Ferrara, buses run 11 times daily to Comacchio (€4.10, one hour).

racks that are thick with a healthy coating of Ferrara dust.

Trattoria de Noemi TRATTORIA €€
(✆0532 76 90 70; www.trattoriadanoemi.it; Via Ragno 31; meals €25-35) All of Ferrara's classic dishes are delivered *con molto amore* (with much love) here. Arrive early (yes, it's busy) to get the city's best *cappellacci di zucca*, grilled meats and macaroni pie. Enough said!

Il Sorpasso TRATTORIA €
(www.trattoriailsorpasso.it; Via Sarceno 120; meals €20-25) Funky yellow signage beckons you into this laid-back trattoria, which tries out creative interpretations of traditional Emiliano dishes. Pride of place is the lasagne: al dente layers of red, green and black pasta under-laid with moist chunks of pork. Assorted cookbooks and kids games shorten the wait.

Il Don Giovanni GASTRONOMIC €€€
(✆0532 24 33 63; www.ildongiovanni.com; Corso Ercole I d'Este 1; meals €45-75; ⊙dinner Mon-Sat) Open only for dinner, this highly acclaimed eatery specialises in fresh-caught fish from the Adriatic, vegetables harvested from the restaurant's own garden, eight varieties of bread baked daily and a wine list featuring over 600 Italian and international labels. The menu is an imaginative feast of unconventional concoctions; guinea-fowl-stuffed pasta and roast eel stand out.

Osteria Quattro Angeli TRADITIONAL ITALIAN €€
(www.osteriaquattroangeli.it; Piazza della Repubblica; meals €25; ⊙Tue-Sun) Relax beneath fat sausage-shaped salamis opposite the castle and demolish enormous portions of Ferranese classics supplemented by some complementary cuts of the local cured meat. Come 6pm, the tented section out front becomes a busy street bar, upping the noise levels and heightening the atmosphere.

☆ Entertainment

Jazz Club NIGHTCLUB, LIVE MUSIC
(www.jazzclubferrara.com; Via Rampari di Belfiore 167; admission €5-15; ⊙7.30pm) Enjoy the sounds of bebop and jazz-funk in a tower built into Ferrara's old city walls. Concerts start at 9.30pm and Monday nights are free.

ⓘ Information

Police station (✆0532 29 43 11; Corso Ercole I d'Este 26)

Post office (Viale Cavour 27)

Tourist office (✆0532 20 93 70; www.ferrarainfo.com; ⊙9am-1pm & 2-6pm Mon-Sat, 9.30am-1pm & 2-5pm Sun) In Castello Estense's courtyard.

URP Informacittà (Via Spadari 2/2; ⊙8.30am-1pm & 2-5.30pm Mon-Thu, 8.30am-1pm Fri, 9am-noon Sat) Free wi-fi and one public computer provided by the municipal government.

ⓘ Getting There & Around

ACFT (www.acft.it, in Italian) buses operate within the city and to surrounding towns such as Comacchio (€4.10, one hour, 11 daily), as well as to the Adriatic beaches. Long-distance buses originate at the bus station on Via Rampari San Paolo, then swing by the train station on their way out of town. The train is the better option for Bologna (€4, 30 to 50 minutes, half-hourly) and Ravenna (€5.70, 1¼ hours, 14 daily).

Most traffic is banned from the city centre. Overnight parking (€3 per 24 hours) is available at a large car park off Via Darsena (just outside the *centro storico*).

Get in the saddle and join the hundreds of other pedallers in one of Italy's most cycle-friendly city. Many places rent bikes (per day €7 to €10) including **Romanelli** (Via Aldighieri 28a; ⊙9.30am-12.30pm & 3.15-7pm).

RAVENNA
POP 153,400

Stray a few blocks from its diminutive train station and Ravenna feels immediately different, even by multi-layered Italian standards. Historically it fills a little-known void between the fall of the Roman Empire and the advent of the High Middle Ages, an era when the Ravennese were enjoying a protracted golden age while the rest of the Italian peninsula flailed in the wake of Barbarian invasions. Between 402 and 476 Ravenna was briefly capital of the Western Roman Empire and a fertile art studio for skilled Byzantine craftsmen, who left their blindingly colourful mosaics all over the terracotta-bricked Christian churches.

No matter how impervious you might have become to zealous religious art, Ravenna's brilliant 4th- to 6th-century gold, emerald and sapphire masterpieces will leave you struggling for adjectives. A suitably impressed Dante once described them as a 'symphony of colour' and spent the last few years of his life admiring them. Romantic toff Lord Byron added further weight to Ravenna's literary credentials when he spent a couple of years here before decamping to Greece. In 1996 the mosaics were listed as Unesco World Heritage Sites.

⊙ Sights

Ravenna's essential business is its eight Unesco World Heritage Sites, most of which lie scattered around the town (with one situated 5km outside). Five of them must be visited on the same ticket (€8.50). One is free. The other two can be paid for separately. The website www.ravennamosaici.it gives more information.

TOP CHOICE **Basilica di San Vitale** CHURCH **443**
(Via Fiandrini, entrance on Via San Vitale; ⊙9am-7pm Apr-Sep, to 5.30pm Mar & Oct, 9.30am-5pm Nov-Feb) Sometimes, after weeks of trolling around dark Italian churches you can lose your sense of wonder. Not here! The lucid mosaics that adorn the altar of this ancient church consecrated in 547 by Archbishop Massimiano invoke a sharp intake of breath in most visitors. Gaze in wonder at the rich greens, brilliant golds and deep blues bathed in shafts of soft yellow sunlight. The mosaics on the side and end walls represent scenes from the Old Testament: to the left, Abraham prepares to sacrifice Isaac in the presence of three angels, while the one on the right portrays the death of Abel and the offering of Melchizedek. Inside the chancel, two magnificent mosaics depict the Byzantine emperor Justinian with San Massimiano and a particularly solemn and expressive Empress Theodora, who was his consort.

Mausoleo di Galla Placidia
(Via Fiandrini; ⊙9am-7pm Apr-Sep, to 5.30pm Mar & Oct, 9.30am-5pm Nov-Feb) In the same complex as Basilica di San Vitale, the small but equally candescent Mausoleo di Galla Placidia was constructed for Galla Placidia, the half-sister of Emperor Honorius, who initiated construction of many of Ravenna's grandest buildings. The mosaics here are the oldest in Ravenna, probably dating from around AD 430.

Museo Arcivescovile MUSEUM
(Piazza Arcivescovado; ⊙9am-7pm Apr-Sep, 9am-5.30pm Oct-Mar) A museum with a difference, this recently renovated religious gem on the 2nd floor of the Archiepiscopal Palace hides two not-to-be-missed exhibits: an exquisite ivory throne carved for Emperor Maximilian by Byzantium craftsmen in the 6th century (the surviving detail is astounding); and Ravenna's most improbable mosaics displayed in the 5th-century chapel of San Andrea that has been cleverly incorporated into the museum's plush modern interior.

Battistero Neoniano BAPTISTERY
(Piazza del Duomo; ⊙9am-7pm Apr-Sep, 9.30am-5.30pm Mar & Oct, 10am-5pm Nov-Feb) Roman ruins aside, this is Ravenna's oldest intact building, constructed over the site of a former Roman baths in the late 4th century. Built in an octagonal shape as was the

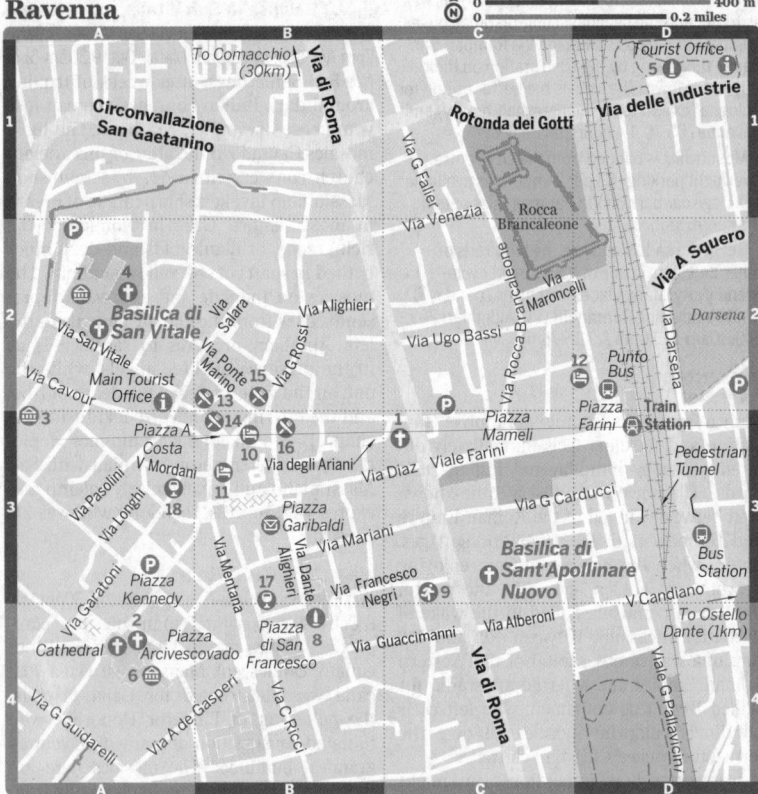

Ravenna

custom with all Christian baptistries of this period, it was originally attached to a church (since destroyed). The mosaics, which thematically depict Christ being baptised by St John the Baptist in the River Jordan, were added at the end of the 5th century.

Basilica di Sant'Apollinare Nuovo   CHURCH

(Via di Roma; ⊙9am-7pm Apr-Sep, 9.30am-5.30pm Mar & Oct, 10am-5pm Nov-Feb) An old legend states that Pope Gregory the Great once ordered the Apollinare's mosaics to be blackened as they were distracting worshippers from prayer. A millennium-and-a-half later and the dazzling Christian handiwork is still having the same effect. It's almost impossible to take your eyes off the 26 white-robed martyrs heading towards Christ with his apostles on the right (south) wall. On the opposite side, an equally expressive procession of virgins bear similar offerings for the Madonna. The basilica dates originally from the 560s and its architectural fusion of Christian east and west can be seen in its marble porticoes and distinctive conical bell tower.

FREE Tomba di Dante   MAUSOLEUM

(Via D Alighieri 9; ⊙9.30am-6.30pm) A son of Florence, Italy's Sommo Poeta (supreme poet), Dante Alighieri, was expelled from the city of his birth in 1302 for political reasons and spent many years 'on the run'. He finally sought refuge in Ravenna, where he died in 1321. As a perpetual act of penance, Florence still supplies the oil for the lamp that burns continually in his tomb.

Mausoleo di Teodorico   MAUSOLEUM

(Via delle Industrie 14; admission €3; ⊙8.30am-7pm) Historically and architecturally separate from the other Unesco sites (there are no mosaics here), this two-storey mausoleum was built in 520 for Gothic king Teodorico, who ruled Italy as a viceroy for the Byzantines. It is notable for its Gothic design features (rare for the time) and throwback Roman construction techniques: the huge blocks of stone were not cemented by any mortar. At the heart of the mausoleum is a Roman basin of porphyry that was recycled as a sarcophagus. It's 2km from the city centre. Take bus 2 or 5.

Basilica di Sant'Apollinare in Classe   CHURCH

(Via Romea Sud, Classe; admission €3; ⊙8.30am-7.30pm Mon-Sat, 1-7.30pm Sun) More magnificent mosaics this time in a signature early-Christian Ravennese church situated 5km to the southeast of town in the small village of Classe. Fear not; the (small) effort to get here is worth it. Lighter than other Ravenna churches, the brilliant star-spangled triumphal arch mosaic displays symbols of the four evangelists: Matthew, Mark, Luke and John. Other mosaics in the apse depict Byzantium Emperor Constantine IV (652–685) and biblical figures such as Abel and Abraham. The basilica – architecturally the city's most 'perfect' – was built in the early 6th century on the burial site of Ravenna's patron saint, who converted the city to Christianity in the 2nd century. To get there take bus 4 to Classe or take the train one stop in the direction of Rimini.

Museo Nazionale   MUSEUM

(Via Fiandrini; adult/reduced €4/2; ⊙8.30am-7.30pm Tue-Sun) Next door to the Basilica di San Vitale, housed in the cloisters of a former Benedictine monastery, this museum has pottery, bronzes and more Madonna-and-child portraits than you can shake a halo at. Strangely it's not included in the Vitale joint ticket.

FREE Battistero degli Ariani   BAPTISTERY

(Via degli Ariani; ⊙8.30am-4.30pm Oct-Mar, to 7.30pm Apr-Sep) Aside from its breath-taking dome mosaic depicting the baptism of Christ, the Ariani's main quirk is that it's the only Unesco site you can enter for free. But the gratis entry is no reflection on the quality of the artistry inside, a vivid display of Christ being baptised encircled by the 12 apostles. The Ariani's mosaics were completed over a period of years beginning in the 5th century. You can clearly detect slight variations in colour on some of the green stones.

Domus dei Tappeti di Pietra   MUSEUM

(Via B Gianbattista; adult/reduced €4/3; ⊙10am-5pm Tue-Fri, to 6pm Sat & Sun) More mosaics, but noticeably different ones, these 6th-century floor mosaics from a 14-room late-Roman palace were only unearthed in 1993/94. Now fully restored, they show considerable artistic merit, and are decorated with geometric and floral designs.

Courses

The following outfits run mosaic courses catering to everyone from beginners to artists.

Gruppo Mosaicisti MOSAICS

(www.gruppomosaicisti.com; Via Fiandrini; beginners course €550)

Mosaic Art School MOSAICS

(www.mosaicschool.com; Via Francesco Negri 14; 1-week course €660-760)

Festivals & Events

Ravenna hosts one of Italy's top classical music events and jazz fans are well served.

Ravenna Festival MUSIC

(www.ravennafestival.org) Renowned Italian conductor Riccardo Muti has close ties with Ravenna and is intimately involved each year with this festival. Concerts are staged from June to late July at venues all over town, including the Teatro Alighieri (www.teatroalighieri.org; Via Mariani 2). Ticket prices start at around €15.

Ravenna Jazz MUSIC

In late October, stars of the jazz firmament descend on town.

Sleeping

TOP CHOICE **Hotel Centrale Byron** HOTEL €

(☑0544 21 22 25; www.hotelbyron.com; Via IV Novembre 14; s €45-55, d €70-90; ❋@🖘) Locations don't get much better than this, especially in the car-free, wonderfully ingratiating streets of central Ravenna. It's no lie to say you could lob a football from the window of your clean modern Centrale Byron window into pivotal (and beautiful) Piazza del Popolo. Regularly updated and improved, Byron keeps ahead of the game. So what if the great poet never stayed here.

Albergo Cappello BOUTIQUE HOTEL €€€

(☑0544 21 98 13; www.albergocappello.it; Via IV Novembre 41; s €150-180, d €180-260; P❋@🖘) Colour-themed rooms are called 'suites' at this finely coiffed hotel where Murano glass chandeliers, original 15th-century frescoes and coffered ceilings are set against modern fixtures and flat-screen TVs. The ample breakfast features pastries from Ravenna's finest *pasticceria* (pastry shop). There's also an excellent restaurant and wine bar attached.

Ostello Dante HOSTEL €

(☑0544 42 11 64; www.hostelravenna.com; Via Nicolodi 12; dm/s/d €16/25/44; @🖘) Ravenna's handy HI hostel is in a modern building 1km east of the train station. There's a noon

to 2.30pm lock-up but for €1 you can hire a 'night key', allowing you to come and go freely. Take bus 80 or the red 'Metrobus' from the train station.

Hotel Ravenna HOTEL €

(☑0544 21 22 04; www.hotelravenna.ra.it; Via Maroncelli 12; s €45-55, d €60-90; P❋🖘) A stone's throw from the train station, Hotel Ravenna is a safe bet. The bland rooms feature fading beige and gold decor and unexceptional furniture, but they're large and comfortable enough. Parking is free; wi-fi costs €4 per hour.

Eating

Self-caterers and sandwich-fillers should load up at the city's covered market (Piazza Andrea Costa).

TOP CHOICE **Osteria La Mariola** MODERN ITALIAN €€

(☑0544 20 14 45; Via P Costa 1; meals €35-40) Trying to fancy up Italian food is a precarious profession in a country where tradition and simplicity rule. All the more reason to offer kudos to new kid on the block La Mariola, which opened in February 2011 in the 16th century Palazzo Grossi. Three trendy purple-accented rooms divide into wine bar/restaurant/*enoteca* (wine bar). Food is a shade more artistic than the usual homespun fare and wine can be ordered by the *quartino* (quarter-litre measure).

La Gardela TRATTORIA €

(☑0544 21 71 47; Via Ponte Marino 3; meals €20; ☉Thu-Tue) Economical prices and formidable home cooking mean La Gardela can be crowded, but in a pleasant gregarious way. Professional waiters glide by with plates full of the Italian classics: thin-crust pizza, *ragù*, fried fish. Lap it up.

Babaleus PIZZERIA €

(www.ristorantebabaleus.com; V Gabbiani 7; pizzas from €4, meals €20-25; ☉dinner Thu-Tue, lunch Mon, Tue, Thu & Fri) Remember the days before TV chefs went viral, when hard-working cooks in white hats used to sit down with their diners and sip glasses of wine between courses? True to the tradition, cheap and cheerful Babaleus still ensures its fresh-from-the-oven pizza is brought to your table by congenial kitchen helpers in well-used pinnies armed with plenty of early-evening banter.

Ristorante Cappello GASTRONOMIC €€€

(☑0544 21 98 76; Via IV Novembre 41; meals €40-50; ☉closed Sun dinner & Mon) Under the hotel of the same name, this refined restaurant takes its food very seriously. The menu changes weekly, but seafood always figures prominently, in dishes such as *strozzapreti con calamaretti, zucchine, fiori di zucca e zafferano* (pasta with cuttlefish, zucchini, pumpkin flowers and saffron).

Drinking

TOP CHOICE **Ca' de Vèn**   BAR

(www.cadeven.it; Via Corrado Ricci 24; ⊙Tue-Sun) Old men with canine companions mix with wine snobs swapping oenological tips in this atmospheric wine bar-cum-restaurant (meals €25 to €35) beautified with floor-to-ceiling shelves stuffed with bottles, books and other curiosities. Use it for its excellent *aperitivi* and, when the frescoed ceiling starts to spin, make tracks for your main course elsewhere.

Cabiria   PUB

(Via Mordani 8; ⊙6pm-3am Mon-Sat) A wine bar that hums like a Friday-night pub, Cabiria is a local favourite, popular with the 30-something crowd.

ℹ Information

Multimediateca (Via Guido da Polenta 4; per hr €2; ⊙3-7pm Mon-Fri, 9am-1pm & 3-6pm Sat) Internet access on the 1st floor of Palazzo Farini.

Police station (☎0544 48 29 99; Piazza Mameli)

Post office (Piazza Garibaldi 1)

Tourist offices (www.turismo.ravenna. it) Via delle Industrie (Via delle Industrie 14; ⊙9.30am-12.30pm & 3-6pm); Via Salara (Via Salara 8-12; ⊙8.30am-6pm Mon-Sat, 10am-4pm Sun Oct-Mar, 8.30am-7pm Mon-Sat, 10am-6pm Sun Apr-Sep) The main office is in the centre, on Via Salara.

ℹ Getting There & Around

ATM (www.atm.ra.it, in Italian) local buses depart from Piazza Farini. Intercity buses for Ferrara and towns along the coast leave from the bus station on the east side of the railroad tracks (reached by a pedestrian underpass). **Punto Bus** (⊙6.30am-7.30pm, from 7.30am Sun), on the piazza, is ATM's information and ticketing office.

Ravenna is on a branch (A14 dir) of the main east-coast A14 autostrada. The SS16 (Via Adriatica) heads south to Rimini and on down the coast. The main car parks are east of the train station and north of the Basilica di San Vitale.

Trains connect with Bologna (€6.20, 1¼ hours, hourly), Ferrara (€5.70, 1¼ hours, 14 daily), Rimini (€4, one hour, hourly) and the south coast.

In town, cycling is popular. The main (Via Salara) branch of the tourist office offers a free bike-hire service for visitors. Register by presenting a photo ID, then simply grab a yellow bike from one of the cycle stalls outside and return it to the same rack within normal business hours.

Just outside Ravenna's train station, **Cooperativa Sociale la Formica** (Piazza Farini; bikes per hr/day €1.10/8.50; ⊙7am-7pm Mon-Fri) also rents out bikes.

RIMINI
POP 138,500

Fellini followers trip over lounging sunbathers in Italy's largest and most hedonistic beach resort, a city immortalised in its native son's movies (*Amacord*, if you're an aficionado) and – more recently – internationally renowned nightclubs. Although there's been a settlement here for over 2000 years, Rimini's coast was just sand dunes until 1843 when the first bathing establishments took root next to the ebbing Adriatic. The beach huts quickly morphed into a mega-resort that was sequestered by a huge nightclub scene in the 1990s. It hasn't looked back since.

One wonders if the Romans would have approved. Once a thriving Latin colony known as Ariminum, Rimini changed hands like a well-worn library book in the Middle Ages when periods of Byzantine, Lombard and Papal rule culminated in the roguish reign of Sigismondo Malatesta in the 15th century. But the worst was to come. Rimini got whacked more than any other Italian city during WWII when bombing raids were followed by the brutal 'Battle of Rimini', during which an estimated 1.5 million rounds of allied ammunition were fired on the German-occupied city.

⊙ Sights

Piazza Cavour is Rimini's main square, containing the city's finest *palazzi* including the 16th-century **Palazzo del Municipio**, reconstructed after being razed during WWII, and the 14th-century Gothic **Palazzo del Podestà**.

Tempio Malatestiano   CHURCH

(Via IV Novembre 35; ⊙8.30am-12.30pm & 3.30-7pm Mon-Sat, 9am-1pm & 3.30-7pm Sun) Rimini's cathedral is the result of a medieval love story with a rather ambiguous ending. Built originally in Gothic style in the 1200s and dedicated to St Francis, it was transformed in the 15th century into a kind of Renaissance 'Taj Mahal' for the tomb of Isotta

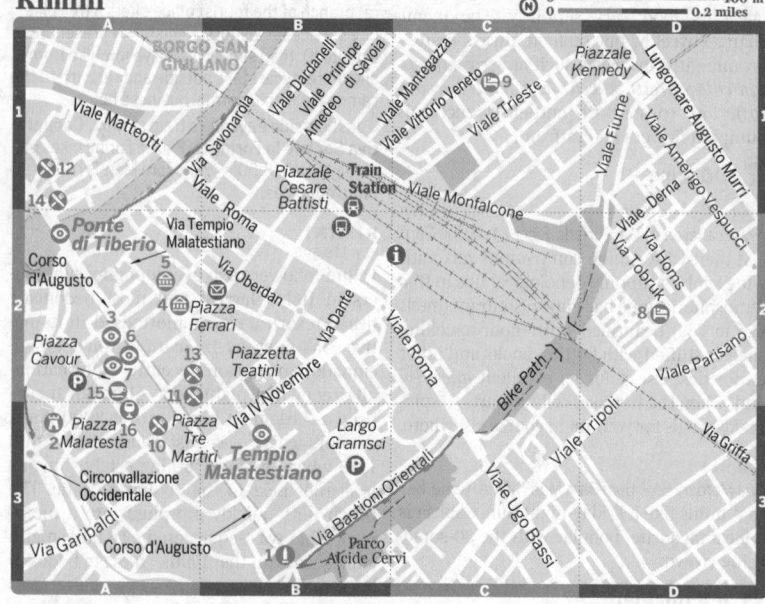

Rimini

degli Atti, the beloved mistress of roguish ruling clansman Sigismondo Malatesta. Sigismondo, known disparagingly as the 'Wolf of Rimini', gave Leon Battista Alberti, a Florentine architect with grandiose Roman ideas, the job of redesigning the church in 1450, but it was a task he never finished. Sigismondo, thanks to his aggressive military campaigns, had fallen out with the pope, Pius II (himself no angel), who burned his effigy in Rome and condemned him to hell for a litany of sins that included rape, mur-

der, incest, adultery and severe oppression of the people. With his credibility dented, Sigismondo's popularity waned, though some people still superstitiously think he defaced the cathedral with pagan undertones. Judge for yourself. Sigismondo and Isotta's sarcophagi reside inside.

Castel Sismondo   MUSEUM

(Piazza Malatesta; admission €2; ⊗8.30am-1.30pm) Also known as the Rocca Malatestiana, Rimini's classic Renaissance castle was designed by the great military leader himself, Sigismondo Malatesta. One small subterranean room displays information on the region's castles and natural parks.

Museo della Città
MUSEUM

(Via Tonini 1; adult/child incl Domus del Chirurgo €5/3, admission free Sun; ⊙10am-12.30pm & 4.30-7.30pm Tue-Sat, 4.30-7.30pm Sun) The town's main museum displays paintings upstairs, including a haunting *Pietà* by Giovanni Bellini and an altarpiece by Domenico Ghirlandaio. However, the museum's centrepiece is the archaeological section on the ground floor. Spread over several rooms with excellent bilingual (Italian/English) signage are finds from two nearby Roman villas, including splendid mosaics, a rare and exquisite representation of fish rendered in coloured glass, and the world's largest collection of Roman surgical instruments. You can walk through a life-sized reconstruction of the surgeon's offices, then visit the original excavation site across the street at the glass-floored Domus del Chirurgo, with some fine floor mosaics still intact.

Ponte di Tiberio
LANDMARK

The start of the arterial Roman road, the Via Emilia, no less, the majestic five-arched Tiberius' Bridge dates from AD 21. It still links the city centre to the old fishing quarter of Borgo San Giuliano and rests on its original foundations consisting of an ingenious construction of wooden stilts.

Arco di Augusto
LANDMARK

Rimini's other great Roman ruin was commissioned by Emperor Augustus in 27 BC and stands 17m high on modern-day Corso d'Augusto. It was once the end point of the ancient Via Flaminia that linked Rimini with Rome. Buildings that had grown up around the arch were demolished in 1935 to improve its stature.

Borgo San Giuliano
NEIGHBOURHOOD

Just over the Ponte di Tiberio, Rimini's old fishing quarter has been freshened up and is now a colourful patchwork of cobbled lanes, trendy trattorias, wine bars and trim terraced houses (read: prime real estate). Look out for the numerous murals.

Activities

Beaches
BEACH

Rimini beaches are Italy's proverbial California. Spend 10 minutes on the promenade in August and you'll realise that all kinds of

new trends kick off here – wacky or otherwise. Earnest Nordic beach-walkers, office girls getting a reiki massage, gym meatheads pumping iron, clubbers in search of a hangover cure, computer geeks surfing on their sunloungers, and more.

In peak season, it's hard to see the sand through all the assembled umbrellas, sun loungers, amusement parks and crowded beach bars. Suffice to say there's 40km of it mostly backed by clamorous hotel development.

Theme Parks
AMUSEMENT PARK

In a beach resort, garish theme parks are an inevitable by-product and Rimini has its fair share. The truly committed can buy a Fantasticket (see www.larivieradeiparchi.it/fantasticket.php) granting reduced-price admission to multiple parks. The tourist office can provide a full list. Major ones include Fiabilandia (www.fiabilandia.it; Via Cardano 15, Rivazzurra; adult/child €22/15; ﹙﹚), which focuses on fun for kids, and Aquafàn (www.aquafan.it; Via Ascoli Piceno 6, Riccione; adult/child €24/18; ⊙10am-6.30pm Jun–mid-Sep), a huge water-park in Riccione; take bus 42 or 45 from Riccione station.

Festivals & Events

Gradisca
CARNIVAL

On 21 June Rimini celebrates with dancing, fireworks and eating – it's estimated that revellers consume some two tonnes of grilled sardines and 12,000L of Sangiovese wine in one night.

Rimini Jazz Festival
MUSIC

(www.rimini jazz.it, in Italian) In summer this is held beside the main Marina Centro beach area.

Sleeping

Ironically for a city with more than 1200 hotels, accommodation can be tricky. In July and August places can be booked solid and prices are sky-high, especially as many proprietors insist on full board; in winter a lot of places simply shut up shop.

TOP CHOICE Grand Hotel
LUXURY HOTEL €€€

(☑0541 5 60 00; www.grandhotelrimini.com; Parco Federico Fellini; s €120-255, d €160-330; P ﹡ @ ﹫﹚) Rimini's only five-star hotel is as much a monument as a place to stay. Despite a 1920 fire and serious damage incurred during WWII, it has remained true to its 1908 roots with rooms clad in authentic 18th-century Venetian antiques. Beloved by

THE PEARL & THE OYSTER

All art is autobiographical; the pearl is the oyster's autobiography.
Federico Fellini

If Fellini was a pearl, Rimini would be his oyster. Few film directors have crammed more autobiographical material into their work than Italy's greatest movie maestro, born in the ancient Roman city-turned-beach resort in January 1920.

Fragments of Rimini, both dreamt and real, crop up in much of Fellini's early work including *La Strada*, *I Vitelloni* and his Magnus opus, *8½*, but his greatest film memoir appeared in 1973 with the movie *Amacord* (the title is a corruption of *a m'acord* meaning 'I believe' in Romagnolo), a bawdy, comic, at times convoluted tale of a group of boys growing up in a typical 1930s Italian town known as 'Borgo' – a thinly disguised version of pre-war Rimini. In the movie, many of the city's famous sights such as the Grand Hotel and the Cinema Fulgor make cameo appearances.

Fellini's legacy is preserved by the Rimini-based **Fondazione Fellini** (Fellini Foundation; www.federicofellini.it, in Italian), which was in the process of opening a new museum dedicated to the director at the time of writing. The museum will be encased in the **Cinema Fulgor** (Corso d'Augusto 162), where Fellini used to watch films as a boy. It was due to open in late 2011 and will display artefacts from the foundation's extensive archive.

The Foundation also organises regular expositions, talks and events; check its website for details.

Fellini, the hotel has lured many other celebs with its pool, private beach and elegant communal areas.

Hotel Villa Lalla   HOTEL €

(✆0541 5 51 55; www.villalalla.com; Viale V Veneto 22; d €56-98; P❋@) One of the better hotels in the leafy residential district between the beach and the train station. Its smart white rooms are fresh and cool and, in winter, its rates are a snip. From mid-June to mid-September when the restaurant's open, it's a good idea to invest in half-board or full board (a mere €8 extra per meal). Bikes are free for guests.

Camping Italia Rimini   CAMPGROUND €

(✆0541 73 28 82; www.campingitaliarimini.it; Via Toscanelli 112, Viserba; camping per adult/child/tent/car €10/5.50/11/5; ☉Jun-Sep) One of numerous campgrounds along the coast, this tree-shaded place 2km northwest of the city centre has all the requisite facilities. Take bus 4 from the train station and get off at stop 14.

Sunflower City Backpacker Hostel HOSTEL €

(✆0541 2 51 80; www.sunflowerhostel.com; Via Dardanelli 102; dm €18-27, s €26-49, d €46-79; @) Run by three ex-backpackers, the chilled-out Sunflower welcomes travellers with laundry and cooking facilities, spacious lockers, retro Austin Powers–style wallpaper, pool tables, a bar and free bike hire. There's another one on Viale Siracusa 25 near the beach.

Hotel Aurora Centro   HOTEL €

(✆0541 39 10 02; Via Tobruk 6; s/d €35/60;P) A homely *pensione* with threadbare carpets and children's toys cheerfully littered around the breakfast room. You get no airs and graces here, just clean, simple rooms and but kindly welcome. The beach is a quick hop away.

🍴 Eating

Rimini's cuisine is anchored by the *piadina* (a form of wrap) and *pesce azzurro* (oily fish), especially sardines and anchovies. The favourite tipple is Sangiovese wine

🏆 Osteria Dë Börg   OSTERIA €€

(www.osteriadeborg.it; Via Forzieri 12; meals €25-35; ☉lunch & dinner) A homey *osteria* in the old fishing quarter, this place is what eating in Italy is all about: simple, honest food made with local ingredients and served in unpretentious surroundings. Second courses revolve around meat, from stuffed rabbit to steaks grilled on an open fire and seasoned with rosemary and sea salt.

Casina del Bosco   SNACKS €

(Via Beccadelli 15; piadine €4-7; ☉noon-late) It's very simple (isn't all good food?). It's called a *piadina* – a toasted half-moon of unleavened bread with a savoury filling – and it's Romagna's retort to the wrap. You can get them in many places, but they're rarely as consistent or wide-ranging as they are at this fast and efficient alfresco joint overlooking Parco Federico Fellini near the beach.

Tonino Il Lurido
SEAFOOD €€€
(www.ristoranteillurido.com; Via Ortaggi 7; meals €45) When Fellini said it was 'easier to be faithful to a restaurant than a woman', he might have been talking about this place. The great film director's (allegedly) favourite eating establishment in Rimini has been in operation since 1949. Can it still cut it? Sample the small, tasty portions of fresh fish and decide.

Picnic
TRADITIONAL ITALIAN €€
(Via Tempio Malatestiano 30; meals €30; ⊘closed Mon Sep-May) In business for nearly half a century, Picnic has a wide-ranging menu of traditional favourites like *salsiccia fagioli con polenta* (sausage with beans and polenta), supplemented with whatever's freshest from the market – grilled fish of the day, for example, or local strawberries with whipped cream.

Brodo di Giuggiole
TRADITIONAL ITALIAN €€
(www.brododigiuggiole.info; Via Soardi 11; meals €35; ⊘dinner Tue-Sun; 🛜) Tucked down an alley off Piazza Tre Martiri, this intimate spot is great for an elegant night out, with its wood-panelled dining room, lantern-lit plank terrace and an ever-changing menu featuring some of the freshest, best-prepared fish in town. Reservations are recommended, especially on live-jazz Tuesdays.

Gelateria Pellicano
GELATERIA €
(www.gelateriapellicano.com; Via S Mentana 10; ⊘7.30am-7.30pm Mon-Sat) This Rimini-based, five-store chain makes some seriously good ice cream. Try the *pinoli* (pine nut), with toasted whole nuts on top.

🍷 Drinking
Most Italian drinking trends begin life in Rimini – or so the locals claim – from street bars to free aperitifs. The action spins on two hubs: the old *pescheria* (fish market) through the brick triple archway off Piazza Cavour, and the seafront around Marino Centro.

Caffè Cavour
CAFE
(Piazza Cavour 12; ⊘7am-midnight) Early risers bump into the remnants of last night's dance marathons in this swish cafe on Rimini's main square. Mornings are for cappuccinos, evenings for *aperitivi*, the plush leather seats inside for anytime.

Rock Island
BAR
(www.rockislandrimini.net; Piazzale Boscovich) Perched on stilts over the Adriatic on the pier next to the marina, Rock Island is the place for beer, sunset cocktails, live rock music and bikers with beards.

Barge
BAR
(Lungomare C Tintori 13; ⊘closed Mon winter) A magnet for modish 20-somethings, this seafront pub offers an irresistible combo: draught Guinness, regular DJs and frequent live music.

Taverna della Vecchia Pescheria
BAR
(Via Pisacane 10; ⊘6pm-2am) In the historic fish market, this rustic pub with little wooden tables and chairs is elbow-to-elbow with locals enjoying draught beer and free snacks at *aperitivo* time.

☆ Entertainment
Rimini's club scene is legendary. Bank on paying €15 to €30 for entrance to the bigger clubs.

Discoteca Baia Imperiale
NIGHTCLUB
(www.baiaimperiale.net; Via Panoramica 195, Gabicce Mare; ⊘10pm-4am) A Rimini legend overlooking the Adriatic, the Baia likes to brag that it is one of the 10 most beautiful discos in the world. Get an eyeful of the marble staircase, pool, and assorted obelisks and statues of Roman emperors, and even the stone-cold sober might be inclined to agree. Forty-somethings won't feel out of place here.

Cocoricò
NIGHTCLUB
(www.cocorico.it; Viale Chieti 44, Riccione; ⊘11pm-5.30am) Dance under a glass pyramid with 2000 clammy strangers who'll quickly become your friends at this fount of techno, house and underground 12km south of town in Riccione. Look out for Fatboy Slim behind the sound system.

Paradiso
NIGHTCLUB
(Viale Covignano 260; ⊘9pm-5am) Words like 'hip', 'chic' and 'trendy' are bandied around liberally when discussing Paradiso, one of Italy's most famous clubs with cocktails, celeb sightings and de rigueur dancing.

Velvet Club
NIGHTCLUB, LIVE MUSIC
(www.velvet.it; Via Sant'Aquilina 21; ⊘9pm-late) The Velvet, located 8km southwest of the centre, features DJs, big-name rock acts and dancing till dawn. The adjacent Velvet Factory is a live-work space for international visual and performing artists.

Disco Bar Coconuts BAR, LIVE MUSIC
(www.coconuts.it; Lungomare C Tintori 5;
⊙11.30pm-4am) Flaunting its prime waterfront location, Rimini's most centrally located disco exudes a summer-beach-party
atmosphere, with palm trees sprouting from
the wooden deck and a 'flower power' VW
convertible parked out the front.

❶ Information

Hospital (☑0541 70 51 11; Viale L Settembrini
2) Located 1.2km southeast of the centre.

Police station (☑0541 35 31 11; Corso
d'Augusto 192)

Post office (Via Gambalunga 40)

Tourist offices (www.riminiturismo.it) Parco
Federico Fellini (Parco Federico Fellini 3;
⊙8.30am-7pm Mon-Sat, to 2pm Sun); train station (Piazzale Cesare Battisti; ⊙8.30am-7pm
Mon-Sat, to 1.30pm Sun)

Ufficio Relazioni con il Pubblico (☑0541
70 47 04; Corso d'Augusto 158; ⊙9am-1pm &
2.30-6pm Mon-Wed & Fri, 9am-6pm Thu, to
1pm Sat) Free internet provided by Rimini's
town government.

❶ Getting There & Away

Ryanair offers thrice-weekly direct flights from
London Stansted to Rimini's Federico Fellini

airport, 8km south of the city centre. Alitalia also
flies nonstop to/from Rome.

There are regular buses from Rimini's train
station to San Marino (return €7.40, 45 minutes,
11 daily).

By car, you have a choice of the A14 (south into
Le Marche or northwest towards Bologna and
Milan) or the toll-free but very busy SS16.

Hourly trains run down the coast to the ferry
ports of Ancona (regional/Eurostar €5.15/14,
one to 1¼ hours) and Bari (€31/58, five to six
hours). Up the line, they serve Ravenna (€4, one
hour, hourly) and Bologna (regional/Eurostar
€8.40/13, one to 1½ hours, half-hourly).

❶ Getting Around

TRAMServizi (www.tramservizi.it, in Italian)
buses operate throughout the city. Local bus
9 runs between Rimini's train station and the
airport (€1, 25 minutes). For Riccione (€1.50,
30 minutes), catch local bus 11 from the train
station or along the *lungomare* (seafront
promenade); it leaves every eight to 15 minutes
between 6am and 2am.

You can hire bikes and scooters from various
kiosks on Piazzale Kennedy. Free bikes are also
available from Rimini's municipal offices (Corso
d'Augusto 158).

FROM ROMANS TO RAVES

Early-morning insomniacs and late-night clubbers mention Rimini in the same breath
as London, Berlin and Ibiza, and even the leery acknowledge that the city is far more
than a here-today-gone-tomorrow stag weekend. Grabbing at the coat-tails of rave,
acid house and the Second Summer of Love, Rimini first established itself as a club city
in the early 1990s. Fortunes have fluctuated in the years since but, with a far classier
reputation than other Mediterranean megaresorts, the nightlife here has created a
definitive niche, with the clubs now seemingly as entrenched as the Roman relics that
preceded them.

Classic Rimini evenings start early and end late. Warm-ups can kick off any time after
6pm in the vicinity of the Marino Centro and the Parco Federico Fellini. Another popular
meeting place is in the old fish market just off Piazza Cavour for an aperitif, free snacks
and maybe a live band.

Most of Rimini's famous clubs are in the hills of Misano Monte and Riccone several
kilometres to the south of the city centre, and a proverbial Beverley Hills for the fash-
ionista set. You'll find none of the disused aircraft hangars or muddy cow fields of rave-
scene yore here. Instead, the Italians have designed their clubs rather like they make
their cars – with effortless panache. Dance in a mansion with slick stylish furnishings, or
recline in a regal garden next to a swimming pool where the only thing brighter than the
stars is the bling.

Part of the fabric (and fun) of Rimini's club scene is the **Blue Line** (www.bluelinebus.
com; tickets €4; ⊙10pm-6am), a fleet of multicoloured disco buses that ferry clubbers
from Piazzale Kennedy in the city centre to and from the various nightclubs to the south.
Blue Line buses don't just serve as safe, secure public transport tools; they also carry
DJs, coffee shops and music systems, and deposit clubbers in town for that other classic
Rimini innovation, the dawn breakfast.

SAN MARINO

Of the world's 193 independent countries, San Marino is the fifth smallest and – arguably – the most curious. How it exists at all is something of an enigma. A sole survivor of Italy's once powerful city-state network, this landlocked micro-nation clung on long after the more powerful kingdoms of Genoa and Venice folded. And still it clings, secure in its status as the world's oldest surviving sovereign state and its oldest republic (since AD 301). San Marino also enjoys the lowest unemployment rate in Europe and one of the planet's highest GDPs.

Measuring 61 sq km, the country is larger than many outsiders imagine, being made up of nine municipalities each hosting its own settlement. The largest 'town' is Dogana (on the bus route from Italy), a place 99.9% of the two million annual visitors skip on their way through to the Città di San Marino, the medieval settlement on the slopes of 749m Monte Titano that was added to the Unesco World Heritage list in 2008.

Though San Marino is old and commands some astounding views, it retains a curious lack of intimacy and (for want of a better word) soul.

⊙ Sights & Activities

San Marino's highlights are its spectacular views, its Unesco-listed streets, and a stash of rather bizarre museums dedicated to vampires, torture, wax dummies and strange facts. Ever popular is the half-hourly changing of the guard (⊙May-Sep) in Piazza della Libertà.

Castello della Cesta   CASTLE
(admission €4.50; ⊙8am-8pm mid-Jun–mid-Sep, 9am-5pm mid-Sep–mid-Jun) Dominating the skyline and offering superb views towards Rimini and the coast, the Cesta dates from the 13th century and sits atop 750m Monte Titano. Today you can walk its ramparts and peep into a small museum devoted to medieval armaments. The admission price also includes entry to the Castello della Guaita, the older of San Marino's castles, dating from the 11th century; it was still being used as a prison until as recently as 1975.

Museo delle Curiosità   MUSEUM
(www.museodellecuriosita.sm; Salità alla Rocca 26; adult/reduced €7/4; ⊙10am-6pm) If you're overtly curious or just a little bored, you can brush up on your Trivial Pursuit skills at this shrine to throwaway facts.

FREE Museo di Stato   MUSEUM
(www.museidistato.sm; Piazza Titano 1; ⊙8am-8pm mid-Jun–mid-Sep, 9am-5pm mid-Sep–mid-Jun) San Marino's best museum by far is the well-laid-out if disjointed state museum displaying art, history, furniture and culture.

Azienda Filatelica-Numismatica   STORE
(www.aasfn.sm; Piazza Garibaldi 5; ⊙8.15am-6pm Mon & Thu, to 2.15pm Tue, Wed & Fri) Collectors can pick up rare San Marino stamps and coins at this small shop.

🛏 Sleeping & Eating

Albergo Diamond   PENSIONE €
(☎0549 99 10 03; Contrada del Collegio 50; r €50) Few of the two million annual visitors stay overnight in San Marino, but if they checked out the Diamond's giveaway prices they might be tempted. Cute, modest rooms look like something your grandma put together and there's a large, busy restaurant below.

Hotel Titano   HOTEL €€
(☎0549 99 10 07; www.hoteltitano.com; Contrada del Collegio 31; r with/without view €115/88; P@🖥) The Titano is San Marino's best all-rounder, with a tearoom, fine view restaurant (La Terraza), and enough mod cons to justify a three-star rating.

Caffè Titano   INTERNATIONAL €
In the eponymous square and not directly connected to its namesake hotel, the Titano appears to be San Marino's sleekest inexpensive option. Seating is in cool booths, there's a bit of local action and the plates of sliced beef, rocket and *parmigiano* are delicious.

❶ Information

Post office (Viale A Onofri 87) Vital for sending those 'proved-you've-been-there' postcards.

Tourist office (www.visitsanmarino.com; Contrada del Collegio 40; ⊙10am-5pm) You can get your passport stamped with a San Marino visa for a rip-off €5 here.

❶ Getting There & Away

Buses run to/from Rimini (return €7.40, 45 minutes, 11 daily), arriving at Piazzale Calcigni. The SS72 leads up from Rimini.

Leave your car at one of the numerous car parks and walk up to the *centro storico*. If necessary, park at car park 11 and take the **funivia** (cable car; return €4.50; ⊙7.50am-sunset Sep-Jun, to 1am Jul & Aug).

Florence & Tuscany

POP 1.03 MILLION

Why Go?

Laden with grand-slam sights and experiences, Tuscany (Toscana in Italian) offers the perfect introduction to Italy's famed *dolce vita*. Despite incessant praise, its beauty and charm defy description. It has extraordinary art and architecture; vibrant festivals; a seasonal cuisine emulated the world over; and never-ending, picture-perfect landscapes of olive groves, vineyards and poplars. There are few places in the world where food, fashion, art and nature intermingle so effortlessly and to such magnificent effect.

Then there is that over-abundance of things to do and see: visit a World Heritage Site in the morning, drive through a national park in the afternoon and bunk down in stylish vineyard accommodation at night. Medieval sculptures, Renaissance paintings and Gothic cathedrals? Check. Spectacular trekking and sensational Slow Food? Yep. Hills laden with vines, ancient olive groves...what more could one possibly desire?

Best Places to Eat

- » Il Santo Bevitore (p484)
- » L'Osteria di Giovanni (p482)
- » Filippo (p508)
- » Osteria di Passignano (p528)
- » Enoteca I Terzi (p521)

Best Places to Stay

- » Hotel L'Orologio (p479)
- » Barbialla Nuova (p508)
- » Tenuta La Chiusa (p515)
- » Campo Regio Relais (p520)

When to Go

Florence

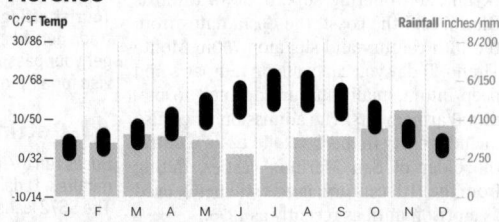

May-Jun Spring, strewn with wildflowers, begs outdoor action be it walking, cycling or horse riding.

Jul It's not as mad-busy as August (avoid) and its music festivals are magnificent.

Sep & Oct Grapes and olives are harvested, porcini mushrooms and chestnuts fill forests.

The Tuscan Table

'To cook like your mother is good; to cook like your grandmother is better', says the Tuscan proverb. And indeed, it is age-old recipes passed between generations that form the backbone of Tuscan cuisine today. Originally cooked up over an open wood fire in *la cucina contadina* (the farmer's kitchen), it is essentially a peasant fare built around beans, bread and other cheap, abundant essentials. The basic premise of Tuscany's so-called *mangiafagioli* (bean eaters): don't waste a crumb. Fresh local seasonal produce is key, fussy execution eschewed, and the result – a stunning feast of gastronomic experiences. Be it by sinking your teeth into a brilliantly blue *bistecca alla fiorentina* (T-bone steak), sampling wafer-thin pig fat marinated in marble vats near Carrara, savouring flavoursome fish stew in Livorno or hunting white truffles in San Miniato, Tuscany is foodie paradise.

LESS-TRODDEN ROADS

Few regions in Italy have so many big hitters as Tuscany – which means crowds. Yet even in top-drawer destinations like Florence, Pisa and Siena, with savvy planning it is still possible to get away from it all along a less-trodden road. In Florence enjoy extraordinary art in lesser-known museums like **Museo del Bargello** (early Michelangelos), **Museo di San Marco** (superb frescoes) and **Chiesa di Orsanmichele** (medieval statuary) or hidden treasures such as Michelangelo's curvaceous staircase and vestibule in the **Biblioteca Laurenziana Medicea**. In Pisa save the Leaning Tower for sunset when the coach loads have gone for the day and indulge in peaceful meanderings along the Arno river, over its bridges and through Pisa's medieval heart – or trade the over-touristed town for unknown **Pietrasanta** with its outstanding contemporary art and dining. Wedged between Siena and the coast, hilltop town **Massa Marittima** is a particular less-tourist-trodden fave, while in busy San Gimignano, a **guided nature walk** in the hills is just the ticket – or what about a peaceful walk to **Abbazia di Sant'Antimo** near Montalcino?

Top Five Wine Tastings

» Vernaccia in San Gimignano (p528)

» Brunello in Montalcino (p536)

» Chianti in guess where (p523)

» Vino Nobile in Montepulciano (p536)

» Vin Santo in the company of *cantuccini* (crunchy, almond-studded biscuits), anywhere in the region

CYCLING TUSCANY

Italy's most eminently cycle-able region is not only for pros. Guided tours in Florence (p477) are big, or consider a two-wheeler foray fuelled only by wine around Chianti (p523).

Blogs to Excite

» Emiko Davies: www.emikodavies.com

» Tuscan Traveler: http://tuscantraveler.com

Advance Planning

» Book tickets/accommodation for Siena's Palio (p520) one year in advance!

» Buy tickets for the Uffizi and Leaning Tower 15 days in advance and earlier for the Vasari Corridor (p473).

» Tuscany's key music festivals – Maggio Musicale Fiorentino (p477) and Settimana Musicale Senese and Estate Musicale Chigiana (p520) – need advance planning; snag tickets early or miss out.

» Work out which Florence museum pass suits you best (p463) and purchase online.

Resources

» Regione Toscana (www.turismo.intoscana.it)

» The Florentine (www.theflorentine.com)

» Florence Museums (www.firenzemusei.it)

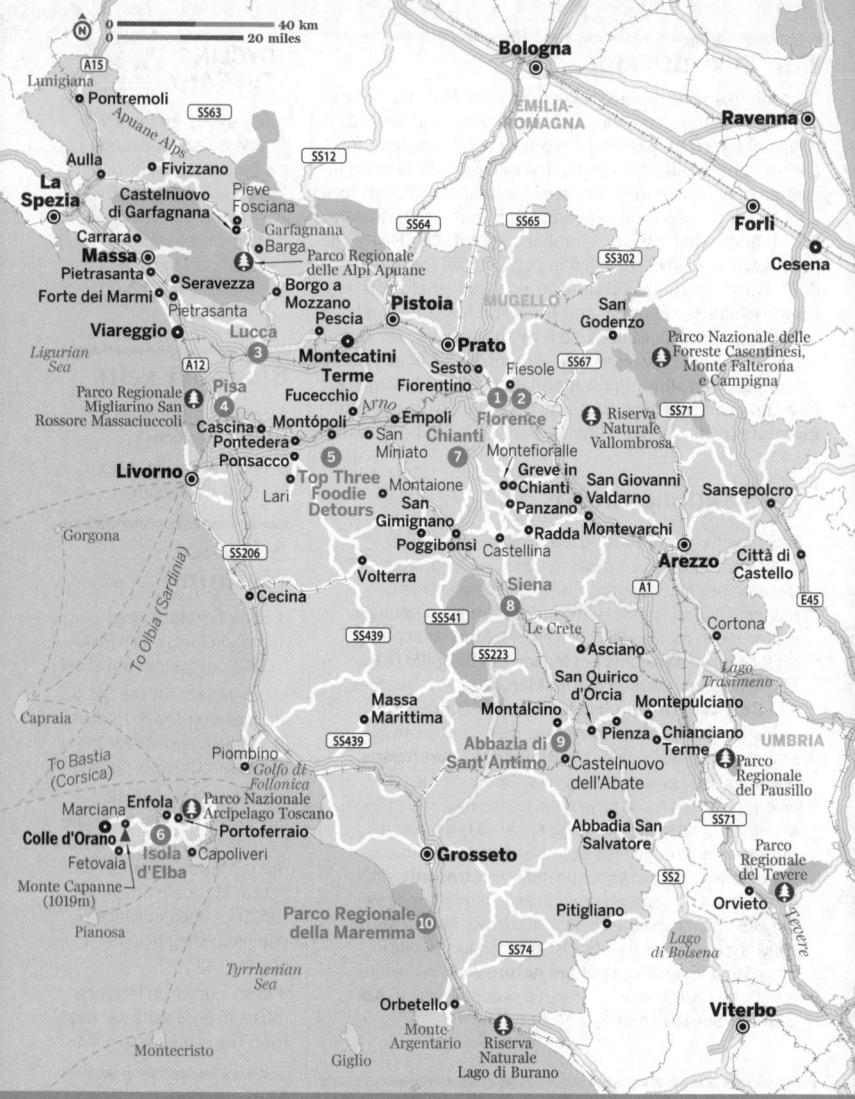

Florence & Tuscany Highlights

1 Discover Renaissance treasures in Florence's **Uffizi Gallery** (p463)

2 Follow in the footsteps of the Medicis along Florence's mysterious **Vasari Corridor** (p473)

3 Pedal and picnic atop Lucca's lovely Renaissance **city walls** (p503)

4 Fall in love with medieval Pisa; scale its iconic **Leaning Tower** (p496) at sunset

5 Flee the crowds: watch spaghetti being handmade, cook Tuscan and hunt white truffles (p508)

6 Sleep between groves and seashore on the island of Elba's oldest **wine estate** (p515)

7 Explore the world-famous wine region of **Chianti** (p523)

8 Gorge on Gothic architecture in **Siena** (p516)

9 Hear Gregorian chants in **Abbazia di Sant'Antimo** (p537)

10 Play cowboy for the day in the **Parco Regionale della Maremma** (p540)

FLORENCE

POP 368,900

Return time and again and you still won't see it all. Stand on a bridge over the Arno several times in a day and the light, mood and view will always vary. Surprisingly small as it is, this city is like no other. Cradle of the Renaissance and home of Machiavelli, Michelangelo and the Medici, Florence (Firenze) is magnetic, romantic, unrivalled and – above all – busy. Its historic streets teem with tourists, who flock year-round to feast on the city's world-class art and extraordinary architecture.

Yet there's more to this intensely absorbing place than priceless masterpieces. Towers and palaces evoke a thousand tales of its medieval past; designer boutiques and artisan workshops stud its streets; there's a buzzing cafe and bar scene; and – when the summer heat simply gets too stifling – vine-laden hills and terrace restaurants are only a short drive away.

History

Controversy continues over who founded Florence. The most commonly accepted story tells us that Emperor Julius Caesar founded Florentia around 59 BC. Archaeological evidence suggests the presence of an earlier village founded by the Etruscans of Fiesole around 200 BC.

In the 12th century Florence became a free *comune* (town council), ruled by 12 *priori* (consuls) assisted by the Consiglio di Cento (Council of One Hundred), drawn mainly from the merchant class. Agitation among differing factions led to the appointment of a foreign governing *podestà* (magistrate) in 1207.

The first conflicts between two of the factions, the pro-papal Guelphs (Guelfi) and the pro-imperial Ghibellines (Ghibellini), started in the mid-13th century, with power passing between the two groups for almost a century.

In the 1290s the Guelphs split into two: the Neri (Blacks) and Bianchi (Whites). When the Bianchi were defeated, Dante was among those driven into exile in 1302. As the nobility lost ground the Guelph merchant class took control, but trouble was never far away. The plague of 1348 halved the city's population and the government was rocked by agitation from the lower classes.

In the 14th century Florence was ruled by a caucus of Guelphs under the leadership of the Albizi family. Among the families opposing them were the Medici, who substantially increased their clout when they became the papal bankers.

Cosimo il Vecchio (the Elder, also known simply as Cosimo de' Medici) emerged as head of the opposition to the Albizi in the 15th century and became Florence's ruler. His eye for talent saw a constellation of artists such as Alberti, Brunelleschi, Lorenzo Ghiberti, Donatello, Fra' Angelico and Fra' Filippo Lippi flourish.

The rule of Lorenzo il Magnifico (1469–92), Cosimo's grandson, ushered in the most glorious period of Florentine civilisation and of the Italian Renaissance. His court fostered a flowering of art, music and poetry, turning Florence into Italy's cultural capital. Not long before Lorenzo's death, the Medici bank failed and the family was driven out of Florence. The city fell under the control of Savonarola, a Dominican monk who led a puritanical republic, burning the city's wealth on his 'bonfire of vanities'. But his lure was short-lived and after falling from favour he was tried as a heretic and executed in 1498.

After the Spanish defeated Florence in 1512, Emperor Charles V married his daughter to Lorenzo's great-grandson Alessandro de' Medici, whom he made duke of Florence in 1530. Seven years later Cosimo I, one of the last truly capable Medici rulers, took charge, becoming grand duke of Tuscany after Siena fell to Florence in 1569 and ushering in more than 150 years of Medici domination of Tuscany.

In 1737 the grand duchy of Tuscany passed to the French House of Lorraine, which retained control, apart from a brief interruption under Napoleon, until it was incorporated into the Kingdom of Italy in 1860. Florence briefly became the national capital but Rome assumed the mantle permanently in 1870.

The city was severely damaged during WWII, ravaged by floods in 1966, and in 1993 the Mafia exploded a massive car bomb, destroying a part of the Uffizi Gallery. The current renovation and expansion of the gallery, official end date not yet known, is the biggest (and longest) ever.

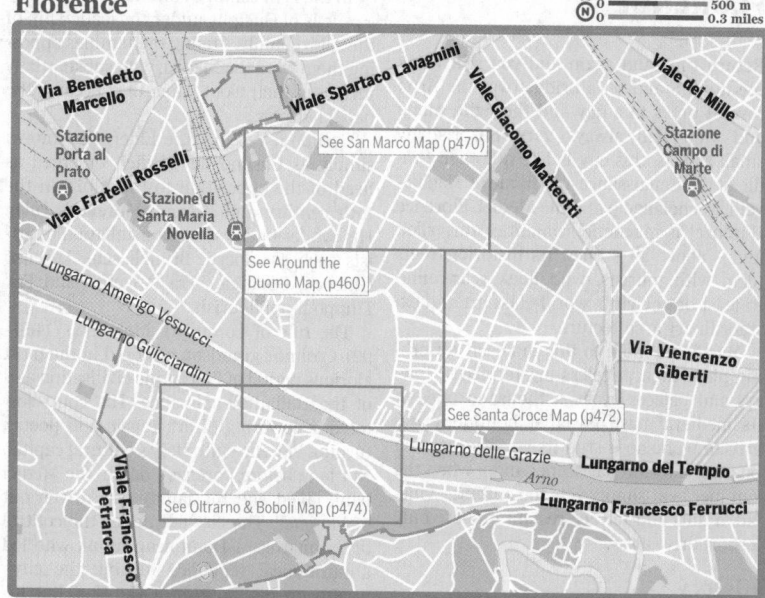

◉ Sights

Florence's big-hit sights lie in the geographic, historic and cultural heart of the city – the tight grid of streets between Piazza del Duomo and cafe-strung Piazza della Signoria.

PIAZZA DEL DUOMO

Duomo   CATHEDRAL
(Map p460; Cattedrale di Santa Maria del Fiore or St Mary of the Flower; www.duomofirenze.it; ◷10am-5pm Mon-Wed & Fri, to 3.30pm Thu, to 4.45pm Sat, to 3.30pm 1st Sat of month, 1.30-4.45pm Sun, mass in English 5pm Sat) The city's most iconic landmark with its famous red-tiled dome, graceful bell tower and breathtaking pink, white and green marble facade has wow factor in spades. Begun in 1296 by Sienese architect Arnolfo di Cambio, the cathedral took almost 150 years to complete. Its neo-Gothic facade was designed in the 19th century by architect Emilio de Fabris to replace the uncompleted original, torn down in the 16th century.

After the visually tumultuous facade, the sparse decoration of the cathedral's vast interior, 155m long and 90m wide, is surprising. Scaling the 463 steep stone steps up to the **dome** (admission €8; ◷8.30am-7pm Mon-Fri, to 5.40pm Sat) is a must. No supporting frame was used in its construction – it's actually two concentric domes built from red brick to designs by Filippo Brunelleschi. The climb rewards you with an unforgettable 360-degree panorama of one of Europe's most beautiful cities.

Equally physical is the 414-step climb up the neighbouring 82m-high **campanile** (adult/child €6/free; ◷8.30am-7.30pm daily).

Battistero   BAPTISTERY
(Map p460; Piazza di San Giovanni; admission €4; ◷12.15-7pm Mon-Sat, 8.30am-2pm 1st Sat of month & Sun) Lorenzo Ghiberti designed the famous gilded bronze bas-reliefs adorning the eastern doors of Florence's 11th-century Romanesque baptistry, an octagonal striped structure of white and green marble. Dante counts among the famous dunked in its baptismal font.

The baptistry has three sets of doors, conceived as a series of panels in which the story of humanity and the Redemption would be told. Andrea Pisano executed the southern doors (1330) illustrating the life of St John the Baptist, and Ghiberti won a public competition in 1401 to design the northern doors, but it is his gilded bronze doors at the eastern entrance, known as the Gate of Paradise (Porta del Paradiso), that are the most celebrated. What you see today are copies of the panels.

Museo dell'Opera di Santa Maria del Fiore
MUSEUM
(Cathedral Museum; Map p460; www.operaduomo.firenze.it; Piazza del Duomo 9; admission €6; ⊗9am-6.50pm Mon-Sat, 9am-1pm Sun) Surprisingly overlooked by the crowds, the Cathedral Museum safeguards treasures that once adorned the Duomo, Baptistry and campanile. Make a beeline for the glass-topped courtyard with its awe-inspiring display of seven of the original 10 panels from Ghiberti's glorious masterpiece the *Porta del Paradiso* (Gate of Paradise), designed for the Baptistry. Afterwards search out Michelangelo's *Pietà,* intended for his own tomb.

PIAZZA DELLA SIGNORIA
The hub of the city's political life and surrounded by some of its most celebrated buildings, this lovely cafe-lined piazza is a favourite *passeggiata* (evening stroll) choice for Florentines who saunter around it in the early evening and all day on weekends.

It was on this crowd-packed square, pierced at its centre by an equestrian statue of Cosimo I by Giambologna, that preacher-leader Savonarola set light to the city's art – books, paintings, musical instruments, mirrors, fine clothes and so on – on his famous bonfire of vanities in 1497. A year later the Dominican monk was burnt as a heretic on the same spot, marked by a bronze plaque in front of Ammannati's monumental but ugly Fontana di Nettuno (Neptune Fountain).

Palazzo Vecchio
PALAZZO
(Map p460; www.palazzovecchio-museoragazzi.it; Piazza della Signoria; adult/reduced €6/4.50; ⊗9am-7pm Mon-Wed & Fri-Sun, 9am-2pm Thu) As much a symbol of the city as the Duomo is the striking 94m-tall **Torre d'Arnolfo** that crowns the 'Old Palace', the traditional seat of Florentine government. Built by Arnolfo di Cambio between 1298 and 1314 for the Signoria, the highest level of Florentine republican government, the palace became the residence of Cosimo I in the 16th century. It remains the mayor's office today, guarded at its western entrance by a much-photographed copy of Michelangelo's **David** (the original, now in the Galleria dell'Accademia, stood here until 1873).

The series of lavish apartments created for the Medici is well worth seeing, as is the **Salone dei Cinquecento** (16th-Century Room), created within the original building in the 1490s to accommodate the Consiglio dei Cinquecento (Council of Five Hundred)

FLORENCE IN...

Two Days

Start with a coffee on Piazza della Repubblica before hitting the **Uffizi Gallery**. After lunch, head to **Piazza del Duomo** to visit the **cathedral**, **baptistry** and **Museo dell'Opera del Duomo**. After this, you'll deserve an *aperitivo* and dinner. Next morning, follow the walk outlined in the Duomo to Palazzo Strozzi section, then head to San Marco to visit the **Galleria dell'Accademia** and **Museo di San Marco**. For *aperitivo* and dinner, venture across the Arno to the Oltrarno, stopping en route to admire the sunset from the **Ponte Vecchio**, and later **Piazzale Michelangelo**.

Four Days

On day three, explore **Palazzo Pitti**, the **Giardino di Boboli** and the **Giardino di Bardini**. Alternatively, visit the city's major basilicas – **San Lorenzo**, **Santa Croce** and **Santa Maria Novella**. For dinner, enjoy good food and entertainment at **Teatro del Sale**. On day four, take a guided tour of **Palazzo Vecchio** in the morning and explore the city's specialist **shops** in the afternoon.

One Week

With three extra days, you'll be able to fit in gems such as **Cappella Brancacci**, **Cappella di Benozzo** at **Palazzo Medici-Riccardi** and the **Museo del Bargello**. Or take a day trip to **Fiesole**.

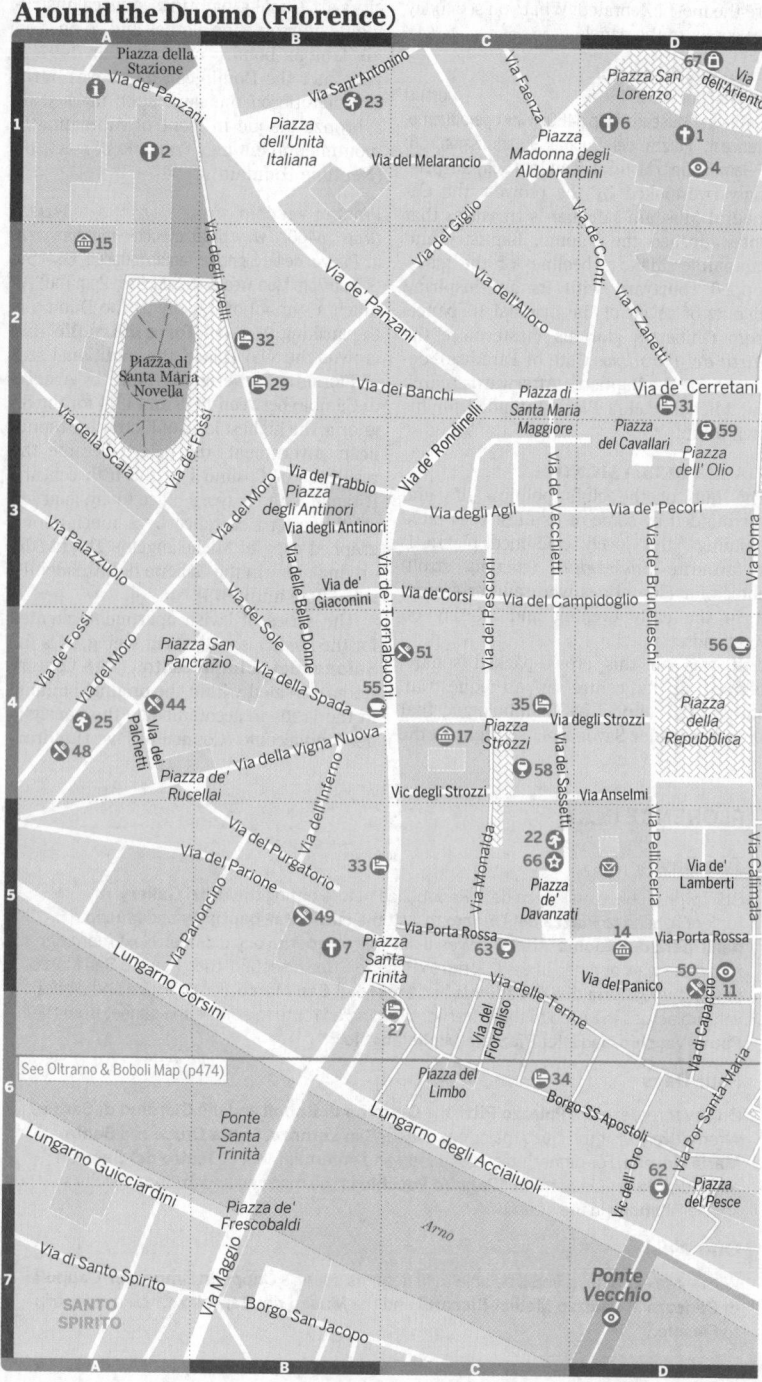

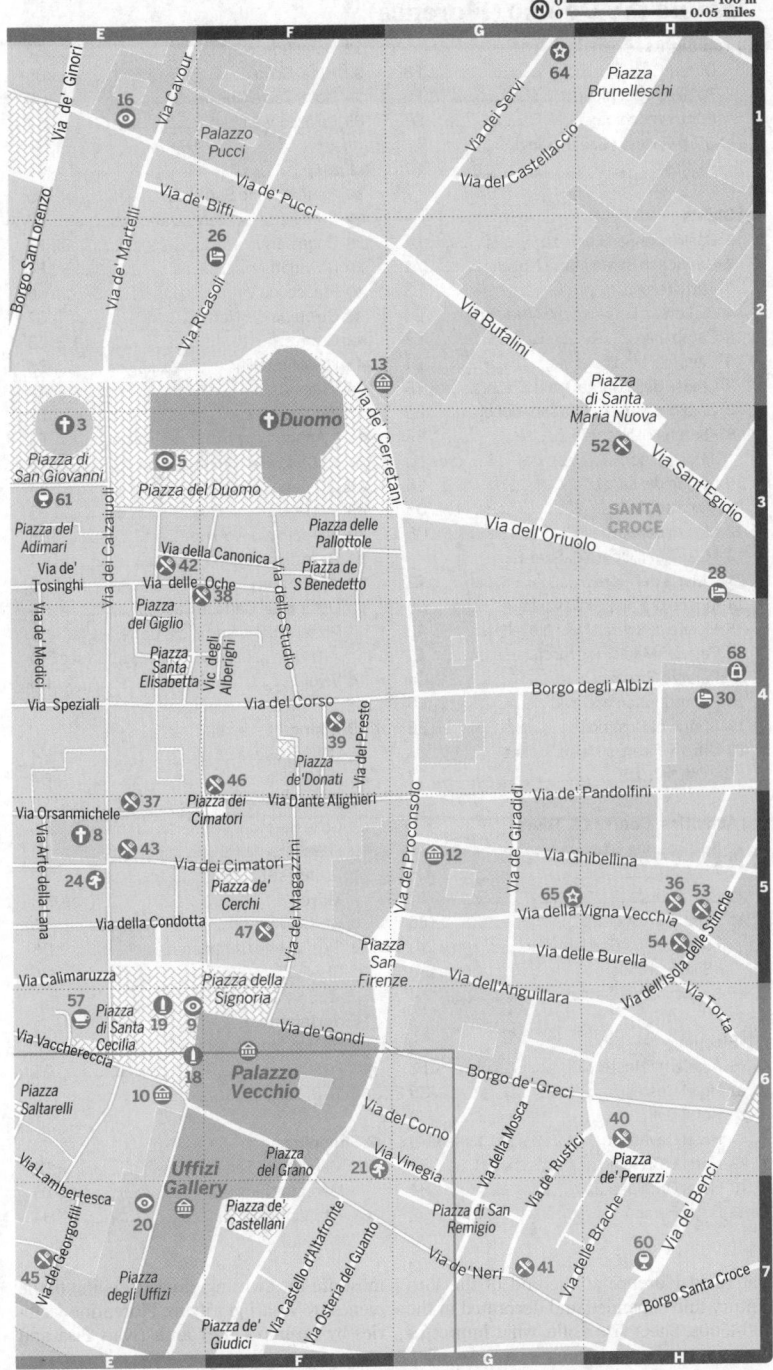

Map labels:

0   100 m
0   0.05 miles

Via de' Ginori
Via Cavour
Borgo San Lorenzo
Palazzo Pucci
Via de' Pucci
Via de' Biffi
Via de' Martelli
Via de' Ricasoli
Via dei Servi
Via del Castellaccio
Piazza Brunelleschi
Via Bufalini
Piazza di Santa Maria Nuova
SANTA CROCE
Via Sant'Egidio
Duomo
Via de' Cerretani
Piazza di San Giovanni
Piazza del Duomo
Via del'Oriuolo
Piazza del Adimari
Via de' Tosinghi
Via della Canonica
Via delle Oche
Piazza delle Pallottole
Piazza de S Benedetto
Via dello Studio
Via de' Medici
Via de' Calzaiuoli
Piazza del Giglio
Piazza Santa Elisabetta
Vic. degli Alberighi
Via Speziali
Via del Corso
Borgo degli Albizi
Via Orsanmichele
Piazza dei Cimatori
Via Dante Alighieri
Via del Presto
Piazza de' Donati
Via de' Pandolfini
Via de' Giraldi
Via Ghibellina
Via Arte della Lana
Via dei Cimatori
Piazza de' Cerchi
Via del Proconsolo
Via della Vigna Vecchia
Via delle Burella
Via della Condotta
Via de' Magazzini
Piazza San Firenze
Via dell'Anguillara
Via dell'Isola delle Stinche
Via Torta
Via Calimaruzza
Piazza della Signoria
Via de' Gondi
Piazza di Santa Cecilia
Via Vaccherecci
Palazzo Vecchio
Borgo de' Greci
Piazza Saltarelli
Via del Corno
Via della Mosca
Piazza de' Peruzzi
Uffizi Gallery
Via Vinegia
Piazza del Grano
Piazza di San Remigio
Via de' Rustici
Via delle Brache
Via de' Benci
Via Lambertesca
Piazza de' Castellani
Via de' Georgofili
Piazza degli Uffizi
Via Castello d'Altafronte
Via Osteria del Guanto
Via de' Neri
Borgo Santa Croce

Numbered markers: 16, 26, 64, 13, 3, 5, 61, 52, 28, 42, 38, 68, 30, 39, 46, 37, 12, 8, 43, 24, 65, 36, 53, 54, 57, 19, 9, 40, 18, 10, 21, 45, 20, 41, 60, 47

that ruled Florence at the end of the 15th century, and expanded and decorated in the mid-1500s. Sheer size aside, what impresses most are the swirling, floor-to-ceiling battle scenes by Vasari glorifying Florentine victories by Cosimo I over arch rivals Pisa and

MUSEUM PASSES

The all-new Firenze Card (www.firenzecard.it; €50) is valid for 72 hours and covers admission to 33 museums (it covers all the biggies), villas and gardens in Florence as well as unlimited use of public transport. Buy it online (and collect upon arrival in Florence) or in Florence at tourist offices or ticketing desks of the Uffizi (Entrance 2), Palazzo Pitti, Palazzo Vecchio, Museo Nazionale del Bargello, Cappella Brancacci, Museo di Santa Maria Novella and Giardini Bardini. If you're an EU citizen your card also covers under-18s travelling with you.

The big downside of the Firenze Card is it only allows one admission per museum. So, for example, if you want to split your Uffizi forays into a couple of visits and/or you're not from the EU and are travelling with kids, the annual Friends of the Uffizi Card (www.amicidegliuffizi.it; adult/under 26yr/family of 4 €60/40/100) is a better deal. Valid for a calendar year (expires 31 December), it covers admission to 22 Florence museums (including Galleria dell'Accademia, Museo Nazionale del Bargello and Palazzo Pitti) and allows as many return visits as you fancy (have your passport on you as proof of ID to show at each museum with your card). Buy online or from the Amici degli Uffizi Welcome Desk (☑055 21 35 60; ⊘10am-5pm Tue-Sat) next to Entrance 2 at the Uffizi.

Siena: unlike the Sienese, the Pisans are depicted bare of armour (play 'Spot the Leaning Tower'). To top off this unabashed celebration of his own power, Cosimo had himself portrayed as a god in the centre of the exquisite panelled ceiling – but not before commissioning Vasari to raise the original ceiling 7m in height. Also in this room is Michelangelo's sculpture *Genius of Victory,* destined for Rome and Pope Julius II's tomb, but left unfinished when he died.

The best way to see this building is by guided tour (obligatory reservations ☑055 276 82 24; info.museoragazzi@comune.fi.it). Around one hour long, these are conducted by English-speaking guides and take you into parts of the building that are not otherwise accessible. Its themed tours for children are particularly appealing.

FREE Loggia dei Lanzi   MUSEUM
(Map p460) What makes this gorgeous square so agreeable is, in part, its wealth of fountains and statues, climaxing with this 14th-century loggia where works such as Giambologna's *Rape of the Sabine Women* (c 1583), Benvenuto Cellini's bronze *Perseus* (1554) and Agnolo Gaddi's *Seven Virtues* (1384–89) are displayed. The loggia owes its name to the Lanzichenecchi (Swiss bodyguards) of Cosimo I, who were stationed here, and the present-day guards live up to this heritage, sternly monitoring crowd behaviour and promptly banishing anyone carrying food or drink.

Galleria degli Uffizi;
Uffizi Gallery   ART GALLERY
(Map p460; www.uffizi.firenze.it; Piazza degli Uffizi 6; adult/reduced €6.50/3.25, incl temporary exhibition €11/5.50; ⊘8.15am-6.50pm Tue-Sun) Housed inside Palazzo degli Uffizi, built between 1560 and 1580 as a government office building, this world-class art museum safeguards the Medici family's private art collection. It was bequeathed to the city in 1743 on the condition that it never leaves Florence.

An ongoing and vastly overdue €65 million refurbishment and redevelopment project will see the addition of a new exit loggia designed by Japanese architect Arato Isozaki and the doubling of exhibition space. In true Italian fashion no one, including architect Antonio Godoli, will commit to a final completion date (originally 2013), but until the so-called Nuovi Uffizi (www.nuoviuffizi. it) project is finished you can expect some rooms to be temporarily closed and the contents of others changed.

The world-famous collection spans the gamut of art history from ancient Greek sculpture to 18th-century Venetian paintings, arranged in chronological order by school. But its core is the masterpiece-rich Renaissance collection.

Visits are best kept to three or four hours max. When it all gets too much, head to the rooftop cafe (aka the terraced hanging garden where the Medici clan listened to music performances on the square below) for fresh air and fabulous views.

The Uffizi

JOURNEY INTO THE RENAISSANCE

Navigating the Uffizi's main art collection, chronologically arranged in 45 rooms on one floor, is straightforward; knowing which of the 1500-odd masterpieces to view before gallery fatigue strikes is not. Swap coat and bag (travel light) for floor plan and audioguide on the ground floor, then meet 16th-century Tuscany head-on with a walk up the palazzo's magnificent bust-lined staircase (skip the lift – the Uffizi is as much about masterly architecture as art).

Allow four hours for this journey into the High Renaissance. At the top of the staircase, 2nd floor, show your ticket, turn left and pause to admire the full length of the first corridor sweeping south towards the river Arno. Then duck left into room 2 to witness first steps in Tuscan art – shimmering altarpieces by **Giotto** 1 et al. Journey through medieval art to room 8 and **Piero della Francesca's** 2 impossibly famous portrait, then break in the corridor with playful **ceiling art** 3. After Renaissance heavyweights **Botticelli** 4 and **da Vinci** 5, meander past the Tribuna (potential detour) and enjoy the daylight streaming in through the vast windows and panorama of the **riverside second corridor** 6. Lap up soul-stirring views of the Arno, crossed by Ponte Vecchio and its echo of four bridges drifting towards the Apuane Alps on the horizon. Then saunter into the third corridor, pausing between rooms 25 and 34 to ponder the entrance to the enigmatic Vasari Corridor. End on a high with High Renaissance maestros **Michelangelo** 7 and **Raphael** 8.

© THE ART ARCHIVE / ALAMY

The Ognissanti Madonna
Room 2
Draw breath at the shy blush and curvaceous breast of Giotto's humanised Virgin (*Maestà;* 1310) – so feminine compared to those of Duccio and Cimabue painted just 25 years before.

Diptych of Duke & Duchess of Urbino
Room 8
Revel in realism's voyage with these uncompromising, warts-and-all portraits (1465–72) by Piero della Francesca. No larger than A3 size, they originally slotted into a portable, hinged frame that folded like a book.

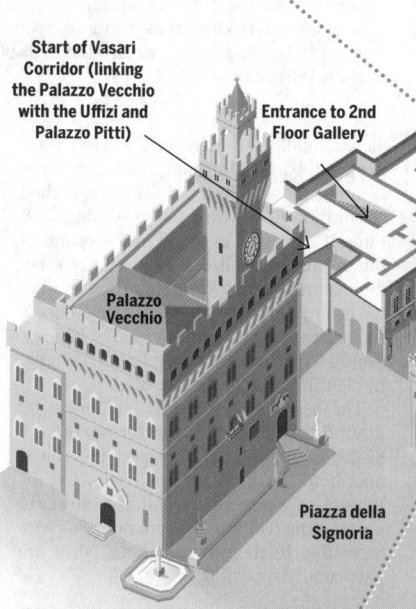

Start of Vasari Corridor (linking the Palazzo Vecchio with the Uffizi and Palazzo Pitti)

Entrance to 2nd Floor Gallery

Palazzo Vecchio

Piazza della Signoria

Grotesque Ceiling Frescoes
First Corridor
Take time to study the make-believe monsters and most unexpected of burlesques (spot the arrow-shooting satyr outside room 15) waltzing across this eastern corridor's fabulous frescoed ceiling (1581).

IMAGE REPRODUCED WITH THE PERMISSION OF MINISTERO PER I BENI E LE ATTIVITÀ CULTURALI

ALINARI ARCHIVES, FLORENCE

The Genius of Botticelli
Room 10–14

The miniature form of *The Discovery of the Body of Holofernes* (c 1470) makes Botticelli's early Renaissance masterpiece all the more impressive. Don't miss the artist watching you in *Adoration of the Magi* (1475), left of the exit.

View of the Arno

Indulge in intoxicating city views from this short glassed-in corridor – an architectural masterpiece. Near the top of the hill, spot one of 73 outer towers built to defend Florence and its 15 city gates below.

Second Corridor

Tribuna

First Corridor

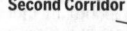

Arno River

Entrance to Vasari Corridor

Third Corridor

Portrait of Pope Leo X
Room 26

Stare into the eyes of the trio in this Raphael masterpiece (1518) and work out what the devil they're thinking – a perfect portrayal of High Renaissance intrigue.

> **Matter of Fact**
>
> The Uffizi collection spans the 13th to 18th centuries, but its 15th- and 16th-century Renaissance works are second to none.

Doni Tondo
Room 25

David's creator, Michelangelo, was essentially a sculptor and no painting expresses this better than *Doni Tondo* (1506–08). Mary's muscular arms against a backdrop of curvaceous nudes are practically 3D in their shapeliness.

Annunciation
Room 15

Admire the exquisite portrayal of the Tuscan landscape in this painting (c 1475–80), one of few by Leonardo da Vinci to remain in Florence.

> **Value Lunchbox**
>
> Try the Uffizi rooftop cafe or – better value – gourmet *panini* at 'Ino (www.ino-firenze.com; Via dei Georgofili 3-7r).

Tuscan Masters: 12th to 14th Centuries

The first room to the left of the staircase (Room 2) highlights 13th-century Sienese art and is designed like a medieval chapel (look up to admire those great wooden ceiling trusses) to reflect its fabulous contents: three large altarpieces from Florentine churches by Tuscan masters Duccio di Buoninsegna, Cimabue and Giotto. These clearly reflect the transition from the Gothic to the nascent Renaissance style. Note the overtly naturalistic realism overtones in Giotto's portrayal of the Madonna and child among angels and saints.

The next room stays in Siena but moves into the 14th century. The highlight is Simone Martini's shimmering *Annunciation* (1333), painted with Lippo Memmi and setting the Madonna in a sea of gold. Also of note is the *Madonna with Child and Saints* triptych (1340) by Pietro Lorenzetti, which demonstrates a realism similar to Giotto's; unfortunately both Pietro and his artistic brother Ambrogio died from the plague in Siena in 1348.

Masters in 14th-century Florence paid as much attention to detail as their Sienese counterparts, as works in the next room demonstrate: savour the realism of *San Reminio Pietà* (1360–65) by gifted Giotto pupil, Giottino.

Renaissance Pioneers

A concern for perspective was a hallmark of the early-15th-century Florentine school (room 7) that pioneered the Renaissance. One panel (the other two are in the Louvre and London's National Gallery) from Paolo Uccello's striking *Battle of San Romano* shows the artist's efforts to create perspective with amusing effect as he directs the lances, horses and soldiers to a central disappearing point. The painting celebrates Florence's victory over Siena.

In room 8, the highlights are Piero della Francesca's famous profile portraits of the crooked-nosed, red-robed Duke and Duchess of Urbino (1465–72) – the former always painted left-side after losing his right eye in a jousting accident and the latter painted a deathly white, reflecting the fact that the portrait was painted posthumously.

Carmelite monk Fra' Filippo Lippi had an unfortunate soft spot for earthly pleasures, scandalously marrying a nun from Prato. Search out his self-portrait as a podgy friar in *Coronation of the Virgin* (1439–47) and don't miss his later *Madonna and Child*

with Two Angels (1460–65), an exquisite work that clearly influenced his pupil, Sandro Botticelli.

Another related pair, brothers Antonio and Piero del Pollaiolo, fill room 9, where their seven cardinal and theological values of 15th-century Florence – commissioned for the merchant's tribunal in Piazza della Signoria – ooze energy.

Botticelli Room

The spectacular Sala del Botticelli, numbered 10 to 14 but in fact one large hall, is one of the Uffizi's most popular rooms and is always packed. Of the 15 works by the Renaissance master, *Birth of Venus* (c 1485), *Primavera* (Spring; c 1482), the deeply spiritual *Cestello Annunciation* (1489–90), the *Adoration of the Magi* (1475) featuring the artist's self-portrait (look for the blonde-haired guy, extreme right, dressed in yellow) and *The Madonna of the Magnificat* (1483) are the best known, but true aficionados rate his twin set of miniatures depicting a sword-bearing Judith returning from the camp of Holofernes and the discovery of the decapitated Holofernes in his tent (1495–1500) as being among his finest works.

Leonardo Room

Room 15 displays two early Florentine works by Leonardo da Vinci: the incomplete *Adoration of the Magi* (1481–82), drawn in red earth pigment, and his *Annunciation* (c 1475–80).

High Renaissance to Mannerism

In the third corridor, Michelangelo dazzles with the *Doni Tondo,* a depiction of the Holy Family that steals the High Renaissance show in room 25. The composition is unusual – Joseph holding an exuberant Jesus on his muscled mother's shoulder as she twists round to gaze at him, the colours as vibrant as when they were first applied in 1506–08.

Raphael (1483–1520) and Andrea del Sarto (1486–1530) rub shoulders in room 26, where Raphael's charming *Madonna of the Goldfinch* (1505–06) holds centre stage.

Previous works by Tuscan masters can be compared with the greater naturalism inherent in the work of their Venetian counterparts in room 28, where 11 Titians are displayed. Masterpieces include the sensual nude *Venus of Urbino* (1538), the seductive *Flora* (1515) and the striking portrait of *Eleonora Gonzaga, Duchess of Urbino* (1536–37).

CUT THE QUEUE: PRE-BOOKED TICKETS

In July, August and other busy periods such as Easter, unbelievably long queues are a fact of life at Florence's key museums – if you haven't pre-booked your ticket in advance you could well end up standing in line queuing for four hours or so.

For a fee of €3 per ticket (€4 for the Uffizi and Galleria dell'Accademia), tickets to all 13 *musei statali* (state museums) can be reserved, including the Uffizi, Galleria dell'Accademia (where *David* lives), Palazzo Pitti, Museo del Bargello and the Medicean chapels (Cappelle Medicee). In reality, the only museums where pre-booking is vital are the Uffizi and Accademia – to organise your ticket, go to www.firenzemusei.it or call **Firenze Musei** (Florence Museums; ☎055 29 48 83; ☺telephone booking line 8.30am-6.30pm Mon-Fri, 8.30am-12.30pm Sat), with **ticketing desks** (☺8.30am-7pm Tue-Sun) at the Uffizi and Palazzo Pitti.

At the Uffizi, signs point pre-booked-ticket holders to the building opposite the gallery where pre-booked tickets can be collected; once you've got the ticket you go to Door One of the museum (for pre-booked tickets only) and queue again to enter the gallery. It's annoying, but you'll still save hours of queuing time overall.

Many hotels in Florence also pre-book museum tickets for guests.

AROUND PIAZZA DELLA REPUBBLICA

Piazza della Repubblica   CITY SQUARE

(Map p460) Originally the site of a Roman forum and the heart of medieval Florence, this busy civic space was created in the late 1880s as part of a controversial plan of 'civic improvements' involving the demolition of the old market, Jewish ghetto and surrounding slums, and the relocation of nearly 6000 residents. Fortunately, Vasari's lovely Loggia del Pesce (Fish Market) was saved and re-erected on Via Pietrapiana. Today, the piazza is known for its concentration of historic cafes.

⌂ TOP CHOICE Chiesa e Museo di Orsanmichele   CHURCH, MUSEUM

(Map p460; Via dell'Arte della Lana; admission free; ☺church 10am-5pm daily, museum 10am-5pm Mon) This unique church was created when the arcades of an old grain market (1290) were walled in and two storeys added during the 14th century. A real must-see, its exterior is exquisitely decorated with niches and tabernacles bearing statues. Representing the patron saints of Florence's many guilds, they were commissioned in the 15th and 16th centuries after the *signoria* (city government) ordered the city's guilds to finance the church's decoration.

These statues represent the work of some of the greatest Renaissance artists. Only copies adorn the building's exterior today but all the originals except one are beautifully displayed in the church's impressive, little-known and thoroughly inspirational **museum**, open just one day a week in two floors above the church.

Museo di Palazzo Davanzati   HISTORICAL RESIDENCE

(Map p460; Via Porta Rossa 13; adult/reduced €2/1; ☺8.15am-1.50pm, closed 1st, 3rd & 5th Mon, 2nd & 4th Sun of month) Tucked inside a 14th-century warehouse and home of the wealthy Davanzati merchant family from 1578, this palace-museum is a less-visited gem. Peep at the carved faces of the original owners on the pillars in the inner courtyard and don't miss the 1st-floor reception room with its painted wooden ceiling or the exquisitely decorated Sala dei Pappagalli (Parrot Room) and Camera dei Pavoni (Peacock Bedroom).

Palazzo Strozzi   PALAZZO, MUSEUM

(Map p460; Via de' Tornabuoni; admission prices & opening hr vary) Aplomb on Florence's most legendary fashion street, **Via de' Tornabuoni**, often called the 'Salotto di Firenze' (Florence's Drawing Room), sits this magnificent 15th-century palace with wonderful interior courtyard where seemingly half of Florence meets and mingles. The palace was built for wealthy merchant Filippo Strozzi and hosts blockbuster exhibitions. There's always a buzz around this place, with young Florentines congregating in the courtyard cafe.

⌂ TOP CHOICE Museo del Bargello   ART GALLERY

(Map p460; Via del Proconsolo 4; adult/reduced €7/3.50; ☺8.15am-5pm Tue-Sun & 1st & 3rd Mon of month) It was behind the stark exterior of Palazzo del Bargello, Florence's earliest public building, that the *podestà* meted out justice from the late 13th century until 1502. Today the building is home to Italy's most

GUARANTEED RETURN

To ensure a return trip to Florence local legend says you must rub the bronze snout of **Il Porcellino** (The Piglet), aka the bronze statue of a wild boar on the southern side of Florence's 16th-century marketplace, **Mercato Nuovo** (Map p460; Piazza di Mercato Nuovo).

comprehensive collection of Tuscan Renaissance sculpture.

Crowds clamour to see *David* in the Galleria dell'Accademia but few rush to see his creator's early works, many of which are on display in the Bargello's downstairs **Sala di Michelangelo**. The artist was just 21 when a cardinal commissioned him to create the drunken, grape-adorned *Bacchus* (1496–97) displayed here. Other Michelangelo works to look out for include the marble bust of *Brutus* (c 1539–40), the *David/Apollo* from 1530–32 and the large, uncompleted roundel of the *Madonna and Child with the Infant St John* (1503–05, aka the *Tondo Pitti*).

On the 1st floor, to the right of the staircase, is the Sala di Donatello where Donatello's two versions of *David* fascinate: Donatello fashioned his slender, youthful, dressed image in marble in 1408 and his fabled bronze between 1440 and 1450. The latter is extraordinary – the more so when you consider it was the first free-standing naked statue to be sculpted since classical times.

SANTA MARIA NOVELLA AREA

Basilica di Santa Maria Novella CHURCH
(Map p460; Piazza di Santa Maria Novella; admission €3.50; ⊗9am-5.50pm Mon-Thu, 11am-5.30pm Fri, 9am-5pm Sat, 1-5pm Sun) Just south of the central train station, this church was begun in the mid-13th century as the Dominican order's Florentine base. The lower section of the marble facade is transitional from Romanesque to Gothic, while the upper section (1470) and main doorway were designed by Alberti. The highlight of the Gothic interior, halfway along the north aisle, is Masaccio's superb fresco *Trinity* (1424–25), one of the first art works to use the then newly discovered techniques of perspective and proportion. Close by, hanging in the nave, is a luminous painted *Crucifix* by Giotto (c 1290).

Museo di Santa Maria Novella MUSEUM
(Map p460; Piazza di Santa Maria Novella; adult/reduced €2.70/2; ⊗9am-5pm Mon-Thu & Sat) The indisputable highlight of this museum – arranged around the monastery's tranquil **Chiostro Verde** (Green Cloister; 1332–62) which takes its name from the green earth base used for the frescoes on three of the cloister's four walls – is the spectacular **Cappellone degli Spagnoli** (Spanish Chapel). The chapel is covered in extraordinary frescoes (c 1365–67) by Andrea di Bonaiuto. The vault features depictions of the *Resurrection, Ascension* and *Pentecost* and on the altar wall are scenes of the *Via Dolorosa, Crucifixion* and *Descent into Limbo*. On the right wall is a huge fresco of *The Militant and Triumphant Church* – look in the foreground for a portrait of Cimabue, Giotto, Boccaccio, Petrarch and Dante. Other frescoes in the chapels depict the *Triumph of Christian Doctrine,* 14 figures symbolising the Arts and Sciences and the *Life of St Peter*.

On the west side of the cloister, a passage leads to the 14th-century **Cappella degli Ubriachi** and a large **refectory** featuring ecclesiastical relics and a 1583 *Last Supper* by Alessandro Allori.

FREE **Officina Profumo-Farmaceutica di Santa Maria Novella** PHARMACY
(www.santamarianovella.com.br; Via della Scala 16; ⊗9.30am-7.30pm Mon-Sat, 10.30am-8.30pm Sun, museum 10am-5.30pm Mon-Fri) In business since 1612, this perfumery-pharmacy is famed for the remedies and sweet-smelling unguents it concocts using medicinal herbs cultivated in the monastery garden. The shop has changed little over the centuries and is an absolute treasure. After a day battling crowds at the Uffizi or Accademia, you may want to come here to source some Acqua di Santa Maria Novella, said to cure hysterics.

Chiesa della Santa Trìnita CHURCH
(Map p460; Piazza Santa Trìnita; admission free; ⊗8am-noon & 4-6pm Mon-Sat, 4-6pm Sun) This 14th-century church was rebuilt in Gothic style and later graced with a mannerist facade. Eye-catching frescoes by Domenico Ghirlandaio depict the life of St Francis of Assisi in the south transept's Cappella Sassetti. Lorenzo Monaco, Fra' Angelico's master, painted the altarpiece in the fourth chapel on the south aisle and the frescoes on the chapel walls.

SAN LORENZO AREA

Basilica di San Lorenzo CHURCH

(Map p460; Piazza San Lorenzo; admission €3.50, incl biblioteca €6; ⏱10am-5.30pm Mon-Sat year-round, 1.30-5.30pm Sun Mar-Oct) In 1425 the Medici commissioned Brunelleschi to re-build what would become the family's parish church and funeral chapter: 50-odd Medici are buried inside this church, one of the most harmonious examples of Renaissance architecture. However, it looks nothing from the outside: Michelangelo was commissioned to design the facade in 1518 but his design in white Carrara marble was never executed, hence its rough unfinished appearance.

Inside, columns of *pietra serena* (soft grey stone) crowned with Corinthian capitals separate the nave from the two aisles. Donatello, who was still sculpting the two bronze pulpits adorned with panels of the Crucifixion when he died, is buried in the chapel featuring Fra' Filippo Lippi's *Annunciation* (c 1450). Left of the altar is the **Sagrestia Vecchia** (Old Sacristy), designed by Brunelleschi and decorated in the main by Donatello.

Biblioteca Laurenziana Medicea LIBRARY

(Map p460; www.bml.firenze.sbn.it; Piazza San Lorenzo 9; admission €3, incl basilica €6; ⏱9.30am-1.30pm Mon-Fri) To the left of the basilica's entrance are peaceful cloisters, off which an extraordinary staircase designed by Michelangelo leads to the Biblioteca Laurenziana Medicea, commissioned by Giulio de' Medici (Pope Clement VII) in 1524 to house the extensive Medici library that had been started by Cosimo the Elder and greatly added to by Lorenzo il Magnifico.

Cappelle Medicee MAUSOLEUM

(Map p460; Piazza Madonna degli Aldobrandini; adult/reduced €6/3; ⏱8.15am-4.50pm Tue-Sat & 1st, 3rd Sun & 2nd, 4th Mon of month) Nowhere is Medici conceit expressed so explicitly as in this mausoleum. Principal burial place of the Medici rulers, it's sumptuously adorned with granite, the most precious marble, semiprecious stones and some of Michelangelo's most beautiful sculptures. Francesco I lies in the **Cappella dei Principi** (Princes' Chapel) alongside Ferdinando I and II and Cosimo I, II and III. From here, a corridor leads to the stark but graceful **Sagrestia Nuova** (New Sacristy), Michelangelo's first architectural work and showcase for three of his most haunting sculptures: *Dawn and Dusk, Night and Day* and *Madonna and Child*.

Palazzo Medici-Riccardi PALAZZO, CHAPEL

(Map p460; www.palazzo-medici.it; Via Cavour 3; adult/reduced €7/4; ⏱9am-7pm Thu-Tue) Just off Piazza San Lorenzo is this lovely palace, the principal Medici residence until 1540 and the prototype for other *palazzi* (mansions) in the city. Inside, the **Capella di Benozzo** (Chapel of the Magi) houses one of the supreme achievements of Renaissance painting and is an absolute must-see for art lovers. The tiny space is covered in a series of wonderfully detailed and recently restored frescoes (c 1459-63) by Benozzo Gozzoli, a pupil of Fra' Angelico. His ostensible theme of *Procession of the Magi to Bethlehem* is but a slender pretext for portraying members of the Medici clan in their best light; try to spy Lorenzo il Magnifico and Cosimo the Elder in the crowd. Only 10 visitors are allowed into the chapel at a time, for a maximum of just five minutes; reserve your slot in advance at the palace ticket desk.

Central Market MARKET

(Piazza del Mercato Centrale; ⏱7am-2pm Mon-Fri, to 5pm Sat) Housed in a 19th-century iron-and-glass structure, Florence's oldest and largest food market is noisy, smelly and full of wonderful fresh produce to cook and eat.

SAN MARCO AREA

This part of the city boasts far more than the city's most famous resident, one Sig David.

Galleria dell'Accademia ART GALLERY

(Map p470; ☏055 294 883; Via Ricasoli 60; adult/reduced €6.50/3.25; ⏱8.15am-6.50pm Tue-Sun) A lengthy queue marks the door to this gallery where Michelangelo's *David* is displayed. Fortunately, the most famous statue in the world is worth the long wait. Carved from a single block of marble, the statue of the nude warrior assumed its pedestal in front of Palazzo Vecchio on Piazza della Signoria in 1504, providing Florentines with a powerful emblem of power, liberty and civic pride.

Adjacent rooms contain paintings by Andrea Orcagna, Taddeo Gaddi, Domenico Ghirlandaio, Filippino Lippi and Sandro Botticelli.

Museo di San Marco MUSEUM

(Map p470; Piazza San Marco 1; adult/reduced €4/2; ⏱8.15am-1.50pm Mon-Fri, 8.15am-4.50pm Sat & Sun, closed 1st, 3rd, 5th Sun & 2nd, 4th Mon of month) At the heart of Florence's univer-

San Marco (Florence)

sity area sits the Chiesa di San Marco and adjoining 15th-century Dominican monastery where gifted painter Fra' Angelico (c 1395–1455) and sharp-tongued Savonarola piously served God. Today, the monastery showcases the work of Fra' Angelico. It is one of Florence's most spiritually uplifting museums.

Enter via Michelozzo's **Cloister of Saint Antoninus** (1440). Turn immediately right to enter the **Sala dell'Ospizio** (Pilgrims' Hospital), where Fra' Angelico's attention to perspective and the realistic portrayal of nature comes to life in a number of major paintings, including the *Deposition of Christ* (1432). On the 1st floor, Fra' Angelico's most famous work, *Annunciation* (c 1450), commands all eyes, and a stroll around the monks' living quarters reveals snippets of many more fine religious reliefs by the Tuscan-born friar, who decorated the cells between 1440 and 1441 with deeply devotional frescoes to guide the meditation of his fellow friars. Among several masterpieces is the magnificent *Adoration of the Magi* in the cell used by Cosimo the Elder as a meditation retreat (No 38 & 39). Quite a few frescoes are extremely gruesome – check out the cell of San Antonino Arcivescovo, which features a depiction of Jesus pushing open the door of his sepulchre, squashing a nasty-looking devil in the process.

Piazza della Santissima
Annunziata
CITY SQUARE

(Map p470) Giambologna's equestrian statue of Grand Duke Ferdinando I de' Medici commands the scene from the centre of this square, which teems with students.

Across the street **Chiesa della Santissima Annunziata** was established in 1250 by the founders of the Servite order, and rebuilt by Michelozzo and others in the mid-15th century.

The **Spedale degli Innocenti** (Hospital of the Innocents) was founded on the south-eastern side of the piazza in 1421 as Europe's first orphanage. Brunelleschi designed the classically influenced portico, which Andrea della Robbia (1435–1525) famously decorated with terracotta medallions of babies in swaddling clothes. At the north end of the portico, the false door surrounded by railings was once a revolving door where unwanted children were left.

Inside, the **Museo dello Spedale degli Innocenti** (Map p470; www.istitutodeglinnocenti. it; Piazza della Santissima Annunziata 12; adult/reduced €5/4; ⊙10am-7pm) displays works by Florentine artists, including Domenico Ghirlandaio's striking *Adoration of the Magi* (1488), two wonderfully serene wooden sculptures of the *Madonna* and *St Joseph* by Marco della Robbia (c 1505) and a *Madonna with Holy Child and Angel* (1465–66) by Botticelli. Less valuable, but even more moving, is the display case of 19th-century markers left on the clothing of abandoned babies to allow for eventual reunification with their mothers.

Museo Archeologico

(Map p470; Via della Colonna 38; adult/reduced €4/2; ⊙8.30am-7pm Tue-Fri) About 200m southeast of the piazza is this museum, whose rich collection of finds, including most of the Medici hoard of antiquities, plunges you deep into the past and offers an alternative to Renaissance splendour.

SANTA CROCE

Presided over by the massive Franciscan basilica of the same name on the neighbourhood's main square, this area has a slightly rough veneer to it.

Basilica di Santa Croce   CHURCH
(Map p472; Piazza di Santa Croce; adult/reduced incl Museo dell'Opera di Santa Croce €5/3, audioguide 1/2 people €5/7; ⊙9.30am-5.30pm Mon-Sat, 1-5.30pm Sun) When Lucy Honeychurch, the heroine of EM Forster's *A Room With a View,* is stranded in Santa Croce without a Baedeker, she panics and then, looking around, wonders why the basilica is thought to be such an important building. After all, doesn't it look just like a barn ('a black and white facade of surprising ugliness')? On

entering, many visitors to this massive Franciscan church share the same sentiment. The austere interior *is* a shock after the magnificent neo-Gothic facade.

Though most visitors come to see the tombs of famous Florentines buried inside this church – including Michelangelo, Galileo, Ghiberti and Machiavelli – it's the frescoes by Giotto and his school in the chapels to the right of the altar that are the real highlight. Some of these are substantially better preserved than others.

From the transept chapels a doorway designed by Michelozzo leads into a corridor, off which is the **Sagrestia**, an enchanting 14th-century room dominated on the left by Taddeo Gaddi's fresco of the Crucifixion. There are also a few relics of St Francis on show, including his cowl and belt. Through the next room, the church bookshop, you can access the **Scuola del Cuoio**, a leather school and shop.

The second of Santa Croce's two serene **cloisters** was designed by Brunelleschi just before his death in 1446. His unfinished **Cappella de' Pazzi** at the end of the first cloister is notable for its harmonious lines and restrained terracotta medallions of the Apostles by Luca della Robbia, and is a masterpiece of Renaissance architecture.

Located off the first cloister, the **Museo dell'Opera di Santa Croce** features a *Crucifixion* by Cimabue; a wonderful terracotta bust of St Francis receiving the stigmata by the della Robbia workshop; and frescoes by Taddeo Gaddi, including *The Last Supper* (1333).

THE OLTRARNO
Literally 'Beyond the Arno', the atmospheric Oltrarno takes in all of Florence south of the river.

Ponte Vecchio   LANDMARK
(Map p460) Florence's iconic bridge has twinkled with the glittering wares of jewellers since the 16th century when Ferdinando I de' Medici ordered them here to replace the often malodorous presence of the town butchers, who were wont to toss unwanted leftovers into the river.

The bridge as it stands was built in 1345 and was the only one in Florence saved from destruction by the retreating Germans in 1944. At the southern end of the bridge is the medieval **Torre dei Mannelli**, which looks rather odd, as the **Corridoio Vasariano** was built around it – not

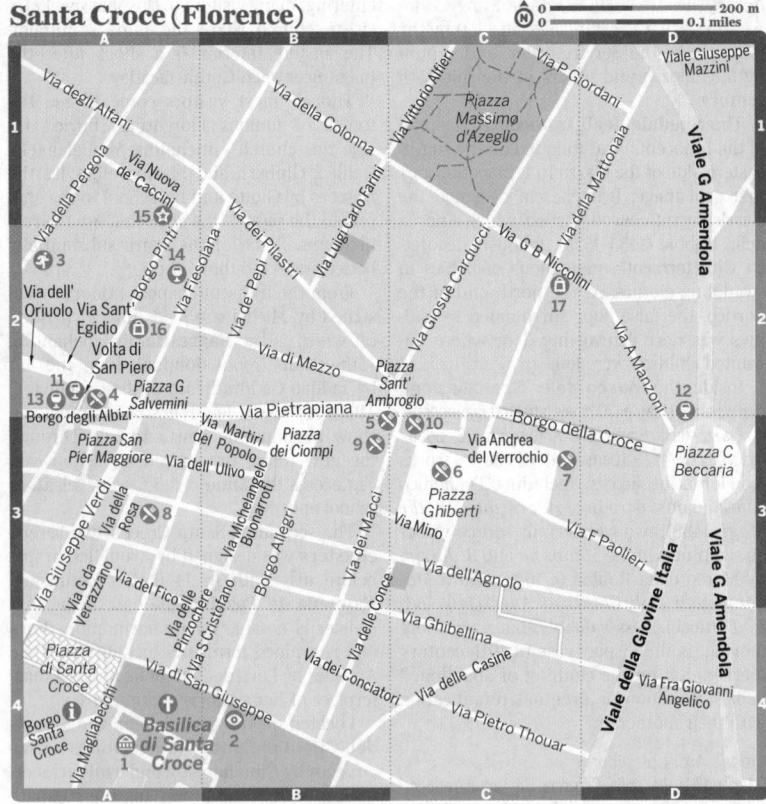

Santa Croce (Florence)

simply straight through it as the Medici would have preferred.

Palazzo Pitti PALAZZO, MUSEUM
(Map p474; Piazza de' Pitti 1; adult €7-12, 3-day ticket valid when no temporary exhibition €11.50) This vast palace was begun in 1458 for the Pitti family, rivals of the Medici. Cosimo I and Eleonora di Toledo acquired it in 1549 and it remained the official residence of Florence's rulers until 1919 when the Savoys gave it to the state.

The ground-floor **Museo degli Argenti** (Silver Museum; ⊙8.15am-7.30pm Jun-Aug, shorter hr rest of year, closed 1st & last Mon of month) hosts temporary exhibitions in its elaborately frescoed audience chambers.

Raphaels and Rubens vie for centre stage in the enviable collection of 16th- to 18th-century art amassed by the Medici and Lorraine dukes in the 1st-floor **Galleria Palatina** (⊙8.15am-6.50pm Tue-Sun). Highlights include Filippo Lippi's *Madonna and Child with Stories from the Life of St Anne* (aka the *Tondo Bartolini;* 1452–53) and Botticelli's *Madonna with Child and a Young Saint John the Baptist* (c 1490–95) in the Sala di Prometeo; Raphael's *Madonna of the Window* (1513–14) in the Sala di Ulisse; and Caravaggio's *Sleeping Cupid* (1608) in the Sala dell'Educazione di Giove. Don't miss the Sala di Saturno, full of magnificent works by Raphael. The sentimental favourite, Tiberio Titi's charming portrait of the young Prince Leopoldo de' Medici, hangs in the Sala di Apollo and the Sala di Venere shines with Titian's *Portrait of a Lady* (c 1536).

Past the Sala di Venere are the **Appartamenti Reali** (Royal Apartments; ⊙8.15am-6.50pm Tue-Sun Feb-Dec), a series of rooms presented as they were c 1880–91, when they were occupied by members of the House of Savoy. The style and division of tasks assigned to each room is reminiscent of Spanish royal palaces, all heavily bedecked with drapes, silk and chandeliers.

Forget about Marini, Mertz or Clemente – the collection of the 2nd-floor **Galleria d'Arte Moderna** (Gallery of Modern Art; ⊙8.15am-6.50pm Tue-Sun) is dominated by late-19th-century works by artists of the

THE EXTRAORDINARY VASARI CORRIDOR

Look above the jewellery shops on the eastern side of Ponte Vecchio and what you see, most dramatically at sunset, is the infamous and enigmatic **Corridoio Vasariano** (Vasari Corridor; Map p474), an extraordinary elevated covered passageway joining the Palazzo Vecchio on Piazza della Signoria with the Uffizi and Palazzo Pitti on the other side of the river. Around 1km long, it was designed by Vasari for Cosimo I in 1565 to allow the Medicis and court's high dignitaries to wander between the two palaces in privacy and comfort. From the 17th century, the Medicis strung it wiith self-portraits – a collection of 700-odd art works today that includes self-portraits of Andrea del Sarto (the oldest), Rubens, Rembrandt, Canova and others.

The original promenade incorporated tiny windows (facing the river) and circular apertures (facing the street) to ensure the safety of those who used it. But when Hitler visited Florence in 1941, his mate and fellow dictator Benito Mussolini had big new windows punched into the corridor walls on Ponte Vecchio so that his guest could enjoy an expansive view down the Arno from the famous Florentine bridge.

On the Oltrarno the corridor passed by **Chiesa di Santa Felicità** (Map p474; Piazza di Santa Felicità; admission free; ⊙9.30am-noon & 1.30-5.30pm Mon-Sat), thereby providing the Medici with a private balcony in the church where they could likewise attend Mass without mingling with the minions.

The Vasari Corridor is open to just a privileged few – see p464 for spots in the Uffizi and elsewhere where you can get a sneak peek at it. To visit it, either join a guided tour of just five people (in Italian only) sporadically organised by **Firenze Musei** (p467; €15 incl Uffizi admission & booking fee) – tours are advertised in advance on the Uffizi website (www.uffizi.firenze.it); or pay the price for an English-language tour in a group of 15 organised by **Florence Town** (☑055 012 39 94; www.florencetown.com; Via de' Lamberti 1; adult/6-12yr incl Uffizi admission €89/45; ⊙two to three times weekly). Whichever option you plump for, reserve well in advance.

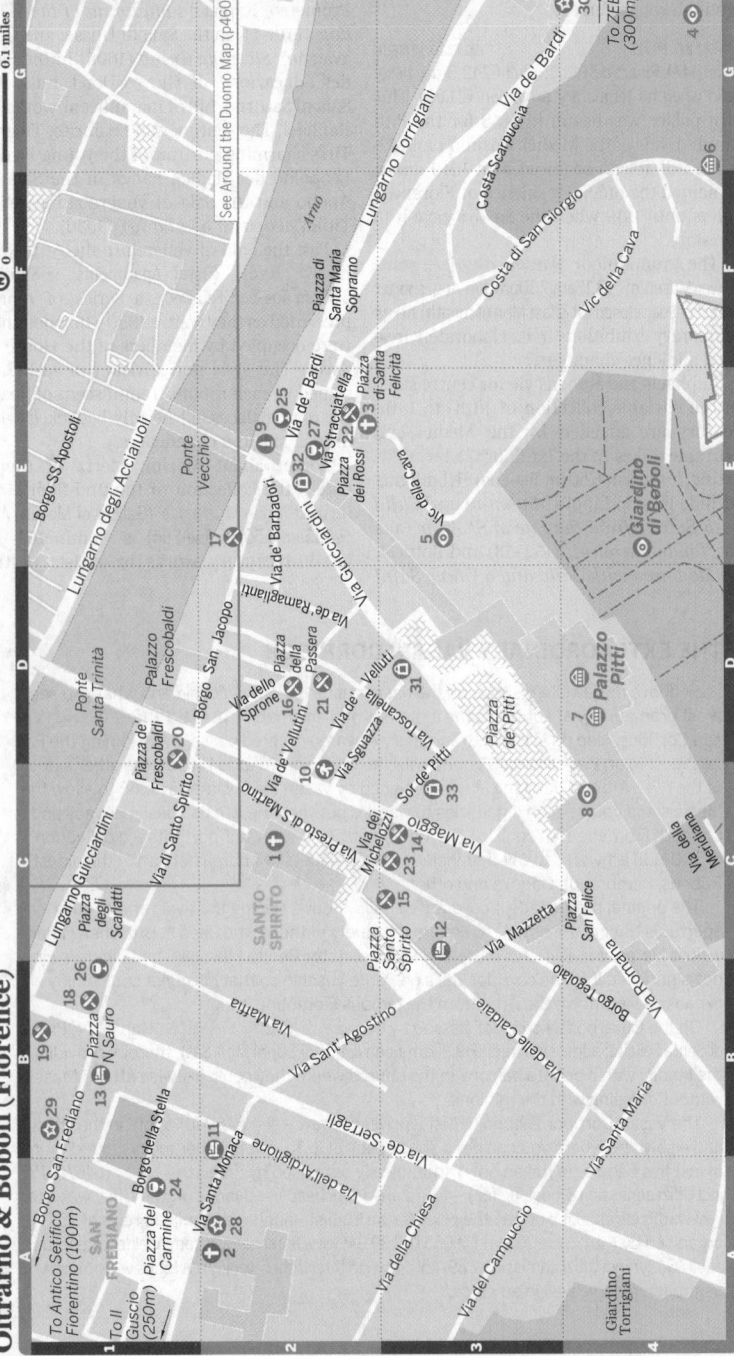

FLORENCE & TUSCANY SIGHTS

Florentine Macchiaioli school (the local equivalent of Impressionism).

Few visitors visit the **Galleria del Costume** (Costume Gallery; ◷8.15am-7.30pm Jun-Aug, shorter hr rest of year, closed 1st & last Mon of month), thus missing its fascinating, if somewhat macabre, display of the semi-decomposed burial clothes of Cosimo I, his wife Eleonora di Toledo and their son Don Garzia.

FREE **Giardino di Boboli**   PALAZZO, GARDEN
(Piazza Pitti; ◷8.15am-sunset) The palace's expansive gardens were laid out in the mid-16th century according to a design by architect Niccolò Pericoli, aka Il Tribolo.

Boboli is a prime example of a formal Tuscan garden and is fun to explore: skip along **Cypress Alley**; let the imagination rip with a gallant frolic in the walled **Giardino del Cavaliere** (Knights' Garden); dance around 170-odd statues; meditate next to the **Isoletto**, a gorgeous ornamental pond; discover species and birdsong in the garden along the signposted **nature trail**; or watch a fleshy *Venere* (Venus) by Giambologna rise from the waves in the **Grotta del Buontalenti** (guided visits hourly).

At the upper, southern limit of the gardens, fantastic views over the palace complex and Florentine countryside fan out beyond the box-hedged **rose garden**, overlooked by the **Museo delle Porcellane**, home to Sèvres, Vincennes, Meissen, Wedgwood and other porcelain pieces collected by Palazzo Pitti's wealthy tenants.

Giardino di Bardini   GARDEN
(Map p474; www.bardinipeyron.it; entrances at Via de' Bardi 1r & Costa San Giorgio 2; adult/reduced incl Museo delle Porcellane €10/5; ◷8.15am-sunset) Florence's little-known Giardino Bardini was named after art collector Stefano Bardini (1836–1922), who bought the villa in 1913. Smaller and more manicured than the Boboli, it has all the features of a quintessential Tuscan garden – artificial grottos, orangery, marble statues, fountains, loggia, amphitheatre and a monumental baroque stone staircase staggering up the beautiful tiered gardens – but not the crowds. A springtime stroll is an extra-special joy when its azaleas, peonies, wisteria (April and May)

and irises (June) are all in bloom. Its somewhat idyllic, summer **cafe terrace**, set in a stone loggia overlooking the Florentine skyline, is a wonderful spot for a *panino* lunch, ice cream or afternoon tea.

Inside the villa the **Museo Bardini** (www. bardinipeyron.it, in Italian; adult/reduced €6/4; ⊘10am-6pm Wed-Sun Apr-Sep, to 4pm Wed-Fri, to 6pm Sat & Sun Oct-Mar) hosts a collection of Roberto Capucci–designed haute couture and temporary exhibitions.

Piazzale Michelangelo   VIEWPOINT

Turn your back on the bevy of ticky-tacky souvenir stalls flogging *David* boxer shorts and take in the soaring city panorama from this vast square, pierced by one of Florence's two *David* copies. Sunset here is dramatic. It's a 10-minute uphill walk along the serpentine road, paths and steps that scale the hillside from the river and Piazza Giuseppe Poggi; from Piazza San Nicolò walk uphill and bear left up the long flight of steps signposted Viale Michelangelo; by bus, take No 13 from Stazione di Santa Maria Novella.

Chiesa di San Miniato al Monte   CHURCH, VIEWPOINT

(Via Monte alle Croce; ⊘8am-7pm May-Oct, 8am-noon & 3-6pm Nov-Apr) The real point of your exertions up to Piazzale Michelangelo is five minutes further uphill to this wonderful Romanesque church. It is dedicated to St Minius, an early-Christian martyr in Florence who is said to have flown to this spot after his death down in the town (or, if you want to believe an alternative version, walked up the hill head tucked underneath his arm).

The church dates to the early 11th century, although its typical Tuscan multicoloured marble facade was tacked on a couple of centuries later. Inside, 13th- to 15th-century frescoes adorn the south wall and intricate inlaid marble designs line the nave, leading to a fine Romanesque crypt. The **sacristy** in the southeast corner features frescoes by Spinello Arentino depicting the life of St Benedict. Slap-bang in the middle of the nave is the bijou **Capella del Crocefisso**, to which Michelozzo, Agnolo Gaddi and Luca della Robbia all contributed.

Cappella Brancacci   CHURCH

(Map p474; Piazza del Carmine; ✍advance reservations 055 276 82 24; admission €4; ⊘10am-5pm Wed-Fri & Sat, 1-5pm Sun) The 13th-century **Basilica di Santa Maria del Carmine** might have been all but destroyed by fire in the late 18th century, but the magnificent frescoes in its chapel were not. Entered next to the basilica on the square, the vibrantly coloured frescoes by Masaccio are considered the painter's finest work and had an enormous influence on 15th-century Florentine art. Masaccio painted them in his early 20s but interrupted the task to go to Rome, where he died aged only 28. Filippino Lippi completed the cycle some 60 years later. Masaccio's contribution includes the *Expulsion of Adam and Eve from Paradise* and *The Tribute Money* on the chapel's upper left wall.

Visits to the chapel are strictly by guided tour, which must be booked in advance.

Basilica di Santo Spirito   CHURCH

(Map p474; Piazza Santo Spirito; ⊘9.30am-12.30pm & 4-5.30pm Thu-Tue) One of Brunelleschi's last commissions, this church is beautifully planned with a colonnade of 35 columns and a series of semicircular chapels. The chapels' works of art include a poorly lit *Madonna and Saints* (1493–94) by Filippo Lippi in the Cappella Nerli in the right transept. Ask an attendant to show you the **sacristy**, where you'll find a poignant wooden crucifix attributed by some critics to Michelangelo.

⌖ Courses

Florence has zillions of schools running courses in Italian language, culture and cuisine.

Scuola del Cuoio   LEATHER-WORKING

(Map p472; ✍055 24 45 34; www.scuoladelcuoio. com; Via San Giuseppe 5r) Held here are leatherworking courses in a leather school created by Franciscan friars after WWII.

In Tavola   COOKING

(Map p474; ✍055 21 76 72; www.intavola.org; Via deiVelluti 18r) Take your pick from dozens of carefully crafted courses for beginners and professionals: pizza and gelato, pasta-making, easy Tuscan dinners etc.

Food & Wine Academy   COOKING

(Map p460; ✍055 012 39 94; www.florencecookingclasses.com; Via de' Lamberti 1; 1-day classes incl lunch €79) Shop at the market with charismatic chef Giovanni, learn how to cook what you've bought, then eat it.

La Cucina del Garga   COOKING

(Map p460; ✍055 21 13 96; www.divinacucina.com; Via del Moro 48r; 1-day classes incl lunch €155) Delve into the secrets of Florentine trattoria cuisine with American-born Sharon Oddson.

Florence for Fun COOKING
(Map p472; ☑055 247 66 05; www.florenceforfun.
org; Via della Pergola 10Ar) Mainstream cookery
classes and pizza-, gelato- and sorbet-making
workshops are run here.

 **Tours**

Bus
CAF Tours COACH
(Map p460; ☑055 21 06 12; www.caftours.com; Via
Sant'Antonino 6r) Half- and full-day city coach
tours (€45 to €190), including designer-outlet
shopping tours (€35, six hours).

City Sightseeing Firenze BUS
(Map p470; ☑055 29 04 51; www.firenze.city-sight
seeing.it; Piazza Stazione 1; tickets incl audioguide
adult/5-15yr €22/11) Explore Florence by red
open-top bus, hopping on and off at 15 bus
stops around the city. Tickets, sold by the
driver, are valid for 24 hours.

Car
TOP CHOICE 500 Touring Club VINTAGE CAR
(Map p460; ☑334 996 5836; www.500touringclub.
com; Via Vinegia 23r) Hook up with Florence's
500 Touring Club for a guided tour in a vintage
motor – with you behind the wheel!
Every car has a name in this outfit's fleet of
gorgeous vintage Fiat 500s from the 1960s
(Giacomo is the playboy, Sergio the speed-
fiend king, Anna the girl with style and so
on). Motoring tours are guided – hop in your
car and follow the leader – and themed;
families love the picnic trip, couples wine
tasting. March to November tours need to
be booked well in advance.

Cycling
I Bike Florence BIKE
(☑055 012 39 94; www.ibikeflorence.com; Via de'
Lamberti 1) Guided history tours of Florence
by bike (€29, two hours) and guided day
trips to Chianti (€80 including lunch and
wine tasting).

Tuscany Bike Tours BIKE
(☑055 386 04 95; www.tuscany-biketours.com;
Via Ghibellina 34r) One-day, 23km-long bike
tours in Chianti with lunch, castle tour, wine
and oil tasting (€75); transfer to Chianti by
minibus.

Walking
ArtViva WALKING
(Map p460; ☑055 264 50 33, 329 6132730; www.
italy.artviva.com; Via de' Sassetti 1) Marketed as
the 'Original & Best', these excellent one-
to three-hour city walks (€25 to €39) are

led by historians or art history graduates;
tours include the Uffizi, the Original David
tour and an Evening Walk/Murder Mystery
Tour. ArtViva also runs trips further afield
to Chianti (wine tasting) and a Renaissance
villa outside Florence (villa lunch and
swim).

Faith Willinger – Lessons & Tours WALKING
(www.faithwillinger.com) Food lovers' walking
tour, a market stroll, gelato crawl and much
more by American-born, Florence-based
food writer Faith Willinger who runs cooking courses, hands-on 'market to table' sessions, tastings, demonstrations and culinary
visits including meaty field trips to Panzano
in Chianti.

Accidental Tourist WALKING
(☑055 69 93 76; www.accidentaltourist.com) Become an Accidental Tourist (membership
€10) then sign up for a wine tour (€50),
cooking class (€60), picnic (€70) and so on;
tours happen in and around Florence.

Freya's Florence WALKING
(☑349 0748907; www.freyasflorence.com; €60/hr)
A recommended Australian-born, Florence-
based private tour guide; pay admission fees
on top of guiding fee.

✦ Festivals & Events
Festa di Anna Maria Medici HISTORICAL EVENT
(18 February) Florence's Feast of Anna Maria Medici marks the death in 1743 of the
last Medici, Anna Maria, with a costumed
parade from Palazzo Vecchio to her tomb in
the Cappelle Medicee.

Scoppio del Carro EASTER
A cart of fireworks is exploded in front of
the cathedral at 11am on Easter Sunday – get
there at least two hours early to grab a good
position.

Maggio Musicale Fiorentino ARTS
(www.maggiofiorentino.com) This month-long
arts festival – Italy's oldest – held in Florence's Teatro del Maggio Musicale Fiorentino (p490) stages world-class performances
of theatre, classical music, jazz and dance;
April to June.

Festa di San Giovanni RELIGIOUS
Florence celebrates its patron saint, John,
with a *calcio storico* match on Piazza di
Santa Croce and fireworks over Piazzale Michelangelo; 24 June.

Sant'Ambrogio Summer Festival
ARTS

(www.firenzejazz.it) The streets between Borgo La Croce and Piazza Beccaria become an evening stage for art, dance, jazz and theatre; June to July.

Jazz & Co
MUSIC

(www.santissima.it) On summer nights, Piazza della Santissima Annunziata is filled with tables of people enjoying an *aperitivo* or dinner catered by Slow Food International while listening to jazz musicians from Italy and overseas perform; late June to Septemer.

Festival Firenze Classica
MUSIC

(www.orcafi.it) July sees Florence's highly regarded Orchestra da Camera Toscana performing classical music in the atmospheric settings of the Oratorio di San Michele a Castello and Palazzo Strozzi.

Festa delle Rificolone
RELIGIOUS

During the Festival of the Paper Lanterns children carrying lanterns, accompanied by drummers, *sbandieratori* (flag throwers), musicians and others in medieval dress, process through the streets from Piazza di Santa Croce to Piazza della Santissima Annunziata to celebrate the Virgin Mary's birthday; 7 September.

🛏 Sleeping

The city has hundreds of hotels, some excellent hostels and a burgeoning B&B scene. Places in this section have been selected for their good value for money.

Too many hotels and boutique B&Bs competing for too little business means great deals for the traveller, especially in winter when there are bargains to be had in all price ranges – a midrange double in a gorgeous 16th-century *palazzo* can cost as little as €45.

Tourist offices don't recommend or reserve places, but carry lists of what is available.

PIAZZA DEL DUOMO & PIAZZA DELLA SIGNORIA

Incredibly, for such a dead-central part of Florence, this area has some excellent budget addresses. And if your hotel lacks an internet connection, free wi-fi hot spot Palazzo Strozzi, with its wonderfully airy and very hip courtyard, is just a minute's walk away.

TOP CHOICE Hotel Scoti
HOTEL €

(Map p460; ☑055 29 21 28; www.hotelscoti.com; Via de' Tornabuoni 7; s €29-75, d €45-125, tr €75-150, q €85-175; 🛜🛗) Wedged between Prada and McQueen, this *pensione* is a splendid mix of old-fashioned charm and value for money. Run with smiling aplomb by Australian Doreen and Italian Carmello, the hotel is enthroned in a 16th-century *palazzo* on Florence's smartest shopping strip. Its 16 rooms are clean and comfortable, but the star of the show is the frescoed living room (1780). Breakfast costs €5.

Hotel Cestelli
BOUTIQUE HOTEL €

(Map p460; ☑055 21 42 13; www.hotelcestelli. com; Borgo SS Apostoli 25; s without bathroom €40-60, d €50-100; ☺closed 4 weeks Jan-Feb, 3 weeks Aug) Located a stiletto-hop and a skip from the Arno and fashionable Via de' Tornabuoni, this eight-room hotel is a gem. Its large, quiet rooms ooze understated style – think washbasin with silk screen, vintage art and original wood-slat shutters. Before stepping out quiz Italian photographer Alessio and Japanese wife Asumi on the latest best addresses to drink, dine and shop. No breakfast.

Hotel Torre Guelfa
HOTEL €€

(Map p460; ☑055 239 63 38; www.hoteltorreguelfa. com; Borgo SS Apostoli 8; d €70-170, tr €130-210; ✹@🛜) If you want to kip in a Real McCoy Florentine *palazzo* without breaking the bank, this 31-room hotel with fortress-style facade is the address. Scale its 13th-century, 50m-tall tower – Florence's tallest privately owned *torre* – for a sundowner overlooking Florence and you'll be blown away. A couple of its spacious rooms, all with high ceilings and faded period furnishings, share the same staggering panorama.

Hotel Dalí
HOTEL €

(Map p460; ☑055 234 07 06; www.hoteldali.com; Via dell'Oriuolo 17; s/d €40/85, d without bathroom €70, apt 2/4/6 guests €90/140/200; 🅿@🛜🛗) This overwhelmingly friendly hotel with 10 spacious rooms goes from strength to strength. Run with unrelenting dynamism by world travellers-turned-parents Marco and Samanta ('running the hotel is like travelling without moving'), Dalí now has a kettle in every room, new bathrooms, microwave for shared use and three gorgeous self-catering apartments – one with Duomo view – sleeping two, four and six. No breakfast, but free parking in the leafy inner courtyard. Low-season rates 20% less.

Hotel Orchidea
HOTEL €

(Map p460; ☑055 248 03 46; www.hotelorchi deaflorence.it; Borgo degli Albizi 11; s €30-55, d €50-75, tr €65-90, q €75-110, all without bathroom) This old-fashioned *pensione* in the mansion where the Donati family roosted in the 13th century (Dante's wife, Gemma, was allegedly born in the tower) is charm itself. Its seven rooms with sink and shared bathroom are simple but their outlook over a gorgeous garden or old stone terrace is five-star. Many guests return to enjoy the 100-year-old wisteria in bloom (May to June). No breakfast, but free tea- and coffee-making facilities.

Hotel Davanzati
HOTEL €€

(Map p460; ☑055 286 666; www.hoteldavanzati. it; Via Porta Rossa 5; s €72-122, d €122-189, q €222-342; ❋@🛜🛗) Don't be put off by the 26 steps leading up to this 1st-floor hotel snug against Palazzo Davanzati. It is a beguiling labyrinth of enchanting rooms, unexpected frescoes and up-to-the-minute comforts run by irresistibly charismatic Florentine debonair Tommaso and father Fabrizio.

Palazzo Vecchietti
HISTORIC RESIDENCE €€€

(Map p460; ☑055 230 28 02; www.palazzovecchi etti.com; Via degli Strozzi 4; d €284-734; ❋@🛜🛗) Wow, and wow again! This *residenza d'epoca* with 14 hopelessly romantic rooms and loggia in a 15th-century *palazzo* is a buzzword for hotel chic. Every room has coffee machine and kitchenette, and three have a terrace between rooftops. No surprise: this is the handiwork of Florentine interior designer Michele Bönan.

Hotel Perseo
HOTEL €

(Map p460; ☑055 21 25 04; www.hotelperseo.it; Via de' Cerretani 1; s €50-125, d €80-165, tr €80-185, q €90-220; ❋@🛜🛗) Twenty-room Perseo is a great family choice with its large rooms and unpretentious decor. Family rooms have bunk beds and those on the top floor smooch with the rooftops and gorgeous views of the Duomo. Should you have trouble tracking down (black) No 1 on the street, look for red No 23.

SANTA MARIA NOVELLA AREA
TOP CHOICE Hotel L'Orologio
DESIGN HOTEL €€€

(Map p460; ☑055 27 73 80; www.hotelorologio florence.com; Piazza di Santa Maria Novella 24; d €178-450; P❋@🛜) The type of seductive, superstylish address James Bond would feel right at home in, this elegant new hotel oozes panache. Designed to be something of a showcase for the (very wealthy) owner's (exceedingly expensive) luxury wristwatch

collection, the hotel has four stars, five floors, 54 rooms named after watches, and clocks pretty much everywhere you look. Room 501 has a perfect balcony view of the Duomo.

Ostello Archi Rossi
HOSTEL €

(Map p470; ☑055 29 08 04; www.hostelarchirossi. com; Via Faenza 94r; s €40-60, d €60-90, tr €75-105, dm €21-27, all incl breakfast & sheets; ⊙closed 2 weeks Dec; @🛜) Guests' paintings and graffiti pattern the walls at this ever-busy private hostel near Stazione di Santa Maria Novella. Bright white dorms have three to 12 beds (those across the garden are quieter); there are washing machines, frozen meal dispensers and microwaves for guests to use. No curfew (knock to get in after 2am).

Hotel Rosso 23
BOUTIQUE HOTEL €€

(Map p460; ☑055 27 73 00; www.hotelrosso23. com; Piazza di Santa Maria Novella 23; s €79-100, d €85-195; ❋@🛜) The entrance is so discreet you might well walk straight pass this stylish town house with a beautiful facade and smart, oyster-grey and red interior colour scheme. Rooms, all 42 of them, are thoroughly modern, and breakfast is served in a bijou interior courtyard.

Ostello Gallo d'Oro
HOSTEL €

(☑055 552 29 64; www.ostellogallodoro.com; 1st fl, Via Cavour 104; dm €28-32, s/d/tr €40/70/96; @🛜) Silvia and Max are the energy behind this popular, curfew-free hostel. Rooms max at five beds, all have private bathroom and TV, and three have a balcony. Breakfast is buffet-style and the bubbly Silvia cooks up dinner twice a week.

SAN LORENZO AREA
TOP CHOICE Academy Hostel
HOSTEL €

(Map p460; ☑055 239 86 65; www.academyhostel. eu; Via Ricasoli 9; s & d incl breakfast per person €35-42, dm €34-40; ❋@🛜) Cheap accommodation shouldn't compromise on comfort is the much-appreciated philosophy of this small modern hostel, snug on the 1st floor of a 17th-century *palazzo*. Dorms with four beds are crisp white with brightly coloured lockers and chic flower-adorned screens. Rates include breakfast. No credit cards for payments under €150.

Sette Angeli Rooms
B&B, SELF-CATERING €

(Map p470; ☑393 939490810; www.setteangeli rooms.com; Via Nazionale 31; s €45-60, d €85-110, tr €95-135; ❋🛜) Tucked behind the central market on a mainstream shopping street, Seven Angels is a tantalising mix of great value and recent renovation. Its rooms are perfectly comfortable and guests can pay an extra €10 to use the self-catering kitchen corner.

Johanna & Johlea
B&B €€

(☑055 463 32 92/48 18 96; www.johanna.it; s €50-90, d €70-170; ✦🎇🎐) One of the most established B&Bs in town, J&J has more than a dozen tasteful, impeccable, individually decorated rooms split between five historic residences, some with wi-fi connections. Those desiring total luxury can ask about the suite apartments.

SAN MARCO AREA

Hotel Morandi alla Crocetta
HOTEL €€

(Map p470; ☑055 234 47 47; www.hotelmorandi. it; Via Laura 50; s €70-140, d €110-220, tr €130-195; q €150-370; ☐🎇🎐) This medieval convent-turned-hotel away from the madding crowd is a stunner. A couple of rooms have handkerchief-sized gardens to laze in, but the pièce de résistance is frescoed No 29, the former chapel.

THE OLTRARNO

Palazzo Magnani Feroni
HOTEL €€€

(Map p474; ☑055 239 95 44; www.florence palace.com; Borgo San Frediano 5; d €310-720; ☐🎇@🎐) This old palace is the stuff of dreams. Its 12 suites are vast, ooze elegance and the 360-degree city view from the rooftop is magnificent and unforgettable.

Ostello Santa Monaca
HOSTEL €

(Map p474; ☑055 26 83 38; www.ostello.it; Via Santa Monaca 6; d/q per person €24.50/20.50, dm €17.50-19.50; @🎐) Once a convent, this large hostel comes warmly recommended. There is a bright kitchen with washing machine for guests' use, free safe deposits and two computers to surf. Single-sex dorms sleep four to 22 (closed for cleaning 10am to 2pm). Curfew 2am. Low-season rates €1 less. Breakfast/dinner is €3.50/12.

Palazzo Guadagni Hotel
HOTEL

(Map p474; ☑055 265 83 76; www.palazzoguad agni.com; Piazza Santo Spirito 9; d €100-150, f per person €35; 🎇🎐) Plump above Florence's most buzzing summertime square, this hotel, with impossibly romantic loggia, is legendary – Zefferelli shot several scenes of Tea with Mussolini here. Known for years as the shabby, over-priced but wholly irresistible Pensione Bandini (since shut), the Renaissance 16th-century palace has been brought back to life – in the most fabulous

of manners – by local Florentines Laura and Ferdinando. Spacious rooms tastefully mix old and new, and that loggia terrace with wicker garden furniture is, well, dreamy...

Campeggio Michelangelo
CAMPGROUND €

(☑055 681 19 77; www.ecvacanze.it; Viale Michelangelo 80; camping adult €9.50-11.40, car & tent €11.40-13.80; ☐@) Just off Piazzale Michelangelo, this large and comparatively leafy site has lovely city views. Take bus 13 from Stazione di Santa Maria Novella or walk – steeply uphill!

OUT OF TOWN

Should you want to flee the Florentine crowd and stay out of town, two remarkable 'prince and pauper' addresses leap out.

In a 17th-century villa framed by extensive grounds, HI-affiliated Villa Camerata (☑055 60 14 51; www.ostellofirenze.it; Viale Augusto Righi 2-4; dm €20, d/tr/q with bathroom €65/75/88; ☐@🎐) is among Italy's most beautiful hostels (and oh so typically Tuscan!). Bus 17 from Stazione di Santa Maria Novella stops 400m from the hostel; count on 30 minutes' travel time.

Then there's five-star Grand Hotel Villa Cora (☑055 22 87 90; www.villacora.it; Viale Machiavelli 18; d from €310; ☐@🎐🎇), a glorious 19th-century mansion guaranteed to make your head spin with its sumptuous frescoes, fabrics, chandeliers and art works just steps from Boboli Gardens.

🍴 Eating

Quality ingredients and simple execution are the hallmarks of Florentine cuisine, climaxing with the fabulous bistecca alla fiorentina, a huge slab of prime T-bone steak rubbed with olive oil, seared on the char grill, garnished with salt and pepper and served beautifully al sangue (bloody).

Other typical dishes include crostini (toasts topped with chicken-liver pâté or other topping), ribollita (a thick vegetable, bread and bean soup), pappa al pomodoro (bread and tomato soup) and trippa alla fiorentina (tripe cooked in a rich tomato sauce).

PIAZZA DEL DUOMO & PIAZZA DELLA SIGNORIA

TOP CHOICE Obikà
CHEESE BAR €€

(Map p460; ☑055 277 35 26; www.obika.it; Via de' Tornabuoni 16; 3/5 mozzarellas €19.50/30, pizzas €9-14.50; ⊙lunch & dinner Mon-Sat, 10am-11pm Sun) Given its exclusive location in Palazzo Tornabuoni, this designer address is naturally

FLORENCE & TUSCANY FLORENCE

TOP FIVE GELATERIE

Florentines take gelato seriously and there's healthy rivalry among local *gelaterie artigianale* (makers of handmade gelato) who strive to create the city's creamiest, most flavourful and freshest ice cream. Flavours are seasonal and a cone or tub costs €2/3/4/5 per small/medium/large/maxi.

» **Vivoli** (Map p460; Via dell'Isola delle Stinche 7; ☺7.30am-midnight Mon-Sat, 9am-midnight Sun Apr-Oct, to 9pm Nov-Mar) Inside seating tea-salon style alongside coffee, tea and cakes make this ice-cream shop stand out. Pay at the cash desk then trade receipt for ice. No cones, only tubs.

» **Grom** (Map p460; www.grom.it; cnr Via del Campanile & Via delle Oche; ☺10.30am-midnight Apr-Sep, to 11pm Oct-Mar) Rain, hail or shine, queues halfway down the street are a constant at this sweet address; flavours are all delectable and many ingredients organic. Rather tasty hot chocolate and milkshakes too.

» **La Carraia** (Map p474; Piazza N Sauro 25r; ☺11am-11pm) Take one look at the constant queue out the door of this bright green-and-citrus shop with its exciting flavours and you know you're at a real Florentine favourite. Ricotta and pear anyone?

» **Gelateria dei Neri** (Map p460; Via de' Neri 22r; ☺9am-midnight) Semifreddo-style gelato that is cheaper than its competitors; known for its coconut, gorgonzola and ricotta and fig flavours.

» **Carabé** (Map p470; www.gelatocarabe.com; Via Ricasoli 60r; ☺10am-midnight, closed mid-Dec–mid-Jan) Sicilian gelato, *granita* (sorbet) and *brioche* (ice-cream sandwich); handy while waiting in line to see *David*.

ubertrendy. Taste different mozzarella cheeses with basil, organic veg or sun-dried tomatoes in the cathedral-like interior or snuggle beneath heaters in the star-topped courtyard. The mozzarella pizzas are particularly creative – as is the copious *aperitivi* salad buffet (€9 including one drink) and cheesy Sunday brunch.

Cantinetta dei Verrazzano WINE CELLAR, BAKERY €

(Map p460; Via dei Tavolini 18-20; platters €4.50-12, focaccias €3-3.50, panini €2.50-4; ☺noon-9pm Mon-Sat) Together, a *forno* (baker's oven) and *cantinetta* (small cellar) equal a match made in heaven. Sit down at one of just five marble-topped tables, admire prized vintages displayed behind glass in wall-to-ceiling wooden cabinets and sip a glass of wine (€3.50 to €8) produced on the Verrazzano estate in Chianti. The focaccia, perhaps topped with caramelised radicchio or *porcini* mushrooms, is a must – as is a mixed cold-meat platter (try to ignore the bristly boar legs strung in the small open kitchen).

TOP CHOICE Mariano SANDWICH SHOP €

(Map p460; Via del Parione 19r; ☺8am-3pm & 5-7.30pm Mon-Fri, 8am-3pm Sat) Our favourite for its simplicity, around since 1973. Sun-

rise to sunset this brick-vaulted, 13th-century cellar gently buzzes with Florentines propped at the counter sipping coffee, wine or eating salads and *panini*. Come here for a coffee-and-pastry breakfast, light lunch, *aperitivo* or *panino* to eat on the move.

'Ino SANDWICH SHOP €

(Map p460; Via dei Georgofili 3r-7r; ☺11am-8pm Mon-Sat, noon-5pm Sun) Artisan ingredients are sourced locally and creatively mixed at this stylish address near the Uffizi. Create your own combination or pick a house special and scoff on the spot with a glass of wine (included in the sandwich price).

I Due Fratellini SANDWICH SHOP €

(Map p460; www.iduefratellini.com; Via dei Cimatori 38r; ☺9am-8pm Mon-Sat, closed Fri & Sat 2nd half of Jun & all Aug) This hole in the wall has been in business since 1875. Wash *panini* down with a beaker of wine and leave the empty on the wooden shelf outside.

Oil Shoppe SANDWICH SHOP €

(Map p460; www.oleum.it; Via Sant'Egidio 22r) Queue at the back of the shop for hot subs, at the front for cold, at this busy student favourite. Choose your own or let chef Alberto Scorzon take the lead with his 10-filling wonder.

Coquinarius WINE BAR €€

(Map p460; ☑055 230 21 53; www.coquinarius. com; Via delle Oche 15r; meals €35; ☺noon-10.30pm daily) Nestled within the shadow of the Duomo, this *enoteca* (wine bar) is extremely popular with tourists – try the justly famous ravioli with cheese and pear. Bookings essential.

La Canova di Gustavino WINE BAR €

(Map p460; ☑055 239 98 06; Via della Condotta 29r; meals €35; ☺noon-midnight daily) The emphasis at this atmospheric *enoteca* is on Tuscan classics, but it's perfectly fine to plump for a lighter cheese/salami platter or bruschetta too.

SANTA MARIA NOVELLA AREA

^{TOP}_{CHOICE} **L'Osteria di Giovanni** TUSCAN €€

(Map p460; ☑055 28 48 97; www.osteriadigiovanni. it; Via del Moro 22; meals €45; ☺lunch & dinner Fri-Mon, dinner Tue-Thu) It's not the decor or eclectic choice of wall art that stands out at this wonderfully friendly neighbourhood eatery. It's the cuisine, staunchly Tuscan and stunningly creative. Think chickpea soup with octopus or pear- and ricotta-stuffed *tortelli* (ravioli) bathed in a leek-and-almond cream. Throw in the complimentary glass of sparkling *prosecco* as aperitif and subsequent Vin Santo (with homemade *cantuccini* – crunchy, almond-studded biscuits – to dunk in) at the end of the meal and you'll return time and again.

Osteria dei Centopoveri TRATTORIA €€

(☑055 21 88 46; Via Palazzuolo 31r; meals €30; ☺lunch & dinner daily) The 'hostel of the hundred poor people' is no soup kitchen, rather a modern dining option recommended in practically every guidebook. Creative Tuscan is its culinary spin.

Il Latini TRATTORIA €€

(Map p460; ☑055 21 09 16; www.illatini.com; Via dei Palchetti 6r; meals €40; ☺lunch & dinner Tue-Sun) Another guidebook favourite built around melt-in-your-mouth crostini, Tuscan meats, fine pasta and roasted meats served at shared tables. There are two dinner seatings (7.30pm and 9pm), bookings mandatory.

SAN LORENZO & SAN MARCO AREAS

^{TOP}_{CHOICE} **Trattoria Mario** TRATTORIA €

(Map p470; www.trattoriamario.com; Via Rosina 2; meals €15-25; ☺noon-3.30pm Mon-Sat, closed 3 weeks Aug) Arrive at noon to ensure a stool around a shared table at this noisy, busy trattoria – a Florentine legend. The charming Fabio, whose grandfather Mario opened the place in 1953, is front of house and big brother Romeo and nephew Francesco cook with speed and skill in the kitchen. Monday and Thursday is tripe, Friday fish and Saturday the day locals flock here for a brilliantly blue *bistecca alla fiorentina* (€35/kg). No advance reservations, no credit cards.

Nerbone MARKET STALL €

(Map p470; Mercato Centrale, Piazza del Mercato Centrale; primi €4, secondi €5-9; ☺7am-2pm Mon-Sat) Forge your way past cheese, meat and sausage stalls in Florence's central market to join the lunchtime queue at Nerbone,

---

TIP-TOP PIZZERIAS

Expect to pay around €8 for a pizza at these Florentine-recommended addresses:

» **Gustapizza** (Map p474; Via Maggio 46r; ☺11.30am-3pm & 7-11pm Tue-Sun) Wow! This unpretentious pizzeria by Piazza Santa Spirito gives a new meaning to the word 'packed'. Arrive early to grab a bar stool at a wooden-barrel table and pick from eight pizza types.

» **Pizzeria del' Osteria del Caffè Italiano** (Via dell'Isola delle Stinche 11-13r; ☺7.30-11.30pm Tue-Sun) Simplicity is the buzzword at this pocket-sized pizzeria that makes just three pizza types: Margherita, Napoli and Marinara. No credit cards.

» **PizzaMan** (Map p472; Via dell'Agnolo 79; ☺noon-2.30pm & 6.30pm-midnight Mon-Fri, 6.30pm-midnight Sat & Sun) This cheap and cheerful pizzeria with booth-style seating gets rave reviews for its Naples-style pizza (baked in a wood-burning oven) and bargain-basement prices. To lunch cheap, go for the PizzaMan's €6 pizza-and-fries deal or €8 menu.

» **Il Pizzaiuolo** (Map p472; Via dei Macci 113r; pizzas €5-10, pastas €6.50-12; ☺lunch & dinner Mon-Sat, closed Aug) Young Florentines flock to the Pizza Maker to nosh Neapolitan thick-crust pizzas hot from the wood-fired oven. Bookings are essential for dinner.

in the biz since 1872. Go local and order *trippa alla fiorentina* or *panini con bollito* (boiled-beef bun, dunked in the meat's juices before serving). Eat standing up or fight for a table.

La Mescita WINE BAR €
(Map p470; Via degli Alfani 70r; mains €5-10; ☺10.30am-4pm Mon-Sat, closed Aug) Conveniently close to *David* and the Galleria dell'Accademia, this part *enoteca* part *fiaschetteria* (wine seller) is an unapologetically old-fashioned place from 1927. It serves Tuscan specialities such as *maccheroni* with sausage and *insalata di farro* (spelt salad), and has a great marble-topped bar propped up by noontime tipplers.

Il Vegetariano VEGETARIAN €
(off Map p470; www.il-vegetariano.it; Via delle Ruote 30r; meals €15-20; ☺lunch & dinner Tue-Fri, dinner Sat & Sun) This self-service veggie restaurant cooks up a great selection of Tuscan vegetable dishes, build-your-own salads and mains eaten around shared wooden tables.

SANTA CROCE

TOP CHOICE Teatro del Sale TRADITIONAL ITALIAN €€
(Map p472; ☎055 200 14 92; www.teatrodelsale. com; Via dei Macci 111r; breakfasts/lunches/dinners €7/20/30; ☺9-11am, 12.30-2.30pm & 7-11pm Tue-Sat Sep-Jul) Aptly set in an old Florentine theatre, this members-only club is the brainchild of larger-than-life Florentine chef Fabio Picchi. Teatro del Sale serves breakfast, lunch and dinner, culminating at 9.30pm in a live performance of drama, music or comedy arranged by artistic director and famous comic actress (and Picchi's wife) Maria Cassi. Dinners are hectic affairs and advance reservations are essential: grab a chair, serve yourself water, wine and antipasti and wait for Picchi to yell out what's just about to be served before queuing at the glass hatch for your *primo* (first course) and *secondo* (second course). Dessert and coffee are laid out buffet-style just prior to the performance.

TOP CHOICE Trattoria Cibrèo TRATTORIA €€
(Map p472; Via dei Macci 122r; meals €35; ☺12.50-2.30pm & 6.50-11.15pm Tue-Sat Sep-Jul) Dine here and you'll instantly understand why a queue gathers outside before it opens. Once in, revel in top-notch Tuscan cuisine: perhaps ricotta and potato flan with a rich meat sauce, puddle of olive oil and grated Parmesan (divine!) or a simple plate of polenta, followed by homemade sausages, beans in

DON'T MISS

PIAZZA DELLA PASSERA

483

This bijou square with no passing traffic is a gourmet gem. Pick from cheap wholesome tripe in various guises at **Il Magazzino** (Map p474; ☎055 21 59 69; www.tripperiailmagazzino.com; Piazza della Passera 2/3; meals €25; ☺lunch & dinner daily) or pricier Tuscan classics at **Trattoria 4 Leoni** (Map p474; ☎055 21 85 62; www.4leoni.com; Piazza della Passera 2/3; meals from €35; ☺lunch & dinner daily), known for its *bistecca all fiorentina* (T-bone steak) that it's cooked up since 1550; reservations essential.

a spicy tomato sauce and braised celery. No advance reservations, no credit cards, no coffee and arrive early to snag a table.

Pin Gusto ASIAN FUSION €
(Map p472; ☎055 23 44 397; www.pingusto.com; Via della Mattonaia 2-18; lunches/dinners €10/20; ☺lunch & dinner daily) A great cheap-eat recommended by several savvy Florentines, this modern dining address behind Sant' Ambrogio market cooks up a bottomless lunch buffet (€10) built around hot and cold sushi, wok and fusion dishes. Dinner – a busy affair hence best to reserve one of two sittings (7.30pm and 9.30pm) – sees grilled meats added to the excellent-value, eat-as-much-as-you-can equation.

Francesco Vini TUSCAN €€
(Map p460; ☎055 21 87 37; www.francescovini. com; Piazza de' Peruzzi 8r; meals €40, pizzas €6-10; ☺lunch & dinner daily) Built on top of Roman ruins, this surprise address with striking glass facade sits on one of Florence's quintessentially quiet, stumble-upon-by-accident squares. Winter dining is between bottle-lined wall and red brick and in summer everything spills outside. But it is the wine list, packed with all the Tuscan greats, that is Francesco's real pride and joy.

Antico Noè OSTERIA €
(Map p472; Volta di San Piero 6r; meals €25; ☺noon-midnight Mon-Sat) Don't be put off by the dank alley in which this old butcher's shop with white marble-clad walls and wrought-iron meat hooks is found. The drunks loitering outside are generally harmless and the down-to-the-earth Tuscan fodder served is a real joy. For a quick bite, go for a *panini* from the adjoining *fiaschetteria*. No credit cards.

APERI-CENA

Aperi-cena, a brilliant cent-saving trick and trend among students and 20-somethings in Florence, translates as an *aperitif* buffet so copious it doubles as *cena* (dinner). Firm Florentine favourites are Kitsch (p486), Slowly (p486) and Obikà (p480).

Osteria del Caffè Italiano
TRADITIONAL TUSCAN €€

(Map p460; ☎055 28 90 20; www.caffeitaliano.it; Via dell'Isola delle Stinche 11-13r; meals €40; ☺lunch & dinner Tue-Sun) The menu at this cosy *osteria* (casual tavern or eatery presided over by a host) – a veteran in the Florence dining scene – is packed with simple classics such as *mozzarella di bufala* (buffalo mozzarella) with Parma ham, ravioli stuffed with ricotta and *cavolo nero* (black cabbage), and the city's famous *bistecca alla fiorentina* (per kg €50). Find it on the ground floor of 14th-century Palazzo Salviati.

Caffè Italiano Sud
ITALIAN €€

(Map p460; ☎055 28 93 68; Via della Vigna Vecchia; meals €25; ☺7.30-11pm Tue-Sun) Fronted by two potted olive trees, chef Umberto Montano's ode to southern Italy is a change from the Tuscan norm. Loads of homemade pasta, including unusual dishes from his native Puglia, stars on the menu and house wine comes in pitchers drawn from traditional 58L straw-cushioned glass flasks.

THE OLTRARNO

TOP CHOICE Il Santo Bevitore
MODERN TUSCAN €€

(Map p474; ☎055 21 12 64; www.ilsantobevitore.com; Via di Santo Spirito 64-66r; meals €35; ☺lunch & dinner daily Sep-Jul) Reserve in advance or arrive at 7.30pm to snag the last of the remaining tables at this raved-about address, an understated ode to stylish dining where gastronomes dine by candlelight in a cavernous whitewashed, wood- and bottle-lined interior. The menu is a creative reinvention of seasonal classics, and different for lunch and dinner: hand-chopped beef tartare, chestnut millefeuille and lentils, puréed purple cabbage soup with mozzarella cream and anchovy syrup, acacia honey *bavarese* (type of firm, creamy mousse) with Vin Santo–marinated dried fruits…

TOP CHOICE Il Ristoro
TUSCAN €

(Map p474; ☎055 26 45 569; Borgo San Jacopo 48r; meals €20; ☺noon-4pm Mon, noon-10pm Tue-Sun) A disarmingly simple address not to be missed, this two-room restaurant with deli counter is a great budget choice. Pick from classics like *pappa al pomodoro* (tomato and bread soup) or a plate of cold cuts and swoon at views of the Arno swirling beneath your feet.

TOP CHOICE Gustpanino
SANDWICH SHOP €

(Map p474; Piazza Santa Spirito; ☺11am-8pm Mon-Sat, noon-5pm Sun) It's dead simple to spot what many Florentines rate as the city's best *enopaninoteca* (hip wine and sandwich stop), with no seating but bags of square space and church steps outside – just look for the long line in front.

Trattoria La Casalinga
TRATTORIA €

(Map p474; ☎055 21 86 24; Via de' Michelozzi 9r; meals €25; ☺lunch & dinner Mon-Sat) Family run and locally loved, this busy unpretentious place is one of Florence's cheapest trattorias. You'll be relegated behind locals in the queue – it's a fact of life and not worth protesting – with the eventual reward being hearty peasant dishes such as *bollito misto con salsa verde* (mixed boiled meats with green sauce).

Trattoria Bordino
TRATTORIA €

(Map p474; ☎055 21 30 48; www.trattoriabordino. it; Via Stracciatella 9r; meals €25; ☺lunch & dinner Mon-Sat) If eat cheap is your mantra, Bordino is your address. Hidden behind Chiesa di Santa Felicità, not far from Ponte Vecchio, this pocket-sized trattoria cooks up all the classics and a great-value €7 lunch.

Olio & Convivium
TUSCAN €€

(Map p460; ☎055 265 81 98; Via di Santo Spirito 4; meals €40; ☺lunch & dinner Tue-Sat, lunch Mon) A key address on any gastronomy agenda: your taste buds will tingle at the sight of the legs of ham, conserved truffles, wheels of cheese, artisan-made bread and other delectable delicatessen products sold in its shop. Dine out back.

Il Guscio
TUSCAN €€

(off Map p474; ☎055 22 44 21; www.ristoranteilguscio firenze.com; Via dell'Orto 49; meals €40; ☺lunch & dinner Tue-Sat) Exceptional dishes come out of the kitchen of this family-run gem in San Frediano. Meat and fish are given joint billing, with triumphs such as white-bean soup with prawns and fish joining superbly executed mains, including guinea fowl breast in balsamic vinegar, on the sophisticated menu.

SELF-CATERING

Mercato Centrale
MARKET €

(Map p470; Piazza del Mercato Centrale; ⊙7am-2pm Mon-Fri, to 5pm Sat) Central food market inside an iron-and-glass structure dating to 1874.

Mercato di Sant'Ambrogio
MARKET €

(Map p472; Piazza Ghiberti; ⊙7am-2pm Mon-Sat) Outdoor food market with intimate, local flavour.

Drinking

Florence's drinking scene is split between *enoteche* (increasingly hip wine bars that invariably make great eating addresses too), trendy bars with lavish *aperitivo* buffets, and traditional cafes that double as lovely lunch venues.

Nothing whets one's appetite for Florentine lifestyle better than hanging out in an *enoteca*, glass of Chianti in hand.

The other bars listed have that all-essential *aperitivo* (predinner drinks from around 7pm to 10pm) and/or late-night cocktails (around midnight before clubbing), two trends embraced with gusto by Florentines. Live music is the common denominator.

If you visit one of the historic cafes, remember, a coffee taken sitting down at a table is three to four times more expensive than one standing up at the bar: a cappuccino costs around €1.40/5.50 standing up/sitting down and a hot chocolate €2.50/6.

TOP Le Volpi e l'Uva
CHOICE
WINE BAR

(Map p474; www.levolpieluva.com; Piazza dei Rossi 1; ⊙11am-9pm Mon-Sat) The city's best *enoteca con degustazione* (wine bar with tasting) bar none: this intimate address chalks up an impressive list of wines by the glass (€3.50 to €8). To attain true bliss indulge in crostini (toasted breads; €6.50) topped with honeyed speck or *lardo* (pork fat), or a platter of boutique Tuscan cheeses (cheese or meat platters €8 to €12).

TOP Il Santino
CHOICE
WINE BAR

(Map p474; Via Santo Spirito 34; ⊙daily) Just a few doors down from one of Florence's best gourmet addresses is this pocket-sized wine bar, run by the same gastronomic folk and packed every evening. Inside, squat modern stools contrast with old brick walls but the real action is outside, from around 9pm, when the buoyant wine-loving crowd spills onto the street.

Clubhouse
BAR

(Map p470; ☑055 21 14 27; www.theclubhouse.it; Via de' Ginori 6r; ⊙noon-midnight daily) Rave reviews from Florentines as well as resident and visting Anglophones is all this thoroughly modern American bar, pizzeria and restaurant in San Marco gets. Handily close to *David*, it is the perfect drinking-dining hybrid any time of day, and that includes Sunday brunch. Design buffs will love its faintly industrial, cavernous vibe.

TOP Sky Lounge Continentale
CHOICE
BAR

(Map p460; www.continentale.it; Vicolo dell Oro 6r; ⊙2.30-11.30pm daily Apr-Sep) This rooftop bar with wooden decking terrace accessible from the 5th floor of the Ferragamo-owned Hotel Continentale is as chic as one would expect from a fashion-house hotel. Its evening *aperitivo* buffet might be a modest affair, but who cares with that fabulous, drop-dead-gorgeous panorama of one of Europe's most beautiful cities. Dress the part or feel out of place.

Caffè Giacosa
CAFE

(Map p460; www.caffegiacosa.com; Via della Spada 10r) This small cafe is as famous for what it

---

TRIPE: FAST-FOOD FAVOURITE

When Florentines fancy a fast munch on the move, they flit by a *trippaio* – a cart on wheels or mobile stand – for a tripe *panini*. Think cow's stomach chopped up, boiled, sliced, seasoned and bunged between bread.

One of those great bastions of good old-fashioned Florentine tradition, *trippai* still going strong include the cart on the southwest corner of **Mercato Nuovo** (Map p460); **L'Antico Trippaio** (Map p460; Piazza dei Cimatori); **Pollini** (Map p471; Piazza Sant' Ambrogio); and hole-in-the-wall **Da Vinattieri** (Map p460; Via Santa Margherita 4). Pay €3.50 for a *panini* with tripe doused in *salsa verde* (pea-green sauce of smashed parsley, garlic, capers and anchovies) or garnished with salt, pepper and ground chilli. Alternatively, opt for a bowl of *lampredotto* (cow's fourth stomach chopped and simmered for hours).

was – an 1815 child, Negroni inventor and hub of Anglo-Florentine sophistication during the interwar years – as what it is today (hip cafe of local hotshot designer Roberto Cavalli, whose flagship boutique is next door). Giacosa is known for its reasonable prices and also runs the equally hip cafe across the street in the courtyard of **Palazzo Strozzi**.

Caffè Rivoire   CAFE
(Map p460; Piazza della Signoria 4) The golden oldie in which to refuel after an Uffizi or Palazzo Vecchio visit, this pricey little number with unbeatable people-watching terrace has produced the city's most exquisite chocolate since 1872. Black-jacketed barmen with ties set the formal tone.

Golden View Open Bar   BAR
(Map p474; www.goldenviewopenbar.com; Via de' Bardi 58; ⊙7.30am-1.30am) Of course it is touristy given its prime location near Ponte Vecchio, but it is worth a pit stop – preferably at *aperitivo* hour when chic Florentines sip cocktails (€10/12 at bar/table), slurp oysters (€15) and watch the Arno swirling below their feet. Art exhibitions and live jazz from 8.30pm.

Eby's Bar   BAR
(Map p472; Via dell' Oriuolo 5r; ⊙10am-3am Mon-Sat) A lively student crowd packs out this young, fun address with wooden bench tucked outside in an alleyway. The kitchen is Mexican – think great-value lunch platters and all-day salads, crêpes, burritos and so on – and the drinks menu laden with fruity cocktails.

Slowly   BAR
(Map p460; www.slowlycafe.com; Via Porta Rossa 63r; ⊙9pm-3am Mon-Sat, closed Aug) Sleek and sometimes snooty, Slowly is known for its glam interior, Florentine Lotharios and lavish fruit-garnished cocktails – €10 including buffet during *aperitivo* hour, which lasts until 10.30pm. Ibiza-style lounge tracks dominate the turntable.

Kitsch   BAR
(Map p470 & Map p472; www.kitsch-bar.com; Piazza Beccaria & Via San Gallo 22r; ⊙6.30pm-2.30am;) Known among every cent-conscious Florentine for its lavish *aperitivi* spread (€8.50 including a drink, 6.30pm to 10pm), this hipster American-styled bar lures a 20s- to early-30s crowd out for a good time. The second Kitsch on Via San Gallo has a lovely,

chandelier-lit shabby-chic exterior and animal-print seating. Live bands.

Lochness Lounge   BAR
(Map p460; www.lochnessfirenze.com; Via de' Benci 19r; ⊙7pm-2am) Lochness is a sassy, vintage-cool music-and-cocktail venue with an Andy Warhol twist to its bold interior. Dane-turned-native Trine West is the creative force behind the place and DJs spin alternative sounds most nights. Drinks cost €5 during the daily 7pm to 10pm 'happy hour'; check Facebook for the week's line-up.

Moyo   BAR
(Map p460; www.moyo.it; Via de' Benci 23r; ⊙8am-2am Mon-Sat, 9am-3am Sun;) Free wi-fi until 7.30pm pulls in the crowds at this trendy all-rounder, popular for breakfast (€7 to €10), lunch (€8), *aperitivi* or late-night drinks. Cocktails (€7) are big – cranberry martini with lemon juice and triple sec is the house speciality – and DJs spin tip-top tunes Thursday to Saturday. And the decor? Think chandelier and bamboo!

Caffè Gilli   CAFE
(Map p460; Piazza della Repubblica 3r) The most famous of a trio of historic cafes atop the city's old Roman forum, Gilli has been serving utterly delectable cakes, chocolates, fruit tartlets and *millefoglie* (sheets of puff pastry filled with rich vanilla or chocolate chantilly cream) since 1733. It moved here in 1910 and has a beautifully preserved art nouveau interior.

Sei Divino   WINE BAR
(Borgo Ognissanti 42r; ⊙daily) This stylish 'wine gallery' hosts one of Florence's most happening *aperitivo* scenes, complete with music, the odd exhibition and plenty of pavement action.

Fiaschetteria Nuvoli   WINE BAR
(Map p460; Piazza dell'Olio 15r; ⊙7am-9pm Mon-Sat) Pull up a stool on the street and chat with a regular over a glass of *vino della casa* (house wine) at this old-fashioned *fiaschetteria*, a street away from the Duomo.

ZEB   WINE BAR
(off Map p474; www.zebgastronomia.com; Via San Miniato 2r; ⊙9.30am-8pm Thu, Mon & Tue, to 10.30pm Fri & Sat) This modern, minimalist *enoteca* with a lovely choice of cold cuts at the deli-style counter sits afoot the hill leading up to Piazzale Michelangelo – enter the perfect pit stop post-panorama.

Dolce Vita
BAR

(Map p474; www.dolcevitaflorence.com; Piazza del Carmine 6r; ☺5pm-2am Tue-Sun, closed 2 weeks Aug) For the city's hip set the other side of the river, this 1980s favourite remains *the* address.

Lion's Fountain
IRISH PUB

(Map p472; www.thelionsfountain.com; Borgo degli Albizi 34r; ☺10am-2am) If you have the urge to hear more English than Italian – or local bands play – come here. In summer the beer-loving crowd spills across most of the square.

Colle Bereto
BAR

(Map p460; www.collebereto.com; Piazza Strozzi 5; ☺8am-2am Tue-Sun; 🛜) The local fashion scene's bar of choice, uberstylish Colle Bereto is where the bold and the beautiful come to see or be seen.

The Old Stove
IRISH PUB

(Map p460; Piazza di San Giovanni 3; ☺11am-2am) A firm favourite among expats and foreign students, this tiny packed space has a wooden terrace facing the baptistry and a sought-after terrace for two up top.

Rex Caffé
BAR

(Map p472; Via Fiesolana 25r; ☺6pm-3am Sep-May) Another firm long-term favourite, down-to-earth Rex sports great drinks and an artsy Gaudi-inspired interior.

☆ Entertainment

Hanging out on warm summer nights on cafe and bar terraces aside, Florence enjoys a vibrant entertainment scene thanks in part to its substantial foreign-student population. The city has highly regarded theatres, a bounty of festivals (p477) and – from around midnight once *aperitivi* and dinner are done – a fairly low-key but varied dance scene.

Nightclubs

To savour the best of Florentine clubs, don't arrive before midnight – dance floors generally fill by 2am. June to September everything grinds to a halt when most clubs – bar Central Park and Meccanò Club, which have outdoor dance floors – shut. Admission, variable depending on the night, is usually more expensive for males than females and is sometimes free if you arrive early (between 9.30pm and 11pm).

YAB
DISCO

(Map p460; www.yab.it; Via Sassetti 5r; ☺9pm-4am Oct-May) It's crucial to pick your night

according to your age and tastes at Florence's busiest disco club, around since the 1970s behind Palazzo Strozzi. Thursdays is the evening the over-30s hit the dance floor – otherwise, the set is predominantly student.

Central Park
NIGHTCLUB

(Via Fosso Macinante 1; ☺11pm-4am Wed-Sat) Flit between a handful of different dance floors at this mainstream club in city park Parco delle Cascine where everything from Latin to pop, house to drum and bass plays. From May the dance floor moves outside beneath the stars.

Cavalli Club
NIGHTCLUB

(Map p474; www.cavalliclub.com; Piazza del Carmine 8r; ☺7.30pm-2.30am Tue-Sun) Incongruously wedged beside 13th-century Basilica di Santa Maria del Carmine, designer Robert Cavalli's club – in a deconsecrated church, look for the shiny red door – is glitzy, glam, wildly theatrical and over the top. Love it or hate it. Dine upstairs or sip cocktails with seafood *antipastissimo* (€38) downstairs. Dinner is €50.

Montecarla Club
NIGHTCLUB

(Map p474; Via de' Bardi 2; ☺10pm-6am) With its fearsome bouncers, boudoir furnishings and multi-level leopard-skin mosh pits, this small hip club exudes Late Empire decadence – and clubbing elitism. Dress to kill.

Cargo Club
NIGHTCLUB

(http://cargoclub.wordpress.com; Via dell'Erta Canina 12r; ☺11pm-4am Wed-Sat) Ex-Jaragua, this club prides itself on being a tad underground; DJs spin all sounds.

Full Up
DISCO

(Map p460; Via della Vigna Vecchia 21r; ☺11pm-4am Mon-Sat Sep-Jun) A variety of sounds energise the crowd at this popular Florentine nightclub where 20-somethings dance until dawn.

Meccanò
DISCO

(Viale degli Olmi 10; ☺11pm-5am Tue-Sat) Big-crowd disco in the city park with three dance floors spinning house, funk and standard commercial music to a mainstream youthful set.

Live Music

Most venues are outside town and closed in July and/or August.

1. Gelato and other desserts
Tuscany is a paradise for foodies.

2. Eating out in Lucca (p501)
At almost every turn there is a pavement terrace to dine alfresco.

3. Central Market (p469), Florence
Florence's oldest and largest food market is full of wonderful fresh produce.

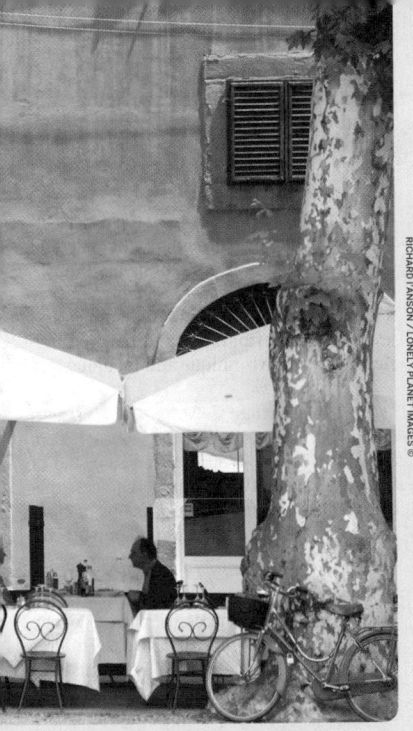

4. Wheatfield, Siena (p516)
Classic Tuscan countryside: gently rolling hills, sun-kissed vineyards and avenues of cypress trees.

5. Duomo (p458), Florence
The city's most iconic landmark took almost 150 years to complete.

RICHARD I'ANSON / LONELY PLANET IMAGES ©

3

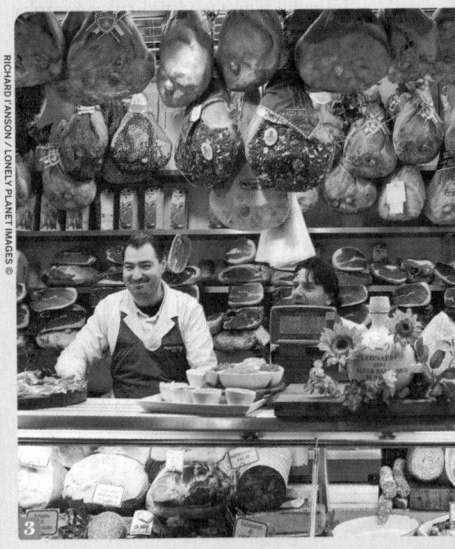

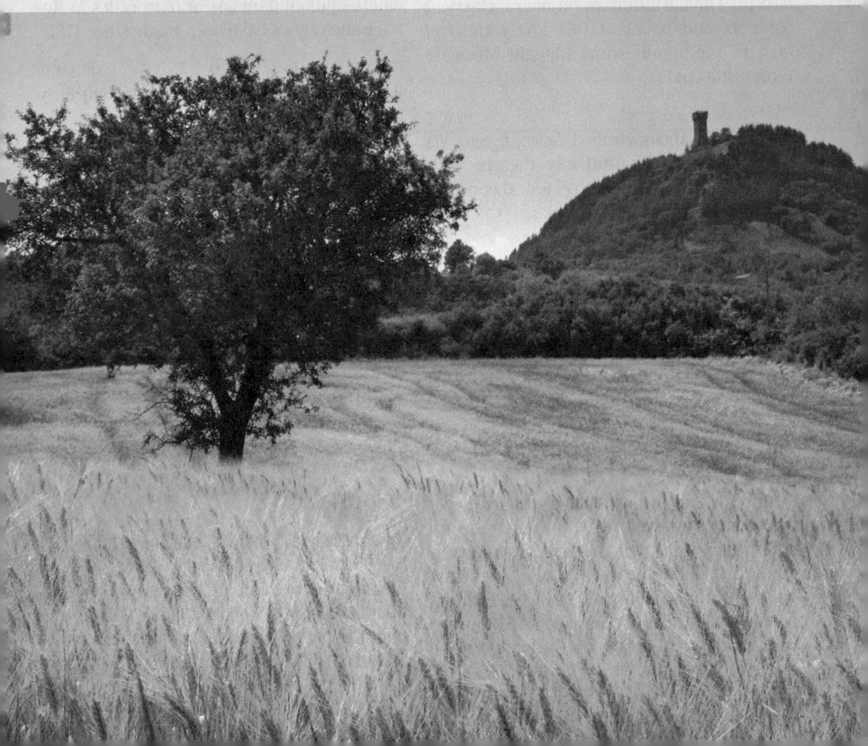

La Cité
LIVE MUSIC

(Map p474; www.lacitelibreria.info; Borgo San Frediano 20r; ⊙10am-1am Mon-Sat, 4pm-1am Sun; 🛜) By day this cafe-bookshop is a hip cappuccino stop with an eclectic choice of vintage seating to flop down on and surf. By night, the intimate bookshelf-lined space morphs into a vibrant live-music space: think swing, fusion, jam-session jazz...the staircase next to the bar hooks up with mezzanine seating up top.

Jazz Club
JAZZ CLUB

(Map p471; www.jazzclubfirenze.com; Via Nuovo de' Caccini 3; ⊙9pm-2am Tue-Sat, closed Jul & Aug) Catch salsa, blues, Dixieland and world music as well as jazz at Florence's top jazz venue.

Be Bop Music Club
LIVE MUSIC

(Map p460; Via dei Servi 76r; admission free; ⊙8pm-2am) Inspired by the Swinging Sixties, this beloved retro venue features everything from Led Zeppelin and Beatles cover bands to swing jazz and 1970s funk.

Theatre, Classical Music & Ballet

Teatro del Maggio Musicale Fiorentino
THEATRE

(☎055 287 222; www.maggiofiorentino.com; Corso Italia 16) The curtain rises on opera, classical concerts and ballet at this lovely theatre, host to the summertime Maggio Musicale Fiorentina (p477).

Teatro della Pergola
THEATRE

(☎055 2 26 41; www.teatrodellapergola.com; Via della Pergola 18) Beautiful city theatre with stunning entrance; host to classical concerts October to April.

🔒 Shopping

Tacky mass-produced souvenirs (boxer shorts emblazoned with *David*'s packet) are everywhere, not least at the city's two main markets: Mercato de San Lorenzo (Map p460; Piazza San Lorenzo; ⊙9am-7pm Mon-Sat); and Mercato Nuovo (Map p460; Loggia Mercato Nuovo; ⊙8.30am-7pm Mon-Sat), awash with cheap imported handbags and other leather goods.

But for serious shoppers keen to delve into a city synonymous with craftsmanship since medieval times, there are ateliers and studios to visit. Leather goods, jewellery, hand-embroidered linens, designer fashion, perfume, marbled paper, wine and gourmet foods are among the distinctively Florentine treats to take home.

In addition to the places listed below, try recommended address Scuola del Cuoio behind Basilica di Santa Croce (p471) for leather and Officina Profumo-Farmaceutica di Santa Maria Novella (p468) for perfume.

TOP CHOICE Mrs Macis
FASHION

(Map p472; Borgo Pinti 38r; ⊙3-7.30pm Mon-Sat) Workshop and showroom of the talented Carla Macis, this eye-catching boutique – dollhouse-like in design – specialises in very feminine 1950s, '60s and '70s clothes and jewellery made from new and recycled fabrics. Every piece is unique and fabulous.

TOP CHOICE Pitti Vintage
FASHION

(Map p460; Borgo degli Albizi 72r; ⊙10am-1.30pm & 3-7.30pm Tue-Sat 4-7.30pm Mon & Sun) One of the city's most stylish vintage choices, this creative boutique is a Pandora's box of carefully selected couture pieces and one-off collectables.

Antico Setifico Fiorentino
ARTISANAL

(off Map p474; www.anticosetificiofiorentino.com; Via Bartoini 4; ⊙9am-1pm & 2-5pm Mon-Fri) Precious silks, velvets and other luxurious fabrics are woven on 18th- and 19th-century looms at this world-famous fabric house where opulent damasks and brocades in Renaissance styles have been made since 1786.

Guilo Giannini e Figlio
ARTISANAL

(Map p474; www.guilogiannini.it; Piazza Pitti) Easy to miss, this quaint old shopfront has watched Palazzo Pitti turn pink with the evening sun since 1856. One of Florence's oldest artisan families, the Gianninis – bookbinders by trade – make and sell marbled paper, beautifully bound books, stationery and so on. Don't miss the workshop upstairs.

Société Anonyme
FASHION

(Map p472; www.societeanonyme.it; Via Niccolini 3f) Near Sant'Ambrogio food market, this urban concept store turns to London's Brick Lane, Berlin's Mitte and other hip neighbourhoods for inspiration. Look for its list of brands chalked on the board outside (and the Shared Platform design gallery next door).

TOP CHOICE Dolce Forte
FOOD

(www.dolceforte.it; Via della Scala 21; ⊙3.30-7.45pm Tue, 10am-1pm & 3.30-7.45pm Wed-Sat & Mon) Elena is the passion and knowledge behind this astonishing chocolate shop, which sells only the best. Think black-truffle chocolate, a cherry soaked in grappa and wrapped in

Florence is the birthplace of Gucci, Emilio Pucci, Roberto Cavalli and Ermanno Scervino alongside a bevy of lesser-known designers who beaver away to ensure Florence's continuing reputation as a city synonymous with beauty, creativity and skilled craftsmanship.

Which is precisely what Florence's Department of Tourism and Fashion strives to promote with its outstanding website www.florenceartfashion.com, an authoritative guide to the city's fashion studios and workshops. Themed itineraries walk you through small ateliers and boutiques that design and craft footwear, women's fashion, jewellery, and so on; and you can also sign up for an on-the-ground **guided fashion tour**.

To DIY shop, legendary **Via de' Tornabuoni** – a fashionably quaint street with a pharmacy, bookshop, several cafes and so on until Florence Fashion dug in her manicured claws and turned it into the glittering catwalk of designer boutiques it is today – is the place to start. **Via della Vigna Nuova**, the street where icon of Florence fashion Gucci started out as a tiny saddlery shop in 1921, is Florence's other fashion-hot street.

white chocolate or – for the ultimate taste sensation – *formaggio di fossa* (a cheese from central Italy) soaked in sweet wine and enrobed in dark chocolate.

 Slow ECO DESIGN
(Map p474; www.slow-design.it; Sdruccioli dei Pitti 13r) Beautiful objects for the home, all crafted from natural or recycled materials by local designers.

Obsequium WINE
(www.obsequium.it; Borgo San Jacopo 17-39r) Fine Tuscan wines, wine accessories and gourmet foods, including truffles.

Madova FASHION
(Map p474; www.madova.com; Via Guicciardini 1r; ⊙Mon-Sat) Cashmere-lined, silk-lined, lambswool-lined, unlined – gloves in whatever size, shape, colour and type of leather you fancy by Florentine glovemakers in the biz since 1919.

Barberino Designer Outlet FASHION
(www.mcarthurglen.it; Via Meucci, Barberino di Mugello; ⊙10am-8pm Tue-Fri, to 9pm Sat & Sun, 2-8pm Mon Jan, Jun-Sep & Dec) Previous season's collections at discounted prices, 40km north. A shuttle bus (return €12, 35 minutes) departs from Piazza Stazione at 10am or 2.30pm, returning at 1.30pm or 6pm.

Mall FASHION
(www.themall.it; Via Europa 8, Leccio; ⊙10am-7pm or 8pm daily) Find this busy designer outlet 35km from Florence; buses (€3.30, up to four daily) from the SITA bus station.

Information

Emergency
Police station (Questura; ☑055 4 97 71; http://questure.poliziadistato.it; Via Zara 2; ⊙24hr)

Tourist Police (Polizia Assistenza Turistica; ☑055 20 39 11; Via Pietrapiana 50r; ⊙8.30am-6.30pm Mon-Fri, to 1pm Sat) English-speaking service for filing reports of thefts etc.

Medical Services
24-hour pharmacy (Stazione di Santa Maria Novella) In the main train station.

Dr Stephen Kerr: Medical Service (☑055 28 80 55, 335 8361682; www.dr-kerr.com; Piazza Mercato Nuovo 1; ⊙3-5pm Mon-Fri, or by appointment) Resident British doctor.

Tourist Information
Amerigo Vespucci airport (☑055 31 58 74; ⊙8.30am-8.30pm)

Train station (Map p460; ☑055 21 22 45; Piazza della Stazione 4; ⊙8.30am-7pm Mon-Sat, 8.30am-2pm Sun) Baby changing facilities.

Santa Croce (Map p472; ☑055 234 04 44; www.comune.fi.it, in Italian; Borgo Santa Croce 29r; ⊙9am-7pm Mon-Sat, 9am-2pm Sun)

San Lorenzo (Map p470; ☑055 29 08 32; www.firenzeturismo.it; Via Cavour 1r; ⊙8.30am-6.30pm Mon-Sat)

Websites
Firenze Spettacolo (www.firenzespettacolo.it)
The Florentine (www.theflorentine.net)
Notte Fiorentina (www.nottefiorentina.it)
Viva Notte Firenze (www.vivanotte.it)
ViviFirenze (www.vivifirenze.it)

ℹ Getting There & Away

Air

Florence airport (www.aeroporto.firenze.it) Also known as Amerigo Vespucci or Peretola airport, 5km northwest of the city centre; domestic and a handful of European flights.

Pisa airport (www.pisa-airport.com) Tuscany's main international airport named after Galileo Galilei is nearer Pisa, but well linked with Florence by public transport.

Bus

Services from the **SITA bus station** (www.sitabus.it; Via Santa Caterina da Siena 17r; ⊘information office 8.30am-12.30pm & 3-6pm Mon-Fri, 8.30am-12.30pm Sat), just west of Piazza della Stazione, go to the following towns.

Siena (€7.10, 1¼ hours, at least hourly)

San Gimignano via Poggibonsi (€6.25, 50 minutes, at least hourly).

Greve in Chianti (€3.30, one hour, hourly)

Car & Motorcycle

Florence is connected by the A1 northward to Bologna and Milan, and southward to Rome and Naples. The Autostrada del Mare (A11) links Florence with Pistoia, Lucca, Pisa and the coast, but most locals use the FI-PI-LI – a *superstrada* (dual carriageway, hence no tolls); look for blue signs saying FI-PI-LI (as in Firenze-Pisa-Livorno). Another dual carriageway, the S2, links Florence with Siena.

Train

Florence's central train station is **Stazione di Santa Maria Novella** (Map p458; Piazza della Stazione). The **train information counter** (⊘7am-7pm) faces the tracks in the main foyer. The **left-luggage counter** (Deposito Bagagliamano; first 5hr €4, then €0.60 per hr; ⊘6am-11.50pm) is located on platform 16 and the Assistenza Disabili (Disabled Assistance) office is on platform 5. International train tickets are sold in the **ticketing hall** (⊘6am-9pm). For domestic tickets, skip the queue and buy your tickets from the touch-screen automatic ticket-vending machines; machines have an English option and accept cash and credit cards.

Florence is on the Rome–Milan line. Services include the following:

Lucca (€5.10, 1½ hours to 1¾ hours, half-hourly)

Pisa (€5.80, 45 minutes to one hour, half-hourly)

Pistoia (€3.10, 45 minutes to one hour, half-hourly)

Rome (€17.25, 1¾ hours to 4¼ hours)

Bologna (€10.50 to €25, one hour to 1¾ hours)

Milan (€29.50 to €53, 2¼ hours to 3½ hours)

Venice (€24 to €43, 2¾ hours to 4½ hours)

ℹ Getting Around

To/From the Airport

BUS A shuttle (single/return €5/8, 25 minutes) travels between Florence airport and Florence's Stazione di Santa Maria Novella train station every 30 minutes between 6am and 11.30pm. **Terravision** (www.terravision.eu) runs daily services (single/return €10/16, 1¼ hours, 13 daily) between the bus stop outside Florence's Stazione di Santa Maria Novella on Via Alamanni and Pisa's Galileo Galilei airport – buy tickets online, on board or from the **Terravision desk** (Via Alamanni 9r; ⊘6am-7pm) inside the Deanna Bar; at Galileo Galilei airport, the Terravision ticket desk dominates the arrival hall.

TAXI A taxi between Florence airport and town costs a flat rate of €20, plus surcharges of €2 on Sunday and holidays, €3 between 10pm and 6am and €1 per bag. Exit the terminal building, bear right and you'll come to the taxi rank.

TRAIN Regular trains link Florence's Stazione di Santa Maria Novella with Pisa's Galileo Galilei airport (€5.80, 1½ hours, at least hourly from 4.30am to 10.25pm).

Bicycle & Scooter

Biciclette a Noleggio (Piazza della Stazione; per hr/day €1.50/8; ⊘7.30am-7pm Mon-Sat, 9am-7pm Sun, to 6pm Nov-Jan) Royal-blue bikes to rent in front of the train station.

Rental Point Ghiberti (Piazza Sant'Ambrogio; per hr/day €1.50/8; ⊘8.30am-7pm Mon-Sat May-Sep, shorter hr Oct-Apr) Open-air stand behind Sant'Ambrogio market.

Florence by Bike (www.florencebybike.com; Via San Zanobi 120r; city bike/scooter €14.50/68 per day; ⊘9am-1pm & 3.30-7.30pm Mon-Sat) Top-notch bike shop, itinerary suggestions, bike routes and rental outlet.

Car & Motorcycle

Most traffic is banned from the historic centre and motorists risk a hefty fine if they breach the rules.

There is free street parking around Piazzale Michelangelo (park within blue lines; white lines are for residents only). Pricey underground parking can be found in the area around the Fortezza da Basso and in the Oltrarno beneath Piazzale di Porta Romana. Otherwise, many hotels arrange parking for guests.

Public Transport

Buses and electric *bussini* (minibuses) run by **ATAF** (☎800 424500; from mobiles ☎199 104245; www.ataf.net, in Italian) serve the city. Most start/terminate at the ATAF bus stops opposite the southeastern exit of Stazione di Santa Maria Novella.

Tickets valid for 90 minutes (no return journeys) cost €1.20 (€2 on board) and are sold at kiosks, tobacconists and the **ATAF ticket & information office** (⊗7.30am-7.30pm) adjoining the train station.

A carnet of 10 tickets costs €10, a handy *biglietto multiplo* (four-journey ticket) is €4.70 and a travel pass valid for 1/3/7 days is €5/12/18. Passengers caught travelling without a time-stamped ticket (punch it on board) are fined.

If you prefer the speed and convenience of an SMS bus ticket, you'll need to first register your credit card (Visa or MasterCard) with Bemoov (www.bemoov.com). After that it's plain sailing: before hopping aboard send a text with the message 'ataf' to ☑339 9941264 and receive within seconds a reply containing an alphanumeric code that will keep any ticket controller happy. SMS tickets cost the same as paper tickets.

Taxi

Hailing a taxi in the street is not easy given stands are not always marked. Pick one up at the train station or ring for one by telephone:
☑055 42 42
☑055 43 90

NORTHERN & WESTERN TUSCANY

Travel through this part of Tuscany and you will be left with a true understanding of what the term 'slow travel' really means. Lingering over lunches of rustic regional specialities swiftly becomes the norm, as do activities such as meandering through medieval hilltop villages, taking leisurely bike rides along coastal wine trails with spectacular scenery or hiking on an island where Napoleon was once exiled. Even the larger towns here – including the university hub of Pisa and 'love at first sight' Lucca – have an air of tranquillity and tradition about them that positively begs the traveller to stay for a few days of cultural R&R.

Pisa

POP 87,440

Once a maritime power to rival Genoa and Venice, Pisa now draws its fame from an architectural project gone terribly wrong. But the world-famous Leaning Tower is just one of many noteworthy sights in this compact and compelling city. Education has fuelled the local economy since the 1400s, and students from across Italy still compete for

ⓘ
TOWER & COMBO TICKETS

Reserve and buy tickets for the Leaning Tower from one of two well-signposted **ticket offices** (www.opapisa.it; Piazza dei Miracoli; ⊗8am-7.30pm Apr-Sep, 8.30am-7pm Oct, 9am-5pm Nov & Feb, 9.30am-4.30pm Dec-Jan, 8.30am-6pm Mar): the main ticket office behind the tower or the smaller office inside Museo delle Sinópie. To guarantee your visit to the Tower, book tickets via the website at least 15 days in advance.

The ticket offices also sell combination tickets covering admission to the Baptistry, Camposanto, Museo dell'Opera del Duomo and Museo delle Sinópie: buy a ticket covering one/two/five admissions costing €5/6/10 (reduced €2/3/5, under 10 years free) and pick which sights to visit.

places in its elite university and research schools. This endows the centre of town with a vibrant and affordable cafe and bar scene, and balances what is an enviable portfolio of well-maintained Romanesque buildings, Gothic churches and Renaissance piazzas with a lively street life dominated by locals rather than tourists.

Sure, the iconic Leaning Tower is Pisa's raison d'être and the reason everyone wants to go to Pisa. But once you've put yourself through the whole Piazza del Miracoli madness (overzealous souvenir sellers, boisterous school groups, photo-posing pandemonium, you get the picture...) most people simply want to get out of town.

To avoid leaving Pisa feeling oddly deflated by one of Europe's great landmarks, save the Leaning Tower and its miraculous square for the latter part of the day – or, better still, an enchanting visit after dark (mid-June to August), when the night casts a certain magic on the glistening white monuments and the tour buses have long gone.

Upon arrival, indulge instead in peaceful meanderings along the Arno river, over its bridges and through Pisa's medieval heart. Enjoy low-key architectural and art genius at the Chiesa di Santa Maria della Spina and Palazzo Blu, and lunch with locals at Sottobosco.

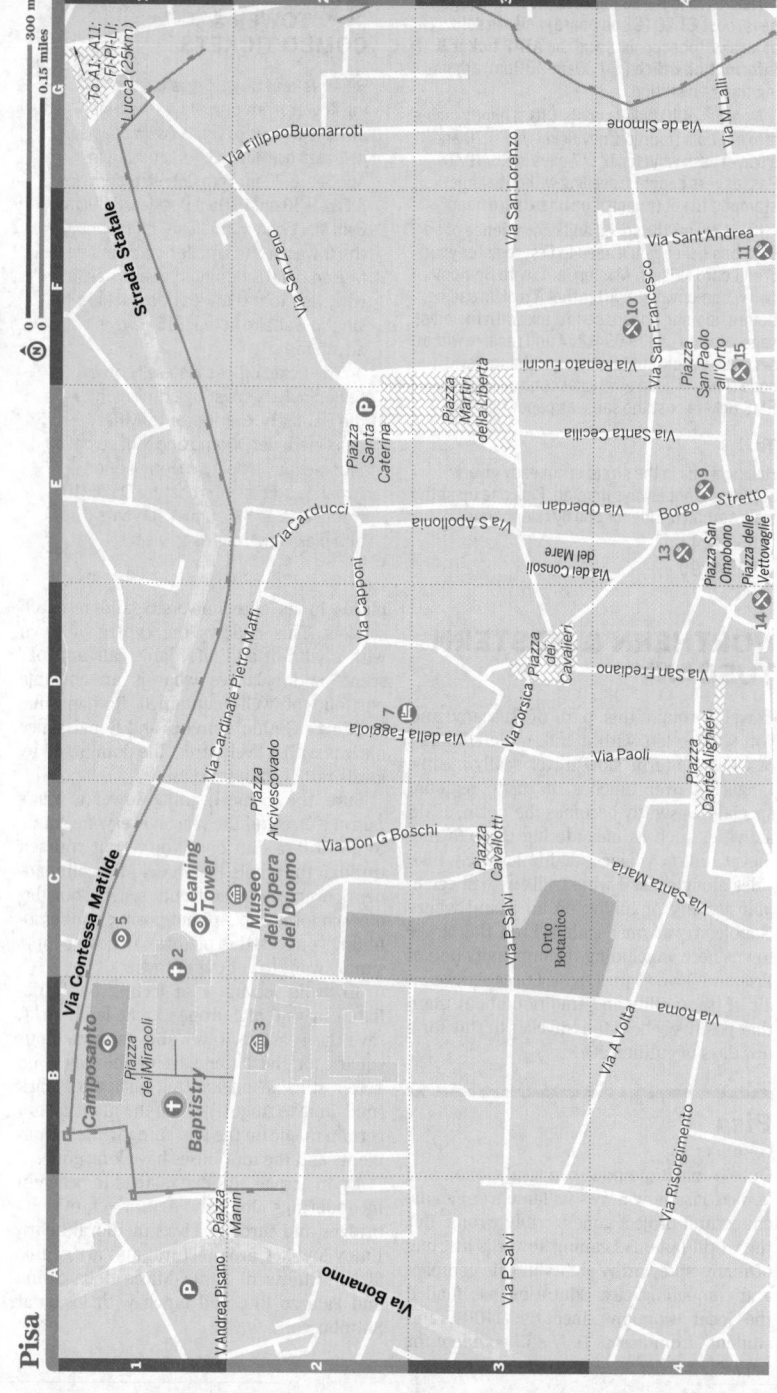

FLORENCE & TUSCANY NORTHERN & WESTERN TUSCANY

Pisa

To A1, A11;
FI-PI-LI;
Lucca (25km)

300 m
0.15 miles

Strada Statale

Via Filippo Buonarroti

Via San Zeno

Via Contessa Matilde

Camposanto

Piazza
dei Miracoli

Baptistry

V Andrea Pisano

Piazza
Manin

Via Bonanno

Via Andrea Pisano

Leaning
Tower

Museo
dell'Opera
del Duomo

Piazza
Arcivescovado

Via Cardinale Pietro Maffi

Via Carducci

Piazza
Santa
Caterina

Via San Lorenzo

Via de Simone

Via M Lalli

Via Sant'Andrea

Via San Francesco

Via Renato Fucini

Piazza
San Paolo
all'Orto

Piazza
Martiri
della Libertà

Via Santa Cecilia

Via Oberdan

Via S Apollonia

Via del Consoli
del Mare

Borgo Stretto

Piazza San
Omobono

Piazza delle
Vettovaglie

Via della Faggiola

Via Don G Boschi

Via Capponi

Piazza
dei
Cavalieri

Via Corsica

Via San Frediano

Piazza
Cavallotti

Via Paoli

Piazza
Dante Alighieri

Via P Salvi

Orto
Botanico

Via Santa Maria

Via Roma

Via A Volta

Via P Salvi

Via Risorgimento

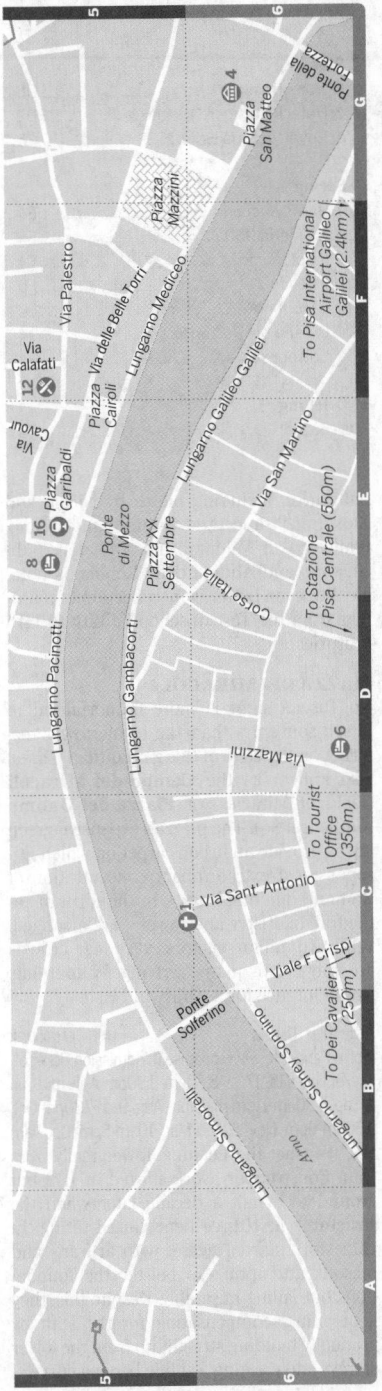

And only then, once you've fallen in love with the other Pisa, should you head for its tower.

History

Possibly of Greek origin, Pisa became an important naval base under Rome and remained a significant port for many centuries. The city's so-called golden days began late in the 9th century when it became an independent maritime republic and a rival of Genoa and Venice. The good times rolled on into the 12th and 13th centuries, by which time Pisa controlled Corsica, Sardinia and most of the mainland coast as far south as Civitavecchia. Most of the city's finest buildings date from this period, when the distinctive Pisan-Romanesque architectural style flourished.

Pisa's support for the Ghibellines during the tussles between the Holy Roman Emperor and the pope brought the city into conflict with its mostly Guelph Tuscan neighbours, including Siena, Lucca and Florence. The real blow came when Genoa's fleet defeated Pisa in devastating fashion at the Battle of Meloria in 1284. After the city fell to Florence in 1406, the Medici encouraged great artistic, literary and scientific endeavours and re-established Pisa's university. Galileo Galilei, the city's most famous son, later taught at the university.

⊙ Sights

ALONG THE ARNO

Away from the crowded heavyweights of Piazza dei Miracoli, along the Arno river banks, Pisa comes into its own. Splendid *palazzo,* painted a multitude of hues, line the southern *lungarno* (riverside embankment) from where Pisa's main shopping boulevard, **Corso Italia**, legs it south to the train station.

Pisa's medieval heart lies north of the water. From riverside **Piazza Cairoli** with its evening bevy of bars and gelaterie, meander along **Via Cavour** and get lost in the surrounding narrow lanes and alleys. A daily fresh-produce market fills **Piazza delle Vettovaglie**, ringed with 15th-century porticoes and popular *aperitivo* bar and cafe terraces. And marvel at graffiti on the facade of **Chiesa di San Michele in Borgo** (Borgo Stretto) that dates all the way back to a 15th-century election for the rector of a local school.

Chiesa di Santa Maria della Spina   CHURCH
(Lungarno Gambacorti; adult/reduced €2/1.50; ☉11am-12.45pm & 3-5.45pm Tue-Fri, 11am-12.45pm & 3-6.45pm Sat & Sun) A Pisan architectural gem, this exquisite church plump on the Arno's southern bank, is a fine example of Pisan-Gothic style. The now-deconsecrated church, built between 1230 and 1223 to house a reliquary of a *spina* (thorn) from Christ's crown, is refreshingly intimate. Its ornate, triple-spired exterior is encrusted with tabernacles and statues. The focal point inside is Andrea and Nino Pisano's *Madonna and Child* (aka Madonna of the Rose; 1345–48), a masterpiece of Gothic sculpture that still bears traces of its original colours and gilding.

FREE **Palazzo Blu**   ART GALLERY
(www.palazzoblu.it; Lungarno Gambacorti 9; ☉10am-7pm Tue-Fri, 10am-8pm Sat & Sun) Facing the river is this magnificently restored, 14th-century building with striking dusty-blue facade. Inside, its over-the-top 19th-century interior decoration is the perfect backdrop for the Foundation CariPisa's art collection – Pisan works from the 14th to the 20th century, plus various temporary exhibitions.

Museo Nazionale di San Matteo   ART GALLERY
(Piazza San Matteo in Soarta, Lungarno Mediceo; adult/reduced €5/2; ☉8.30am-7.30pm Tue-Sat, 8.30am-1.30pm Sun) This repository of medieval masterpieces sits in a 13th-century Benedictine convent on the Arno's northern waterfront boulevard. The gallery's collection of 14th- and 15th-century Pisan sculptures, including pieces by Nicola and Giovanni Pisano, Andrea and Nino Pisano, Francesco di Valdambrino, Donatello, Michelozzo and Andrea della Robbia, is notable. But even better is its collection of paintings from the Tuscan school (c 12th to 14th centuries).

PIAZZA DEI MIRACOLI
No Tuscan sight is more immortalised in kitsch souvenirs than the iconic tower teetering on the edge of this gargantuan piazza, also known as the **Campo dei Miracoli** (Field of Miracles) or **Piazza del Duomo** (Cathedral Sq). The piazza's expansive green lawns provide an urban carpet on which Europe's most extraordinary concentration of Romanesque buildings – in the form of cathedral, baptistry and tower – are arranged. With two million visitors every year, crowds are the norm, many arriving by tour bus from Florence for a whirlwind visit.

Leaning Tower   LANDMARK
(Torre Pendente; www.opapisa.it; admission ticket office/online €15/17; ☉8.30am-8.30pm Apr–mid-Jun & Sep, 8.30am-11pm mid-Jun–Aug, 9am-7.30pm Oct, 9.30am-6pm Nov & Feb-Mar, 10am-5pm Dec-Jan) Yes, it's true: the Leaning Tower really *does* lean. Construction work started in 1173 but ground to a halt a decade later when the structure's first three tiers started tilting. In 1272 work started again, with artisans and masons attempting to bolster the foundations but failing miserably. Despite this, they kept going, compensating for the lean by gradually building straight up from the lower storeys and creating a subtle banana curve.

Over the centuries, the tower has tilted an extra 1mm each year. By 1993 it was 4.47m out of plumb, more than five degrees from the vertical. The most recent solution saw steel braces slung around the third storey that were then joined to steel cables attached to neighbouring buildings. This held the tower in place as engineers began gingerly removing soil from below the northern foundations. After some 70 tonnes of earth had been extracted from the northern side, the tower sank to its 18th-century level and, in the process, rectified the lean by 43.8cm. Experts believe that this will guarantee the tower's future (and a fat tourist income) for the next three centuries.

Access to the Leaning Tower is limited to 40 people at one time – children under eight are not admitted. To avoid disappointment, book in advance online or go straight to a ticket office when you arrive in Pisa to book a slot for later in the day. Visits last 30 minutes and involve a steep climb up 294 occasionally slippy steps. All bags, handbags included, must be deposited at the free left-luggage desk next to the central ticket office – cameras are about the only thing you can take up.

Duomo

(Piazza dei Miracoli; adult/reduced €2/1, admission free Nov-Mar & Sun year-round; ☉10am-8pm mid-Mar–Sep, 10am-7pm Oct, 10am-1pm & 2-5pm Nov-Feb, 10am-6 or 7pm early–mid-Mar) Pisa's cathedral was paid for with spoils brought home after Pisans attacked an Arab fleet entering Palermo in 1063. Begun a year later, the cathedral, with its striking cladding of alternating bands of green and cream marble, became the blueprint floor for Romanesque churches throughout Tuscany. The elliptical dome, the first of its kind in Europe at the time, was added in 1380.

The cathedral was Europe's largest when it was constructed; its breathtaking proportions were designed to demonstrate Pisa's domination of the Mediterranean. Its main facade – not completed until the 13th century – has four exquisite tiers of columns diminishing skywards, while the vast interior is propped up by 68 hefty granite columns in classical style. The wooden **ceiling** decorated with 24-carat gold is a legacy from the period of Medici rule.

Inside, don't miss the extraordinary early-14th-century octagonal **pulpit** in the north aisle. Sculpted from Carrara marble by Giovanni Pisano and featuring nude and heroic figures, its depth of detail and heightening of feeling brought a new pictorial expressionism and life to Gothic sculpture. Pisano's work forms a striking contrast to the modern pulpit and altar by Italian sculptor Giuliano Vangi, which were controversially installed in 2001.

Baptistry

BAPTISTERY

(Piazza dei Miracoli; adult/reduced €5/2; ☉8am-8pm Apr-Sep, 9am-7pm Oct, 10am-5pm Nov-Feb,

FLORENCE & TUSCANY PISA

TOP FIVE FACTS YOU NEVER KNEW ABOUT THE TOWER

» In 1160 Pisa boasted 10,000-odd towers – but no bell tower for its cathedral. Loyal Pisan Berta di Bernardo righted this in 1172 when she died, leaving a legacy of 60 *soldi* in her will to the city to get cracking on a *campanile* (bell tower).

» The Leaning Tower – a whimsical folly of its inventors – was built to lean: hotly debated in the early 19th century, this theory was blown to shreds in 1838 when a clean-up job to remove muck oozing from its base revealed the true nature of its precarious foundations.

» It is not the only tower in Pisa to lean: the neighbouring Duomo tilts 25cm to the north and the Baptistry, 51cm north. Away from the square, the octagonal bell tower of Chiesa di San Nicola (Via Santa Maria) by Nicola Pisano and that of Chiesa di San Michele degli Scalzi (Via San Michele degli Scalzi), a wonky red-brick square tower north of the centre, both lean too.

» Moscow will help restore the city of Pisa, shipping in construction workers by train from Odessa, Tashkent and Dushanbe to build skyscrapers around the cathedral and a vast car park beneath the Leaning Tower to resolve traffic congestion around one of Italy's most visited sights – the April Fools run by the *Moscow Times* on 1 April 2004.

» Seven bells, each sounding a different musical note and rung from the ground by 14 men, were added to the completed tower in 1370 but silenced in the 1950s for fear of a catastrophic collapse.

FIESOLE DAY TRIPPER

One of the joys of Florence is leaving it behind and Fiesole provides the perfect excuse. This hilltop village, 9km northeast of the city, has seduced for centuries with its cooler air, olive groves, scattering of Renaissance-styled villas and spectacular views of the plain. Boccaccio, Marcel Proust, Gertrude Stein and Frank Lloyd Wright, among others, all raved about it.

10am

Hop aboard ATAF bus 7 (€1.20) from Florence's Piazza San Marco and alight 30 minutes later on Fiesole's central square, Piazza Mino di Fiesole. Founded in the 7th century BC by the Etruscans, Fiesole was the most important city in northern Etruria and its **Area Archeologica** (www.fiesolemusei.it; Via Portigiani 1; adult/reduced €12/8; ⊙10am-7pm Apr-Sep, to 6pm Mar & Oct, 10am-2pm Wed-Mon Nov-Feb), a couple of doors down from the **tourist office** (☑055 596 13 23; www.comune.fiesole.fi.it; Via Portigiani 3; ⊙10.30am-1pm & 1.30-4pm Mar-Oct, shorter hr rest of year), provides the perfect flashback to its fabulous past. Meander around the ruins of a small Etruscan temple, Roman baths and an archaeological museum with exhibits from the Bronze Age to the Roman period. Later, take a break alfresco on one of the stone steps of the 1st-century-BC Roman amphitheatre where musicians, actors and artists take to the stage in summer during Italy's oldest open-air festival, **Estate Fiesolana** (www.estatefiesolana.it). July's **Vivere Jazz Festival** (www.viverejazz.it) is the other hot date at this atmospheric theatre.

Afterwards, pop into the neighbouring **Museo Bandini** (Via Dupré; adult/reduced €5/3 or free with Area Archeologica ticket; ⊙9.30am-7pm Apr-Sep, 9.30am-6pm Oct & Mar, 10am-5pm Wed-Mon Nov-Dec, 11am-5pm Thu-Mon Jan & Feb) to view early Tuscan Renaissance art, including fine medallions (c 1505–20) by Giovanni della Robbia and Taddeo Gaddi's luminous *Annunciation* (1340–45).

Noon

From the museum, a 300m walk along Via Giovanni Dupré brings you to the lavish villa of **Museo Primo Conti** (www.fondazioneprimoconti.org; Via Dupré 18; admission €3; ⊙9am-1pm Mon-Fri) where the eponymous avant-garde 20th-century artist lived and worked. Inside hang over 60 of his paintings and the views from the garden are inspiring. Ring to enter.

1pm

Meander back to main square, **Piazza MinoFiesole**, host to an antiques market the first Sunday of each month, where cafe and restaurant terraces tempt on all sides. The pagoda-covered terrace of four-star hotel-restaurant **Villa Aurora** (☑055 5 93 63; www.villaurora.net; Piazza Mino Fiesole 39; meals €50; ⊙lunch & dinner, closed Mon winter), around since 1860, is the classic choice, not so much for the gourmet cuisine but rather for the spectacular panoramic view of Florence it cooks up. For a wholly rustic and typical Tuscan lunch built around locally produced salami and cheese, homemade pasta and Chianina T-bones eaten at a shared table, *enoteca*-cum-bistro **Vinandro** (☑055 5 91 21; www.vinandrofiesole.com; Piazza Mino Fiesole 33; meals €25; ⊙lunch & dinner Tue-Sun) is the hot spot on the square to grab a table.

3pm

Stagger around **Cattedrale di San Romolo** (Piazza Mino Fiesole; ⊙7.30am-noon & 3-5pm), the central square's centrepiece, begun in the 11th century but renovated in the 19th. A terracotta statue of San Romolo by Giovanni della Robbia guards the entrance inside.

Afterwards, from the far end of the square, make your way up steep walled **Via San Francesco** and be blown away by the beautiful panorama of Florence that unfolds from the terrace adjoining 15th-century **Basilica di Sant'Alessandro**. (If you're lucky, the church might be open and have a temporary exhibition inside.) Grassy-green afternoon-nap spots abound and the tourist office has brochures outlining several short trails (1km to 3.5km) fanning out from here, should you prefer to carry on walking.

9am-6pm Mar) The unusual round Baptistry has one dome piled on top of another. Construction began in 1152, but it was notably remodelled and continued by Nicola and Giovanni Pisano more than a century later and was finally completed in the 14th century – hence its hybrid architectural style: the lower level of arcades is Pisan-Romanesque; the pinnacled upper section and dome are Gothic.

Inside, the beautiful hexagonal marble **pulpit** carved by Nicola Pisano between 1259 and 1260 is the undisputed highlight. Inspired by the Roman sarcophagi in the Camposanto, Pisano used powerful classical models to enact scenes from biblical legend. His figure of Daniel, who supports one of the corners of the pulpit on his shoulders, is one of the earliest heroic nude figures in Italian art, often cited as the inauguration of a tradition that would reach perfection with Michelangelo's *David*.

Pisan scientist Galileo Galilei (who, so the story goes, came up with the laws of the pendulum by watching a lamp in Pisa's cathedral swing) was baptised in the **octagonal font** (1246).

Don't leave the baptistry without (a) admiring the Islamic floor, (b) climbing up to the gallery for a stunning overview, (c) risking a whisper and listening to it resound; otherwise, the custodian demonstrates the double dome's remarkable acoustics and echo effects every half-hour.

Camposanto CEMETERY

(Piazza dei Miracoli; adult/reduced €5/2; ⌚8.30am-8pm Apr–mid-Jun & Sep, to 11pm mid-Jun–Aug, 9am-7pm Oct, 10am-5pm Nov-Feb, 9am-6pm Mar) Soil shipped from Calvary during the Crusades is said to lie within the white walls of this hauntingly beautiful cemetery, a beautiful final resting place for many prominent Pisans, arranged around a garden in a cloistered quadrangle.

During WWII, Allied artillery destroyed many of the cloisters' precious frescoes. Those that survived are the focus of the Museo delle Sinópie.

Museo delle Sinópie MUSEUM

(Piazza dei Miracoli; adult/reduced €5/2; ⌚8am-8pm Apr-Sep, 9am-7pm Oct, 10am-5pm Nov-Feb, 9am-6pm Mar) Home to some wonderful pieces of wall art, this museum safeguards those precious few 14th- and 15th-century frescoes not destroyed by Allied artillery during WWII. Most notable is the *Triumph of Death,* a remarkable illustration of Hell attributed to 14th-century painter Buonamico Buffalmacco.

Museo dell'Opera del Duomo MUSEUM

(Piazza dei Miracoli; adult/reduced €5/2; ⌚8am-8pm Apr-Sep, 9am-7pm Oct, 10am-5pm Nov-Feb, 9am-6pm Mar) No museum provides a better round-up of Piazza dei Miracoli's trio of architectural masterpieces than this museum inside the cathedral's former chapter house. Highlights include Giovanni Pisano's ivory carving of the *Madonna and Child* (1299), made for the cathedral's high altar, and his mid-13th-century *Madonna del colloquio,* originally from a gate of the Duomo. Legendary booty includes various pieces of Islamic art including the griffin that once topped the cathedral and a 10th-century Moorish hippogriff.

Festivals & Events

Luminaria FIREWORKS

The night before Pisa's patron saint's day is magical: thousands upon thousands of candles and blazing torches light up the river and riverbanks while fireworks bedazzle the night sky; 16 June.

Regata Storica di San Ranieri SPORT

The Arno comes to life with a rowing regatta to commemorate the city's patron saint; 17 June.

Gioco del Ponte MEDIEVAL

(Game of the Bridge) Two teams in medieval costume battle it out over the Ponte di Mezzo; last Sunday in June.

Palio delle Quattro Antiche Repubbliche Marinare SPORT

(Regatta of the Four Ancient Maritime Republics) The four historical maritime rivals – Pisa, Venice, Amalfi and Genoa – meet each year in June for a procession of boats and dramatic race; the next to be held in Pisa will be in 2014.

Sleeping

TOP CHOICE **Royal Victoria Hotel** HOTEL €

(☎050 94 01 11; www.royalvictoria.it; Lungarno Pacinotti 12; s without bathroom €30-45, d without bathroom €40-55, d €65-80, tr €80-120, q €120-175; P❄📶👪) This doyen of Pisan hotels has been run with pride by the Piegaja family since 1837. The word on the street says rooms vary, but those we saw were the perfect shabby-chic mix of Grand Tour antique and modern-day comfort. The unquestionable highlight is an aperitif flopped on a sofa on the flowery 4th-floor terrace.

Hotel Bologna
HOTEL €€

(℡050 50 21 20; www.hotelbologna.pisa.it; Via Mazzini 57; s €59-99, d €79-179, tr €99-199, q €119-259; P❄@🖥👪) A pleasant 1km walk or bike ride from the Piazza dei Miracoli mayhem, this four-star choice is a 68-room oasis of peace and tranquillity. Rooms for four make it a practical, if pricey, family choice. Kudos to the small terrace garden out back – perfect for a summer breakfast!

Hotel Relais dell'Orologio
HOTEL €€€

(℡050 83 03 61; www.hotelrelaisorologio.com; Via della Faggiola 12-14; d €200-800; P❄🖥) Something of a honeymoon venue, Pisa's dreamy five-star hotel occupies a tastefully restored 14th-century fortified tower house in a quiet street.

Dei Cavalieri
B&B €

(℡050 99 10 597, 291 22 880; www.deicavalieri.pisa.it; Piazza Sant'Antonio 4; s/d/tr/q €45/65/89/99; @🖥) Hidden in a 4th-floor apartment, views of the Pisan rooftops are lovely here. Count €10 less a night for rooms with shared bathroom.

✕ Eating

Being a university town, Pisa has a good range of eating places, especially around Borgo Stretto and south of the river in the trendy San Martino quarter.

⌜TOP⌟CHOICE Sottobosco
CAFE €

(www.sottoboscocafe.it; Piazza San Paolo all'Orto; lunches €15; ⊙10am-midnight Tue-Fri, noon-1am Sat, 7pm-midnight Sun) What a tourist-free breath of fresh air this creative cafe with a few books for sale is! Tuck into a sugary ring doughnut and cappuccino at a glass-topped table filled with artists' crayons perhaps, or a collection of buttons. Lunch dishes (salads, pies and pasta) are simple and homemade and come dusk, jazz bands play or DJs spin tunes.

Il Crudo
SANDWICH SHOP €

(Piazza Cairoli 7; panini €4.50-6; ⊙11am-3.30pm & 6pm-1am Mon-Thu, to 2pm Fri, 11am-2am Sat, 11am-1am Sun) Grab a well-filled *panini* to munch on the move or enjoy one alfresco with a glass of wine at this pocket-sized *panineria* and *vineria* strung with ham legs. Find it by the river on one of Pisa's prettiest squares.

⌜TOP⌟CHOICE Il Montino
PIZZERIA

(Vicolo del Monte 1; pizzas €4.20-7.50; ⊙10.30am-3pm & 5-10pm Mon-Sat) There is nothing flash or fancy about this place, a brilliantly down-to-earth pizzeria with iconic status among Pisans, student or sophisticate. Order pizza to take away or grab one of a handful of tightly packed tables, inside or out, and munch on house specialities like *cecina* (chickpea pizza), *castagnacci* (chestnut cake) and *spuma* (sweet, nonalcoholic drink). Or go for a *foccacine* (flat roll) filled with salami, pancetta or *porchetta* (suckling pig). Hidden in a back alley, the quickest way to find Il Montino is to head west along Via Ulisse Dini from the northern end of Borgo Stretto (opposite the Lo Sfizio cafe at Borgo Stretto 54) to Piazza San Felice, where it is easy to spot, on your left, a telling blue neon 'Pizzeria' sign.

Il Colonnino
OSTERIA €€

(℡050 313 84 30; Via Sant'Andrea 37-41; meals €30; ⊙lunch & dinner Tue-Sun) Hidden in the warren of medieval streets between Piazza San Francesco and the river, Il Colonnino is the sort of lunch, *aperitivo* or dinner spot that locals like. Modern-accented Italian is the cuisine. Go for spaghetti-like *tagliolini* sprinkled with San Miniato truffles, pork fillet in a balsamic and pink peppercorn sauce or – for the springtime vegetarian in you – white asparagus with boiled-egg sauce. The fixed €25 menu is excellent value.

🌿 biOsteria 050
ORGANIC, TUSCAN €

(℡050 54 31 06; www.zerocinquanta.com; Via San Francesco 36; meals €25; ⊙12.30-2.30pm & 7.45-10.30pm Mon & Wed-Sat, 7.45-10.30pm Sun) What a clever concept Zero Cinquante (Zero Fifty) is. 'Tradition and fantasy' is its strapline and the produce it uses to cook up its seasonal Tuscan dishes is strictly local and organic. There is ample choice for vegetarians and coeliac-sufferers too. Try black cabbage, nut and gorgonzola risotto, rabbit with sweet mustard perhaps, or one of the excellent-value daily lunch specials chalked on the board outside.

Osteria del Porton Rosso
OSTERIA €€

(℡050 58 05 66; Vicolo del Porton Rosso 11; meals €35; ⊙lunch & dinner Mon-Sat) Two menus – one from the land and one from the sea – tempt at this old-fashioned but excellent *osteria* at the end of an alley; from riverside Lungarno Pacinotti look for the incongruous neon-sign-lit doorway with red fly curtain. Pisan specialities such as fresh ravioli with salted cod and chickpeas happily coexist with Tuscan classics such as grilled fillet steak.

Bar Pasticceria Salza PASTRIES & CAKES €
(Borgo Stretto 44; ⊘8am-8.30pm Apr-Oct, shorter hr Tue-Sun Nov-Mar) This old-fashioned cake shop has been tempting Pisans off Borgo Stretto and into sugar-induced wickedness since the 1920s.

Drinking

Most of the student drinking action is in and around Piazza delle Vettovaglie and the university on cafe-ringed Piazza Dante Alighieri – always packed with students.

Bazeel BAR
(www.bazeel.it, in Italian; Lungarno Pacinotti 1; ⊘5pm-2am) This bar draws a mixed clientele and is famous for its *aperitivo* spread. After 9pm there's usually live music or a DJ. Check its Twitter feed for what's on.

❶ Information

Tourist office (www.pisaunicaterra.it) airport (☑050 50 25 18; ⊘9.30am-11.30pm); train station (☑050 4 22 91; Piazza Vittorio Emanuele II 13; ⊘9am-7pm Mon-Sat, 9am-4pm Sun); town centre (☑050 91 03 50; touristpoint@comune.pisa.it; Piazza XX Settembre; ⊘8.30am-12.30pm)

❶ Getting There & Away

AIR Galileo Galilei airport (www.pisa-airport.com) Tuscany's main international airport, 2km south of town; flights to most major European cities.

BUS From its hub on Piazza Sant'Antonio, Pisan bus company **CPT** (www.cpt.pisa.it, in Italian) runs buses to/from Volterra (€6.10, two hours, up to 10 daily) and Livorno (€2.75, 55 minutes, half-hourly to hourly).

CAR Pisa is close to the A11 and A12. The SCG FI-PI-LI (SS67) is a toll-free alternative for Florence and Livorno, while the north–south SS1, the Via Aurelia, connects the city with La Spezia and Rome.

TRAIN

Florence (€5.80, 1¼ hours, frequent)

Livorno (€1.90, 15 minutes, frequent)

Lucca (€2.40, 30 minutes, every 30 minutes)

Viareggio (€2.40, 15 minutes, every 20 minutes)

Rome (€16.85, 2½ to four hours, 16 daily)

❶ Getting Around

To/From the Airport

BUS The LAM Rossa (red) bus line (€1.10, 10 minutes, every 10 to 20 minutes) passes through the city centre and the train station en route to/from the airport.

TAXI A taxi between the airport and city centre costs around €10. To book, call **Radio Taxi Pisa** (☑050 54 16 00; www.cotapi.it).

TRAIN Services run to/from Stazione Pisa Centrale (€1.10, five minutes, 33 per day); be sure to purchase and validate your ticket before you get on the train.

Bicycle

Most hotels rent bikes. Otherwise, stands at the northern end of Via Santa Maria and other streets off Piazza dei Miracoli rent four-wheel bikes (€5 per 40 minutes), quad bikes seating up to 3/6 people (€10/15 per hour) and regular bicycles (€2/3 per 30/60 minutes).

Car & Motorcycle

Parking costs up to €2 per hour, but be careful the car park you choose is not in the city's exclusion zone. There's a free car park outside the zone on Lungarno Guadalongo near the Fortezza di San Gallo on the south side of the Arno.

Lucca
POP 84,640

This beautiful old city elicits love at first sight with its rich history, handsome churches and excellent restaurants. Hidden behind imposing Renaissance walls, it is an essential stopover on any Tuscan tour and a perfect base for exploring the Apuane Alps and the Garfagnana.

Founded by the Etruscans, Lucca became a Roman colony in 180 BC and a free *comune* (self-governing city) during the 12th century, when it enjoyed a period of prosperity based on the silk trade. In 1314 it briefly fell under the control of Pisa but under the leadership of local adventurer Castruccio Castracani degli Antelminelli, the city regained its freedom and remained an independent republic for almost 500 years.

Napoleon ended all this in 1805, when he created the principality of Lucca and placed his sister Elisa in control. Twelve years later the city became a Bourbon duchy, before being incorporated into the Kingdom of Italy. It miraculously escaped being bombed during WWII, so the fabric of the historic centre has remained unchanged for centuries.

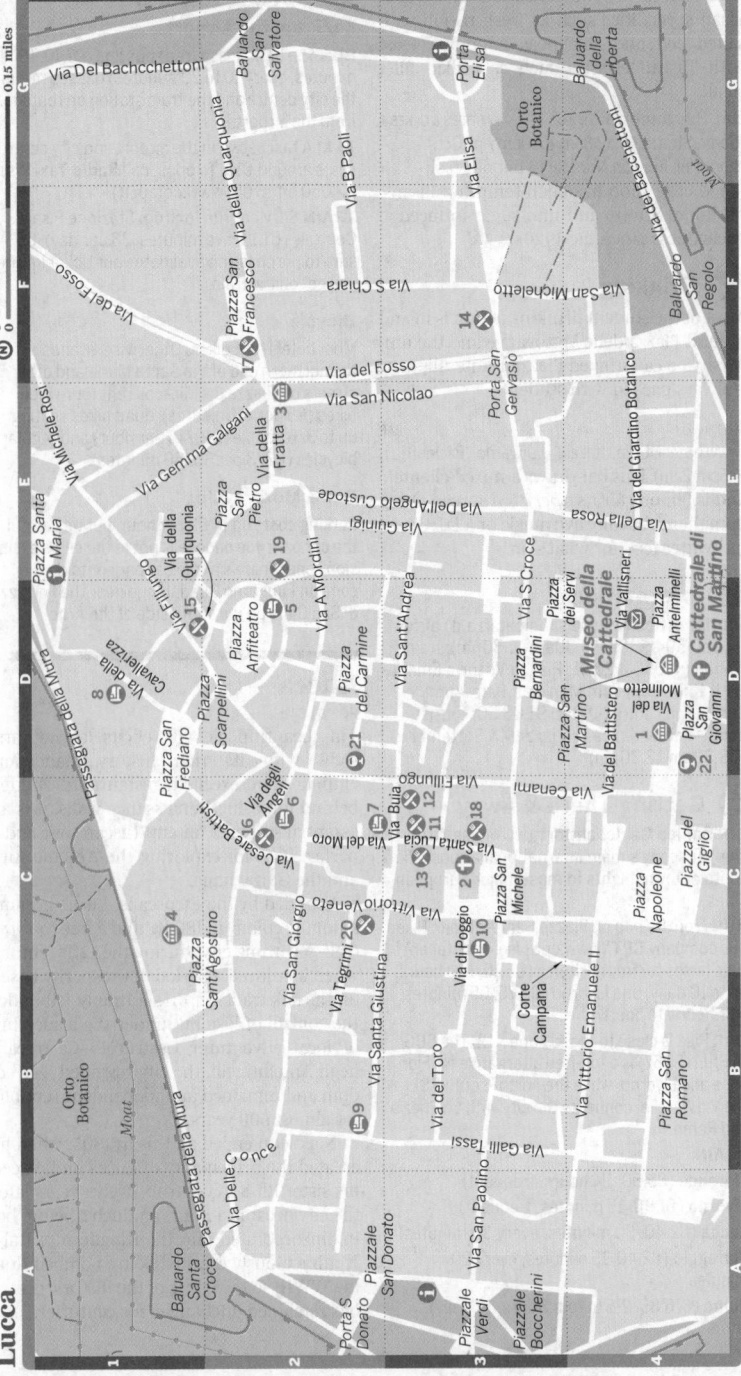

Lucca

◎ Sights

Threading its way through the medieval heart of the old city, cobbled Via Fillungo is full of sleek, modern boutiques housed in great old buildings – cast your eyes above the street-level bustle to appreciate ancient awnings and architectural details.

East of Via Fillungo is one of Tuscany's loveliest piazzas, oval cafe-studded Piazza Anfiteatro, so called after the amphitheatre that was located here in Roman times. Look closely to spot remnants of the amphitheatre's brick arches and masonry on the exterior walls of the medieval houses ringing the piazza.

City Walls   CITY WALLS
Lucca's monumental mura (walls), built around the old city in the 16th and 17th centuries and defended by 126 cannons, remain in almost perfect condition. Twelve metres high and 4km in length, the ramparts are crowned with a tree-lined footpath that looks down on the old town and out towards the Apuane Alps – the perfect spot to stroll, cycle, run and inhale shot after shot of local Lucchesi life. Children's playgrounds, swings and picnic tables beneath shady plane trees add a buzz of activity to three of the 11 bastions studding the way.

Cattedrale di San Martino   CATHEDRAL
(Piazza San Martino; ⊙9.30am-5.45pm Mon-Fri, to 6.45pm Sat, 9.30-10.45am & noon-6pm Sun) Lucca's predominantly Romanesque cathedral dates to the start of the 11th century. Its stunning facade was constructed in the prevailing Lucca-Pisan style and designed to accommodate the pre-existing *campanile*. The reliefs over the left doorway of the portico are believed to be by Nicola Pisano.

The interior was rebuilt in the 14th and 15th centuries with a Gothic flourish. The **Volto Santo** (literally, Holy Countenance) is not to be missed. Legend has it that this simply fashioned image of a dark-skinned, life-sized Christ on a wooden crucifix was carved by Nicodemus, who witnessed the Crucifixion. In fact, the Volto Santo has recently been dated to the 13th century. A major object of pilgrimage, the sculpture is carried in procession through the streets on 13 September each year at dusk during the Luminaria di Santa Croce, a solemn torchlit procession marking its miraculous arrival in Lucca.

The cathedral's many other works of art include a magnificent *Last Supper* by Tintoretto above the third altar of the south aisle and Domenico Ghirlandaio's 1479 *Madonna Enthroned with Saints* in the sacristy (adult/reduced €2/1.50). Opposite lies the exquisite, gleaming marble memorial to Ilaria del Carretto carved by Jacopo della Quercia in 1407. The young second wife of the 15th-century lord of Lucca, Paolo Guinigi, Ilaria died in childbirth aged only 24. At her feet lies her faithful dog.

WORTH A TRIP

VESPA TOUR

There's a certain romance to touring Tuscany on the back of a Vespa, Italy's iconic scooter that revolutionised travel when Piaggio launched it from its factory in **Pontedera**, 25km southeast of Pisa, in 1946. The 'wasp' as the two-wheeled utility vehicle was affectionately known, has been restyled 120 times since, culminating most recently in Piaggio's vintage-inspired GTV and LXV models. Yet the essential design remains timeless.

The complete Vespa story, from the Genovese company's arrival in Tuscany in 1921 to its manufacturing of four-engine aircraft and hydroplanes, WWII destruction and rebirth as Europe's exclusive Vespa producer, is grippingly told in Pontedera's **Museo Piaggio** (www.museopiaggio.it; Viale Rinaldo Piagio 7; admission free; ☺10am-6pm Tue-Sat), in a former factory building.

Should Vespa's free-wheeling, carefree spirit take hold, hook up with Florence-based **Tuscany by Vespa** (☑055 0123 994; www.tuscanybyvespa.com; Via de' Lamberti 1; 1-day tour incl lunch & winery €120) for your very own Hepburn-style one-day tour of Chianti on the back of a Vespa.

Museo della Cattedrale MUSEUM
(www.museocattedralelucca.it; Piazza San Martino; adult/reduced €4/2.50; ☺10am-6pm daily) Next door to the cathedral, this museum safeguards elaborate gold and silver decorations made for the Volto Santo, including a 17th-century crown and a 19th-century sceptre. A combined ticket covering museum and cathedral sacristy costs €6/4.

Chiesa dei SS Giovanni e Reparata CHURCH
(Piazza San Giovanni; adult/reduced €2.50/1.50; ☺10am-6pm mid-Mar–Oct, 10am-5pm Sat & Sun Nov–mid-Mar) The 12th-century interior of this deconsecrated church is a hauntingly atmospheric setting for summertime opera recitals staged by **Puccini e la sua Lucca** (☑340 8106042; www.puccinielasualucca.com; adult/reduced €17/13; ☺7pm daily mid-Mar–Oct, 7pm Fri-Wed Nov–mid-Mar). Professional singers present a one-hour program of arias and duets dominated by the music of Puccini but also featuring works by Verdi, Mozart, Mascagni and Cilea. Tickets are sold inside the church.

In the north transept of the church is a **baptistry** crowning an archaeological area comprising five building levels going back to the Roman period.

Chiesa di San Michele in Foro CHURCH
(Piazza San Michele; ☺7.40am-noon & 3-6pm daily Apr-Oct, 9am-noon & 3-5pm Nov-Mar) This dazzling Romanesque church marks the spot where the city's Roman forum was. The present building with exquisite wedding-cake facade was constructed on the site of its 8th-century precursor over a period of nearly 300 years. Crowning the structure is

a figure of the archangel Michael slaying a dragon. Inside, don't miss Filippino Lippi's 1479 painting of Sts Helen, Jerome, Sebastian and Roch (complete with plague sore) in the south transept.

Lucca Center of Contemporary Art ART GALLERY
(☑0583 57 17 12; www.luccamuseum.com; Via della Fratta 36; adult/reduced €7/5; ☺10am-7pm Tue-Sun) A refreshing change from the historic Tuscan norm, Lucca's contemporary art museum hosts some riveting temporary exhibitions.

Palazzo Pfanner PALAZZO
(www.palazzopfanner.it; Via degli Asili 33; palace or garden adult/reduced €4/3.50, both €5.50/4.50; ☺10am-6pm Apr-Oct) Fire the romantic in you with a stroll around this privately owned 17th-century palace where parts of *Portrait of a Lady* (1996) starring Nicole Kidman and John Malkovich were shot. Take the outdoor staircase to the frescoed and furnished *piano nobile* (main Floor), then visit the ornate, statue-studded 18th-century garden – the only one of substance within the city walls. (Felix Pfanner, may God rest his soul, was an Austrian émigré who first brought beer to Italy – and brewed it in the mansion's cellars.) From August to October, watch out for the lovely chamber music concerts Palazzo Pfanner hosts.

🎭 Festivals & Events

Puccini Festival MUSIC
(www.puccinifestival.it) Hosted by the nearby village of Torre del Lago in July and August, this festival has been going for more than 50 years.

Summer Festival
MUSIC

(www.summer-festival.com) Top international artists perform in a variety of musical genres at this July fest.

🛏 Sleeping

Tourist offices have accommodation lists and, if you visit in person, can make reservations for you (free of charge); pay 10% of the room price as on-the-spot deposit and the remainder at the hotel.

Ostello San Frediano
HOSTEL €

(☎0583 46 99 57; www.ostellolucca.it; Via della Cavallerizza 12; dm with/without bathroom €21/19, d/tr/q €60/78/100; P@🛜; reception ⊙7am-midnight) In a staggeringly historic building, hostellers won't get closer to the action than this. Top notch in comfort and service, this Hostelling International–affiliated hostel with 141 beds in voluminous rooms is serviced with a bar and grandiose dining room (breakfast €3, lunch or dinner €11). Non-HI members can buy a €3 one-night stamp.

Piccolo Hotel Puccini
HOTEL €

(☎0583 55 42 1; www.hotelpuccini.com; Via di Poggio 9; d €75-95, tr €95-120, q €120-140; ❄🛜) Snug around the corner from the great man himself (or at least a bronze copy of him) and the house where he was born, this elegant address is an ode to Puccini. Decor is an unobtrusive mix of period furnishings and historic collectables. From April to October, breakfast costs €3.50.

La Boheme
B&B €€

(☎0583 46 24 04; www.boheme.it; Via del Moro 2; d €90-140; ❄@) A hefty dark-wood door located on a peaceful backstreet heralds the entrance to this five-room B&B, which is run with charm and style by former architect Ranieri. Rooms are furnished in antique Tuscan style; some have breathtaking high ceilings and all have decent-sized bathrooms. Breakfast is generous.

Alla Corte degli Angeli
BOUTIQUE HOTEL €€

(☎0583 46 92 04; www.allacortedegliangeli.com; Via degli Angeli 23; s €80-110, d €110-160; ❄@🛜) Occupying three floors of a 15th-century town house, this four-star boutique hotel with 10 rooms and an old-fashioned rocking horse in its wood-beamed lounge oozes charm. Beautifully frescoed rooms are named after flowers: lovers in the hugely romantic Rosa room can lie beneath a pergola and swallow-filled sky.

2italia
APARTMENT €€

(☎3355 208251; www.2italia.com; Via della Anfiteatro74; apt for 2 adults & up to 4 kids €150-170; 🛜🍴) Not a hotel but a clutch of family-friendly self-catering apartments overlooking Piazza Anfiteatro. Available on a nightly basis (minimum two nights), the project is the brainchild of well-travelled parents of three Kristin (English) and Kaare (Norwegian). Spacious apartments sleep up to six, have fully equipped kitchen and washing machine, and come with sheets and towels. Kristin and Kaare also organise cycling tours, cooking courses, wine tastings and olive pickings.

Palazzo Alexander
BOUTIQUE HOTEL €€

(☎0583 58 35 71; www.hotelpalazzoalexander.it; Via Santa Giustina 48; s €80-120, d €90-150; P❄@🛜) This exuberant palace hotel has plenty of oversized mirrors, ornate gold-gilt bedheads and floor-to-ceiling drapes to woo history aficionados. Each of its 14 rooms is named after a Puccini or Verdi opera and the pièce de résistance is Bohème with frescoed ceiling and Tosca with rooftop balcony. Parking costs €14 per night.

🍴 Eating

TOP CHOICE Da Felice
PIZZERIA €

(www.pizzeriadafelice.com; Via Buia 12; focaccias €1-3.50, pizza slices €1.30; ⊙10am-8.30pm Mon-Sat) This buzzing local favourite behind Piazza San Michele is easy to spot – come noon look for the crowd packed around two tiny tables inside, spilling out the door or squatting on one of two streetside benches. *Cecina,* a salted chickpea pizza served piping-hot from the oven, and *castagnacci* (chestnut cakes) are Felice's raison d'être.

Pecora Nera
TRATTORIA €

(☎0583 46 97 38; www.lapecoraneralucca.it; Piazza San Francesco 4; pizzas €5-9, meals €20; ⊙Wed-Sat, lunch Sun) Plump on a big empty piazza, well away from the madding crowds, the Black Sheep – the only Lucca restaurant recommended by the Slow Food Movement – scores extra brownie points for social responsibility (its profits fund workshops for young people with Down syndrome). Thirty-odd different pizza types and a handful of Tuscan classics are what's cooking in the kitchen.

Gli Orti di Via Elisa
TUSCAN €€

(☎0583 49 12 41; Via Elisa 17; meals €20; ⊙lunch & dinner Mon, Tue & Thu-Sat, lunch Wed; 🍴) Don't

A WALLTOP PICNIC

Picnicking atop Lucca's city walls, on grass or at a wooden picnic table, is as lovely and typical a Lucchesi lunch as any.

Buy fresh-from-the-oven pizza and focaccia with choice of fillings and toppings from fabulous and famed bakery **Forno Amedeo Giusti** (Via Santa Lucia 20; pizzas & filled focaccias €8-16 per kg; ⏰7am-7.30pm Mon, Tue & Thu-Sat, 7am-1.30pm Wed, 4-7.30pm Sun), then nip across the street for a bottle of Lucchesi wine and Garfagnese *biscotti al farro* (spelt biscuits) at **Antica Bodega di Prospero** (Via Santa Lucia 13; ⏰9am-1pm & 4-7.30pm); look for the old-fashioned shop window fabulously stuffed with sacks of beans, lentils and other local pulses.

be surprised to see *'Siamo Completo'* (fully booked) chalked on the board outside this eating address, well away from the tourist action and busy! Gorge on gnocchi in zucchini-flower sauce or bean soup with salt cod followed by grilled meat while the kids radiate happiness with pre-meal drawings to colour in, games and so on.

Taddeucci　　　　　PASTRIES & CAKES
(www.taddeucci.com; Piazza San Michele 34; ⏰8.30am-7.45pm, closed Thu winter) The perfect accompaniment to a mid-morning or -afternoon espresso and gift to take home, *buccellato* is a traditional sweet bread loaf with sultanas and aniseed seeds, baked in Lucca since 1881. Taddeucci is the *pasticceria* (pastry shop) to ogle at and shop for this traditional Lucchesi sweet treat. Pay €4/8/12 for a 300/600/900g loaf.

Osteria del Manzo　　　　TUSCAN €€
(📞0583 49 06 49; Via Battisti 28; meals €30; ⏰lunch & dinner Mon-Sat) Quite often the local favourites are strictly inside, and this – simplicity in the making – is one of them. Enjoy typical local dishes beneath a beamed ceiling, watched on, oddly enough, by a collection of garden gnomes. Someone clearly collects bottle miniatures too.

Trattoria Canuleia　　　　TUSCAN €€
(📞0583 46 74 70; Via Canuleia 14; meals €40; ⏰lunch & dinner Mon-Sat) What makes this dining address stand out from the crowd is

its secret walled garden out back – the perfect spot to escape the tourist hordes and listen to birds tweet over partridge risotto, artichoke and shrimp spaghetti or a traditional *peposa* (beef and pepper stew).

Osteria Baralla　　　　OSTERIA €€
(📞0583 44 02 40; www.osteriabaralla.it; Via Anfiteatro 5; meals €32; ⏰lunch & dinner Mon-Sat) Feast on local specialities beneath huge red-brick vaults at this busy *osteria* from 1860. Thursday is *bollito misto* (mixed boiled meats) day, Saturday roast pork.

Trattoria da Leo　　　　TRATTORIA €
(📞0583 49 22 36; Via Tegrimi 1; meals €25; ⏰lunch & dinner Mon-Sat) Another address everyone knows and goes to, Leo is famed Lucca-wide for its friendly ambience and cheap food – which ranges from acceptable to delicious. No credit cards.

Drinking

At almost every turn within the walls there is a pavement terrace to sit down at and savour a coffee or *aperitivo* – those on Piazza San Frediano are a favourite and not as tourist-packed as the cafe- and wine-bar terraces of Piazza Anfiteatro.

Caffè di Simo　　　　CAFE
(Via Fillungo 58; ⏰9am-8pm & 8.30pm-1am) For a respite from the sun's glare, immerse yourself in the chic Liberty (art nouveau) interior of Lucca's famous coffee shop. Its cakes are masterpieces.

Enoteca Calasto　　　　WINE BAR
(www.lucca-wine-treasures.com; Piazza San Giovanni 5; ⏰11am-11pm) A Brit and a Dane are the creative duo behind this *enoteca* with terracotta-pot terrace overlooking the baptistry. Its wine list only features local Lucchesi production and Thursday evening ushers in wine tasting (€5) with a local producer.

ⓘ Information

Tourist office (www.luccatourist.it) Piazza Santa Maria 35 (📞0583 91 99 31; ⏰9am-7pm daily); Piazzale Verdi (📞0583 58 31 50; ⏰9am-7pm daily Apr-Sep, to 5pm Oct-Mar); Via Elisa67 (⏰9am-1pm & 2-6pm Wed-Mon Apr-Sep)

ⓘ Getting There & Away

BUS From the bus stops around Piazzale Verdi, **Vaibus** (www.vaibus.it) runs services throughout the region.

Pisa airport (€3.20, 45 minutes to one hour, 30 daily).

Castelnuovo di Garfagnana (€4.20, 1½ hours, eight daily)

Bagni di Lucca (€3.40, one hour, eight daily).

CAR & MOTORCYCLE The A11 runs westward to Pisa and Viareggio and eastward to Florence. To access the Garfagnana, take the SS12 and continue on the SS445.

TRAIN The station is south of the city walls: take the path across the moat and through the tunnel under Baluardo San Colombano.

Florence (€5.30, 1¼ to 1¾ hours, hourly)

Pisa (€2.40, 30 minutes, every 30 minutes)

Viareggio (€2.40, 25 minutes, hourly).

❶ Getting Around

BICYCLE Rent regular wheels (€2.50/12 per hour/day; ID required) from the Piazzale Verdi tourist office or a city/mountain bike (€3/4 per hour), racer (€5 per hour) or tandem (€6.50 per hour).

Cicli Bizzarri (☑0583 49 66 82; www.ciclibizzarri.net, in Italian; Piazza Santa Maria 32; ⊙9am-7pm)

Biciclette Poli (☑0583 49 37 87; www.biciclettepoli.com, in Italian; Piazza Santa Maria 42; ⊙9am-7pm)

SCOOTER & VESPA **Scooter Tuscany Rentals** (☑0583 95 41 39; www.scootertuscany.com; Via della Cavallerizza 23; ⊙9am-7pm daily) Rent two motorised wheels from €55/210 per day/week; opposite Lucca's hostel.

Versilian Riviera

Italy's beach-loving hoi polloi pack out this coastal strip that legs it north from Viareggio to the regional border with Liguria. Grand Duke Giancarlo Leopold I was the first in Italy to decriminalise homosexuality here in 1863, and roads from the coastal towns snake their way deep into the Apuane Alps.

Frolicking on the long sandy beach and lapping up the seafront's gorgeous line-up of 1920s art nouveau facades aside, the main reason to visit Viareggio is for its flamboyant, four-week Mardi Gras Carnevale (www.viareggio.ilcarnevale.com) in February. Second only to Venice for party spirit, it lasts four weeks and sees the city go wild with a festival of floats.

PIETRASANTA

Often overlooked by Tuscan travellers, this refined art town – an easy day trip by train from Pisa (€3.10, 25 minutes) – is a real unexpected surprise. Its bijou historic heart, originally walled, is car-free and loaded with tiny art galleries, workshops and fashion boutiques – perfect for a day's amble broken only by lunch.

Founded by Guiscardo da Pietrasanta, *podestà* (governing magistrate) of Lucca in 1255, Pietrasanta was seen as a prize by Genoa, Lucca, Pisa and Florence, all of whom jostled for possession of its marble quarries and bronze foundries. Florence predictably won and Leo X (Giovanni de' Medici) took control in 1513, putting the town's famous quarries at the disposal of Michelangelo, who came here in 1518 to source marble for the facade of Florence's San Lorenzo. The artistic inclination of Pietrasanta dates from this time, and today it is the home of many artists, including internationally lauded Colombian-born sculptor Fernando Botero, whose work can be seen here.

⊙ Sights

From Pietrasanta train station (Piazza della Stazione) head straight across Piazza Carducci to the old city gate and onto central square Piazza del Duomo, where the attractive Duomo di San Martino (1256) with red-brick, 36m-tall bell tower and neighbouring 13th-century Chiesa di Sant'Agostino (⊙4-7pm Tue-Sun) – deconsecrated and a wonderfully evocative venue for art exhibitions – awaits. Next, dip into Pietrasanta's art heritage with dozens of moulds of famous sculptures cast or carved in Pietrasanta, at the Museo dei Bozzetti (www.museodei bozzetti.it; Via S Agostino 1; admission free; ⊙2-7pm Tue-Sat, 4-7pm Sun), inside the convent adjoining the church.

Cross to the other side of the square and meander along Via Giuseppe Mazzini, the town's main shopping strip bookended by contemporary street sculptures. Tucked between boutiques at No 103 is the superb Chiesa della Misericordia, frescoed with the *Gate of Paradise* and *Gate of Hell* by Botero (the artist portrays himself in Hell).

⌷ Sleeping

Should you find yourself totally smitten with Pietrasanta and unable to leave, art-filled Albergo Pietrasanta (☑0584 79 37 26; www.albergopietrasanta.com; Via Garibaldi 35; d €203-264; P❄@❅) is one of Tuscany's loveliest boutique town hotels. Otherwise Filippo has fantastic, design-driven rooms.

TOP THREE FOODIE DETOURS

Flee the crowd from Florence, Pisa or Lucca with these insider day trips built around a quintessentially Tuscan, food-driven experience:

» **Watch spaghetti being made** at Tuscany's oldest pasta-making factory, **Martelli** (✆0587 68 42 38; www.famigliamartelli.it; Lari; admission free; ☉10am-noon & 3-4pm Mon-Sat), run by the same family in the village of Lari since 1926 and famed for its gourmet spaghetti, spaghettini, penne and macaroni packaged in canary-yellow paper bags. Simply knock on the door and ask to be shown around.

» **Learn how to cook Tuscan** at San Miniato's much-lauded restaurant, **Pepenero** (✆0571 41 95 23; www.pepenerocucina.it; Via IV Novembre 13, San Miniato; incl lunch & wine €60; ☉Wed). New breed of innovative chef and TV star Gilberto Rossi uses traditional products to create modern, seasonally driven dishes.

» **Hunt white truffles** at **Barbialla Nuova** (✆0571 67 70 04; www.barbiallanuova.it; Via Casastada 49, Montaione; per person for groups of 6 to 8 €60, per group of 5 or less €300), a heavily wooded, 500-hectare organic farm where creamy Chianina cows, reared for their beef, graze on the hillside. The hunting season runs mid-October to mid-December and, should you fall in love with the place (highly probable), Barbialla has a clutch of stylish self-catering apartments and houses to rent (minimum three nights; from €270/420 for two/four people). Guests pay 50% less for truffle hunts. There's parking, a swimming pool and it's kid friendly.

Eating

The historic heart spoils for choice with its many artsy addresses spilling onto flowerpot-adorned summer terraces. Pedestrian Via Stagio Stagi, parallel to Via Giuseppe Mazzini, has several particularly appealing restaurants, including thoroughly modern **Filippo** (✆0584 70 00 10; http://ristorantefilippo. com; Via Stagio Stagi 22; meals €30; ☉lunch & dinner daily, closed Mon winter), flowery **Quarantuno** (✆0584 77 25 07; www.quarantunopietrasanta. com; Via Stagio Stagi 41; ☉lunch & dinner Thu-Sun) and contemporary fish restaurant **Pinocchio** (✆0584 70 510; Vicolo San Biagio 5; meals €50; ☉lunch & dinner Tue-Sun).

Piazza del Duomo is the alfresco spot for an atmospheric coffee or sundowner; **Caffè del Teatro** on the corner of Via dei Piastroni apparently being Botero's favourite hang-out. Or try **Enoteca Marcucci** (www. enotecamarcucci.it; Via Garibaldi 40; ☉10am-1pm & 5pm-1am Tue-Sun), a fabulous *enoteca* with great wine and a wonderfully contemporary decor.

Apuane Alps & Garfagnana

Rearing up from the Versilian Riviera are the Apuane Alps, a relatively undiscovered mountain range and area of raw beauty protected by the **Parco Regionale delle Alpi Apuane** (www.parcapuane.it). Head east and a trio of stunning valleys formed by the Serchio river and its tributaries – the low-lying Lima and Serchio valleys and the higher Garfagnana valley – kick in. Collectively known as the **Garfagnana**, this vast inland valley, easy to reach from Lucca, is known for its invigorating outdoor activities and rustic cuisine sourced from local fruits of the forest: chestnuts (often ground into flour), *porcini* mushrooms and honey.

In **Castelnuovo di Garfagnana** (population 6109), the main town in the valley, the **Centro Visite Parco Alpi Apuane** (✆0583 6 51 69; www.turismo.garfagnana.eu; Piazza delle Erbe 1; ☉9.30am-1pm & 3-7pm Jun-Sep, to 5.30pm Oct-May) and the **tourist office** (✆0583 64 10 07; www.castelnuovagarfagnana.org; Piazza delle Erbe; ☉9.30am-1pm & 3.30-6.30pm Mon-Sat), on the same square opposite, have bags of information on walking, mountain biking and horse riding in the park. The visitor centre also sells hiking maps and has lists of local guides, *agriturismi* and *rifugi* off any beaten track.

If photogenic hilltop villages are more your thing, drive 12km south to **Barga** (population 10,307), an apologetically lovely, go-slow patchwork of narrow streets, archways, ancient walls and crumbling piazzas staggering steeply uphill to the forbidding village church and prison-turned-museum.

CARRARA

POP 65,588

Many first-time visitors assume the snowy-white mountain peaks forming Carrara's backdrop are capped with snow. In fact, the vista provides a breathtaking illusion – the white is 2000 hectares of marble gouged out of the foothills of the Apuane Alps in vast quarries that have been worked since Roman times.

The texture and purity of Carrara's white marble (derived from the Greek *marmaros*, meaning shining stone) is unrivalled and it was here that Michelangelo selected marble for masterpieces including *David* (actually sculpted from a dud veined block). These days it's a multi-billion-euro industry.

The quarries, 5km north of Carrara in Colonnata and Fantiscritti, have long been the area's biggest employers. It's hard, dangerous work and on Carrara's central Piazza XXVII Aprile a monument remembers workers who lost their lives up on the hills. Discover the full story of marble at the **Museo del Marmo** (Marble Museum; Viale XX Settembre; adult/child €4/free; ☉9am-12.30pm & 2.30-5pm Mon-Sat), opposite the **tourist office** (☑0585 84 41 36; Viale XX Settembre; ☉8.30am-5.30pm Jun-Aug, 9am-4pm Sep-May), then make your way up the mountain to visit **Cave di Fantiscritti**. Pick from a 30-minute **guided tour** (www.marmotour.com; adult/child €8/4; ☉11am-6pm daily Apr-Oct, 10.30am-5.30pm Jun-Aug, 9am-4pm Sep-May) by minibus/on foot of the marble quarry inside the mountain; or a **4WD tour** (www.carraramarbletour.it; adult/child €8/4; ☉11am-6pm daily Apr-Oct 10.30am-5.30pm Jun-Aug, 9am-4pm Sep-May) of the open-cast quarry. Both are dramatic.

Livorno

POP 160,742

Tuscany's second-largest city is a quintessential port town. Though first impressions are rarely kind, this is a 'real' city that really does grow on you. Its seafood is the best on the Tyrrhenian coast, its shabby historic quarter threaded with Venetian-style canals is ubercool, and pebbly beaches stretch south from the town's belle époque seafront. Be it a short stay between ferries or a day trip from Florence or Pisa, Livorno (Leghorn in English) is understated and agreeable.

From the main train station bus 1 heads along the coast road, stopping en route in front of the cathedral on Piazza Grande.

If tasting wine on the seashore or pedalling between olive groves is your cup of tea, then consider a trip along the Costa degli Etruschi (Etrsucan Coast) – the chunk of coast stretching south from Livorno to just beyond **Piombino** and onwards by ferry to the gorgeous island of Elba. Its entire length is covered by the **Strada del Vino e dell'Olio** (Wine & Oil Rd; www.lastradadelvino. com), a 150km itinerary that maps out cellars, wine estates and farms where you can taste and buy local wine and olive oil; and recommends places to stay and eat en route.

⊙ Sights & Activities

Piccola Venezia   HISTORICAL CENTRE
'Little Venice' is crossed with small canals built during the 17th century. Canals link **Fortezza Nuova** (New Fort; admission free), built for the Medici court in the 16th century, with the crumbling **Fortezza Vecchia** (Old Fort; admission free). What the area lacks in gondolas and tourists, it makes up for with tow paths intersected with hip waterside cafes and wine bars. Buy tickets for a 45-minute **boat tour** (adult/child €10/5; ☉11am, noon & 4pm daily Apr-Sep) from the tourist office.

TOP CHOICE **Terrazza Mascagni**   PROMENADE
(Viale Italia) No trip to Livorno is complete without a stroll along (and photo shoot of) this dazzling art work – an elegant 1920s terrace that sweeps gracefully along the seafront in a chessboard flurry of black-and-white checks.

Nearby, **Bagni Pancaldi** (www.pancal diacquaviva.it; Viale Italia 56; adult/child €5/4; ☉8.30am-noon & 3-6pm Sat & Sun Apr-Sep) are old-fashioned baths – the height of sophistication in 1846 – where you can swim and hang out in coloured canvas cabins.

The thoroughly modern **Acqvario Livorno** (☑0586 26 91 11; www.acquariodilivorno.it; Piazzale Mascagni 1; adult/child €15/8; ☉11am-10pm Tue-Sun, daily Jul & Aug, to 7pm Tue-Sun Jun & Sep, shorter hr rest of year), overlooking the terrace's northern end, swims with Etruscan and Mediterranean marine life.

Museo Civico Giovanni Fattori   ART GALLERY
(Via San Jacopo in Acquaviva 65; admission €4; ☉10am-1pm & 4-7pm Tue-Sun) This art museum, in a pretty park, features works by the 19th-century Macchiaioli (Italian Impressionist) school.

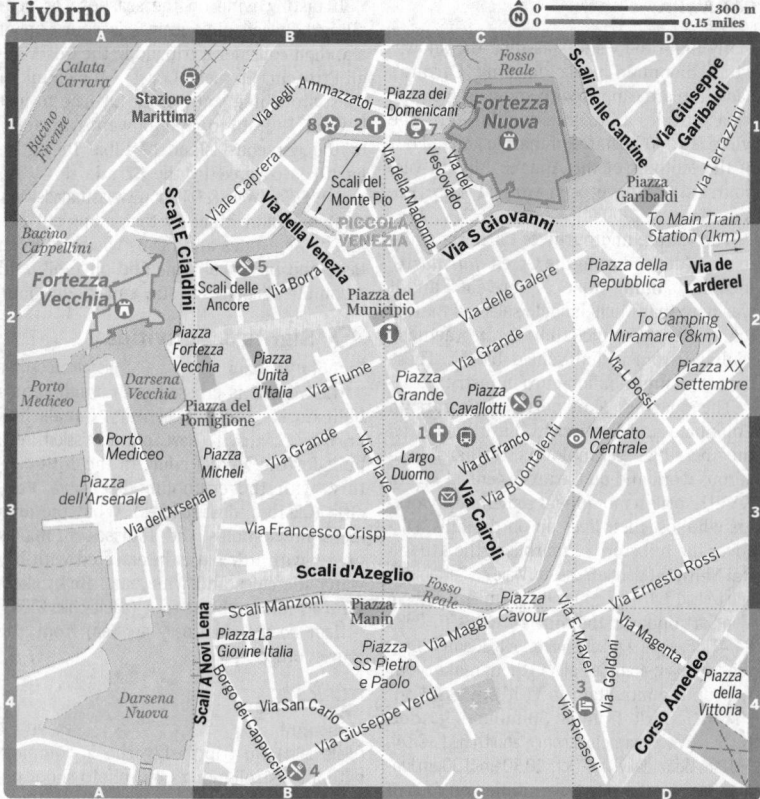

Livorno

◎ Top Sights	**⊗ Eating**
Fortezza Nuova................................C1	4 Cantina Senese...........................B4
Fortezza Vecchia...........................A2	5 La Barrocciaia............................C2
	6 L'Ancora....................................B2
◎ Sights	
1 Cathedral....................................C3	**⊖ Drinking**
2 Chiesa di Santa Catarina............B1	7 La Bodeguita..............................C1
⊟ Sleeping	**⊛ Entertainment**
3 Hotel al Teatro...........................D4	8 Teatrofficina Refugio..................B1

Museo di Storia Naturale del Mediterraneo MUSEUM
(Via Roma 234; adult/child €10/5; ☺9am-1pm Wed & Fri, 9am-1pm & 3-7pm Tue, Thu & Sat, 3-7pm Sun) Livorno's friendly and hands-on Natural History Museum is an exhaustive, first-rate museum experience for the natural sciences. Highlight of the permanent collection: Anne, the 20m-long common whale skeleton.

🛏 Sleeping

TOP **Hotel al Teatro** BOUTIQUE HOTEL €€
(☎0586 89 87 05; www.hotelalteatro.it; Via Mayer 42; s €80, d €95-145; P❄@🛜) One of Tuscany's loveliest urban hotels, this bijou eight-room

address is irresistible. Lounge on green wicker furniture beneath a breathtakingly beautiful, 350-year-old magnolia tree in the gravel garden out back and enjoy!

Camping Miramare
CAMPGROUND €

(✆0586 58 04 02; www.campingmiramare.it; Via del Littorale 220; camping 2 people, car & tent €26-88; ⛵) Be it tent pitch beneath trees or deluxe version with wooden terrace and sun-loungers on sandy beach, this site – open all year thanks to its village of mobile homes, maxi caravans and bungalows – has it all. Find it 8km south of town in Antignano.

Hotel Gran Duca
HOTEL €

(✆0586 89 10 24; www.granduca.it; Piazza Micheli 16; s/d €90/110; ❄@🛜) Embedded in the little that survives of Livorno's 16th-century city walls, this hotel across from the fishing docks is unique. Its 62 rooms are classic; those on the 2nd floor with private terrace aplomb in the red-brick ramparts of the Medici wall are straight out a film.

✖ Eating

Sampling traditional *cacciucco,* a remarkable mixed seafood stew, is reason enough to visit Livorno.

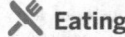 **L'Ancora**
SEAFOOD €€

(✆0586 88 14 01; Scali delle Ancore 10; meals €25-35; ⊙Wed-Mon) This canalside terrace is the white-hot ticket in good weather, though settling for a table in the Medici-built,

barrel-ceilinged, brick boat house is hardly a hardship. The *carbonara di mare* (seafood and pasta in white sauce) is the family's pride and joy.

La Barrocciaia
OSTERIA €

(✆0586 88 26 37; Piazza Cavallotti 13; meals €20; ⊙11am-2.30pm & 6-11pm Tue-Sat, 6-11pm Sun) Locating Barrocciaia takes a careful eye given its inconspicuous facade swamped by market stalls. With luck and timing, score a table to discover why every local speaks of La Barrocciaia with such reverence.

Cantina Senese
OSTERIA €

(✆0586 89 02 39; Borgo dei Cappuccini 95; meals €20; ⊙Mon-Sat) Food- and value-conscious harbour workers are the first to fill the long wooden tables at this unpretentious eatery. The mussels are exceptional, as is the *cacciucco di pesce,* both served with piquant garlic bread.

❶ Information

Tourist office (✆0586 20 46 11; www. costadeglietruschi.it; Piazza del Municipio; ⊙7.30am-6.30pm daily Jun-Nov, shorter hr rest of yr)

❶ Getting There & Away

Boat

Regular ferries for Sardinia and Corsica depart from Calata Carrara, beside the **Stazione Marittima**; and ferries to Capraia and Gorgona use the smaller **Porto Mediceo** near Piazza

---

DON'T MISS

A TRUE TASTE OF GARFAGNANA

If there is one address that stands out in this gastronomic valley for its staunchly local cuisine, top-quality products and unwavering commitment to culinary tradition, it is Castelnuovo di Garfagnana's 160-year-old **Osteria Vecchio Mulino** (✆0583 6 21 92; www.vecchiomulino.info; Via Vittorio Emanuele 12; tasting menus incl wine €25; ⊙lunch Tue-Sun, evening with advance reservation), run with passion and humour by the fun-loving, gregarious Andrea Bertucci. There is no menu, rather a symphony of cold dishes crafted strictly from local products and brought out to shared tables one at a time.

Then there is Castelnuovo di Garfagnana's bright, modern ice-cream shop, **Fuori dal Centro** (Piazza Dini 1f; 1/2/3/4/5 balls €1/1.70/2.20/2.70/3.20), with regional-inspired flavours such as chestnut, fig, honey, pine kernel and – to die for – meringue or *gusto italiano.* Look for the amber-coloured canopied entrance just near Castelnuovo's main city gate.

Feasting over for the day, the tastiest place to stay in the Garfagnana thanks to superb dinners of farm-grown *farro* (spelt) salad, homemade pasta and handsome meats cooked to perfection by Rosa is **Pradaccio di Sopra** (✆0583 66 69 66; www.agriturismo-pradaccio.it; Pieve Fosciana; d €50-70, q €100; P⛵🍴), a family farm ensnared by chestnut woods and spelt fields a five-minute drive from Castelnuovo di Garfagnana in Pieve Fosciana.

dell'Arsenale. Boats to Spain and Sicliy, plus some Sardinia services, use **Porto Nuovo**, 3km north along Via Salvatore Orlando.

Ferry companies running these services include the following:

Toremar (☏199 117733; www.toremar.it, in Italian) Daily services to Capraia (€14.70, 2½ hours).

Corsica Ferries/Sardinia Ferries (☏199 400500; www.corsicaferries.com, www.sardiniaferries.com) Two or three services per week (daily in summer) to Bastia, Corsica (deck class €28 to €36, four hours), and four services per week (daily in summer) to Golfo Aranci, Sardinia (deck class €32 to €40, six hours express, nine hours regular).

Moby (☏199 303040; www.moby.it) Boats to/from Bastia, Corsica (€32 to €46, four hours) and Olbia, Sardinia (€44 to €67, six to 10½ hours).

Grand Navi Veloci (☏010 2094591; www.gnv.it) Sailings three times weekly to/from Palermo, Sicily (€92, 19 hours).

Grimaldi Lines (☏0586 42 66 82; www.grimaldi-ferries.com) Sailings three times weekly to/from Barcelona (€235, 21 hours) and every four days to/from Valencia, Spain (32 hours).

Train

From the **central train station** (Piazza Dante) walk westward along Viale Carducci, Via de Larderel, then Via Grande into central Piazza Grande, Livorno's main square. Trains are less frequent to **Stazione Marittima**, the station for the ports.

Florence (€6.70, 1½ hours, 16 daily)

Pisa (€1.90, 15 minutes, frequent)

Rome (€17.05 to €43, three to four hours, 12 daily)

❶ Getting Around

ATL (www.atl.livorno.it; Largo Duomo 2) Bus 1 runs from central train station to Porto

Mediceo (€1.20, on board €1.70), via Piazza Grande. To reach Stazione Marittima, take bus 1 to Piazza Grande then bus 5 from Via Cogorano, just off Piazza Grande.

Isola d'Elba

POP 31,000

Napoleon would think twice about fleeing from the island of Elba were he exiled here today. Substantially more congested now than when he arrived in 1814 (he engineered an escape in less than a year), the island is nonetheless an ever-glorious setting of rocky beach-laced coves, vineyards, blue waters, thoroughly fabulous hairpin-bend motoring and mind-bending views crowned by the highest peak of Monte Capanne (1019m). Predictably, given the rugged terrain, hiking and biking are big here.

Elba is the largest and most heavily populated island in the **Parco Nazionale Arcipelago Toscano** (www.islepark.it), Europe's largest marine protected area. Over a million visitors a year take the one-hour ferry cruise here, and in the island's main town and port Portoferraio in August it feels decidedly like everyone's turned up the same weekend. Avoid coming then!

But come in springtime and early summer, or autumn for grape and olive harvests, and you'll find plenty of tranquil nooks in this stunningly picturesque, 28km-long, 19km-wide island that beg the question: why on earth did Napoleon ever want to leave?

◉ Activities

A dizzying network of walking and mountain-biking trails blanket Elba. Though some start right at Portoferraio, walkers can easily get to/from better, far-flung trailheads

---

DON'T MISS

PIAZZA DEI DOMENICANI

End 'Little Venice' explorations on this gorgeous piazza, across the bridge at the northern end of Via Borra. Chiesa di Santa Catarina, with its thick stone walls, stands sentry on the western side of the square as it did for the Medicis four centuries ago. Follow its walls along canalside Scala del Refugio to Teatrofficina Refugio (http://teatrofficinarefugio.blogsome.com), a crumbling stone building with gargantuan wooden doors and a fabulous calendar of theatre, music and cultural events.

Or stroll down the causeway by the bridge to La Bodeguita (Scala Rosciano 9), an equally hip address with red-brick cellar and sun-drenched wooden decking terrace afloat the canal. Lunch on pasta (€10), salads (€7) and generously topped bruschetta (€7) while members of the local rowing club ply the water with oars in front of you or, come dark, enjoy live music from 10pm.

TOP FIVE BEACH SPOTS

It pays to know your *spiaggia* (beach) given that the beaches along Elba's 147km of coastline embrace every shade of sand, pebble and rock. The quietest, most select beaches are tucked in bijou rocky coves and involve a steep clamber down from the street. Predictably, parking is invariably roadside and scant. Surf Info Elba (www.infoelba.com) for a complete lowdown.

ENFOLA

Just 6km west of Portoferraio, it's not so much the grey pebbles as the outdoor action that lures the crowds here in the shape of pedalos to rent, beachside Enfola Diving Center (www.enfoladivingcenter.it), and a family-friendly 2.5km-long circular **hiking trail** around the green cape. The Parco Nazionale Arcipelago Toscano (☑0565 91 94 11; ⊙9am-1pm Mon & Fri, 2.30-4pm Tue & Thu) also has an information centre here.

PROCCHIO

This small bustling beach town, 10km west of Portoferraio, has one of Elba's longest stretches of golden sand and the island's best gelato and Sicilian *granita* at Scalo 70 (Via del Mare 10; cones €2-4); try the rice ice cream or nut, fig and caramel.

SANSONE & SORGENTA

This twinset of cliff-ensnared, white-shingle and pebble beaches stands out for its turquoise, crystal-clear waters just made for **snorkelling** and the naturally pretty campground, Camping La Sorgenta (☑0565 91 71 39; www.campinglasorgente.it; camping adult/tent/car €14/3/14, 4-person bungalows €60-150; ⊙reception 9am-9pm Apr–mid-Sep), which staggers up the terraced hillside from the shore of Sorgenta. By car from Portoferraio, follow the SP27 to Enfola.

MORCONE, PARETI & INNAMORATA

Find this trio of charming sandy-pebble coves framed by sweet-smelling pine and eucalyptus trees some 3km south of Capoliveri, on the southeastern part of the island. Rent a kayak and paddle out to sea on Innamorata, the wildest of the three; or dine fine and overnight on Pereti beach at Hotel Stella Maris (☑0565 96 84 25; www.albergostellamaris.com; half-board d €68-120 per person; P❄), one of the few island hotels to be found plump on the sand.

COLLE D'ORANO & FETOVAIA

Standout highlight of these two gorgeous swaths of golden sand on Elba's western coast is the **dramatic drive** – not to be missed – along the SP25 that links the two. Legend has it that Napoleon frequented Colle d'Orano to sit and swoon over his native Corsica visible across the water. A heavenly scented, maquis-covered promontory protects sandy Fetovaia, where nudists flop on nearby granite rocks dubbed 'le piscine'.

using the island's robust bus network. Buy trail maps and guides in Portoferraio from Il Libraio (Calata Mazzini 10) or, should you rather not DIY, hook up with a guide through the national park office in Portoferraio. The following are recommended walks.

San Lucia to San Martino A low-impact, 90-minute walk, starting just outside Portoferraio at the church of San Lucia, traversing meadows and former farmland being repossessed by nature for about 2.2km and terminating at Napoleon's villa in San Martino.

Marciana to Chiessi A 12km trek starting high in Marciana, dribbling downhill, past ancient churches, sea vistas and granite boulders for about six hours to the seaside in Chiessi.

The Great Elba Crossing A three-to-four day, 60km east–west island crossing, including Monte Capanne, Elba's highest point (1019m), overnighting down on the coast as camping is not allowed on the paths. The highlight is the final 19km leg from Poggio to Pomonte, passing the Sanctuary of Madonna del Monte and the Masso dell'Aquila rock formation.

ℹ️ Getting There & Away

Regular car and foot passenger ferries (every half-hour) sail from Piombino to Elba operated by **Moby** (www.mobylines.com) and **Toremar** (www.toremar.it) – most dock at Portoferraio but a handful in high season call at smaller ports on the island.

Unless it is a summer weekend or August, when queues can form, there is no need to buy a ticket in advance. Simply buy a ticket at the port. Fares (from €15/45 one way per person/car) vary according to the season. Sailing time is one hour.

ℹ️ Getting Around

Don't bother with a vehicle in high season – the island's few roads are far too clogged with cars. Opt for a mountain bike, scooter or bike instead, available for rent in Portoferraio from **Two Wheels Network** (📞0565 91 46 66; www.twn-rent.it; Viale Elba 32, Portoferraio), or take an ATL bus from **Portoferraio bus station** (Viale Elba 20, Portoferraio), almost opposite the Toremar jetty.

PORTOFERRAIO
POP 12,182

Known to the Romans as Fabricia and later Ferraia (since it was a port for iron exports), this small harbour was acquired by Cosimo I de' Medici in the mid-16th century, when the fortifications took shape.

It can be a hectic place in high season, but wandering the streets and steps of the historic centre, indulging in the exceptional eating options and bargaining for sardines with fishermen at the old port more than makes up for the squeeze.

👁️ Sights & Activities

Old Town   HISTORICAL CENTRE
From the ferry terminal, it's a bit less than a kilometre along the foreshore to the old

DON'T MISS

SCALINATA MEDICI

From Portoferraio's central square, Piazza Cavour, head uphill along Via Giuseppe Garibaldi to the foot of this monumental staircase, a fabulous mirage of 140 wonky stone steps cascading up through every sunlit hue of amber to the dark, dimly lit church of 17th-century **Chiesa della Misericordia** (Via della Misericordia) guardian to Napoleon's death mask. Continue to the top to reach the forts and Napoleonic villa.

town, a spiderweb of narrow streets and alleys held firmly in place by the town's defining twinset of forts, **Forte Falcone** (closed) and the salmon-pink **Forte Stella** (Via della Stella; adult/child €2/1.50; ⏰9am-7pm Easter-Sep) with deserted 16th-century ramparts to wander and scores of freewheeling seagulls.

Back by the water, Napoleon was 'imprisoned' in 1814 at the start of his fleeting exile on Elba in the 15th-century **Torre del Martello** by the port entrance – contemporary guide to the modest **Museo Archeologica della Linguelle** (Archaeological Museum; admission €3; ⏰10am-1pm & 3.30-7.10pm Fri-Wed Apr-Oct).

Museo Nazionale della Residenza Napoleoniche   HISTORICAL RESIDENCE
(Piazzale Napoleone; adult/child €3/1.50; ⏰9am-7pm Mon & Wed-Sat, 9am-1pm Sun) Up on the bastions, between the two forts, is Villa dei Mulini or Palazzo dei Mulini, home to Napoleon during his stint as emperor of this small isle. With its splendid library, Italianate gardens and sea view, the emperor certainly didn't want for creature comforts during his brief Elban exile – contrast his Elba lifestyle with the simplicity of his camp bed and travelling trunk when he was on the campaign trail.

Museo Villa Napoleonica di San Martino   HISTORICAL RESIDENCE
(San Martino; adult/parking €3/3; ⏰9am-7pm Wed-Sat, 9am-1pm Sun) Set in hills about 5km southwest of town in San Martino, this villa – a remodelled farmhouse topped by a roof terrace with Napoleonic stone eagles – was where Napoleon occasionally dropped in to escape the city heat. After his death in 1851 a Russian nobleman had the rather overbearing gallery built at its base, now host to temporary Napoleon-related exhibitions.

A combined ticket covering both villas costs €5 and is valid for three days.

🛏️ Sleeping

Half-board is usually the only option in August and many hotels only open April to October. The best places to stay are a short drive from the town centre.

Rosselba Le Palme   CAMPGROUND €
(📞0565 93 31 01; www.rosselbalepalme.it; camping adult/tent/car €10.40/12.10/3.80; ⏰Apr–mid-Oct; 🅿️🛜🏊🐕) Set around a botanical garden and considered one of Europe's best campgrounds, this 'camping village' 9km east of Portoferraio town centre along the SP26

and SP28 is a green oasis of tropical palms. Among its many activities is diving taught by Jean-Jacques Mayol, son of legendary free diver Jacques Mayol of *Big Blue* fame.

Villa Ombrosa
HOTEL €€
(☎0565 91 43 63; www.villaombrosa.it; Via de Gasperi 3; d from €95; P🅟🛜) One of the very few Portoferraio hotels open year-round, Ombrosa has a great location overlooking the sea (ask for a sea-facing room; those overlooking the back garden aren't half as nice) and Spiaggia delle Ghiaie (Ghiaie Beach).

🍴 Eating

TOP CHOICE Osteria Libertaria
OSTERIA €€
(☎0565 91 49 78; Calata Matteotti 12; meals €30; ⊙Apr-Oct) Plump on the waterfront across from the fishing boats, this stylish dining address cooks up an outstanding fish-driven cuisine. Dishes are simple – think a simple mixed platter of marinated fish, fried calamari or *tonno in crosta di pistacchi* (pistachio-encrusted tuna fillet) – but fresher than fresh and cooked to perfection every time. Dine at one of two tile-topped tables on the traffic-noisy street outside or on the back-alley terrace. No coffee.

Il Castagnacciao
PIZZERIA €
(Via del Mercato Vecchio 5; pizzas €4.50-8; ⊙9am-2.30pm & 4.40-11pm Thu-Tue) Hidden in an alley near central square Piazza Cavour, this iconic address with bench seating at wooden tables centre is tantamount to no-frills pizza bliss. Watch your thin-crust, rectangular-shaped pizza go in and out the wood-fired oven and make sure you save space for dessert – *castagnacci* baked in the same oven. Big appetites can kick off the lip-smacking feast with *torta di ceci* (chickpea 'cake').

❶ Information
Info Park Are@ (☎0565 91 94 14; www.islepark.it; cnr Viale Elba & Calata Italia; ⊙9.30am-1.30pm & 3.30-7.30pm, closed Sun winter) Parco Nazionale Arcipelago Toscano information centre.

Tourist office (☎0565 91 46 71; www.isoleditoscana.it; Calata Italia 43; ⊙9am-7pm Mon-Fri, 9am-1pm Sat & Sun, shorter hr winter) Near the ferry port.

AROUND PORTOFERRAIO
Now this is what you call style: a walled estate on the seashore with a 17th-century farmhouse, an 18th-century villa, almost eight hectares of vineyards tumbling towards the sea, olive groves, palm trees and

---

❶ MAKING THE MOST OF YOUR EURO

If you are planning on visiting Siena's major monuments, be sure to purchase a money-saving combined pass:

» SIA Summer (Museo Civico, Santa Maria della Scala, Museo dell'Opera, Battistero di San Giovanni, Oratorio di San Bernadino and Chiesa di San Agostino; €17, valid for seven days during period 15 March to 31 October)

» OPA SI Pass (Duomo, Museo dell'Opera, Battistero di San Giovanni, Cripta and Oratorio di San Bernardino; €10, valid for three days)

» SIA Winter (Museo Civico, Santa Maria della Scala, Duomo, Museo dell'Opera and Battistero di San Giovanni; €14, valid for seven days during period 1 November to 14 March)

» Museo Civico and Torre del Mangia (€13)

» Musei Comunali (Museo Civico and Santa Maria della Scala; €11, valid for two days)

The OPA SI Pass can be booked in advance at www.operaduomo.siena.it; all other passes are purchased directly from the museums.

---

10 self-catering apartments – some on the beach in former peasant-worker cottages. Upon landing on the island of Elba in 1814 it was at **Tenuta La Chiusa** (☎0565 93 30 46; www.tenutalachiusa.it; Magazzini 93, Portoferraio; d €65-120, up to 5 people €110-185, d per week €450-850, up to 5 people €750-1300; P🅟) that Napoleon stayed the night before heading into Portoferraio to be received by the crowd.

Elba's oldest winemaking estate, La Chuisa, 8km east of Portoferraio along the SP26 and SP28, really is unique. It arranges **winetasting** (⊙8.30am-12.30pm & 4-8pm, shorter hr low season) and accommodation (minimum two/five nights September to July/August) and has a simple charm: guests can buy olive oil and wine direct from reception; and, should you not fancy cooking, beachside **Ristorante Mare**, open for breakfast, lunch and dinner, is a wonderful two-minute stroll away along the pebbly seashore.

MARCIANA
POP 2236

From Portoferraio cruise 20km west along the coast to Marciana Marina, from where it's another 9km inland to the island's highest (375m) and oldest village. Park at the entrance to Marciana and follow Via delle Fonti and its continuation, Via delle Coste, out of the village to the Santuario della Madonna del Monte (627m) – a 40-minute uphill hike through scented parasol pine and chestnut forest. Fourteen Stations of the Cross pave the old mule track up to the pilgrimage site and the coastal panorama that unfolds as you get higher is remarkable. Play I Spy Corsica.

Back down in Marciana village, lunch à la Slow Food at Osteria del Noce (☑0565 90 12 85; Via della Madonna 27; meals €30; ☉lunch & dinner daily), a simple family-run place that cooks up a mean spaghetti laced with Granseolo Elbano (a large crab typical to Elba) and *fritto del pescatore* (local deep-fried fish served in brown paper). End the typical Elban feast with a wander around the village, past arches, flowerboxes and petite balconies to drop-offs revealing views of Marciana Marina and neighbouring Poggio below.

MONTE CAPANNE

If you only have time for just one road trip from Portoferraio, it has to be this: Some 750m south of Marciana on the road to Poggio, the Cabinovia Monte Capanne (Cableway; ☑0565 90 10 20; single/return €12/18; ☉10am-12.50pm & 2.20-5pm Easter-Nov) whisks walkers in open, barred cabins – akin to canary-yellow parrot cages – up the mountain to the summit of Elba's highest point, Monte Capanne (1019m). Alight 20 minutes later at the top and hike a little further around the peak to savour an astonishing 360-degree panorama of the entire island, surrounding Tuscan archipelago, Etruscan Coast and Corsica.

CENTRAL TUSCANY

When people imagine classic Tuscan countryside, they usually conjure up images of central Tuscany. However, there's more to this popular region than gently rolling hills, sun-kissed vineyards and artistically planted avenues of cypress trees. Truth be told, the real gems here are the medieval towns and cities, most of which are Gothic and Renaissance time capsules magically transported to the modern day.

Siena
POP 54.414

The rivalry between historic adversaries Siena and Florence continues to this day, and participation isn't limited to the locals – most travellers tend to develop a strong preference for one over the other. These allegiances often boil down to aesthetic preference: while Florence saw its greatest flourishing during the Renaissance, Siena's enduring artistic glories are largely Gothic.

History

Legend tells us that Siena was founded by the son of Remus, and the symbol of the wolf feeding the twins Romulus and Remus is as ubiquitous in Siena as it is in Rome. In reality the city was probably of Etruscan origin, although it didn't begin to grow into a proper town until the 1st century BC, when the Romans established a military colony here called Sena Julia.

In the 12th century, Siena's wealth, size and power grew along with its involvement in commerce and trade. Its rivalry with neighbouring Florence grew proportionately, leading to numerous wars during the first half of the 13th century between Guelph Florence and Ghibelline Siena. Eventually, Siena was forced to ally with its rival in 1270.

In the ensuing century the city was ruled by the Council of Nine (a bourgeois group constantly bickering with the aristocracy) and enjoyed its greatest prosperity.

A plague outbreak in 1348 killed two-thirds of Siena's 100,000 inhabitants and led to a period of decline that culminated in the city being handed over to Cosimo I de' Medici, who barred the inhabitants from operating banks and thus severely curtailed its power.

This centuries-long economic downturn in the wake of the Medici takeover was a blessing in disguise, as lack of funds meant that its city centre was subject to very little redevelopment or new construction. This has led to the historic centre's listing on Unesco's World Heritage list as the living embodiment of a medieval city.

◉ Sights

Piazza del Campo
PIAZZA

This sloping piazza, popularly known as Il Campo, has been Siena's civic and social centre for nearly 600 years. In the upper part of the square is the Fonte Gaia (Happy Fountain), now clad in reproductions of the original white marble figures (1419) by Sienese sculptor Jacopo della Quercia. The recently restored originals are on show in the Complesso Museale Santa Maria della Scala.

The Campo is the undoubted heart of the city. Its magnificent pavement acts as an urban carpet on which students and tourists picnic and relax, and the cafes around the perimeter are the most popular *aperitivo* spots in town.

Palazzo Comunale
TOWN HALL

This restrained early-14th century building is also known as the Palazzo Pubblico. Entry to the ground-floor central courtyard is free. From the *palazzo* soars its graceful bell tower, the Torre del Mangia (admission €8; ☺10am-7pm Mar–mid-Oct, to 4pm mid-Oct–Feb), 102m high and with 500-odd steps. The views from the top are magnificent.

Museo Civico
MUSEUM

(Palazzo Comunale; adult/reduced €8/4.50; ☺10am-7pm mid-Mar–Oct, to 6pm Nov–mid-Mar) Many visitors enter the courtyard of the Palazzo Comunale and climb the Torre del Mangia, but end up bypassing this museum on the 1st floor. Make sure you don't do the same.

The collection includes Simone Martini's famous *Maestà* (Virgin Mary in Majesty; 1315–16), the artist's first known canvas. Opposite it is another work attributed to Martini, his oft-reproduced fresco (1328–30) of Guidoriccio da Fogliano, a captain of the Sienese army.

Next door, in the Sala della Pace where the Council of Nine was based, is the most important secular painting of the Renaissance, Ambrogio Lorenzetti's fresco cycle known as the *Allegories of Good and Bad Government* (c 1337–40). In it, Lorenzetti contrasts the harmony and prosperity that arises from good government with an – alas, much deteriorated – depiction of the privations and trials of those subject to bad rule.

Opera della Metropolitana di Siena
DUOMO

Siena's *duomo* is one of one of Italy's greatest Gothic churches, and is the focal point of this important group of ecclesiastical buildings (www.operaduomo.siena.it; Piazza del Duomo).

Construction of the duomo (admission €3, audioguide adult/child €5/3; ☺10.30am-8pm Mon-Sat, 1.30-6pm Sun Jun-Aug, shorter hr rest of year) started in 1215 and work continued well into the 14th century. The magnificent facade of white, green and red polychrome marble was designed by Giovanni Pisano (the statues of philosophers and prophets are copies; you'll find Pisano's originals in the Museo dell'Opera Metropolitana).

The interior features a magnificent inlaid marble floor decorated with 56 panels depicting historical and biblical subjects. The most valuable are kept covered and are revealed only from late August to late October each year (admission is €6 during this period).

Other drawcards include the exquisitely crafted marble and porphyry pulpit by Nicola Pisano, assisted by Arnolfo di Cambio, who later designed the *duomo* in Florence.

Through a door from the north aisle is the enchanting **Libreria Piccolomini**, built to house the books of Enea Silvio Piccolomini, better known as Pius II. The walls of the small hall are decorated with vividly coloured narrative frescoes (1502–07) painted by Bernardino Pinturicchio.

On the right-hand (eastern) side of the *duomo* is the Museo dell'Opera (admission €6; ☺9.30am-7pm Mar-May & Sep-Oct, to 8pm Jun-Aug, 10am-7pm Nov-Feb). Its highlight is Duccio di Buoninsegna's striking *Maestà* (1311), which was painted on both sides as a screen for the *duomo*'s high altar. The main painting portrays the Virgin surrounded by angels, saints and prominent Sienese citizens of the period; the rear panels (sadly incomplete) portray scenes from the Passion of Christ.

Behind the *duomo* and down a steep flight of steps is the Battistero di San Giovanni (Baptistry; Piazza San Giovanni; admission €3; ☺9.30am-7pm Mar-May, to 8pm Jun-Aug, to 7pm Sep-Oct), richly decorated with frescoes and featuring a hexagonal marble font by Jacopo della Quercia. The font is decorated with bronze panels depicting the life of St John the Baptist by artists including Lorenzo Ghiberti and Donatello.

Accessed through the baptistry is the Cripta (Crypt; admission incl audioguide €6; ☺9.30am-7pm Mar-May, to 8pm Jun-Aug, to 7pm Sep-Oct), a room below the cathedral's pulpit that was discovered in 1999. Its walls are

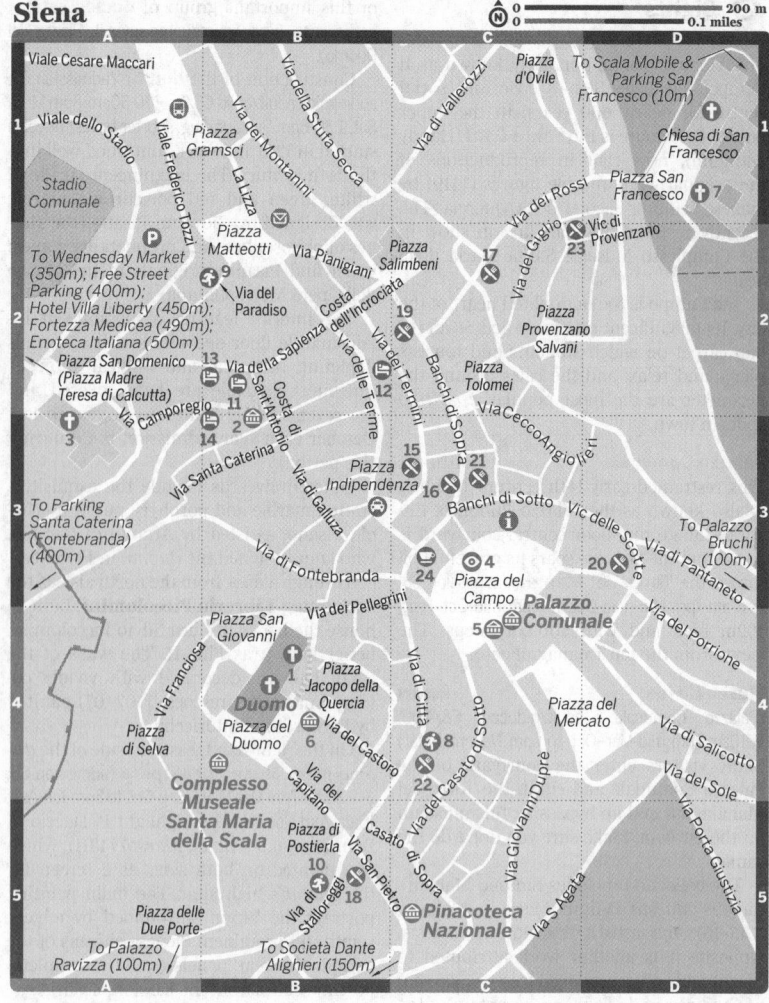

completely covered with *pintura a secco* ('dry painting') dating back to the 1200s.

Complesso Museale Santa Maria della Scala

CULTURAL CENTRE

(www.santamariadellascala.com; Piazza del Duomo 1; adult/reduced €6/3.50; ☉10.30am-6.30pm) This former hospital, parts of which date to the 13th century, was built as a hospice for pilgrims travelling the Via Francigena but soon expanded its remit to shelter abandoned children and care for the poor. Located directly opposite the *duomo,* it now functions as a cultural centre and houses

three museums – the Archaeological Museum, Art Museum for Children and Center of Contemporary Art (SMS Contemporanea) – as well as a variety of historic halls, chapels and temporary exhibition spaces. Though the atmospheric **Archaeological Museum** housed in the basement tunnels is impressive, the complex's undoubted highlight is the upstairs **Pellegrinaio** (Pilgrim's Hall), with vivid 15th-century frescoes by Lorenzo Vecchietta, Priamo della Quercia and Domenico di Bartolo lauding the good works of the hospital and its patrons. The building's medieval *fienile* (hayloft) on level three houses Jacopo della Quercia's original *Fonte Gaia* sculptures.

Pinacoteca Nazionale   ART GALLERY
(Via San Pietro 29; adult/reduced €4/2; ⊘8.15am-7.15pm Tue-Sat, 9am-1pm Sun & Mon) Occupying the once grand but now sadly dishevelled 14th-century Palazzo Buonsignori, this labyrinthine gallery showcases what is probably the world's most impressive collection of Sienese art work. The highlights are all on the 2nd floor: oom 3 has Duccio's polyptych *Madonna col Bambino e I Santi* (Madonna with Child and Saints, 1305) and Simone Martini's *Madonna col Bambino* (Madonna with Child, c1321); Room 5 has Martini's *Il Beato Agostino* altarpiece (The Blessed Agostino, 1324); Room 7 houses Ambrogio Lorenzetti's luminous *Annunciazione* (Annunciation, 1343–44); and Room 11 has Taddeo di Bartolo's *Annunciazione di Maria Vergine* (The Annunciation of the Virgin Mary, 1409).

Chiesa di San Domenico   CHURCH
(Piazza San Domenico; ⊘9am-12.30pm & 3-7pm) The city's patron saint was welcomed into the Dominican fold within this imposing church, and its **Cappella di Santa Caterina** is adorned with frescoes by Sodoma depicting events in her life. Catherine died in Rome, where most of her body is preserved,

but her head was returned to Siena (it's in a 15th-century tabernacle above the altar in the *cappella*), as was her desiccated thumb (in a small window box to the right of the chapel).

For more of Santa Caterina – figuratively speaking – visit the **Casa Santuario di Santa Caterina** (Costa di Sant'Antonio 6; admission free; ⊘9am-6.30pm Mar-Nov, 10am-6pm Dec-Feb), where the saint was born and where she lived with her parents and, according to legend, 24 siblings. As the locals say, her mother must have been a saint, too!

For information about guided and self-guided walking tours of St Catherine's Siena, go to www.viaesiena.it

Oratorio di San Bernardino   ART GALLERY
(www.operaduomo.siena.it; Piazza San Francesco 9; admission €3; ⊘1pm-7pm mid-Mar-Oct) Nestled in the shadow of the huge Gothic church of San Francesco is this 15th-century oratory, which is dedicated to another Sienese saint and decorated with mannerist frescoes by Sodoma, Beccafumi and Pacchia. Upstairs, the small Museo Diocesano di Arte Sacra has some lovely paintings, including a Madonna del Latte (Nursing Madonna, c 1340) by Ambrogio Lorenzetti. Note that admission to the oratory is included in the OPA SI Pass.

Courses

Accademia Musicale Chigiana MUSIC
(📞0577 2 20 91; www.chigiana.it; Via di Città 89) Offers competitive-entry classical music masterclasses and workshops every summer.

Fondazione Siena Jazz MUSIC
(📞0577 27 14 01; www.sienajazz.it; Fortezza Medicea 1) One of Europe's foremost institutions of its type offering courses and workshops for experienced jazz musicians.

Scuola Leonardo da Vinci LANGUAGE
(📞057 724 90 97; www.scuolaleonardo.com; Via del Paradiso 16) Italian-language school with supplementary cultural programs.

Società Dante Alighieri LANGUAGE
(📞057 74 95 33; www.dantealighieri.com; Via Tommaso Pendola 37) Language and cultural courses southwest of the city centre.

Tuscan Wine School WINE
(📞333 7229716; www.tuscanwineschool.com; Via Stalloreggi 26) Two-hour wine-tasting classes introducing Italian and Tuscan wines (€40).

Università per Stranieri LANGUAGE
(University for Foreigners; 📞0577 24 03 02; www.unistrasi.it; Piazza Carlo Rosselli 27/28) Offers various courses in Italian language and culture. You'll find it near the train station.

Tours

Ninety-minute **walking tours** in English and Spanish leave from Piazza Gramsci at 1pm daily (€15 per person). From Easter through to October there are also extra two-hour tours in English and Italian (€20 including entry ticket to the *duomo*) departing from outside the tourist office in the Campo. Advance bookings aren't necessary. For details contact the tourist office.

Festivals & Events

The Accademia Musicale Chigiana presents three highly regarded series of concerts featuring classical musicians from around the world: **Micat in Vertice** from April to May, **Settimana Musicale Senese** in July and **Estate Musicale Chigiana** between July and September.

The **Associazione Musicale Quattro Quarti** (www.quattroquarti.org) stages the **Musica Senese – La Primavera Senese** chamber music festival in April and May.

For more information about events, go to www.informacitta.net and download the Siena-specific PDF on the home page.

Sleeping

TOP CHOICE Campo Regio
Relais BOUTIQUE HOTEL €€€
(📞0577 22 20 73; www.camporegio.com; Via della Sapienza 25; s €150-220, d €190-250, ste €250-450; ❋@🛜) Siena's most charming hotel has only six rooms, all of which are individually decorated and luxuriously equipped. Breakfast is served in the sumptuously decorated lounge or on the terrace, which has a sensational view of the *duomo* and Torre del Mangia.

Palazzo Ravizza HOTEL €€
(📞0577 28 04 62; www.palazzoravizza.com; Pian dei Mantellini 34; r €75-230, ste €150-320;

IL PALIO

Dating from the Middle Ages, this colourful annual event stages a series of colourful pageants and a wild horse race on 2 July and 16 August. Ten of Siena's 17 *contrade* (town districts) compete for the coveted *palio* (silk banner). Each *contrada* has its own traditions, symbol and colours plus its own church and *palio* museum.

From about 5pm, representatives from each *contrada* parade around the Campo in historical costume, all bearing their individual banners.

The race is held at 7.45pm in July and 7pm in August. For scarcely one exhilarating minute, the 10 horses and their bareback riders tear three times around a temporary dirt racetrack with a speed and violence that makes spectators' hair stand on end.

Join the crowds in the centre of the Campo at least four hours before the start if you want a place on the rails, but be aware that once there you won't be able to leave until the race has finished. Alternatively, the cafes in the Campo sell places on their terraces; these cost between €350 and €400 per ticket, and can be booked through the tourist office up to one year in advance.

Note that during the Palio, hotels raise their rates between 10% and 50% and enforce a minimum-stay requirement.

P✱@🛜) Occupying a Renaissance-era *palazzo* located in a quiet but convenient corner of the city, this impressive hotel offers rooms with frescoed ceilings, huge beds and small but well-equipped bathrooms. Suites are even more impressive, with views over the delightful rear garden. The three cheapest rooms are in the attic, with small windows and even smaller bathrooms.

Hotel Alma Domus   HOTEL €

(🖉0577 4 41 77; www.hotelalmadomus.it; Via Camporegio 37; s €40-45, d €65-75; ✱@🛜) Owned by the Catholic diocese and still home to eight Dominican nuns who act as guardians at the Casa Santuario di Santa Caterina (located in the same complex), this convent is now privately operated as a budget hotel. Most of the simple but spotlessly clean rooms have views over the narrow green Fontebranda valley across to the *duomo*. There's a 1am curfew.

Hotel Villa Liberty   HOTEL €€

(🖉0577 4 49 66; www.villaliberty.it; Viale Vittorio Veneto 11; s €55-85, d €89-159; ✱🛜) Located in a tree-lined boulevard opposite the Fortezza Medicea, this Liberty-style villa has been converted into a 17-room hotel and is one of the city's best midrange choices. Though the Campo is only a 15-minute walk away, the area is less touristy than the historic centre and there is free (but highly contested) parking right outside the hotel. Rooms are light and modern.

Antica Residenza Cicogna   B&B €€

(🖉0577 28 56 13; www.anticaresidenzacicogna.it; Via dei Termini 67; s €70-75, d €85-100, ste €120-130; ✱@🛜) Charming host Elisa supervised the recent restoration of this 13th-century building and will happily recount its history (it's been owned by her family for generations). The seven rooms are clean and well maintained, with comfortable beds, painted ceilings and tiled floors.

Albergo Bernini   PENSIONE €

(🖉0577 28 90 47; www.albergobernini.com; Via della Sapienza 15; s €78, d without bathroom €75, d €85, f without bathroom €115; 🛜) A welcoming, family-run hotel with clean and neat rooms and a gorgeous terrace sporting views across to the *duomo* and Chiesa di San Domenico. The downsides are uncomfortable beds and the fact that only two rooms – the single and triple – have air-con. Rates are negotiable in winter and payment is cash only; breakfast costs €3 to €7.50.

Palazzo Bruchi   B&B €€

(🖉0577 28 73 42; www.palazzobruchi.it; Via di Pantaneto 105; s €80-90, d €90-150; @🛜) Host Camilla Masignani goes out of her way to make guests feel at home at her six-roomed B&B in a 17th-century *palazzo* close to the Campo. It's one of the few places in Siena where one wakes up to church bells and chirping birds rather than street noise (rooms overlook the Fontebranda valley).

Camping Colleverde Siena   CAMPGROUND €

(🖉0577 33 25 45; www.campingcolleverde.com; Strada di Scacciapensieri 47; camping 2 people, tent & car €33.70, tw mobile home €45-65; ☺Mar–early Jan; P🅿🛆) Three kilometres north of the historical centre, this popular place rents standard campsites as well as mobile homes, some with full kitchens. Buses 3 and 8 travel between the campground, the train station and the city centre. Wi-fi is €4 per day.

🍴 Eating & Drinking

TOP
CHOICE Enoteca I Terzi   MODERN ITALIAN €€

(🖉0577 4 43 29; www.enotecaiterzi.it; Via dei Termini 7; meals €39; ☺11am-1am Mon-Sat) Close to the Campo but off the well-beaten tourist trail, this classy modern *enoteca* is a favourite with bankers from the nearby headquarters of the Monte dei Paschi di Siena bank, who love to linger over their working lunches of light-as-air fried *baccalá* (cod), handmade pasta, flavoursome risotto and succulent grilled meats.

Tre Cristi   SEAFOOD €€

(🖉0577 28 06 08; www.trecristi.com; Vicola di Provenzano 1-7; 4-course tasting menus €35-40, 6-course menus €60; ☺closed Sun) Seafood restaurants are thin on the ground in this meat-obsessed region, so the long existence of Tre Cristi (it's been around since 1830) should be heartily celebrated. The menu here is as elegant as the decor, and added touches such as a complimentary glass of *prosecco* (dry sparkling wine) at the start of the meal add to the experience. Dishes are delicate and delicious, and the tasting menus offer excellent value.

Morbidi   DELI €

(Via Banchi di Sopra 75; ☺9am-8pm Mon-Sat) Local gastronomes shop here, as the range of cheese, cured meats and imported delicacies is the best in Siena. If you are self-catering you can join them, but make sure you also investigate the downstairs lunch buffet

(€12; ⏱12.30-2.30pm), which offers fantastic value. Choose from platters of antipasti, salads, pastas and a dessert of the day – it's perfectly acceptable to return for second helpings.

Osteria Le Logge
MODERN ITALIAN €€€

(✆0577 4 80 13; www.osterialelogge.it; Via del Porrione 33; meals €55; ⏱closed Sun) This place changes its menu of creative Tuscan cuisine almost daily. The best tables are in the downstairs dining room – once a pharmacy and still retaining its handsome display cabinets – or on the streetside terrace. The antipasti and *primi* are consistently delicious, but mains can be disappointing. There's a wonderful wine list.

Enoteca Italiana
WINE BAR €€

(www.enoteca-italiana.it; Fortezza Medicea; ⏱noon-1am Mon-Sat Apr-Sep, to midnight Oct-Mar) The former munitions cellar and dungeon of this Medici fortress has been artfully transformed into a classy *enoteca* that carries over 1500 Italian labels. You can take a bottle with you, ship a case home or enjoy a glass or two in the attractive courtyard or atmospheric vaulted interior.

Grom
GELATERIA €

(www.grom.it; Via Banchi di Sopra 11-13; gelati €2.50-5; ⏱11am-midnight Sun-Thu, to 1am Fri & Sat summer, 11am-11pm Sun-Thu, to midnight Fri & Sat winter) Delectable gelato with flavours that change with the season; many of the ingredients are organic or Slow Food–accredited. Also serves milkshakes.

Kopa Kabana
GELATERIA €

(www.gelateriakopakabana.it; Via dei Rossi 52-55; gelati €1.70-2.30; ⏱11am-midnight mid-Feb–mid-Nov) Come here for fresh gelato made by self-proclaimed ice-cream master, Fabio (we're pleased to concur). There's a second location at Via San Pietro 20, close to the Pinacoteca Nazionale.

Pizzicheria de Miccoli
DELI €

(Via di Città 93-95; ⏱8am-8pm) Richly scented, de Miccoli has windows festooned with sausages, stacks of cheese and *porcini* mushrooms by the sackful. It also sells filled *panini* to go.

Pasticceria Nannini
CAFE €

(24 Via Banchi di Sopra; ⏱7.30am-11pm) Come here for the finest *cenci* (fried sweet pastry), *panforte* (a rich cake of almonds, honey and candied fruit) and *ricciarelli* (almond biscuits) in town, enjoyed with a coffee.

Caffè Fiorella
CAFE €

(www.torrefazionefiorella.it; Via di Città 13; ⏱7am-8pm Mon-Sat) Squeeze into this tiny space behind the Campo to enjoy Siena's best coffee. In summer, the coffee granita with a dollop of cream is a wonderful indulgence.

🛍 Shopping

Wednesday market
MARKET

(⏱7.30am-1pm) Spreading around Fortezza Medicea and towards the Stadio Comunale, this is one of Tuscany's largest markets and is great for foodstuffs and cheap clothing.

❶ Information

Hospital (✆0577 58 51 11; Viale Bracci) Just north of Siena at Le Scotte.

Police station (✆0577 20 11 11; Via del Castoro 6)

Tourist office (✆0577 28 05 51; www.terresiena.it; Piazza del Campo 56; ⏱9am-7pm) Reserves accommodation, sells a map of Siena (€0.50), organises car and scooter hire, and sells train tickets.

❶ Getting There & Away

Bus

Siena Mobilità (✆800 570530; www.sienamobilita.it), part of the **Tiemme** (✆0577 20 42 46; www.tiemmespa.it) network, runs services between Siena and other parts of Tuscany. It has a **ticket office** (⏱6.30am-7.30pm Mon-Fri, 7am-7.30pm Sat & Sun) underneath the main bus station in Piazza Gramsci; there's also a left-luggage office here (per 24 hours €5.50).

Frequent 'Corse Rapide' (Express) buses race up to Florence (€7.10, 1¼ hours); they are a better option than the 'Corse Ordinarie' services, which stop in Poggibonsi and Colle di Val d'Elsa en route. Other regional destinations include the following.

San Gimignano (€5.50, one to 1½ hours, 10 daily either direct or changing in Poggibonsi)

Montalcino (€3.65, 1½ hours, six daily)

Poggibonsi (€3.95, 50 minutes, every 40 minutes)

Montepulciano (€5.15, 1¾ hours)

Arezzo (€5.40, 1½ hours, eight daily)

Colle di Val d'Elsa (€2.70, 30 minutes, hourly) Connections for Volterra (€2.75)

Sena (✆861 1991900; www.sena.it) buses run to/from Rome (€21, 3½ hours, eight daily), Milan (€35, 4¼ hours, four daily), Venice (€28, 5¼ hours, two daily) and Perugia (€12, 90 minutes, one daily). Its **ticket office** (✆8.30am-7.45pm Mon-Sat) is also underneath the bus station.

Car & Motorcycle

For Florence, take the RA3 (Siena–Florence *superstrada*) or the more attractive SR222.

Train

Siena isn't on a major train line so buses are generally a better alternative. You'll need to change at Chiusi for Rome and at Empoli for Florence.

ⓘ Getting Around

TO/FROM THE AIRPORT A Siena Mobilità bus travels between Pisa airport and Siena (one way/return, €14/26, two hours), leaving Siena at 7.10am and Pisa at 1pm. Tickets should be purchased at least one day in advance from the bus station or online.

My Tour (☑0577 23 63 30; www.mytours.it) operates a shuttle service between Florence airport and Siena twice daily (one way/return, €30/50, two hours). Tickets can be booked through the tourist office.

BUS Siena Mobilità operates city bus services (€1 per 90 minutes). Buses 9 and 10 run between the train station and Piazza Gramsci.

CAR & MOTORCYCLE There's a ZTL (Zona a Traffico Limitato) in the historic centre, although visitors can drop off luggage at their hotel, then get out (don't forget to have reception report your licence number or risk receiving a hefty fine).

There are large, conveniently located car parks at the Stadio Comunale and around the Fortezza Medicea, both just north of Piazza San Domenico. Some free street parking (look for white lines) is available in Viale Vittorio Veneto, on the southern edge of the Fortezza Medicea, but it is hotly contested. The paid car parks at San Francesco and Santa Caterina (aka Fontebranda) each have a *scala mobile* (escalator) to take you up into the centre.

All paid car parks charge €1.60 per hour. For more information on parking, go to www.siena parcheggi.com (in Italian).

Chianti

The ancient vineyards in this postcard-perfect part of Tuscany produce the grapes used in Chianti Classico, a Sangiovese-dominated drop sold under the Gallo Nero (Black Cockerel/Rooster) trademark.

Split between the provinces of Florence (Chianti Fiorentino) and Siena (Chianti Sienese), Chianti is usually accessed via the SR222 (Via Chiantigiana) and is crisscrossed by a picturesque network of *strade provinciale* (provincial roads) and *strade secondaria* (secondary roads), some of which are unsealed. You'll pass immaculately maintained vineyards and olive groves, honey-coloured stone farmhouses, graceful Romanesque *pieve* (rural churches), handsome Renaissance villas and imposing castles built by Florentine and Sienese warlords during the Middle Ages.

For information about the Consorzio Vino Chianti Classico (the high-profile consortium of local producers), go to www.chiant classico.com. For a handy guide to events in the region, go to www.classico-e.it.

GREVE IN CHIANTI
POP 14,304

Located 26km south of Florence, Greve is the main town in the Chianti Fiorentino. As well as being the hub of the local wine industry, it is home to the enthusiastic and entrepreneurial Falorni family, who operate the town's three main tourist attractions.

Greve's annual wine fair is held in the first or second week of September – make sure that you book accommodation well in advance if you plan to visit at this time.

◉ Sights & Activities

Museo del Vino   MUSEUM
(www.museovino.it; Piazza Nino Tirinnanzi 10; adult/reduced €5/4; ⊙11am-6pm Mon-Sat mid-Mar–mid-Oct) Opened in 2010, this privately established and operated museum is a labour of love by Lorenzo and Stefano Falorni, who have spent over 40 years documenting the history of the local wine industry and adding to their father's collection of artefacts and materials associated with it. The audioguide (included in entry fee) provides a fascinating narrative, as does an interview-based audiovisual presentation.

Le Cantine di Greve in Chianti   WINE BAR
(www.lecantine.it; Piazza delle Cantine 2; ⊙10am-7pm) Another Falorni family enterprise, this vast commercial *enoteca* stocks more than 1200 varieties of wine. To indulge in some of the 140 different wines available for tasting here (including Super Tuscans, top DOCs and DOCGs, Vin Santo and grappa), buy a prepaid wine card costing €10 to €25 from the central bar, stick it into one of the many taps and out trickles your tipple of choice. Any unused credit will be refunded when you return the card. It's fabulous fun, though somewhat distressing for designated drivers. To find the *cantine*, look for the supermarket on the main road – it's down a staircase opposite the supermarket entrance.

Wine Tour of Chianti

A Four-Day Itinerary

Tuscany has more than its fair share of highlights, but few can match the glorious indulgence of a leisurely drive through Chianti. On offer is an intoxicating blend of scenery, acclaimed restaurants and ruby-red wine.

» Heading south from Florence along the SR222 (Via Chiantigiana), stop to prime your palate with a wine tasting or lunch at the historic **Castello di Verrazzano** (p526). Continue to the major town in Chianti Fiorentino, **Greve in Chianti** (p523). Visit its Museo del Vino to learn about the history of Chianti's centuries-old wine industry and then test your newfound knowledge over a self-directed tasting in the nearby Cantine di Greve in Chianti.

» Next day, head to the idyllically located wine estate of **Badia di Passignano** (p526) to enjoy a tour and tasting followed by lunch in the acclaimed restaurant Osteria di Passignano. In the late afternoon, watch the sun set over the vineyards at La Cantinetta di Passignano.

» On day three, carnivores may wish to head to **Panzano in Chianti** to enjoy lunch at one of Dario Cecchini's acclaimed eateries (p528). Alternatively, meander along the narrow roads west of the Via Chiantigiana, visiting the late-Renaissance sanctuary of the **Madonna di Pietracupa** and small medieval towns such as **San Donato in Poggio**, where you can sample award-winning modern Tuscan cuisine at La Locanda di Pietracupa (p528).

» On the final leg to **Siena**, travel via the scenic SP76 to **Castellina in Chianti** (p526), the major town in the Chianti Senese, where you can sample and purchase acclaimed local wines in a number of *enoteche* (wine shops).

Clockwise from top left
1. Chianti Classico 2. Vineyard, Badia di Passignano
3. Dario Cecchini, Panzano in Chianti 4. Wine barrels

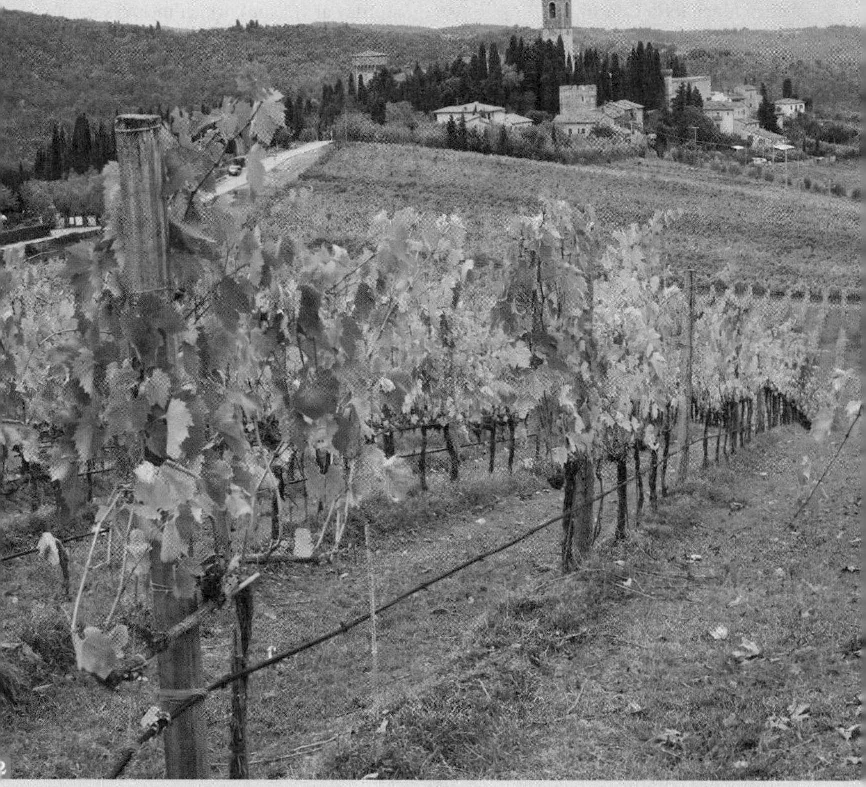

2

3

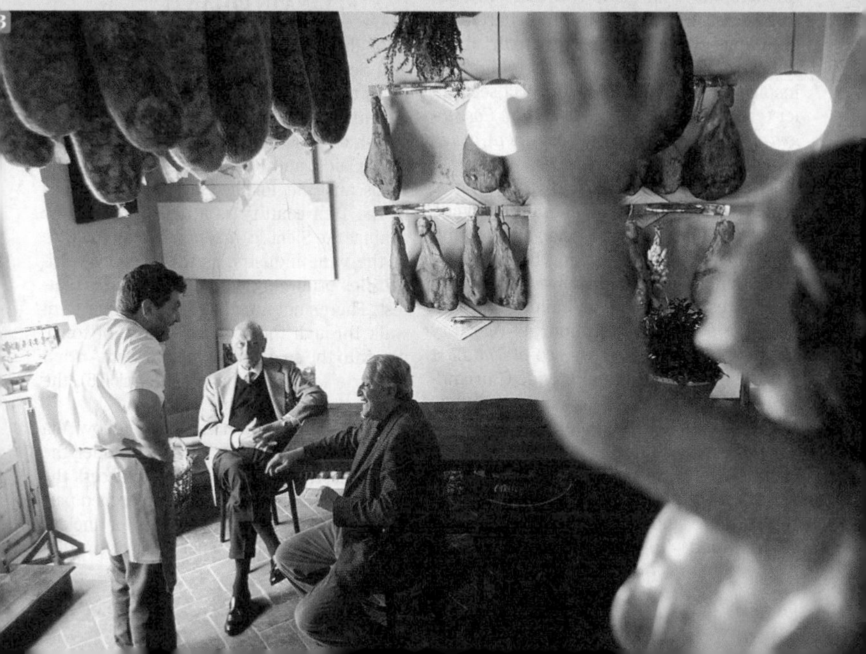

Antica Macelleria Falorni   FOOD
(www.falorni.it; Piazza Matteotti 71; ☉8am-1pm
& 3.30-7.30pm Mon-Sat, 10am-1pm & 3.30-7pm
Sun) This atmospheric *macelleria* (butcher
shop) in the main square was established
by the Fallornis way back in 1729. Known
for its *finocchiona briciolona* (pork salami
made with fennel seeds and Chianti), it's
the perfect pit stop if you're after picnic
provisions.

❶ Information

Tourist office (☑055 854 62 99; www.com
une.greve-in-chianti.fi.it/ps/s/info-turismo;
Piazza Matteotti 11; ☉10am-1pm & 2-7pm Mon-
Fri, & Sat May-Sep) Reasonably helpful but only
open over summer.

❶ Getting There & Around

BUS SITA buses travel between Greve and Florence (€3.30, one hour, hourly).

CAR & MOTORCYCLE Be sure to purchase a
copy of *Le strade del Gallo Nero* (€2), a useful
map of the wine-producing zone that's sold by
local tourist offices.

There is free parking in the two-level open-air
car park on Piazza della Resistenza, on the opposite side of the main road to Piazza Matteotti.

AROUND GREVE IN CHIANTI

A narrow and very steep road leads from
Greve up to the medieval village of **Montefioralle**, the ancestral home of Amerigo Vespucci (1415–1512). An explorer, navigator and
cartographer who made two early voyages
to America following the route charted by
Columbus, Vespucci wrote excitedly about
the New World on his return to Europe,
inspiring cartographer Martin Waldseemül-
ler (creator of the 1507 *Universalis Cosmo-
graphia*) to name the new continent in his
honour.

The 11th-century **Badia di Passignano**
located 6km west of Montefioralle is owned
by the Antinoris, one of Tuscany's oldest and
most prestigious winemaking families, and
is surrounded by vines and olive trees. At the
time of research, the main building was undergoing a major restoration; its refectory
(home to a 15th-century fresco of *The Last
Supper* by Domenico and Davide Ghirlandaio) and cloisters will be open to the public
when the restoration is complete.

There are a number of options if you are
keen to take a **guided wine tour** (☑055 807
12 78; www.osteriadipassignano.com), including
the 'Antinori and Badia a Passignano' tour
(€150; Monday to Wednesday and Friday to

Saturday at 11.15am), which includes a tasting of four estate wines followed by a three-
course lunch in the estate's restaurant; and
the 'Antinori and the Osteria' tour (€200;
Monday to Wednesday and Friday to Saturday at 5.45pm), which includes a tasting of
four estate wines plus a five-course dinner.
Alternatively, you can enjoy a tour of the cellars and a paid tasting of four wines (€80;
Monday to Saturday at 4pm). Bookings for
all of these tours are essential. It's also possible to taste and purchase Antinori wines
and olive oil at **La Bottega** (☉10am-6.30pm
Mon-Sat), the estate's wine shop. You don't
need to make a reservation for this.

The castle at **Castello di Verrazzano**
(☑055 85 42 43; www.verrazzano.com) wine estate 3km north of Greve was once home to
Giovanni da Verrazzano (1485–1528), who
explored the North American coast and is
commemorated in New York by the Verra-
zano Narrows bridge (the good captain lost
a 'z' from his name somewhere in the mid-
Atlantic). Today, the castle presides over a
220-hectare historic estate where Chianti
Classico, Vin Santo, grappa, honey, olive oil
and balsamic vinegar are produced. There
are four guided tours on offer (€14 to €110),
including one that transports you to and
from Florence and includes a private guide
and lunch with estate wines. Details are on
the website.

CASTELLINA IN CHIANTI
POP 2966

Though it is now the major town in the Chianti Senese, Castellina was once one of the
three towns in the Lega del Chianti, a military and administrative alliance within the
city-state of Florence (the others members
were Gaiole and Radda). Established by the
Etruscans and fortified by the Florentines
in the 15th century as a defensive outpost
against the Sienese, it is now a major centre
of the wine industry, as the huge cylindri-
cal silos brimming with Chianti Classico at-
test. There's not much to do here other than
walk through the compact centre of town,
pop into the small museum and visit **Antica
Fattoria la Castellina** (Via Ferruccio 26), the
town's best-known wine shop.

From the southern car park, follow Via
Ferruccio or the panoramic path under the
town's eastern defensive walls to access the
atmospheric **Via delle Volte**, an arched passageway that was originally used for ancient
sacred rites and later enclosed with a roof

CYCLING CHIANTI

Exploring Chianti by bicycle is a highlight for many travellers. You can rent bicycles from **Ramuzzi** (☎055 85 30 37; www.ramuzzi.com; Via Italo Stecchi 23; touring bike/125cc scooter per day €20/55; ⏰9am-1pm & 3-7pm Mon-Fri, 9am-1pm Sat) in Greve in Chianti.

A number of companies offer guided cycling tours leaving from Florence.

» **Florence by Bike** (☎055 48 89 92; www.florencebybike.it; Via San Zanobi 120r) Day tour of northern Chianti including lunch and wine tasting (March to October, €74).

» **I Bike Florence** (☎055 012 39 94; www.ibikeflorence.com; Via de' Lamberti 1) Two-day guided tour from Florence to Siena (including one night's accommodation, two lunches and one dinner, €329) every Monday and Thursday between April and October.

» **I Bike Italy** (☎055 012 39 94; www.ibikeflorence.com; Via de' Lamberti 1) Jointly runs the two-day tour with I Bike Florence, but also offers a day tour including lunch at a winery (March to October, €80). Students receive a 10% discount.

» **I Bike Tuscany** (☎335 8120769; www.ibiketuscany.com) Year-round one-day tours (€110 to €140) for riders at every skill level. The company transports you from your Florence hotel to Chianti by minibus, where you join the tour. Both hybrid and electric bikes are available, as is a support vehicle.

and incorporated into the Florentine defensive structure.

◎ Sights

Museo Archeologico del Chianti Sienese   MUSEUM
(www.museoarcheologicochianti.it; Piazza del Comune 18; adult/reduced €5/3; ⏰11am-7pm daily Apr-Oct, 11am-5pm Sat & Sun Nov-Mar) Etruscan archaeological finds from the local area are on display at this museum located in the town's medieval *roccca* (fortress). Room 4 showcases artefacts found in the 7th-century-BC Etruscan tombs of **Monte-calvario** (Ipogeo Etrusco di Monte Calvario; admission free; ⏰always open), which are located on the northern edge of town off the SR222.

❶ Information

The helpful **InCHIANTI tourist office** (☎0577 74 13 92; www.essenceoftuscany.it; Via Ferruccio 40; ⏰9am-1pm Mon-Sat, 2-6pm Mon-Tue & Thu-Sat mid-Mar–Oct, closed Nov–mid-Mar) can book visits to wineries and cellars. It also provides maps, accommodation suggestions and other information.

❶ Getting There & Around

BUS **Siena Mobilità** (www.sienamobilita.it) buses travel between Castellina and Siena (€2.55, 35 minutes, 10 daily).

CAR & MOTORCYCLE The most convenient car park is at the southern edge of town off Via IV Novembre (€1/5 per hour/day).

TRAIN It's possible to access Castellina from Florence by train (€5.80, 90 minutes, hourly), but you'll need to change trains in Empoli.

⛏ Sleeping

Fattoria di Rignana   AGRITURISMO €€
(☎055 85 20 65; www.rignana.it; Val di Rignana 15, Rignana; s/d in fattoria €100/110, s/d in villa €120/140; P@☒) This old farmstead and noble villa 3.8km from Badia di Passignano has everything you'll need for the perfect Chianti experience – an historic setting, glorious views, a large swimming pool and walking access to a decent local *cantina*. Two accommodation options are on offer: elegant rooms in the 17th-century villa and more rustic rooms in the adjoining *fattoria* (farmhouse).

Villa I Barronci   HOTEL €€
(☎055 82 05 98; www.villaibarronci.com; Via Sorripa 10, San Casciano in Val di Pesa; s €85-150, d €115-230; P✳@☎☒♨) Located on the northwestern edge of Chianti between Florence and Pisa, this extremely comfortable modern country hotel offers exemplary service and amenities. You can relax in the bar and restaurant, rejuvenate in the spa, laze by the pool or head off for easy day trips to Volterra, San Gimignano and Siena.

⃠ Agrifuturismo   AGRITURISMO €
(☎339 501 9849; www.agrifuturismo.com; Strada San Silvestro 11, Barberino Val d'Elsa; 2-/4-/6-person apt €70/120/140; ☎) Woods filled with oak, juniper, cypress and pine trees sit next to ancient terraces of olive trees on this farm estate 13km southwest of Greve. The apartments are charming, with a strong and attractive design ethos, and sustainable

features such as solar panels, rain collection and recycling are utilised. No credit cards; and minimum three-night stay.

Ostello del Chianti HOSTEL €
(☎055 805 02 65; www.ostellodelchianti.it; Via Roma 137, Tavernelle Val Di Pesa; dm €16.50, d without bathroom €39, d €50; ☺reception 8.30-11am & 4pm-midnight, hostel closed mid-Mar–Oct; P@) This is one of Italy's oldest hostels (it's been going strong since the 1950s). Staff members are extremely friendly, dorms max out at six beds and bike hire can be arranged for €10 per day. Breakfast costs €2. Florence is easily accessed by SITA bus (one hour; €3.30).

Eating & Drinking

TOP CHOICE **Osteria di Passignano** GASTRONOMIC €€€
(☎055 807 12 78; www.osteriadipassignano.com; Via di Passignano 33; meals €70, tasting menus €65; ☺closed Sun) This elegant dining room on the Antinori Estate at Badia di Passignano is one of Tuscany's most impressive restaurants. The delectable food utilises local produce and is decidedly Tuscan in inspiration, but its execution is refined rather than rustic.

L'Antica Macelleria Cecchini TRADITIONAL ITALIAN €€
(www.dariocecchini.com, Via XX Luglio 11, Panzano in Chianti; ☺9am-2pm Mon-Thu & Sun, to 6pm Fri & Sat) The small town of Panzano southwest of Greve is known throughout Italy for this *macellerìa,* which is owned and run by extrovert butcher Dario Cecchini. This Tuscan celebrity has carved out a niche for himself as a poetry-spouting guardian of the *bistecca* (steak) and other Tuscan meaty treats, and he operates three eateries here as well as the *macellerìa* **Officina della Bistecca** (☎055 85 21 76; set menus €50; ☺dinner 8pm Tue, Fri & Sat, lunch 1pm Sun), with a simple set menu built around the famous *bistecca;* **Solociccia** (☎055 85 27 27; set menus €30; ☺dinner Thu, Fri & Sat 7pm & 9pm, lunch 1pm Sun), where guests share a communal table to sample meat dishes other than *bistecca;* and **Dario +** (burger with vegetables & potatoes €10, light menus €20; ☺lunch Mon-Sat), his casual lunchtime-only eatery. Book ahead for the Officina and Solociccia.

La Locanda di Pietracupa GASTRONOMIC €€
(☎055 807 24 00; www.locandapietracupa.com; Via Madonna di Pietracupa 31, San Donato in Poggio;

meals €40; ☺closed Tue) The prices at this restaurant near the late-Renaissance sanctuary of the Madonna di Pietracupa are remarkably reasonable considering the quality of the modern Tuscan cuisine on offer. You can enjoy a long lunch on the pretty outdoor terrace, or book one of the four **B&B rooms** (s/d €70/80; P) in advance and settle in for an indulgent dinner in the elegant dining room.

La Cantinetta di Passignano WINE BAR €€
(☎055 807 19 75; www.lacantinettadipassignano. com; Via di Greve 1a, Badia di Passignano; meals €30; ☺closed Wed) Lolling on a designer couch in the garden of this recently opened wine bar/restaurant is a perfect way to while away an hour or two in the late afternoon. The vineyard views are gorgeous, and the antipasto platters are a perfect accompaniment to the wines and designer beers on offer.

Il Giglio GELATERIA €
(Via del Giglio 13, San Donato in Poggio; gelati €1.50-4; ☺3pm-midnight Mon-Fri, 11.30am-midnight Sat & Sun) The fortified medieval village of San Donato is on the RA3 (Siena–Florence *superstrada*), close to Tavarnelle in Val di Pesa and a short drive from Badia di Passignano. It has three claims to fame: a charming main street with a Renaissance palace; a beautiful 12th-century *pieve;* and this gelateria (try the fig and ricotta flavour).

Val d'Elsa

A convenient base for visiting the rest of Tuscany, this valley stretching from Chianti to the Maremma can be relied upon to tick many of the boxes on your Tuscan 'must-do' list, with plenty of opportunities to enjoy food, wine, museums and scenery.

SAN GIMIGNANO
POP 7770

As you crest the hill coming from the east, the 15 towers of this walled hill town look like a medieval Manhattan. Originally an Etruscan village, the town was named after the bishop of Modena, San Gimignano, who is said to have saved the city from Attila the Hun. It became a *comune* in 1199 and was very prosperous due in part to its location on the Via Francigena – building a tower taller than those built by one's neighbour (there were originally 72) became a popular way for the town's prominent families to flaunt their power and wealth. In 1348 plague wiped out much of the population and weakened the local economy, leading to the town's submission to Florence in 1353. Today, not even the plague would deter the swarms of summer day trippers, who are lured by the town's palpable sense of history, intact medieval streetscapes and enchanting rural setting.

◉ Sights & Activities

The two most important sights in town are the Collegiata and the Palazzo Comunale. You can purchase individual entry tickets for both, or choose to take advantage of two money-saving combined entry tickets. The first (adult/child six to 18 years €7.50/5.50) gives admission to the Palazzo Comunale and two other museums in town (the Archaeological Museum complex and the Ornithological museum). The second (adult/child six to 18 years €5.50/2.50) gets you into the Collegiata and the Museo d'Arte Sacra.

Collegiata CHURCH
(Piazza del Duomo; adult/child €3.50/1.50; ⊘10am-7.10pm Mon-Fri, to 5.10pm Sat, 12.30-7.10pm Sun Apr-Oct, shorter hr rest of year, closed second half of Nov & Jan) San Gimignano's Romanesque cathedral, officially titled the Duomo Collegiata o Basilica di Santa Maria Assunta but commonly known as the Collegiata (referring to the college of priests who originally managed it), has a bare facade that belies the remarkably vivid frescoes inside.

Parts of the building date back to the second half of the 11th century, but the frescoes, which resemble a vast medieval comic strip, are later (14th century). Entry is via the side stairs and through a loggia that was originally covered and functioned as the baptistry. Inside, along the northern aisle, are frescoes of key moments from the Old Testament by Bartolo di Fredi. Opposite, covering the walls of the south aisle, are illustrated New Testament scenes by artists from the workshop of Simone Martini (probably led by Lippo Memmi, Martini's brother-in-law). On the inside wall of the facade, extending onto adjoining walls, is Taddeo di Bartolo's gruesome *Last Judgment* (c1410).

Off the south aisle, near the main altar, is the **Cappella di Santa Fina**, a Renaissance chapel adorned with naive and touching frescoes by Domenico Ghirlandaio depicting events in the life of one of the town's patron saints. The chapel featured in Franco Zeffirelli's 1999 film *Tea with Mussolini*.

Palazzo Comunale ART GALLERY
(Piazza del Duomo; art gallery & tower admission €5; ⊘9.30am-7pm Apr-Sep, 10am-5.30pm Oct-Mar) This 12th-century *palazzo* has always been the centre of local government; its **Sala del Consiglio**, which contains an early-14th-century fresco of the *Maestà* by Lippo Memmi, is where the great poet Dante addressed the town's council in 1299, urging it to support the Guelph cause.

Above the Sala del Consiglio is the small but charming **Pinacoteca**, which features paintings from the Sienese and Florentine schools of the 12th to 15th centuries. Highlights of its collection are *Angel Annunciate* (1482) by Filippino Lippi, *Madonna and Child with Saints* (1466) by Benozzo Gozzoli and an altarpiece by Taddeo di Bartolo (1401) illustrating the life of Saint Gimignano.

In the **Camera del Podestà**, at the top of the stairs, is a recently restored cycle of frescoes by Memmo di Filippuccio illustrating a moral history (check out the somewhat saucy scenes of the rewards of marriage!).

After visiting the Pinacoteca, be sure to climb up the *palazzo's* **Torre Grossa** for a spectacular view of the town and surrounding countryside.

Museo del Vino WINE BAR
(Wine Museum; Parco della Rocca; admission free; ⊘11.30am-6.30pm) More a wine bar than a museum, this operation is housed in an unmarked gallery next to the *rocca* and exists to celebrate San Gimignano's famous white wine, Vernaccia. There's a small exhibition on the history of the varietal (Italian language only) and an *enoteca* where you can enjoy a paid tasting (four/six wines €6/10) or purchase a glass (€3 to €5) to enjoy on the terrace, which has a panoramic view.

San Gimignano del 1300 MUSEUM
(www.sangimignano1300.com; Via Berignano 23; adult/child €5/3; ⊘9am-7pm) San Gimignano's newest tourist attraction is particularly popular with young children, A handmade ceramic recreation of the medieval city, it shows houses, streets, towers and people as they would have looked in 1300. It's bound to inspire junior visitors to attempt bigger and better LEGO projects on their return home.

Museo Archeologico & Speziera di Santa Fina MUSEUM
(Via Folgore da San Gimignano 11; both museums adult/reduced €3.50/2.50; ⊘11am-5.45pm mid-Mar–Dec) There are actually two museums

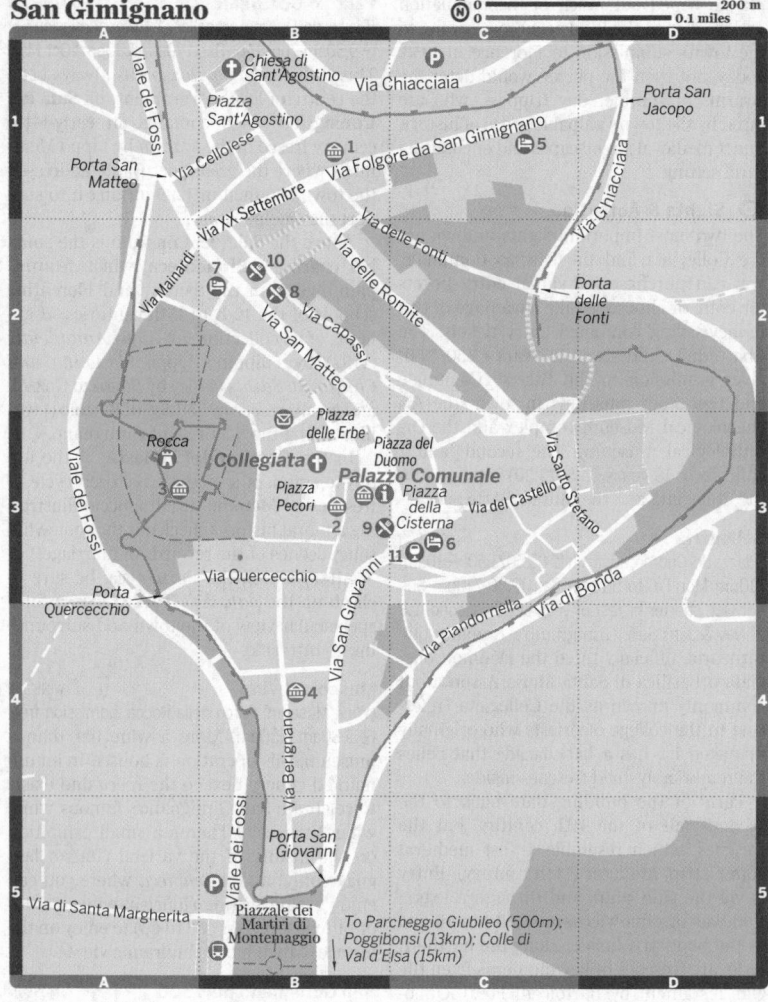

and a gallery in this complex. The Speziera section includes ceramic and glass storage vessels from the 16th-century Speziera di Santa Fina, a reconstructed 16th-century pharmacy and herb garden. Many are beautifully painted and still contain curative concoctions. Follow your nose to the side room in Gallery 7, called 'the kitchen', which is filled with herbs and spices used for elixirs. Beyond here is a small archaeological museum divided into Etruscan/Roman and medieval sections with exhibits found locally. Upstairs is the Galleria d'Arte Moderna e Contemporanea, a modern art gallery that in itself merits a visit. Permanent works include Renato Guttuso's impressive Marina (1970).

Museo d'Arte Sacra   MUSEUM
(Piazza Pecori 1; adult/under 6 yr €3.50/1.50; ⊙10am-7.10pm Mon-Fri, to 5.10pm Sat, 12.30-7.10pm Sun Apr-Oct, shorter hr rest of year, closed 2nd half of Nov & Jan) Works of religious art from the Collegiata and other churches in the town are on display in this modest museum. Those who are interested in medieval religious objects will appreciate the items made from precious metals, including

San Gimignano

beautifully crafted chalices and thuribles (censers), as well as some exquisitely embroidered textiles.

🖐 Tours

The tourist office offers a range of tours: from mid-April to October it conducts a **guided walking tour** (adult/under 12 yr incl entrance to Palazzo Comunale €20/free) of the town on Saturday and Sunday at 11am. Advance bookings aren't necessary. Other activities include a **Vernaccia di San Gimignano Vineyard Visit** (adult €20; ☉Tue & Thu Apr-Oct) that involves tastings of local foods and wines; and **nature walks** (€20) through the hills surrounding San Gimignano on Wednesday at 3pm and through Riserva Naturale di Castelvecchio, southwest of town, on Friday at 3pm. Advance bookings are essential for these.

🎊 Festivals & Events

San Gimignano Estate   CULTURAL
(www.terresiena.it) Includes performances of opera in Piazza Duomo, films in the *rocca*, concerts, theatre and dance. Held between June and September.

Ferie delle Messi   CULTURAL
Held in June (usually the third weekend), this pageant evokes the town's medieval past through re-enacted battles, archery contests and plays.

Festival Barocco di San Gimignano   MUSIC
A season of baroque music concerts in September and early October.

🛏 Sleeping

Hotel L'Antico Pozzo   BOUTIQUE HOTEL €€
(☎0577 94 20 14; www.anticopozzo.com; Via San Matteo 87; s €85-100, d €110-180; ☉closed first 2 weeks Nov & Jan; ✳@🛜) The town's best hotel is named after the old, softly illuminated *pozzo* (well) just off the lobby. Each room in the 15th-century building features high ceilings, simple but elegant decor and good-sized bathrooms; the superior rooms are particularly attractive. There's a handsome breakfast room, but in summer most guests choose to enjoy the first meal of the day in the charming rear courtyard.

Foresteria Monastero di San Girolamo   HOSTEL €
(☎0577 94 05 73; www.monasterosangirolamo.it; Via Folgore da San Gimignano 26-32; per person €27) This is an excellent budget choice. Run by friendly nuns, it has basic but comfortable rooms with attached bathrooms, sleeping two to five people. If you don't have a reservation, arrive between 9am and 12.30pm or between 3.30pm and 5.45pm and ring the monastery bell (not the Foresteria one, which is never answered). Kitchen use €3 per day, breakfast €3 and parking €2 per day.

La Cisterna   HOTEL €€
(☎0577 94 03 28; www.hotelcisterna.it; Piazza della Cisterna 24; s €64-78, d €85-160; ✳@🛜) Although it is in sore need of a renovation, the Cisterna is worth considering due to its setting (a splendid 14th-century building on the piazza of the same name) and its rooftop breakfast room/restaurant, which has panoramic views. The cheaper rooms have cramped bathrooms and can be dark – opt for a superior or deluxe version if possible. Internet €1 per 24 hours but wi-fi is free.

🍴 Eating & Drinking

San Gimignano is known for its *zafferano* (saffron), which features on many restaurant menus. You can purchase fresh produce at the **Thursday morning market** (Piazza della Erbe).

TOP CHOICE Dal Bertelli SANDWICH SHOP €

(Via Capassi 30; panini €3-5, glasses of wine €1.50; ⊙1-7pm Mar–early Jan) The Bertelli family has lived in San Gimignano since 1779, and its current patriarch is fiercely proud of both his heritage and his sandwiches. Sig Brunello Bertelli sources his salami, cheese, bread and wine from local artisan producers and sells his generously sized offerings from an atmospheric space as far away from what he calls the town's 'tourist grand bazaar' as possible. Fabulous.

Gelateria di Piazza GELATERIA €

(www.gelateriadipiazza.com; Piazza della Cisterna 4; gelati €1.80-2.50; ⊙8.30am-11pm Mar–mid-Nov) Master gelato-maker Sergio Dondoli uses only the choicest ingredients to create his creamy and icy delights. Get into the local swing of things with a Crema di Santa Fina (saffron cream) gelato or a Vernaccia sorbet.

Perucà TRADITIONAL ITALIAN €€

(✆0577 94 31 36; www.peruca.eu; Via Capassi 16; meals €34; ⊙Mar–mid-Jan) The lady owner here is as knowledgeable about regional food and wine as she is enthusiastic, and the food is excellent. Try the house speciality of *fagottini del contadino* (ravioli with pecorino, pears and saffron cream) with a glass of Fattoria San Donato's Vernaccia – it's a match made in heaven.

Da Nisio MODERN ITALIAN €€

(✆0577 94 10 29; www.danisio.com; Località Sovestro 32; meals €41; ⊙dinner Wed-Mon) The location's not the best (it's on the road to Poggibonsi, 1.5km before town, and is attached to the unattractive Le Colline hotel), but the chef/owner grows all of the vegetables he uses in his imaginative dishes, and results are both light and full of flavour. The antipasti *'specialità'* changes according to what is in season, all pasta and bread is homemade, and meats are cooked on a wood grill, imparting excellent flavour.

DiVinorum WINE BAR €

(Piazza della Cisterna 30; ⊙11am-8pm Mar-Oct, to 4pm Nov-Dec) As cool as San Gimignano comes, this wine bar is housed in cavernous former stables and has a few outdoor tables with views over the historic town walls. There's a decent array of antipasti (cheese, meats, bruschettas, salads) on offer, and an excellent selection of wine by the glass.

ⓘ Information

The extremely helpful **tourist office** (✆0577 94 00 08; www.sangimignano.com; Piazza Duomo 1; ⊙9am-1pm & 3-7pm Mar-Oct, 9am-1pm & 2-6pm Nov-Feb) organises tours, supplies maps and can book accommodation. It also has a wealth of material on the *Strada del Vino Vernaccia di San Gimignano* (Vernaccia Wine Rd of San Gimignano).

ⓘ Getting There & Away

BUS The bus station is beside Porta San Giovanni, the main entrance to town. Buy tickets at the tourist office.

Buses run to/from Florence (€6.50, 1¼ hours, 14 daily) but almost always require a change at Poggibonsi. Buses also run to/from Siena (€5.50, one to 1½ hours, 10 daily Monday to Saturday).

For Volterra you need to go to Colle di Val d'Elsa (€2.40, 35 minutes, four daily) and then buy a ticket for Volterra (€2.75, 50 minutes, four daily).

CAR & MOTORCYCLE From Florence or Siena, take the SP1 to Poggibonsi, then the SR2 and finally the RA3 (Siena–Florence *superstrada*). From Volterra, take the SR68 east and follow the turn-off signs north to San Gimignano on the SP47.

Parking is expensive here. The cheapest option (per hour/24 hours €1.50/6) is at Parcheggio Giubileo (P1) on the southern edge of town; the most convenient is at Parcheggio Montemaggio (P2) next to Porta San Giovanni (per hour/24 hours €2/20).

TRAIN Poggibonsi (by bus €1.95, about 30 minutes, frequent) is the closest train station.

VOLTERRA
POP 11,136

Volterra's well-preserved medieval ramparts give the windswept town a proud, forbidding air that author Stephanie Meyer deemed ideal for the discriminating tastes of the planet's principal vampire coven in her wildly popular book series *Twilight*. Fortunately, the reality is considerably more welcoming, as any wander through the winding cobbled streets attests.

⊙ Sights

Though it's a relatively small town, Volterra has a lavish array of museums, churches and archaeological sites to visit. If you plan on visiting a number of these, it's worth purchasing the discount tickets on offer. One of these gives admission to the Museo Etrusco Guarnacci, the Pinacoteca Comunale and the Museo Diocesano d'Arte Sacra (adult/reduced/family €10/6/20) and another (€3.50)

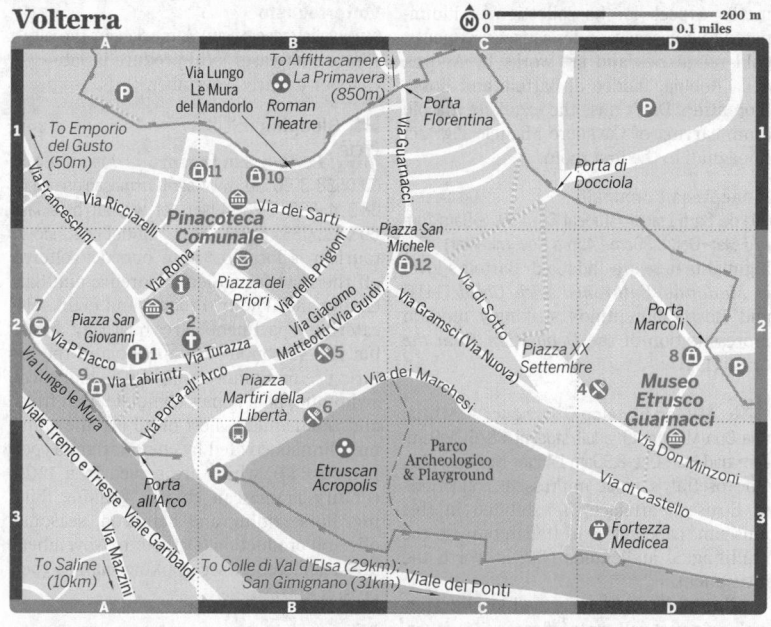

Volterra

gives entry to both the Roman Theatre and the acropolis at the Parco Archeologico. Truth be told, the second ticket isn't really necessary as there is a great view over the theatre from Via Lungo Le Mura del Mandorlo and the acropolis isn't a compelling attraction.

Cattedrale di Santa Maria Assunta CHURCH
(Piazza San Giovanni; ☺8am-12.30pm & 3-6pm) Built in the 12th and 13th centuries, the *duomo*'s interior was remodelled in the 16th century and features a handsome coffered ceiling. The **Chapel of Our Lady of Sorrows** on the left as you enter from Piazza San Giovanni has two sculptures by Andrea della Robbia and a small fresco of the *Procession of the Magi* by Benozzo Gozzoli – please don't damage it by throwing a coin behind the glass, as some visitors do.

In front of the cathedral, a 13th-century **baptistry** features a small marble font (1502) by Andrea Sansovino.

Museo Diocesano d'Arte Sacra MUSEUM
(Via Roma 1; admission by cumulative ticket; ☺9am-1pm & 3-6pm mid-Mar–Oct, 9am-1pm Nov–mid-Mar) Close to the *duomo*, this tiny museum

merits a peek for its collection of illuminated manuscripts, ecclesiastical vestments, gold reliquaries and art works by Andrea della Robbia, Taddeo di Bartolo and Rosso Fiorentino. Don't miss the exquisite marble tomb carving of Cavaliere Michele Pigi dei Bonaguidi in the first room.

Pinacoteca Comunale ART GALLERY
(Via dei Sarti 1; adult/student €6/4.50; ⊙9am-7pm mid-Mar–Oct, 8.30am-1.45pm Nov–mid-Mar) The highlights here are Taddeo di Bartolo's lovely *Madonna Enthroned with Child* (1411) and Rosso Fiorentino's strikingly modern representation of the *Deposition from the Cross* (1521).

TOP CHOICE **Museo Etrusco Guarnacci** MUSEUM
(Via Don Minzoni 15; adult/student €8/6; ⊙9am-7pm mid-Mar–Oct, 8.30am-1.45pm Nov–mid-Mar) One of Italy's most impressive collections of Etruscan artefacts is exhibited in this museum. Labelling is in Italian only, so the multilingual audioguide (€3) is worth the investment.

All exhibits were unearthed locally. They include a vast collection of some 600 funerary urns carved mainly from alabaster and tufa and displayed according to subject and period. The best examples (those dating from later periods) are on the 2nd and 3rd floors; don't miss the *Urn of the Sposi,* a strikingly realistic terracotta rendering of an elderly couple.

Other exhibits to search out include a crested helmet excavated from the Tomba del Guernero at nearby Poggio alle Croci; and the *L'Ombra della Sera* (Shadow of the Evening), an elongated bronze nude figurine that bears a striking resemblance to the work of the Italian sculptor Alberto Giacometti.

☞ Tours

Volterra Walking Tour WALKING
(☑0588 08 62 01; www.volterrawalkingtour.com) A one-hour English-language tour of the city by foot costs only €5 per person (minimum four participants or €20 for tour to operate). It leaves from Piazza Martiri della Libertà at 6pm daily from April to July and September to October. Bookings aren't necessary and payment is cash only.

✲✲ Festivals & Events

Volterra AD 1398 CULTURAL
(www.volterra1398.it, in Italian; day pass €9) Medieval festival held on the third and fourth Sundays of August.

Volterragusto FOOD
(www.volterragusto.com) A market in the city centre showcases local produce in late October to early November.

☞ Sleeping

TOP CHOICE **Podere San Lorenzo** AGRITURISMO €€
(☑0588 3 90 80; www.agriturismosanlorenzo.it; B&B d €90, 2-/3-/4-bed apt without breakfast €98/118/138; ☏☀☻) This model of 'slow' tourism is located 3.4km outside Volterra off the road from Siena, Florence and San Gimignano. The two rooms and eight self-catering apartments are relatively basic, but the surrounds are bucolic and the alluring mountain-spring-fed biological swimming pool comes complete with frogs and salamanders. Best of all are the gourmet dinners created by chef Marianna (per person €28), which are served in a 12th-century Franciscan chapel. Walking, biking, horse riding and hands-on, seasonal olive-oil production (October to November) are available, as are cooking classes (per person €90).

Chiosco delle Monache HOSTEL €
(☑0588 8 66 13; www.ostellovolterra.it; Via delle Teatro 4; dm €16-18, B&B s €42-53, d €53-69; ⊙Apr-Sep; ℗☏) Opened in 2009 after a major renovation, this excellent private hostel occupies a 13th-century monastery complete with a frescoed refectory where breakfast is served. It's outside town, near the hospital, but the historic centre is only a 30-minute (albeit steep) walk away and local buses from Piazza Martiri della Libertà stop right outside the entrance (€1). Airy rooms overlook the cloisters and have good beds and bathrooms; dorms sleep up to six. Reception is open 8am to noon and 5pm to 11pm, but often stays open for the full day in high summer. Wi-fi is €1 per hour; breakfast (for those in dorms) €6.

Affittacamere La Primavera B&B €
(☑0588 8 72 95; www.affittacamere-laprimavera.com; Via Porta Diana 15; d €70; ℗☏) Just outside the walls (near the Roman Theatre), this family-run place offers four pleasantly decorated rooms and a generous breakfast. An additional bed costs only €10.

✗ Eating & Drinking

TOP CHOICE **La Carabaccia** TRADITIONAL ITALIAN €€
(☑0588 8 62 39; Piazza XX Settembre 4-5; meals €20; ⊙closed Mon) A trio of local women – Sara, Lala and Patrizia – have put their

heart and soul into this fantastic trattoria, which is the city's best lunch option. Named after a humble Tuscan vegetable soup, it has a small menu that changes daily according to what local producers are offering and always has vegetarian options. Sit on the front terrace or head indoors to enjoy the Italian folk music played on the sound system.

Emporio del Gusto
DELI €

(Via San Lino 2; ☺9.30am-1pm & 4.30-8pm Mon-Fri) This food co-op is sponsored by the *comune* and sells produce from around the region. It stocks olive oil products (including toiletries), fresh milk and yoghurt, cheese, vegetables, locally grown saffron, truffles, pasta, bread and wine.

L'Incontro
CAFE €

(Via Matteotti 18; sandwiches €2.50-3.50; ☺6.30am-1am Thu-Tue) Come here for excellent coffee, delectable home-baked biscuits and great savoury snacks. The rear *salone* is a great spot to grab a quick antipasto plate or *panino* for lunch, and the long front bar is always crowded with locals enjoying a coffee or *aperitivo*.

Ristorante-Enoteca Del Duca
TRADITIONAL ITALIAN €€

(☑0588 8 15 10; www.enoteca-delduca-ristorante.it; Via di Castello 2; 5-course tasting menus €42; ☺closed Tue) Volterra's best restaurant serves traditional Tuscan dishes in its vaulted dining areas and lovely rear courtyard. It has an excellent wine list – not surprising considering the owner has his own vineyard (try his Giusto Alle Balze Merlot).

Caffè dei Fornelli
CAFE €

(Piazza dei Fornelli; ☺9am-11pm Tue-Sat, 9am-6pm Sun) The city's bohemian set congregates here. Poetry readings and exhibitions are regular occurrences, and the streetside terrace is the only place in town where you can enjoy a coffee or glass of wine while enjoying a view over the surrounding countryside.

🛍 Shopping

For information about artisans in Volterra, see www.arteinbottegavolterra.it.

Fabula Etrusca
JEWELLERY

(www.fabulaetrusca.it; Via Lungo Le Mura del Mandorlo 10; ☺10am-7pm daily Easter-Christmas) Distinctive pieces in 18-carat gold – many based on Etruscan designs – are handmade in this workshop on the city's northern walls.

Alabaster Workshops
ARTISANAL

Volterra is known as the city of alabaster, and has a number of shops specialising in hand-carved alabaster items; many of these double as ateliers where the artisans work. Among the best are **Opus Artis** (www.opusartis.com; Piazza Minucci 1); **Paolo Sabatini** (www.paolosabatini.com; Via Matteotti 56); and the atelier of sculptor **Alessandro Marzetti** (www.alessandromarzetti.it; Via dei Labirinti). To watch alabaster being carved, head to **alab'Arte** (Via Orti San Agostino 28).

❶ Information

The efficient **tourist office** (☑0588 8 72 57; www.volterratur.it; Piazza dei Priori 19-20; ☺10am-1pm & 2-6pm) provides free maps, offers a free hotel-booking service, runs a guided *New Moon*–themed walking tour and rents out an audioguide tour of the town (€5).

❶ Getting There & Around

BUS The bus station is in Piazza Martiri della Libertà. **CPT** (☑800 570530; www.cpt.pisa.it) buses connect the town with Saline (€2, 20 minutes, frequent) and its train station.

You'll need to go to Colle di Val d'Elsa (€2.75, 50 minutes, four daily) to catch connecting services to San Gimignano (€2.40, 35 minutes, four daily) and Siena (€2.70, two hours). For Florence, you'll need only one ticket (€7.85, two hours, three to four daily), but you'll usually need to change buses at Colle di Val d'Elsa.

CAR & MOTORCYCLE Volterra is accessed via the SR68, which runs between Cecina on the coast and Colle di Val d'Elsa, just off the RA3 (Siena–Florence *superstrada*).

A ZTL applies in the historic centre. The most convenient car park is beneath Piazza Martiri della Libertà (P1; per hour/day €1.50/11), but there are other car parks around the circumference – P2, P3, P6 and P8 are free.

Val d'Orcia & Val di Chiana

These two valleys offer a feast of classic Tuscan images, including ridgelines adorned with cypress trees and hills silhouetted one against another as they fade into the misty distance. In fact, the landscape of the Val d'Orcia is so magnificent that it is protected as a Unesco World Heritage Site. An added extra is that the local food and wine scenes in both valleys are among the best in Italy.

MONTALCINO
POP 5278

This placid medieval hill town is known throughout the world for its coveted wine, Brunello. In February each year, the new vintage is celebrated at **Benvenuto Brunello**, a weekend of tastings and award presentations organised by the Consorzio del Vino Brunello di Montalcino (www.consorzio brunellodimontalcino.it), the association of local producers.

⊙ Sights

The main activity in town is visiting *enoteche*. For non-alcoholic diversion, consider popping into the modest **Musei di Montalcino** (Via Ricasoli 31; adult/under 12 yr €4.50/3; ⊙10am-1pm & 2-5.50pm Tue-Sun), just off Piazza Sant'Agostino. It has a fine collection of painted wooden sculptures by the Sienese school.

Within the 14th-century **fortezza** (courtyard free, ramparts adult/under 12 yr €4/2; ⊙9am-8pm Apr-Oct, 9am-6pm Nov-Mar) is an *enoteca* where you can sample and buy local wines. The view is almost as magnificent from the courtyard as it is from the ramparts.

A combined ticket giving full access to the museum and fortress costs €6.

✯✯ Festivals & Events

Montalcino stages the following annual music festivals: **Festa della Musica** (www. montalcinofestadellamusica.com), held in mid-June; the **International Chamber Music Festival** (www.musica-reale.com), staged in July; and the **Jazz & Wine Festival** (www. montalcinojazzandwine.com), also in July.

🛏 Sleeping

Hotel Vecchia Oliviera   HOTEL €€
(☎0577 84 60 28; www.vecchiaoliviera.com; Via Landi 1; s €70-85, d €120-190; ⊙closed Dec–mid-Feb; 🅿✳🅰🛆) Just beside the Porta Cerbaia, this former olive mill has been tastefully restored and converted into a stylish hotel with 11 individually decorated rooms. The garden terrace has a spectacular view.

Hotel Il Giglio   HOTEL €€
(☎0577 84 81 67; www.gigliohotel.com; Via Soccorso Saloni 5; s €88, d €130-140, annexe s/d €60/95, apt €100-140; 🅿🛆) The comfortable wrought-iron beds here are each gilded with a painted *giglio* (lily), and all doubles have panoramic views. Room 1 has a private terrace with a fantastic view, and the small single is very attractive.

✗ Eating & Drinking

For a quick and delicious snack, head to **Pizzeria La Torre** (€1 per slice; ⊙11am-9pm Tue-Sun) on Piazza del Popolo. The best cafe in town, **Alle Logge di Piazza** (⊙7am-1am Thu-Tue; 🛆), is on the opposite side of the piazza.

The **Friday market** on and around Via della Libertà sells fresh local produce.

Osticcio   OSTERIA €€
(www.osticcio.it; Via Matteoti 23; antipasto plates €10, meals €36; ⊙11am-11pm Fri-Wed) A huge selection of Brunello and its more modest – but still very palatable – sibling Rosso di Montalcino joins dozens of bottles of wine from around the world at this excellent *enoteca/osteria*. After browsing the selection downstairs, claim a table in the upstairs dining room for a glass of wine accompanied by an antipasto plate or a full meal. You can also enjoy a tasting session here (three Brunello €14.50, one Rosso and one Brunello €8).

Ristorante di Poggio Antico   MODERN ITALIAN €€
(☎0577 84 92 00; www.poggioantico.com; meals €48, 6-/7-course tasting menus €50/70; ⊙lunch & dinner Tue-Sun Apr-Oct, lunch Tue-Sun Nov-Mar) It's obligatory to visit at least one vineyard when in this world-famous wine region, and combining an excellent meal with a tasting is the way to do this in style. Located 4.5km outside town on the road to Grosseto, Poggio Antico makes award-winning wines (try its Brunello or Madre IGT), conducts tours of the winery (free), offers paid tastings (€22 for five wines) and has one of the area's best restaurants.

ℹ Information

The **tourist office** (☎0577 84 93 31; www.prolo comontalcino.it, in Italian; Costa del Municipio 1; ⊙10am-1pm & 2-5.50pm daily Apr-Oct, closed Mon Nov-Mar) is just off the main square. It can supply information about vineyard visits and book accommodation.

ℹ Getting There & Away

BUS Regular Siena Mobilità buses (€3.65, 1½ hours, six daily) run to/from Siena.

CAR & MOTORCYCLE From Siena, take the SR2 (Via Cassia) and exit onto the SP14 at Lama. There's free parking next to the *fortezza*.

MONTEPULCIANO
POP 14,506

You'll acquire a newfound appreciation for the term 'hotel restaurant' after a day of climbing Montepulciano's steep streets.

ABBAZIA DI SANT'ANTIMO

The beautiful **Abbazia di Sant'Antimo** (www.antimo.it; Castelnuovo dell'Abate; admission free; ☉10.30am-12.30pm & 3-6.30pm Mon-Sat, 9.15-10.45am & 3-6pm Sun) lies in an isolated valley just below the village of Castelnuovo dell'Abate, 10.5km from Montalcino. Its Romanesque exterior, built in pale travertine stone, features stone carvings set in the bell tower and apsidal chapels. Monks perform Gregorian chants in the abbey during daily services – check times on the website.

Three to four daily buses (€1.35, 15 minutes, Monday to Saturday only) connect Montalcino with the village of Castelnuovo dell'Abate.

It's a two-hour walk from Montalcino to the abbey. The route starts next to the police station near the main roundabout in town; many visitors choose to walk there and return by bus – check the timetable with the tourist office.

The abbey has a **guesthouse** (foresterie@antimo.it) offering simple accommodation for pilgrims.

When your quadriceps reach their failure point, self-medicate with a generous pour of the highly reputed Vino Nobile while drinking in the views over the Val di Chiana and Val d'Orcia.

◉ Sights

Montepulciano's streets harbour a wealth of *palazzi*, fine buildings and churches.

The main street, called in stages Via di Gracciano nel Corso, Via di Voltaia del Corso and Via dell'Opio nel Corso ('the Corso'), climbs uphill from Porta dal Prato, near the car park on Piazza Don Minzoni. Halfway along its length are Michelozzo's **Chiesa di Sant'Agostino** (Piazza Michelozzo; ☉9am-noon & 3-6pm) and the **Torre di Pulcinella**, a medieval tower house topped by the hunched figure of Pulcinella (Punch of Punch and Judy fame), who strikes the hours on the town clock.

After passing historic **Caffè Poliziano**, which has been operating since 1868, the Corso eventually does a dog-leg at Via del Teatro, continuing uphill (ouch!) past **Cantine Contucci** (www.contucci.it; Via del Teatro 1; admission free, paid tastings; ☉8.30am-12.30pm & 2.30-6pm Mon-Fri, from 9.30am Sat & Sun), housed underneath the handsome *palazzo* of the same name. You can visit the historic cellars and taste local tipples here. Palazzo Contucci fronts onto **Piazza Grande**, the town's highest point and the location for the main crowd scene in *New Moon*. Also here are the 14th-century **Palazzo Comunale** (€2 to access panoramic terrace; ☉9am-6pm Mon-Sat) and the late-16th-century **duomo** (☉9am-noon & 4-7pm), with its unfinished facade. Behind the high altar is Taddeo di Bartolo's lovely *Assumption* triptych (1401).

From Piazza Grande, Via Ricci runs downhill (phew!) past **Palazzo Ricci** (www.palazzoricci.com; Via Ricci 9-11); a festival of classical music is held here in June and the lovely main salon hosts occasional concerts during the year; see the website for details. From the *palazzo*'s courtyard, stairs lead down to another historic wine cellar, **Cantina del Redi** (www.vecchiacantinadimontepulciano.com; admission free, paid tastings; ☉10.30am-7.30pm mid-Mar–early Jan, Sat & Sun only early Jan–mid-Mar). Via Ricci continues past the **Museo Civico** (admission €5; ☉10am-1pm & 3-6pm Tue-Sun), home to an eclectic collection of art works and artefacts, and terminates in Piazza San Francesco, where you can admire a panoramic view of the Val di Chiana.

☞ Tours & Courses

The office of the **Strada del Vino Nobile di Montepulciano** (www.stradavinonobile.it) organises a range of tours and courses, including cooking courses (€60 to €180), vineyard tours (€18 to €48), Slow Food tours (€100 to €155), wine-tasting lessons (€37) and walking tours in the vineyards culminating in a wine tasting (€45 to €60). You can make bookings at its information office in Piazza Grande.

🛏 Sleeping

Locanda San Francesco   B&B **€€€**
(📞349 6721302; www.locandasanfrancesco.it; Piazza San Francesco 5; r €195-215, ste €235; ☉closed mid-Jan–mid-Feb; [P][❄][@][🕏]) Four handsome rooms (two with magnificent views) and an elegantly furnished lounge/breakfast room await at this luxury B&B. Host Cinzia Caporali runs both it and

E Lucevan Le Stelle (antipasto plates €4.50-8, piadinas €6, pastas €6.50-9; ⊙11.30am-11pm Easter–mid-Nov; 🕿), the on-site bistro/wine bar, with friendly efficiency.

Camere Bellavista HOTEL €
(☑347 8232314; www.camerebellavista.it; Via Ricci 25; s €65-70, d €75; 🅿🕿) Nearly all of the 10 high-ceilinged double rooms at this excellent budget hotel have fantastic views; room 6 also has a private terrace (€100). No one lives here, so phone ahead in order to be met and given a key (if you've omitted this stage, there's a phone in the lobby from where you can call). No breakfast.

✖ Eating & Drinking

TOP CHOICE La Grotta TRADITIONAL ITALIAN €€
(☑0578 75 74 79; www.lagrottamontepulciano.it; Via San Biagio 15; 6-course set menus €48; ⊙closed Wed) Facing the High Renaissance Tempio di San Biago on the road to Chiusi, La Grotta has elegant dining rooms and a gorgeous courtyard garden that's perfect for summer dinners. The food is simple but delicious, and service is exemplary. A hint: don't skip dessert.

Osteria Acquacheta OSTERIA €
(☑0578 71 70 86; www.acquacheta.eu; Via del Teatro 22; meals €19; ⊙closed Tue) Hugely popular with locals and tourists alike, this bustling place specialises in *bistecca alla fiorentina*, which comes to the table in huge, lightly seared and exceptionally flavoursome slabs (don't even *think* of asking for it to be served otherwise). Lunch sittings are at 12.15pm and 2.15pm; dinner at 7.30pm and 9.15pm – book ahead.

Enoteca a Gambe di Gatto TRADITIONAL ITALIAN €€
(☑0578 75 74 31; Via dell Opio nel Corso 34; meals €34; ⊙closed Jan-Easter & Wed) Renowned throughout the region, the exacting husband-and-wife team of Emanuel (front of house) and Laura (kitchen) travels the country each winter to acquire the best products from organic producers. The daily menu fluctuates wildly, depending on market offerings, and meals start with a complimentary tasting of wine and olive oil. Unfortunately, service here gives a whole new meaning to the term 'Slow Food'.

❶ Information

Strada del Vino Nobile di Montepulciano Information Office (☑0578 71 74 84; www.stradavinonobile.it; Piazza Grande 7;

⊙10am-1pm & 3-6pm Mon-Fri) Books accommodation and arranges courses and tours.

Tourist office (☑0578 75 73 41; www.prolo comontepulciano.it; Piazza Don Minzoni; ⊙9.30am-12.30pm & 3-8pm Mon-Sat, 9.30am-12.30pm Sun) Reserves accommodation, offers internet access (€3.50 per hour), sells a map of the town (€0.50), rents bikes and scooters and sells bus and train tickets.

❶ Getting There & Around

BUS The bus station is next to Car Park No 5, outside the Porta al Prato. Siena Mobilità runs four buses daily between Siena and Montepulciano (€5.15, 1½ hours) stopping at Pienza en route. To get here from Florence, you need to catch a Tiemme service to Bettolle (€7.90, 90 minutes, three daily) and connect with a Siena Mobilità bus (€1.95, 40 minutes, one daily).

Regular buses connect with Chiusi-Chianciano Terme (€2.55, 40 minutes), from where you can catch a train to Florence (€9.30, two hours, frequent) via Arezzo (€4.70, 50 minutes).

CAR & MOTORCYCLE Coming from Florence, take the Valdichiana exit off the A1 (direction Bettolle-Sinalunga) and then follow the signs; from Siena, take the Siena–Bettolle–Perugia autostrada.

A 24-hour ZTL applies in the historic centre between June and September; between October and May it applies from 7am to 5pm. Your hotel can usually supply a permit. The most convenient car park is at Piazza Minzoni (P1, €1.20 per hour), from where minibuses (€1) weave their way up the hill to Piazza Grande.

SOUTHERN TUSCANY

With its landscape of lush rumpled hills, dramatic coastlines, mysterious Etruscan sites and medieval hilltop villages, this little-visited pocket of the region offers contrasts galore.

Massa Marittima
POP 8820

This medieval hill town is set in the Colline Metallifere (metal-producing hills) located between Siena and the coast. Its lack of tourists is puzzling, as there's an eccentric yet endearing array of museums here and the central piazza is one of the most magnificent in Tuscany.

Briefly under Pisan domination, Massa became an independent *comune* in 1225 but was swallowed up by Siena a century later. The 1348 plague, followed by the decline of its lucrative mining industry 50 years later, reduced the town to the brink of extinction. It was brought back to life by the draining of surrounding marshes (formerly a malarial risk) and the re-establishment of mining in the 18th century.

Massa's big event of the year is the **Balestro del Girifalco**, a medieval crossbow competition held twice yearly, in May and either July or August.

◉ Sights

The *città vecchia* (old town) is dominated by the impressive bulk of the **duomo** (⊙8am-noon & 3-5pm), which presides over photogenic **Piazza Garibaldi** (aka Piazza Duomo). Cleverly set asymmetrical to the square to better show off its splendour, it dates from 1260 and is dedicated to St Cerbonius, Massa's patron saint, who is always depicted surrounded with a flock of geese; carved panels on the facade depict scenes from his life. Inside, beware the self-appointed custodian (an elderly lady), who firmly believes that the cathedral is for worship rather than sightseeing.

The *duomo* was once home to a splendid *Maestà* by Ambrogio Lorenzetti, now the central exhibit in the diminutive **Museo di Arte Sacra** (Corso Diaz 36; adult/child €5/3; ⊙10am-1pm & 3-6pm Apr-Sep, 11am-1pm & 3-5pm Oct-Mar) in the *città nuova* (new town).

Next to the *duomo,* the Palazzo del Podestà houses Massa's musty **Museo Archeologico** (Piazza Garibaldi 1; adult/child €3/2; ⊙10am-12.30pm & 3.30-7pm Tue-Sun Apr-Oct, 10am-12.30pm & 3-5pm Tue-Sun Nov-Mar), whose only truly noteworthy exhibit is *La Stele del Vado all'Arancio,* a simple but compelling stone stela (funeral or commemorative marker) dating from the 3rd millennium BC.

Downhill from Piazza Garibaldi, opposite the main car park, is a 13th-century building that was once used to store wheat. Under its loggia is a disused public drinking fountain topped by an extraordinary fresco of the *Albero della Fecondità* (Fertility Tree). Look closely to see what type of fruit the tree bears!

A cumulative ticket (adult/six to 16 years €15/10) gives access to all of Massa's museums (www.massamarittimamusei.it).

🛏 Sleeping

Massa's hotels leave a lot to be desired, but there are fabulous villas and *agriturismi* dotted around the surrounding area.

TOP CHOICE **Pieve di Caminino** AGRITURISMO €€
(☑0564 56 97 37; www.caminino.com; Via Provinciale di Peruzzo, Roccatederighi; ste/apt from €110/90; P❄🌐⛱) Be prepared for an atmosphere overload at this magical 11th-century monastery 30km southeast of Massa. Set on a 200-hectare estate planted with olive trees and vines, it offers charmingly decorated suites and apartments sleeping up to five people. All have sitting rooms and basic kitchenettes, two have air-con.

Montebelli Agriturismo & Country Hotel AGRITURISMO €€
(☑0566 88 71 00; www.montebelli.com; Località Molinetto Caldana; s €62-190, d €180-240, ste €180-270; ⊙closed Jan-end Mar; P❄🌐⛱🐾) A country-club feel prevails on this sprawling wine and olive-oil estate 28km south of Massa. The facilities are sensational – tennis court, indoor and outdoor swimming pools, horse-riding lessons, restaurant (five-course dinner adult/child €30/15) and sleek health centre. Rooms are extremely comfortable, but air-con is only available in the newly constructed country house. Wi-fi is €4 per hour.

🍴 Eating & Drinking

L'Osteria da Tronca TRADITIONAL ITALIAN €€
(☑0566 90 19 91; Vicolo Porte 5; meals €26; ⊙closed Wed & mid-Dec–Feb) Squeezed into a side street behind Hotel Il Sole, this stone-walled restaurant serves the rustic dishes of the Maremma. Specialities include *acquacotta* (a hearty vegetable soup with bread and egg) and *tortelli alla maremma* (pasta parcels filled with ricotta and a type of spinach).

Il Bacchino WINE BAR €
(Via Moncini 8; ⊙daily Mar-Jan, Tue-Sun Feb) Owner Magdy Lamei may not be a local (in fact, he's from Cairo), but it would be hard to find anyone else as knowledgeable and passionate about local artisanal produce. Come here to stock up on wine, honey, jams, cheese and meats, and while you're here settle in for a tasting in the upstairs wine bar (€12 for three glasses of wine and a tasting plate).

ℹ Information

The **tourist office** (☑0566 90 47 56; www.turismoinmaremma.it; Via Todini 5-7; ⊙9.30am-1pm & 2-6.30pm Tue-Sun) is down a side street beneath the Museo Archeologico.

ℹ Getting There & Away

BUS The bus station is at Piazza del Risorgimento, 800m down the hill from Piazza Garibaldi. There is one bus daily to Grosseto (€3.30, one hour), two to Siena (€4.70, two hours) at 7.05am and 4.40pm, and around four to Volterra (changing at Monterotondo).

CAR & MOTORCYCLE From Siena, take the SP73bis and the SP441. From Volterra, take the SR151 and SR439. There's a car park (€1 per hour) at Piazza Mazzini, close to the *duomo*.

TRAIN The nearest train station is Massa-Follonica in Follonica, 22km southwest of Massa, served by a regular shuttle bus (€2.30, 25 minutes, 10 daily).

Parco Regionale della Maremma

This spectacular **nature park** (www.parco-maremma.it; adult €6-15, student €4-12) includes the Monti dell'Uccellina, which drops to a magnificent stretch of unspoiled coastline. The main **visitor centre** (☑0564 40 70 98; ☉8.30am-5.30pm) is in Alberese, on the park's northern edge.

Park access is limited to 11 signed walking trails, varying in length from 2.5km to 13km; the most popular is A2 ('Le Torri'), a 5.8km trek to the beach. The entry fee (paid at the visitor centre) varies according to whether a park-operated bus transports you from the visitor centre to your chosen route.

Bicycles (per half-/full day €7/11 can be hired from the main visitor centre, and there are free tastings of local food and wine four times daily (June to September) in the upstairs *degustazione* (tasting) room.

Parts of the park are farmed as they have been for centuries (mainly to graze the famous Maremma breed of cattle). **Agienza Regionale Agricola di Alberese** (☑0564 40 71 80; www.alberese.com; Via della Spergolaia) produces beef, wine, olive oil and its own organic pasta and is a regional headquarters for the Slow Food organisation. It offers a **Farm Experience** (€25-40; ☉10am-1pm Thu summer) including an introduction to the work of the Maremma's famed *butteri* (traditional cowboys) and tastings of farm produce. Experienced horse riders can also sign up for a full day's work experience with a *buttero* (€50; ☉daily 7am-7pm). The farm's **fattoria** (☉8.30am-12.30pm & 4.30-7.30pm Tue, Thu & Fri-Sun), located near the park visitor centre in Alberese, sells its own products and those of other Slow Food–accredited producers. It's a

great place to stock up on supplies if you're self-catering (its Morellino di Scansano – a robust red wine – costs a mere €1.55 per litre, so bring a couple of bottles to fill!).

The *agienza* offers accommodation at the **Fattoria Granducale** (www.alberese.com/ita/villa; B&B d per weekend €180, self-catering apt €255-310), a 15th-century villa once owned by Grand Duke Leopoldo II of Lorraine. It also has simple **apartments** (d/t/q €150/200/250) in surrounding farm buildings.

EASTERN TUSCANY

There are two good reasons why so many local and international directors have chosen this part of Tuscany as a film location: its scenery offers oh-wow moments galore, and the excellent food, wine and accommodation on offer is the perfect bribe to ensure happy cooperation on a shoot.

Up until now, visitor numbers have been limited to domestic tourists and these film crews. We highly recommend that you buck this trend.

Arezzo

POP 99.503

Arezzo may not be a Tuscan centrefold, but those parts of its historic centre that survived merciless WWII bombings are as compelling as any destination in the region. The setting for much of Roberto Benigni's Oscar-winning film *La vita è bella* (Life is Beautiful), it's well worth a visit.

Once an important Etruscan town, Arezzo was later absorbed into the Roman Empire. A free republic as early as the 10th century, it supported the Ghibelline cause in the violent battles between pope and emperor and was eventually subjugated by Florence in 1384.

Today, the city is known for its churches, museums and shopping – Arentini (residents of Arezzo) flock to the huge antiques fair held in Piazza Grande on the first weekend of every month, and love nothing more than combining the *passeggiata* with a spot of upmarket retail therapy on Corso Italia.

Fans of the work of Renaissance painter Piero della Francesca can follow a trail of his paintings through the city and to the towns of Sansepolcro and Monterchi. Check http://turismo.provincia.arezzo.it for details or pick up the *Piero della Francesca: In and Around Arezzo* brochure from museums and tourist offices in the city.

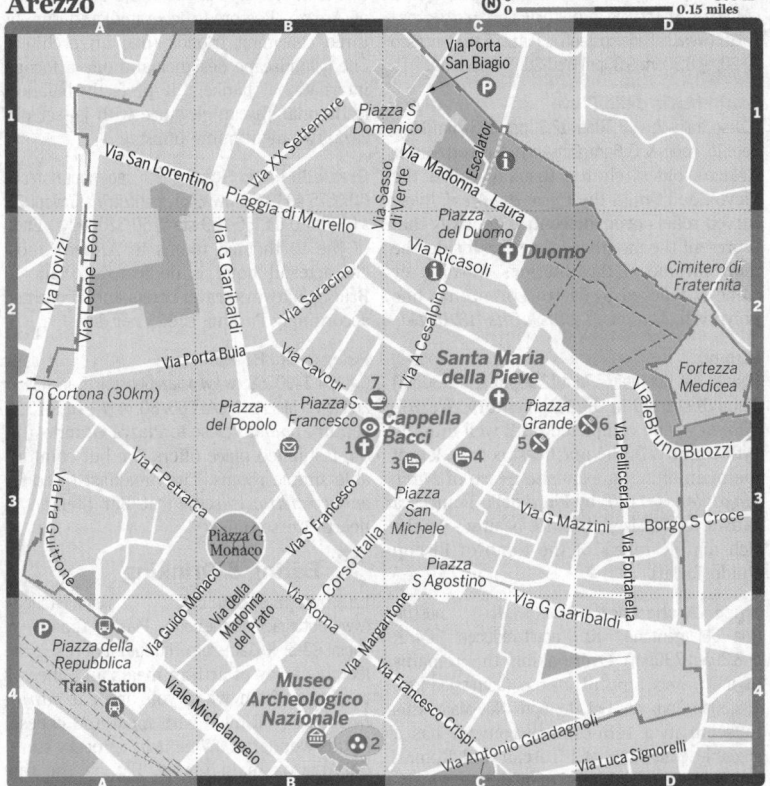

◉ Sights

A combined ticket (€10) gives entry to the Cappella Bacci, Museo Archeologico and two other museums.

Cappella Bacci   CHURCH
(www.pierodellafrancesca.it; Piazza San Francesco; adult/reduced €6/4. ⊘9am-6.30pm Mon-Fri, to 5.30pm Sat & 1-5.30pm Sun Apr-Oct, 9am-5.30pm Mon-Fri, 9am-5pm Sat & 1-5pm Sun Nov-Mar) Gracing the apse of the 14th-century **Chiesa di San Francesco** is one of the greatest works of Italian art, Piero della Francesca's fresco cycle of the *Legend of the True Cross* (1452–66).

Only 25 people are allowed into the chapel every half-hour (maximum 30-minute visit). At the time of research the ticket office was at Piazza San Francesco 4, to the right of the church's main entrance, but there was talk of this changing.

After your visit, consider stopping for a coffee or *aperitivo* at historic **Caffè dei Costanti** (www.caffedeicostanti.it; Piazza San Francesco 19-20; ☺8.30am-9.30pm Wed-Sun), opposite.

Santa Maria della Pieve CHURCH
(Corso Italia 7; ☺8.30am-12.30pm & 3-7pm May-Sep, to noon & 3-6pm Oct-Apr) As you enter Arezzo's oldest church (usually called the Pieve), don't miss the *Cyclo dei Mesi,* lively carved reliefs over the central doorway that represent the months of the year. Inside, the monochrome of the interior's warm, grey stone is relieved by Pietro Lorenzetti's fine polyptych, *Madonna and Saints* (1320–24).

Duomo DUOMO
(Piazza del Duomo; ☺7am-12.30pm & 3-6.30pm) Though started in the 13th century, Arezzo's *duomo* wasn't completed until well into the 15th century. In the northeast corner, left of the main altar, an exquisite fresco of *Mary Magdalene* (c1460) by Piero della Francesca is dwarfed in size – but not beauty – by the rich marble reliefs of the tomb of Bishop Guido Tarlati.

Museo Archeologico Nazionale MUSEUM
(Via Margaritone 10; adult/reduced €4/2; ☺8.30am-7.30pm) Overlooking the remains of a **Roman amphitheatre** (admission free; ☺8.30am-7pm Apr-Oct, to 6pm Nov-Mar), this museum in a 14th-century convent has a sizeable collection of Etruscan and Roman artefacts, the highlight of which is an extraordinary Roman miniature on glass in a gallery on the upper floor.

Tours

Two-hour guided English-language **walking tours** (☎0575 2 66 77; www.coloritoscani.com; adult/under 12 yr €10/free) are held every Thursday from 3pm between May and September. Bookings are essential.

✯ Festivals & Events

Giostra del Saracino MEDIEVAL
(www.giostradelsaracino.arezzo.it, in Italian) This medieval jousting competition is held in Piazza Grande on the third Saturday of June and first Sunday of September each year.

⌂ Sleeping

ᵀᴼᴾCHOICE Villa Fontelunga BOUTIQUE HOTEL €€
(☎0575 66 04 10; www.fontelunga.com; Via Cunicchio 5, Foiano della Chiana; r €179-265, ste €210-280; closed mid-Nov–late Mar; P꘡❄⬤⬤) Gorgeous is the only word to use when describing this 19th-century villa 30 minutes southwest of Arezzo. Restored, decorated and run by three charming friends (one an architect, one a landscape designer and one a former international banker), it perfectly balances traditional Tuscan elegance with jet-set pizzazz. Two-night minimum stay.

Graziella Patio Hotel BOUTIQUE HOTEL €€
(☎0575 40 19 62; www.hotelpatio.it; Via Cavour 23; s €100-180, d €150-250, ste €250-320; ❄⬤) Each of the 10 themed rooms in Arezzo's most characterful hotel is dedicated to one of Bruce Chatwin's travel books and decorated accordingly. Parking is €22 per day.

Palazzo dei Bostoli B&B €
(☎334 1490558; www.palazzobostoli.it, in Italian; 2nd fl, Via Mazzini 1; s/d €60/80; ❄⬤) In a 13th-century *palazzo* close to Piazza Grande, this old-fashioned place offers five but comfortable simple rooms. The breakfast (a coffee and *cornetto*) is served at Bar Stefano in nearby Corso Italia.

Eating & Drinking

La Bottega di Gnicche SANDWICH SHOP €
(www.bottegadignicche.com; Piazza Grande 4; panini €3-5; ☺11am-8pm Thu-Tue) There's a delectable array of artisan meats and cheeses to choose from when you order a *panini imbottiti* (roll filled with meat and cheese) at this wonderful *alimentari* (grocery store) on Arezzo's main piazza. Eat on the tiny front terrace, or on a stool inside.

La Torre di Gnicche TRATTORIA €€
(☎0575 35 20 35; Piaggia San Martino 8; meals €28; ☺closed Wed) Just off Piazza Grande, this is a fine traditional restaurant offering a rich variety of antipasti. Choose from the ample range of local *pecorino* cheeses, accompanied by a choice red from the extensive wine list.

ⓘ Information

Centro di Accoglienza Turistica Benvenuti ad Arezzo (☎0575 40 19 45; www.turismo.provincia.arezzo.it; Palazzo Comunale, Via Ricasoli; ☺10am-7pm), the region's main tourist office is opposite the *duomo.* **Na Vetrina per Arezzo e Le Sue Vallate** (☎0575 1822770; ☺9.30am-7pm) is a private office located on the *scala mobile* leading up to Piazza del Duomo.

Getting There & Away

BUS Tiemme/Siena Mobilità buses depart Piazza della Repubblica for Siena (€5.40, 1½ hours, eight daily) and Cortona (€3.10, one hour, more than 10 weekdays).

CAR & MOTORCYCLE To drive here from Florence, take the A1. The SS73 heads west to Siena.

There is free car parking at Via Pietri, from where a *scala mobile* takes you up to Piazza del Duomo. Parking at the train station costs €1.50 per hour.

TRAIN Arezzo is on the Florence–Rome train line with frequent services to Rome (€23, 2½ hours) and Florence (€5.80, 1½ hours). Trains also call by Cortona (€2.40, 20 minutes, hourly).

Sansepolcro

Sansepolcro was the birthplace of the 15th-century artist Piero della Francesca, and its **Museo Civico** (www.museocivicosansepolcro.it; Via Aggiunti 65; adult/reduced €6/4.50; ⊙9.30am-1.30pm & 2.30-7pm mid-Jun–mid-Sep, 9.30am-1pm & 2.30-6pm mid-Sep–mid-Jun) is home to four of his masterpieces, including the *Resurrection* and the *Madonna della Misericordia* (Madonna of Mercy).

Art isn't the only reason to come here, though. The historical centre ('Il Borgo') is full of handsome Renaissance churches and *palazzi*. In the second Sunday of September, the town hosts the **Palio della Ballestra**, a crossbow tournament between local archers and rivals from the nearby Umbrian town of Gubbio. Contestants and the crowd dress in medieval costumes, and a great time is had by all.

There are a number of excellent restaurants too, including **Ristorante Fiorentino** (📳0575 74 20 33; www.ristorantefiorentino.it; meals €35; ⊙closed Wed & 1 week Nov, Jul & Feb) and **Ristorante Da Ventura** (📳0575 74 25 60; albergodaventura; Via Pacioli 60; meals €23; ⊙closed Mon & dinner Sun). Both also offer B&B rooms.

The **tourist office** (📳0575 74 05 36; infosansepolcro@apt.arezzo.it; Via Matteotti 8; ⊙9.30am-1pm & 3.30-7pm) is packed with multilingual information.

SITA/Baschetti buses link Sansepolcro with Arezzo (€3.50, one hour, frequent). You'll find free parking outside the historic walls. A ZTL applies inside the walls.

Cortona

POP 23,083

Rooms with a view are the rule rather than the exception in this spectacularly sited hilltop town. In the late 14th century Fra' Angelico lived and worked here, and fellow artists Luca Signorelli and Pietro da Cortona were

both born within the walls – all are represented in the Museo Diocesano's collection. More recently, large chunks of *Under the Tuscan Sun*, the soap-in-the-sun film of the book by Frances Mayes, were shot here.

A **produce market** is held on Saturday mornings and an **antique and collectable fair** on the fourth Sunday of the month.

◉ Sights

Brooding over lopsided Piazza della Repubblica is the **Palazzo Comunale**, built in the 13th century. To the north is attractive **Piazza Signorelli** and, on its north side, the 13th-century **Palazzo Casali**, whose rather plain facade was added in the 17th century. Inside is the **Museo dell'Accademia Etrusca e della Città di Cortona** (MAEC; www.cortonamaec.org; Piazza Signorelli 9; adult/6-12 yr €8/4; ⊙10am-7pm daily Apr-Oct, to 5pm Tue-Sun Nov-Mar), which displays substantial local Etruscan and Roman finds, Renaissance globes, 18th-century decorative arts and contemporary paintings. The well-presented Etruscan collection is the highlight, particularly those objects excavated from the tombs at Sodo, just outside town.

For the most effective cardiovascular workout in Tuscany, head up through the sleepy warren of steep cobbled lanes in the eastern part of town to the largely 19th-century **Chiesa di Santa Margherita** (Piazza Santa Margherita; ⊙8am-noon & 3-7pm Apr-Oct, 9am-noon & 3-6pm Nov-Mar). The remains of St Margaret, the patron saint of Cortona, are on display in an ornate, 14th-century, glass-sided tomb above the main altar.

Climb further still and you'll reach the forbidding **Fortezza Medicea** (adult/child €3/1.50; ⊙10am-1.30pm & 2.30-6pm May, Jun & Sep, to 7pm Jul & Aug), Cortona's highest point, from where there's a stupendous view over the surrounding countryside to Lake Trasimeno in Umbria.

ⓒ Tours

Two-hour, guided English-language **walking tours** (📳0575 2 66 77; www.coloritoscani.com; adult/under 12 yr €10/free) are held every Monday from 11am between April and October. The ticket includes entrance to MAEC. Bookings are essential.

✷ Festivals & Events

Giostra dell'Archidado CULTURAL
A full week of medieval merriment in May or June (the date varies to coincide with

MUSEO DIOCESANO

Little is left of the Romanesque character of Cortona's *duomo*, northwest of Piazza Signorelli, as it was completely rebuilt late in the Renaissance and again, indifferently, in the 18th century. Its true wealth lies in the **Museo Diocesano** (Piazza del Duomo 1; adult/child €5/3, audioguide €3; ☺10am-7pm Tue-Sun Apr-Oct, to 5pm Tue-Sun Nov-Mar) located in the former church of Gesù opposite, which has a small but particularly fine collection including *Crucifixion* (1320) by Pietro Lorenzetti and two beautiful works by Fra' Angelico: *Annunciation* (1436) and *Madonna with Child and Saints* (1436–37).

A combined ticket (adult/child €10/6) gives entry to the Museo Diocesano and the Museo dell'Accademia Etrusca della Città di Cortona (MAEC).

Ascension Day) culminates in a crossbow competition.

Festival of Sacred Music   MUSIC
(www.cortonacristiana.it) This festival is held in early July each year.

Tuscan Sun Festival   CULTURAL
(www.tuscansunfestival.com) Annual music and art festival held in late July/early August each year.

🛏 Sleeping

TOP
CHOICE **Casa Chilenne**   B&B €
(☏0575 60 33 20; www.casachilenne.com; Via Nazionale 65; s €80-85, d €88-110; ❄@⊕🐾) Run by American-born Jeanette and her Cortonese husband Luciano, this wonderfully welcoming B&B has it all – great hosts, a central location, comfortable rooms, a lavish breakfast spread and keen prices. There's also a communal lounge with a cooking corner (great for families).

Hotel San Michele   HOTEL €€
(☏0575 60 43 48; www.hotelsanmichele.net; Via Guelfa 15; d €99-250; ☺closed Jan–mid-Mar; P❄@⊕) This is Cortona's finest hotel. Primarily Renaissance, but with elements dating from the 12th century and modifications over subsequent centuries, it's like a little history of Cortona in stone. Rooms are airy and comfortable, if a little faded. Parking is €20 per night and wi-fi is only in the foyer.

🍴 Eating & Drinking

Taverna Pane e Vino   WINE BAR €
(www.pane-vino.it; Via Dardano 24; bruschetta €3.50, meat & cheese platters €6-10, pastas €7.50-10; ☺closed Mon) Serving over 900 wines, this casual place is a perfect spot for a light lunch, afternoon drink or rustic dinner. Claim a table in the front courtyard or vaulted interior, settle back over a glass or two of wine and relax with the local bon vivants.

La Bucaccia   TRADITIONAL ITALIAN €€
(☏0575 60 60 39; www.labucaccia.it; Via Ghibellina 17; meals €35) Set in a medieval stable that was incorporated into a Renaissance *palazzo*, this family-run place is an atmospheric and enjoyable dinner venue, but is a bit dark at lunchtime. The set menu (€29) of four courses, one glass of wine and water offers good value.

ℹ Information

The **tourist office** (☏0575 63 72 23; infocortona@apt.arezzo.it; Palazzo Comunale; ☺9am-1pm & 3-6pm Mon-Sat, 9am-1pm Sun May-Sep, 9am-1pm & 3-6pm Mon-Fri, to 1pm Sat Oct-Apr) stocks maps and brochures and can book accommodation.

ℹ Getting There & Around

BUS From Piazza Garibaldi, Tiemme buses connect the town with Arezzo (€3.10, one hour, frequent).

CAR & MOTORCYCLE The city is on the north-south SR71 that runs to Arezzo. It's also close to the Siena–Bettolle–Perugia autostrada, which connects to the A1.

There are free car parks around the circumference of the city walls; the most convenient is at Porta San Agostino. A ZTL applies inside the walls.

TRAIN The nearest train station is located about 6km away at Camucia, and can be accessed via a local bus (€1.20, 15 minutes, hourly). Destinations include Arezzo (€2.40, 20 minutes, hourly), Florence (€7.30, 1½ hours, hourly), Rome (€10.25, 2½ hours, eight daily) and Perugia (€3.85, 50 minutes, six daily).

Note that Camucia station has no ticket office, only machines. If you need assistance purchasing or booking tickets, you'll need to go to the station at Terontola, south of Camucia, instead.

Umbria & Le Marche

Best Places to Eat

» Ristorante Vespasia (p580)

» L'Antico Forziere (p559)

» Ristorante I Sette Consoli (p584)

Best Places to Stay

» Hotel Fortino Napoleonico (p590)

» Palazzo Seneca (p580)

» Palazzo Guiderocchi (p598)

Why Go?

If you've fallen for Tuscany's charms, then Umbria and Le Marche will also entice, offering a similar landscape and attractions but in a less hectic form. The soft olive- and vine-clad hills, jagged mountains and ancient towns are all there, but without the incessant crowds. Both regions are proud of their agricultural traditions and have transitioned easily into Slow Food destinations.

Not everything is sleepy and bucolic, however. The Umbrian capital, Perugia, has a surprisingly vibrant student-fuelled nightlife, while Spoleto's annual festival brings together some of the finest dance and music performances. In summer, myriad sun seekers flock to Le Marche's coast. The mystical peaks of the Monti Sibillini offer all the hiking you could ever want, while labyrinthine medieval villages such as Todi, Gubbio and the religious centre of Assisi inspire visitors to put on their stoutest walking shoes and explore.

When to Go
Perugia

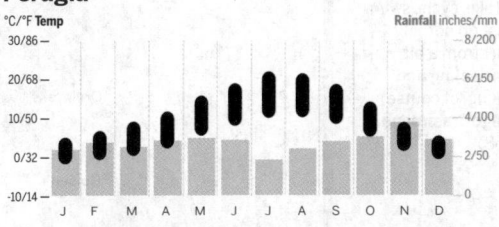

February Celebrate all things truffle at Norcia's Mostra Mercato del Tartufo Nero

May Head to Le Marche's beaches, as wildflowers bloom on the Piano Grande

June & July Indulge music passions at the Spoleto Festival and Perugia's Umbria Jazz

Umbria & Le Marche Highlights

1 See where the best 13th-century art, religion and history intersect at the **Basilica di San Francesco** (p562) in Assisi

2 Meander through fields of wildflowers or trek up the snow-capped peaks of **Monti Sibillini** (p599)

3 Spelunk your way through a glistening forest of stalactites at **Grotte di Frasassi** (p595), Europe's largest cave

4 Dine off the beaten path in one of any number of excellent fish restaurants in the stunning **Parco del Conero** (p590)

5 Enjoy some of Umbria's most towering views on a rickety ride up Monte Ingino aboard Gubbio's **Funivia Colle Eletto** (p570)

6 Cash in your golden ticket for a tour of the **Perugina Chocolate Factory** (p551)

7 Hike, cycle, swim or just do nothing (apart from a bit of fine eating and drinking, of course) at **Lago Trasimeno** (p558)

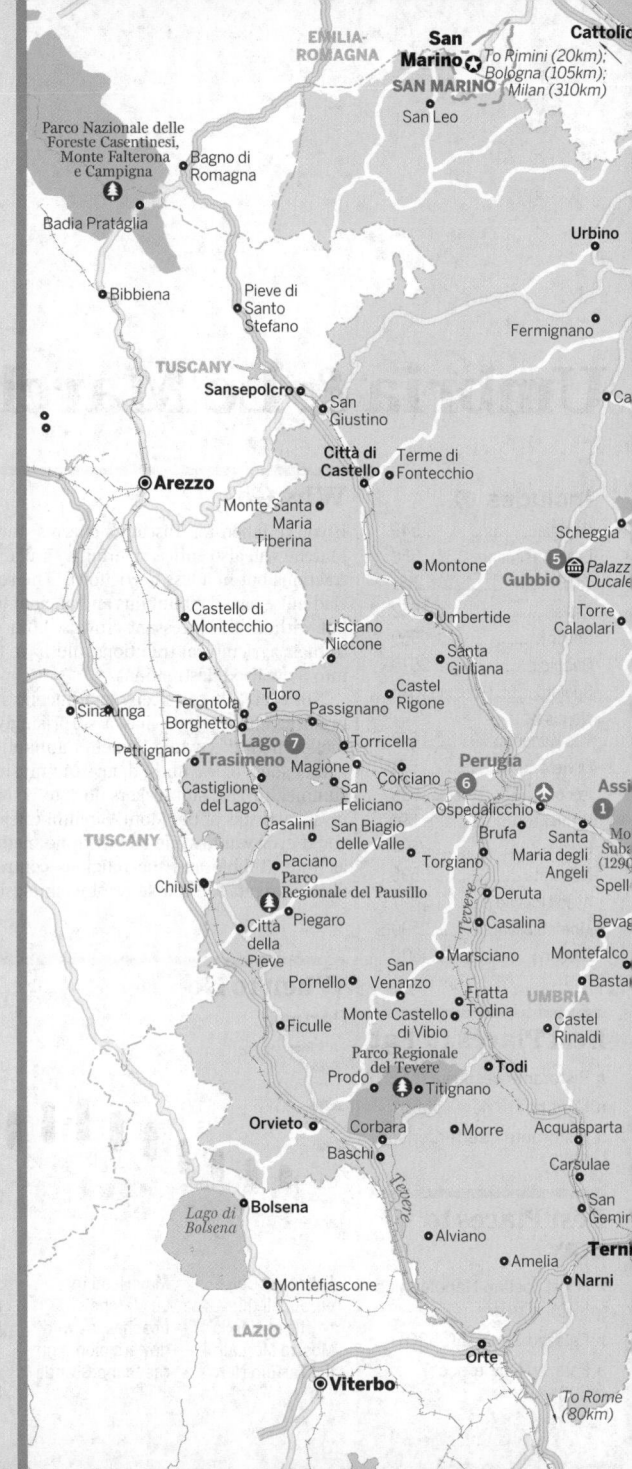

UMBRIA

Known as 'the green heart of Italy', Umbria is a land unto itself, the only Italian region that borders neither the sea nor another country. Removed from outside influences, it has kept alive many of Italy's old-world traditions. You'll see grandmothers in aprons making pasta by hand and front doors that haven't been locked in a century. It's a beautiful place (in spring the countryside is splashed with colourful wildflowers) but also a richly entertaining one. An Umbrian adventure can span everything from dancing the night away at a Perugian nightclub to making a solemn pilgrimage to Assisi, home town of St Francis. Holidaying foodies will delight in the region's food and wine. The earthy, addictive *tartufo* (truffle) finds its way onto every menu, while pork from the Norcia area is so well respected that quality pork butchers throughout Italy are known as *norcineria*.

History

Umbria is named in honour of its first inhabitants, the Umbri tribe who settled the land east of the Tiber around 1000 BC, establishing the towns of Spoleto, Gubbio and Assisi. They jockeyed for regional supremacy with the Etruscans to the west of the river – the founders of Perugia and Orvieto – until the 3rd century BC when the Romans came marching through, conquering them both.

Following the collapse of the Western Roman Empire, the region spent much of the Middle Ages being fought over by supporters of the Holy Roman Empire (known as Ghibellines) and supporters of the Pope (known as Guelphs). Intriguingly, it was during this most troubled of periods that Umbria's most famous – and most peaceful – son, St Francis, came to prominence in Assisi.

Eventually the region became one of the Papal States, though this was not to its long-term benefit. Indeed, historians like to say that time stopped in Umbria in 1540 when the pope imposed a salt tax. The resulting war brought Umbrian culture to a standstill. The Renaissance didn't flourish here like it did in neighbouring Tuscany, which is partly why the medieval hearts of many Umbrian towns are so well preserved.

ℹ️ Getting Around

Getting around Umbria on public transport requires some forethought. Conversely having a car is a hindrance in the narrow streets of the congested hill towns. The best way to see Umbria is to take the train or bus to towns such as Assisi, Spoleto, Perugia, Orvieto, Spello and Gubbio and then rent a car for a week and wander through the countryside.

Buses head from Perugia to every town in this chapter; check at the tourist office or the bus station for exact details. The **state train**

TOP FIVE UMBRIAN DELICACIES

While considered a backwater region for years, much of the world is now striving to catch up with Umbria's natural culinary commitment to Slow Food. For hundreds of years, three-hour dinners, organic ingredients and locally grown peasant cuisine have remained Umbria's culinary claim to fame. Here are a few of our favourite ingredients you might want to try while you're here:

Cinghiale Wild boar is ubiquitous on Umbrian menus, and rightfully so. Richly gamey but tender, the flavoursome meat often comes served over pasta or stewed in sauce.

Tartufi Umbrian black truffles (preferably the stronger *nero* variety) are a menu mainstay, especially in the autumn harvest months. The earthy fungus is especially delicious sliced over long, thick pasta like Umbrian *strangozzi*.

Lenticchie These small, thin lentils from Castelluccio (or Colfiorito) are partially responsible for the Piano Grande's floral explosion each spring and summer, and are at their best in a thick soup topped with bruschetta and virgin olive oil.

Piccione English uses the euphemistic 'squab', but Umbrians readily order pigeon, often from the highest-end restaurants. The delicate poultry was a mainstay for townsfolk under siege in the Middle Ages when hunting and farming were too dangerous.

Farro Spelt was the daily staple in ancient times, and still graces many Umbrian menus. Classic *zuppa di farro* is a rich, nutty, distinctly Umbrian experience, perfect for a warm lunch on a cold, misty day in the hills.

USEFUL WEBSITES ON UMBRIA

Bella Umbria (www.bellaumbria.net, in Italian, English, German, French & Spanish) A comprehensive site that lists almost all accommodation in Umbria, while the 'Events and Traditions' page allows you to search for festivals by both town or date.

Regione Umbria (www.regioneumbria.eu, in Italian, English & German) The official Umbrian tourist website.

Sistema Museo (www.sistemamuseo.it, in Italian) Detailed information about Umbria's museums with constantly updated lists of upcoming events.

Umbria Online (www.umbriaonline.com, in Italian & English) A privately run website with information on accommodation, events and itineraries for all major and minor tourist towns in Umbria.

system (Ferrovie dello Stato; ☑892021; www.fsitaliane.it) sparsely criss-crosses Umbria, but the private **Ferrovia Centrale Umbra** (FCU; ☑075 57 54 01; www.fcu.it, in Italian) and several bus companies fill in the blanks.

Perugia

POP 166,667

Perugia is as close as Umbria gets to a heaving metropolis – which is not all that close. A large well-preserved hill town replete with museums and churches, Perugia's two universities give it a vibrancy lacking in many of its more sleepy neighbours. The presence of a large student population ensures a thriving arts scene and plenty of nightlife. However, for all its cultural modernism, little has changed here architecturally for over 400 years.

History

Although the Umbri tribe once inhabited the surrounding area and controlled land stretching from present-day Tuscany into Le Marche, it was the Etruscans who founded the city, which reached its zenith in the 6th century BC. It fell to the Romans in 310 BC and was given the name Perusia.

During the Middle Ages the city was racked by the feuding of noble families, and 1538 was incorporated into the Papal States where it remained for almost three centuries.

Perugia has a strong artistic tradition. In the 15th century it was home to fresco painters Bernardino Pinturicchio and his master Pietro Vannucci (known as Perugino), who would later teach Raphael. Its cultural tradition continues to this day in the form of the University of Perugia and several other institutions of learning, including the famous Università per Stranieri (University for Foreigners), which teaches Italian, art and culture to thousands of students from around the world.

☉ Sights

The centre of Perugia is **Piazza IV Novembre**. For thousands of years, it was the meeting point for the ancient Etruscan and Roman civilisations. In the medieval period, it was the political centre of Perugia. Now both students and tourists gather here to eat gelato. As long as you're planning on visiting a number of sights, savings can be made on most of the attractions listed below by purchasing a **Perugia Città Museo Card** (€10), which provides admission to five museums of your choice. It's available at all the participating sights and the tourist office. For more information, see www.perugiacittamuseo.it.

Palazzo dei Priori   PALAZZO

The palace, constructed between the 13th and 14th centuries and formerly the headquarters of the city's magistrature, now houses some of the best museums in Perugia, including Umbria's foremost art gallery, the stunning **Galleria Nazionale dell'Umbria** (☑800 69 76 16; Palazzo dei Priori, Corso Vannucci 19; adult/reduced €6.50/3.25; ☺8.30am-7.30pm Tue-Sun) Entered via Corso Vannucci, it's an art historian's dream, with 30 rooms of works featuring everything from Byzantine art from the 13th century to the 16th-century creations of home town heroes Pinturicchio and Perugino.

The same building also holds what some consider the most beautiful bank in the world, the **Nobile Collegio del Cambio** (Exchange Hall; ☑075 572 85 99; Corso Vannucci 25; adult/reduced €4.50/2.60; ☺9am-12.30pm & 2.30-5.30pm Mon-Sat, 9am-1pm Sun, closed Mon afternoon winter), whose rooms have

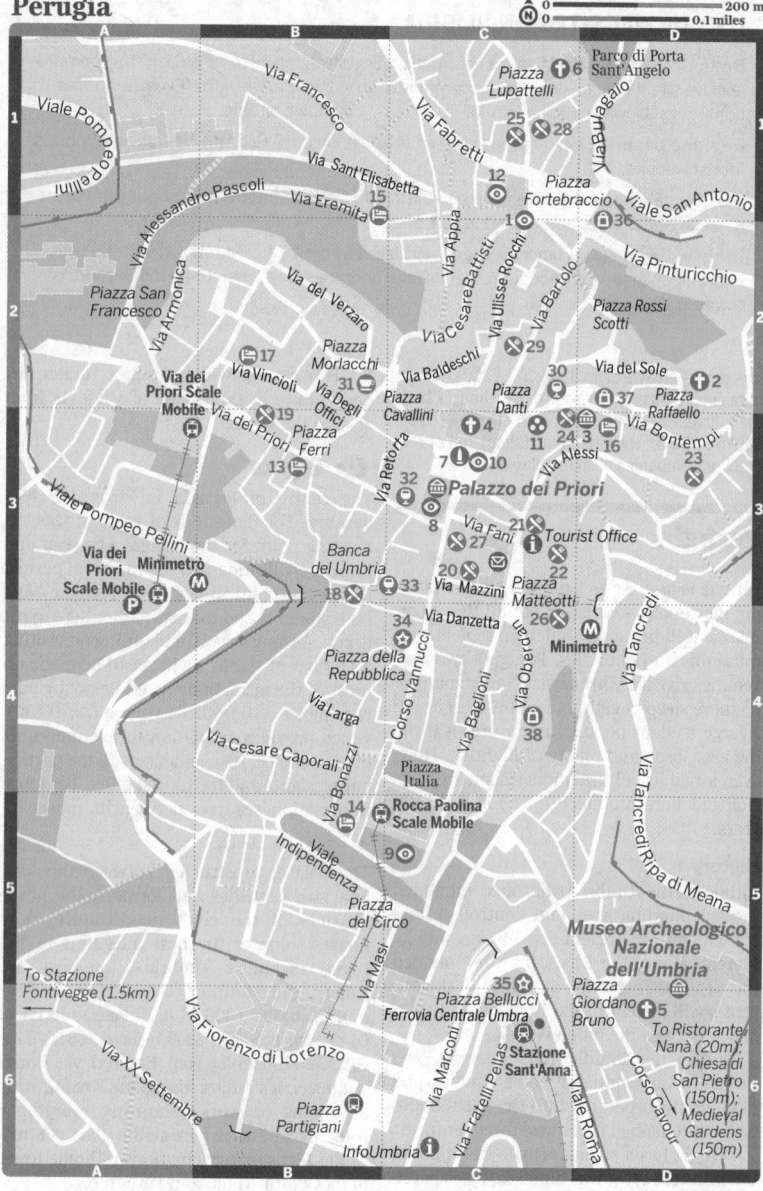

17th-century wooden stalls carved by Giampiero Zuccari and frescoes by Perugino. Also there is the **Nobile Collegio della Mercanzia** (Merchant's Hall; ☎075 573 03 66; Corso Vannucci 15; admission €3.10; ☺9am-1pm & 2.30-5.30pm Tue-Sun summer, often closed afternoon winter), which showcases an audience chamber from the 13th century, with wood panelling carved by northern craftsmen.

The **Sala dei Notari** (Notaries' Hall; ☎075 577 23 39; Piazza IV Novembre, Palazzo dei Priori; admission free; ☺9am-1pm & 3-7pm Tue-Sun) was built from 1293 to 1297 and is where the nobility met. The arches supporting the vaults are Romanesque, covered with frescoes depicting biblical scenes and Aesop's fables. To reach the hall, walk up the steps from Piazza IV Novembre.

Museo Archeologico Nazionale
dell'Umbria
MUSEUM

(☏075 572 71 41; Piazza Giordano Bruno 10; adult/reduced €4/2; ⏰8.30am-7.30pm Tue-Sun, 10am-7.30pm Mon) The convent adjoining the Chiesa di San Domenico is home to a superior collection of Etruscan and prehistoric artefacts – carved funerary urns, coins and Bronze Age statuary – dating as far back as the 16th century BC. The *Cippo Perugino* (Perugian Memorial Stone) has the longest Etruscan-language engraving ever found, offering a rare window into this obscure culture.

FREE **Perugina Chocolate Factory** MUSEUM
(☏075 527 67 96; www.perugina.it; Van San Sisto; ⏰9am-1pm & 2-5.30pm Mon-Fri year-round, also

9am-1pm Sat Oct-Jan & Mar-May; ⏰) The trick for independent travellers visiting this Wonka-esque experience is to either call ahead to arrange a guided tour, or simply latch on to a tour group (conducted in either Italian or English). After visiting the simple museum, you'll wend your way through an enclosed sky bridge, watching as the white-outfitted Oompa, er, factory workers go about their chocolate-creating business. Drive through the gates of the humorously nondescript factory entrance marked Nestlé, or take the bus to San Sisto.

Cattedrale di San Lorenzo
CHURCH

(☏075 572 38 32; Piazza IV Novembre; ⏰10am-12.30pm & 3-5.30pm Tue-Sun) Although a church has been on this land since the 900s, the version you see at the northern end of Piazza IV Novembre was begun in 1345 from designs created by Fra Bevignate. Building of the cathedral continued until 1587, although the main facade was never completed. Inside you'll find dramatic Gothic architecture, an altarpiece by Signorelli and sculptures by Duccio. The steps in front of the pink facade are where seemingly all of Perugia congregates.

Just outside the cathedral, at the very centre of the piazza, stands the **Fontana Maggiore** (Great Fountain). It was also designed by Fra Bevignate, and built between 1275 and 1278. Along the edge are bas-relief statues representing scenes from the Old Testament, the founding of Rome, the 'liberal arts', and a griffin and lion. Look for the griffin all over Perugia – it's the city's symbol. The lion is the symbol for the Guelphs, the Middle Ages faction that favoured rule by the papacy over rule by the Holy Roman Empire.

Chiesa di San Pietro   CHURCH

(☑075 3 47 70; Borgo XX Giugno; ☉8am-noon & 4pm-sunset) South of the town centre, past the Porta di San Pietro, this 10th-century church's interior is an incredible mix of gilt and marble, and contains a *pietà* (a painting of the dead Christ supported by the Madonna) by Perugino. For a glimpse into gardens past, take a stroll or picnic at the **Medieval Gardens** (☑075 585 64 32; Borgo XX Giugno 74; ☉8am-6.30pm Mon-Fri), behind the church. During the medieval period, monasteries often created gardens reminiscent of the Garden of Eden and biblical stories, with plants that symbolised myths and sacred stories. Numbered locations through this garden include the Cosmic Tree, symbolising the forefather of all trees; the Tree of Light and Knowledge; and the Tree of Good and Evil.

FREE Rocca Paolina   HISTORICAL BUILDING

(main entrance Piazza Italia, entrances on Via Marzia, Via Masi & Viale Indipendenza; ☉8am-7pm) At the southern end of Corso Vannucci is the tiny **Giardini Carducci**, which has towering views of the countryside. The gardens stand atop a once-massive 16th-century fortress (Palazzo della Provincia), now known as the Rocca Paolina. Pope Paolo III Farnese built the monstrosity in the 1540s, wiping out entire sections of what had been a wealthy neighbourhood. Now used as the throughway for the *scale mobili*, its nooks and crannies are now venues for art exhibits and the last weekend of the month sees Perugia's antiques market held here.

Casa Museo di Palazzo Sorbello   MUSEUM

(☑075 573 27 75; Piazza Piccinino 9; adult €5; ☉noon-1.30pm Mon, 11am-1.30pm Tue-Sun)

Perugia's latest attraction lies a few steps from the Piazza IV Novembre. This grand city-centre mansion, once owned by the noble Sorbello family, has recently been restored to its frescoed, gilt-clad 18th-century prime. Guided tours (in Italian) let you admire the family's almost ludicrously opulent collection of art, porcelain and manuscripts.

Capella di San Severo   CHURCH

(☑075 573 38 64; Piazza Raffaello, Porta Sole; adult/reduced €3/2; ☉10am-1.30pm & 2.30-6pm Tue-Sun May-Jul & Sep-Oct, 10.30am-1.30pm & 2.30-5pm Tue-Sun Nov-Mar, 10am-1.30pm & 2.30-6pm daily Apr & Aug) Walking for a couple of minutes northeast from Piazza IV Novembre brings you to this rather bland, boxy-looking church. Your efforts will be rewarded, however, once you step inside and find the chapel decorated with Raphael's lush *Trinity with Saints* (thought by many to be his first fresco), painted during the artist's residence in Perugia (1505–08).

Ipogeo dei Volumni   HISTORICAL SITE

(☑075 39 33 29; Via Assisana 53; adult/reduced €3/1.50; ☉9am-1pm & 3.30-6.30pm Sep-Jun, 9am-12.30pm & 4.30-7pm Jul & Aug) About 5km southeast of the city, the Ipogeo dei Volumni is a 2nd-century-BC underground Etruscan burial site, holding the funerary urns of the Volumni, a local noble family. The surrounding grounds are a massive expanse of partially unearthed burial chambers, with several buildings housing the artefacts that haven't been stolen over the years. Take a train or APM bus 3 from Piazza Italia to Ponte San Giovanni and walk west from there. By car, take the Bonanzano exit heading south on the E45.

Pozzo Etrusco   HISTORICAL SITE

(Etruscan Well; ☑075 573 36 69; Piazza Danti 18; adult/reduced €3/2; ☉10am-1.30pm & 2.30-6pm Wed-Mon May-Jul & Sep-Oct, 10.30am-1.30pm & 2.30-5pm Wed-Mon Nov-Mar, 10am-1.30pm & 2.30-6pm daily Apr & Aug) Just north of Piazza IV Novembre, you can venture down into a 36m-deep well. Dating from the 3rd century BC, it was the main water reservoir of the Etruscan town, and, more recently, a source of water during WWII bombing raids.

Chiesa di San Domenico   CHURCH

(☑075 573 15 68; Piazza Giordano Bruno; ☉8am-noon & 4pm-sunset) Erected in the early 14th century, the city's largest church has a Romanesque interior lit by immense stained-glass windows. Pope Benedict XI, who died after eating poisoned figs in 1325, lies buried here.

Arco Etrusco
HISTORICAL SITE

(Etruscan Arch) At the end of Ulisse Rocchi, facing Piazza Fortebraccio and the Università per Stranieri, are the ancient city's Etruscan gates dating from the 3rd century BC. The upper part is Roman and bears the inscription 'Augusta Perusia'.

Chiesa di Sant'Agostino
CHURCH

(Piazza Lupattelli; ⊗8am-noon & 4pm-sunset) North of the Università per Stranieri, along Corso Giuseppe Garibaldi, this formerly magnificent church still boasts a beautiful 16th-century choir by sculptor Baccio d'Agnolo. However, small signs forlornly mark the places where art works once hung before they were carried off to France by Napoleon's troops.

Chiesa di Sant'Angelo
CHURCH

(☑075 57 22 64; Via Sant'Angelo; ⊗10am-noon & 4-6pm) Further north along Corso Garibaldi, Via del Tempio branches off to one of Italy's oldest churches, the Romanesque Chiesa di Sant'Angelo, parts of which date back to the 5th century. It stands on the foundations of an even older Roman temple.

Museo delle Porte
e delle Mura Urbiche
MUSEUM

(Museum of the City Walls and Gates; ☑075 4 16 70; Porta Sant'Angelo, Corso Garibaldi; ⊗10.30am-1.30pm & 3-6pm Tue-Sun May-Jul & Sep-Oct, 11am-1pm & 3-5pm Tue-Sun Nov-Mar, 10.30am-1.30pm & 3-6pm daily Apr & Aug) Next door to the Chiesa di Sant'Angelo, in the 14th-century Porta Sant'Angelo (the city's largest medieval gateway), the museum describes the history of the city's defences, although the panoramic view facing back onto Perugia is the main reason to come out here.

🐾 Courses

Check with the tourist office for lists of all current classes in and around Perugia.

Università per Stranieri
LANGUAGE

(☑075 5 74 61; www.unistrapg.it; Palazzo Gallenga, Piazza Fortebraccio 4) This is Italy's foremost academic institution for foreigners, offering courses in language, literature, history, art, music, opera and architecture. One-, three- and six-month intensive language courses start at €400 a month.

🎊 Festivals & Events

Perugia – and Umbria in general – has gazillions of events, festivals, concerts, summer outdoor films and *sagre* (traditional festivals). Check www.bellaumbria.net or www.regioneumbria.eu for details.

Umbria Jazz
MUSIC

(☑800 462311, 075 500 11 07; www.umbriajazz.com) This attracts top-notch international performers for 10 days each July, usually around the middle of the month. The main venue is the Arena Santa Giuliana, outside the centre, where tickets start at €18 (and rapidly rise), but events take place across the city, including the Teatro del Pavone (tickets from €10). There are also free performances at Piazza IV Novembre and Giardini Carducci.

Eurochocolate
FOOD

(☑075 502 58 80; www.eurochocolate.com) Perugia hosts a slightly overwhelming celebration of the cocoa bean over nine days in mid-October. More than a million chocolate lovers arrive to visit chocolate-themed exhibitions, take part in chocolate cookery classes, admire giant chocolate sculptures and (the real reason everyone is here) hoover up the free samples. The local Perugina chocolate factory always has a big presence. Plan your hotel stay months in advance and don't even think of driving.

🛏 Sleeping

Perugia has a good number of hotels and *pensioni,* but few stand out. However, Perugia is a transport hub and is a good place to lay your head if you'd like to do day trips around the region.

TOP CHOICE Torre Colombaia
AGRITURISMO €

(☑075 878 73 41; www.torrecolombaia.it; San Biagio delle Valle; per person incl breakfast €40, apt €85-135, dinner €23; ⊗dinner Fri-Sun; Ｐ🖘) The iron staircase curling around the tree-draped fairy-tale cottage will make any urban dweller's heart instantly melt. Just 15 minutes from downtown Perugia, the former hunting farm now offers well-equipped antique-strewn rooms, an organic restaurant (supplied by the first organic farm in Umbria), a meditation room and plentiful wildlife-spotting opportunities in the surrounding woodland.

Primavera Minihotel
HOTEL €

(☑075 572 16 57; www.primaveraminihotel.it; Via Vincioli 8; s €45-55, d €65-90; ❄@☎) Though not quite the bargain it once was, this central hotel run by a dedicated English- and French-speaking mother-daughter team is still a great find, tucked in a quiet corner. The magnificent views complement the bright and airy rooms. Breakfast costs €3 to €6.

Hotel Brufani Palace
LUXURY HOTEL €€€

(☑075 573 25 41; www.sinahotels.com; Piazza Italia 12; s/d €99/205, ste €105-260; P❄@☎☷) One of Umbria's few five-star hotels and a truly spectacular experience, the palace's special touches include frescoed public rooms, impeccably decorated bedrooms, a garden terrace for summer dining, and helpful trilingual staff. Swim over Etruscan ruins in the subterranean fitness centre. Access for disabled guests.

Albergo Anna
HOTEL €

(☑/fax 075 573 63 04; www.albergoanna.it; Via dei Priori 48; s €30-50, d €50-80, all incl breakfast) If you want central and quiet, aren't too fussed about the up-to-dateness of your facilities and don't mind carrying your luggage up four floors, this option is a fabulous bet. You'll feel like you're staying in the private apartment of your great aunt (assuming she's a quirky Italian ceramics teacher with a penchant for knick-knacks and whipping up a mean espresso for breakfast).

Ostello di Perugia
HOSTEL €

(☑075 572 28 80; www.ostello.perugia.it; Via Bontempi 13; dm €15, sheets €2; ☉mid-Jan–mid-Dec; @) Having mellowed slightly in its old age, the hostel now only locks its guests out from 11am to 3.30pm (as opposed to 10am to 4pm), making it practically welcoming. It's actually rather charming inside, with 16th-century frescoed ceilings, tidy four- to six-person dorms and sweeping countryside views from the terrace. No credit cards.

Camping Il Rocolo
CAMPGROUND €

(☑/fax 075 518 16 35; www.ilrocolo.it; Str Fontana 1/n, Loc Colle della Trinità; per person €6.50-8, per car €3-4, per tent €5.50-6.50; ☉Easter-Sep & during Eurochocolate; @) International newspapers, Skype telephone connection, 24-hour hot showers and 100 shaded sites make this a good choice, and there's also an on-site restaurant, friendly multilingual staff and plenty of extras (barbecue pit, TV area, market and proximity to a bus into Perugia).

Etruscan Chocohotel
HOTEL €€

(☑075 583 73 14; www.chocohotel.it; Via Campo di Marte 134; s €54-73, d €88-140; P❄@☎☷) It's hard to believe, but this is the world's only chocolate-themed hotel. Once you've unpacked in your (brown, obviously) room, you can gorge on items from the restaurant's 'chocomenu', shop at the 'chocostore' or swim in the rooftop pool (sadly, filled with water). Access for disabled guests. It's located around a 20-minute walk due south of the old town.

Hotel San Sebastiano
HOTEL €€

(☑075 573 78 65; www.hotelsansebastiano.it; Via San Sebastiano 4; s €40-50, d €50-70, s without bathroom €25-40) Near Perugia's university is an old-school family-style *pensione*. Its side-street location guarantees a good night's sleep in its sparse rooms.

✖ Eating

Because of the great number of students and tourists, the amount of places to eat in Perugia is staggering. The first days the mercury rises above 15°C or so (usually in March), dozens of open-air locales spring up along and around Corso Vannucci.

TOP CHOICE Sandri
PASTRIES & CAKES €

(☑075 572 41 12; Corso Vannucci 32; ☉10am-8pm Tue-Sun) When you enter into your third century of business, you must be doing something right. This place is known for delectable chocolate cakes, candied fruit, espresso and pastries. Staff wrap all take-home purchases, no matter how small, in beautiful red paper with a ribbon bow.

Ristorante Nanà
TRADITIONAL ITALIAN €

(☑075 573 35 71; Corso Cavour 206; mains €15-18; ☉Mon-Sat) It's a good sign when approximately 47 members of the same family run a 15-table restaurant (it's actually only four, but it seems like more). Simply furnished with a small menu, the food is rustic – try the pigeon with capers (€16) – but done in a refined *nuovo* style.

Caffè di Perugia
CAFE €

(☑075 573 18 63; Via Mazzini 10; mains €14-20; ☉noon-3pm & 7pm-midnight Wed-Mon) The fanciest sit-down cafe in town, its desserts are worth the high prices. It also serves a fine choice of basic pasta and meat dishes and offers outdoor seating in summer.

Pizzeria Mediterranea
PIZZERIA €

(☎075 572 13 22; Piazza Piccinino 11/12; pizzas €4-8; ☺Wed-Mon) Perugians know to come here for the best pizza in town. A spaceship-sized wood-fired brick oven heats up pizzas from the simplest *margherita* to the 12-topping 'his and hers'. It gets busy enough to queue, especially Thursday and Saturday nights.

Al Mangiar Bene
PIZZERIA €

(☎075 573 10 47; Via della Luna 21; pizzas €5-8) Proudly flying the organic flag in Perugia, this subterranean restaurant at the end of a narrow alley sources nearly all its ingredients locally from organic suppliers. Pizzas and calzones are baked in a hearth-like brick oven. Even the beer and wines are organic.

Il Gufo
TRADITIONAL ITALIAN €€

(☎075 573 41 26; Via della Viola 18; meals €29; ☺8pm-1am Tue-Sat) The owner-chef gathers ingredients from local markets and cooks up whatever is fresh and in season. Try dishes such as wild boar with fennel (€12.50) or pappardelle with rabbit *ragù* (€9). A two-course set menu is €15. No credit cards.

Wine Bartolo Hosteria
OSTERIA €€

(☎075 571 60 27; Via Bartolo 30; meals €32; ☺Thu-Tue) Descend a staircase into a hobbit-like burrow where walls of wine bottles surround a handful of cosy tables underneath a low brick ceiling. Staff do beautiful things with Chianina beef stewed with Sangiovese.

Ristorante dal Mi'Cocco
TRADITIONAL ITALIAN €

(☎075 573 25 11; Corso Garibaldi 12; set meals €13; ☺Tue-Sun) Don't ask for a menu because there isn't one at this most traditional Perugian restaurant. Diners get a set menu of a starter, main course, side dish and dessert. You may receive asparagus risotto in May or *tagliatelle* with peas and ham in November. Extremely popular with students, it's best to call ahead.

Tuttotesto
TRADITIONAL ITALIAN €

(☎075 573 66 66; Corso Garibaldi 15; crêpes €3.90-5.50; ☺Tue-Sun) A change from Perugia's usual pasta-and-meat combos, this casual university spot sees professors and students debate Nietzsche over sweet and savoury crêpes and *torta al testo* (Umbrian flatbread sandwiches). Gluten-free options available.

Ristorante Il Sole
TRADITIONAL ITALIAN €€

(☎075 573 50 31; Via delle Rupe 1; meals €32; ☺Tue-Sun) Even if the food here was world-class, it would still play second fiddle to the views of the countryside from the terrace, which are simply stupendous. As it is, the food is pretty decent with a few inventive choices, such as smoked duck carpaccio with truffles, in among the usual fare.

Covered Market
MARKET

(Piazza Matteotti; ☺7am-1.30pm Mon-Sat) Found below a rather desultory craft and tourist-tat market, you can buy fresh produce, bread, cheese and meat here. Head through the arched doorway labelled 18A to the immediate right of the tourist office.

Coop
SUPERMARKET

(Piazza Matteotti; ☺9am-8pm Mon-Sat) The largest grocery store in the historical centre sells all the staples, fruits and vegetables, and also has a deli counter with fresh pasta and cheeses.

Bangladeshi Alimentari
SUPERMARKET

(Via dei Priori 71; ☺11am-10pm daily) This grocery just sells the basics, but check out those opening hours.

🍷 Drinking

Caffè Morlacchi
CAFE

(☎075 572 17 60; Piazza Morlacchi 6/8; ☺8am-1am Mon-Sat) Bring your bongo drums and leftist rhetoric to this most hip of establishments. Students, professors and expats nosh on international fare, sipping tea or hot chocolate during the day and cocktails at night.

Lunabar Ferrari
BAR

(Via Scura 1/6; ☺8am-2am Tue-Sun) Atmospherically equidistant between New York and Umbria, the city-centre lounge off Corso Vannucci spins together frescoed plaster walls and luxuriant rugs with modern art, crazy chandeliers and space-age restrooms. The hungry will appreciate the good snack selection.

Bottega del Vino
WINE BAR

(Via del Sole 1; ☺7pm-1am Mon-Sat) A fire or candles burn romantically on the terrace, while inside live jazz and hundreds of bottles of wine lining the walls add to the romance of the setting. You can taste dozens of Umbrian wines, which you can purchase with the help of sommelier-like experts.

Gold
WINE BAR

(Via dei Priori 7; ☺6pm-1am) This lounge bar-cum-restaurant is maybe trying a bit too hard to be classy with its endless 'gold' and 'luxury' theming. Still, it attracts a fun crowd, has plenty of wine choices and sells *torta al testo* for €2.50. Happy hour from 6pm.

☆ Entertainment

Much of Perugia's nightlife parades outside the cathedral and around Fontana Maggiore. Hundreds of local and foreign students congregate here practically every night, playing guitars and drums and chatting with friends. Tourists mix in easily, slurping gelati and enjoying this fascinating version of outdoor theatre. When the student population grows, some of the clubs on the outskirts of town run a bus to Palazzo Gallenga, starting around 11pm. Students get paid to hand out flyers on Corso Vannucci, so check with them or ask at the steps. Most clubs get going around midnight, so be warned on your way back into town: the *scale mobili* stop running at about 1am.

Cinema Teatro del Pavone   CINEMA
(☎075 572 49 11; www.teatrodelpavone.it; Corso Vannucci 67) Dating back to 1717, the grand theatre plays host to not only films but also musical performances and special events.

Velvet Fashioncafè   NIGHTCLUB
(☎075 572 06 07; www.velvetfashioncafe.com; Viale Roma 20; ⊘Tue-Sun) Come to the club where the beautiful people play. It opens around 10pm, but the well-dressed party here until the wee hours.

AC Perugia   SPORTS
(☎075 500 66 41; www.perugiacalcio.it; Renato Curi Stadium, Via Piccolpasso 48; tickets €2-40) Having been a mainstay of Serie A (Italy's topflight football competition) for decades, Perugia Calcio has fallen on hard times of late, having been disbanded after filing for bankruptcy in 2010. The team has since been refounded and, as of 2011, was playing in lowly Lega Pro Seconda Divisione (formerly Serie C). Take bus 9, 11 or 13 to the stadium.

🛍 Shopping

Look for the banner reading 'Via Oberdan – Shopping Street'. It's the place for boutiques, jewellery, shoes and music shops.

If you're lucky enough to be in Perugia on the fourth weekend of the month, spend a few hours in the Mercato Mensile Antiquariato (Antiques Market; ⊘9am-6pm or 7pm) around Piazza Italia and in Giardini Carducci. It's a great place to pick up old prints, frames, furniture, jewellery, postcards and stamps.

Umbria Terraviva   MARKET
(☎075 835 50 62; Piazza Piccinino) On the first Sunday of the month, check out this organic market along the side of the Duomo heading towards Via Bonanzi. You'll find all sorts of organic fruits and vegetables, and fabulous canned or packaged items to take home as gifts.

Augusta Perusia Cioccolato e Gelateria   CHOCOLATE
(www.cioccolatoaugustaperusia.it, in Italian; Via Pinturicchio 2; ⊘10.30am-11pm Mon-Sat, 10.30am-1pm & 4-8pm Sun) Giordano worked for Perugina for 25 years. In 2000, he opened his own shop, creating delectable morsels from the old tradition, including *baci* (hazelnut 'kisses' covered in chocolate) from the original Perugian recipe.

ℹ Information

Little Blue What-to-Do is a free English-language booklet that's a must-have for anyone staying longer than a few hours. Known as the 'little blue book', it lists restaurants, housing suggestions, side trips and a description of local characters. It's available at Cinema Teatro del Pavone, the tourist office and news stands.

Banks line Corso Vannucci. All have ATMs.

Emergency doctor (☎075 3 65 84; ⊘weekends & nights)

InfoUmbria (☎075 57 57; www.infoumbria.com, in Italian; Piazza Partigiani Intercity bus station, Largo Cacciatori delle Alpi 3; ⊘9am-1pm & 2.30-6.30pm Mon-Fri, 9am-1pm Sat) Also known as InfoTourist, it offers information on all of Umbria, and is a fantastic resource for *agriturismi*.

Ospedale Silvestrini (☎075 57 81; S Andrea delle Frate) Hospital.

Post office (Piazza Matteotti; ⊘8am-6.30pm Mon-Fri, 8am-noon Sat)

Tempo Reale (Via del Forno 17; per hr €1.80; ⊘10am-11.30pm Mon-Sat, 10am-10pm Sun) On a small easy-to-miss alley, this offers internet access, plus phone, fax and photocopying services.

Tourist office (☎075 573 64 58; info@iat.perugia.it; Piazza Matteotti 18; ⊘8.30am-6.30pm) Plenty of maps and tourist pamphlets for hotels, activities, events etc. Also has the most up-to-date bus and train timetables.

ℹ Getting There & Away

Air

Aeroporto Sant'Egidio (PEG; ☎075 59 21 41; www.airport.umbria.it), 13km east of the city, offers at least three daily **Alitalia** (www.alitalia.it) flights to Milan, plus a **Ryanair** (www.ryanair.co.uk) service to London Stansted thrice weekly.

Bus

Intercity buses leave from Piazza Partigiani in the city's south (take the *scale mobili* through the Rocca Paolina from Piazza Italia). Services go to the following destinations.

TO	FARE (€)	DURATION	FREQUENCY
Assisi	3.20	45min	9 daily
Castiglione del Lago	5.10	1hr	9 daily
Deruta	2.80	30min	13 daily
Florence	10.50	2½hr	2 daily
Gubbio	4.60	1¼hr	10 daily
Todi	5.50	1¼hr	9 daily
Torgiano	1.90	30min	9 daily

Most routes within Umbria are operated by **APM** (☑800 512141; www.apmperugia.it) in the north and **SSIT** (☑0743 21 22 11; www.spoletina.com) or **ATC Terni** (☑0744 40 94 57; www.atcterni.it) in the south. For the latest details pick up the monthly *Viva Perugia* (€1) from the tourist office.

Car & Motorcycle

From Rome, leave the A1 at the Orte exit and follow the signs for Terni. Once there, take the SS3bis/E45 for Perugia. From the north, exit the A1 at Valdichiana and take dual-carriageway SS75 for Perugia. The SS75 to the east connects the city with Assisi.

Rental companies have offices at the airport and train station.

Train

In the southwest of town, Perugia's main **train station** (Piazza Vittorio Veneto) is officially named 'Stazione Fontivegge', though the sign simply reads 'Perugia'. Trains run to the following destinations.

TO	FARE (€)	DURATION	FREQUENCY
Arezzo	6-9	1hr	every 2 hours
Assisi	2.50	30min	hourly
Florence	11-16	2hr	8 daily
Gubbio	5.50	1½hr	7 daily
Orvieto	7	1¼hr	every 2 hours
Rome	11-35	2¼-3hr	15 daily
Spello	3	30min	hourly

The adorably graffitied 'Thomas the Tank Engine' trains of the **Ferrovia Central Umbra** (FCU;

ARRIVING FROM ROME?

It's quite easy to take a direct bus from Rome's Fiumicino (FCO) airport to Perugia. Pick up a blue **Sulga** (☑800 099661; www.sulga.it) bus across the street from international terminal C. From Monday to Saturday there are four or five daily buses to Perugia (€21, 3½ to four hours), and two daily on Sunday and holidays. Several buses stop in Assisi. Check the website for details.

☑075 57 54 01; www.fcu.it, in Italian; Stazione Sant'Anna, Piazzale Bellucci) head to Rome (change in Terni, €5.30, 1¼ hours, 10 daily), Deruta (€1.25, 25 minutes, 11 daily), Todi (€2.55, 50 minutes, 17 daily) and Terni (€4.40, 1½ hours, 17 daily). Validate your ticket on board.

❶ Getting Around

If you're not carrying too much luggage, the simplest way of getting from Perugia's intercity bus station to the centre of town is by hopping aboard the series of escalators (known as *scale mobili*) linking Piazza Pargigiani with Piazza Italia. There are also *scale mobili* taking arrivals from the car park at the Piazzale della Cuppa outside the city walls up to the Via dei Priori.

To/From the Airport

A white shuttle bus (€3.50) leaves from Piazza Italia for the airport about two hours before each flight, stopping at the train station. From the airport, buses leave once everyone is on board.

A taxi costs approximately €30.

Bus

It's a steep 1.5km climb from Perugia's train station, so a bus is highly recommended (and essential for those with luggage). The bus takes you to Piazza Italia. Tickets cost €1.50 from the train-station kiosk or €2 on board. Validate your ticket on board to avoid a fine. A 10-ticket pass costs €12.90.

Car & Motorcycle

Perugia is humorously difficult to navigate and most of the city centre is only open to residential or commercial traffic (although tourists may drive to their hotels to drop off luggage).

Perugia has several fee-charging car parks (€0.80 to €1.60 per hour, 24 hours a day). Piazza Partigiani and the Mercato Coperto are the most central and convenient. There's also a free car park at Piazza Cupa.

Call the **information line** (☑ 075 577 53 75) if your car has been towed or for general parking information.

Minimetrò

These single-car people-movers traverse between the train station and Pincetto (just off Piazza Matteotti) every minute. The same €1.50 tickets work for the bus and Minimetrò. From the train station facing the tracks, head right up a long platform.

Taxi

Taxi services are available from 6am to 2am (24 hours a day in July and August); call ☑ 075 500 48 88 to arrange pick-up. A ride from the city centre to the main train station, Stazione Fontivegge, will cost about €10 to €15. Tack on €1 for each suitcase.

Torgiano

POP 6479

In little Torgiano, a 25-minute bus ride from Perugia, olive oil is treated with a reverence usually reserved for wine, and wine with a devotion bordering on the sacred. It's home to the most important wine museum in Europe, the Museo del Vino (☑ 075 988 02 00; Corso Vittorio Emanuele 31; adult/reduced €4.50/2.50, incl Museo dell'Olivo e dell'Olio €7, audioguide €2; ☺10am-1pm & 3-7pm summer, to 6pm winter), housed in a 20-room former palace, which traces the history of the region's wine production through displays of utensils, graphic art, wine containers and production techniques.

You'll also find the Museo dell'Olivo e dell'Olio (☑ 075 988 03 00; Via Garibaldi 10; adult/reduced €4.50/2.50; ☺10am-1pm & 3-7pm summer, to 6pm winter), which documents the use of olives and how they relate to the economy, the landscape and the general culture of the region.

Despite its small size, there's a distinct air of sleepy self-importance about Torgiano, born in part of its status as a 'company' town. The Lungarottis, who operate most of the wineries around here, are the closest thing Umbria has to a ruling noble family these days.

🛏 Sleeping & Eating

Al Grappolo d'Oro HOTEL €€

(☑ 075 98 22 53; www.algrappolodoro.net; Via Principe Umberto 24; s €50, d €90-105, all incl breakfast; P✳☀) One of the best hotel deals in Umbria, it is worth a stay just for the vineyard view from the pool. Smartly furnished 19th-

century rooms have been upgraded with DSL, satellite TV, DVD players, hairdryers and towel warmers.

Ristorante Siro TRADITIONAL ITALIAN €€

(☑ 075 98 20 10; Via Giordano Bruno 16; meals €26) This old-school eatery is one of those spots where waiters and customers all know each other by name. The *antipastone al tagliere* (large plate of mixed antipasti; €15 for two) starter would feed a hungry family.

ℹ Getting There & Away

APM Perugia (☑ 800 512141; www.apmperugia.it) *extraurbano* buses head to Perugia (€1.90, 25 minutes, nine daily).

Lago Trasimeno

It would have been easy for drop-dead gorgeous Lago Trasimeno to become a holiday haven for busloads of northern European sun seekers, à la the coast of Le Marche. Thankfully the majority of the area – outside Passignano and a strip leaving San Feliciano – has eschewed the Stalinist high-rise mono-architecture of such Adriatic holiday villages. *Agriturismi* cover the hills like the omnipresent sunflower, historic Castiglione del Lago folds travellers in gently to allow room for all, and everyone respects the delicate ecology of the precious lake.

◉ Sights & Activities

Popular activities at the lake include trekking, wine tasting, camping, water sports and *dolce far niente* (the sweet enjoyment of doing nothing). Many also go for the culinary delights. The locals are very proud of their excellent produce, most notably their high-quality DOC wines and DOP olive oils. If you are interested in following the Strade del Vino (Wine Route) of the Colli del Trasimeno (Trasimeno Hill district), the Associazione Strada del Vino Colli del Trasimeno (www.stradadelvinotrasimeno.it/en) produces a brochure with suggested itineraries, which you can also pick up at the tourist office in Castiglione del Lago, the area's main town.

Castiglione del Lago's attractions include the Palazzo della Corgna (☑ 075 965 82 10; Piazza Gramsci; admission incl Rocca del Leone adult/reduced €3/2; ☺10am-1pm & 4-7.30pm summer, 9.30am-4.30pm Sat & Sun winter), an ancient ducal palace. A covered passageway connects the palace with the 13th-century

POT LUCK IN DERUTA

If Torgiano is a two-note town, then Deruta (a few kilometres to the south) has just the one – majolica ceramics – but it doesn't half blast it out loudly. The blue and yellow metallic-oxide glazing technique was imported here from Majorca in the 15th century and has been the mainstay of the local industry ever since. Giant pots and plates advertising Deruta's many factories and workshops proudly line the approach roads, while the centre of town is packed with so many businesses as to seem almost like one giant shop with many entrances.

For the best-quality stuff, head to the smaller places that follow centuries-old traditions. The pieces in the larger operations are mass-produced in a factory. The prices will be lower, but so will the quality.

Maioliche Nulli (☎/fax 075 97 23 84; Via Tiberina 142; ☉daily) is one of the better operations, specialising in intricate medieval designs, and you can explore the history of the town's business in depth at the Museo Regionale della Ceramica (☎/fax 075 971 10 00; www.museoceramicaderuta.it; Largo San Francesco; adult/reduced €7/5; ☉10.30am-1pm & 3-6pm or 7pm daily, closed Tue afternoon Oct-Mar).

Just south of Deruta, in the village of Casalina, foodies come from far and wide to sample the tasty creations at L'Antico Forziere (☎075 972 43 14; www.anticoforziere.it; Via della Rocca 2, Loc Casalina di Deruta; r €65-150, meals €32; P✳☒). Twin-brother chefs, who also have a sideline as TV personalities (imagine two identical, slightly less sweary Gordon Ramsays), present beautifully prepared dishes (lots of towers, drizzling and artful arrangements). Inventive mains include turnip pasta with leeks and poppy seeds, and there's also a huge wine list. The highlight, however, is the dessert sampler, comprising 10 elegantly crafted sweet creations. Yet another brother works front of house at the fine adjoining hotel.

APM buses connect the town with Perugia (€2.80, 25 minutes, 13 daily).

Rocca del Leone, an excellent example of medieval military architecture.

The lake's main inhabited island – Isola Maggiore, near Passignano – was reputedly a favourite with St Francis. The hilltop Chiesa di San Michele Arcangelo contains a crucifixion painted by Bartolomeo Caporali dating from around 1460. You can also visit the mostly uninhabited island and environmental lab at Isola Polvese on a day trip with Fattoria Il Poggio (see below).

Ask at any of the tourist offices around the lake or in Perugia for a booklet of walking and horse-riding tracks. Horse-riding centres include La Rosa Canina (☎075 835 06 60; www.larosacanina.com; Via dei Mandorli 23, Casalini), to the south of the lake.

🛏 Sleeping

For a full list of hundreds of places to stay, check out www.regioneumbria.eu, www.bellaumbria.net or any of the tourist offices around the lake or in Perugia.

Fattoria Il Poggio   HOSTEL €
(☎075 965 95 50; www.fattoriaisolapolvese.com; Isola Polvese; s €15-18, dm €22-28, d apt €70-110, meals from €12; ☉Mar-Oct, reception closed 3-7pm; @) You would hardly know you're in an HI youth hostel. Dorm, doubles and family rooms all have views of the surrounding lake. Those who don't mind catching a ferry back by 7pm will be rewarded handsomely with a family-style meal (full meals €10) in a former barn outfitted with many eco-friendly additions on its own private island. Kayaks, private beaches, games, DVDs, laundry room, 14th-century ruins and a nearby environmental lab are just some of the offerings.

La Casa sul Lago   HOSTEL €
(☎075 840 00 42; www.lacasasullago.com; Via del Lavoro 25, Torricella di Magione; dm €18, r per person €25-30, all incl breakfast; @☎) This is one of the top-rated hostels in central Italy, and for a very good reason. The private rooms could be in a three-star hotel, and guests have access to every amenity known to hostelkind: laundry, bicycles and wi-fi (both free!), home-cooked group meals, bar, football pitch, foosball table, pedal boat and private garden...all within 50m of the lake. It's a short walk from the Torricella train station, but use the bicycles to get around the lake.

Il Torrione
B&B €

(☎075 95 32 36; www.iltorrionetrasimeno.com; Via delle Mura 4, Castiglione del Lago; s €50, d €60-70, all incl breakfast; ☺1 Mar-10 Nov) Romance abounds at this artistically minded tranquil retreat. Each room is decorated with art work painted by the owner, and a private flower-filled garden overlooks the lake, complete with chaises longues from which to watch the sunset and a 16th-century tower. Rent the tower room (up a flight of pirate-ship stairs) for a romantic private apartment.

Camping Badiaccia
CAMPGROUND €

(☎075 965 90 97; www.badiaccia.com; Via Trasimeno I 91, Bivia Borghetto; per person €5.50-7.50, tent €4.50-5.50, car €2-2.50, dog €2, 2- to 6-person bungalow €38-110; P@☼⊛) Practise your Dutch while playing tennis, table tennis or bocce, eating at the surprisingly good *ristorante*, or swimming in one of three pools. The campsite is paradise for families, but the childless will equally enjoy renting a kayak, bicycle or paddleboat and the beachfront location.

La Torre
HOTEL €

(☎075 95 16 66; www.trasinet.com/latorre; Via Vittoria Emanuele 50, Castiglione del Lago; r €45-90; ⊛) The price is right at this central three-star hotel, a renovated palace. The rooms are a tad sterile but fully outfitted with TV, minibar and telephone, and the owners run the yummy bakery below (breakfast is delicious but costs €6 extra).

✕ Eating

Specialities of the Trasimeno area include *fagiolina* (little white beans), carp in *porchetta* (cooked in a wood oven with garlic, fennel and herbs) and *tegamaccio,* a kind of soupy stew of the best varieties of local fish, cooked in olive oil, white wine and herbs.

La Cantina
TRADITIONAL ITALIAN €€

(☎075 965 24 32; Via Vittoria Emanuele, Castiglione del Lago; meals €27; ☺Tue-Sun) Not only is the well-priced restaurant fabulous – a stately interior with a lovely outdoor terrace for summer dining – but there's also an adjacent *magazzino* (shop) where you can buy the area's best wine and olive oil. Try the delicious trout with local *fagiolina* (€9).

Il Lido Solitario
TRADITIONAL ITALIAN €€

(☎075 95 18 91; Via Lungolago 16, Castiglione del Lago; meals €28) It isn't often we recommend a heavily trafficked waterfront restaurant, but it isn't often you get to try a delicate fish cake topped with sweet Castelluccian lentils or a tender Chianina beef infused with Sagrantino wine. Grab a front porch table overlooking the nearby lake for a true summer experience.

Ristorante L'Acquario
TRADITIONAL ITALIAN €€

(☎075 965 24 32; Corso Vittorio Emanuele 69, Castiglione del Lago; meals €27; ☺Fri-Wed Jan-Oct; P⊛) L'Acquario has been open more than 20 years, and is still serving much the same menu. But if it ain't broke... the restaurant relies on time-honoured methods of good ingredients (many of them fished out of the lake), good cooking and reasonable prices rather than fancy flavour combinations. It's a great place to take your time over a meal. Try the eel *tegamaccio.*

☆ Entertainment

Hotel Faliero (Da Maria)
FOLK DANCING

(☎075 847 63 41; www.hotelfaliero.it; Loc Montebuono di Magione; s €35-38, d €60-65; ☺to midnight daily in season) Dine, dance and sleep it off at Lago Trasimeno's most famous institution. For Umbrians, a trip to the lake simply isn't complete without a visit to this temple of folk dancing. Il Faliero is hopping with dancers on most summer weekends, but the casual, counter-service restaurant has garnered just as much fame. In a pinch, 13 business-casual hotel rooms are far enough from the noise for a good night's sleep.

ⓘ Information

Tourist office (☎075 965 24 84; info@iat. castiglione-del-lago-pg.it; Piazza Mazzini 10, Castiglione del Lago; ☺8.30am-1pm & 3.30-7pm Mon-Sat, 9am-1pm Sun) Advises on *agriturismi* and activities like cycling and water sports, and has an impressive collection of maps.

ⓘ Getting There & Around

BICYCLE You can hire bikes at most campsites or at **Cicli Valentini** (☎/fax 075 95 16 63; www. ciclivalentini.it; Via Firenze 68b, Castiglione del Lago; per hr/day €2/14).

BUS APM (☎800 512141; www.apmperugia. it) connects Perugia with Passignano (€3.20, 70 minutes, 10 daily) and Castiglione del Lago (€5.10, one hour, nine daily).

CAR & MOTORCYCLE Two major highways skirt the lake: the SS71, which heads from Chiusi to Arezzo on the west side (in Tuscany); and SS-75bis, which crosses the north end of the lake, heading from the A1 in Tuscany to Perugia.

FERRY APM services run from Easter to the end of September. Hourly ferries head from San

Feliciano to Isola Polvese (€6.90 return, 20 minutes), Tuoro to Isola Maggiore (€6.90 return, 20 minutes) and Castiglione del Lago or Passignano to Isola Maggiore (€6.90 return, 30 minutes). Ferries stop running at 7pm.

TRAIN Services run about hourly from Perugia to Torricella (€2.40 to €4.80, 25 minutes), Passignano (€3, 35 minutes) and Castiglione del Lago (€4.40 to €8.90, 50 minutes).

Todi

POP 17,282

Todi embodies all that is good about a central Italian hill town. Ancient structures line even more ancient roads, and the pace of life inches along, keeping time with the fields of wildflowers that languidly grow with the seasons. Foreign artists share Todi's cobblestone streets with families who have lived here for generations.

Like rings around a tree, Todi's history can be read in layers: the interior walls show Todi's Etruscan and even Umbrian influence, the middle walls are an enduring example of Roman know-how, and the 'new' medieval walls boast of Todi's economic stability and prominence during the Middle Ages.

◉ Sights

Just try to walk through the **Piazza del Popolo** (Piazza of the People) without feeling compelled to sit on the medieval building steps and write a postcard home. The 13th-century **Palazzo del Capitano** links to the Palazzo del Popolo to create what is now the **Museo Pinacoteca e Museo della Città di Todi** (☎075 895 62 16; Piazza del Popolo; admission €3.10; ⊙10am-1.30pm & 3-6pm Mar-Oct, 10.30am-1pm & 2.30-5pm Tue-Sun Nov-Feb), holding a fine (if hardly overwhelming) collection of paintings, and a rather more successful archaeological section – lots of old coins and ceramics.

The **cathedral** (☎075 894 30 41; Piazza del Popolo; ⊙8.30am-1pm & 3.30-6.30pm), at the northwestern end of the square, has a magnificent rose window. You can skip it, however, to visit two of Umbria's most impressive churches. The lofty **Tempio di San Fortunato** (Piazza Umberto 1; ⊙10am-1pm & 2.30-7pm Mar-Oct, 10am-1pm & 2.30-5pm Wed-Mon Nov-Feb) has frescoes by Masolino da Panicale and holds the tomb of Beato Jacopone, Todi's beloved patron saint. Inside, make it a point to climb the **Campanile di San Fortunato** (adult/reduced €1.50/1; ⊙10am-1pm & 3-6.30pm Apr-Oct, 10.30am-1pm & 2.30-5pm Nov-Mar, closed

Mon), where views of the hills and castles surrounding Todi awaits.

The postcard you've just written from the Piazza del Popolo? Most likely it's of Todi's famed church, the late-Renaissance masterpiece **Chiesa di Santa Maria della Consolazione** (Via della Consolazione; ⊙9.30am-12.30pm & 2.30-6.30pm Mar-Oct, 9.30am-12.30pm & 2.30-5pm Wed-Mon Nov-Feb). Inside, architecture fans can admire its geometrically perfect Greek cross design.

🎭 Festivals & Events

Todi Arte Festival CULTURAL
(www.todiartefestival.com, in Italian) Held for 10 days each September, this is a mixture of classical and jazz concerts, theatre, ballet and cinema. Ask at the tourist office for details.

🛏 Sleeping

San Lorenzo Tre B&B €
(☎075 894 45 55; www.sanlorenzo3.it; Via San Lorenzo 3; s/d €75/95, s/d without bathroom €55/75, all incl breakfast; ⊙Mar-Dec) Five generations of the same family have lived at this historical residence. Awaiting guests are home-cooked breakfasts, a stunning rooftop view and atmospheric, romantic rooms.

Todi Castle HOTEL €€
(☎0744 95 20 04; www.todicastle.com; Vocabolo Capecchio, Morre; villa r €70-120, castle r incl breakfast €100-200, weekly rates available; P 🗢 ☀) Here's your chance to live in an honest-to-goodness castle, or in one of three equally perfect (and more affordable) private villas. With on-site private pools, medieval ruins, a deer park and the most attentive staff in Umbria, you'll feel positively royal.

Fonte Cesia BOUTIQUE HOTEL €€
(☎075 894 46 77; www.fontecesia.it; Via Lorenzo Leonj 3; s €80-120, d €90-219, all incl breakfast; P @) Just south of the main square, this renovated 17th-century palazzo has great old-world charm. The rooms are a bit small, but come with elegant antique touches, and some have views of the surrounding hills. There's also a very good restaurant, Le Palme.

🍴 Eating

Antica Hosteria de la Valle OSTERIA €
(☎075 894 48 48; Via Ciuffelli; mains €12-20; ⊙Tue-Sun) Art vies with food for top billing at this most creative of restaurants. Every few months, local artists not only display their work, but also illustrate the seasonal menus. Truffles find their way onto plenty

NARNI – THE MAGICAL HEART OF ITALY

Like Greenwich or the North Pole, Narni is a place best known for where it is rather than what it is, lying as it does almost slap-bang at the geographical centre of Italy. You can walk to a stone marking the exact spot just outside the town. But Narni has a lot more going for it than merely being the answer to a trivia question. It boasts one of the finest medieval town centres in Umbria (and that's against some pretty stiff competition) with a collection of churches, piazzas, palazzos and fortresses that are quite magical – and fittingly so given that CS Lewis used the Roman name for the town (plucked at random from an ancient atlas) for his own fictional magical kingdom: Narnia.

The town lies 21km south of Todi, just east of the A1 autostrada (from the south take the Magliano Sabina exit; from the north the Orte exit) and is well served by buses from Terni and Orvieto; contact ATC Terni (☑0744 71 52 07; www.atcterni.it).

of dishes: you can try them with *tagliolini* (€14) or *filetto di manzo* (€20).

Pizzeria Ristorante Cavour　　PIZZERIA €€
(☑075 894 37 30; Coro Cavour 21; meals €30; ☺Tue-Sun) Even by Umbrian hill-town standards, Todi is pretty steep. The upside to all that lactic acid build-up is the many towering views – with none better than here. It's a huge place with several rooms, but if it's a fine day, ignore them all and head straight outside to the terrace, order a plate of fettuccine with goose *ragù* (€8) and take it all in.

Bar Pianegiani　　ICE CREAM €
(☑075 894 23 76; Corso Cavour 40; ☺6am-midnight Tue-Sun) Just like Clark Kent, this nondescript neighbourhood bar puts on an innocent front to conceal its superpowers, but 50 years of tradition has created the world's most perfect gelato. Try the black cherry (*spagnola*) or hazelnut (*nocciola*).

❶ Information

Biblioteca Comunale Lorenzo Leonj (☑075 895 67 10; ☺8.30am-2pm Mon-Fri, 3-6pm Tue & Thu) Free high-speed internet (take your passport to register).

Post office (☑075 894 24 26; Piazza Garibaldi; ☺8am-6.30pm Mon-Fri, 8am-12.30pm Sat)

Tourist office (☑075 894 54 18; Piazza del Popolo 37; ☺9.30am-1pm & 3.30-6.30pm Mon-Sat, 10am-1.30pm Sun & holidays summer, reduced hours winter)

❶ Getting There & Away

APM (☑800 512141; www.apmperugia.it) buses head from Perugia's Piazza Partigiani (€5.50, 1½ hours) every hour or so to either Piazza Jacapone or Piazza Consolazione. There is one daily service to Spoleto (€5.50, 1½ hours, 6.50am).

By car, Todi is easily reached on the SS3bis-E45, which runs between Perugia and Terni, or take the Orvieto turn-off from A1 (the Milan–Rome–Naples route).

FCU (☑075 57 54 01; www.fcu.it in Italian) trains run to Perugia (€2.55, 50 minutes, 18 daily). Although the train station is 3km away, city bus C (€0.90, eight minutes) coincides with arriving trains, and every other hour on Sunday.

Assisi

POP 27,740

The spiritual capital of Umbria is Assisi, a town tied to its most famous son – St Francis of Assisi was born here in 1181 and preached his message throughout Umbria until his death in 1226.

To visit Assisi now is to see it almost as Francis himself saw it. Except, of course, for the millions of pilgrims and tourists now attempting to share in the same tranquillity as you.

◉ Sights

Basilica Di San Francesco　　CHURCH
(☑075 81 90 01; Piazza di San Francesco) St Francis asked his followers to bury him here on a hill known as Colle d'Inferno (Hell Hill), where people were executed at the gallows until the 13th century, so as to be in keeping with Jesus, who had died on the cross among criminals and outcasts. He also asked that his followers refrain from all forms of ostentation in their places of worship. Well, one out of two ain't bad.

The upper church (☺8.30am-6.45pm Easter-Oct, to 6pm Oct-Easter) was built just after the lower church, between 1230 and 1253, and is a terribly grand place. Circling the inner walls is one of the most famous pieces of art in the world, a giant multi-part fresco usually attributed to Giotto (though there is some debate within the art-historian community) depicting 28 scenes from St Francis's life below corresponding images from the Old and New Testaments. It revolutionised art in the Western world, with the standard gold-leaf and flat iconic images of the Byzantine and Romanesque periods eschewed for natural backgrounds and a human, suffering Jesus. These fresco painters were the storytellers of their day, turning biblical passages into *Bibliae Pauperum:* open public Bibles for the poor, who were mostly illiterate.

The **lower church** (⊗6am-6.45pm Easter-Oct, to 6pm Oct-Easter) was built between 1228 and 1230. In the centre above the main altar are four frescoes attributed to Maestro delle Vele, a pupil of Giotto, that represent what St Francis called 'the four greatest allegories'. The first is the victory of Francis over evil, and the other depict the precepts his order was based on: poverty, obedience and chastity. Lorenzetti's triptych in the left transept ends with his famous and controversial *Madonna Who Celebrates Francis.* Mary is seen holding the baby Jesus and indicating with her thumb towards St Francis. On the other side of Mary is the Apostle John, whom we assume is being unfavourably compared with Francis. In 1234 Pope Gregory IX decided that the image was not heretical because John had written the gospel, but Francis had lived it. Cimabue was the most historically important painter who worked in this church because he was the only artist to get a first-hand account from St Francis' two nephews, who had personally known the saint. In the *Madonna in Majesty,* in the right transept, Cimabue's depiction of St Francis is considered the most accurate.

Downstairs from the lower church is the **Tomb of St Francis**, where the saint's body has been laid to rest, and the **Reliquary Chapel** (⊗9am-6pm daily, 1-4.30pm holidays), which contains items from St Francis' life, including his simple, much-patched tunic and fragments of his celebrated *Canticle of the Creatures.*

The basilica has its own **information office** (☑075 819 00 84; www.sanfrancesco assisi.org; ⊗9am-noon & 2-5pm Mon-Sat), which can be found opposite the entrance to the lower church. Here you can schedule a tour in English or Italian, led by a resident Franciscan friar.

Rocca Maggiore HISTORICAL BUILDING

(☑075 81 52 92; Via della Rocca; adult/reduced €5/3.50; ⊗10am-sunset) Dominating the city is the massive 14th-century Rocca Maggiore, an oft-expanded, pillaged and rebuilt hill-fortress offering 360-degree views of Perugia to the north and the surrounding valleys below. Walk up winding staircases and claustrophobic passageways to reach the archer slots that served Assisians as they went medieval on Perugia.

Basilica di Santa Chiara CHURCH

(☑075 81 22 82; Piazza Santa Chiara; ⊗6.30am-noon & 2-7pm summer, to 6pm winter) Built in the 13th century in a Romanesque style, with steep ramparts and a striking white and pink facade, the basilica was raised in honour of St Clare, a spiritual contemporary of St Francis and founder of the Sorelle Povere di Santa Chiara (Order of the Poor Ladies), now known as the Poor Clares. She is buried in the church's crypt. The Byzantine cross that is said to have spoken to St Francis is also housed here.

Basilica di Santa Maria degli Angeli CHURCH

(☑075 8 05 11; Santa Maria degli Angeli; ⊗6.15am-12.50pm & 2.30-7.30pm) That enormous domed church you can see as you approach Assisi along the Tiber Valley is the 16th-century Basilica di Santa Maria degli Angeli, the centrepiece of the new town, some 4km west and several hundred metres further down the hill from old Assisi. Built between 1565 and 1685, its vast ornate confines house the tiny, humble Porziuncola Chapel, where St Francis first took refuge having found his vocation and given up his worldly goods, and which is generally regarded as the place where the Franciscan movement started. St Francis died at the site of the **Cappella del Transito** on 3 October 1226.

FREE Eremo delle Carceri HISTORICAL SITE

(☑075 81 23 01; ⊗6.30am-7pm Easter-Oct, to sunset Oct-Easter) In around 1205 St Francis chose this set of caves above Assisi as his hermitage where he could retire to contemplate spiritual matters. The *carceri* (isolated places, or 'prisons') along the forest slopes of Monte Subasio are as peaceful today as in St Francis' time, albeit now surrounded by various religious buildings. Many visitors use the locale as a jumping-off point for contemplative walks or picnics under the oaks. It's a 4km drive (or walk) east, and a dozen nearby hiking trails are well signposted.

The Saint of Assisi

That someone could found a successful movement based on peace, love and understanding in any age is remarkable; that Francis Bernardone was able to do it in war-torn 13th-century Umbria was extraordinary. But then again, in his early years Francis was very much a man of the times – and anything but saintly. Born in Assisi in 1181, the son of a wealthy merchant, he spent his youth carousing. However, following a holy vision in his early 20s, Francis decided to give up his possessions in order to live a humble, 'primitive' life in imitation of Christ, preaching and helping the poor. He travelled widely around Italy (and beyond), performing miracles (curing the sick, communicating with animals) and setting up monasteries.

Today various places claim links with St Francis, including Greccio in Lazio where he supposedly created the first (live) nativity scene in 1223, Bevagna in Umbria where he is said to have preached to the birds, and La Verna in Tuscany where he received the stigmata shortly before his death at the age of 44. He was canonised just two years later, after which the business of 'selling' St Francis began in earnest. Modern Assisi, with its glorious churches and thriving souvenir industry, seems an almost wilfully ironic comment on Francis' ascetic and spiritual values.

TOP ST FRANCIS SITES

» **Assisi** (p562) His home town and the site of his birth and death, his hermitage, his chapel, the first Franciscan monastery and the giant basilica containing his tomb.

» **Gubbio** (p570) Where the saint supposedly brokered a deal between the townsfolk and a man-eating wolf.

» **Rome** (p93) Francis was given permission by Pope Innocent III to found the Franciscan order at the Basilica di San Giovanni in Laterano.

Clockwise from top left
1. Basilica di San Francesco, exterior 2. Basilica di San Francesco and town of Assisi 3. Basilica di San Giovanni, Rome, birthplace of the Franciscan order 4. Basilica Di San Francesco, interior.

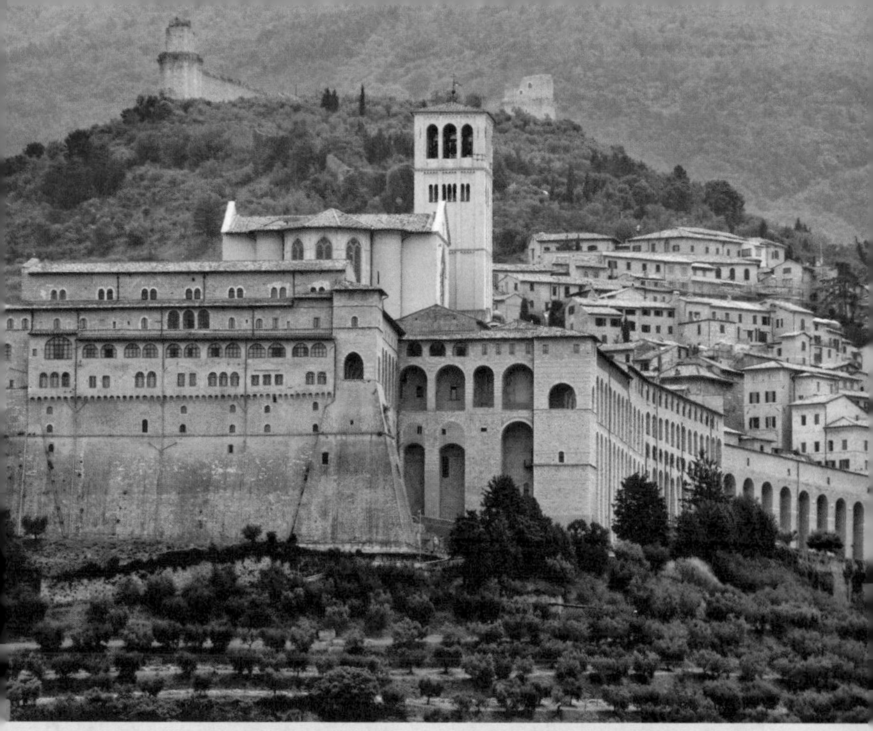

MARTIN MOOS / LONELY PLANET IMAGES ©

3

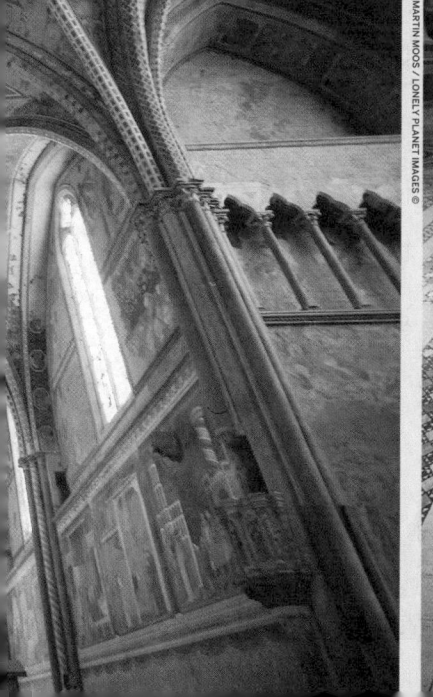

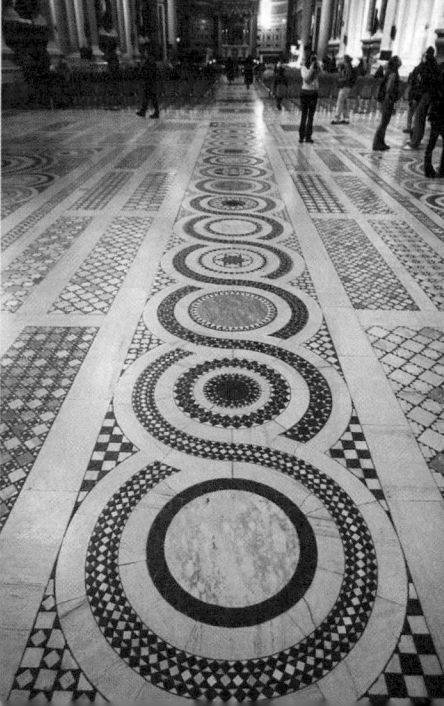

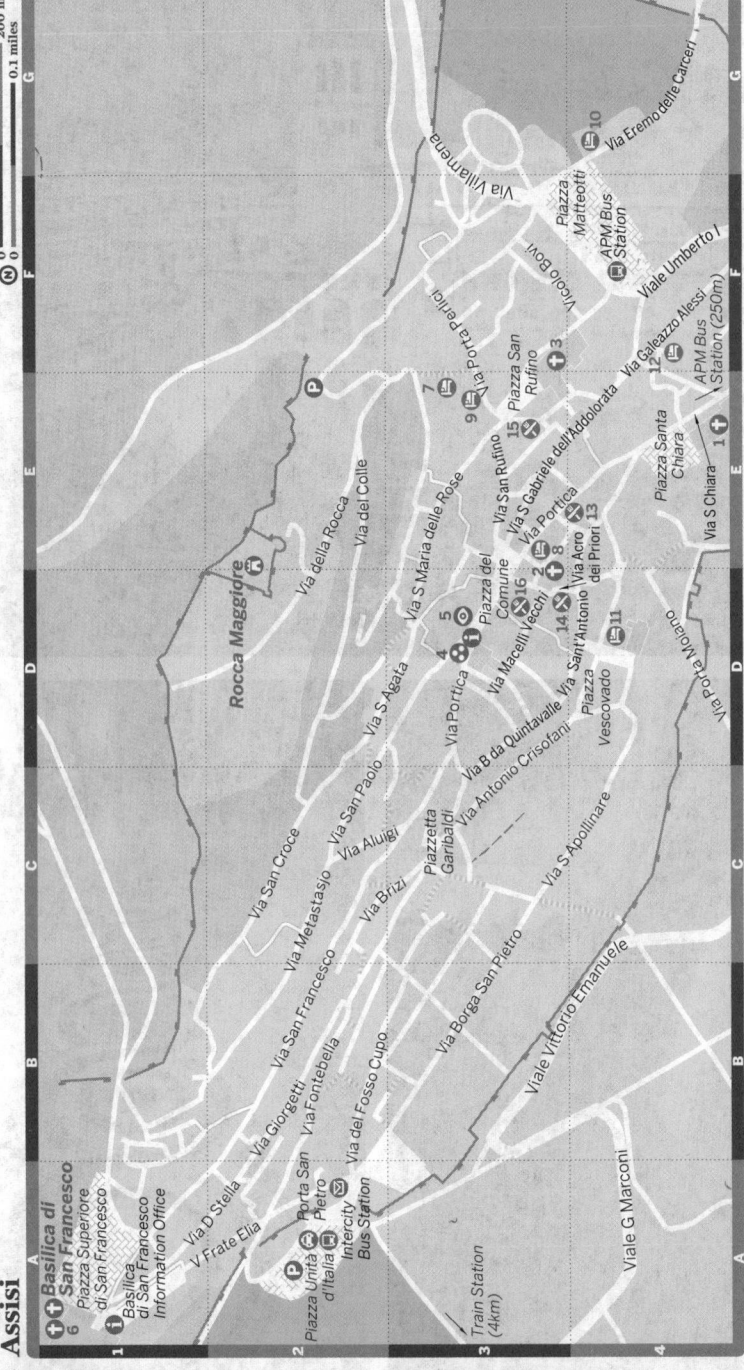

Assisi

Santuario di San Damiano   CHURCH
(☑075 81 22 73; ◷10am-noon & 2-6pm summer, 10am-noon & 2-4.30pm winter, vespers 7pm summer, 5pm winter) It's a 1.5km olive tree–lined stroll to the church where St Francis first heard the voice of God and where he wrote his *Canticle of the Creatures*. The serene surroundings are popular with pilgrims.

Foro Romano   HISTORICAL SITE
(Roman Forum; ☑075 81 30 53; Via Portica; adult/reduced incl Pinacoteca €4/2.50, with Rocca Maggiore €8/5; ◷10am-1pm & 2.30-6pm summer, to 5pm winter) On Piazza del Comune, just round the corner from the tourist office, is the entrance to the town's partially excavated Roman Forum, while on the piazza's northern side is the well-preserved facade of a 1st-century Roman temple, the **Tempio di Minerva** (Temple of Minerva; Piazza del Comune; admission free; ◷7.30am-noon & 2-7pm Mon-Sat, 8.30am-noon & 2-7pm Sun), hiding a rather uninspiring 17th-century church.

Duomo di San Rufino   CHURCH
(☑075 81 60 16; Piazza San Rufino; ◷7.30am-12.30pm & 2.30-7pm, to 6pm in winter) The 13th-century Romanesque church, remodelled by Galeazzo Alessi in the 16th century, contains the fountain where St Francis and St Clare were baptised. The facade is festooned with grotesque figures and fantastic animals.

Chiesa Nuova   CHURCH
(☑075 81 23 39; Piazza Chiesa Nuova; ◷6.30am-noon & 2.30-6pm summer, 6.30am-noon & 2-5pm winter) Just southeast of the Piazza del Comune, the 'New Church' was built by King Philip III of Spain in the 1600s on the spot reputed to be the house of St Francis' family.

🏃 Activities

St Francis devotees and nature buffs will appreciate the plethora of strolls, day hikes and overnight pilgrimage walks leading into and out of Assisi. Many make the trek to Eremo delle Carceri or Santuario di San Damiano on foot. The tourist office has several maps, including a route that follows in St Francis' footsteps to Gubbio (18km). A popular spot for hikers is nearby **Monte Subasio**. Local bookshops sell all sorts of walking and mountain-biking guidebooks and maps for the area. The tourist office can help with brochures and maps as well.

Bicycle rentals are available at **Angelucci Andrea Cicli Riparazione Noleggio** (☑075 804 25 50; www.angeluccicicli.it; Via Risorgimento 54a) in Santa Maria degli Angeli.

🎉 Festivals & Events

The **Festa di San Francesco** falls on 3 and 4 October and is the main religious event in the city. **Settimana Santa** (Easter Week) is celebrated with processions and performances.

Festa di Calendimaggio   CULTURAL
This colourful festival celebrates spring in medieval fashion and starts the first Thursday after 1 May.

Marcia della Pace   CULTURAL
Europe's largest peace march began in 1961 and attracts more than 150,000 pilgrims the first week in October, who walk the 24km route between Perugia and Assisi.

🛏 Sleeping

Assisi has a phenomenal amount of rooms, which ensures good prices. Keep in mind that in peak periods such as Easter, August and September, and during the Festa di San Francesco, you will need to book accommodation well in advance.

The tourist office has a complete list of private rooms, religious institutions (of which there are 17), flats and *agriturismi* options in and around Assisi.

Nun Assisi
LUXURY HOTEL €€€

(075 815 51 50; www.nunassisi.com; Via Eremo delle Carceri 1a; s €180-325, d €220-480, all incl breakfast; P@) The latest addition to the Assisi hotel scene is also its fanciest. An elegant restored former convent, this has just enough of the original features to be charming, and just the right level of mod-cons to be luxurious. The rooms are beautiful, the restaurant a cut above and the spa is set within 1st-century Roman ruins (and it's not every spa that can say that).

Alla Madonna del Piatto
AGRITURISMO €€

(075 819 90 50; www.incampagna.com; Via Petrata 37, Pieve San Nicolo; d incl breakfast €85-105; Mar–mid-Nov; P) As beautiful as it is seemingly isolated, this *agriturismo* is less than 15 minutes from the basilica. Each of the six Moroccan- or Indian-themed guest chambers is truly a room with a view. But the real reason to stay here is the intimate cooking classes Letizia runs (in Italian or English). Start the day in local markets and finish it off with a feast of your own creation. Two-night minimum.

Ostello della Pace
HOSTEL €

(075 81 67 67; www.assisihostel.com; Via Valecchie 177; dm incl breakfast €15-18, r from €20; 1 Mar-8 Nov & 27 Dec-6 Jan; P@) Student groups, couples appreciating the handful of private rooms, backpackers and pilgrims all can find their bliss at Assisi's HI hostel. Beautiful and quiet, it's just off the road coming in from Santa Maria degli Angeli. Thrifty travellers will appreciate the dinners (€10.50), hikers will appreciate the boxed lunches (€7) and everyone will appreciate the idyllic setting.

St Anthony's Guesthouse
B&B €

(075 81 25 42; atoneassisi@tiscali.it; Via Galeazzo Alessi 10; s/d/tr incl breakfast €40/60/80; P) Look for the iron statue of St Francis feeding the birds and you've found your Assisian oasis. Rooms are austere but welcoming and six have balconies with breathtaking views. Gardens, ample parking and an 800-year-old breakfast salon make this a heavenly choice. Like most religious accommodation, it has a two-night minimum stay and an 11pm curfew.

Residenza D'Epoca San Crispino
HOTEL €€€

(075 815 51 24; www.assisibenessere.it; Via Sant'Agnese 11; ste incl breakfast €170-340; @) Rooms are medieval old but have been upgraded with armoire kitchenettes to become blissful apartment suites named after St Francis' *Canticle of the Creatures* – Brother Fire, Sister Water etc. It's a short stroll to the Basilica di Santa Chiara.

Hotel Alexander
B&B €€

(075 81 61 90; http://hotelalexanderassisi.it; Piazza Chiesa Nuova 6; s €60-80, d €78-140, all incl breakfast;) Right by the Chiesa Nuova, this has just a few rooms and they do vary in size. Try to get the one on the top floor, which is huge and has great countryside views. It can get a bit noisy at times owing both to the location and the sparse, modern decor (wooden floors, no rugs), which provides a nice contrast to all the carefully preserved antiquity all around.

Hotel San Rufino
HOTEL €

(075 81 28 03; www.hotelsanrufino.it; Via Porta Perlici 7; s €42-50, d €52-65, breakfast €4-5; P) With rooms in two locations (those at the **Albergo Il Duomo** round the corner are slightly smaller), this hotel is as quiet as it is comfortable. Stairs to the hotel can be tricky, but once you arrive at the San Rufino, a lift comes in handy. Sweetly decorated rooms all come with private bathrooms and TVs.

✖ Eating

Trattoria Pallotta
TRATTORIA €

(075 81 26 49; Vicolo della Volta Pinta; mains €9-16; Wed-Mon) Head through the Volta Pinta (Painted Vault) off Piazza del Comune – being careful not to bump into someone as you gaze at the 16th-century frescoes above you – into this gorgeous setting of vaulted brick walls and wood-beamed ceilings. They cook all the Umbrian classics here: rabbit, homemade *strangozzi* and pigeon. Slightly less traditionally, they also offer a three-course vegetarian menu for €25.

Medio Evo
TRADITIONAL ITALIAN €€

(075 81 30 68; Via Arco dei Priori 4; meals €33; Thu-Tue) Traditional Umbrian dishes are served in fabulous vaulted 13th-century surroundings, including lamb stew with artichokes (€13.50) and truffle omelettes (€11). The early 6.45pm opening time is geared for, and highly appreciated by, non-Italian tourists.

Gran Caffè
PASTRIES & CAKES €

(☎075 815 51 44; Corso Mazzini 16; ☺8am-midnight) This elegant place has the most fabulous gelati, mouth-watering pastries and cakes, and a great selection of drinks. Try the *tè freddo alla pesca* (iced tea with peach) on a hot day, or choose from a selection of delicious hot chocolates and coffee when the weather is cool. Remember it costs much more to sit.

Pozzo della Mensa
OSTERIA €€

(☎075 815 52 36; Via del Pozzo della Mensa; meals €30; ☺Fri-Wed) Just far enough off the main sightseeing routes to be more of a local than a tourist restaurant, this is presided over by two friends who serve up a small menu of regional favourites, such as *torta al testa* (try the sausage and wild greens), *crostini misti* and ravioli with white truffle sauce. A roof terrace opens in summer.

Shopping

Open-air markets take place in Piazza Matteotti on Saturday and Santa Maria degli Angeli on Monday.

ⓘ Information

Bar Sabatini Sandro (☎075 81 62 46; Via Portica 29b; per 30min €3; ☺8am-8pm) Internet access.

Ospedale di Assisi (☎075 8 13 91; Via Fuori Porta Nuova) Hospital about 1km southeast of Porta Nuova.

Police station (☎075 81 28 20; Piazza del Comune)

Post office Porta Nuova (☺8am-1.30pm Mon-Fri, 8am-12.30pm Sat); Porta San Pietro (☺8.10am-6.30pm Mon-Fri, 8am-1pm Sat & Sun)

Tourist office (☎075 813 86 80; www.assisi.regioneumbria.eu; Piazza del Comune 22; ☺8am-2pm & 3-6pm Mon-Sat, 10am-1pm & 2-5pm Sun summer, 9am-1pm Sun winter) Also has a branch outside Porta Nuova open Easter to October.

ⓘ Getting There & Around

BUS APM (☎800 512141; www.apmperugia.it) buses run to Perugia (€3.20, 45 minutes, nine daily) and Gubbio (€5.50, 70 minutes, 11 daily) from Piazza Matteotti. **Sulga** (☎800 099661; www.sulga.it) buses leave from Porta San Pietro for Florence (€11, 2½ hours, one daily at 7am) and Rome's Stazione Tiburtina (€16.50, 3¼ hours, three daily).

CAR & MOTORCYCLE From Perugia take the SS75, exit at Ospedalicchio and follow the signs.

In town, daytime parking is all but banned. Six car parks dot the city walls, where you can leave your car for €1.60/12 per hour/day; they are connected to the centre by orange shuttle buses.

TAXI For a cab, call ☎075 81 31 00.

TRAIN Assisi is on the Foligno–Terontola train line with regular services to Perugia (€2.50, 30 minutes, hourly). You can change at Terontola for Florence (€11.75 to €19, 1¾ to 2¾ hours, hourly) and at Foligno for Rome (€9.40 to €14.30, two to 2½ hours, hourly). Assisi train station is 4km west in Santa Maria degli Angeli; shuttle bus C (€1) runs between the train station and Piazza Matteotti every 30 minutes. Buy tickets from the station *tabacchi* or in town.

Spello
POP 8673

Sometimes it seems like it's just not possible for the next Umbrian town to be any prettier than the last. And then you visit Spello. It's often passed by as tourists head to nearby Assisi or Perugia, but the proliferation of arched stone walkways and hanging flowerpots make it well worth a visit, especially in spring when the whole bloomin' town smells of flowers.

Sights

Spello isn't known for any one sight; a leisurely stroll is the best way to see the town. Begin at **Porta Consolare**, which dates from Roman times, then head towards Piazza Matteotti, the heart of Spello, where the impressive 12th-century **Chiesa di Santa Maria Maggiore** (Piazza Matteotti; ☺8.30am-12.30pm & 3-7pm Mar-Oct, to 6pm Nov-Feb) houses the town's real treat. In its **Cappella Baglioni**, Pinturicchio's beautiful frescoes of the life of Christ are in the right-hand corner as you enter. Even the floor, dating from 1566, is a masterpiece. Stay in the same piazza for the gloomier **Chiesa di Sant'Andrea** (Piazza Matteotti; ☺8am-7pm), where you can admire Pinturicchio's *Madonna with Child and Saints*.

To see the view of all views, head up past the **Arco Romano** to the **Chiesa di San Severino**. The active Capuchin monastery is closed to the public but its exterior Romanesque facade is so stunning you'll have trouble deciding whether you'd like to gaze at its architecture or the bucolic countryside view below.

★ Festivals & Events

Corpus Domini
RELIGIOUS

The people of Spello celebrate this feast in June (the Sunday 60 days after Easter) by skilfully decorating stretches of the main street with fresh flowers in colourful designs. Come on the Saturday evening before the Sunday procession to see the floral fantasies being laid out (from about 8.30pm). The Corpus procession begins at 11am on Sunday.

⏚ Sleeping

Hotel Ristorante La Bastiglia
HOTEL €€

(☎0742 65 12 77; www.labastiglia.com; Via Salnitraria 15; s €80-105, d €80-155, all incl breakfast; P✳☎⛱) Welcoming well-heeled pilgrims, bicyclists and tour participants for decades, it has three classes of rooms that open the stunning grounds to the travelling public, all of whom enjoy seasonal breakfast (Italian style) on the terrace. The restaurant is one of Umbria's best.

Del Prato Paolucci
B&B €

(☎0742 30 10 18; www.hoteldelpratopaolucci.it; Via Brodolini 4; s/d/tr incl breakfast €40/60/80; P⛱) This modest family-run spot just outside the centre offers a reasonable level of comfort and a swimming pool in summer. Plus, you'll have a perfectly acceptable bathroom, TV and phone, and a few rooms have views.

Residence San Jacopo
APARTMENT €

(☎0742 30 12 60, 333 2232899; www.residence sanjacopo.com, in Italian; Via Borgo di Via Giulia 1; apt for 2/3 people €75/105) This holiday house saw its first incarnation in 1296 as the hospice of San Jacopo, a way station for pilgrims heading to Santiago de Compostela in Galicia. Ten mini-apartments feature a kitchenette, bathroom and TV, and are furnished with rustic antiques.

✗ Eating & Drinking

Osteria del Buchetto
OSTERIA €€

(☎0742 30 30 52; Via Cappuccini 19; meals €25; ⏰Tue-Sun) Right at the top of town near the Roman arch – only the hardiest travellers make it up here – you eat at a raised platform while enjoying romantic views of the valley towards Assisi. The food is proudly local, and you're encouraged to take your time. Perhaps start with the bruschetta and move on to the *strangozzi* with truffles (or, if in season, asparagus), but be sure to make room for the speciality – grilled steaks.

Enoteca Properzio
WINE BAR

(☎0742 30 45 11; www.enoteche.it; Palazzo dei Canonici, Piazza Matteotti 8/10; ⏰9am-11pm Apr-Oct, 9am-8pm Nov-Mar) Umbrian wineries aren't usually open to the public, so one of the only chances visitors have of tasting several wines at once without breaking the bank is to stop off at an *enoteca* in town. And there's no better place in Umbria to do so than here, where for €30 you can try a half-dozen Umbrian wines while snacking on cheese, prosciutto and bruschetta.

ⓘ Information

Tourist office (Pro Loco; ☎0742 30 10 09; www.prospello.it; Piazza Matteotti 3; ⏰9.30am-12.30pm & 3.30-5.30pm) Has town maps, a list of accommodation options and walking maps, including an 8km walk across the hills to Assisi.

ⓘ Getting There & Away

CAR & MOTORCYCLE Spello is on the SS75 between Perugia and Foligno.

TRAIN There are services at least hourly to Perugia (€3, 30 minutes) and Assisi (€1.70, 10 minutes). The station is often unstaffed, so buy your tickets at either the self-service ticket machine or at the news stand **Rivendita Giornali** (Piazza della Pace 1). It's a 10-minute walk into town.

Gubbio

POP 32,985

While most of Umbria feels soft and rounded by the millennia, Gubbio is angular, sober and imposing. Perched on the steep slopes of Monte Ingino, the Gothic buildings wend their way up the hill towards Umbria's closest thing to an amusement park ride, its open-air *funivia*. During the holidays, the side of the mountain becomes the world's largest Christmas tree.

The small town is easy to reach by bus or car, easy to explore on foot and has plenty of good low-cost accommodation. Gothic architecture buffs shouldn't miss it.

⦿ Sights

Funivia Colle Eletto
LOOKOUT

Although the **Basilica di Sant'Ubaldo**, perched high up on Monte Ingino, is a perfectly lovely church, the adventure is reaching it. Take the **Funivia** (☎075 922 11 99; adult/reduced €5/4; ⏰9am-7pm daily summer, 10am-5pm Thu-Tue winter; ♿), surely the most fun you can have getting to church. While the

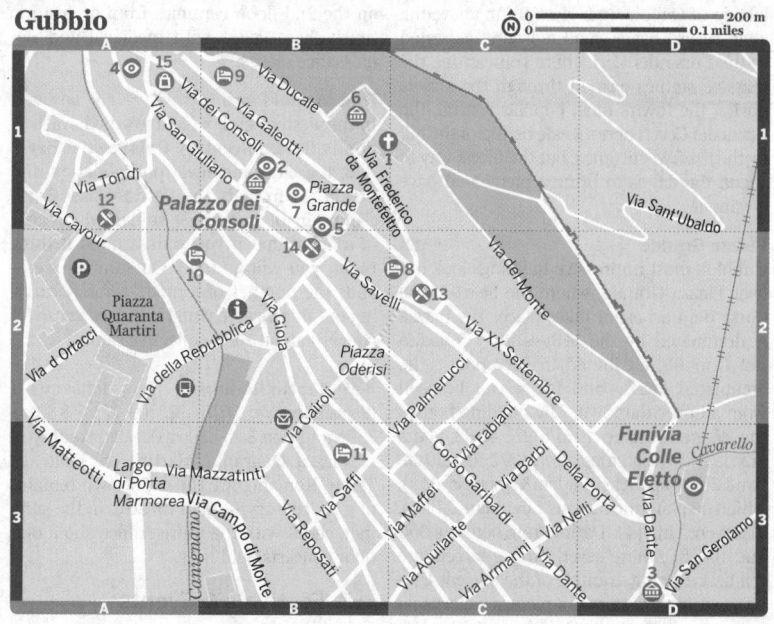

Gubbio

word '*funivia*' (and indeed the signs to it) suggests an enclosed cable car, the reality is a contraption like a ski lift that whisks visitors up the mountain in precarious-looking metal baskets. The *funivia* never stops during its operating hours (it's best to call ahead in poor weather, as hours can change), so in order to board you have to stand on a red dot and then get sort of thrown into a basket by the operator as it whizzes past – it's not

recommended for the old, the very young or the infirm. Once the initial disorientation has worn off, you can watch Gubbio – which moments before had seemed so impossibly hilly – gradually transform into a flat little toy town far below. The views from the top are simply stupendous.

The basilica, which can't help but come as a bit of an anti-climax after the approach, displays the body of St Ubaldo, the 12th-century bishop of Gubbio, in a glass coffin above the altar. It also has a small museum dedicated to the Corsa dei Ceri where you can see the massive statues carried through the streets during the town's most popular festival, the Corsa dei Ceri. There's a cafe on top of the hill by the *funivia* entrance, but the nicest way to spend the day is to bring a picnic and have a wander.

Piazza Grande   PIAZZA
Gubbio's most impressive buildings look out over Piazza Grande, where the heart of the Corsa dei Ceri event takes place. The piazza is dominated by the 14th-century **Palazzo dei Consoli**, attributed to Gattapone – its crenulated facade and tower can be seen from all over the town. The building houses the **Museo Civico** (☑075 927 42 98; Piazza Grande; adult/reduced incl gallery €4/2.50; ☺10am-1pm & 3-6pm Apr-Oct, 10am-1pm & 2-5pm Nov-Mar), which displays the famous Eugubian Tablets, discovered in 1444. Dating from between 300 and 100 BC, these seven bronze tablets are the best existing example of the ancient Umbrian script. Upstairs is a picture gallery featuring works from the Gubbian school, while downstairs – and accessed round the back – is a small archaeological museum. Across the square is the **Palazzo del Podestà**, built along similar lines to its grander counterpart, and now the active town hall.

Via Federico da Montefeltro   STREET
Walk up Via Ducale to the Via Federico da Montefeltro where you'll encounter a triumvirate of ancientness, beginning at the 13th-century pink **cathedral** (donations welcome; ☺10am-5pm), with a fine 12th-century stained-glass window and a fresco attributed to Bernardino Pinturicchio. Opposite, the 15th-century **Palazzo Ducale** (☑075 927 58 72; adult/reduced €2/1; ☺9am-7.30pm Tue-Fri & Sun, 9am-10.30pm Sat) was built by the Duke of Montefeltro's family as a scaled-down version of their grand *palazzo* in Urbino. Next door is the **Museo Diocesano** (☑075 922 09 04; ☺10am-7pm summer, 10am-6pm Mon-Sat winter, 10am-6pm Sun & holidays year-round), a homage to Gubbio's medieval history.

Museo della Mailoca a Lustro e Torre Medioevale di Porta Romana   MUSEUM
(Ceramic Museum and Medieval Tower; ☑075 922 11 99; Via Dante 24; admission €2.50; ☺10.30am-1pm & 3.30-7pm) Just below the Funivia Colle Eletto, this museum is dedicated to the *a lustro* ceramic style, which has its origins in 11th-century Muslim Spain. Up in the tower,

on the 2nd floor, ceramics from prehistoric times share space with medieval and Renaissance pieces.

Fontana dei Pazzi   MONUMENT
In the western end of Gubbio's medieval section is the 13th-century **Palazzo del Bargello**, the city's medieval police station and prison. In front is the **Fontana dei Pazzi** (Fountain of Lunatics), so-named because of a belief that if you walk around it three times, you will go mad. On summer weekends the number of tourists actually carrying out this bizarre ritual is indeed cause for concern about their collective sanity.

FREE Teatro Romano   HISTORICAL SITE
(Roman Theatre; ☑075 922 09 22; ☺8.30am-7.30pm Apr-Sep, 8am-1.30pm Oct-Mar) Southwest of Piazza Quaranta Martiri, off Viale del Teatro Romano, are the overgrown remains of a 1st-century Roman theatre. In the summer, check with the tourist office about outdoor concerts held here.

Festivals & Events

Corsa dei Ceri   CULTURAL
The 'Candles Race' is a centuries-old event held each year on 15 May to commemorate the city's patron saint, Sant'Ubaldo. It starts at 5.30am and involves three teams, each carrying a *cero* (massive wooden pillars weighing about 400kg, each bearing a statue of a 'rival' saint) and racing through the city's streets. This is one of Italy's liveliest festivals and has put Gubbio on the map.

Palio della Balestra   CULTURAL
On the last Sunday in May, Gubbio gets out its medieval crossbows for its annual archery competition with regional rival Sansepolcro. The festival carries over all year in tourist shops alive with rather scary looking crossbow paraphernalia.

Sleeping

Residenza di Via Piccardi   HOTEL €
(☑075 927 61 08; www.agriturismocolledelsole.it; Via Piccardi 12; s/d/apt incl breakfast €30/55/60; ☺closed Jan & Feb) Step through the arched gate into the romantic garden of this period residence. Share an amorous breakfast for two in the garden or cook up a simple dinner in the mini-apartment's kitchenette. Family-owned, the medieval stone building has cosy rooms decorated in cheery florals with all the basic comforts.

Bosone Palace
HOTEL €€

(☎075 922 06 88; www.hotelbosone.com; Via XX Settembre 22; s €56-74, d €80-130, all incl breakfast; P❄@) Fancy looking at a fresco during breakfast? How about staying in a room once frequented by Dante Alighieri? All rooms have minibars, satellite TV and phones in the bathroom, and many have gorgeous views of the surrounding valley.

Relais Ducale
HOTEL €€

(☎075 922 01 57; www.relaisducale.com; Via Galleoti 7; s €80-116, d €90-150) You'll need to be in shape, as this hotel is a stiff walk up the hill (and, as it doesn't have a restaurant, a stiff walk down again every night), but the accommodation is worth it. Set in a converted annex of the Ducale Palace, it boasts antique-strewn rooms and a terrace overlooking the Piazza della Signoria – perfect for relaxing after all that luggage hauling.

Città di Gubbio & Villa Ortoguidone
CAMPGROUND €

(☎075 927 20 37; www.gubbiocamping.com; Loc Ortoguidone 49; per person €6.50-9.50, tent €7-9.50, car €2.50, 2- to 4-person apt €36-100; ☉Easter-Sep; ☀) Just a few minutes from Gubbio's centre, this full-service, four-star campsite has a tennis court, Jacuzzi, pool and snack bar. Stunning apartments in an old stone manor house offer TVs, beautiful wooden furnishings and private bathrooms. July and August visits require a one-week stay. From the SS298, follow the signs for 3km to 'Agriclub Villa Ortoguidone'.

Ristorante Hotel Grotta dell'Angelo
HOTEL €

(☎075 927 17 47; www.grottadellangelo.it; Via Gioia 47; s €38-42, d €55-60; ☉closed 2-3 weeks Jan) While it is mostly a popular restaurant with all sorts of truffle dishes and a beautiful garden, the Grotta dell'Angelo also serves up a few basic rooms for rent.

 Eating

Ristorante Ulisse e Letizia
TRADITIONAL ITALIAN €€

(☎075 922 19 70; Via Mastro Giorgio 2; meals €32; ☉Wed-Mon) Taking over one of the town's most respected restaurants is never easy, but this place has done a fine job. In the stylish setting provided by a restored ceramics workshop, most of the food (including the olive oil and pasta) is either made in-house or (in the case of the mushrooms and truffles) sourced locally. It's a place to take your time and explore the menu (including the 500-item wine list).

Taverna del Lupo
TRADITIONAL ITALIAN €€€

(☎075 927 43 68; Via Ansidei 21; meals €45; ☉Tue-Sun) Il Lupo was the wolf that St Francis domesticated, and which supposedly came back to this restaurant to dine. He made an excellent choice. The atmosphere is sophisticated, if a bit stiff, and diners will feel more comfortable smartly dressed. Most ingredients are locally produced, including cheese, truffles and olive oil. The à la carte prices are steep, but it does set menus for €23.50, €27.50 and €29.50.

Ristorante Fabiani
PIZZERIA €€

(☎075 927 46 39; Piazza Quaranta Martiri 26; meals €28; ☉Wed-Mon) This is a fabulous spot to sit on a back patio and enjoy the garden for a few hours. The selection here is vast, including more than 30 pizzas, and there is a rotating €16 tourist menu. Stop in on Thursday or Friday for the fish specials.

🛍 Shopping

A weekly market selling all kinds of everything – including fresh produce, clothes and flowers – takes place every Tuesday morning on the Piazza Quaranta Martiri.

Leo Grilli Arte
ARTISANAL

(Via dei Consoli 78) In the Middle Ages, ceramics were one of Gubbio's main industries and there are some fabulous contemporary samples on sale in this crumbly 15th-century mansion.

ℹ Information

Hospital (☎075 927 08 01; Località Branca) About 2km from the city centre.

Police station (☎075 927 37 70; Via Mazzatinti)

Post office (☎075 927 39 25; Via Cairoli 11; ☉8am-6.30pm Mon-Fri, 9am-12.30pm Sat)

Tourist office (☎075 922 06 93; www.gubbio -altochiascio.regioneumbria.eu; Via della Reppublica 15; ☉8.30am-1.45pm & 3-6pm Mon-Fri, 9am-1pm & 3-6pm Sat, Sun & holidays)

ℹ Getting There & Around

Gubbio has no train station but **APM** (☎800 51 21 41; www.apmperugia.it) buses run to Perugia (€4.60, one hour and 10 minutes, 10 daily) from Piazza Quaranta Martiri.

By car, take the SS298 from Perugia or the SS76 from Ancona, and follow the signs.

Walking is the best way to get around, but APM buses connect Piazza Quaranta Martiri with the funicular station and most main sights.

1. **Pecorino (p36)**
Weekly morning markets take place at towns across Umbria.

2. **Barley field near Gubbio (p570)**
Soft olive- and vine-clad hills, jagged mountains and ancient towns, without the crowds.

3. **Old town, Perugia (p549)**
Although culturally modern, little has changed architecturally in Perugia for over 400 years.

FRANK WING / LONELY PLANET IMAGES ©

3

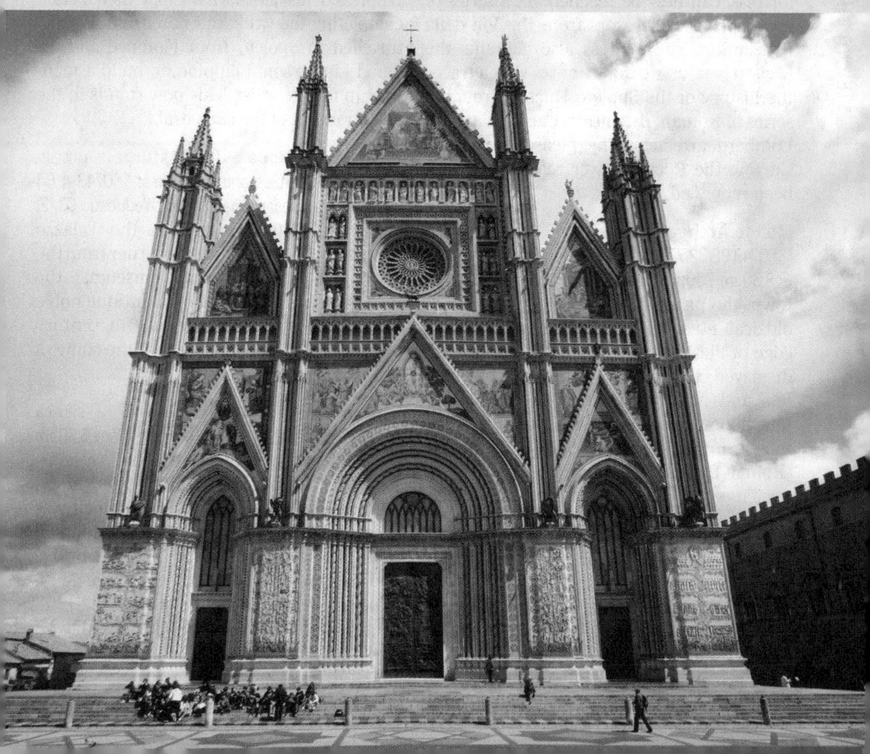

Spoleto

POP 39,339

Spoleto was once a typically sleepy Umbrian hill town until, in 1958, Italian-American composer Gian Carlo Menotti founded the Festival dei Due Mondi, now known around the world as simply the Spoleto Festival. Combining theatre, dance, music, spoken word and other art forms, the festival has gained a reputation as one of the best of its kind in the world and has put this town – historically important since Roman times and once the capital of the Lombardy Duchy and part of the Holy Roman Empire – firmly back on the map. However, even outside of festival season, Spoleto has more than enough museums, Roman ruins, restaurants and wanderable streets to keep you busy for a good day or two.

◉ Sights

Rocca Albornoziana   HISTORICAL BUILDING
(☑/fax 0743 22 30 55; Piazza Campello; adult/reduced €7.50/6.50; ☺8.30am-7.30pm Tue-Sun) Previously a long and rather arduous walk up the hill from the centre of town, the Rocca, a glowering 14th-century former papal fortress, can now be reached via a series of escalators and elevators from the Via della Ponzianina. The fortress also contains the **Museo Nazionale del Ducato**, which traces the history of the Spoleto Duchy through a series of Roman, Byzantine, Carolingian and Lombard artefacts. The pleasant walkway skirting the Rocca's lower reaches has also been reopened.

Museo Archeologico   MUSEUM
(☑0743 22 32 77; Via S Agata; adult/reduced €4/2; ☺8.30am-7.30pm) Down in the centre of town, the prime draw is the town's archaeological museum, located on the western edge of Piazza della Libertà. It holds a well-displayed collection of Roman and Etruscan bits and bobs from the area spread over four floors. You can step outside to view the mostly intact 1st-century **Teatro Romano** (Roman theatre), which often hosts live performances during the summer; check with the museum or the tourist office.

Museo Carandente   MUSEUM
(☑0743 4 64 34; Piazza Collicola; adult/reduced €4/3; ☺10.30am-1pm & 3.30-7pm Wed-Sun) Formerly the Galleria D'Arte Moderna, the town's premier collection of modern art has been renamed after its late former director

and noted art critic, Giovanni Carandente, and significantly revamped. The collection is dominated by works of late-20th-century Italian artists, including the sculptor Leonardo Leoncillo.

Casa Romana   HISTORICAL BUILDING
(Roman House; ☑/fax 0743 23 42 50; Via di Visiale; adult/reduced €2.50/2; ☺10.30am-5.30pm) This excavated Roman house isn't exactly Pompeii, but it gives visitors a peek into what a typical home of the area would have looked like in the 1st century BC. Just to the south, near the Piazza Fontana, stands the remains of the **Arco di Druso e Germanico** (Arch of Drusus and Germanicus, named for the sons of Emperor Tiberius), which once marked the entrance to the Roman forum.

Cattedrale di Spoleto   CHURCH
(☑0743 4 43 07; Piazza Duomo; ☺8.30am-12.30pm & 3.30-7pm summer, 8.30am-12.30pm & 3.30-5.30pm winter) The town's cathedral was initially constructed in the 11th century, utilising huge blocks of salvaged stones from Roman buildings for its rather sombre belltower. A 17th-century remodelling saw a striking Renaissance porch added. Mosaic frescoes in the domed apse were executed by Filippo Lippi and his assistants. Lippi died before completing the work and Lorenzo de Medici travelled to Spoleto from Florence and ordered Lippi's son, Filippino, to build a mausoleum for the artist. This now stands in the right transept of the cathedral.

Museo del Tessile e del Costume   MUSEUM
(Museum of Textiles and Costumes; ☑0743 4 64 34; Palazzo Rosari-Spadi; adult/reduced €3/2; ☺3-6pm Wed-Sun) Housed in the Palazzo Rosari-Spada, just round the corner from the revamped modern art museum, the museum holds a collection of antique noble finery from the 15th to the 20th century donated from the wardrobes of the some of the area's leading families.

Chiesa di San Pietro   CHURCH
(☑0743 4 48 82; Loc San Pietro; ☺9am-6.30pm summer, 9am-noon & 3.30-5pm winter) An hour-long stroll can be made along the Via del Ponte to the **Ponte delle Torri**, which was erected in the 14th century on the foundations of a Roman aqueduct. Cross the bridge and follow the lower path, Strada di Monteluco, to reach the church where the 13th-century facade is liberally bedecked with sculpted animals.

THE MARKET WEEK

Weekly morning markets selling everything (fresh local produce, hot food, clothes, shoes, flowers, household goods, antiques – you name it) take place at towns across Umbria, usually in the main square. They can be intense, densely packed affairs swarming with locals on the hunt for bargains, but are a great way to immerse yourself in the life and culture of the region. They take place between 8.30am and 1pm at the following locations: Assisi (Monday), Gubbio (Tuesday), Castiglione del Lago (Wednesday), Città di Castello (Thursday), Bastia Umbria (Friday), Todi (Saturday), Passignano (Sunday) and Spoleto (second Sunday of the month). Plan your trip carefully and you could visit a market every day of the week. These are complemented by a number of monthly antique markets, such as the one held in Perugia on the last weekend of the month. If driving, be sure to set off early as parking – though often free on market morning – can be difficult to track down once the commerce is in full swing.

✦✦ Festivals & Events

Spoleto Festival
ARTS

The Italian-American composer Gian Carlo Menotti conceived the Festival dei Due Mondi (Festival of Two Worlds) in 1958. Now simply known as the Spoleto Festival, it has given the town a worldwide reputation.

Events at the festival, held over three weeks from late June to mid-July, range from opera and theatre performances to ballet and art exhibitions, which take place in the Rocca Albornoziana, the Teatro Romano at the archaeological museum and the cathedral, among other places. Tickets cost €5 to €200, but most are in the €20 to €30 range. There are also usually several free concerts in various churches.

For details and tickets, contact the **Spoleto Festival Box Office** (☎800 565600; Piazza della Libertà; ⊙10.30am-1.30pm & 4-7pm Fri & Sat 1 May-24 June, 10.30am-12.30pm & 4-7pm daily 25 June-12 July) next to the tourist office or book online at www.festivaldispoleto.it.

🛏 Sleeping

The city is well served by cheap hotels, *affittacamere* (rooms for rent), hostels and campsites. Expect significantly higher prices during the festival.

Hotel Aurora
B&B €

(☎0743 22 03 15; www.hotelauroraspoleto.it; Via Apollinare 3; s/d incl breakfast from €55/80; 🅿@) Just off Piazza della Libertà, the bright yellow Aurora is very central and fabulous value. Staff are friendly and will help you plan your Spoleto itinerary. From a few rooms, you can enjoy a private balcony view over the Roman amphitheatre below.

Hotel Charleston
HOTEL €

(☎0743 22 00 52; www.hotelcharleston.it; Piazza Collicola 10; s/d incl breakfast from €59/79; ❄@🛜) With a sauna, fireplace and an outdoor terrace, the Charleston is an enticing location in both winter and summer. The 17th-century building has been thoroughly renovated with double-paned windows, parquet floors and handsome modern furniture. It's named after Charleston, South Carolina, the home of a sister Spoleto Festival. Parking costs €10.

Hotel dei Duchi
HOTEL €€

(☎/fax 0743 44 54 1; www.hoteldeiduchi.com; Viale Giacomo Matteotti; s €75, d €100-175; ❄) Next to a tidy park just outside the old town, this is a purpose build rather than a renovation. So although the rooms are a good size (and some of the bathrooms have bathtubs), it's not exactly reeking of old-world charm – think clean, well-equipped and professionally run. Its slightly elevated position gives it good views of the countryside and, slightly closer to home, the Roman theatre.

Ostello Villa Redenta
HOSTEL €

(☎0743 22 49 36; www.villaredenta.com; Via di Villa Redenta 1; dm €20-24, s €28-35, d €52-75, all incl breakfast; 🅿) Pope Leone XII slept here. Literally. The 17th-century hostel is set within a quiet park just outside the historic centre and comes complete with a bar, breakfast and private bathroom in each room. Reception is open 8am to 1pm and 3.30pm to 8pm.

Hotel San Carlo Borromeo
HOTEL €

(☎0743 22 53 20; www.hotelsancarloborromeo.it; Via San Carlo 13; s €30-45, d €60-90, all incl breakfast; 🅿❄@) It's not hugely atmospheric,

UMBRIA & LE MARCHE UMBRIA

Piazza della
Vittoria

Piazza
Garibaldi

Via Cacciatori delle Alpi

Via Flaminia

Viale Martiri della Resistenza

Corso Garibaldi

Via dell'Anfiteatro

Tessino

Via del Trivio
12

Anfiteatro
Romano

Via Salara Vecchia

Via Filitteria

Andrea
Largo
B Gigli

Via Viata S

Via Adriano Belli

Piazza
Mentana

Piazza
Pianciani

Via del Duomo

Piazza
della
Signoria

Piazza S
Domenico

Piazza
Collicola

4

Via Plinio il Giovane

Via di Fontesecca

Via A Saffi

Piazza
del Duomo

3

Via Matteo Gattaponi

Piazza
Sordini

9

5

Corso Giuseppe Mazzini

Via del Mercato

2

Piazza del
Municipio

Piazza
Campello

Rocca
Albornoziana

6

Museo
Archeologico

8

13

Via della Trattoria

Piazza del
Mercato

Via di Visiale

Via S Agata

7

Via delle Terme

14

Piazza
Fontana

1

Via Brignone

Via degli Eremiti

Via del Ponte

Piazza della
Libertà

10

Largo
Possenti

Viale Giacomo
Matteotti

11

Via
Benedetto
Egio

Via Monterone

Via Sant'Angelo

Via Flaminia

Tessino

To Hotel San
Carlo Borromeo
(250m); Chiesa di
San Pietro (450m)

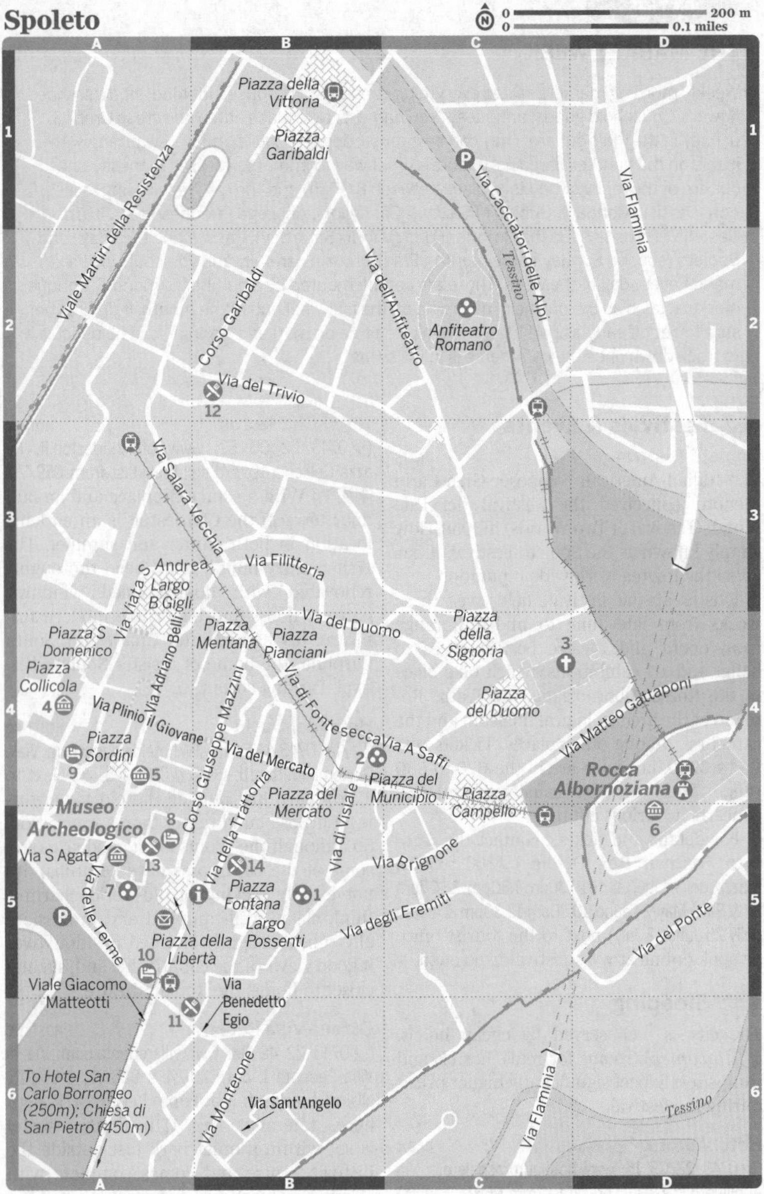

but the convenience, price and free car park make it a safe bet. The back rooms are quieter and have a view of the countryside around Monteluco, but all are clean, functional and spacious.

✗ Eating

Taverna la Lanterna   TRADITIONAL ITALIAN **€€**
(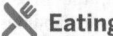0743 4 98 15; Via della Trattoria 6; meals €29; ⊙Thu-Tue) Popular with the locals – always a good sign – this informal little place is

Spoleto

hidden away on a gloomy backstreet. The mains consist mainly of various varieties of grilled meat (steak, pork chops, spicy sausages) and omelettes (with black truffles for €10). Watch the old ladies cooking up a storm in the kitchen.

Osteria del Trivio   OSTERIA €€
(☑0743 4 43 49; Via del Trivio 16; meals €28; ☺Wed-Mon, closed Jan) Strings of garlic and dried peppers grace the walls of this most homey of home-style restaurants run by a husband-and-wife team. This is a great place to try the *strangozzi alla spoletina* (local pasta in a tangy tomato sauce), and the stuffed artichokes are legendary.

Ristorante Apollinare   TRADITIONAL ITALIAN €€
(☑0743 22 32 56; Via S Agata 14; tasting menus incl veg €30-50; ☺Wed-Sun) California cuisine meets Umbrian tradition: somehow this restaurant manages to figure out that squid-ink pasta does go with pesto and crayfish, and rabbit feels quite at home in a black olive sauce. No matter what, save room for dessert. The menu changes seasonally but you are constantly enveloped in low wood-beamed ceilings and candlelight flickering against brick.

La Locanda del Passero   TRADITIONAL ITALIAN €€
(☑0743 67 06 51; Via Benedetto Egio 3/5; meals €40; ☺Wed-Mon) A recent addition to the restaurant scene, having replaced a much-loved stalwart, this clean, bright dining room does a mean line in fish, including scampi risotto, tuna carpaccio and a sea-food *frittura mista*. There's a good selection of wine and it offers a set three-course menu for €30.

❶ Information

Ospedale San Mateo (☑0743 21 01; Via Madonna di Loreto) Hospital.

Pizzeria Zeppelin (☑0743 4 77 67; Corso Giuseppe Mazzini 81; per hr €3; ☺10.30am-9.30pm) Internet access.

Police station (☑0743 2 32 41; 191 Via Marconi)

Post office (☑0743 20 15 20; Piazza della Libertà 12; ☺8am-6.30pm Mon-Fri, 8am-12.30pm Sat)

Tourist office (☑0743 23 89 20/1; www.visitspoleto.it; Piazza della Libertà 7; ☺8.30am-1.30pm & 4-7pm Mon-Fri, 9.30am-12.30pm & 4-7pm Sat & Sun Apr-Oct, 8.30am-1.30pm & 3.30-6.30pm Mon-Sat, 9.30am-12.30pm Sun Nov-Mar)

❶ Getting There & Around

SSIT (☑0743 21 22 09; www.spoletina.com) buses run to Norcia (€4.80, one hour, six daily).

Trains from the main station connect with Rome (€8 to €12.30, 1½ hours, hourly), Perugia (€4.80, one hour, nine daily) and Assisi (€3.24, 40 minutes, hourly). From the train station, about 1km from the centre, take city bus A, B or C for €1 to the Piazza dell Libertà (make sure the bus reads 'Centro').

By car, the city lies on the E45 and an easy connection via the SS209 to the Valnerina.

Norcia & the Valnerina

After all the thigh-challenging hill towns of western and northern Umbria, the flatter, less elevated prospects of Norcia, right on Umbria's eastern boundaries, can come as a bit of a relief. You'll still need to do something to work up an appetite, however, as there are probably more things to eat in Norcia than anywhere else in the region. Norcia is the cured-meat capital of Italy and its streets, particularly the main Piazza San Benedetto, are filled with shops selling all manner of acorn-fed pig products. Giant hams, salamis, strings of sausages and (as a marketing ploy rather than to eat) stuffed boars' heads are everywhere you look. In fact, the word 'Norcineria' has become synonymous with 'butcher' throughout Italy. The surrounding area is also one of the region's largest producers of the elusive black truffle. Suitably fortified, you can then tackle the town's other great draw – its proximity to the glorious Monti Sibillini, which many consider the most beautiful area in the region. We heartily agree. Although near impossible to reach by public transport (the nearest train station is in Spoleto), those with a car could easily fill an entire week here. Almost as scenic is Norcia's own valley, the Valnerina, which is best explored on a meandering drive along the SS209.

✴✴ Festivals & Events

Mostra Mercato del Tartufo Nero   FOOD

(www.neronorcia.it) Truffle lovers, foodies and mooches should head to Norcia on the last weekend in February and the first weekend in March to join thousands of visitors from all over the world as they sift through dozens of booths, tasting, of course, all things truffle from Norcia, but also candies from Sicily, cheese from Tuscany and other goodies. The entrance and most tastings are free and any gifts will be well loved.

🛏 Sleeping & Eating

Palazzo Seneca   HOTEL €€

(☎0743 81 74 34; www.palazzoseneca.com; Via Cesare Battisti 12; s €100-120, d €150-199; 🅿❄🀄) Sometimes you truly feel like you live in a palace, even just for a night or two. Perhaps it's as you play chess in an overstuffed leather chair in front of the fireplace or maybe it's while you're enjoying your Thai massage in the subterranean spa. Four-poster beds and marble bathrooms meld seamlessly with ancient stone walls, and the accompanying practically perfect Ristorante Vespasia means you never have to leave.

Hotel Grotta Azzura   HOTEL €

(☎0743 81 65 13; www.bianconi.com; Via Alfieri 12; s €39-86, d €59-113, all incl breakfast; ❄) This 18th-century *palazzo* with suits of armour in the reception offers fabulous deals during the week and in low season. Cross-vaulted rooms are stately if a bit dark, complete with carved ceilings and recently upgraded bathrooms. Its restaurant has been open daily for 150 years. It is a tad touristy, but the food is still excellent and comes in great piles of porcini mushrooms, sausages and prosciutto.

Residenza San Pietro in Valle   HOTEL €€

(☎0744 78 01 29; www.sanpietroinvalle.com; SS209 Valnerina km20; s €98-109, d €129-139, all incl breakfast; ⊙Easter-Oct; 🅿) Around 30km southwest of Norcia, this medieval convent beckons travellers with its historical charm and delicious cuisine. The rooms have been upgraded quite a bit since their days as medieval nunnery cells, but the stone fireplaces and breathtaking view over the cloisters are the same. Ask for hiking maps and activity suggestions, or start a leisurely morning with freshly baked bread and homemade preserves on the abbey's outdoor patio.

Ristorante Vespasia   TRADITIONAL ITALIAN €€€

(☎0743 81 65 13; Via Cesare Battisti 10; restaurant/lounge meals €55/32; ⊙lunch & dinner) Set in a 16th-century *palazzo*, the elegantly simple furnishings complement the understated gourmet cuisine. A simple organically grown egg is topped with a generous helping of Norcia black truffles, or locally grown saffron accompanies risotto and local pork. Herbs come from their own garden. In warmer months, dine in the garden to jazz or blues.

Trattoria dal Francese   TRATTORIA €€

(☎0743 81 62 90; Via Riguardati 16; meals €32; ⊙Sat-Thu) Perhaps it's its presence in many of the Italian 'best restaurant' guides that keeps this trattoria permanently packed (and often turning away custom when other places are struggling for trade) or perhaps it's the quality of the food, which is a cut above even for this renowned foodie town. It's in Norcia, so expect a menu packed with piggy products (salami, ham, sausages), truffles and cheese.

❶ Information

Casa del Parco (☎344 222 76 98; www.sibillini.net; Piazza San Benedetto, Norcia; ⊙9.30am-12.30pm & 3.30-6.30pm) Has tourist information about the area, including Monti Sibillini.

❶ Getting There & Around

SSIT (☎0743 21 22 09; www.spoletina.com) buses run to and from Spoleto (€4.60, one hour, five daily) and Perugia (€6.90, two hours, one daily).

By car, from Spoleto, take the SS209 to the SS396. The closest train station is in Spoleto.

Orvieto

Orvieto is placed precariously on a cliff made of tufaceous stone, a craggy porous limestone that seems imminently ready to crumble under the weight of the magnificent Gothic cathedral (or at least under all the people who come to see it). Just off a main autostrada, Orvieto can get a bit crowded with summer bus tours, but they're all here for good reason.

◉ Sights

Cattedrale di Orvieto   CHURCH
(☎0763 34 11 67; www.opsm.it; Piazza Duomo; admission €2, incl Cappella di San Brizio €3; ⊙9.30am-7.30pm Apr-Oct, 9.30am-1pm & 2.30-5pm Nov-Mar) Little can prepare you for the visual feast that is the Orvieto's cathedral. Started in 1290, this remarkable edifice was originally planned in the Romanesque style, but as work proceeded and architectural styles changed, Gothic features were incorporated into the structure. The black-and-white marble banding of the main body of the church is overshadowed by the rich rainbow colours of the facade. A harmonious blend of mosaic and sculpture, plain stone and dazzling colour, it has been likened to a giant outdoor altar screen.

The building took 30 years to plan and three centuries to complete. It was probably started by Fra Bevignate and later additions were made by Lorenzo Maitani (responsible for Florence's cathedral), Andrea Pisano and his son Nino Pisano, Andrea Orcagna and Michele Sanicheli.

Inside, Luca Signorelli's fresco cycle *The Last Judgement* shimmers with life. Look for it to the right of the altar in the **Cappella di San Brizio** (⊙closed during Mass). Signorelli began work on the series in 1499, and Michelangelo is said to have taken inspiration from it. Indeed, to some, Michelangelo's masterpiece runs a close second to Signorelli's work. The **Cappella del Corporale** houses a 13th-century altar cloth stained with blood that miraculously poured from the communion bread of a priest who doubted the transubstantiation.

Next to the cathedral is the **Museo dell'Opera del Duomo** (☎0763 34 24 77; Palazzo Soliano, Piazza Duomo; admission €4, with cathedral €5; ⊙9.30am-7pm Apr-Oct, 9.30am-1pm & 3-5pm Nov-Mar, closed Tue in winter), which houses a clutter of religious relics from the

cathedral, as well as Etruscan antiquities and works by artists such as Simone Martini and the three Pisanos: Andrea, Nino and Giovanni.

Orvieto Underground   HISTORICAL SITE
(☎0763 34 48 91; www.orvietounderground.it; Parco delle Grotte; adult/reduced €5.50/4.50; ⊙tours 11am, 12.15pm, 4pm & 5.15pm daily Mar-Jan, Sat & Sun Feb) The coolest place in Orvieto – literally – this series of 440 caves has been used for millennia by locals for various purposes, including as WWII bomb shelters, refrigerators, wells and, during many a pesky Roman or barbarian siege, as dovecotes to trap the usual one-course dinner: pigeon (still seen on local restaurant menus as *palombo*). Tours (with English-speaking guides) leave from in front of the tourist office.

Museo Claudio Faina e Civico   MUSEUM
(☎0763 34 15 11; www.museofaina.it; Piazza Duomo 29; adult/reduced €8/5; ⊙9.30am-6pm Apr-Sep, 10am-5pm Tue-Sun Oct-Mar) This fantastic museum opposite the cathedral houses one of Italy's most important collection of Etruscan archaeological artefacts – including plenty of stone sarcophagi and terracotta pieces – as well as some significant Greek ceramic works.

Torre del Moro   HISTORICAL BUILDING
(Moor's Tower; ☎0763 34 45 67; Corso Cavour 87; adult/reduced €2.80/2; ⊙10am-8pm May-Aug, 10am-7pm Mar, Apr, Sep & Oct, 10.30am-1pm & 2.30-5pm Nov-Feb) From the Piazza Duomo, head northwest along Via del Duomo to Corso Cavour and the 13th-century Torre del Moro. Climb all 250 steps for sweeping views of the city.

Chiesa di San Giovenale   CHURCH
(Piazza San Giovenale; ⊙8am-12.30pm & 3.30-6pm) North of Corso Cavour, the 12th-century Romanesque-Gothic **Palazzo del Popolo** presides over the piazza of the same name. At the western end of town is this stout little church, constructed in the year 1000. Its Romanesque-Gothic art and frescoes from the later medieval Orvieto school are an astounding contrast. Just to the north, you can enjoy towering views of the countryside from the town walls.

Museo Archeologico Nazionale   MUSEUM
(☎/fax 0763 34 10 39; Palazzo Papale, Piazza Duomo; adult/reduced €3/1.50; ⊙8.30am-7.30pm) Though not quite in the same league as the other attractions on the Piazza Duomo, the

UMBRIA & LE MARCHE ORVIETO

Orvieto

UMBRIA & LE MARCHE UMBRIA

N

0   400 m
0   0.2 miles

To Train
Station (150m)

Tourist Office -
Piazza Cahen

Funicular Station

Piazza
Cahen

Corso Cavour

Via Belisario

Via San Stefano

Via Roma

Via Postierla

Via Montemarte

Via Porcari

Piazza
Angelo da
Orvieto

8

Via da Orvieto

Via Solana

Piazza Marconi

Parco
delle
Grotte

Corso Cavour

15

Via Cavallotti

Piazza
XXIX Marzo

Via degli Orti

Via Nebbia

14 20

3

Cathedral

11

4

Viale G Carducci

Via di Loreto

Fracassini
Piazza

21

12

Museo Claudio Faina
e Civico

Tourist
Office

Orvieto
Underground

Via del Popolo

5

Piazza del
Popolo

6

17

7

Via Gualtieri

9

Via Lorenzo Maitani

Piazza
di Febei

Via della Misericordia

10

Via Angelico

Piazza Duomo

Via del Duomo

Piazza
Clementini

18

2

Via Pecorelli

Piazza della
Repubblica

Via Garibaldi

16

Via dell'Olmo

Via Magalotti

Via Malabranca

19

13

Piazza San
Giovenale

1

Via della Cava

Via Ripa
Serancia

archaeological museum nonetheless holds plenty of interesting artefacts, some over 2500 years old, even if the displays are a little bit jumbled and unfocused.

Chiesa di Sant'Andrea CHURCH

(Piazza della Repubblica; ⊗8.30am-12.30pm & 3.30-7.30pm) This 12th-century church, with its curious decagonal bell tower, presides over the Piazza della Repubblica, once Orvieto's Roman Forum and now lined with cafes. It lies at the heart of what remains of the medieval city.

 Festivals & Events

Palombella RELIGIOUS

Orvieto's most famous festival is held every year on Pentecost Sunday. For traditionalists, this sacred rite has been celebrating the Holy Spirit and good luck since 1404. For animal rights activists, the main event celebrates nothing more than scaring the living crap out of a bewildered dove.

For six centuries, the ritual has gone like this: take one dove, cage it, surround the cage with a wheel of exploding fireworks, and hurtle the cage 300m down a wire towards the cathedral steps. If the dove lives (which it usually does), the couple most recently married in the cathedral becomes its caretakers (and, presumably, the ones who pay for post-traumatic stress disorder counselling for the dove).

Umbria Jazz Winter MUSIC

Appropriately enough, this celebration of the coolest of musical styles takes place at the coldest time of year, from the end of December to early January, with a great feast and party on New Year's Eve to warm things up. Ask at the tourist office for a program of events. See p553 for details of the summer jazz festival in Perugia.

🛌 Sleeping

Orvieto does not lack for hotels, and visitors will benefit from the highly competitive pricing. It's always a good idea to book ahead in summer, on weekends or if you're planning to come over New Year when the Umbria Jazz Winter festival is in full swing.

Hotel Maitani HOTEL €€

(☑0763 34 20 11; www.hotelmaitani.com; Via Lorenzo Maitani 5; s/d €77/126, breakfast €10; ⓟ🛜) Every detail is covered, from a travel-sized toothbrush and toothpaste in each room to chocolates (Perugino, of course) on your pillow. Several rooms have cathedral or countryside views. Rooms are pin-drop quiet, as they come with not one but two double-glazed windows.

Hotel Corso HOTEL €€

(☑/fax 0763 34 20 20; www.hotelcorso.net; Corso Cavour 343; s €60-72, d €80-108; 🌐@) Set a bit further away from the cathedral than most other hotels, this is nevertheless an excellent choice. Several rooms boast wood-beamed ceilings, terracotta bricks and antique cherry furniture, allowing one to describe them as snug rather than tiny. The breakfast buffet is an extra €6.50 but it's worth it to sit on the outdoor terrace.

B&B La Magnolia
B&B €

(☑0763 34 28 08, 338 9027400; www.bblamagnolia.it; Via del Duomo 29; r €65-75, apt for 2 people €75) In the centre of Orvieto, next to a small cafe north of the Duomo (the sign is small and easy to miss), this light-filled historic residence has six delightful rooms, an English-speaking owner and a large shared kitchen.

Villa Mercede
B&B €

(☑0763 34 17 66; www.argoweb.it/casareligiosa_villamercede; Via Soliana 2; s/d incl breakfast €50/70; ⓟ) Heavenly close to the Duomo, with 23 rooms there's space for a gaggle of pilgrims. The building dates back to the 1500s, so the requisite frescoes adorn several rooms. High ceilings, a quiet garden and free parking seal the deal. Vacate rooms each morning by 9.30am or you'll earn the housekeepers' wrath.

Hotel Posta
B&B €

(☑0763 34 19 09; www.orvietohotels.it; Via Luca Signorelli 18; d with/without bathroom €56/43; ⓟ) A restored 16th-century palace it may be, but 'palatial' it is not. However, after a full renovation, the mustiness is (mostly) gone but the historical touches remain. Quiet garden-view guest rooms, breakfast on the centuries-old patio and a convenient lift bump up the quality. Its sibling, the Hotel Reale on Piazza del Popolo, is a bit grander (and a bit more expensive).

MAKING THE MOST OF YOUR EURO

The **Orvieto Unica Card** (adult/reduced valid 1 year €18/15) permits entry to the town's nine main attractions (including the Cappella di San Brizio in the cathedral, Museo Claudio Faina e Civico, Orvieto Underground, Torre del Moro and Museo dell'Opera del Duomo) and a round trip on the funicular and city buses. It can be purchased at many of the attractions, the tourist office, the Piazza Cahen tourist office and the railway station.

Eating

Ristorante I Sette Consoli
MODERN ITALIAN €€€

(☑0763 34 39 11; Piazza Sant'Angelo 1/a; meals €45; ⓨThu-Tue) With its inventive, artfully presented dishes, such as guinea fowl stuffed with chestnuts, this get foodies flocking in all the way from Rome and Milan. In good weather, try to get a seat in the garden. Reservations highly recommended for dinner.

Trattoria dell'Orso
TRATTORIA €€

(☑0763 34 16 42; Via della Misericordia 18; meals €32; ⓨWed-Sun) As the owner of Orvieto's oldest restaurant, Gabriele sees no need for such modern fancies as written menus, instead reeling off the day's dishes at you as you walk in the door (in either Italian or English, depending on how bemused your look). Go with his recommendations – perhaps the *zuppa di farro* followed by fettuccine with porcini – as he knows what he's talking about. And be prepared to take your time.

Ristorante Zeppelin
TRADITIONAL ITALIAN €€

(☑0763 34 14 47; Via Garibaldi 28; meals €36; ⓨMon-Sat, lunch Sun) This natty place has a cool 1920s atmosphere, jazz on the stereo and a long wooden bar where Ingrid Bergman would have felt right at home. It serves creative Umbrian food, including well-priced tasting menus for vegetarians (€25) and children (€18), as well as a set Etruscan menu (€32). Ask about its day-long cooking courses.

Le Grotte del Funaro
TRADITIONAL ITALIAN €€

(☑0763 34 32 76; Via Ripa Serancia 41; meals €35; ⓨTue-Sun) Orvieto's numerous cellars cut out of the soft tufa have played a variety of roles over the years – as wartime hideouts, wine stores and even pigeon coops. Today they are being put to new uses, and none better than here where a wide range of pizzas (€6 to €8.50) and traditional Umbrian dishes, such as Chianina beef with balsamic vinegar, are served in a cool, elegant space.

Cantina Foresi
WINE BAR €

(☑/fax 0763 34 16 11; Piazza Duomo 2; snacks from €4.50; ⓨ9.30am-7.30pm) This family-run *enoteca* and cafe serves up panini and sausages, washed down with dozens of local wines from the ancient cellar.

ORVIETO'S WINE COUNTRY

Now famed for its white DOC vintages, the Orvieto region's wine-growing potential was first spotted by the Etruscans more than 2000 years ago. They were attracted not just by the ideal soil and climate, but also by the soft tufa rock that underpins much of the landscape from which deep cool cellars could be (and indeed still are) cut to allow the grapes to ferment. From the Middle Ages onwards, Orvieto became known across Italy and beyond for its super-sweet gold-coloured wines. Today these have largely given way to drier vintages, such as Orvieto and Orvieto Classico.

If you want to see (and more importantly taste) what the fuss is about, head to Orvieto's **Enoteca Regionale dell'Umbria** (☑0763 34 18 18; www.ilpalazzodelgusto.it; Via Ripa Serancia I 16; ⏰11am-1pm & 5-7pm Mon-Fri summer, 11am-1pm & 3-5pm winter) in the Palazzo del Gusto where you can sample a huge range of wines for between €8 and €30.

If you really want to immerse yourself in the world of viticulture, you could spend a night or two at the **Locanda Palazzone** (☑0763 39 36 18; www.locandapalazzone.com; Loc Rocca Ripesena; d €45-105; P@🐕), a highly respected winery a few kilometres outside Orvieto that also rents out rather good rooms in a restored medieval farmhouse.

Sosta   TRADITIONAL ITALIAN €
(☑0763 34 30 25; Corso Cavour 100a; pizzas €4.50-7) This extremely simple self-service *(tavola calda)* restaurant rustles up decent pizza, pasta and panini, with dishes changing throughout the week according to a set schedule. Two mains and a side dish go for €9.50 (or €8.50 if you're a student).

Pasqualetti   GELATERIA €
(☑0763 34 10 34; Piazza Duomo 14) This gelateria serves mouth-watering gelato, plus there are plenty of tables on the piazza for you to gaze at the magnificence of the cathedral while you gobble.

 Drinking

Vinosus   WINE BAR
(Piazza Duomo 15; meals €35; ⏰Tue-Sun) In photo-op range of the cathedral's northwest wall is this wine bar and eatery. Try the cheese platter with local honey and pears (€8) for an elegant addition to wine. Open until the wee hours.

☆ **Entertainment**

Teatro Mancinelli   THEATRE
(☑0763 34 04 22; Corso Cavour 122; adult/reduced €2/1, tickets €15-60; ⏰10am-1pm & 4-7pm Mon-Sat, 4-8pm Sun) The theatre plays host to Umbria Jazz in winter but offers everything from ballet and opera to folk music and Pink Floyd tributes throughout the year. If you're not able to catch a performance, it's worth a visit to see the allegorical frescoes and tufa walls.

 Information

Farmacia del Moro (☑0763 34 41 00; Corso Cavour 89; ⏰9am-1pm & 4.30-7.30pm Mon-Sat) Posts 24-hour pharmacy information.

Ospedale (☑0763 30 71) Hospital in the Ciconia area, east of the train station.

Police station (☑0763 3 92 11; Piazza Cahen)

Post office (☑0763 3 98 31; Via Largo M Ravelli; ⏰8.10am-6pm Mon-Fri, 8.10am-12.30pm Sat)

Tourist office Piazza Duomo (☑0763 34 17 72; info@iat.orvieto.tr.it; Piazza Duomo 24; ⏰8.15am-1.50pm & 4-7pm Mon-Fri, 10am-1pm & 3-6pm Sat, Sun & holidays); Piazza Cahen (☑0763 34 01 68; ⏰9am-4pm summer) In summer, you can buy funicular, bus and Carta Unica tickets here.

 Getting There & Away

BUS Bargagli (☑057 778 62 23) runs a daily bus service to Rome's Tiburtina station (€8, one hour and 20 minutes, 8.10am and 7.10pm on Sunday). Buses depart from the station on Piazza Cahen, stopping at the train station.

TRAIN Connections include Rome (€7.10 to €14.50, 1¼ hours, hourly), Florence (€11.20 to €19, 1½ to 2½ hours, hourly) and Perugia (€7, 1¼ hours, every two hours).

CAR & MOTORCYCLE Orvieto is on the Rome–Florence A1, while the SS71 heads north to Lago Trasimeno. There's plenty of metered parking on Piazza Cahen and in designated areas outside the city walls, including Campo della Fiera.

 Getting Around

A century-old **cable car** (€1.80; ⏰every 10min 7.05am-8.25pm Mon-Fri, every 15min 8.15am-8pm Sat & Sun) connects Piazza Cahen with the train station west of the centre. The fare includes a bus ride from Piazza Cahen to Piazza Duomo.

Bus 1 runs up to the old town from the train station (€1), ATC bus A connects Piazza Cahen with Piazza Duomo and bus B runs to Piazza della Repubblica.

For a taxi, dial ☑0763 30 19 03 for the train station or ☑0763 34 26 13 for Piazza della Repubblica.

LE MARCHE

Le Marche is Italy in microcosm: from the beachside resorts along the Adriatic through sloped hill towns in the centre and the jagged mountain range of Monti Sibillini. You'll want to pick and choose carefully, however. While Monte Conero offers an unhurried coastal holiday and Pesaro teems with history (and, from June to September, holidaymakers), much of Le Marche's coast is lined with rows of rather depressing high-rise hotels and apartment buildings, which in turn give way to the industrial functionalism of Ancona, the region's major ferry port.

It's further inland where Le Marche really shines. Urbino, perhaps Le Marche's most famous town to outsiders, boasts an impressive display of Renaissance art and history up and down its vertical streets. Ascoli Piceno is filled with a history rivalling any Italian city but remains relatively undiscovered. Equally walkable is the quaint Macerata, with a famous open-air opera theatre and festival. Covering its western reaches, and bleeding over into neighbouring Umbria, is the region's greatest natural wonder: the stunning peaks of the Parco Nazionale dei Monti Sibillini.

History

The first settlers of Le Marche we know much about were the Piceni tribe, whose 3000-year-old artefacts can be seen in the Museo Archeologico in Ascoli Piceno. The Romans invaded the region early in the 3rd century BC, and dominated it for almost 700 years. After they fell, Le Marche was sacked by the Goths, Vandals, Ostrogoths and, finally, the Lombards.

In the middle of the 8th century AD, Pope Stephen II decided to call upon foreigners to oust the ungodly Lombards. The first to lead the charge of the Frankish army was Pepin the Short, but it was his rather tall son Charlemagne who finally took back control from the Lombards for good. On Christmas Day AD 800, Pope Leo III crowned him Emperor of the Holy Roman Empire. However, he was never recognised as such by the Eastern Byzantine church, which had control of much of Le Marche's Adriatic coast at the time.

After Charlemagne's death, Le Marche entered into centuries of war, anarchy and general Dark Ages mayhem. In central Italy, two factions developed: the Guelphs (who backed papal rule) and the Ghibellines (who supported the emperor). The Guelph faction eventually won out and Le Marche became part of the Papal States. It stayed that way until Italian unification in 1861.

❶ Getting There & Around

Drivers have two options on the coastline: the A14 autostrada (main highway) or the SS16 *strada statale* (state highway). Inland roads are either secondary or tertiary and much slower. Regular trains ply the coast on the Bologna–Lecce line and spurs head to Macerata and Ascoli Piceno, but it requires some forethought and help from the tourist board to travel between inland towns.

Ancona

POP 102,521

A port town through and through, the main tourist draw of Ancona is leaving Ancona. Embarrassingly lacking in good accommodation, Italy's largest mid-Adriatic ferry port is trying to develop a tourist infrastructure. Although fairly grimy and tattered around the port and train station, the town does have a fascinating history, and a handful of sights to warrant an extra day or two.

Indeed, there are two distinct parts to Ancona: the front where you'll find the ugly, modern sprawl of the city's travel infrastructure; and the much more pleasant old town, just back from the water and rising up the hill. The part-pedestrianised and rather elegant *corsos* of Garibaldi and Mazzini are the main shopping and eating streets, and are where you should head if you've just got an hour or so to kill before your ferry. East of Piazza Cavour, the Corso Garibaldi turns into the Viale della Vittoria, which you can follow all the way to Ancona's artificial concrete beach, the Passetto, about a 20-minute walk away.

Sights

Chiesa di San Domenico
CHURCH

(☎071 20 67 04; Piazza del Plebiscito; ☺10am-noon & 4-8pm) Flanked by cafes, the elegant Piazza del Plebiscito has been Ancona's meeting spot since medieval times. It's dominated by this baroque church, containing the superb *Crucifixion* by Titian and *Annunciation* by Guercino. That gigantic statue in front is Pope Clement XII, who was honoured by the town for giving it free port status. The nearby fountain is from the 19th century, but head instead along Corso Mazzini, where you will see the 16th-century **Fontana del Calamo**, 13 masked spouts of satyrs and fauns designed in 1560 by architect Pellegrino Tibaldi.

Cattedrale di San Ciriaco
CHURCH

(☎071 5 26 88; Piazzale del Duomo; ☺8am-noon & 3-7pm summer, to 6pm winter) A hefty climb from Via Giovanni XXIII up Monte Guasco – or, if you don't fancy the exercise, a short hop on Bus 11 – takes you to Piazzale del Duomo, from where there are sweeping views of the city and the port. From up here, the ferry port looks almost picturesque. The cathedral sits grandly atop the site of an ancient pagan temple, with Byzantine, Romanesque and Gothic features.

Museo Archeologico Nazionale delle Marche
MUSEUM

(☎071 20 26 02; Via Ferretti 6; adult/reduced €4/2; ☺8.30am-7.30pm Tue-Sun, closed Mon except holidays) Up the hill above the port, the museum is housed in the 16th-century Palazzo Ferretti, where the ceilings are covered with original frescoes and bas-reliefs. Although not the most thoughtfully laid-out display, artefacts range from Greek and Etruscan back to the Bronze and Neolithic Ages.

Ancona's Arches
MONUMENT

North of Piazza Dante Alighieri, at the far end of the port, is the **Arco di Traiano** (Trajan's Arch), erected in 115 BC by Apollodorus of Damascus in honour of the Roman Emperor Trajan. Luigi Vanvitelli's grand **Arco Clementino** (Clementine's Arch), inspired by Apollodorus' arch and dedicated to Pope Clement XII, is further on, near Molo Rizzo. Head south along the coastal road and, after about 750m, you'll come across the enormous **Mole Vanvitelliana**, designed by Luigi Vanvitelli in 1732 for Pope Clementine. Just past the pentagonal building, on Via XXIX Settembre, is the baroque **Porta Pia**, built as a monumental entrance to the town in the late 18th century at the request of Pope Pius VI.

Teatro delle Muse
THEATRE

(☎071 5 25 25; www.teatrodellemuse.org; Via della Loggia) On Piazza della Republica, this ornate theatre was built in 1826 and has a neoclassical facade that melds with Greek friezes portraying Apollo and the Muses.

Sleeping

There are several cheap, bare-bones hotels near the station; it's a grimy area but busy enough to be safe during the day. If you want something a little fancier, you'll have to head into town.

Grand Hotel Passetto
HOTEL €€

(☎071 3 13 07; www.hotelpassetto.it; Via Thaon de Revel 1; s/d incl breakfast €120/195; P❋❀) Near Ancona's concrete beach, a 20-minute walk from the centre, the rooms all come with a combination of sea view, terrace, Jacuzzi or four-poster iron bed. Stroll to the *ascensore* to get to the beach or cross the road to the restaurant, one of the best in town. Substantial discounts can be had on weekends and around holidays.

Residence Vanvitelli
APARTMENT €€

(☎071 20 60 23; www.residencevanvitelli.it; Piazza Saffi; studio per night/week €65/375, 1-room apt €80/475, 2-room apt €95/575; P@) Tucked away in a tiny piazza a few minutes' walk from most of Ancona's sights is this comfortable, quiet and modern rental. All flats include kitchenettes, Sky TV (€5/10/16 per day/three days/week) and high-speed internet (€2/10 per day/week). The flat is cleaned twice a week and the bed linen is changed weekly.

Grand Hotel Palace
HOTEL €€

(☎071 20 18 13; www.hotelancona.it; Lungomare Vanvitelli 24; s €88-98, d €90-110, all incl breakfast; ☎) 'Grand' is a bit of an overstatement: 'convenient' or 'adequate' would probably be more fitting. The rooms are a little small and the decor and fittings have seen better days, but everything is clean and orderly, and it's well placed for the ferries (which you can watch come and go from the top-floor breakfast room) and exploring the old town.

Ostello della Gioventù
HOSTEL €

(☎071 4 22 57; www.ostelloancona.it; Via Lamaticci 7; dm €17) Ancona's HI youth hostel is divided into male and female floors with spotless

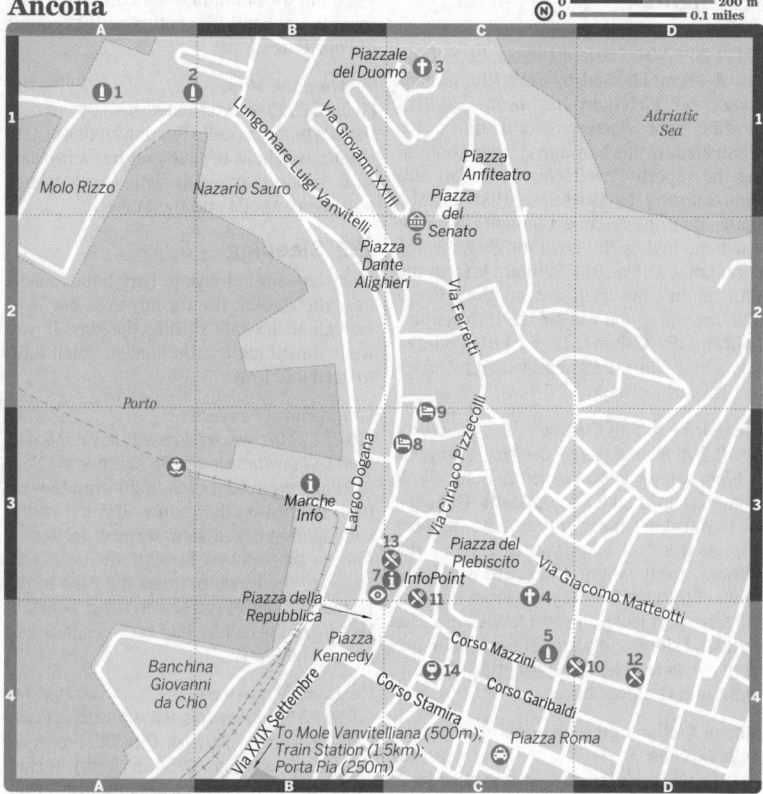

four- to six-bed dorms with separate bathrooms. What they lack in character they make up for in proximity to the train station and...well, that's it, actually. Open 24 hours a day.

🍴 Eating

Ancona is no Slow Food destination. The numerous eateries on and around Corso Garibaldi and Corso Mazzini are used to serving people hurrying either to get somewhere else or back to work. Restaurants can be fiercely packed at lunchtime (aim to arrive early) and queues at the various pizza-by-the-slice places can be long. *'Prossima, prossima!'* comes the hectoring cry of the harassed waiting staff trying to process the great wedge of hungry humanity.

Enopolis   TRADITIONAL ITALIAN €€
(☑071 207 15 05; Corso Mazzini 7; meals €40; ⊙Wed-Mon) A visit to this restaurant and

international wine establishment is worth it simply for the tour of the labyrinthine cellars of the 18th-century Palazzo Jona. With fresh fish as the main event (besides, of course, the wine), you can sit among contemporary art or next to an ancient well as you sample the fixed-price menus (€25 to €45) along with recommended wines for each course.

Osteria del Pozzo   OSTERIA €€
(☑071 207 39 96; Via Bonda 2; meals €36; ⊙Mon-Sat) The sea bass ravioli with zucchini and clam sauce (€10) alone deserves a trip to this Ancona favourite. Most locals go for the fixed-price multicourse offers, which range from €23 to €130.

Cremeria Rosa   ICE CREAM €
(☑071 20 34 08; Corso Mazzini 61) A cafeteria, bar and gelateria all in one, it's also on the main drag – perfect for people-watching while eating an ice cream (€2 gets you a

Ancona

cornet with three scoops). The adjoining place serves up pizza for €4.50 to €8.

Mercato delle Erbe   MARKET €

(Corso Mazzini 130; ⊙7.30am-12.45pm & 5-8pm summer, 4.30-7.30pm Mon-Sat winter) A picnickers' mecca, dozens of booths line this green metal-and-glass-enclosed bazaar. Freshly baked pastries and bread, locally produced cheese and meat, and everything else you would need for a picnic (including plastic cups) are sold here.

Drinking

Liberty Cocktail Lounge   BAR

(Via Traffico 7-10; ⊙11.30am-2am Thu-Tue, 5pm-2am holidays) Hidden on a back alley and identified only by a discreet sign (you get the feeling the owners don't want too many people discovering it), this art deco–inspired cafe would have made Picasso feel right at home. Asian-influenced art work, Tiffany glass lamps and a bohemian crowd will make you want to paint the scene and sell it as a framed poster.

Information

Farmacia Centrale (⊠071 20 27 46; Corso Mazzini 1)

InfoPoint (⊠320 0196321; Via Gramsci; ⊙10am-1pm & 4-8pm May-Oct) Tourist office for the city of Ancona.

Internet Point/Phone Centre (⊠071 5 42 33; Piazza Roma 26-27; per 15min/hr €1/2; ⊙9.30am-9.30pm)

Marche Info (⊠071 35 89 91; www.comune. ancona.it; Via della Loggia 50; ⊙9am-2pm & 3-7pm Mon-Sat) Within the ferry terminal; the tourist office for Le Marche province.

Ospedale Umberto I (⊠071 59 61; Piazza Capelli 1) Hospital.

Police station (⊠071 2 28 81; Via Giovanni Gervasoni 19) South of the city centre.

Post office (Largo XXIV Maggio; ⊙8am-6.30pm Mon-Fri, 8am-12.30pm Sat)

Getting There & Away

Air

At **Falconara airport** (Raffaello Sanzio Airport; AOI; ⊠071 2 82 71; www.ancona-airport.com) flights arrive from Dusseldorf, London, Rome, Madrid, Paris and Brussels. Major airlines include Lufthansa, Alitalia and Ryanair.

Bus

Most buses leave from Piazza Cavour, inland from the port (it's a five-minute walk east of the seafront along Corso Giuseppe Garibaldi), except for a few going to Falconara and Portonovo, which originate at the train station.

TO	FARE (€)	DURATION	FREQUENCY
Falconara airport	1.80	45min	every 45min
Jesi	2.60	45min	hourly
Macerata	3.75	1½hr	12 daily
Numana	2.10	45min	hourly
Portonovo	1.50	30min	9 daily Jun-Aug
Recanati	2.85	1¼hr	hourly
Senigallia	2.40	1hr	hourly

Car & Motorcycle

Ancona is on the A14, which links Bologna with Bari. The SS16 coastal road runs parallel to the autostrada and is pleasant, toll-free alternative if you're not looking to get anywhere fast. The SS76 connects Ancona with Perugia and Rome.

There's plenty of parking, which gets steadily more expensive the closer to the centre you get (€1.20 to €2.70 per hour). At the multistorey Parcheggio Degli Archi near the train station it's just €2 to park all day.

You'll find **Europcar** (⊠071 20 31 00) across from the train station and **Maggiore** (⊠071 4 26 24) 40m to the left as you walk out. At the airport, there are **Avis** (⊠071 5 22 22; www.avis. com) and **Hertz** (⊠071 207 37 98; www.hertz. com) desks.

Ferry

Ferry operators have booths at the ferry terminal or check with any of a dozen agencies in town. Ferries operate to Greece, Croatia, Albania and Turkey.

Train

Ancona is on the Bologna–Lecce line. Check whether you're taking a Eurostar service, as there can be a substantial supplement.

TO	FARE (€)	DURATION	FREQUENCY
Bari	37.50-51	4hr	8 daily
Bologna	13	2-3hr	hourly
Florence	16-34.50	3½hr	every 2hr
Milan	25-71.50	3-4hr	hourly
Pesaro	3.50	30-45min	hourly
Rome	15-33	3-4hr	every 2hr

ⓘ Getting Around

TO/FROM THE AIRPORT Conero bus J runs roughly hourly from the train station to the airport (6.05am to 8.15pm Monday to Saturday); bus S runs five times a day on Sunday and public holidays. The trip costs €1.80 and takes 25 to 45 minutes. From the airport to Ancona, line J runs until 11.30pm. The airport **taxi consortium** (☑334 154 88 99) can take you to central Ancona (€34 to €38) and Portonovo (€52 to €57).

BUS About six **Conero Bus** (www.conerobus. it) services, including bus 1/3, 1/4 and 1/5, connect the main train station with the centre (Piazza Cavour), while bus 12 connects the main station with the ferry port (€1.20); look for the bus stop with the big signpost displaying Centro and Porto.

TAXI Call ☑071 4 33 21 at the train station or ☑071 20 28 95 in the town centre.

Parco del Conero

Only minutes from Ancona but a world unto itself, Monte Conero is tiny but visually stunning. One of the only sections of unspoilt Adriatic coastline in Le Marche, this park encompasses 58 sq km, taking in Portonovo (9.5km south of Ancona), Sirolo (22km from Ancona) and Numana (a further 2km southeast).

Tiny Portonovo is its own mini-retreat, with a smattering of fancy restaurants and hotels. Sirolo is even more upmarket, surrounded by town walls with gorgeous ocean views, though it's not directly on the water.

Numana starts off well at its northern end, but slips into the tacky waterfront that the rest of Le Marche seems to favour.

🛏 Sleeping

Hotel Fortino Napoleonico LUXURY HOTEL €€€
(☑071 80 14 50; www.hotelfortino.it; Via Poggio 166, Portonovo; s €130-150, d €180-250, all incl breakfast; ✳@≊) One of Le Marche's most stunning beachfront hotels, this former Napoleonic fort practically begs for a romantic tryst. Its stone-built walls, antique furnishings and plush sitting rooms might be enough to bring you inside from the ocean-fronted terrace, and the gilded restaurant (open lunch and dinner daily; meals €50) specialising in fresh fish might make you linger even longer.

Rocco Locanda & Ristorante BOUTIQUE HOTEL €€
(☑071 933 05 58; www.locandarocco.it; Via Torrione 1, Sirolo; d incl breakfast €125-210; ✳) In town rather than on the beach, the elegant seven-room hotel above the eponymous restaurant feels more intimate than stuffy. Feather-soft sheets and period details like wrought-iron beds and stone walls make this a romantic town hideaway.

Camping Internazionale CAMPGROUND €
(☑071 933 08 84; www.campinginternazionale. com; Via San Michele 10, Sirolo; per person €5-11, tent €10-16, car €2-6, chalets & mobile homes €50-150; ☺Easter-Sep; @≋≊♠) Shaded in the trees just a few metres from the scenic beaches below Sirolo, this full-service campsite is replete with hot showers, caravan hook-ups and a children's playground. Free walking tours of the park are offered in summer.

✗ Eating

Some of Le Marche's best restaurants are in Parco Naturale del Monte Conero.

 Susci Bar al Clandestino SEAFOOD €€
(☑071 80 14 22; Via Portonovo, Loc Poggio, Portonovo; meals €38; ☺May–mid-Sep) Beyond cool, the Caribbean blue-coloured Susci Bar al Clandestino serves food that is highly recommended by Italy's food critics. There's no formality here and, after a swim in the beautiful Baia di Portonove, you can drop in for a taste of its Mediterranean sushi or some tapas.

La Torre

SEAFOOD €€

(☎071 933 07 47; Via la Torre 1, Numana; meals €40) Leave behind quaint stone walls and wood-beamed ceilings for open ducts and metal furnishings. Fight for a seat by the giant oceanfront window and enjoy freshly caught fish served according to your preference: fried, grilled or in a casserole. It also does a mean tiramisu. It's hugely popular with the locals.

Rocco

SEAFOOD €€

(☎071 933 05 58; Via Torrione 1, Sirolo; meals €35; ⊗Wed-Mon Easter–mid-Oct) This Slow Food restaurant is run by passionate young cooks who base their excellent dishes on the freshest ingredients. With a leafy outdoor veranda, it serves up, not surprisingly, many fish and shellfish meals.

Ristorante Acquamarina

SEAFOOD €€€

(☎071 739 08 70; Via Litoranea 209, Numana; meals €55; ⊗Tue-Sun Mar–mid-Dec) Even with all the stiff local competition, this beachfront establishment is generally regarded as one of the area's top seafood choices. Diners come from far and wide to sample its elegantly presented dishes. The mixed-fish antipasti provides a perfect introduction.

Il Molo

SEAFOOD €€

(☎071 80 10 40; Spiaggia di Portonovo, Portonovo; meals €30; ⊗Apr-Oct) If you can find it in the ocean within a few kilometres of Monte Conero, it's on the menu at Il Molo, where most items are courtesy of the fishermen who show up here each morning with their fresh catches. Expect various inventive combinations of pasta and shellfish.

❶ Information

Tourist office (☎071 933 11 61; www.parcodel conero.com; Via Peschiera 30, Sirolo; ⊗9am-1pm & 4-7pm mid-Jun–mid-Sep, 9am-1pm Mon-Sat mid-Sep–mid-Jun) For information on the park or to arrange guided tours.

❶ Getting There & Away

Buses from Ancona run sporadically throughout the year, peaking in July and August (see p589).

Urbino

POP 15,627

Urbino is most people's first stop on a trip to Le Marche, and it's not hard to understand why. The patriarch of the Montefeltro family, Duca Federico da Montefeltro, created

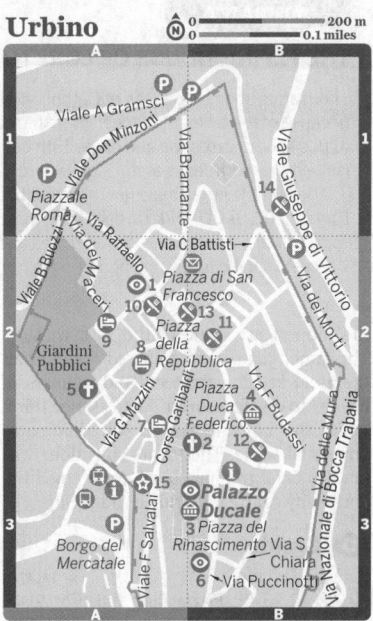

Urbino

Urbino

THE FLYING HOUSE OF LORETO

Thousands upon thousands of Catholic pilgrims travel to Loreto every year, possibly because of the belief that angels transferred the house of the Virgin Mary from Palestine to this spot towards the end of the 13th century, and possibly because they can't find glow-in-the-dark Jesus statues anywhere else.

The humble little house now sits within the gloriously OTT **Basilica della Santa Casa** (☎071 97 01 04; Piazza della Madonna; ⊙6.15am-8pm Apr-Sep, 6.45am-12.30pm & 2.30-7pm Oct-Mar), a riot of religious frescoes and gilt.

Loreto can be easily reached by train from Ancona (€2.05, 15 minutes, seven daily).

the hippest art scene of the 15th century. The famed art patron gathered together all the great artists, architects and scholars of his day to create a sort of Renaissance think tank. The university here still dominates any social scene. The town's splendour was made official by Unesco, which deemed the entire city centre a World Heritage Site.

◉ Sights

Palazzo Ducale PALAZZO
(☎0722 2 76 01; Piazza Duca Federico; adult/reduced €5/2.50; ⊙8.30am-7.15pm Tue-Sun, 8.30am-2pm Mon) A microcosm of Renaissance architecture, art and history, the Palazzo Ducale houses the **Galleria Nazionale delle Marche**, **Museo Archeologico** and **Museo della Ceramica**. The museum triptych is housed within Federico da Montefeltro's Renaissance palace, which is a work of art in itself, as the duke employed some of the greatest artists and architects of the Renaissance to create what was then a modern masterpiece.

A monumental staircase, one of Italy's first, leads to the *piano nobile* (literally 'noble floor') and the Ducal Apartments. Piero della Francesca was one of the artists employed by the duke, and his work, *The Flagellation,* adorns the duke's library. The collection also includes a large number of drawings by Federico Barocci, as well as works by Raphael, Titian and Signorelli.

From Corso Garibaldi you get the best view of the complex, with its unusual Facciata dei Torricini, a three-storey loggia in the form of a triumphal arch, flanked by circular towers.

Cattedrale di Urbino CHURCH
(Piazza Duca Federico; ⊙7.30am-1pm & 2-7pm) Rebuilt in the early 19th century in neoclassical style, the interior of Urbino's Duomo commands much greater interest than its austere facade. Particularly memorable is Federico

Barocci's *Last Supper*. The basilica's **Museo Albani** (☎0722 65 00 24; admission €3; ⊙9.30am-1pm & 2.30-6.30pm Wed-Mon) contains religious artefacts, vestments and more paintings, including Andrea da Bologna's *Madonna del Latte* (Madonna Breastfeeding).

Casa Natale di Raffaello HISTORICAL BUILDING
(☎0722 32 01 05; Via Raffaello 57; adult/reduced €2/1; ⊙9am-1pm & 3-7pm Mar-Oct, 9am-2pm Nov-Feb) North of the Piazza della Repubblica you'll find the 15th-century house where Raphael spent his first 16 years. On the 1st floor is possibly one of Raphael's first frescoes, a Madonna with child.

FREE **Museo della Città** MUSEUM
(☎0722 30 92 70; Via Valerio 1; ⊙9.30am-1.30pm Mon & Wed-Fri, 10am-6pm Sat & Sun) South of the piazza, the museum in the Renaissance Palazzo Odasi has displays on Urbino's history, including a scale model of the city (useful for finding your bearings) and various archaic signs.

Oratorio di San Giovanni CHURCH
(☎347 6711181; Via Barocci; admission €2.50; ⊙10am-12.30pm & 3-5.30pm Mon-Sat, 10am-12.30pm Sun) The 14th-century oratorio features brightly coloured frescoes by Lorenzo and Giacomo Salimbeni.

✱ Festivals & Events

Urbino has a full calendar of festivals.

In May, Urbino decks itself out in blooms for its annual flower festival, **Urbino Città Fiorita**. In June, **Urbino Jazz Festival** sees performances taking place all over town, followed by the **International Festival of Ancient Music** in July and the **Festa dell'Aquilone**, a kite festival, on the first Sunday in September.

Festa dell'Duca CULTURAL
The city goes all medieval on the second Sunday in August, when the town's streets become the setting for a costume procession and the re-enactment of a tournament on horseback.

🛏 Sleeping

TOP CHOICE Locanda della Valle Nuova AGRITURISMO €€
(☏/fax 0722 33 03 03; www.vallenuova.it; La Cappella 14, Sagrata di Fermignano; per person incl breakfast €56; ⊙Jun-Nov; P@☀) Ecology and comfort coexist in perfect balance at this working *agriturismo*. There are six rooms plus a couple of self-catering apartments, if you can resist the temptation of the cooked meals. Enjoy a horse ride or a home-grown truffle. It is about 20 minutes from Urbino, but the English-speaking owners will assist you with transport and visiting the local towns. Minimum stay is three nights.

Albergo Italia HOTEL €€
(☏0722 27 01; www.albergo-italia-urbino.it; Corso Garibaldi 32; s €50-70, d €80-120, all incl breakfast; ❀@) Set behind the Palazzo Ducale, the Italia could not be better positioned. Modern but well designed, the multistorey building is restfully quiet while offering all the amenities of a business hotel. In warmer months, take breakfast on the balcony.

Hotel Raffaello HOTEL €€
(☏0722 47 84; www.albergoraffaello.com; Via Santa Margherita 40; s €50-70, d €70-120, all incl breakfast; ❀) The imposing marbled entrance of this former seminary makes way for plain but comfortable rooms outfitted with TVs, minibars and radios. Some rooms have fantastic views of the palace.

Albergo San Giovanni HOTEL €
(☏0722 28 72; www.albergosangiovanniurbino.it; Via Barocci 13; s/d €39/60, without bathroom €29/46; ⊙closed 10-30 Jul & 20 Dec-10 Jan) Fittingly for a university town, these dormitory-looking rooms are good value for the price. Despite the slightly musty smell, beds are comfy enough and the shared bathrooms are clean. There's a decent restaurant next door.

Campeggio Pineta CAMPGROUND €
(☏0722 47 10; www.camping-pineta-urbino.it; Via Ca' Mignone 5, San Donato; per person €10-12, per tent €12-14; ⊙Easter-Sep) Only 2km from the city centre, this campsite is located amid luscious treed surrounds. Hot showers, a bar and market await campers. Take the shuttle bus into town.

🍴 Eating & Drinking

Don't miss Italy's only homicidal pasta – *strozzapreti* (priest stranglers) – available in most restaurants. One legend has it that the shredded pasta was designed to choke priests who would eat for nothing at local restaurants, so if you happen to wear the collar – be careful.

La Trattoria del Leone TRATTORIA €
(☏0722 32 98 94; Via Cesare Battisti 5; meals €24; ⊙dinner nightly, lunch Sat & Sun) This city-centre trattoria specialises in inventive Marchigiani cuisine such as ravioli with the local Casciotta d'Urbino cheese (€8) or baked rabbit with olives, bacon and sausages (€10). It offers a set menu for €20.

La Balestra OSTERIA €
(☏0722 29 42; Via Valerio 16; meals €24; ⊙dinner till midnight) Urbino's literati and university students congregate below a historical vaulted brick ceiling or outside at the convivial decking area. The food goes back in time as well, with medieval recipes a big hit. Try the speciality, *pappardelle del duca*, or the famous *strozzapreti*.

Antica Osteria de la Stella OSTERIA €€
(☏0722 32 02 28; Via Santa Margherita 1; meals €26) A modern update of a 15th-century inn once patronised by the likes of Piero de la Francesca, the de la Stella serves some unusual takes on traditional cuisine (such as lasagne with asparagus) and a delicious range of homemade breads in a simple, elegant dining space.

Osteria L'Angolo Divino OSTERIA €€
(☏0722 32 75 59; Via Sant'Andrea 14; meals €32; ⊙lunch & dinner Tue-Sat year-round & lunch Sun Jun–mid-Dec) This subterranean *osteria* just oozes atmosphere. Arched brick alcoves overflow with wine bottles, which are available for tastings. Even teetotallers will enjoy this place as the menu boasts simple but perfectly flavoured pasta specialities, including the much-better-tasting-than-it-sounds *pasta nel sacco* (pasta in a sack), which is fresh pasta coated with eggs and breadcrumbs.

Caffè Centrale CAFE €
(☏0722 24 48; Piazza della Repubblica; ⊙6.30am-2am) Popular with Urbino's students, this

is the best of the piazza cafes. Its outdoor tables get a relaxing dose of afternoon sun. Pastries, sandwiches and gelato are served any time of day, and *aperitivi* accompany late-afternoon drinks.

☆ Entertainment

Teatro Sanzio THEATRE
(☎0722 22 81; Corso Garibaldi) This grand old 19th-century theatre hosts plays and concerts, particularly from July to September. Pick up a brochure at the tourist office.

❶ Information

Ospedale Civile (☎0722 30 11; Via Bonconte da Montefeltro) Hospital 1.5km north of the city centre.

Police station (☎0722 3 51 81; Piazza Mercatale)

Post office (☎0722 3 77 91; Via Bramante 28; ☉8.30am-6.30pm Mon-Fri, 8.30am-12.30pm Sat)

Tourist information point (Piazza Mercatale; ☉6.30am-8.30pm) At the entrance of the lift into town.

Tourist office (☎0722 26 13; fax 0722 24 41; Via Puccinotti 3; ☉9am-1pm Mon-Sat, 3-6pm Tue-Fri) Pick up a free map and the miniguide *Urbino City of Art* for €5.

❶ Getting There & Around

BUS Adriabus (☎0800 66 43 32, 0722 37 67 38; www.adriabus.eu, in Italian) runs up to 15 services daily between Urbino and Pesaro (€2.80, 55 minutes) where you can pick up a train for Bologna.

CAR & MOTORCYCLE Most vehicles are banned from the walled city. There are car parks outside the city gates, including the main one at Borgo del Mercatale.

TAXIS Call ☎0722 25 50; shuttle buses operate from Piazza della Repubblica and Piazza Mercatale.

TRAIN There is no train service to Urbino (pick up trains in Pesaro, about 35km away). Locally, a land train service, **Tren Urbino** (€1.05), trundles its way round the main sights (pay on board). It's a bit cheesy, but worth it if you're beginning to get hilltop-town fatigue.

Pesaro

POP 94,799

Geographically the town of Pesaro is practically perfect. Its beachfront locale adds to the beauty of its winding, ancient pedestrian zone and backdrop of undulating hills. It's too bad that tens of thousands of Speedo-clad northern Europeans come here for five months out of the year to do a sardine impression on the beach, and that this beach is backed by a Soviet-looking strip of high-rise concrete hotels. However, the charming historical centre deserves an entire day to wander, and the composer Gioachino Rossini loved his home town so much he willed Pesaro all of his possessions when he died (be sure to check out Casa Rossini while you're here).

◉ Sights & Activities

In 1792 famed composer Rossini was born in a typical Pesaro house that is now known as the **Casa Rossini** (☎0721 38 73 57; Via Rossini 34; adult/reduced €4/3, incl entry to Musei Civici €7/4; ☉9.30am-12.30pm Tue-Sun, 4-7pm Thu-Sun Sep-Jun, to 10.30pm Tue & Thu Jul-Aug). Follow the history of Rossini and opera through the early 19th century via a series of prints, personal effects and portraits.

Opened in 1860 just after Italian reunification, the town's original art gallery is now the **Musei Civici** (☎0721 38 75 41; www.museicivicipesaro.it; Piazza Toschi Mosca 29; adult/reduced €4/2, incl entry to Casa Rossini €7/4; ☉10am-1pm Tue-Sun, 4-7pm Tue & Thu-Sun), which also showcases Pesaro's 700-year-old pottery tradition with one of Italy's best collections of majolica ceramics.

Pesaro has four major beach areas – **Levante**, **Ponente**, **Baia Flaminia** and the **free beach**. Levante and Ponente are the jam-packed hotel-fronted beaches on either side of the tourist office, so for more elbow room head to the free (open) beach to the south of the city, under Monte Ardizio.

⁜ Festivals & Events

Rossini Opera Festival MUSIC
(☎0721 380 02 94; www.rossinioperafestival.it; Via Rossini 24; ☉box office 10am-1pm & 3-6pm Mon-Fri) In honour of its most famous son, Pesaro hosts this festival round town each summer. Tickets cost anywhere from €10 to €125, with substantial student and last-minute discounts.

⌂ Sleeping & Eating

The majority of hotels close down from October until around Easter. Most places are square concrete blocks from the 1960s, uninspiring but close to or on the beach. For a room, contact the **Associazione Pesarese** di Albergatori (☎0721 6 79 59; www.apahotel.it, in Italian and English; Viale Marconi 57) or try the tourist office.

Marinella CAMPGROUND €
(☎0721 5 57 95; www.campingmarinella.it; SS Adriatica Nord km244; per person €6.50-9.50, per tent €5-7, per car €3-5, d bungalow €55-75; ☺Easter-Sep; 🄰) Drift off to the sound of waves breaking on the beach in your seaside tent. A casual restaurant is on site, as well as a market, beach volleyball, washing machines, showers and lots of child-friendly activities.

Felici e Contenti SEAFOOD €€
(☎0721 3 20 60; Via Cattaneo 37; meals €26; ☺Tue-Sat, dinner Sun) When a restaurant names itself 'Happily Ever After', you can bet you'll retire for the evening both happy and content. Its speciality is fish, but pasta also makes a memorable entrance on the menu. The atmosphere is more sophisticatedly urban than many other Pesaro restaurants and it's located on a quiet side street in the medieval centre.

☆ **Entertainment**

Teatro Rossini THEATRE
(☎0721 3 24 82; www.enteconcerti.it; Via Rossini) This theatre was renamed in the composer's honour, and its grand ceiling and ornate box seats make it a breathtaking spot to catch a concert, especially during the Rossini Opera Festival.

ℹ **Information**

Pesaro Urbino Tourism (www.turismo.pesarourbino.it) Has excellent information in English, with maps, hotels and sights.

Tourist office (☎0721 6 93 41; www.comune.pesaro.ps.it, in Italian; Piazzale della Libertà 11; ☺9am-1pm & 3-7pm Mon-Sat, 9am-1pm Sun summer, 9am-1pm Mon, Wed, Fri & Sat, 3-6pm Tue & Thu winter)

ℹ **Getting There & Around**

BUS The main bus station is on Piazza Matteotti. **Bucci** (☎0721 3 24 01) has buses to Ancona (€3.10, 1¼ hours, four daily) and Rome (€20, 4¾ hours). **Adriabus** (☎0800 664332, 0722 37 67 38; www.adriabus.eu, in Italian) runs up to 15 buses daily to Urbino (€2.80, 55 minutes).

TRAIN Pesaro is on the Bologna–Lecce train line and you can reach Rome (€17.05 to €43, four hours, nine daily) by changing trains at Falconara Marittima, just before Ancona. There

are hourly services to Ancona (€3.40, 30 to 50 minutes), Rimini (€3.30, 20 to 40 minutes) and Bologna (€9.50 to €12, two hours). The train station is on the western edge of town, about 2km from the beach.

Grotte di Frasassi

In September 1971 a team of climbers stumbled across a hole in the hill country around Genga, which upon further exploration turned out to be nothing less than the biggest known cave in Europe.

The **grotte** (☎0732 9 00 80; www.frasassi.com; adult/reduced €15.50/13.50; ☺10am-6pm Mar-Oct, 11am & 4pm Mon-Fri, 11am-6pm weekends & holidays Nov-Feb, closed 10-30 Jan) now has a 1.5km trail through five chambers where professional guides take you on a 70-minute tour.

Ancona Abyss, the first chamber, is almost 200m high, 180m wide and 120m long, which (as your guide will point out) would allow it to comfortably accommodate Milan Cathedral. However, the wonder of the caves is not so much their size, impressive as it is, but their contents – an undulating mass of glistening stalactites and stalagmites, some 1.4 million years in the making, which have an almost flesh-like quality to them, like giant candles of melting fat. The tour can be a little slow (sadly you're not allowed to wander off on your own), but the lighting is very well done. The whole area deserves an entire day, as you can also check out a Romanesque temple and enjoy one of many beautiful hiking trails.

To reach the caves from Ancona, take the SS76 off the A14 and look for the signs to the dedicated car park, 1.5km east of the cave entrance at San Vittore Terme. The car park is where you buy your tickets and catch the shuttle bus to the caves. The closest train station, Genga San Vittore Terme, is also next to the official car park and ticket office.

Macerata

POP 43,002

Macerata is well off the tourist radar, but offers charming hill-town scenery, great accommodation, one of Italy's most famous opera festivals and several days' worth of sights.

EXTREME CAVING

If the basic 70-minute tour through the dripping forest of stalactites and stalagmites at the Grotte di Frasassi leaves you hungering for something a little more challenging, you could sign up for a *Speleo Avventura*. This will up the adventure level considerably as you pass across 30m chasms and crawl on your hands and knees along narrow passages and tunnels. There are two versions: blue (easy-ish), which lasts two hours and costs €35 and red (hard, as you'll be going right into the cave's bowels), which lasts three to four hours and costs €45. Book in advance and happy spelunking.

◉ Sights & Activities

One of Europe's most stunning outdoor theatres is the Arena Sferisterio (☑0733 23 07 35; www.sferisterio.it; Piazza Mazzini 10; adult/reduced €3/2, shows €15-150; ◷tours noon & 5pm summer, noon & 4pm Mon-Sat winter), which resembles an ancient Roman arena but was built in the early 19th century. Between 15 July and 15 August every year it's a venue for the Stagione Lirica, one of Italy's most prestigious musical events, which attracts big operatic names.

The city centre starts at the Loggia dei Mercanti, next to the tourist office in the Piazza della Libertà. Built in the 16th century, the open-air building housed travelling merchants selling their wares to the area's villagers. Across the square is the Teatro Lauro Rossi (☑0733 23 35 08; www.sferisterio.it; Piazza della Libertà 21; admission from €10; ◷tours 9am-1pm & 5-8pm Mon-Fri), an elegant theatre built in 1774 for the musical enjoyment of the nobility, which now allows well-dressed riff-raff to attend. It's operated by the same management as the Sferisterio.

Macerata's main museums have recently moved home from the Palazzo Ricci to the Palazzo Buonaccorsi just down the road and have been renamed the Musei Civici di Palazzo Buonaccorsi (☑0733 25 63 61; www.maceratamusei.it; Via Don Minzoni 24; admission free; ◷9am-1pm & 4-7.30pm Tue-Sat, 9am-1pm Sun). The collections are now spread over three floors. On the ground floor is the Museo delle Carozza (carriage museum) housing an extensive collection of 18th- to 20th-century coaches. Above this, on the

1st floor, is the city's Arte Antica collection, with works dating from the 13th to the 19th centuries, while the 2nd floor is dedicated to Arte Moderna, with several rooms given over to the painter Ivo Pannaggi as well as Macerata's 'Secondo Futurismo' movement of the 1930s.

🛏 Sleeping

Albergo Arena   HOTEL €

(☑0733 23 09 31; www.albergoarena.com; Vicolo Sferisterio 16; s €45-65, d €65-95, all incl breakfast; P✱) Serving one of the best breakfasts of any three-star hotel around, Arena has a beautiful display of fresh fruit, juice and pastries. Comfortable rooms include spotless bathrooms with hairdryer and towel warmer.

Hotel Arcadia   HOTEL €

(☑0733 23 59 61; www.harcadia.it; Via Matteo Ricci 134; s €40-65, d €65-95, all incl breakfast; P✱) Owned by the Albergo Arena folks but a step up in comfort, this business-bland hotel on a quiet street not far from the cathedral gives three-star comfort at very reasonable prices. All come with 'frigobar', and a few have minibalconies over the cobblestone streets below.

Hotel Claudiani   HOTEL €€

(☑0733 26 14 00; www.hotelclaudiani.it; Via Ulissi 8; s/d incl breakfast €70/105; P🛜) Macerata's only four-star hotel is tucked into a quiet side street, just a stone's throw from the heartbeat of the historical centre. Although laid out for efficient business travellers, the building is a recently restored *palazzo* of the noble Claudiani family.

✖ Eating & Drinking

Da Secondo   TRATTORIA €€

(☑0733 26 09 12; Via Pescheria Vecchia 26/28; meals €36; ◷Tue-Sun) At *the* place in Macerata to try the local cuisine, you can follow the town's history through both photos covering the walls and the regional ingredients in your meal: *pecorino* (sheep's-milk cheese), *tartufo* (truffles) and osso buco with porcini mushrooms. In summer dine on the romantic outdoor terrace. Its famed warm chocolate torte caps off a perfect meal.

Osteria dei Fiori   OSTERIA €

(☑0733 26 01 42; Via Lauro Rossi 61; meals €23; ◷Mon-Sat) For an atmosphere that is subdued, warm and homey, this is the place. Try the typical *maceratese* cuisine and, in the warmer months, sit outside on the welcoming patio.

Caffè Venanzetti CAFE €

(☏0733 23 60 55; Galleria Scipione, Via Gramsci 21/23) Locals have assured us this is the best coffee shop in town. High ceilings and an old-style wood and mirror decor is a visual treat to go along with a delectable pastry case and one of the best cappuccinos in Le Marche.

❶ Information

Internet centre (☏0733 26 44 04; Piazza Mazzini 52; per hr €4; ☺10am-1pm & 5-8pm Mon-Sat)

Macerata Incoming (☏0733 23 43 33; www. macerataincoming.it; Porta Picena 1; ☺10am-1pm & 3-6pm winter, 3-7pm Tue-Sun summer) Private tourist information centre that opens on Sundays.

Post office (☏0733 27 30 53; Via Gramsci 44; ☺8am-6.30pm Mon-Fri, 8am-1pm Sat)

Tourist office (☏0733 23 48 07; iat. macerata@regione.marche.it; Piazza della Libertà 12; ☺9am-1pm & 3-6pm Mon-Fri, 9am-1pm Sat Sep-Jun, 9am-6pm Mon-Sat Jul & Aug)

❶ Getting There & Around

BUS Services head to Rome (€21, four hours, three daily) and Civitanova Marche (€2.25, one hour, hourly). Timetables are available at the bus terminal behind **Giardini Diaz** (☏0733 26 15 94).

CAR & MOTORCYCLE The SS77 connects the city with the A14 to the east and roads for Rome in the west. There is paid parking (8am to 8pm) skirting the city walls and free parking at the Giardini Diaz where the buses arrive.

TAXI You'll find **taxis** (☏0733 23 35 70) for hire at Piazza della Libertà, the **train station** (☏0733 24 03 53) and **Giardini Diaz** (☏0733 23 13 39).

TRAIN From the **train station** (☏0733 24 03 54; Piazza XXV Aprile 8/10) there are good connections to Ancona (€4.35, 1¼ hours, hourly) and Rome (€14.50 to €30, four to 5½ hours, eight daily). To reach Ascoli Piceno (€5.85, two hours, 10 daily) change trains in San Benedetto del Tronto and Civitanova Marche. Bus 6 links the station with the Piazza della Libertà in the city centre.

Ascoli Piceno

POP 51,203

With a continuous history dating from the Sabine tribe in the 9th century, Ascoli (as it's known locally) is like the love child of ancient Rome and a small Marchigiani village, heavy on the history and food. Weary legs will appreciate its lack of hills and all travellers will appreciate its historical riches, excellent pinacoteca, one of Italy's unsung perfect piazzas and a veal-stuffed fried olive treat (*olive all'ascolana*) good enough to plan a heart attack around.

⊙ Sights

Chiesa di San Francesco CHURCH

(☏0736 25 94 46; Piazza del Popolo; ☺7am-12.30pm & 3.30-8pm) This beautiful church was started back in 1262 as homage to a visit from St Francis himself. In the left nave is a 15th-century wooden cross that miraculously made it through a 1535 fire at the Palazzo dei Capitani, and has since reputedly spilled blood twice. Virtually annexed to the church is **Loggia dei Mercanti**, built in the 16th century by the powerful guild of wool merchants to hide their rough-and-tumble artisan shops.

The church stands on the imposing Piazza del Popolo, which since Roman times has been Ascoli's *salotto* (sitting room). The square, which is rectangular, is flanked on the west by the 13th-century **Palazzo dei Capitani del Popolo**. Built in the same famed travertine stone used throughout the region for centuries, the 'Captain's Palace' was the headquarters for the leaders of Ascoli. The statue of Pope Paul III above the main entrance was erected in recognition of his efforts to bring peace to the town.

Pinacoteca MUSEUM

(☏0736 29 82 13; www.ascolimusei.it; Piazza Arringo; adult/reduced €8/5; ☺10am-7pm Tue-Sun Mar-Sep, 10.30am-5pm Oct-Feb) The second-largest art gallery in Le Marche is inside the 17th-century **Palazzo Comunale**. It boasts an outstanding display of art, sculpture and religious artefacts; there's 400 works in total, including paintings by Van Dyck, Titian and Rembrandt, and a stunning embroidered 13th-century papal cape worn by Ascoli-born Pope Nicholas IV. Your ticket also gives you entry to two small collections in Ascoli's old quarter: the **Galleria d'Arte Contemporanea** (☏0736 25 07 60; Corso Mazzini; ☺10am-7pm Tue-Sun Mar-Sep, 10am-7pm Mon-Fri, 10am-5pm Sat & Sun Oct-Feb) and the **Museo dell'Arte Ceramica** (☏0736 29 82 13; Piazza San Tommaso; ☺10am-7pm Tue-Sun Mar-Sep, 10am-7pm Mon-Fri, 10am-5pm Sat & Sun Oct-Feb), which has displays on the major Italian pottery towns, including Deruta, Faenza and Genoa.

Duomo della Città di Ascoli Piceno
CHURCH

(☎0736 25 97 74; Piazza Arringo; ⊙7am-6pm) On the eastern flank of Piazza Arringo, Ascoli's Duomo was built in the 15th century over a medieval building and dedicated to St Emidio, patron saint of the city. In the **Cappella del Sacramento** is the *Polittico*, a polyptych executed in 1473 by Carlo Crivelli and considered by critics to be his best work. The **crypt of Sant Emidio** has a set of mosaics any ceramicist will appreciate.

Next to the cathedral and something of a traffic barrier today, the **battistero** (baptistry) has remained unchanged since it was constructed in the 11th century.

Vecchio Quartiere
NEIGHBOURHOOD

The town's Vecchio Quartiere (Old Quarter) stretches from Corso Mazzini (the main thoroughfare of the Roman-era settlement) to Castellano river. Its main street is the picturesque Via delle Torri, which eventually becomes Via Solestà; it's a perfect spot to wander round. On Via delle Donne (Street of Women) is the 14th-century **Chiesa di San Pietro Martire** (☎0736 25 52 14; Piazza Ventidio Basso; ⊙7.30am-12.30pm & 3.30-7pm), dedicated to the saint who founded the Dominican community at Ascoli. The chunky Gothic structure houses the **Reliquario della Santa Spina**, containing what is claimed to be a thorn from Christ's crown.

Museo Archeologico
MUSEUM

(☎0736 25 35 62; Piazza Arringo; adult/reduced €2/1; ⊙8.30am-7.30pm Tue-Sun) Ascoli's archaeological museum holds a small collection of tribal artefacts from Piceni and other European people dating back to the first centuries AD.

Torre degli Ercolani
HISTORICAL BUILDING

The 40m-high tower located on Via dei Soderini, west of the Chiesa di San Pietro Martire, is the tallest of the town's medieval towers. **Palazzetto Longobardo**, a 12th-century Lombard-Romanesque defensive position and now the Ostello dei Longobardi youth hostel abuts the tower. Just to the north is the well-preserved **Ponte Romano**, a single-arched Roman bridge.

🎉 Festivals & Events

Fritto Misto all'Italiana
FOOD

This four-day festival of fried food held in late April aims is to 'de-bunk the prejudice that fried food is unhealthy'. However, after a few hours spent grazing stalls packed with heavy-duty treats – *cannoli* from Sicily, *panzerotti* from Puglia and, of course, fried stuffed Ascoli olives – your body may not agree, but your taste buds will have had a nice time.

Quintana
CULTURAL

With all the medieval festivals in Italy, when one of them receives an accolade for best historical re-enactment, there's probably a pretty good reason. Held the second Saturday in July and the first Sunday in August, Quintana brings out thousands of locals dressed in the typical costume of the 12th and 13th centuries: knights in suits of armour and ladies in velvet and lace. Processions and flag-waving contests take place throughout July and August, but the big draw is the Quintana joust, when the town's six *sestier*s (quarters) face off.

🛏 Sleeping

For a town with not many hotels, Ascoli has a good range of accommodation. The tourist office has lists of other accommodation options, including rooms and apartments, *agriturismi* and B&B options in outlying districts.

Palazzo Guiderocchi
BOUTIQUE HOTEL €€

(☎0736 25 97 10; www.palazzoguiderocchi.com; Via Cesare Battisti 3; r incl breakfast €69-199; P🅿✳@) Not many places offer the history, atmosphere and comfort of this 16th-century palace. Fully restored, it maintains the romance of 6m vaulted ceilings on the 1st floor, low wood-beamed ceilings on the 2nd, and frescoes and several original doors throughout. During slow months, palatial rooms can be an absolute steal.

Albergo Piceno
BOUTIQUE HOTEL €€

(☎0736 25 30 17; www.albergopiceno.it; Via Minucia 10; s € 59-95, d €74-110; ✳@) Just round the corner from the Duomo on a narrow street, this is a great boutique place in a converted 17th-century *palazzo* with large rooms decorated in a bright modern style (but with the odd bit of rustic stone poking out here and there to give it character). It offers a generous breakfast plus a gym to help you work it off.

Ostello dei Longobardi
HOSTEL €

(☎0736 26 18 62; longoboardoascoli@libero.it; Via dei Soderini 26; dm €18) Atmosphere aside, remember that comfort and warmth were invented after the Middle Ages, so when staying at an 11th-century stone palace-turned-youth hostel, don't expect much from the plumbing, and ask for an extra blanket in the winter. Two single-sex rooms sleep just eight each.

Eating

Rua dei Notari TRADITIONAL ITALIAN €€
($\boxed{?}$0736 26 36 30; Via Cesare Battisti 3; meals €30) Perfect for a special meal, this elegant restaurant possesses old-world charm in a modern setting. Dishes, which include plenty of fried goods, are presented as artfully as the contemporary paintings covering the walls.

Cafe Lorenz SNACKS €
($\boxed{?}$0736 25 99 59; Piazza del Popolo 5; snacks & gelati €2-7; ⊘7am-2pm) Head upstairs for a convivial drink (drinks and wine €2 to €5) or a light dinner. But the main reason to come here is the takeaway *olive all'ascolana* (olives from Ascoli) for €3.

Gallo D'Oro TRADITIONAL ITALIAN €€
($\boxed{?}$0736 25 35 20; Corso Vittorio Emanuele 54; meals €26; ⊘Mon-Sat) A bit outside the tourist area and popular with long-time Ascoli residents, this business-casual restaurant has been serving up local fare for decades. Try the appetiser selection of fried goodies.

Drinking

Caffè Meletti CAFE
(Piazza del Popolo 20; ⊘8am-7pm) From the shade of the ancient portico you can sip a coffee or the famous *anisette* (made on site) as you gaze onto the perfect Italian piazza. The cafe, founded in 1907 and once a popular haunt for the likes of Ernest Hemingway and Jean-Paul Sartre, fell into disrepair for a time but has since been restored to its former glory.

Information

Hospital ($\boxed{?}$0736 35 81; Monticelli) Located 4km east of town.

Internet point ($\boxed{?}$/fax 0736 25 23 70; Piazza Bonfine 6; per hr €2; ⊘9am-12.45pm & 4-9pm Mon-Sat, 2-9pm Sun, closed Tue morning)

Police station ($\boxed{?}$0736 35 51 11; Viale della Repubblica 8)

Post office ($\boxed{?}$0736 24 22 85; Via Crispi; ⊘8am-6.30pm Mon-Fri, 8am-12.30pm Sat)

Tourist office ($\boxed{?}$0736 25 23 91; iat. ascolipiceno@regione.marche.it; Palazzo del Popolo, Piazza del Popolo; ⊘9am-6.30pm Mon-Fri, 9.30am-6.30pm Sat & Sun)

ℹ Getting There & Away

BUS Services leave from Piazzale della Stazione, in front of the train station in the new part of town, east of the Castellano river. **Start** ($\boxed{?}$800 218692; www.startspa.it) runs buses to Rome (€14.50, three hours, four daily) and Civitanova Marche (€4.95, two hours, 12 daily). At 6.30am daily, **Amadio** ($\boxed{?}$0736 34 23 40) runs a service to Perugia (€17) and on to Siena (€25) from in front of the train station.

TRAIN There are connections to Ancona (€6.45, 70 minutes), and Macerata (€5.85, two hours, 10 daily). The station is a 15-minute walk east of the centre.

Monti Sibillini

Straddling the Le Marche–Umbria border, the beautiful **Parco Nazionale dei Monti Sibillini** covers some of the most scenic mountains in central Italy. The area is filled with mystical valleys, ancient hamlets, infinite expanses of wildflowers and soaring peaks (10 are more than 2000m high).

The area is a paradise for anyone interested in outdoor activities and wildlife. Walking trails criss cross the area. *Rifugi* (mountain huts) welcome hikers every few kilometres with a restaurant and a warm bed (most open summer only; maps with phone numbers and opening details are available at all local tourist offices).

There's a good driving loop around the mountains, which visitors can easily reach from Norcia (in Umbria) or Ascoli Piceno, Macerata or Ancona. From the southwest, start in Norcia, heading to Castelluccio. Follow signs to Montemonaco, Montefortino and Amandola. Just past **Montefortino**, take the road marked for Madonna dell'Ambro, which will take you to the **Gola dell'Infernaccio**, Monti Sibillini's waterfall masterpiece. Backtrack to Montefortino and continue on the circle.

Although not technically in the Monti Sibillini national park, the largest and prettiest town is **Sarnano**, on the SS78, which leads to **Sasso Tetto**, the main ski area in Monti Sibillini. From the main ski area, the road drops down to Lago Fiastra. To continue on an equally stunning drive, circle around to the SS209 through the Valnerina in Umbria.

Activities

The tiny hilltop village of **Castelluccio**, which is technically in Umbria (although only just) is perhaps the best base from which to explore the park. It's famous for its *lenticchie,* and *pecorino* and ricotta cheeses, but it's the location that brings in visitors. The town is surrounded by the **Piano Grande**, a wide open expanse that blooms with gazillions of wildflowers every spring and fills with snow each winter. The Casa del Parco (p580) in Norcia has information on walking and other activities in the surrounding area.

To learn hang-gliding or paragliding, contact **Pro Delta** (☑0743 82 11 56; www.prodelta. it; Via delle Fate 3) in Castelluccio; it opens in summer only. Readers have heartily recommended the courses. A beginner's course of five days will cost about €400.

🛏 Sleeping & Eating

La Quercia della Memoria
AGRITURISMO €

(☑0733 69 44 31; www.querciadellamemoria.it; Contrada Vellato, San Ginesio; per person €30-40, meals €25; ℗) Follow the pandas to this one-in-a-million find. It's about 15 minutes off the Monti Sibillini route, but is so worth the drive. On the weekends, dine in the *biologico* (organic) restaurant on home-grown and home-ground wheat bread or stay in the refurbished stone houses, where dozens of sustainable building touches include radiant floor heating made from wine bottles, a grey-water system and solar power.

Casa Sibillini
B&B €

(☑0736 85 90 44; www.casasibillini.com; Via dei Tiratori 11, Montefortino; s/d/apt incl breakfast €40/60/80; 🛜) This English-owned B&B is a gracious home appointed with appreciated touches: an indoor brick oven, a comfortable living-room area filled with books, and a home-cooked breakfast each morning. Fountains of information about the area, the owners can help you plan your day or trip around the mountain.

Hotel Paradiso
HOTEL €

(☑0737 84 74 68; www.sibillinihotels.it; Piazza Umberto I, Amandola; s €40, d €62-100; ℗) It's not easy to find or to reach, but this private retreat hamlet is worth the slog for the view alone. With 40 comfortable rooms (most with balconies), an impressive restaurant (breakfast €5, lunch and dinner €20), tennis courts and romantic arched walkway, the unassuming-looking hotel offers everything you need in a mountain holiday.

La Citadella
AGRITURISMO €

(☑0736 84 42 62; www.cittadelladeisibillini.it; Loc Citadella, Montemonaco; r €40, meals €15) The 18 rooms at this friendly *agriturismo* just north of the village of Montemonaco are pretty simple, but with a great restaurant serving local dishes (many made with home-grown ingredients), a swimming pool and easy access to the walks of the Monti Sibillini, you probably won't be spending too much time in them. Minimum stay two nights.

Albergo Sibilla
HOTEL €

(☑/fax 0743 82 11 13; www.sibillacastelluccio.com; Via Pian Grande 2, Castelluccio; s €50, d € 65-70; ☺Apr-Oct; ℗) The Albergo Sibilla is the sole hotel in Castelluccio and has 11 rooms, some views to die for, and a good restaurant downstairs. Since the nightlife consists mostly of chasing goats around dilapidated stone buildings, a good night's sleep is practically guaranteed.

❶ Information

The official park website (www.sibillini.net) has a wealth of information on where to say, what to do and how to get around. There are also 15 'Casa del Parco' visitor information centres, including at Norcia (p580) and **Amandola** (☑/fax 0736 84 85 98; Via Indipendenza 73; ☺9.30am-12.30pm & 4-6pm Easter-Sep).

❶ Getting There & Away

Monti Sibillini is best reached by bus from Ascoli Piceno or Macerata. The services are busiest when school is in session, so can be spotty for tourists. Check with tourist offices in Ascoli or Macerata, or with the bus companies: **Contram** (☑800 443040) in Macerata and **Start** (☑800 037737) in Ascoli Piceno.

The nearest train stations are in Ascoli Piceno to the south and Tolentino to the north.

Sarnano

Though not technically in Monti Sibillini, Sarnano is the largest town near the range, and the most hospitable. Its red-brick facades charm all who visit.

The bench in the flower-filled garden at **Albergo La Villa** (☑0733 65 72 18; www.hrlavilla.com; Viale della Rimembranza 46; s €35, d €52-55; ℗🐾) is reason enough to stay, but the dead silence, five-minute walk into town, price (rooms with shared bathroom are less expensive), adjoining restaurant with local treats (rabbit, truffles, lamb etc) and children's play space make this an excellent choice for families or couples.

On the Sassotetto road lies the sparklingly modern **Novidra** (☑0733 65 71 97; www.novidra.com; Via DeGasperi 26; s €50-65, d €90-120, all incl breakfast; P@🛜🆒) serving weary skiers, view seekers and spa aficionados. Although the long corridors feel a bit spooky, rooms are comfortably designed for those visiting the next-door spa, with soft sheets, plush bathrobes and a full complement of toiletries.

The stone staircase leading to the cavernous interior of **Ristorante Il Vicolo** (☑0733 65 85 65; Vicolo Brunforte 191a; meals €23; ☺Thu-Tue) is a hint as to the history found in the restaurant's dishes – hare, wild boar and grilled pork. The house antipasto *della nonna* is a mix of Marchigiani specialities and international flavours, such as chickpeas with curry.

The **Sarnano tourist office** (☑0733 65 71 44; iat.sarnano@regione.marche.it; Largo Ricciardi 1; ☺9am-1pm Mon-Sat, plus 3-6pm Tue-Fri) has walking and climbing information and details of accommodation in the park.

Abruzzo & Molise

Includes »

Why Go?

A stunning mountain region little known to foreign visitors, Abruzzo is an area of unspoiled natural beauty and rural, back-country charm. Only an hour from Rome, it feels like a world apart with its great Apennines peaks, still, silent valleys and pretty hilltop towns. To the south, Molise offers more of the same, albeit on a smaller, less dramatic scale.

The landscape is extraordinary. In the region's three national parks, thick forests and flowering meadows give way to high barren plains and snowcapped granite peaks, and wolves and bears roam free in the vast beech woods. A mecca for outdoor enthusiasts, it offers wonderful hiking, skiing and mountain biking, while the coast boasts some beautiful sandy beaches.

Nestled in this verdant land, cultural gems await discovery. Pescocostanzo's baroque centre and Sulmona's historic *palazzi* (mansions) testify to past glories, while isolation has ensured the survival of age-old customs such as Cocullo's bizarre snake charmers' procession.

Best Places to Eat

» Locanda Sotto gli Archi (p607)

» Hosteria dell'Arco (p607)

» Il Panzotto (p614)

» Ristorante Clemente (p607)

Best Places to Stay

» Sextantio (p607)

» Locanda Alfieri (p616)

» Le Torri Hotel (p608)

» B&B Villa del Pavone (p613)

» Residenza Sveva (p616)

When to Go

L'Aquila

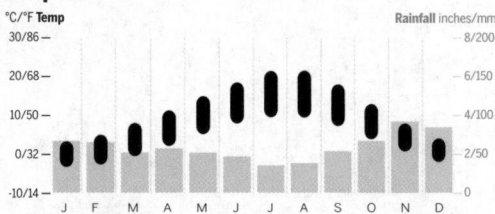

May Cocullo's bizarre snake festival involves a statue, procession and writhing nest of snakes.

Jul Sulmona's square fills with prancing horses and jousting during this medieval tournament.

Jun–Sep Spring wildflowers, summer sun and autumn leaves – perfect conditions for hiking.

ABRUZZO

Best known for its dramatic mountain scenery, Abruzzo's landscape is surprisingly diverse. A vast plain extends east of Avezzano, the coastline is flat and sandy, and there are ancient forests in the Parco Nazionale d'Abruzzo, Lazio e Molise.

Many towns retain a medieval look, while the numerous hilltop castles and isolated, sometimes abandoned, *borghi* (medieval towns) exude a sinister charm, lending credence to Abruzzo's fame as an ancient centre of magic, and the land of a thousand castles.

Parco Nazionale del Gran Sasso e Monti della Laga

About 20km northeast of L'Aquila, the Gran Sasso massif is the centrepiece of the Parco Nazionale del Gran Sasso e Monti della Laga, one of Italy's largest national parks. The park's predominant feature is its jagged rocky landscape through which Europe's southernmost glacier, the Calderone, cuts its course. It's also a haven for wildlife, home to an estimated 40 wolves, 350 chamois and six pairs of royal eagles. Hiking trails criss-cross the park and atmospheric castles and medieval hill towns crown the foot hills.

TOP CHOICE **Rocca Calascio**, six kilometres west of Santo Stefano di Sessanio, is one such imposing castle dominating the skyline above the Navelli Plain. There's not much to see inside, but the views are stupendous, and from a distance the castle makes an impressive photograph.

Fonte Cerreto is the main gateway to the Gran Sasso and **Campo Imperatore** (2117m), a high windswept plateau 27km long and known as 'Italy's Little Tibet'. A **funivia** (cable car; ☎0862 60 61 43; €14 Mon-Fri, €16 Sat & Sun; ☉8am-5pm Mon-Sat, to 6pm Sun, closed May) runs up to the Campo from Fonte Cerreto. Up top, there's hiking in summer and skiing in winter (see the boxed text, p609).

For more information contact the **park office** (☎0862 6 05 21; www.gransassolagapark.it, in Italian; Via del Convento 1; ☉10.30am-1pm Mon-Fri & 4-6pm Tue & Thu) in **Assergi**.

One of the most popular trekking routes is the surprisingly straightforward climb up **Corno Grande** (at 2912m, it's the Apennines' highest peak). The 9km *via normale* (normal route) starts in the main parking area

L'AQUILA: AFTER THE SHOCK WAVE

Destruction from the devastating earthquake that struck northern Abruzzo in 2009 – 10km from the regional capital **L'Aquila** – is still very much in evidence. After three years, much of L'Aquila's *centro storico* (historic center) is still off limits to visitors: rubble surrounds buildings damaged beyond repair, scaffolding fronts those slowly undergoing restoration, and the military patrols cordoned-off streets. Many of the 65,000 made homeless by the earthquake remain in housing estates built to accommodate them on the edge of the city.

Abruzzo and neighbouring Molise are particularly vulnerable to earthquakes as they sit on a major fault line that follows the Apennines from Sicily up to Genoa.

At the time of research there was no indication as to when restorations to L'Aquila's historic centre would be complete.

at Campo Imperatore and heads to the summit. The trail should be clear of snow from early June to late September/early October. If attempting the ascent, or any other serious route, be sure to arm yourself with the CAI 1:25,000 map *Gran Sasso d'Italia* (€10).

The park has a network of *rifugi* (mountain huts) for walkers. Otherwise, you can bed down at **Camping Funivia del Gran Sasso** (☎0862 60 61 63; Fonte Cerreto; camping per person/tent/car €7/8/1.50; ☉mid-May–mid-Sep), a modest camp ground in Fonte Cerreto. At the top of the cable-car lift, the **Hotel Campo Imperatore** (☎0862 40 00 00; Campo Imperatore; half-board from €70), where Mussolini was briefly imprisoned in 1943, also has a **hostel** (dm per person €30, incl dinner €45) that offers basic year-round digs.

Fonte Cerreto is just off the A24 motorway (clearly signposted). It's best to have your own transport to navigate the park.

Sulmona

POP 25,220

Sulmona lies in a picturesque location, nestled in a valley with the Morrone massif as a backdrop. A lively and prosperous provincial

Abruzzo & Molise Highlights

1 Breathe in the pure mountain air of **Pescocostanzo** (p608), one of Abruzzo's hidden jewels

2 Drive or hike the high windswept plateau of **Campo Imperatore** (p603), Italy's 'Little Tibet'

3 Feel the call of the wild as you climb the **Corno Grande** (p603), summit of the Gran Sasso and the Apennine's highest peak

4 Travel back in time as you walk the ancient Roman town of **Saepinum** (p615)

5 Drive through the breathtaking **Gole di Sagittario** (p612) between Sulmona and Scanno

6 Laze on the beaches at **Termoli** (p616), a cheerful and unpretentious Adriatic resort

7 Marvel at the many imposing hilltop castles, such as **Rocca Calascio** (p603)

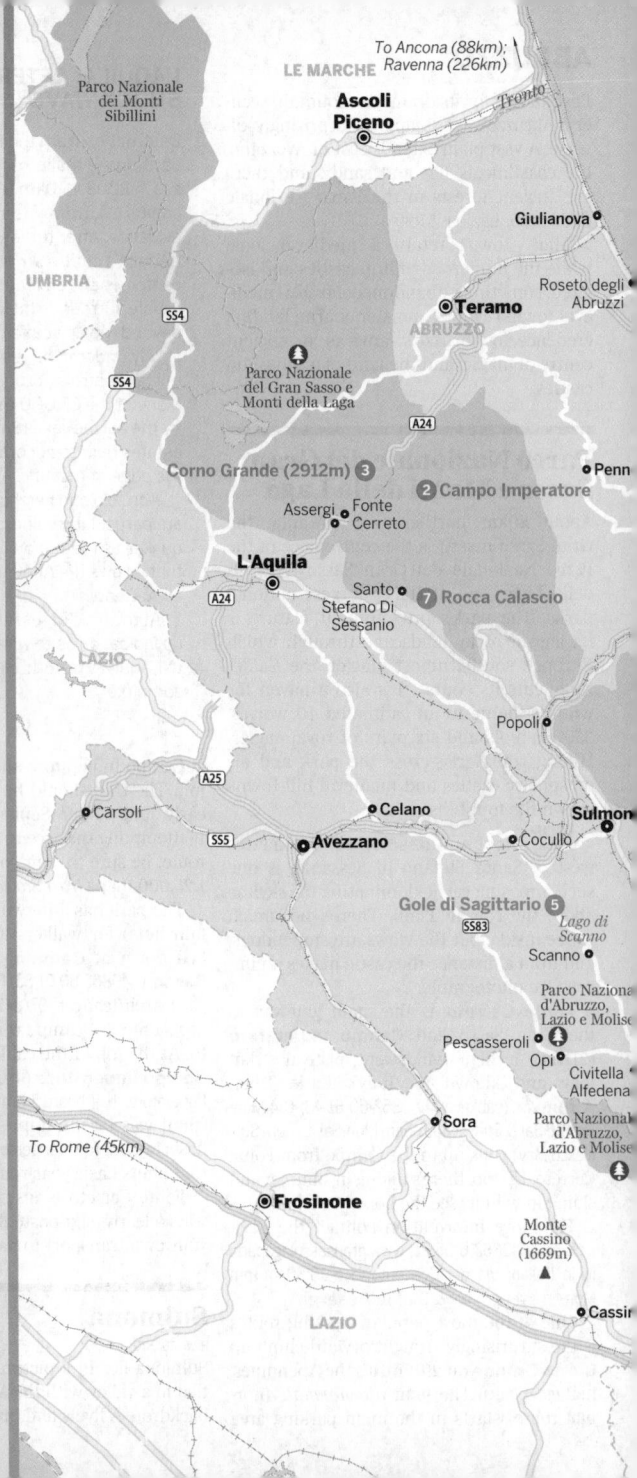

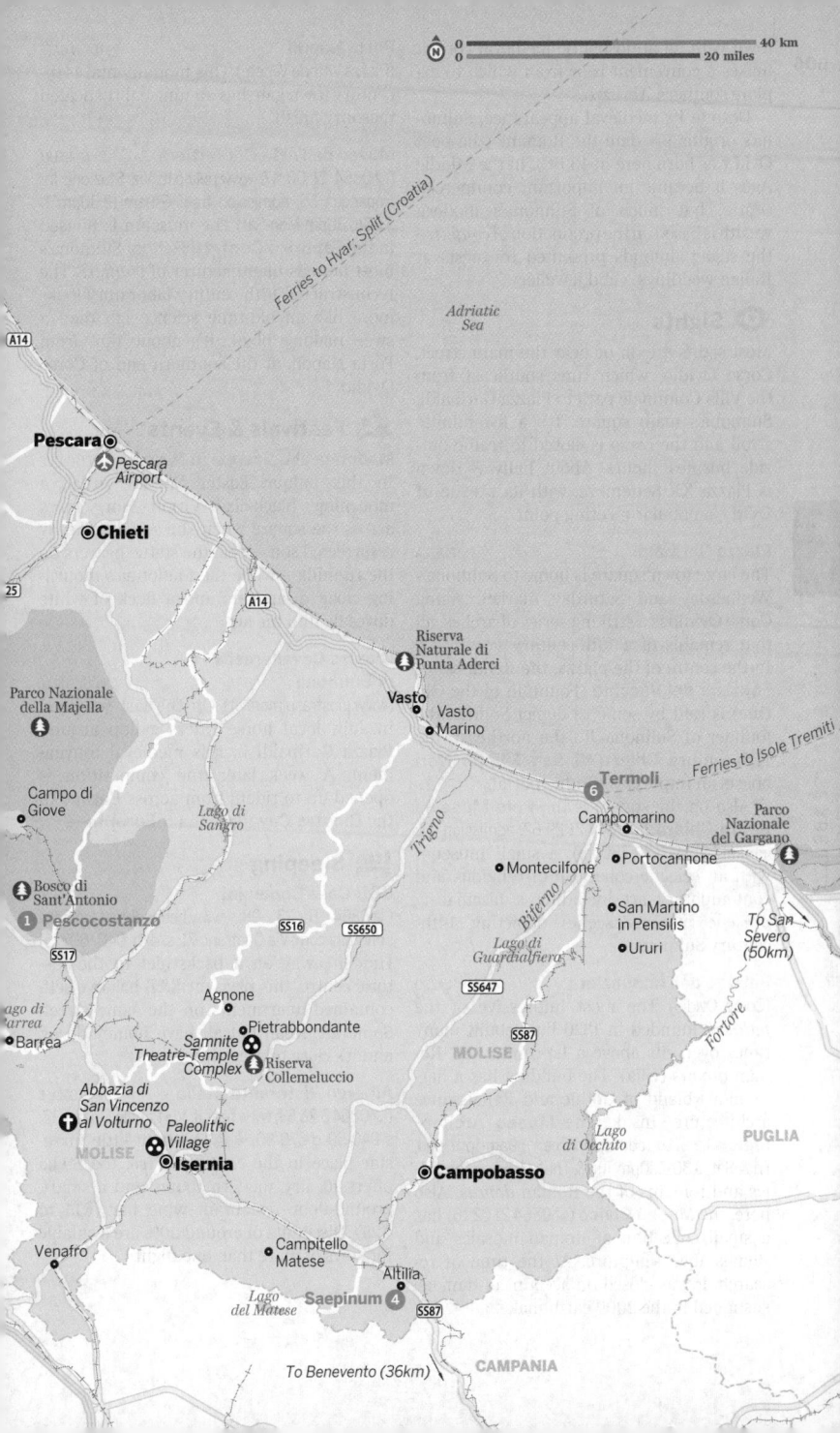

town with an atmospheric medieval core, it makes a convenient base from which to explore southern Abruzzo.

Despite its medieval appearance, Sulmona's origins pre-date the Romans (the poet Ovid was born here in 43 BC). In the Middle Ages it became an important commercial centre, but much of Sulmona's modern wealth is based on the production of *confetti* – the sugar almonds presented to guests at Italian weddings – and jewellery.

⊙ Sights

Most sights are on or near the main street, Corso Ovidio, which runs southeast from the Villa Comunale park to Piazza Garibaldi, Sulmona's main square. It's a five-minute stroll and the *corso* is closed to traffic outside business hours. About halfway down is Piazza XX Settembre, with its **statue of Ovid** – a popular meeting point.

Piazza Garibaldi PIAZZA
The large town square is home to Sulmona's Wednesday and Saturday market. Along Corso Ovidio is a striking series of arches, all that remains of a 13th-century **aqueduct**. In the centre of the piazza, the Renaissance **Fontana del Vecchio** (Fountain of the Old One) is said by some to depict Solimo, the founder of Sulmona. To the northeast, the 14th-century **Chiesa di San Filippo Neri** boasts an impressive Gothic portal.

Also on the square is the **Polo Museale Santa Chiara** (☑0864 21 29 62; admission €3; ⊙9am-1pm & 3.30-7.30pm), a small museum with an eclectic collection of religious and contemporary art including a fascinating *presepe* (nativity scene) depicting 19th-century Sulmona.

Palazzo dell'Annunziata PALAZZO
(Corso Ovidio) The most impressive of the *palazzi,* founded in 1320 but rebuilt many times over, sits above a 1st-century-BC Roman *domus* (villa). The building has a harmonious blend of Gothic and Renaissance architecture. Inside, the **Museo Archeologico in situ** (admission free; ⊙9am-1pm Wed, Fri & Sat, 3.30-7.30pm Tue & Thu) showcases relics and remains of the Roman *domus.* Also here, the **Museo Civico** (☑0864 21 02 16) has a small collection of Roman mosaics and Renaissance sculpture. At the time of research, it was closed on account of damage sustained in the 2009 earthquake.

Porta Napoli TOWN GATE
(Piazza Vittorio Veneto) This monumental 14th-century town gate has an unusual rusticated masonry finish.

Museo dell'Arte Confettiera MUSEUM
(☑0864 21 00 47; www.pelino.it; Via Stazione Introdacqua 55; admission free; ⊙9am-12.30pm & 3.30-6.30pm Mon-Sat) The museum is housed in the **Fabbrica Confetti Pelino**, Sulmona's most famous manufacturer of *confetti.* The reconstructed 16th-century laboratory looks more like an old-time science lab than a sweet-making plant. It's about 1km from Porta Napoli, at the southern end of Corso Ovidio.

⚜ Festivals & Events

Madonna che Scappa in Piazza RELIGIOUS
In this unique Easter Sunday ritual, a mourning, black-clad Virgin Mary races across the square when she sees her newly resurrected son – well, the statue bearers do the running – while the Madonna's mourning cloak disappears and a flock of white doves fly into the air.

Giostra Cavalleresca di Sulmona CULTURAL
(www.giostrasulmona.it) On the last weekend in July, local horse riders gallop around Piazza Garibaldi in this medieval tournament. A week later, the competition is opened up to riders from across Europe in the **Giostra Cavalleresca d'Europa**.

🛏 Sleeping

B&B Case Bonomini B&B €
(☑0864 5 23 08; www.bedandbreakfastcasebonomini.com; Via Quatrario 71; s/d/tr €40/60/75) Hidden away on a backstreet in the historic centre, this pleasant B&B has five self-contained apartments on the same street. Some are small but all have homey decor, and it's close to everything.

Albergo Ristorante Stella HOTEL €
(☑0864 5 26 53; www.hasr.it; Via Panfilo Mazara 18; s €40-50, d €70-80; ❋@) A bright little three-star place in the *centro storico,* the Stella offers 10 airy, modern rooms and a smart, ground-floor restaurant–wine bar (€15 to €25). Discounts of around 20% are available for stays of more than one night.

SANTO STEFANO DI SESSANIO

Known as Sextantio in Roman times, this atmospheric hilltop village has a commanding position overlooking two valleys. Although the 2009 earthquake that struck L'Aquila damaged a number of buildings in Santo Stefano, including the iconic 18m-high watchtower (which now lies in ruins), a stroll through the *centro storico* (historic centre) reveals why the village is regarded as one of Gran Sasso's most picturesque, and why it made the list as a *borghi piu belli d'Italia* (one of the most beautiful towns in Italy).

The town flourished in the 16th century under the rule of the Medici family, and the Medici coat of arms can still be seen on the entrance portal to the main piazza. The collapsed tower, although constructed in the 13th century, became known as the Medici Tower as it, too, bore the family's coat of arms. Renovations to the tower last century – when reinforced concrete replaced the wooden observation platform (making the tower top-heavy) – may have rendered it vulnerable to collapse.

Sextantio (☎0862 89 91 12; www.sextantio.it; Via Principe Umberto; r €150-450; 🖢) is an enchanting *albergo diffuso* (diffused hotel), which has a number of rooms and apartments scattered throughout the *centro storico*. Rooms capture the authenticity of the past with handmade blankets and rustic furniture made in the village, yet remain refined thanks to modern conveniences such as underfloor heating, mood lighting and divinely deep bathtubs.

In Sextantio's restaurant, **Locanda Sotto gli Archi** (meals €50; ☉dinner daily, lunch Sat & Sun), tables adorned with soft candlelight evoke a medieval mood for a fixed menu of traditional Abruzzese dishes.

Taking the SS 17, Santo Stefano di Sessanio is 27km from L'Aquila, but a more scenic route takes you through Fonte Cerreto on the 17bis and across the grand plateau of Campo Imperatore before turning south to Santo Stefano (about 50km).

Eating & Drinking

TOP CHOICE **Hosteria dell'Arco** TRADITIONAL ITALIAN € (☎0864 21 05 53; Via M D'Eramo 20; meals €20-25; ☉closed Mon evening & Sun) Superb food, lovely, rustic surroundings, laid-back atmosphere and friendly service – what more could you ask for? First up is the fabulous antipasto buffet, prepared from scratch every night, followed by delicious grilled lamb and scrumptious homemade desserts.

Ristorante Clemente TRADITIONAL ITALIAN €€ (☎0864 21 06 79; Vico Quercia 5; meals €25; ☉Fri-Wed) Photos of family members on the wall remind you this is a proud, family-run restaurant – and it feels it. The menu is based on the cornerstones of Abruzzese cooking using seasonal products to produce delicious meals.

La Cantina di Biffi TRADITIONAL ITALIAN €€ (☎0864 3 20 25; www.cantinadibiffi.it; Via Barbato 1; meals €25; ☉closed Sun evening & Mon) Just off Corso Ovidio, this is a charming and atmospheric bistro–wine bar. Exposed-stone walls and the arched, vaulted ceiling set the stage for excellent homemade food and local wine (served by the glass from €4).

Gran Caffè dell'Annunziata CAFE € (☎0864 21 11 21; Piazza SS Annunziata 2; ☉9am-1pm daily, 4-8pm Mon-Sat) Grab an outdoor table and sip something cool as you watch the evening parade on Corso Ovidio.

ℹ Information

Tourist office (☎0864 5 32 76; www.abruzzo turismo.it; Corso Ovidio 208; ☉9am-1pm & 4-7pm Mon-Sat, 9am-1pm Sun mid-May–mid-Sep, 9am-1pm Mon-Sat, 3-6pm Mon, Wed & Fri mid-Sep–mid-May)

ℹ Getting There & Away

BUS ARPA (☎800 762 622; www.arpaonline.it) buses go to/from L'Aquila (€5.50, 1½ hours, nine daily), Pescara (€5.50, one hour, 11 daily), Scanno (€2.90, one hour, 12 daily) and other nearby towns. **SATAM** (☎0871 34 49 69) runs three daily services to Naples (€15, 2½ hours). Buses leave from a confusing array of points, including Villa Comunale, the hospital, train station and beneath Ponte Capograssi. Find out which stop you need when you get your ticket from **Agenzia Fai** (☎0864 3 33 49; Via Circonvallazione Orientale 3; ☉9am-1pm & 4-7.30pm Mon-Sat) near Porta Napoli.

TRAIN Trains link with L'Aquila (€3.90, one hour, 10 daily), Pescara (€3.90, 1¼ hours, 16 daily) and

SNAKES IN COCULLO

A one-horse hamlet in the hills west of Sulmona, Cocullo is the unlikely setting for one of Italy's weirdest festivals. The Processione dei Serpari (Snake Charmers' Procession) is the highlight of celebrations to honour San Domenico, Cocullo's patron saint and protector against snake bites. Events kick off at noon on the first Thursday of May when villagers gather in the main square to adorn a statue of St Dominic with jewellery, banknotes and dozens of writhing snakes. Once dressed, the saint is paraded through the streets by a team of fearless *serpari*. Local lore holds that if the snakes twist around the saint's head it's good news for the year ahead; if they crawl up the arms, the omens are bad.

Despite the religious element of the festivities, its origins are said to be pagan. Before the arrival of Christianity, locals worshipped a goddess called Angizia, who supposedly had powers to cure snake bites. As Christianity spread, the ancient deities were substituted by Christian saints and San Domenico inherited Angizia's mantle.

The serpents used for the festival are harmless *cervoni* and *saettoni*. They are caught in the surrounding countryside in late March and released back into the hills once the festivities are over.

Cocullo is accessible by a daily bus from Sulmona (€1.40, 30 minutes), although on festival day extra services are laid on – ask at Sulmona tourist office (p607) for details.

Rome (€8.80, 2½ to three hours, seven daily). The train station is 2km northwest of the historic centre; the half-hourly bus A runs between the two.

Parco Nazionale della Majella

Monte Amaro (2793m), the Apennines' second-highest peak, lies in a dramatic landscape of ominous mountains and empty valleys. Over half of Parco Nazionale della Majella's 750 sq km is at an altitude of over 2000m. Wolves roam in the woods and over 500km of paths and cycling trails criss-cross the area.

From Sulmona the two easiest access points are Campo di Giove (elevation 1064m), a small skiing village 18 tortuous kilometres to the southeast, and the lovely town of Pescocostanzo, 33km south of Sulmona along the SS17.

Sights & Activities

Set amid verdant highland plains, Pescocostanzo (elevation 1400m) is a real gem, a hilltop town whose historical core has changed little in over 500 years. Much of the cobbled centre dates from the 16th and 17th centuries when it was an important town on the 'Via degli Abruzzi', the main road linking Naples and Florence. Of particular note is the Collegiata di Santa Maria del Colle, an atmospheric church that combines a superb Romanesque portal with a lavish baroque

interior. Nearby, Piazza del Municipio is flanked by a number of impressive *palazzi*, including Palazzo Comunale with its distinctive clock tower and Palazzo Fanzago, designed by the great baroque architect Cosimo Fanzago in 1624.

History apart, Pescocostanzo also offers skiing on Monte Calvario and summer hiking in the Bosco di Sant'Antonio.

Sleeping & Eating

TOP CHOICE Le Torri Hotel   HOTEL €€
(☎0864 64 20 40; www.letorrihotel.it; Via Roma 21; d €100-160; ❄@) This stylish hotel, in a *palazzo* once owned by a baron, has large, comfortable rooms with wooden floors, antique furnishings and inviting white bedspreads.

Albergo La Rua   HOTEL €
(☎0864 64 00 83; www.larua.it; Via Rua Mozza 1; d €70-100; ☎) Hikers should head straight for this charming little hotel in the historic centre. The look is country cosy with low wood-beamed ceilings and a stone fireplace, and the superfriendly owners are a mine of local knowledge.

Il Gallo di Pietra   TRADITIONAL ITALIAN €€
(☎0864 64 20 40; www.ilgallodipietra.it; Via del Vallone 4; meals €35; ☉lunch & dinner) Attached to Le Torri Hotel, you can dine alfresco in the garden or beside the fire in the cosy indoor restaurant. The menu features the enticing flavours of Abruzzese and Neapolitan cuisine.

ℹ Information

Tourist office (☑0864 64 14 40; Vico delle Carceri; ⊘9am-1pm & 3-6pm Mon-Fri Sep-Jun, 9am-1pm & 4-7pm daily Jul & Aug) In Pescocostanzo, off the central Piazza del Municipio. Also see the park's comprehensive website (www.parcomajella.it).

ℹ Getting There & Away

Buses run from Sulmona to Pescocostanzo (€3.60, one hour, three daily) via Castel di Sangro, and to Campo di Giove (€1.90, 45 minutes, three daily).

Scanno

POP 1990

A tangle of steep alleyways and sturdy, greystone houses, picture-pretty Scanno is an atmospheric medieval *borgo,* and is known for its finely worked filigree gold jewellery. For centuries a centre of wool production, it is one of the few places in Italy where you can still see women wearing traditional dress – especially during the week-long costume festival (www.costumediscanno.org) held at the end of April.

Be sure to take the exhilarating drive up from Sulmona through the rocky Gole di Sagittario (Sagittarius Gorge) and past tranquil Lago di Scanno.

🛏 Sleeping & Eating

Il Palazzo B&B €
(☑0864 74 78 60; www.ilpalazzo.it; Via Ciorla 25; r €60-80; ℗🖧) This elegant B&B spans seven rooms on the 2nd floor of an old *palazzo* in the *centro storico.* The rooms are stylishly decorated with antique furnishings.

Hotel Belvedere HOTEL €
(☑0864 7 43 14; www.belvederescanno.it; Piazza Santa Maria della Valle 3; r per person incl breakfast €35-50) In a good location on Scanno's main piazza, this cracking hotel offers spick-and-span modern rooms decked out with parquet and polished wood trimmings. Also offers half and full board.

Pizzeria Trattoria Vecchio Mulino TRATTORIA €
(☑0864 74 72 19; Via Silla 50; pizzas/meals €7/25; ⊘closed Wed winter) This old-school eatery is a good bet for a classic wood-fired pizza, cheesy antipasti and char-grilled hunks of pork and lamb. In summer the pretty streetside terrace provides a good perch to people-watch.

Ristorante Gli Archetti TRADITIONAL ITALIAN €€
(☑0864 7 46 45; www.gliarchetti.it; Via Silla 8; meals €35-40; ⊘closed Wed) Housed in the cellar of a Renaissance *palazzo,* this smart restaurant is highly rated. The menu is seasonal;

TAKE TO THE PISTES

Abruzzo and Molise might lack the glamour of the northern Alps, but skiing is enthusiastically followed and there are resorts across the regions (bank on about €35 for a daily ski pass).

» **Campitello Matese** In Molise's Monti del Matese, Campitello offers 40km of pistes, including 15km for cross-country skiers.

» **Campo di Giove** At the foot of the Parco Nazionale della Majella, this resort offers Abruzzo's highest skiing, at 2350m.

» **Campo Felice** A small resort 40km south of L'Aquila with 40km of pistes (30km downhill, 10km cross-country).

» **Campo Imperatore** Twenty-two kilometres of mainly downhill pistes, and over 60km of cross-country trails in the Parco Nazionale del Gran Sasso e Monti della Laga.

» **Ovindoli** Abruzzo's biggest ski resort, with 30km of downhill pistes and 50km of cross-country trails.

» **Pescasseroli** A popular outpost deep in the Parco Nazionale d'Abruzzo with 30km of downhill slopes.

» **Pescocostanzo** Good for ski hiking as well as downhill, it's celebrated for its medieval architecture.

» **Rivisondoli-Roccaraso** Near Pescocostanzo, this is one of the best equipped, with 28 ski lifts, two cable cars and over 100km of ski slopes.

in winter try the *spaghetti alla pastora* (pasta with chopped pig's cheeks, pepper and ripe *pecorino* – sheep's milk cheese).

❶ Information

Tourist office (☎0864 7 43 17; Piazza Santa Maria della Valle 12; ☉9am-1pm & 4-7pm Mon-Sat, 9am-1pm Sun Jun-Sep, 9am-1pm & 3-6pm Mon-Sat Oct–mid-May) In the village centre.

❶ Getting There & Away

ARPA (☎800 762 622; www.arpaonline.it) buses run to/from Sulmona (€2.90, one hour, 12 daily).

Parco Nazionale d'Abruzzo, Lazio e Molise

Encompassing 1100 sq km of spectacular mountain scenery, the Parco Nazionale d'Abruzzo, Lazio e Molise is the oldest and most popular of Abruzzo's national parks. It is also an important natural habitat and home to the native Marsican brown bear and Apennine wolf. If you're very lucky you might also spot one of the very few lynx still in the wild.

The park offers superb hiking as well as skiing, mountain biking and other outdoor pursuits.

◉ Sights & Activities

The park's main centre is lively Pescasseroli, an attractive village about 80km southwest of Sulmona. Situated on a hilltop six kilometres from Pescasseroli is Opi, a *borghi più belli d'Italia* (one of the most beautiful towns in Italy). It's one of the highest settlements in the park and worth a stroll through its pretty centre.

On the park's eastern edge and about 17km from Opi is the picturesque Lago di Barrea with the ancient town of Barrea positioned on a rocky spur above the lake.

At nearby Civitella Alfedena you can study the local flora and fauna at the Centro Lupo (Wolf Centre; ☎0864 89 01 41; admission €3; ☉10am-2pm & 2.30-5.30pm) and spy on a couple of wolves at the free Area Faunistica del Lupo. To see a rare lynx follow the signs to the Area Faunistica delle Lince.

Hiking opportunities abound, whether you want to go it alone or with an organised group. There are numerous outfits offering guided excursions, including Ecotur (☎0863 91 27 60; www.ecotur.org; Via Piave 9, Pes-

casseroli), which organises treks, bike rides and various other excursions.

Between May and October, the Centro Ippico Vallecupa (☎0863 91 04 44; www.agriturismomaneggiovallecupa.it; Via della Difesa; rides 1hr/full day €20/80) offers guided horse rides in the park.

For skiing information see the boxed text, p609.

🛏 Sleeping

B&B La Sosta   B&B €

(☎0863 91 60 57; Via Marsicana 17, Opi; r per person €25; Ⓟ) This delightful B&B in Opi is run with passionate care by a hospitable elderly couple. There are six very clean, smart rooms, a sunny terrace, and excellent access to the nearby mountains. The breakfasts are quite special too, with cakes and lashings of homemade jam. Excellent value.

Hotel La Conca   HOTEL €

(☎0863 91 05 62; Via Vicenne, Pescasseroli; d incl breakfast €65-100; Ⓟ) In a quiet location but still close to the action, this three-star hotel has spacious, comfortable rooms and solid wooden doors. It's a good-value, no-frills affair.

Albergo Antico Borga La Torre   HOTEL €

(☎0864 89 01 21; www.albergolatorre.com; Via Castello 3, Civitella Alfedena; s €30-40, d €45-60; Ⓟ@) Housed in an atmospheric 18th-century *palazzo* in Civitella Alfedena's medieval centre, this basic hotel is popular with hikers. There's also a small restaurant serving hot, fortifying food.

Campeggio Wolf   CAMPGROUND €

(☎0864 89 03 60; Via Sotto i Cerri, Civitella Alfedena; camping per person €5-6.50, tent €5-6, car €3-4; ☉May-Sep) This camp ground is a fairly simple affair but has free hot showers.

🍴 Eating

Trattoria da Armando   TRATTORIA €

(☎0863 91 23 86; Piazza Vittorio Veneto 11, Pescasseroli; meals €18-20; ☉Fri-Wed) This no-fuss trattoria has simple yet delicious meals with a range of *panini* as well as the usual pasta and meat dishes.

Pizzeria Trattoria da Laura   PIZZERIA €

(☎334 5252587; Via Pave 8, Pescasseroli; pizzas €6; ☉dinner) For a quick pizza, head to this laid-back pizzeria just off the main square. It's cosy and the pizza smell is delicious.

With about 150 well-marked routes, the Parco Nazionale d'Abruzzo, Lazio e Molise is a mecca for hikers. Trails range from easy family jaunts to multiday hikes over rocky peaks and exposed highlands. The best time to go is between June and September, although access to some of the busier routes around Pescasseroli is often limited in July and August. To book entry to trails contact the Centro di Visita in Pescasseroli or the Centro Lupo in Civitella Alfedena.

Two of the area's most popular hikes are the climbs up Monte Amaro (2793m; Route F1) and Monte Tranquillo (1841m; Route C3). The Monte Amaro route, a 2¼-hour hike, starts from a car park 7km southeast of Pescasseroli (follow the SS83 for about 2km beyond Opi) and rises steeply up to the peaks where you're rewarded with stupendous views over the Valle del Sangro. There's quite a good chance of spotting a chamois on this walk.

The Monte Tranquillo route takes about 2½ hours from a starting point about 1km south of Pescasseroli (follow signs for the Hotel Iris and Centro Ippico Vallecupa). If you still have your breath at the top, you can continue northwards along the Rocca Ridge before descending down to Pescasseroli from the north. This beautiful but challenging 19.5km circuit takes six or seven hours.

❶ Information

Centro di Visita (☑0863 911 32 21; Viale Colli d'Oro, Pescasseroli; ⊙9am-7.30pm Apr-Aug, 10am-5.30pm Sep-Mar)

Tourist office (☑0863 91 04 61; Via Principe di Napoli, Pescasseroli; ⊙9am-1pm & 3-6pm Mon-Sat Sep-Jun, 9am-1pm & 4-7pm daily Jul & Aug)

❶ Getting There & Away

Pescasseroli, Civitella Alfedena and other villages in the national park are linked by daily buses to Avezzano (€4.70, 1½ hours), from where you can change for L'Aquila, Pescara and Rome; and to Castel di Sangro (€3.60, 1¼ hours) for connections to Sulmona and Naples.

Pescara

POP 123,100

Abruzzo's largest city is a heavily developed seaside resort with one of the largest marinas on the Adriatic. The city was heavily bombed during WWII and much of the city centre was reduced to rubble. However, it's a lively place with an animated seafront, especially in summer, but unless you're coming for the 16km of sandy beaches there's really no great reason to hang around.

◉ Sights

Pescara's main attraction is its long stretch of beachfront, and the shopping precinct around pedestrianised Corso Umberto. From Piazzale della Repubblica, the beach is a short walk down Corso Umberto. There's also a few sights worth a quick look.

Museo delle Genti d'Abruzzo   MUSEUM
(☑085 451 00 26; www.gentidabruzzo.it; Via delle Caserme 24; adult/reduced €6/3; ⊙9am-1.30pm Mon-Sat, 5-8pm Sun Sep-Jun, to midnight Fri & Sat Jul & Aug) Illustrates local peasant culture.

Museo Casa Natale Gabriele D'Annunzio   MUSEUM
(☑0865 6 03 91; Corso Manthonè 116; admission €2; ⊙9am-1.30pm) Birthplace of controversial fascist poet Gabriele D'Annunzio.

Museo d'Arte Moderna Vittoria Colonna   ART GALLERY
(☑085 428 37 59; Via Gramsci 26; adult/reduced €6/4; ⊙9.30am-1.30pm & 4-8pm) Near the seafront, it boasts a Picasso and Miró among its small collection of modern art.

☞ Tours

Absolutely Abruzzo Tours   CULTURAL
(☑0699 197460; www.absolutelyabruzzo.com; day tours from €250; ⊙May-Oct) Australian-Italian Luciana Masci leads private small-group tours from one day to a week (including cooking courses and cultural and hiking tours) and offers specialised heritage services to retrace one's ancestral family village. Bookings essential.

🎉 Festivals

Pescara Jazz   MUSIC
(www.pescarajazz.com) This international jazz festival is held in mid-July at the Teatro D'Annunzio.

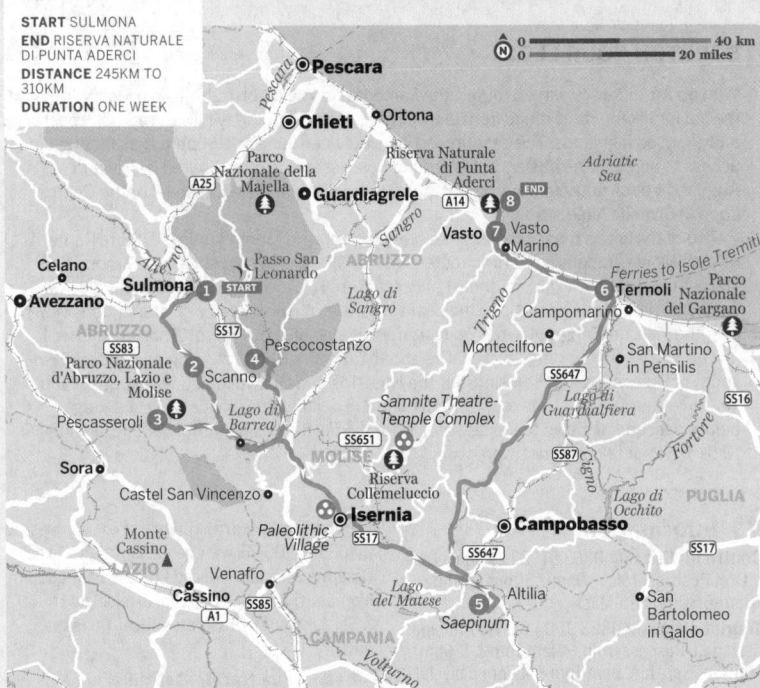

START SULMONA
END RISERVA NATURALE DI PUNTA ADERCI
DISTANCE 245KM TO 310KM
DURATION ONE WEEK

Driving Tour
Cut to the Heart

❯ An oasis in the mountainous terrain of southern Abruzzo, ① **Sulmona** is the place to start. With its attractive historic centre, welcoming vibe and great trattorias, it's the archetypal Italian town. Check out the market stalls on Piazza Garibaldi and join the locals on their *passeggiata* (evening stroll) along Corso Ovidio. After a night in Sulmona, push on southward to hilltop ② **Scanno**. It's a slow, scenic ride that takes you through the breathtaking **Gole di Sagittario**, a rocky gorge that squeezes the road like a natural vice, and up past the beautiful Lago di Scanno. Scanno's biscuit-tin beauty has made it something of a tourist attraction, but visit out of high summer and you'll find it a tranquil spot.

From Scanno, the next leg takes you into the national parks. From Lago di Barrea either head deep into the magnificent Parco Nazionale d'Abruzzo, Lazio e Molise, the most popular of Abruzzo's three national parks and set up camp in ③ **Pescasseroli**, or head north and take the long way round to pretty ④ **Pescocostanzo** in the Parco Nazionale

della Majella. Either way, spend a couple of days exploring the surrounding mountains. Once you've recharged your batteries, continue on past Isernia to the well-preserved Roman ruins at ⑤ **Saepinum**.

After the mountains, it's time to hit the coast and top up your tan at ⑥ **Termoli**, or further up the road at ⑦ **Vasto**, both popular Adriatic resorts. From Termoli, the Isole Tremiti are just a day trip away. But if the crowds get too much (and they might well in summer), go north to the Spiaggia di Punta Penna, a lovely beach in the ⑧ **Riserva Naturale di Punta Aderci**.

Sleeping & Eating

B&B Villa del Pavone
B&B €

(☑085 421 17 70; www.villadelpavone.it; Via Pizzoferrato 30; d €70-80; P❄️🛜) Over the tracks on a quiet residential street about 300m behind the train station, this gorgeous B&B is a home away from home. A model of old-fashioned pride, it's laden with gleaming antiques and chichi knick-knacks. Outside, the lush garden is presided over by a resident peacock.

Hotel Alba
HOTEL €

(☑085 38 91 45; www.hotelalba.pescara.it; Via Michelangelo Forti 14; s €50-80, d €75-120; P❄️@) A businesslike three-star place, the Alba provides anonymous comfort and a central location. Rooms vary but the best sport polished wood, firm beds and plenty of sunlight. Note that rates are lowest at weekends and that garage parking costs €10.

Osteria La Lumaca
OSTERIA €€

(☑085 451 08 80; www.osterialalumaca.com; Via delle Caserme 51; lunch menus €8-15, meals €35; ⊙closed Sat lunch & Sun) They take their food seriously at this warm wood-panelled restaurant. Particularly outstanding are the cured meats and ricotta, and the Abruzzo lamb. The fixed-price lunch menus are good value.

Ristorante Marechiaro da Bruno
SEAFOOD €€

(☑085 421 38 49; www.ristorantemarechiaro.eu; Lungomare Matteotti 70; pizzas €6.50-9, meals €30; ⊙Thu-Tue) With a prime position on the seafront, the speciality is bound to be seafood – in all shapes and sizes. It's a lively place and there's an impressive array of pizzas at night.

Caffè Letterario
CAFE €

(☑085 6 42 43; Via delle Caserme 22; lunch menus €7-12; ⊙9am-6pm Sun-Wed, 9am-3am Thu-Sat) With its huge floor-to-ceiling windows and exposed-brick walls, this is a popular lunchtime spot. The menu is chalked up on a daily board, but typically comprises a few mains and several vegetable side dishes. There's live music Thursday to Saturday nights.

❶ Information

Tourist office Piazzale della Repubblica (☑085 422 54 62; www.proloco.pescara.it; ⊙9am-1pm & 3-6pm Oct-May, 9am-1pm & 4-7pm Jun-Sep); airport (☑085 432 21 20; ⊙with flight arrivals).

❶ Getting There & Away

AIR Pescara airport (☑899 130 310; www.abruzzo-airport.it) is 3km out of town and easily reached by bus 38 (€1, 20 minutes, every 15 minutes) from in front of the train station. Ryanair and Alitalia are the main airlines flying to Pescara.

BOAT Throughout August, a daily **SNAV** (☑071 207 61 16; www.snav.it) jetfoil runs to the Croatian island of Hvar and on to Split (Spalato in Italian). One-way tickets for the 5¾-hour journey cost €120 per person and per car. See **Agenzia Sanmar** (☑0854 451 08 73; www.sanmar.it; Stazione Marittima Banchina Sud) at the port.

BUS ARPA (☑800 762 622; www.arpaonline.it) buses leave from Piazzale della Repubblica for L'Aquila (€7.80, two hours, 10 daily), Sulmona (€5.50, one hour, 11 daily), Naples (€24, 4½ hours, four daily), Rome (€15, 2¾ hours, 11 daily) and towns throughout Abruzzo and Molise.

TRAIN Direct trains run to Ancona (€7.50 to €20, 1¼ to two hours, 20 daily), Bari (€27 to €37, three hours, 16 daily), Rome (€11.70, four hours, six daily) and Sulmona (€3.90, 1¼ hours, 16 daily).

Chieti

POP 54,300

Overlooking the Aterno valley, Chieti is a hilltop town with roots dating back to pre-Roman times when, as capital of the Marrucini tribe, it was known as Teate Marrucinorum. Later, in the 4th century BC, it was conquered by the Romans and incorporated into the Roman Republic. These days the main reason to stop by is to the visit the town's two fascinating archaeology museums.

TOP CHOICE **Museo Archeologico Nazionale dell'Abruzzo** (☑0871 40 43 92; www.archeoabruzzo.beniculturali.it; Villa Frigerj; adult/reduced €4/2; ⊙9am-7.30pm Tue-Sun) is housed in a neoclassical villa in the Villa Comunale park. Displays include a comprehensive collection of local finds, with the star event the 6th-century-BC *Warrior of Capestrano,* considered the most important pre-Roman find in central Italy. Mystery surrounds the identity of the warrior, but there are some who reckon it to be Numa Pompilo, the second king of Rome and successor to Romulus. The museum also showcases 5th-century-BC funerary steles, an impressive coin collection, and some colossal statues – including that of a seated Hercules – dating from the 1st century BC.

TOP FIVE HILLTOP TOWNS IN ABRUZZO

In Abruzzo's mountainous terrain, the hills are crowned with ruined castles and medieval villages. Wander through these pretty and atmospheric hilltop towns:

» **Pescocostanzo** (p608)

» **Scanno** (p609)

» **Vasto** (p614)

» **Chieti** (p613)

» **Sulmona** (p603) OK, it's not exactly hilltop, but Ovid's birthplace makes an attractive base for exploring the Parco Nazionale della Majella.

Nearby is the **Complesso Archeologico la Civitella** (☎0871 6 31 37; www.lacivitella.it; Via Pianell; adult/reduced €4/2; ⊙9am-7.30pm Tue-Sun), a modern museum built round a Roman amphitheatre. Exhibits chart the history of Chieti and include weapons and pottery dating back to the Iron Age.

About 3km downhill from the historic centre, **Agriturismo Il Quadrifoglio** (☎0871 63 4 00; www.agriturismoilquadrifoglio.com; Strada Licini 22, Località Colle Marcone; s/d €40/50; Ⓟ) is a picturesque farmhouse with rustic rooms, panoramic views and a lovely, overflowing garden. Meals are €15 to €20. To get here follow signs to Colle Marcone.

Chieti's helpful **tourist office** (☎0871 6 36 40; Via Spaventa 47; ⊙8am-1pm & 4-7pm Mon-Sat Jul-Sep, 8am-1pm Mon-Sat & 3-6pm Tue, Thu & Fri Oct-Jun) can provide information and accommodation lists for the town and surrounding area.

Regular buses (€2, 20 minutes) link Chieti with Pescara.

Vasto

POP 39,820

On Abruzzo's southern coast, the hilltop town of Vasto has an atmospheric medieval quarter and superb sea views. Much of the *centro storico* dates from the 15th century, a golden period in which the city was known as 'the Athens of the Abruzzi'.

Two kilometres downhill is the blowsy resort of **Vasto Marina**, a strip of hotels, restaurants and camp grounds fronting a long sandy beach. About 5km further north along the coast is the beautiful **Spiaggia di Punta Penna** and the **Riserva Naturale di Punta Aderci** (www.puntaderci.it), a 285-hectare area of uncontaminated rocky coastline, ideal for long beach walks, swimming and diving.

Sights & Activities

In summer, the action is on the beach at Vasto Marina. Up in the old town, interest centres on the small historic centre.

From the landmark **Castello Caldoresco** on Piazza Rossetti, Corso de Parma leads down to the 13th-century **Cattedrale di San Giuseppe** (☎0873 36 71 93; Piazza Pudente; ⊙8.30am-noon & 4.30-7pm), a lovely low-key example of Romanesque architecture. Nearby, the Renaissance Palazzo d'Avalos houses the **Museo Civico Archaeologica** (☎0873 36 77 73; Piazza Pudente; admission €1.50; ⊙9.30am-12.30pm & 4.30-7.30pm Tue-Sun) with its eclectic collection of ancient bronzes, glasswork and paintings, as well as three other museums – the **Pinacoteca Comunale** (admission €3.50), the **Galleria d'Arte Moderna** (admission free) and the **Museo del Costume** (admission €1.50). A combined ticket to see all museums costs €4.50.

Sleeping & Eating

Hotel San Marco HOTEL €
(☎0873 6 05 37; www.hotelsanmarcovasto.com; Via Madonna dell'Asilo 4; s €42-52, d €66-86; ❄️📶) Just off Corso Garibaldi in the upper town, this cracking little three-star place is excellent value for money, offering slick modern rooms at far from designer prices.

Il Panzotto PIZZERIA €
(☎0873 6 93 41; Loggia Amblingh 51; pizzas €6.50-9; ⊙Wed-Mon) If the panoramic views of the sea weren't enough, the excellent pizza (with over 40 choices) will win you over. Also has a selection of pasta and meat dishes.

Information

Tourist office (☎0873 36 73 12; Piazza del Popolo 18; ⊙9am-1pm daily & 4-7pm Mon-Sat Jul–mid-Sep, 9am-1pm Mon-Fri & 3-6pm Tue, Thu & Fri mid-Sep–Jun) In the *centro storico*.

Getting There & Away

The train station (Vasto-San Salvo) is about 2km south of Vasto Marina. Trains run frequently to Pescara (€4.30, one hour) and Termoli (from €2.30, 15 minutes). From the station take bus 1 or 4 for Vasto Marina and the town centre (€1).

MOLISE

One of Italy's forgotten regions, Molise is one of the few parts of the country where you can still get off the beaten track. And while it lacks the grandeur of its northern neighbour, the lack of a slick tourist infrastructure and the raw, unspoiled countryside ensure a gritty authenticity that's so often missing in more-celebrated areas.

To get the best out of Molise, you really need your own transport.

Campobasso

POP 51,000

Molise's regional capital and main transport hub is a sprawling, uninspiring city with little to recommend it. However, if you do find yourself passing through, the pocket-sized *centro storico* is worth a quick look.

Although rarely open, the Romanesque churches of San Bartolomeo (Salita San Bartolomeo) and San Giorgio (Viale della Rimembranza) are fine examples of their genre. Further up the hill, at the top of a steep tree-lined avenue, sits Castello Monforte (0874 6 32 99; admission free; 9am-1pm & 3.30-6.30pm Tue-Sun). Ceramics found in the castle are now on show at the small Museo Samnitico (Samnite Museum; 0874 41 22 65; Via Chiarizia 12; admission free; 9am-5.30pm), along with artefacts from local archaeological sites.

For a spot of lunch, Trattoria La Grotta di Zi Concetta (0874 31 13 78; Via Larino 9; meals €25; lunch & dinner Mon-Fri) is an old-school trattoria serving delicious homemade pasta and superb meat dishes.

The tourist office (0874 41 56 62; Piazza della Vittoria 14; 8.30am-1.30pm Mon-Fri, 3-5.30pm Mon & Wed) can provide further information on the city and surrounding province.

Unless you're coming from Isernia, Campobasso is best reached by bus. Services link with Termoli (€3.30, 1¼ hours, 10 daily), Naples (€9.60, 2¾ hours, four daily weekdays), and Rome (€11.90, three hours, five daily). Up to 14 daily trains run to/from Isernia (€2.80, one hour).

Around Campobasso

One of Molise's hidden treasures, the Roman ruins of Saepinum (admission free) are among the best preserved and least visited in the country. Unlike Pompeii and Ostia Antica, which were both major ports, Saepinum was a small provincial town of no great importance. It was originally established by the Samnites but the Romans conquered it in 293 BC, paving the way for an economic boom in the 1st and 2nd centuries AD. Some 700 years later, it was sacked by Arab invaders. The walled town retains three of its four original gates and its two main roads, the *cardus maximus* and the *decamanus*. Highlights include the forum, basilica and theatre, near to which the Museo Archeologico Vittoriano (admission €2; 9.30am-1pm & 3-6.30pm Tue-Sun) displays artefacts unearthed on the site.

It's not easy to reach Saepinum by public transport, but the Larivera (0874 6 47 44; www.lariverabus.it) bus from Campobasso to Sepinio (€1.20, six daily weekdays) generally stops near the site at Altilia, although it's best to ask the driver.

Looming over the ruins are the Monti del Matese (Matese Mountains). Campitello Matese (elevation 1430m) is a popular ski resort with facilities for winter and summer sports. Outside of the ski season and summer holiday period, the resort pretty much shuts up shop.

Between December and March, Autolinee Micone (0874 78 01 20) runs three daily buses from Campobasso up to Campitello Matese (one hour).

Isernia

POP 22,000

Surrounded by remote, scarcely populated hills, Isernia doesn't make a huge impression. Earthquakes and a massive WWII bombing raid spared little of its original *centro storico* and the modern centre is a drab, workaday place. The one reason to stop over is to visit the site of one of Europe's oldest human settlements, a 700,000-year-old village unearthed by road workers in 1978. Excavations are ongoing, although you can visit by calling the site office (0865 41 35 26; Contrada Ramiera Vecchia 1, Localita La Pineta).

If you don't make it to the site, the dusty Museo Santa Maria delle Monache (0865 41 05 00; Corso Marcelli 48; admission €2; 8.30am-7pm) houses many of its finds, including piles of elephant and rhino bones, fossils and stone tools.

If you want to stay the night, Hotel Sayonara (0865 5 09 92; www.sayonara.is.it; Via G Berta 131; s/d €55/85; [*]) is the most centrally located hotel. It's an anonymous business-style set-up, but rooms are comfortable and there's a convenient restaurant.

Isernia's **tourist office** (📞0865 39 92; 6th fl, Palazzo della Regione, Via Farinacci 9; ⏰8am-2pm Mon-Sat) can provide accommodation lists but little more in the way of practical help.

From the bus terminus next to the train station on Piazza della Repubblica, **Trasporti Molise** (📞0874 49 30 80; www.molisetrasporti.it) runs buses to Campobasso (€2.80, 50 minutes, five daily) and Termoli (€7, 1¾ hours, three daily). Get tickets from Bar Ragno d'Oro on the square.

Trains connect Isernia with Sulmona (€7.10, three to four hours, two daily), Campobasso (€2.80, one hour, 14 daily), Naples (€6, two hours, five daily) and Rome (€10.50, two hours, six daily).

Around Isernia

The hills around Isernia are peppered with places of interest. About 30km northeast of town, outside **Pietrabbondante**, the remains of a 2nd-century-BC **Samnite theatre-temple complex** (📞0865 7 61 29; adult/reduced €2/1; ⏰10am-6pm) reward a visit, as much for its panoramic setting high above the rolling green countryside than anything else.

En route, the 350-hectare **Riserva Collemeluccio** (⏰9.30am-7pm Jun-Sep, to 5.30pm Apr-May, to 4.30pm Oct-Mar) is a prime picnic venue. It also offers good walking, with several trails leading off from the roadside visitors centre.

Further north, **Agnone** is an ancient hilltop town famous for its bell making. For more than 1000 years, local artisans have been producing church bells for some of Italy's most famous churches, including St Peter's Basilica in Rome. Learn all about it at the **Marinelli Pontificia Fonderia di Campane** (📞0865 7 82 35; www.campanemarinelli.com; Via D'Onofrio 14; adult/reduced €5/3.50; ⏰guided tours 11am, noon, 4pm & 6pm Mon-Sat & 11am Sun Aug, noon & 4pm Mon-Sat & noon Sun Sep-Jul). For further information and details of accommodation in the area, ask at the helpful **tourist office** (📞0865 7 72 49; www.prolocoagnone.com; Corso Vittorio Emanuele 78; ⏰9.30am-12.30pm & 3.30-6pm).

A 30km drive northwest of Isernia, near Castel San Vincenzo, the **Abbazia di San Vincenzo al Volturno** (📞0865 95 52 46; ⏰by appointment) is famous for its cycle of 9th-century frescoes by Epifanio (824–42). The abbey, one of the foremost monastic and cultural centres in 9th-century Europe, is now home to a community of Benedictine nuns.

From Isernia, **SATI** (📞0874 60 52 20) buses serve Pietrabbondante (€1.50, 35 minutes, two daily) and Agnone (€2.05, one hour, nine daily). Buy tickets on the bus. **Larivera** (📞0874 6 47 44; www.lariverabus.it) buses run between Isernia and Castel San Vincenzo (€1.20, 45 minutes, two daily), a 1km walk from the abbey.

Termoli

POP 32,600

Despite its touristy trattorias and brassy bars, Molise's top beach resort retains a winning, low-key charm. At the eastern end of the seafront, the pretty *borgo antico* (old town) juts out to sea atop a natural pier, dividing the sandy beach from Termoli's small harbour. From the port, year-round ferries sail for the Isole Tremiti.

The town's most famous landmark, Frederick II's 13th-century **Castello Svevo** (📞0875 71 23 54; ⏰on request) guards entry to the tiny *borgo* – a tangle of narrow streets, pastel-coloured houses and souvenir shops. From the castle, follow the road up and you come to Piazza Duomo and Termoli's majestic 12th-century **cathedral** (📞0875 70 80 25). A masterpiece of Puglian-Romanesque architecture, the cream-coloured facade features a striking round-arched central portal.

🛏 Sleeping

Locanda Alfieri ALBERGO DIFFUSO €€
(📞0875 70 81 13; www.locandalfieri.com; Via Duomo 39; s incl breakfast €40-55, d incl breakfast €75-110; ❄🛜) A 'diffused hotel' with rooms scattered throughout the *centro storico*, this is a great base from which to explore Termoli, the Isole Tremiti and Molise. Room styles vary from 'creative' traditional to modern-chic (some with ubercool chromatherapy showers).

Residenza Sveva ALBERGO DIFFUSO €€
(📞0875 70 68 03; www.residenzasveva.com; Piazza Duomo 11; s €50-80, d €89-180; ❄🛜) This elegant *centro storico* 'diffused hotel' has its reception on Piazza Duomo, near the cathedral, but the 21 rooms are squeezed into several *palazzi* in the *borgo*. The style is summery with plenty of gleaming blue tiles

and traditional embroidery. There's also an elegant seafood restaurant (open Wednesday to Sunday) on site.

Coppola Villaggio Camping Azzurra
CAMPGROUND €

(☎0875 5 24 04; www.camping.it/molise/azzurra; SS16 km538; camping per person €5-9, tent €9-15, car €3, 4-person bungalow €60-120; ☺mid-May-Sep; ℗) Termoli's only camp ground is a modern, beachfront affair 2km outside town on the SS16 coastal road. As well as shady tent pitches and bungalows, on-site facilities include a minimarket and restaurant.

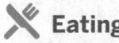 Eating

La Sacrestia
TRADITIONAL ITALIAN €

(☎0875 70 56 03; Via Ruffini 48-50; meals €25, pizzas €7-8; ☺daily summer, Wed-Mon winter) This is one of the better restaurants in the lively area between Corso Nazionale and Via Fratelli Brigida. Sit streetside or in the brick vaulted interior and chow down on knock-out pizza or fresh-off-the-boat seafood.

Ristorante Da Nicolino
SEAFOOD €€

(☎0875 70 68 04; Via Roma 3; meals €35; ☺Fri-Wed) Well regarded by locals, this discreet restaurant serves the best seafood in town. Highly recommended is the *brodetto di pesce* (fish soup).

Sognadoro
PIZZERIA €

(☎0875 70 64 42; Via F Mugnano Rocca 3; pizzas €7-8; ☺Wed-Mon) The extensive range of delicious pizza warrants a return visit at this friendly and homey pizzeria in the old town.

❶ Information

Tourist office (☎0875 70 39 13; www.termoli.net; 1st fl, Piazza Bega 42; ☺8am-2pm Mon-Fri & 3-6pm Mon & Wed-Fri) Helpful but hard to find, it's tucked away in a dodgy-looking car park behind a small shopping gallery, 100m east of the train station.

❶ Getting There & Away

BOAT Termoli is the only port with year-round ferries to the Isole Tremiti. **Tirrenia Navigazione** (☎0875 70 53 43; www.tirrenia.it; tickets €15.80-17.70) runs a year-round ferry and **Navigazione Libera del Golfo** (☎0875 70 48 59; www.navlib.it; tickets €15-19; ☺Apr-Sep) operates a quicker hydrofoil. Buy tickets at the port.

BUS Termoli's bus station is beside Via Martiri della Resistenza. Various companies have services to/from Campobasso (€3.30, 1¼ hours, 10 daily), Isernia (€7, 1¾ hours, three daily), Pescara (€6.20, 1¼ hours, four daily), Naples (€14, 3½ hours, four daily) and Rome (€15, four hours, frequent).

TRAIN Direct trains serve Bologna (from €36.50, four to 5½ hours, 10 daily), Lecce (from €23.10, 3½ to 4½ hours, 10 daily) and stations along the Adriatic coast.

Albanian Towns

Several villages to the south of Termoli form an Albanian enclave that dates back to the 15th century. These include Campomarino, Portocannone, San Martino in Pensilis and Ururi. Although the inhabitants shrugged off their Orthodox religion in the 18th century, they still use a version of Albanian that's incomprehensible to outsiders. However, it's for their *carressi* (chariot races) that the villages are best known. Each year Ururi (3 May), Portocannone (the Monday after Whit Sunday) and San Martino in Pensilis (30 April) stage a no-holds-barred chariot race. The chariots (more like carts) are pulled by bulls and hurtle round a traditional course, urged on by villagers on horseback.

Getting to these villages is quite a trial without your own transport, but Larivera runs daily buses to all four from Termoli.

Naples & Campania

POPULATION: 5.8 MILLION

Includes »

Why Go?

Campania could be a multi–Academy Award winner, swooping everything from Best Cinematography to Best Original Screenplay. Strewn with three millennia worth of temples, castles and palaces, it heaves with legend – Icarus plunged to his death in the Campi Flegrei, sirens lured sailors off Sorrento, and Wagner put quill to paper in lofty Ravello. Campania's cast includes some of Europe's most fabled destinations, from haunting Pompeii to Med-chic Capri. At its heart thumps bad-boy Naples, a love-it-or-loathe-it sprawl of operatic *palazzi*, mouth-watering markets, and art-crammed museums. Home to Italy's top coffee and pizza, it's also one of the country's gastronomic superstars. Beyond its pounding streets lies a wonderland of lush bay islands, faded fishing villages and wild mountains. Welcome to Italy at its nail-biting best.

Best Places to Eat

- » Ristorante Il Buco (p665)
- » Lo Scoglio (p666)
- » Ristorante Radici (p637)

Best Places to Stay

- » Hotel San Francesco al Monte (p636)
- » Hotel Piazza Bellini (p635)
- » Hotel Luna Convento (p671)
- » Casale Giancesare (p681)

When to Go
Naples

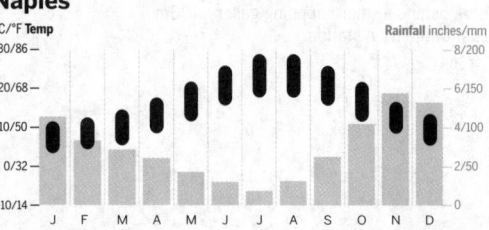

Easter Follow the faithful at Sorrento and Procida's mystical Easter processions.

May Naples celebrates culture with its event-packed Maggio dei Monumenti festival.

September Hit the coast for warm, languid days without the August crowds.

The Subterranean City

Mysterious shrines, secret passageways, forgotten burial crypts: it might sound like the set of an *Indiana Jones* film, but it's actually what lurks beneath Naples' loud and greasy streets. Subterranean Naples is one of the world's most thrilling urban wonderlands; a silent, mostly undiscovered sprawl of cathedral-like cisterns, pin-sized conduits, catacombs and ancient ruins.

Speleologists (cave specialists) estimate that about 60% of Neapolitans live and work above this network, known in Italian as the *sottosuolo* (underground). Since the end of WWII, some 700 cavities have been discovered, from original Greek-era grottoes, to palaeo-Christian burial chambers and royal Bourbon escape routes. According to the experts, this is simply a prelude, with another 2 million sq metres of troglodytic treats to unfurl.

Naples' dedicated caving geeks are quick to tell you that their underworld is one of the largest and oldest on earth. Sure, Paris might claim a catacomb or two, but its subterranean offerings don't come close to this giant's 2500-year history.

And what a history it is. Naples' most famous saint, San Gennaro, was interred in the Catacombe di San Gennaro in the 5th century. A century later, in 536, Belisario and his troops caught Naples by surprise by storming the city through the city's ancient tunnels. According to legend, Alfonso of Aragon used the same trick in 1442, undermining the city walls by using an underground passageway leading into a tailor's shop and straight into town. Even the city's dreaded Camorra has got in on the act. In 1992, the notorious Stolder clan was busted for running a subterranean drug lab, with escape routes heading straight to the clan boss' pad.

Don't Miss

Naples' Cappella Sansevero is home to the astounding Cristo Velato (Veiled Christ), its marble veil so translucent it baffles to this day.

Hold the Prawns

Order a pizza marinara in Naples and you'll get a simple affair of tomato, garlic and olive oil. And the seafood? There is none. The pizza was named after fishermen who took it out to sea for lunch.

Resources

» Turismo Regione Campania (www.incampania.it) Up-to-date events, as well as articles and itineraries.

» Italy Traveller (www.italytraveller.com) Luxe and boutique hotel listings, themed itineraries and travel ideas.

Naples' Top Museums

» Museo Archeologico Nazionale (p628) A veritable treasure chest of ancient art, propaganada and erotica

» Museo di Capodimonte (p634) From Caravaggio to Warhol.

» Museo del Novecento, Castel San't Elmo (p632) A stylish ode to Naples' 20th-century art scene

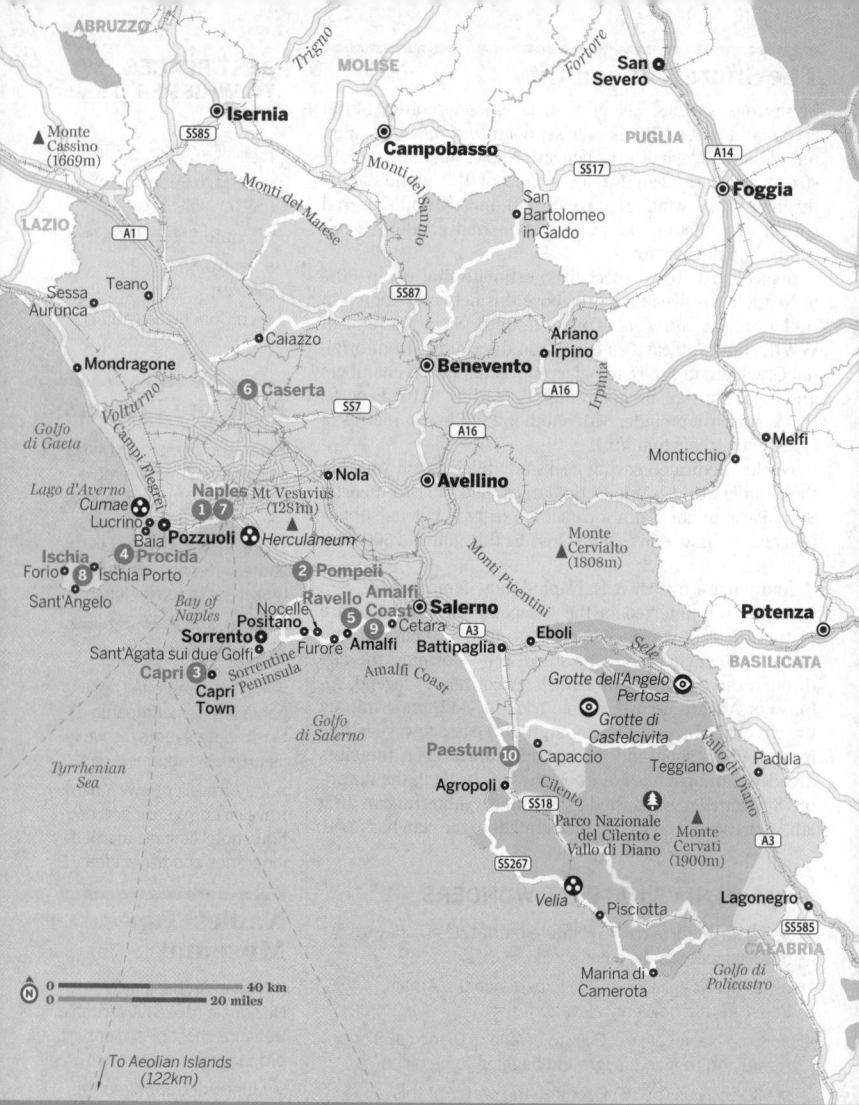

Naples & Campania Highlights

① Explore Naples' labyrinthine underworld on a **Napoli Sotterranea (p634)** tour

② Channel the ancients on the ill-fated streets of **Pompeii** (p657)

③ Be bewitched by Capri's ethereal **Grotta Azzurra** (p645)

④ Lunch by the waves on pastel-hued **Procida** (p654)

⑤ Treat your senses to a concert at Ravello's dreamy **Villa Rufolo** (p675)

⑥ Pretend you're royalty at **Palazzo Reale** (p644)

⑦ Whet your appetite at Naples' produce-packed **Mercato di Porta Nolana** (p628)

⑧ Indulge in a little thermal therapy on **Ischia** (p651)

⑨ Walk with the gods on the **Amalfi Coast** (p674)

⑩ Admire Hellenic ingenuity at the World Heritage–listed temples of **Paestum** (p680)

NAPLES

POP 3,079,000

Italy's most misunderstood city is also one of its finest – an exhilarating mess of bombastic baroque churches, bellowing baristas and electrifying street life. Contradiction is the catchphrase here; a place where anarchy, pollution and crime sidle up to lavish palaces, mighty museums and aristocratic tailors.

First stop for many is the Unesco World Heritage–listed *centro storico* (historic city centre). It's here, under the washing lines, that you'll find Naples' arabesque street life – cocky kids playing football in noisy piazzas, overloaded Vespas hurtling through cobbled alleyways and clued-up *casalinghe* (homemakers) bullying market vendors. Once the heart of Roman Neapolis, this intoxicating warren of Dickensian streets groans with ancient churches, citrus-filled cloisters, and rough'n'tumble pizzerias.

By the sea the cityscape opens up. Imperious palaces flank show-off squares as Gucci-clad shoppers strut their stuff and lunch in chandeliered cafes. This is Royal Naples, the Naples of the Bourbons that so impressed the 18th-century grand tourists.

History

According to legend, traders from Rhodes established the city on the island of Megaris (where Castel dell'Ovo now stands) in about 680 BC. Originally called Parthenope in honour of the siren whose body had earlier washed up there (she drowned herself after failing to seduce Ulysses), it was eventually incorporated into a new city, Neapolis, founded by Greeks from Cumae (Cuma) in 474 BC. However, within 150 years it was in Roman hands, becoming something of a VIP resort favoured by emperors Pompey, Caesar and Tiberius.

After the fall of the Roman Empire, Naples became a duchy, originally under the Byzantines and later as an independent dukedom, until it was captured in 1139 by the Normans and absorbed into the Kingdom of the Two Sicilies. The Normans, in turn, were replaced by the German Swabians, whose charismatic leader Frederick II injected the city with new institutions, including its university.

The Swabian period came to a violent end with the victory of Charles I of Anjou at the 1266 battle of Benevento. The Angevins did much for Naples, promoting art and culture, building Castel Nuovo and enlarging the port, but they were unable to stop the Spanish Aragons taking the city in 1442. Naples continued to prosper, though. Alfonso I of Aragon, in particular, introduced new laws and encouraged the arts and sciences.

In 1503 Naples was absorbed by Spain, which sent viceroys to rule as virtual dictators. Despite Spain's heavy-handed rule, Naples flourished artistically and acquired much of its splendour. Indeed, it continued

---

NAPLES IN...

Two Days

Kick-start with espresso at **Caffè Mexico** before taking in the frescoes inside **Chiesa del Gesù Nuovo**, the majolica-tiled cloisters of **Basilica di Santa Chiara** and the sculptures inside **Cappella Sansevero**. Lunch at **Pizzeria Gino Sorbillo** before taking the funicular up to Vomero and the **Certosa di San Martino**. When the sun sets, nibble on aperitivo at **Nàis** and dine at **Ristorante Radici**. Start day two with a *sfogliatella* from **Pintauro** before tackling the **Museo Archeologico Nazionale**. Refuel with cheese and wine at **La Stanza del Gusto** then go underground on a **Napoli Sotterranea** tour. Catch an evening sea breeze at **Castel dell'Ovo** before drinks and a bite with the culture crowd at **Penguin Cafè**.

Four Days

Spend day three among the ruins at **Pompeii** or **Herculaneum**, dining at **President** before heading back to town for a nightcap at elegant, piazza-side **Intra Moenia**. On day four, grab some picnic provisions at **La Pignasecca** and devour them in leafy **Capodimonte**. Fed, catch Caravaggio's moving *Flagellazione* at the art-crammed **Museo di Capodimonte**, then cap off your stay with a night of encores at the luscious **Teatro San Carlo**.

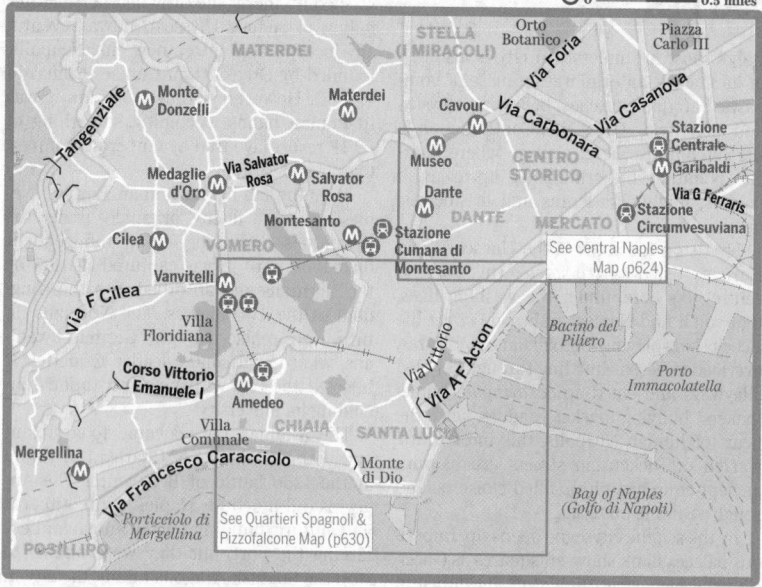

to bloom when the Spanish Bourbons re-established Naples as the capital of the Kingdom of the Two Sicilies in 1734. Aside from a Napoleonic interlude under Joachim Murat (1806–15), the Bourbons remained until unseated by Garibaldi and the Kingdom of Italy in 1860.

MODERN STRUGGLES & HOPES

Naples was heavily bombed in WWII, and the effects can still be seen on many monuments around the city. Since the war, Campania's capital has continued to suffer. Endemic corruption and the re-emergence of the Camorra have plagued much of the city's postwar resurrection, reaching a nadir in the 1980s after a severe earthquake in 1980.

In 2011, the city's sporadic garbage-disposal crisis flared up again, leading frustrated residents to set fire to uncollected rubbish in the streets.

More encouraging has been the recent inauguration of the poptastic Università metro station (designed by Karim Rashid and the first of four new stations on the nearly completed extension of Linea 1) and the city's upcoming role as host of the Universal Forum of Cultures in 2013.

◉ Sights

CENTRO STORICO

The three east-west *decumani* (main streets) of Naples' historic centre follow the original street plan of ancient Neapolis. Most of the major sights are grouped around the busiest two of these classical thoroughfares: 'Spaccanapoli' (consisting of Via Benedetto Croce, Via San Biagio dei Librai and Via Vicaria Vecchia) and Via dei Tribunali. North of Via dei Tribunali, Via della Sapienza, Via Anticaglia and Via Santissimi Apostoli make up the quieter third *decumanus*.

Duomo — DUOMO, MUSEUM
(Map p624; ☎081 44 90 97; Via Duomo; ◷8.30am-1.30pm & 2.30-8pm Mon-Sat, 8.30am-1.30pm & 4.30-8pm Sun) This is Naples' spiritual centrepiece, sitting on the site of earlier churches, themselves preceded by a temple to the god Neptune. Begun by Charles I of Anjou in 1272 and consecrated in 1315, it was largely destroyed by an earthquake in 1456. Copious nips and tucks over the centuries, including the addition of a late-19th-century neo-Gothic facade, have created a melange of styles and influences.

Topping the huge central nave is a gilded coffered ceiling studded with late mannerist art. The high sections of the nave and the transept were decorated by Luca Giordano.

The 17th-century baroque **Cappella di San Gennaro** (Chapel of St Januarius; also known as the Chapel of the Treasury; ⊙8.30am-12.30pm & 4.30-6.30pm Mon-Sat, 8.30am-1pm & 5-7pm Sun) features a fiery painting by Giuseppe Ribera and a bevy of silver busts and bronze statues. Above them, a heavenly dome glows with frescoes by Giovanni Lanfranco. Hidden away behind the altar is a 14th-century silver bust containing the skull of St Januarius and the two phials that hold his miraculous blood. Naples' patron saint was martyred at Pozzuoli in AD 305, and according to legend, his blood liquefied in these phials when his body was transferred back to Naples. For information on the mysterious San Gennaro festival, see p634.

The next chapel eastwards contains an urn with the saint's bones, cupboards full of femurs, tibias and fibulas, and a stash of other grisly relics. Below the high altar is the Renaissance **Cappella Carafa**, also known as the Crypt of San Gennaro.

Halfway down the north aisle and beyond the 17th-century Basilica di Santa Restituta is the fascinating **archaeological zone** (⊙morning hours vary & 4.30-7pm Mon-Sat, 9am-noon Sun), where tunnels burrow into the remains of the site's original Greek and Roman buildings. At the time of research, the archaeological zone was closed for restoration, although the **baptistry** (admission €1.50; ⊙8.30am-12.30pm & 4.30-7pm Mon-Sat, 8.30am-1.30pm Sun), the oldest in western Europe, with remarkably fresh 4th-century mosaics, remained open.

At the *duomo's* southern end, the **Museo del Tesoro di San Gennaro** (✆081 29 49 80; Via Duomo 149; admission €6; ⊙10am-5pm Thu-Tue) glimmers with gifts made to St Januarius over the centuries, from bronze busts and sumptuous paintings to silver ampullas and a gilded 18th-century sedan chair.

Cappella Sansevero CHURCH
(Map p624; ✆081 551 84 70; www.museosansevero.it; Via de Sanctis 19; admission €7; ⊙10am-5.40pm Mon & Wed-Sat, 10am-1.10pm Sun) Don't be fooled by the Plain Jane exterior: awaiting inside is some of the city's most sumptuous sculpture, including Corradini's erotically charged, ironically named *Pudicizia* (Modesty). The centrepiece, however, is *Cristo Velato* (Veiled Christ), Giuseppe Sanmartino's jaw-dropping depiction of Jesus covered by a veil so realistic that it's tempting to try and lift it. The air of mystery continues downstairs, where two meticulously preserved human arterial systems are a testament to the bizarre obsession of alchemist Prince Raimondo di Sangro, the man who financed the chapel's 18th-century makeover.

Basilica di Santa Chiara CHURCH, MUSEUM
(Map p624; ✆081 551 66 73; www.monastero disantachiara.eu; Via Benedetto Croce; ⊙7.30am-1pm & 4.30-8pm) What you see today is not

THE DARK PRINCE OF NAPLES

While Naples' history bubbles with tales of miraculous and magical characters, few rev up the rumour mill like Raimondo di Sangro (1710–71). Inventor, scientist, soldier and alchemist, the so-called Prince of Sansevero reputedly imported freemasonry into the Kingdom of Naples, resulting in a temporary excommunication from the Catholic Church.

Yet even a papal rethink couldn't quell the salacious stories surrounding Raimondo, which spanned everything from castrating promising young sopranos to knocking off seven cardinals and making furniture with their skin and bones. According to Italian philosopher Benedetto Croce (1866–1952), who wrote about Di Sangro in his book *Storie e Leggende Napoletane* (Neapolitan Stories and Legends), the alchemist held a Faustian fascination for the *centro storico's* masses. To them, his supposed knack for the dark arts saw him master everything from replicating the miracle of San Gennaro's blood to reducing marble to dust with a simple touch.

To this day, rumours surround the two perfect anatomical models in the crypt of the Di Sangro funerary chapel, the Cappella Sansevero. Believed to be the preserved bodies of his defunct domestics, some believe that they were far from dead when the prince got started on the embalming. Tall tale or not, the exact method of preservation still confounds scientists today.

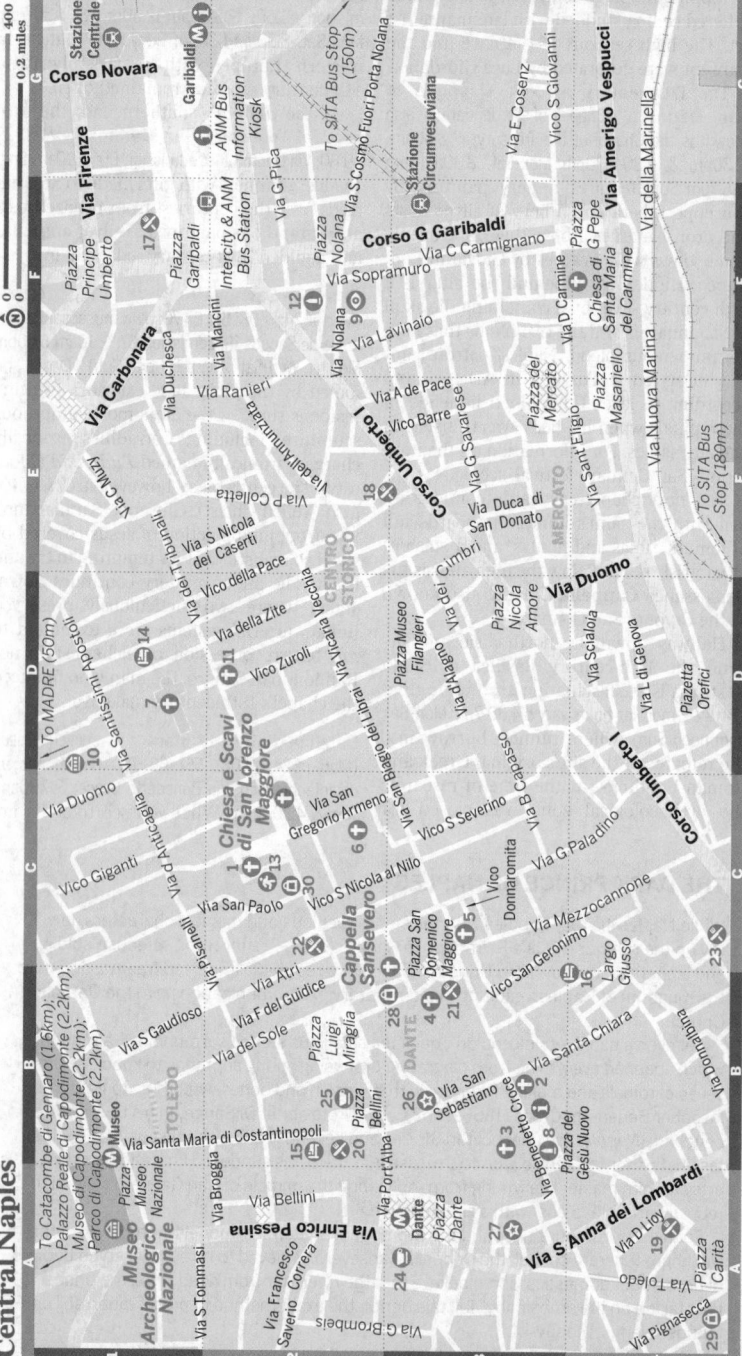

the original 14th-century Angevin church but a brilliant re-creation – the original was all but destroyed by Allied bombing in August 1943. The real attraction, however, is the adjacent **nuns' cloisters** (adult/concession €5/3.50; ⊙9.30am-5.30pm Mon-Sat, 10am-2.30pm Sun, last entry 30min before closing), a long parapet lavished with decorative ceramic tiles depicting scenes of rural life, from hunting to posing peasants. The four internal walls are covered with softly coloured 17th-century frescoes of Franciscan tales. Adjacent to the cloisters, an elegant **museum** of mostly ecclesiastical props also features the excavated ruins of a 1st-century spa complex.

Chiesa del Gesù Nuovo　　　　　CHURCH
(Map p624; ☑081 557 81 11; Piazza del Gesù Nuovo; ⊙7am-1pm & 4.15-7.30pm Mon-Sat, 7am-1.45pm Sun) One of Naples' finest Renaissance buildings, this 16th-century church actually sports the 15th-century, pyramid-shaped facade of Palazzo Sanseverino, converted to create the church. Awaiting inside is a lavish 17th-century makeover, with works by a trio of Naples' mightiest baroque artists – Cosimo Fanzago, Luca Giordano and Francesco Solimena.

Puncturing the Piazza del Gesù outside is the soaring **Guglia dell'Immacolata**, an 18th-century obelisk.

Chiesa e Scavi di San Lorenzo Maggiore　　CHURCH, HISTORICAL SITE
(Map p624; ☑081 211 08 60; Via dei Tribunali 316; church admission free, excavations & museum adult/child €9/6; ⊙9.30am-5.30pm Mon-Sat, to 1.30pm Sun) A masterpiece of French Gothic architecture, this late 13th-century church features the 14th-century mosaic-covered tomb of Catherine of Austria. You can also pass through to the cloisters of the neighbouring convent, where the poet Petrarch stayed in 1345.

Beneath the complex are some remarkable *scavi* (excavations) of the original Graeco-Roman city. Stretching the length of the underground area is a road lined with ancient bakeries, wineries and communal laundries.

Historical Riches

Few Italian regions can match Campania's historical legacy. Colonised by the ancient Greeks and loved by the Romans, it's a sun-drenched repository of A-list antiquities, from World Heritage wonders to lesser-known archaeological gems.

Campi Flegrei

1 The Phlegraean Fields simmer with ruins. Seek out the Sybil (mythical prophetess) at the Acropoli di Cuma (p643), ponder ancient booty at the Museo Archeologico dei Campi Flegrei (p643) or spare a thought for panicked martyrs at the Anfiteatro Flavio (p643).

Paestum

2 Great Greek temples never go out of vogue and those at Paestum (p680) are among the greatest outside of Greece. With the oldest structures stretching back to the 6th century BC, this place makes Rome's Colosseum feel positively modern.

Herculaneum

3 A bite-sized Pompeii, Herculaneum (p655) is even better preserved than its nearby rival. This is the place to delve into the details, from once-upon-a-time shop advertisements and furniture, to quirky mosaics and even an ancient security device.

Pompeii

4 Short of stepping into the Tardis, Pompeii (p657) is your best bet for a little time travel. Snap-locked in ash for centuries, its excavated streetscapes offer a tangible, 3D encounter with the ancients and their daily lives.

Subterranean Naples

5 Eerie aqueducts, mysterious burial crypts and ancient streetscapes: beneath Naples' hyperactive streets lies a wonderland of Graeco-Roman ruins. For a taste, head below the Chiesa di San Lorenzo Maggiore (p622) or follow the leader on a Napoli Sotterranea (p634) tour.

Clockwise from top left
1. Museo Archeologico dei Campi Flegrei 2. Tempio di Nettuno, Paestum 3. Ruins of Herculaneum 4. Ruins of Pompeii.

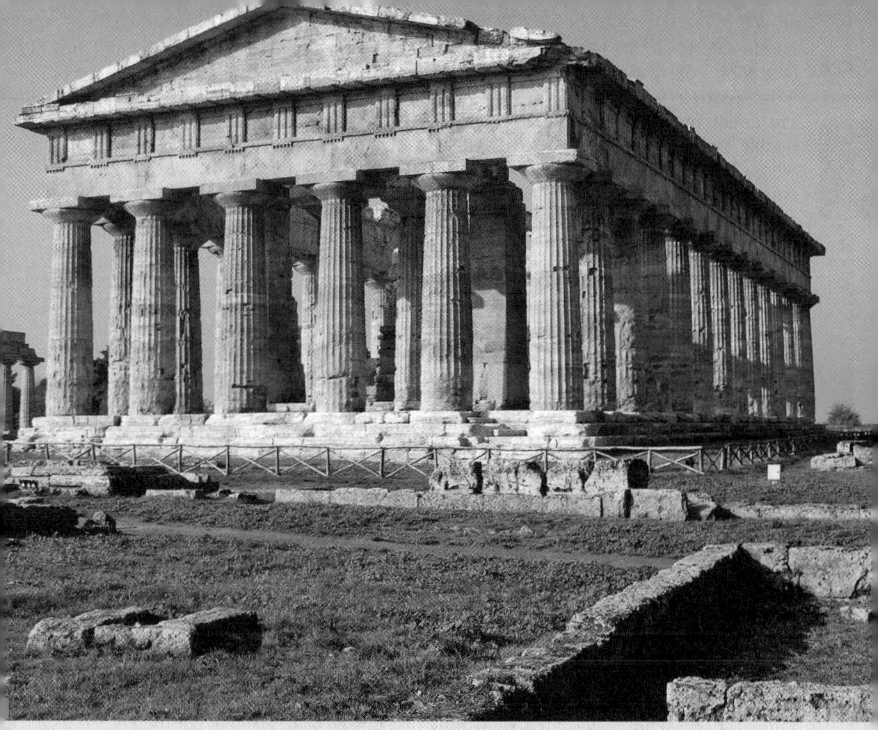

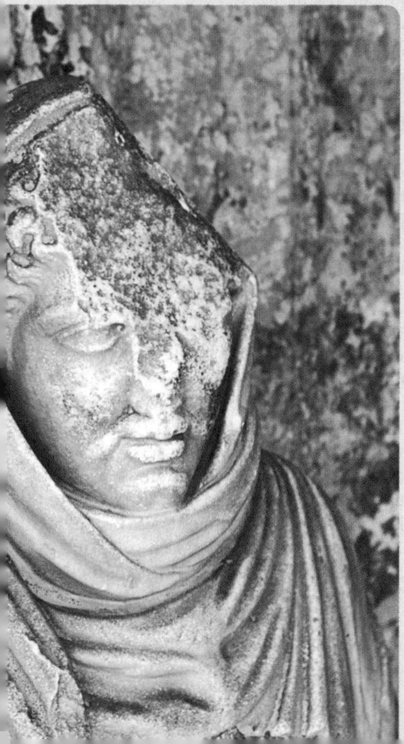

STOCK ITALIA / ALAMY ©

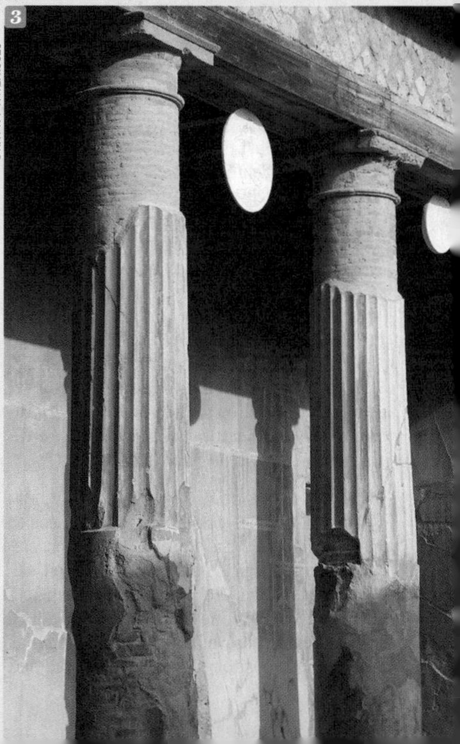

Basilica di San Paolo Maggiore CHURCH
(Map p624; ☑081 45 40 48; Piazza San Gaetano 76; ⊙9am-6pm Mon-Sat, 10am-12.30pm Sun) Across the street on Via dei Tribunali, a grand double staircase leads up to this basilica, whose huge gold-stuccoed interior features paintings by Massimo Stanzione, as well as frescoes by Francesco Solimena in the exquisite sacristy.

Pio Monte della Misericordia CHURCH, ART GALLERY
(Map p624; ☑081 44 69 44; Via dei Tribunali 253; admission €5; ⊙9am-2pm Thu-Tue) Caravaggio's masterpiece *Le sette opere di Misericordia* (The Seven Acts of Mercy) is considered by many to be the single most important painting in Naples. And it's here that you'll see it, hung above the main altar of this small octagonal church. The small 1st-floor art gallery boasts a fine collection of Renaissance and baroque paintings.

MADRE MUSEUM
(off Map p624; Museo d'Arte Contemporanea Donnaregina; ☑081 1931 3016; www.museomadre.it; Via Settembrini 79; admission €7, Mon free; ⊙10.30am-2.30pm Wed-Mon) In a city overwhelmed by the classical, Naples' top contemporary museum makes for a refreshing change. Permanent collection highlights include Jeff Koons' uberkitsch *Wild Boy and Puppy,* Rebecca Horn's eerie *Spirits,* and a perspective-warping installation by Anish Kapoor.

Mercato di Porta Nolana MARKET
(Map p624; ⊙8am-6pm Mon-Sat, to 2pm Sun) A heady spectacle of sing-song fishmongers, fragrant bakeries, industrious Chinese traders and contraband cigarette stalls, this street market is Naples at its vociferous, gut-rumbling best. Dive in for anything from buxom tomatoes and mozzarella to golden-fried street snacks, cheap luggage and bootleg CDs. The market's namesake, **Porta Nolana,** is one of Naples' medieval city gates. Standing at the head of Via Sopramuro, its arch features a bas-relief of Ferdinand I of Aragon on horseback.

Museo Diocesano di Napoli MUSEUM
(Map p624; ☑081 557 13 65; www.museodiocesanonapoli.it; Chiesa di Santa Maria Donnaregina Nuova, Largo Donnaregina; admission €6; ⊙9.30am-4.30pm Mon & Wed-Sat, 9.30am-2pm Sun) Once a baroque church, the Chiesa di Donnaregina Nuova has reinvented itself as a superb repository of religiously themed art, from Renaissance triptychs and 19th-century wooden sculptures to works from baroque greats like Fabrizio Santafede, Andrea Vaccaro and Luca Giordano.

Chiesa di San Domenico Maggiore CHURCH
(Map p624; ☑081 557 32 04; Piazza San Domenico Maggiore 8a; ⊙8.30am-noon & 4-7pm Mon-Sat, 9am-1pm & 4.30-7.15pm Sun) Backing on to lively Piazza San Domenico Maggiore, this Gothic beauty was completed in 1324 and much favoured by the Angevin nobility. The interior, a cross between baroque and 19th-century neo-Gothic, features some fine 14th-century frescoes by Pietro Cavallini and, in the sacristy, 45 coffins of Aragon princes and other nobles.

Chiesa di Sant'Angelo a Nilo CHURCH
(Map p624; ☑081 420 12 22; Vico Donnaromita 15; ⊙9am-1pm daily plus 4-6pm Mon-Sat) Nudging at the southeastcorner of Piazza San Domenico Maggiore is the 14th-century Chiesa di Sant'Angelo a Nilo, home to Cardinal Brancaccio's monumental Renaissance tomb, created by Donatello and others.

Via San Gregorio Armeno STREET, CHURCH
Connecting Spaccanapoli with Via dei Tribunali, the *decumanus maior* (main road) of ancient Neapolis, this narrow street is the heart of the city's *presepe* (nativity scene) obsession, its clutter of shops selling everything from doting donkeys to tongue-in-cheek caricatures of Silvio Berlusconi.

Amidst the kitsch sits the 16th-century **Chiesa e Chiostro di San Gregorio Armeno** (Map p624; ☑081 420 63 85; Via San Gregorio Armeno 44; ⊙9.30am-noon Mon-Sat, to 1pm Sun), a blast of bombastic baroque. Highlights include lavish frescoes by Paolo de Matteis and Luca Giordano.

TOLEDO & QUARTIERI SPAGNOLI

Museo Archeologico Nazionale MUSEUM
(Map p624; ☑081 44 01 66; Piazza Museo Nazionale 19; admission €6.50; ⊙9am-7.30pm Wed-Mon) Head here for one of the world's finest collections of Graeco-Roman artefacts. Originally a cavalry barracks and later the seat of the city's university, the museum was established by the Bourbon king Charles VII in the late 18th century to house the rich collection of antiquities he had inherited from his mother, Elisabetta Farnese, as well as treasures that had been looted from Pompeii and Herculaneum. The museum also contains the Borgia collection of Etruscan and Egyptian relics.

To avoid getting lost in its rambling galleries (numbered in Roman numerals), invest €7.50 in the green quick-guide *National Archaeological Museum of Naples* or, to concentrate on the highlights, €5 for an audioguide in English. It's also worth calling ahead to ensure the galleries you want to see are open, as staff shortages often mean that sections of the museum close for part of the day.

While the basement houses the Borgia collection of Egyptian relics and epigraphs, the ground floor is given over to the **Farnese collection** of Greek and Roman sculpture. The two highlights are the colossal *Toro Farnese* (Farnese Bull) in Room XVI and gigantic *Ercole* (Hercules) in Room XIII. Sculpted in the early 3rd century AD, the *Toro Farnese,* probably a Roman copy of a Greek original, depicts the death of Dirce, Queen of Thebes, who was tied to a bull and torn apart over rocks. The sculpture, carved from a single block, was discovered in Rome in 1545 and restored by Michelangelo before being shipped to Naples in 1787. *Ercole* was discovered in the same Roman excavations. It was found legless, but the Bourbons had his original pins, which turned up at a later dig, fitted.

On the mezzanine floor is a small but stunning collection of **mosaics**, mostly from Pompeii. Of the series taken from the Casa del Fauno at Pompeii, it's the awe-inspiring *La Battaglia di Alessandro Contro Dario* (The Battle of Alexander against Darius) that stands out. Measuring 20 sq metres, it's the best-known depiction of Alexander the Great in existence.

Beyond the mosaics is the **Gabinetto Segreto** (Secret Room), home to the museum's ancient porn. The climax, so to speak, is an intriguing statue of Pan servicing a nanny goat, originally found in Herculaneum. The erotic paintings depicting sexual positions once served as a menu for brothel clients.

On the 1st floor, the vast **Sala Meridiana** contains the *Farnese Atlante*, a statue of Atlas carrying a globe on his shoulders. The rest of the floor is largely devoted to discoveries from Pompeii, Herculaneum, Stabiae and Cuma. Items range from huge murals and frescoes to a pair of gladiator helmets, household items, ceramics and glassware.

La Pignasecca MARKET
(Map p624; Via Pignasecca; ☺8am-1pm) Slap bang in the lively Quartieri Spagnoli, Naples' oldest street market offers a multisensory escapade into a world of wriggling seafood, drool-inducing delis and clued-up *casalinghe*. It's a great place to soak up the city's trademark street life and pick up a few bargains.

VOMERO
Visible from all over Naples, the stunning Certosa di San Martino is the one compelling reason to take the funicular (p642) up to Vomero (*vom*-e-ro), an area of spectacular views, Liberty mansions, and middle-class manners.

Museo Nazionale di San Martino MONASTERY, MUSEUM
(Map p630; ☑848 80 02 88; Largo San Martino 5; admission €6; ☺8.30am-7.30pm Thu-Tue, last entry 6.30pm) The high point (quite literally) of Neapolitan baroque, this charterhouse-turned-museum was founded as a Carthusian monastery in the 14th century. The Certosa owes most of its present look to facelifts in the 16th and 17th centuries, the latter by baroque maestro Cosimo Fanzago. The **church** contains a feast of frescoes and paintings by Naples' greatest 17th-century artists – Francesco Solimena, Massimo Stanzione, Giuseppe de Ribera and Battista Caracciolo.

Adjacent to the church, the elegant **Chiostro dei Procuratori** is the smaller of the monastery's two cloisters. A grand corridor on the left leads to the larger **Chiostro Grande**, considered one of Italy's finest. Originally designed by Giovanni Antonio Dosio in the late 16th century and added to by Fanzago, it's a sublime composition of white Tuscan-Doric porticoes, camelias and marble statues. The skulls mounted on the balustrade were a light-hearted reminder to the monks of their own mortality.

Just off the Chiostro dei Procuratori, the **Sezione Navale** focuses on the history of the Bourbon navy from 1734 to 1860, and features a small collection of beautiful royal barges.

To the north of the Chiostro Grande, the **Sezione Presepiale** houses a whimsical collection of rare Neapolitan *presepi* (nativity scenes) carved in the 18th and 19th centuries.

The **Quarto del Priore** (Prior's Quarter) in the southern wing houses the bulk of the picture collection, as well as one of the museum's most famous pieces, Pietro Bernini's tender *La Vergine col Bambino e San Giovannino* (Madonna and Child with the Infant John the Baptist).

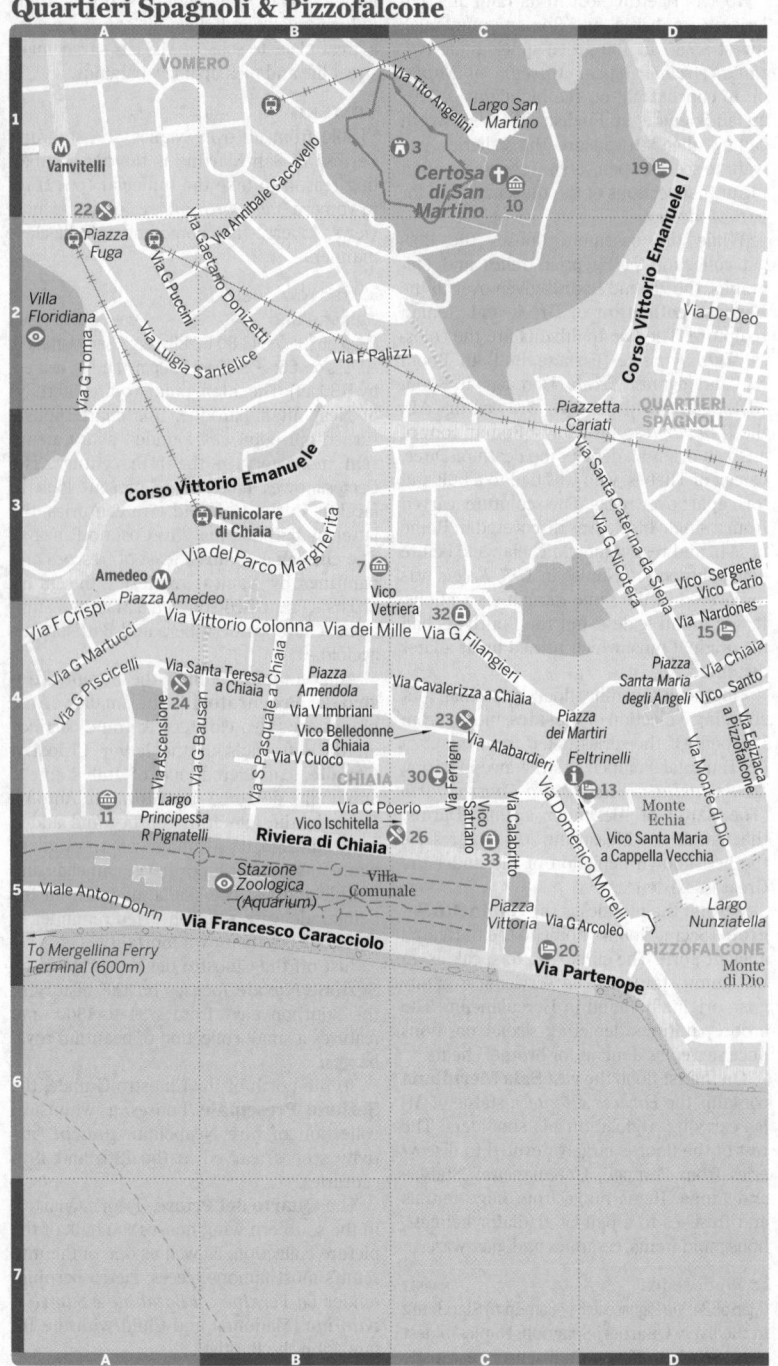

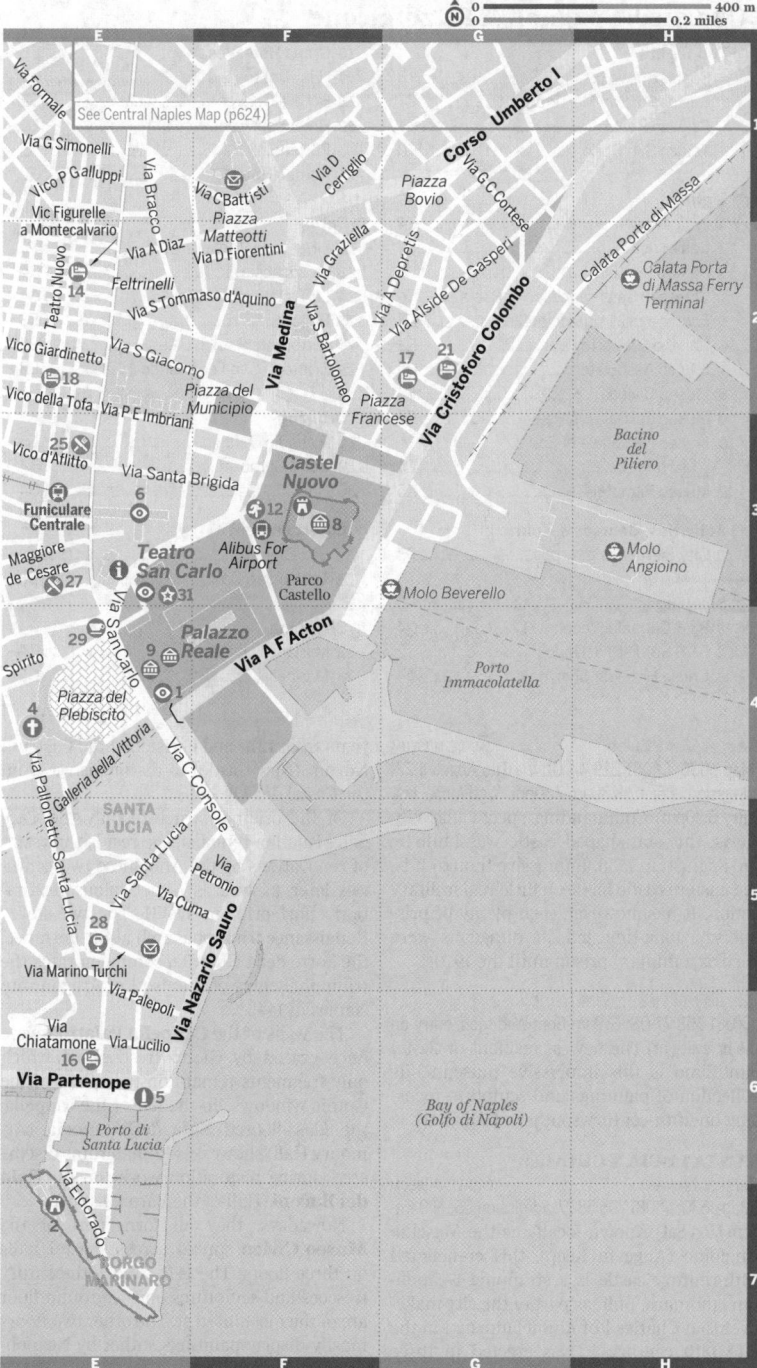

See Central Naples Map (p624)

Quartieri Spagnoli & Pizzofalcone

Castel Sant'Elmo CASTLE, MUSEUM
(Map p630; ☑081 229 44 01; Via Tito Angelini 22; admission €5; ☺8.30am-7.30pm Wed-Mon, last entry 6.30pm) Commanding spectacular city views, this star-shaped castle was built by the Spanish in 1538. Impressive though it is, the austere castle has seen little real military action. It has, however, seen plenty of prisoners: a long-time jail, its dungeons were used as a military prison until the 1970s.

Museo del Novecento Napoli
(☑081 558 77 08; ☺9am-6pm Wed-Mon, entry on the hr, every hr) The newest resident of Castel Sant'Elmo is this impressive museum, its collection of paintings and sculpture focussing on 20th-century southern Italian art.

SANTA LUCIA & CHIAIA
Castel Nuovo CASTLE, MUSEUM
(Map p630; ☑081 795 58 77; admission €5; ☺9am-7pm Mon-Sat) Known locally as the Maschio Angioino (Angevin Keep), this crenellated 13th-century castle is a strapping Neapolitan landmark. Built as part of the city makeover that Charles I of Anjou launched in the late 13th century, it was erected in three

years from 1279 and christened the Castrum Novum (New Castle) to distinguish it from the Castel dell'Ovo.

Of the original structure only the Cappella Palatina remains; the rest is the result of renovations by the Aragonese two centuries later, as well as a meticulous restoration effort prior to WWII. The two-storey Renaissance triumphal arch at the entrance, the Torre della Guardia, commemorates the triumphal entry of Alfonso I of Aragon into Naples in 1443.

The walls of the **Cappella Palatina** were once graced by Giotto frescoes, of which only fragments remain on the splays of the Gothic windows. To the left of the cappella, the glass-floored **Sala dell'Armeria** (Armoury Hall) showcases Roman ruins discovered during restoration works on the **Sala dei Baroni** (Hall of the Barons) above.

Nowadays, they all form part of the **Museo Civico** spread across several halls on three floors. The 14th- and 15th-century frescoes and sculptures on the ground floor are of the most interest. The other two floors mostly display paintings, either by Neapolitan artists, or with Naples or Campania as subjects, covering the 17th to the early 20th centuries. Worth looking out for is Guglielmo Monaco's 15th-century bronze door, complete with a cannonball embedded in it.

Teatro San Carlo THEATRE
(Map p630; ☑box office 081 797 23 31, guided tours 081 553 45 65; www.teatrosancarlo.it; Via San Carlo 98; tours €5; ☉10am-5.30pm Mon-Sat, call ahead to book). Famed for its perfect acoustics, Italy's largest opera house was built in 1737, predating its northern rival, Milan's La Scala, by 41 years. Severely damaged by a fire in 1816 it was rebuilt by Antonio Niccolini, the same architect who a few years before had added the facade.

Across Via San Carlo is one of the four entrances to the palatial glass atrium of the **Galleria Umberto I** shopping centre. Opened in 1900 as a twin arcade to the Galleria Vittorio Emanuele II (p233) in Milan, it's worth a quick look for its beautiful marble floor and elegant engineering.

Palazzo Reale PALAZZO, MUSEUM
(Map p630; Royal Palace; ☑081 40 05 47; Piazza Trieste e Trento; admission €4; ☉9am-7pm Thu-Tue) Flanking Piazza del Plebiscito, this former royal residence traces its birthdate to around 1600. Revamped in 1841 and extensively damaged during WWII, its monumental double staircase leads to the royal apartments, now home to the **Museo del Palazzo Reale** and its rich collection of baroque and neoclassical furnishings, porcelain, tapestries, statues and paintings. There's also a lavish private theatre, the Teatrino di Corte (1768), and a colossal 18th-century *presepe* in the Cappella Reale (Royal Chapel).

The palace also houses the **Biblioteca Nazionale** (National Library; Map p630; ☑081 781 91 11; ☉8.30am-7.30pm Mon-Fri, to 1.30pm Sat), which includes at least 2000 papyruses discovered at Herculaneum and fragments of a 5th-century Coptic Bible. Bring photo ID.

Chiesa di San Francesco di Paola CHURCH
(Map p630; ☑081 74 51 33; Piazza del Plebiscito; ☉8.30am-noon & 4-7pm) This church is a neoclassical copy of Rome's Pantheon. A later addition to the colonnade that formed the highlight of Joachim Murat's original piazza (1809), the church was commissioned by Ferdinand I in 1817 to celebrate the restoration of his kingdom after the Napoleonic interlude.

Castel dell'Ovo CASTLE
(Map p630; ☑081 240 00 55; Borgo Marinaro; admission free; ☉8.30am-7.30pm Mon-Sat, to 1.45pm Sun) Marking the eastern end of the 2.5km *lungomare* (seafront promenade), Naples' oldest castle sits atop the rocky Borgo Marinaro. Built by the Normans in the 12th century, it became a key fortress in the defence of Campania. According to myth, the castle owes its improbable name (Castle of the Egg) to Virgil, who was said to have buried an egg on the site where the castle now stands, warning that when the egg breaks, the castle (and Naples) will fall.

Nearby, the **Fontana dell'Immacolatella** dates from the 17th century and features statues by Bernini and Naccherini.

ISI Arti Associate ART GALLERY
(Map p630; ☑081 658 63 81; www.isiartiassociate. net; Vico del Vasto a Chiaia 47; ☉during exhibitions, check website) This hip art space exhibits anything from contemporary painting and photography, to sculpture and multimedia installations from Italy and abroad. From September to May, special Friday night events might include DJ sessions, live music or performance art. There's even an intimate bistro (meals €15, open for lunch Tuesday to Saturday, September to May), serving honest, well-executed dishes at bohemian prices. Check the website for upcoming exhibitions, performances and themed culinary tastings.

Museo Pignatelli MUSEUM
(☑081 761 23 56; Riviera di Chiaia 200; admission €2; ☉8.30am-1.30pm Wed-Mon) Housed in a neoclassical villa once belonging to the Rothschilds, this chichi museum contains mostly 19th-century furnishings, china and other mildly interesting knick-knacks. A pavilion set in the villa's handsome gardens houses a coach museum, currently closed.

CAPODIMONTE
Palazzo Reale di Capodimonte PALAZZO, MUSEUM, PARK
On the northern edge of the city, this colossal palace took more than a century to build. It was originally intended as a hunting lodge for Charles VII of Bourbon, but as construction got under way in 1738, the plans got grander and grander. The result was the monumental *palazzo* that since 1759 has housed the art collection that Charles inherited from his mother Elisabetta Farnese.

Museo di Capodimonte

(☏081 749 91 11; www.museo-capodimonte.it; Parco di Capodimonte; admission €7.50; ⏰8.30am-7.30pm Thu-Tue, last entry 90min before closing) This museum is spread over three floors and 160 rooms. You'll never see the whole place in one day, but a morning should be enough for an abridged best-of tour.

On the 1st floor you'll find works by Bellini, Botticelli, Caravaggio, Masaccio and Titian. Highlights are numerous, but look out for Masaccio's *Crocifissione* (Crucifixion), Bellini's *Trasfigurazione* (Transfiguration) and Parmigianino's *Antea*.

Also on the 1st floor, the **royal apartments** are a study in regal excess. The Salottino di Porcellana (Room 51) is an outrageous example of 18th-century Chinoiserie, its walls and ceiling crawling with whimsically themed porcelain 'stucco'. Originally created between 1757 and 1759 for the Palazzo Reale in Portici, it was transferred to Capodimonte in 1867.

Upstairs, the 2nd-floor galleries display work by Neapolitan artists from the 13th to the 19th centuries, plus some spectacular 16th-century Belgian tapestries. The piece that many come to Capodimonte to see, Caravaggio's *Flagellazione* (Flagellation; 1607–10), hangs in reverential solitude in Room 78, at the end of a long corridor.

If you have any energy left, the small **gallery of modern art** on the 3rd floor is worth a quick look, if for nothing else than Andy Warhol's poptastic *Mt Vesuvius*.

Parco di Capodimonte

(admission free; ⏰9am to 1hr before sunset) Once you're finished in the museum, this adjoining 130-hectare park provides a much-needed breath of fresh air.

Catacombe di San Gennaro CATACOMB
(☏081 744 37 14; www.catacombedinapoli.it; Via di Capodimonte 13; admission €8; ⏰1hr tours every hr 10am-5pm Mon-Sat, to 1pm Sun) The oldest and most famous of Naples' ancient catacombs date to the 2nd century. Spread over two levels and decorated with early Christian frescoes, they contain a mix of tombs, corridors and broad vestibules held up by columns and arches. They were an important pilgrimage site in the 5th century, when St Januarius' body was brought here.

☞ Tours

Napoli Sotterranea WALKING
(Underground Naples; Map p624; ☑081 29 69 44; www.napolisotterranea.org; Piazza San Gaetano 68; tours €9; ⏰tours noon, 2pm & 4pm Mon-Fri, extra tours Thu, Sat & Sun) This outfit runs 1½-hour guided tours of the city's underworld. Visits take you 40m below the city to explore a network of creepy passages and caves. The passages were originally hewn by the Greeks to extract tufa stone used in construction and to channel water from Mt Vesuvius. Extended by the Romans, the network of conduits and cisterns was more recently used as air-raid shelters in WWII. Part of the tour takes place by candlelight via extremely narrow passages – not suitable for expanded girths!

City Sightseeing Napoli BUS
(☑081 551 72 79; www.napoli.city-sightseeing. it; adult/child €22/11) A hop-on, hop-off bus service with four routes across the city. All depart from Piazza del Municipio Parco Castello, and tickets, available on board, are valid for 24 hours for each of the routes. Tour commentaries are provided in English.

⭐ Festivals & Events

Festa di San Gennaro RELIGIOUS
Naples' main festival honours St Januarius. On the first Sunday in May and then on 19 September and 16 December, thousands of people gather in the *duomo* to witness the saint's blood liquefy – a miracle believed to save the city from potential disasters. In 1944 the miracle failed and Mt Vesuvius

---

MAKING THE MOST OF YOUR EURO

If you're planning to blitz the sights, the Campania artecard (☎800 600601; www. campaniartecard.it) is an excellent investment. A cumulative ticket that covers museum admission and transport, it comes in various forms. The Naples and Campi Flegrei three-day ticket (adult/EU citizens 18-25 yrs €16/10) gives free admission to three participating sites, a 50% discount on others and free transport in Naples and the Campi Flegrei. Other options range from €12 to €30 and cover sites as far afield as Pompeii and Paestum. The tickets can be bought at the Stazione Centrale (Central Station) infopoint, participating museums and archaeological sites, online, or through the call centre.

erupted; in 1980 it failed again and the city was struck by an earthquake.

Maggio dei Monumenti — CULTURAL
In May, Naples premier cultural event ensures a month-long menu of exhibitions, concerts, dance performances, guided tours and more.

Napoli Teatro Festival Italia — THEATRE
(www.teatrofestivalitalia.it) Usually in June and July, the Napoli Teatro Festival Italia serves up over three weeks of local and international theatre in venues across the city.

Madonna del Carmine — RELIGIOUS
Held on 16 July, Madonna del Carmine culminates in a fabulous fireworks display on Piazza del Carmine.

Neapolis Rock Festival — MUSIC
(www.neapolis.it) Southern Italy's top rock fest, it attracts top international acts in July/August.

Festa di Piedigrotta — CULTURAL
(www.festadipiedigrotta.it) In early to mid-September, Naples' Piedigrotta combines folk tunes with floats and fireworks around the Chiesa di Piedigrotta in Mergellina.

🛌 Sleeping

Spanning funky B&Bs and cheery hostels, to luxe seafront piles, slumber options in Naples are varied, plentiful and relatively cheap.

For maximum atmosphere, consider the *centro storico*, where you'll have many of the city's sights on your doorstep.

Seaside Santa Lucia is home to some of the city's most prestigious hotels, and Chiaia is cool and chic. For lofty views and a chilled-out vibe, hit Vomero.

CENTRO STORICO & PORT AREA

Hotel Piazza Bellini — BOUTIQUE HOTEL €€
(Map p624; ☑081 45 17 32; www.hotelpiazzabellini. com; Via Costantinopoli 101; s €70-125, d €80-150, tr €100-170; ❄@🛜) Naples' newest art hotel inhabits a 16th-century *palazzo*, its cool white spaces spiked with original majolica tiles and the work of emerging artists. Rooms offer pared-back cool, with designer fittings, chic bathrooms and mirror frames drawn straight on the wall. Rooms on the 5th and 6th floor feature panoramic balconies.

Romeo Hotel — DESIGN HOTEL €€€
(☑081 017 50 01; www.romeohotel.it; Via Cristoforo Colombo 45; r €165-330; ❄@🛜) Naples' top design hotel combines Artesia stone with A-list art and furniture, a fabulous rooftop restaurant, and a super-sleek spa centre. 'Classic' category rooms are small but luxe, with De-Longhi espresso machines and sleek bathrooms. Up a notch, 'Deluxe' rooms (€225 to €450) offer the same perks but with added space and bay views.

B&B Cerasiello — B&B €
(☑081 033 09 77, 338 9264453; www.cerasiello. it; Via Supportico Lopez 20; s €40-60, d €55-80, tr €70-95; ❄🛜) Technically in the Sanità district but a short walk north of the *centro storico*, this gorgeous B&B has four rooms, an enchanting communal terrace, stylish kitchen and an ethno-chic look. Bring €0.10 for the lift.

Costantinopoli 104 — BOUTIQUE HOTEL €€€
(Map p624; ☑081 557 10 35; www.costantinopoli 104.it; Via Santa Maria di Costantinopoli 104; s/d/ste €170/220/250; ❄@🛜🏊) Sprinkled with books and antiques, Costantinopoli 104 is set in a chic neoclassical villa in the city's bohemian heartland. Although showing a bit of wear in places, rooms remain elegant and clean – those on the 1st floor open on to a sun terrace, while ground-floor rooms face the small, palm-fringed pool. The suites are simply gorgeous.

Hostel of the Sun — HOSTEL €
(Map p630; ☑081 420 63 93; www.hostelnapoli. com; Via Melisurgo 15; dm €16-18, s with bathroom €30-35, d with bathroom €60-70; ❄@🛜) Recently renovated and constantly winning accolades, HOTS is an ultrafriendly hostel near the port. Located on the 7th floor (have €0.05 handy for the lift), it's a bright, sociable place with multicoloured dorms, a cute in-house bar, and, a few floors down, a series of hotel-standard private rooms, two with private bathroom.

Decumani Hotel de Charme — BOUTIQUE HOTEL €€
(Map p624; ☑081 551 81 88; www.decumani.it; Via San Giovanni Maggiore Pignatelli 15; s €90-105, d €105-130, deluxe d €130-150; ❄@🛜) Don't be fooled by the scruffy staircase; this boutique hotel is fresh, elegant and located in the former *palazzo* of Cardinal Sisto Riario Sforza, the last bishop of the Bourbon Kingdom. The simple yet stylish rooms have high ceilings, 19th-century furniture and modern bathrooms. Deluxe rooms have a Jacuzzi, and the restored baroque hall hosts cultural soirées.

B&B DiLetto a Napoli
B&B €

(Map p624; ☎081 033 09 77, 338 9264453; www.dilettoanapoli.it; Vicolo Sedil Capuano 16; s €35-55, d €50-75, tr €65-90; P❖📶) Four rooms with vintage *cotto* (fired clay) floor tiles, organza curtains and artisan decor set a stylish scene at this B&B set in a 15th-century *palazzo*. The urbane communal lounge comes with a kitchenette and dining table for convivial noshing and lounging.

TOLEDO & VOMERO

Hotel San Francesco al Monte
LUXURY HOTEL €€€

(Map p630; ☎081 423 91 11; www.hotelsanfrancesco.it; Corso Vittorio Emanuele I 328; s €160-190, d €170-225; P❖@📶🏊) The monks in this 16th-century monastery never had it as good as the hotel's pampered guests. The cells have been converted into stylish rooms, the ancient cloisters house an open-air bar and the barrel-vaulted corridors are cool and atmospheric. Topping it all off is the 7th-floor swimming pool.

B&B Sui Tetti di Napoli
B&B €

(Map p630; ☎081 033 09 77, 338 9264453; www.suitettidinapoli.net; Vico Figuerelle a Montecalvario 6; s €35-60, d €45-80, tr €60-95; ❖📶) A block away from Via Toledo, this B&B is more like four apartments atop a thigh-toning stairwell. While two apartments share a terrace, the rooftop option has its own, complete with mesmerising views. All apartments include a kitchenette (the cheapest two share a kitchen), bright, simple furnishings and a homey vibe.

Hotel Il Convento
HOTEL €€

(Map p630; ☎081 40 39 77; www.hotelilconvento.com; Via Speranzella 137a; s €55-90, d €65-160; ❖📶) Taking its name from the neighbouring convent, this lovely hotel blends antique Tuscan furniture, erudite book collections and candlelit stairs. Rooms are cosy and elegant, with creamy tones, dark woods and patches of 16th-century brickwork. For €80 to €180 you get a room with a private roof garden.

SANTA LUCIA & CHIAIA

Chiaja Hotel de Charme
BOUTIQUE HOTEL €€

(Map p630; ☎081 41 55 55; www.hotelchiaia.it; Via Chiaia 216; s €95-105, d €99-145, superior d €140-165; ❖@📶) Encompassing a former brothel and an aristocratic town house, this refined, peaceful hotel lives up to its name. The look is effortlessly noble – think gilt-framed portraits on pale lemon walls, opulent table lamps and heavy fabrics. Rooms facing pedestrianised shopping strip Via Chiaia come with a Jacuzzi.

B&B Cappella Vecchia
B&B €

(Map p630; ☎081 240 51 17; www.cappellavecchia11.it; Vico Santa Maria a Cappella Vecchia 11; s €50-70, d €75-100; ❖@📶) Run by a super helpful young couple, this B&B has six simple, witty rooms with funky bathrooms and different Neapolitan themes, from *mal'occhio* (evil eye) to *peperoncino* (chilli). There's a spacious communal area for breakfast, and free internet available 24/7.

Parteno
B&B €€

(Map p630; ☎081 245 20 95; www.parteno.it; Via Partenope 1; s €80-99, d €100-125; ❖@📶) Six chic rooms are exquisitely decorated with period furniture, vintage Neapolitan prints and silk bedding. The azalea room (€130 to €165) steals the show with its seamless view of sea, sky and Capri. Hi-tech touches include satellite TV and free calls to Italian mobile numbers and to landlines in Europe, USA and Canada.

Grand Hotel Vesuvio
LUXURY HOTEL €€€

(Map p630; ☎081 764 00 44; www.vesuvio.it; Via Partenope 45; s €230-370, d €290-450; ❖@📶) Known for bedding legends – past guests include Rita Hayworth and Humphrey Bogart – this five-star heavyweight is a wonderland of dripping chandeliers, period antiques and opulent rooms. Count your lucky stars while drinking a martini at the rooftop restaurant.

🍴 Eating

Pizza and pasta are the staples of Neapolitan cuisine. Pizza was created here and nowhere will you eat it better. Seafood is another local speciality and you'll find mussels and clams served in many dishes.

Neapolitan street food is equally brilliant. *Misto di frittura* – zucchini flowers, deep-fried potato and eggplant – makes for a great snack, especially if eaten from paper outside a tiny streetside stall.

Many eateries close for two to four weeks in August.

AROUND STAZIONE CENTRALE & MERCATO

Attanasio
STREET FOOD €

(Map p624; Vico Ferrovia 1-4; snacks from €1.10; ⏱6.30am-7.30pm Tue-Sun) This retro pastry peddler makes one mighty *sfogliatella* (sweetened ricotta pastry), not to mention creamy *cannoli siciliani* (pastry shells with a sweet filling of ricotta) and runny, rummy *babà* (rum-soaked yeast cake). Savoury fiends shouldn't miss the hearty *pasticcino rustico* (savoury bread), stuffed with *provola* (provolone), ricotta and salami.

Da Michele
PIZZERIA €

(Map p624; Via Cesare Sersale 1; pizzas from €4; ⊙Mon-Sat) As hard core as it gets, Naples' most famous pizzeria takes the no-frills ethos to its extremes. It's dingy and old-fashioned and serves only two types of pizza: *margherita* (tomato, basil and mozzarella) and *marinara* (tomatoes, garlic and oregano). Grab a ticket and join the queue.

CENTRO STORICO

[TOP CHOICE] Pizzeria Gino Sorbillo
PIZZERIA €

(Map p624; Via dei Tribunali 32; pizzas from €2.30; ⊙Mon-Sat) The clamouring crowds say it all: Gino Sorbillo is king of the pizza pack. Head in for gigantic, wood-fired perfection, best followed by a velvety *semifreddo;* the chocolate and *torroncino* (almond nougat) combo is divine.

Palazzo Petrucci
MODERN ITALIAN €€€

(Map p624; ☑081 552 40 68; www.palazzo petrucci.it, in Italian; Piazza San Domenico Maggiore 4; 5-course degustation menu €50; ⊙Mon-Sat) Progressive Petrucci is a breath of fresh air, exciting palates with mostly successful new-school creations like raw prawn and mozzarella 'lasagne' or poached egg onion soup. Balancing fine-dining elegance and a relaxed air, it's a fine choice if you plan on celebrating something special.

La Stanza del Gusto
CHEESE BAR, MODERN ITALIAN €€

(Map p624; ☑081 40 15 78; www.lastanzadelgusto. com, in Italian; Via Costantinopoli 100; lunch special €13, 5-/7- course tasting menu €45/65; ⊙cheese bar 3.30pm-midnight Mon, 11am-midnight Tue-Sat; restaurant dinner Mon-Sat) Creative and eclectic, the 'Taste Room' is divided into a casual ground-floor 'cheese bar' and a more formal upstairs dining room. Kick back with fabulous wine and rare *formaggi* (cheeses), or taste-test the mod-twist fare (think almond and saffron soup). Servings are small but the food is fab.

Trattoria Mangia e Bevi
TRATTORIA €

(Map p624; Via Sedile di Porto 92; meals €10; ⊙lunch Mon-Fri) Everyone from pierced students to bespectacled *professori* squeeze around the lively, communal tables for bril-

liant home cooking at rock-bottom prices. Scan the daily-changing menu, jot down your choices and brace for gems like juicy *salsiccia di maiale* (pork sausage) and *peperoncino*-spiked *friarielli* (local broccoli).

TOLEDO & VOMERO

Trattoria San Ferdinando
TRATTORIA €€

(Map p630; Via Nardones 117; meals €30; ⊙lunch Mon-Sat, dinner Wed-Fri) Hung with theatre posters and playbills, saffron-hued San Ferdinando pulls in well-spoken theatre types and intellectuals. For a Neapolitan taste trip, ask for a rundown of the day's antipasti and choose your favourites for an *antipasto misto*. Seafood standouts include a delicate *seppia ripieno* (stuffed squid), while the homemade desserts make for a satisfying dénouement.

Il Garum
TRADITONAL ITALIAN €€

(Map p624; Piazza Monteoliveto 2A; meals €39) In the soft glow of wrought-iron lanterns, regulars tuck into made-with-love gems like rigatoni with shredded zucchini and mussels, and an exquisite grilled calamari stuffed with vegetables, cherry tomatoes and Parmesan. All the desserts are made on-site.

Friggitoria Vomero
STREET FOOD €

(Map p630; Via Cimarosa 44; snacks from €1; ⊙9.30am-2.30pm & 5-9.30pm Mon-Fri, 9.30am-2.30pm & 5-11pm Sat) The Brits don't have a monopoly on fried food served in paper. Here you'll find piles of crunchy deep-fried eggplants and artichokes, croquets filled with prosciutto and mozzarella, and a whole lot more.

Pintauro
PASTRIES & CAKES €

(Map p630; Via Toledo 275; sfogliatelle €2; ⊙8am-2pm & 2.30-8pm Mon-Sat, 9am-2pm Sun Sep-May) Another local institution, the cinnamon-scented Pintauro peddles perfect *sfogliatelle* to shopped-out locals.

SANTA LUCIA & CHIAIA

Ristorante Radici
MODERN ITALIAN €€€

(Map p630; ☑081 248 11 00; www.ristoranteradici. it, in Italian; Via Riviera di Chiaia 268; meals €50; ⊙dinner Mon-Sat) Elegant yet warm, Radici offers respite from the tried-and-tested standards on most local menus. Here, prime local produce is revamped in dishes like melt-in-your-mouth *spigola* (European sea bass) patties topped with tomatoes and served in a delicate broth. Book ahead.

La Trattoria dell'Oca
TRATTORIA €€

(Map p630; Via Santa Teresa a Chiaia 11; meals €35; ⊙closed dinner Sun Oct-May, closed all day Sun Jun-Sep) Refined yet relaxed, this softly lit trattoria celebrates beautifully cooked classics, which may include *gnocchi al ragù* or a superb *baccalà* (salted cod) cooked with succulent cherry tomatoes, capers and olives.

La Focaccia
PIZZA BY SLICE €

(Map p630; Vico Belledonne a Chiaia 31; focaccia from €1.50; ⊙11am-late Mon-Sat, 5pm-late Sun) Head to this funky, no-fuss bolt-hole for fat focaccia squares stacked with combos like artichokes and *provola,* or eggplant with *pecorino* cheese and smoked ham. Best of all, there isn't a microwave oven in sight.

 Drinking

The city's student and alternative drinking scene is around the piazzas and alleyways of the *centro storico.* For a chicer vibe, hit the cobbled lanes of upmarket Chiaia. While some bars operate from 8am, most open from around 6.30pm and close around 2am.

Penguin Café
WINE BAR

(Map p630; Via Santa Lucia 88; ⊙7.30pm-late) Not just a snug wine bar, Penguin sells cinema-themed books, hosts literary events, and offers live music Thursday to Saturday. The 100-plus wine list includes six fine drops by the glass, perfectly paired with quality cheeses, *salumi* (charcuterie), salads and a handful of heartier, seasonal dishes.

Caffè Mexico
CAFE

(Map p624; Piazza Dante 86; ⊙7am-8.30pm Mon-Sat) Make a beeline for Naples' best-loved espresso bar, where old-school baristas serve up the city's mightiest espresso. Don't forget to ask for *un bicchiere di acqua, per favore* (a glass of water, please), which you should drink *before* your coffee.

Intra Moenia
CAFE

(Map p624; Piazza Bellini 70) Of the squareside hang-outs on bohemian Piazza Bellini, this cafe-cum-bookshop remains our top choice. Favoured by local writers, artists and people who prefer an erudite air with their Negroni, it's the perfect spot to wile away a lazy afternoon.

Nàis
BAR

(Map p630; Via Ferrigni 29) Slap bang on *aperitivo* strip Via Ferrigni, Nàis oozes a warm, convivial air with friendly bartenders, comfy suede banquettes and a book-lined shelf. Order a glass of vino, pick at the *aperitivo,* and eye-up the candy crowd.

Caffè Gambrinus
CAFE

(Map p630; Via Chiaia 12) Tourists and over-dressed visitors self-consciously sip coffee and overpriced cocktails at Naples' most venerable cafe. Oscar Wilde and Bill Clinton count among the celebs who have graced its lavish art nouveau interior.

 Entertainment

Options run the gamut from world-class opera and jazz to rock festivals and cavernous clubbing. For cultural listings check www.incampania.it; for the latest club news check out the free minimag *Zero* (www.zero.eu, in Italian), available from many bars.

You can buy tickets for most cultural events at the box office inside **Feltrinelli** (☏081 764 21 11; Piazza dei Martiri; ⊙4.30-8pm Mon-Sat).

The month-long **Maggio dei Monumenti** festival in May offers concerts and cultural activities in various museums and monuments around town, most of which are free. From May until September, al fresco concerts are common throughout the city. Tourist offices have details.

Football

Naples' football team, Napoli, is the third-most supported in the country after Juventus and Milan, and watching it play at the **Stadio San Paolo** (Piazzale Vincenzo Tecchio) is a highly charged rush. The season runs from September to May and you can expect to pay between €20 to €100 for a seat. Tickets can be purchased from **Azzurro Service** (☏081 593 40 01; www.azzurroservice.net, in Italian; Via Francesco Galeota 19; ⊙9am-1pm & 3.30-7.30pm Mon-Fri, also Sat & Sun on match days); and **Box Office** (Map p630; ☏081 551 91 88; www.boxofficenapoli.it, in Italian; Galleria Umberto I 17; ⊙9.30am-8.30pm Mon-Fri, 9.30am-1.30pm & 4.30-8pm Sat), as well as from some tobacconists. Tickets are best booked two weeks in advance and don't forget to take photo ID.

Nightclubs & Live Music

Clubs usually open at 10.30pm or 11pm but don't fill up until after midnight. Many close in summer (July to September), some transferring to out-of-town beach locations. Admission charges vary, but expect to pay between €5 and €30, which may or may not include a drink.

Galleria 19 — NIGHTCLUB

(Map p624; www.galleria19.it; Via San Sebastiano 19; ⊙Tue-Sat) Set in a long, cavernous cellar scattered with chesterfields and industrial lamps, this cool and edgy club draws a uni crowd early in the week and 20/30-somethings with its Friday electronica sessions and Saturday live music gigs. Resident mixologist Gianluca Morziello is one of the city's best (order his Cucumber Slumber to understand why).

Kinky Klub — LIVE MUSIC, NIGHTCLUB

(Map p624; www.kinkyjam.com; Vicolo della Quercia 26; ⊙Tue-Sun mid-Sep–mid-Jun) Don't come here expecting latex and leather. Despite the name, Kinky's speciality is both live and DJ-spun reggae, rocksteady ska and dance-hall tunes. Acts span local to global names. Check the website for upcoming gigs.

Arenile Reload — LIVE MUSIC/CLUB

(www.arenilereload.com, in Italian; Via Coroglio 14, Bagnoli) The biggest of Naples' beachside clubs, head in for poolside cocktails, see-and-be-seen *aperitivo* sessions, live bands and dancing under the stars. The club is a short walk south of Bagnoli station on the Cumana rail line.

Around Midnight — LIVE MUSIC

(☎081 742 32 78; www.aroundmidnight.it, in Italian; Via Bonito 32A; ⊙Tue-Sun Sep-Jun) One of Naples' oldest and most famous jazz clubs, this tiny swinging bolt-hole features mostly home-grown live gigs, with the occasional blues band putting in a performance. Check the website for the week's line-up.

Theatre

Teatro San Carlo — THEATER

(Map p630; ☎081 797 23 31; www.teatrosancarlo.it; Via San Carlo 98; ⊙box office 10am-7pm Tue-Sat, 10am-3.30pm Sun) One of Italy's premier opera venues, the theatre stages a year-round programme of opera, ballet and concerts, though tickets can be fiendishly difficult to get. For opera, count on at least €50 for a place in the sixth tier and around €140 for a seat in the stalls.

Shopping

Colourful markets, artisan studios, and heirloom tailors – shopping in Naples is highly idiosyncratic.

For a gastronomic souvenir, head to **Limonè** (Map p624; Piazza San Gaetano 72), where you'll be able to try the organic *limoncello* (lemon liqueur) before buying a bottle. If it goes to your head, grab some lemon pasta as well.

For organic, handmade soaps and beauty products, try **Kiphy** (Map p624; www.kiphy.it, in Italian; Vico San Domenico Maggiore 3), while those after quality, handcrafted nativity-scene figurines shouldn't miss **La Scarabattola** (Map p624; www.lascarabattola.it; Via dei Tribunali 50).

Elegant Chiaia is home to several legendary Neapolitan tailors, including **Mariano Rubinacci** (Map p630; www.marianorubinacci.net; Via Filangieri 26) and **Marinella** (Map p630; www.marinellanapoli.it; Via Riviera di Chiaia 287); the latter's made-to-measure ties were once worn by Aristotle Onassis.

Information

Dangers & Annoyances

Petty crime can be a problem in Naples but with a little common sense you shouldn't have a problem. Leave valuables in your hotel room and never leave bags unattended. Be vigilant for pickpockets in crowded areas and carry bags across your body. Car and motorcycle theft is rife, so think twice before bringing a vehicle into town and never leave anything in your car. Use only marked, registered taxis and ensure the meter is running. Be careful if walking alone late at night, particularly near Stazione Centrale.

Emergency

Police station (☎081 794 11 11; Via Medina 75) To report a stolen car, call ☎113.

Internet Access

Navig@ndo (Via Santa Anna di Lombardi 28; per hr €2; ⊙10am-7.30pm Mon-Fri, 10am-1.30pm Sat)

Internet Resources

I Naples (www.inaples.it) The city's official tourist board site.

Napoli Unplugged (www.napoliunplugged.com) Attractions, up-to-date listings, news, articles and blog entries.

Turismo Regione Campania (www.turismoregionecampania.it) Up-to-date events listings, as well as audio clips and itineraries.

Medical Services

Ospedale Loreto-Mare (☎081 20 10 33; Via Amerigo Vespucci 26)

Pharmacy (Stazione Centrale; ⊙7am-10pm)

Post

Post office (Piazza Matteotti; ⊙8am-6.30pm Mon-Sat)

DESTINATION (FROM NAPLES – MOLO BEVERELLO)	FERRY COMPANY	PRICE (€)	DURATION (MINS)	DAILY FREQUENCY (HIGH SEASON)
Capri	Caremar	16	50	18
	Gescab-Navigazione Libera del Golfo	17	40	8-12
	Gescab-SNAV	17	45	12
Ischia (Casamicciola Terme & Forio)	Caremar	16	50	5
	Gescab-Alilauro	17	50-65	10
	Gescab-SNAV	16	55	4
Procida	Caremar	13	40	5
	Gescab-SNAV	13	35	4
Sorrento	Gescab-Alilauro	11	35	5
	SNAV	11	35	7

Tourist Information

Head to the following tourist bureaus for information and a map of the city.

Tourist Information Office Piazza del Gesù Nuovo 7 (Map p624; ☉9am-7pm Mon-Sat, 9am-2pm Sun); Stazione Centrale (Map p624; ☉9am-8pm Mon-Sat, to 6pm Sun); Via San Carlo 9 (Map p630; ☉9.30am-1.30pm & 2.30-6.30pm Mon-Sat, 9am-1.30pm Sun)

Travel Agencies

CTS (☎081 033 19 48; Via Luigi Settembrini 86) Student travel centre.

ℹ Getting There & Away

Air

Capodichino airport (NAP; ☎081 751 54 71; www.gesac.it), 7km northeast of the city centre, is southern Italy's main airport, linking Naples with most Italian and several major European cities, as well as New York. Airlines include Alitalia and British Airways, and budget carrier easy-Jet, the latter's connections including London, Paris (Orly) and Berlin.

Boat

Naples, the bay islands and the Amalfi Coast are served by a comprehensive ferry network. Catch fast ferries and hydrofoils for Capri, Sorrento, Ischia (both Ischia Porto and Forio) and Procida from Molo Beverello in front of Castel Nuovo; hydrofoils for Capri, Ischia and Procida also sail from Mergellina.

Ferries for Sicily, the Aeolian Islands and Sardinia sail from Molo Angioino (right beside Molo Beverello) and neighbouring Calata Porta di Massa. Slow ferries to Ischia and Procida also depart from Calata Porta di Massa.

Ferry services are pared back considerably in the winter, and adverse sea conditions may affect sailing schedules.

The tables list hydrofoil and ferry destinations from Naples. The fares, unless otherwise stated, are for a one-way, high-season, deck-class single.

Tickets for shorter journeys can be bought at the ticket booths on Molo Beverello and at Mergellina. For longer journeys try the offices of the ferry companies or a travel agent.

The following is a list of hydrofoil and ferry companies:

Caremar (☎081 551 38 82; www.caremar.it, in Italian)

Gescab-Alilauro (☎081 497 22 22; www.alilauro.it)

Gescab-Navigazione Libera del Golfo (NLG; ☎081 552 07 63; www.navlib.it, in Italian)

Gescab-SNAV (☎081 428 55 55; www.snav.it)

Medmar (☎081 333 44 11; www.medmargroup.it)

Siremar (☎199 118866; www.siremar.it, in Italian)

Tirrenia (☎081 720 11 11; www.tirrenia.it)

Suspended indefinitely in 2011, **Metrò del Mare** (☎199 600700; www.metrodelmare.net, in Italian) normally runs summer-only ferry services between Naples and Ercolano, Sorrento, Positano, Amalfi and Salerno, as well as between the main Amalfi Coast towns. It also sails from Naples to Pozzuoli and Baia/Bacoli in the Campi Flegrei. Check the website for updates.

Bus

Most national and international buses leave from Piazza Garibaldi.

Regional bus services are operated by numerous companies, the most useful of which is **SITA** (☎089 405 145; www.sitabus.it, in Italian).

Connections from Naples include the following.

Amalfi (€4, two hours, five daily Monday to Saturday)

Pompeii (€2.80, 30 minutes, half-hourly)

Positano (€4, two hours, one daily Monday to Saturday)

Salerno (€4, one hour 10 minutes, every 25 minutes).

You can buy SITA tickets and catch buses either from Porto Immacolatella, near Molo Angioino, or from Via Galileo Ferraris, near Stazione Centrale.

Miccolis (☎081 20 03 80; www.miccolis-spa. it, in Italian) connects Naples to the following destinations.

Taranto (€19, four hours, three daily)

Brindisi (€26.60, five hours)

Lecce (€29, 5½ hours)

Marino (☎080 311 23 35; www.marinobus.it) runs to the following.

Bari (€19, three hours, three to six daily)

Matera (€19, 4½ hours, two to three daily)

Car & Motorcycle

Naples is on the Autostrada del Sole, the A1 (north to Rome and Milan) and the A3 (south to Salerno and Reggio di Calabria). The A30 skirts Naples to the northeast, while the A16 heads across the Apennines to Bari.

On approaching the city, the motorways meet the Tangenziale di Napoli, a major ring road around the city. The ring road hugs the city's northern fringe, meeting the A1 for Rome in the east, and continuing westwards towards the Campi Flegrei and Pozzuoli.

Train

Naples is southern Italy's main rail hub. Most national trains arrive at or depart from Stazione Centrale or underneath the main station, Stazione Garibaldi. Some services also stop at Mergellina station. There are up to 42 trains daily to Rome. Travel times and prices vary. Options to/from Rome are as follows.

Frecciarossa (High Velocity; 2nd class one-way €45; 70 minutes)

ES (Eurostar; 2nd class one-way €36; 1¾ hours)

IC (InterCity; 2nd class one-way €22; two hours)

Regionale (Regional; one-way €10.50; 2¾ to 3½ hours)

Stazione Circumvesuviana (☎081 772 24 44; www.vesuviana.it; Corso Garibaldi), southwest of Stazione Centrale (follow the signs from the main concourse), connects Naples to Sorrento (€4, 65 minutes, around 40 trains daily). Stops along the way include: Ercolano (€2.10, 15 minutes) and Pompeii (€2.80, 35 minutes).

Ferrovia Cumana and **Circumflegrea** (☎800 053939; www.sepsa.it, in Italian), based at Stazione Cumana di Montesanto on Piazza Montesanto, 500m southwest of Piazza Dante, operate services to Pozzuoli (€1.20, 20 minutes, every 25 minutes).

FERRIES

DESTINATION (FROM NAPLES – CALATA PORTA DI MASSA & MOLO ANGIOINO)	COMPANY	PRICE (€)	DURATION	FREQUENCY (HIGH SEASON)
Capri	Caremar	9.60	80 mins	3 daily
Ischia	Caremar	11	80 mins	7 daily
	Medmar	11	75 mins	6 daily
Procida	Caremar	9.60	45 mins	7 daily
Aeolian Islands	Siremar	from 50	13½ hrs	2 weekly
	Gescab-SNAV (summer only)	from 65	4½-6hrs	1 daily
Milazzo (Sicily)	Siremar	from 50	16 hrs	2 weekly
Palermo (Sicily)	Gescab-SNAV	from 35	10¼-11¾ hrs	1 to 2 daily
	Tirrenia	from 45		1 daily
Cagliari (Sardinia)	Tirrenia	from 45	16¼ hrs	2 weekly

ⓘ Getting Around

To/From the Airport

By public transport you can take either the regular **ANM** (☎800 639525; www.unicocampania.it) bus 3S (€1.20, 45 minutes, every 20 minutes) from Piazza Garibaldi or the **Alibus** (☎800 639525) airport shuttle (€3, 45 minutes, every 20 minutes) from Piazza del Municipio or Piazza Garibaldi.

Official taxi fares to the airport are as follows: €23 from a seafront hotel or from the Mergellina hydrofoil terminal; €19 from Piazza del Municipio; and €15.50 from Stazione Centrale.

Bus

In Naples, buses are operated by the city transport company **ANM** (☎800 639525; www.unicocampania.it). There's no central bus station, but most buses pass through Piazza Garibaldi, the city's chaotic transport hub. To locate your bus stop you'll probably need to ask at the information kiosk in the centre of the square.

Useful bus services:

140 Santa Lucia to Posillipo via Mergellina.

152 From Piazza Garibaldi to Fuorigrotta via Molo Beverello, Piazza Vittoria and Mergellina.

N3 A night bus operating from midnight to 4.50am (hourly departures) from Via Brin to Stazione Centrale, Piazza del Municipio, Piazza Dante and Vomero, and then back down to Stazione Centrale and Via Brin.

C28 From Piazza Vittoria to Piazza Vanvitelli in Vomero via Via dei Mille.

E1 From Piazza del Gesù, along Via Costantinopoli, to Museo Archeologico Nazionale, Via Tribunali, Via Duomo, Piazza Nicola Amore, along Corso Umberto I and Via Mezzocannone.

R1 From Piazza Medaglie D'Oro to Piazza Carità, Piazza Dante and Piazza Bovio.

R2 From Stazione Centrale, along Corso Umberto I, to Piazza Bovio, Piazza del Municipio and Piazza Trieste e Trento.

R4 From Capodimonte down past Via Dante to Piazza Municipio and back again.

Car & Motorcycle

Vehicle theft and anarchic traffic make driving in Naples a bad option.

Officially much of the city centre is closed to nonresident traffic for much of the day. Daily restrictions are in place in the *centro storico*, in the area around Piazza del Municipio and Via Toledo, and in the Chiaia district around Piazza dei Martiri. Hours vary but are typically from 8am to 6.30pm, possibly later.

East of the city centre, there's a 24-hour car park at Via Brin (€1.30 for the first four hours, €7.20 for 24 hours).

If renting a car, expect to pay around €60 per day for an economy car or a scooter. The major car-hire firms are all represented in Naples.

Avis (☎081 28 40 41; www.avisautonoleggio.it; Corso Novara 5) Also at Capodichino airport.

Hertz (☎081 20 62 28; www.hertz.it; Via Giuseppe Ricciardi 5) Also at Capodichino airport and Mergellina.

Maggiore (☎081 28 78 58; www.maggiore.it; Stazione Centrale) Also at Capodichino airport.

Rent Sprint (☎081 764 13 33; Via Santa Lucia 36) Scooter hire only.

Funicular

Unico Napoli tickets (see boxed text, p644) are valid on the funiculars. Three of Naples' four funicular railways connect the centre with Vomero (the fourth, Funicolare di Mergellina, connects the waterfront at Via Mergellina with Via Manzoni).

Funicolare Centrale Ascends from Via Toledo to Piazza Fuga.

Funicolare di Chiaia From Via del Parco Margherita to Via Domenico Cimarosa.

Funicolare di Montesanto From Piazza Montesanto to Via Raffaele Morghen.

Metro

Naples' **Metropolitana** (☎800 568866; www.metro.na.it) metro system is covered by Unico Napoli tickets (see boxed text, p644).

Line 1 Runs north from Università (Piazza Bovio), stopping at Toledo (projected station opening 2012), Piazza Dante, Museo (for Piazza Cavour and Line 2), Materdei, Salvator Rosa, Cilea, Piazza Vanvitelli, Piazza Medaglie D'Oro and seven stops beyond. In 2012, the line is also expected to connect Università to Garibaldi (Stazione Centrale).

Line 2 Runs from Gianturco, just east of Stazione Centrale, with stops at Piazza Garibaldi (for Stazione Centrale), Piazza Cavour, Montesanto, Piazza Amedeo, Mergellina, Piazza Leopardi, Campi Flegrei, Cavalleggeri d'Aosta, Bagnoli and Pozzuoli.

Taxi

Official taxis are white and have meters. There are taxi stands at most of the city's main piazzas or you can call one of the five taxi cooperatives: **Napoli** (☎081 556 44 44), **Consortaxi** (☎081 22 22), **Cotana** (☎081 570 70 70), **Free** (☎081 551 51 51) or **Partenope** (☎081 556 02 02).

The minimum taxi fare is €4.50, of which €3 is the starting fare. There's also a baffling range of additional charges: €1 for a radio taxi call, €2.50 extra between 10pm and 7am and all day on Sundays, €2.60 to €4 for an airport run and €0.50 per piece of luggage in the boot. Guide dogs for the blind and wheelchairs are carried free of charge.

Always ensure the meter is running.

AROUND NAPLES

CAMPI FLEGREI

Stretching west from Posillipo to the Tyrrhenian Sea, the Campi Flegrei (Phlegraean – or 'Fiery' – Fields) is a pockmarked area of craters, lakes and fumaroles, one of the world's most geologically unstable. Here, archaeological ruins stand in the midst of modern eyesores, and history merges with myth. This is where Greek colonists first settled in Italy – Cuma dates to the 8th century BC.

Before exploring the area it's worth stopping at Pozzuoli's tourist office for updated information on the area's sights and opening times. Also a good idea is the two-day €4 cumulative ticket that covers the archaeological sites of Baia and Cuma.

Pozzuoli

The first town that emerges beyond Naples' dreary western suburbs is Pozzuoli, a workaday place whose attractions are not immediately apparent. However, nose around and you'll find some impressive Roman ruins and a steaming volcanic crater. The town was established by the Greeks around 530 BC and later renamed Puteoli (Little Wells) by the Romans, who turned it into a major port. It was here that St Paul is said to have landed in AD 61 and that screen goddess Sophia Loren spent her childhood.

The **tourist office** (📞081 526 66 39; Piazza G Matteotti 1a; ☉9am-3.30pm Mon-Fri) is beside the Porta Napoli gate, around 700m downhill from the metro station.

SIGHTS

Anfiteatro Flavio   AMPHITHEATRE
(📞081 526 60 07; Via Terracciano 75; admission €4; ☉9am to 1hr before sunset Wed-Mon) Head northeast along Via Rosini to the ruins of this 1st-century-BC amphitheatre. Italy's third-largest, it could hold over 20,000 spectators and was occasionally flooded for mock naval battles. Head under the main arena and get your head around the complex mechanics involved in hoisting the caged wild beasts up to their waiting victims. In AD 305 seven Christian martyrs, including St Januarius, were thrown to the animals here. They survived only to be beheaded later.

Solfatara Crater   NATURE RESERVE
(📞081 526 23 41; www.solfatara.it; Via Solfatara 161; admission €6; ☉8.30am to 1hr before sunset) Some 2km up Via Rosini, which becomes Via Solfatara, this was known to the Romans as

the Forum Vulcani (home of the god of fire). At the far end of the steaming, malodorous crater are the **Stufe**, in which two ancient grottoes were excavated at the end of the 19th century to create two brick *sudatoria* (sweat rooms). Christened Purgatory and Hell, they both reach temperatures of up to 90°C. To get to the crater, catch any city bus heading uphill from the metro station and ask the driver to let you off at Solfatara.

Tempio di Serapide   HISTORICAL SITE
Despite its name, the Temple of Serapis wasn't a temple at all, but an ancient *macellum* (town market). Named after a statue of the Egyptian god Serapis found here in 1750, its toilets (at either side of the eastern apse) are considered works of ancient ingenuity. Badly damaged over the centuries by bradyseism (the slow upward and downward movement of the earth's crust), the temple is occasionally flooded by sea water. You'll find it just east of the port in a leafy piazza.

Baia

About 7km southwest of Pozzuoli, Baia was an upmarket Roman holiday resort with a reputation as a sordid centre of sex and sin. Today much of the ancient town is underwater, and modern development has left what is effectively a built-up, ugly and uninspiring coastal road.

Between April and October, CYMBA runs glass-bottom-boat tours of the underwater ruins of ancient Baia Sommersa (📞349 4974183; www.baiasommersa.it; tours €12; ☉10am, noon & 3pm Sat & Sun). All year round, however, you can admire the elaborate *nymphaeum* (shrine to the water nymph), complete with statues, jewels, coins and decorative pillars dredged up and reassembled in the little-known but worthy Museo Archeologico dei Campi Flegrei (📞081 523 37 97; Via Castello; admission €4; ☉varies, usually 9am to 1hr before sunset Tue-Sun). The 15th-century castle that houses the museum was built by Naples' Aragon rulers as a defence against possible French invasion.

Cuma & Lucrino

Located 3km northwest of Baia, the quaint town of Cuma was the earliest Greek colony on the Italian mainland. Just to the east, Lucrino is where you'll find a peaceful lake with a sinister mythical past.

The highlight of ancient Cumae's Acropoli di Cuma (📞081 854 30 60; Via Montecuma; admission €4; ☉9am to 1hr before sunset) is the haunting **Antro della Sibilla Cumana**

(Cave of the Cuman Sybil). Hollowed out of the tufa bank, its eerie 130m-long trapezoidal tunnel leads to the vaulted chamber where the Sybil was said to pass on messages from Apollo. The poet Virgil writes of Aeneas coming here to seek the oracle, who directs him to Hades (the underworld), entered from nearby Lago d'Averno (Lake Avernus).

🛈 Getting There & Away

Boat There are frequent car and passenger ferries from Pozzuoli to Ischia and Procida, run by a variety of companies. Typical prices are €6.60 to Procida and €7.60 to Ischia – more if you take a hydrofoil.

Bus AMN bus 152 links Naples to Pozzuoli.

Car Take the Tangenziale ring road from Naples and swing off at the Pozzuoli exit. Less swift but more scenic is taking Via Francesco Caracciolo along the Naples waterfront to Posillipo, then on to Pozzuoli.

Train Both the Ferrovia Cumana (📞800 001616; www.sepsa.it) and the Naples metro (line 2) serve Pozzuoli. To reach Cuma, take the Ferrovia Cumana train to Fusaro station, walk 150m north to Via Fusaro and jump on a Cuma-bound EAV bus (www.eavbus.it, in Italian), which runs roughly every 30 minutes Monday to Saturday and every hour on Sunday. For Baia, jump on a Miseno-bound EAV bus from the opposite side of the street.

CASERTA
POP 78,670

The one compelling reason to stop at this otherwise nondescript town, 22km north of Naples, is to visit the colossal Palazzo Reale.

One of the greatest – and last – achievements of Italian baroque architecture, its film credits include *Mission Impossible III* and the interior shots of Queen Amidala's royal residence in *Star Wars: Episode 1 – The Phantom Menace* and *Star Wars: Episode 2 – Attack of the Clones*.

Caserta was founded in the 8th century by the Lombards on the site of a Roman emplacement atop Monte Tifata, expanding onto the plains below from the 12th century onwards.

Caserta's **tourist office** (📞0823 32 11 37; www.eptcaserta.it; Corso Trieste; ⊗9am-1pm Mon-Fri) is 600m east of the palace.

👁 Sights

Palazzo Reale   PALAZZO & GARDENS
(📞0823 44 80 84; Viale Douhet 22; admission €12; ⊗8.30am-7pm Wed-Mon) Known to Italians as the Reggia di Caserta, this Unesco-listed palace began life in 1752 after King Charles VII of Bourbon ordered a palace to rival Versailles. Neapolitan Luigi Vanvitelli was commissioned for the job and built a palace bigger than its French rival. With its 1200 rooms, 1790 windows, 34 staircases and a 250m-long facade, it was reputedly the largest building in 18th-century Europe.

You enter by Vanvitelli's immense staircase, a masterpiece of vainglorious baroque, and follow a route through the royal apartments, richly decorated with tapestries, furniture and crystal. Beyond the library is a room containing a vast collection of *presepi* composed of hundreds of hand-carved nativity pieces.

TICKETS PLEASE

Tickets for public transport in Naples and the surrounding Campania region are managed by Unico Campania (www.unicocampania.it) and sold at stations, ANM booths and tobacconists. There are various tickets, depending on where you plan to travel. The following is a rundown of the various tickets on offer:

» **Unico Napoli** (90 minutes €1.20; 24 hours €3.60 weekdays, €3 weekends) Unlimited travel by bus, tram, funicular, metro, Ferrovia Cumana or Circumflegrea.

» **Unico 3T** (72 hours €20) Unlimited travel throughout Campania, including the Alibus, EAV buses to Mt Vesuvius and transport on the islands of Ischia and Procida.

» **Unico Ischia** (90 minutes €1.40; 24 hours €5.40) Unlimited bus travel on Ischia.

» **Unico Capri** (60 minutes €2.40; 24 hours €8.40) Unlimited bus travel on Capri. The 60-minute ticket also allows a single trip on the funicular connecting Marina Grande to Capri Town; the daily ticket allows for two funicular trips.

» **Unico Costiera** (45 minutes €2.40; 90 minutes €3.60; 24 hours €7.20; 72 hours €18) A money-saver if you plan on much travelling by SITA or EAV bus and/or Circumvesuviana train in the Bay of Naples and Amalfi Coast area. The 24- and 72-hour tickets also cover the City Sightseeing tourist bus between Amalfi and Ravello, and Amalfi and Maiori, which runs from April to October.

To clear your head afterwards, explore the elegant landscaped park (☺8.30am-6pm Jun-Aug, to 5.30pm May & Sep, to 5pm Apr, to 4.30pm Oct, to 4pm Mar, to 2.30pm Nov-Feb). It stretches for some 3km to a waterfall and fountain of Diana and the famous Giardino Inglese (English Garden; ☺Wed-Mon) with its intricate pathways, exotic plants, pools and cascades.

The weary can cover the same ground in a pony and trap (from €5), or for €1 you can bring a bike into the park. A picnic is another good idea. Within the palace there's also the Mostra Terrea Motus (admission free with palace ticket; ☺9am-6pm Wed-Mon), illustrating the 1980 earthquake that devastated the region.

❶ Getting There & Away

Bus CTP buses connect Caserta with Naples' Piazza Garibaldi (€2.90) about every 20 to 60 minutes between 4.30am and 11.30pm. Some Benevento services also stop in Caserta.

Train The town is on the main train line between Rome (IC €21, around 2½ hours) and Naples (€3.40, 40 minutes). Both bus and train stations are near the Palazzo Reale entrance. If you're driving, follow signs for the Reggia.

BAY OF NAPLES

Capri

POP 14,050

A stark mass of limestone rock that rises sheerly through impossibly blue water, Capri (pronounced *ca*-pri) is the perfect microcosm of Mediterranean appeal – a smooth cocktail of chichi piazzas and cool cafes, Roman ruins and rugged seascapes. It's also a hugely popular day-trip destination and a summer favourite of holidaying VIPs. Inevitably, the two main centres, Capri Town and its uphill rival, Anacapri, are almost entirely given over to tourism and high prices. But explore beyond the designer boutiques and pointedly traditional trattorias and you'll find that Capri's hinterland retains an unspoiled rural charm with grand villas, overgrown vegetable plots, sun-bleached peeling stucco and banks of brilliantly coloured bougainvillea.

◉ Sights

Grotta Azzurra   GROTTO
(Blue Grotto; Map p646; admission €11.50; ☺9am to 1hr before sunset) Long known to local fishermen, this stunning sea cave was re-discovered by two Germans, Augustus Kopisch and Ernst Fries, in 1826. Subsequent research, however, revealed that Emperor Tiberius had built a quay in the cave around AD 30, complete with a *nymphaeum*. You can still see the carved Roman landing stage towards the rear of the cave.

Far from being an overblown tourist attraction, the grotto's iridescent blue light is pure magic. It's caused by the refraction of sunlight off the sides of the 1.3m-high entrance, coupled with the reflection off the white sandy bottom.

The easiest way to visit is to take a boat tour from Marina Grande. A return trip will cost €23.50, comprising a return motorboat to the cave, a rowing boat into the cave and admission fee; allow a good hour. The singing 'captains' are included in the price, so don't feel any obligation if they push for a tip.

The grotto is closed if the sea is too choppy, so before embarking check that it's open at the Marina Grande tourist office.

Capri Town   TOWN
With its whitewashed stone buildings and tiny car-free streets, Capri Town evokes a film set. In summer its toy-town streets swell with camera-wielding day trippers and the glossy rich. Central to the action is Piazza Umberto I (aka the Piazzetta), the showy, open-air salon where tanned tourists pay eye-watering prices to sip at one of four squareside cafes. Nearby, the 17th-century Chiesa di Santo Stefano (Map p648; Piazza Umberto I; ☺8am-8pm) has a well-preserved marble floor (taken from Villa Jovis) and a statue of San Costanzo, Capri's patron saint. Beside the northern chapel is a reliquary with a saintly bone that reputedly saved Capri from the plague in the 19th century.

Across the road, Museo Cerio (Map p648; ✆081 837 66 81; Piazzetta Cerio 5; adult/concession €2.50/1; ☺10am-1pm Tue-Sat) harbours a library of books and journals about the island (mostly in Italian) and a collection of locally found fossils.

To the east of the Piazzetta, Via Vittorio Emanuele and its continuation, Via Serena, lead down to the picturesque Certosa di San Giacomo (Charterhouse of San Giacomo; Map p648; ✆081 837 62 18; Viale Certosa 40; admission free; ☺9am-2pm Tue-Sun), a 14th-century monastery with two cloisters and some fine 17th-century frescoes in the chapel.

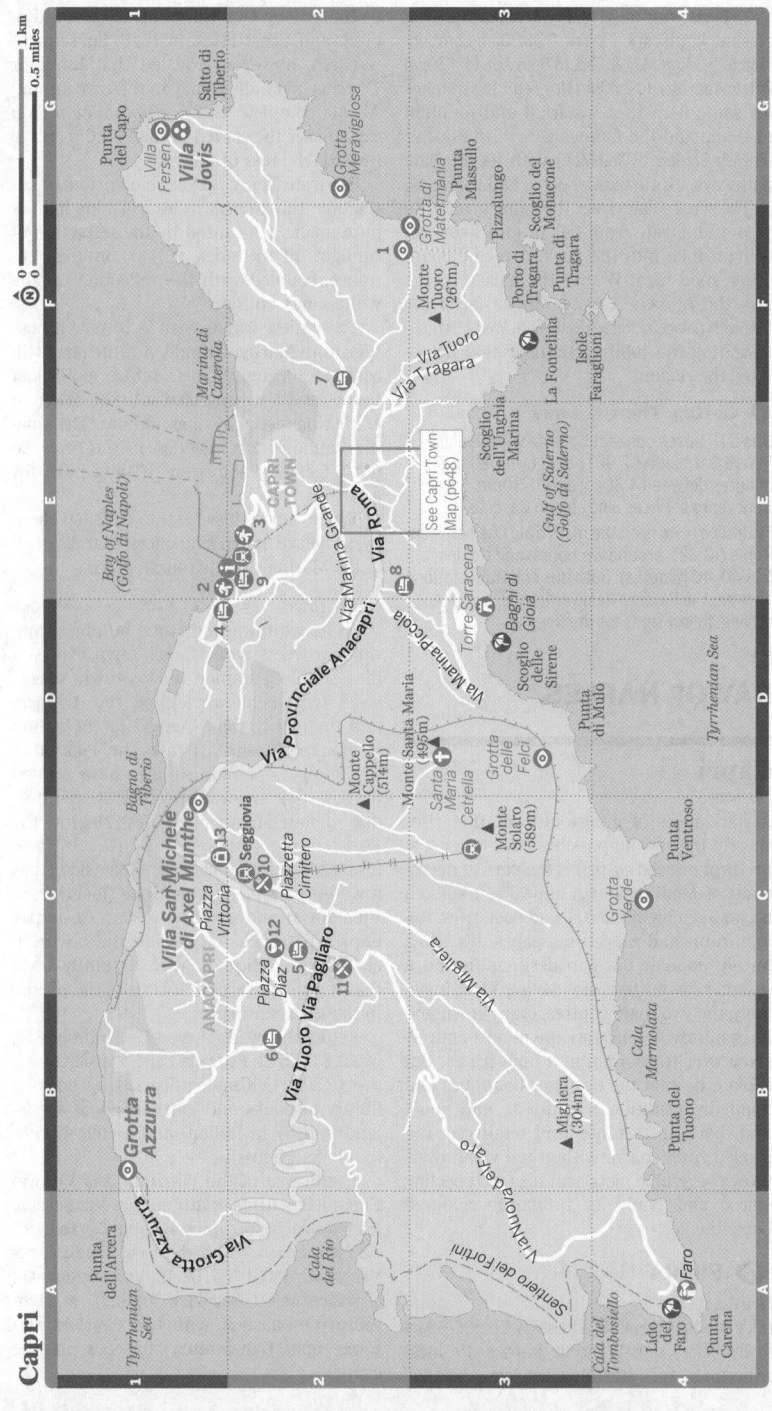

Capri

From the *certosa* (charterhouse), Via Matteotti leads down to the colourful Giardini di Augusto (Gardens of Augustus; Map p648; ⊙dawn-dusk), founded by the Emperor Augustus. The view from the gardens is breathtaking, looking over to the Isole Faraglioni (Map p646), three limestone pinnacles that rise vertically out of the sea.

Villa Jovis   VILLA

(Jupiter's Villa; Map p646; ☎081 837 06 34; Via Tiberio; admission €2; ⊙9am to 1hr before sunset) East of Capri Town, a comfortable 2km walk along Via Tiberio, is Villa Jovis (aka Palazzo di Tiberio). Standing 354m above sea level, this was the largest and most sumptuous of the island's 12 Roman villas and Tiberius' main Capri residence. It's not in great nick today, but the size of the ruins gives an idea of the scale at which Tiberius liked to live. His private rooms, with superb views over to the Punta Campanella, were on the northern and eastern sides of the complex.

The stairway behind the villa leads to the 330m-high Salto di Tiberio (Tiberius' Leap), a sheer cliff from where Tiberius had out-of-favour subjects hurled into the sea.

A 1.5km walk from the villa, down Via Tiberio and Via Matermània, is the Arco Naturale (Map p646), a huge rock arch formed by the pounding sea.

Villa San Michele di Axel Munthe   MUSEUM, GARDEN

(Map p646; ☎081 837 14 01; www.villasanmichele. eu; Via Axel Munthe; admission €6; ⊙9am-6pm May-Sep, 9am-3.30pm Nov-Feb, 9am-4.30pm Mar, 9am-5pm Apr & Oct) A short walk from Anacapri's Piazza Vittoria awaits the former home

of self-aggrandising Swedish doctor Axel Munthe. The story behind the villa, built on the ruined site of a Roman villa, is told by Munthe himself in his autobiography *The Story of San Michele* (1929). Other than the collection of Roman sculpture, the villa's best feature is the beautifully preserved gardens and their superb views. If you are here in July or August, you may be able to catch one of the classical concerts that take place in the gardens. Check the website for programme and reservation information.

Beyond the villa, Via Axel Munthe continues to the 800-step stairway leading down to Capri Town. Built in the early 19th century, this was the only link between Anacapri and the rest of the island until the present mountain road was constructed in the 1950s. Traditionally, the people of Capri and Anacapri have been at loggerheads, and they are always ready to trot out their respective patron saints to ward off the *malocchio* (evil eye) of their rivals.

Seggiovia   VIEWPOINT

(Map p646; ☎081 837 14 28; Piazza Vittoria; single/return €7.50/10; ⊙9.30am-4.30pm Apr-Oct, 9.30am-3.30pm Nov-Mar) Hop onto this chairlift and head up to the summit of Monte Solaro (589m), Capri's highest point. The views from the top are utterly unforgettable – on a clear day you can see the entire Bay of Naples and the islands of Ischia and Procida.

Faro   LIGHTHOUSE

(Map p646) Rising above Punta Carena, Capri's rugged southwesterly point, is Italy's second-tallest and most powerful lighthouse.

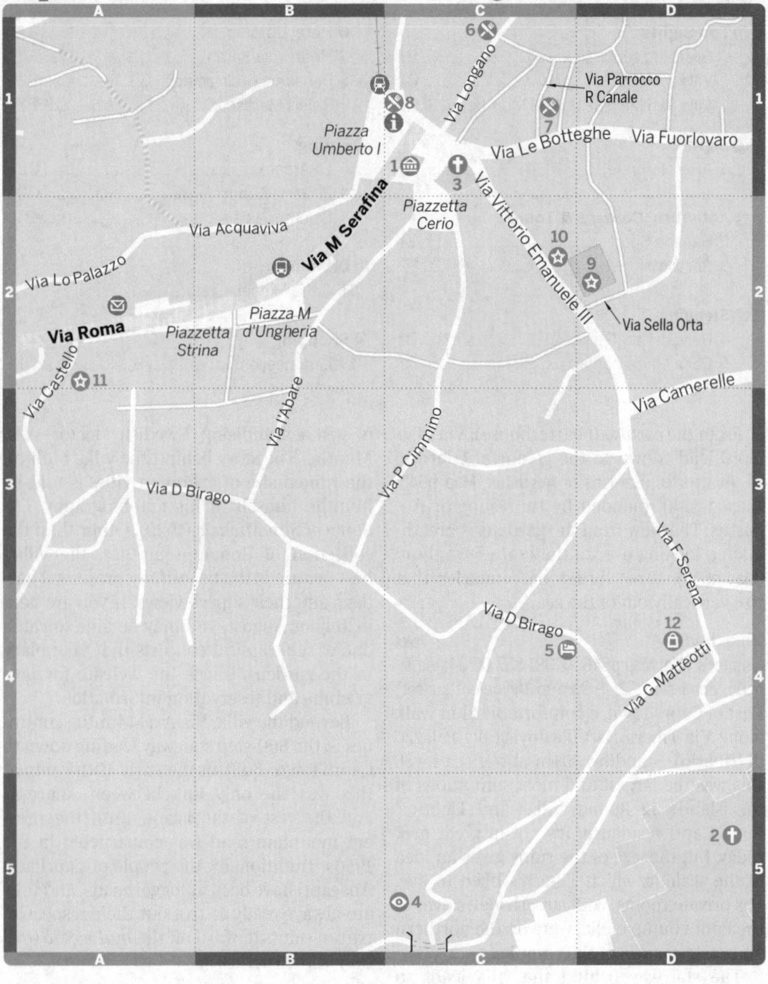

N 0 —————— 100 m
0 —————— 0.05 miles

Via Parrocco R Canale

Via Longano

Via Le Botteghe *Via Fuorlovaro*

Piazza Umberto I

Via Acquaviva

Via Lo Palazzo

Via M Serafina

Piazzetta Cerio

Via Vittorio Emanuele III

Via Roma

Piazzetta Strina

Piazza M d'Ungheria

Via Sella Orta

Via Castello

Via l'Abate

Via Camerelle

Via P Cimmino

Via D Birago

Via F Serena

Via D Birago

Via G Matteotti

From Anacapri a bus runs to the Faro every 20 minutes from April to October and every 30 to 40 minutes from November to March.

🏃 Activities

Top swimming spots include **La Fontelina** (Map p646), reached along Via Tragara. Access to the private beach will set you back €19 but it's right beside Capri's craggy Faraglioni stacks and is one of the few beaches exposed to the sun until late in the day. On the west coast, **Lido del Faro** (Map p646) at Punta Carena is another good option; €20 will get you access to the private beach, complete with swimming pool and a pricey but fabulous restaurant. Otherwise, opt for the neighbouring public beach, and grab a decent bite at snack bar Da Antonio. To get here, catch the bus to Faro and follow the steps down to the beach.

Capri also offers some memorable hiking. Favourite routes link the Arco Naturale with Punta di Tragara, and Monte Solaro with Anacapri. Running along the island's oft-overlooked western coast, the Sentiero dei Fortini (Path of the Small Forts) leads from Punta Carena up to the Grotta Azzurra.

Capri Town

Marina Grande is the hub of Capri's thriving water-sports business.

Sercomar DIVE CENTRE
(Map p646; ☎081 837 87 81; www.caprisub.com, in Italian; Via Colombo 64; ⊙closed Nov) Offers various diving packages, costing from €100 for a single dive to €350 for a four-session beginners' course.

Bagni di Gioia CANOEING
(Map p646; ☎081 837 77 02) You can hire single/double canoes here for €8/14 per hour.

Banana Sport BOATING
(Map p646; ☎081 837 51 88, 330 227064; ⊙mid-May–Oct) Operating out of a kiosk to the west of the port, Banana Sport hires out five-person motorised dinghies for €70 to €90 for two hours or €150 to €190 for the day.

🛏 Sleeping

Capri's accommodation is top-heavy, with plenty of four- and five-star hotels but few budget options. Cheaper *pensioni* do exist, but they tend to be at the top of their price bracket. Although there are a growing number of B&Bs, they're rarely much of a saving. As a general rule, the further you go from Capri Town, the less you'll pay. Camping is forbidden.

Always book ahead. Hotel space is at a premium during the summer, and many places close in winter, typically between November and March.

TOP CHOICE Casa Mariantonia BOUTIQUE HOTEL €€
(Map p646; ☎081 837 29 23; www.casamariantonia .com; Via G Orlandi 80, Anacapri; r €100-260, ste €180-400; Ⓟ❉🕏🏊) With past guests including Jean-Paul Sartre and Alberto Moravia, you might just find your own muse by the pool at this gorgeous boutique retreat. Rooms deliver restrained elegance in soothing hues, as well as a private terrace with garden views.

Relais Maresca HOTEL €€
(Map p646; ☎081 837 96 19; www.relaismaresca .it; Via Marina Grande 284, Marina Grande; r incl breakfast €130-250; ⊙Apr-Oct; ❉🕏) A delightful four-star, this is the top choice in Marina Grande, with acres of gleaming ceramic in turquoise, blue and yellow. There's a range of rooms (and corresponding prices); the best have balconies and sea views. There's also a lovely flower-filled 4th-floor terrace. Minimum two-day stay on weekends in July and August.

Hotel Villa Sarah HOTEL €€
(Map p646; ☎081 837 78 17; www.villasarahcapri .com; Via Tiberio 3a, Capri Town; s €95-155, d €145-225; ⊙Easter-Oct; ❉🕏) Villa Sarah retains a rustic appeal that so many of the island's hotels have long lost. Surrounded by its own fruit-producing gardens, it has 20 airy rooms, all decorated in classical local style with ceramic tiles and old-fashioned furniture. Best of all, though, is the small swimming pool.

Hotel Bussola HOTEL €€
(Map p646; ☎081 838 20 10; www.caprihotel bussola.com; Traversa La Vigna 14, Anacapri; s €50-120, d €70-140; ❉@🕏) This hotel has moved up several elegant notches from its days as a hostel-cum-hotel. The sun-filled rooms have luxurious drapes and a blue-and-white colour scheme, while the public spaces are a Pompeii-esque combo of columns, statues and vaulted ceilings. To get here take the bus up to Piazza Vittoria and call for the hotel shuttle service.

Hotel La Tosca HOTEL €€
(Map p648; ☎081 837 09 89; www.latoscahotel .com; Via Birago 5, Capri Town; s €50-100, d €75-160; ⊙Apr-Oct; ❉🕏) This charming one-star *pensione* is hidden away down a quiet back lane overlooking the Certosa di San Giacomo and the surrounding mountains. The rooms

are plain but comfortable, with cool white-washed walls and large bathrooms; several have private terraces. The genial owner extends a warm welcome. It's popular, so book ahead!

Belvedere e Tre Re   HOTEL €€

(Map p646; ☎081 837 03 45; www.belvedere-tre-re.com; Via Marina Grande 264, Marina Grande; s €80-120, d €100-140; ⊙Apr-Oct; ❄) Five minutes' walk from the port with superb boat views, this fairly modest two-star offers comfortable rooms, complete with private covered balconies. There's a sun-bronzing terrace on the top floor. Breakfast is an extra €5 per person.

Pensione Guarracino   PENSIONE €€

(Map p646; ☎/fax 081 837 71 40; guarracino@capri.it; Via Mulo 13; s €70-85, d €90-130; ❄) A short walk from the centre of Capri Town and within easy striking distance of Marina Piccola, this small, family-run *pensione* has 13 modest rooms, each decked out with a comfy bed, decent shower and independent air-con.

✖ Eating

Traditional food in traditional trattorias is what you'll find on Capri. The island's culinary gift to the world is *insalata caprese*, a salad of fresh tomato, basil and mozzarella bathed in olive oil. Also look out for *caprese* cheese, a cross between mozzarella and ricotta, and *ravioli caprese*, ravioli stuffed with ricotta and herbs.

Many restaurants, like the hotels, close over winter.

TOP CHOICE Pulalli   WINE BAR €€

(Map p648; Piazza Umberto I 4, Capri Town; meals €40; ⊙Wed-Mon Easter-Oct) Climb the clock-tower steps to the right of Capri Town's tourist office and your reward is a laid-back local hang-out, where fabulous vino meets a discerning selection of cheeses, *salumi* (charcuterie) and more substantial fare like spaghetti with zucchini flowers. Try for a seat on the terrace or, if you're feeling lucky, the coveted table on its own petite balcony.

Buca di Bacco   TRATTORIA, PIZZERIA €€

(Map p648; Via Longano 35, Capri Town; pizzas €6-15, meals €40; ⊙Thu-Tue Mar-Oct) A famous hang-out for artists early last century, this hidden Capri Town treasure is now better known for its solid local cooking, bubbling pizzas and amiable staff. The seafood is especially good, as is the window table with dreamy sea views.

Le Arcate   TRADITIONAL ITALIAN €€

(Map p646; Via de Tommaso 24, Anacapri; meals €40) This is the restaurant that the locals recommend – and frequent. An unpretentious place with hanging baskets of ivy and well-aged terracotta tiles, it specialises in delicious *primi* (first courses) and pizzas. A real show-stopper is the *risotto con polpa di granchio, rughetta e scaglie di parmigiano* (risotto with crab meat, rocket and shavings of Parmesan).

Capri Pasta   TAKE AWAY €

(Map p648; Via Parrocco R. Canale 12, Capri Town; meals €8; ⊙closed Mon) In-the-know locals come here for a cheap, tasty takeaway lunch. The just-cooked soul food might include *parmigiana di melanzana* (eggplant parmigiana) and *friarelle* (local broccoli). The house ravioli is legendary and offered fresh or ready-to-eat in dishes like *ravioli fritti* (fried ravioli) stuffed with Caciotta cheese and marjoram.

Salemeria da Aldo   DELI €

(Map p646; Via Cristoforo Colombo 26, Marina Grande; sandwiches from €3.50) Ignore the restaurant touts and head straight to this honest portside deli, where bespectacled Aldo will make you his legendary *panino alla Caprese* (crusty bread stuffed with silky mozzarella and tomatoes from his own garden). Grab a bottle of Falanghina and you're set for a day at the beach.

Pizzeria Aumm Aumm   PIZZERIA €

(Map p646; Via Caprile 18, Anacapri; pizzas €5-9; ⊙dinner Tue-Sun) Usually open until 1am, this is the locals' late-night option, complete with TV screen to capture any soccer goals. The wood-fired pizzas are seriously good, made with only fresh produce.

🍷 Drinking & Entertainment

The main evening activity is styling up and hanging out, ideally on Capri Town's Piazzetta. There are few nightclubs to speak of and just a few upmarket taverns. Most places open around 10pm (don't expect a crowd until midnight), charging anywhere between €30 and €40 for admission. Many close between November and Easter.

Anema e Core   LIVE MUSIC, NIGHTCLUB

(Map p648; Via Sella Orta 39e) In Capri Town, celebs head for this self-styled tavern, the island's most famous nightspot.

O Guarracino LIVE MUSIC
(Map p648; ☎081 837 05 14; Via Castello 7, Capri Town) Somewhat more casual.

Number One LIVE MUSIC, NIGHTCLUB
(Map p648; Via Vittorio Emanuele III 55, Capri Town) The latest hot spot, it offers live music and a small dance floor.

Caffè Michelangelo CAFE
(Map p646; Via Orlandi 138) Up in Anacapri, Michelangelo is a laid-back cafe good for people-watching.

🛍 Shopping

If you're not in the market for a new Rolex or Prada bag, look out for ceramic work, lemon-scented perfume and *limoncello* (lemon liqueur). For perfume don't miss Carthusia I Profumi di Capri (Map p648; Via F Serena 28) in Capri Town; for *limoncello* head up to Anacapri and Limoncello Capri (Map p646; Via Capodimonte 27).

If you *are* in the market for a new Rolex or Prada bag, head to Via Vittorio Emanuele and Via Camerelle.

ℹ Information

Emergency
Police station (☎081 837 42 11; Via Roma 70, Capri Town)

Internet Access
Capri Internet Point (☎081 837 32 83; Piazzetta Cimitero, Anacapri; per hr €2; ⏰9am-9pm Mon-Sat, to 2.30pm Sun May-Oct, shorter hrs Nov-Apr) Also sells international newspapers.

Internet Resources
Capri Island (www.capri.net) Excellent website with listings, itineraries and ferry schedules.
Capri Tourism (www.capritourism.com) Official website of Capri's tourist office.

Medical Services
Farmacia Internazionale (Via Roma 45, Capri Town)
Hospital (☎081 838 12 05; Via Provinciale Anacapri 5)

Post
Post office Capri Town (Map p648; Via Roma 50); Anacapri (Via de Tommaso 8)

Tourist information
Tourist office Marina Grande (Map p646; ⏰9.15am-1pm & 3-6.15pm Mon-Sat, 9am-3pm Sun Apr-Sep); Capri Town (Map p648; Piazza Umberto I; ⏰9am-1pm & 4-7.15pm Mon-Sat, to 3pm Sun Apr-Sep, 9.15am-1.15pm & 3-6.15pm

Mon-Sat Oct-Mar); Anacapri (Via Orlandi 59; ⏰9am-3pm Mon-Sat Apr-Sep) Each tourist office can provide a free map of the island with town plans of Capri and Anacapri, and a more detailed one for €1. For hotel listings and other useful information, ask for a free copy of *Capri è*.

ℹ Getting There & Away

See Naples (p640) and Sorrento (p665) for details of ferries and hydrofoils to the island.

In summer hydrofoils connect with Positano (€17, 30 to 40 minutes) and Ischia (€16.50, one hour).

Note that some companies require you to pay a small supplement for luggage, typically around €2.

ℹ Getting Around

The best way to get around Capri is by bus. There's no car-hire service on the island, and between Easter and October you can bring a vehicle to the island only if it's registered outside Italy.

Sippic (☎081 837 04 20) runs regular buses between Capri Town and Marina Grande, Anacapri and Marina Piccola. It also operates buses from Marina Grande to Anacapri and from Marina Piccola to Anacapri.

From Anacapri bus terminal, **Staiano Autotrasporti** (www.staiano-capri.com, in Italian) buses serve the Grotta Azzurra and Faro.

Single tickets cost €1.60 on all routes, as does the funicular that links Marina Grande with Capri Town.

You can hire a scooter from **Ciro dei Motorini** (☎081 837 80 18; Via Marina Grande 55) at Marina Grande. Rates are about €30 per two hours or €65 per 24 hours.

From Marina Grande, a **taxi** (☎in Capri Town 081 837 05 43, in Anacapri 081 837 11 75) costs around €20 to Capri and €25 to Anacapri; from Capri to Anacapri costs about €15.

Ischia

POP 62,030

Sprawling over 46 sq km, Ischia is the biggest and busiest island in the bay. It's a lush concoction of sprawling spa towns, mud-wrapped Germans and ancient booty. Also famous for its thermal waters, it has some fine beaches and spectacular scenery.

Most visitors stay on the touristy north coast, but go inland and you'll find a rural landscape of chestnut forests, dusty farms and earthy hillside towns. On the tranquil south coast, Sant'Angelo is a blissful blend of twisting laneways, cosy harbour and bubbling beaches.

⊙ Sights

Castello Aragonese CASTLE, MUSEUM
(☑081 99 28 34; Rocca del Castello; admission €10; ☺9am-1 hr before sunset) Ischia's imposing, iconic castle sits on a rocky islet just off Ischia Ponte. A sprawling complex comprising a 14th-century cathedral and several smaller churches, it largely dates to the 1400s, when King Alfonso of Aragon gave an older Angevin fortress a makeover. Inside, the **Museo delle Armi** (Weaponry Museum) has a curious collection of torture tools, kinky illustrations and medieval armoury.

La Mortella GARDEN
(☑081 98 62 20; www.lamortella.it; Via F Calese 39, Forio; admission €12; ☺9am-7pm Tue, Thu, Sat & Sun Apr-Oct) More than 1000 rare and exotic plants flourish in this veritable Garden of Eden on Ischia's west coast. Designed by Russell Page and inspired by the Moorish gardens of Granada's Alhambra in Spain, they were established by Sir William Walton, the late British composer, and his wife, who made La Mortella their home in 1949. Classical music concerts are staged on the premises; check the website.

🏃 Activities

Unlike Capri, Ischia has some great beaches. From chic Sant'Angelo on the south coast, water taxis reach the sandy **Spiaggia dei Maronti** (€5 one way; ☺Apr-Oct) and the intimate cove of **Il Sorgeto** (€7 one way; ☺Apr-Oct), with its steamy thermal spring. Sorgeto can also be reached on foot down a poorly signposted path from the village of Panza.

Negombo HOT SPRING, BEACH
(☑081 98 61 52; www.negombo.it; Baia di San Montano, Lacco Ameno; admission all-day €25; ☺8.30am-7pm Apr-Oct) Part spa resort, part botanical wonderland, Negombo's Zen-like thermal pools, hammam, contemporary sculpture and private beach make for a serious day of R&R. There's a decent *tavola calda* (snack bar) and a full range of pampering treatments and massages. Admission charges get cheaper the later in the day you arrive.

Monte Epomeo WALK
A strenuous uphill walk from the village of Fontana brings you to Ischia's highest point

(788m), with superb views of the Bay of Naples. The little church near the summit is the 15th-century **Cappella di San Nicola di Bari**, which features a pretty majolica floor.

Ischia Diving Center DIVE CENTRE
(☑081 98 18 52; www.ischiadiving.net; Via Iasolino 106, Ischia Porto) Offers diving equipment and courses. A single dive will typically cost from €38.

🛏 Sleeping

Most hotels close in winter, and prices normally drop considerably among those that stay open.

Albergo Il Monastero BOUTIQUE HOTEL €€
(☑081 99 24 35; www.albergoilmonastero.it; Castello Aragonese, Ischia Ponte; s €75-90, d €100-170, ste €250-300; ☺Easter-Oct; ❄@☏) For sheer location, it's hard to beat this lofty ex-convent inside the Castello Aragonese. Rooms are small but comfortable, some with vaulted ceilings and all with heavenly views. The spacious two-bedroom suite has been recently renovated, while the terrace restaurant serves tasty Ischian fare with produce from the garden.

Hotel Semiramis HOTEL €€
(☑081 90 75 11; www.hotelsemiramisischia.it; Spiaggia di Citara, Forio; r €94-142; ☺Apr-Sep; P❄☷) This bright, friendly hotel has a tropical-oasis feel, with its central pool surrounded by palms. Rooms, the best of which have distant sea views, are large and beautifully tiled in the traditional yellow-and-turquoise pattern.

Hotel Casa Celestino HOTEL €€
(☑081 99 92 13; www.casacelestino.it; Via Chiaia di Rose 20, Sant'Angelo; s €70-145, d €100-230; ☺Jan-Oct; ❄) This chic little number is a soothing blend of vibrant furnishings, whitewashed walls and contemporary art. Bedrooms have majolica-tiled floors, modern bathrooms and balconies overlooking the sea. There's a good restaurant across the way.

Camping Mirage CAMPGROUND €
(☑081 99 05 51; www.campingmirage.it; Via Maronti 37, Spiaggia dei Maronti, Barano d'Ischia; camping 2 people & tent €29.50-36.50; P) On Spiaggia dei Maronti is this shady campsite with pitches under a panoply of eucalyptus trees. On-site facilities include showers, a laundry, a bar and a restaurant serving great seafood pasta.

Albergo Macrì
HOTEL €

(☑/fax 081 99 26 03; Via Iasolino 78a, Ischia Porto; s €38-46, d €65-78; ℙ🅿️) Down a blind alley near the main port, this place oozes a friendly vibe. While the pine and bamboo furnishings won't snag any design awards, rooms are clean, bright and comfy. All first-floor rooms have terraces, and the small downstairs bar serves a mean espresso.

✗ Eating

Seafood aside, Ischia is famed for its rabbit, which is bred on inland farms. Another local speciality is *rucolino* – a green liquorice-flavoured liqueur made from *rucola* (rocket) leaves.

TOP CHOICE **Il Focolare**
TRATTORIA €€

(☑081 90 29 44; Via Cretaio 36, Casamicciola Terme; meals €40; ☺lunch Fri-Sun, dinner Mon-Sun, closed Wed Nov-May) Turf upstages surf at this rustic Slow Food favourite, tucked away in the hills above Casamicciola Terme. Complete with crackling fire, it's one of the best spots to sample the island's legendary *coniglio all'ischitana* (claypot-cooked local rabbit with garlic, onion, tomatoes, wild thyme and white wine).

Lo Scoglio
TRADITIONAL ITALIAN €€

(☑081 99 95 29; Via Cava Ruffano 58, Sant'Angelo; meals €32; ☺Apr-Oct) Jutting out over the sea beside a gorgeous beach cove, Lo Scoglio dishes up brilliant seafood. The ingredients are as fresh as the day's catch, appearing in dishes like mussel soup and grilled sea bass. Sunday lunchtime is a popular weekly event.

Pantera Rosa
TRADITIONAL ITALIAN €€€

(Via Porto 53, Ischia Porto; meals €50) Of Ischia Porto's string of harbourside restaurants, the 'Pink Panther' is our choice for good food and genuine, honest service. Tuck into gems like pappardelle pasta with seafood, followed by one of the homemade desserts and a frosty fix of the house *limoncello*.

❶ Information

Ischia Online (www.ischiaonline.it) Website with hotels, sights, activities and events.

Tourist office (www.infoischia procida.it; Via Sogliuzzo 72, Ischia Porto; ☺9am-2pm & 3-8pm Mon-Sat)

❶ Getting There & Away

See p640 for details of hydrofoils and ferries to/from Naples. You can also catch hydrofoils direct to Capri (€15) and Procida (€9).

❶ Getting Around

There are two principal bus lines: the CS (Circo Sinistra; Left Circle) and CD (Circo Destra; Right Circle), which circle the island in opposite directions, passing through each town and leaving every 30 minutes. Buses pass near all hotels and campsites. A single ticket, valid for 90 minutes, costs €1.40, while a 24-hour, multi-use ticket is €4.50. Taxis and microtaxis (scooter-engined three-wheelers) are also available.

Help the island avoid congestion and pollution by not bringing your car.If you want to hire one (or a scooter), there are plenty of rental firms, including **Fratelli del Franco** (☑081 99 13 34; Via A De Luca 127, Ischia Ponte), which hires out cars (from €30 per day), scooters (€25 to €35) and mountain bikes (around €10 per day). You can't take a rented vehicle off the island.

Procida

POP 10,620

Dig out your paintbox: the Bay of Naples' smallest island (and its best-kept secret) is a soulful blend of hidden lemon groves, weathered fishers and pastel-hued houses.

August aside – when beach-bound mainlanders flock to its shores – its narrow sun-bleached streets are the domain of the locals: wiry young boys clutch fishing rods, weary mothers clutch wiry young boys and wizened old seafarers swap tales of malaise.

◉ Sights & Activities

The best way to explore the island – a mere 4 sq km – is on foot or by bike. However, the island's narrow roads can be clogged with cars – one of its few drawbacks.

From panoramic Piazza dei Martiri, the village of Corricella tumbles down to its marina in a riot of pinks, yellows and whites. Further south, a steep flight of steps leads down to Chiaia beach, one of the island's most beautiful.

All pink, white and blue, little Marina di Chiaiolella has a yacht-stocked marina, old-school eateries and a languid disposition. Nearby the Lido is a popular beach.

Castello d'Avalos
HISTORICAL BUILDING

Clinging on to Procida's highest point is the crumbling 16th-century former Bourbon hunting lodge and ex-prison.

Abbazia di San Michele Arcangelo
MUSEUM

(☑081 896 76 12; Via Terra Murata 89; admission €3; ☺9.45am-12.45pm Mon-Sat year-round, plus 3.30-6pm May-Oct) Next door to Castello d'Avalos, this one-time Benedictine abbey contains a church, a small museum with some arresting paintings, and a honeycomb of catacombs.

Procida Diving Centre
DIVE CENTRE

(☎081 896 83 85; www.vacanzeaprocida.it/frame diving01-uk.htm; Via Cristoforo Colombo 6, Marina di Chiaiolella) This outfit runs diving courses and hires out equipment. The price ranges from €45 for a single dive to €130 for a snorkelling course and €350 for more advanced open-water diving.

Blue Dream
BOATING

(☎081 896 05 79, 339 572 08 74; www.bluedream charter.com; Via Ottimo 3) You can charter a yacht from Blue Dream, from €70 per person per day (minimum of six people).

★ Festivals & Events

Procession of the Misteri
RELIGIOUS

Good Friday sees a colourful procession of the Misteri. A wooden statue of Christ and the Madonna Addolorata, along with life-sized tableaux of plaster and papier-mâché illustrating events leading to Christ's crucifixion, is carted across the island. Men dress in blue tunics with white hoods, while many of the young girls dress as the Madonna.

🛏 Sleeping

Campsites are dotted around the island and open from April/May to September/October. Typical prices are €10 per site plus €10 per person. Reliable places include La Caravella (☎081 810 18 38; Via IV Novembre).

TOP CHOICE Hotel La Vigna
BOUTIQUE HOTEL €€

(☎081 896 04 69; www.albergolavigna.it; Via Principessa Margherita 46; s €75-150, d €90-180, ste €140-230; ❀❁@⊛) A cliff-side, vine-fringed garden and an in-house spa make this 18th-century villa a top choice. Five of the spacious, simply furnished standard rooms offer direct access to the garden. Superior rooms (€110 to €200) feature family-friendly mezzanines, while the suite comes with a bedside Jacuzzi.

Casa Giovanni da Procida
B&B €

(☎081 896 03 58; www.casagiovannidaprocida.it; Via Giovanni da Procida 3; d €65-110, tr €90-130; ❁closed Feb; ℙ❀⊛) This chic farmhouse B&B basks in the shade of a centuries-old magnolia tree and has split-level rooms with low-rise beds and contemporary furniture.

Bathrooms are small but slick, with funky mosaic tiling and cube basins.

Hotel La Corricella
HOTEL €€

(☎081 896 75 75; www.hotelcorricella.it; Via Marina Corricella 88; s €60-110, d €80-140; ❁mid-Mar–mid-Nov) One bookend to Marina Corricella, La Corricella offers comfy, low-fuss rooms with fans (air-con rooms cost an extra €10 to €20). The terrace offers gorgeous harbour views, the restaurant serves local specialities, and there's a boat service to the nearby beach.

✗ Eating

Ristorante Scarabeo
TRADITIONAL ITALIAN €€

(☎081 896 99 18; Via Salette 10; meals €35; ❁daily Jun-Oct, weekends only Dec-Feb & Mar-May, closed Nov) Behind a veritable jungle of lemon trees, Signor Francesco whips up classics like *fritelle di basilico* (fried patties of bread, egg, Parmesan and basil) and *ravioli di provola e melanzana* (ravioli stuffed with provola cheese and eggplant). Best of all, it's all yours to devour under a pergola of bulbous lemons.

La Conchiglia
TRADITIONAL ITALIAN €€

(☎081 896 76 02; Via Pizzaco 10; meals €30; ❁lunch Mar-Oct, dinner May–mid-Sep) Topaz waves at your feet, pastel Corricella in the distance – this is what you come to Procida for. Up against the views, the food holds its own with dishes such as *spaghetti alla povera* (spaghetti with *peperoncino*, green peppers, cherry tomatoes and anchovies). To get here, take the steep steps down from Via Pizzaco or book a boat from Corricella.

Gorgonia
TRADITIONAL ITALIAN €

(Via Marina Corricella; meals €24; ❁Mar-Oct) Along unpretentious Marina Corricella, with its old fishing boats, piles of fishing nets and sleek, lazy cats, any restaurant will provide you with a memorable experience. That said, this place peddles particularly fine smoked-seafood dishes, including swordfish and tuna steaks.

❶ Information

Procida Holidays (☎081 896 95 94; www.isoladiprocida.it; Via Roma 117; ❁9am-1pm & 4-8pm Mon-Sat Apr-Oct, closed Sat afternoon Nov-Mar) can organise accommodation (single/double from €40/50) and boat trips (about €15 for a two-hour tour), and also has a free map of the island.

Getting There & Around

Procida is linked by boat and hydrofoil to Ischia (€9), Pozzuoli (€9) and Naples (see p640).

There is a limited bus service (€1), with four lines radiating out from Marina Grande. Bus L1 connects the port and Marina di Chiaiolella.

Microtaxis can be hired for two to three hours for about €35, depending on your bargaining prowess. Contact **Sport & Company** (Via Roma 137; ⊘closed Sun) for bike hire (per day €18).

SOUTH OF NAPLES

Ercolano & Herculaneum

Ercolano is an uninspiring Neapolitan suburb that's home to one of Italy's best-preserved ancient sites – Herculaneum. A superbly conserved Roman fishing town, Herculaneum is smaller and less daunting than Pompeii, allowing you to visit without that nagging itch that you're bound to miss something.

History

In contrast to modern Ercolano, classical Herculaneum was a peaceful fishing and port town of about 4000 inhabitants, and something of a resort for wealthy Romans and Campanians.

Herculaneum's fate paralleled that of nearby Pompeii. Destroyed by an earthquake in AD 63, it was completely submerged in the AD 79 eruption of Mt Vesuvius. However, as it was much closer to the volcano than Pompeii, it drowned in a 16m-thick sea of mud rather than in the lapilli (burning pumice stone) and ash that rained down on Pompeii. This essentially fossilised the town, ensuring that even delicate items, like furniture and clothing, were discovered remarkably well preserved.

The town was rediscovered in 1709, and amateur excavations were carried out intermittently until 1874, with many finds being carted off to Naples to decorate the houses of the well-to-do or to end up in museums. Serious archaeological work began again in 1927 and continues to this day, although with much of the ancient site buried beneath modern Ercolano, it's slow going.

◉ Sights

Ruins of Herculaneum   RUINS
(🖉081 732 43 38; Corso Resina 6; adult/EU national 18-25yr/EU national under 18yr & over 65yr

€11/5.50/free; ⊘8.30am-7.30pm Apr-Oct, to 5pm Nov-Mar) Pompeii may be much larger, but the ruins of Herculaneum are better preserved, offering an unrivalled insight into ancient Roman life.

From the site's main gateway on Corso Resina, head down the wide boulevard, where you'll find the **ticket office** on the left. Pick up a free map and guide booklet here, and then follow the boulevard right to the actual entrance into the ruins themselves. Here you can hire the useful audioguide (€6.50).

To enter the ruins you pass through what appears to be a moat around the town but is in fact the ancient shoreline. It was here in 1980 that archaeologists discovered some 300 skeletons, the remains of a crowd that had fled to the beach only to be overcome by boiling surge clouds sweeping down from Vesuvius.

As you begin your exploration northeast along Cardo III you'll stumble across Casa d'Argo (Argus House), a well-preserved example of a Roman noble family's house, complete with porticoed garden and triclinium (dining area).

Across the street sits the Casa dello Scheletro (House of the Skeleton), a modest-size house with five styles of mosaic flooring and the remnants of an ancient security grill protecting the original skylight.

Across the Decumano Inferiore (one of ancient Herculaneum's main streets), the Terme Maschili was the men's section of the Terme del Foro (Forum Baths). Note the ancient latrine to the left of the entrance before stepping into the *apodyterium* (changing room). To the left is the *frigidarium* (cold bath), to the right the *tepadarium* (tepid bath), *caldarium* (hot bath) and an exercise area.

At the end of Cardo III, Decumano Massimo (Herculaneum's main thoroughfare) is lined with ancient shops and advertising, such as that adorning the wall to the right of the Casa del Salone Nero.

Further east along Decumano Massimo, a crucifix found in an upstairs room of the Casa del Bicentenario (Bicentenary House) provides possible evidence of a Christian presence in pre-Vesuvius Herculaneum.

Turn into Cardo IV from Decumano Massimo and you'll find the Casa del Bel Cortile (House of the Beautiful Courtyard), which houses three of the 300 skeletons discovered on the ancient shore in 1980.

Next door, the Casa di Nettuno e Anfitrite (House of Neptune and Amphitrite) is named after the extraordinary mosaic in the *nymphaeum*.

Over the road, the Terme Femminili was the women's section of the Terme del Foro; note the finely executed floor mosaic of a naked Triton in the *apodyterium*.

Further southwest on Cardo IV, the Casa dell'Atrio a Mosaico (House of the Mosaic Atrium; closed for restoration) is an impressive mansion with extensive floor mosaics, including a black-and-white chessboard design in the atrium.

Backtrack up Cardo IV and turn right at Decumano Inferiore. Here you'll find the Casa del Gran Portale (House of the Large Portal), whose main entrance is flanked by elegant brick Corinthian columns. Inside are some well-preserved wall paintings.

Accessible from Cardo V, Casa dei Cervi (House of the Deer) is an imposing example of a Roman noble family's house. The two-storey villa, around a central courtyard, contains murals and still-life paintings. In the courtyard is a diminutive pair of marble deer assailed by dogs and an engaging statue of a peeing Hercules.

Marking the site's southernmost tip, the 1st-century-AD Terme Suburbane (Suburban Baths; closed for restoration) is one of the best-preserved bath complexes in existence, with deep pools, stucco friezes and bas-reliefs looking down upon marble seats and floors.

Northwest of the ruins, Villa dei Papiri was a vast four-storey, 245m-long complex owned by Julius Caesar's father-in-law. At the time of research, the villa was closed for restoration. For updates, contact www.arethusa.net.

MAV

(Museo Archeologico Virtuale; ☑081 1980 6511; www.museomav.com; Via IV Novembre; admission €7.50; ☺9am-5.30pm Tue-Sun) On the main street linking the ruins and the train station, child-friendly MAV is a virtual-reality archaeology museum bringing the region's ruins back to life through holograms and computer-generated video.

ℹ Information

En route, you'll pass the **tourist office** (Via IV Novembre 82; ☺9am-6pm Mon-Sat) on your right.

ℹ Getting There & Away

The best way to get to Ercolano is by Circumvesuviana train (get off at Ercolano-Scavi). Trains run regularly to/from Naples (€2.10), Pompeii (€1.50) and Sorrento (€2.10).

By car take the A3 from Naples, exit at Ercolano Portico and follow the signs to car parks near the site's entrance.

Mt Vesuvius

Towering darkly over Naples and its environs, Mt Vesuvius (Vesuvio; 1281m) is the only active volcano on the European mainland. Since it exploded into history in AD 79, burying Pompeii and Herculaneum and pushing the coastline out several kilometres, it has erupted more than 30 times. The most devastating of these was in 1631, the most recent in 1944. And while there's little evidence to suggest any imminent activity, observers worry that the current lull is the longest in the past 500 years.

A full-scale eruption would be catastrophic. Some 600,000 people live within 7km of the crater and, despite incentives to relocate, few are willing to go.

Established in 1995, Parco Nazionale del Vesuvio (Vesuvius National Park; www.parco nazionaledelvesuvio.it) attracts some 400,000 visitors annually. From a car park at the summit, an 860m path leads up to the volcano's crater (admission incl tour €8; ☺9am-6pm Jul & Aug, to 5pm Apr-Jun & Sep, to 4pm Mar & Oct, to 3pm Nov-Feb). It's not a strenuous walk, but it's more comfortable in trainers than in sandals or flip-flops.

You'd also do well to take sunglasses – useful against swirling ash – and a sweater, as it can be chilly up top, even in summer.

About halfway up the hill, the Museo dell'Osservatorio Vesuviano (Museum of the Vesuvian Observatory; ☑081 610 84 83; www. ov.ingv.it; admission free; ☺10am-2pm Sat & Sun) tells the history of 2000 years of Vesuvius-watching.

EAV Bus (☑800 053 939; www.eavbus.it) runs two daily services from Naples to Vesuvius (€14.60 return, 90 minutes), stopping at Piazza Garibaldi at 9.25am and 10.40am. Two return services depart Vesuvius at 12.30pm and 2pm. It also runs eight to 10 daily buses to Vesuvius from Piazza Anfiteatro in Pompeii (€10, one hour). Buses terminate in the crater car park.

By car, exit the A3 at Ercolano Portico and follow signs for the Parco Nazionale del Vesuvio.

Note that when weather conditions are bad the summit path is shut and bus departures are suspended.

Pompeii

POP 25,760

A stark reminder of the malign forces that lie deep inside Vesuvius, Pompeii (Pompei in Italian) is Europe's most compelling archaeological site. Each year about 2.5 million people pour in to wander the ghostly shell of what was once a thriving commercial centre.

Its appeal goes beyond tourism, though. From an archaeological point of view, it's priceless. Much of the value lies in the fact that it wasn't simply blown away by Vesuvius: rather it was buried under a layer of lapilli (burning pumice stone), as Pliny the Younger describes in his celebrated account of the eruption.

History

The eruption of Vesuvius wasn't the first disaster to strike the Roman port of Pompeii. In AD 63, a massive earthquake hit the city, causing widespread damage and the evacuation of much of the 20,000-strong population. Many had not returned when Vesuvius blew its top on 24 August AD 79, burying the city under a layer of lapilli and killing some 2000 men, women and children.

The origins of Pompeii are uncertain, but it seems likely that it was founded in the 7th century BC by the Campanian Oscans. Over the next seven centuries the city fell to the ancient Greeks and the Samnites before becoming a Roman colony in 80 BC.

After its catastrophic demise, Pompeii receded from the public eye until 1594, when the architect Domenico Fontana stumbled across the ruins while digging a canal. However, short of recording the find, he took no further action.

Exploration proper began in 1748 under the Bourbon king Charles VII and continued into the 19th century. In the early days, many of the more spectacular mosaics were siphoned off to decorate Charles' palace in Portici; thankfully, though, most were subsequently moved up to Naples, where they now sit in the Museo Archeologico Nazionale (p628).

Work continues today and although new discoveries are being made, the emphasis is now on restoring what has already been unearthed rather than raking for new finds. Given the spate of recent government funding cuts, this has been a challenging task, the shock collapse of the Casa dei Gladiatori (House of the Gladiators) in November 2010 bringing to light the challenges faced in protecting this fragile site.

◎ Sights

Ruins of Pompeii RUINS
(☏081 861 90 03; entrances at Porta Marina & Piazza Anfiteatro; adult/EU national 18yr-25yr/ EU national under 18yr & over 65yr €11/5.50/free; ◎8.30am-7.30pm Apr-Oct, 8.30am-5pm Nov-Mar) Of Pompeii's original 66 hectares, 44 have now been excavated. Of course, that doesn't mean that you'll have unhindered access to every inch of the Unesco World Heritage–listed site: you'll come across areas cordoned off for no apparent reason, the odd stray dog and a noticeable lack of clear signs. Audioguides (€6.50) are a sensible investment, and a good guidebook will help – try the €10 *Pompeii* published by Electa Napoli.

If visiting in summer, note that there's not much shade on-site, so bring a hat and sunscreen. To do justice to the site, allow at least three or four hours, longer if you want to go into detail.

The site's main entrance is at **Porta Marina**, the most impressive of the seven gates that punctuated the ancient town walls. A busy passageway, now as then, it originally connected the town with the nearby harbour. Just outside the wall is the impressive **Terme Suburbane**. Accessible subject to prior booking at www.arethusa.net (click on 'Prenotazioni e Prevendite'), these baths are famed for the risqué frescoes in the *apodyterium* (changing room), which include a rare homoerotic scene involving two women.

Immediately on the right as you enter Porta Marina is the 1st-century-BC **Tempio di Venere** (Temple of Venus), formerly one of the town's most opulent temples.

Continuing down Via Marina you come to the **basilica**, the 2nd-century-BC seat of the city's law courts and exchange. Opposite, the **Tempio di Apollo** (Temple of Apollo) is the oldest and most important of Pompeii's religious buildings, dating to the 2nd century BC. The grassy **foro** (forum) adjacent to the temple was the city's main piazza – a huge traffic-free rectangle flanked by limestone columns.

Tragedy in Pompeii

24 AUGUST AD 79

8am Buildings including the **Terme Suburbane** 1 and the **foro** 2 are still undergoing repair after an earthquake in AD 63 caused significant damage to the city. Despite violent earth tremors overnight, residents have little idea of the catastrophe that lies ahead.

Midday Peckish locals pour into the **Thermopolium di Vetutius Placidus** 3. The lustful slip into the **Lupanare** 4, and gladiators practise for the evening's planned games at the **anfiteatro** 5. A massive boom heralds the eruption. Shocked onlookers witness a dark cloud of volcanic matter shoot some 14km above the crater.

3pm–5pm Lapilli (burning pumice stone) rains down on Pompeii. Terrified locals begin to flee; others take shelter. Within two hours, the plume is 25km high and the sky has darkened. Roofs collapse under the weight of the debris, burying those inside.

25 AUGUST AD 79

Midnight Mudflows bury the town of Herculaneum. Lapilli and ash continue to rain down on Pompeii, bursting through buildings and suffocating those taking refuge within.

4am–8am Ash and gas avalanches hit Herculaneum. Subsequent surges smother Pompeii, killing all remaining residents, including those in the **Orto dei Fuggiaschi** 6. The volcanic 'blanket' will safeguard frescoed treasures like the **Casa del Menandro** 7 and **Villa dei Misteri** 8 for almost two millennia.

TOP TIPS

» **Visit** in the afternoon
» **Allow** three hours
» **Wear** comfortable shoes and a hat
» **Bring** drinking water
» **Don't** use flash photography

CRISTIAN BONETTO

Terme Suburbane
The *laconicum* (sauna), *caldarium* (hot bath) and large, heated swimming pool weren't the only sources of heat here; scan the walls of this suburban bathhouse for some of the city's raunchiest frescoes.

Villa di Diomede
Casa dei Vettii
Casa del Poeta Tragico
Porta Ercolano
Casa de Fauno
Tempio di Apollo
Basilica
Porta Marina 1
2
4
Terme del Foro
Macellum
Teatro Grande
Quadriportico dei Teatri
Porta di Stabia
Teatro Piccolo

Foro
An ancient Times Square of sorts, the forum sits at the intersection of Pompeii's main streets and was closed to traffic in the 1st century AD. The plinths on the southern edge featured statues of the imperial family.

CRISTIAN BONETTO

Villa dei Misteri

Home to the world-famous *Dionysiac Frieze* fresco. Other highlights at this villa include *trompe l'oeil* wall decorations in the *cubiculum* (bedroom) and Egyptian-themed artwork in the *tablinum* (reception).

Lupanare

The prostitutes at this brothel were often slaves of Greek or Asian origin. Mattresses once covered the stone beds and the names engraved in the walls are possibly those of the workers and their clients.

Thermopolium di Vetutius Placidus

The counter at this ancient snack bar once held urns filled with hot food. The *lararium* (household shrine) on the back wall depicts Dionysus (the god of wine) and Mercury (the god of profit and commerce).

Eyewitness Account

Pliny the Younger (AD 61–c 112) gives a gripping, first-hand account of the catastrophe in his letters to Tacitus (AD 56–117).

Porta del Vesuvio

Porta di Nola

Casa della Venere in Conchiglia

Porta di Sarno

3

7

6

Grande Palestra

5

Tempio di Iside

Casa del Menandro

This dwelling most likely belonged to the family of Poppaea Sabina, Nero's second wife. A room to the left of the atrium features Trojan War paintings and a polychrome mosaic of pygmies rowing down the Nile.

Orto dei Fuggiaschi

The Garden of the Fugitives showcases the plaster moulds of thirteen locals seeking refuge during Vesuvius' eruption – the largest number of victims found in any one area. The huddled bodies make for a moving scene.

Anfiteatro

Magistrates, local senators and the games' sponsors and organisers enjoyed front-row seating at this veteran amphitheatre, home to gladiatorial battles and the odd riot. The parapet circling the stadium featured paintings of combat, victory celebrations and hunting scenes.

North of the forum stands the **Tempio di Giove** (Temple of Jupiter), one of whose two flanking triumphal arches remains, and the **Granai del Foro** (Forum Granary), now used to store hundreds of amphorae and a number of body casts. These casts were made in the late 19th century by pouring plaster into the hollows left by disintegrated bodies. Nearby, the **macellum** was the city's main meat and fish market.

From the market follow Via degli Augustali until Vicolo del Lupanare. Halfway down this narrow alley is the **Lupanare**, an ancient brothel. A tiny two-storey building with five rooms on each floor, it's lined with some of Pompeii's raunchiest frescoes.

At the end of Via dei Teatri, the green **Foro Triangolare** would originally have overlooked the sea. The main attraction here was, and still is, the 2nd-century-BC **Teatro Grande**, a huge 5000-seat theatre. Behind the stage, the porticoed **Quadriportico dei Teatri** was initially used for the audience to stroll between acts and later as a barracks for gladiators. Next door, the **Teatro Piccolo**, also known as the Odeion, was once an indoor theatre, while the pre-Roman **Tempio di Iside** (Temple of Isis) was a popular place of cult worship.

Just to the east, Via dell'Anfiteatro (which becomes Vico Meridionale) is where you'll find **Casa del Menandro**. One of Pompeii's grander private homes, its highlights include an elegant peristyle (colonnaded garden) and a striking mosaic floor in the *caldarium* (hot room).

Back on Via dell'Abbondanza, the **Terme Stabiane** is a typical 2nd-century-BC bath complex. Entering from the vestibule, bathers would stop off in the vaulted *apodyterium* (changing room) before passing through to the *tepidarium* and *caldarium*. Further northeast along Via dell'Abbondanza, the **Thermopolium di Vetutius Placidus** is a fine example of a Roman snack bar, while the **Casa della Venere in Conchiglia** (House of the Venus Marina) harbours a lovely peristyle looking on to a small, manicured garden. It's here that you'll find the striking Venus fresco after which the house is named.

Nearby, the grassy **anfiteatro** is the oldest-known Roman amphitheatre in existence. Built in 70 BC, it was at one time capable of holding up to 20,000 bloodthirsty spectators. Over the way, the **Grande Palestra** is an athletics field with an impressive portico and, at its centre, the remains of a swimming pool.

From here, double back along Via dell'Abbondanza and turn right into Via Stabiana to see some of Pompeii's grandest houses. Turn left into Via della Fortuna for the **Casa del Fauno** (House of the Faun), Pompeii's largest private house. Named after the small bronze statue in the *impluvium* (rain tank), it was here that early excavators found Pompeii's greatest mosaics, most of which are now in Naples' Museo Archeologico Nazionale. A couple of blocks away, the **Casa del Poeta Tragico** (House of the Tragic Poet) features the world's first 'beware of the dog' – *cave canem* – warnings. To the north, on Vicolo di Mercurio, the **Casa dei Vettii** is home to a famous depiction of Priapus with his gigantic phallus balanced on a pair of scales.

From here follow the road west and turn right into Via Consolare, which takes you out of the town through **Porta Ercolano**. Continue past **Villa di Diomede**, turn right, and you'll come to the **Villa dei Misteri**, one of the most complete structures left standing in Pompeii. The *Dionysiac Frieze*, the most important fresco still on-site, spans the walls of the large dining room. One of the world's largest ancient paintings, it depicts the initiation of a bride-to-be into the cult of Dionysus, the Greek god of wine.

The **Museo Vesuviano** ([📞]081 850 72 55; Via Bartolomeo 12; admission free; [⏱]9am-1pm Mon-Fri), southeast of the excavations, contains an interesting array of artefacts.

[👉] Tours

You'll almost certainly be approached by a guide outside the *scavi* ticket office. Authorised guides wear identification tags and you can expect to pay between €100 and €120 for a two-hour tour, whether you're alone or in a group. Reputable tour operators include **Yellow Sudmarine** ([📞]329 1010 328; www.yellowsudmarine.com), **Torres Travel** ([📞]081 856 78 02; www.torrestravel.it) and **Pompeii Cast** ([📞]081 850 49 12; www.pompeiicast.it), all of whom offer tours of the ruins, as well as excursions to other regional highlights, including Naples, Capri and the Amalfi Coast.

[🛏] Sleeping & Eating

There's really no need to stay overnight in Pompeii. The ruins are best visited on a day trip from Naples, Sorrento or Salerno, and once the excavations close for the day, the area around the site becomes decidedly seedy.

Old Pompeii

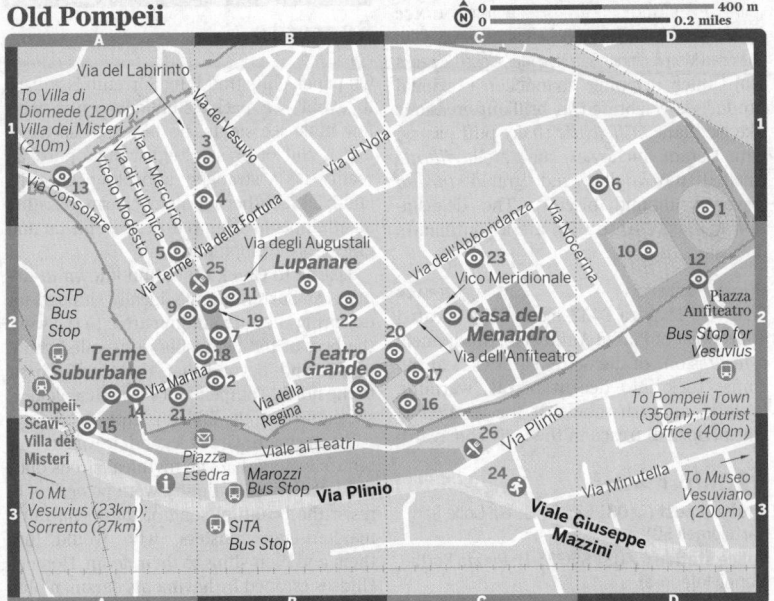

Old Pompeii

Most of the restaurants near the ruins are characterless affairs set up for feeding busloads of tourists. Wander down to the modern town and it's a little better, with a few decent restaurants serving excellent local food.

If you'd rather stay at the ruins, the onsite **cafeteria** (Via di Mercurio) peddles the standard choice of panini, pizza slices, salads, hot meals and gelato. You'll find it near the Tempio di Giove.

TOP CHOICE President MODERN ITALIAN €€

(☑081 850 72 45; Piazza Schettini 12; meals €40; ◎closed Mon & dinner Sun Nov-Mar, closed 2 weeks Jan) Under dripping chandeliers, regional produce is celebrated in brilliant creations like eggplant *millefoglie* (flaky puff pastry) with Cetara anchovies, mozzarella *filante* (melted mozzarella) and grated *tarallo* (savoury almond biscuit). The degustation menus (€40 to €70) are a gourmand's delight.

Plinio Hostaria OSTERIA, PIZZERIA €€

(Via Plinio 12; pizza €4-12, meals €30) Located 450m west of Piazza Anfiteatro, this homely *osteria* is one of the better eateries near the ruins. Tuck into decent pizzas, warming lasagne, or fresh salads. If the weather is warm, nosh al fresco in the leafy courtyard.

ℹ Information

First-aid post (☑081 535 91 11; Via Colle San Bartolomeo 50)

Police station (☑081 856 35 11; Piazza Porta Marina Inferiore)

Pompeii Sites (www.pompeiisites.org) A comprehensive website covering Pompeii and Herculaneum.

Post office (Piazza Esedra)

Tourist office Porta Marina (☑081 536 32 93; www.pompeiturismo.it; Piazza Porta Marina Inferiore 12; ◎8am-3.45pm Mon-Sat); Pompeii town (☑081 850 72 55; Via Sacra 1; ◎8am-3.30pm Mon-Fri, to 1.30pm Sat)

ℹ Getting There & Away

Frequent Circumvesuviana trains run from Pompeii-Scavi-Villa dei Misteri station to Naples (€2.80, 35 minutes) and Sorrento (€2.10, 30 minutes).

Otherwise, **SITA** (☑089 405 145; www.sita bus.it, in Italian) operates buses half-hourly to/from Naples (€2.80, 30 minutes); and **CSTP** (☑800 016 659; www.cstp.it, in Italian) bus 4 runs to/from Salerno (€2.10, one hour).

For Rome, **Marozzi** (☑080 579 01 11; www.marozzivt.it) has one to two daily buses (€16.50, three hours), departing from Piazza Esedra.

For information on getting to/from Vesuvius see p656. Buses to Vesuvius depart from Piazza Anfiteatro.

To get here by car, take the A3 from Naples. Use the Pompeii exit and follow signs to Pompeii Scavi. Car parks (approximately €5 per hour) are clearly marked and vigorously touted.

Sorrento

POP 16,610

On paper, cliff-straddling Sorrento is a place to avoid – a package-holiday centre with few must-see sights, no beach to speak of and a glut of brassy English-style pubs. In reality, it's a strangely appealing place, its laid-back southern Italian charm resisting all attempts to swamp it in souvenir tat and graceless development.

Dating to Greek times and known to Romans as Surrentum, it's ideally situated for exploring the surrounding area: to the west, the best of the peninsula's unspoiled countryside and, beyond that, the Amalfi Coast; to the north, Pompeii and the archaeological sites; offshore, the fabled island of Capri.

According to Greek legend, it was in Sorrento's waters that the mythical sirens once lived. Sailors of antiquity were powerless to resist the beautiful song of these charming maidens-cum-monsters, who would lure them and their ships to their doom. Homer's Ulysses escaped by having his oarsmen plug their ears with wax and by strapping himself to his ship's mast as he sailed past.

◎ Sights

Spearing off from Piazza Tasso, Corso Italia (closed to traffic from 7pm to 1am daily during the summer, as well as from 10am to 1pm on Sundays and public holidays) cuts through the *centro storico*, whose narrow streets throng with tourists on summer evenings. An attractive area, it's thick with loud souvenir stores, cafes, churches and restaurants.

Chiesa di San Francesco CHURCH

(☑081 878 12 69; Via San Francesco; ◎8am-1pm & 2-8pm) The real attraction here is not the church but its beautiful medieval cloisters. A harmonious marriage of architectural styles – two sides are lined with 14th-century crossed arches, the other two with round arches supported by octagonal pillars – they are often used to host exhibitions and summer concerts.

Next door, the **Villa Comunale park** (◎8am-8pm mid-Oct–mid-Apr, 8am-midnight mid-Apr–mid-Oct) commands grand views over the water to Mt Vesuvius.

Museo Correale MUSEUM

(☑081 878 18 46; www.museocorreale.com; Via Correale 50; admission €7; ◎9.30am-1.30pm Wed-Mon) Sorrento's main museum, it houses

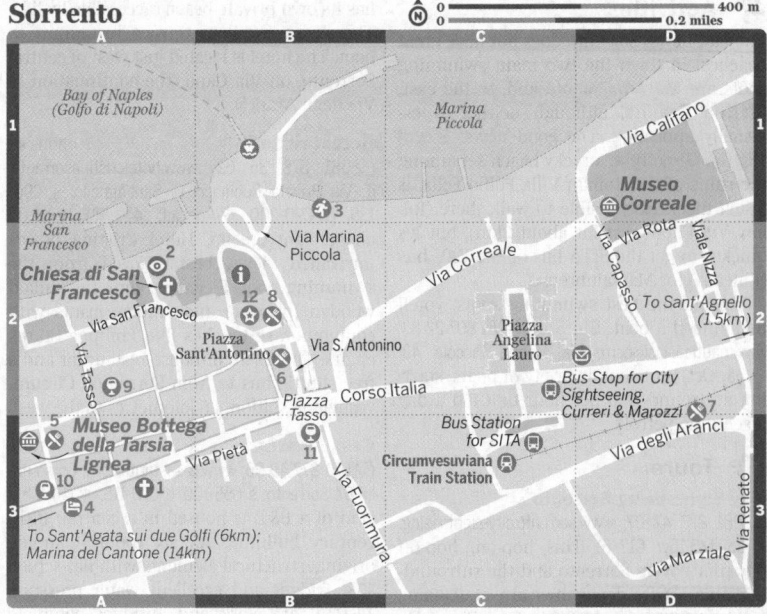

Sorrento

a rich collection of 17th- and 19th-century Neapolitan art, Japanese, Chinese and European ceramics, clocks and furniture, as well as Greek and Roman artefacts. The museum's gardens are equally impressive, with heavenly bay views.

Museo Bottega della Tarsia Lignea MUSEUM
(☑081 877 19 42; Via San Nicola 28; admission €8; ⊙10am-1pm & 3-6.30pm) Further west, the palatial Bottega della Tarsia Lignea showcases some fabulous examples of *intarsio* (mar-

quetry) furniture – a craft Sorrento has been famous for since the 18th century.

Duomo   DUOMO
(☑081 878 22 48; Corso Italia; ⊙8am-noon & 6-8pm) The gleaming white exterior of Sorrento's spiritual centrepiece gives no hint of its inner exuberance. Of particular note are the marble bishop's throne and the beautiful wooden choir stalls. Outside, the tripletiered bell tower rests on an archway into which three classical columns have been set.

🏃 Activities

The bad news: Sorrento does not have great beaches. In town the two main swimming spots are **Marina Piccola** and, to the east, **Marina Grande**, although neither is especially appealing. The good news: **Bagni Regina Giovanna**, a rocky beach set among the ruins of the Roman Villa Pollio Felix, is much nicer. It's possible to walk there (follow Via Capo west for about 2km), but it's quicker to get the SITA bus or the EAV bus (Linea A) for Massalubrense.

To find the best swimming spots, you'll really need a boat. **Sic Sic** (☑081 807 22 83; www.nauticasicsic.com; Via Marina Piccola 43; ☺May-Oct) rents out a variety of boats, starting at around €50 per hour or €150 a day (excluding petrol).

👉 Tours

City Sightseeing Sorrento BUS
(☑081 877 47 07; www.sorrento.city-sightseeing. it; adult/6-15yr €12/6) This hop-on, hop-off bus tour covers Sorrento and the surrounding area. Daily departures are at 9.30am, 11.30am, 1.30pm and 3.30pm from Piazza De Curtis (Circumvesuviana station). English-language commentaries are provided, and tickets, available on board, are valid for six hours.

🎉 Festivals & Events

The city's patron saint, Sant'Antonino, is remembered on 14 February each year with processions and huge markets. The saint is credited with having saved Sorrento during WWII, when Salerno and Naples were heavily bombed.

Sorrento's **Settimana Santa** Easter processions are famous throughout Italy. There are two main processions: one at midnight on the Thursday preceding Good Friday, the second on Good Friday.

🛏️ Sleeping

Most accommodation is in the town centre or clustered along Via Capo, the coastal road west of the centre. Be sure to book early for the summer season.

La Tonnarella HOTEL €€€
(☑081 878 11 53; www.latonnarella.it; Via Capo 31; d €112-225, ste €300-400; ☺Apr-Oct; P ❊ @ ☎) A dazzling combo of blue-and-yellow majolica tiles, antiques, chandeliers and statues. Most of the classically themed rooms have their own balcony or small terrace, and the hotel

has its own private beach (accessible by lift). There's an excellent terrace restaurant to boot. The hotel is located just west of central Sorrento, on Via Capo (the continuation of Via degli Aranci).

Hotel Cristina HOTEL €€
(☑081 878 35 62; www.hotelcristinasorrento. it; Via Privata Rubinacci 6, Sant'Agnello; s €90-135, d €90-200; ☺Apr-Oct; ❊ ☎ ☻) Perched above Sant'Agnello, Hotel Cristina boasts unrivalled views, best enjoyed from the swimming pool. Elegant rooms fuse inlaid wooden furniture and vintage prints with contemporary touches like Philippe Starck chairs. There's an in-house restaurant and a free shuttle bus to/from Sorrento's Circumvesuviana station, 1.5 kilometres to the west.

Casa Astarita B&B €
(☑081 877 49 06; www.casastarita.com; Corso Italia 67, Sorrento; s €55-100, d €70-115; ❊ @) This gem of a B&B is housed in a central, 16th-century building. All six rooms combine original structural elements with flat-screen TVs, fridges and excellent water pressure. Tasteful art work and antiques complete the eclectic look. Rooms surround a central parlour where breakfast is served on a large rustic table.

Seven Hostel HOSTEL €
(☑081 878 67 58; www.sevenhostel.com; Via Iommella Grande 99, Sant'Agnello; dm €20-32, s €50-80, d €60-100; ❊ @ ☎) Seven sexes up 'budget' with its sleek spaces, chic rooftop terraces, and weekend live-music gigs. Dorms are spacious and contemporary (some with en suite bathroom), private rooms small but smart, and the on-site laundry is a welcome bonus. It's 800m north of the Sant'Agnello Circumvesuviana train station, one stop from Sorrento.

Nube d'Argento CAMPGROUND €
(☑081 878 13 44; www.nubedargento.com; Via Capo 21; camping 2 people, tent & car €25-37, 2-person bungalows €50-85; ☺Mar-Dec; ☎ ☻ ❉) This inviting campsite is an easy 1km drive west of the Sorrento town centre. Pitches and wooden chalet-style bungalows are spread out beneath a canopy of olive trees, and the facilities, including an open-air swimming pool, are excellent.

🍴 Eating

A local speciality to look out for is *gnocchi alla sorrentina* (gnocchi baked in tomato sauce with mozzarella).

Inn Bufalito CHEESE BAR €€

(Via Fuoro 21; meals €30; ☺Apr-Oct) A brilliant Slow Food mozzarella bar-restaurant. Head here for sterling local produce – think Sorrento-style cheese fondue, buffalo meat carpaccio and *salsiccia* (local sausage) with broccoli. There's regular cheese tastings, as well as the odd art exhibitions or live-music act.

Ristorante Il Buco GASTRONOMIC €€€

(✆081 878 23 54; Rampa Marina Piccola 5; meals €70, 6-course degustation menu €75-85; ☺Thu-Tue Feb-Dec) Hardly the hole its name suggests, this Michelin-starred restaurant is housed in a former monks' wine cellar. The emphasis is on innovative regional cooking, so expect revived classics such as cheese tartlet with tomato tartare and rucola pesto. Reservations recommended.

La Basilica MODERN ITALIAN, PIZZERIA €€

(Via S Antonino 12; pizzas €6-11, meals €50; ☺noon-midnight) Elegant without the attitude, barrel-vaulted Basilica serves regional nosh with subtle yet confident twists (think house-made black scialatielli pasta with calamari and pomodorini or a decadent dark chocolate and whiskey tart). For a cheaper feed, dig into the excellent wood-fired pizzas.

Mondo Bio VEGETARIAN €

(Via degli Aranci 146; snacks €3, pasta from €6.50; ☺8.30am-8.30pm Mon-Sat) Flying the banner for organic vegetarian food, this bright shop-cum-restaurant serves a limited range of meat-free antipasti, mains and sweets. The menu, chalked up outside, changes daily but might include *zuppa di soia verde* (soybean soup) and *polpette di tofu* (tofu balls).

🍷 Drinking

From wood-panelled wine bars to cocktail-centric cafes, you'll find no shortage of drinking dens in Sorrento.

Café Latino CAFE, BAR

(Vico I Fuoro 4a) A romantic choice, this is the place to sit among orange and lemon trees and gaze into your lover's eyes over a chilled cocktail. If you can't drag yourselves away, you can also eat here (meals around €30).

Fauno Bar CAFE, BAR

(Piazza Tasso) This elegant cafe covers half of Piazza Tasso and offers the best people-watching in town. Expect stiff drinks at stiff prices – cocktails start at around €8.50.

Snacks and sandwiches are also available (from €7).

Bollicine WINE BAR

(Via dell'Accademia 9; ☺closed Tue) An unpretentious wine bar with a dark wooden interior and boxes of bottles littered around the place. The wine list includes all the big Italian names and a selection of local labels – the amiable bartender will happily advise you. There's also a menu of rustic dishes, including pizza and homemade salami.

☆ Entertainment

In the summer, concerts are held in the cloisters of Chiesa di San Francesco.

Teatro Tasso LIVE MUSIC, THEATRE

(✆081 807 55 25; www.teatrotasso.com; Piazza Sant'Antonino) Head here for a good old sing-along. The southern Italian equivalent of a cockney music hall, it's home to the Sorrento Musical (€25), a sentimental revue of Neapolitan classics such as 'O Sole Mio'. The 75-minute performances start at 9.30pm every evening from Monday to Saturday from Easter to October.

Fauno Notte Club LIVE MUSIC, THEATRE

(✆081 878 10 21; www.faunonotte.it; Piazza Tasso 1) Teatro Tasso's direct competitor offers 'a fantastic journey through history, legends and folklore'. In other words, 500 years of Neapolitan history set to music.

ℹ Information

Hospital (✆081 533 11 11; Corso Italia 1)

Police station (✆081 807 53 11; Via Capasso 11)

Post office (Corso Italia 210)

Sorrento Tour (www.sorrentotour.it) Extensive website with tourist and transport information on Sorrento and environs.

Tourist office (Via Luigi De Maio 35; ☺8.30am-4.15pm Mon-Fri) In the Circolo dei Forestieri (Foreigners' Club). Has printed material and can offer accommodation advice. From May to September, you'll also find information kiosks (open 10am to 1pm and 4pm to 9pm) at the train station, ferry terminal and in the centre of town.

ℹ Getting There & Away

Boat

Sorrento is the main jumping-off point for Capri and also has excellent ferry connections to Naples, Ischia and Amalfi coastal resorts. **Alilauro** (✆081 878 14 30; www.alilauro.it) runs up to five daily hydrofoils between Naples and Sorrento

(€11, 35 minutes). The slower **Metrò del Mare** (☑199 600700; www.metrodelmare.net) covers the same route but was suspended indefinitely in 2011. **Gescab-Linee Marittime Partenopee** (☑081 704 19 11; www.consorziolmp.it) runs hydrofoils from Sorrento to Capri from April to November (€15, 20 minutes, 15 daily).

All ferries and hydrofoils depart from the port at Marina Piccola, where you buy your tickets.

Bus

Curreri (☑081 801 54 20; www.curreriviaggi.it) runs six daily services to Sorrento from Naples' Capodichino airport, departing from outside the arrivals hall and arriving in Piazza Tasso. Buy tickets (€10) for the 75-minute journey on the bus.

SITA (☑089 405 145; www.sitabus.it, in Italian) buses serve the Amalfi Coast and Sant'Agata sui due Golfi, leaving from outside the Circumvesuviana train station. Buy tickets at the station bar or from shops bearing the blue SITA sign. Around 30 buses run daily between Sorrento and Amalfi (€2.80, 1¾ hours), looping around Positano (€1.50, one hour). Change at Amalfi for Ravello.

Marozzi (☑080 579 01 11; www.marozzivt.it) operates one to two daily buses to/from Rome (€17.50).

Train

Circumvesuviana (☑081 772 24 44; www. vesuviana.it) trains run every half-hour between Sorrento and Naples (€4), via Pompeii (€2.10) and Ercolano (€2.10).

🛈 Getting Around

Local bus Line B runs from Piazza Sant'Antonino to the port at Marina Piccola (€1).

Jolly Service & Rent (☑081 877 34 50; www. jollyrent.eu; Via degli Aranci 180) has Smart cars from €53 a day and 50cc scooters from €27.

For a taxi, call ☑081 878 22 04.

West of Sorrento

The countryside west of Sorrento is the very essence of southern Italy. Tortuous roads wind their way through hills covered in olive trees and lemon groves, passing through sleepy villages and tiny fishing ports. There are magnificent views at every turn, the best from Sant'Agata sui due Golfi and the high points overlooking Punta Campanella, the westernmost point of the Sorrentine Peninsula.

SANT'AGATA SUI DUE GOLFI

Perched high in the hills above Sorrento, sleepy Sant'Agata sui due Golfi commands spectacular views of the Bay of Naples on one side and the Bay of Salerno on the other (hence its name, Saint Agatha on the two Gulfs). The best viewpoint is the Deserto (☑081 878 01 99; Via Deserto; ⊙gardens 7am-7pm, panoramic lookout 5-8pm Apr-Sep, 3-4pm Oct-Mar), a Carmelite convent 1.5km uphill from the village centre. The convent (s incl breakfast, lunch & dinner €45) also offers simple, peaceful accommodation for those who find the peace and panorama too hard to leave.

Agriturismo Le Tore (☑081 808 06 37; www.letore.com; Via Pontone 43; s €50-80, d €90-110, dinner €25-30; ⊙Easter–mid-Nov; ℗) is a working organic farm with eight barnlike rooms and an apartment that sleeps six (€600 to €1000 per week). A short drive, or a long walk, from the village, the setting is lovely, a rustic farmhouse hidden among fruit trees and olive groves.

From Sorrento, there's a pretty 3km (approximately one hour) trail up to Sant'Agata. Otherwise, hourly SITA buses leave from the Circumvesuviana train station.

MARINA DEL CANTONE

From Sorrento, follow the coastal road round to Termini. Stop a moment to admire the views before continuing on to Nerano, from where a beautiful hiking trail leads down to the stunning Bay of Ieranto, one of the coast's top swimming spots, and Marina del Cantone. This unassuming village with its small pebble beach is a lovely, tranquil place to stay and a popular diving destination.

Nettuno Diving (☑081 808 10 51; www. sorrentodiving.com; Via Vespucci 39) Padi Dive Resort leads underwater activities, including snorkelling excursions, beginner courses and cave dives. Adult rates start at €25 for a daylong outing to the Bay of Ieranto.

Set among olive groves by the village entrance, Villaggio Residence Nettuno (☑081 808 10 51; www.villaggionettuno.it, www. torreturbolo.com; Via Vespucci 39; camping 2 people, tent & car €15-31, bungalow €35-80, apt €60-250; ⊙Mar-early Nov; ℗❄@🛜🏊) offers tent pitches, bungalows for two to eight people, mobile homes for two to four people, and apartments in a 16th-century tower for two to five people.

The village has a reputation as a gastronomic hot spot and VIPs regularly boat over from Capri to dine here. A favourite is Lo Scoglio (☑081 808 10 26; Marina del Cantone; meals €55), which serves superlative seafood tempters like a €30 antipasto of raw seafood and a celestial *spaghetti al riccio* (spaghetti with sea urchins).

SITA runs regular bus services between Sorrento and Marina del Cantone (on time-tables as Nerano Cantone; €2.10, one hour).

AMALFI COAST

Stretching about 50km along the southern side of the Sorrentine Peninsula, the Amalfi Coast (Costiera Amalfitana) is one of Europe's most breathtaking. Cliffs terraced with scented lemon groves sheer down into sparkling seas; sherbet-hued villas cling precariously to unforgiving slopes while sea and sky merge in one vast blue horizon.

Yet its stunning topography has not always been a blessing. For centuries after the passing of Amalfi's glory days as a maritime superpower (from the 9th to the 12th centuries), the area was poor and its isolated villages regular victims of foreign incursions, earthquakes and landslides. But it was this very isolation that first drew visitors in the early 1900s, paving the way for the advent of tourism in the latter half of the century. Today the Amalfi Coast is one of Italy's premier tourist destinations, a favourite of cashed-up jet-setters and love-struck couples.

The best time to visit is in spring or early autumn. In summer the coast's single road (SS163) gets very busy and prices are inflated; in winter much of the coast simply shuts down.

❶ Getting There & Away

Boat

Boat services to the Amalfi Coast towns are generally limited to the period between April and October.

Gescab-Alicost (☑089 87 14 83; www.alicost.it, in Italian) operates one daily ferry and one daily hydrofoil from Salerno to Amalfi (€7/9), Positano (€11/13) and Capri (€18.50/20) from mid-April to October. Services from Amalfi and Positano to Capri run twice daily. It also runs two daily ferries from Sorrento to Positano (€13) and Amalfi (€14).

TraVelMar (☑089 87 29 50; www.travelmar.it, in Italian) connects Salerno with Amalfi (€7, six daily) and Positano (€11, six daily) from April to October.

Metrò del Mare (☑199 600700; www.metrodelmare.net, in Italian) was suspended indefinitely in 2011 but normally runs summer-only services to various Amalfi Coast destinations, including Sorrento, Positano, Amalfi and Salerno.

Bus

SITA (☑089 405 145; www.sitabus.it, in Italian) operates a frequent, year-round service along the SS163 between Sorrento and Salerno (€3.30), via Amalfi.

Car & Motorcycle

If driving from the north, exit the A3 autostrada at Vietri sul Mare and follow the SS163 along the coast. From the south leave the A3 at Salerno and head for Vietri sul Mare and the SS163.

Train

From Naples you can take either the Circumvesuviana to Sorrento or a Trenitalia train to Salerno, then continue along the Amalfi Coast, eastwards or westwards, by SITA bus.

Positano

POP 3985

The pearl in the pack, Positano is the coast's most photogenic and expensive town. Its steeply stacked houses are a medley of peaches, pinks and terracottas, and its near-vertical streets (many of which are, in fact, staircases) are lined with voguish shop displays, jewellery stalls, elegant hotels and smart restaurants. Look closely, though, and you'll find reassuring signs of everyday reality – crumbling stucco, streaked paintwork and even, on occasion, a faint whiff of drains.

An early visitor, John Steinbeck, wrote: 'Positano bites deep. It is a dream place that isn't quite real when you are there and becomes beckoningly real after you have gone' (*Harper's Bazaar*, May 1953). More than 50 years on, his words still ring true.

◉ Sights

Chiesa di Santa Maria Assunta   CHURCH
(Piazza Flavio Gioia; ⊗8am-noon & 4-9pm) The lofty, ceramic-tiled dome of this church is the town's most famous, and pretty much only, major sight. Inside the building, classical lines are broken by pillars topped with gilded Ionic capitals, while winged cherubs peek from above every arch. Above the main altar is a 13th-century Byzantine *Black Madonna and Child*.

⚑ Activities

Spiaggia Grande   BEACH
Although it's no one's dream beach, with greyish sand covered by legions of brightly coloured umbrellas, the water's clean and the setting *is* memorable. Hiring a chair

Positano

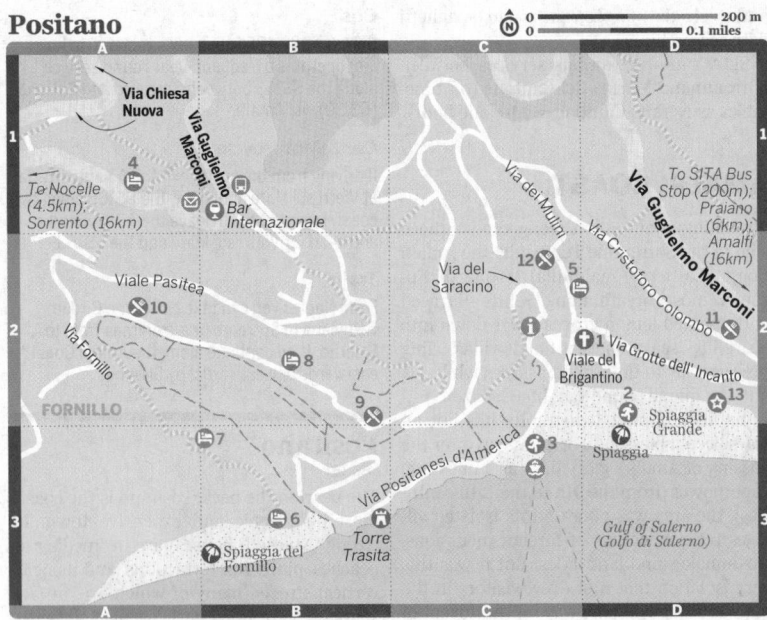

Positano

and umbrella in the fenced-off areas costs around €20 per person per day, but the crowded public areas are free.

Blue Star   BOATING, TOURS
(📞329 622 44 04; www.bluestarpositano.it; Spiaggia Grande; ⊙9am-9pm Apr-Nov) Operating out of a kiosk on Spiaggia Grande, Blue Star hires out small motorboats for around €55 per hour and also organises excursions to Capri, the Grotta dello Smeraldo and all along the Amalfi Coast.

L'Uomo e il Mare   BOATING, TOURS
(📞089 81 16 13; www.gennaroesalvatore.it; ⊙8am-8pm Easter-Nov) A similar company to Blue

Star, this outfit operates from a kiosk near the ferry terminal and offers a range of tours, including day trips to Capri (€50, including *prosecco* and cakes) and along the Amalfi Coast (€80, including lunch), and a romantic sunset cruise to the Li Galli islands (€30).

🛏 Sleeping

Most hotels are three-star and above and prices are universally high. Cheaper accommodation is more limited and must usually be booked well in advance for summer. Ask at the tourist office about rooms or apartments in private houses.

TOP CHOICE Pensione Maria Luisa   PENSIONE €

(☎089 87 50 23; www.pensionemarialuisa.com; Via Fornillo 42; s €50, d €70-85; @🛜) The best budget choice in town, Maria Luisa's rooms and bathrooms have recently been updated with shiny new blue tiles and fittings; those with private terraces are well worth the extra €10 to €15 for the bay view. Other perks include a sunny communal area and a jovial, helpful owner. Payment is by cash only.

Hotel Palazzo Murat   LUXURY HOTEL €€€

(☎089 87 51 77; www.palazzomurat.it; Via dei Mulini 23; s €130-315, d €150-370; ☺late Mar-Oct; ❄@🛜) This upmarket treat is housed in the *palazzo* that Gioacchino Murat, Napoleon's brother-in-law and one-time king of Naples, used as his summer residence. Beyond the lush gardens, rooms are traditional, with antiques, original oil paintings and plenty of lavish marble.

Hotel Ristorante Pupetto   HOTEL €€

(☎089 87 50 87; www.hotelpupetto.it; Via Fornillo 37; s €90-100, d €130-170; ☺Apr-Oct; @🛜) Overlooking Spiaggia del Fornillo, this is as close to the beach as you can get without sleeping on a sun-lounge. A bustling, cheerful place, the hotel forms part of a rambling beach complex with a popular terraced restaurant (meals €25), a nautical-theme bar and sunny, renovated guest rooms with sea views.

Villa Nettuno   PENSIONE €

(☎089 87 54 01; www.villanettunopositano.it; Viale Pasitea 208; s €70, d €80-95; ❄) Hidden behind a barrage of foliage, Villa Nettuno oozes charm. Rooms in the 300-year-old part of the building have heavy rustic decor, frescoed wardrobes and a communal terrace; those in the renovated part are still good value but less interesting. That said, you probably won't be thinking of the furniture as you lie in bed gazing out to sea.

Hostel Brikette   HOSTEL €

(☎089 87 58 57; www.brikette.com; Via Marconi 358; dm €23-25, d €65-85, apt €115-180; ☺late Mar-Nov; @🛜) Not far from the Bar Internazionale bus stop on the coastal road is this bright and cheerful hostel offering the cheapest accommodation in town. There are various options: six- to eight-person dorms (single-sex and mixed), double rooms, and apartments for two to five people. There are also laundry and left-luggage facilities.

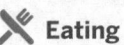 Eating

Most restaurants, bars and trattorias, many of which are unashamedly touristy, close over winter, making a brief reappearance for Christmas and New Year.

TOP CHOICE Da Vincenzo   TRATTORIA €€

(☎089 87 51 28; Viale Pasitea 172-178; meals €40; ☺dinner daily, lunch Wed-Mon Apr-Nov) The best of the town's trattorias, Da Vincenzo has been serving *cucina di territorio* (cuisine of the territory) since 1958. Simple dishes sing with flavour, from fresh fish to a triumphant starter of grilled octopus skewers with fried artichokes.

Ristorante Bruno   TRADITIONAL ITALIAN €€

(Via Colombo 157; meals €40; ☺closed Nov-Jan) Don't let the underwhelming decor fool you: this unassuming restaurant serves superb seafood. Bag a table across the street and enjoy *the* view of Positano while swooning over house specialities like the antipasto of marinated fish with vegetables, orange and Parmesan; for a main course try the grilled fish with a wedge of local lemon.

Ristorante Max   TRADITIONAL ITALIAN €€€

(☎089 87 50 56; Via dei Mulini 22; meals €45; ☺Mar-Nov) Peruse the art work while choosing your dish at this perennial favourite of 'ladies who lunch'. Eavesdrop over dishes like ravioli with clams and asparagus, and buttery eggplant *melanzana*. Cooking courses are offered in the summer months.

Il Saraceno d'Oro   TRADITIONAL ITALIAN €€

(Viale Pasitea 254; pizzas from €7, meals €35; ☺Mar-Oct) A busy, bustling place, the Saracen's blend of cheery service, uncomplicated food and reasonable prices continues to please the punters. The pizzas are good, the pasta's tasty and the desserts are sticky and sweet. The complimentary end-of-meal glass of *limoncello* makes for a pleasing epilogue.

☆ Entertainment

Generally speaking, Positano's nightlife is genteel, sophisticated and safe.

Music on the Rocks   BAR/CLUB

(www.musicontherocks.it; Via Grotte dell'Incanto 51; ☺Easter-Oct) Carved into the tower at the eastern end of Spiaggia Grande, this uber-chic nightclub attracts a good-looking crowd and some of the region's best DJs. Sounds are mainstream house and disco.

❶ Information

La Brezza (☏089 87 58 11; Via del Brigantino 1; per 15min €3; ⊙10am-10pm Mar-Nov) Small ceramics shop with internet access.

Police station (☏089 87 50 11; cnr Via Marconi & Viale Pasitea)

Positano (www.positano.com) A slick website with hotel and restaurant listings, itineraries and transport information.

Post office (Via Marconi 318)

Tourist office (www.aziendaturismopositano. it; Via del Saracino 4; ⊙8.30am-7.30pm Mon-Sat Apr-Oct, 8.30am-4.30pm Mon-Fri Nov-Mar)

❶ Getting There & Away

Boat

Between April and October, ferries link Positano with Amalfi (€7, seven daily), Sorrento (€9 to €13, six daily), Salerno (€7 to €11, seven daily), and Capri (€15.50, 45 minutes, four daily).

Bus

SITA runs frequent buses to/from Amalfi (€1.50, 40 to 50 minutes) and Sorrento (€1.50, one hour). Buses drop you off at one of two main bus stops: coming from Sorrento and the west, opposite Bar Internazionale; arriving from Amalfi and the east, at the top of Via Colombo. When departing, buy bus tickets at Bar Internazionale or, if headed eastwards, from the tobacconist at the bottom of Via Colombo.

❶ Getting Around

Getting around Positano is largely a matter of walking. If your knees can handle them, there are dozens of narrow alleys and stairways that make walking relatively easy and joyously traffic-free. Otherwise, an orange bus follows the lower ring road every half-hour, passing along Viale Pasitea, Via Colombo and Via Marconi. Buy your ticket (€1.60) on board or at a *tabaccaio* (tobacconist's shop). It passes by both SITA bus stops.

Praiano & Furore

An ancient fishing village, Praiano has one of the coast's most popular beaches, Marina di Praia. From the SS163 (next to the Hotel Continental), take the steep path that leads down the side of the cliffs to a tiny inlet with a small stretch of coarse sand and deep-blue water.

The **Centro Sub Costiera Amalfitana** (☏089 81 21 48; www.centrosub.it; Via Marina di Praia) runs beginner to expert dives (€80 to €130) exploring the area's coral, marine life and grottoes.

On the coastal road east of Praiano, **Hotel Pensione Continental** (☏089 87 40 84; www.continental.praiano.it; Via Roma 21; camping 2 people, tent & car €35-40, s €45-65, d €70-90, apt per week €500-1500; ⊙camping Easter-Oct, r & apt year-round) offers the full gamut of accommodation: cool, white rooms with sea views, apartments sleeping up to six people, and 12 tent sites on a series of grassy terraces. From the lowest of these a private staircase leads down to a rocky platform on the sea. Transport is no problem, either, as there's a bus stop just outside the hotel.

A few kilometres further on, **Marina di Furore** sits at the bottom of what's known as the fjord of Furore, a giant cleft that cuts through the Lattari mountains. The main village, however, stands 300m above, in the upper Vallone del Furore. A one-horse place that sees few tourists, it breathes a distinctly rural air despite the colourful murals and unlikely modern sculpture.

To get to upper Furore by car follow the SS163 and the SS366 signposted to Agerola; from Positano, it's 15km. Otherwise, regular SITA buses depart from the bus terminus in Amalfi (€1.20, 30 minutes, five times daily).

Amalfi

POP 5340

It is hard to grasp that pretty little Amalfi, with its sun-filled piazzas and small beach, was once a maritime superpower with a population of more than 70,000. For one thing, it's not a big place – you can easily walk from one end to the other in about 20 minutes. For another, there are very few historical buildings of note. The explanation is chilling – most of the old city, and its populace, simply slid into the sea during an earthquake in 1343.

Today, although the resident population is fairly modest, the numbers swell significantly during summer, when day trippers pour in by the coachload.

Just around the headland, neighbouring Atrani is a picturesque tangle of white-washed alleys and arches centred on a lively, lived-in piazza and popular beach.

◉ Sights

Cattedrale di Sant'Andrea DUOMO, MUSEUM (☏089 87 10 59; Piazza del Duomo; ⊙9am-6.45pm Apr-Jun, 9am-7.45pm Jul-Sep, reduced hrs off season) Dominating Piazza del Duomo, Amalfi's iconic cathedral makes an imposing sight at the top of its sweeping flight of stairs. The cathedral dates in part from the early 10th century, although its distinctive striped facade has been rebuilt twice, most recently at the end of the 19th century. It's a melange of architectural styles: the two-toned masonry is largely Sicilian Arabic-Norman while the interior is pure baroque. The exquisite **crypt** is home to the reliquary of St Andrew the Apostle. The fresco facing the crypt's altar is by Neapolitan baroque maestro Aniello Falcone. Between 10am and 5pm, entrance to the cathedral is through the adjacent Chiostro del Paradiso.

To the left of the cathedral's porch, the pint-sized **Chiostro del Paradiso** (☎089 87 13 24; adult/11-17yrs €3/1; ⏲9am-6.45pm Apr-Jun, 9am-7.45pm Jul-Sep, reduced hrs off season) was built in 1266 to house the tombs of Amalfi's prominent citizens. From here you enter the **Basilica del Crucifisso**, Amalfi's original 9th-century cathedral, itself built on the remains of an earlier palaeo-Christian temple. It's home to a small, yet fascinating collection of ecclesial treasures, including a jewel-studded, 13th-century Angevin mitre.

Museo della Carta MUSEUM
(Paper Museum; ☎089 830 45 61; www.museodellacarta.it; Via delle Cartiere; admission €4; ⏲10am-6.30pm Apr–mid-Nov, 10am-3pm Tue, Wed & Fri-Sun mid-Nov–Mar). Housed in a 13th-century paper mill (the oldest in Europe), this fascinating museum lovingly preserves the original paper presses, which are still in full working order, as you'll see during the 15-minute guided tour (in English).

Museo Arsenale Amalfi MUSEUM
(☎089 87 11 70; Largo Cesareo Console 3; admission €2; ⏲10am-2pm & 4.30-8.30pm) Amalfi's other museum of note is home to the *Tavole Amalfitane,* an ancient manuscript draft of Amalfi's maritime code, and other historical documents. Harking back to Amalfi's days as a great maritime republic, the museum is housed in the cavernous **Arsenale**, once the town's main shipbuilding depot.

Activities

For all its seafaring history, Amalfi's main beach is not a particularly appealing swimming spot. If you're intent on a dip, think about hiring a boat. You'll find a number of operators along Lungomare dei Cavalieri, charging about €50 for a couple of hours.

Grotta dello Smeraldo GROTTO
(admission €5; ⏲9am-4pm Mar-Oct, 9am-3pm Nov-Feb) Four kilometres west of Amalfi, Conca dei Marini is home to this haunting cave, named after the eerie emerald colour that emanates from the seawater. SITA buses regularly pass the car park above the cave entrance (from where you take a lift or stairs down to the rowing boats). Alternatively, **Coop Sant'Andrea** (☎089 87 31 90; www.coopsantandrea.it; Lungomare dei Cavalieri 1) runs hourly boats from Amalfi (€14 return) between 9am and 3pm daily from May to October. Allow around one hour for the round trip.

> WORTH A TRIP
>
> ### NOCELLE
>
> A tiny, still-isolated mountain village, Nocelle (450m) affords some of the most spectacular views on the entire coast. A world apart from touristy Positano, it's a sleepy, silent place where not much ever happens and none of the few residents would ever want it to.
>
> The easiest way to get here is by local bus from Positano (€1.10, 30 minutes, 17 daily). Hikers tackling the Sentieri degli Dei (see p674) might fancy lunch at the **Ristorante Santa Croce** (Via Nocelle 19; meals €25; ⏲summer) as they pass through.

Festivals & Events

Every 24 December and 6 January, divers from all over Italy make a pilgrimage to the ceramic *presepe* (nativity scene) submerged in the Grotta dello Smeraldo.

The **Regatta of the Four Ancient Maritime Republics**, which rotates between Amalfi, Venice, Pisa and Genoa, is held on the first Sunday in June. Amalfi's turn comes round again in 2013.

Sleeping

TOP CHOICE **Hotel Luna Convento** HOTEL €€€
(☎089 87 10 02; www.lunahotel.it; Via Pantaleone Comite 33; s €220-280, d €240-300; P❄@🛜≋) This former convent was founded by St Francis in 1222. Rooms in the original building are in the former nuns' cells, but there's nothing pokey about the bright tiles, balconies and sea views. The newer wing is equally beguiling, with religious frescoes over the bed (to stop any misbehaving). The cloistered courtyard is magnificent.

KARL BLACKWELL / LONELY PLANET IMAGES ©

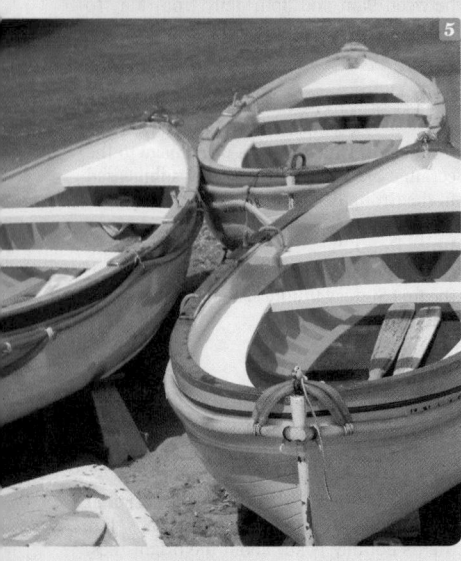

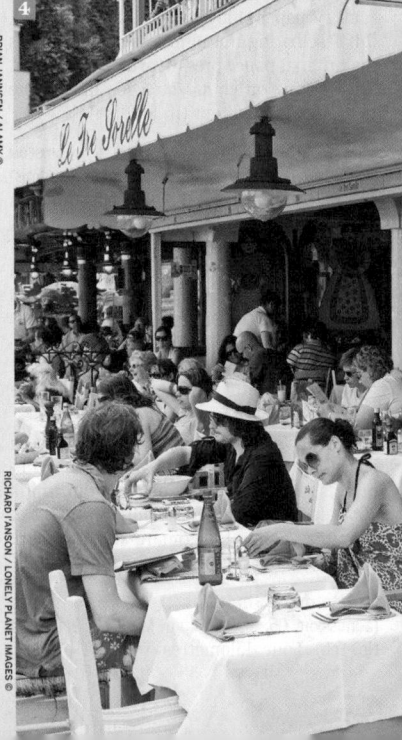

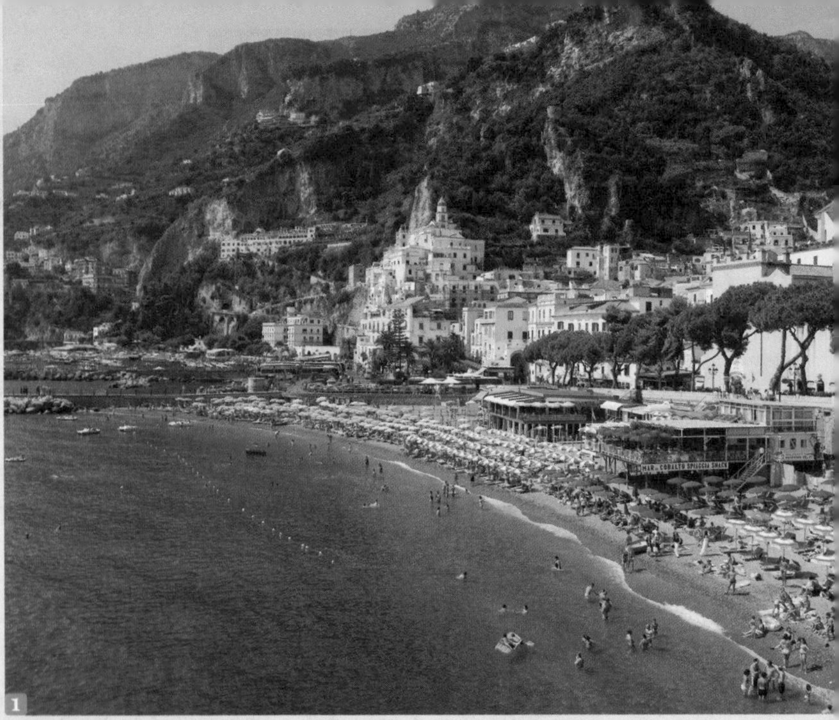

BRIAN JANNSEN / ALAMY ©

RICHARD I'ANSON / LONELY PLANET IMAGES ©

1. Amalfi beach (p670)
A small beach, but popular with daytrippers in summer.

2. Capri (p645)
Capri's chichi piazzas and cool cafes make it a favourite destination for holidaying VIPs.

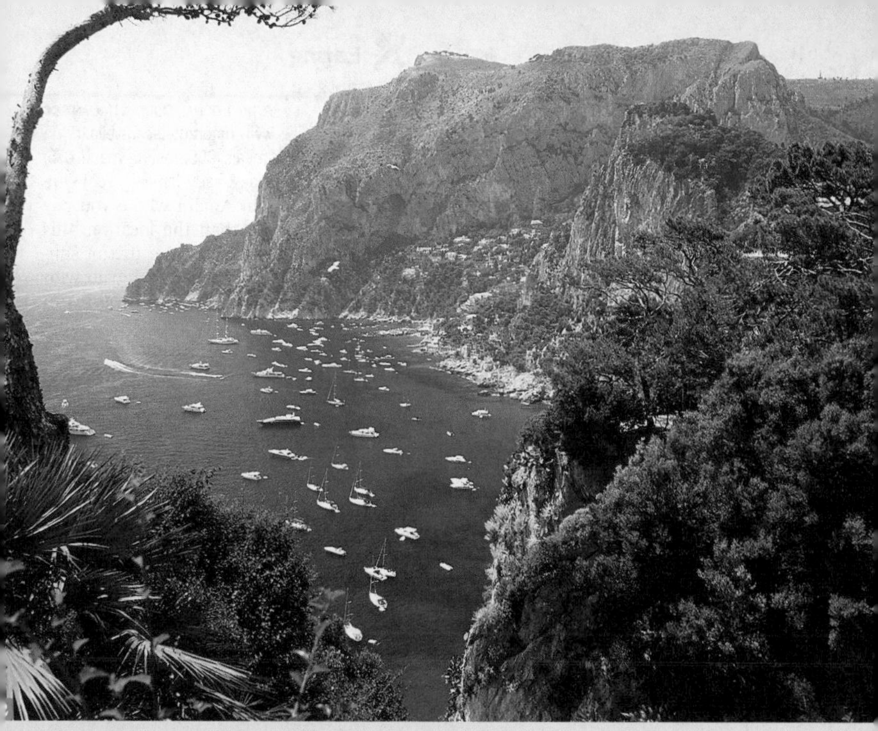

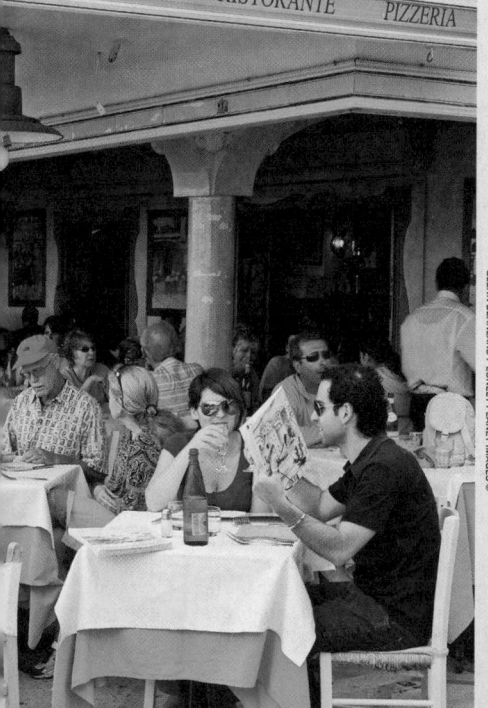

RISTORANTE
PIZZERIA

GLENN BEANLAND / LONELY PLANET IMAGES ©

3. View from Villa Rufolo (p675)
This villa in Ravello is famous for its romantic 19th-century gardens.

4. Restaurant, Positano (p667)
Diners take a break in this incredibly photogenic Amalfi town.

5. Boats on beach at Capri (p645)
Boating is another popular activity for visitors to the Amalfi Coast.

3

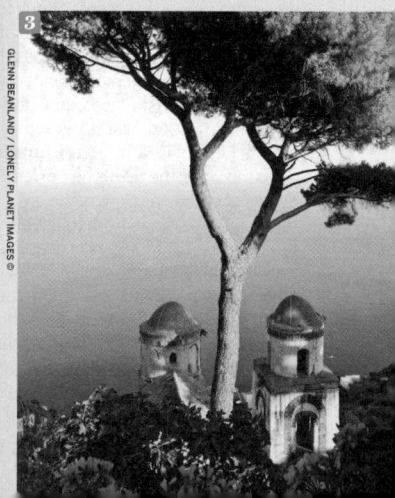

Hotel Lidomare
HOTEL €€

(☏089 87 13 32; www.lidomare.it; Largo Duchi Piccolomini 9; s/d €50/120; ❄) This old-fashioned, family-run hotel has real character. The spacious rooms have an air of gentility, with their appealingly haphazard decor, old-fashioned tiles and fine old antiques. Some rooms have Jacuzzi bathtubs, others boast sea views.

Hotel Centrale
HOTEL €€

(☏089 87 26 08; www.amalfihotelcentrale.it; Largo Duchi Piccolomini 1; s €60-120, d €70-140; ❄@☐) This is one of the best-value hotels in Amalfi. The entrance is on a tiny piazza in the *centro storico*, but many rooms actually overlook Piazza del Duomo (No 24 is a good choice). The bright green and blue tile work gives the place a vibrant, fresh look, and the views from the rooftop terrace are magnificent.

A'Scalinatella Hostel
HOSTEL €

(☏089 87 14 92; www.hostelscalinatella.com; Piazza Umberto I, Atrani; dm €20-25, s €35-50, d €70-90) This bare-bones operation, just round the headland in Atrani, has dorms, rooms and apartments scattered across the village. Breakfast is included in the price, and there's a laundry to boot.

 Eating

Ristorante La Caravella
TRADITIONAL, MODERN ITALIAN €€€

(☏089 87 10 29; www.ristorantelacaravella.it; Via Matteo Camera 12; meals €65, tasting menu €75; ⊙Wed-Mon, closed Nov & early Jan-early Feb) One of the few places in Amalfi where you pay for the food rather than the location, this celebrated dining den serves a mix of simple, soulful classics and regional grub with a nouvelle twist – think lemon risotto with cooked and raw prawns and Grey mullet roe. The 1750-plus wines are an aficionado's dream.

Trattoria Il Mulino
TRATTORIA €€

(Via delle Cartiere 36; pizzas €6, meals €29) A TV-in-the-corner, kids-running-between-the-tables sort of place, this is about as authentic a trattoria as you'll find in Amalfi. The menu features the usual pizzas, pasta and seafood, but the food is tasty and the prices honest. The *scialatiella alla pescatore* (pasta ribbons with prawns, mussels, tomato and parsley) is fabulous.

Pasticceria Pansa
PASTRIES & CAKES €

(Piazza Duomo 40; pastries from €1.50) Compromising waistlines since 1830, this vintage pastry peddler is a must for gluttons. Must-trys

---

WALK THE COAST

Rising steeply from the coast, the densely wooded Lattari mountains provide some stunning walking opportunities. An extraordinary network of paths traverses the craggy precipitous peaks, climbing to remote farmhouses through wild and beautiful valleys. It's tough going, though – long ascents up seemingly endless flights of steps are almost unavoidable.

Probably the best-known walk, the 12km Sentiero degli Dei (Path of the Gods; 5½ to six hours) follows the steep, often rocky paths linking Positano to Praiano. It's a spectacular trail passing through some of the area's least developed countryside. The route is marked by red-and-white stripes daubed on rocks and trees, although some of these have become worn in places and might be difficult to make out. Pick up a map of the walk at local tourist offices, included in a series of three excellent booklets containing the area's most popular hikes, including the equally famed, and lyrically named, Via degli Incanti (Trail of Charms) from Amalfi to Positano.

To the west, the tip of the Sorrentine Peninsula is another hiking hot spot. Some 110km of paths criss-cross the area, linking the spectacular coastline with the rural hinterland. These range from tough all-day treks – such as the 14.1km Alta Via dei Monti Lattari from the Fontanelle hills near Positano down to the Punta Campanella – to shorter walks suitable for the family. Tourist offices throughout the area can provide maps detailing the colour-coded routes. With the exception of the Alta Via dei Monti Lattari (marked in red and white), long routes are shown in red on the map; coast-to-coast trails in blue; paths connecting villages in green; and circular routes in yellow.

If you're intent on trying one of the more demanding routes in the region, invest in a detailed map such as the CAI's (Club Alpino Italiano) *Monti Lattari, Penisola Sorrentina, Costiera Amalfitana: Carta dei Sentieri* (€8) at 1:30,000 scale.

include chocolate-dipped candied citrus peels (the fruit is grown at the family's own estate), *torta setteveli* (a multi-layered chocolate and hazelnut cake) and the *limoncello*-laced local *delizia al limone*.

Le Arcate
TRADITIONAL ITALIAN €€

(Largo Orlando Buonocore Atrani; pizzas from €6, meals €40; ⊘closed early Jan–mid-Feb & Mon Sep-Jun) On a sunny day it's hard to beat the dreamy harbourside location. Beyond the sprawl of al fresco tables is a cavernous, stone-lined interior. Pizzas are served at night, while daytime fare includes the house speciality, *scialatielli* pasta with shrimp and zucchini.

Supermercato Decò
SUPERMARKET €

(Salita dei Curiali 6) Self-caterers and picnickers can stock up here.

❶ Information

Amalfi Servizi Express (Piazza dei Dogi 8; internet per 15min €3; ⊘9.30am-1.30pm & 4.30-8pm Mon-Sat, closed Thu evening)

Post office (Corso delle Repubbliche Marinare 31) Next door to the tourist office.

Tourist office (www.amalfitouristoffice.it; Corso delle Repubbliche Marinare 27; ⊘9am-1pm & 2-6pm Mon-Sat, 9am-1pm Sun, closed Sun Apr, May & Sep, closed Sat & Sun Oct-Mar) Good for bus and ferry timetables.

❶ Getting There & Away

Boat

Between April and October there are daily ferry sailings to Salerno (€7, seven daily), Positano (€7, seven daily) and Capri (€17, one daily). There is also a hydrofoil service to Capri (€19, one daily).

Bus

SITA buses run from Piazza Flavio Gioia to Sorrento (€2.80, 1½ hours, around 30 daily) via Positano (€1.50, 40 minutes), and also to Ravello (€1.20, 25 minutes, every 30 minutes), and Salerno (€2.10, 1¼ hours, hourly). There are only two daily connections to Naples (€4, two to three hours depending on the route), so you're better off catching a bus to Sorrento and then the Circumvesuviana train to Naples. Buy tickets and check schedules at **Bar Il Giardino delle Palme** (Piazza Flavio Gioia), opposite the bus stop.

Ravello

POP 2475

Sitting high in the hills above Amalfi, refined Ravello is a polished town almost entirely dedicated to tourism. Boasting impeccable bohemian credentials – Wagner, DH Lawrence and Virginia Woolf all lounged here – it's today known for its ravishing gardens and stupendous views, the best in the world according to former resident Gore Vidal.

Most people visit on a day trip from Amalfi – a nerve-tingling 7km drive up the Valle del Dragone – although to best enjoy Ravello's romantic otherworldly atmosphere you'll need to stay overnight.

The **tourist office** (www.ravellotime.it; Via Roma 18bis; ⊘9.30am-7pm Apr-Oct, to 5pm Nov-Mar) has some general information on the town, plus a handy map with walking trails.

⊙ Sights & Activities

Cathedral
DUOMO, MUSEUM

(⊘8am-noon & 5.30-8.30pm) Forming the eastern flank of Piazza del Duomo, Ravello's cathedral was originally built in 1086 but has since undergone various facelifts. The facade is 16th century, even if the central bronze door is an 1179 original; the interior is a late-20th-century interpretation of what the original must once have looked like. The pulpit is particularly striking, supported by six twisting columns set on marble lions and decorated with flamboyant mosaics of peacocks, birds and dancing lions. Note also how the floor is tilted towards the square – a deliberate measure to enhance the perspective effect. To the right of the central nave, stairs lead down to the cathedral **museum** (admission €2; ⊘9am-7pm) and its modest collection of religious artefacts.

Villa Rufolo
GARDEN

(☑089 85 76 21; admission €5; ⊘9am-sunset) To the south of the cathedral, Villa Rufolo is famous for its romantic 19th-century gardens. Commanding mesmerising views, they are packed with exotic colours, artistically crumbling towers and luxurious blooms. On seeing them in 1880, Wagner wrote that he had found the garden of Klingsor (setting for the second act of his opera *Parsifal*). Today the gardens are used to stage concerts during the town's celebrated festival.

Villa Cimbrone
GARDEN

(☑089 85 74 59; adult/under 12yr & over 65yr €6/4; ⊘9am-sunset) If Villa Rufolo's gardens leave you longing for more, seek out the 20th-century Villa Cimbrone for the vast views from the delightfully ramshackle gardens. The best viewpoint is the Belvedere of Infinity, an awe-inspiring terrace lined with fake classical busts. The villa is some 600m south of Piazza del Duomo.

 Festivals & Events

Ravello Festival CULTURAL
(☎089 85 83 60; www.ravellofestival.com) Between June and mid-September the Ravello Festival turns much of the town centre into a stage. Events ranging from orchestral concerts and chamber music to ballet performances, film screenings and exhibitions are held in various locations.

Ravello Concert Society MUSIC
(☎089 85 81 49; www.ravelloarts.org) Ravello's program of classical music actually begins in April and continues until late October. Performances are world class, and the two venues of Villa Rufolo and the Convento di Santa Rosa in Conca dei Marini (the latter was closed for restoration at the time of research) are unforgettable. Tickets are bookable by fax (☎089 85 82 49) or online on the website.

Sleeping

Agriturismo Monte Brusara AGRITURISMO €
(☎089 85 74 67; www.montebrusara.com; Via Monte Brusara 32; s €42-45, d €84-90) It's a tough half-hour walk from Ravello's centre, but this authentic mountainside *agriturismo* (farm-stay accommodation) is the real McCoy. It's an ideal spot to escape the crowds and offers three comfortable but basic rooms, fabulous food and some big views. Half-board is also available.

Hotel Villa Amore PENSIONE €
(☎/fax 089 85 71 35; www.villaamore.it; Via dei Fusco 5; s €50-60, d €75-100; ☎) This welcoming *pensione* is the best budget choice in town. Tucked away down a quiet lane, it has modest, homey rooms and sparkling bathrooms. All rooms have their own balcony and some have bathtubs. The garden restaurant (meals about €25) is a further plus.

Hotel Toro HOTEL €€
(☎089 85 72 11; www.hoteltoro.it; Via Roma 16; s/d €85/118; ⊘mid-Apr–Nov; ❀☎) A hotel since the late 19th century, the Toro is just off Piazza del Duomo, within easy range of the clanging cathedral bells. The not-huge rooms are decked out in traditional style with terracotta or light-marble tiles and soothing cream furnishings. Outside, the walled garden is the perfect place for a sundowner.

 Eating

Cumpà Cosimo TRADITIONAL ITALIAN, PIZZERIA €€
(☎089 85 71 56; Via Roma 44-46; pizzas €6-12, meals €45) Netta Bottone's rustic cooking is so good that even US celebrity Rosie O'Donnell tried to get her on her show. Netta didn't make it to Hollywood but she still rules the roost at this historic trattoria. Order the *piatto misto* (mixed plate), which may include Ravello's trademark *crespolini* (cheese and prosciutto-stuffed crepes). Evening options include pizza.

Da Salvatore TRADITIONAL & MODERN ITALIAN €€
(www.salvatoreravello.com; Via della Republicca 2; meals €35; ⊘restaurant lunch & dinner Tue-Sun, pizzeria dinner Thu-Tue, both open daily Aug) Located just before the bus stop and the Garden Hotel, this average-looking nosh spot has an exceptional view, not to mention creative dishes like mixed Gragnano pasta with potato and calamari. In the evening, head in for some of the best wood-fired pizza this side of Naples.

Take Away da Nino STREET FOOD €
(Viale Parco della Rimembranza 41) Fast food Ravello-style – come here for takeaway pizza and crunchy fried nibbles.

❶ Getting There & Away

SITA operates hourly buses from the eastern side of Piazza Flavio Gioia in Amalfi (€1.20, 25 minutes). By car, turn north about 2km east of Amalfi. Vehicles are not permitted in Ravello's town centre, but there's plenty of space in supervised car parks on the perimeter.

South of Amalfi

FROM AMALFI TO SALERNO
The 26km drive to Salerno, though less exciting than the 16km stretch westwards to Positano, is exhilarating and dotted with a series of small towns, each with their own character and each worth a brief look.

Three and a half kilometres east of Amalfi, or a steep 1km-long walk down from Ravello, **Minori** is a small, workaday town, popular with holidaying Italians. Further along, **Maiori** is the coast's biggest resort, a brassy place full of large seafront hotels, restaurants and beach clubs.

Just beyond **Erchie** and its beautiful beach, **Cetara** is a picturesque tumbledown fishing village with a reputation as a gastronomic highlight. Tuna and anchovies are the local specialities, appearing in various guises at **Al Convento** (📞089 26 10 39; Piazza San Francesco 16; meals €25; ⊗closed Wed Oct–mid-May), a sterling seafood restaurant near the small harbour. For your money, you'll probably not eat better anywhere else on the coast; the *puttanesca con alici fresche* (pasta with fresh anchovies, chilli and garlic) sings with flavour.

Shortly before Salerno, the road passes through **Vietri sul Mare**, the ceramics capital of Campania. Its not-unattractive historic centre is packed to the gills with ceramics shops, the most famous of which is **Ceramica Artistica Solimene** (www.solimene.com; Via Madonna degli Angeli 7; ⊗8am-7pm Mon-Fri, 8am-1.30pm & 4-7pm Sat), a vast factory outlet with an extraordinary glass-and-ceramic facade.

SALERNO
POP 139,700

Upstaged by the glut of postcard-pretty towns along the Amalfi Coast, Campania's second-largest city is actually a pleasant surprise. A decade of civic determination has turned this major port and transport hub into one of southern Italy's most liveable cities, and its small but buzzing *centro storico* is a vibrant mix of medieval churches, tasty trattorias and good-spirited, bar-hopping locals.

Originally an Etruscan and later a Roman colony, Salerno flourished with the arrival of the Normans in the 11th century. Robert Guiscard made it the capital of his dukedom in 1076 and, under his patronage, the Scuola Medica Salernitana was renowned as one of medieval Europe's greatest medical institutes. More recently, it was left in tatters by the heavy fighting that followed the 1943 landings of the American 5th Army, just south of the city.

⊙ Sights

Cathedral
DUOMO
(📞089 23 13 87; Piazza Alfano; ⊗9.30am-6pm Mon-Sat, 1-6pm Sun) Salerno's cathedral is the highlight of the *centro storico*. Built by the Normans under Robert Guiscard in the 11th century and remodelled in the 18th century, it sustained severe damage in the 1980 earthquake. It's dedicated to San Matteo (St Matthew), whose remains were reputedly brought to the city in 954 and now lie beneath the main altar in the exquisite vaulted crypt. In the right-hand apse, the **Cappella delle Crociate** (Chapel of the Crusades) was so named because crusaders' weapons were blessed here. Under the altar stands the tomb of the 11th-century pope Gregory VII.

Scuola Medica Salernitana Museo Virtuale
MUSEUM
(📞089 257 32 13; www.museovirtualescuolamedicasalernitana.it; Via Mercanti 74; donation €1) Slap bang in Salerno's historic centre, this engaging museum deploys 3D and touch-screen technology to explore the teachings and wince-inducing procedures of Salerno's once-famous, now-defunct medical institute. Established in the 9th century and surviving 10 centuries, the school was Europe's first and most prestigious centre of medicine.

Castello di Arechi
CASTLE, MUSEUM
(📞089 285 45 33; Via Benedetto Croce; admission €3; ⊗9am-7pm Tue-Sun May-Sep, to 5pm Oct-Apr) Salerno's lofty *castello* is spectacularly positioned 263m above the city. Originally a Byzantine fort, it was built by the Lombard duke of Benevento, Arechi II, in the 8th century and subsequently modified by the Normans and Aragonese. Today it houses a permanent collection of ceramics, arms and coins. To get there take bus 19 from Piazza XXIV Maggio in the city centre.

Museo Pinacoteca Provinciale
MUSEUM
(📞089 258 30 73; Via Mercanti 63; admission free; ⊗9am-7.45pm Tue-Sun) Facing the Scuola Medica Salernitana Museo Virtuale, this small but interesting art collection dates from the Renaissance right up to the first half of the 19th century.

🛏 Sleeping

Ostello Ave Gratia Plena
HOSTEL €
(📞089 23 47 76; www.ostellodisalerno.it; Via dei Canali; dm/s/d €15/33/47; @☎) Housed in a 16th-century convent, Salerno's HI hostel is right in the heart of the *centro storico*. Inside there's a charming central courtyard and a range of bright rooms, from dorms to doubles with private bathroom. The 2am curfew is for dorms only.

Hotel Plaza
HOTEL €
(📞089 22 44 77; www.plazasalerno.it; Piazza Vittorio Veneto 42; s/d €65/100; ❄@☎) The Plaza is convenient and comfortable, a stone's throw from the train station. It's a friendly place and the decent-size rooms, complete with gleaming bathrooms, are pretty good value for money. Those facing the station have terraces overlooking the city and, beyond, the mountains.

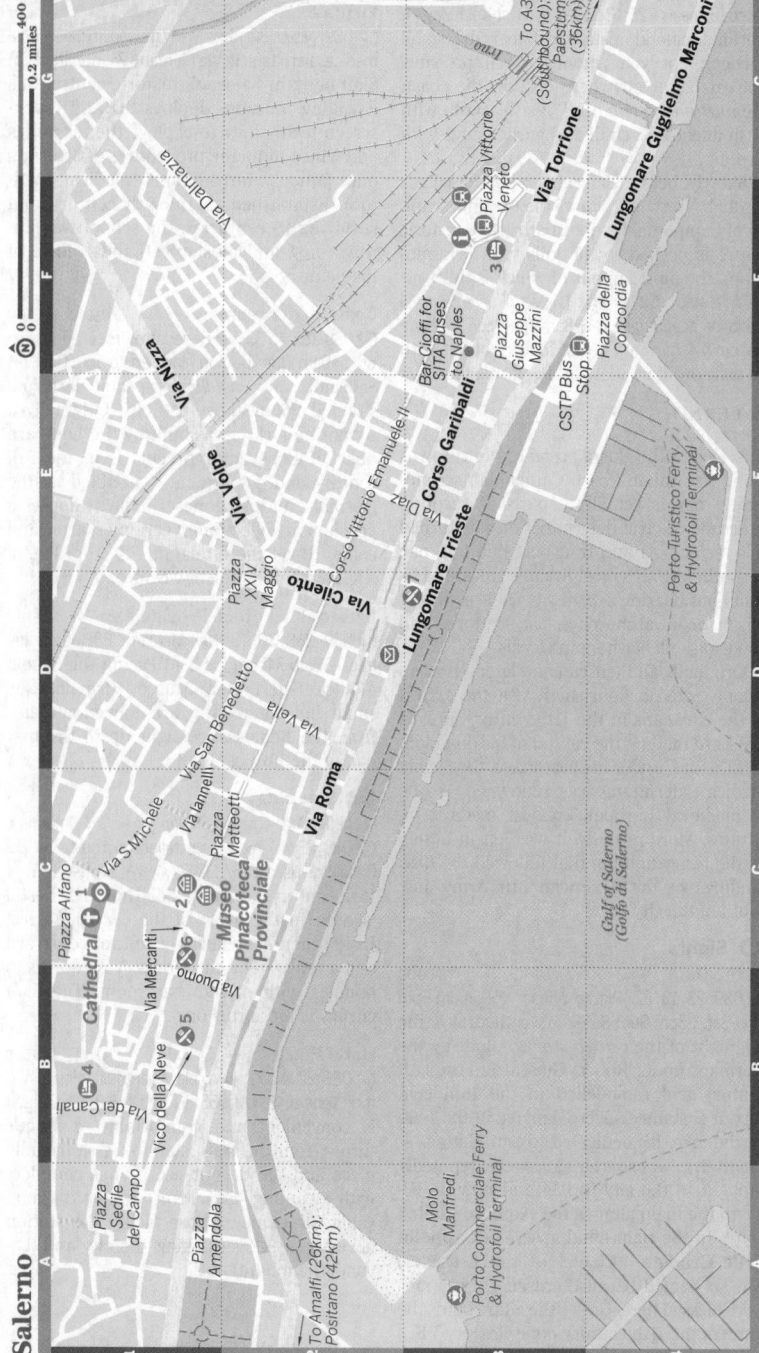

Salerno

✕ Eating

Head to Via Roma and Via Mercanti in the lively medieval centre, where you'll find everything from traditional, family-run trattorias and gelaterie to wine bars, pubs and restaurants.

La Cucina di Edoardo   TRADITIONAL ITALIAN €
(☑089 296 26 67; Vico della Neve 14; meals €25; ⊘closed Mon & dinner Sun) Snugly tucked away in a *centro storico* side street, Edoardo's Kitchen is one of those cheap, scrumptious finds any local *buongustaio* (foodie) will direct you to. The focus is on tasty, regional grub, with standout dishes including the *antipasto misto* and *zuppa di cipolle* (onion soup). Leave room for the *flan al cioccolato* (chocolate flan) and don't forget to book ahead on weekends.

Ristorante Lazzarella   TRADITIONAL ITALIAN €€
(Lungomare Trieste 92; meals €28; ⊘closed Mon Sep-Jul, dinner Sun Oct-Easter & lunch Mon-Sun Aug) Bright, intimate and youthful, head here for top-tasting local dishes like *lagane e ceci* (pasta with chickpeas). Particularly fabulous is the *Lazzarella di mare,* a tasting plate of seafood specialities like *calamaro imbottito* (stuffed calamari) and *seppia in agrodolce* (cuttlefish with sautéed onion). The dish can be upsized from three to five *assaggi* (tastings) on request.

Pasticceria Pantaleone   PASTRIES & CAKES €
(Via Mercanti 75; pastries from €1.50; ⊘closed Tue) Where better to commit dietary sins than in a deconsecrated church? It's now home to Salerno's finest pastry shop, best known for

inventing the *scazzetta,* a pastry of *pan di spagna* sponge, fresh berries and Chantilly cream, soaked in Strega liqueur and finished with a strawberry glacé. Wash away the guilt with a glass of the house liqueur, Elisir, made with aromatic herbs and orange.

ⓘ Information

Ospedale Ruggi D'Aragona (☑089 67 11 11; Via San Leonardo)

Post office (Corso Garibaldi 203)

Tourist infopoint (Corso Vittorio Emanuele 193; ⊘9.30am-1.30pm & 4.30-8.30pm Mon-Sat) Inside the Galleria Capitol Cinema shopping centre, has brochures, bus and ferry timetables and accommodation information.

Tourist office (Piazza Vittorio Veneto 1; ⊘9am-1pm & 3.15-7.15pm Mon-Sat)

ⓘ Getting There & Away

BOAT

Gescab-Alicost (☑089 87 14 83; www.alicost. it, in Italian) operates one daily ferry and one daily hydrofoil from Salerno to Amalfi (€7/9, two daily), Positano (€11/13) and Capri (€18.50/20) from mid-April to October.

Gescab-Linee Marittime Partenopee (☑081 704 19 11; www.consorziolmp.it, in Italian) runs hydrofoils and fast ferries from Salerno to Capri (€20/18.50, one each daily) from April to October.

TraVelMar (☑089 87 29 50; www.travelmar. it, in Italian) runs ferries from Salerno to Amalfi (€7, six daily) and Positano (€11, six daily) from April to October.

Metrò del Mare (☑199 600700; www.metro delmare.net, in Italian) operates regular ferries to/from Naples and Sorrento. The service was suspended temporarily in 2011, so check the website for updates.

Departures are from the Porto Turistico, 200m down the pier from Piazza della Concordia. You can buy tickets from the booths by the embarkation point.

Departures for Capri leave from Molo Manfredi at the Porto Commerciale.

BUS

SITA buses for Amalfi (€2.10, 1¼ hours, at least hourly) depart from Piazza Vittorio Veneto, beside the train station, stopping en route at Vietri sul Mare, Cetara, Maiori and Minori. The Naples service, however, departs from Piazza G Mazzini, 50m east of **Bar Cioffi** (Corso Garibaldi 134), where you buy your €4 ticket. Tickets are also available inside the train station.

CSTP (☑800 016 659; www.cstp.it, in Italian) bus 4 runs from Piazza Vittorio Veneto to Pompeii (€2.10, one hour, 17 daily) from Monday to Saturday. On Sunday, bus 4 will get you there in 90 minutes. For Paestum (€3.30, one hour, hourly) take bus 34 from Piazza della Concordia.

Buonotourist (📋089 79 50 68; www.buono tourist.it) runs daily services (excluding Sunday and public holidays) to Naples' Capodichino airport, departing from the train station. Tickets (€7) can be bought on board; journey time is one hour.

CAR & MOTORCYCLE

Salerno is on the A3 between Naples and Reggio di Calabria, which is toll-free from Salerno southwards.

TRAIN

Salerno is a major stop on southbound routes to Calabria and the Ionian and Adriatic coasts. From the station in Piazza Vittorio Veneto there are regular trains to Naples (IC €7.50, 40 minutes, 44 services daily), Rome (Eurostar €39, 2½ hours, hourly), and Reggio di Calabria (IC €36.50, 4½ hours, nine daily).

❶ Getting Around

Walking is the most sensible option; from the train station it's a 1.2km walk along Corso Vittorio Emanuele II to the historic centre.

If you want to hire a car there's a **Europcar** (📋089 258 07 75; www.europcar.com; Via Clemente Mauro 18) agency not far from the train station.

PAESTUM

Paestum's Unesco-listed temples are among the best-preserved monuments of Magna Graecia, the Greek colony that once covered much of southern Italy. An easy day trip from Salerno or Agropoli, they are one of the region's most iconic sights and absolutely unmissable.

Paestum, or Poseidonia as the city was originally called (in honour of Poseidon, the Greek god of the sea), was founded in the 6th century BC by Greek settlers and fell under Roman control in 273 BC. It became an important trading port and remained so until the fall of the Roman Empire, when periodic outbreaks of malaria and savage Saracen raids led its weakened citizens to abandon the town.

Its temples were rediscovered in the late 18th century by road builders – who proceeded to plough their way right through the ruins. However, the road did little to alter the state of the surrounding area, which remained full of malarial swamps, teeming with snakes and scorpions, until well into the 20th century.

The tourist office (www.infopaestum.it; Via Magna Grecia 887; ⏱9am-1pm & 2-4pm) has

practical information on Paestum and the Costiera Cilentana.

◉ Sights

Ruins of Paestum   RUINS
(📋0828 81 10 23; admission €4, incl museum €6.50; ⏱8.45am-2hrs before sunset) Tickets to the ruins are sold at the main entry point, near the tourist office, or, in winter, from the museum, where you can also hire an audioguide (€5).

The first temple you encounter on entering from the main entrance is the 6th-century-BC **Tempio di Cerere** (Temple of Ceres). The smallest of the three temples, it served for a time as a Christian church.

Heading south, you pass the **agorà** (piazza), which contained the city's most important monument, a shrine to Poseidon known as the **heroon**. Nearby, a sunken area marks where once a public **swimming pool** stood, part of a larger sports campus.

The grassy rectangular area south of the pool is the **foro** (forum), the heart of the Roman city. Among the partially standing buildings are a vast domestic housing area, an Italic temple, the Bouleuterion (where the Roman Senate used to meet) and, further south, the amphitheatre.

The **Tempio di Nettuno** (Temple of Neptune), dating from about 450 BC, is the largest and best preserved of the three temples; only parts of its inside walls and roof are missing. Although originally attributed to Neptune, recent studies have claimed that it was, in fact, dedicated to Apollo.

Next door, the **basilica** (in reality, a temple to the goddess Hera) is Paestum's oldest surviving monument. Dating to the middle of the 6th century BC, and with nine columns across and 18 along the sides, it's a majestic building. Just to its east you can, with a touch of imagination, make out remains of the temple's sacrificial altar.

In its time the city was ringed by an impressive 4.7km of walls, subsequently built and rebuilt by both Lucanians and Romans. The most intact section is south of the ruins themselves.

Just east of the ruins, the **museum** (📋0828 81 10 23; admission €4, incl ruins €6.50; ⏱8.30am-7.30pm, last entry 6.45pm, closed 1st & 3rd Mon of month) houses a collection of much-weathered metopes (bas-relief friezes), including 33 of the original 36 from the **Tempio di Argiva Hera** (Temple of Argive Hera), 9km north of Paestum, of which virtually nothing else remains. The star exhibit is the

5th-century-BC Tomba del Truffatore (Tomb of the Diver), whose depiction of a diver in mid-air reputedly represents the passage of life to death.

Sleeping & Eating

TOP CHOICE Casale Giancesare   B&B €

(☑0828 72 80 61, 333 189 77 37; www.casale -giancesare.it; Via Giancesare 8; s €45-75, d €65-120, apt per wk €600-1300; P✱@🛜🛆♣) A converted 19th-century farmhouse, this charming stone-clad B&B is 2.5km from Paestum. Surrounded by vineyards and olive and mulberry trees, the views are stunning, particularly from the swimming pool. Delightful owners Anna, Enzo and son Antonino are passionate about food, producing (and selling) their own olives, jams, *limoncello* and wine. Beware of road signs advertising another bed and breakfast, called Residence Giancesere.

Nonna Sceppa   TRADITIONAL ITALIAN €€

(Via Laura 53, località Laura; meals €39; ⊙lunch & dinner Easter-Sep, lunch Fri-Wed & dinner Sat rest of yr) Worth seeking out as an alternative to the mediocre, overpriced on-site restaurants. Dishes are robust, strictly seasonal and, during the summer, concentrate on fresh seafood like the refreshingly simple grilled fish with lemon. The risotto with zucchini and artichokes is equally inspired.

🛈 Getting There & Away

The best way to get to Paestum by public transport is to take CSTP (☑800 016 659; www.cstp. it, in Italian) bus 34 from Piazza della Concordia in Salerno (€3.30, one hour 20 minutes, 12 daily) or, if approaching from the south, the same bus from Agropoli (€1.20, 15 minutes, 12 daily).

If you're driving you could take the A3 from Salerno and exit for the SS18 at Battipaglia. Better, and altogether more pleasant, is the Litoranea, the minor road that hugs the coast. From the A3 take the earlier exit for Pontecagnano and follow the signs for Agropoli and Paestum.

COSTIERA CILENTANA

Southeast of the Gulf of Salerno, the coastal plains begin to give way to wilder, jagged cliffs and unspoilt scenery, a taste of what lies further on in the stark hills of Basilicata and the wooded peaks of Calabria. Inland, dark mountains loom over the remote highlands of the Parco Nazionale del Cilento e Vallo di Diano, one of Campania's best-kept secrets.

On the coast 75km south of Salerno, the Greek settlement of Elea (now Velia) was founded in the 6th century BC and later became a popular resort for wealthy Romans. The ruins (☑0974 97 23 96; Contrada Piana di Velia; admission €2; ⊙9am to 1hr before sunset), topped by a tower visible for miles around, are not in great nick but merit a quick look if you're passing through.

Several destinations on the Cilento coast are served by the main rail route from Naples to Reggio di Calabria. Check Trenitalia (www.trenitalia.it) for fares and information.

By car take the SS18, which connects Agropoli with Velia via the inland route, or the SS267, which hugs the coast.

Agropoli

POP 21,035

The main town on the southern stretch of the coast, Agropoli makes a good base for Paestum and the beaches to the northwest. Popular with holidaying Italians, it's an otherwise tranquil place with a ramshackle medieval core on a promontory overlooking the sea.

The tourist office (☑0974 82 74 19; Piazza della Repubblica 3; ⊙9am-1pm Mon-Fri, also 3-6pm Tue & Thu) can provide you with a city map.

Sleeping & Eating

Anna   B&B €

(☑0974 82 37 63; www.bbanna.it; Via S Marco 28-32; s €35-50, d €50-70; ✱) Across from Agropoli's sweeping sandy beach, Anna has bright, cheerful rooms with white walls, smart striped fabrics, and balconies; request a sea view. Sunbeds and bicycles are available for a minimal price, and the popular downstairs restaurant (pizzas from €3, meals €18) serves gluten-free meals.

Ostello La Lanterna   HOSTEL €

(☑/fax 0974 83 83 64; lanterna@cilento.it; Via Lanterna 8; dm €18-19, d with bathroom €40-50, tr €58-65, q €80-85; ⊙mid-Mar–Oct) Agropoli's friendly hostel offers dorms, doubles and four-bed family rooms, as well as a garden and optional evening meals (€10). The beach is a two-minute walk away.

U'Sghiz   TRADITIONAL ITALIAN, PIZZERIA €

(Piazza Umberto I; pizzas from €3, meals €22; ⊙closed Tue Oct-May) In a 17th-century building on the headland, U'Sghiz specialises in seafood dishes like *spaghetti a vongole* (with mussels), and also has an extensive pizza menu. We suggest you ditch the quarter carafe of house red wine (€2) for one of the marginally more expensive drops.

Parco Nazionale del Cilento e Vallo di Diano

Stretching from the coast up to Campania's highest peak, Monte Cervati (1900m), and beyond to the regional border with Basilicata, the Parco Nazionale del Cilento e Vallo di Diano is Italy's second-largest national park. A little-explored area of barren heights and empty valleys, it's the perfect antidote to the holiday mayhem on the coast. To get the best out of it, you will, however, need a car – either that or unlimited patience and a masterful grasp of local bus timetables.

For further information stop by the tourist office in Paestum (p680). For guided hiking opportunities, contact Gruppo Escursionistico Trekking (☑0975 725 86; www.getvallodidiano.it; Via Provinciale 29, Sassano) or Associazione Trekking Cilento (☑0974 84 33 45; www.trekkingcilento.it, in Italian; Via Cannetiello 6, Agropoli).

About 25km northeast of Paestum, the Oasi Naturalistica di Persano (☑0828 97 46 84; persano@wwf.it; ⊙9am-5pm Wed, Sat & Sun Jun-Sep, 10am-3pm Wed, Sat & Sun Oct-May) covers 110 hectares of wetlands on the river Sele. A favourite of ornithologists, it's home to a wide variety of birds, both resident and seasonal. Signs direct you there from the SS18. Visits should be booked a day in advance. Guided tours should be booked two days ahead.

There are also two cave systems worth exploring. Located about 20km northeast of Paestum, the Grotte di Castelcivita (☑0828 77 23 97; www.grottedicastelcivita.com; Castelcivita; admission €10; ⊙six daily tours mid-Mar–Sep, four daily Oct–mid-Mar) complex is

where Spartacus is said to have taken refuge following his slave rebellion in 71 BC. There are longer 3½-hour tours (€25) between June and September, when the water deep within the cave complex has dried up. Hard hats and a certain level of fitness and mobility are required. Visits should be booked a day in advance.

There is a De Rosa (☑0828 94 10 65) bus that departs from Capaccio (6km east of Paestum) at 9.20am and a return service departing Castelcivita at 3.20pm, Monday to Saturday. A one-way ticket costs €2.50. By car take the SS18 from Paestum towards Salerno and follow the signs.

On the eastern edge of the park, the Grotte dell'Angelo Pertosa (☑0975 39 70 37; www.grottedipertosa.it; Pertosa; tours €10; ⊙9am-7pm Mar-Oct, 10am-4pm Nov-Feb) is a 2.5km-long system bristling with stalactites and stalagmites. Although SITA buses from Salerno to Pertosa (€5) run Monday to Saturday, their inconvenient running times make the possibility of a day trip redundant. By car take the A3 southbound from Salerno, exit at Petina and follow the SS19 for 9km.

Continuing south on the A3 autostrada, Padula harbours one of the region's hidden jewels, the magnificent Certosa di San Lorenzo (☑0975 777 45; Viale Certosa, Padula; admission €4; ⊙9am-7pm Wed-Mon). Also known as the Certosa di Padula, this is one of Europe's biggest monasteries, with a huge central courtyard, wood-panelled library and sumptuously frescoed chapels. Begun in the 14th century and modified over time, it was abandoned in the 19th century, then suffered further degradation as a children's holiday home and later a concentration camp.

Lamanna (☑0975 52 04 26) buses run four to six times daily from Salerno to Padula.

Puglia, Basilicata & Calabria

Includes »

Why Go?

Southern Italy is the land of the *mezzogiorno* – the midday sun – which sums up the Mediterranean climate and the languid pace of life. From the heel to the toe of Italy's boot, the landscape reflects the individuality of its people. Basilicata is a crush of mountains and rolling hills with a dazzling stretch of coastline. Calabria is Italy's wildest area with fine beaches and a mountainous landscape with peaks frequently crowned by ruined castles. Puglia is the sophisticate of the south with charming seaside villages along its 800km of coastline, lush flat farmlands, thick forests and olive groves.

The south's violent history of successive invasions and economic hardship has forged a fiercely proud people and influenced its distinctive culture and cuisine. A hotter, edgier place than the urbane north of Italy, this is an area that still feels like it has secret places to explore, although you will need your own wheels (and some Italian) if you plan to seriously sidestep from the beaten track.

Best Places to Eat

» Cucina Casareccia (p710)
» La Locanda di Federico (p688)
» Il Frantoio (p703)
» Taverna Al Cantinone (p695)

Best Places to Stay

» Sotto Le Cummerse (p701)
» Palazzo Rollo (p707)
» Locanda delle Donne Monache (p729)

When to Go

Bari

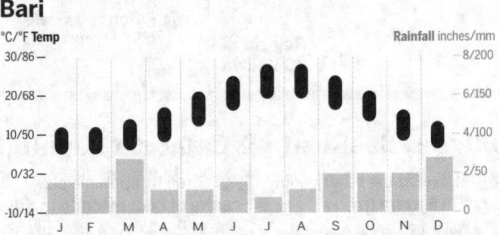

| April-June Spring wildflowers are blooming: the perfect time for hiking in the mountains. | July & August Summer is beach weather and the best party time for festivals and events. | September & October No crowds, mild weather and wild mushrooms galore. |

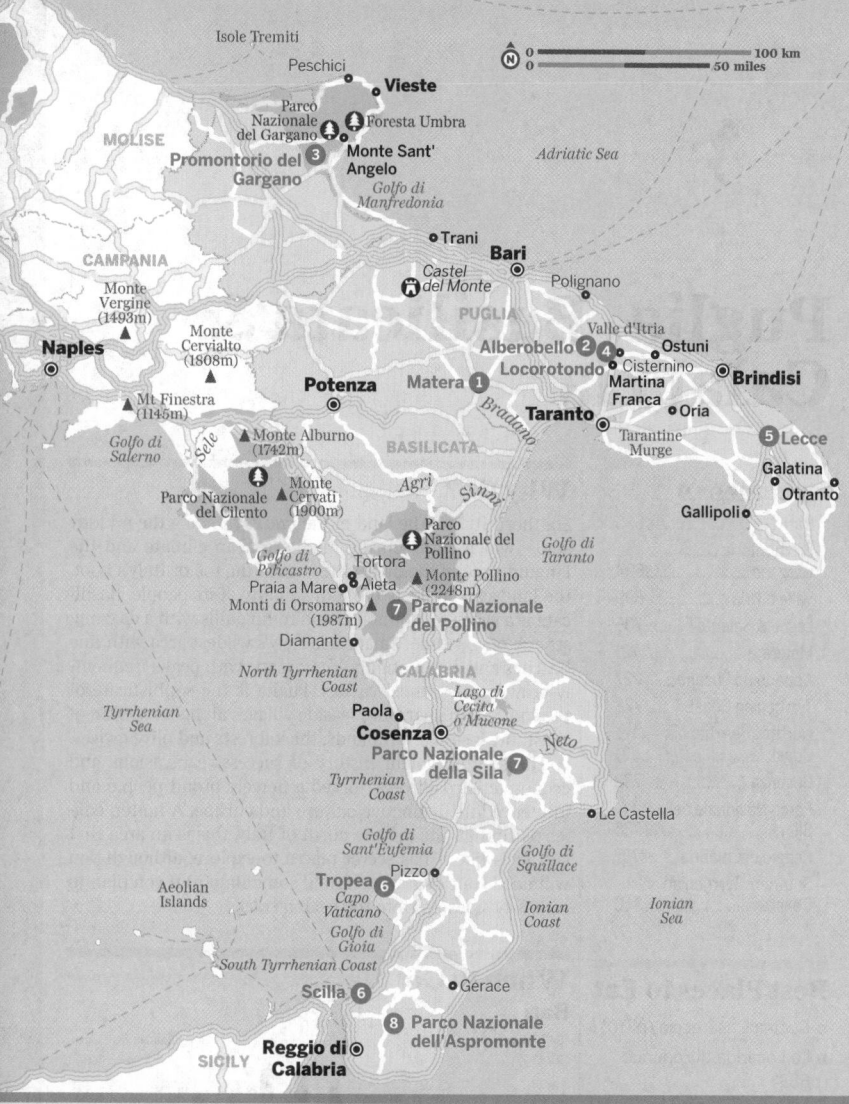

Puglia, Basilicata & Calabria Highlights

① Marvel at the otherworldly *sassi* of **Matera** (p721)

② Dip into the Disney-style scenario of the gnome-size *trulli* dwellings in **Alberobello** (p700)

③ Hike in shady forests and swim in aqua-blue seas in the **Promontorio del Gargano** (p694)

④ Stroll through the old centre of **Locorotondo** (p701), one of Puglia's prettiest towns

⑤ Wonder at ornate baroque facades in **Lecce** (p705)

⑥ Discover Calabria's picturesque seaside villages of **Tropea** (p741) and **Scilla** (p740)

⑦ Vanish into the vast hills of the **Parco Nazionale della Sila** (p735) or the **Parco Nazionale del Pollino** (p733)

⑧ Drive or trek into the wilds of the mysterious **Parco Nazionale dell'Aspromonte** (p737)

PUGLIA

Puglia is sun-bleached landscapes, silver olive groves, seascapes, and hilltop and coastal towns. It is a lush, largely flat farming region, skirted by a long coast that alternates between glittering limestone precipices and long sandy beaches. The heel of Italy juts into the Adriatic and Ionian Seas and the waters of both are stunningly beautiful, veering between translucent emerald-green and dusky powder blue. Its extensive coastline bears the marks of many conquering invaders: the Normans, the Spanish, the Turks, the Swabians and the Greeks. Yet, despite its diverse influences, Puglia is authentic.

In a land where the cuisine is all-important, Puglia's *cucina povera* is legendary. Olive oil, grapes, tomatoes, eggplants, artichokes, peppers, salami, mushrooms, olives and fresh seafood strain its table. Although boasting some of Italy's best food and wines, in some places it's rare to hear a foreign voice. But in July and August Puglia becomes a huge party, with *sagre* (festivals, usually involving food), concerts and events, and thousands of Italian tourists heading down here for their annual break.

History

At times Puglia feels Greek – and for good reason. This tangible legacy dates from when the Greeks founded a string of settlements along the Ionian coast in the 8th century BC. A form of Greek dialect (Griko) is still spoken in some towns southeast of Lecce. Historically, their major city was Taras (Taranto), settled by Spartan exiles who dominated until they were defeated by the Romans in 272 BC.

The long coastline made the region vulnerable to conquest. The Normans left their fine Romanesque churches, the Swabians their fortifications and the Spanish their flamboyant baroque buildings. No one, however, knows exactly the origins of the extraordinary 16th-century, conical-roofed stone houses, the *trulli,* unique to Puglia.

Apart from invaders and pirates, malaria was long the greatest scourge of the south, forcing many towns to build away from the coast and into the hills. After Mussolini's seizure of power in 1922, the south became the frontline in his 'Battle for Wheat'. This initiative was aimed at making Italy self-sufficient when it came to food, following the sanctions imposed on the country after its conquest of Ethiopia. Puglia is now covered in wheat fields, olive groves and fruit arbours.

Bari

POP 320,150

Once regarded as the Bronx of southern Italy, Bari's reputation has gradually improved and the city, Puglia's capital and one of the south's most prosperous, deserves more than a cursory glance. Spruced up and rejuvenated, Bari Vecchia, the historic old town, is an interesting and atmospheric warren of streets. In the evenings, the piazzas buzz with trendy restaurants and bars, but there are still parts of the old town that carry a gritty undertone.

Dangers & Annoyances

Petty crime can be a problem, so take all the usual precautions: don't leave anything in your car; don't display money or valuables; and watch out for bag-snatchers on scooters. Be careful in Bari Vecchia's dark streets at night.

⊙ Sights

Most sights are in or near the atmospheric old town, Bari Vecchia, a medieval labyrinth of tight alleyways and graceful piazzas, which fills a small peninsula between the new port to the west and the old port to the southeast; it crams in 40 churches and more than 120 shrines.

Castello Svevo CASTLE
(Swabian Castle; ☑083 184 00 09; Piazza Federico II di Svevia; admission adult/reduced €2/1; ⊙8.30am-7.30pm Thu-Tue) The Normans originally built over the ruins of a Roman fort, then Frederick II built over the Norman castle, incorporating it into his design – the two towers of the Norman structure still stand. The bastions, with corner towers overhanging the moat, were added in the 16th century during Spanish rule, when the castle was a magnificent residence.

Basilica di San Nicola BASILICA
(Piazza San Nicola; www.basilicasannicola.it; ⊙7am-1pm & 4-7pm Mon-Sat, 7am-1pm & 4-9pm Sun) One of the south's first Norman churches, the basilica is a splendid example of Puglian-Romanesque style, built to house the relics of St Nicholas (better known as Father Christmas), which were stolen from Turkey in 1087 by local fishermen. His remains are said to emanate a miraculous

Puglia

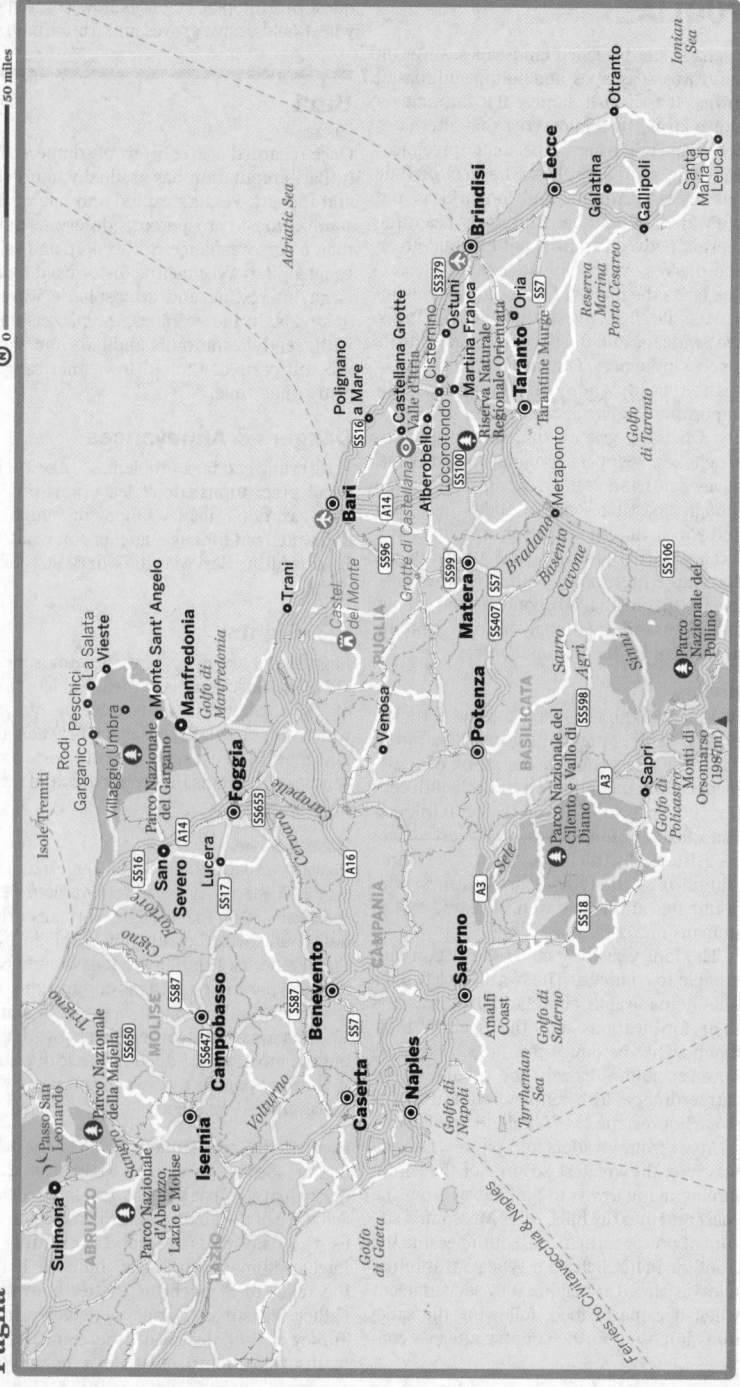

manna liquid with special powers. For this reason – and because he is also the patron saint of prisoners and children – the basilica remains an important place of pilgrimage. The interior is huge and simple with a decorative 17th-century wooden ceiling. The magnificent 13th-century ciborium over the altar is Puglia's oldest. The shrine in the crypt, lit by hanging lamps, is beautiful.

Cathedral
CATHEDRAL

(Piazza Odegitria; ⊙8am-12.30pm & 4-7.30pm Mon-Fri, 8am-12.30pm & 5-8.30pm Sat & Sun) Built over the original Byzantine church, the 11th-century Romanesque cathedral retains its basilica plan and Eastern-style cupola. The plain walls are punctuated with deep arcades and the eastern window is a tangle of plant and animal motifs.

Piazza Mercantile
PIAZZA

This beautiful piazza is fronted by the Sedile, the headquarters of Bari's Council of Nobles. In the square's northeast corner is the Colonna della Giustizia (Column of Justice), where debtors were once tied and whipped.

★✩ Festivals

Festa di San Nicola
RELIGIOUS

The Festival of St Nicholas, held around 7 to 9 May, is Bari's biggest annual shindig, celebrating the 11th-century arrival of St Nicholas' relics from Turkey. On the first evening a procession leaves Castello Svevo for the Basilica di San Nicola. The next day a fleet of boats carries the statue of St Nicholas along the coast and the evening ends with a massive fireworks competition.

🛏 Sleeping

Accommodation here tends to be bland and overpriced, aimed at business clientele.

B&B Casa Pimpolini
B&B €

(✆080 521 99 38; www.casapimpolini.com; Via Calefati 249; s/d €60/80; ❇ @) This lovely B&B in the new town is within easy walking distance to shops, restaurants and Bari Vecchia. The rooms are warm and welcoming, and the homemade breakfast a treat. Great value.

Hotel Adria
HOTEL €€

(✆080 524 66 99; www.adriahotelbari.com; Via Zuppetta 10; s/d €70/110; P❇@) A dusky-pink building fronted by wrought-iron balconies, this is a good choice near the train station. Rooms are comfortable, bright and modern.

Palace Hotel
HOTEL €€€

(✆080 521 65 51; www.dominahotels.com; Via Lombardi 13; s/d €195/260; P❇@🤶) A large

---

PUGLIA ON YOUR PLATE

Puglia is home to Italy's most uncorrupted, brawniest, least known vernacular cuisine. It has evolved from *cucina povera* – literally 'cooking of the poor' or peasant cooking: think of pasta made without eggs and dishes prepared with wild greens gathered from the fields.

Most of Italy's fish is caught off the Puglian coast, 80% of Europe's pasta is produced here and 80% of Italy's olive oil originates in Puglia and Calabria. Tomatoes, broccoli, chicory, fennel, figs, melons, cherries and grapes are all plentiful in season and taste better than anywhere else. Almonds, grown near Ruvo di Puglia, are packed into many traditional cakes and pastries, which used to be eaten only by the privileged.

Like their Greek forbears, the Pugliese eat *agnello* (lamb) and *capretto* (kid). *Cavallo* (horse) has only recently galloped to the table while *trippa* (tripe) is another mainstay. Meat is usually roasted or grilled with aromatic herbs or served in tomato-based sauces.

Raw fish (such as anchovies or baby squid) are marinated in olive oil and lemon juice. *Cozze* (mussels) are prepared in multitudinous ways, with garlic and breadcrumbs, or as *riso cozze patata,* baked with rice and potatoes – every area has its variations on this dish.

Bread and pasta are close to the Pugliese heart, with per capita consumption at least double that of the USA. You'll find *orecchiette* (small ear-shaped pasta, often accompanied by a small rod-shaped variety, called *strascinati* or *cavatelli*), served with broccoli or *ragù* (meat sauce), generally topped by the pungent local cheese *ricotta forte*.

Previously known for quantity rather than quality, Pugliese wines are now developing apace. The best are produced in Salento (the Salice Salentino is one of the finest reds), in the *trulli* (conical houses) area around Locorotondo (famous for its white wine), around Cisternino (home of the fashionable heavy red Primitivo) and in the plains around Foggia and Lucera.

impersonal hotel, the Palace has classical rooms and a renowned rooftop restaurant, the Murat.

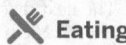 **Eating**

TOP CHOICE **La Locanda di Federico**　TRATTORIA €€
(☑080 522 77 05; www.lalocandadifederico.com; Piazza Mercantile 63-64; meals €30; ⊙lunch & dinner) With domed ceilings, archways and medieval-style art work on the walls, this restaurant oozes atmosphere. The menu is typical Pugliese, the food delicious and the price reasonable. *Orecchiette con le cime di rape* ('little ears' pasta with turnip greens) is highly recommended.

Vini e Cucina　OSTERIA €
(☑338 212 03 91; Strada Vallisa 23; meals €10; ⊙lunch & dinner) Run by the same family for more than a century, this boisterous *osteria* chalks up its daily specials of well-prepared and filling Pugliese dishes. Grab a seat in the brick-flanked tunnel of a dining room and wait (and wait) to be served by the one impressively indefatigable waiter.

Caffè Borghese　CAFE €
(☑080 524 21 56; Corso Vittorio Emanuele II 22; dishes €6-10; ⊙8am-2am Tue-Sun) You'll experience genuine hospitality and friendly service in this small cafe. Its understated charm and simple dishes will have you returning for breakfast, lunch and *aperitivi*.

Alberosole　TRADITIONAL ITALIAN €€
(☑080 523 54 46; www.alberosole.com; Corso Vittorio Emanuele II 13; meals €40; ⊙Tue-Sun) Dine alongside bankers in Brioni suits at this elegant restaurant. The contemporary menu is complemented by a traditional dining room, complete with an old stone floor and cathedral ceiling. Highly recommended by locals.

 **Drinking**

Barcollo　BAR
(☑080 521 38 89; Piazza Mercantile 69/70; cocktails €7; ⊙8am-3am) Lounge on brilliant-red banquettes or sit outside on the twinkling square supping a cocktail and nibbling work-of-art hors d'oeuvres.

Ferrarese　BAR
(☑392 074 44 74; Piazza Ferrarese 1) Overlooking the harbour on Piazza Ferrarese, this is a popular hang-out for university students.

🛍 Shopping

Designer shops and the main Italian chains line Via Sparano da Bari, while delis and gourmet food shops are located throughout the city.

Il Salumaio　FOOD
(☑080 521 93 45; www.ilsalumaio.it; Via Piccinni 168; ⊙8.30am-2pm & 5.30-9.30pm Mon-Sat) Breathe in the delicious scents of fine regional produce at this venerable delicatessen.

Enoteca de Pasquale　WINE
(☑080 521 31 92; Via Marchese di Montrone 87; ⊙8am-2pm & 4-8.30pm Mon-Sat) Stock up on Puglian wines.

❶ Information

From Piazza Aldo Moro, in front of the main train station, streets heading north will take you to Corso Vittorio Emanuele II, which separates the old and new parts of the city.

CTS (☑080 521 88 73; Via Garriba 65-67) Good for student travel and discount flights.
Hospital (☑080 559 11 11; Piazza Cesare)
Morfimare Travel Agency (☑080 578 98 26; www.morfimare.it; Corso de Tullio 36-40) Ferry bookings.
Police station (☑080 529 11 11; Via Murat 4)
Post office (Piazza Umberto 33/8)
Tourist office (☑080 990 93 41; www.viaggiareinpuglia.it; 1st fl, Piazza Moro 33a; ⊙8.30am-1pm & 3-6pm Mon-Fri, 10am-1pm Sat); **information kiosk** (⊙9am-7pm May-Sep) in front of the train station in Piazza Aldo Moro.

❶ Getting There & Away

Air
Bari's Palese **airport** (☑080 580 03 58; www.aeroportidipuglia.it) is served by a host of international and budget airlines, including British Airways, Alitalia and Ryanair.

Pugliairbus (☑080 580 03 58; http://pugliairbus.aeroportidipuglia.it) connects the airports of Bari, Brindisi, Taranto and Foggia. It also has a service from Bari airport to Matera (€5, 1¼ hours, four daily), and to Vieste (€20, 3½ hours, four daily May to September).

Boat
Ferries run from Bari to Albania, Croatia, Greece and Montenegro. All boat companies have offices at the ferry terminal, accessible on bus 20 from the main train station. Fares vary considerably between companies and it's easier to book with a travel agent such as **Morfimare** (☑080 578 98 26; booking office 080 578 98 11; www.morfimare.it; Corso de Tullio 36-40).

START VIESTE
END MARATEA
DISTANCE 650KM TO 700KM
DURATION ONE WEEK

Driving Tour
Italy's Authentic South

❯ Consider a gentle start in lovely, laid-back ❶ **Vieste** with its white sandy beaches and medieval backstreets, but set aside half a day to hike or bike in the lush green forests of the ❷ **Parco Nazionale del Gargano**. Follow the coast road past dramatic cliffs, salt lakes and flat farming land to ❸ **Trani** with its impressive seafront cathedral and picturesque port. The next day, dip into pretty ❹ **Polignano a Mare** with its dramatic location above the pounding surf before heading to ❺ **Alberobello,** home to a dense neighbourhood of extraordinary cone-shaped stone homes called *trulli*. Shake your head in wonder and consider an overnight *trulli* stay.

Stroll around one of the most picturesque *centro storico's* in southern Italy at ❻ **Locorotondo**. Hit the road and cruise on to a delightful gem of a city: ❼ **Lecce**, where you can easily chalk up a full day exploring the sights, the shops and the flamboyantly fronted *palazzi* and churches, including the **Basilica di Santa Croce**.

Day five will be one to remember. Nothing can prepare you for Basilicata's ❽ **Matera** where the *sassi* (former cave dwellings) are a dramatic, albeit harrowing, reminder of the town's poverty-stricken past. After days of pasta, *fave* beans and *cornetti* (Italian croissants), it's high time you laced up those hiking boots and checked out the trails and activities on offer in the spectacular ❾ **Parco Nazionale del Pollino**. Finally, wind up the trip and soothe those aching muscles with a dip in the sea at postcard-pretty ❿ **Maratea** with its surrounding seaside resorts, medieval village and cosmopolitan harbour offset by a thickly forested and mountainous interior.

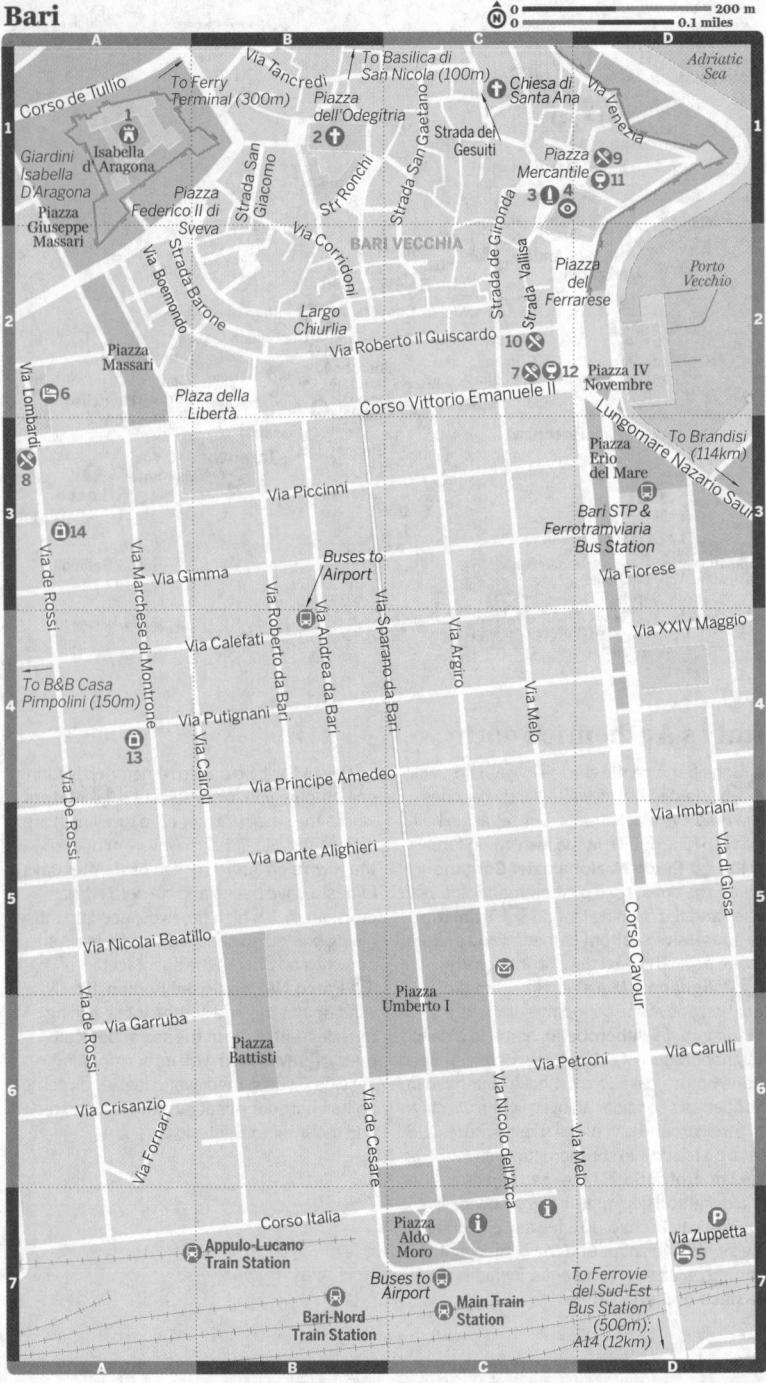

PUGLIA, BASILICATA & CALABRIA PUGLIA

0 — 200 m
0 — 0.1 miles

Adriatic Sea

Corso de Tullio
To Ferry Terminal (300m)
Via Tancredi
To Basilica di San Nicola (100m)
Piazza dell'Odegitria
Chiesa di Santa Ana
Via Venezia

Giardini Isabella D'Aragona
Isabella d'Aragona
Strada San Giacomo
Strada San Gaetano
Strada dei Gesuiti
Piazza Mercantile

Piazza Giuseppe Massari
Piazza Federico II di Sveva
Str Ronchi
Via Corridoni
BARI VECCHIA
Strada de Gironda

Via Boemondo
Strada Barone
Largo Chiurlia
Via Roberto il Guiscardo
Strada Vallisa
Piazza del Ferrarese
Porto Vecchio

Piazza Massari
Plaza della Libertà
Corso Vittorio Emanuele II
Piazza IV Novembre

Via Lombardi
Piazza Erio del Mare
Lungomare Nazario Sauri
To Brandisi (114km)

Via Piccinni
Bari STP & Ferrotramviaria Bus Station

Via de Rossi
Buses to Airport
Via Gimma
Via Roberto da Bari
Via Andrea da Bari
Via Sparano da Bari
Via Argiro
Via Fiorese

Via Marchese di Montrone
Via Calefati
Via XXIV Maggio

To B&B Casa Pimpolini (150m)
Via Putignani
Via Cairoli
Via Melo

Via Principe Amedeo
Via Imbriani

Via De Rossi
Via Dante Alighieri
Via di Giosa

Via Nicolai Beatillo
Corso Cavour

Via de Rossi
Via Garruba
Piazza Umberto I

Piazza Battisti
Via de Cesare
Via Nicolo dell'Arca
Via Petroni
Via Carulli

Via Crisanzio
Via Fornari
Via Melo

Corso Italia
Piazza Aldo Moro
Via Zuppetta

Appulo-Lucano Train Station
Buses to Airport
Main Train Station
To Ferrovie del Sud-Est Bus Station (500m); A14 (12km)

Bari-Nord Train Station

Bari

The main companies and their routes are as follows:

Agoudimos Lines (www.agoudimos-lines.com) To Cephalonia, Corfu, Igoumenista in Greece.

Jadrolinija (www.jadrolinija.hr) To Dubrovnik in Croatia.

Montenegro Lines (☎382 30 311 164; www. montenegrolines.net) To Bar in Montenegro; Cephalonia, Corfu, Igoumenista in Greece; and Durrës in Albania.

Superfast (☎080 528 28 28; www.superfast. com) To Corfu, Igoumenista, Patras in Greece. Departures at 7pm or 8pm depending on the route.

Ventouris Ferries (☎for Greece 080 521 76 99, for Albania 521 27 56; www.ventouris. gr) Regular ferries to Corfu and Igoumenitsa (Greece) and daily ferries to Durrës (Albania).

Bus

Intercity buses leave from three main locations. From Via Capruzzi, south of the main train station, **SITA** (☎080 579 01 11; www.sitabus.it, in Italian) covers local destinations. **Ferrovie Appulo-Lucane** (☎080 572 52 29; www.fal-srl. it, in Italian) buses serving Matera also depart from here, plus **Marozzi** (☎080 556 24 46; www.marozzivt.it) buses for Rome (€35, eight hours, eight daily – note that the overnight bus departs from Piazza Moro) and other long-distance destinations.

Piazza Eroi del Mare is the terminal for **STP** (☎080 505 82 80; www.stpspa.it) buses

serving Trani (€2.95, 45 minutes, frequent). **Ferrotramviaria** (☎080 529 93 52; www. ferrovienordbarese.it) runs frequent buses to Andria (€3.90, one hour) and Ruvo di Puglia (€2.60, 40 minutes).

Buses operated by **Ferrovie del Sud-Est** (FSE; ☎080 546 21 11; www.fseonline.it, in Italian) leave from Largo Ciaia, south of Piazza Aldo Moro.

Alberobello €3.90, 1¼ hours; continues to **Locorotondo** and **Martina Franca**

Brindisi €7.70, 23 to 24 hours, four daily Monday to Saturday

Grotte di Castellana €2.90, one hour, five daily

Ostuni €5.20, two hours, four daily

Taranto €5.80, 1¾ to 2¼ hours, frequent

Train

A web of train lines spreads out from Bari. Note that there are fewer services on the weekend.

From the **main train station** (☎080 524 43 86) trains go to Puglia and beyond:

Brindisi from €15, one hour

Foggia from €18, one hour

Milan from €85, about eight hours

Rome from €51, four hours

Ferrovie Appulo-Lucane (☎080 572 52 29; www.fal-srl. it) serves two main destinations:

Matera €4.50, 1½ hours, 12 daily

Potenza €9.70, four hours, four daily

FSE (☎080 546 21 11; www.fseonline.it, in Italian) trains leave from the station in Via Oberdan – cross under the train tracks south of Piazza Luigi di Savoia and head east along Via Capruzzi for about 500m. They serve the following towns:

Alberobello €4.50, 1½ hours, hourly

Martina Franca €5.20, two hours, hourly

Taranto from €7.70, 2½ hours, nine daily

ⓘ Getting Around

Central Bari is compact – a 15-minute walk will take you from Piazza Aldo Moro to the old town. For the ferry terminal take bus 20 from Piazza Moro (€1.50).

Street parking is migraine-inducing. There's a large parking area (€1) south of the main port entrance; otherwise, there's a large multistorey car park between the main train station and the Ferrovie del Sud-Est (FSE) station. Another car park is on Via Zuppetta opposite Hotel Adria.

To/From the Airport

For the airport, take the Tempesta shuttle bus (€4.14, 30 minutes, hourly) from the main train station, with pick-ups at Piazza Garibaldi and the

TRAVELLING EAST

Puglia is the main jumping-off point for onward travel to Greece, Croatia and Albania. The two main ports are Bari and Brindisi, from where you catch ferries to Vlore in Albania, Bar in Montenegro, and Cephalonia, Corfu, Igoumenista and Patras in Greece. Fares from Bari to Greece are generally more expensive than those from Brindisi. Taxes are usually from €9 to €12 per person and car. High season is generally the months of July and August, with reduced services in low season. Tariffs can be up to one-third cheaper in low season.

corner of Via Andrea da Bari and Via Calefati. A taxi trip from the airport to town costs around €24.

Ferrovia Bari-Nord (☑080 529 93 52; www.ferrovianordbarese.it) has frequent train services to the airport (€1.10, 10 minutes).

Around Bari

The Terra di Bari, or 'land of Bari', surrounding the capital is rich in olive groves and orchards, and the region has an impressive architectural history with some magnificent cathedrals, an extensive network of castles along its coastline, charming seaside towns like Trani and Polignano a Mare, and the mysterious inland Castel del Monte.

TRANI
POP 53,860

Known as the 'Pearl of Puglia', beautiful Trani has a sophisticated feel, particularly in summer when well-heeled visitors pack the diminutive array of marina-side bars. The marina is the place to promenade and watch the white yachts and fishing boats in the harbour, while the historic centre, with its medieval churches, glossy limestone streets and faded yet charming *palazzi* is an enchanting area to explore. But it's the cathedral, white against the deep-blue sea, that is the town's most arresting sight.

👁 Sights

Cathedral   CATHEDRAL
(Piazza del Duomo; ⊙9am-12.30pm & 3-6.30pm) The dramatic seafront cathedral is dedicated to St Nicholas the Pilgrim, famous for being foolish. The Greek Christian wandered through Puglia, crying '*Kyrie eleison*' (Greek for 'Lord, have mercy'). First thought to be

a simpleton, he was revered after his death (aged 19) after several miracles attributed to him occurred. The cathedral was started in 1097 on the site of a Byzantine church and completed in the 13th century. The magnificent original bronze doors (now displayed inside) were cast by Barisano da Trani, an accomplished 12th-century artisan.

The interior of the cathedral reflects typical Norman simplicity and is lined by colonnades. Near the main altar are the remains of a 12th-century floor mosaic, stylistically similar to that in Otranto. Below the church is the crypt, a forest of ancient columns where the bones of St Nicholas are kept beneath the altar. You can also visit the **campanile** (admission €3).

Castle   CASTLE
(☑0883 50 66 03; www.castelloditrani.beniculturali.it; Piazza Manfredi 16; admission €2; ⊙8.30am-7.30pm) Two hundred metres north of the cathedral is Trani's other major landmark, the vast, almost modernist Swabian castle built by Frederick II in 1233. Charles V later strengthened the fortifications; it was used as a prison from 1844 to 1974.

Ognissanti Church   CHURCH
(Via Ognissanti; ⊙hours vary) Built by the Knights Templar in the 12th century, Norman knights swore allegiance here to Bohemond I of Antioch, their leader, before setting off on the First Crusade.

Scolanova Church   CHURCH
(☑0883 48 17 99; Via Scolanova 23; ⊙hours vary) This church was one of four former synagogues in the ancient Jewish quarter, all of which were converted to churches in the 14th century. Inside is a beautiful Byzantine painting of Madonna dei Martiri.

🛏 Sleeping

Albergo Lucy   HOTEL €
(☑0883 48 10 22; www.albergolucy.com; Piazza Plebiscito 11; d/tr/q €65/85/105; 🖭) In a restored 17th-century *palazzo* overlooking a leafy square and close to the shimmering port, this family-run place oozes charm. Bike hire and guided tours available. Great value.

B&B Centro Storico Trani   B&B €
(☑0883 50 61 76; www.bbtrani.it; Via Leopardi 28; s €35-50, d €50-70) This simple, old-fashioned B&B inhabits an old backstreet monastery and is run by an elderly couple. It's basic, but the rooms are large and 'Mama' makes a mean *crostata* (jam tart).

Hotel Regia
HOTEL €€

(📞0883 58 44 44; www.hotelregia.it; Piazza del Duomo 2; s €120-130, d €130-150; ❀🅿🛜) A lone building facing the cathedral, the understated grandeur of 18th-century Palazzo Filisio houses a charming hotel. Rooms are sober and stylish.

✖ Eating

U'Vrascir
TRATTORIA €

(📞0883 49 18 40; www.uvrascir.it; Piazza Cesare Battisti 9; meals €25; ⊙Wed-Mon) With a cosy atmosphere, friendly service, and a menu written in dialect, this inviting trattoria and pizzeria is sure to satisfy. Good value.

Corteinfiore
SEAFOOD €€

(📞0883 50 84 02; www.corteinfiore.it; Via Ognissanti 18; meals €30; ⊙Tue-Sun) Romantic, urbane, refined. The wooden decking, buttercup-yellow tablecloths and marquee-conservatory setting is refreshing. The wines are excellent and the cooking delicious.

La Darsena
SEAFOOD €€

(📞0883 48 73 33; Via Statuti Marittimi 98; meals €30; ⊙Tue-Sun) Renowned for its seafood, La Darsena is housed in a waterfront *palazzo*. Outside tables overlook the port while inside photos of old Puglia cover the walls beneath a huge wrought-iron dragon chandelier.

ℹ Information

From the train station, Via Cavour leads through Piazza della Repubblica to Piazza Plebiscito and the public gardens. Turn left for the harbour and cathedral.

The **tourist office** (📞0883 58 88 30; www.traniweb.it; 1st fl, Palazzo Palmieri, Piazza Trieste 10; ⊙8.30am-1.30pm Mon-Fri, plus 3.30-5.30pm Tue & Thu) is 200m south of the cathedral.

ℹ Getting There & Away

STP (📞0883 49 18 00; www.stpspa.it) has frequent services to Bari (€2.95, 45 minutes). Services depart from **Bar Stazione** (Piazza XX Settembre 23), which also has timetables and tickets.

Trani is on the main train line between Bari (€4.40, 40 to 60 minutes, frequent) and Foggia (€9.50, one hour, frequent).

CASTEL DEL MONTE

You'll see **Castel del Monte** (📞0883 56 99 97; www.casteldelmonte.beniculturali.it; admission adult/reduced €5/2.50; ⊙9am-6pm Oct-Feb, 10.15am-7.45pm Mar-Sep), an unearthly geometric shape on a hilltop, from miles away. Mysterious and perfectly octagonal, it's one of southern Italy's most talked-about landmarks and a Unesco World Heritage Site.

No one knows why Frederick II built it. Nobody has ever lived here – note the lack of kitchens – and there's no nearby town or strategic crossroads. It was not built to defend anything, as it has no moat or drawbridge, no arrow slits, and no trapdoors for pouring boiling oil on invaders.

Some theories claim that, according to mid-13th-century beliefs in geometric symbolism, the octagon represented the union of the circle and square, of God-perfection (the infinite) and human-perfection (the finite). The castle was therefore nothing less than a celebration of the relationship between humanity and God.

The castle has eight octagonal towers. Its interconnecting rooms have decorative marble columns and fireplaces, and the doorways and windows are framed in coral-lite stone. Many of the towers have washing rooms – Frederick II, like the Arab world he admired, set great store by cleanliness.

It's difficult to reach here by public transport. By car, it's about 35km from Trani.

POLIGNANO A MARE

Dip into this spectacularly positioned small town if you can. Located around 34km south of Bari on the S16 coastal road, **Polignano a Mare** is built on the edge of a craggy ravine pockmarked with caves.

On Sunday the *logge* (balconies) are crowded with day trippers from Bari who come here to view the crashing waves, visit the caves and crowd out the *cornetterias* (shops specialising in Italian croissants) in the atmospheric *centro storico*. The town is thought to be one of the most important ancient settlements in Puglia and was later inhabited by successive invaders ranging from the Huns to the Normans. There are several baroque churches, an imposing Norman monastery and the medieval **Porta Grande**, the only access to the historic centre until the 18th century. You can still see the holes that activated the heavy drawbridge and the openings from where boiling oil was poured onto any unwelcome visitors to town.

La Balconata (📞080 424 17 12; Vico Lapergola 10; meals €16; ⊙lunch & dinner) has the best position on a balcony overlooking the sea. It's a restaurant, pizzeria, sandwich bar and gelateria all in one.

Several operators organise boat trips to the grottoes, including **Dorino** (📞329 646 59 04), costing around €20 per person.

Although there is a twice-daily bus service from Bari, your own car is the best way to reach Polignano.

Promontorio del Gargano

The coast surrounding the promontory seems permanently bathed in a pink-hued, pearly light, providing a painterly contrast to the sea, which softens from intense to powder blue as the evening draws in. It's one of Italy's most beautiful areas, encompassing white limestone cliffs, fairy-tale grottoes, sparkling sea, ancient forests, and tangled, fragrant maquis. Once connected to what is now Dalmatia (in Croatia), the 'spur' of the Italian boot has more in common with the land mass across the sea than with the rest of Italy. Creeping urbanisation was halted in 1991 by the creation of the Parco Nazionale del Gargano. Aside from its magnificent national park, the Gargano is home to pilgrimage sites and the lovely seaside towns of Vieste and Peschici.

Along the coast you'll spot strange cat's-cradle wood-and-rope arrangements, unique to the area. These are *trabucchi,* ancient fishing traps (possibly Phoenician in origin) from which fishermen cast their nets, 'walk the plank', and haul in their catch.

VIESTE
POP 13,890

Vieste is an attractive whitewashed town jutting off the Gargano's easternmost promontory into the Adriatic Sea. It's the Gargano capital and sits above the area's most spectacular beach, a gleaming wide strip backed by sheer white cliffs and overshadowed by the towering rock monolith, Scoglio di Pizzomunno. It's packed in summer and ghostly quiet in winter.

◎ Sights

Vieste is primarily a beach resort. The castle built by Frederick II is occupied by the military and closed to the public.

Chianca Amara   HISTORICAL SITE
(Bitter Stone; Via Cimaglia) Vieste's most gruesome sight is this stone where thousands were beheaded when Turks sacked Vieste in the 16th century.

FREE Museo Malacologico   MUSEUM
(☑0884 70 76 88; Via Pola 8; ☺9.30am-12.30pm & 4.30-9pm) This impressive shell museum has four rooms of fossils and molluscs, some

enormous and all beautifully patterned and coloured.

Cathedral   CATHEDRAL
(Via Duomo) Built by the Normans on the ruins of a Vesta temple, the cathedral is in Puglian-Romanesque style with a fanciful tower that resembles a cardinal's hat. It was rebuilt in 1800.

La Salata   HISTORICAL SITE
(admission adult/child €4/free; ☺5.30-6.15pm Jun-Aug, 4-4.45pm Sep, Oct-May on request) This palaeo-Christian graveyard dating from the 4th to 6th centuries AD is 9km out of town. Inside the cave, tier upon tier of narrow tombs are cut into the rock wall; others form shallow niches in the cave floor. Guided tours are essential. Book with Agenzia Sinergie (☑338 840 62 15; www.agenziasinergie. it), which can also arrange customised tours of the Gargano.

✦ Activities

Superb sandy beaches surround the town: in the south are Spiaggia del Castello, Cala San Felice and Cala Sanguinaria; due north, head for the area known as La Salata. Diving is popular around the promontory's rocky coastline, filled with marine grottoes.

From May to September fast boats zoom to the Isole Tremiti.

Boat hire and tours can be arranged at the port:

Centro Ormeggi e Sub   BOAT HIRE
(☑0884 70 79 83) Offers diving courses and rents out sailing boats and motorboats.

Leonarda Motobarche   BOAT TOUR
(☑0884 70 13 17; www.motobarcheleonarda.it; per person €15; ☺Apr-Sep) Boat tours of marine caves.

☞ Tours

Agenzia Sol (☑0884 70 15 58; www.solvieste.it; Via Trepiccioni 5; ☺9.20am-1.15pm & 5-9pm winter, to midnight in summer) organises hiking, cycling and 4WD tours in the Foresta Umbra; boat tours around the Gargano; and gastronomic tours and small group tours into Puglia. It also sells bus tickets and ferry tickets for the Isole Tremiti.

⊨ Sleeping

B&B Rocca sul Mare   B&B €
(☑0884 70 27 19; www.roccasulmare.it; Via Mafrolla 32; per person €25-70; ☎) In a former convent in the old quarter, this popular place has charm, with large, comfortable high-ceilinged rooms. There's a vast rooftop

LUCERA

Lovely Lucera has one of Puglia's most impressive castles and a handsome old town centre with mellow sand-coloured brick and stone work, and chic shops lining wide, shiny stone streets. Founded by the Romans in the 4th century BC, it was abandoned by the 13th century. Following excommunication by Pope Gregory IX, Frederick II decided to bolster his support base in Puglia by importing 20,000 Sicilian Arabs, simultaneously diminishing the headache Arab bandits were causing him in Sicily. It was an extraordinary move by the Christian monarch, even more so because Frederick allowed Lucera's new Muslim inhabitants the freedom to build mosques and practise their religion a mere 290km from Rome. History, however, was less kind; when the town was taken by the rabidly Christian Angevins in 1269, every Muslim who failed to convert was slaughtered.

Frederick II's enormous **castle** (admission free; ⏰9am-2pm year-round & 3-7pm Apr-Sep), shows just what a big fish Lucera once was in the Puglian pond. Built in 1233, it's 14km northwest of the town on a rocky hillock surrounded by a perfect 1km pentagonal wall, guarded by 24 towers.

On the site of Lucera's Great Mosque, Puglia's only Gothic **cathedral** (⏰8am-noon & 4-7pm May-Sep, 5-8pm Oct-Apr) was built in 1301 by Charles II of Anjou. The altar was once the castle banqueting table.

Dominated by a huge rose window, the contemporaneous Gothic **Chiesa di San Francesco** (⏰8am-noon & 4-7pm) incorporates recycled materials from Lucera's 1st-century-BC **Roman amphitheatre** (admission free; ⏰9am-2pm & 3.15-6.45pm Tue-Sun Apr-Sep). The amphitheatre was built for gladiatorial combat and accommodated up to 18,000 people.

The **tourist office** (☎0881 52 27 62; ⏰9am-2pm & 3-8pm Tue-Sun Apr-Sep, 9am-2pm Oct-Mar) is near the cathedral.

Ferrovie del Gargano trains run to Lucera from Foggia (€1.30, 20 minutes, three daily) which is on the east coast train line between Bari and Pescara.

terrace with panoramic views and a suite with a steam bath. Meals and bike hire available.

Hotel Seggio HOTEL €€
(☎0884 70 81 23; www.hotelseggio.it; Via Veste 7; d €80-150; ⏰Apr-Oct; P✳@🛜🏊) A butter-coloured *palazzo* in the town's historic centre with steps that spiral down to a pool and sunbathing terrace with a backdrop of the sea. The rooms are modern and plain but it's family run.

Campeggio Capo Vieste CAMPGROUND €
(☎0884 70 63 26; www.capovieste.it; Litoranea Vieste–Peschici Km 8; camping 2 people, car & tent €33, 1-bedroom bungalow €77-164; ⏰Mar-Oct; 🏊) This tree-shaded campground is right by a sandy beach at La Salata, around 8km from Vieste and accessible by bus. Activities include tennis and a sailing school.

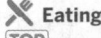

✖ Eating

TOP CHOICE Taverna
Al Cantinone TRADITIONAL ITALIAN €€
(☎0884 70 77 53; Via Mafrolla 26; meals €25-30; ⏰lunch & dinner Wed-Mon) Run by a charming Italian-Spanish couple who have a passion for cooking; the food is exceptional and exquisitely presented. The menu changes with the seasons.

Osteria Al Duomo OSTERIA €
(☎0884 70 82 43; www.osterialduomo.it; Via Alessandro lll 23; meals €25; ⏰lunch & dinner Mar-Nov) Tucked away in a narrow alley in the heart of the old town, this *osteria* has a cosy cave interior and outdoor seating under a shady arbour. Homemade pastas with seafood sauces feature prominently.

Enoteca Vesta TRADITIONAL ITALIAN €€
(☎0884 70 64 11; Via Duomo 14; meals €30-35) Housed in a cool vaulted cave, you can savour a magnificent selection of Puglian wines here to accompany innovative seafood dishes.

❶ Information
Post office (Via Vittorio Veneto)

Tourist office (☎0884 70 88 06; Piazza Kennedy; ⏰8am-8pm Jun-Sep, 8am-1.30pm Mon-Fri & 4-7pm Tue-Thu Oct-May)

PADRE PIO: SAINT OF THE GARGANO

Pilgrims flock to San Giovanni Rotondo, home to Padre Pio, a humble and pious Capuchin priest 'blessed' with the stigmata and a legendary ability to heal the sick. Pio (1887–1968) was canonised in 2002 and immortalised in the vast numbers of prefabricated statues to be found throughout the Gargano. There's even a statue of Pio beneath the waters off the Isole Tremiti.

The ailing Capuchin priest arrived in San Giovanni Rotondo, then a tiny isolated medieval village, in 1916. As Pio's fame grew, the town too underwent a miraculous transformation. These days, it's a mass of functional hotels and restaurants catering to eight million pilgrims a year. It's all overlooked by the palatial Home for the Relief of Suffering, one of Italy's premier hospitals (established by Pio in 1947).

The Convent of the Minor Capuchin Friars (☑0882 41 71; www.conventopadrepio. com; Piazza Santa Maria delle Grazie) includes Padre Pio's cell (⏱7am-7pm summer, 7.30am-6.30pm winter), a simple room containing mementos such as his blood-stained socks. The old church, where he used to say Mass, dates from the 16th century. The spectacular new church, designed by Genovese Renzo Piano (who also designed Paris' Pompidou Centre), resembles a huge futuristic seashell, with an interior of bony vaulting. Padre Pio's body now lies in the geometric perfection of the semicircular crypt.

SITA buses run daily to San Giovanni Rotondo from Monte Sant'Angelo (€1.90, 50 minutes) and Vieste (€5.80, 2½ hours).

ⓘ Getting There & Around

Boat

Vieste's port is to the north, about a five-minute walk from the tourist office. In summer, several companies, including **Navigazione Libera del Golfo** (☑0884 70 74 89; www.navlib.it), head to the Isole Tremiti. Tickets can be bought portside and there are several daily boats (€16.50 to €20, 1½ hours).

Several companies also offer tours of the caves which pock the Gargano coast – a three-hour tour costs around €13.

Bus

From Piazzale Manzoni, where intercity buses terminate, a 10-minute walk east along Viale XXIV Maggio, which becomes Corso Fazzini, brings you into the old town and the Marina Piccola's attractive promenade. In summer, buses terminate at Via Verdi.

SITA (☑0881 35 20 11; www.sitabus.it) buses run between Vieste and Foggia (€6.50, 2¾ hours, four daily) via Manfredonia. There are also services to Monte Sant'Angelo (€4.90) via Manfredonia but **Ferrovie del Gargano** (☑0881 58 72 11; www.ferroviedelgargano.com) buses have a direct daily service to Monte Sant'Angelo (€5.80, two hours), and frequent services to Peschici (€1.60, 35 minutes).

From May to September, **Pugliairbus** (☑080 580 03 58; http://pugliairbus.aeroportidipuglia. it) runs a service to the Gargano, including Vieste, from Bari airport (€20, 3½ hours, four daily).

MONTE SANT'ANGELO
POP 13,250 / ELEV 796M

One of Europe's most important pilgrimage sites, this isolated mountaintop has an extraordinary atmosphere. Pilgrims have been coming here for centuries – and so have the hustlers, pushing everything from religious kitsch to parking spaces.

The object of devotion is the Santuario di San Michele. Here, in AD 490, St Michael the Archangel is said to have appeared in a grotto to the Bishop of Siponto. He left behind his scarlet cloak and instructions not to consecrate the site as he had already done so.

During the Middle Ages, the sanctuary marked the end of the Route of the Angel, which began in Mont St-Michel (in Normandy) and passed through Rome. In 999 the Holy Roman Emperor Otto III made a pilgrimage to the sanctuary to pray that prophecies about the end of the world in the year 1000 would not be fulfilled. His prayers were answered, the world staggered on and the sanctuary's fame grew.

⊙ Sights

The town's serpentine alleys and jumbled houses are perfect for a little aimless ambling. Look out for the different shaped *cappelletti* (chimney stacks) on top of the neat whitewashed houses.

FREE Santuario di
San Michele
GROTTO
(Via Reale Basilica; ◎7.30am-7.30pm Jul-Sep, 7.30am-12.30pm & 2.30-7pm Apr-Jun & Oct, to 5pm Nov-Mar) Look for the 17th-century pilgrims' graffiti as you descend the steps. St Michael is said to have left a footprint in stone inside the grotto, so it became customary for pilgrims to carve outlines of their feet and hands. Etched Byzantine bronze and silver doors, cast in Constantinople in 1076, open into the grotto itself. Inside, a 16th-century statue of the archangel covers the site of St Michael's footprint.

Tomba di Rotari
HISTORICAL SITE
(admission €0.60; ◎10am-1pm & 3-7pm Apr-Oct) A short flight of stairs opposite the sanctuary leads not to a tomb, but to a 12th-century baptistry with a deep sunken basin for total immersion. You enter the baptistry through the facade of the Chiesa di San Pietro with its intricate rose window squirming with serpents – all that remains of the church, destroyed in a 19th-century earthquake. The Romanesque portal of the adjacent 11th-century Chiesa di Santa Maria Maggiore has some fine bas-reliefs.

Castle
HISTORICAL SITE
(Largo Roberto Giuscardo 2; admission €2; ◎9.30am-1pm & 2.30-7pm) At the highest point is this rugged bijou, a Norman castle with Swabian and Aragonese additions as well as panoramic views.

🛏 Sleeping & Eating
Hotel Michael
HOTEL €
(☑0884 56 55 19; www.hotelmichael.com; Via Basilica 86; s €50-60, d €70-80; 🐝) A small hotel with shuttered windows on the main street, across from the sanctuary, this traditional place has spacious rooms with extremely pink bedspreads. Ask for a room with a view.

Casa li Jalantuúmene
TRATTORIA €€
(☑0884 56 54 84; www.li-jalantuumene.it; Piazza de Galganis 5; meals €40; ◎lunch Wed-Mon Feb-Dec) This renowned restaurant has an entertaining and eccentric chef, Gegè Mangano, and serves excellent fare. It's intimate, there's a select wine list and, in summer, tables spill into the piazza. Accommodation (d €80-110), decorated in traditional Pugliese-style, should be available by 2012.

❶ Getting There & Away
SITA (☑0881 35 20 11; www.sitabus.it, in Italian) buses run from Foggia (€4.50, 1¾ hours, four daily) and Vieste via Manfredonia; **Ferrovie del Gargano** has a direct service from Vieste (€5.80, two hours, five daily). Buy your tickets from Bar Esperia next to the sanctuary.

PESCHICI
POP 4400
Perched above a turquoise sea and tempting beach, Peschici clings to the hilly, wooded coastline. It's a pretty resort area with a tight-knit old walled town of Arabesque whitewashed houses. The small town gets crammed in summer, so book in advance. Boats zip across to the Isole Tremiti in high season.

🛏 Sleeping & Eating
Locanda al Castello
B&B €
(☑0884 96 40 38; Via Castello 29; s €35-70, d €70-100; 🅿🌂🐝) Staying here is like entering a large, welcoming family home. It's by the cliffs with fantastic views. Enjoy hearty home cooking in the restaurant (meals €18).

Baia San Nicola
CAMPGROUND €
(☑0884 96 42 31; www.baiasannicola.it; camping €21.50-36.50, 2-person bungalow per week €320-360; ◎mid-May–mid-Oct) The best campground in the area, 2km south of Peschici towards Vieste, Baia San Nicola is on a pine-shaded beach, offering camping, bungalows, apartments and myriad amenities.

Porto di Basso
SEAFOOD €€
(☑0884 91 53 64; www.portodibasso.it; Via Colombo 38; meals €30-40; ◎Fri-Wed) Superb views of the ocean drop away from the floor-length windows beside the intimate alcove tables in this elegant clifftop restaurant. The menu of fresh local seafood changes daily. Close to the restaurant, two stylish suites with fantastic sea views were under construction at time of research. When ready they should be the pick of Peschici's accommodation choices.

Il Trabucco da Mimi
SEAFOOD €€
(0884 96 25 56; Localita Punta San Nicola; meals €30-40; ◎lunch & dinner Easter-Oct) For the ultimate in fresh fish you can't beat eating in a *trabucco*, the traditional wooden fishing platforms lining the coast. Watch the process in operation and dine on the catch. The decor is simple and rustic and you'll pay for the experience – but it's worth it.

ℹ Information

Tourist office (☎0884 91 53 62; Via Magenta 3; ⊘8am-2pm & 5-9pm Mon-Fri summer, 8am-2pm Mon-Fri & 9am-noon & 4-7pm Sat in winter).

ℹ Getting There & Away

The bus terminal is beside the sportsground, uphill from the main street, Corso Garibaldi.

Ferrovie del Gargano (☎0881 58 72 11; www.ferroviedelgargano.com, in Italian) buses run frequent daily services between Peschici and Vieste (€1.60, 35 minutes).

From April to September, ferry companies including **MS&G Societá di Navigazione** (☎0884 96 27 32; www.msgnavigazioni.it; Corso Umberto I 20) and **Navigare SRL** (☎0884 96 42 34; Corso Garibaldi 30) serve the Isole Tremiti (adult €28 to €32, child €16 to €20, one to 1½ hours).

FORESTA UMBRA

The 'Forest of Shadows' is the Gargano's enchanted interior – thickets of tall, epic trees interspersed with picnic spots bathed in dappled light. It's the last remnant of Puglia's ancient forests: Aleppo pines, oaks, yews and beech trees shade the mountainous terrain. More than 65 different types of orchid have been discovered here; the wildlife includes roe deer, wild boar, foxes, badgers and the increasingly rare wild cat. Walkers and mountain bikers will find plenty of well-marked trails within the forest's 5790 sq km.

The small visitors centre in the middle of the forest houses a **museum and nature centre** (www.ecogargano.it; €1.20; ⊘9am-7pm mid-Apr–mid-Oct) with fossils, photographs and stuffed animals and birds. Half-day guided hikes (per person €10), bike hire (per hour/day €5/25), and walking maps (€2.50) are available.

Specialist tour operators organise hiking, biking and 4WD excursions in the park. These include **Agenzia Sol** (☎0884 70 15 58; www.solvieste.it; Via Trepiccioni 5) and **Explora Gargano** (☎0884 70 22 37; www.exploragargano.it) in Vieste, and **Soc Cooperative Ecogargano** (☎0884 56 54 44) in Monte Sant'Angelo.

La Chiusa delle More (☎330 54 37 66; www.lachiusadellemore.it; Vallo dello Schiaffo; B&B per person €80-100; ⊘May-Sep; 🅿❄🅿🛜) offers an escape from the cramped coast. An attractive stone-built *agriturismo* (farmstay) only 1.5km from Peschici, it's set in a huge olive grove. You can dine on homegrown produce, borrow mountain bikes and enjoy panoramic views from your poolside lounger. Note there is a three-night minimum stay.

Isole Tremiti

POP 500

This beautiful archipelago of three islands, 36km offshore, is a picturesque sight of raggedy cliffs, sandy coves and thick pine woods, surrounded by the glittering dark-blue sea.

Unfortunately the islands are no secret, and in July and August some 100,000 holidaymakers descend on the archipelago. At this time it's noisy, loud and hot. If you want to savour the islands' tranquillity visit

---

CAMPING IN STYLE

If your experience of camping is the Boy Scout version of flapping tents, freezing nights and eating cold baked beans out of a tin, you will be delighted at the five-star quality of the typical campsites in this southern region of Italy. They are also prolific, particularly in and around the national parks. In the Gargano region alone there are an astonishing 100 campsites, compared to the relatively modest number of *pensioni* and hotels. If you don't fancy sleeping under canvas (or need a plug for those heated rollers) then consider a bungalow rental.

Virtually all these camping *villaggios* (villages) include well-furnished and equipped bungalows. This means you can really economise on eating out, as well as having the advantages of the campsite facilities, which often include tennis courts, a swimming pool, a children's playground and small supermarket. Bungalows (normally only available for week-long rentals) start from around €200/500 (low/high season) for a two-person bungalow or mobile-home rental. Traditional under-canvas campers can expect to pay a daily rate of approximately (low/high season) €15/25, which includes camping for two people, tent and car parking space.

Check the following websites for more information and camping listings: www.camping.it; www.camping-italy.net and www.caravanandcampsites.eu.

during the shoulder season. In the low season most tourist facilities close down and the few permanent residents resume their quiet and isolated lives.

The islands' main facilities are on San Domino, the largest and lushest island, which was formerly used to grow crops. It's ringed by alternating sandy beaches and limestone cliffs, while the inland is covered in thick maquis flecked with rosemary and foxglove. The centre harbours a nondescript small town with several hotels.

Easily defended, the small San Nicola island is the traditional administrative centre – a castle-like cluster of medieval buildings rises up from the rocks. The third island, Capraia, is uninhabited.

Most boats arrive at San Domino. Small boats regularly make the brief crossing to San Nicola (€6 return) in high season – from October to March a single boat makes the trip after meeting the boat from the mainland.

⊙ Sights & Activities

Head to **San Domino** for walks, grottoes and coves. It has a pristine, marvellous coastline and the islands' only sandy beach, **Cala delle Arene**. Alongside the beach is the small cove **Grotta dell'Arene**, with calm clear waters for swimming. You can also take a boat trip (€12 to €15 from the port) around the island to explore the grottoes: the largest, **Grotta del Bue Marino**, is 70m long. A tour around all three islands costs €15 to €17. Diving in the translucent sea is another option with **Tremiti Diving Center** (☎337 64 89 17; www.tremitidivingcenter.com; Via Federico 2, San Domino).

There's an undemanding, but enchanting, walking track around the island, starting at the far end of the village. Alternatively, you could hire wheels from **Jimmy Bike** (☎338 897 09 09; www.jimmybike.com; bicycle/scooter per day €20/50) at Piazzetta San Domino.

Medieval buildings thrust out of **San Nicola's** rocky shores, the same pale-sand colour as the barren cliffs. In 1010, Benedictine monks founded the **Abbazia e Chiesa di Santa Maria** here; for the next 700 years the islands were ruled by a series of abbots who accumulated great wealth. Although the church retains a weather-worn Renaissance portal and a fine 11th-century floor mosaic, its other treasures have been stolen or destroyed throughout its troubled history. The only exceptions are a painted wooden Byzantine crucifix brought to the island

in AD 747 and a black Madonna, probably transported here from Constantinople in the Middle Ages.

The third of the Isole Tremiti, **Capraia**, (named after the wild caper plant) is uninhabited. Birdlife is plentiful, with impressive flocks of seagulls. There's no organised transport, but trips can be negotiated with local fishermen.

🛏 Sleeping & Eating

In summer you'll need to book well ahead and many hotels insist on full board. Camping is forbidden.

La Casa di Gino   B&B €€
(☎0882 46 34 10; www.hotel-gabbiano.com; San Nicola; r €100-180; ❄) A tranquil accommodation choice on San Nicola, away from the frenzy of San Domino, this newly opened B&B run by the Hotel Gabbiano has stylish white-on-white rooms.

Hotel Gabbiano   HOTEL €€
(☎0882 46 34 10; www.hotel-gabbiano.com; Piazza Belvedere, San Domino; s €45-105, d €90-210, incl breakfast; ❄🌐) An established icon on the island and run for more than 30 years by a Neapolitan family, this smart hotel has pastel-coloured rooms with balconies overlooking San Nicola and the sea. It also has a seafood restaurant.

Architiello   SEAFOOD €€
(☎0882 46 30 54; San Nicola; meals €25; ⊙Apr-Oct) A class act with a seaview terrace, this specialises in – what else? – fresh fish.

❶ Getting There & Away

Boats for the Isole Tremiti depart from several points on the Italian mainland: Manfredonia, Vieste and Peschici in summer, and Termoli in nearby Molise year-round (see p617).

Valle d'Itria

Between the Ionian and Adriatic coasts rises the great limestone plateau of the Murgia (473m). It has a strange karst geology; the landscape is riddled with holes and ravines through which small streams and rivers gurgle, creating what is, in effect, a giant sponge. At the heart of the Murgia lies the idyllic Valle d'Itria. Here you will begin to spot curious circular stone-built houses dotting the countryside, their roofs tapering up to a stubby and endearing point. These are *trulli,* Puglia's unique rural architecture.

It's unclear why the architecture developed in this way; one popular story says that it was so the dry-stone constructions could be quickly dismantled, to avoid payment of building taxes.

The rolling green valley is criss-crossed by dry-stone walls, vineyards, almond and olive groves and winding country lanes. This is the part of Puglia most visited by foreign tourists and is the best served for hotels and luxury *masserias* or manor farms. Around here are also many of Puglia's self-catering villas; to find them, try websites such as www.tuscanynow.com, www.ownersdirect.co.uk, www.holidayhomesinitaly.co.uk and www.trulliland.com.

GROTTE DI CASTELLANA

Don't miss these spectacular limestone caves (☎800 23 19 76, 080 499 82 11; www.grottedicastellana.it; Piazzale Anelli; ☉9.30am-7pm Apr-Oct, 9.30am-12.30pm Nov-Mar), 40km southeast of Bari and Italy's longest natural subterranean network. The interlinked galleries, first discovered in 1938, contain an incredible range of underground landscapes, with extraordinary stalactite and stalagmite formations – look out for the jellyfish, the bacon and the stocking. The highlight is the Grotta Bianca (White Grotto), an eerie white alabaster cavern hung with stiletto-thin stalactites.

There are two tours in English: a 1km, 50-minute tour that doesn't include the Grotta Bianca (€10, on the half-hour); and a 3km, two-hour tour (€15, on the hour) that does include it. The temperature inside the cave averages 18°C so take a light jacket. Visit, too, the Museo Speleologico Franco Anelli (☎080 499 82 30; admission free; ☉9.30am-1pm & 3.30-6.30pm mid-Mar–Oct, 10am-1pm Nov–mid-Mar) or the Osservatorio Astronomico Sirio (☎080 499 82 11; admission €3), with its telescope and solar filters allowing for maximum solar-system visibility. Guided visits only with advance notification.

The grotto can be reached by rail from Bari on the FSE Bari-Taranto train line but not all trains stop at Grotte di Castellana. However, all services stop at Castellana Grotte (€2.90, 50 minutes, roughly hourly), 2km before the grotto, from where you can catch a local bus (€1) from the station to the caves.

ALBEROBELLO
POP 11,000

Unesco World Heritage Site Alberobello resembles a mini urban sprawl – for gnomes.

The Zona dei Trulli on the western hill of town is a dense mass of 1500 beehive-shaped houses, white-tipped as if dusted by snow. These dry-stone buildings are made from local limestone; none are older than the 14th century. Inhabitants do not wear pointy hats, but they do sell anything a visitor might want, from miniature *trulli* to woollen shawls.

The town is named after the primitive oak forest *Arboris Belli* (beautiful trees) that once covered this area. It's an amazing area, but is also something of a tourist trap – from May to October busloads of tourists pile into *trullo* homes, drink in *trullo* bars and shop in *trullo* shops.

If you park in Lago Martellotta, follow the steps up to the Piazza del Popolo where Belvedere Trulli offers fabulous views over the whole higgledy-piggledy picture.

◉ Sights
Alberobello spreads across two hills. The new town is perched on the eastern hilltop; the Zona dei Trulli lies on the western hill and consists of two adjacent neighbourhoods, the Rione Monti and the Rione Aia Piccola.

Sightseeing in Alberobello mainly consists of wandering around admiring its eccentricity. Within the old town quarter of Rione Monti over 1000 *trulli* cascade down the hillside, most of which are now souvenir shops. To its east, on the other side of Via Indipendenza, is Rione Aia Piccola. This neighbourhood is much less commercialised, with 400 *trulli*, many still used as family dwellings. You can climb up for a rooftop view at many shops, although most do have a strategically located basket for a donation.

In the modern part of town, the 18th-century Trullo Sovrano (☎080 432 60 30; www.trullosovrano.it; Piazza Sacramento; admission €1.50; ☉10am-6pm) is the only two-floor *trullo*, built by a wealthy priest's family. It's a small museum giving something of the atmosphere of *trullo* life, with sweet, rounded rooms which include a re-created bakery, bedroom and kitchen. The souvenir shop here has a wealth of literature on the town and surrounding area.

🛏 Sleeping
It's a unique experience to stay in your own *trullo*, though some people might find Alberobello too touristy to use as a base.

Trullidea
APARTMENT €€

(📞080 432 38 60; www.trullidea.it; Via Monte San Gabriele 1; 2-person trullo €63-149) A series of 15 renovated *trulli* in Alberobello's Trulli Zone, these are quaint, cosy and atmospheric. They're available on a self-catering, B&B, or half- or full-board basis.

Camping dei Trulli
CAMPGROUND €

(📞080 432 36 99; www.campingdeitrulli.com; Via Castellana Grotte, Km 1.5; camping 2 people, car & tent €26.50, bungalows per person €22-35, trulli €30-40; P@🏊) This campsite is 1.5km out of town and has some nice tent sites. It has a restaurant, market, two swimming pools, tennis courts and bicycle hire and you can also rent *trulli* off the grounds.

✖ Eating

Trattoria Amatulli
TRATTORIA €

(📞080 432 29 79; Via Garibaldi 13; meals €16; ⏰Tue-Sun) Excellent trattoria with a cheerily cluttered interior papered with photos of smiley diners, plus superb down-to-earth dishes like *orecchiette scure con cacioricotta pomodoro e rucola* ('little ears' pasta with cheese, tomato and rucola). Wash it down with the surprisingly drinkable house wine, costing the lordly sum of €4 a litre.

La Cantina
TRADITIONAL ITALIAN €

(📞080 432 34 73; www.ilristorantelacantina.it; cnr Corso Vittorio Emanuele & Vico Lippolis; meals €25; ⏰Wed-Mon) Although tourists have discovered this place, it has maintained the high standards established back in 1958. There are just seven tables and one frenetic waiter serving delicious meals made with fresh seasonal produce.

Il Poeta Contadino
TRADITIONAL ITALIAN €€€

(📞080 432 19 17; www.ilpoetacontadino.it; Via Indipendenza 21; meals €65; ⏰Tue-Sun Feb-Dec) The dining room here has a medieval banqueting feel with its sumptuous decor and chandeliers. Dine on a poetic menu which includes the signature dish, fava bean purée with *cavatelli* and seafood.

ⓘ Information

The **tourist office** (📞080 432 51 71; Via Garibaldi; ⏰8am-1pm Mon-Fri, plus 3-6pm Tue & Thu) is just off the main square. In the Zona dei Trulli is another **tourist information office** (📞080 432 28 22; www.prolocoalberobello.it; Monte Nero 1; ⏰9am-7.30pm).

ⓘ Getting There & Away

Alberobello is easily accessible from Bari (€4.10, 1½ hours, hourly) on the FSE Bari-Taranto train

line. From the station, walk straight ahead along Via Mazzini, which becomes Via Garibaldi, to reach Piazza del Popolo.

LOCOROTONDO
POP 14,200

Locorotondo has an extraordinarily beautiful and whisper-quiet *centro storico*, where everything is shimmering white aside from the blood-red geraniums that tumble from the window boxes. Situated on a hilltop on the Murge Plateau, it's a *borghi più belli d'Italia* (www.borghitalia.it) – that is, it's rated as one of the most beautiful towns in Italy. The streets are paved with smooth ivory-coloured stones, with the church of Santa Maria della Graecia as their sunbaked centrepiece.

From Villa Comunale, a public garden, you can enjoy panoramic views of the surrounding valley. You enter the historic quarter directly across from here.

Not only is this deepest *trulli* country, but it's also the liquid heart of the Puglian wine region. Sample some of the local spumante at Cantina del Locorotondo (📞080 431 16 44; www.locorotondodoc.com; Via Madonna della Catena 99; ⏰9am-1pm & 3-7pm).

🛏 Sleeping

TOP CHOICE Sotto le Cummerse
APARTMENT €€

(📞080 431 32 98; www.sottolecummerse.it; Via Vittorio Veneto 138; apt €82-230 incl breakfast; ❄) As an *albergo diffuso* (diffused hotel), you stay in tastefully furnished apartments scattered throughout the *centro storico*. The apartments are traditional buildings that have been beautifully restored and furnished. Excellent value and a great base for exploring the region.

Truddhi
COTTAGE €€

(📞080 443 13 26; www.trulliresidence.it; C da Trito 292; d €65-80, apt €100-150, per week €450-741; P❄) This charming cluster of 10 self-catering *trulli* in the hamlet of Trito near Locorotondo is surrounded by olive groves and vineyards. It's a tranquil place and you can take cooking courses (per day €80) with Mino, a lecturer in gastronomy.

✖ Eating

TOP CHOICE Quanto Basta
PIZZERIA €

(📞080 431 28 55; Via Morelli 12; pizza €6-7; ⏰dinner Tue-Sun) With its wooden tables, soft lighting and stone floors this pizzeria is cosy and welcoming. The pizzas are delicious and the beer list extensive.

La Taverna del Duca TRATTORIA €€

(☑080 431 30 07; Via Papadotero 3; meals €35; ⊙lunch & dinner, closed Sun night in winter), In a narrow side street next to an ancient tunnel, this well-regarded trattoria serves local classics such as *orecchiette* with various vegetable sidekicks.

ℹ Information

Tourist office (☑080 431 30 99; www.proloco locorotondo.it; Piazza Vittorio Emanuele 27; ⊙10am-1pm & 3-6pm Mon-Fri, 10am-1pm Sat)

ℹ Getting There & Away

Locorotondo is easily accessible via frequent trains from Bari (€4.50, 1½ to two hours) on the FSE Bari-Taranto train line.

CISTERNINO
POP 12,000

An appealing, whitewashed hilltop town, slow-paced Cisternino has a charming *centro storico* beyond its bland modern outskirts. Beside its 13th-century **Chiesa Matrice** and **Torre Civica** there's a pretty communal garden with rural views. If you take Via Basilioni next to the tower you can amble along an elegant route right to the central piazza, Vittorio Emanuele.

Just outside the historic centre, the **tourist office** (☑080 444 66 61; www.proloccis ternino.it; Via San Quirico 18 ⊙10.15am-12.15pm & 4.30-7.30pm Mon-Sat) can advise on B&Bs in the historic centre, but it's not always open.

Cisternino has a grand tradition of *fornello pronto* (ready-to-go roast or grilled meat) and in numerous butchers' shops and trattorias you can select a cut of meat, which is then promptly cooked on the spot. Try it under rustic whitewashed arches at **Trattoria La Botte** (☑080 444 78 50; Via Santa Lucia 47; meals €20; ⊙lunch & dinner, closed Thu in winter), which also serves up Pugliese favourites such as *fave e verdura* (beans and greens).

Cisternino is accessible by regular trains from Bari (€4.50, 45 minutes).

MARTINA FRANCA
POP 49,800

The old quarter of this town is a picturesque scene of winding alleys, blinding white houses and blood-red geraniums. There are graceful baroque and rococo buildings here too, plus airy piazzas and curlicue iron-work balconies that almost touch above the narrow streets. This town is the highest in the Murgia, and was founded in the 10th century by refugees fleeing the Arab invasion of Taranto. It only started to flourish in the 14th century when Philip of Anjou granted tax exemptions (*franchigie,* hence Franca); the town became so wealthy that a castle and defensive walls complete with 24 solid bastions were built.

◉ Sights & Activities

The beauty of Martina Franca is to wander around the *centro storico*'s narrow lanes and alleyways.

Passing under the baroque **Arco di Sant'Antonio** at the western end of pedestrianised Piazza XX Settembre, you emerge into Piazza Roma, dominated by the imposing, elegant 17th-century **Palazzo Ducale**, built over an ancient castle and now used as municipal offices.

From Piazza Roma, follow the fine Corso Vittorio Emanuele, with baroque town houses, to reach Piazza Plebiscito, the centre's baroque heart. The piazza is overlooked by the 18th-century **Basilica di San Martino**, its centrepiece city patron, St Martin, swinging a sword and sharing his cloak with a beggar.

Walkers can ask for the *Carta dei Sentieri del Bosco delle Pianelle* (free) from the tourist office, which maps out 10 walks in the nearby **Bosco delle Pianelle** (around 10km west of town). This lush woodland is part of the larger 1206-hectare **Riserva Naturale Regionale Orientata** – populated with lofty trees, wild orchids and a rich and varied bird life with kestrels, owls, buzzards, hoopoe and sparrow hawks.

✳ Festivals & Events

Festival della Valle d'Itria is an annual music festival (late July to early August) featuring international performances of opera, classical and jazz. For information, contact the **Centro Artistico Musicale Paolo Grassi** (☑080 480 51 00; www.festivaldellavalle ditria.it; ⊙10am-1pm Mon-Fri) in the Palazzo Ducale.

🛏 Sleeping

Villaggio In APARTMENT €€

(☑080 480 59 11; www.villaggioin.it; Via Arco Grassi 8; apt per night €75-170, per week €335-1030) These charming arched apartments are located in original *centro storico* homes. The rooms are large, painted in pastel colours and decorated with antiques and country frills. A variety of apartments are on offer, sleeping from two to six people.

B&B San Martino B&B €

(☑080 48 56 01; http://xoomer.virgilio.it/bed-and -breakfast-sanmartino; Via Abate Fighera 32; d €40-120; ❄) A stylish B&B in an historic palace

Masserie (or *masserias*) are unique to southern Italy. Modelled on the classical Roman villa, these fortified farmhouses – equipped with oil mills, cellars, chapels, storehouses and accommodation for workers and livestock – were built to function as self-sufficient communities. These days, they still produce the bulk of Italy's olive oil, but many have been converted into luxurious hotels, *agriturismi,* holiday apartments or restaurants. Staying in a *masseria* is a unique experience, especially when you can dine on local home-grown produce.

The following *masserias* are recommended:

Il Frantoio (☎0831 33 02 76; www.trecolline.it; SS16, Km 874; d €139-259, apt €319-350; P@) Stay in a charming, whitewashed farmhouse, where the owners still live and work, producing high-quality organic olive oil. (Or else book yourself in for one of the marathon eight-course lunches; the food is superb.) Armando takes guests for a tour of the farm each evening in his 1949 Fiat. Il Frantoio lies 5km outside Ostuni along the SS16 in the direction of Fasano. You'll see the sign on your left-hand side when you reach the Km 874 sign.

Masseria Torre Coccaro (☎080 482 93 10; www.masseriatorrecoccaro.com; Contrada Coccaro 8, Savelletri di Fasano; d €278-1339; ✳@🛜🏊) For pure luxury, stay in this super-chic yet countrified *masseria*. There's a glorious spa set in a cave, a beach-style swimming pool, cooking courses on offer and a restaurant (meals €90) dishing up home-grown produce.

Masseria Maizza (www.masseriatorremaizza.com; €278-1493; ✳@🛜🏊) Next door to Masseria Torre Coccaro and run by the same people, you know luxury is assured. The two *masserias* share a balmy beach club (about 4km away) and a neighbouring golf course.

Borgo San Marco (☎080 439 57 57; www.borgosanmarco.it; Contrada Sant'Angelo 33; s €130-140, d €180-230; P✳🛜🏊) Once a *borgo* (small village), this *masseria* has 16 rooms, a Jacuzzi in the orchard and is traditional with a bohemian edge. Nearby are some frescoed rock churches. It's 8km from Ostuni; to get here take the SS379 in the direction of Bari, exiting at the sign that says SC San Marco–Zona Industriale Sud Fasano, then follow the signs. Note that there's a one-week minimum stay in August.

with rooms overlooking gracious Piazza XX Settembre. The apartments have exposed stone walls, shiny parquet floors, wrought-iron beds and small kitchenettes.

✗ Eating

Il Ritrovo degli Amici TRADITIONAL ITALIAN €€
(☎080 483 92 49; www.ilritrovodegliamici.it; Corso Messapia 8; meals €35; ⏲lunch & dinner Tue-Sat, lunch Sun Mar-Jan) This excellent restaurant, with stone walls and vaulting, has a convivial atmosphere oiled by the region's spumante. Dishes are traditional, with salamis and sausages the specialities.

Ciacco TRADITIONAL ITALIAN €€
(☎080 480 04 72; Via Conte Ugolino; meals €30; ⏲lunch & dinner Tue-Sun) Dive into the historic centre to find Ciacco, a traditional restaurant with white-clad tables and a cosy fireplace, serving up Puglian cuisine in a modern key. It's tucked down a narrow pedestrian lane a couple of streets in from the Chiesa del Carmine.

La Piazzetta Garibaldi OSTERIA €€
(☎080 430 49 00; Piazza Garibaldi; meals €20-30; ⏲lunch & dinner Thu-Tue) A highly recommended *osteria* in the *centro storico*. Delicious aromas entice you into the cavernous interior and the menu doesn't disappoint. Worthy of a long lunch.

❶ Information

The **tourist office** (☎080 480 57 02; Piazza Roma 37; ⏲9am-1pm Mon-Sat, 4.30-7pm Tue & Thu, 9am-12.30pm Sat) is within Palazzo Ducale (part of the Bibliotece Comunal).

❶ Getting There & Around

The FSE train station is downhill from the historic centre. Go right along Viale della Stazione, continuing along Via Alessandro Fighera to Corso Italia; continue to the left along Corso Italia to Piazza XX Settembre.

FSE (☎080 546 21 11) trains run to/from the following destinations:

Bari €5.20, two hours, hourly
Lecce €7.10, two hours, five daily

OUR TOP FIVE CENTRO STORICOS (HISTORIC CENTRES) IN PUGLIA

» **Locorotondo** (p701)

» **Ostuni**

» **Vieste** (p694)

» **Martina Franca** (p702)

» **Lecce** (p705)

Taranto €2.40, 50 minutes, frequent

FSE buses run to Alberobello (€1.50, 30 minutes, five daily, Monday to Saturday).

OSTUNI
POP 32,500

Ostuni shines like a pearly white tiara, extending across three hills with the magnificent gem of a cathedral as its sparkling centrepiece. It's the end of the *trulli* region and the beginning of the hot, dry Salento. Chic, with some excellent restaurants, stylish bars and swish yet intimate places to stay, it's packed in summer.

Sights

Ostuni is surrounded by olive groves, so this is the place to buy some of the region's DOC 'Collina di Brindisi' olive oil – either delicate, medium or strong – direct from producers.

Cathedral   CATHEDRAL
(Via Cattedrale) Ostuni's dramatic 15th-century cathedral has an unusual Gothic-Romanesque facade with a frilly rose window and an inverted gable.

FREE **Museo di Città**
Preclassiche della Murgia   MUSEUM
(☎0831 33 63 83; Via Cattedrale 15) Located in the Convento delle Monacelle, the museum's most famous exhibit is the 25,000-year-old star of the show: Delia. She was pregnant at the time of her death and her well-preserved skeleton was found in a local cave. Many of the finds here come from the Palaeolithic burial ground, now the **Parco Archeologico e Naturale di Arignano** (☎0831 30 39 73), which can be visited by appointment. The museum was closed for restoration at time of research. Check with the tourist office for the opening hours.

Activities
The surrounding countryside is perfect for cycling. **Ciclovagando** (☎330 98 52 55; www.

ciclovagando.com; Via di Savoia 19, Mesagne; half-day/full-day €30/40) organise guided tours. Each tour covers approximately 20km and departs daily from various towns in the district, including Ostuni and Brindisi. For an extra €15 you can sample typical Apulian foods on the tour.

Festivals & Events
La Cavalcata   RELIGIOUS
Ostuni's annual feast day is held on 26 August, when processions of horsemen dressed in glittering red-and-white uniforms (resembling Indian grooms on their way to be wed) follow the statue of Sant'Oronzo around town.

Sleeping
La Terra   HOTEL €€
(☎0831 33 66 51; www.laterrahotel.it; Via Petrarolo; d €130-170; ⓟ❄️🛜) This former 13th-century palace offers atmospheric and stylish accommodation with original niches, dark-wood beams and furniture, and contrasting light stonework and whitewash. The result is a cool contemporary look. The bar is as cavernous as they come – it's tunnelled out of a cave.

Le Sole Blu   B&B €
(☎0831 30 38 56; www.webalice.it/solebluostuni; Corso Vittorio Emanuele II 16; s €30-40, s €50, d €60-80) Located in the 18th-century (rather than medieval) part of town, Le Sole Blu only has one room available: it's large and has a separate entrance, but the bathroom is tiny. However, the two self-catering apartments (double €60 to €80) nearby are excellent value.

Eating
Osteria Piazzetta Cattedrale   OSTERIA €€
(☎0831 33 50 26; www.piazzettacattedrale.it; Via Arcidiacono Trinchera 7; meals €25-30; ☺Wed-Mon) Just beyond the arch opposite Ostuni's cathedral is this tiny little hostelry serving up magical food in an atmospheric setting. The menu includes plenty of vegetarian options.

Osteria del Tempo Perso   OSTERIA €€
(☎0831 30 33 20; www.osteriadeltempoperso.com; Gaetano Tanzarella Vitale 47; meals €30; ☺Tue-Sun) A sophisticated rustic restaurant in a former bakery, this laid-back place serves great Pugliese food, specialising in roasted meats. To get here, face the cathedral's south wall and turn right through two archways into Largo

Giuseppe Spennati, then follow the signs to the restaurant.

Porta Nova
TRADITIONAL ITALIAN €€

(☎0831 33 89 83; www.ristoranteportanova.com; Via G Petrarolo 38; meals €45) This restaurant has a wonderful location on the old city wall. Revel in the rolling views from the terrace or relax in the elegant interior while you feast on top-notch local cuisine, with fish and seafood the speciality.

❶ Information

Tourist office (☎0831 30 12 68; Corso Mazzini 8; ☯9am-1pm & 5-9pm Mon-Fri, 5.30-8.30pm Sat & Sun) Located off Piazza della Libertà; can organise guided visits of the town in summer and bike rental.

❶ Getting There & Around

STP buses run to Brindisi (€2.90, 50 minutes, six daily) and to Martina Franca (€2, 45 minutes, three daily), leaving from Piazza Italia in the newer part of Ostuni.

Trains run frequently to Brindisi (€4, 25 minutes) and Bari (€9, 50 minutes). A half-hourly local bus covers the 2.5km between the station and town.

Lecce & Salento

The Penisola Salentina, better known simply as Salento, is hot, dry and remote, retaining a flavour of its Greek past. It stretches across Italy's heel from Brindisi to Taranto and down to Santa Maria di Leuca. Here the lush greenery of Valle d'Itria gives way to flat, ochre-coloured fields, hazy with wildflowers in spring, and endless olive groves. Lecce is the cultural heart of the region and a great base from which to savour Salento's endless sunshine, sandy beaches and some of Puglia's (and perhaps, Italy's) finest wines.

LECCE
POP 95,000

Historic Lecce is a beautiful baroque town; a glorious architectural confection of palaces and churches intricately sculpted from the soft local sandstone. It is a city full of surprises: one minute you are perusing sleek designer fashions from Milan, the next you are faced with a church, dizzyingly decorated with asparagus column tops, decorative dodos and cavorting gremlins. Swooning 18th-century traveller Thomas Ashe thought it 'the most beautiful city in Italy', but the less-impressed Marchese Grimaldi said the facade of Santa Croce made him think a lunatic was having a nightmare.

Either way, it's a lively, graceful university town packed with upmarket boutiques, antique shops, restaurants and bars. Both the Adriatic and Ionian Seas are within easy access and it's a great base from which to explore the Salento.

◎ Sights

Lecce has more than 40 churches and at least as many *palazzi*, all built or renovated between the 17th and 18th centuries, giving the city an extraordinary cohesion. Two of the main proponents of *barocco leccese* (Lecce baroque – the craziest, most lavish decoration imaginable) were brothers Antonio and Giuseppe Zimbalo, who both had a hand in the fantastical Basilica di Santa Croce.

TOP CHOICE / Basilica di Santa Croce CHURCH

(☎0832 24 19 57; www.basilicasantacroce.eu; Via Umberto I; ☯9am-noon & 5-8pm) It seems that hallucinating stonemasons have been at work on the basilica. Sheep, dodos, cherubs and beasties writhe across the facade, a swirling magnificent allegorical feast. Throughout the 16th and 17th centuries, a team of artists under Giuseppe Zimbalo laboured to work the building up to this pitch. Look for Zimbalo's profile on the facade.

The interior is more conventionally Renaissance and deserves a look, once you've finished swooning outside. Zimbalo also left his mark in the former Convento dei Celestini, just north of the basilica, which is now the **Palazzo del Governo**, the local government headquarters.

Piazza del Duomo
PIAZZA

Piazza del Duomo is a baroque feast, the city's focal point and a sudden open space amid the surrounding enclosed lanes. During times of invasion the inhabitants of Lecce would barricade themselves in the square, which has conveniently narrow entrances. The 12th-century **cathedral** (☯8.30am-noon & 4-6.30pm) is one of Giuseppe Zimbalo's finest works – he was also responsible for the towering 68m-high bell tower. The cathedral is unusual in that it has two facades, one on the western end and the other, more ornate, facing the piazza. It's framed by the 15th-century **Palazzo Vescovile** (Episcopal Palace) and the 18th-century **Seminario** (☯exhibitions only), designed by Giuseppe Cino.

Lecce

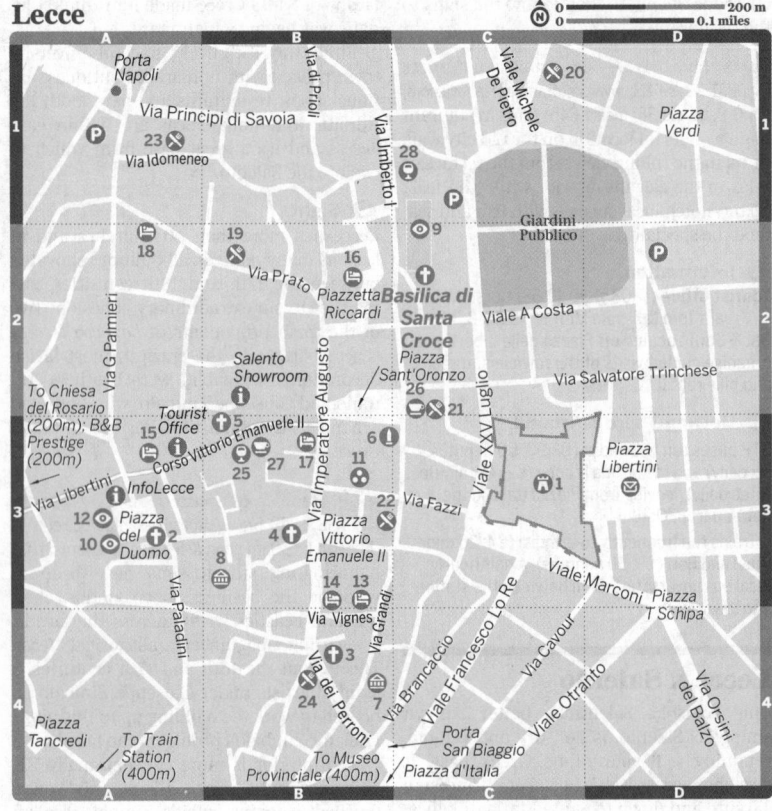

Lecce

Museo Faggiano
MUSEUM

(☑360 72 24 48; www.museofaggiano.it; Via Grandi 56/58; admission €3; ☺9.30am-1pm & 4-8pm) Breaking the floor to replace sewer pipes led the owner of this private home to the chance discovery of an archaeological treasure trove. Layers of history are revealed beneath the floors and in the walls. Look out for what appears to be the Knights Templar symbol in the rooftop tower.

FREE Museo Provinciale
MUSEUM

(☑0832 68 35 03; Via Gallipoli 28; ☺8.30am-7.30pm Mon-Sat, 8.30am-1.30pm Sun) The museum stylishly covers 10,000 years of history, from Palaeolithic and Neolithic bits and bobs to a handsome display of Greek and Roman jewels, weaponry and ornaments. The stars of the show are the Messapians, who were making jaunty jugs and bowls centuries before the Greeks arrived to give them any pottery lessons.

Roman Amphitheatre
HISTORICAL SITE

(Piazza Sant'Oronzo; admission adult/reduced €2/1; ☺10am-noon & 5-7pm May-Sep) Below the ground level of the piazza is this restored 2nd-century-AD amphitheatre, discovered in 1901 by construction workers. It was excavated in the 1930s to reveal a perfect horseshoe with seating for 15,000.

Colonna di Sant'Oronzo
MONUMENT

(Piazza Sant'Oronzo) A statue of Lecce's patron saint perches precariously on a column in the piazza. The column, originally from Brindisi, marked the end of the Via Appia – the Roman road that stretched from Rome to Brindisi.

Museo Teatro Romano
HISTORICAL SITE

(☑0832 27 91 96; Via Ammirati; admission adult/reduced €3/2; ☺9.30am-1.30pm Mon-Sat, 5-7.30pm Mon-Fri) Uncovered in the 1930s, this small Roman theatre has well-preserved russet-coloured Roman mosaics and frescoes.

FREE Castello di Carlo V
CASTLE

(☑0832 24 65 17; admission free; ☺9am-1pm & 5-9pm) This 16th-century castle was built around a 12th-century Norman tower to the orders of Charles V and consists of two concentric trapezoidal structures. It's been used as a prison, a court and military headquarters; now you can wander around the baronial spaces and visit the occasional art exhibition.

OTHER CHURCHES

On Corso Vittorio Emanuele, the interior of 17th-century Chiesa di Sant'Irene contains a magnificent pair of mirror-image baroque altarpieces, facing each other across the transept. Other notable baroque churches include Chiesa di Santa Chiara (Piazza Vittorio Emanuele; ☺9.30-11.30am daily, 4.30-6.30pm Mon-Sat), with every niche a swirl of twisting columns and ornate statuary; the Chiesa di San Matteo (Via dei Perroni 29; ☺7.30-11am & 4-6pm), 200m to its south; and the last work of Giuseppe Zimbalo, Chiesa del Rosario (Via Libertini). Instead of the intended dome roof, it ended up with a quick-fix wooden one following Zimbalo's death before the building was completed. The Chiesa dei SS Nicolò e Cataldo (Via San Nicola; ☺9am-noon Sep-Apr), near Porta Napoli, was built by the Normans in 1180. It got caught up in the city's baroque frenzy and was revamped in 1716 by the prolific Cino, who retained the Romanesque rose window and portal.

🍳 Courses

Awaiting Table
COOKING

(www.awaitingtable.com; day/week-long course €300/1995) Silvestro Silvestori's splendid culinary and wine school provides day or week-long courses with tours, tastings and noteworthy lecturers. Book well in advance as courses fill up rapidly.

🛏 Sleeping

Risorgimento Resort
HOTEL €€

(☑0832 24 63 11; www.risorgimentoresort.it; Via Imperatore Augusto 19; d €145-165, ste €190-290; P❄@🛜) A warm welcome awaits at this stylish five-star hotel in the centre of Lecce. The rooms are spacious and refined with high ceilings, modern furniture and contemporary details reflecting the colours of the Salento. The bathrooms are enormous. There's a restaurant, wine bar and rooftop garden.

Palazzo Rollo
B&B €€

(☑0832 30 71 52; www.palazzorollo.it; Via Vittorio Emanuelell; 14; d €90-120, 4-person studio €100; P❄@) Stay in a 17th-century palace – the family seat for over 200 years. The three grand B&B suites (with kitchenettes) have high curved ceilings and chandeliers. Downstairs, contemporary-chic studios open onto an ivy-hung courtyard. The rooftop garden has wonderful views.

Surprises of the South

In the Mezzogiorno, the sun shines on a magical landscape: dramatic cliffs and sandy beaches fringed with turquoise seas; wild rocky mountains and gentle forested slopes; rolling green fields and flat plains. Sprinkled throughout are elegant *palazzi* (mansions), *masserias* (working farms), ancient cave-dwellings and gnome-like stone huts.

Promontorio del Gargano

1 Along with its charming seaside villages, sandy coves and crystalline blue waters, the Gargano is also home to the Parco Nazionale del Gargano (p694). Perfect for hikers, nature trippers and beach fiends alike.

Valle d'Itria

2 In a landscape of rolling green hills, vineyards, orchards and picture-pretty fields, conical stone huts called *trulli* sprout from the ground en masse in the Disneyesque towns of Alberobello (p700) and Locorotondo (p701).

Salento

3 Here, hot, dry plains covered in wildflowers and olive groves reach towards the gorgeous beaches and waters of the Ionian and Adriatic Seas. It's the unspoilt 'heel', with Lecce (p705) its sophisticated capital.

Sassi of Matera

4 The ancient cave city of Matera has been inhabited since Palaeolithic times. Explore the tangled alleyways, admire frescoes in rock churches, and sleep in millennia-old *sassi* (former cave dwellings) (p721).

Parco Nazionale dell'Aspromonte

5 In this wild park, narrow roads lead to hilltop villages like semi-deserted Pentidàttilo (p737). Waterfalls, wide riverbeds, jagged cliffs and sandstone formations form the backdrop to a landscape made for hiking.

Clockwise from top left
1. Parco Nazionale del Gargano 2. *Trulli*, Puglia 3. Basilica di Santa Croce, Lecce 4. *Sassi*, Matera.

GREG ELMS / LONELY PLANET IMAGES ©

Suite 68
BOUTIQUE HOTEL €

(📞0832 30 35 06; www.kalekora.it; Via Prato; s €60-80, d €80-120; ❄) Strong colours, abstract canvases and vividly patterned rugs in the large, bright rooms give this place a contemporary feel. It's simple and stylish. Bikes available.

B&B Prestige
B&B €

(📞349 775 12 90; www.bbprestige-lecce.it; Giuseppe Libertini 7; s €60-70, d €70-90; 🅿@🛜) On the corner of Via Santa Maria del Paradiso in the historic centre, the rooms in this lovely B&B are light, airy and beautifully finished. The communal sun-trap terrace has views over San Giovanni Battista church. There's also an apartment downstairs.

Patria Palace Hotel
HOTEL €€

(📞0832 24 51 11; www.patriapalacelecce.com; Piazzetta Riccardi 13; s €106-210, d €165-350; 🅿❄@🛜) This sumptuous hotel is traditionally Italian with large mirrors, dark-wood furniture and wistful murals. The location is wonderful, the bar gloriously art deco with a magnificent carved ceiling, and the shady roof terrace has views over the Basilica di Santa Croce.

Casa Elisabetta
B&B €

(📞0832 30 70 52; www.beb-lecce.com; Via Vignes 15; s €30-45, d €50-80; ❄🛜) An elegant mansion that's centred on a graceful courtyard close to Piazza Vittorio Emanuele II, this has a warren of corridors and plain functional rooms.

Centro Storico B&B
B&B €

(📞338 588 12 65; www.bedandbreakfast.lecce.it; Via Vignes 2b; s €35-40, d €70-100; 🅿❄🛜)

Recently refurbished, this B&B has big rooms, double-glazed windows and coffee-and-tea-making facilities. The rooftop terrace has sunloungers and views.

🍴 Eating

TOP CHOICE Cucina Casareccia
TRATTORIA €€

(📞0832 24 51 78; Viale Costadura 19; meals €20-25; ⏱lunch Tue-Sun, dinner Tue-Sat) Ring the bell to gain entry into a place that feels like a private home, with its patterned cement floor tiles, desk piled high with papers, and charming owner Carmela Perrone. In fact, it's known locally as *le Zie* (the aunts). Here you'll taste the true *cucina povera* (cooking of the poor), including horsemeat done in a *salsa piccante* (spicy sauce). Booking is a must.

Trattoria di Nonna Tetti
TRATTORIA €

(📞0832 24 60 36; Piazzetta Regina Maria 28; meals €15-20; ⏱lunch & dinner daily) A warmly inviting restaurant, popular with all ages and budgets, this trattoria serves a wide choice of traditional dishes. Try the most emblematic Pugliese dish here – braised wild chicory with a purée of boiled dried fava beans, along with *contorni* (side dishes) like *patate casarecce* (homemade thinly sliced fries).

Alle due Corti
TRATTORIA €

(📞0832 24 22 23; www.alleduecorti.com; Via Prato 42; meals €22; ⏱lunch & dinner daily) For a taste of sunny Salento, check out this no-frills, fiercely traditional restaurant. The seasonal menu is classic Pugliese, written in a dialect that even some Italians struggle with. Go for the real deal with a dish of *ciceri e tria* (crisply fried pasta with chickpeas).

LECCE IN ...

One Day

Start the day with a cappuccino and *pasticciotto* (custard-filled pastry) at **Caffè Alvino** on Piazza Sant'Oronzo. All that sugar and froth should be good preparation for the fanciful **Basilica di Santa Croce**, worth at least an hour of your time.

To get a sense of Lecce's history visit the fascinating **Museo Faggiano,** then come back to the present with a spot of window-shopping and browsing through the entertaining mix of shops on Corso Vittorio Emanuele II. Be sure to stop for a campari and soda at one of the many bars in town before lunching on typical Pugliese fare at firmly traditional **Alle due Corti**.

Walk off the pasta and beans by heading across town to the excellent **Museo Provinciale**. Or, for more fancy facades, Lecce's baroque feast of *palazzi*-flanked streets (like Via Palmieri), **churches** and the **cathedral** will keep you simpering happily till dinner time. Crown your day with a meal at **Cucina Casareccia**, where you'll feel like one of the family. Stroll back to your hotel via the Basilica, which is spectacularly lit up at night.

Picton
TRADITIONAL ITALIAN €€

(☎0832 33 23 83; www.acena.it/picton; Via Idomeneo 14; meals €35-40; ☺Mon-Sat) This elegant backstreet restaurant is housed in an old *palazzo* with a cool barrel-vaulted interior and a refreshing internal garden. The cuisine is traditional with a twist.

Mamma Lupa
OSTERIA €

(☎340 783 27 65; Via Acaja 12; meals €20-25; ☺lunch Sun-Fri, dinner daily) Looking and tasting suitably rustic, this *osteria* serves proper peasant food – such as roast tomatoes, potatoes and artichokes, or horse meatballs – in snug surroundings with just a few tables surrounded by dark ochre walls.

Gelateria Natale
GELATERIA €

(Via Trinchese 7a) Lecce's best ice-cream parlour also has an array of fabulous confectionery.

🍷 Drinking

Via Imperatore Augusto is full of bars, and on a summer's night it feels like one long party. Wander along to find somewhere to settle.

All'Ombra del Barocco
CAFE, WINE BAR

(www.allombradelbarocco.it; Corte dei Cicala 9; ☺8am-1am) Next door to Il Caffè di Liberrima, this cool restaurant/cafe/wine bar has a range of teas, cocktails and *aperitivi*. It's open for breakfast and also hosts musical events.

Caffè Alvino
CAFE

(Piazza Sant'Oronzo; ☺Wed-Mon) Treat yourself to good coffee and *pasticciotto* at this iconic cafe in Lecce's main square.

Il Caffè di Liberrima
CAFE

(Corte dei Cicala) Tables fill the little square next to the bookshop and *enoteca* (wine bar) on the central pedestrianised strip – an ideal place to watch the world amble past.

Shui 13 Wine Bar
WINE BAR

(Via Umberto I 21; ☺10am-late summer, 10am-3pm & 6pm-midnight winter) A popular and atmospheric wine bar with a range of Pugliese wines.

ℹ Information

The train station is 1km southwest of Lecce's historic centre. The centre's twin main squares are Piazza Sant'Oronzo and Piazza del Duomo, linked by pedestrianised Corso Vittorio Emanuele II.

CTS (☎0832 30 18 62; Via Palmieri 89; ☺9am-1pm daily & 4-7.30pm Sun-Mon) Good for student travel.

Hospital (☎0832 66 11 11; Via San Cesario) About 2km south of the centre on the Gallipoli road.

InfoLecce (☎0832 52 18 77; www.infolecce.it; Piazza Duomo 2; ☺9.30am-1.30pm & 3.30-7.30pm Mon-Sat, from 10am Sun) Independent and helpful tourist information office. Has guided tours and bike rental (per hour/day €3/15).

Police station (☎0832 69 11 11; Viale Otranto 1)

Post office (Piazza Libertini)

Salento Showroom (☎0832 17 90 357; www.salentotime.it; Via Revina Isabella 22; ☺9.30am-1.30pm & 3.30-7.30pm Mon-Sat, from 10am Sun) Independent tourist office which can provide help with accommodation and car hire. Has internet access (per hour €3).

Tourist office (☎0832 24 80 92; www.viaggiareinpuglia.it; Corso Vittorio Emanuele II 24; ☺9am-1pm Mon-Sat, 4-7pm Mon-Thu)

www.thepuglia.com Voted the most popular blog on Puglia in Italy, this informative site run by Fabio Ingrosso has articles on culture, history, food, wine, accommodation and travel in Puglia

❶ Getting There & Away

BUS

STP (☎0832 35 91 42) runs buses to Brindisi (€6, 35 minutes, nine daily) and throughout Puglia from the STP bus station.

FSE (☎0832 66 81 11) runs buses to Gallipoli (€3.50, one hour, four daily), Otranto (€2.60, 1½ hours, two daily) and Brindisi (€3.30, 45 minutes, two daily), leaving from Largo Vittime del Terrorismo.

Pugliairbus (http://pugliairbus.aeroportidipuglia.it) runs to Brindisi airport (€7, 40 minutes, nine daily). **SITA** also has buses to Brindisi airport (€6, 45 minutes, nine daily), leaving from Viale Porte d'Europa.

TRAIN

The main train station runs frequent services to the following destinations:

Bari from €14.50, 1½ to two hours

Bologna from €75, 7½ to 9½ hours

Brindisi from €9.40, 30 minutes

Naples from €62, 5½ hours (transfer in Caserta)

Rome from €63, 5½ to nine hours

FSE trains head to Otranto and Martina Franca.

BRINDISI
POP 89,800

Like all ports, Brindisi has its seamy side, but it's also surprisingly slow-paced and balmy, particularly the palm-lined Corso Garibaldi linking the port to the train station and the promenade stretching along the interesting seafront.

The town was the end of the ancient Roman road Via Appia, down whose weary length trudged legionnaires and pilgrims, crusaders and traders, all heading to Greece and the Near East. These days little has changed except that Brindisi's pilgrims are sun-seekers rather than soul-seekers.

◉ Sights & Activities

TOP CHOICE Museo Archeologico Provinciale Ribezzo   MUSEUM

(☑0831 56 55 08; Piazza del Duomo 8; admission free; ⊙9.30am-1.30pm Tue-Sat, 3.30-6.30pm Tue, Thu & Sat) This superb museum covers several floors with well-documented exhibits (in English) including some 3000 bronze sculptures and fragments in Hellenistic Greek style, terracotta figurines from the 7th century, underwater archeological finds, and Roman statues and heads (not always together).

Chiesa di Santa Maria del Casale   CHURCH

(☑0831 41 85 45; Via Ruggero de Simone; ⊙8am-8pm) Located 4km north of town towards the airport, this church was built by Prince Philip of Taranto around 1300. The church mixes up Puglian Romanesque, Gothic and Byzantine styles, with a Byzantine banquet of interior frescoes. The immense *Last Judgement* on the entrance wall, full of blood and thunder, is the work of Rinaldo di Taranto.

Roman Column   MONUMENT

(Via Colonne) The gleaming white column above a sweeping set of sun-whitened stairs leading to the waterfront promenade marks the imperial Via Appia terminus at Brindisi. Originally there were two, but one was presented to the town of Lecce back in 1666 as thanks to Sant'Oronzo for having relieved Brindisi of the plague.

Cathedral   CATHEDRAL

(Piazza del Duomo; ⊙8am-9pm Mon-Fri & Sun, 8am-noon Sat) This 11th-century cathedral was substantially remodelled about 700 years later. You can see how it may have looked from the nearby Porta dei Cavalieri Templari, a fanciful portico with pointy arches – all that remains of the Knights Templar's main church.

Tempio di San Giovanni al Sepolcro   CHURCH

(Via San Giovanni) The Knights Templar's other church is a square brown bulk of Norman

stone conforming to the circular plan the Templars so loved.

Monument to Italian Sailors   MONUMENT

For a wonderful view of Brindisi's waterfront, take one of the regular boats (return €1.80) on Viale Regina Margherita across the harbour to the monument erected by Mussolini in 1933.

⌂ Sleeping

Hotel Orientale   HOTEL €€

(☑0831 56 84 51; www.hotelorientale.it; Corso Garibaldi 40; s/d €99/130; P❋☏) This sleek, modern hotel overlooks the long palm-lined *corso*. Rooms are pleasant, the location is good and it has a small fitness centre, private car park and (rare) cooked breakfast option.

Grande Albergo Internazionale   HOTEL €€€

(☑0831 52 34 73; www.albergointernazionale.it; Viale Regina Margherita 23; s/d €100/250; P❋☏) Built in 1870 for English merchants en route to Bombay and the Raj, the hotel is proud of its grand past. It has great harbour views, large rooms with grandly draped curtains and an ideal location across the street from the waterfront promenade.

✖ Eating

Trattoria Pantagruele   TRATTORIA €€

(☑0831 56 06 05; Via Salita di Ripalta 1; meals €30; ⊙lunch & dinner Mon-Fri, dinner Sat) Named after French writer François Rabelais' satirical character, this charming trattoria three blocks from the waterfront serves up excellent fish and grilled meats.

Il Giardino   TRADITIONAL ITALIAN €€

(☑0831 56 40 26; Via Tarantini 14-18; meals €30; ⊙lunch & dinner Tue-Sat, lunch Sun) Established more than 40 years ago in a restored 15th-century *palazzo*, sophisticated Il Giardino serves refined seafood and meat dishes in a delightful garden setting.

❶ Information

The new port is east of town, across the Seno di Levante at Costa Morena, in a bleak industrial wilderness.

The old port is about 1km from the train station along Corso Umberto I, which leads into Corso Garibaldi where there are numerous cafes, shops, ferry companies and travel agencies.

Ferries (www.ferries.gr) Details of ferry fares and timetables to Greek destinations.

Hospital (☑0831 53 71 11; SS7 for Mesagne)

Police station (☑0831 54 31 11; Via Perrino 1)

Post office (Piazza Vittoria)

Brindisi

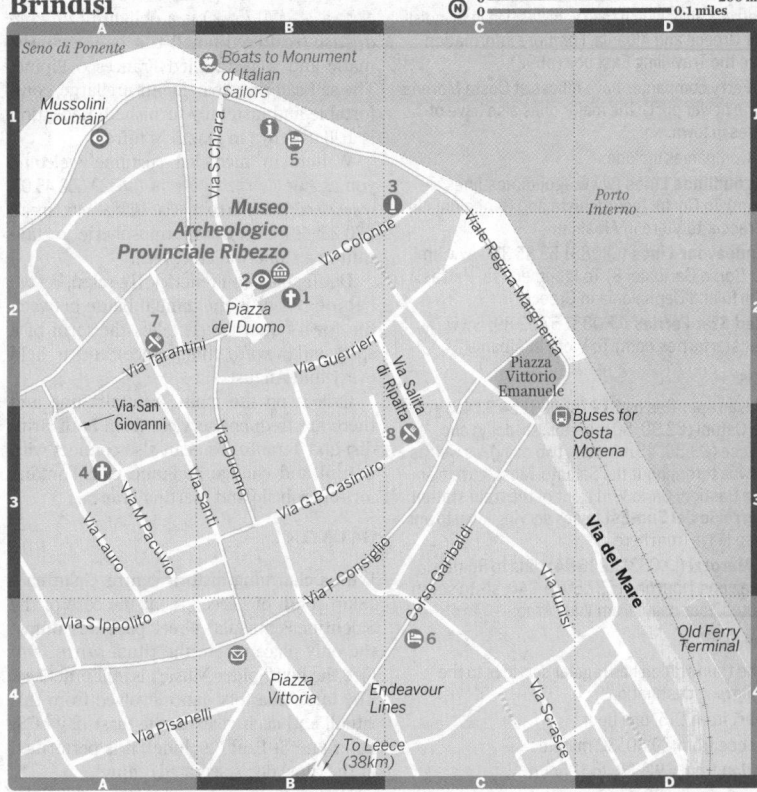

Tourist office (☑0831 52 30 72; www. viaggiareinpuglia.it; Viale Regina Margherita 44; ☺9am-1pm & 2-8pm Mon-Sat summer, 8.30am-2pm Mon-Sat & 3.30-7pm Mon-Fri winter)

❶ Getting There & Away

AIR

From **Papola Casale** (BDS; www.aeroportidipug lia.it), Brindisi's small airport, there are domestic flights to Rome, Naples and Milan. Airlines include Alitalia, AirOne and easyJet. There are also direct flights from London Stansted with Ryanair.

Major and local car-rental firms are represented at the airport and there are regular SITA buses to Lecce (€6, 45 minutes, nine daily) and STP buses to central Brindisi (€1.50, 15 to 30 minutes, every 30 minutes).

Pugliairbus (http://pugliairbus.aeroportidi puglia.it) has services to Bari airport (€8, 1¾ hours) and Lecce (€7, 40 minutes).

Brindisi

◉ Top Sights

◉ Sights

▣ Sleeping

✖ Eating

BOAT

Ferries, all of which take vehicles, leave Brindisi for Greece and Albania. For more information see the Travelling East box (p692).

Ferry companies have offices at Costa Morena (the newer port); the major ones also have offices in town.

Companies include:

Agoudimos Lines (www.agoudimos-lines. com) To Corfu, Igoumenista and Cephalonia in Greece; to Vlore in Albania.

Endeavour Lines (☑0831 52 85 31; www.hml. it; Corso Garibaldi 8) To Igoumenitsa, Patras, Corfu and Cephalonia in Greece.

Red Star Ferries (☑0831 57 52 89; www. redstarferries.com) To Vlore in Albania.

BUS

Buses operated by **STP** (☑0831 54 92 45) go to Ostuni (€2.90, 50 minutes, six daily) and Lecce (€3.30, 45 minutes, two daily), as well as towns throughout the Salento. Most leave from Via Bastioni Carlo V, in front of the train station. **Ferrovie del Sud-Est** buses serving local towns also leave from here.

Marozzi (☑0831 52 16 84) runs to Rome's Stazione Tiburtina (€37.50 to €40, six to seven hours, four daily) from Viale Arno.

TRAIN

The train station has regular services to the following destinations:

Bari from €15, one hour

Lecce from €9.40, 30 minutes

Milan from €92, 8½ to 11 hours

Rome from €58, five to seven hours

Taranto from €5.10, 1¼ hours

ⓘ Getting Around

A free minibus connects the train station and old ferry terminal with Costa Morena. It departs two hours before boat departures. You'll need a valid ferry ticket.

To reach the airport take the STP-run Cotrap bus from Via Bastioni Carlo V.

ORIA
POP 15,400

The multicoloured dome of Oria's cathedral can be seen for miles around, surrounded by the narrow streets of this appealing medieval town. An intriguing, if ghoulish, sight is the cathedral's Cripta delle Mummie (Crypt of the Mummies), where 11 mummified corpses of former monks are still preserved. Surmounting the town, the Frederick II castle, built in a triangular shape, has been carefully restored. It is privately owned.

Borgo di Oria (☑329 2307506; www.borgo dioria.it; ste €70-75; ❄) is a delightful *albergo diffuso* (scattered hotel) run by the charismatic and well-travelled Francesco Pipino. The self-catering apartments are large, comfortable and tastefully furnished. Reception is at Bar Kenya in Piazza Manfredi.

Waiters in medieval costume welcome you at Alle Corte di Hyria (☑329 662 45 07; www.allecortedihyria.com; Via Milizia 146; meals €20-25; ◷Thu-Tue), an atmospheric restaurant in a stone-walled cavern.

Dating back to Frederick II's reign, Il Torneo dei Rioni is the annual battle between the town's quarters. It takes the form of a spectacular *palio* (horse race) and is held every mid-August.

Oria is on the main Trenitalia line and there are frequent services from both Brindisi and Taranto. You can also connect with Ostuni and change at Francavilla Fontana for Alberobello and Martina Franca.

GALATINA
POP 27,320

With a charming historic centre, Galatina – 18km south of Lecce – is at the core of the Salentine Peninsula's Greek past. It is almost the only place where the ritual *tarantismi* (see the box 'Spider Music') is still practised. The tarantella folk dance evolved from this ritual, and each year on the feast day of St Peter and St Paul (29 June), it is performed at the (now deconsecrated) church.

However, most people come to Galatina to see the incredible 14th-century Basilica di Santa Caterina d'Alessandria (◷8am-12.30pm & 4.30-6.45pm Apr-Sep, 8am-12.30pm & 3.45-5.45pm Oct-Mar), its interior a kaleidoscope of fresco. It was built by the Franciscans, whose patroness was the Frenchwoman Marie d'Enghien de Brienne. Married to Raimondello Orsini del Balzo, the Salentine's wealthiest noble, she had plenty of cash to splash on interior decoration. The gruesome story goes that Raimondello (who is buried here) climbed Mt Sinai to visit relics of Santa Caterina (St Catherine). Kissing the dead saint's hand, he bit off a finger and brought it back as a holy relic.

The church is absolutely beautiful, with a pure-white altarpiece set against the frenzy of frescoes. It is not clear who the artists Marie employed really were; they could have been itinerant painters down from Le Marche and Emilia, or southerners who'd absorbed the latest Renaissance innovations on trips north. Bring a torch.

Soothe the soul further with a stay at nearby Samadhi (☑0836 60 02 84; www.agricolasamadhi.com; Via Stazione 116; per person from €40, per week from €390-995; ✱☎✉) located around 7km east of here in tiny Zollino. It's on a 10-hectare organic farm and the owners are multilingual. As well as ayurvedic treatments and yoga courses, there's a vegan restaurant offering organic meals. Check the website for upcoming retreats and courses.

FSE runs frequent trains between Lecce and Galatina (€1.90, 30 minutes), and Zollino (€1.30, 20 minutes).

OTRANTO
POP 5540

Otranto overlooks a pretty harbour on the blue Adriatic coast. In the historic centre, looming golden walls guard narrow car-free lanes, protecting countless pretty little shops selling touristic odds and ends. In July and August it's one of Puglia's most vibrant towns.

Otranto was Italy's main port to the East for 1000 years and suffered a brutal history. There are fanciful tales that King Minos was here and St Peter is supposed to have celebrated the first Western Mass here.

A more definite historical event is the Sack of Otranto in 1480, when 18,000 Turks led by Ahmet Pasha besieged the town. The townsfolk were able to hold the Turks at bay for 15 days before capitulating. Eight hundred survivors were subsequently led up the nearby Minerva hill and beheaded for refusing to convert.

Today the only fright you'll get is the summer crush on Otranto's scenic beaches and in its narrow streets.

◉ Sights

TOP CHOICE **Cathedral** CATHEDRAL
(☑0836 80 27 20; Piazza Basilica; ◷8am-noon daily, 3-6pm Apr-Sep, 3-5pm Oct-Mar) This cathedral was built by the Normans in the 11th century, though it's been given a few facelifts since. On the floor is a vast 12th-century mosaic of a stupendous tree of life balanced on the back of two elephants. It was created by a young monk called Pantaleone (who had obviously never seen an elephant, whose vision of Heaven and Hell encompassed an amazing (con)fusion of the classics, religion and plain old superstition, including Adam and Eve, Diana the huntress, Hercules, King Arthur, Alexander the Great, and a menagerie of monkeys, snakes and sea monsters. Don't forget to look up; the cathedral also boasts a beautiful wooden coffered ceiling.

It's amazing that the cathedral survived at all, as the Turks stabled their horses here when they beheaded the martyrs of Otranto on a stone preserved in the altar of the chapel (to the right of the main altar). This **Cappella Mortiri** (Chapel of the Dead) is a ghoulishly fascinating sight, with the skulls and bones of the martyrs arranged in neat patterns in seven tall glass cases.

Castle CASTLE
(www.castelloaragoneseotranto.it; Piazza Castello; adult/child €2/free; ◷10am-1pm & 3-5pm Oct-Mar, 10am-1pm & 3-7pm Apr-May, 10am-1pm & 3-10pm Jun & Sep, 10am-midnight Aug) This squat thick-walled fort, with the Charles V coat of arms above the entrance, has great views from the ramparts. There are some faded original murals and original cannonballs on display.

Chiesa di San Pietro CHURCH
(Via San Pietro; ◷10am-noon & 3-6pm Apr-Sep, 10am-noon & 3-6pm Oct-Mar) Vivid Byzantine frescoes decorate the interior of this church. If it's closed, ask for the key at the cathedral.

🏃 Activities

There are some great beaches north of Otranto, especially **Baia dei Turchi**, with its translucent blue water. South of Otranto a spectacular rocky coastline makes for an

---

SPIDER MUSIC

In August, one of Salento's biggest festivals is a frenzied night of *pizzica* dancing at La Notte della Taranta (www.lanottedellataranta.it) in Melpignano, about 30km south of Lecce. *Pizzica* developed from the ritual *tarantismi,* a dance meant to rid the body of tarantula-bite poison. It's more likely the hysterical dancing was symbolic of a deeper societal psychosis and an outlet for individuals living in bleak, repressed conditions to express their pent-up desires, hopes and unresolved grief. Nowadays, *pizzica* (which can be quite a sensual dance) means party, with all-night dances held in various Salento towns throughout summer, leading up to Melpignano's humdinger affair.

impressive drive down to Castro. To see what goes on underwater, Scuba Diving Otranto (☑0836 80 27 40; www.scubadiving.it; Via Francesco di Paola 43) offers day or night dives as well as introductory courses and diving courses.

🛏 Sleeping

TOP CHOICE Palazzo Papaleo HOTEL €€

(☑0836 80 21 08; www.hotelpalazzopapaleo.com; Via Rondachi 1; r €119-490; P✳@🛜) Located next to the cathedral, this sumptuous hotel was the first to earn the EU Eco-label in Puglia. Aside from its ecological convictions, the hotel has magnificent rooms with original frescoes, exquisitely carved antique furniture and walls washed in soft greys, ochres and yellows. Soak in the panoramic views while enjoying the rooftop Jacuzzi. The staff are exceptionally friendly.

Balconcino d'Oriente B&B €

(☑0836 80 15 29; www.balconcinodoriente.com; Via San Francesco da Paola 71; s €40-70, d €60-110; P✳) This B&B has an African-cum–Middle Eastern theme throughout with colourful bed linens, African prints, Moroccan lamps and orange colour washes on the walls. The downstairs restaurant serves traditional Italian meals.

Palazzo de Mori BOUTIQUE HOTEL €€

(☑0836 80 10 88; www.palazzodemori.it; Bastione dei Pelasgi; r €120-150; ☉Apr-Oct; ✳@) In Otranto's historic centre, this charming B&B serves breakfast on the sun terrace overlooking the port. The rooms are decorated in soothing white-on-white.

🍴 Eating

La Bella Idrusa PIZZERIA €

(☑0836 80 14 75; Via Lungomare degli Eroi; pizza €5; ☉dinner Thu-Tue) You can't miss this pizzeria right by the huge Porta Terra in the historic centre. Outdoor seating is great for people-watching while indoors is atmospheric and romantic. And it's not just pizzas on offer.

Laltro Baffo SEAFOOD €€

(☑0836 80 16 36; www.laltrobaffo.com; Cenobio Basiliano 23; meals €30-35; ☉Tue-Sun) This elegant modern restaurant near the castle dishes up seafood with a contemporary twist. Try the *polipo alla pignata* (octopus stew).

Acmet Pasica TRADITIONAL ITALIAN €€

(☑0836 80 12 82; Via Lungomare degli Eroi; meals €40; ☉Tue-Sun) Trading on Otranto's macabre history with the Turks, this restaurant is in a prime position overlooking the sea. As well as a large selection of seafood, there are other traditional meals on the menu.

🍷 Drinking

A number of bars along the city wall overlook the sea, including the popular Il Covo dei Mori (☑0836 80 20 33; Via Leon Dari).

❶ Information

Tourist office (☑0836 80 14 36; Piazza Castello; ☉9am-1pm & 3-8pm Mon-Fri Jun-Sep, 9am-1pm Mon-Fri Oct-May) Faces the castle.

❶ Getting There & Away

Otranto can be reached from Lecce by FSE train (€2.60, 1½ hours) or bus (€2.60, 1½ hours). **Marozzi** (☑0836 80 15 78) has daily bus services to Rome (€47, 10 hours, three daily).

For travel information and reservations, head to **Ellade Viaggi** (☑0836 80 15 78; www.ellade viaggi.it, in Italian; Via del Porto) at the port.

GALLIPOLI
POP 21,040

The old medieval centre of Gallipoli (meaning 'beautiful town' in Greek) fills an island in the Ionian Sea and is connected by a bridge to the mainland and modern city. It's a picturesque town surrounded by high walls which were built to protect it against attacks from the sea. An important fishing centre, it feels like a working Italian town, unlike more seasonal coastal places. In the summer, bars and restaurants make the most of the island's ramparts, looking out to sea.

◉ Sights & Activities

Gallipoli has some fine beaches, including the Baia Verde, just south of town while nature enthusiasts will want to take a day trip to Parco Regionale Porto Selvaggio, about 20km north – a protected area of wild coastline with walking trails amid the trees and diving off the rocky shore.

Cattedrale di Sant'Agata CATHEDRAL

(Via Antonietta de Pace; ☉hours vary) In the centre, on the highest point of the island, is this 17th-century baroque cathedral, lined with paintings by local artists. Zimbalo, who imprinted Lecce with his crazy baroque styles, also worked on the facade.

Frantoio Ipogeo
HISTORICAL SITE

(☎338 136 30 63; Via Antonietta de Pace 87; ⏰10am-12.30pm & 4-6.30pm Jun-Sep, to midnight Jun & Jul) This is only one of some 35 olive presses buried in the tufa rock below the town. It's here that they pressed Gallipoli's olive oil, which was then stored in one of the 2000 cisterns carved out beneath the old town.

Museo Civico
MUSEUM

(☎0833 26 42 24; Via Antonietta de Pace 108; adult €3; ⏰9am-1pm & 4-9pm Mon-Fri, 10am-1pm Sat) Founded in 1878, the museum is a 19th-century time capsule featuring fish heads, ancient sculptures, a 3rd-century-BC sarcophagus and other weird stuff.

Farmacia Provenzana
PHARMACY

(Via Antonietta de Pace; ⏰8.30am-12.30pm & 4.30-8.30pm Sun-Fri) A beautifully decorated pharmacy dating from 1814.

🛏 Sleeping

La Casa del Mare
B&B €

(☎333 474 57 54; www.lacasadelmare.com; Piazza de Amicis 14; d €60-110; ❄@🛜) This butter-coloured 16th-century building on a little square in the town centre is a great choice. Helpful and friendly Federico has also restored a beautiful 18th-century *palazzo* nearby, Palazzo Flora (www.palazzoflora.com; Via d'Ospina 19; d €65-120, house €150-300), which sleeps four to six and has fantastic views, especially from the rooftop terrace. During the summer Federico cooks a sumptuous buffet feast for his guests every Friday night (per person €35).

Insula
B&B €

(☎366 346 83 57; www.bbinsulagallipoli.it; Via de Pace 56; d €60-120; ⏰Apr-Oct; ❄@) A magnificent 15th-century building houses this memorable B&B. The five rooms are all different but share the same princely atmosphere with exquisite antiques, vaulted high ceilings and cool pastel paintwork.

Relais Corte Palmieri
HOTEL €€

(☎0833 26 53 18; www.relaiscortepalmieri.it; Corte Palmieri 3; s €130-185, d €165-195; ❄🛜) This cream-coloured, well-kept hotel in the historic centre has elegant rooms accentuated by traditional painted furniture, wrought-iron bedheads and crisp red-and-white linen.

🍴 Eating

La Puritate
TRATTORIA €€

(☎0833 26 42 05; Via S Elia 18; meals €40-45; ⏰Thu-Tue) A great place for fish in the old

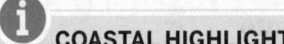

COASTAL HIGHLIGHT

For a scenic road trip, the drive south from **Otranto** to **Castro** takes you along a wild and beautiful coastline. The coast here is rocky and dramatic, with cliffs falling down into the sparkling, azure sea. When the wind is up you can see why it is largely treeless. Many of the towns here started life as Greek settlements, although there are few monuments to be seen. Further south, the resort town of **Santa Maria di Leuca** is the tip of Italy's stiletto and the dividing line between the Adriatic and Ionian Seas.

town with picture windows and sea views. Follow the excellent antipasti with delicious *primi* (first courses) such as seafood spaghetti, then see what's been caught that day – the swordfish is usually a good bet.

Al Pescatore
SEAFOOD €€

(☎0833 26 36 56; Riviera Colombo 39; meals €25-30; ⏰Tue-Sun) In a hotel of the same name, this restaurant has no views but is recommended by locals for its good seafood dishes at reasonable prices.

ℹ Information
Tourist office (☎0833 26 25 29; Via Antonietta de Pace 86; ⏰8am-9pm summer, 8am-1pm & 4-9pm Mon-Sat winter) Near the cathedral in the old town.

ℹ Getting There & Away
FSE buses and trains head to Lecce (€3.90, one hour, four daily).

TARANTO
POP 193,140

According to legend, the city was founded by Taras, son of Poseidon, who arrived on the back of a dolphin (as you do). Less romantically, the city was actually founded in the 7th century BC by exiles from Sparta to become one of the wealthiest and most important colonies of Magna Graecia. The fun finished, however, in the 3rd century BC when the Romans marched in, changed its name to Tarentum and set off a two-millennia decline in fortunes. Its cultural heyday may be over but Taranto still remains an important naval base, second only to La Spezia.

Once a Roman citadel, the collapsing historic medieval centre is gritty and dirty but

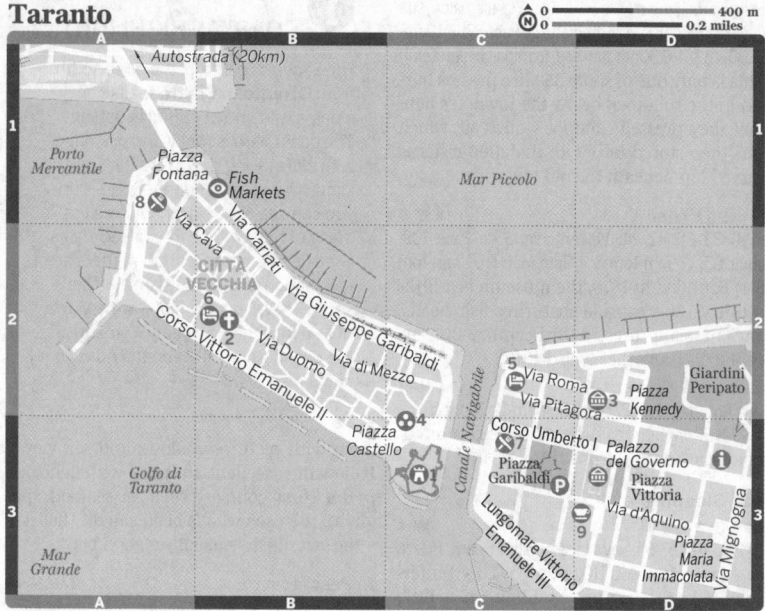

Taranto

◎ **Sights**

🛏 **Sleeping**

🍴 **Eating**

☕ **Drinking**

has a lovely seaside promenade. However, the mainland industrial centre, with Italy's largest steel plant, dominates the skyline.

◉ **Sights**

Although Taranto's medieval town centre is run-down and has a gritty undertone, it's gradually being tastefully renovated. It is perched on the small island dividing the Mar Piccolo (Small Sea; an enclosed lagoon) and the Mar Grande (Big Sea). This peculiar geography means that blue sea and sky surround you wherever you go.

Museo Nazionale Archeologico   MUSEUM
(☎099 453 21 12; www.museotaranto.it, in Italian; Via Cavour 10; adult/child €5/free; ⊙8.30am-7.30pm) In the new town is one of Italy's most important archaeological museums. It houses, among other ancient artefacts, the largest collection of Greek terracotta figures in the world. Also on exhibit are fine collections of 1st-century-BC glassware, classic black-and-red Attic vases and stunning jewellery such as a 4th-century-BC bronze and terracotta crown.

Cathedral   CATHEDRAL
(Via del Duomo) The 11th-century cathedral is one of Puglia's oldest Romanesque buildings and an extravagant treat. It's dedicated to San Cataldo; the Capella di San Cataldo is a baroque riot of frescoes and polychrome marble inlay.

Castello Aragonese   CASTLE
(Piazza Castello; ☎099 775 34 38; ⊙by appointment 9am-noon Mon-Fri) Guarding the swing bridge that joins the old and new parts of town, this impressive 15th-century structure was once a prison and is currently occupied by the Italian navy. Opposite are

the remaining columns of Taranto's ancient Temple of Poseidon.

✴ Festivals & Events

Le Feste di Pasqua RELIGIOUS
Taranto is famous for its Holy Week celebrations – the biggest in the region – when bearers in Ku Klux Klan–style robes carry icons around the town. There are three processions: the Perdoni, celebrating pilgrims; the Addolorata (which lasts 12 hours but covers only 4km); and the Misteri (even slower at 14 hours to cover 2km).

🛏 Sleeping

Hotel Akropolis HOTEL €€
(☑099 470 41 10; www.hotel akropolis.it; Vico I Seminario 3; s/d €105/145; ❋@) A converted medieval *palazzo* in the crumbling old town, this luxurious hotel sits grandly beside the cathedral. There are 13 stylish cream-and-white rooms, original majolica-tiled floors and tremendous views from the rooftop terrace. The downstairs bar and restaurant is enclosed in stone, wood and glass and has atmospheric curtained alcoves.

Europa Hotel HOTEL €€
(☑099 452 59 94; www.hoteleuropaonline.it; Via Roma 2; s €80-105, d €135-190; ❋🐾) On the seafront next to the swing bridge, this hotel has comfortable rooms (some with kitchenettes) overlooking the old town. A good choice.

🍴 Eating & Drinking

Trattoria da Ugo TRATTORIA €€
(☑329 141 58 50; cnr Via Cataldo de Tulio & Via Fontana; meals €18-25; ☺lunch & dinner Mon-Fri, lunch Sat) This deeply traditional Tarantine trattoria is known for its seafood, which includes grilled mussels, octopus with lemon and olive oil, and fried prawns and squid.

Balzi Blu PIZZERIA €
(☑347 465 32 11; Corso Due Mari 22; pizza from €6.50, meals €15; ☺Wed-Mon) A local favourite on the *corso*, serving excellent pizza with an exceptional crust made from 13 different types of flour. There are great views of the old city from the summer terrace.

Caffè Italiano CAFE
(Via D'Aquino 86a; ☺5am-2am) Swish as you might wish, this is a Taranto hot spot, with outside seating on the pedestrianised street. Great for an evening aperitif.

ℹ Information

Taranto splits neatly into three. The old town is on a tiny island, lodged between the northwest

port and train station and the new city to the southeast. Italy's largest steel plant occupies the city's entire western half. The grid-patterned new city contains the banks, most hotels and restaurants and the **tourist office** (☑099 453 23 97; Corso Umberto I 113; ☺9am-1pm & 4.30-6.30pm Mon-Fri, 9am-noon Sat).

ℹ Getting There & Around

BUS
Buses heading north and west depart from Porto Mercantile. FSE buses go to Bari (€5.80, 1¾ to 2¼ hours, frequent). Infrequent **SITA** (☑899 32 52 04; www.sitabus.it) buses leave for Matera (€5.20, 1¾ hours, one daily). STP and FSE buses go to Lecce (€7.70, two hours, five daily).

Marozzi (☑080 579 90 111) has express services serving Rome's Stazione Tiburtina (€41.50, six hours, three daily). **Autolinee Miccolis** (☑099 470 44 51) serves Naples (€19, four hours, three daily) via Potenza (€10.50, two hours).

The bus **ticket office** (☺6am-1pm & 2-7pm) is at Porto Mercantile.

TRAIN
Trenitalia and **FSE** trains go to the following destinations:
Bari €7.40, 2½ hours, frequent
Brindisi €5.10, 1¼ hours, frequent
Rome from €41, six to 7½ hours, five daily

AMAT (☑099 4 52 67 32) buses run between the train station and the new city.

BASILICATA

Basilicata has an otherworldly landscape of tremendous mountain ranges, dark forested valleys and villages so melded with the rockface that they seem to have grown there. Its isolated yet strategic location on routes linking ancient Rome to the eastern Byzantine empire has seen it successively invaded, pillaged, plundered, abandoned and neglected.

In the north the landscape is a fertile zone of gentle hills and deep valleys – once covered in thick forests, now cleared and cultivated with wheat, olives and grapes. The purple-hued mountains of the interior are impossibly grand and a wonderful destination for hikers and naturalists, particularly the soaring peaks of the Lucanian Apennines and the Parco Nazionale del Pollino.

On the coast, Maratea is one of Italy's most chic seaside resorts. However, Matera is Basilicata's star attraction, the famous

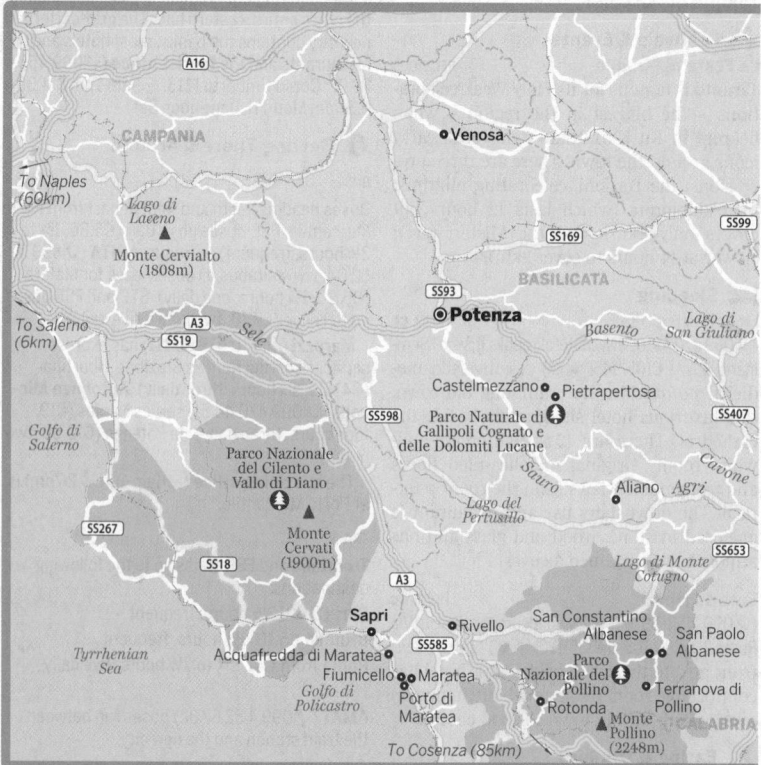

sassi of the cave city presiding over a rugged landscape of ravines and caves. Its ancient cave dwellings tell a tale of poverty, hardship and struggle, its history best immortalized in writer Carlo Levi's superb book *Christ stopped at Eboli* – a title suggesting Basilicata was beyond the hand of God, a place where pagan magic still existed and thrived.

Today, Basilicata is attracting a slow but steadily increasing trickle of tourists. For those wanting to experience a raw and unspoilt region of Italy, Basilicata's remote atmosphere and wild landscape will appeal.

History

Basilicata spans Italy's instep with slivers of coastline touching the Tyrrhenian and Ionian Seas. It was known to the Greeks and Romans as Lucania (a name still heard today) after the Lucani tribe who lived here as far back as the 5th century BC. The Greeks

also prospered, settling along the coastline at Metapontum and Erakleia, but things started to go wrong under the Romans, when Hannibal, the ferocious Carthaginian general, rampaged through the region.

In the 10th century, the Byzantine Emperor Basilikòs (976–1025) renamed the area, overthrowing the Saracens in Sicily and the south and reintroducing Christianity. The pattern of war and overthrow continued throughout the Middle Ages as the Normans, Hohenstaufens, Angevins and the Bourbons constantly tussled over its strategic location, right up until the 19th century. As talk of the Italian unification began to gain ground, Bourbon-sponsored loyalists took to Basilicata's mountains to oppose political change. Ultimately, they became the much-feared bandits of local lore who make scary appearances in writings from the late 19th and early 20th centuries. In the 1930s, Basilicata was used as a kind of open prison for political

Matera is said to be one of the world's oldest towns, inhabited since the Palaeolithic Age. The simple natural grottoes that dotted the gorge were adapted to become homes, and an ingenious system of canals regulated the flow of water and sewage. The prosperous town became the capital of Basilicata in 1663, a position it held until 1806 when the power moved to Potenza. In the decades that followed, an unsustainable increase in population led to the habitation of unsuitable grottoes – originally intended as animal stalls – even lacking running water.

By the 1950s over half of Matera's population lived in the *sassi*, a typical cave sheltering an average of six children. The infant mortality rate was 50%. In his book, *Christ Stopped at Eboli,* Carlo Levi describes how children would beg passers-by for quinine to stave off the deadly malaria. Such publicity finally galvanised the authorities into action and in the late 1950s about 15,000 inhabitants were forcibly relocated to new government housing schemes. In 1993 the *sassi* were declared a Unesco World Heritage Site. Ironically, the town's history of outrageous misery has transformed it into Basilicata's leading tourist attraction.

◉ Sights & Activities

There are two *sasso* districts: the more restored, northwest-facing Sasso Barisano and the more impoverished, northeast-facing Sasso Caveoso. Both are extraordinary, riddled with serpentine alleyways and staircases, and dotted with frescoed *chiese rupestri* (cave churches) created between the 8th and 13th centuries. Matera contains some 3000 habitable caves.

The *sassi* are accessible from several points. There's an entrance off Piazza Vittorio Veneto, or take Via delle Beccherie to Piazza del Duomo and follow the tourist itinerary signs to enter either Barisano or Caveoso. Sasso Caveoso is also accessible from Via Ridola.

For a great photograph, head out of town for about 3km on the Taranto-Laterza road and follow signs for the *chiese rupestri*. This takes you up on the Murgia Plateau to the Belvedere, the location of the crucifixion in Mel Gibson's 2004 film, *The Passion of the Christ,* from where you have fantastic views of the plunging ravine and Matera.

dissidents – most famously Carlo Levi – sent into exile to remote villages by the fascists.

Matera

POP 60,530 / ELEV 405M

Approach Matera from virtually any direction and your first glimpse of its famous *sassi* (stone houses carved out of the caves and cliffs) is sure to be etched in your memory forever. Haunting and beautiful, the *sassi* sprawl below the rim of a yawning ravine like a giant nativity scene. The old town is simply unique and warrants at least a day of exploration and aimless wandering. Although many buildings are crumbling and abandoned, many have been restored and transformed into cosy abodes, restaurants and swish cave-hotels. On the cliff top, the new town is a lively place, with its elegant churches, *palazzi* and especially the pedestrianised Piazza Vittorio Veneto.

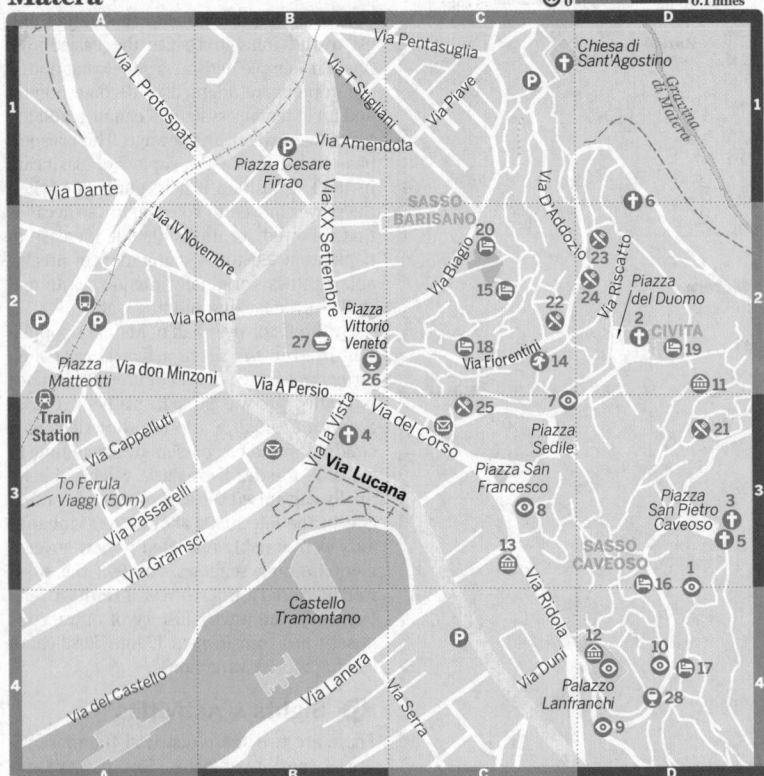

Sasso Barisano

Chiesa di Madonna delle Virtù & Chiesa di San Nicola del Greci   CHURCH

(Via Madonna delle Virtù; ⊙10am-7pm Sat & Sun) This monastic complex is one of the most important monuments in Matera and is composed of dozens of caves spread over two floors. The church of the Chiesa Madonna delle Virtù was built in the 10th or 11th century and restored in the 17th century. Above it, the simple church of Chiesa di San Nicola del Greci is rich in frescoes. The complex was used in 1213 by Benedictine monks of Palestinian origin.

Sasso Caveoso

Chiesa di San Pietro Caveoso   CHURCH

(Piazza San Pietro Caveoso) The only church in the *sassi* not dug into the tufa rock, it was originally built in 1300 and has a 17th-century Romanesque-baroque facade.

Chiesa di Santa Maria d'Idris   CHURCH

(Piazza San Pietro Caveoso; admission adult/reduced €3/2; ⊙10am-1pm & 2.30-7pm Tue-Sun Apr-Oct, 10.30am-1.30pm Tue-Sun Nov-Mar) Dug into the Idris rock, this church has an unprepossessing facade, but the narrow corridor communicating with the recessed church of San Giovanni in Monterrone is richly decorated with 12th- to 17th-century frescoes. Purchase a joint ticket for this site and Chiesa di Santa Lucia alle Malve for €5/3.50.

Chiesa di Santa Lucia alle Malve   CHURCH

(Via la Vista; admission adult/reduced €3/2; ⊙10am-1pm & 2.30-7pm Apr-Oct, 10.30am-1.30pm Tue-Sun Nov-Mar) Built in the 8th century to house a Benedictine convent, this church has an ornate entrance door and a number of 12th-century frescoes.

Matera

La Raccolta delle Acque HISTORICAL SITE
(☏340 665 91 07; www.laraccoltadelleacque matera.it; Via Bruno Buozzi 67; admission €2.50; ☺9.30am-1pm & 2-7pm Apr-Oct, 9.30am-1pm Nov-Mar) Matera's fascinating water-storage system can be better understood when you visit this ancient complex of underground cisterns and canals which was used to collect rainwater from roofs, streets and houses in the vicinity. The largest cistern is nearly 15m deep and 5m long.

Casa-Grotta di Vico Solitario HISTORICAL SITE
(admission €1.50) For a glimpse of life in old Matera visit this refurbished *sasso* off Via Bruno Buozzi. There's a bed in the kitchen, a room for manure and a section for a pig and a donkey.

Museo della Scultura Contemporanea MUSEUM
(MUSMA, ☏366 935 77 68; www.musma.it; Via San Giacomo; adult/reduced €5/3.50; ☺10am-2pm Tue-Sun & 4-8pm Sat & Sun) Housed in Palazzo Pomarici, MUSMA is a fabulous contemporary sculpture museum. Some of the exhibits are artfully displayed in atmospherically lit caves. You can also book a tour to visit the **Cripta del Peccato Originale** (the Crypt of Original Sin), which has well-preserved frescoes from the late 8th century. It's known as

the Sistine Chapel of the cave churches and the frescoes depict dramatic Old Testament scenes.

The New Town

The focus of the town is Piazza Vittorio Veneto, an excellent, bustling meeting point for an evening *passeggiata* (stroll). It's surrounded by elegant churches and richly adorned *palazzi,* with their backs to the *sassi;* an attempt by the bourgeois to block out the shameful poverty the *sassi* once represented. Further excavations here have yielded more ruins of Byzantine Matera, including a rock church, a castle, a large cistern and numerous houses. You can gaze down to the site from the piazza.

Museo Nazionale d'Arte Medievale e Moderna della Basilicata MUSEUM
(☏0835 31 42 35; Palazzo Lanfranchi; adult/reduced €2/1; ☺9am-8pm Thu-Tue) The stars of the show are Levi's paintings, including the enormous mural *Lucania '61* depicting peasant life in biblical Technicolor.

Cathedral CATHEDRAL
(Piazza del Duomo; ☺closed for renovation) Set high up in town, the subdued, graceful exterior of the 13th-century Puglian-Romanesque cathedral makes the neobaroque excess within all the more of a surprise: ornate capitals, sumptuous chapels and tons of gilding.

Pediments mounted on its altars came from the temples at Metaponto. Matera's patron saint, the Madonna della Bruna, is hidden within the older church, **Santa Maria di Costantinopoli**, which can be accessed from the cathedral if it's open.

Museo Nazionale Ridola MUSEUM
(☑0835 31 00 58; Via Ridola 24; adult/concession €2.50/1.25; ☺9am-8pm Tue-Sun, 2-8pm Mon) The impressive collection includes some remarkable Greek pottery, such as the *Craterea Mascheroni,* a huge urn over 1m high.

☞ Tours

There are plenty of official guides for the sassi – try www.sassiweb.it. Alternatively, contact the Cooperativa Amici del Turista (☑0835 33 03 01; www.amicidelturista.it; Via Fiorentini 28-30) or English-speaking guide Amy Weideman (☑339 282 3618; half-day tour for 2 people €40).

For excellent and informative guided visits, Ferula Viaggi (see Information) has tours of the *sassi,* classic tours, underground tours, tours that include tastings or cookery courses, longer trips to the Pollino or into Puglia, and also hiking and cycling tours. Hikes range from short walks to week-long trips. For a detailed list of walks see Ferula Viaggi's Walk Basilicata (www.walkbasilicata. it). Ferula Viaggi also runs Bike Basilicata (www.bikebasilicata.it), which rents bikes and helmets and supplies a road book and map

so you can head off on your own; guided bike tours include a seven-night 500km odyssey across Puglia and Basilicata.

★☆ Festivals & Events

Sagra della Madonna della Bruna RELIGIOUS
On 2 July the colourful Procession of Shepherds parades ornately decorated papiermâché floats around town. The finale is the *assalto al carro,* when the crowd descends on the main cart and tears it to pieces.

Gezziamoci MUSIC
(☑0835 33 02 00; www.gezziamocimatera.onyx jazzclub.it) This jazz festival in the *sassi* and surrounding Murgia park kicks off in the last week of August.

🛏 Sleeping

TOP CHOICE **Hotel in Pietra** BOUTIQUE HOTEL €€
(☑0835 34 40 40; www.hotelinpietra.it; Via San Giovanni Vecchio 22, Barisano; s €70, d €110-150, ste €220; ❄@) The lobby is set in a former 13th-century chapel complete with soaring arches, while the eight rooms combine soft golden stone with the natural cave interior. Furnishings are Zen-style with low beds, while the bathrooms are super stylish and include vast sunken tubs.

Locanda di San Martino HOTEL €€
(☑0835 25 66 00; www.locandadisanmartino.it; Via Fiorentini 71; d €89-200; ❄@🌐) A sumptuous hotel where you can swim in a cave – in a

---

MATERA IN...

One Day

Zip out to the **Belvedere** for a photo-snap of the *sassi* before any heat haze sets in. Back in the *sassi,* approach Sasso Barisano via Via Fiorentini and wind your way along to the monastic complex of **Madonna delle Virtù and San Nicola dei Greci** with its original frescoes. Then head for more frescoes in Sasso Caveoso's rock churches of **San Pietro Caveoso, Santa Maria d'Idris** and **Santa Lucia alle Malve**. Wander through the *sassi,* imagining life in a cave, stopping to learn about Matera's fascinating system of underground cisterns at **La Raccolta delle Acque**. Early evening, enjoy a sassy cocktail in lively Piazza Vittorio Veneto at **Caffe Tripoli** followed by dinner at **Ristorante Il Cantuccio**.

Two Days

On day two, allow a couple of hours to visit the **Cripta del Peccato Originale**, with its magnificent frescoes. Then either spend the rest of the day hiking in the **gorge** or squeeze in a few museums in town, including the **Museo Nazionale d'Arte Moderna**, which showcases Carlo Levi's bold *Lucania '61*. In the heart of Sasso Caveoso the **Casa-Grotte di Vico Solitario** may sound a tad contrived but really *does* provide a vivid picture of former living conditions here. For contemporary sculptures, visit the **Museo della Scultura Contemporanea**. Finish off with dinner in a cave at stylish **Baccanti**.

EXPLORING THE GORGE

In the picturesque landscape of the Murgia Plateau, the Matera Gravina cuts a rough gouge in the Earth, a 200m-deep canyon pockmarked with abandoned caves and villages. You can hike from the *sassi* into the gorge and then up to the Belvedere in one to two hours, but a hike along the canyon rim gives you a better appreciation of the termite-like network of caves that gave birth to the *sassi*. Ferula Viaggi (www.ferulaviaggi.it) offers excellent guided hikes into the gorge, as well as a range of hiking and cycling tours throughout Basilicata and Puglia.

subterranean underground swimming pool. The cave accommodation, complete with niches and rustic brick floors, is set around a warren of cobbled paths and courtyards.

La Dolce Vita B&B
B&B €

(☑0835 31 03 24; www.ladolcevitamatera.it; Rione Malve 51; s €40-60, d €60-80; 🐾) This delightful eco-friendly B&B in Sasso Caveoso has self-contained apartments with solar panels and recycled rainwater for plumbing. They're cool, comfortable and homey. Vincenzo is passionate about Matera and is a mine of information on the *sassi*.

Palazzo Viceconte
HOTEL €€

(☑0835 33 06 99; www.palazzoviceconte.it; Via San Potito 7; d €95-140, ste €139-350; ✳@) Rooms in this 15th-century *palazzo* near the cathedral have superb views of the *sassi* and *gravina*. The hotel is elegantly furnished and the rooftop terrace has panoramic views.

Il Vicinato
B&B €

(☑0835 31 26 72; www.ilvicinato.com; Piazzetta San Pietro Caveoso 7; s/d €60/70; ✳🐾) This B&B enjoys a great, easy-to-find location. Rooms are decorated in clean modern lines, with views across to Idris rock and the Murgia Plateau. There's a room with a balcony and a small apartment, each with independent entrances.

Sassi Hotel
HOTEL €

(☑0835 33 10 09; www.hotelsassi.it; Via San Giovanni Vecchio 89; s/d incl breakfast €70/90; ✳@) The first hotel in the *sassi* is set in an 18th-century rambling edifice in Sasso Barisano with some rooms in caves and some not. Singles are small but doubles are gracefully furnished. The balconies have superb views of the cathedral.

✗ Eating

TOP CHOICE Ristorante Il Cantuccio
TRATTORIA €€

(☑0835 33 20 90; Via delle Becchiere 33; meals €25; ☻Tue-Sun) This quaint, homey trattoria

near Piazza Vittorio Veneto is as welcoming as its chef and owner, Michael Lella. The menu is seasonal and the dishes traditional and delicious.

Baccanti
TRADITIONAL ITALIAN €€€

(☑0835 33 37 04; www.baccantiristorante.com; Via Sant'Angelo 58-61; meals €50; ☻lunch & dinner Tue-Sat, lunch Sun) As classy as a cave can be. The design is simple glamour against the low arches of the cavern; the dishes are delicate and complex, using local ingredients. This is where stars go to twinkle when in town.

Oi Marì
PIZZERIA €

(☑0835 34 61 21; Via Fiorentini 66; pizzas from €6.50; ☻dinner nightly, lunch Sat & Sun) In Sasso Barisano, this big convivial cavern is styled as a Neapolitan pizzeria – and has a great cheery atmosphere and excellent substantial pizzas to match.

La Talpa
TRADITIONAL ITALIAN €

(☑0835 33 50 86; Via Fiorentini 167; meals €15-20; ☻Wed-Mon) Down the road from Oi Marì, the cavernous dining rooms are moodily lit and atmospheric. A popular spot for romancing couples.

Le Botteghe
TRADITIONAL ITALIAN €€

(☑0835 34 40 72; Piazza San Pietro Barisano; meals €40; ☻lunch & dinner Mon-Sat, lunch Sun) In Sasso Barisano, this is a classy but informal restaurant in arched whitewashed rooms. Try delicious local specialities like *fusilli mollica e crusco* (pasta and fried bread with local sweet peppers).

Drinking

Caffe Tripoli
CAFE

(Piazza Vittorio Veneto; ☻Tue-Sun) This is a good people-watching spot for morning coffee or evening aperitifs.

19a Buca Winery? WINE BAR
(☑0835 33 35 92; www.diciannovesimabuca.com; Via Lombardi 3; ☉11am-midnight Tue-Sun) The question mark says it all – 13m below Piazza Vittorio Veneto the past takes a futuristic twist. This ultra-chic wine bar–restaurant-cafe-lounge has white space-pod chairs, a 19-hole indoor golf course surrounding an ancient cistern and an impressive wine cellar and degustation menu (meals €30).

Morgan Pub PUB
(www.morganpub.com; Via Buozzi 2; ☉Wed-Mon) A hip and cavernous cellar pub with outside tables in the summer.

ℹ Information

The maps *Carta Turistica di Matera* and *Matera: Percorsi Turistici* (€1.50), available from various travel agencies, bookstores and hotels around town, describe a number of itineraries through the *sassi* and the gorge.

Basilicata Turistica (www.aptbasilicata.it) Official tourist website with useful information on history, culture, attractions and sights.

Ferula Viaggi (☑0835 33 65 72; www.materaturismo.it; Via Cappelluti 34; ☉9am-1.30pm & 3.30-7pm Mon-Sat) Excellent information centre and travel agency. Runs walking tours (www.walkbasilicata.it), cycling tours (www.bikebasilicata.it), cooking courses, and other great tours through Basilicata and Puglia.

Hospital (☑0835 25 31 11; Via Montescaglioso) About 1km southeast of the centre.

Internet point (☑0835 34 41 66; Via San Biagio 9; per hr €3; ☉10am-1pm & 3.30-8.30pm)

Maruel Viaggi (☑0835 33 31 35; www.maruelviaggi.com; Via Dante; ☉9am-1.30pm & 4-8pm) Private travel agency and information centre with good information on buses. Can organise tours.

Parco Archeologico Storico Naturale delle Chiese Rupestri del Materano (☑0835 33 61 66; www.parcomurgia.it; Via Sette Dolori) For info on the Murgia park.

Police station (☑0835 37 81; Via Gattini)

Post office (Via Passerelli; ☉8am-6.30pm Mon-Fri, 8am-12.30pm Sat)

Sassiweb (www.sassiweb.it) Informative website on Matera.

ℹ Getting There & Away

Bus

The bus station is north of Piazza Matteotti, near the train station. **SITA** (☑0835 38 50 07; www.sitabus.it) goes to Taranto (€5.50, two hours, six daily) and Metaponto (€2.70, one hour, up to five daily) and many small towns in the province.

Buy tickets from newspaper kiosks on Piazza Matteotti.

Grassani (☑0835 72 14 43) serves Potenza (€5.30, 1½ hours, four daily). Buy tickets on the bus.

Marozzi (☑06 225 21 47; www.marozzivt.it) runs three daily buses to Rome (€34, 6½ hours). A joint SITA and Marozzi service leaves daily for Siena, Florence and Pisa, via Potenza. Advance booking is essential.

Pugliairbus (☑080 580 03 58; http://pugliairbus.aeroportidipuglia.it) operates a service to Bari airport (€5, 1¼ hours, four daily).

Train

Ferrovie Appulo-Lucane (FAL; ☑0835 33 28 61; www.fal-srl.it) runs regular trains (€4.50, 1½ hours, 12 daily) and buses (€4.50, 1½ hours, six daily) to Bari. For Potenza, take a FAL bus to Ferrandina and connect with a Trenitalia train, or head to Altamura to link up with FAL's Bari-Potenza run.

Potenza

POP 68,600 / ELEV 819M

Basilicata's regional capital, Potenza, has been ravaged by earthquakes (the last in 1980) and also has some brutal housing blocks. If that wasn't enough, as the highest town in the land, it broils in summer and shivers in winter. You may find yourself here, however, as it's a major transport hub.

The centre straddles east to west across a high ridge. To the south lie the main Trenitalia and Ferrovie Appulo-Lucane train stations, connected to the centre by buses 1 and 10.

Potenza's few sights are in the old centre, at the top of the hill. To get there, take the elevators from Piazza Vittorio Emanuele II. The ecclesiastical highlight is the cathedral, erected in the 12th century and rebuilt in the 18th. The elegant Via Pretoria, flanked by a boutique or two, makes a pleasant traffic-free stroll, especially during the *passeggiata*.

In central Potenza, **Al Convento** (☑097 12 55 91; www.alconvento.eu; Largo San Michele Arcangelo 21; s €50-55, d €80-90; ❄@) is a great accommodation choice housing a mix of polished antiques and design classics.

Grassani (☑0835 72 14 43) has buses to Matera (€5.30, 1½ hours, four daily). SITA (☑0971 50 68 11; www.sitabus.it) has daily buses to Melfi, Venosa and Maratea. Buses leave from Via Appia 185 and also stop near the Scalo Inferiore Trenitalia train station. **Liscio** (☑097 15 46 73) buses serve cities

MAGNA GRAECIA MUSEUMS OF THE IONIAN COAST

In stark contrast to the dramatic Tyrrhenian coast, the Ionian coast is a listless, flat affair dotted with large tourist resorts. However, the Greek ruins at Metaponto and Policoro, with their accompanying museums, bring alive the enormous influence of Magna Graecia in southern Italy.

Metaponto's Greek ruins are a rare site where archaeologists have managed to map the entire ancient urban plan. Settled by Greeks in the 8th and 7th centuries BC, Metapontum's most famous resident was Pythagoras, who founded a school here after being banished from Crotone (in Calabria) in the 6th century BC. After Pythagoras died, his house and school were incorporated into the Temple of Hera. The remains of the temple – 15 columns and sections of pavement – are Metaponto's most impressive sight. They're known as the Tavole Palatine (Palatine Tables), since knights, or paladins, are said to have gathered here before heading to the Crusades. It's 3km north of town, just off the highway – to find it follow the slip road for Taranto onto the SS106.

In town, the Museo Archeologico Nazionale (☑0835 74 53 27; Via Aristea 21; admission €2.50; ☉9am-8pm Tue-Sun, 2-8pm Mon) houses artefacts from Metapontum and other sites while in the Parco Archeologico (admission free), 2km northeast of the train station, are the remains of a Greek theatre and the Doric Tempio di Apollo Licio.

In Policoro, 21km southwest of Matera, the Museo della Siritide (☑0835 97 21 54; Via Colombo 8; admission €2.50; ☉9am-8pm Wed-Mon, 2-8pm Tue) has a fabulous display of artefacts from 7000 BC through to Lucanian ornaments, Greek mirrors and Roman spears and javelins.

SITA buses run from Matera to Metaponto (€2.70, one hour, up to five daily) and on to Policoro. Metaponto is on the Taranto-Reggio line; trains connect with Potenza, Salerno and occasionally Naples.

---

including Rome (€23, 4½ hours, three daily), Naples (€7.40, two hours, four daily) and Salerno (€5.30, 1½ hours, four daily).

There are regular train services from Potenza to Foggia (from €6, 2¼ hours), Salerno (from €6, two hours) and Taranto (from €8.50, two hours). For Bari (from €14, three to four hours, four daily), use the Ferrovie Appulo-Lucane (☑0971 41 15 61) at Potenza Superiore station.

Appennino Lucano

The Appenino Lucano (Lucanian Apennines) bite Basilicata in half like a row of jagged teeth. Sharply rearing up south of Potenza, they protect the lush Tyrrhenian Coast and leave the Ionian shores gasping in the semi-arid heat. Careering along its hair-raising roads through the broken spine of mountains can be arduous, but if you're looking for drama, the drive could be the highlight of your trip.

The fascists exiled writer and political activist Carlo Levi to this isolated region in 1935. He lived and is buried in the tiny hilltop town of Aliano, where remarkably little seems to have changed since he

wrote his dazzling *Christ Stopped at Eboli,* which laid bare the boredom, poverty and hypocrisy of village life. The Pinacoteca Carlo Levi (☑0835 56 83 15; Piazza Garibaldi; admission €3; ☉10am-1pm & 4-7.30pm in summer, 10am-12.30pm & 3.30-6.30pm Thu-Tue in winter) also houses the Museo Storico di Carlo Levi, featuring his papers, documents and paintings. Admission to the pinacoteca (art gallery) includes a tour of Levi's house and entry to the museum.

More spectacular than Aliano are the two mountaintop villages of Castelmezzano (elevation 985m) and Pietrapertosa (elevation 1088m), ringed by the Lucanian Dolomites. They are Basilicata's highest villages and are often swathed in cloud, making you wonder why anyone would build here, in territory best suited to goats. Castelmezzano is surely one of Italy's most dramatic villages; the houses huddle along an impossibly narrow ledge that falls away in gorges to the Caperrino river. Pietrapertosa is even more amazing: the Saracen fortress at its pinnacle is difficult to spot as it is carved out of the mountain.

You can spend an eerie night in Pietrapertosa at a delightful B&B, La Casa di

POETIC VENOSA

About 70km north of Potenza, pretty Venosa used to be a thriving Roman colony, owing much of its prosperity to being a stop on the Appian Way. It was also the birthplace of the poet Horace in 65 BC. The main reason to come here is to see the remains of Basilicata's largest monastic complex.

Venosa's main square, Piazza Umberto I, is dominated by a 15th-century Aragonese castle with a small **Museo Archeologico** (☑0972 3 60 95; Piazza Umberto I; admission €2.50; ☉9am-8pm Wed-Mon, 2-8pm Tue) that houses finds from Roman Venusia and human bone fragments dating back 300,000 years.

Admission to the museum also gets you into the ruins of the **Roman settlement** (☉9am-1hr before dusk Wed-Mon, 2pm-1hr before dusk Tue) and the graceful later ruins of **Abbazia della Santissima Trinità** (☑0972 3 42 11). At the northeastern end of town, the *abbazia* (abbey) was erected above the Roman temple around 1046 by the Benedictines and predates the Norman invasions. Within the complex is a pair of churches, one unfinished. The earlier church contains the tomb of Robert Guiscard, a Norman crusader, and his fearsome half-brother Drogo. The other unfinished church was begun in the 11th century using materials from the neighbouring Roman amphitheatre. A little way south are some Jewish and Christian catacombs.

Hotel Orazio (☑0972 3 11 35; www.hotelorazio.it; Vittorio Emanuele II 142; s/d €50/65) is a 17th-century palace complete with antique majolica tiles and marble floors, and is overseen by a pair of grandmotherly ladies.

Venosa can be reached by taking the S658 north from Potenza and exiting at Barile onto the S93. Buses run Monday to Saturday from Potenza (€3.10, two hours, two daily).

Penelope e Cirene (☑0971 98 30 13; Via Garibaldi 32; d from €70). Dine at the authentic Lucano restaurant **Al Becco della Civetta** (☑0971 98 62 49; www.beccodellacivetta.it; Vicolo I Maglietta 7; meals €25; ☉Wed-Mon) in Castelmezzano, which also offers traditionally furnished, simple whitewashed rooms (double €80).

Aliano is accessible by SITA bus (€5.40) from Potenza. You'll need your own vehicle to visit Castelmezzano and Pietrapertosa.

Tyrrhenian Coast

Resembling a mini-Amalfi, Basilicata's Tyrrhenian coast is short (about 20km) but sweet. Squeezed between Calabria and Campania's Cilento peninsula, it shares the same beguiling characteristics: hidden coves and pewter sandy beaches backed by majestic coastal cliffs. The SS18 threads a spectacular route along the mountains to the coast's star attraction, the charming seaside settlements of Maratea.

MARATEA
POP 5220

Maratea is a charming, if confusing, place at first, being comprised of several distinct localities ranging from a medieval village to a stylish harbour. The setting is lush and dramatic, with a coastal road (narrower even than the infamous Amalfi Coast road!) that dips and winds past the cliffs and pocket-size beaches that line the sparkling Golfo di Policastro. Studded with elegant hotels, Maratea's attraction is no secret and you can expect tailback traffic and fully booked hotels in July and August. Conversely, many hotels and restaurants close from October to March.

◉ Sights & Activities

Your first port of call should be the pretty **Porto di Maratea**, a harbour where sleek yachts and bright-blue fishing boats bob in the water, overlooked by bars and restaurants. Then there's the enchanting 13th-century medieval *borgo* (small town) of **Maratea Inferiore**, with pint-sized piazzas, wriggling alleys and interlocking houses, offering startling coastal views. It's all overlooked by a 21m-high, gleaming white statue of **Christ the Redeemer** – if you have your own transport, don't miss the roller-coaster road and stupendous views from the statue-mounted summit – below which lie the ruins of **Maratea Superiore**, all that remains of the original 8th-century-BC Greek colony.

The deep green hillsides that encircle this tumbling conurbation offer excellent walking trails and there are a number of easy day trips to the surrounding hamlets of **Acquafredda di Maratea** and **Fiumicello**, with its small sandy beach. The **tourist office** (☎0973 87 69 08; Piazza Gesù 40; ⏰8am-2pm & 5-8pm Mon-Fri, 9am-1pm & 5-8pm Sat & Sun Jul & Aug, 8am-2pm Sep-Jun) is in Fiumicello.

Centro Sub Maratea (☎0973 87 00 13; www.web.tiscali.it/csmaratea; Via Santa Caterina 28, Maratea) offers diving courses and boat tours that include visits to surrounding grottoes and coves.

A worthwhile day trip via car is to pretty **Rivello** (elevation 479m). Perched on a ridge and framed by the southern Apennines, it is a centre for arts and crafts and has long been known for its exquisite working of gold and copper. Rivello's interesting Byzantine history is evident in the tiny tiled cupolas and frescoes of its gorgeous churches.

Sleeping

Locanda delle Donne Monache HOTEL €€
(☎0973 87 74 87; www.locandamonache.com; Via Mazzei 4; r €130-310; ⏰Apr-Oct; P❄@📶🏊) Overlooking the medieval *borgo,* this exclusive hotel is in a converted 18th-century convent with a suitably lofty setting. It's a hotchpotch of vaulted corridors, terraces and gardens fringed with bougainvillea and lemon trees. The rooms are elegantly decorated in pastel shades, while the Sacello restaurant prepares delicate dishes drawing on the regional flavours of Lucania.

B&B Nefer B&B €
(☎0973 87 18 28; www.bbnefer.it; Via Cersuta; r €60-90; P❄@) This B&B set in a small hamlet 5km northwest of Maratea has four rooms decorated in sea greens, blues and pinks. Rooms open onto a lush green lawn complete with deckchairs for contemplating the distant sea view. There's a simple outdoor kitchen area for guest use and a small beach a short walk away along narrow seaside paths.

Hotel Villa Cheta Elite HOTEL €€
(☎0973 87 81 34; www.villa cheta.it; Via Timpone 46; r €140-264; ⏰Apr-Oct; P❄📶) A charming art nouveau villa at the entrance to the hamlet of Acquafredda, this hotel has a broad terrace with spectacular views, a fabulous restaurant and large rooms decorated with antiques.

Eating

Taverna Rovita TRADITIONAL ITALIAN €€
(☎0973 87 65 88; www.tavernarovitamaratea.it; Via Rovita 13; meals €35; ⏰Mar-Oct) This tavern is just off Maratea Inferiore's main piazza. Rovita is excellent value and specialises in hearty local fare, with Lucanian specialities involving stuffed peppers, game birds, local salami and fine seafood.

Lanterna Rossa SEAFOOD €€
(☎0973 87 63 52; Maratea Porto; meals €40; ⏰Wed-Mon Feb-Dec, daily Jul & Aug) Head for the terrace overlooking the port to dine on exquisite seafood. Highly recommended is the signature dish, *zuppa di pesce* – fish soup.

La Caffetteria CAFE €
(Piazza Buraglia, Maratea; panini from €3; ⏰7.30am-2am summer, 7.30am-10pm winter) The outdoor seating at this delightful cafe in Maratea's central piazza is ideal for dedicated people watching.

Getting There & Away

SITA (☎0971 50 68 11; www.sitabus.it) operates a comprehensive network of routes including up the coast to Sapri in Campania (€1.60, 50 minutes, six daily). Local buses (€1) connect the coastal towns and Maratea train station with Maratea Inferiore, running frequently in summer. InterCity and regional trains on the Rome-Reggio line stop at Maratea train station, below the town.

CALABRIA

Tell a non-Calabrese Italian that you're going to Calabria and you will probably elicit some surprise, inevitably followed by stories of the 'ndrangheta – the Calabrian Mafia – notorious for smuggling and kidnapping wealthy northerners and keeping them hidden in the mountains.

But Calabria contains startling natural beauty and spectacular towns that seem to grow out of the craggy mountaintops. It has three national parks: the Pollino in the north, the Sila in the centre and the Aspromonte in the south. It's around 90% hills, but skirted by some 780km of Italy's finest coast (ignore the bits devoured by unappealing holiday camps). Bergamot grows here, and it's the only place in the world where the plants are of sufficient quality to produce the essential oil used in many perfumes and

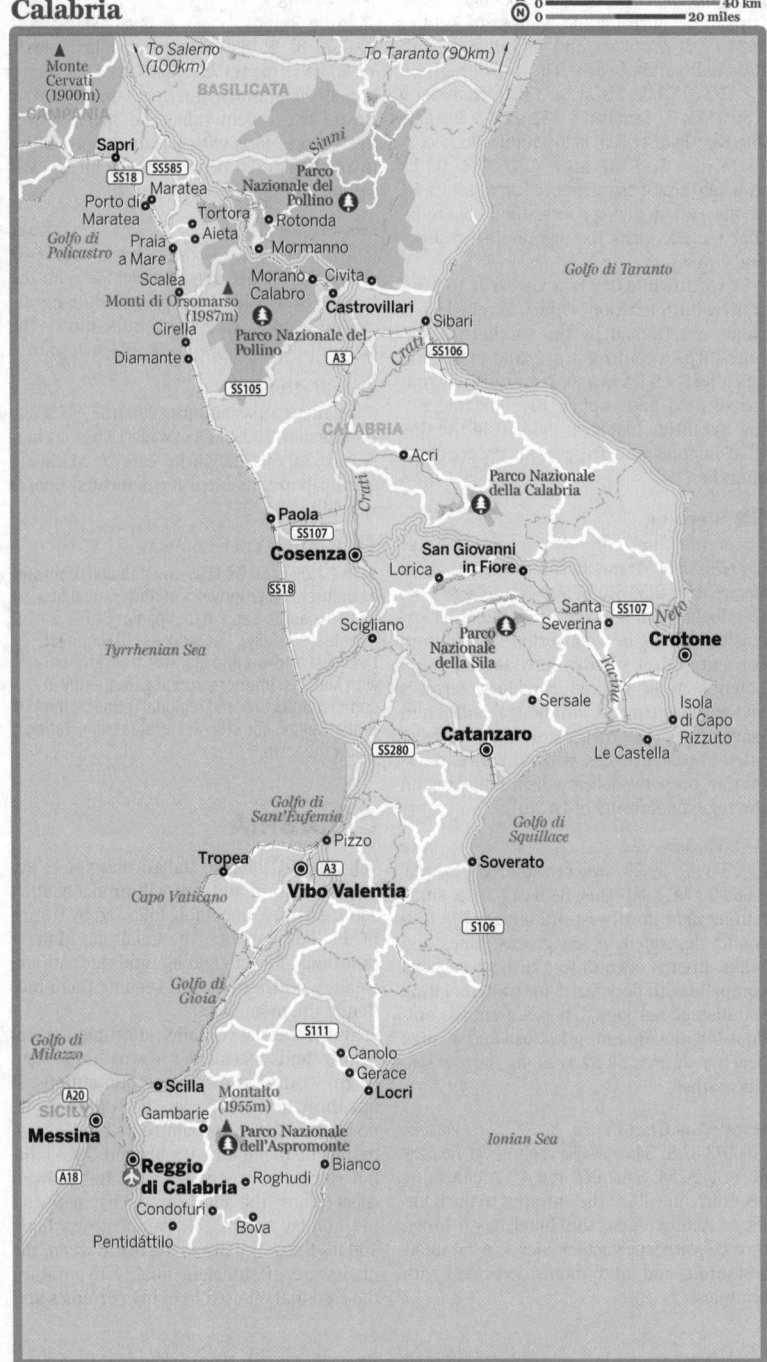

to flavour Earl Grey tea. As in Puglia, there are hundreds of music and food festivals here year-round, reaching a fever pitch in July and August.

Admittedly, you sometimes feel as if you have stepped into a 1970s postcard, as its towns, destroyed by repeated earthquakes, are often surrounded by brutal breeze-block suburbs. The region has suffered from the unhealthy miscegenation between European and government subsidies (aimed to develop the south) and dark Mafia opportunism. Half-finished houses often mask well-furnished flats where families live happily, untroubled by invasive house taxes.

This is where to head for an adventure into the unknown.

History

Traces of Neanderthal, Palaeolithic and Neolithic life have been found in Calabria, but the region only became internationally important with the arrival of the Greeks in the 8th century BC. They founded a colony at what is now Reggio di Calabria. Remnants of this colonisation, which spread along the Ionian coast with Sibari and Crotone as the star settlements, are still visible. However, the fun didn't last for the Greeks and in 202 BC the cities of Magna Graecia all came under Roman control. Destroying the countryside's handsome forests, the Romans did irreparable geological damage. Navigable rivers became fearsome *fiumare* (torrents) dwindling to wide, dry, drought-stricken riverbeds in high summer.

Calabria's fortified hilltop communities weathered successive invasions by the Normans, Swabians, Aragonese and Bourbons, and remained largely undeveloped. Although the 18th-century Napoleonic incursion and the arrival of Garibaldi and Italian unification inspired hope for change, Calabria remained a disappointed, feudal region and, like the rest of the south, was racked by malaria.

A by-product of this tragic history was the growth of banditry and organised crime. Calabria's Mafia, known as the 'ndrangheta (from the Greek for heroism/virtue), inspires fear in the local community, but tourists are rarely the target of its aggression. For many, the only answer has been to get out and, for at least a century, Calabria has seen its young people emigrate in search of work.

Northern Tyrrhenian Coast

The good, the bad and the ugly line the region's western seashore.

The Autostrada del Sole (A3) is one of Italy's great coastal drives. It twists and turns through mountains, past huge swathes of dark-green forest and flashes of cerulean-blue sea. But the Italian penchant for cheap summer resorts has taken its toll here and certain stretches are blighted by shoddy hotels and soulless stacks of flats.

In the low season most places close. In summer many hotels are full, but you should have an easier time with the camping sites.

PRAIA A MARE
POP 6820

Praia a Mare lies just short of Basilicata, the start of a stretch of wide, pebbly beach that continues south for about 30km to Cirella and Diamante. This flat, leafy grid of a town sits on a wide pale-grey beach, looking out to an intriguing rocky chunk off the coast: the Isola di Dino.

Just off the seafront is the **tourist office** (☑0985 7 25 85; Via Amerigo Vespucci 6; ☺8am-1pm) with information on the Isola di Dino, famed for its sea caves. To visit the caves expect to pay around €5 for a guided tour from the old boys who operate off the beach. Alternatively, ask at the tourist office.

Autolinee Preite (☑0984 41 30 01) operates buses to Cosenza (€5.20, two hours, 10 daily). SITA (☑0971 50 68 11; www.sitabus.it, in Italian) goes north to Maratea and Potenza. Regular trains also pass through for Paola and Reggio di Calabria.

AIETA & TORTORA

Precariously perched, otherworldly Aieta and Tortora must have been difficult to reach pre-asphalt. Rocco (☑0973 22 943; www.roccosrl.it) buses serve both villages, 6km and 12km from Praia respectively. Aieta is higher than Tortora and the journey constitutes much of the reward. When you arrive, walk up to the 16th-century Palazzo Spinello at the end of the road and take a look into the ravine behind it – it's a stunning view.

DIAMANTE
POP 5400

This fashionable seaside town, with its long promenade, is central to Calabria's famous *peperoncino* – the conversation-stalling spice that so characterises its cuisine. In early September a hugely popular chilli-eating competition takes place. Diamante is also famed for the bright murals that contemporary local and foreign artists have painted on the facades of the old buildings. For the best seafood restaurants head for the seafront at Spiaggia Piccola.

Autolinee Preite (☑0984 41 30 01) buses between Cosenza and Praia a Mare stop at Diamante.

PAOLA
POP 16,900

Paola is worth a stop to see its holy shrine. The large pilgrimage complex is above a sprawling small town where the dress of choice is a tracksuit and the main activity is hanging about on street corners. The 80km of coast south from here to Pizzo is mostly overdeveloped and ugly. Paola is the main train hub for Cosenza, about 25km inland.

Watched over by a crumbling castle, **Santuario di San Francesco di Paola** (☑0982 58 25 18; admission free; ⊘6am-1pm & 2-6pm) is a curious, empty cave with tremendous significance to the devout. The saint lived and died in Paola in the 15th century and the sanctuary that he and his followers carved out of the bare rock has attracted pilgrims for centuries. The cloister is surrounded by naïve wall paintings depicting the saint's truly incredible miracles. The original church contains an ornate reliquary of the saint. Also within the complex is a modern basilica, built to mark the second millennium. Black-clad monks hurry about.

There are several hotels near the station, but you'll be better off staying in towns further north along the coast.

Cosenza
POP 69,800 / ELEV 238M

Cosenza's medieval core is Calabria's best-preserved historic centre, the one piece of history that has managed to escape the constant earthquakes that have levelled almost everything else in the region. It rises above the confluence of the Crati and Busento rivers, its narrow lanes winding ever upwards to the hilltop castle. Legend states that Alaric, a Visigoth king, was killed and buried at the confluence of the two rivers.

In the past, Cosenza was a sophisticated and lively city but nowadays there's a gritty feel to the old town with its dark streets and fading, once-elegant *palazzi*. It's the gateway to La Sila's mountains, home to Calabria's most important university and a major transport hub – but there's not much to see or do here.

⊙ Sights

In the new town, pedestrianised Corso Mazzini provides a pleasant respite from the chaotic traffic and incessant car honking. There are a number of sculptures lining the *corso*.

In the old town, head up the winding, charmingly dilapidated Corso Telesio which has a raw Neapolitan feel to it and is lined with ancient hung-with-washing tenements, antiquated shopfronts and a worrying number of funeral parlours. At the top, the 12th-century **cathedral** (Piazza del Duomo; ⊘8am-noon & 3-7.30pm) has been rebuilt in restrained baroque style in the 18th century. In a chapel off the north aisle is a copy of an exquisite 13th-century Byzantine Madonna.

From the cathedral, you can walk up Via del Seggio through a little medieval quarter before turning right to reach the 13th-century **Convento di San Francesco d'Assisi**. Otherwise head along the *corso* to Piazza XV Marzo, an appealing square fronted by the Palazzo del Governo and the handsome neoclassical **Teatro Rendano**.

South of the piazza stretches the lovely **Villa Vecchia** park with lofty mature trees providing welcome shade.

From Piazza XV Marzo, follow Via Paradiso, then Via Antonio Siniscalchi for the route to the down-at-heel Norman **castle** (Piazza Frederico II), left in disarray by several earthquakes. It's closed for restoration, but the view merits the steep ascent.

🛏 Sleeping

B&B Via dell'Astrologo   B&B €
(☑338 920 53 94; www.viadellastrologo.com; Via Rutilio Benincasa 16; s €35-40, d €60-70, tr €90; ☎) A gem in the historical centre, this small B&B is tastefully decorated with polished wooden floors, white bedspreads, and good quality art work. Brothers Mario and Marco are a mine of information on Cosenza and Calabria in general.

Royal Hotel   HOTEL €€
(☑0984 41 21 65; www.hotelroyalsas.it; Via Molinella 24; €100; P ❄ @ ☎) One of the few decent

Italy's largest national park, the Pollino National Park (www.parcopollino.it), straddles Basilicata and Calabria and covers 1960 sq km. It acts like a rocky curtain separating the region from the rest of Italy and has the richest repository of flora and fauna in the south.

The park's most spectacular areas are Monte Pollino (2248m), Monti di Orsomarso (1987m), and the canyon of the Gole del Raganello. The mountains, often snowbound, are blanketed by forests of oak, alder, maple, beech, pine and fir. The park is most famous, however, for its ancient *pino loricato* trees, which are only found here and in the Balkans. The oldest specimens reach 40m in height.

The park has a varied landscape, from deep river canyons to alpine meadows, and is home to rare stocks of roe deer, wild cats, wolves, birds of prey (including the golden eagle and Egyptian vulture) and the endangered otter, *Lutra lutra*.

In Basilicata, the park's main centre is Rotonda (elevation 626m) and is home to the official park office, Ente Parco Nazionale del Pollino (☎0973 66 93 11; Via delle Frecce Tricolori 6; ☺8am-2pm Mon-Fri, 3-5.30pm Mon & Wed). Interesting villages to explore include the unique Albanian villages of San Paolo Albanese and San Costantino Albanese. These isolated and unspoilt communities fiercely maintain their mountain culture and the Greek liturgy is retained in the main churches. For local handicrafts visit Terranova di Pollino for wooden crafts, Latronico for alabaster, and Sant'Arcangelo for wrought iron.

In Calabria, Civita was founded by Albanian refugees in 1746. Other towns worth visiting are Castrovillari, with its well-preserved 15th-century Aragonese castle, and Morano Calabro – look up the beautiful MC Escher woodcut of this town. Naturalists should also check out the wildlife museum Centro Il Nibbio (☎0981 3 07 45; Vico II Annunziata 11; admission €4; ☺10am-1pm & 3-6pm winter, 10am-1pm & 4-8pm summer) in Morano, which explains the Pollino ecosystem.

Good hiking maps are scarce. The *Carta Excursionistica del Pollino Lucano* (scale 1:50000), produced by the Basilicata tourist board, is a useful driving map. The large-scale *Parco Nazionale del Pollino* map shows all the main routes and includes some useful information on the park, its flora and fauna and the park communities. Both maps are free and can be found in local tourist offices.

For an English-speaking guide, contact Giuseppe Cosenza from Asklepios, who arranges trekking, mountain-biking and rafting trips in the Pollino and throughout Basilicata. Ferula Viaggi in Matera also runs mountain-bike excursions and treks into the Pollino. For guided trips in Calabria visit www.guidapollino.it.

White-water rafting down the spectacular Lao river is popular in the Calabrian Pollino. Centro Lao Action Raft (☎0985 2 14 76; www.laoraft.com; Via Lauro 8) in Scalea can arrange rafting trips as well as canyoning, trekking and mountain-biking trips.

The park has a number of *agriturismi*. Agriturismo Colloreto (☎347 323 69 14; www.colloreto.it; Fratelli Coscia; s/d €28/56), near Morano Calabro, is in a remote rural setting, gorgeous amid rolling hills. Rooms are comfortable and old-fashioned with polished wood and flagstone floors. Also in Calabria, Locanda di Alia (☎0981 4 63 70; www.alia.it; Via letticelle 55; s/d €90/120; P❋☾), in Castrovillari, offers bungalow-style accommodation in a lush green garden.

In Basilicata, Asklepios (☎0973 66 92 90, 347 263 14 62; www.asklepios.it; Contrada Barone 9, Rotonda; s/d €30/50) has basic accommodation but is the place to stay for walkers as it's run by hiking guide Giuseppe Cosenza. Otherwise, the chalet-style Picchio Nero (☎0973 9 31 70; www.picchionero.com; Via Mulino 1; s/d incl breakfast €60/73; P) in Terranova di Pollino, with its Austrian-style wooden balconies and recommended restaurant, is a popular hotel for hikers.

Two highly recommended restaurants include Luna Rossa (☎0973 9 32 54; Via Marconi 18; meals €35; ☺Thu-Tue) in Terranova di Pollino, and Da Peppe (☎0973 66 12 51; Corso Garibaldi 13; meals €25-35; ☺lunch & dinner Tue-Sun) in Rotonda.

You'll need your own vehicle to visit the Pollino.

N 0 ————————— 200 m
0 ————————— 0.1 miles

Map area with labels:

To Corso Mazzini (100m) | To Royal Hotel (800m)

Busento

Via Garibaldi

Piazza dei Valdesi

Corso Telesio

7

Grotte Di San Francesco D'Assisi

Vico II Giuseppe Marini Serra

3

Lungo Crati de Seta

Crati

8

Piazza del Duomo

Via G Campagna

Via del Seggio

Via Giostra Vecchia

Corso Vittorio Emanuele

Via Paoloisi

Corso Telesio

6

Via Cafarone

Via Rutilio Benincasa

5

Piazza Luigi Cribari

Via Dei Normanni

Via F Pettrarca

1

Via Argento

Piazza XV Marzo

Villa Vecchia

4

Via Paradiso

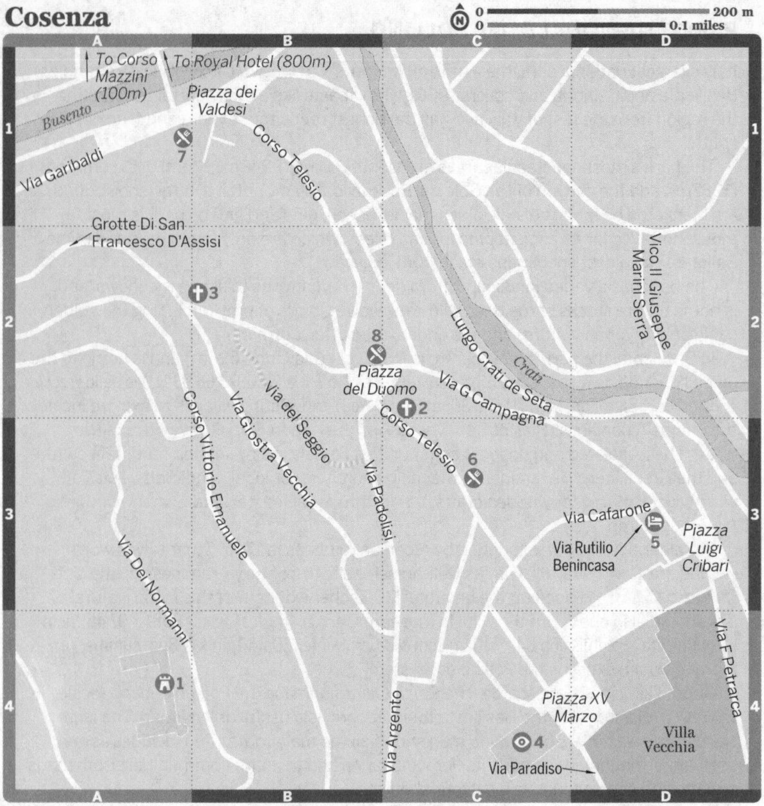

Cosenza

◎ Sights
1 Castle..A4
2 Cathedral...C2
3 Convento di San Francesco
   d'Assisi...B2
4 Teatro Rendano................................C4

🛏 Sleeping
5 B&B Via dell'Astrologo.....................D3

🍴 Eating
6 Gran Caffè Renzelli...........................C3
7 Per... Bacco!!.....................................A1
8 Ristorante Calabria Bella.................B2

options in town, the Royal is a short stroll from Corso Mazzini. Rooms are impersonal but comfortable. Stay in the new section of the hotel, around the corner from its older sister.

✗ Eating

Gran Caffè Renzelli　　　　　CAFE €

(Corso Telesio 46) This venerable cafe behind the *duomo* has been run by the same family since 1803 when the founder arrived from Naples and began baking gooey cakes and desserts (cakes start at around €1.20). Sink your teeth into *torroncino torrefacto* (a confection of sugar, spices and hazelnuts) or *torta telesio* (made from almonds, cherries, apricot jam and lupins).

**Ristorante Calabria
Bella**　　　　　TRADITIONAL ITALIAN €€

(📞0984 79 35 31; www.ristorantecalabriabella.it; Piazza del Duomo; meals €25; ⊗noon-3pm & 7pm-midnight) Traditional Calabrian cuisine, such as *grigliata mista di carne* (mixed grilled meats), is regularly dished up in this cosy restaurant in the old town.

Per... Bacco!! TRATTORIA €€
(📞0984 79 55 69; www.perbaccowinebar.it; Piazza dei Valdesi; meals €25) This smart yet informal restaurant has windows onto the square. Inside are exposed stone walls, vines and heavy beams. The reassuringly brief menu includes a generous and tasty antipasto (€8).

ℹ Information

The main drag, Corso Mazzini, runs south from Piazza Bilotti (formerly known as Piazza Fera), near the bus station, and intersects Viale Trieste before meeting Piazza dei Bruzi. Head further south and cross the Busento river to reach the old town.

ℹ Getting There & Around

Air

Lamezia Terme airport (Sant'Eufemia Lamezia, SUF; 📞0968 41 43 33; www.sacal.it), 63km south of Cosenza, at the junction of the A3 and SS280 motorways, links the region with major Italian cities. The airport is also served by Ryanair, easyJet and charters from northern Europe. A shuttle leaves the airport every 20 minutes for the airport train station where there are frequent trains to Cosenza (€4.60, one hour).

Bus

The main **bus station** (📞0984 41 31 24) is northeast of Piazza Bilotti. Services leave for Catanzaro (€4.60, 1¾ hours, eight daily) and towns throughout La Sila. **Autolinee Preite** (📞0984 41 30 01) has buses heading daily along the north Tyrrhenian coast; **Autolinee Romano** (📞0962 2 17 09) serves Crotone as well as Rome and Milan.

Train

Stazione Nuova (📞0984 2 70 59) is about 2km northeast of the centre. Regular trains go to Reggio di Calabria (from €11.60, three hours) and Rome (from €44, four to six hours), both usually with a change at Paola, and Naples (from €26.40, three to four hours), as well as most destinations around the Calabrian coast.

Amaco (📞0984 30 80 11) bus 27 links the centre and Stazione Nuova, the main train station.

Parco Nazionale della Sila

'La Sila' is a big landscape, where wooded hills create endless rolling views. It's dotted with small villages and cut through with looping roads that make driving a test of your digestion.

It's divided into three areas covering 130 sq km: the Sila Grande, with the highest mountains; the strongly Albanian Sila Greca (to the north); and the Sila Piccola (near Catanzaro), with vast forested hills.

The highest peaks, covered with tall Corsican pines, reach 2000m – high enough for thick snow in winter. This makes it a popular skiing destination. In summer the climate is coolly alpine with carpets of spring wildflowers and mushroom hunting in autumn. At its peak is the Bosco di Gallopani (Forest of Gallopani). There are several beautiful lakes, the largest of which is Lago di Cecita o Mucone near Camigliatello Silano. There is also plenty of wildlife here, including the light-grey Apennine wolf, a protected species.

Good-quality information in English is scarce. You can try the national park **visitors centre** (📞0984 53 71 09) at Cupone, 10km from Camigliatello, or the **Pro Loco tourist office** (📞0984 57 81 59; Via Roma; ⏰9.30am-12.30pm & 3.30-6.30pm Wed-Mon) in Camigliatello. A useful internet resource is the official park website: www.parcosila.it. The people who run B&B Calabria in the park are extremely knowledgeable and helpful.

For maps, you can use *Carta del Parco Nazionale della Sila* (€8) which has walking trails (in Italian). *The Sila for 4* is a miniguide in English which outlines a number of walking trails in the park. The booklet is available in tourist offices and from the privately run **New Sila Tourist Service Agency** (📞0984 57 81 25; Via Roma 16, Camigliatello) – a good source of information on the park.

Valli Cupe (📞333 698 88 35, 864 36 01; www.vallicupe.it) runs hiking trips in the area around Sersale (in the southeast), where there are myriad waterfalls and the dramatic Canyon Valli Cupe. Trips cost only €8 per person per day. Specialising in botany, the guides (who speak Italian and French) also visit remote monasteries and churches. Stay in their rustic accommodation in the town.

During August, **Sila in Festa** takes place, featuring traditional music. Autumn is mushroom season, when you'll be able to frequent mushroom festivals, including the **Sagra del Fungo** in Camigliatello.

◉ Sights

La Sila's main town, **San Giovanni in Fiore** (1049m), is named after the founder of its beautiful medieval **abbey**. The town has an attractive old centre, once you've battled through the suffocating suburbs, and is famous for its Armenian-style handloomed carpets and tapestry. You can visit the studio and shop of Domenico Caruso (☑0984 99 27 24; www.scuolatappeti.it), but ring ahead.

A popular ski-resort town, with 6km of slopes, Camigliatello Silano (1272m) looks much better under snow. A few lifts operate on Monte Curcio, about 3km to the south. Around 5.5km of slopes and a 1500m lift can be found near Lorica (1370m), on gloriously pretty Lago Arvo – the best place to camp in summer.

Scigliano (620m), in Sila Piccola, is a small hilltop town and has a superb B&B; from Sersale (739m), further south, you can go trekking with Valli Cupe guides.

🛏 Sleeping

TOP CHOICE B&B Calabria
B&B €

(☑349 878 18 94; www.bedandbreakfastcalabria.it; Via Roma 9, Frazione Diano, Scigliano; s/d €40/60; ☺Apr-Nov) In the mountains, this B&B has five comfortable rooms, all with separate entrances. Raffaele is a great source of information on the region and can recommend places to eat, visit and go hiking. Rooms have character and clean modern lines and there's a wonderful terrace overlooking endless forested vistas. Mountain bikes available.

Hotel Aquila & Edelweiss
HOTEL €

(☑0984 57 80 44; www.hotelaquilaedelweiss.com; Viale Stazione 15, Camigliatello; s €60-80, d €80-100; P❄@) This three-star hotel in Camigliatello has a stark and anonymous exterior but it's in a good location and the rooms are cosy and comfortable.

Valli Cupe
B&B €

(☑333 698 88 35; www.vallicupe.it; Sersale; per person €20) Valli Cupe can arrange a stay in a charming rustic cottage in Sersale, complete with an open fireplace (good for roasting chestnuts) and kitchen. All bookings via its website.

Park Hotel 108
HOTEL €€

(☑0521 64 81 08; www.hotelpark108.it; Via Nazionale 86, Lorica; r €90-130; P🖥) Situated on the hilly banks of Lago Arvo, surrounded by dark-green pines, the rooms here are decorated in classic bland-hotel style – but who cares about decor with views like this!

Camping del Lago Arvo
CAMPGROUND €

(☑0984 53 70 60; camping 2 people, tent & car €10-14, bungalow €40-60) Lorica's lakeside is a particularly great place to camp. Try this large comfortable spot, near the Calabrian National Park office.

🛍 Shopping

La Sila's forests yield wondrous wild mushrooms, both edible and poisonous. Sniff around the Antica Salumeria Campanaro (Piazza Misasi 5) in Camigliatello Silano; it's a temple to all things fungoid, as well as an emporium of fine meats, cheeses, pickles and wines.

ℹ Getting There & Away

You can reach Camigliatello Silano and San Giovanni in Fiore via regular Ferrovie della Calabria buses along the SS107, which links Cosenza and Crotone.

Ionian Coast

With its flat coastline and wide sandy beaches, the Ionian coast has some fascinating stops from Sibari to Santa Severina, with some of the best beaches on the coast around Soverato. However, the coast has borne the brunt of some ugly development and is mainly a long, uninterrupted string of resorts, thronged in the summer months and shut down from October to May.

It's worth taking a trip inland to visit Santa Severina, a spectacular mountaintop town, 26km northwest of Crotone. The town is dominated by a Norman castle and is home to a beautiful Byzantine church.

LE CASTELLA

The town is named for its impressive 16th-century Aragonese castle (admission €3; ☺9am-1pm & 3-6pm winter, 9am-midnight summer), a vast edifice linked to the mainland by a short causeway. The philosopher Pliny said that Hannibal constructed the first tower. Evidence shows it was begun in the 4th century BC, designed to protect Crotone in the wars against Pyrrhus.

Le Castella is south of a rare protected area (Capo Rizzuto) along this coast, rich not only in nature but also in Greek history. For further information on the park try www.riservamarinacaporizzuto.it.

With around 15 camp sites near Isola di Capo Rizzuto to the north, this is the Ionian coast's prime camping area. Try **La Fattoria** (☑0962 79 11 65; Via del Faro; camping 2 people, car & tent €23, bungalow €60; ⊙Jun-Sep), 1.5km from the sea, with bungalows also available. Otherwise, **Da Annibale** (☑0962 79 50 04; Via Duomo 35; s/d €50/70; ℗✳@🛜) is a pleasant hotel in town with a splendid fish **restaurant** (meals €30; ⊙lunch & dinner).

For expansive sea views dine at bright and airy **Ristorante Micomare** (☑0962 79 50 82; Via Vittoria 7; meals €20-25; ⊙lunch & dinner).

GERACE
POP 2830

A spectacular medieval hill town, Gerace is worth a detour for the views alone – on one side the Ionian Sea, on the other dark, interior mountains. About 10km inland from Locri on the SS111, it has Calabria's largest Romanesque **cathedral**. Dating from 1045, later alterations have robbed it of none of its majesty.

For a taste of traditional Calabrian cooking, the modest and welcoming **Ristorante a Squella** (☑0964 35 60 86; Viale della Resistenza 8; meals €20) makes for a great lunchtime stop serving reliably good dishes, specialising in seafood and pizzas. Afterwards you can wander down the road and admire the views.

Further inland is **Canolo**, a small village seemingly untouched by the 20th century. Buses connect Gerace with Locri and also Canolo with Siderno, both of which link to the main coastal railway line.

Parco Nazionale dell'Aspromonte

Most Italians think of the **Parco Nazionale dell'Aspromonte** (www.parcoaspromonte.it, in Italian) as a hiding place used by Calabrian kidnappers in the 1970s and '80s. It's still rumoured to contain 'ndrangheta strongholds, but as a tourist you're unlikely to encounter any murky business. The national park, Calabria's second-largest, is startlingly dramatic, rising sharply inland from Reggio. Its highest peak, **Montalto** (1955m), is dominated by a huge bronze statue of Christ and offers sweeping views across to Sicily.

Subject to frequent mudslides and carved up by torrential rivers, the mountains are nonetheless awesomely beautiful. Underwater rivers keep the peaks covered in coniferous forests and ablaze with flowers in spring. It's wonderful walking country and the park has several colour-coded trails.

Extremes of weather and geography have resulted in some extraordinary villages, such as **Pentidàttilo** and **Roghudi**, clinging limpet-like to the craggy, rearing rocks and now all but deserted. It's worth the drive to explore these eagle-nest villages. Another mountain eyrie with a photogenic ruined castle is **Bova**, perched at 900m above sea level. The drive up the steep, dizzying road to Bova is not for the faint hearted, but the views are stupendous.

Maps are scarce. Try the **national park office** (☑0965 74 30 60; www.parcoaspromonte. it; Via Aurora; ⊙9am-1pm Mon-Fri, 3-5pm Tue & Thu) in **Gambarie**, the Aspromonte's main town and the easiest approach to the park. The roads are good and many activities are organised from here – you can ski and it's also the place to hire a 4WD; ask around in the town.

It's also possible to approach from the south, but the roads aren't as good. The cooperative **Naturaliter** (☑347 3046799; www. naturaliterweb.it), based in **Condofuri**, is an excellent source of information, and can help arrange walking and donkey treks and place you in B&Bs throughout the region. **Co-operativa San Leo** (☑347 3046799), based in Bova, also provides guided tours and accommodation. In Reggio di Calabria, you can book treks and tours with **Misafumera** (☑0965 67 70 21; www.misafumera.it; Via Nazionale 306d).

Stay on a bergamot farm at **Azienda Agrituristica Il Bergamotto** (☑347 601 23 38; Via Amendolea, Condofuri; per person €25) where Ugo Sergi can also arrange excursions. Hiking trails pass nearby so it's a good hiking base. The rooms are simple but it's in a lovely rural location and the food is delicious.

To reach Gambarie, take ATAM city bus 127 from Reggio di Calabria (€1, 1½ hours, up to six daily). Most of the roads inland from Reggio eventually hit the SS183 road that runs north to the town.

Reggio di Calabria

POP 185,900

Reggio is the main launching point for ferries to Sicily, which sparkles temptingly across the Strait of Messina. It is also home to the spectacular Bronzi di Riace and has

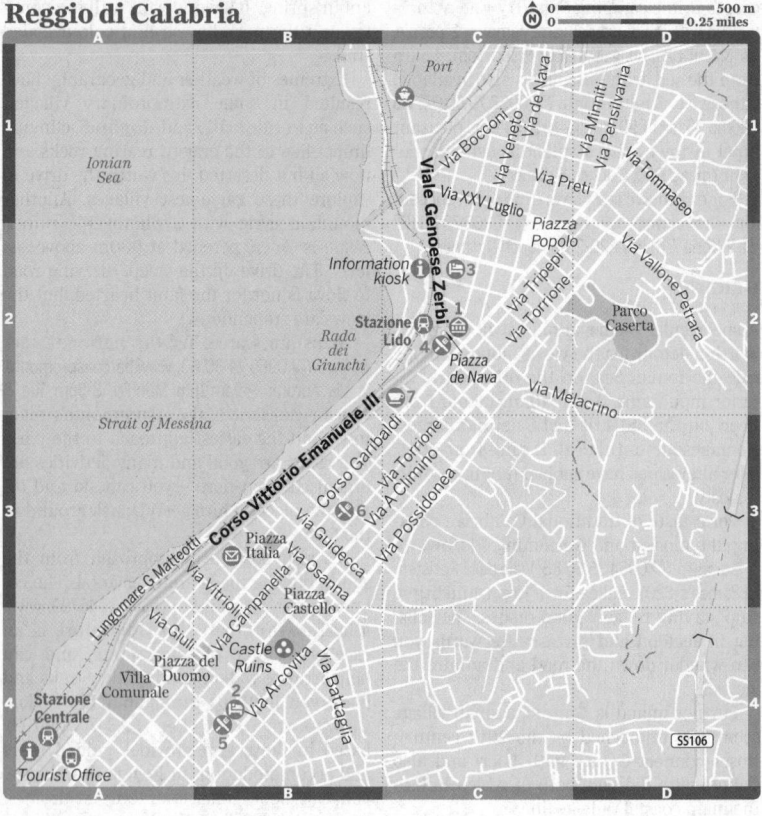

Ionian
Sea

Port

Information
kiosk

Stazione
Lido

Rada
dei
Giunchi

Strait of Messina

Viale Genoese Zerbi

Corso Vittorio Emanuele III

Corso Garibaldi

Via Bocconi
Via Veneto
Via de Nava
Via Minniti
Via Pensilvania
Via Tommaseo

Via XXV Luglio
Via Preti

Piazza
Popolo

Via Tripepi
Via Torrione

Parco
Caserta

Via Vallone Petrara

Piazza
de Nava

Via Melacrino

Via Torrione
Via A. Climino
Via Possidonea

Lungomare G Matteotti

Piazza
Italia

Via Guidecca

Via Osanna

Via Vitriolf
Via Campanella

Piazza
Castello

Via Giuli

Castle
Ruins

Piazza del
Duomo

Villa
Comunale

Via Arcovita

Via Battaglia

Stazione
Centrale

Tourist Office

SS106

Reggio di Calabria

◎ Sights

1 Museo Nazionale della Magna
   Grecia C2

🛏 Sleeping

2 B&B Casa Blanca.................................. B4
3 Hotel Lungomare.................................. C2

🍴 Eating

4 Cèsare...C2
5 La Cantina del Macellaio B4
6 Le Rose al Bicchiere...............................B3

🍷 Drinking

7 Caffe Matteoti..C2

a long, impressive seafront promenade –
packed during the evening *passeggiata*.
Otherwise, the city's grid system of dusty
streets has the slightly dissolute feel shared
by most ports.

Beyond the seafront, the centre gives way
to urban sprawl. Ravaged by earthquakes,
the most recent in 1908, this once-proud
ancient Greek city has plenty of other woes.

As a port and the largest town close to the
'ndrangheta strongholds of Aspromonte, organised crime is a major problem, with the
associated corrosive social effect.

On a lighter note, there are plenty of
festivals in Reggio – early August sees the
Festival dello Stretto (www.festivaldello
stretto.it), featuring the traditional music of
the south.

⦿ Sights

Museo Nazionale della Magna Grecia
MUSEUM

(☏0965 81 22 55; www.museonazionalerc.it; Piazza de Nava 26; adult/child €7/3; ☺9am-7.30pm Tue-Sun) The museum's prides are the world's finest examples of ancient Greek sculpture: the Bronzi di Riace, two exquisite bronze statues discovered on the seabed near Riace in 1972. Larger than life, they depict the Greek obsession with the body: inscrutable, determined and fierce, their perfect form more godlike than human. No one knows who they are – whether man or god – and even their provenance is a mystery. They date from around 450 BC; it's believed they're the work of two artists.

Aside from the bronzes, there are other magnificent ancient exhibits. Look for the 5th-century-BC bronze *Philosopher's Head,* the oldest-known Greek portrait in existence.

🛏 Sleeping

Finding a room should be easy, even in summer, since most visitors pass straight through en route to Sicily.

B&B Casa Blanca
B&B €

(☏347 9459210; www.bbcasablanca.it; Via Arcovito 24; s €40-50, d €65-80; ❄🔊) A little gem in Reggio's heart, this 19th-century *palazzo* has spacious rooms gracefully furnished with romantic white-on-white decor. There's a self-serve breakfast nook, a small breakfast table in each room and two apartments available. Great choice.

Hotel Lungomare
HOTEL €€

(☏0965 2 04 86; www.hotellungomare.rc.it; Viale Genoese Zerbi 13; s/d €85/130; P❄@🔊) The ornate wedding-cake exterior is a welcome reprise from Reggio's faceless modern blocks. Rooms are plain and nothing special, but the staff are friendly and courteous. Ask for a room with a sea view.

🍴 Eating & Drinking

Le Rose al Bicchiere
TRADITIONAL ITALIAN €€

(☏0965 2 29 56; Via Demetrio Tripepi 118; meals €30; ☺lunch Mon-Fri, dinner Mon-Sat Oct-Jun) A wine bar with some delicious fresh local and organic produce on offer to accompany wines so inviting you'll have to pour yourself onto the ferry. The local cheeses and desserts are particularly good.

La Cantina del Macellaio
TRATTORIA €€

(☏0965 2 39 32; www.lacantinadelmacellaio.it; Via Arcovito 26; meals €25; ☺dinner nightly, lunch Sun) This popular trattoria, recommended by locals, dishes up typical Calabrese cuisine with an emphasis on meat dishes. The wine cellar is extensive and impressive.

Caffe Matteotti
CAFE €

(www.caffematteotti.it; Corso Vittorio Emanuele 39; ☺7am-2am Tue-Sun) The tables along the *corso* offer sea views with your *aperitivi* and it's a prime spot for people watching.

Cèsare
GELATERIA €

(Piazza Indipendenza; ☺6am-1am) The most popular gelateria in town is in a green kiosk at the end of the *lungomare* (seafront).

ℹ Information

Stazione Centrale, the main train station, is at the town's southern edge. Walk northeast along Corso Garibaldi for the tourist office, shopping and other services. The *corso* has long been a de facto pedestrian zone during the ritual *passeggiata*.

Hospital (☏0965 39 71 11; Via Melacrino)

Police station (☏0965 41 11 11; Corso Garibaldi 442)

Post office (Via Miraglia 14)

Tourist information kiosk (Viale Genovese Zerbi; ☺9am-noon & 4-7pm); airport (☏0965 64 32 91); Stazione Centrale (☏0965 2 71 20)

ℹ Getting There & Away

Air

Reggio's **airport** (REG; ☏0965 64 05 17; www.aeroportodellostretto.it) is at Ravagnese, about 5km south.

Boat

Boats for Messina (Sicily) leave from the port (just north of Stazione Lido), where there are three adjacent ferry terminals. In high season there are up to 20 hydrofoils daily; in low season there are as few as two. Some boats continue to the Aeolian Islands.

Services are run by various companies, including **Meridiano** (☏0965 81 04 14; www.meridianolines.it). Prices for cars are €12 one way and for foot passengers €1.50 to €2.80. The crossing takes 20 minutes.

Bus

Most buses terminate at Piazza Garibaldi, in front of the Stazione Centrale. Several different companies operate to towns in Calabria and beyond. **ATAM** (☏800 43 33 10; www.atam-rc.it) serves the Aspromonte Massif, with bus 127 to Gambarie (€1, 1½ hours, six daily). **Lirosi** (☑0966 5 79 01) serves Rome (€46, eight hours, two daily). Regional trains are more convenient than bus services to Scilla and Tropea.

Car & Motorcycle

The A3 ends at Reggio. If you are continuing south, the SS106 hugs the coast round the 'toe', then heads north along the Ionian Sea. Reggio has a weirdly complex parking system – buy a parking permit (€0.50 per hour) from newspaper kiosks or from a parking representative, if you can find one.

Train

Trains stop at **Stazione Centrale** (☑0965 89 20 21) and less frequently at Stazione Lido, near the museum. There are frequent trains to Milan (from €140, 9½ to 11½ hours), Rome (from €69, 7½ hours) and Naples (from €56, 4½ to 5½ hours). Regional services run along the coast to Scilla and Tropea, and also to Catanzaro and less frequently to Cosenza and Bari.

ℹ Getting Around

Orange local buses run by **ATAM** (☑800 433310; www.atam-rc.it) cover most of the city. For the port, take bus 13 or 125 from Piazza Garibaldi outside Stazione Centrale. The Porto-Aeroporto bus (125) runs from the port via Piazza Garibaldi to the airport and vice versa (25 minutes, hourly). Buy your ticket at ATAM offices, tobacconists or news stands.

Southern Tyrrhenian Coast

North of Reggio, along the coast-hugging Autostrada del Sole (A3), the scenery rocks and rolls to become increasingly beautiful and dramatic, if you ignore the shoddy holiday camps and unattractive developments that sometimes scar the land. Like the northern part of the coast, it's mostly closed in winter and packed in summer.

SCILLA
POP 5160

In Scilla, cream-, ochre- and earth-coloured houses cling on for dear life to the jagged promontory, ascending in jumbled ranks to the hill's summit, which is crowned by a castle and, just below, the dazzling white confection of the Chiesa Arcipretale Maria Immacolata. Lively in summer and serene in low season, the town is split in two by the tiny port. The fishing district of Scilla Chianalea, to the north, harbours small hotels

and restaurants off narrow lanes, lapped by the sea. It can only be visited on foot.

Scilla's highpoint is a rock at the northern end, said to be the lair of Scylla, the mythical six-headed sea monster who drowned sailors as they tried to navigate the Strait of Messina. Swimming and fishing off the town's glorious white sandy beach is somewhat safer today. Head for Lido Paradiso from where you can squint up at the castle while sunbathing on the sand.

◉ Sights

Castello Ruffo   CASTLE
(☑0956 70 42 07; admission €1.50; ⊙8.30am-7.30pm) An imposing hilltop fortress, the castle has at times been a lighthouse and a monastery. It houses a *luntre*, the original black boat used for swordfishing, and on which the modern-day *passarelle* is based.

🛏 Sleeping

Le Piccole Grotte   B&B €
(☑338 2096727; www.lepiccolegrotte.it; Via Grotte 10; d €90-120; ❄) In the picturesque Chianalea district, this B&B is housed in a 19th-century fishermen's house beside steps leading to the crystal-clear sea. Rooms have small balconies facing the cobbled alleyway or the sea.

La Locandiera   B&B €
(☑0965 75 48 81; www.lalocandiera.org; Via Zagari 27; d €60-100; ❄🅰) Run by the same people who own Le Piccole Grotte, this B&B is just as picturesque with large, comfortable rooms and views over the sea.

🍴 Eating & Drinking

Bleu de Toi   SEAFOOD €€
(☑0965 79 05 85; www.bleudetoi.it; Via Grotte 40; meals €30-35; ⊙Wed-Mon) Soak up the Chianalea atmosphere at this little restaurant. It has a terrace over the water and excellent seafood dishes, including Scilla's renowned swordfish.

Dali City Pub   BAR
(Via Porto) On the beach in Scilla town, this popular bar has a Beatles tribute corner (appropriately named The Cavern) and has been going since 1972.

CAPO VATICANO

There are spectacular views from this rocky cape, with its beaches, ravines and limestone sea cliffs. Birdwatchers' spirits should soar. Around 7km south of Tropea, Capo Vaticano has a lighthouse, built in

1885, which is close to a short footpath from where you can see as far as the Aeolian Islands. Capo Vaticano beach is one of the balmiest along this coast.

TROPEA
POP 6780

Tropea, a puzzle of lanes and piazzas, is famed for its captivating prettiness, dramatic position and sunsets the colour of amethyst. It sits on the Promontorio di Tropea, which stretches from Nicotera in the south to Pizzo in the north. The coast alternates between dramatic cliffs and icing-sugar-soft sandy beaches, all edged by translucent sea. Unsurprisingly, hundreds of Italian holidaymakers descend here in summer. If you hear English being spoken it is probably from Americans visiting relatives: enormous numbers left the region for America in the early 20th century.

Despite the mooted theory that Hercules founded the town, it seems this area has been settled as far back as Neolithic times. Tropea has been occupied by the Arabs, Normans, Swabians, Anjous and Aragonese, as well as attacked by Turkish pirates. Perhaps they were after the town's famous sweet red onions.

☉ Sights

The town overlooks Santa Maria dell'Isola, a medieval church with a Renaissance makeover, which sits on its own island, although centuries of silt have joined it to the mainland.

The beautiful Norman cathedral (☺6.30-11.30am & 4-7pm) has two undetonated WWII bombs near the door: it's believed they didn't explode due to the protection of the town's patron saint, Our Lady of Romania.

⌸ Sleeping

Donnaciccina B&B €€
(☎0963 6 21 80; www.donnaciccina.com; Via Pelliccia 9; s €40-75, d €80-150; ❇ @) Overlooking the main *corso*, this delightful B&B has retained a tangible sense of history with its carefully selected antiques, canopy beds and exposed stone walls. There's also a self-catering apartment perfectly positioned on the cliff overlooking the sea.

Residence il Barone B&B €€
(☎0963 60 71 81; Largo Barone; www.residenceilbarone.com; r €70-180; ❇@☎) This graceful *palazzo* has six suites decorated in masculine neutrals and tobacco-browns, with

dramatic modern paintings by the owner's brother adding pizazz to the walls. There's a computer in each suite and you can breakfast on the small roof terrace with views over the old city and out to sea.

✗ Eating

Al Pinturicchio TRADITIONAL ITALIAN €
(☎0963 60 34 52; www.ristorantiitaliani-it/pinturicchio; Via Dardona, cnr Largo Duomo; meals €16-22) Recommended by the locals, this restaurant in the old town has a romantic ambience, candlelit tables and a menu of imaginative dishes.

Osteria del Pescatore SEAFOOD €
(☎0963 60 30 18; Via del Monte 7; meals €20-25; ☺dinner Thu-Tue) Swordfish rates highly on the menu at this simple seafood place tucked away in the backstreets.

❶ Information

CST Tropea (☎0963 6 11 78; www.csttropea.it; Largo San Michele 7; ☺9am-1pm & 4-7.30pm, to 10pm Jul & Aug) Helpful tourist office at the entrance to the old town. Can organize trekking, mountain biking, diving and cultural tours.

Tourist office (☎0963 6 14 75; Piazza Ercole; ☺9am-1pm & 4-8pm) In the old town centre.

❶ Getting There & Away

Trains run to Pizzo (30 minutes), Scilla (one hour 20 minutes) and Reggio (two hours). SAV (☎0963 611 29) buses connect with other towns on the coast.

PIZZO
POP 9240

Stacked high up on a sea cliff, pretty little Pizzo is the place to go for *tartufo,* a death-by-chocolate ice-cream ball, and to see an extraordinary rock-carved grotto church. It's a popular tourist stop. Piazza della Repubblica is the epicentre, set high above the sea with great views. Settle here at one of the many gelateria terraces for an ice-cream fix.

A kilometre north, the Chiesa di Piedigrotta (admission €2.50; ☺9am-1pm & 3-7.30pm) is an underground cave full of carved stone statues. It was carved into the tufa rock by Neapolitan shipwreck survivors in the 17th century. Other sculptors added to it and it was eventually turned into a church. Later statues include the less-godly figures of Fidel Castro and JFK. It's a bizarre, one-of-a-kind mixture of mysticism, mystery and kitsch.

In town, the 16th-century Chiesa Matrice di San Giorgio (Via Marconi), with its dressed-up Madonnas, houses the tomb of Joachim Murat, brother-in-law of Napoleon and one-time king of Naples. Although he was the architect of enlightened reforms, the locals showed no great concern when Murat was imprisoned and executed here. At the neat little 15th-century Castello Murat (☎0963 53 25 23; adult/reduced admission €2.50/1.50; ☺9am-1pm & 3pm-midnight Jun-Sep, 9am-1pm & 3-7pm Oct-May), south of Piazza della Repubblica, you can see Murat's cell. His last days and death by firing squad are graphically illustrated by waxworks.

Good accommodation is hard to find. Armonia B&B (☎0963 53 33 37; www.casaarmonia.com; Via Armonia 9; d without bathroom €50-75; @), run by the charismatic Franco, has a number of rooms (with shared bathroom). Eat at Pizzeria Ruota (☎0963 53 24 27; Piazza della Republica 36; pizzas from €4-6; ☺11am-3.30pm & 7.30pm-midnight Thu-Tue), which has splendid, big pizzas.

Sicily

POPULATION: 5 MILLION

Best Places to Eat

» Trattoria Ai Cascinari (p756)

» Quattro Gatti (p791)

» Il Liberty (p789)

» Il Gallo e l'Innamorata (p800)

Best Places to Stay

» Isoco Guest House (p772)

» Pensione Tranchina (p804)

» Villa Athena (p797)

Why Go?

More of a sugar-spiked espresso than a milky cappuccino, Sicily rewards visitors with an intense bittersweet experience. Here it seems the sun shines brighter, the shadows are darker, and life is lived full-on and for the moment. Overloaded with art treasures and natural beauty, undersupplied with infrastructure and continuously struggling against Mafia-driven corruption, Sicily's complexities sometimes seem unfathomable. To really appreciate this place, come with an open mind – and a healthy appetite. Despite the island's perplexing contradictions one factor remains constant: the uncompromisingly high quality of the cuisine.

After 25 centuries of foreign domination, Sicilians are heirs to an impressive cultural legacy, from the refined architecture of Magna Graecia to the Byzantine splendour and Arab craftsmanship of the island's Norman cathedrals and palaces. This cultural richness is matched by a startlingly diverse landscape that includes bucolic farmland, smouldering volcanoes and kilometres of island-studded aquamarine coastline.

When to Go
Palermo

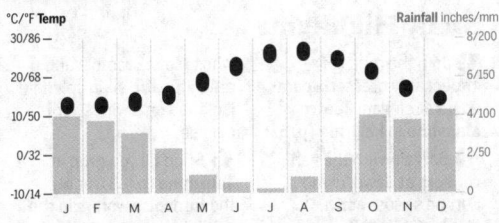

February Almond blossoms float over temples and orchard-covered hills during Sagra del Mandorlo.

Easter Impassioned religious processions and marzipan lambs in every bakery window.

May Spring weather, wildflowers and fewer crowds; a dreamy time for coastal walking.

History

Sicily's most deeply ingrained cultural influences originate from its first inhabitants – the Sicani from North Africa, the Siculi from Latium (Italy) and the Elymni from Greece. The subsequent colonisation of the island by the Carthaginians (also from North Africa) and the Greeks, in the 8th and 6th centuries BC respectively, compounded this cultural divide through decades of war when powerful opposing cities, such as Palermo and Catania, struggled to dominate the island.

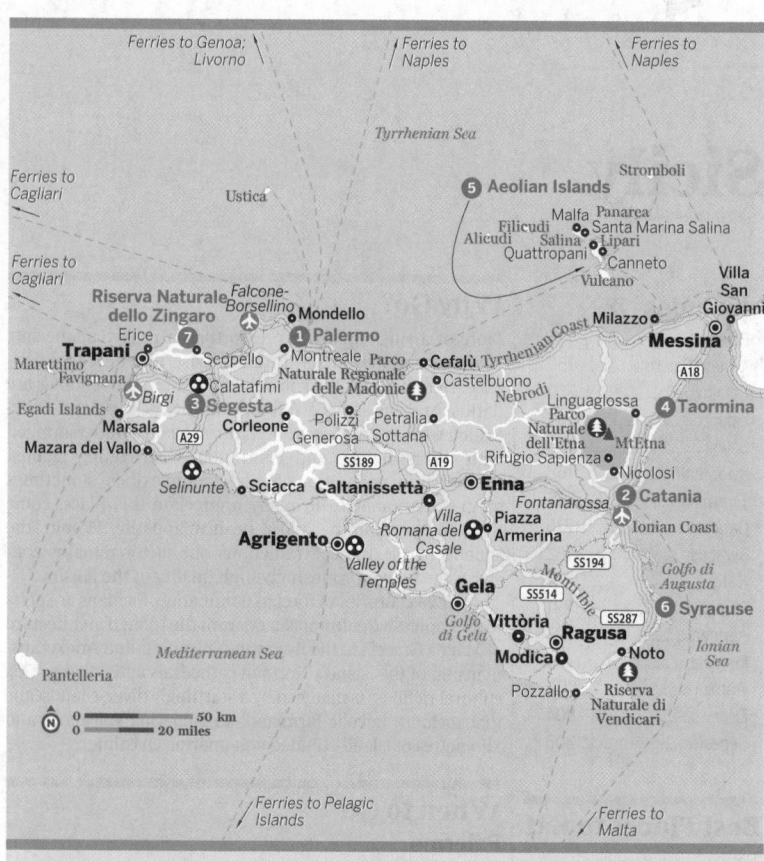

Sicily Highlights

❶ Join the ranks of impeccably dressed opera-goers at elegant **Teatro Massimo** in Palermo (p757)

❷ Bargain with the fish vendors at dawn, climb Europe's most active volcano in the afternoon and enjoy Sicily's best nightlife in constantly buzzing **Catania** (p775)

❸ Marvel at the majesty of **Segesta** (p805), whose Greek temple and amphitheatre sit in splendid isolation on a windswept hillside

❹ Shop till you drop in **Taormina** (p769), or ply the turquoise waters in the sparkling coves below

❺ Soak up the sun, watch Stromboli's volcanic fireworks and hike to your heart's content on the stunningly scenic **Aeolian Islands** (p762)

❻ Wander aimlessly in Ortygia's atmospheric alleys before settling in for an evening of classical drama at the fabled Greek theatre in **Syracuse** (p785)

❼ Hike the rugged, undeveloped coastline and scan the sky for eagles at **Riserva Naturale dello Zingaro** (p804)

Although inevitably part of the Roman Empire, it was not until the Arab invasions of AD 831 that Sicily truly came into its own. Trade, farming and mining were all fostered under Arab influence and Sicily soon became an enviable prize for European opportunists. The Normans, desperate for a piece of the pie, invaded in 1061 and made Palermo the centre of their expanding empire and the finest city in the Mediterranean.

Impressed by the cultured Arab lifestyle, King Roger squandered vast sums on ostentatious palaces and churches and encouraged a hedonistic atmosphere in his court. But such prosperity – and decadence (Roger's grandson, William II, even had a harem) – inevitably gave rise to envy and resentment and, after 400 years of pleasure and profit, the Norman line was extinguished and the kingdom passed to the austere German House of Hohenstaufen with little opposition from the seriously eroded and weakened Norman occupation. In the centuries that followed, Sicily passed to the Holy Roman Emperors, Angevins (French), Aragonese (Spanish) and Austrians in a turmoil of rebellion and revolution that continued until the Spanish Bourbons united Sicily with Naples in 1734 as the Kingdom of the Two Sicilies. Little more than a century later, on 11 May 1860, Giuseppe Garibaldi planned his daring and dramatic unification of Italy from Marsala.

Reeling from this catalogue of colonisers, Sicilians struggled in poverty-stricken conditions. Unified with Italy, but no better off, nearly one million men and women emigrated to the USA between 1871 and 1914 before the outbreak of WWI.

Ironically, the Allies (seeking Mafia help in America for the reinvasion of Italy) helped in establishing the Mafia's stranglehold on Sicily. In the absence of suitable administrators, they invited the undesirable *mafioso* (Mafia boss) Don Calógero Vizzini to do the job. When Sicily became a semi-autonomous region in 1948, Mafia control extended right to the heart of politics and the region plunged into a 50-year silent civil war. It only started to emerge from this after the anti-Mafia maxi-trials of the 1980s, in which Sicily's revered magistrates Giovanni Falcone and Paolo Borsellino hauled hundreds of Mafia members into court, leading to important prosecutions against members of the massive heroin and cocaine network between Palermo and New York, known as the 'pizza connection'.

Today most Sicilians remain less than enthralled by an organisation that continues to grow rich on money from the illegal drugs trade, human trafficking and – that old, ubiquitous cash-flow booster – extortion and protection which, experts say, many businesses in Sicily still pay. At least the thuggery and violence of the 1980s has diminished and there have been some important arrests, serving as encouragement for those who would speak out against Mafia influence.

❶ Getting There & Away

For additional transport details and local telephone contacts, see the Getting There & Away sections under individual cities.

AIR

An increasing number of airlines fly direct to Sicily's three international airports – Palermo (PMO), Catania (CTA) and Trapani (TPS) – although many still require a transfer in Rome or Milan. **Alitalia** (www.alitalia.com) is the main Italian carrier, while **Ryanair** (www.ryanair.com) is the leading low-cost airline carrier serving Sicily.

BOAT

Regular car and passenger ferries cross the strait between Villa San Giovanni (Calabria) and Messina, while hydrofoils connect Messina with Reggio di Calabria.

Sicily is also accessible by ferry from Naples, Civitavecchia, Livorno, Genoa, Cagliari, Malta and Tunisia. Prices rise between June and September, when advanced bookings may also be required.

BUS

SAIS (✆ 091 617 11 41; www.saistrasporti.it) runs long-haul services to Sicily from Rome and Naples.

TRAIN

Direct trains run from Milan, Florence, Rome, Naples and Reggio di Calabria to Messina and on to Palermo, Catania and other provincial capitals – the trains are transported from the mainland by ferry from Villa San Giovanni.

For travellers originating in Rome and points south, InterCity trains cover the distance from mainland Italy to Sicily in the least possible time, without a change of train. If coming from Milan, Bologna or Florence, your fastest option is to take the ultra-high-speed Frecciarossa as far as Naples, then change to an InterCity train for the rest of the journey.

SICILY FERRY CROSSINGS

ROUTE	COST € (HIGH SEASON ADULT FARE)	DURATION (HOURS)
Genoa-Palermo	117	20
Malta-Catania	108	3
Naples-Catania	60	11
Naples-Palermo	55	11
Naples-Trapani	90	7
Reggio di Calabria-Messina	2	35min
Tunis-Palermo	69	10

If saving money is your top priority, Espresso or InterCity night trains will still get you to Sicily relatively fast, and won't take such a big bite out of your budget.

 Getting Around

AIR

Regular domestic flights serve the offshore islands of Pantelleria and Lampedusa. Local carriers include Alitalia, Meridiana and Air One.

BUS

Bus services within Sicily are provided by a variety of companies. Buses are usually faster if your destination involves travel through the island's interior; trains tend to be cheaper (and sometimes faster) on the major coastal routes. In small towns and villages tickets are often sold in bars or on the bus.

CAR & MOTORCYCLE

Having your own vehicle is advantageous in the interior, where public transit is often slow and limited. Roads are generally good and autostradas connect most major cities. There's a cheap and worthwhile toll road running along the Ionian coast. Drive defensively; the Sicilians are some of Italy's most aggressive drivers, with a penchant for overtaking on blind corners, holding a mobile phone in one hand while gesticulating wildly with the other!

TRAIN

The coastal train service is very efficient. Services to towns in the interior tend be infrequent and slow, although if you have the time the routes can be very picturesque. IC trains are the fastest and most expensive, while the *regionale* is the slowest.

PALERMO

POP 656,000

Palermo is a city of decay and of splendour and – provided you can handle its raw energy,

deranged driving and chaos – has plenty of appeal. Unlike Florence or Rome, many of the city's treasures are hidden, rather than scrubbed up for endless streams of tourists. This giant treasure trove of palaces, castles and churches has a unique architectural fusion of Byzantine, Arab, Norman, Renaissance and baroque gems.

While some of the crumbling *palazzi* (mansions) bombed in WWII are being restored, others remain dilapidated; turned into shabby apartments, the faded glory of their ornate facades is just visible behind strings of brightly coloured washing. The evocative history of the city remains very much part of the daily life of its inhabitants, and the dusty web of backstreet markets in the old quarter has a Middle Eastern feel.

The flip side is the modern city, a mere 15-minute stroll away, parts of which could be neatly jigsawed and slotted into Paris with its grid system of wide avenues lined by seductive shops and handsome 19th-century apartments.

At one time an Arab emirate and seat of a Norman kingdom, Palermo became Europe's grandest city in the 12th century, but in recent years its fame (or notoriety) has originated from the Mafia's pervasive influence. Many judges require 24-hour police surveillance and, despite a growing campaign of public resistance, protection payoffs remain commonplace.

Sights

Via Maqueda is the main street, running north from the train station, changing names to Via Ruggero Settimo as it passes the landmark Teatro Massimo, then finally widening into leafy Viale della Libertà north of Piazza Castelnuovo, the beginning of the city's modern district.

AROUND THE QUATTRO CANTI

The busy intersection of Corso Vittorio Emanuele and Via Maqueda is known as the **Quattro Canti**. Forming the civic heart of Palermo, this crossroads neatly divides the historic nucleus into four traditional quarters – Albergheria, Capo, Vucciria and La Kalsa.

Fontana Pretoria   FOUNTAIN

This huge and ornate fountain, with tiered basins and sculptures rippling in concentric circles, forms the centrepiece of **Piazza Pretoria**, a spacious square just south of the Quattro Canti. The city bought the fountain in 1573; however, the flagrant nudity of the provocative nymphs proved too much for Sicilian church-goers attending Mass next door, and they prudishly dubbed it the Fountain of Shame.

La Martorana   CHURCH

(Chiesa di Santa Maria dell'Ammiraglio; Piazza Bellini 3; ⊘8.30am-1pm & 3.30-5.30pm Mon-Sat, 8.30am-1pm Sun) This lovely 12th-century church was originally planned as a mosque by King Roger's Syrian Emir, George of Antioch. In 1433 the church was donated to an aesthetically challenged order of Benedictine nuns who demolished most of the stunning mosaics executed by Greek craftsmen and replaced them with gaudy baroque ornamentation. The few remaining original mosaics include two magnificent portraits of George of Antioch and Roger II that are well worth seeking out; unfortunately both were indefinitely off limits due to restoration at the time of research.

Chiesa Capitolare di San Cataldo   CHURCH

(Piazza Bellini 3; admission €2; ⊘9.30am-1.30pm & 3.30-5.30pm Mon-Sat, 9.30am-1.30pm Sun) This 12th-century church in Arab-Norman style is one of Palermo's most striking buildings, with its dusky-pink bijoux domes, solid square shape, blind arcading and delicate tracery. Disappointingly, it's almost bare inside.

ALBERGHERIA

Southwest of the Quattro Canti is Albergheria, a rather shabby, run-down district once inhabited by Norman court officials, now home to a growing number of immigrants who are attempting to revitalise its dusty backstreets.

Palazzo dei Normanni   PALAZZO, CHAPEL

(Palazzo Reale; ☑091 626 28 33; www.federico secondo.org; Piazza Indipendenza 1; Cappella Palatina only adult/reduced €7/5, combined ticket incl palace rooms & Cappella Palatina adult/reduced €8.50/6.50) This austere fortified palace was once the centre of a magnificent medieval court. Today it remains in regular use as the seat of the Sicilian parliament. Four days a week government officials vacate the building, allowing visitors access to the **parliamentary chambers and royal apartments** (⊘8.15am-5pm Fri, Sat & Mon, 8.15am-12.15pm Sun), including the sumptuous **Sala di Ruggero II**, the king's former bedroom, which is decorated with stunning mosaics of Persian peacocks, palm trees and leopards.

Cappella Palatina

(Palatine Chapel; ⊘8.15am-5pm Mon-Sat, 8.15-9.45am & 11.15am-12.15pm Sun) On the middle level of the palace's three-tiered loggia is Palermo's premier tourist attraction. This mosaic-clad jewel of a chapel, designed by Roger II in 1130, has been returned to its original splendour thanks to restoration work completed in 2008. Swarming with figures in glittering, dreamy gold, these exquisite mosaics recount tales of the Old and New Testaments, capturing expression, detail and movement with extraordinary grace. The harmony of the chapel's decoration is further enhanced by the inlaid marble floors and the wooden *muqarnas* ceiling, a masterpiece of honeycomb carving in Arabic style that reflects the cultural complexity of Norman Sicily.

Mercato di Ballarò   MARKET

Snaking for several city blocks southeast of Palazzo dei Normanni is Palermo's busiest street market, which throbs with activity well into the early evening. It's a fascinating mix of noises, smells and street life, and the cheapest place for everything from Chinese padded bras to fresh produce, fish, meat, olives and cheese – smile nicely for a taste.

CAPO

Northwest of Quattro Canti is the Capo neighbourhood, another densely packed web of interconnected streets and blind alleys.

Cattedrale   CATHEDRAL

(www.cattedrale.palermo.it; Corso Vittorio Emanuele; ⊘8am-5.30pm Mon-Sat, 7am-1pm & 4-7pm Sun) A feast of geometric patterns, ziggurat

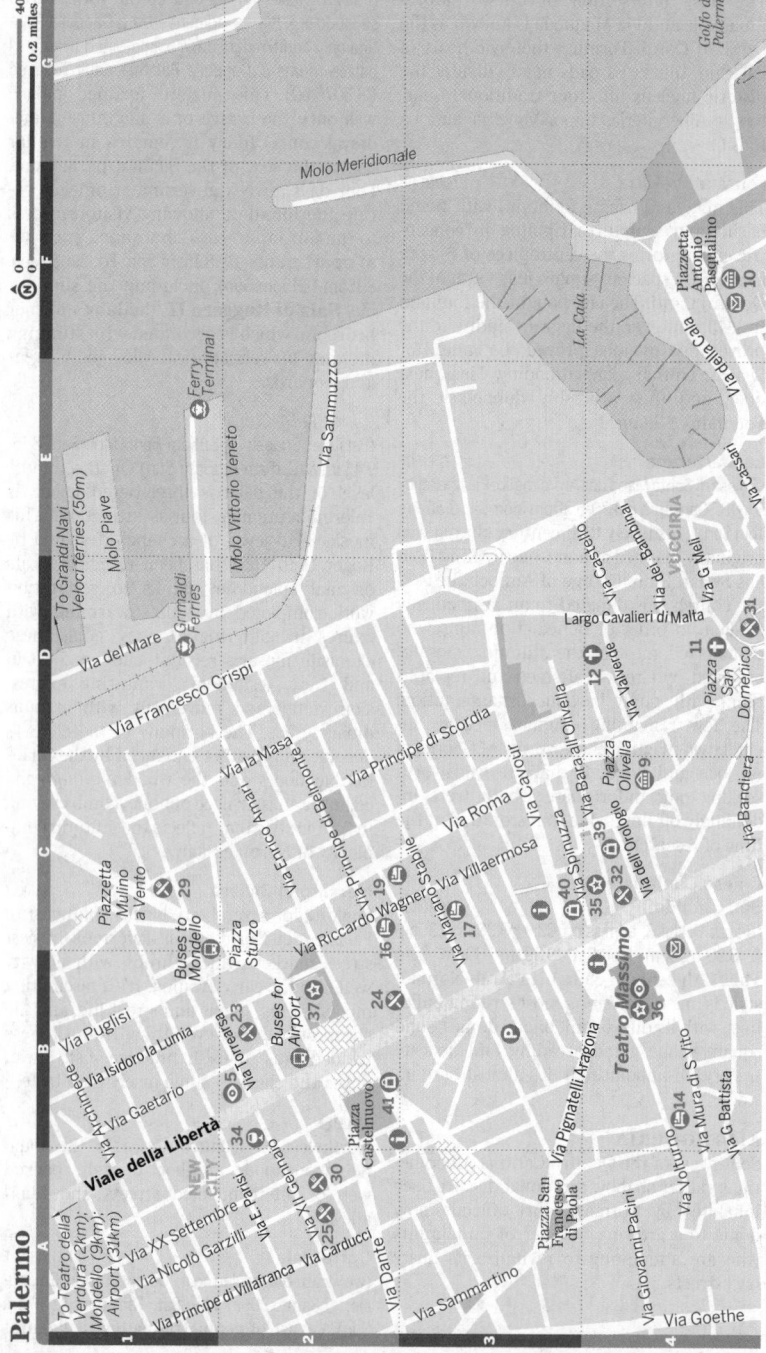

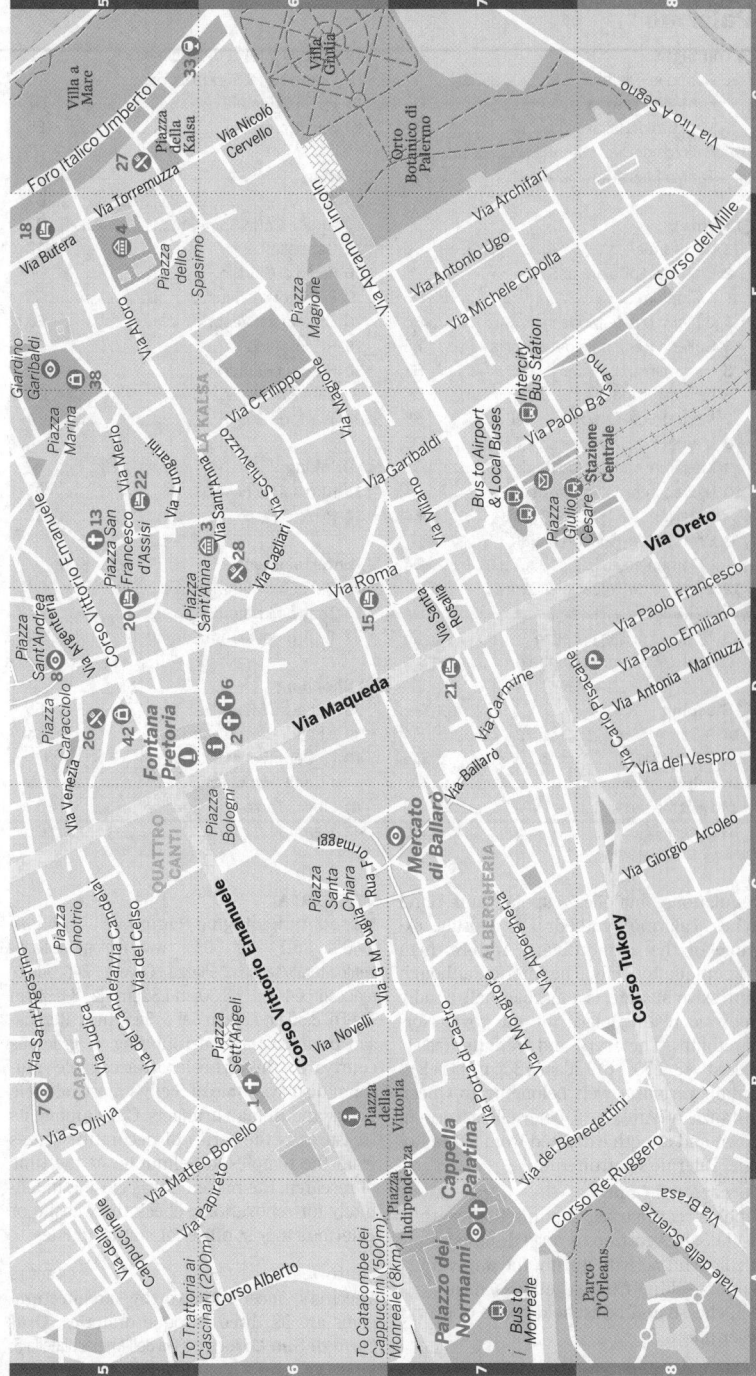

crenulations, majolica cupolas and blind arches, Palermo's cathedral is a prime example of the extraordinary Arab-Norman style unique to Sicily. The interior, although impressive in scale, is a marble shell, a sadly un-exotic resting place for the royal Norman tombs. The **crypt** and **treasury** (adult/reduced €3/1.50; ⊙9.30am-5.30pm Mon-Sat) contain various jewels belonging to Queen Costanza of Aragón, a bejewelled Norman crown and a tooth extracted from Santa Rosalia, Palermo's patron saint.

Mercato del Capo   MARKET
Capo's street market, running the length of Via Sant'Agostino, is a seething mass of colourful activity during the day, with vendors selling fruit, vegetables, meat, fish, cheese and household goods of every description.

VUCCIRIA

Museo Archeologico Regionale   MUSEUM
(☎091 611 68 05; www.regione.sicilia.it/beniculturali/salinas; Piazza Olivella 24; adult/reduced €4/2; ⊙8.30am-1.30pm & 3-6.30pm Tue-Fri, 8.30am-1.30pm Sat & Sun) In a Renaissance monastery surrounding a gracious courtyard, this wheelchair-accessible museum displays some of Sicily's most valuable Greek and Roman artefacts. Chief among its treasures is the series of decorative friezes from the temples at Selinunte. At the time of research, the museum was closing indefinitely for renovations; check the website or Palermo's tourist office for status updates.

Oratories   ORATORIES
Vucciria's most noteworthy architectural gems are its three baroque oratories: **Oratorio di San Lorenzo** (Via dell'Immacolatella 5;

adult/reduced €2.50/1.50; ⏱10am-6pm), **Oratorio del Rosario di Santa Zita** (Via Valverde) and **Oratorio del Rosario di San Domenico** (Via dei Bambinai 2). The latter two are known collectively as the **Tesori della Loggia** (combined ticket €5; ⏱9am-1pm Mon-Sat) and can be visited on a single ticket, together with a cluster of nearby churches: covered in ornate stuccowork, these former social clubs for the celebs of their time are ostentatious displays of 17th-century status and wealth.

Mercato della Vucciria   MARKET
(Piazza Caracciolo) The market here was once a notorious den of Mafia activity but is a muted affair today, compared to the spirited Ballarò and Capo markets.

LA KALSA
Due to its proximity to the port, La Kalsa was subjected to carpet bombing during WWII, leaving it derelict and run down. Mother Teresa considered it akin to the shanty towns of Calcutta and established a mission here. Thankfully, this galvanised embarrassed authorities into action and the quarter is now undergoing extensive restoration.

Galleria d'Arte Moderna   ART GALLERY
(☎091 843 16 05; www.galleriadartemoderna palermo.it, in Italian; Via Sant'Anna 21; adult/reduced €7/5; ⏱9.30am-6.30pm Tue-Sun, to 11pm Fri & Sat) This lovely museum is housed in a 15th-century *palazzo*, which metamorphosed into a convent in the 17th century. The wide-ranging collection of 19th- and 20th-century Sicilian art is beautifully displayed, and there's a regular program of modern-art exhibitions here, as well as an excellent bookshop and gift shop.

Galleria Regionale della Sicilia   ART GALLERY
(☎091 623 00 11; www.regione.sicilia.it/benicul turali/palazzoabatellis; Via Alloro 4; adult/reduced €8/4; ⏱9am-5.30pm Tue-Fri, 9am-1pm Sat & Sun) Tucked down a side street in the stately 15th-century Palazzo Abatellis, this recently reopened museum has a wide-ranging collection featuring works by Sicilian artists from the Middle Ages to the 18th century.

Museo Internazionale delle Marionette   MUSEUM
(☎091 32 80 60; www.museomarionettepalermo.it, in Italian; Piazzetta Antonio Pasqualino 5; adult/reduced €5/3; ⏱9am-1pm & 2.30-6.30pm Mon-Sat, 10am-1pm Sun) Housing over 3500 puppets and marionettes from Italy, Japan, southeast Asia, Africa, China and India, this whimsical museum also stages delightful puppet shows most Tuesdays and Fridays at 5.30pm from October through June. For more on Sicily's famous puppet tradition, see the boxed text, p757.

19TH-CENTURY PALERMO
North of Piazza Giuseppe Verdi, Palermo elegantly slips into cosmopolitan mode. Here you'll find fabulous neoclassical and art nouveau buildings hailing from the last golden age of Sicilian architecture, along with late-19th-century mansion blocks lining the broad boulevard of Viale della Libertà.

Teatro Massimo   OPERA HOUSE
(☎tour reservations 091 605 32 67; www.teatro massimo.it; Piazza Giuseppe Verdi; guided tours adult/reduced €7/5; ⏱10am-2.30pm Tue-Sun) An iconic Palermo landmark, this grand neoclassical opera house took more than 20 years to complete and has become a symbol of the triumph and tragedy of the city. Appropriately, the closing scene of *The Godfather: Part III,* with its visually stunning juxtaposition of high culture, low crime, drama and death, was filmed here.

Teatro Politeama Garibaldi   THEATRE
(Piazza Ruggero Settimo) Designed by architect Giuseppe Damiani Almeyda between 1867 and 1874, Palermo's second theatre has the same imposing circular layout as the Teatro Massimo and features a striking facade resembling a triumphal arch topped by a huge bronze chariot.

Hammam   BATHHOUSE
(☎091 32 07 83; www.hammam.pa.it; Via Torrearsa 17d; admission €40; ⏱women only 2-9pm Mon & Wed, 11am-9pm Fri, men only 2-9pm Tue & Thu, 10am-8pm Sat) For a sybaritic experience, head to this luxurious marble-lined Moorish bathhouse, where you can indulge in a vigorous scrub-down, a steamy sauna and many different types of massages and therapies. There's a one-off charge (€10) for slippers and a hand glove.

OUTSIDE CITY CENTRE
Catacombe dei Cappuccini   CATACOMB
(☎091 21 21 17; Piazza Cappuccini; admission €3; ⏱9am-1pm & 3-6pm) These catacombs house the mummified bodies and skeletons of some 8000 Palermitans who died between the 17th and 19th centuries. Earthly power,

gender, religion and professional status are still rigidly distinguished, with men and women occupying separate corridors, and a first-class section set aside for virgins. From Piazza Independenza, it's a 15-minute walk.

 Festivals & Events

Settimana Santa   RELIGIOUS
Holy Week (the week leading up to Easter) is the year's major religious festival, celebrated all over the island. In Palermo there are Greek Orthodox celebrations at La Martorana (p747).

U Fistinu   RELIGIOUS
From 10 to 15 July, Palermo's biggest annual festival celebrates the patron saint of the city, Santa Rosalia, with fireworks, parades and four days of partying.

Festa di Morgana   PUPPET
(www.museomarionettepalermo.it, in Italian) In November, puppeteers from all over the world gather at Museo Internazionale delle Marionette.

Sleeping

Most budget options can be found around Via Maqueda and Via Roma in the vicinity of the train station. Midrange and top-end hotels are concentrated further north. Parking usually costs an extra €10 to €15 per day.

Butera 28   APARTMENT €
(333 3165432; www.butera28.it; Via Butera 28; 2-/4-/8-person apt per day from €50/100/150, per week €300/650/950;) Delightful bilingual owner Nicoletta offers 11 well-equipped and comfortable apartments in her elegant old *palazzo* near Piazza della Kalsa. Units range in size from 30 to 180 sq metres, most sleeping a family of four or more. Four apartments face the sea (No 9 is especially nice), and all have CD and DVD players, plus kitchens stocked with basic essentials. Nicoletta also offers cooking classes in her gorgeous blue-and-white-tiled kitchen.

A Casa di Amici   HOSTEL €
(091 58 48 84; www.acasadiamici.com; Via Volturno 6; dm €17-23, s €30-45, d €50-72, tr €60-96;) In a renovated 19th-century *palazzo* with high ceilings and decorative tile floors, this artsy, hostel-type place behind Teatro Massimo has four colourful rooms sleeping two to four, with shared bathrooms and a guest kitchen. The annexe across the street,

ideal for families or anyone seeking more peace and quiet, has four additional rooms, including one with private bath and terrace. Multilingual owner Claudia and her staff provide helpful maps and information displays, plus friendly advice to help newcomers navigate the city.

San Francesco   B&B €
(091 888 83 91, 328 5516242; www.sanfrancesco palermo.it; Via Merlo 30; s €50-60, d €80-90;) On a side street near Piazza Marina is this lovingly restored old house with stone walls, beamed ceilings and only three rooms, run by the friendly young couple Vanessa and Filippo. The quiet, central location and the breakfast win rave reviews from guests.

B&B Amélie   B&B €
(091 33 59 20; www.bb-amelie.it; Via Prinicipe di Belmonte 94; s €40-60, d €60-80, tr €90-100;) In an unbeatable new city location on a pedestrianised street a stone's throw from Teatro Politeama, the affable, multilingual Angela has converted her grandmother's spacious 6th floor flat into a cheery B&B. Rooms are colourfully decorated, and the corner triple has a sunny terrace. Angela, a native Palermitan, generously shares her wealth of local knowledge. People with allergies needn't worry about the cat on the logo; the place is spotless, with no pets or fur in sight!

Hotel Orientale   HOTEL €
(091 616 57 27; www.albergoorientale.191.it; Via Maqueda 26; s €30-50, d €45-70;) This *palazzo*'s grand marble stairway and arcaded courtyard, complete with rusty bicycles, stray cats and strung-up washing, is an evocative introduction to an atmospheric if faded hotel. Rooms have wrought-iron beds, tall windows and heavy wooden furniture; the cheapest come with shared bathrooms. Breakfast is served under the lovely frescoed ceiling in the library. Rooms 8 and 9 overlook the tail end of the Ballaró market, close enough to hear the vendors singing in the morning.

B&B Maxim   B&B €€
(091 976 54 71; www.bbmaxim.it; Via Mariano Stabile 136a; s €80-90, d €110-130, ste €160-190;) Owner Massimo has spared no expense in creating this little B&B with restrained tones of cream, beige and brown. Perks include ambient sound, chromotherapy lighting in the showers, and state-of-the-art designer

If you were taught that it was bad manners to eat in the street, you can break the rule in good company here. The mystery is simply how Palermo is not the obesity capital of Europe given just how much eating goes on! Palermitans are at it all the time: when they're shopping, commuting, discussing business, romancing...basically at any time of the day. What they're enjoying is the *buffitieri* – little hot snacks prepared at stalls and meant to be eaten on the spot, just as they were in the marketplaces of Sicily's Greek-settled cities.

Kick off the morning with a *pane e panelle*, Palermo's famous chickpea fritters – great for vegetarians and a welcome change from a sweet custard-filled croissant. Later in the day, you might want to go for the potato croquettes, the *sfincione* (a spongy, oily pizza topped with onions and *caciocavallo* cheese) or *scaccie* (discs of bread dough spread with a filling and rolled up into a pancake). In summer, locals enjoy a freshly baked brioche filled with a type of ice cream flavoured with fruits, coffee or nougat.

From 4pm onwards the snacks become decidedly more carnivorous and you may just wish you hadn't read the following translations: how about some barbecued *stigghiola* (goat intestines filled with onions, cheese and parsley), for example? Or a couple of *pani ca meusa* (bread roll stuffed with sautéed beef spleen). You'll be asked if you want it '*schietta o maritata*' ('single or married'). If you choose *schietta*, the roll will only have ricotta in it before being dipped into boiling lard; choose *maritata* and you'll get the beef spleen as well. Somewhat tamer, and a favourite in Catania, are all manner of *impanata* (bread-dough snacks) stuffed with meat, vegetables or cheese, and the unique *arancino* (a deep-fried rice ball stuffed with meat, tomato and vegetables).

fixtures throughout. It's on the 6th floor, high above the surrounding urban bustle, yet only a five-minute walk from Teatro Massimo and Teatro Politeama.

Grand Hotel Piazza Borsa　　HOTEL €€
(☎091 32 00 75; www.piazzaborsa.com; Via dei Cartari 18; s €115-181, d €154-208, ste €340-569; P ☀ @ ☎) This grand new four-star opened in 2010 in Palermo's former stock exchange. Three separate buildings house the 127 rooms; the nicest ones are the high-ceilinged suites with Jaccuzi tubs and windows facing Piazza San Francesco. Internet access costs €10 extra.

Grand Hotel et des Palmes　　HOTEL €€€
(☎091 602 81 11; www.hotel-despalmes.it; Via Roma 398; r €230-265; P ☀ @ ☎) Dating from 1874, this is one of Palermo's most historically fascinating hotels. Like a royal court, it has been the scene of intrigue, liaisons and double-dealings. The grand salons still impress with their chandeliers and gigantic mirrors, while the rooms are regally luxurious. The official rates listed above are often slashed in half during slow periods; look online for special deals.

B&B 900　　B&B €
(☎091 976 11 94; www.novecentopalermo.com; Via Roma 62; s €30-60, d €50-100; ☀ ☎) Convenient to the train station, this welcoming B&B on the 5th floor of a Via Roma *palazzo* wins guests over with owners Elisa and Dario's warm hospitality and a breakfast emphasizing organic ingredients.

🍴 Eating

Sicily's ancient cuisine is a mixture of spicy and sweet flavours, epitomised in the ubiquitous eggplant-based *caponata* and the Palermitan classic *bucatini con le sarde* (hollow tube-shaped noodles with sardines, wild fennel, raisins, pine nuts and breadcrumbs). Cakes, marzipan confections and pastries are all works of art – try the *cannoli* (tubes of pastry filled with sweetened ricotta).

Restaurants rarely start to fill up until 9.30pm. For cheap eats, visit Palermo's markets, wander the tangle of alleys east and south of Teatro Massimo, or spend a Saturday evening snacking with locals on grilled sausages, *stigghiola, panelle* and *crocchè* at the outdoor food carts in Piazza Caracciolo in the Vucciria district.

Delightful Desserts

From citrus-scented pastries filled with sheep's-milk ricotta, to ice cream served on a brioche, to the marzipan fruits piled high in every confectioner's window, Sicily celebrates the joys of sugar morning, noon and night.

Peoples from the Arabs to the Aztecs have influenced Sicily's culture of sweets: the former introduced sugar cane to the island; the latter's fiery-hot chocolate so impressed the Spaniards that they brought the recipe across the Atlantic to their Sicilian kingdom. The Romans also left their mark, legendarily mixing snow from Mt Etna into precursors of the famous *granita* (Italian ice).

The all-star list of Sicilian desserts starts with *cannoli*, crunchy pastry tubes filled with lightly sweetened ricotta cheese, then finished off with chocolate, a dusting of crumbled pistachios or a spike of candied citrus. Vying for the title of Sicily's most famous dessert is *cassata*, a coma-inducing concoction of sponge cake, cream, marzipan, chocolate and candied fruit. Feeling more adventurous? How about an *'mpanatigghiu*, a traditional Modican pastry stuffed with minced meat, almonds, chocolate and cinnamon?

A SUGAR-FUELLED ISLAND CIRCUIT

» **Cappello** (p753) Home to Palermo's famous *setteveli*, a velvety seven-layer chocolate cake.

» **Da Alfredo** (p767) Dreamy *granite* made with coffee and wild strawberries.

» **Grand Cafè Tabbacco** (p778) Perfect *cannoli* and sidewalk tables facing Mt Etna.

» **Dolceria Bonajuto** (p790) Aztec-influenced chocolate with vanilla and hot peppers.

» **Gelati DiVini** (p791) Outlandish ice-cream flavours including Marsala wine, wild fennel and olive oil.

» **Maria Grammatico** (p805) Marzipan fruit, almond pastries and toasted-nut *torrone* (nougat).

Clockwise from top left
1. Cakes 2. Traditional sweets 3. *Granita* and brioche
4. *Cannoli*.

Trattoria Ai Cascinari SICILIAN €

(☑091 651 98 04; Via d'Ossuna 43/45; meals €20-23; ⊙lunch Tue-Sun, dinner Wed-Sat) Friendly service, simple straw chairs and blue-and-white-checked tablecloths set the relaxed tone at this Slow Food–recommended neighbourhood trattoria, 1km north of the Cappella Palatina. Locals pack the labyrinth of back rooms, while waiters perambulate non-stop with plates of scrumptious seasonal antipasti and divine main dishes. Save room for homemade ice cream and outstanding desserts brought in from Palermo's beloved Pasticceria Cappello.

Piccolo Napoli SEAFOOD €€

(☑091 32 04 31; Piazzetta Mulino a Vento 4; meals €25-35; ⊙lunch Mon-Sat, dinner Thu-Sat) Known throughout Palermo for its fresh seafood, this Slow Food–recommended eatery is another hot spot for serious foodies. Nibble on toothsome sesame bread and plump olives while perusing the menu for a pasta dish that takes your fancy, then head to the seafood display (often still wriggling) to choose a second course. The atmosphere is bustling and the genial owner greets his many regular customers by name.

Trattoria Basile TRATTORIA €

(☑091 33 56 28; Via Bara all'Olivella 76; meals €9-13; ⊙noon-3.30pm Mon-Sat) This unpretentious trattoria offers an unforgettable, authentic Palermitan eating experience. Pay first, take a number at the window for your pasta (€2.50 to €4) or main course (€3.50 to €5), then sidle over to the antipasti bar and choose three items for €2 or six items for €4. While enjoying your appetisers, listen for your number – they'll bellow it out (in Italian) when the rest of your food is ready. Avoid the busy period between 1pm and 2pm when every workman in town is elbowing in for his plate of pasta.

Osteria dei Vespri GASTRONOMIC €€€

(☑091 617 16 31; www.osteriadeivespri.it; Piazza Croce dei Vespri 6; meals €55-70, tasting menu €80; ⊙lunch & dinner Mon-Sat) This sophisticated Michelin-star restaurant has a stone-vaulted ceiling and intimate dining space. In the summer, sit out under the shadow of the *palazzo* and tuck into dishes such as pasta with fennel and red prawns or spicy tuna with nutmeg-potato croquettes and mint-flavoured rice. Top it all off with a hazelnut waffle, lemon-scented ricotta and kiwis in red fruit-and-wine jam.

Ferro di Cavallo TRATTORIA €

(☑091 33 18 35; Via Venezia 20; meals €18-20; ⊙lunch Mon-Sat, dinner Thu-Sat) Religious portraits beam down from bright-red walls upon the bustling mixed crowd of tourists and locals at this cheerful little trattoria near the Quattro Canti. Nothing costs more than €8 on the straightforward à la carte menu of Sicilian classics, but hungry diners can still 'splurge' on the fixed-price menu for €19, including drinks.

Sant'Andrea MODERN SICILIAN €€

(☑091 33 49 99; www.ristorantesantandrea.eu; Piazza Sant'Andrea 4; meals €30-35; ⊙dinner Mon-Sat) Tucked into the corner of a ruined church in a shabby piazza, Sant'Andrea's location doesn't inspire much confidence, but its superbly creative Sicilian dishes and congenial high-ceilinged dining room keep well-heeled customers picking their way across the broken flagstones nightly.

Cappello PASTRIES & CAKES

(Via Nicolò Garzilli 10; cake slices €2.50) Famous for the *setteveli* (seven-layer chocolate cake) that was invented here – and has long since been copied all over Palermo – this hole-in-the-wall creates splendid desserts of all kinds. Not to be missed is the dreamy *delizia di pistacchio*, a granular pistachio cake topped with creamy icing and a chocolate medallion.

Antico Caffè Spinnato CAFE

(☑091 32 92 20; Via Principe di Belmonte 107-15; snacks €4-8) At this sophisticated cafe dating back to 1860, Palermitans throng the sidewalk tables daily to enjoy afternoon piano music, coffee, cocktails, ice cream, sumptuous cakes and snacks.

Friggitoria Chiluzzo SANDWICH SHOP €

(Piazza della Kalsa; sandwiches €1.50; ⊙lunch Mon-Sat) This beloved street vendor makes some of Palermo's best *pane, panelle e crocchè* (sesame bread with chickpea fritters and potato croquettes). Add fried eggplant and a squeeze of lemon and call it lunch!

Pizzeria Biondo PIZZERIA €

(☑091 58 36 62; Via Nicolò Garzilli 27; pizzas €5-14; ⊙dinner Thu-Tue) Made with super-fresh *mozzarella di bufala* (buffalo-milk mozzarella), Biondo's pizza is often recognised as the best in Palermo. An animated crowd fills the sidewalk tables and inside rooms every night.

Acanto

MODERN SICILIAN €€

(☎091 32 04 44; Via Torrearsa 10; meals €30-35; ⊙dinner Tue-Sun) New-town elegance together with inventive cooking make this one of the most fashionable restaurants among the designer-chic crowd. In the summer tables are set out on the romantic back patio.

🍷 Drinking

Palermo's liveliest cluster of bars can be found in the Champagneria district east of Teatro Massimo, centred on Piazza Olivella, Via Spinuzza, and Via Patania. Other hot spots include Via Alessandro Paternostro in the Kalsa neighbourhood and Via dei Candelai, a short stagger of a street flanked by pubs, bars and discos catering to a younger, rowdier crowd. Higher-end bars and dance venues are concentrated in the newer part of Palermo. In summer, many Palermitans decamp to Mondello by the sea.

 **Kursaal Kalhesa**

BAR

(☎091 616 00 50; www.kursaalkalhesa.it, in Italian; Foro Umberto I 21; ⊙noon-3pm & 6pm-1am Tue-Sun) Recline on plump sofas with silk cushions and sip a cocktail beneath the high vaulted ceilings. There's a roaring fire in winter, plus art exhibits and a bookstore with foreign newspapers. A lively unpretentious crowd is attracted by the good program of music and literary events. Meals (from €30) are served upstairs on the leafy patio flanked by 15th-century walls.

Pizzo & Pizzo

WINE BAR

(☎091 601 45 44; www.pizzoepizzo.com; Via XII Gennaio 5; ⊙closed Sun) Sure, this sophisticated wine bar is a great place for *aperitivi*, but the buzzing atmosphere and the tempting array of cheeses, cured meats, and smoked fish may just convince you to stick around for dinner.

☆ Entertainment

The daily paper *Il Giornale di Sicilia* has a listing of what's on. The tourist office and information booths also have programs and listings.

Teatro Massimo

OPERA HOUSE

(☎091 605 35 80; www.teatromassimo.it; Piazza Verdi 9) Ernesto Basile's art nouveau masterpiece stages opera, ballet and music concerts. The theatre's program runs from October to May.

Teatro Politeama Garibaldi

THEATRE

(☎091 637 37 43; www.amicidellamusicapalermo.it; Piazza Ruggero Settimo) Another grandiose theatre for opera, ballet and classical music, staging afternoon and evening concerts from November through May.

Teatro della Verdura

OPEN-AIR THEATRE

(☎091 688 41 37; Viale del Fante) A summer-only program of ballet and music in the lovely gardens of the Villa Castelnuovo.

Cuticchio Mimmo

PUPPET THEATRE

(☎091 32 34 00; www.figlidartecuticchio.com; Via Bara all'Olivella 95; ⊙6.30pm Sat & Sun Sep-Jul) This theatre is a charming low-tech choice for children (and adults), staging traditional shows with fabulous handcrafted puppets.

IL TEATRO DEI PUPI

Since the 18th century the traditional Sicilian puppet theatre has been enthralling adults and children alike. The shows are a mini theatrical performance with some puppets standing 1.5m high – a completely different breed from the Pooh Bear–style of glove puppet popular in the West. These characters are intricately carved from beech, olive or lemon wood with realistic-looking glass eyes and distinct features. And, to make sure that they will have no problem swinging their swords or beheading dragons, their joints have flexible wire.

Effectively the soap operas of their day, Sicilian puppet shows expounded the deepest sentiments of life – unrequited love, treachery, thirst for justice and the anger and frustration of the oppressed. The swashbuckling tales centre on the legends of Charlemagne's heroic knights, Orlando and Rinaldo, with an extended cast including the fair Angelica, the treacherous Gano di Magonza and forbidding Saracen warriors. Good puppeteers are judged on the dramatic effect they can create – lots of stamping feet and a gripping running commentary – and on their speed and skill in directing the battle scenes.

Shopping

Via Bara all'Olivella is good for arts and crafts. Check out the puppet workshop of the Cuticchio family, Il Laboratorio Teatrale (Via Bara all'Olivella 48-50).

For ceramics and pottery (albeit at higher prices than you'd find in Sicily's hinterland) stop by Le Ceramiche di Caltagirone (caltagironeceramiche@alice.it; Via Cavour 114) or Mercurio (www.casamerlo.it; Corso Vittorio Emanuele 231).

For edible souvenirs with a dollop of social consciousness, consider buying some wine, olive oil or pasta – all grown on land confiscated from the Mafia – at Libera Terra (www.liberapalermo.org; Piazza Castelnuovo 13), an organization actively working to resist the Mafia's influence in Sicilian society.

On Sundays, there's a good antiques market on Piazza Marina south of the port.

Information

Emergency
Ambulance (☎118)

Police station (☎091 21 01 11; Piazza della Vittoria) For reporting theft and other petty crimes.

Internet Access
There are countless internet points in the old centre, particularly around Via Maqueda where they double as phone centres for the city's immigrant population.

Aboriginal Café (☎091 662 22 29; www.aboriginalcafe.com; Via Spinuzza 51; per hr €3.50; ⊙9am-3am) A lively Australian-style bar and internet cafe.

Medical Services
Farmacia Inglese (☎091 33 44 82; Via Mariano Stabile 177; ⊙4.30-1pm Mon-Fri, 8pm-8.30am Sat & Sun) All-night pharmacy service, seven days a week.

Ospedale Civico (☎091 666 11 11; www.ospedalecivicopa.org; Via Carmelo Lazzaro) Emergency facilities.

Money
ATMs are plentiful. There are exchange offices open outside normal banking hours at the airport.

Post
Main post office (Via Roma 322) Smaller branch offices can be found at the train station and on Piazza Verdi.

Tourist Information
CIT tourist information booths (☎091 611 78 87; www.comune.palermo.it/comune/assessorato_turismo, in Italian; ⊙9am-1pm &

3-7pm) At several locations throughout town, including Piazza Bellini, the port, Via Cavour and Piazza della Vittoria.

Tourist office (www.palermotourism.com) airport (☎091 59 16 98; ⊙8.30am-7.30pm Mon-Sat); city centre (☎091 605 83 51; Piazza Castelnuovo 34; ⊙8.30am-2pm & 2.30-6pm Mon-Fri) Has friendly, multilingual staff and abundant brochures.

Getting There & Away

Air
Falcone-Borsellino airport (PMO; ☎091 702 01 11; www.gesap.it) is at Punta Raisi, 31km west of Palermo.

Several no-frills airlines operate between major European cities and Palermo. Falcone-Borsellino is also the hub airport for regular domestic flights to the islands of Pantelleria and Lampedusa.

Boat
The ferry terminal is located off Via Francesco Crispi. Ferries depart regularly from Molo Vittorio Veneto for Cagliari and Naples. Ferries for Genoa leave from Molo S Lucia.

Grandi Navi Veloci (☎091 58 74 04; www.gnv.it; Calata Marinai d'Italia) Ferries from Palermo to Civitavecchia (€78 to €95, 12 hours, three weekly), Naples (€45 to €64, 12 hours, daily), Tunis (€37 to €42, 10 hours, weekly), Livorno (€72 to €92, 18 hours, three weekly), Malta (€62, 10 hours, weekly) and Genoa (€83 to €117, 20 hours, daily).

Grimaldi Ferries (☎091 611 36 91; www.grimaldi-lines.com; Via Emerico Amari 8) Ferries from Palermo to Tunis (€69, 10 hours, twice weekly).

Siremar (☎091 749 31 11; www.siremar.it, in Italian; Via Francesco Crispi 118) Ferries (€16.55, 2½ hours, one daily) and summer-only hydrofoils (€22.95, 1¼ hours, two daily) from Palermo to Ustica.

SNAV (☎091 601 42 11; www.snav.it; Calata Marinai d'Italia) Overnight service to Naples (€55, 10½ hours, one daily). The office is located at the port to the left of the main entrance.

Tirrenia (☎091 976 07 73; www.tirrenia.it; Calata Marinai d'Italia) Services from Palermo to Cagliari (€55, 13 hours, one weekly) and an overnight ferry to Naples (€50, 10 hours, one daily). The office is located at the port to the right of the main entrance.

Ustica Lines (☎0923 87 38 13; www.usticalines.it) Summer-only hydrofoil service to Lipari (€39.30, 4½ hours, two daily) and other points on the Aeolian Islands.

Bus

The main intercity bus station is on Via Paolo Balsamo, one block east of the train station. Several bus companies maintain independent offices here.

Azienda Siciliana Trasporti (AST; ☑091 680 00 32; www.aziendasicilianatrasporti.it; Via Rosario Gregorio 46) Services to southeastern destinations including Ragusa (€12.80, four hours, four daily Monday to Saturday, two on Sunday).

Cuffaro (☑091 616 15 10; www.cuffaro.info; Via Paolo Balsamo 13) Services to Agrigento (€8.10, two hours, three to nine daily).

SAIS (☑091 616 60 28, 091 617 11 41; www.saisautolinee.it, www.saistrasporti.it; Via Paolo Balsamo 16) Services to Catania (€14.20, 2¾ hours, at least nine daily), Messina (€15.10, 2¾ hours, three to seven daily), Naples (€37.50, 10 hours, one nightly) and Rome (€45.50, 10½ hours, one nightly).

Segesta (☑091 616 90 39; www.segesta.it; Via Paolo Balsamo 26) Services to Trapani (€8.60, two hours, at least 10 daily). Also sells Interbus tickets to Syracuse (€11, 3¼ hours, two to three daily).

Car & Motorcycle

Palermo is accessible on the A20-E90 toll road from Messina and the A19-E932 from Catania via Enna. Trapani and Marsala are also easily accessible from Palermo by motorway (A29), while Agrigento and Palermo are linked by the SS121, a good state road through the island's interior.

Car hire is not cheap in Sicily. Renting on site will typically set you back €250 to €500 per week. It's often more economical to book your rental online before leaving home. One dependable low-budget choice in downtown Palermo is **Auto Europa** (☑091 58 10 45; www.autoeuropa.it; Via Mariano Stabile 6a). **Avis** (www.avis.com) airport (☑091 59 16 84); port (☑091 58 69 40; Via Francesco Crispi 250) also has a downtown branch and is among the many larger car-hire companies represented at the airport.

Train

From Palermo Centrale station, just south of the centre at the foot of Via Roma, regular trains leave for Messina (€11.60 to €27.50, three to 3½ hours, nine to 15 daily), Agrigento (€8.10, 2¼ hours, seven to 12 daily) and Cefalù (€5, one hour, 10 to 19 daily). There are also InterCity trains to Reggio di Calabria, Naples and Rome.

For Catania or Syracuse, you're generally better off taking the bus. There's only one direct train to Catania (€12.30, three hours, weekday mornings only); all the others require a time-consuming change at Messina.

❶ Getting Around

To/From the Airport

Prestia e Comandè (☑091 58 63 51; www.prestiaecomande.it) runs a half-hourly bus service from the airport to the centre of town (€5.80), with stops outside Teatro Politeama Garibaldi (30 minutes) and Palermo Centrale train station (45 minutes). Buses are parked to the right as you exit the arrivals hall. Buy tickets on the bus. Return journeys to the airport run with similar frequency, picking up at the same points.

The Trinacria Express train (€5.80, one hour) from the airport (Punta Raisi station) to Palermo takes longer and runs less frequently than the bus. At the time of research, due to track work, trains were only running as far as Notarbartolo station 3km northwest of downtown Palermo, making this an even less appealing option.

A taxi from the airport to downtown Palermo costs €45.

Bus

Palermo's orange, white and blue **city buses** (AMAT; ☑848 80 08 17; www.amat.pa.it, in Italian) are frequent but often crowded and slow. The free map handed out at Palermo tourist offices details all the major bus lines; most stop at the train station. Tickets (per 1½ hours €1.30, per day €3.50) must be purchased before you get on the bus, from *tabacchi* (tobacconists) or AMAT booths at major transfer points.

Three small buses – Linea Gialla, Linea Verde and Linea Rossa (€0.52 for 24-hour ticket) – operate in the narrow streets of the *centro storico* (historic centre) and can be useful if you're moving between tourist sights.

Car & Motorcycle

Driving is frenetic in the city and best avoided, if possible. Theft of, and from, vehicles is also a problem; use one of the attended car parks around town (€12 to €20 per day) if your hotel lacks parking.

Around Palermo

Just outside Palermo's city limits, the beach town of Mondello and the dazzling cathedral of Monreale are both worthwhile day trips. Just offshore, Ustica makes a great overnight or weekend getaway.

Mondello's long, sandy beach became fashionable in the 19th century, when people came to the seaside in their carriages, prompting the construction of the huge art nouveau pier that still graces the waterfront. Most of the beaches near the pier are private (two sun lounges and an umbrella cost €10 to €20); however, there's a wide swath of public beach opposite the centre of town with all the prerequisite pedaloes and jet skis for hire. Given its easy-going seaside feel, Mondello is an excellent base for families. To get here, take bus 806 (€1.30, 30 minutes) from Piazza Sturzo in Palermo.

Cattedrale di Monreale (☎091 640 44 03; Piazza del Duomo; ◷8am-6pm), 8km southwest of Palermo, is considered the finest example of Norman architecture in Sicily, incorporating Norman, Arab, Byzantine and classical elements. Inspired by a vision of the Virgin, it was built by William II in an effort to outdo his grandfather Roger II, who was responsible for the cathedral in Cefalù and the Cappella Palatina in Palermo. The interior, completed in 1184 and executed in shimmering mosaics, depicts 42 Old Testament stories. Outside the cathedral, the **cloister** (admission €6; ◷9am-7pm) is a tranquil courtyard with a tangible oriental feel. Surrounding the perimeter, elegant Romanesque arches are supported by an exquisite array of slender columns alternately decorated with mosaics. To reach Monreale take bus 389 (€1.30, 35 minutes, half-hourly) from Piazza Indipendenza in Palermo.

The 8.7-sq-km island of **Ustica** was declared Italy's first marine reserve in 1986. The surrounding waters are a feast of fish and coral, ideal for snorkelling, diving and underwater photography. In July the island hosts the **Rassegna Internazionale di Attività Subacquee** (International Festival of Underwater Activities), drawing divers from around the world. To enjoy Ustica's wild coastline and dazzling grottoes without the crowds try visiting in June or September. **Profondo Blu** (☎091 844 96 09; www.ustica-diving.it) is among the better-established dive centres on the island, and also offers accommodation.

To get here from Palermo, take the once-daily car ferry (€18.35, 2½ hours) operated by **Siremar** (☎091 844 90 02; www.siremar.it); or the faster hydrofoils (€23.55, 1½ hours) operated by both Siremar and **Ustica Lines** (☎091 844 90 02; www.usticalines.it).

TYRRHENIAN COAST

The coast between Palermo and Milazzo is studded with popular tourist resorts attracting a steady stream of holidaymakers, particularly between June and September.

The best of these include the two massive natural parks of the Madonie and Nebrodi mountains, the sweeping beaches around Capo d'Orlando and Capo Tindari, and Cefalù, a resort second only to Taormina in popularity.

Cefalù

POP 13,800

This popular holiday resort wedged between a dramatic mountain peak and a sweeping stretch of sand has the lot: a great beach; a truly lovely historic centre with a grandiose cathedral; and winding medieval streets lined with restaurants and boutiques. Avoid the height of summer when prices soar, beaches are jam-packed and the charm of the place is tainted by bad-tempered drivers trying to find parking.

From the train station, turn right into Via Moro to reach Via Matteotti and the old town. If heading for the beach, turn left and walk along Via Gramsci, which in turn becomes Via V Martoglio.

◉ Sights

Duomo   DUOMO
(Piazza del Duomo; ◷8am-5.30pm winter, to 7.30pm summer) Cefalù's imposing cathedral is the final jewel in the Arab-Norman crown alongside the Cappella Palatina and Monreale. Inside, a towering figure of Christ Pantocrator is the focal point of the elaborate 12th-century Byzantine mosaics. Framed by the steep cliff, the twin pyramid towers of the cathedral stand out above the magnificent **Piazza del Duomo**, which swarms with camera-snapping tourists among the pavement cafes and restaurants.

La Rocca   VIEWPOINT
Looming over the town, the craggy mass of La Rocca appears a suitable home for the race of giants that are said to have been Sicily's first inhabitants. It was here that the Arabs built their citadel, occupying it until the Norman conquest in 1061 forced the locals down from the mountain to the port below. An enormous staircase, the **Salita Saraceno**, winds up through three tiers of city walls, a 30-minute climb nearly to the summit. There are stunning views of the town below and the ruined 4th-century **Tempio di Diana** provides a quiet and romantic getaway for young lovers.

CEFALÙ'S BACKYARD PLAYGROUND

Due south of Cefalù, the 40,000-hectare **Parco Naturale Regionale delle Madonie** incorporates some of Sicily's highest peaks, including the imposing Pizzo Carbonara (1979m). The park's wild, wooded slopes are home to wolves, wildcats, eagles and the near-extinct ancient Nebrodi fir trees that have survived since the last ice age. Ideal for hiking, cycling and horse trekking, the park is also home to several handsome mountain towns, including **Castelbuono**, **Petralia Soprana** and **Petralia Sottana**.

The region's distinctive rural cuisine includes roasted lamb and goat, cheeses, grilled mushrooms and aromatic pasta with *sugo* (meat sauce). A great place to sample these specialities is **Nangalarruni** (☑0921 67 14 28; Via delle Confraternite 5/7, Castelbuono; meals €25-45) in Castelbuono.

For park information, contact the **Ente Parco delle Madonie** (www.parcodelle madonie.it, in Italian) in **Cefalù** (☑0921 92 33 27; Corso Ruggero 116; ☉8am-8pm) or **Petralia Sottana** (☑0921 68 40 11; Corso Paolo Agliata 16).

Bus service to the park's main towns is limited; to fully appreciate the Madonie, you're better off hiring a car for a couple of days.

Activities

Cefalù's crescent-shaped beach, just west of the medieval centre, is lovely, but in the summer get here early to find a patch for your brolly and towel. You can escape with a boat tour along the coast or to the Aeolian Islands (from €60) during the summer months with several agencies located along Corso Ruggero.

Sicilia Divers   DIVING
(☑347 6853051; www.sicilia-divers.com; Hotel Kalura, Via Vincenzo Cavallaro 13; dives from €45, courses from €60) Organises dives and courses for all ages.

Scooter for Rent   BIKE RENTAL
(☑0921 42 04 96; www.scooterforrent.it; Via Vittorio Emanuele 57) Rents out bicycles (€10 per day) and scooters (from €35 per day).

🛏 Sleeping

Cheap accommodation is generally scarce year-round. Bookings are essential.

B&B Casanova   B&B €
(☑0921 92 30 65; www.casanovabb.it; Via Porpora 3; s €35-55, d €50-100, q €70-140; ❀🛜) This B&B on the waterfront has rooms of varying size, from a cramped single with one minuscule window to the Ruggero room, a palatial space sleeping up to four, with a vaulted frescoed ceiling, decorative tile floors and French doors offering grand views of Cefalù's medieval centre. All guests share access to a small terrace overlooking the sea.

Hotel Kalura   HOTEL €€
(☑0921 42 13 54; www.hotel-kalura.com; Via Vincenzo Cavallaro 13; d €89-159; P❀@≋) East of town on a rocky outcrop, this German-run, family-oriented hotel has its own pebbly beach, restaurant and fabulous pool. Most rooms have sea views, and the hotel arranges loads of activities, including mountain biking, hiking, canoeing, pedaloes, diving and dance nights. It's a 20-minute walk into town.

La Plumeria   HOTEL €€
(☑0921 92 58 97; www.laplumeriahotel.it; Corso Ruggero 185; s €70-180, d €90-220; P❀🛜) Newly opened in 2010, this hotel's big selling point is its perfect location between the *duomo* and the waterfront, with free parking a few minutes away. Rooms are unexceptional, but clean and well-appointed. The single on the top floor is the sweetest of the lot, a cosy eyrie with checkerboard tile floors and a small terrace looking up to the *duomo*.

B&B Dolce Vita   B&B €
(☑0921 92 31 51; www.dolcevitabb.it; Via Bordonaro 8; r €60-120; ❀@🛜) This popular B&B has a lovely terrace with deck chairs overlooking the sea and a barbecue for warm summer evenings. Rooms are airy and light, with comfy beds, but the staff's lackadaisical attitude can detract from the charm. Breakfast is via a voucher system at a nearby cafe.

Eating & Drinking

There are dozens of restaurants, but the food can be surprisingly mundane and the ubiquitous tourist menus can quickly pall.

Al Porticciolo
SEAFOOD, PIZZERIA €€

(☑0921 92 19 81; Via Carlo Ortolani di Bordonaro 66/86/90; pizzas €5-12, meals €20-35; ☺closed Wed Oct-Apr) Dine in a five-star setting without shifting your credit card into overdrive at this popular waterfront eatery; in summer everyone piles out onto the ample outdoor terrace. There's pizza day and night, and fixed-price menus start at €20.

La Brace
INTERNATIONAL €€

(☑0921 42 35 70; Via XXV Novembre 10; meals €20-30; ☺lunch Wed-Sun, dinner Tue-Sun) This Dutch-Indonesian-run eatery has won a following over the past several decades for its eclectic, reasonably priced menu, where Italian classics rub elbows with international favourites like chile con carne, *shashlik* (marinated skewers of chicken) and roast rabbit with chestnuts.

La Galleria
BAR, FUSION €€

(☑0921 42 02 11; www.lagalleriacefalu.it; Via Mandralisca 23; cocktails €5, meals €30-40; ☺noon-3pm & 7pm-midnight Fri-Wed) Here you'll find a literary cafe, sophisticated cocktail bar, and tasteful art gallery combined into a super-cool, one-of-a-kind venue. Start or end your evening here, or stick around for dinner on its outdoor patio.

❶ Information

ATMs are concentrated along Corso Ruggero.

Hospital (☑0921 92 01 11; Contrada Pietra-pollastra) On the main road out of town in the direction of Palermo.

La Galleria (☑0921 42 02 11; Via Mandralisca 23; internet per hr €6; ☺noon-3pm & 7pm-midnight Fri-Wed) Cocktail bar with two fast internet computers and free wi-fi.

Police station (☑0921 92 60 11; Via Roma 15)

Post office (Via Vazzana 2) Just in from the *lungomare* (seafront promenade).

Tourist office (☑0921 42 10 50; strcefalu@regione.sicilia.it; Corso Ruggero 77; ☺9am-1pm & 3-7.30pm Mon-Sat) English-speaking staff, lots of leaflets and good maps.

❶ Getting There & Away

BOAT From June to September, **Ustica Lines** (www.usticalines.it) runs daily hydrofoils at 8.15am from Cefalù to the Aeolian Islands; destinations include Alicudi (€20.25, 1¼ hours), Filicudi (€23.40, 1¾ hours), Salina (€25.70, 2¾ hours) and Lipari (€29.10, 3¼ hours).

TRAIN The best way of getting to and from Cefalù is by rail. Hourly trains link Cefalù with Palermo (€5, one hour) and other towns along the Tyrrhenian coast.

AEOLIAN ISLANDS

The Aeolian Islands are a little piece of paradise. Stunning cobalt sea, splendid beaches, some of Italy's best hiking, and an awe-inspiring volcanic landscape are just part of the appeal. The islands also have a fascinating human and mythological history that goes back several millennia; the Aeolians figured prominently in Homer's *Odyssey*, and evidence of the distant past can be seen everywhere, most notably in Lipari's excellent archaeological museum.

The seven islands of Lipari, Vulcano, Salina, Panarea, Stromboli, Alicudi and Filicudi are part of a huge 200km volcanic ridge that runs between the smoking stack of Mt Etna and the threatening mass of Vesuvius above Naples. Collectively, the islands exhibit a unique range of volcanic characteristics, which earned them a place on Unesco's World Heritage list in 2000. The islands are mobbed with visitors in July and August but out of season things remain remarkably tranquil.

❶ Getting There & Away

In summer, ferries and hydrofoils leave regularly from Milazzo and Messina, the two mainland cities closest to the islands. Peak season is from June to September with winter services much reduced and sometimes cancelled due to heavy seas. All of the following prices are one-way high-season fares.

Ferry

Siremar (www.siremar.it) and **NGI Traghetti** (☑090 928 40 91; www.ngi-spa.it) both run car ferries from Milazzo to the islands; they're slightly cheaper, but slower and less regular than the summer hydrofoils.

Hydrofoil

Both **Ustica Lines** (www.usticalines.it) and Siremar run hydrofoils from Milazzo to Lipari (€16.80, one hour), and then on to the other islands. From 1 June to 30 September hydrofoils depart every hour or two for Lipari, stopping en route at Vulcano (€16, 45 minutes) and continuing onward to Santa Marina or Rinella (€17.55, 1½ to two hours) on Salina island. Beyond Salina, boats either branch off east to Panarea (€18.80, 2¼ hours) and Stromboli (€21.95, three hours), or west to Filicudi (€23.25, 2½ hours) and Alicudi (€28.70, 3¼ hours).

Ustica Lines also operates year-round hydrofoils to Lipari from Messina (€23.90, 1½ to 3½ hours, one to five daily) and Reggio di Calabria (€24.90, 1½ to 3½ hours, one to four daily).

DESTINATION	COST (€) HYDROFOIL/FERRY	DURATION HYDROFOIL/FERRY
Alicudi	18.85/13.95	2/4hr
Filicudi	15.80/12.40	1¼/2¾hr
Panarea	10.40/7.50	1/2hr
Salina (Rinella)	9.60/7.30	40min/1½hr
Salina (Santa Marina)	8.80/6.70	25/45min
Stromboli	17.80/12.40	1¾/4hr
Vulcano	5.80/4.70	10/25min

In summer, Ustica Lines adds service to Lipari from Cefalù (€29.10, 3¼ hours, one daily) and Palermo (€39.30, four hours, two daily).

Getting Around

Boat

Regular hydrofoil and ferry services operate between the islands. On Lipari all hydrofoil and ferry services arrive at and depart from Marina Lunga, where Siremar and Ustica Lines both have ticket offices. On the other islands, ticket offices are at or close to the docks. Timetables are posted at all offices.

Car & Scooter

You can take your car to Lipari, Vulcano or Salina by ferry, or garage it on the mainland from €12 per day. The islands are small, with narrow, winding roads. You'll often save money (and headaches) by hiring a scooter on site, or better yet, exploring the islands on foot.

Lipari

POP 11,300 / ELEV 602M

Lipari is the Aeolians' thriving hub, both geographically and functionally, with regular ferry and hydrofoil connections to all other islands. Lipari town, the largest urban centre in the archipelago, is home to the islands' only tourist office and most dependable banking services, along with enough restaurants, bars and year-round residents to offer a bit of cosmopolitan buzz. Meanwhile, the island's rugged shoreline offers excellent opportunities for hiking, boating and swimming.

Lipari has been inhabited for some 6000 years. The island was settled in the 4th millennium BC by Sicily's first known inhabitants, the Stentillenians, who developed a flourishing economy based on obsidian, a

glassy volcanic rock. Commerce subsequently attracted the Greeks, who used the islands as ports on the east-west trade route, and pirates such as Barbarossa (or Redbeard), who coveted Lipari's lucrative obsidian and pumice mines.

Today trade is still flourishing. Lipari's two harbours, Marina Lunga (where ferries and hydrofoils dock) and Marina Corta (700m south, used by smaller boats) are linked by a bustling main street, Corso Vittorio Emanuele, flanked by shops, restaurants and bars. Overlooking the colourful snake of day trippers is Lipari's clifftop citadel, surrounded by 16th-century walls.

◉ Sights

Museo Archeologico Eoliano　　MUSEUM
(☑090 988 01 74; www.regione.sicilia.it/beniculturali/museolipari; Castello di Lipari; adult/reduced €6/3; ⓢ9am-1pm & 3-6pm Mon-Sat, 9am-1pm Sun) Within the citadel's fortifications is one of Sicily's best museums, tracing the volcanic and human history of the islands. It is divided into three sections: an archaeological section devoted to artefacts from the Neolithic period and Bronze Age to the Roman era; a classical section with finds from Lipari's necropolis (including the most complete collection of miniature Greek theatrical masks in the world); and a section on vulcanology and finds from the other islands.

🏃 Activities

Beaches　　BEACHES
On the island's western side, **Spiaggia Valle i Muria** is a secluded rocky beach with gorgeous views south to Vulcano. Closed for a time following an August 2010 earthquake, it has since reopened. The most scenic way to get here is by boat, passing the dramatic

faraglioni (rock towers) and stone arches along Lipari's southwestern shore. Call **Barni** (☎349 1839555) to arrange boat transport (€5/10 one way/return). Alternatively, catch the bus from Marina Lunga towards Quattropani, get off at Quattrochi and walk 15 minutes steeply down towards the water.

On Lipari's eastern shore, sunbathers and swimmers head for Canneto, a few kilometres north of Lipari town, to bask on the pebbly **Spiaggia Bianca**. Further north are the **pumice mines** of Pomiciazzo and Porticello, where there's another beach, **Spiaggia della Papesca**, dusted white by the fine pumice that gives the sea its limpid turquoise colour.

Coastal Hikes

WALKING

Lipari's rugged northwestern coastline offers excellent walking opportunities. Most accessible is the pleasant hour-long stroll from Quattropani to Acquacalda along Lipari's north shore, which affords spectacular views of Salina and a distant Stromboli. Take the bus to Quattropani (€1.90), then simply proceed downhill on the main road 5km to Acquacalda, where you can catch the bus (€1.55) back to Lipari.

More strenuous, but equally rewarding in terms of scenery, is the three- to four-hour hike descending steeply from Pianoconte, down past the old Roman baths of Terme di San Calogero to the western shoreline, then skirting the clifftops along a flat stretch before climbing steeply back to the town of Quattropani.

Diving Center La Gorgonia

DIVING

(☎090 981 26 16; www.lagorgoniadiving.it; Salita San Giuseppe, Marina Corta; dive/night dive/beginner course €30/40/55) Offers courses, boat transport and equipment hire for scuba diving and snorkelling in Lipari's crystal-clear waters.

☞ Tours

You can take boat tours to the surrounding islands (€15 to €45), or arrange a day trip to hike up Stromboli (€80) with agencies throughout town, including the following friendly, English-speaking organisations:

Avventurisole

BOAT

(☎090 988 02 74; www.avventurisole.com, in Italian; Via Maurolico 10)

Da Massimo/Dolce Vita

BOAT

(☎090 981 30 86; www.damassimo.it; Via Maurolico 2)

Popolo Giallo

BOAT

(☎090 981 12 10; www.popologiallo.it; Salita San Giuseppe)

☷ Sleeping

Lipari is the Aeolians' best-equipped base for island-hopping, with plenty of places to stay, eat and drink. Touts besiege arriving passengers at the port, and the tourist office can sometimes help arrange accommodation in private homes. Note that prices soar in summer; avoid August if possible.

Diana Brown

B&B €

(☎090 981 25 84; www.dianabrown.it; Vico Himera 3; s €30-90, d €40-100; ❄️@🛜) Tucked down a narrow alley, South African Diana has delightful rooms decorated in contemporary style with tile floors, abundant hot water, bright colours and welcome extras such as kettles, fridges, clothes-drying racks and satellite TV. Darker rooms downstairs are compensated for by built-in kitchenettes. There's a sunny breakfast terrace and solarium with deck chairs, plus book exchange and laundry service. Optional breakfast per person is €5 extra.

Villa Diana

HOTEL €€

(☎090 981 14 03; www.villadiana.com; Via Tufo 1; s €43-80, d €76-145; 🅿️❄️🛜) Swiss artist Edwin Hunziker converted this Aeolian house into a bohemian-spirited hotel in the 1950s. It stands above Lipari town in a garden of citrus trees and olives and offers panoramic views from the terrace. Amenities include free wi-fi (in the reception area only) and use of the tennis court.

Hotel Oriente

HOTEL €

(☎090 981 14 93; www.hotelorientelipari.com; Via Marconi 35; s €40-60, d €60-95; 🅿️❄️🛜) You'll either love this place for its quirkiness or hate it for its clutter. Just 100m west of the centre, its rooms are rather bland and faded, but the common spaces drip with character, from the spacious citrus-filled courtyard, to the eclectically decorated breakfast room and bar, to the in-house museum of Sicilian antique paraphernalia. Breakfast goes above and beyond the norm, with marinated veggies and cheese supplementing the usual bread and coffee.

Enzo Il Negro

GUESTHOUSE €

(☎090 981 31 63; www.enzoilnegro.com; Via Garibaldi 29; s €40-50, d €60-90; ❄️) Run by an older couple, this simple guesthouse near Marina Corta sports spacious, tiled, pine-furnished rooms with fridges. Two panoramic terraces overlook the rooftops, the harbour and the castle walls.

Eating & Drinking

Fish abound in the waters of the archipelago and include tuna, mullet, cuttlefish and sole, all of which end up on local menus. Try *pasta all'eoliana,* a simple blend of the island's excellent capers with olive oil, anchovies and basil.

Bars are concentrated along Corso Vittorio Emanuele and down by Marina Corta. In peak season everything stays open into the wee hours.

E Pulera MODERN SICILIAN €€
(☑090 981 11 58; Via Isabella Vainicher Conti; meals €30-45; ⓧdinner May-Oct) With its serene garden setting, low lighting, artsy tile-topped tables and exquisite food, E Pulera makes an upscale but relaxed choice for a romantic dinner. Start with a carpaccio of tuna with blood oranges and capers, choose from a vast array of Aeolian and Sicilian meat and fish dishes, then finish it all off with *cassata* or biscotti and sweet Malvasia wine.

Kasbah MODERN SICILIAN €€
(☑090 981 10 75; Via Maurolico 25; pizzas €6-9, meals €30-35; ⓧdinner, closed Wed Oct-Mar) Choose the environment that suits you best: the sleek, contemporary interior dining room or the vine-covered, candlelit garden out back. The food is superb, including delicious pizzas and seafood delicacies (order from the menu or select your fish from the display case).

Bar Pasticceria Subba PASTRIES & CAKES €
(☑090 981 13 52; Corso Vittorio Emanuele 92; pastries from €1; ⓧ7am-10pm) Feed your sweet tooth with fabulous pastries at this long-established bakery (since 1930) on Lipari's main drag.

La Piazzetta PIZZERIA €
(☑090 981 25 22; pizzas €5.50-9.50; ⓧdinner, closed Thu Sep-Jun) A lively pizzeria with vine-draped outdoor seating that has served the likes of Audrey Hepburn. It's off Corso Vittorio Emanuele, behind Pasticceria Subba.

Shopping

You simply can't leave these islands without a small pot of capers and a bottle of sweet Malvasia wine. You can get both, along with tuna, meats, cheeses and other delicious

goodies, at **La Formagella** (Corso Vittorio Emanuele 250) or **Fratelli Laise** (www.fratelli laise.com; Corso Vittorio Emanuele 118).

 Information

Corso Vittorio Emanuele is lined with ATMs. The other islands have few facilities, so sort out your finances here before moving on.

Internet Point (Corso Vittorio Emanuele 185; per hr €5; ⓧ9.30am-1pm & 5-8.30pm Mon-Sat winter, 9am-1pm & 5.30pm-midnight summer)

Ospedale Civile (☑090 988 51 11; Via Sant'Anna) Operates a first-aid service.

Police (☑090 981 13 33; Via Guglielmo Marconi)

Post office (Corso Vittorio Emanuele 207)

Tourist office (☑090 988 00 95; www.aas teolie.191.it, in Italian; Corso Vittorio Emanuele 202; ⓧ9am-1pm & 4.30-7pm Mon-Fri year-round, 9am-1pm Sat summer) Lipari's office provides information covering all the islands.

ⓘ Getting There & Around

BUS Autobus Guglielmo Urso (☑090 981 10 26; www.ursobus.com) runs frequent buses around the island from Marina Lunga (€1.55 to €1.90 depending on destination). One main route serves the island's eastern shore, from Canneto to Acquacalda, while the other serves the western highland settlements of Quattrochi, Pianoconte and Quattropani. Multi-ride booklets (six/10/20 rides €7/10.50/20.50) will save you money if you're here for several days.

BOAT See p762 for ferry and hydrofoil details.

CAR & MOTORCYCLE Several places around town rent scooters (€15 to €30) and cars (€30 to €50), including **Da Luigi** (☑090 988 05 40; Marina Lunga) down at the ferry dock.

Vulcano

POP 720 / ELEV 500M

Vulcano is a memorable island, not least because of the vile smell of sulphurous gases. Once you escape the drab and dated tourist centre, Porto di Levante, there's a delightfully tranquil, unspoilt quality to the landscape. Following the well-marked trail to the looming Fossa di Vulcano, the landscape gives way to rural simplicity with vineyards, birdsong and a surprising amount of greenery. The island is worshipped by Italians for its therapeutic mud baths and hot springs, and its black beaches and weird steaming landscape make for an interesting day trip.

Boats dock at Porto di Levante. To the right, as you face the island, are the mud baths and the small Vulcanello peninsula, to the left is the volcano. Straight ahead is Porto di Ponente, 700m west, where you will find the Spiaggia Sabbia Nera (Black Sand Beach).

🏃 Activities

Fossa di Vulcano   WALKING
(admission €3) The island's top attraction is the trek up its 391m volcano, easily manageable without a guide. Start early in the day if possible and don't forget a hat, sunscreen and water. Follow the signs south along Strada Provinciale, then turn left onto the zigzag gravel track that leads to the summit. It's about an hour's scramble to the lowest point of the crater's edge (290m). From here, the sight of the steaming crater encrusted with red and yellow crystals is reward enough, but it's well worth lingering up top for a while. You can descend steeply to the crater floor, or better yet, continue climbing around the rim for stunning views of all the islands lined up to the north.

Laghetto di Fanghi   BATHS
(admission €2) Vulcano's large harbourside pit of thick, smelly, sulphurous gloop has long been considered an excellent treatment for arthritis, rheumatism and skin disorders. Don't wear your designer swimsuit (you'll never get the smell out), keep the mud away from your eyes (it burns!), and be sure to leave your gold chains behind (they will tarnish). Afterwards, you can hop into the water at the adjacent beach where *acque calde* (hot springs) create a natural Jacuzzi effect.

Beaches   BEACHES
At Porto di Ponente, on the far side of the peninsula from Porto di Levante, the dramatic and only mildly commercialised black-sand beach of Spiaggia Sabbia Nera curves around a pretty bay. It is one of the few sandy beaches in the archipelago. A smaller, quieter black-sand beach, Spiaggia dell'Asina, can be found on the island's southern side near Gelso.

🛏 Sleeping & Eating

Unless you're here for the walking and the mud baths, Vulcano is not a great place for an extended stay; the town is pretty soulless, the hotels are expensive and the mud baths really do smell. If you do stay, the best hotels are situated around Spiaggia Sabbia Nera.

La Forgia Maurizio   SICILIAN, INDIAN €€
(🎧 339 137 91 07; Strada Provinciale 45; meals €25-30) The owner of this devilishly good restaurant spent 20 winters in Goa, India; Eastern influences sneak into a menu of Sicilian specialities, all prepared and presented with flair. Don't miss the *liquore di kumquat e cardamom,* Maurizio's home-made answer to *limoncello.* The tasting menu is an excellent deal at €25 including wine and dessert.

Trattoria Maniaci Pina   SEAFOOD €€
(🎧 368 66 85 55; Gelso; meals €25-35; ⊙ May–mid-Oct) On the south side of the island, beside a black-sand beach, this atmospheric, down-to-earth trattoria serves hefty portions of fresh-caught fish at affordable prices. Two local men do the fishing, and their moms do the cooking.

❶ Getting There & Around

BOAT Vulcano is an intermediate stop between Milazzo and Lipari; both Siremar and Ustica Lines run multiple vessels in both directions throughout the day. See p762 for more details.

You can hire boats locally at **Centro Nautico Baia di Levante** (🎧 339 337 27 95; www.baia levante.it; ⊙ Apr-Oct), in a shed on the beach to the left of the hydrofoil dock.

CAR & MOTORCYCLE Scooters (per day €15 to €40), bicycles (€5 to €10) and small cars (€25 to €78) can be rented from **Sprint** (🎧 090 985 22 08), well signposted near the hydrofoil dock. Friendly multilingual owners Luigi and Nidra also offer helpful tourist info and rent out an apartment in Vulcano's tranquil interior.

Salina

POP 2300 / ELEV 962M

In stark contrast to Vulcano's barren landscape, Salina's twin craters of Monte dei Porri and Monte Fossa delle Felci are lushly wooded, a result of the numerous freshwater springs on the island. Wildflowers, thick yellow gorse bushes and serried ranks of grapevines carpet the hillsides in vibrant colours and cool greens, while its high coastal cliffs plunge dramatically towards beaches. The famous Aeolian capers grow plentifully here, as do the grapes used for making Malvasia wine.

◉ Sights & Activities

Fossa delle Felci   VIEWPOINT
For jaw-dropping views of Salina and the surrounding islands, climb to Salina's

highest point (962m). The trail starts at Valdichiesa, in the valley that separates Salina's two volcanoes, at the Santuario della Madonna del Terzito, a popular pilgrimage site. From the church, follow the track (signposted) up through a nature reserve all the way to the peak (about two hours), where you'll have unparalleled views of the entire archipelago. To get to the trailhead, take the bus from Santa Marina Salina to Malfa, then change for a Rinella-bound bus and ask the driver to let you off at Valdichiesa.

Pollara
BEACH

Don't miss a trip to Pollara, sandwiched dramatically between the sea and the steep slopes of an extinct volcanic crater on Salina's western edge. The gorgeous beach here was used as a location in the 1994 film *Il Postino*. Although the land access route to the beach has since been closed due to landslide danger, you can still descend the steep stone steps at the northwest end of town and swim across, or simply admire the spectacular view, with its backdrop of volcanic cliffs.

Nautica Levante
BOAT

(✆090 984 30 83; www.nauticalevante.it, in Italian; Via Lungomare, Santa Marina Salina; ⓧEaster-Sep) Boat hire (from €65).

🛏 Sleeping & Eating

The island remains relatively undisturbed by mass tourism, yet still offers some fine hotels and restaurants. Accommodation can be found in Salina's three main towns: Santa Marina Salina on the east shore, Malfa on the north shore and Rinella on the south shore, as well as in Lingua, a village adjoining ancient salt ponds 2km south of Santa Marina.

Capo Faro
BOUTIQUE HOTEL €€€

(✆090 984 43 30; www.capofaro.it; Via Faro 3; d €150-380; ⓧApr-Sep; ❄@🏮🏊) Immerse yourself in luxury at this five-star boutique resort halfway between Santa Marina and Malfa, surrounded by well-tended Malvasia vineyards and a picturesque lighthouse. The 20 rooms all have sharp white decor and terraces looking straight out to smoking Stromboli. Tennis courts, poolside massages, wine tasting, vineyard visits and occasional cooking courses complete this perfect vision of island chic.

Signum
BOUTIQUE HOTEL €€€

(✆090 984 42 22; www.hotelsignum.it; Via Scalo 15, Malfa; d €130-280; ⓧmid-Mar–early Nov; ❄🏮🏊) Hidden in the hillside lanes of Malfa is this alluring labyrinth of antique-clad rooms, peach-coloured stucco walls, tall blue windows, and vine-covered terraces. There's a lovely pool, a wellness centre complete with natural spa baths and one of the island's best-regarded restaurants on site (meals €35 to €50). Check the website for offers.

Hotel Mamma Santina
BOUTIQUE HOTEL €€

(✆090 984 30 54; www.mammasantina.it; Via Sanità 40, Santa Marina Salina; d €110-190; ⓧApr-Oct; ❄@🏮🏊) A labour of love for its architect owner, this boutique hotel has inviting rooms decorated with pretty tiles in traditional Aeolian designs. Many of the sea-view terraces come equipped with hammocks, and on warm evenings the attached restaurant has outdoor seating overlooking the glowing blue pool and landscaped garden.

Campeggio Eolie
CAMPGROUND €

(✆090 980 90 52; www.campeggioeolie.it; Rinella; campsite per person €9-14; ⓧlate Jun–mid-Sep) This campground has lovely terraced sites amid olive and eucalyptus trees overlooking the sea, plus a mini-market, bar and pizzeria. It's a five-minute walk from Rinella's hydrofoil dock.

TOP CHOICE Da Alfredo
SANDWICH SHOP €

(Piazza Marina Garibaldi, Lingua; granite €2.50, sandwiches €7-10) The most atmospheric place on Salina for an affordable snack, Alfredo's place is renowned all over Sicily for its *granite:* ices made with coffee, fresh fruit or locally grown pistachios and almonds. It's also worth a visit for its *pane cunzato* – open-faced sandwiches piled high with tuna, ricotta, eggplant, tomatoes, capers and olives; split one with a friend – they're huge!

Porto Bello
SEAFOOD €€

(✆090 984 31 25; Via Bianchi 1, Santa Marina Salina; meals €30-45; ⓧTue-Sun) This award-winning seafood restaurant with a terrace overlooking the harbour dates back to 1978 with the same family at the helm. Aside from fish, it's famous for its *pasta al fuoco* (fiery pasta with hot peppers).

Al Cappero
SICILIAN €

(✆090 984 41 33; www.alcappero.it; Pollara; meals €20-25; ⓧlunch May, lunch & dinner Jun–mid-Sep) This family-run place specialises in old-fashioned Sicilian home-cooking, including several vegetarian options. It also sells home-grown capers and rents out simple rooms down the street (€20 to €35 per person).

'nni Lausta MODERN ITALIAN €€
(☑090 984 34 86; Via Risorgimento, Santa Marina Salina; meals €35-40) This stylish modern eatery with its cute lobster logo serves superb food based on fresh local ingredients. The downstairs bar is popular for *aperitivi* and late-night drinking.

❶ Information

Banco di Sicilia (Via Risorgimento, Santa Marina Salina) ATM on Santa Marina's main pedestrian street.
Post office (Via Risorgimento, Santa Maria Salina)

❶ Getting There & Around

BOAT Hydrofoils and ferries service Santa Marina Salina and Rinella from Lipari. You'll find ticket offices in both places.
BUS CITIS (☑090 984 41 50) buses run roughly half-hourly (every 90 minutes in low season) from Santa Marina Salina to Lingua, Malfa, Rinella, Pollara, Valdichiesa and Leni (€1.70 to €2.40 depending on destination). Timetables are posted at the ports and bus stops.
CAR & MOTORCYCLE Above Santa Marina Salina's port, **Antonio Bongiorno** (☑090 984 34 09; Via Risorgimento 240) rents bikes (per day from €8), scooters (from €26) and cars (from €50). Several agencies in Rinella offer similar services – look for signs at the ferry dock.

Stromboli

POP 400 / ELEV 924M

Stromboli's perfect triangle of a volcano juts dramatically out of the sea. It's the only island whose smouldering cone is permanently active, thus attracting both experts and amateurs, like moths to a massive flame. Volcanic activity has scarred and blackened one side of the island, while the eastern side is untamed, ruggedly green and dotted with low-rise whitewashed houses. A youngster among the Aeolians, Stromboli was formed a mere 40,000 years ago and its gases continue to send up an almost constant spray of liquid magma. The most recent major eruptions took place in February 2007 when two new craters opened on the volcano's summit, producing two scalding lava flows. Although seismic activity,

including rock falls, continued for several days, fortunately no mass evacuation was deemed necessary.

Boats arrive at Porto Scari-San Vincenzo, downhill from the town. Most accommodation, as well as the meeting point for guided hikes up the volcano, is a short walk up the Scalo Scari to Via Roma.

 Activities

Volcano WALKING
Note that you're legally required to hire a guide to climb higher than 400m on the volcano.

The path to the summit (920m) is a demanding three-hour climb (rest stops every 40 minutes), but the atmosphere is charged and you will be rewarded with tremendous views of the **Sciara del Fuoco** (Trail of Fire) and the constantly smoking crater. Fiery explosions usually occur every 20 minutes or so and are preceded by a loud belly-roar as gases force the magma into the air. Departure times for organised treks vary from 3.30pm to 6pm, depending on the season; treks are always timed so you can observe sunset from the mountaintop, then ooh and aah over the crater's fireworks for about 45 minutes as night falls.

To undertake the climb you'll need heavy shoes; clothing for cold, wet weather; a torch (flashlight); a backpack that allows free movement of both arms; and a good supply of water. **Totem Trekking** (☑090 986 57 52; Piazza San Vincenzo 4) hires out all the necessary equipment, including headlamps (€3), trekking boots (€6) and windbreakers (€5).

Two other great ways to see the volcano, with less huffing and puffing, are the hike up to L'Osservatorio and the nightly boat tours to Sciara del Fuoco. To reach the pizzeria, follow the waterfront 2km west from the hydrofoil dock to the community of Piscità, then climb the gradual, winding path 1km further, following the signs.

Beaches BEACH
The most accessible swimming and sunbathing is at Ficogrande, a beach of rocks and black volcanic sand 10 minutes by foot from the hydrofoil dock. Further-flung beaches worth exploring are at Piscità to the west and Forgia Vecchia to the south.

La Sirenetta Diving Club DIVING
(☑347 596 14 99; www.lasirenettadiving.it; Via Marina 33; ☉Jun–mid-Sep) Offers diving courses and accompanied dives.

Tours

Magmatrek (☎090 986 57 68; www.magma trek.it; Via Vittorio Emanuele) has experienced, multilingual vulcanological guides who lead regular treks (maximum group size 20) up to the crater every afternoon (per person €28). It can also put together tailor-made treks for individual groups. Other agencies charging identical prices include **Il Vulcano a Piedi** (☎090 98 61 44; www.stromboliguide.it; Via Roma) and **Stromboli Adventures** (☎090 98 62 64; www.stromboliadventures.it, in Italian; Via Vittorio Emanuele).

Società Navigazione Pippo (☎090 98 61 35; pipponav.stromboli@libero.it) and **Antonio Caccetta** (☎090 98 60 23) are among the numerous boat companies at Porto Scari offering daytime circuits of the island and sunset excursions to watch the Sciara del Fuoco from the sea (each €20 per person).

Sleeping & Eating

Over a dozen places offer accommodation, including B&Bs, guesthouses and full-fledged hotels.

TOP CHOICE Casa del Sole GUESTHOUSE €
(☎090 98 63 00; www.casadelsolestromboli.it; Via Domenico Cincotta; dm €25-30, s €30-50, d €60-100) This cheerful Aeolian-style guesthouse is only 100m from a sweet black-sand beach in Piscitá, the tranquil neighbourhood at the far end of town. Dorms, private doubles and a guest kitchen all surround a sunny patio, overhung with vines, fragrant with lemon blossoms, and decorated with the masks and stone carvings of sculptor-owner Tano Russo. Call for free pickup (low season only) or take a taxi (€10) from the port 2km away.

Il Giardino Segreto B&B €
(☎090 98 62 11; www.giardinosegretobb.it; Via Francesco Natoli; d €60-120) In a 'secret garden' framed by picturesque rows of cypresses, this sweet little B&B offers stylishly decorated rooms and a rooftop terrace five minutes' walk above the church on the way to the volcano.

L'Osservatorio PIZZERIA €
(☎090 98 63 60; pizzas €6.50-10.50; ☺lunch & dinner) Sure, you could eat a pizza in town, but come on – you're on Stromboli! Make the 45-minute uphill trek to this pizzeria and you'll be rewarded with exceptional volcano views, best after sundown.

La Bottega del Marano GROCERY €
(Via Vittorio Emanuele; snacks from €1.50; ☺8.30am-1pm & 4.30-7.30pm Mon-Sat) The perfect source for volcano-climbing provisions or a self-catering lunch, this reasonably priced neighbourhood grocery, five minutes west of the trekking-agency offices, has a well-stocked deli, shelves full of wine and awesomely tasty mini-focaccias (€1.50).

Locanda del Barbablù SICILIAN €€€
(☎090 98 61 18; www.barbablu.it; Via Vittorio Emanuele 17; tasting menus excl drinks €40-56; ☺dinner Apr-Oct) This dusky-pink Aeolian inn houses the island's classiest restaurant, serving multicourse tasting menus of traditional Sicilian recipes, with a strong emphasis on fresh-caught seafood.

❶ Information

Bring enough cash for your stay on Stromboli. Many businesses don't accept credit cards, and the village's lone ATM is often out of service. Internet access is virtually non-existent.

Police station (☎090 98 60 21; Via Picone) Just on the left as you walk up from the port.

Post office (Via Roma)

❶ Getting There & Away

It takes four hours to reach the island from Lipari by ferry, or 1½ to two hours by hydrofoil. Ticket offices for **Ustica Lines** (☎090 98 60 03) and **Siremar** (☎090 98 60 16) are at the port.

IONIAN COAST

Magnificent, overdeveloped, crowded – and exquisitely beautiful – the Ionian coast is Sicily's most popular tourist destination and home to 20% of the island's population. Moneyed entrepreneurs have built their villas and hotels up and down the coastline, eager to bag a spot on Sicily's version of the Amalfi Coast. Above it all towers the muscular peak of Mt Etna (3329m), puffs of smoke billowing from its snow-covered cone.

Taormina

POP 11,100 / ELEV 204M

Spectacularly situated on a terrace of Monte Tauro, with views westwards to Mt Etna, Taormina is a beautiful small town, reminiscent of Capri or an Amalfi coastal resort. Over the centuries, Taormina has seduced an exhaustive line of writers and artists,

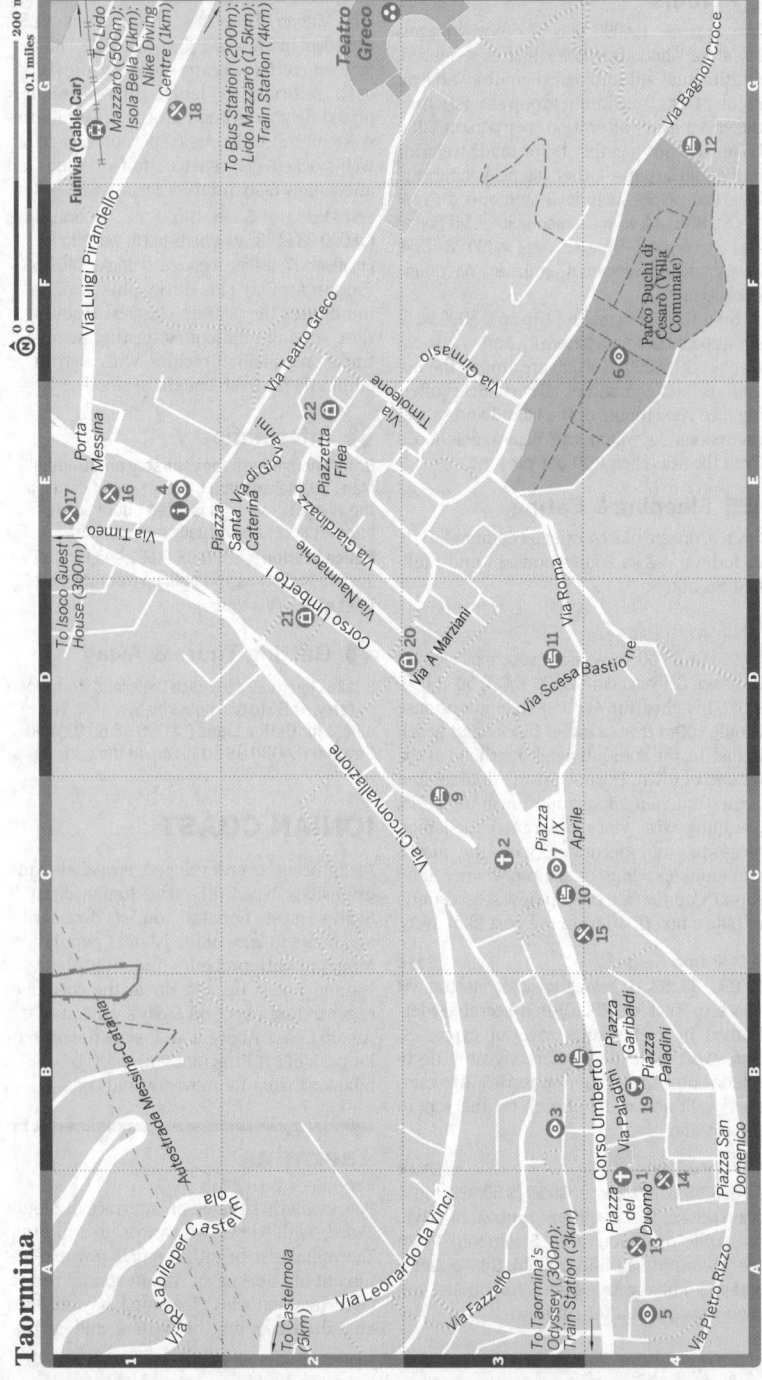

aristocrats and royalty, and these days it's host to a summer arts festival that packs the town with international visitors.

Perched on its eyrie, Taormina is sophisticated, chic and comfortably cushioned by some serious wealth – very far removed from the banal economic realities of other Sicilian towns. But the charm is not manufactured. The capital of Byzantine Sicily in the 9th century, Taormina is an almost perfectly preserved medieval town, and if you can tear yourself away from the shopping and sunbathing, it has a wealth of small but perfect tourist sites. Taormina is also a popular resort with gay men.

Be warned that in July and August the town and its surrounding beaches are swarming with tourists.

◎ Sights

A short walk uphill from the bus station brings you to Corso Umberto I (abbreviated below as Corso Umberto), a pedestrianised thoroughfare that traverses the length of the medieval town and connects its two historic town gates, Porta Messina and Porta Catania.

Teatro Greco   AMPHITHEATRE
(✆0942 2 32 20; Via Teatro Greco; adult/reduced €8/4; ◷9am-1hr before sunset) Taormina's premier attraction is this perfect horseshoe-shaped theatre, suspended between sea and sky, with Mt Etna looming on the southern horizon. Built in the 3rd century BC, it's the most dramatically situated Greek theatre in the world and the second largest in Sic-

ily (after Syracuse). In summer the theatre is used as the venue for international arts and film festivals. In peak season the site is best explored early in the morning to avoid the crowds.

Corso Umberto   PROMENADE
One of the chief delights of Taormina is wandering along its pedestrian-friendly medieval main avenue, Corso Umberto I, lined with antique and jewellery shops, delis and designer boutiques. Midway down, pause to revel in the stunning panoramic views of Mt Etna and the seacoast from Piazza IX Aprile and pop your head into the charming rococo church, Chiesa San Giuseppe (Piazza IX Aprile; ◷9am-7pm). Continue west through the 12th-century clock tower, Torre dell'Orologio, into the Borgo Medievale, the oldest quarter of town. A few blocks further along is Piazza del Duomo, where teenagers congregate around the ornate baroque fountain (built 1635), which sports a two-legged centaur with the bust of an angel, the symbol of Taormina. On the eastern side of this piazza is the 13th-century cathedral (Piazza del Duomo; ◷9am-8pm). It survived much of the Renaissance-style remodelling undertaken throughout the town by the Spanish aristocracy in the 15th century. The Renaissance influence is better illustrated in various palaces along the Corso, including Palazzo Duca di Santo Stefano with its Norman-Gothic windows, Palazzo Corvaja (the tourist office) and Palazzo Ciampoli (now the Hotel El Jebel).

OFFSHORE ISLANDS

Sicily is an island lover's paradise, with more than a dozen offshore islands scattered in the seas surrounding the main island. Beyond the major islands of Lipari, Vulcano, Stromboli and Salina, covered in detail here, you can detour to the less visited Aeolian islands of **Panarea**, **Filicudi** and **Alicudi**. Off Sicily's western coast are the slow-paced **Egadi Islands** (see p801) and the remote, rugged volcanic island of **Pantelleria** (see p803). South of Agrigento, the sand-sprinkled **Pelagic Islands** of Lampedusa, Linosa and Lampione offer some fantastic beaches but are temporarily off limits to tourists because of an influx of refugees fleeing the conflicts in North Africa – check locally to see if trips have resumed. Ustica Lines (www.usticalines.it) and Siremar (www.siremar.it) provide hydrofoil and/or ferry service to all of the islands listed above; see their websites for details.

Villa Comunale — PARK
(Parco Duchi di Cesarò; Via Bagnoli Croce; ⏱9am-midnight summer, 9am-10pm winter) To escape the crowds, wander down to these stunningly sited public gardens. Created by Englishwoman Florence Trevelyan, they're a lush paradise of tropical plants and delicate flowers. There's also a children's play area.

Castelmola — HILLTOP VILLAGE
For eye-popping views of the coastline, head 5km up Via Leonardo da Vinci to this hilltop village crowned by a ruined castle. The walk will take you around an hour along a well-paved route. Alternatively, Interbus runs an hourly service (one way/return €1.70/2.80) up the hill.

Activities

Lido Mazzarò — BEACH
Many visitors to Taormina come only for the beach scene. To reach Lido Mazzarò, directly beneath Taormina, take the cable car (Via Luigi Pirandello; one way/return €2/3.50; ⏱8.45am-1am, every 15min). This beach is well serviced with bars and restaurants; private operators charge a fee for umbrellas and deck chairs (€10 per person per day, discountable at some hotels).

Isola Bella — NATURE RESERVE
Southwest of the beach is the minuscule Isola Bella, set in a stunning cove with fishing boats. You can walk here in a few minutes but it's more fun to rent a small boat from Mazzarò and paddle round Capo Sant'Andrea.

Nike Diving Centre — DIVING
(☎339 1961559; www.diveniketaormina.com; dive from €35) Opposite Isola Bella, this dive centre offers a wide range of courses for children and adults.

Gole dell'Alcàntara — SWIMMING
Perfect for cooling off on a hot summer day, this series of vertiginous lava gorges with swirling rapids is 20km west of town; take Interbus from Taormina (€4.60 return, one hour).

Festivals & Events

Taormina FilmFest — FILM
(www.taorminafilmfest.it) Hollywood big shots arrive in mid-June for a week of film screenings, premieres and press conferences at the Teatro Greco.

Taormina Arte — ARTS
(www.taormina-arte.com) In July and August, this festival features opera, dance, theatre and music concerts from an impressive list of international names.

Giuseppe Sinopoli Festival — MUSIC
(www.sinopolifestival.it) First held in 2005, this three-day classical music festival attracts important Italian orchestras and enthusiastic audiences in early October. Concerts are held in Palazzo Corvaja and the Teatro Greco.

🛏 Sleeping

Taormina has plenty of luxurious accommodation; the following represents a range of what's available, including some less expensive places. Many hotels offer discounted pricing (from €10) at Taormina's two public parking lots.

TOP CHOICE Isoco Guest House — B&B €
(☎0942 2 36 79; www.isoco.it; Via Salita Branco 2; s €65-120, d €85-120; ⏱Mar-Nov; P❄@) Every room in this exceptionally welcoming, gay-friendly B&B is dedicated to an artist – from Botticelli to the sculpted buttocks

and pant-popping thighs on the walls of the Herb Ritts room. The excellent breakfast, free internet access, sundecks and outdoor Jacuzzi are great as well. Multi-course dinners available on the terrace (€25 per person including drinks) in summer. German and English spoken.

B&B Le Sibille
B&B €

(☑349 726 28 62; www.lesibille.net; Corso Umberto 187a; d €60-100, apt per week without breakfast €400-600; ☺Apr-Oct; @☎) This B&B wins points for its prime location on Taormina's pedestrian thoroughfare, its rooftop breakfast terrace and its cheerful, artistically tiled self-catering apartments, newly added in 2011. Light sleepers beware: Corso Umberto can get noisy with holidaymakers! English spoken.

Villa Belvedere
HOTEL €€

(☑0942 2 37 91; www.villabelvedere.it; Via Bagnoli Croce 79; d with inland view €124-184, with sea view €144-236; ☺Mar-Nov; P ✴@☎☎) Built in 1902, adjacent to the Villa Comunale, the jaw-droppingly pretty Villa Belvedere oozes class. Rooms are simple but refined with cream linens and terracotta floors, and the luxurious garden commands majestic sea views. There's even a swimming pool with a 100-year-old palm tree rising from a small island in the middle. Wi-fi costs extra.

Casa Turchetti
B&B €€€

(☑0942 62 50 13; www.casaturchetti.com; Salita dei Gracchi 18/20; d €200-250, jr ste €350; ✴☎) Every detail is perfect in this painstakingly restored former music school, recently converted to a luxurious B&B on a back alley just above Corso Umberto. Vintage furniture and fixtures, handcrafted woodwork, fine homespun sheets and modern bathrooms all contribute to the elegant feel; the spacious rooftop terrace is just icing on the cake.

Hotel Villa Schuler
HOTEL €€

(☑0942 2 34 81; www.hotelvillaschuler.com; Via Roma, Piazzetta Bastione; s €128, d €142-202; P ✴@☎) Surrounded by shady terraced gardens and with views of Mt Etna, the rose-pink Villa Schuler has been run by the same family for over a century (longer than any other Taormina hotel) and preserves a homely atmosphere. A lovely breakfast is served on the panoramic terrace.

Hotel Metropole
LUXURY HOTEL €€€

(☑0942 62 54 17; www.hotelmetropoletaormina. it; Corso Umberto 154; d/ste €374/770; ✴@☎☎) In a lavishly renovated *palazzo* that incorporates ancient Roman columns and 14th-century monastery walls, Taormina's newest hotel offers an unparalleled combination of amenities, including a pool, a spa, a prime location just off Piazza IX Aprile and a restaurant and bar with full-on views of Mt Etna and the sea. The eight rooms and 15 suites are filled with designer furniture and top-of-the-line amenities, as reflected in the prices.

Taormina's Odyssey
GUESTHOUSE €

(☑0942 2 45 33, 349 8107733; www.taormina odyssey.com; Via Paternò di Biscari 13; dm €20, d €50-70; @☎) This family-run hostel and guesthouse offers two small dorms and three doubles (one with private bath) five minutes uphill from Porta Catania. There's a nice guest kitchen and internet area downstairs, and the dorm rate is as affordable a sleep as you'll find anywhere in Taormina.

✕ Eating

Eating out in Taormina goes hand in hand with posing. It's essential to make a reservation at the more exclusive choices. Be aware that Taormina's cafes charge extraordinarily high prices even for coffee.

Licchio's
SEAFOOD €€

(☑0942 62 53 27; Via Patricio 10; meals €30-40; ☺lunch & dinner, closed Thu Nov-Mar) The seafood antipasti at this classy little eatery are delicious and varied enough to constitute a meal in themselves, but the menu's full of other enticements: tempura-fried zucchini flowers, fabulously fresh spinach-ricotta gnocchi and divine desserts. Angelo also offers cooking classes (€80 including meal and drinks).

Trattoria Da Nino
TRATTORIA €€

(☑0942 2 12 65; Via Luigi Pirandello 37; meals €27-34; ☺lunch & dinner) Bright and bustling after a recent remodel, this place has been in business under the same family ownership for 50 years. Locals and tourists alike flock here for straightforward, reasonably priced Sicilian home cooking, including an excellent *caponata* plus fresh local fish served grilled, steamed, fried, stewed or rolled up in *involtini* (roulades).

Tiramisù — MODERN ITALIAN €€

(☎0942 2 48 03; Via Cappuccini 1; pizzas €7-10, meals €30-45; ☺closed Tue) This stylish place near Porta Messina makes fabulous meals, from *linguine cozze, menta e zucchine* (pasta with mussels, mint and zucchini) to old favourites like *scaloppine al limone e panna* (veal escalope in lemon cream sauce). When dessert rolls around, don't miss its trademark tiramisu, a perfect ending to any meal here.

Al Duomo — SICILIAN €€

(☎0942 62 56 56; Vico Ebrei 11; meals €40-45; ☺lunch & dinner, closed Mon Nov-Mar) This highly acclaimed restaurant with a romantic terrace overlooking the cathedral puts a modern spin on Sicilian classics like *pesce alla messinese* (fish fillets with tomatoes, capers and olives) and *agnello n'grassatu* (lamb stew with potatoes). For a splurge, indulge in the chef's six-course tasting menu (€60).

Casa Grugno — GASTRONOMIC €€€

(☎0942 2 12 08; www.casagrugno.it; Via Santa Maria dei Greci; meals €70-80; ☺dinner Mon-Sat) With a walled-in terrace surrounded by plants, Taormina's most fashionable restaurant specialises in sublime modern Sicilian cuisine, under the direction of new chef David Tamburini. Multilingual waiters describe the origins of each ultra-fresh local ingredient as they serve up dishes such as red mullet fillets with grilled fennel, orange and saffron or risotto with green peas, candied ginger and marjoram.

Granduca — PIZZERIA €

(☎0942 2 49 83; Corso Umberto 172; pizzas €7-11; ☺dinner) Forget the staid, typically pricey Taormina restaurant upstairs; the best reason to visit Granduca is for pizza on a summer evening, served on a vast outdoor terrace overlooking Mt Etna and the sea – an unbeatable combination of view, quality and price!

 Drinking

Shatulle — BAR

(Piazza Paladini 4; ☺closed Mon) An intimate square just off Corso Umberto, Piazza Paladini is a perennial favourite with Taormina's young, well-dressed night owls. One of the best, and most popular, of the square-side bars is this hip, gay-friendly spot with outdoor seating, an inviting vibe and a fine selection of cocktails (from €5.50).

Bar Turrisi — BAR

(Castelmola; ☺9am-2am) A few kilometres outside Taormina, in the hilltop community of Castelmola, this whimsical bar is built on four levels overlooking the church square. Its decor is an eclectic tangle of Sicilian influences, with everything from painted carts to a giant stone *minchia* (you'll need no translation once you see it). Sip a glass of almond wine, enjoy the view, and don't forget to check out the bathrooms on the way out!

 Shopping

Taormina is a shopper's paradise. The quality in most places is high but don't expect any bargains.

Carlo Mirella Panarello — CERAMIC ART
(Via Antonio Marziani)

Managò & Figlie — CERAMIC ART
(www.manago.it; Via Santa Domenica)

La Torinese — FOOD, WINE
(Corso Umberto 59) Olive oil, capers, jam and wine.

❶ Information

There are plenty of banks with ATMs along Corso Umberto.

British Pharmacy (Corso Umberto 152; ☺8.30am-8pm) One of two pharmacies along Corso Umberto offering emergency night call-out service.

Gustosi Momenti (Salita Alexander Humboldt; internet per 20min €2; ☺10am-9pm Tue-Sun Nov-Mar, 10.30am-midnight Apr-Oct) A slick internet bar with several fast computers, wi-fi and a choice of cocktails.

Ospedale San Vincenzo (☎0942 57 92 97; Contrada Sirina) Downhill and 2km southwest of the centre. Call the same number for an ambulance.

Police station (☎0942 61 02 01; Corso Umberto 219)

Post office (Piazza Sant'Antonio Abate)

Tourist office (☎0942 2 32 43; www.gate2 taormina.com; Palazzo Corvaja, Corso Umberto; ☺8.30am-2.15pm & 3.30-6.45pm Mon-Fri, 9am-12.45pm & 4-6.15pm Sat) Busy, well-staffed tourist office.

❶ Getting There & Around

Bus

The bus is the easiest way to reach Taormina. **Interbus** (☎0942 62 53 01; Via Luigi Pirandello) services leave daily for Messina (€3.90, 55 minutes to 1¾ hours, 10 daily Monday to Saturday, two on Sunday) and Catania (€4.70,

1¼ hours, seven to 11 daily), the latter continuing to Catania's Fontanarossa airport (€7, 1½ hours).

Car & Motorcycle

Taormina is on the A18 autostrada and the SS114 between Messina and Catania. Driving near the historic centre is a complete nightmare and Corso Umberto is closed to traffic. The most convenient place to leave your car is the **Porta Catania car park** (per 24hr €15), at the western end of Corso Umberto. The **Lumbi car park** north of the centre charges the same rates, but from here you'll have to walk five minutes or take the free yellow shuttle bus to get to Porta Messina (at the eastern end of Corso Umberto).

California (☑ 0942 2 37 69; Via Bagnoli Croce 86; Vespa per day/week €30/189, Fiat Panda €60/296) Rents out cars and scooters, just across from the Villa Comunale.

Train

There are regular trains to and from Messina (€3.80, 40 to 75 minutes, hourly) and Catania (€3.80, 40 to 50 minutes, hourly), but the awkward location of Taormina's station (a steep 4km below town) is a strong disincentive. If you arrive this way, catch a taxi (€15) or an Interbus coach (€1.70) up to the town. Buses run roughly every 30 to 90 minutes (less frequently on Sunday).

Catania

POP 296,000

Catania is a true city of the volcano. Much of it is constructed from the lava that poured down the mountain and engulfed the city in the 1669 eruption in which nearly 12,000 people lost their lives. It is also lava-black in colour, as if a fine dusting of soot permanently covers its elegant buildings, most of which are the work of baroque master Giovanni Vaccarini. He almost single-handedly rebuilt the civic centre into an elegant, modern city of spacious boulevards and set-piece piazzas.

Catania is Sicily's second commercial city – a thriving, entrepreneurial centre with a large university and a tough, resilient local population that adheres strongly to the motto of *carpe diem* (seize the day).

◉ Sights

Catania's sights are concentrated within a few blocks of Piazza del Duomo.

Piazza del Duomo   CENTRAL SQUARE
A Unesco World Heritage Site, Catania's central square is a set piece of sinuous buildings and a grand cathedral, all built in the unique local baroque style, with its contrasting lava and limestone. In the centre of the piazza is Catania's most memorable monument, and a symbol of the city, the smiling **Fontana dell'Elefante** (built in 1736). The statue is crowned by a naive black-lava elephant, dating from the Roman period, surmounted by an improbable Egyptian obelisk. Legend has it that it belonged to the 8th-century magician Eliodorus, who reputedly made his living by turning men into animals. The obelisk is believed to possess magical powers that help to calm Mt Etna's restless activity. At the piazza's southwest corner, the **Fontana dell'Amenano** fountain marks the entrance to Catania's fish market and commemorates the Amenano River, which once ran above ground and on whose banks the Greeks first founded the city of Katáne.

Duomo   CATHEDRAL
(☑ 095 32 00 44; Piazza del Duomo; ☺ 8am-noon & 4-7pm) Catania's other defence against Mt Etna is St Agata's cathedral, with its impressive marble facade. Inside the cool, vaulted interior lie the remains of the city's patron saint, the young virgin Agata, who resisted the advances of the nefarious Quintian (AD 250) and was horribly mutilated. The saint's jewel-drenched effigy is ecstatically venerated on 5 February in one of Sicily's largest *feste* (see p777).

La Pescheria   FISH MARKET
(Via Pardo; ☺ 7am-2pm) The best show in Catania is this bustling fish market, where vendors raucously hawk their wares in Sicilian dialect, while decapitated swordfish cast sidelong glances at you across silvery heaps of sardines on ice. Equally colourful is the adjoining **food market** (Via Naumachia; ☺ 7am-3pm), with carcasses of meat, skinned sheep's heads, strings of sausages, huge wheels of cheese and piles of luscious fruits and vegetables all rolled together in a few noisy, jam-packed alleyways.

Graeco-Roman Theatre & Odeon   RUINS
(Via Vittorio Emanuele II 262; adult/reduced €4/2; ☺ 9am-1pm & 2.30pm-1hr before sunset Tue-Sun) These twin theatres west of Piazza del Duomo are the most impressive Graeco-Roman remains in Catania. Both are picturesquely sited in the thick of a crumbling residential neighbourhood, with laundry flapping on the rooftops of vine-covered buildings that appear to have sprouted organically

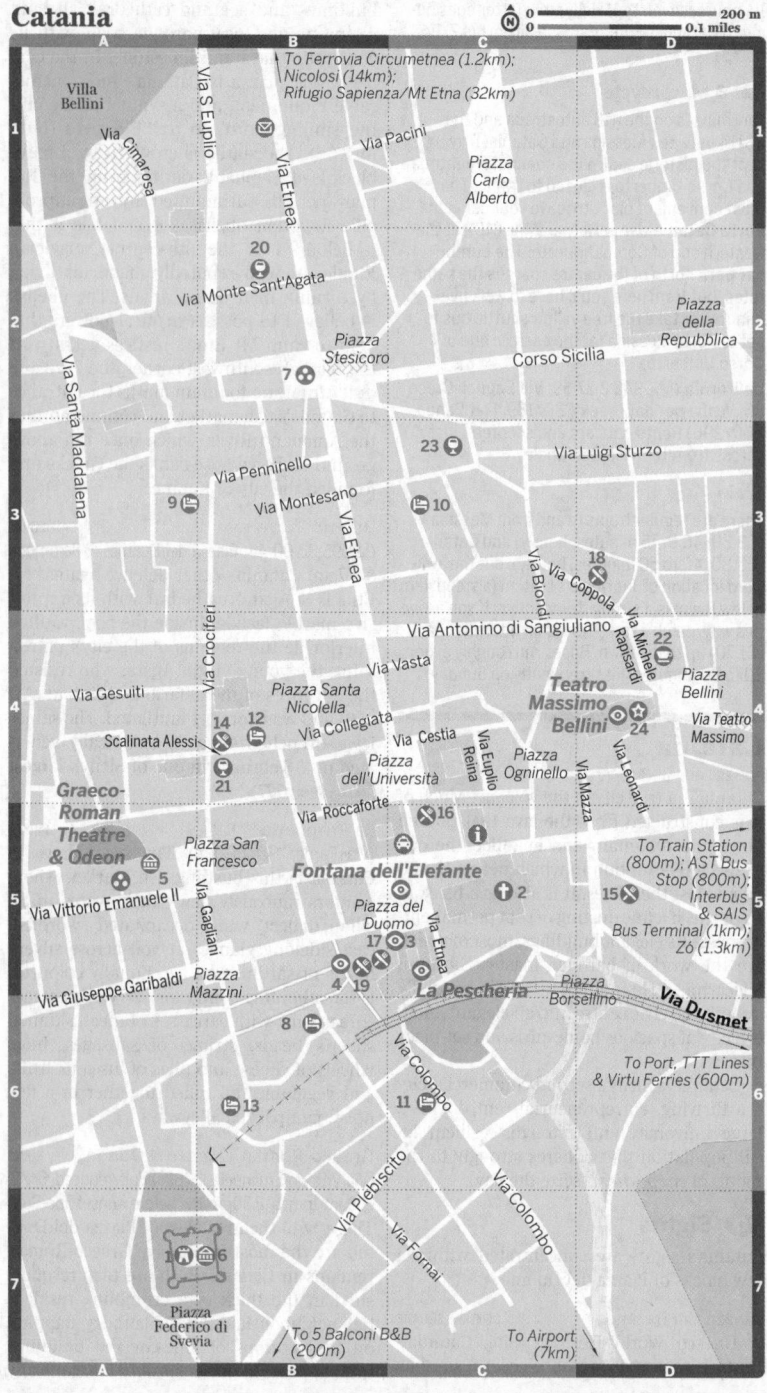

SICILY CATANIA

from the half-submerged stage. Adjacent to the main theatre is the **Casa Liberti** (same admission and opening hours as theatres), an elegantly restored 19th-century *palazzo* with tiled floors and red wallpaper that now houses two millennia worth of artefacts discovered during excavation of the theatres.

Teatro Massimo Bellini   OPERA HOUSE
(☑095 730 61 11; www.teatromassimobellini.it; Via Perrotta 12; guided tours €2; ⊙tours 9.30am & 10.30am Tue, Thu & Sat) A few blocks northeast of the *duomo*, this gorgeous opera house forms the centrepiece of Piazza Bellini. Square and opera house alike were named after composer Vincenzo Bellini, the father of Catania's vibrant modern musical scene.

FREE **Museo Belliniano**   MUSEUM
(☑095 715 05 35; Piazza San Francesco 3; ⊙9am-1pm Mon-Sat) This small museum houses a collection of memorabilia from the composer's life.

Museo Civico   MUSEUM
(☑095 34 58 30; Piazza Federico II di Svevia; ⊙9am-1pm & 3-7pm Mon-Sat, 8.30am-1.30pm Sun) Housed in the grim-looking 13th-century Castello Ursino, Catania's civic museum holds the valuable Biscari archaeological collection, an extensive exhibition of paintings, vases and sculpture, and an impressive coin collection.

Villa Bellini   PARK
(⊙8am-8pm) Escape the madding crowd and enjoy the fine views of Mt Etna from these lovely gardens along Via Etnea.

Roman amphitheatre   AMPHITHEATRE
The modest ruins of this Roman theatre, below street level in Piazza Stesicoro, are worth a quick look.

★ Festivals & Events

Festa di Sant'Agata   RELIGIOUS
In Catania's biggest religious festival (3 to 5 February), one million Catanians follow the Fercolo (a silver reliquary bust of Saint Agata) along the main street of the city accompanied by spectacular fireworks.

Carnevale di Acireale   CARNIVAL
(www.carnevalediacireale.it) Nearby Acireale hosts Sicily's most flamboyant carnival for two weeks every winter. Streets in this baroque coastal resort come alive with gargantuan papier mâché puppets, flowery allegorical floats, confetti and fireworks.

Etnafest   ARTS
From July through December, this arts festival brings classical music, puppet shows and a varied program of rock, pop, blues, reggae and jazz concerts to Le Ciminiere.

🛏 Sleeping

Catania is served by a good range of reasonably priced accommodations, making it an excellent base for exploring the Ionian coast and Etna.

Palazzu Stidda   APARTMENT €

(☑095 34 88 26; www.palazzo-stella.com; Vicolo della Lanterna 5; d €70-100, q €120-140; 🛜📶) A great option for families, these three delightful apartments on a peaceful dead-end alley have all the comforts of home plus a host of whimsical touches. Apartments 2 and 3 each come with a washing machine, kitchen, high chair and stroller, and ample space for a family of four. Apartment 1 is smaller and costs €10 to €20 less. Each has a flowery mini-balcony, and all are decorated with the owners' art work, handmade furniture, family heirlooms and vintage finds from local antiques markets. French and English spoken.

B&B Crociferi   B&B €

(☑095 715 22 66; www.bbcrociferi.it; Via Crociferi 81; s/d/tr €65/85/110; ❋🛜) Affording easy access to the animated nightlife of Catania's historic centre, this B&B in a beautifully decorated family home is one of Catania's most delightful places to stay. With only three rooms, it fills up fast, so book ahead. Rooms are spacious, with high ceilings, antique tiles, frescoes and artistic accoutrements from the owners' travels in India. Each room has its own private bathroom across the hall. Mario (who speaks French) offers tours of the coastline in his private boat, while Teresa (who speaks German and English) makes a delicious, varied breakfast.

5 Balconi B&B   B&B €

(☑095 723 45 34; www.5balconi.it; Via Plebiscito 133; s €30-35, d €50-65, tr €70-75; ❋🛜) You won't find a nicer low-end option than this lovingly remodelled antique *palazzo* in a workaday neighbourhood just south of Castello Ursino. The friendly owners offer three high-ceilinged rooms with a pair of shared bathrooms down the hall, plus a breakfast featuring local organic bread and fresh fruit (delivered to your room upon request). The street out front gets a lot of traffic, but there are views of the castle and Etna in the distance.

BAD   B&B €

(☑095 34 69 03; www.badcatania.com; Via C Colombo 24; s €40-55, d €60-80, apt €90-140; ❋🛜) An uninhibitedly colourful, modern sense of style prevails at this trendy B&B. All rooms feature local art work and TVs with DVD players. The two-level upstairs apartment with full kitchen and private terrace is a fab option for self-caterers, especially since the fish and vegetable markets are right around the corner. Staff is great about suggesting cultural goings-on about town.

Il Principe   HOTEL €€

(☑095 250 03 45; www.ilprincipehotel.com; Via Alessi 24; d €109-189, ste €129-209; ❋@🛜) This boutique-style hotel in an 18th-century building features luxurious rooms on one of the liveliest nightlife streets in town (thank goodness for double glazing!). Perks include international cable TV, free wi-fi and fluffy bathrobes to wear on your way to the Turkish steam bath. Check online for regularly updated special rates. More expensive suites have marble bathrooms with Jaccuzis and spiral staircases leading to a second level.

B&B Faro   B&B €

(☑349 4578856; www.bebfaro.it; Via San Michele 26; s €50, d €70-80, tr €100; ❋@) A stylish B&B with five upstairs rooms incorporating polished wood floors, double-glazed windows, modern bathroom fixtures, antique tiles and bold colours. The two suites are especially nice, and during slower periods can be booked for the price of a double. Additional perks include free cable internet and bikes for guests' use. There's also a studio downstairs where visiting artists are invited to come and paint.

Agorá Hostel   HOSTEL €

(☑095 723 30 10; www.agorahostel.com; Piazza Curró 6; dm €18-21, s €25-30, d €50-55; @🛜) The six- to 10-bed dorms can get loud, and the bathrooms are pretty scuzzy, but the free wi-fi, affordable laundry facilities (€3.50 per wash) and super-cool subterranean bar may still be enough to win over budget-minded solo travellers. Self-caterers will appreciate the location near La Pescheria and the larger guest kitchen under construction at research time.

🍴 Eating

Popular street snacks in Catania include *arancini* (fried rice balls filled with meat, cheese, tomatoes and/or peas) and *seltz* (fizzy water with fresh-squeezed lemon juice and natural fruit syrup). Don't leave town without trying *pasta alla Norma* (pasta with basil, eggplant and ricotta), a dish that originated here.

The **food market** adjacent to La Pescheria is a fantastic place to shop for fruit, cheese, and sandwich fixings (don't let those staring swordfish intimidate you!).

TOP CHOICE **Trattoria di De Fiore** TRATTORIA €
(☑095 31 62 83; Via Coppola 24/26; meals €15-25; ☺closed Mon) This neighbourhood trattoria is presided over by septuagenarian chef Mamma Rosanna, who uses organic flour and fresh, local ingredients to recreate her great-grandmother's recipes, including the best *pasta alla Norma* you'll taste anywhere in Sicily. (Rosanna says her grandmother called this dish Mungibeddu – Sicilian dialect for Mt Etna – in honour of Catania's famous volcano: tomatoes were the red lava, eggplant the black cinders, ricotta the snow and basil leaves the mountain vegetation.) Service is slow and the door doesn't always open promptly at 1pm, but food like this is well worth waiting for. Don't miss the *zeppoline di ricotta* (sweet ricotta fritters dusted with powdered sugar), a dessert invented by Rosanna herself.

Fiaschetteria Biscari SICILIAN €€
(☑095 093 27 61; Via Museo Biscari 8; meals €35-45; ☺closed 1 variable day per week) In the former stables of Palazzo Biscari, this wonderfully atmospheric wine bar and restaurant places a high value on quality; the menu is built around ultra-fresh ingredients from the nearby fish and produce markets.

Osteria Antica Marina SEAFOOD €€
(☑095 34 81 97; Via Pardo 29; meals €35-45; ☺closed Wed) This rustic but classy trattoria behind the fish market is *the* place to come for seafood. A variety of tasting menus showcases everything from swordfish to scampi, cuttlefish to calamari. Decor-wise think solid wooden tables and rough stone walls. Reservations are essential.

Trattoria La Paglia TRATTORIA €
(☑095 34 68 38; Via Pardo 23; meals €15-25; ☺closed Sun) Lacking the lustre and the higher prices of its next-door neighbour, this simple trattoria offers dependably fresh seafood and an in-your-face view of the action around La Pescheria market.

Al Cortile Alessi PIZZERIA €
(☑095 31 54 44; Via Alessi 28; pizzas €6-9; ☺8pm-1am Tue-Sun) Catanians of all ages – but especially students – flock here on

weekend evenings, drawn by the excellent pizzas, draft beer, relaxed atmosphere and outdoor courtyard overhung with banana trees.

Grand Cafè Tabbacco PASTRIES & CAKES €
(Via Etnea 28; ☺7am-midnight) Perfect for people-watching during the *passeggiata* (evening stroll), this old-style *pasticceria* (pastry shop) has sumptuous display cases and outdoor seating on lively Via Etnea, just north of Piazza del Duomo.

🍷 **Drinking**

Not surprisingly for a busy university town, Catania has a reputation for its effervescent nightlife. Fun streets for bar-hopping include (from west to east) Via Alessi, Via Collegiata, Via Vasta, Via Mancini, Via Montesano, Piazza Spirito Santo and Via Teatro Massimo.

Tertulia BOOKSHOP-CAFE
(☑095 715 26 03; Via Michele Rapisardi 1-3; ☺10am-1am Mon-Sat, 5pm-1am Sun) This bookshop-cafe with a stylish teahouse atmosphere hosts occasional live music, plus literary evenings and book presentations.

Agorá Bar BAR
(www.agorahostel.com; Piazza Currò 6) This super-atmospheric bar occupies a neon-lit cave 18m below ground, complete with its own subterranean river. The Romans used it as a spa; nowadays a cosmopolitan crowd lingers over late-night drinks.

Nievski Pub PUB
(Scalinata Alessi 15; ☺8pm-2am Tue-Sun) Popular with Catania's alternative crowd, this place serves affordable food and alcohol with a slightly arch attitude. At night the beer flows freely as students gather on the steps outside.

Energie Cafe BAR-CAFE
(Via Monte Sant'Agata 10) A slick urban cafe with kaleidoscopic '70s-inspired decor, streetside seating and laid-back jazz-infused tunes.

Waxy O'Connor's PUB
(Piazza Spirito Santo 1) One of two Irish pubs on this street, where revellers down pints of Guinness on the sidewalk while listening to occasional live music.

☆ **Entertainment**

Pick up a copy of *Lapis,* a free bi-weekly program of music, theatre and art available throughout the city.

Teatro Massimo Bellini OPERA HOUSE
(☎095 730 61 11; www.teatromassimobellini.it;
Via Perrotta 12; ☺Oct-May) Ernesto Basile's
gorgeous art nouveau theatre stages opera,
ballet and music concerts.

Zò CULTURAL CENTRE
(☎095 53 38 71; www.zoculture.it; Piazzale Asia 6)
Catania's renovated former sulphur works,
Le Ciminiere, now house this very cool
cultural centre featuring films, live music,
dancing, and a bar-cafe-restaurant serving
good food.

❶ Information

Banks with ATMs are concentrated around Pi-
azza del Duomo and along Via Etnea.
Internetteria (Via Penninello 44; per hr €2;
☺9am-11pm Mon-Fri, 5-10pm Sat, 4-10pm Sun)
Fast internet, wi-fi and a great little bar-cafe.
Municipal tourist office (☎095 742 55 73;
bureau.turismo@comune.catania.it; Via Vittorio
Emanuele 172; ☺8.15am-1pm & 2-7pm Mon-Sat)
Ospedale Vittorio Emanuele (☎091 743 54
52; Via Plebiscito 628) Has a 24-hour emer-
gency doctor.
Police station (☎095 736 71 11; Piazza Santa
Nicolella)
Post office (Via Etnea 215)

❶ Getting There & Away

Air
Catania's airport, **Fontanarossa** (☎095 723
91 11; www.aeroporto.catania.it), is 7km southwest of the city centre. To get there, take the
special Alibus 457 (€1, 30 minutes, every 20
minutes) from outside the train station. **Etna
Transporti/Interbus** (☎095 53 03 96; www.
interbus.it) also runs a regular shuttle from
the airport to Taormina (€7, 1½ hours, six to
11 daily). All the main car-hire companies are
represented here.

Boat
The ferry terminal is located southwest of the
train station along Via VI Aprile.
Virtu Ferries (☎095 53 57 11; www.virtu
ferries.com) runs direct ferries from Catania to
Malta (passenger €50 to €108, car €59 to €117,
three hours) every Saturday from May through
September, with more frequent service to Malta
via the southern port of Pozzallo (four hours
including connecting coach from Catania to Pozzallo). Fares quoted above are one-way; substantial discounts are offered for return travel.
TTT Lines (☎800 915365, 095 34 85 86;
www.tttlines.it) runs nightly ferries from Catania
to Naples (seat €38 to €60, cabin per person
€52 to €165, car €75 to €115, 11 hours).

Bus
All intercity buses terminate in the area just
north of Catania's train station. AST buses
leave from Piazza Giovanni XXIII; buy tickets
at Bar Terminal on the west side of the square.
Interbus/Etna and SAIS leave from a terminal
one block further north, with their ticket offices
diagonally across the street on Via d'Amico.
Interbus (☎095 53 03 96; www.interbus.it;
Via d'Amico 187) runs bus services:
Taormina (€4.70, 1¼ to two hours, eight to 17
daily)
Syracuse (€5.70, 1½ hours, hourly Monday to
Friday, fewer on weekends)
Ragusa (€7.50, two hours, five to 10 daily)
SAIS (☎095 53 61 68; www.saisautolinee.it,
www.saistrasporti.it; Via d'Amico 181) also runs
services:
Palermo (€14.20, 2¾ hours, hourly Monday to
Saturday, nine on Sunday)
Agrigento (€12.40, three hours, nine to 15
daily)
Messina (€7.70, 1½ hours, hourly Monday to
Saturday, nine on Sunday)
Rome (€47, 11 hours) Overnight service.
AST (☎095 723 05 35; www.aziendasiciliana
trasporti.it; Via Luigi Sturzo 230) runs to many
smaller towns around Catania.
Nicolosi (€2.20, 50 to 80 minutes, hourly) At
the foot of Mt Etna.

Car & Motorcycle
Catania is easily reached from Messina on the
A18 autostrada and from Palermo on the A19.
From the autostrada, signs for the centre of
Catania will bring you to Via Etnea.

Train
The private Ferrovia Circumetnea train circles
Mt Etna, stopping at towns and villages on the
volcano's slopes.
From Catania Centrale station on Piazza Papa
Giovanni XXIII there are frequent trains.
Messina (€6.80, 1¾ hours, hourly)
Syracuse (€6.20, 1¼ hours, nine daily)
Agrigento (€10.20, 3¾ hours) Two direct daily.
Palermo (€12.30, three hours) One direct daily.

❶ Getting Around

Several useful **AMT city buses** (☎095 751 96
11; www.amt.ct.it, in Italian) terminate in front
of the train station, including buses 1-4 and 4-7
(both running from the station to Via Etnea every
half hour or so) and Alibus 457 (station to airport
every 20 minutes). A 90-minute ticket costs
€1. From mid-June to mid-September, a special
service (bus D-Est) runs from Piazza Raffaello
Sanzio to the local beaches.

SICILY IONIAN COAST

For drivers, some words of warning: there are complicated one-way systems around the city and the centre has now been pedestrianised, which means parking is scarce.

Catania's one-line metro currently has six stops, with more under construction. For tourists, it's mainly useful as a way to get from the central train station to the Circumetnea train that goes around Mt Etna. Tickets cost €1.

For a taxi, call **Radio Taxi Catania** (☑095 33 09 66).

Mt Etna

ELEV 3329M

Dominating the landscape of eastern Sicily and visible from the moon (if you happen to be there), Mt Etna is Europe's largest volcano and one of the world's most active. Eruptions occur frequently, both from the volcano's four summit craters and from its slopes, which are littered with fissures and old craters. The volcano's most devastating eruptions occurred in 1669 and lasted 122 days. Lava poured down Etna's southern slope, engulfing much of Catania and dramatically altering the landscape. More recently, in 2002, lava flows from Mt Etna caused an explosion in Sapienza, destroying two buildings and temporarily halting cable-car service. Less destructive eruptions have continued to occur regularly over the past decade, with 2011 seeing several dramatic instances of lava fountaining – vertical jets of lava spewing from the mountain's southeastern flank. Locals understandably keep a close eye on the smouldering peak.

The volcano is surrounded by the huge Parco dell'Etna, the largest unspoilt wilderness remaining in Sicily. The park encompasses a remarkable variety of environments, from the severe, almost surreal, summit to deserts of lava and alpine forests.

◉ Sights & Activities

The southern approach to Mt Etna presents the easier ascent to the **craters**. The AST bus from Catania drops you off at **Rifugio Sapienza** (1923m) from where **Funivia dell'Etna** (☑095 91 41 41; www.funiviaetna.com; cable car one way/return €14.50/27, incl bus & guide €51; ⊙9am-4.30pm) runs a cable car up the mountain to 2500m. From the upper cable car station it's a 3½- to four-hour return trip up the winding track to the authorised crater zone (2920m). Make sure you leave yourself enough time to get up *and* down before the last cable car leaves at 4.45pm.

Alternatively, you can pay the extra €24 for a guided 4WD tour to take you up from the cable car to the crater zone.

An alternative ascent is from **Piano Provenzano** (1800m) on Etna's northern flank. This area was severely damaged during the 2002 eruptions, as still evidenced by the bleached skeletons of the surrounding pine trees. Regular 4WD excursions climb to the summit from here (around €40 per person). To reach Piano Provenzano you'll need a car, as there's no public transport beyond Linguaglossa, 16km away.

⛰ Tours

Several companies offer private excursions up the mountain.

Volcano Trek   CLIMBING TOURS
(☑333 2096604; www.volcanotrek.com) Run by expert geologists.

Siciltrek   CLIMBING TOURS
(☑095 96 88 82; www.siciltrek.it, in German) Run by multilingual Swiss guide Andrea Ercolani.

**Gruppo Guide Alpine
Etna Sud**   CLIMBING TOURS
(☑095 791 47 55; www.etnaguide.com, in Italian) The official guide service on Etna's southern flank, with an office just below Rifugio Sapienza.

**Gruppo Guide Alpine
Etna Nord**   CLIMBING TOURS
(☑095 777 45 02; www.guidetnanord.com) Offers similar service from Linguaglossa on Etna's northern flank.

🛏 Sleeping & Eating

There's plenty of B&B accommodation around Mt Etna, particularly in the small, pretty town of Nicolosi. Contact Nicolosi's tourist information office for a full list.

Rifugio Sapienza   MOUNTAIN CHALET €€
(☑095 91 53 21; www.rifugiosapienza.com; Piazzale Funivia; per person B&B/half-board/full board €55/75/90) As close to the summit as you can get, this place adjacent to the cable car offers comfortable accommodation with a good restaurant.

ℹ Information

Catania's downtown tourist office provides information about Etna, as do several offices on the mountain itself.

Etna Sud tourist office (☑095 91 63 56; ⊙9am-4pm) Near the summit at Rifugio Sapienza.

Parco dell'Etna (☏095 82 11 11; www.parco etna.ct.it, in Italian; Via del Convento 45; ◷9am-2pm & 4-7.30pm) In Nicolosi, on Etna's southern side.

Proloco Linguaglossa (☏095 64 30 94; www.prolocolinguaglossa.it, in Italian; Piazza Annunziata 5; ◷9am-1pm & 4-7pm Mon-Sat, 9am-noon Sun) In Linguaglossa, on Etna's northern side.

❶ Getting There & Away

Bus

AST (☏095 723 05 35) runs daily buses from Catania to Rifugio Sapienza (one way/return €3.40/5.60, one hour). Buses leave from the car park opposite Catania's train station at 8.15am, travelling via Nicolosi, and return at 4.45pm.

Train

You can circle Etna on the private **Ferrovia Circumetnea** (FCE; ☏095 54 12 50; www.circum etnea.it; Via Caronda 352a) train line. Catch the metro from Catania's main train station to the FCE station at Via Caronda (metro stop Borgo) or take bus 429 or 432 going up Via Etnea and ask to be let off at the Borgo metro stop.

The train follows a 114km trail around the base of the volcano, providing fabulous views. It also passes through many of Etna's unique towns such as Adrano, Bronte and Randazzo (one way/return €4.85/7.80, two hours).

SYRACUSE & THE SOUTHEAST

This is a region of river valleys, fields of olive, almond and citrus trees and magnificent ruins. Within the evocative stone-walled checkerboard lies a series of handsome towns: Ragusa, Modica and Noto. Shattered by a devastating earthquake in 1693, they were rebuilt in the ornate and much-lauded Sicilian baroque style that lends the region a honey-coloured cohesion and collective beauty. Writer Gesualdo Bufalino described the southeast as an 'island within an island' and, certainly, this pocket of Sicily has a remote, genteel air – a legacy of its glorious Greek heritage.

Syracuse

POP 123,800

A dense tapestry of overlapping cultures and civilisations, Syracuse is one of Sicily's most visited cities. Boosted by EU funding, derelict landmarks and ancient buildings lining the slender streets are being aesthetically restored. Settled by colonists from Corinth in 734 BC, Syracuse was considered to be the most beautiful city of the ancient world, rivalling Athens in power and prestige. Under the demagogue Dionysius the Elder, the city reached its zenith, attracting luminaries such as Livy, Plato, Aeschylus and Archimedes, and cultivating the sophisticated urban culture that was to see the birth of comic Greek theatre.

As the sun set on Ancient Greece, Syracuse became a Roman colony and was looted of its treasures. While modern-day Syracuse lacks the drama of Palermo and the energy of Catania, the ancient island neighbourhood of Ortygia continues to seduce visitors with its atmospheric squares, narrow alleyways and lovely waterfront, while the Parco Archaeologico della Neapolis, 2km across town, remains one of Sicily's great classical treasures.

Syracuse's train and bus stations are a block apart from each other, halfway between Ortygia and the archaeological park.

◉ Sights

ORTYGIA

Duomo   DUOMO
(Map p784; Piazza del Duomo; ◷8am-7pm) Despite its baroque veneer, the Greek essence of Syracuse is everywhere in evidence, from the formal civility of the people to disguised architectural relics. The most obvious of these is Syracuse's cathedral, a Greek temple that was converted into a church when the island was evangelised by St Paul. The sumptuous baroque facade, designed by Andrea Palma, barely hides the Temple of Athena skeleton beneath, and the huge 5th-century-BC Doric columns are still visible both inside and out.

Fontana Aretusa   ANCIENT SPRING
(Map p784) Down the winding main street from the cathedral is this ancient spring, where fresh water still bubbles up just as it did in ancient times when it was the city's main water supply. Legend has it that the goddess Artemis transformed her beautiful handmaiden Aretusa into the spring to protect her from the unwelcome attention of the river god Alpheus. Now populated by ducks, grey mullet and papyrus plants, the fountain is the place to hang out on summer evenings.

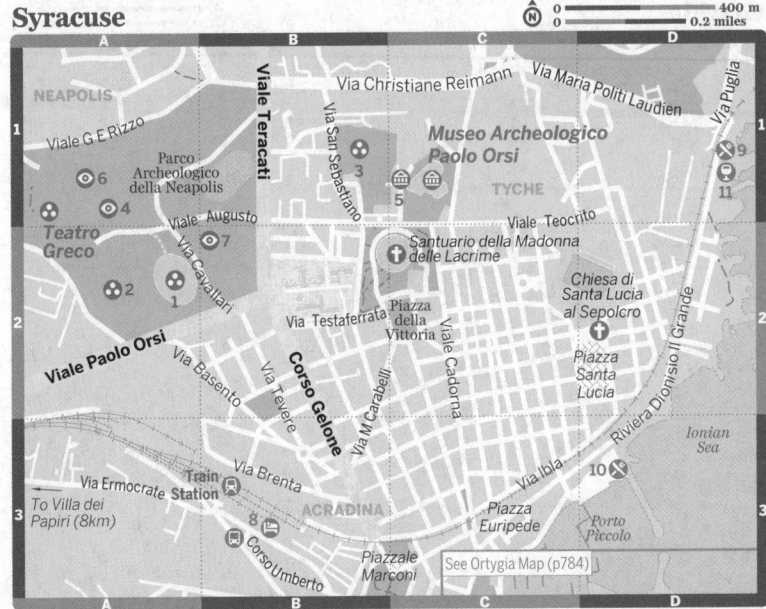

Syracuse

**Galleria Regionale di
Palazzo Bellomo**   ART GALLERY
(Map p784; ☎0931 6 95 11; www.regione.sicilia.
it/beniculturali/palazzobellomo; Via Capodieci 16;
adult/reduced €8/4; ⏰9am-7pm Tue-Sat, 9am-
1pm Sun) Just up Via Capodieci from the
fountain is this art museum, housed in a
13th-century Catalan-Gothic palace. The
eclectic collection ranges from early Byzantine and Norman stonework to 19th-century
Caltagirone ceramics; in between, there's a
good range of medieval religious paintings
and sculpture.

Castello Maniace   CASTLE
(Map p784; ☎0931 46 44 20; adult/reduced €4/2;
⏰9.30am-1pm Tue-Sun) Guarding the island's
southern tip, Ortygia's 13th-century castle
is a lovely place to wander, gaze out over
the water and contemplate Syracuse's past
glories. It also hosts occasional rotating exhibitions.

La Giudecca   NEIGHBOURHOOD
(Map p784) Simply walking through Ortygia's
tangled maze of alleys is an atmospheric
experience, especially down the narrow
lanes of **Via Maestranza**, the heart of the

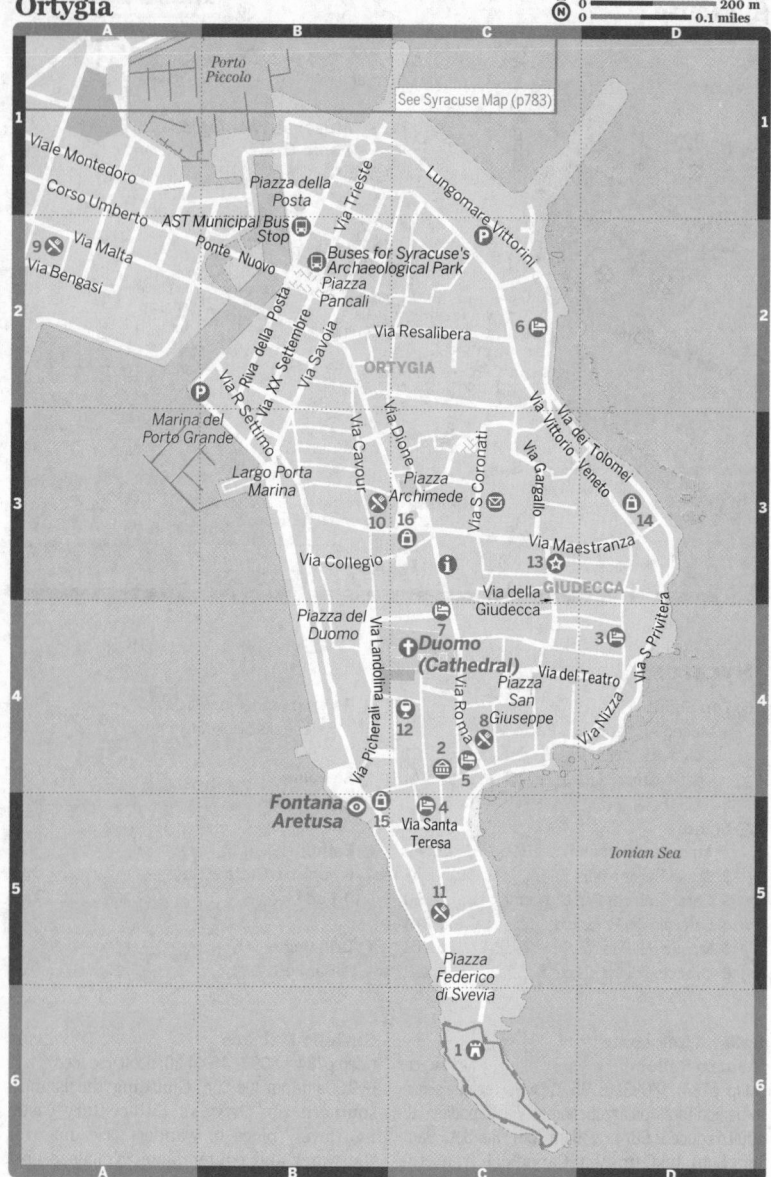

old guild quarter, and the crumbling Jewish ghetto of **Via della Giudecca**. At the Alla Giudecca hotel you can visit an ancient Jewish **miqwe** (ritual bath; ☎0931 2 22 55; Via Alagona 52; hourly tours €5; ⊙11am, noon, 4pm, 5pm & 6pm Mon-Sat, 11am & noon Sun) some 20m below ground level. Blocked up in 1492 when the Jewish community was expelled from Ortygia, the baths were rediscovered during renovation work at the hotel.

MAINLAND SYRACUSE

Parco Archaeologico della Neapolis
ARCHAEOLOGICAL SITE

(Map p783; ☑0931 6 50 68; Viale Paradis; adult/reduced €9/4.50; ☺9am-1hr before sunset, to 4.30pm during theatre festival) For the classicist, Syracuse's real attraction is this archaeological park, with its pearly white, 5th-century-BC Teatro Greco, hewn out of the rock above the city. This theatre saw the last tragedies of Aeschylus (including *The Persians*), which were first performed here in his presence. In summer it is brought to life again with an annual season of classical theatre (see p786).

Just beside the theatre is the mysterious Latomia del Paradiso, deep, precipitous limestone quarries out of which the stone for the ancient city was extracted. These quarries, riddled with catacombs and filled with citrus and magnolia trees, are where the 7000 survivors of the war between Syracuse and Athens in 413 BC were imprisoned. The **Orecchio di Dionisio** (Ear of Dionysius), a grotto 23m by 3m deep, was named by Caravaggio after the tyrant, who is said to have used the almost perfect acoustics of the quarry to eavesdrop on his prisoners.

Back outside this area you'll find the entrance to the 2nd-century AD Anfiteatro Romano, originally used for gladiatorial combats and horse races. The Spaniards, little interested in archaeology, largely destroyed the site in the 16th century, using it as a quarry to build Ortygia's city walls. West of the amphitheatre is the 3rd-century-BC Ara di Gerone II, a monolithic sacrificial altar to Heron II where up to 450 oxen could be killed at one time.

To reach the park, take bus 1, 3 or 12 from Ortygia's Piazza Pancali and get off at the corner of Corso Gelone and Viale Teocrito. Alternatively, the walk from Ortygia will take about 30 minutes. If driving, you can park along Viale Augusto (tickets available at the nearby souvenir kiosks).

Museo Archeologico Paolo Orsi
MUSEUM

(Map p783; ☑0931 46 40 22; Viale Teocrito; adult/reduced €8/4; ☺9am-6pm Tue-Sat, 9am-1pm Sun) In the grounds of Villa Landolina, about 500m east of the archaeological park, the wheelchair-accessible museum contains one of Sicily's largest, best organised and most interesting archaeological collections. Allow plenty of time to get through the museum's four distinct sectors; serious archaeology buffs may even want to consider splitting their visit into two days.

FREE Museo del Papiro
MUSEUM

(Map p783; ☑0931 6 16 16; museodelpapiro.it; Viale Teocrito 66; ☺9am-1pm Tue-Sun) This small museum includes papyrus documents and products, boats and an English-language film about the history of papyrus. The plant grows in abundance around the Ciane River, near Syracuse, and was used to make paper in the 18th century.

Catacombe di San Giovanni
CATACOMB

(Map p783; ☑0931 6 46 94; adult/reduced €6/4; ☺half-hourly tours 9.30am-12.30pm & 2.30-5.30pm) A block north of the archaeological museum, this vast labyrinth of 10,000 underground tombs dates back to Roman times. A 30-minute guided tour ushers visitors through the catacombs as well as the atmospheric ruins of the Basilica di San Giovanni, Syracuse's earliest cathedral.

Activities

Beaches
BEACHES

In midsummer, when Ortygia steams like a cauldron, people flock to the beaches south of town at **Arenella** (take bus 23 from Piazza della Posta) and **Fontane Bianche** (bus 21 or 22); note that there are charges on certain sections. From mid-June to September, there's also great sunbathing (for a fee) and diving off the rocks – but no sand to lay your towel on – adjacent to Bar Zen (p787), 2km north of Ortygia.

Festivals & Events

Ciclo di Rappresentazioni Classiche
THEATRE FESTIVAL

(Festival of Greek Theatre; www.indafondazione.org) Syracuse boasts the only school of classical Greek drama outside Athens, and in May and June it hosts live performances of Greek plays (in Italian) at the Teatro Greco, attracting Italy's finest performers. Tickets (€26 to €62) are available online, from the Via Cavour office in Ortygia or at the ticket booth outside the theatre.

Festa di Santa Lucia
RELIGIOUS

On 13 December, the enormous silver statue of the city's patron saint wends its way from the cathedral to Piazza Santa Lucia accompanied by fireworks.

Sleeping

Stay on Ortygia for atmosphere. Cheaper accommodations are located around the train station.

Villa dei Papiri
AGRITURISMO €€

(☑0931 72 13 21; www.villadeipapiri.it; Contrada Cozzo Pantano, Fonte Ciane; d €70-132, 2-person ste €105-154, 4-person ste €140-208; P🏊@🛜) Immersed in an Eden of orange groves and papyrus reeds 8km outside Syracuse, this lovely *agriturismo* sits next to the Fonte Ciana spring immortalised in Ovid's *Metamorphosis*. Eight family suites are housed in a beautifully converted 19th-century farmhouse, with double rooms dotted around the lush grounds. Breakfast is served in a baronial stone-walled hall, and there are plenty of other perks to keep guests in a holiday mood, including river excursions, bike rentals and an open-door policy towards pets.

B&B dei Viaggiatori, Viandanti e Sognatori
B&B €

(Map p784; ☑0931 2 47 81; www.bedandbreakfast sicily.it; Via Roma 156; s €35-50, d €55-70; 🏊🛜) An old *palazzo* at the end of Via Roma cradles this lovely B&B. Rooms are colourfully and stylishly decorated, with super-comfy beds. The sunny roof terrace with sweeping sea views makes a perfect breakfast spot.

Alla Giudecca
HOTEL €€

(Map p784; ☑0931 2 22 55; www.allagiudecca.it; Via Alagona 52; s €60-100, d €80-120; 🏊@🛜) Located in the old Jewish quarter, this charming hotel boasts 23 suites with warm terracotta-tiled floors, exposed wood beams and lashings of heavy white linen. The communal areas are a warren of vaulted rooms full of museum-quality antiques and enormous tapestries, and feature cosy sofas gathered around huge fireplaces.

Hotel Gutkowski
HOTEL €€

(Map p784; ☑0931 46 58 61; www.guthotel.it; Lungomare Vittorini 26; s €80-90, d €110; 🏊@🛜) Book well in advance for one of the seven sea-view rooms at this charming and friendly hotel on the Ortygia waterfront. Rooms in the original hotel have pretty tiled floors, colourful walls, and retain the building's historic character, while those in the annexe down the street have a more modern feel. There's a nice rooftop sun terrace with sea views, and a cosy internet area with fireplace.

Lol Hostel
HOSTEL €

(Map p783; ☑0931 46 50 88; www.lolhostel.com; Via Francesco Crispi 94; dm €20-26, d €60-75; 🏊@🛜) Around the corner from the train station, this modern, well-kept hostel with its variable-sized dorms and two doubles is a good bet for solo travellers. The pleasant common spaces include an open, airy guest kitchen, an outdoor patio and a sprawling lounge and bar area with four guest computers. It's 10 minutes on foot to Ortygia, or five minutes with one of the hostel's rental bikes.

B&B Aretusa
APARTMENTS €

(Map p784; ☑0931 48 34 84; www.aretusa vacanze.com; Vicolo Zuccalà 1; d €67-86, tr €82-115, q €105-140; P🏊@🛜) This great budget option, elbowed into a tiny pedestrian street, has large rooms and apartments with kitchenettes, computers, satellite TV and small balconies.

Hotel Roma

HOTEL €€

(Map p784; ☎0931 46 56 26; www.hotel romasiracusa.it; Via Roma 66; s €75-105, d €105-149; Ⓟ✴@⍟) Within steps of Piazza del Duomo, this restored *palazzo* has rooms with parquet floors, oriental rugs, wood-beam ceilings and tasteful art work, plus free bike use, a gym and a sauna.

🍴 Eating

Ortygia is teeming with atmospheric eateries, although many are touristy and over-priced; you'll generally find better value on the mainland.

Le Vin de l'Assassin

FRENCH €€

(Map p784; ☎0931 6 61 59; Via Roma 115; snacks €7-15, meals €25-35; ⊘dinner Tue-Sat, lunch & dinner Sun) This gay-friendly French-run bistro provides a classy break from standard Sicilian fare. Offerings scrawled on the chalkboard include French classics like *quiche lorraine* and croque-monsieur, Breton oysters, salads with impeccable vinaigrette dressing, a host of meat and fish mains and a splendid *millefoglie* of eggplant and sweet red peppers. It's also a perfect late-night stop for wine by the glass or one of its home-made, over-the-top creamy and chocolatey desserts.

Red Moon

SEAFOOD €

(Map p783; ☎0931 6 03 56; Riva Porto Lachio 36; meals €25; ⊘lunch & dinner Thu-Tue) Serving some of the best seafood in Syracuse under its tented octagonal roof, this reasonably priced family-run place on the mainland makes a pleasant refuge from Ortygia's well-worn tourist track. Start with *spaghetti ai ricci* (spaghetti with sea urchin roe), move on to *fritto misto* (fried shrimp and squid) or grilled fish from the case, then finish with a refreshing lemon sorbet.

Taberna Sveva

SICILIAN €€

(Map p784; ☎0931 2 46 63; Piazza Federico di Svevia; meals €25-35; ⊘closed Wed) This charming tavern has a cosy terrace on a peaceful cobblestoned square, down near the castle at Ortygia's southern tip. Food is top-notch, from *primi* like *gnocchi al pistacchio* (with olive oil, Parmesan, pepper, garlic and grated pistachios) to a delicious tiramisu to wrap things up.

Jonico-a Rutta 'e Ciauli

SICILIAN €€

(Map p783; ☎0931 6 55 40; Riviera Dionisio il Grande 194; pizzas €4-7, meals €25-35; ⊘closed Tue Oct-May) Inconveniently located but

worth the trek or taxi ride on a sunny afternoon, Jonico's open-air terrace has spectacular views of blue-green sea and sandstone cliffs, while the all-Sicilian menu features pizza at night plus seafood mains such as *orata c'aranci* (gilthead with orange juice, orange peel and black pepper).

Sicilia in Tavola

SICILIAN €

(Map p784; ☎392 4610889; Via Cavour 28; pasta €7-12; ⊘closed Mon) This tiny place with a dozen tables specialises in seafood appetisers and fresh pasta dishes. For dessert, try its *bicchierino* (a sinfully delicious blend of ricotta, chocolate, pistachios and almonds).

Piano B

PIZZERIA €

(Map p784; ☎0931 6 68 51; Via Cairoli 18; pizza €5-9.50, salads €5.50-15, grilled meat €15-22; ⊘closed Mon) Brisk, friendly service complements the trendy, casual atmosphere at this new eatery just west of Ortygia. It's popular with young Syracusans for its pizzas, grilled meat and extensive salad menu.

🍷 Drinking & Entertainment

Syracuse is a vibrant university town, which means plenty of life on the streets after nightfall.

Bar San Rocco

BAR

(Map p784; Piazzetta San Rocco) Heaving till the wee hours, this is the most popular of a cluster of bars with tables sprawled across bustling Piazzetta San Rocco, just south of Piazza del Duomo.

Bar Zen

BAR

(Map p783; ⊘9am-midnight mid-Jun–Sep) At this seaside bar affiliated with Jonico restaurant, you can plunge off the rocks and sunbathe all day, then retire to the outdoor deck for evening drinks and live music.

Piccolo Teatro dei Pupi

PUPPET THEATRE

(Map p784; ☎0931 46 55 40; www.pupari.com; Via della Giudecca 17) Syracuse's thriving puppet theatre hosts regular performances; see its website for a calendar. You can also buy puppets at its workshop next door.

🛍 Shopping

Ortygia is full of quirky little shops.

Circo Fortuna

CERAMICS

(Map p784; www.circofortuna.it; Via dei Tolomei 20) Produces whimsical ceramics.

Massimo Izzo   JEWELLERY
(Map p784; www.massimoizzo.com; Piazza Archimede 25) Specialising in jewellery hand-crafted from Sciacca coral and gold.

Galleria Bellomo   CARDS
(Map p784; www.bellomogalleria.com; Via Capodieci 15) For a more affordable souvenir, check out the hand-painted cards made from local papyrus.

ℹ️ Information

There are numerous banks with ATMs throughout the city.

Biblios Café (Map p784; Via del Consiglio Reginale 11; internet per hr €3, unlimited wireless €2; ☺10am-1.30pm & 5-9pm, closed Wed & Sun mornings) One internet computer, plus wireless access at this comfortable bookstore-cafe.

Ospedale Umberto I (Map p783; ☑0931 72 40 33; Via Testaferrata 1)

Police station (Map p784; ☑0931 6 51 76; Piazza S Giuseppe)

Post office (Map p784; Via dei Santi Coronati 22)

Tourist office (Map p784; ☑0800 05 55 00; infoturismo@provsr.it; Via Roma 31, Ortygia; ☺9am-7pm) English-speaking staff, city maps and lots of good information.

ℹ️ Getting There & Away

Bus

Long-distance buses operate from the bus stop (Map p783) along Corso Umberto, just east of Syracuse's train station. **Interbus** (☑0931 6 67 10; www.interbus.it) runs buses to Catania (€5.70, 1½ hours, 19 daily Monday to Saturday, eight on Sunday) and its airport, and Palermo (€11, 3¼ hours, two to three daily).

AST (☑0931 46 27 11; www.aziendasiciliana trasporti.it) offers services to Noto (€3.20, 55 minutes, 10 daily Monday to Saturday, two on Sunday) and Ragusa (€6.60, 2¾ hours, seven daily Monday to Saturday, one on Sunday).

Car & Motorcycle

The modern A18 and SS114 highways connect Syracuse with Catania and points north. Arriving by car, exit onto the eastbound SS124 and follow signs to Syracuse and Ortygia.

Traffic on Ortygia is restricted; you're better off parking and walking once you arrive on the island. The large Talete parking garage on Ortygia's north side is a bargain – free between 5am and 9pm, and only €1 for overnight parking.

Train

From Syracuse's **train station** (Map p783; Via Francesco Crispi), several trains depart daily for Messina (InterCity/regional train

€16.50/9.50, 2½ to 3¼ hours) via Catania (€8.50/6.20, 1¼ hours). Some go on to Rome, Turin and Milan as well as other long-distance destinations. For Palermo, the bus is a better option. There are also local trains from Syracuse to Noto (€3.30, 30 minutes) and Ragusa (€7.50, 2¼ hours).

ℹ️ Getting Around

For travel between the bus and train stations and Ortygia, catch the free AST shuttle bus 20 (every 20 to 60 minutes). To reach Parco Archeologico della Neapolis from Ortygia, take AST city bus 1, 3 or 12 (two-hour ticket €1.10), departing from Ortygia's Piazza Pancali.

Noto

POP 23,900 / ELEV 160M

Flattened in 1693 by an earthquake, Noto was grandly rebuilt by its nobles. The town's complex of golden-hued sandstone buildings is now a Unesco World Heritage Site and the finest baroque town in Sicily, especially impressive at night when illuminations accentuate the beauty of its intricately carved facades. The baroque masterpiece is the work of Rosario Gagliardi and his assistant, Vincenzo Sinatra, local architects who also worked in Ragusa and Modica.

On 16 March 1996 the town was horrified when the roof and dome of the cathedral collapsed during a thunderstorm – luckily it was 10.30pm and the cathedral was empty. In 2007 the cathedral finally reopened after lengthy reconstruction.

◉ Sights

San Nicoló Cathedral stands in the centre of Noto's most graceful square, Piazza Municipio, surrounded by elegant town houses such as Palazzo Ducezio (Town Hall) and Palazzo Landolina, once home to Noto's oldest noble family.

Recently restored to its former glory and open to visitors is the **Palazzo Nicolaci di Villadorata** (☑320 5568038; www.palazzonico laci.it, in Italian; Via Nicolaci; adult/reduced €4/2; ☺10am-1pm & 3-7.30pm), where wrought-iron balconies are supported by a swirling pantomime of grotesque figures. Although empty of furnishings, its richly brocaded walls and frescoed ceilings give an idea of the sumptuous lifestyle of Sicilian nobles.

Two other piazzas break up the long Corso Vittorio Emanuele: Piazza dell'Immacolata to the east and Piazza XVI Maggio to the west. The latter is overlooked by the beautiful **Chiesa di San Domenico** and the adjacent Dominican monastery, both designed by Rosario Gagliardi. On the same square, Noto's elegant 19th-century **Teatro Comunale** is worth a look, as is the Sala degli Specchi (Hall of Mirrors), opposite the *duomo* in the **Palazzo Ducezio** (admission to either €2, combined ticket €3; ☺9.30am-1.30pm & 2.30-6.30pm). For sweeping rooftop views of Noto's baroque splendour, climb the campanile (bell tower) at **Chiesa di San Carlo al Corso** (admission €2; ☺9am-12.30pm & 4-7pm) or **Chiesa di Santa Chiara** (admission €1.50; ☺9.30am-1pm & 3-7pm).

✨ Festivals & Events

Noto's colourful two-week-long flower festival, **Infiorata**, is celebrated in mid- to late May with parades, historical re-enactments and a public art project in which artists decorate the length of Via Corrada Nicolaci with designs made entirely of flower petals.

🛏 Sleeping

B&Bs are plentiful in Noto; the tourist office keeps a detailed list.

La Corte del Sole   RURAL INN €€
(☎320 820210; www.lacortedelsole.it; Contrada Bucachemi; d €84-206; P❄@🖥🏊) A few kilometres downhill from Noto, overlooking the Vendicari bird sanctuary, is this lovely rural retreat set around a central courtyard. The best of the 34 ceramic-clad, wood-beamed rooms overlook the pool and cost only €8 extra. Other amenities include an in-house restaurant, a lovely breakfast area built around an ancient olive-oil press, bike hire, cooking courses and a shuttle bus to the nearby beach.

Hotel della Ferla   HOTEL €€
(☎0931 57 60 07; www.hoteldellaferla.it; Via A Gramsci; s €48-78, d €84-120; P❄🖥) This friendly family-run hotel in a residential area near the train station offers large, bright rooms with pine furnishings and small balconies, plus free parking.

Ostello Il Castello   HOSTEL €
(☎320 8388869; www.ostellodinoto.it; Via Fratelli Bandiera 1; dm €16) Directly uphill from the centre, this old-school hostel with eight-to 16-bed dorms commands fabulous views over the *duomo* and offers great value for money, despite lacking a guest kitchen.

🍴 Eating

The people of Noto are serious about their food, so take time to enjoy a meal and follow it up with a visit to one of the town's excellent ice-cream shops.

TOP CHOICE **Il Liberty**   MODERN SICILIAN €€
(☎0931 57 32 26; Via Cavour 40; meals €27-35;☺closed Mon) The vaulted dining room at this brand-new eatery makes an atmospheric place to sample Milan-trained chef Giuseppe Angelino's contemporary spin on Sicilian cookery. An excellent local wine list supplements the inspired menu, which moves from superb appetisers like *millefoglie* – wafer-thin layers of crusty cheese and ground pistachios layered with minty sweet-and-sour vegetables – straight through to desserts like warm cinnamon-ricotta cake with homemade orange compote.

TOP CHOICE **Caffè Sicilia**   GELATERIA €
(☎0931 83 50 13; Corso Vittorio Emanuele 125; desserts from €2) Dating from 1892 and especially renowned for its granite, this beloved place vies with its next-door neighbour, Dolceria Corrado Costanzo, for the honours of Noto's best dessert shop. Frozen desserts are made with the freshest seasonal ingredients (wild strawberries in springtime, for example) while the delicious *torrone* (nougat) bursts with the flavours of local honey and almonds.

Ristorante Il Cantuccio   MODERN SICILIAN €€
(☎0931 83 74 64; Via Cavour 12; meals €30-35; ☺dinner Tue-Sun, lunch Sun) Chef Valentina presents a seasonally changing menu that combines familiar Sicilian ingredients in exciting new ways. Try her exquisite *gnocchi al pesto del Cantuccio* (ricotta-potato dumplings with basil, parsley, mint, capers, almonds and cherry tomatoes), then move on to memorable main courses such as lemon-stuffed bass with orange-fennel salad.

Trattoria del Crocifisso   TRATTORIA €€
(☎0931 57 11 51; Via Principe Umberto 48; meals €25-35) This Slow Food–acclaimed trattoria with an extensive wine list is another Noto favourite.

Dolceria Corrado Costanzo   PASTRIES & CAKES €
(☎0931 83 52 43; Via Silvio Spaventa 9) Just around the corner from Caffè Sicilia, Costanzo is famous for its gelati, *torrone*, *dolci di mandorla* (almond sweets) and *cassata* (with ricotta, chocolate and candied fruit).

ℹ Information

Tourist office (☏0931 57 37 79; www.comune. noto.sr.it; Piazza XVI Maggio; ☉9am-1pm & 3-8pm) An excellent and busy information office with multilingual staff and free maps.

ℹ Getting There & Around

BUS From the Giardini Pubblici just east of Noto's historic centre, AST and Interbus serve Catania (€7.70, 1½ to 2½ hours, 11 to 17 Monday to Saturday, six on Sunday) and Syracuse (€3.20, one hour, 16 to 19 Monday to Saturday, four on Sunday).

TRAIN There's frequent service to Syracuse (€3.30, 30 minutes, 10 daily except Sunday), but Noto's station is inconveniently located 1km downhill from the centre.

Modica

POP 55,000 / ELEV 296M

A powerhouse in Grecian times, Modica may have lost its pre-eminent position to Ragusa, but it remains a superbly atmospheric town with its ancient medieval buildings climbing steeply up either side of a deep gorge.

The multilayered town is divided into Modica Alta (Upper Modica) and Modica Bassa (Lower Modica). A devastating flood in 1902 resulted in the wide avenues of Corso Umberto and Via Giarrantana (the river was dammed and diverted), which remain the main axes of the town, lined by *palazzi* and tiled stone houses.

⊙ Sights

Aside from simply wandering the streets and absorbing the atmosphere, a visit to the extraordinary Chiesa di San Giorgio (Modica Alta; ☉9am-noon & 4-7pm) is a highlight. This church, Gagliardi's masterpiece, is a vision of pure rococo splendour, a butter-coloured confection perched on a majestic 250-step staircase. Its counterpoint in Modica Bassa is the Cattedrale di San Pietro (Corso Umberto I), another impressive church atop a rippling staircase lined with life-sized statues of the Apostles.

🛏 Sleeping & Eating

The quality-to-price ratio tends to be excellent, making Modica a top destination for discerning travellers.

TOP CHOICE **Villa Quartarella**   AGRITURISMO €
(☏360 654829; www.quartarella.com; Contrada Quartarella; s €40, d €70-80) Spacious rooms

and welcoming hosts make this converted villa in the countryside south of Modica the obvious choice for anyone travelling by car. Owners Francesco and Francesca are generous in sharing their love and encyclopaedic knowledge of local history, flora and fauna and can suggest a multitude of driving itineraries in the surrounding area. The delicious, ample breakfasts include everything from home-raised eggs to intriguing Modican sweets.

B&B Il Cavaliere   B&B €
(☏0932 94 72 19; www.palazzoilcavaliere.it; Corso Umberto I 259; d €70-80, ste €100-120; ❄@) Stay in aristocratic style at this classy B&B in a 19th-century *palazzo*, just down from the bus station on Modica's main strip. Standard rooms have less character than the beautiful front suite and the large, high-ceilinged common rooms, which retain original tiled floors and frescoed ceilings. The elegant breakfast room has lovely views of San Giorgio church.

Albergo I Tetti di Siciliando   GUESTHOUSE €
(☏0932 94 28 43; www.siciliando.it; Via Cannata 24; s €35-40, d €50-70; ❄📶) A friendly guesthouse just uphill from Corso Umberto, with bright, artistically decorated rooms and balconies with views.

Taverna Nicastro   SICILIAN €
(☏0932 94 58 84; Via S Antonino 28, Modica Alta; meals €14-20; ☉dinner Tue-Sat) With over 60 years of history and a Slow Food recommendation, this is one of the upper town's most authentic and atmospheric restaurants, and a bargain to boot. The carnivore-friendly menu includes grilled meat, boiled veal, lamb stew and pasta specialities such as ricotta ravioli with pork *ragù* (meat sauce).

Dolceria Bonajuto   CHOCOLATE €
(☏0932 94 12 25; www.bonajuto.it; Corso Umberto I 159; ☉9am-1.30pm & 4.30-8.30pm Mon-Sat, 4.30-8.30pm Sun) Sicily's oldest chocolate factory is the perfect place to taste Modica's famous chocolate. Flavoured with cinnamon, vanilla, orange peel and even hot peppers, it's a legacy of the town's Spanish overlords who imported cocoa from their South American colonies.

Osteria dei Sapori Perduti   SICILIAN €
(☏0932 94 42 47; Corso Umberto I 228-230; meals €15-21; ☉closed Tue) On Modica's main drag, this attractive restaurant mixes rustic decor, elegantly dressed waiters, and very

reasonable prices on Sicilian specialities like *cunigghju â stimpirata* (sweet and sour rabbit).

❶ Getting There & Away

BUS Frequent buses run Monday through Saturday from Piazzale Falcone-Borsellino at the top of Corso Umberto I to Syracuse (€6, eight daily), Noto (€3.90, 10 daily) and Ragusa (€2.40, 16 daily); on Sunday, service is limited to two buses in each direction.

TRAIN From Modica's station, 600m southwest of the centre, there are three trains daily (one on Sunday) to Syracuse (€6.80, 1¾ hours) and six (one on Sunday) to Ragusa (€2.10, 25 minutes).

Ragusa

POP 73,300 / ELEV 502M

Like a grand old dame, Ragusa is a dignified and well-aged provincial town. Like every other town in the region, Ragusa collapsed after the 1693 earthquake; a new town called Ragusa Superiore was built on a high plateau above the original settlement. But the old aristocracy were loath to leave their tottering *palazzi* and rebuilt Ragusa Ibla on the original site. The two towns were only merged in 1927.

Ragusa Ibla remains the heart and soul of the town, and has all the best restaurants and the majority of sights. A sinuous bus ride or some very steep and scenic steps connect the lower town to its modern sister up the hill.

◉ Sights

Grand churches and *palazzi* line the twisting, narrow streets of Ragusa Ibla, interspersed with gelaterie and delightful piazzas where the local youth stroll and the elderly gather on benches. Palm-planted Piazza del Duomo, the centre of town, is dominated by the 18th-century **Cattedrale di San Giorgio** (◉10am-12.30pm & 4-6.30pm), with its magnificent neoclassical dome and stained-glass windows.

At the eastern end of the old town is the **Giardino Ibleo** (◉8am-8pm), a pleasant public garden laid out in the 19th century that is perfect for a picnic lunch.

⬛ Sleeping

All places listed here are in Ragusa Ibla, the picturesque lower town.

Risveglio Ibleo GUESTHOUSE €
(☑0932 24 78 11; www.risveglioibleo.com; Largo Camerina 3; r per person €35-45; ⓟ⬤) Housed in an 18th-century Liberty-style villa, this welcoming place has spacious, high-ceilinged rooms, walls hung with family portraits and a flower-flanked terrace overlooking the rooftops. The older couple who run the place go out of their way to share local culture, including their own homemade culinary delights.

Locanda Don Serafino INN €€
(☑0932 22 00 65; www.locandadonserafino.it; Via XI Febbraio 15; s €80-138, d €90-168; ⬛⬤) This historic inn near the *duomo* has beautiful rooms, some with original vaulted stone ceilings, plus a well-regarded restaurant nearby. For €9 extra, guests get access to the Lido Azzurro beach at Marina di Ragusa, 25km away.

L'Orto Sul Tetto B&B €
(☑0932 24 77 85; www.lortosultetto.it; Via Tenente Distefano 56; s €45-59, d €70-100; ⬛⬤) This sweet little B&B behind Ragusa's *duomo* offers an intimate experience, with just three rooms and a lovely roof terrace where breakfast is served.

✖ Eating

⬛ TOP CHOICE Quattro Gatti SICILIAN €
(☑0932 24 56 12; Via Valverde 95; meals €18; ◉dinner, closed Mon Oct-May & Sun Jun-Sep) This fabulous Sicilian-Slovak-run eatery near the Giardini Iblei serves an amazing four-course fixed-price menu bursting with fresh, local flavours. The antipasti spread is especially memorable, as are the seasonally changing specials scribbled on the blackboard up front. Slovak-inspired offerings such as goulash and apple strudel round out a menu of Sicilian classics. The stone-vaulted rooms make a supremely cosy spot to pass away an evening.

Il Barocco TRADITIONAL ITALIAN €
(☑0932 65 23 97; Via Orfanotrofio 29; meals €17-30) This beloved traditional restaurant has an evocative setting in an old stable block, the troughs now filled with wine bottles instead of water. At the *enoteca* (wine bar) next door, you can taste cheeses and olive oils and purchase other exquisite Sicilian edibles.

Gelati DiVini ICE CREAM €
(☑0932 22 89 89; www.gelatidivini.it; Piazza Duomo 20; ice cream from €2; ◉10am-midnight)

This exceptional gelateria makes wine-flavoured ice creams like marsala and muscat, plus unconventional offerings including rose, fennel, wild mint and the surprisingly tasty *gocce verdi*, made with local olive oil.

Ristorante Duomo GASTRONOMIC €€€
(☏0932 65 12 65; Via Capitano Bocchieri 31; meals €90-100, tasting menus €135-140) Hailed by some as Sicily's best restaurant, Duomo serves nouvelle Sicilian cusine in a quintet of small rooms outfitted like private parlours, ensuring a suitably romantic atmosphere.

ℹ Information

Tourist office (☏0932 68 47 80; Piazza della Repubblica; ⊗10am-1pm & 3.30-6.30pm) At the western edge of the lower town.

ℹ Getting There & Around

BUS Long-distance and municipal buses share a terminal on Via Zama in the upper town. Buy tickets at the Interbus/Etna kiosk in the main lot or at cafes around the corner. **Interbus** (www.interbus.it) runs to Catania (€7.50, two hours, six to 10 daily). **AST** (☏0932 68 18 18; www.aziendasicilianatrasporti.it) serves Syracuse (€6.60, three hours, eight daily Monday to Saturday, two on Sunday) via Modica (€2.40, 30 minutes) and Noto (€4.80, 2¼ hours).

City bus 33 (€1.10) runs hourly between the bus terminal and the lower town of Ragusa Ibla. From the train station, bus 11 (bus 1 on Sundays) makes a similar circuit.

TRAIN There are four daily trains to Syracuse (€7.50, two hours) via Noto (€5.60, 1½ hours).

CENTRAL SICILY & THE MEDITERRANEAN COAST

Central Sicily is a land of vast panoramas, undulating fields, severe mountain ridges and hilltop towns not yet sanitised for tourists. Moving towards the Mediterranean, the perspective changes, as ancient temples jostle for position with modern high-rise apartments outside Agrigento, Sicily's most lauded classical site and also one of its busier modern cities.

Agrigento

POP 59,200 / ELEV 230M

Agrigento does not make a good first impression. Seen from a distance, the modern city's rows of unsightly apartment blocks loom incongruously on the hillside, distracting attention from the splendid Valley of the Temples below, where the ancient Greeks once built their great city of Akragas. Never fear: once you get down among the ruins, their monumentality becomes apparent, and it's easy to understand how this impressive complex of temples became Sicily's pre-eminent travel destination, first put on the tourist map by Goethe in the 18th century.

Three kilometres uphill from the temples, Agrigento's medieval core is a pleasant place to pass the evening after a day exploring the ruins. The intercity bus and train stations are both in the upper town, within a few blocks of Via Atenea, the main street of the medieval city.

◉ Sights

VALLE DEI TEMPLI

Parco Archeologico ARCHAEOLOGICAL SITE
(☏0922 49 72 26; adult/reduced/child €8/4/free, incl archaeological museum €10/5/free; ⊗9am-11.30pm Jul & Aug, 9am-7pm Tue-Sat, 9am-1pm Sun & Mon Sep-Jun) Agrigento's Valley of the Temples is one of Sicily's premier attractions. A Unesco World Heritage Site, it incorporates a complex of temples and old city walls from the ancient Greek city of Akragas. Despite the name, the five Doric temples stand along a ridge, designed as a beacon to homecoming sailors. The ruins are divided into two main sections, known as the eastern and western zones. Although in varying states of decay, the temples give a tantalising glimpse of what must truly have been one of the most luxurious cities in Magna Graecia. The most scenic time to come is from February to March when the valley is awash with almond blossom. The main entrance to the Valley of the Temples is at Piazzale dei Templi which also has a large car park. There's a second entrance and ticket office, west of here, at the intersection of Viadotto Akragas and Via Panoramica dei Templi.

Eastern Zone

East of Via dei Templi are the most spectacular temples, the first of which is the **Tempio di Ercole** (Temple of Hercules), built towards the end of the 6th century BC and believed to be the oldest of the temples. Eight of its 38 columns were raised in 1924 to reveal a structure that was roughly the same size as the Parthenon. The magnificent **Tempio della Concordia** (Temple

WORTH A TRIP

SICILY'S BEST-PRESERVED ROMAN MOSAICS

Near the town of Piazza Armerina in central Sicily is the stunning 3rd-century Roman Villa Romana del Casale (☎0935 68 00 36; museo.villacasale@regione.sicilia.it; adult/reduced €10/5; ☺9am-6pm), a Unesco World Heritage Site and one of the few remaining sites of Roman Sicily. This sumptuous hunting lodge is thought to have belonged to Diocletian's co-emperor Marcus Aurelius Maximianus. Buried under mud in a 12th-century flood, it remained hidden for 700 years before its magnificent floor mosaics were discovered in the 1950s. Visit out of season or early in the day to avoid the hordes of motor-coach tourists.

The mosaics cover almost the entire floor (3500 sq metres) of the villa and are considered unique for their narrative style, the range of subject matter and variety of colour – many are clearly influenced by African themes. Along the eastern end of the internal courtyard is the wonderful **Corridor of the Great Hunt**, vividly depicting chariots, rhinos, cheetahs, lions and the voluptuously beautiful Queen of Sheba. Across the corridor is a series of apartments, where floor illustrations reproduce scenes from Homer. But perhaps the most captivating of the mosaics is the so-called **Room of the Ten Girls in Bikinis**, with depictions of sporty girls in scanty bikinis throwing a discus, using weights and throwing a ball; they would blend in well on a Malibu beach. These most famous of Piazza Armerina's mosaics were off limits to the public due to restoration work as of late 2011, but were scheduled to reopen sometime in 2012.

Travelling by car from Piazza Armerina, follow signs south of town to the SP15, then continue 5km to reach the villa.

Getting here without a car is more challenging. Intercity buses run from Catania (Interbus, €8.30, 1¾ hours) and Enna (SAIS, €3.20, 40 minutes) to Piazza Armerina; from here catch a local bus (€0.70, 30 minutes, summer only) or a taxi (€20) the remaining 5km. For an overnight stay that's convenient to public transit, Piazza Armerina's Ostello del Borgo (☎0935 68 70 19; www.ostellodelborgo.it; Largo San Giovanni 6; dm/s/d €17/25/40; ☎) offers good-value accommodation in a converted monastery.

of Concord) is the only temple to survive relatively intact. Built around 440 BC, it was transformed into a Christian church in the 6th century. The Tempio di Giunone (Temple of Juno) stands high on the edge of the ridge, a five-minute walk to the east. Part of its colonnade remains and there's an impressive sacrificial altar.

Western Zone

Across Via dei Templi, to the west, is what remains of the massive Tempio di Giove (Temple of Jupiter), never actually completed and now totally in ruins, allowing you to appreciate the sheer size of the rocks. It covered an area of 112m by 56m with columns 20m high. Between the columns stood *telamoni* (colossal statues), one of which was reconstructed and is now in the Museo Archeologico. A copy lies on the ground among the ruins and gives an idea of the immense size of the structure. Work began on the temple around 480 BC and it was probably destroyed during the Carthaginian invasion in 406 BC. The nearby Tempio di Castore e Polluce (Temple of Castor and Pollux) was

partly reconstructed in the 19th century, although probably using pieces from other constructions.

Tucked into a natural cleft at the far edge of the western zone is the Giardino della Kolymbetra (adult/reduced €2/1; ☺10am-6pm Apr-Jun, 10am-7pm Jul-Sep), a lush garden with more than 300 labelled species of plants and some welcome picnic tables. It's a lovely spot for a break, but note that the climb back up is steep and tiring in hot weather.

All the temples are atmospherically lit up at night.

Museo Archeologico   MUSEUM
(☎0922 4 01 11; Contrada San Nicola; adult/reduced €6/3; ☺9am-7pm Tue-Sat, 9am-1pm Sun & Mon) North of the temples, this wheelchair-accessible museum is one of Sicily's finest, with a huge collection of clearly labelled artefacts from the excavated site. Especially noteworthy are the dazzling displays of Greek painted ceramics and the awe-inspiring reconstructed *telamone*, a colossal statue recovered from the nearby Tempio di Giove.

A Graeco-Roman Legacy

Crossroads of the Mediterranean since the dawn of time, Sicily has seen countless civilisations come and go. The island's classical treasure trove includes Greek temples and amphitheatres, Roman mosaics and a host of fine archaeological museums.

Villa Romana del Casale

1 Bikini-clad gymnasts and wild African beasts prance side by side in a remarkable floor decoration in this ancient Roman hunting lodge (p793). Buried under mud for seven centuries, they're the most extensive mosaics in Sicily and are a Unesco World Heritage Site.

Segesta

2 Segesta's temple (p805) perches on a windswept hilltop above a rugged river gorge.

Taormina

3 With spectacular views of snowcapped Mt Etna and the Ionian Sea, Taormina's Greek theatre (p771) makes the perfect venue for the town's summer film and arts festivals.

Selinunte

4 Selinunte's ruins (p800) poke out of wildflower-strewn fields beside the sparkling Mediterranean.

Valle dei Templi

5 Crowning the craggy heights of Agrigento's Valle dei Templi (p792) are five Doric temples – including stunning Tempio della Concordia, one of the best preserved in all of Magna Graecia. Nearby, the superb archaeological museum makes this Sicily's most cohesive and impressive collection of Greek treasures.

Syracuse

6 Once the most powerful city in the Mediterranean, Syracuse (p782) brims with reminders of its ancient past, from the Greek columns supporting Ortygia's cathedral to the annual festival of classical Greek drama, staged in a 2500-year-old amphitheatre.

Clockwise from top left
1. Mosaic, Villa Romana del Casale 2. Temple, Segesta
3. Greek theatre, Taormina 4. Ruins, Selinunte.

JONAS KALTENBACH / LONELY PLANET IMAGES ©

OLIVER CIRENDINI / LONELY PLANET IMAGES ©

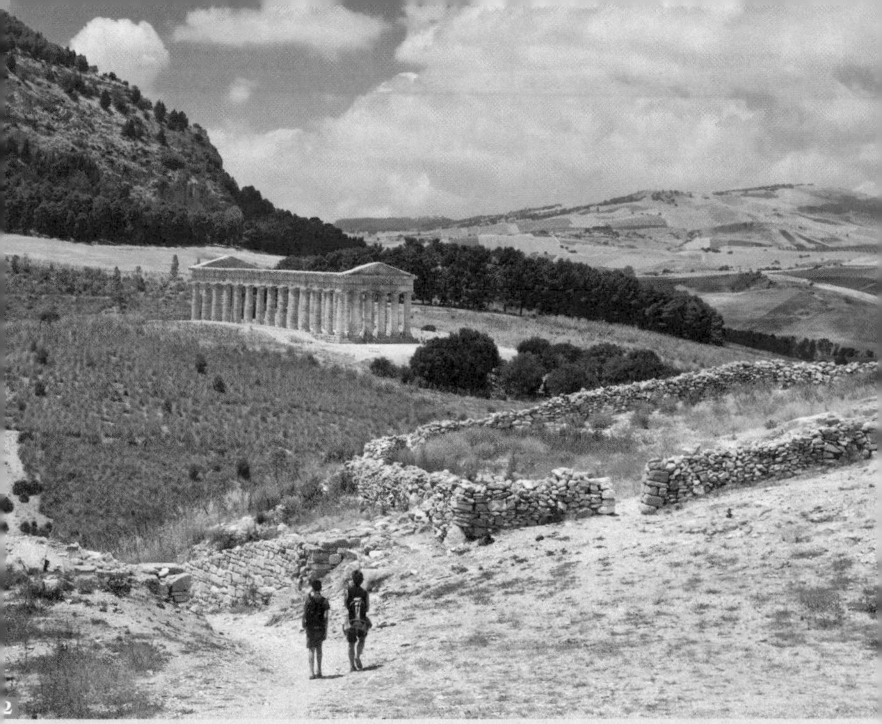

2

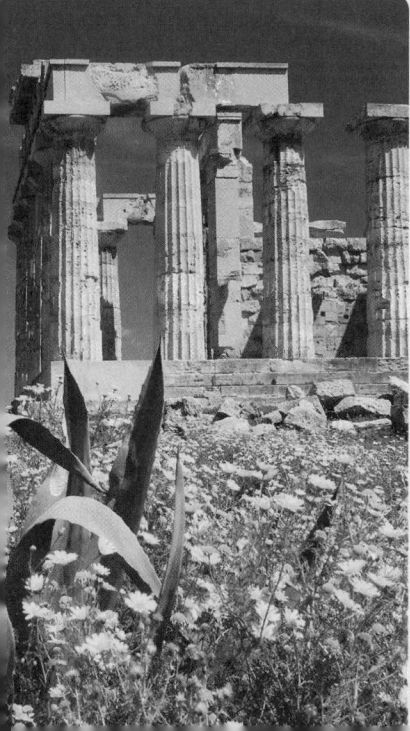

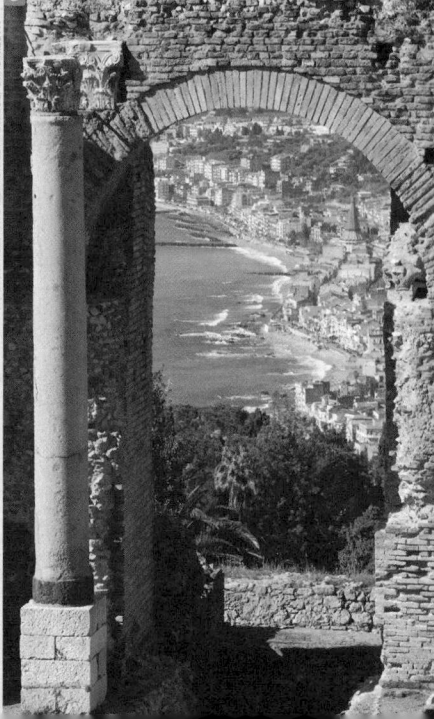

MARTIN CHILD/ROBERT HARDING WORLD IMAGERY/CORBIS ©

3

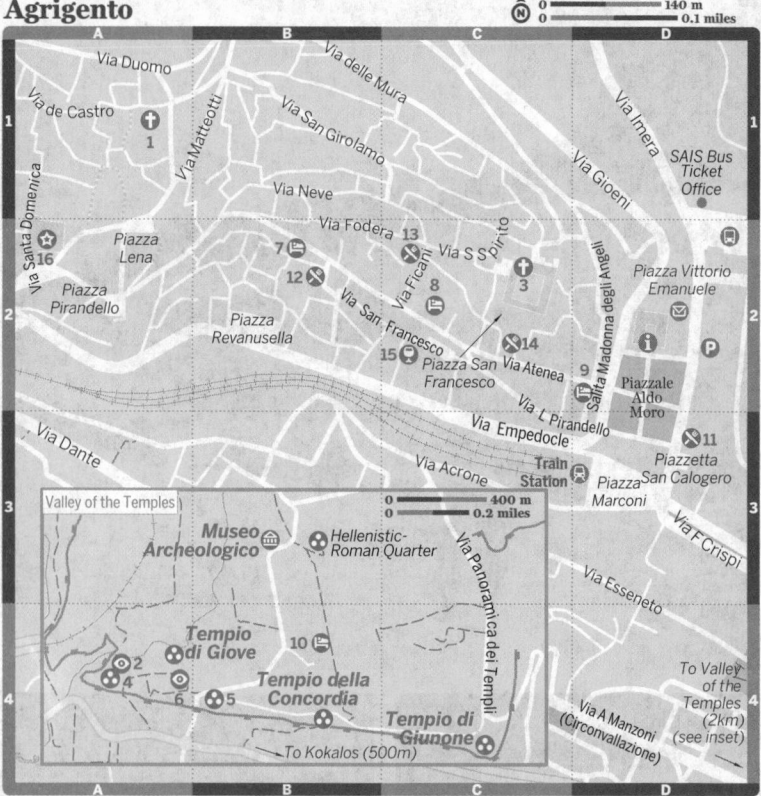

Agrigento

MEDIEVAL AGRIGENTO

Roaming the town's lively, winding streets is relaxing after a day among the temples.

Chiesa di Santa Maria dei Greci `CHURCH`
(Salita Santa Maria dei Greci; ⊙9am-12.30pm & 4-6pm Mon-Sat) Uphill from Via Atenea is this 11th-century Norman church built on the site of a 5th-century-BC temple to Athena. Glass floor panels reveal the temple's foundations, while a narrow passageway left of the church allows you to see the ancient Greek columns.

Monastero del Santo Spirito `CONVENT`
This hillside convent was founded by Cistercian nuns at the end of the 13th century. Ring the buzzer at the door marked No 8, and their modern-day counterparts will sell you a tray of delicious cakes and pastries (€11), including *dolci di mandorla*, *cuscusu* (couscous made of almonds and pistachio) and – at Christmas time – *bucellati* (rolled sweet dough with figs).

☞ Tours

The tourist office maintains a list of multilingual guides. The official rate is €140 for a half-day tour, although discounts can be negotiated.

Michele Gallo (☎0922 40 22 57, 360 397930) is an excellent English-speaking guide offering individual and group itineraries, including a €90, two-hour tour of the temples and a €130, half-day tour of the temples and archaeological museum.

✴ Festivals & Events

Sagra del Mandorlo in Fiore `ALMOND`
A huge folk festival held on the first Sunday in February, when the Valley of the Temples is cloaked in almond blossom.

Festa di San Calògero `RELIGIOUS`
During this week-long festival centred on the first Sunday in July, the statue of St Calògero (who saved Agrigento from the plague) is carried through the town while spectators throw spiced loaves at it.

🛏 Sleeping

The places listed below all offer good value for money.

`TOP CHOICE` Villa Athena `LUXURY HOTEL €€€`
(☎0922 59 62 88; www.hotelvillaathena.it; Via Passeggiata Archeologica 33; d €190-350, jr ste €260-370, ste €300-890; P☀@🖥🌊) With the Tempio della Concordia lit up in the near distance and palm trees lending an exotic Arabian-nights feel, the views from this historic five-star are magnificent. Housed in an aristocratic 18th-century villa, the hotel's interior, gleaming after a recent makeover, is a picture of white, ceramic cool. The Villa Suite, with two cavernous rooms floored in antique tiles, a freestanding Jaccuzi tub and a vast terrace looking straight at the temples, vies for the title of coolest hotel room in Sicily.

Camere a Sud `B&B €`
(☎349 6384424; www.camereasud.it; Via Ficani 6; r €60-70; ☀@🖥) Run by a friendly Agrigentan couple, this extremely cute, comfortable and well-signposted B&B has cheerful rooms and a tiny roof terrace.

Atenea 191 B&B `B&B €`
(☎349 595594; www.atenea191.com; Via Atenea 191; s €35-55, d €50-85) The gregarious, multilingual and well-travelled Sonia runs this B&B on Agrigento's main shopping thoroughfare. The breakfast terrace has sweeping views over the valley, as do some rooms. Sonia is a great source of local travel tips and an entertaining storyteller.

PortAtenea `B&B €`
(☎349 0937492; www.portatenea.com; cnr Via Atenea & Via C Battisti; s €35-50, d €55-70; ☀🖥) Five minutes from the train and bus stations at the entrance to Agrigento's main pedestrian thoroughfare, this B&B wins points for its large roof terrace overlooking the Valley of the Temples. The three double rooms and two triples are spacious and well-appointed, with hairdryers and cheerful decor.

✗ Eating

Kalòs `MODERN SICILIAN €€`
(☎0922 2 63 89; Piazzetta San Calogero; meals €25-40; ⊙closed Mon) This stylish eatery compensates for bland decor by focusing full attention on its well-prepared fish, meat and pasta dishes. The scrumptious offerings include fettucine with prawns and artichokes, grilled lamb chops, citrus shrimp and pear tart with chocolate and hazelnuts.

Kokalos `PIZZERIA €`
(☎0922 60 64 27; Via Magazzeni 3; pizzas €5-11, meals €17-30; ⊙lunch & dinner) This eatery, resembling a Wild West ranch, is the perfect place to enjoy wood-fired pizza on the summer terrace while gazing out over the temples. You will need a car to get here –

it's up a dusty track a couple of kilometres southeast of town.

Trattoria Concordia
TRATTORIA €

(☎0922 2 26 68; Via Porcello 8; meals €18-30; ☺lunch & dinner) Tucked up a side alley, this rustic trattoria with exposed stone and stucco walls specialises in grilled fish along with traditional Sicilian *primi* like *casarecce con pesce spada, melanzane e menta* (pasta with swordfish, eggplant and mint).

Ristorante Per Bacco
SICILIAN €

(☎0922 55 33 69; Vicolo Lo Presti 2; meals from €17; ☺dinner Tue-Sun) The food may not quite live up to the charm of the setting – under stone and brick arches and beamed ceilings – but the service is friendly, and the set menus for under €20 are good value at this restaurant just above Via Atenea.

L'Ambasciata di Sicilia
SICILIAN €€

(☎0922 2 05 26; Via Giambertoni 2; meals €22-33; ☺Mon-Sat) At the 'Sicilian Embassy', they do everything they can to improve foreign relations, plying tourists with tasty plates of traditional Sicilian fare. Try to get a table on the small outdoor terrace, which has splendid views.

Drinking & Entertainment

Mojo Wine Bar
WINE BAR

(☎0922 46 30 13; Piazza San Francesco 11-13; ☺Mon-Sat) A trendy *enoteca* in a pretty piazza. Enjoy a cool white Inzolia, and munch on olives and spicy salami, as you listen to some laid-back jazz.

Teatro Pirandello
THEATRE

(☎0922 2 50 19; www.teatroluigipirandello.it, in Italian; Piazza Pirandello; tickets €18-23) This city-run theatre is Sicily's third largest, after Palermo's Teatro Massimo and Catania's Teatro Massimo Bellini. Works by local hero Luigi Pirandello figure prominently in the program, which runs from November to April.

ℹ Information

There are banks on Piazza Vittorio Emanuele I and Via Atenea.

Internet Point (Cortile Contarini 7; wi-fi/computer access per hr €2/3.20; ☺9.15am-1.15pm & 3.30-9pm Mon-Sat) Internet and international phone service.

Ospedale San Giovanni di Dio (☎0922 44 21 11; Contrada da Consolida) North of the centre.

Police station (☎112; Piazzale Aldo Moro 2)

Post office (Piazza Vittorio Emanuele I)

Provincial tourist office (☎0922 593650, 800 23 68 37; www.provincia.agrigento.it) train station (☺9am-1pm Mon-Fri); Piazzale Aldo Moro (☺8am-2pm Mon-Sat, 2.30-7pm Mon-Fri) Provides both local and regional information.

ℹ Getting There & Away

Bus

The intercity bus station and ticket booths are located on Piazza Rosselli. **Autoservizi Camilleri** (☎0922 2 91 36; www.camilleri argentoelattuca.it) runs buses to Palermo (€8.10, two hours) five times Monday to Saturday and twice on Sunday; **Cuffaro** (☎091 616 15 10; www.cuffaro.info) offers more frequent Palermo service – nine departures Monday to Saturday, three on Sunday. **Lumia** (☎0922 2 91 36; www.autolinealumia.it) has departures to Trapani (€11.30, 3½ to four hours, three daily Monday to Saturday, one on Sunday); and **SAIS** (☎0922 2 93 24; www.saistrasporti.it) runs buses to Catania (€12.40, three hours, 10 to 15 daily).

Car & Motorcycle

The SS189 links Agrigento with Palermo, while the SS115 runs along the coast, northwest towards Trapani and southeast to Syracuse.

Driving in the medieval town is near impossible due to all the pedestrianised streets. There's metered parking at the train station and free parking along Via Esseneto just below.

Train

From Agrigento Centrale station (Piazza Marconi), trains run regularly to Palermo (€8.10, 2¼ hours, eight to 11 daily) and three times daily to Catania (€10.20, 3¾ hours). For other destinations, you're better off taking the bus.

ℹ Getting Around

TUA (Trasporti Urbani Agrigento; ☎0922 41 20 24; www.trasportiurbaniagrigento.it) buses run down to the Valley of the Temples from the Piazza Rosselli bus station, stopping in front of the train station en route. Take bus 1, 2 or 3 (€1.10) and get off at either the museum or the Piazzale dei Templi. Bus 1 continues to Porto Empedocle and bus 2 continues to San Leone. The Linea Verde (Green Line) bus runs hourly from the train station to the cathedral.

WESTERN SICILY

Directly across the water from North Africa and still retaining vestiges of the Arab, Phoenician, and Greek cultures that once prevailed here, western Sicily has a bit of the Wild West about it. There's plenty to

In May 2011, Sicilian art lovers were thrilled to welcome the long-lost **Dea di Morgantina**, an ancient statue of Venus, back to its rightful home in central Sicily. For over two decades, the statue had been on display at the Getty Museum in Los Angeles, California, but when authorities discovered that the Getty's unscrupulous curator had actually smuggled it out of Italy with help from grave robbers, the Italian government initiated moves to repatriate it.

The statue is now proudly back on display in a special gallery at the Museo Archeologico di Aidone (☑0935 8 73 07; www.regione.sicilia.it/beniculturali/deadimorgantina, in Italian; adult/reduced €6/3; ⊙9am-7pm), in Aidone, just outside Piazza Armerina.

stir the senses, from Trapani's savoury fish couscous, to the dazzling views from hilltop Erice, to the wild coastal beauty of Riserva Naturale dello Zingaro.

Marsala

POP 82,500

Best known for its sweet dessert wines, Marsala is an elegant town of stately baroque buildings within a perfect square of walls.

The city was originally founded by Phoenician escapees from the Roman onslaught at nearby Mozia. Not wanting to risk a second attack, they fortified their new home with 7m-thick walls, ensuring that it was the last Punic settlement to fall to the Romans. In AD 830 it was conquered by the Arabs, who gave it its current name, Marsa Allah (Port of God).

It was here in 1860 that Giuseppe Garibaldi, leader of the movement for Italian unification, landed in his rickety old boats with his 1000-strong army – a claim to fame that finds its way into every tourist brochure.

⊙ Sights & Activities

For a taste of local life, take a stroll at sunset around pretty Piazza della Repubblica, heart of the historic centre.

Cantine Florio   WINERY
(☑0923 78 11 11; www.cantineflorio.it; Lungomare Florio; tours €7; ⊙wine shop 9am-1pm & 3-6pm Mon-Fri, 9am-1pm Sat, English-language tours 11am & 4.30pm Mon-Fri, 10.30am Sat) Tipplers shouldn't miss these venerable wine cellars on the road to Mazara del Vallo (bus 16 from Piazza del Popolo). Florio opens its doors to visitors to explain the fascinating history of local viticulture, the process of making Marsala wine and to give you a taste of the goods. Pellegrino, Donnafugata, Rallo, Mavis

and Intorcia are other producers in the same area. Booking is recommended.

Museo Archeologico Baglio Anselmi   MUSEUM
(☑0923 95 25 35; Lungomare Boeo; admission €4; ⊙9am-7pm Tue-Sun, 9am-1.30pm Mon) Marsala's finest treasure is the partially reconstructed remains of a Carthaginian *liburna* (warship) sunk off the Egadi Islands during the first of the Punic Wars nearly 3000 years ago. Displayed alongside other regional archaeological artefacts, the ship's bare bones provide the only remaining physical evidence of the Phoenicians' seafaring superiority in the 3rd century BC; and offer a glimpse of a civilisation that was extinguished by the Romans.

Whitaker Museum   MUSEUM
(☑0923 71 25 98; adult/reduced €9/5; ⊙9.30am-1.30pm & 2.30-6.30pm Mar-Sep) On tiny San Pantaleo island, 5km north of Marsala and connected to the mainland by a submerged Phoenician road, this museum houses a unique collection of Phoenician artefacts assembled over decades by amateur archaeologist Joseph Whitaker. The museum's greatest treasure is *Il Giovinetto di Mozia,* a marble statue of a young man in a pleated robe suggesting Carthaginian influences. The fields around the museum are strewn with ruins from the ancient Phoenician settlement of Mozia. Visitors can wander at will around the island to explore these, following a network of trails punctuated with helpful maps and informational displays. The island is accessible by private boat (€5 return, every 25 minutes) from a pier along the SS115 coast road. The surrounding landscape is quite lovely, with shallow *saline* (salty pools) and softly shimmering heaps of salt presided over by picturesque windmills. The salt from these pans is considered the best in Italy and has been big business since the 12th century.

📖 Sleeping & Eating

Marsala has few hotels within the historic centre.

Hotel Carmine   HOTEL €€
(☎0923 71 19 07; www.hotelcarmine.it; Piazza Carmine 16; s €70-90, d €100-125; 🅿❄@🛜) This lovely hotel in a 16th-century monastery has elegant rooms (especially numbers 7 and 30), with original blue-and-gold majolica tiles, stone walls, antique furniture and lofty beamed ceilings. Enjoy your cornflakes in the baronial-style breakfast room with its historic frescoes and over-the-top chandelier, or sip your drink by the roaring fireplace in winter. Modern perks include a rooftop solarium.

TOP CHOICE Il Gallo e l'Innamorata   MODERN SICILIAN €
(☎0923 195 44 46; Via Bilardello 18; meals €25; ☺lunch & dinner) Warm orange walls and arched stone doorways lend an artsy, convivial atmosphere to this Slow Food–acclaimed eatery with its superb fixed-price menu (€25 including appetisers, pasta, main course, fruit, dessert, water and wine). The à la carte menu is short and sweet, featuring a few well-chosen dishes each day, including the classic scaloppine (veal cooked with marsala wine and lemon).

ℹ Information

Tourist office (☎0923 71 40 97; ufficio turistico.proloco@comune.marsala.tp.it; Via XI Maggio 100; ☺8.30am-1.30pm & 3-8pm Mon-Sat, 9am-1pm Sun) A friendly tourist office with good maps and brochures.

ℹ Getting There & Away

From Marsala, bus operators include **Lumia** (www.autolineelumia.it) to Agrigento (€9.40, 2½ to three hours, one to three daily); and **Salemi** (☎0923 98 11 20; www.autoservizisalemi.it) to Palermo (€8.80, 2¼ hours, at least nine daily).

The train is the best way to get to Trapani (€3.30, 30 minutes, 14 daily, five on Sunday).

Selinunte

The ruins of Selinunte are the most impressively sited in Sicily. The huge city was built in 628 BC on a promontory overlooking the sea, and over two and a half centuries became one of the richest and most powerful in the world. It was destroyed by the Carthaginians in 409 BC and finally fell to the Romans in about 350 BC, at which time it went into rapid decline and disappeared from historical accounts.

The city's past is so remote that the names of the various temples have been forgotten and they are now identified by the letters A to G, M and O. The most impressive, Temple E, has been partially rebuilt, its columns pieced together from their fragments with part of its tympanum. Many of the carvings, particularly from Temple C, are now in the archaeological museum in Palermo (see p750). Their quality is on a par with the Parthenon marbles and clearly demonstrates the high cultural levels reached by many Greek colonies in Sicily.

The **ticket office** (☎0924 4 65 40; adult/reduced €6/3; ☺9am-1hr before sunset) is located near the eastern temples. Try to visit in spring when the surroundings are ablaze with wildflowers.

Selinunte is midway between Agrigento and Trapani, about 10km south of the junction of the A29 and SS115 near Castelvetrano. **Autoservizi Salemi** (☎0924 8 18 26; www.autoservizisalemi.it) runs five buses daily from Selinunte to Castelvetrano (€2.55, 20 minutes), where you can make onward bus connections to Agrigento, or train connections to Trapani (€5.60, 1¼ hours) and Palermo (€7.50, 2½ hours).

TOP CHOICE Vittorio (☎092578381; www.ristorante vittorio.it; meals €25-45), 15km east of Selinunte on the beach at Porto Palo, is a perfect place to end your day if travelling by car. In business for over 40 years, it's earned a reputation as one of Sicily's best seafood eateries, serving hefty portions of the freshest fish and shellfish around. Come here at sunset and dine to the sound of crashing breakers. Rooms (single/double €60/80) are available upstairs for anyone too stuffed to drive home.

Trapani

POP 70,700

The lively port city of Trapani makes a convenient base for exploring Sicily's western tip. Its historic centre is filled with atmospheric pedestrian streets and some lovely churches and baroque buildings, although the heavily developed outskirts are rather bleak. The surrounding countryside is beautiful, ranging from the watery vastness of the coastal salt ponds to the rugged mountainous shoreline north of town.

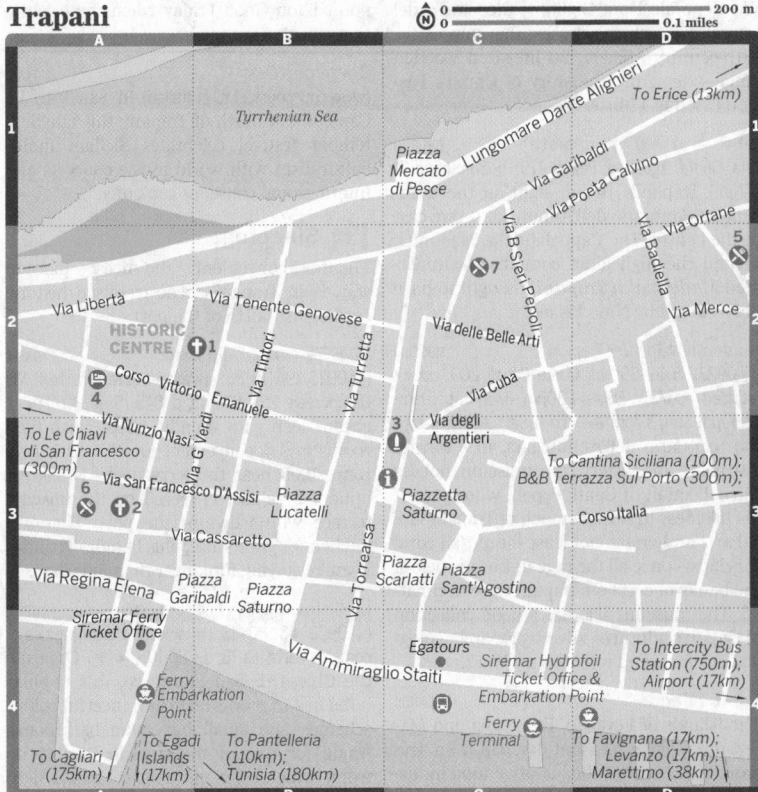

SICILY TRAPANI

Once situated at the heart of a powerful trading network that stretched from Carthage to Venice, Trapani's sickle-shaped spit of land hugs the precious harbour, nowadays busy with a steady stream of tourists and traffic to and from Tunisia, Pantelleria and the Egadi Islands.

⊙ Sights

The narrow network of streets in Trapani's historic centre remains a Moorish labyrinth, although it takes much of its character from the fabulous 18th-century baroque of the Spanish period – a catalogue of examples can be found down the pedestrianised **Via Garibaldi**. The best time to walk down here is in the early evening (around 7pm) when the *passeggiata* is in full swing.

Trapani's other main street is Corso Vittorio Emanuele, punctuated by the huge **Cattedrale di San Lorenzo** (Corso Vittorio Emanuele; ⊙8am-4pm), with its baroque

Trapani

⊙ Sights

1 Cattedrale di San Lorenzo....................B2
2 Chiesa del Purgatorio............................A3
3 Palazzo Senatorio...................................C3

⊜ Sleeping

4 Ai Lumi B&B A2

⊗ Eating

5 La Rinascente..D2
6 Osteria La Bettolaccia..........................A3
7 Tentazioni di Gusto................................C2

facade and stuccoed interior. Facing off the east end of the *corso* is another baroque confection, the **Palazzo Senatorio**.

Chiesa del Purgatorio   CHURCH
(☎0923 56 28 82; Via San Francesco d'Assisi; ⊙4-6.30pm) Just off the *corso*, south along

Via Generale Dom Giglio, is the Chiesa del Purgatorio, which houses the impressive 18th-century *Misteri,* 20 life-sized wooden effigies depicting the story of Christ's Passion (used in I Misteri).

Santuario dell'Annunziata   CHURCH
(Via Conte Agostino Pepoli 179; ⊘8am-noon & 4-7pm) Trapani's major sight is the 14th-century Santuario dell'Annunziata, 4km east of the centre. The Cappella della Madonna, behind the high altar, contains the venerated *Madonna di Trapani,* thought to have been carved by Nino Pisano.

Museo Nazionale Pepoli   MUSEUM
(✆0923 55 32 69; Via Conte Pepoli 200; adult/reduced €6/3; ⊘9am-1.30pm Mon-Sat, 9am-12.30pm Sun, 3-7pm Wed, Fri & Sat) Adjacent to the Santuario dell'Annunziata, in a former Carmelite monastery, the museum houses the collection of Conte Pepoli, who made it his business to salvage much of Trapani's local arts and crafts, not least the garish coral carvings – once all the rage in Europe before the banks of coral off Trapani were decimated. The museum also has a good collection of Gagini sculptures, silverwork, archaeological artefacts and religious art work.

Egadi Islands   ISLANDS
The islands of Levanzo, Favignana and Marettimo make a pleasant day trip from Trapani. For centuries the lucrative tuna industry formed the basis of the islands' economy, but overfishing of the surrounding waters means that the Egadi survives primarily on income from tourists who come to cycle, dive or simply enjoy the relaxed pace of life. The best range of meals and accommodation can be found on Favignana, while the islands' single greatest tourist attraction is Grotta del Genovese on Levanzo, a cave decorated with Mesolithic and Neolithic art work, including a famous image of a prehistoric tuna. Siremar and Ustica Lines (see p803) both run year-round hydrofoil service to the islands.

✯ Festivals & Events

I Misteri   RELIGIOUS
(www.processionemisteritp.it, in Italian, Spanish & French) Sicily's most venerated Easter procession is a four-day festival of extraordinary religious fervour. Nightly processions, bearing life-sized wooden effigies, make their way through the old quarter to a specially erected chapel in Piazza Lucatelli. The high point is on Good Friday when the celebrations reach fever pitch.

Couscous Fest   FOOD
(www.couscousfest.it, in Italian) In San Vito Lo Capo, 40km north of Trapani, this late September festival celebrates Sicilian multiculturalism with world music concerts and international couscous cook offs.

⌇ Sleeping

The most convenient – and nicest – place to stay, is in Trapani's pedestrianised historic centre, just north of the port.

B&B Terrazza Sul Porto   B&B €
(✆0923 194 15 36; www.laterrazzasulporto.it; Via Camporeale 2; s €35-45, d €45-75; ❋ 🐭) For a cheap sleep with friendly hosts, clean tiled rooms and a convenient location, this five-room B&B near the ferry docks is a great option. Breakfast is served on the upstairs terrace with views of the port. There's a kitchen for guests' use, plus laundry facilities if you're staying for longer than four days.

Le Chiavi di San Francesco   HOTEL €
(✆0923 43 80 13; www.lechiavidisanfrancesco.com; Via Tartaglia 18; d €80-105; ❋ 🐭) Opposite the Chiesa di San Francesco, this popular hotel has 16 rooms featuring cheerful colour schemes and small but clean bathrooms. Angle for one of the superior rooms up front, which offer more space, better light and optional kitchen facilities.

Ai Lumi B&B   B&B €
(✆0923 54 09 22; www.ailumi.it; Corso Vittorio Emanuele 71; s €40-70, d €70-100; ❋ 🐭) Housed in an 18th-century *palazzo,* Ai Lumi's greatest asset is its central location. Rooms vary in size and comfort; the best are the small apartments furnished with wrought-iron beds, kitchenettes and balconies overlooking Trapani's most elegant pedestrian street. Guests get a 15% discount at the hotel's atmospheric restaurant next door.

✗ Eating

Sicily's Arab heritage and Trapani's unique position on the sea route to Tunisia have made couscous (*'cuscus'* or *'kuscus'* as they spell it around here) a local speciality.

▯TOP CHOICE Osteria La Bettolaccia   SICILIAN €€
(✆0923 2 16 95; Via Generale Enrico Fardella 25; meals €30-40; ⊘closed Sat lunch & Sun) An unwaveringly authentic, Slow Food-recommended restaurant, this is the perfect

PANTELLERIA

Halfway between Trapani and Tunisia, this volcanic outcrop is Sicily's largest offshore island. Buffeted year-round by winds, Pantelleria is characterised by jagged lava stone, low-slung caper bushes, dwarf vines, steaming fumaroles and mudbaths. There are no true beaches, but Pantelleria's gorgeous, secluded coves – including **Cala Tramontana**, **Cala Levante** and **Balata dei Turchi** – are perfect for snorkelling, diving and boat excursions.

The island has excellent hiking trails, along the coast and in the high vineyard country of **Piana di Ghirlanda**. Near **Mursia** on the west coast, there are signposted but poorly maintained remnants of *sesi* (Bronze Age funerary monuments). Throughout the island you'll also find Pantelleria's famous *dammusi* (houses with thick, whitewashed walls and shallow cupolas). The island's exotic and remote atmosphere has long made it popular with celebrities, including Truman Capote, Sting, Madonna and Giorgio Armani.

Meridiana (www.meridiana.it) and Alitalia (www.alitalia.com) offer regular flights to Pantelleria from Palermo and Trapani. Siremar (www.siremar.it) runs one ferry daily between Trapani and Pantelleria (low/high season €31/35).

For further information about Pantelleria see www.pantelleria.com.

place to try *cous cous con zuppa di mare* (couscous with mixed seafood in a spicy fish sauce, with tomatoes, garlic and parsley).

Tentazioni di Gusto   MODERN SICILIAN **€€**
(☎0923 54 81 65; www.tentazionidigusto.it; Via Badia Nuova 27/29; meals €25-35; ⊘closed Wed Nov-Mar) Young proprietors Piero and Vicenzo have created an instant sensation at this trendy new restaurant-bar, which features a mix of traditional and innovative cuisine, ample outdoor seating on the cobblestones and a newly expanded interior with stone arches and sleek wood floors.

Cantina Siciliana   SICILIAN **€€**
(☎347 690 10 10; Via Giudecca 32; meals €25-35; ⊘lunch & dinner) The reasonably priced regional specialities here are enticing, as are the pretty blue-tiled front rooms. Unfortunately service can range from lacklustre to borderline rude, as owner Pino tends to regale his Italian friends to the exclusion of other guests. Still, it's one of Trapani's better-regarded eateries and worth a visit if you're willing to focus on the food.

La Rinascente   PASTRIES & CAKES **€**
(Via Gatti 3; cannoli €1.60; ⊘9am-1pm & 3-7pm, closed Sun afternoon & Wed) When you enter this bakery through the side door, you'll feel like you've barged into someone's kitchen – and you have! Thankfully, owner Signor Costadura's broad smile will quickly put you at ease, coupled with some of the best *cannoli* on the planet, which you can watch being created on the spot.

ⓘ Information

Trapani has dozens of banks with ATMs.
Ospedale Sant'Antonio Abate (☎0923 80 91 11; Via Cosenza 82)
Police station (☎0923 59 81 11; Piazza Vittoria Veneto)
Post office (Piazza Vittoria Veneto)
Torrepali web cafe (Via Ammiraglio Staiti 69; per hr €3; ⊘8am-2am) Across from the port; six computers with comfortable upstairs seating and bar service.
Tourist office (☎0923 54 45 33; point@ stradadelvinoericedoc.it; Piazzetta Saturno; ⊘9am-1pm & 3-7pm Mon-Sat) For free maps and info about Trapani and local wine routes.

ⓘ Getting There & Around

For bus, plane and ferry tickets, try **Egatours** (☎0923 2 17 54; www.egatourviaggi.it; Via Ammiraglio Staiti 13), a travel agency located opposite the port.

Air

Trapani's small **Vincenzo Florio Airport** (TPS; www.airgest.it) is 17km south of town at Birgi. **Ryanair** (www.ryanair.com) offers direct flights to London Luton and a dozen other European cities; **Meridiana** (www.meridiana.it) serves the Mediterranean island of Pantelleria. AST buses connect Trapani's port and bus station with the airport (€4.50, 45 minutes, hourly).

Boat

Ferry ticket offices are inside Trapani's ferry terminal, opposite Piazza Garibaldi.

SICILY'S OLDEST NATURE RESERVE

Saved from development and road projects by local protests, the tranquil **Riserva Naturale dello Zingaro** (☑0924 3 51 08; www.riservazingaro.it; adult/reduced €3/2; ☺7am-8pm Apr-Sep, 8am-4pm Oct-Mar) is the star attraction on the Golfo di Castellammare, halfway between Palermo and Trapani. Celebrating its 30th anniversary in 2011, this was Sicily's first nature reserve. Zingaro's wild coastline is a haven for the rare Bonelli's eagle along with 40 other species of bird. Mediterranean flora dusts the hillsides with wild carob and bright yellow euphorbia, and hidden coves, such as Capreria and Marinella Bays, provide tranquil swimming spots. The main entrance to the park is 2km north of the village of Scopello. Several walking trails are detailed on maps available free at the entrance or downloadable from the park website (in Italian only). The main 7km trail along the coast passes by the visitor centre and five museums documenting everything from local flora and fauna to traditional fishing methods.

Once home to tuna fishers, Scopello now mainly hosts tourists, although outside of peak summer season it retains some of its sleepy village atmosphere. Its port, 1km below town, has a picturesque rust-red *tonnara* (tuna processing plant) and dramatic *faraglioni* (rock towers) rising from the water.

Pensione Tranchina (☑0924 54 10 99; www.pensionetranchina.com; Via Diaz 7; B&B per person €36-46, half-board per person €55-72; ✳🛰) is the nicest of several places to stay and eat clustered around the cobblestoned courtyard at Scopello's village centre. Superfriendly hosts Marisin and Salvatore offer comfortable rooms, a roaring fire on chilly evenings and delicious home-cooked meals featuring local fish and home-grown fruit and olive oil. Next door, **La Tavernetta** (☑0924 54 11 29; www.albergolatavernetta.it; Via Diaz 3; s €55-70, d €70-96; P✳@🛰) is another good choice.

For Ustica Lines and Siremar hydrofoils, the ticket office and embarkation point is 150m further east along Via Ammiraglio Staiti.

Grimaldi Lines (www.grimaldi-ferries.com) runs weekly services to Tunisia (€95, 7½ hours) and Civitavecchia (€120, 14½ hours).

Tirrenia (☑0923 52 18 96; www.tirrenia.it) runs a weekly service to Cagliari (€52, 10 hours).

Ustica Lines (☑0923 87 38 13; www.ustica lines.it; Via Ammiraglio Staiti) and **Siremar** (☑0923 54 54 55; www.siremar.it; Via Ammiraglio Staiti) both operate hydrofoils year-round to the Egadi Islands. Ustica Lines also offers thrice-weekly summer-only services to Naples (€89.40, seven hours) and Ustica (€26.40, 2½ hours), while Siremar offers nightly ferry service to Pantelleria (€39.50, six hours).

Bus

Intercity buses arrive and depart from the new City Terminal 1km east of the centre (just southeast of the train station).

Segesta (☑0923 2 17 27; www.segesta.it) runs express buses to Palermo (€8.60, two hours, hourly). Board at the bus stop across the street from Egatours or at the bus station.

Lumia (www.autolineelumia.it) buses serve Agrigento (€11.30, three to four hours, one to three daily).

Two free city buses (No 1 and 2) operated by **ATM** (☑0923 55 95 75; www.atmtrapani.it) do circular trips through Trapani, connecting the bus station, the train station and the port.

Car & Motorcyle

To bypass Trapani's vast suburbs and avoid the narrow streets of the city centre, follow signs from the A29 autostrada directly to the port, where you'll find abundant paid parking along the broad waterside avenue Via Ammiraglio Staiti, within walking distance of most attractions.

Train

From Trapani's station on Piazza Umberto I, there are rail links to Palermo (€7.50, 2¼ to 3½ hours, three to six daily) and Marsala (€3.30, 30 minutes, six to 12 daily). At the time of research Palermo-bound trains were only going as far as Notarbartolo station, 3km northwest of downtown Palermo, due to track work between Notarbartolo and Palermo Centrale. Until this work is finished, the bus is a better option.

Erice

POP 28,500 / ELEV 751M

One of Italy's most spectacular hill towns, Erice combines medieval charm with astounding 360-degree views. Erice sits on the legendary Mt Eryx (750m); on a clear day, you can see Cape Bon in Tunisia. Wander the medieval tangle of streets interspersed by churches, forts and tiny cobbled piazzas. The town has a seductive history as a centre for the cult of Venus. Settled by the mysterious Elymians, Erice was an obvious abode for the goddess of love, and the town followed the peculiar ritual of sacred prostitution, with the prostitutes themselves accommodated in the Temple of Venus. Despite countless invasions, the temple remained intact – no guesses why.

Erice's tourist infrastructure is excellent. Posted throughout town, you'll find bilingual (Italian-English) informational displays along with town maps displaying suggested walking routes.

Sights

The best views can be had from Giardino del Balio, which overlooks the rugged turrets and wooded hillsides down to the saltpans of Trapani and the sea. Adjacent to the gardens is the Norman Castello di Venere (Via Castello di Venere), built in the 12th and 13th centuries over the Temple of Venus.

There are several churches and monuments in the small, quiet town and you can purchase a €5 ticket to visit the lot. Especially lovely are the 14th-century Chiesa Matrice (Via Vito Carvini; admission €2; ☺10am-8pm May-Sep, 10am-6pm Oct-Apr), just inside Porta Trapani, and its adjacent bell tower, Torre di Re Federico (admission €2), where climbing the 110 steps rewards you with fabulous views.

Sleeping & Eating

Hotels, many with their own restaurants, are scattered along Via Vittorio Emanuele, Erice's main street. After the tourists have left, the town assumes a beguiling medieval air.

Hotel Elimo HOTEL €€
(☎0923 86 93 77; www.hotelelimo.it; Via Vittorio Emanuele 23; s €80-110, d €90-130, ste €170; P@☺) Communal spaces at this atmospheric historic house are filled with tiled beams, marble fireplaces, intriguing art, knick-knacks and antiques. The bedrooms are more mainstream, although many (along with the hotel terrace and restaurant) have breathtaking vistas.

Erice has a tradition of *dolci ericini* (Erice sweets) made by the local nuns. There are numerous pastry shops in town, the most famous being Maria Grammatico (☎0923 86 93 90; www.mariagrammatico.it; Via Vittorio Emanuele 14), revered for its *frutta martorana* (marzipan fruit) and almond pastries.

ℹ Information

The **tourist office** (☎0923 86 93 88; strerice@regione.sicilia.it; Via Tommaso Guarrasi 1; ☺9am-2pm Mon-Fri) is in the centre of town.

ℹ Getting There & Away

Regular AST buses run to and from Trapani (one way/return €2.40/3.70, 45 minutes). A **funicular** (☎0923 56 93 06; www.funiviaerice.it; one way/return €3.80/6.50; ☺12.30-9pm Mon, 9.30am-9pm Tue-Sun, to midnight Sat) also connects Trapani with Erice. To reach Trapani's funicular terminal, near the corner of Via Manzoni and Via Capua, take AST bus 21 or 23 (€1) eastbound from Trapani's historic centre. The funicular climbs from here to Erice, dropping you opposite the car park at the foot of Erice's Via Vittorio Emanuele.

Segesta

ELEV 304M

Set on the edge of a deep canyon in the midst of wild, desolate mountains, this huge 5th-century-BC temple is a magical site. On windy days its 36 giant columns are said to act like an organ, producing mysterious notes.

The city, founded by the ancient Elymians, was in constant conflict with Selinunte in the south, whose destruction it sought with dogged determination and singular success. Time, however, has done to Segesta what violence inflicted on Selinunte; little remains now, save the theatre and the never-completed Doric temple (☎0924 95 23 56; adult/reduced €6/3; ☺9am-1hr before sunset), the latter dating from around 430 BC and remarkably well preserved. A shuttle bus (€1.50) runs every 30 minutes from the temple entrance 1.5km uphill to the theatre.

In July and August, performances of Greek plays are staged in the theatre during the Festival Calatafimi Segesta (www.festivalsegesta.com).

Tarantola (☎0924 3 10 20; www.tarantolabus.com, in Italian) runs three buses daily from Trapani (one way/return €3.60/6.10, 35 to 50 minutes), plus a single morning bus from Palermo's train station (one way/return €6.40/10.20, 1½ hours); drivers stop just outside the archaeological site upon request. Alternatively, catch a train from Trapani (€3.30, 30 minutes, three daily) to Segesta Tempio station. Exiting the station, turn left under the double underpass, then climb 1.5km (20 minutes) to the site.

Sardinia

Includes »

Best Places to Eat

Best Places to Stay

Why Go?

As DH Lawrence so succinctly put it: 'Sardinia is different.' Indeed, where else but on this 365-village, four-million-sheep island could you travel from shimmering bays to alpine forests, granite peaks to cathedral-like grottoes, rolling vineyards to one-time bandit towns – all in the space of a day? Sardinia baffles with prehistory at 7000 *nuraghic* sites, amazes with its weird and wonderful food (maggoty *pecorino* included), and dazzles with its kaleidoscopic blue waters.

Over millennia islanders have carved out a unique identity, cuisine, culture and language, leaving the forces of nature to work their magic on the landscape. And whether you're swooning over the megayachts in the Costa Smeralda's fjord-like bays or feasting on spit-roasted suckling pig at a rustic *agriturismo* (farm stay accommodation), you can't help but appreciate this island's love of the good life. Earthy and glamorous, adventurous and blissfully relaxed, Sardinia delights in being that little bit different.

When to Go
Cagliari

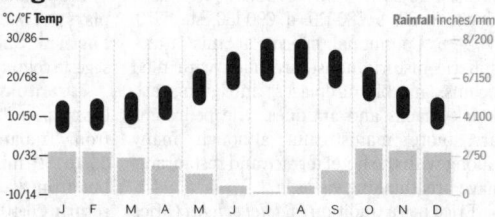

Feb Pre-Lenten shenanigans, from beastly *mamuthones* in Mamoiada to medieval jousting at Sa Sartiglia.

Mar–May Spring wildflowers, Easter parades, and hiking and climbing without the heat and crowds.

Jun–Aug Sun-kissed beaches, open-air festivals and reckless horse races at the S'Ardia.

History

Little is known about Sardinia's prehistory, but the first islanders probably arrived from mainland Italy around 350,000 BC. By the neolithic period (8000 BC to 3000 BC) tribal communities were thriving in north-central Sardinia. Their Bronze Age descendants, known as the *nuraghic* people, dominated the island until the Phoenicians arrived around 850 BC. The Carthaginians came next, followed by the Romans, who took over in the 3rd century BC.

In the Middle Ages, the island was divided into four independent *giudicati* (kingdoms), but by the 13th century the Pisans and Genoese were battling for control. They in turn were toppled by the Catalan-Aragonese from northern Spain, who also had to subdue bitter Sard resistance led by Eleonora d'Arborea (1340–1404), Sardinia's very own Joan of Arc.

Sardinia became Spanish territory after the unification of the Spanish kingdoms in 1479 and today there remains a tangible Hispanic feel to towns such as Alghero and Iglesias. In the ensuing centuries, Sardinia suffered as Spain's power crumbled; in 1720 the Italian Savoys took possession of the island. After Italian unity in 1861, Sardinia found itself under the uninterested boot of Rome.

In the aftermath of WWII, efforts were made to drag the island into the modern era. In 1946 a huge project was launched to rid the island of malaria and in 1948 Sardinia was granted its own autonomous regional parliament.

Coastal tourism arrived in the 1960s and has since become a mainstay of the Sardinian economy. Environmentalists breathed a sigh of relief in 2008 when NATO finally withdrew from the Maddalena islands after a controversial 35-year sojourn.

❶ Getting There & Away

AIR Flights from Italian and European cities serve **Elmas** (☏070 21 12 11; www.sogaer.it) airport in Cagliari; Alghero's **Fertilia** (☏079 93 52 82; www.aeroportodialghero.it); and the **Aeroporto Olbia Costa Smeralda** (☏0789 56 34 00; www.geasar.it) in Olbia. As well as major international carriers, several no-frills airlines operate direct flights, including **Ryanair** (www.ryanair.com), **easyJet** (www.easyjet.com) and **TUIfly** (www.tuifly.com). Some routes are restricted to between April and October.

BOAT Sardinia is accessible by ferry from Genoa, Livorno, Piombino, Civitavecchia and Naples, and from Palermo and Trapani in Sicily. Ferries also run from Bonifacio and Porto Vecchio in Corsica, and from Marseilles via the Corsican ports of Ajaccio and Propriano. The arrival points in Sardinia are Olbia, Golfo Aranci, Santa Teresa di Gallura and Porto Torres in the north; Arbatax on the east coast; and Cagliari in the south. Services are most frequent from mid-June to mid-September, when it is advisable to book well ahead. Useful online resources include www.traghettiweb.it and www.traghettionline.com (in Italian).

FERRY OPERATORS

CMN La Méridionale (☏France 0810 20 13 20; www.cmn.fr) To Porto Torres from Marseille via Corsica.

Corsica Ferries, Sardinia Ferries (☏199 400 500; www.corsica-ferries.co.uk) To Golfo Aranci from Civitavecchia and Livorno. Also Sardinia to Corsica (April to September).

Grandi Navi Veloci (☏010 209 45 91; www.gnv.it) To Olbia and Porto Torres from Genoa.

Moby Lines (☏199 30 30 40; www.moby.it) To Olbia from Civitavecchia, Genoa, Livorno and Piombino; to Porto Torres from Genoa. Also has ferries between Sardinia and Corsica (April to September).

Saremar (☏892 123; www.saremar.it) To Santa Teresa di Gallura from Bonifacio (Corsica).

SNCM (☏079 51 44 77; www.sncm.fr) To Porto Torres from Marseille via Corsica. In July and August some services depart from Toulon.

Tirrenia (☏892 123; www.tirrenia.it) To Cagliari from Civitavecchia, Naples, Palermo and Trapani; to Olbia from Civitavecchia and Genoa; to Arbatax from Civitavecchia and Genoa; to Porto Torres from Genoa.

❶ Getting Around

BUS Sardinia's main bus company, **ARST** (Azienda Regionale Sarda Trasporti; ☏800 865 042; www.arst.sardegna.it, in Italian), runs most local and long-distance services.

CAR & MOTORCYCLE Sardinia is best explored by road. For details about rental agencies in Cagliari, see p816. There are also rental agencies at airports and in major towns.

TRAIN Trenitalia (☏892 021; www.trenitalia.com) services link Cagliari with Oristano, Sassari, Porto Torres, Olbia and Golfo Aranci. Services are slow but generally reliable. Slow **ARST** (☏070 34 31 12; http://arst.sardegna.it, in Italian) trains serve Sassari, Alghero and Nuoro. Between mid-June and early September, ARST also operates a tourist train service known as the **Trenino Verde** (www.trenino verde.com) – see p807.

Sardinia Highlights

❶ Walk on the wild side in the grandiose **Gola Su Gorropu** (p841), Europe's Grand Canyon

❷ Feel the lure of the sea on the dune-backed, windswept beaches of the **Costa Verde** (p821)

❸ Wander the medieval backstreets of **Il Castello** (p810), Cagliari's rocky citadel

❹ Rub bronzed shoulders with the rich and super-famous on the **Costa Smeralda** (p834)

❺ Bone up on prehistory at **Nuraghe Su Nuraxi** (p824), Sardinia's sole World Heritage Site

❻ Drop anchor in the hidden coves of the **Golfo di Orosei** (p844), lapped by

brilliant aquamarine waters

7 Soak up the Spanish vibe of **Alghero** (p827), roaming the cobbled alleyways of its medieval centre

8 Take a scenic drive along the serpentine **SS125** (p844) for captivating views of the mountains and the Med

9 Marvel at the mysterious *nuraghic* ruins of **Tiscali** (p844), high in the limestone Supramonte

10 Explore a forest of stalactites and stalagmites at the fairy-tale **Grotta di Nettuno** (p831)

CAGLIARI

POP 156,951

Forget flying: the best way to arrive in Cagliari is by sea to witness the city rising in a jumble of golden-hued *palazzi* (mansions), domes and facades up to the rocky centrepiece, Il Castello. Cultured and cosmopolitan, Cagliari is Sardinia's most Italian-flavoured city. Vespas buzz down tree-fringed boulevards and locals relax at cafes tucked under the graceful arcades by the seafront. Swing east and you reach Poetto beach, the hub of summer life with its limpid waters and upbeat party scene.

At every turn, Cagliari's gripping history is spelled out, especially through archaeological sites, museums and churches. The city was founded by the Phoenicians in the 8th century BC, but came of age as a Roman port. Later, the Pisans arrived and treated it to a major medieval facelift, the results of which impress to this day.

 Sights

Cagliari's trophy sights cluster in the Castello, Stampace, Marina and Villanova districts.

Il Castello
NEIGHBOURHOOD

Precipitous stone walls enclose Cagliari's medieval citadel, once the fortified home of the city's aristocracy and religious authorities, known to locals as Su Casteddu. Inside the battlements, the old medieval city reveals itself like Pandora's box. The university, cathedral, museums and Pisan palaces are wedged into a jigsaw of narrow high-walled alleys.

FREE Museo Archeologico Nazionale
MUSEUM

(☐070 68 40 00; Piazza dell'Arsenale; ⊙9am-8pm Tue-Sun) The star of the Citadella dei Musei's four museums, this archaeological museum showcases artefacts spanning millennia of ancient history, including pint-sized *nuraghic bronzetti* (bronze figurines). In the absence of any written records, these are a vital source of information on Sardinia's mysterious *nuraghic* culture.

Cattedrale di Santa Maria
DUOMO

(Piazza Palazzo 4) Cagliari's graceful cathedral stands proud on Piazza Palazzo. Apart from the square-based bell tower, little remains of the original 13th-century Gothic structure –

FERRIES TO SARDINIA

Prices quoted here are adult high-season fares for a 2nd-class *poltrona* (reclinable seat) and small car. Children aged four to 12 generally pay around half price; those under four go free. Most companies offer discounts for early booking and online deals – it's always worth checking.

FROM	DESTINATION	FARE (€)	CAR (€)	DURATION (HR)
Bonifacio	Santa Teresa di Gallura	25	68	1
Civitavecchia	Arbatax	49	96	10½
Civitavecchia	Cagliari	58	104	14½
Civitavecchia	Olbia	43	102	4½-10
Civitavecchia	Golfo Aranci*	78	100	5½
Genoa	Arbatax	58	81	19
Genoa	Olbia	59	108	13¼
Genoa	Porto Torres*	107	182	10
Livorno	Golfo Aranci*	83-117	21-90	6
Livorno	Olbia	94	135	7-9
Marseille	Porto Torres	93	121	15-17
Naples	Cagliari	53	94	16¼
Palermo	Cagliari	52	92	14½
Piombino	Olbia	94	135	6½
Trapani	Cagliari	52	92	11

* indicates a high-speed service

TOP FIVE OUTDOOR ACTIVITIES

» **Hiking** Head to the magnificent Parco Nazionale del Golfo di Orosei e del Gennargentu (p839) for exhilarating coastal and mountain trekking.

» **Climbing** The Supramonte, Golfo di Orosei, Ogliastra (p838) and Domusnovas (p819) are rock-climbing wonderlands. For the lowdown on routes, pick up *Arrampicare a Cala Gonone* (€18) by expert climber Corrado Conca in local bookshops, or visit www.sardegnaverticale.it (in Italian) for details of guided climbing excursions.

» **Cycling** Ogliastra offers highly scenic road cycling and jaw-dropping downhill routes on old mule trails. Peter gives invaluable tips at the Lemon House (p846) or visit www.mountainbikeogliastra.it (in Italian).

» **Diving** Sardinia's gin-clear waters are a diver's dream. Check out the Med's largest underwater grotto, Nereo Cave (p830) near Alghero, or the depths of the Parco Nazionale dell'Arcipelago di La Maddalena (p836).

» **Windsurfing** Winds course through the Bonifacio Strait between Sardinia and Corsica, making Porto Pollo (p836) a top venue. Chia (p818) is another favourite spot.

the interior is 17th-century baroque and the Pisan-Romanesque facade is a 20th-century imitation. Inside are two intricate stone pulpits, sculpted by Guglielmo da Pisa and donated to the city in 1312.

Torre dell'Elefante LOOKOUT
(Via Università; adult/reduced €4/2.50; ⊙9am-1pm & 3.30-7.30pm Tue-Sun summer, to 4.30pm winter) One of only two Pisan towers still standing, the Torre dell'Elefante is named after the sculpted elephant by the vicious-looking portcullis. The 42m-high tower became something of a horror show, thanks to its foul decor. The Spaniards beheaded the Marchese di Cea here and left her severed head lying around for 17 years! Climb to the top for far-reaching city views.

Anfiteatro Romano ARCHAEOLOGICAL SITE
(☎070 65 29 56; www.anfiteatroromano.it, in Italian; Viale Sant'Ignazio; adult/reduced €4.30/2.80; ⊙9.30am-1.30pm Tue-Sat, 9.30am-1.30pm & 3.30-5.30pm Sun summer, closed Sun afternoon winter) This amphitheatre is Cagliari's must-see Roman monument. Although much of the original 2nd-century theatre was cannibalised for building material, enough has survived to pique the imagination. In summer, the amphitheatre stages stand-up comedy, music and dance.

Torre di San Pancrazio LOOKOUT
(Piazza Indipendenza; adult/reduced €4/2.50; ⊙9am-1pm & 3.30-7.30pm Tue-Sun summer, to 4.30pm winter) Over by the citadel's northeastern gate, this 36m-high tower is the Torre dell'Elefante's twin. Completed in 1305, it

is built on the city's highest point and has grandstand views of the Golfo di Cagliari.

Bastione San Remy LOOKOUT
The monumental stairway that ascends from busy Piazza Costituzione to Bastione San Remy is the most impressive way to reach Il Castello; save your legs by taking the panoramic elevator. A mix of neoclassical and Liberty styles, the lookout affords sweeping views over Cagliari's higgledy-piggledy rooftops to the glittering Mediterranean.

FREE Pinacoteca Nazionale ART GALLERY
(☎070 68 40 00; www.pinacoteca.cagliari.beniculturali.it, in Italian; Piazza dell'Arsenale; ⊙9am-7.30pm Tue-Sun) Above and behind the archaeological museum, this gallery contains a prized collection of 15th- to 17th-century art, including four outstanding works by Pietro Cavaro, father of the so-called Stampace school and arguably Sardinia's most important artist.

Orto Botanico BOTANICAL GARDEN
(☎070 65 29 56; Viale Sant'Ignazio; admission €3; ⊙8.30am-6pm Mon-Sat, 8.30am-1.30pm Sun) Slightly downhill from the amphitheatre is one of Italy's most famous botanical gardens, bristling with palm trees, cacti, ficus trees and local carobs and oaks. Ancient ruins tastefully litter the gardens.

Galleria Comunale d'Arte ART GALLERY
(☎070 49 07 27; www.galleriacomunalecagliari.it, in Italian; Viale San Vincenzo; adult/reduced €6/2.60; ⊙9am-1pm & 3.30-7.30pm Wed-Mon) Housed in a neoclassical villa north of Il Castello, this

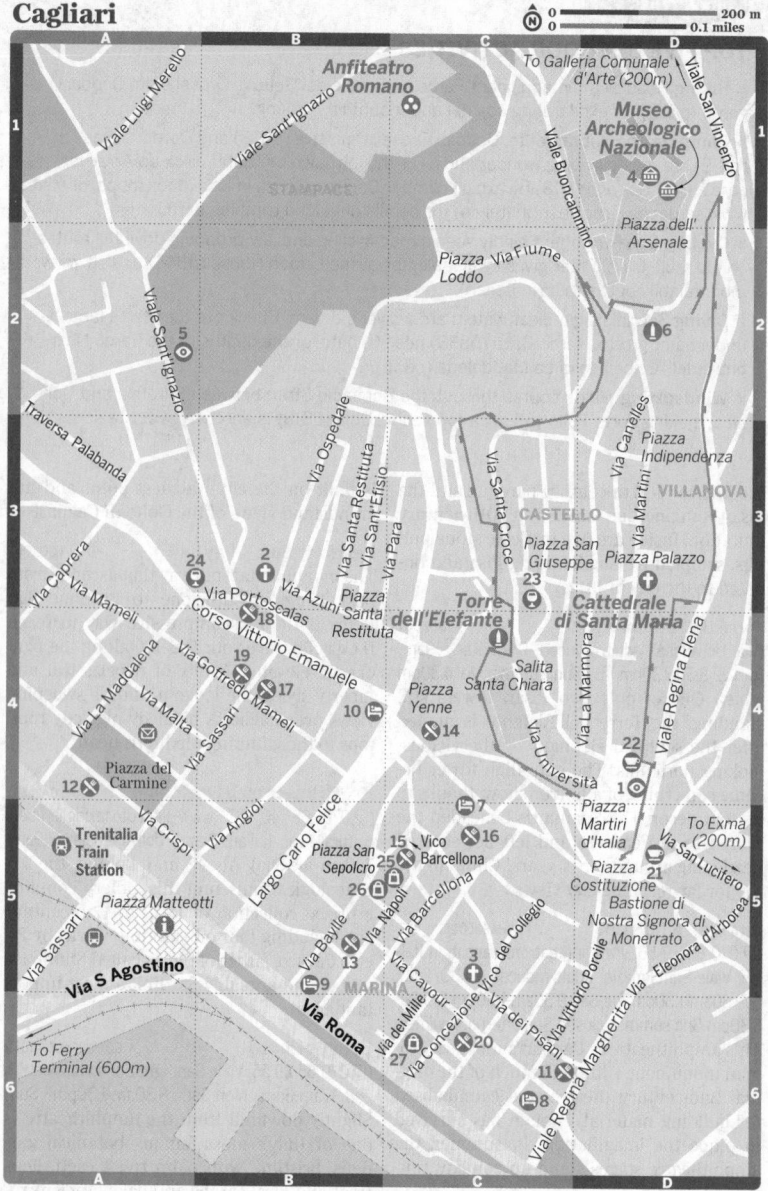

gallery zooms in on modern Sardinian art, including works by island artists such as Tarquinio Sinni (1891–1943).

There are terrific views of Cagliari's skyline from the palm-dotted **garden** (⏱6am-11pm summer, 7am-8pm winter) outside.

Chiesa di San Michele CHURCH
(Via Ospedale 2) This 16th-century church is celebrated for its lavish 18th-century rococo decor. In the atrium, note the four-columned pulpit from which the Spanish emperor Carlos V is said to have delivered a stirring

speech before setting off on a fruitless campaign against Arab corsairs in Tunisia.

Basilica di San Saturnino   CHURCH

(Piazza San Cosimo) A five-minute walk east of Piazza Contituzione, this 5th-century basilica is one of Sardinia's oldest churches and a striking example of palaeo-Christian architecture. It stands over a Roman necropolis where Saturninus, a much-revered local martyr, was buried in AD 304.

Santuario & Basilica di Nostra Signora di Bonaria   CHURCH, LOOKOUT

(Piazza Bonaria 2; donations expected) Around 1km southeast of Via Roma, and crowning the Bonaria hill, is this hugely popular pilgrim site. Devotees come from all over the world to pray to *Nostra Signora di Bonaria*, a statue of the Virgin Mary that is said to have saved a 14th-century Spanish ship during a storm. To the right of the sanctuary, the much larger basilica still acts as a landmark for returning sailors.

Piazza Yenne   PIAZZA

Crowned with a statue of King Carlo Felice, this square is a favourite local hang-out, especially on summer nights when its bars, gelaterie and pavement cafes buzz with young Cagliaritani.

Museo d'Arte Siamese   ART GALLERY

(☑070 65 18 88; Piazza dell'Arsenale; adult/reduced €2/1; ⊙9am-1pm & 3.30pm-7.30pm Tue-Sun) Showcases an eclectic collection of Asian art, crafts and weaponry.

Museo del Tesoro e Area Archeologica di Sant'Eulalia   MUSEUM

(☑070 66 37 24; Vico del Collegio 2; adult/ reduced €5/2.50; ⊙10am-1pm & 4-7pm Tue-Sun) Contains a rich collection of religious art, as well as an archaeological area, which extends for up to 200 sq metres beneath the adjacent Chiesa di Sant'Eulalia.

Exmà   ART GALLERY

(☑070 66 63 99; Via San Lucifero 71; exhibitions €3; ⊙9am-1pm & 4-8pm Tue-Sun) Occupying Cagliari's former abattoir, this cultural centre stages contemporary art exhibitions and summer concerts.

☞ Tours

City Tour Cagliari   BUS

(☑070 66 94 09; adult/reduced €10/5; ⊙9.30am-6.30pm Mon-Sun) This open-topped bus does an hour's loop of the key landmarks and sights, with multilingual commentary available. Departures are hourly from Piazza Yenne.

✳ Festivals & Events

Cagliari puts on a good show for **Carnevale** in February and Easter **Holy Week**, when a hooded procession climbs up to the cathedral in Il Castello.

Festa di Sant'Efisio
RELIGIOUS

(www.festadisantefisio.it, in Italian) Held between 1 and 4 May, on the opening day the saint's effigy is paraded around the city on a bullock-drawn carriage amid an extravagantly costumed procession.

🛏 Sleeping

TOP CHOICE Il Cagliarese
B&B €

(☎070 81 03 46; www.ilcagliarese.com; Via Vittorio Porcile 19; s €40-70, d €60-90; ❄🛜) This wonderfully snug and homey B&B sits in the heart of the Marina district. Mauro gives invaluable sightseeing tips and his sister, Titziana, whips up the delicious cakes and tiramisu served at breakfast.

Hostel Marina
HOSTEL €

(☎070 67 08 18; Scalette S Sepolcro; dm/s/d €22/40/60; ❄@) Housed in a beautifully converted 800-year-old former monastery, this hostel has oodles of historic charm. Many of the well-kept dorms have great city views, and rates include a substantial breakfast.

La Peonia
B&B €

(☎070 51 31 64; www.lapeonia.com; Via Riva Villasanta 77; s €50-60, d €72-88; ❄🛜) Antonello and Vanna are your kindly hosts at this romantic neo-Gothic abode, 2.5km northeast of the centre. Turn-of-the-century interiors with polished wood furnishings are a striking contrast to the sleek monochrome bathrooms.

T Hotel
HOTEL €€

(☎070 4 74 00; www.thotel.it; Via dei Giudicati; s/d/ste/f €139/159/199/249; 🅿❄🛜♨🍴) This hard-to-miss steel and glass tower adds a dash of contemporary design to the cityscape. The rooms reveal a linear, modish look, and the spa invites relaxation with its hydrotherapy pool, jets and treatments. It's a 15-minute walk northeast of Il Castello.

La Ghirlanda
B&B €

(☎070 20 40 610; www.laghirlandacagliari.it; Via Baylle 7; s €48-60, d €75-90, tr €100-120; ❄🛜) Antiques, frescoes and high-ceilinged rooms whisk you back to the 18th century at this handsome town house in the Marina district.

Suite sul Corso
B&B €€

(☎349 4469789; www.locandadelcorso.it; Corso Vittorio Emanuele 8; s €70-90, d €90-110, tr €130-160; ❄🛜🍴) Sleep in style at this boutique B&B just off Piazza Yenne. Exposed stone, floaty fabrics and glass mosaics lend warmth to the minimalist-chic rooms.

🍴 Eating

Dining hot spots include the Marina area, Via Sassari and Corso Vittorio Emanuele. From November to March (mollusc season), *chioschi* (kiosks) serve sea fresh sea urchins and mussels on Poetto beach.

TOP CHOICE Il Fantasma
PIZZERIA €

(☎070 65 67 49; Via San Domenico 94; pizzas €6.50-9; ☉Mon-Sat) A five-minute walk east of Piazza Martiri d'Italia, this boisterous pizzeria does the best pizza in Cagliari. Friendly waiters adroitly navigate the crowded barrel-vaulted interior to deliver bubbling pizzas straight from the wood-fired oven. Book or expect to queue.

Ristorante Ammentos
SARDINIAN €€

(☎070 65 10 75; Via Sassari 120; meals €15-30; ☉Wed-Mon) Dine on authentic Sardinian fare in rustic surrounds at this popular trattoria. *Culurgiones* (ravioli) in herby tomato sauce are a delicious lead-in to succulent meat dishes like wild boar or goat stew.

Monica e Ahmed
SARDINIAN €€

(☎070 640 20 45; Corso Vittorio Emanuele 119; meals around €30; ☉closed dinner Sun) Monica welcomes you with a smile and then plies you with a tempting array of fishy delights, such as *ricci* (sea urchins) and seafood spaghetti at this boho-flavoured restaurant.

Lapola
SARDINIAN €€

(☎070 65 06 04; Vico Barcellona 10; meals around €35; ☉Tue-Sun) Seafood is the star of the menu at this bustling Marina choice, serving taste sensations like octopus carpaccio with rocket and chicory, and sautéed clams in orange juice with *pane carasau*. The €16 lunch including wine and coffee is a bargain.

Trattoria Gennargentu
SARDINIAN €€

(☎070 65 82 47; Via Sardegna 60; meals €20-30; ☉closed Sun winter) Tables fill quickly at this no-frills trattoria that dishes up excellent seafood. Try spaghetti with clams and *bottarga* (mullet roe) or *tonno alla carlofortina* (tuna chunks served cold in a sweet tomato and onion sauce).

FAVOURITE SNACK SPOTS

Le Patate & Co
SNACKS €

(Scalette Santo Sepulcro 1; fries €2.50; ⊗closed dinner Mon) Antonio knocks up the freshest fries in town – cooked in olive oil until crisp, and not overly salty.

Isola del Gelato
ICE CREAM €

(Piazza Yenne 35; ice creams €1.50-4; ⊗9am-2am Tue-Sun) A hugely popular hang-out with ice-creamy treats including semifreddo and sorbet.

Gocce di Gelato e Cioccolato
SWEETS €

(Piazza del Carmine 21; ⊗noon-9pm winter, to 1am summer) Totally divine handmade *gelati*, desserts (try the mille feuille), spice-infused pralines and truffles.

Locanda Caddeo
SNACKS €

(Via Sassari 75; snacks €2.50-8; ⊗daily) A cool, gallery-style haunt for focaccia, pizza and freshly prepared salads.

I Sapori dell'Isola
DELI €

(Via Sardegna 50; ⊗daily) Friendly deli with top-notch Sardinian bread, pastries, salami, cheese, *bottarga (mullet roe)*, olive oil, wine and more.

Dal Corsaro
SARDINIAN €€€

(☏070 66 43 18; www.dalcorsaro.com; Viale Regina Margherita 28; meals €50-55; ⊗daily) At Cagliari's bastion of fine dining, Sardinian ingredients are highlighted in creative dishes such as *raviola di cipolla e pecorino semi stagionato* (onion ravioli with mature *pecorino* cheese) and roast octopus with lemongrass salsa.

 Drinking

Antico Caffè
CAFE

(www.anticocaffe1855.it; Piazza Costituzione 10; ⊗daily) DH Lawrence and Grazia Deledda once frequented this grand old cafe, which opened in 1855. Join locals to chat over leisurely coffees and frilly crêpes.

Caffè Librarium Nostrum
BAR

(Via Santa Croce 33; ⊗Tue-Sun) This modish Castello bar has panoramic seating on top of the city's medieval ramparts and occasional live music in the brick-lined interior.

Caffè degli Spiriti
BAR

(Bastione San Remy; ⊗daily) Grab a hammock, lie back and enjoy the views and vibe at this stylish lounge bar on the Bastione San Remy. If you get the munchies, order pizza (€5 to €8).

Il Merlo Parlante
PUB

(Via Portoscalas 69; ⊗Tue-Sun) Shoehorned into a narrow alley off Corso Vittorio Emanuele, this popular student pub serves lager and rock to a young international crowd.

 Entertainment

Cagliari's nightlife revolves around the city's bars and cafes, which in summer means the beach at Poetto. For the lowdown, ask at the tourist office or pick up a copy of the local newspaper *L'Unione Sarda*. Online, you'll find listings at www.sardegnaconcerti.com (in Italian).

Emerson
NIGHTCLUB

(☏070 37 51 94; Viale Poetto 4) Near the fourth bus stop at Poetto beach, this swanky seafront place is part cocktail lounge, part restaurant and part beach club. It's a chilled spot for a sundowner and occasionally hosts live music.

Teatro Lirico
THEATRE

(☏070 408 22 30; www.teatroliricodicagliari.it; Via Sant'Alenixedda) This is Cagliari's premier venue for classical music, opera and ballet. It's a 15-minute stroll east of Il Castello.

 Shopping

For boutiques and designer labels, head to Via Roma and boutique-studded Via Giuseppe Garibaldi. The Marina district harbours some enticing craft and speciality shops.

TOP CHOICE **Durke**
SWEETS, PASTRIES & CAKES

(www.durke.com; Via Napoli 66) This is an Aladdin's cave of Sardinian sweets and pastries, all prepared according to traditional recipes. Some of the best are made with nothing more than sugar, egg whites and almonds.

Sapori di Sardegna FOOD
(Vico dei Mille 1) Browse this breezy Marina emporium for fine *pecorino,* salami, *bottarga*, bread, wine and pretty-packed *dolci* (sweets).

Loredana Mandas JEWELLERY
(Via Sicilia 31) A jewellery workshop selling the fine gold filigree for which Sardinia is famous.

Mercato di San Benedetto MARKET
(Via San Francesco Cocco Ortu) Seafood, salami, *pecorino* the size of wagon wheels, horse steaks, you name it – it's all at this morning food market in Villanova, a 10- to 15-minute walk east of Il Castello.

ℹ Information

Cagliari is dotted with free wi-fi zones, but annoyingly you can only log on if you have an Italian SIM card (the password is sent to your mobile phone).

Banks and ATMs are widely available, particularly around the port and station, and on Piazza del Carmine and Corso Vittorio Emanuele.

Guardia Medica (☑070 609 52 02; Via Talete) For an emergency call-out doctor.

Lamarù (☑070 66 84 07; Via Napoli 43; per hr €3; ☺9am-8pm Mon-Sat) Speedy internet and wi-fi.

Main post office (Piazza del Carmine 28)

Tourist office (☑070 66 92 55; www.comune.cagliari.it, in Italian; Piazza Matteotti; ☺8.30am-1.30pm & 2-8pm) This friendly tourist office should be your first port of call for city information and maps.

ℹ Getting There & Away

AIR Cagliari's **Elmas airport** (☑070 21 12 11; www.sogaer.it) is 6km northwest of the centre. Flights connect with mainland Italy and European destinations including Barcelona, London, Paris and Stuttgart. In summer, there are additional charter flights.

BOAT Cagliari's ferry port is just off Via Roma. **Tirrenia** (☑892123; www.tirrenia.it; Via dei Ponente 1) is the main operator, with year-round services to Civitavecchia, Naples, Palermo and Trapani. Book tickets at the port or at travel agencies.

BUS From the main bus station on Piazza Matteotti, **Turmo Travel** (☑0789 214 87; www.gruppoturmotravel.com) runs a twice-daily service to Olbia (€19, 4¼ hours) and a daily bus to Santa Teresa di Gallura (€21, 5½ hours). **ARST** (☑800 865042; www.arst.sardegna.it, in Italian) buses serve the following destinations.

DESTINATION	FARE (€)	DURATION (HR)	FREQUENCY
Chia	4	1¼	10 daily
Iglesias	4.50	1-1½	2 daily
Nuoro	15.50	2½-5	2 daily
Oristano	7	1½	2 daily
Pula	3	¾	hourly
Sassari	18.50	3¼	3 daily
Villasimius	4	1½	6-8 daily

CAR & MOTORCYCLE The island's main dual-carriage road, the SS131 Carlo Felice Hwy, links the capital with Porto Torres via Oristano and Sassari, and Olbia via Nuoro. The SS130 leads west to Iglesias.

TRAIN The main **Trenitalia** (www.trenitalia.it) station is on Piazza Matteotti. Trains serve the following destinations.

DESTINATION	FARE (€)	DURATION (HR)	FREQUENCY
Carbonia	4.50	1	7 daily
Golfo Aranci	18	5-7	5 daily
Iglesias	4	1	16 daily
Olbia	17	4	1 daily
Oristano	6	1-2	15 daily
Porto Torres	17	4¼	1 daily
Sassari	16	3¾	3 daily

ℹ Getting Around

TO/FROM THE AIRPORT Buses run from Piazza Matteotti to Elmas airport (€4, 10 minutes, 32 daily) from 5.20am to 10.30pm. Between 9am and 10.30pm, departures are every hour and half past the hour. A taxi costs about €25.

BUS CTM (☑070 209 12 10; www.ctmcagliari.it, in Italian) bus routes cover the city and surrounding area. A standard ticket costs €1.20 and is valid for 90 minutes; a daily ticket is €3.

CAR & MOTORCYCLE On-street parking within the blue lines costs €1 per hour. Alternatively, there's a useful car park next to the train station, which costs €10 for 24 hours. **CIA Rent a Car** (☑070 65 65 03; www.ciarent.it, in Italian; Via S Agostino 13) hires out bikes, cars and scooters from €10/29/30 daily.

TAXI There are taxi ranks at Piazza Matteotti, Piazza della Repubblica and on Largo Carlo Felice. Or call **Quattro Mori** (☑070 400 101) or **Rossoblù** (☑070 66 55).

SAND IN THE CITY

An easy ride on buses PF or PQ from Piazza Matteotti, Cagliari's fabulous Poetto beach extends for 6km beyond the green Promontorio di Sant'Elia, nicknamed the Sella del Diavola (Devil's Saddle). In summer much of the city's youth decamps here to sunbathe and party in the restaurants, bars and discos that line the sand.

Water sports are big and you can hire canoes at the beach clubs. From its base at Marina Piccola, the Windsurfing Club Cagliari (www.windsurfingclubcagliari.org; Viale Marina Piccola) offers a range of courses. A course of six one-hour windsurfing lessons costs €150, while three hours of surfing instruction will set you back €120.

AROUND CAGLIARI

Stretching east and north of Cagliari, the lonely Sarrabus is one of Sardinia's least developed areas. In its centre rise the bushy green peaks of the Monte dei Sette Fratelli, a miraculously wild hinterland.

East of Poetto the SP17 hugs the coast prettily (if precariously) all the way round to Villasimius and then north along the Costa Rei.

A few kilometres short of Villasimius, a road veers south to Capo Carbonara, Sardinia's most southeasterly point. On the western side of the peninsula is a marina and what remains of a Spanish tower, the Fortezza Vecchia. To the south is lovely Spiaggia del Riso. The eastern side is dominated by the Stagno Notteri lagoon, often host to flamingos in winter. On its seaward side is the stunning Spiaggia del Simius beach with its Polynesian-blue waters.

Villasimius

A cheerful summertime resort, Villasimius is a launch pad for exploring the gorgeous sandy bays that necklace the coast. At the Porto Turistico, about 3km outside of town, you can arrange boat tours (about €65 per person) and dives (from €36) to nearby reefs and wrecks.

From May to September, campers converge on Spiaggia del Riso (☎070 79 10 52; www.villaggiospiaggiadelriso.it; Località Campulongu; camping 2 people, car & tent €21-40, 4-bed bungalows €80-160; ⊕) near the Porto Turistico. It has excellent facilities but gets hellishly crowded in summer.

Set in pristine gardens, the attractive, low-slung Hotel Mariposas (☎070 79 00 84; Viale Matteotti; s €74-132, d €96-170, f €116-200; ❋❋❖❖) is just a five-minute stroll from the beach.

Dine alfresco on Sardinian classics like *burrida* (marinated dogfish) and spaghetti with *ricci* at Ristorante Le Anforè (☎070 79 20 32; Localitá Su Cordolinu; meals €30; ⊙Tue-Sun).

ARST buses run to and from Cagliari (€4, 1½ hours, six to eight daily) throughout the year.

Costa Rei

From Villasimius, the SP17 skirts the coast north to the Costa Rei. About 25km out of Villasimius you hit Cala Sinzias, a pretty sandy strand with two campgrounds. Continue for a further 6km and you come to the Costa Rei resort, a holiday village full of villas, shops, bars, clubs and a few indifferent eateries. Spiaggia Costa Rei is a dazzling-white beach lapped by remarkably clear blue-green water.

By the resort's southern entrance and open from May to October, pine-shaded Camping Capo Ferrato (☎070 99 10 12; www.campingcapoferrato.it; camping 2 people, car & tent €16-37.50) has direct access to the beach.

North of the resort, Spiaggia Piscina Rei continues the theme of blinding-white sand and turquoise water. A couple more beaches fill the remaining length of coast up to Capo Ferrato, beyond which drivable dirt trails lead north.

Nora & Around

About 30km southwest of Cagliari, the archaeological zone of Nora (adult/reduced incl Museo Archeologico in Pula €6.50/2.50; ⊙9am-7.30pm) is what's left of a once-powerful ancient city. Founded by Phoenicians in the 11th century BC, it passed into Carthaginian hands before being taken over by the Romans and becoming one of the most important cities on the island. Upon entry,

WORTH A TRIP

TRENINO VERDE

If you're not in a rush, take a slow, nostalgic ride through Sardinia's rugged interior on the narrow-gauge Trenino Verde (www.treninoverde.com). There are four routes: Mandas–Arbatax, Isili–Sorgono, Macomer–Bosa and Sassari–Palau. Of these, the twisting Mandas–Arbatax line is particularly spectacular, crossing the remote highlands of the Parco Nazionale del Golfo di Orosei e del Gennargentu.

From the metro station on Piazza Repubblica in Cagliari, a metro runs to Monserrato where you can connect with trains for Mandas. The Trenino Verde runs between mid-June and early September.

you pass a single melancholy column from a former temple and then a small but beautifully preserved Roman theatre. To the west are the substantial remains of the Terme al Mare (Baths by the Sea). Four columns stand at the heart of what was a patrician villa; the surrounding rooms retain their mosaic floor decoration.

In nearby Pula, the one-room Museo Archeologico (☑070 920 96 10; Corso Vittorio Emanuele 67; admission €2.50, incl Nora €6.50; ⏰9am-8pm Tue-Sun summer to 5.30pm winter) displays finds from Nora, including ceramics found in Punic and Roman tombs, some gold and bone jewellery, and Roman glassware.

For further information about Pula and the surrounding area, ask at the helpful tourist office (☑347 2377842; Piazza del Popolo; ⏰9am-1pm & 3-7pm Mon-Fri, 9am-1pm Sat) just off the town's main hub, Piazza del Popolo.

From Pula, the SS195 follows the coast round to Chia and the stunning Costa del Sud. But unless you're staying at one of the self-contained resort hotels that hog this stretch of coast, you're unlikely to glimpse much sea.

Accommodation tends to be expensive in these parts, but you can still find some affordable, locally run places. Off the road to Santa Margherita di Pula is B&B S'Olivariu (☑339 3674088; SS195 km33, Santa Margherita di Pula; s €35-60, d €70-120; ✷⏩), a lovely, authentic farm B&B surrounded by fragrant fruit trees; and Camping Flumendosa (☑070 920

83 64; www.campingflumendosa.it; SS195 km33, Santa Margherita di Pula; camping 2 people, car & tent €33; ⏩), set in pine and eucalyptus trees near the beach. Camping in this area is blissful in low season, when the temperatures are cooler and the beaches quieter.

Regular buses connect Pula and Cagliari (€3.50, 45 minutes). From Pula there are frequent shuttle buses down to Nora (€1), 4km away.

Costa del Sud & Around

One of the most beautiful stretches of coast in southern Sardinia, the Costa del Sud runs 25km from Chia to Porto Teulada. Popular with windsurfers and kitesurfers, Chia's two ravishing beaches are golden strips of sand divided by a Pisan watchtower, while 3km away there's a magnificent strip of sand at Tueredda. As you wind your way towards the high point of Capo Malfatano there are wonderful views around every corner.

Budget accommodation is available in two camp grounds at either end of the coastal run – this is a fantastic area for camping. At Chia, there's Campeggio Torre Chia (☑070 923 00 54; www.campeggiotorrechia. it; camping 2 people, car & tent €36), a busy spot a few hundred metres back from the beach, while 25km to the west, Portu Tramatzu Camping Comunale (☑070 928 30 27; Località Porto Tramatzu; camping 2 people, car & tent €35; ⏰summer) has modest facilities and an on-site diving centre near Porto Teulada.

Some 25km inland, Le Grotte Is Zuddas (☑0781 95 57 41; www.grotteiszuddas.com, in Italian; adult/reduced €9/6; ⏰9.30am-noon & 2.30-6pm daily summer, noon-4pm Mon-Fri, 9.30am-noon & 2.30-6pm Sat-Sun winter) is a spectacular cave system.

From Cagliari, there are buses to and from Chia (€4, 1¼ hours, 10 daily). Between mid-June and mid-September, two daily buses ply the Costa del Sud.

IGLESIAS & THE SOUTHWEST

Iglesias

POP 27,593

Surrounded by the skeletons of Sardinia's once-thriving mining industry, Iglesias bubbles in the summer and slumbers in the colder months. Its historical centre, an appealing ensemble of lived-in piazzas, sun-bleached buildings and Aragonese-style wrought-iron balconies, creates an atmosphere that is as much Iberian as Sardinian – a vestige of its history as a Spanish colony. Visit at Easter to experience a quasi-Seville experience during the extraordinary drumbeating processions.

The Romans called the town Metalla after the precious metals mined here, especially lead and silver. Mining equipment dating back to the Carthaginian era was discovered in the 19th century.

◉ Sights

Centro Storico HISTORICAL CENTRE

Iglesias' central square, **Piazza Quintino Sella** was laid out in the 19th century in what was at the time a field outside the city walls. Just off the square, scruffy stairs leading up to a stout tower are all that remains of **Castello Salvaterra**, a Pisan fortress built in the 13th century. A stretch of the northwestern perimeter wall survives along Via Campidano.

Dominating the eastern flank of Piazza del Municipio in the heart of the *centro storico* (historic centre), the **Duomo** (Piazza del Municipio) is still closed for renovation, but retains a lovely Pisan-flavoured facade, as does the bell tower, with its chequerboard stonework.

FREE **Museo dell'Arte Mineraria** MUSEUM

(☑0781 35 00 37; www.museoartemineraria.it; Via Roma 47; ☺7-9pm Sat-Sun summer, by appointment rest of year) Bone up on Iglesias' mining history at this former mining school. You can experience the harsh conditions in which miners worked in a series of recreated mine shafts.

🍴 Sleeping & Eating

La Babbajola B&B B&B €

(☑347 614 46 21; www.lababbajola.it; Via Giordano 13; r per person €25-30; ❄) This laid-back, homey B&B is in a gorgeous old mansion, inside the *centro storico*, run by the friendly Carla and her mother. Accommodation is in a mini-apartment or one of three big double rooms, each of which features patterned old floor tiles, bold colours and tasteful furniture. There's a kitchen and TV room for guest use. Two of the three double rooms share a bathroom.

Eurohotel HOTEL €€

(☑0781 226 43; www.eurohoteliglesias.it; Via Fratelli Bandieri 34; s €60-80, d €85-110; ⓟ❄) A five-minute walk from the centre, this welcoming hotel resembles a kitsch Pompeian villa, with its porticoed entrance and gleefully OTT decor. The restaurant is a good bet for a no-nonsense evening meal (€25 to €30).

Pintadera OSTERIA €€

(☑0781 251 864; Viua Mannu 22-24; meals €35-40; ☺daily; ❄) It's a real treat to eat in Pintadera, a welcoming family-run *osteria* (casual tavern or eatery presided over by a host) in the *centro storico*. A mother-and-son outfit, it's where you should focus on the excellent meat, from the sausage-soaked pasta to goat, mutton or beef.

❶ Getting There & Away

Buses for Cagliari (€4.50, 1 to 1½ hours, two daily) arrive at and depart from Via XX Settembre. Get tickets from **Bar Giardini** (Via Oristano 8) across the park. From the train station on Via Garibaldi, a 15-minute walk from the town centre, there are up to 10 daily trains to Cagliari (€3.85, one hour, 16 daily).

Around Iglesias

A winding 15km drive north of Iglesias (follow signs for Fluminimaggiore) brings you to the sand-coloured **Tempio di Antas** (☑0781 58 09 90; adult/reduced €3/2; ☺9.30am-7.30pm summer, 9.30-4.30pm Tue-Sun winter), an impressive Roman temple set in bucolic scenery. The 3rd-century temple was built by the Roman emperor Caracalla over a 6th-century-BC Punic sanctuary, which itself stood over an earlier *nuraghic* settlement. From near the ticket office a path marked Antica Strada Romana, Antas Su Mannau leads to what little remains of this settlement. About 1½ hours further on is the **Grotta di Su Mannau** (☑0781 58 04 11; www.sumannau.it; adult/reduced €6/3.10; ☺9.30am-6.30pm summer, to 5.30pm winter), an 8km-long cave complex with incredible rock formations.

About 10km east of Iglesias, the unremarkable town of **Domusnovas** sits at the centre of one of Sardinia's most exciting rock-climbing areas. The outlying countryside is peppered with limestone rocks, cliffs and caves, many of which are ideal for sports climbing. For technical information, check out www.climb-europe.com/sardinia and www.sardiniaclimb.com.

Four kilometres north of town, the 850m-long **Grotta di San Giovanni** is an impressive sight. Eight daily buses connect Iglesias and Domusnovas (€1, 15 minutes).

Iglesiente Coast

Iglesias' local beach is at **Funtanamare** (also spelt Fontanamare), about 8km west of town. From Funtanamare, the SP83 coastal road affords spectacular views as it dips, bends and climbs its way northward. Dominating the seascape off **Nebida**, 5.5km to the north, is the 133m-high **Scoglio Pan di Zucchero** (Sugarloaf Rock), the largest of several *faraglioni* (sea stacks) that rise out of the glassy blue waters. A small and rather drab village, Nebida is a former mining settlement sprawled along the road high above the sea. Near its southern entrance, **Pan di Zucchero** (⊘0781 4 71 14; www.hotelpandizucchero.it; Via Centrale 365; s/d €50/65, half-board per person €70) is a family-run *pensione* with neat, modestly furnished rooms and a panoramic restaurant (meals €30 to €35).

A few kilometres north, **Masua** is another former mining centre. Seen from above, it looks pretty ugly, but it's not without interest. The main draw is the town's unique mining port, **Porto Flavia** (⊘closed to public). In 1924 two 600m tunnels were dug into the cliffs. In the lower of the two a conveyor belt received zinc and lead ore from the underground deposits and transported it via an ingenious mobile loading arm directly to the ships moored below.

Local buses run between Iglesias and Masua, stopping off at Nebida (€1.50, 30 minutes, 10 daily).

Beyond Masua, and signposted off the SP83, **Cala Domestica** is a cool sandy beach wedged into a natural inlet. **Buggerru**, the biggest village on this stretch of coastline and another former mining settlement, won't delay you long, but it has a useful **tourist office** (⊘0781 5 40 93; SP83; ⊘7am-8.30pm) on the main road. If the office is shut, ask at the adjacent bar.

The road out of Buggerru climbs high along the cliffs for a couple of kilometres before descending down to **Spiaggia Portixeddu**, one of the area's best beaches. At its southern tip, you can dine on pizza and fresh fish at **Ristorante San Nicolò** (⊘0781 5 43 59; Località San Nicolò; pizzas/meals €7/30).

Accommodation in the area is limited, but the **Hotel Golfo del Leone** (⊘0781 549 52; www.golfodelleone.it; Località Caburu de Figu; s €50-110, d €63-180) boasts sunny sea-facing rooms about 1km back from the beach. Service is friendly and the helpful staff can organise horse-riding excursions. The adjacent restaurant serves up decent local food for about €25 to €30 per head.

Inland, there are several *agriturismi*, including **Biologico Fighezia** (⊘348 0698303; www.agriturismofighezia.it; Località Fighezia, Fluminimaggiore; half-board per person €55-60, B&B in winter per person €35-40). Set in tranquil countryside, it offers lush views and cabin-style rooms decorated with terracotta tiles, solid wooden fixtures and private terraces. Dinner is served on a large communal table on the terrace of the main house.

Carbonia & Around

POP 29,821

You won't miss much if you bypass **Carbonia**, a drab town built by Mussolini to house workers from the nearby Sirai-Serbariu coalfield. However, in the vicinity there are a couple of sights worth a detour. The **Museo del Carbone** (⊘0781 67 05 91; www.museodelcarbone.it; Località Grande Miniera di Serbariu; adult/reduced €6/4; ⊘10.30am-7.30pm daily summer, 10am-6pm Tue-Sun winter) offers a chastening look into the life of Carbonia's miners, with an interesting collection of machines, photos and equipment, and guided tours into the claustrophobic mine shafts.

Sant'Antioco & San Pietro

POP 18,330

These islands off Sardinia's southwestern coast display very different characters. Both are popular summer destinations but Isola Sant'Antioco, the larger and more developed of the two, is less obviously picturesque, with a rocky Sardinian landscape and gritty working port. Barely half an hour across the water, the pastel houses and bobbing fishing boats of Isola di San Pietro are much more what you'd expect of a holiday island.

◉ Sights & Activities

The main sights are in Sant'Antioco. Up in the high part of town, the **Basilica di Sant'Antioco Martire** (Piazza Parrocchia 22) is a sublimely simple 5th-century church set over an extensive system of creepy **catacombs** (guided tours €3).

On the outskirts of town, the excellent **Museo Archeologico** (☎0781 821 05; www.archeotur.it, in Italian; admission €6/3.50; ⊙9am-7pm) contains a fascinating collection of local archaeological finds.

For beaches head to **Maladroixa** and **Spiaggia Coa Quaddus** on the eastern coast.

Over on Isola San Pietro the main activity is wandering the streets of laid-back **Carloforte**, the main town. On the seafront, **Cartur Dea** (☎0781 85 43 31; Molo Tagliafico) is one of several outfits offering boat tours. Bank on about €30 per person. In late May or early June, Carloforte's big annual event, the four-day **Girotonno** (www.girotonno.org) festival, is dedicated to the island's traditional tuna kill, known locally as the *mattanza*.

🛏 Sleeping

Hotel California   HOTEL €
(☎0781 85 44 70; www.hotelcaliforniacarloforte.it; Via Cavallera 15, Carloforte; s €35-50, d €45-90) In Carloforte, this superfriendly family-run *pensione* is in a residential street a few blocks back from the *lungomare* (seafront promenade). It's a modest place, but the spacious, sun-filled rooms are more than adequate and its location ensures a good night's sleep.

Hotel Moderno   HOTEL €
(☎0781 8 31 05; www.albergoristorantemoderno.com; Via Nazionale 82, Sant'Antioco; s €45-60, d €70-100; ❄) A bright, welcoming hotel on the main road into Sant'Antioco. Rooms are agreeable with a relaxing cream-and-salmon colour scheme and big, comfy beds. Downstairs, the airy restaurant (open April to October) serves a good line in local fish.

🍴 Eating

Tuna is king of San Pietro cuisine and features on almost all island menus (May to August only).

Ristorante 7 Nani   TRATTORIA €€
(☎0781 84 09 00; Via Garibaldi 139; pizzas/meals €7/30; ⊙Wed-Mon) This laid-back Sant'Antioco trattoria has simple wood tables, a garden dining area and pictures of Snow White's seven dwarves. The wood-fired pizzas are superb, the seafood is fresh and the local *mirto* (a berry-based liqueur) a sweet way to finish off.

Osteria della Tonnara   OSTERIA €€
(☎078 185 57 34; Corso Battellieri 36; meals €35; ⊙Jun-Sep) Run by Isola San Pietro's tuna cooperative, this is the place to try *tonno alla*

> **DON'T MISS**
>
> ## TOP FIVE BEACHES IN SARDINIA
>
> » **Spiaggia Piscinas** (p821)
> » **Chia** (p818)
> » **Spiaggia del Principe** (p834)
> » **Is Aruttas** (p826)
> » **Cala Mariolu** (boxed text, p845)

carlofortina. Bookings are recommended and credit cards are not accepted.

ℹ Information

Tourist office San Pietro (☎0781 85 40 09; www.prolococarloforte.it, in Italian; Piazza Carlo Emanuele III 19; ⊙10am-1pm & 5-8pm); Sant'Antioco (☎0781 8 20 31; Via Roma 43; ⊙10.30am-1pm & 4.30-6.30pm Mon-Fri)

ℹ Getting There & Around

Sant'Antioco is connected to the mainland by a bridge and is accessible by bus from Iglesias (€3, 1¾ hours) and Carbonia (€1, 50 minutes). To get to Isola San Pietro (Carloforte), you'll need to catch a ferry from Portovesme (€6/20 per person/car, 30 minutes, at least 15 daily) or from Calasetta on Isola Sant'Antioco (€1.70/15 per person/car, 13 daily).

Local buses run around Sant'Antioco, and limited summertime services operate on San Pietro. Tickets cost €1.

Costa Verde

One of Sardinia's great untamed coastal stretches, the Costa Verde (Green Coast) extends northward from Capo Pecora to the small resort of Torre dei Corsari. This is an area of wild, exhilarating beauty and spectacular, unspoilt beaches.

To reach the area's two best beaches, head inland from Portixeddu along the SS126 and follow signs for Arbus. Signs off to the left direct you to Gennamari, Bau and **Spiaggia Scivu**, a golden beach backed by 70m-high sand dunes. A further 4km beyond this turn-off is another for the ghost town of **Ingurtosu** and beyond that, the magnificent and untamed **Spiaggia Piscinas**, a broad swath of virgin sand wedged between a desert of imposing dunes and a wild, untamed sea. Note that the route down to the beach involves at least 10km of dirt-track driving.

If you want to stay in the area, there's an excellent *agriturismo* off the SP65 between Montevecchio and Torre dei Corsari. **Agriturismo L'Oasi del Cervo** (📞347 301 13 18; www.oasidelcervo.com; Località Is Gennas Arbus; half-board per person €43-60) is as authentic as it gets, a working farm at the end of a 2.5km dirt track in the middle of silent green hills. Rooms are extremely simple, but the location and the superb homemade food more than compensate.

You'll really need a car to explore the Costa Verde; however, during July and August, a bus runs daily from Oristano to Torre dei Corsari (€4, 1½ hours).

ORISTANO & THE WEST

Oristano

POP 32,156

With its elegant shopping streets, ornate piazzas and popular cafes, Oristano's animated centre makes a great base for exploring this part of the island. The city was founded in the 11th century and became capital of the Giudicato d'Arborea, one of Sardinia's four independent provinces. Eleonora d'Arborea, a heroine in the Joan of Arc mould, became head of the *giudicato*

Oristano

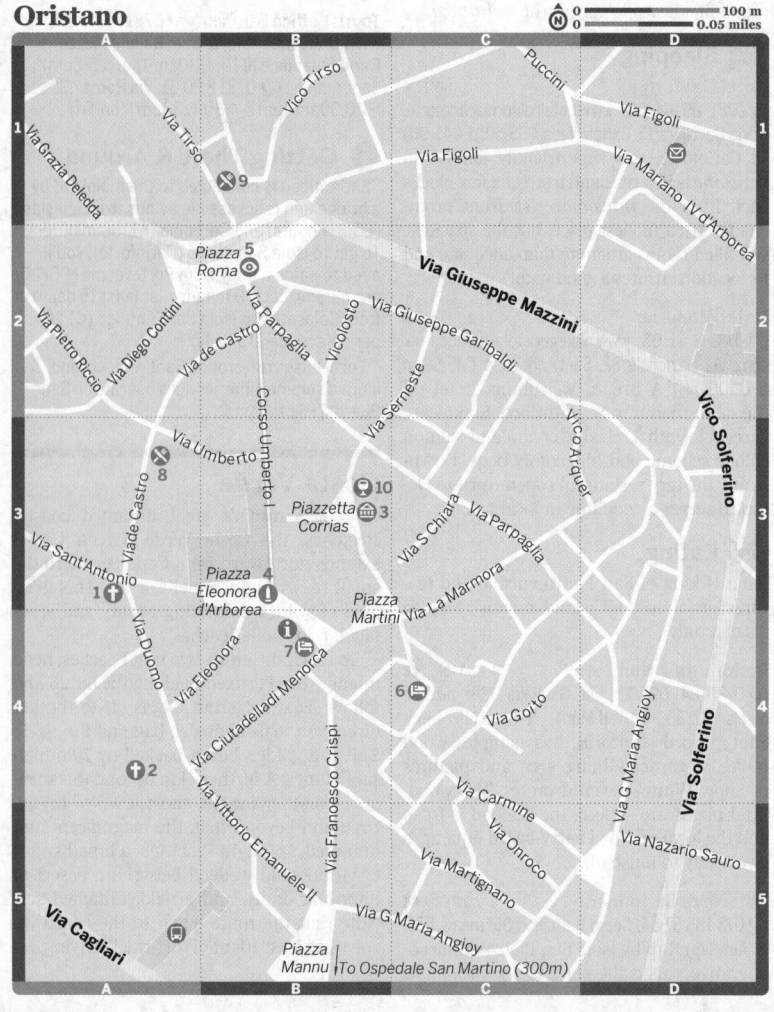

in 1383 and led the fierce resistance against the island's Spanish invaders. But with her death, anti-Spanish opposition crumbled and Oristano was incorporated into the rest of Aragon-controlled Sardinia. Eleonora is also remembered for her celebrated *Carta di Logu* (Code of Laws), an extraordinary law code that tackled land and property legislation as well as introducing a raft of women's rights.

◉ Sights

Centro Storico
HISTORICAL CENTRE

One of the few vestiges of Oristano's medieval past, the 13th-century **Torre di Mariano II** (Piazza Roma) was the town's northern gate and an important part of the city defences. From here, pedestrianised Corso Umberto I leads to Piazza Eleonora d'Arborea, Oristano's elegant outdoor salon. In the centre stands an ornate 19th-century **statue of Eleonora**, raising a finger as if about to launch into a political discourse. Nearby, the neoclassical **Chiesa di San Francesco** (Via Sant'Antonio) harbours a 14th-century wooden sculpture, the *Crocifisso di Nicodemo*, considered one of Sardinia's most precious carvings. Follow Via Duomo to the **Duomo** (Piazza del Duomo), built in the 13th century but remodelled 500 years later. Its freestanding *campanile* (bell tower), topped by a conspicuous majolica-tiled dome, adds an exotic Byzantine look to Oristano's skyline.

Around 3km south of Oristano at Santa Giusta is the 12th-century **Basilica di Santa Giusta**, one of Sardinia's finest Tuscan-style Romanesque churches.

Museo Antiquarium Arborense
MUSEUM

(☑0783 79 12 62; www.antiquariumarborense. it, in Italian; Piazza Corrias; adult/reduced €3/1; ◐9am-2pm & 3-8pm) This museum contains one of the island's major archaeological collections, with prehistoric artefacts from the Sinis Peninsula and finds from Carthaginian and Roman Tharros. There's also a small collection of *retablos* (painted altarpieces), including the 16th-century *Retablo del Santo Cristo,* which depicts a decorative series of Franciscan saints.

✹ Festivals & Events

Sa Sartiglia
RELIGIOUS FESTIVAL

One of Sardinia's top festivals, Oristano's Sa Sartiglia is held over two days: Sunday and *martedì grasso* (Shrove Tuesday or Mardi Gras). It involves a costumed medieval joust and some amazing acrobatic horse riding.

⌨ Sleeping

TOP CHOICE Eleonora B&B
B&B €

(☑0783 7 04 35; www.eleonora-bed-and-breakfast. com; Piazza Eleonora d'Arborea 12; s €35-50, d €60-70, apt €80; ❇🤶) Possibly one of the island's most charming B&Bs, the Eleonora is housed in a medieval *palazzo* on Oristano's central piazza. The rooms are tastefully decorated with antique furniture and the floors are covered in gorgeous old tiles. Wi-fi is available. There's an elegant, two-bedroom loft apartment, ideal for longer stays.

B&B L'Arco
B&B €

(☑0783 7 28 49; www.arcobedandbreakfast.it; Vico Ammirato 12; s/d without bathroom €40/65) Set inside a couple's home, L'Arco sits hidden away in a quiet cul-de-sac near Piazza Martini. There are only two guestrooms but they are spacious and tastefully decorated with exposed-wood beams, terracotta tiles and dark-wood furnishings. Breakfast is served in the family kitchen, and there's a small terrace upstairs.

✗ Eating & Drinking

TOP CHOICE Trattoria Gino
TRATTORIA €€

(☑0783 7 14 28; Via Tirso 13; meals €25-30; ◐Mon-Sat) A wonderful, simple trattoria set in one neat room, the quality of the food in Gino's explains its sustained popularity since the 1930s. Try the simple and fragrant sage and ricotta ravioli, and follow with a char-grilled *seppia* (cuttlefish) studded with fresh cherry tomatoes. Watch out for the lemon *sorbetto* – it's laced with vodka!

Ristorante Craf   OSTERIA €€

(☑0783 7 06 69; Via de Castro 34; meals €35-40;
☺Mon-Sat) This is a place with a huge reputation among the locals. Housed in a former
17th-century granary, the brick-vaulted dining rooms and folksy clutter can feel either
claustrophobic or cosy. Hearty country fare
dominates the menu – try the *panne frattau*
(Sardinian bread soup), pasta with legumes,
grilled meat including *asinello* (donkey),
and homemade *amaretti* (almond biscuits).

Lola Mundo   TRATTORIA €

(Piazzetta Corrias 14; ☺Mon-Sat) With its
piazza seating and relaxing music, Lola
Mundo is a good spot to hang out over an
aperitif. A favourite with the locals.

❶ Information

Farmacia San Carlo (☑0783 7 11 23; Piazza
Eleonora d'Arborea 10/11) For all your medical
needs.

Genius Point (Via Pietro Riccio 4; per hr €4;
☺8.30am-1pm & 4-8pm Mon-Sat) Internet
access.

Ospedale San Martino (☑0783 31 71; Piazza
San Martino) Local hospital.

Post office (Via Mariano IV d'Arborea)

Tourist office (☑0783 368 32 10; turismo@
provincia.or.it; Piazza Eleonora d'Arborea 19;
☺9am-1pm Mon-Fri & 4-6.30pm Mon-Thu)
Friendly and English-speaking staff are eager to
offer information on Oristano and the region.

❶ Getting There & Around

From the bus station on Via Cagliari buses leave
for the following destinations:

TO	FARE (€)	DURATION (HR)	FREQUENCY
Cagliari	7	1½	2 daily
Nuoro	7	2½	6 daily
Santa Giusta	1	¼	half-hourly
Sassari	8-10	2	3 daily

The main train station is in Piazza Ungheria,
east of the town centre. Up to 15 daily trains run
between Oristano and Cagliari (€6, one to two
hours).

City buses on the *azzurra* (blue) line run
from Via Cagliari to the beach at Marina di Tor-
regrande (€1, or €1.20 if bought on bus, 20
minutes).

Barumini & Around

In the heart of voluptuous green countryside
near Barumini, the **Nuraghe Su Nuraxi**
(www.nuraghi.org; adult/reduced €7/5; ☺9am-7pm
summer, to 6pm spring & autumn, to 4pm winter) is
Sardinia's sole World Heritage Site and the
island's most visited *nuraghe* (stone tower).
The focal point is the tower dating from
1500 BC, which originally stood on its own
but was later incorporated into a fortified
compound. The first village buildings were
erected in the Iron Age, and it's these that
constitute the beehive of circular interlocking buildings that spread across the grass.

In Barumini, **Albergo Sa Lolla** (☑070
936 84 19; www.wels.it/salolla; Via Cavour 49; s/d
€50/70; P❊☎) is a tastefully refurbished
farmstead with seven airy rooms and an
excellent restaurant (meals €30). Note that
breakfast costs an extra €6.

Five kilometres west of Barumini, the
village of **Tuili** is a gateway to **La Giara di
Gesturi**, a high basalt plateau famous for its
population of wild *cavallini* (literally 'mini-
horses'), most likely seen by shallow *pauli*
(seasonal lakes) at daybreak or dusk.

To the east, it's a 25km drive to the village
of Serri and the **Santuario Santa Vittoria
di Serri** (adult/concession €4/2; ☺9am-7pm
summer, to 5pm winter), the most extensive
nuraghic settlement unearthed in Sardinia.

Three weekday buses run from Cagliari
to Barumini (€4.50, 1½ hours); otherwise,
you'll need your own transport.

Sinis Peninsula

West of Oristano, the Sinis Peninsula feels
like a world apart with its glassy lagoons,
low-lying countryside and snow-white
beaches. The main sight is the ancient town
of Tharros.

THARROS & AROUND

The blue choppy waters of the Golfo di
Oristano form the ideal backdrop to the
ruins of ancient **Tharros** (☑0783 39 73 06;
admission incl Museo Civico in Cabras €7; ☺9am-
8pm summer, to 5pm winter). Founded by the
Phoenicians in the 8th century BC, Tharros thrived as a Carthaginian naval base
and was later taken over by the Romans.
Much of what you see today dates from the
2nd and 3rd centuries AD, when the basalt
streets were laid and the aqueduct, baths
and other major monuments were built.

To the untrained eye, the strange stone circles that litter Sardinia's interior are mysterious and incomprehensible. But to archaeologists they provide one of the few windows into the dark world of the Bronze Age *nuraghe* people. There are said to be up to 7000 *nuraghi* (stone towers) across the island, most built between 1800 and 500 BC. No one is absolutely certain what they were used for, although most experts think they were defensive watchtowers.

Even before they started building *nuraghi,* the Sardinians were busy digging tombs into the rock, known as *domus de janas* (fairy houses). More elaborate were the common graves fronted by stele called *tombe dei giganti* (giants' tombs).

Evidence of pagan religious practices is provided by *pozzi sacri* (well temples). Built from around 1000 BC, these were often constructed to capture light at the yearly equinoxes, hinting at a naturalistic religion as well as sophisticated building techniques. The well temple at Santa Cristina is a prime example.

On the side of the road just before Tharros, you'll see the 6th-century **Chiesa di San Giovanni di Sinis** (⊙9am-7pm summer, to 5pm winter), one of oldest churches in Sardinia.

Some 4km north, the weird village of **San Salvatore** is worth a quick look. Used as a spaghetti-western film set during the 1960s, it is centred on a dusty town square surrounded by rows of tiny terraced houses, known as *cumbessias*. In the piazza, the 16th-century **Chiesa di San Salvatore** (⊙9.30am-1pm year-round, 3.30-6pm Mon-Sat summer) is built over a pagan sanctuary dating from the *nuraghic* period.

A fantastic place to eat nearby is **Peschiera Pontis** (⚐0783 39 17 74; Strada Provinciale 6; menus €25-30) a restaurant fronting the Pontis fishing cooperative, on the road between Cabras and Tharros. You'll get abundant antipasti, *primo* (first course), *secondo* (second course), desserts and wine in the fixed-price menus, and the freshest fish you're likely to taste on the island.

Just beyond the turn-off for the village, the excellent **Agriturismo Su Pranu** (⚐0783 39 25 61; www.agriturismosupranu.com; Località San Salvatore; half-board per person €52-60; ▣) is a genuine working farm offering six bright guestrooms and superb home-grown food.

In July and August, there are five daily buses for San Giovanni in Sinis from Oristano (€1.50, 35 minutes).

CABRAS
POP 8700
This straggling lagoon town is really only worth stopping at for the **Museo Civico** (⚐0783 29 06 36; www.penisoladelsinis.it, in Italian; Via Tharros 121; adult/reduced incl Tharros €7/3; ⊙9am-1pm & 4-8pm summer, 9am-1pm &

3-7pm winter) at the southern end of the town. It houses finds from the prehistoric site of **Cuccuru Is Arrius**, 3km to the southwest, and Tharros. Buses run every 20 minutes or so from Oristano (€1, 15 minutes).

RIOLA SARDO
POP 2140
The single main reason to stop off at this otherwise drab town is to stay at the wonderful **Hotel Lucrezia** (⚐0783 41 20 78; www.hotellucrezia.it; Via Roma 14a; s €85-100, d €130-160; ▣@). Housed in an ancient family *cortile* (courtyard house), the luxuriously rustic rooms surround an inner courtyard complete with a wisteria-draped pergola, and fig and citrus trees. Free bikes are provided, and the welcoming staff regularly organise cooking, painting and wine-tasting courses.

North Oristano Coast

North of the Sinis Peninsula, there are some superb beaches in and around the popular resort of **Santa Caterina di Pittinuri**. These include **Spiaggia dell'Arco** at **S'Archittu**, and further south, **Is Arenas**, one of the longest beaches in the area. Nearby, **Camping Is Arenas** (⚐0783 5 21 03; www.campingisarenas.it; camping per person €4-6, per tent & car €5-9, 2-person bungalows €50-90) is one of three camping grounds in the vicinity. Large and well-equipped, it has tent sites and bungalows immersed in pine trees.

Inland, the **Monti Ferru** massif (105m) is a beautiful and largely uncontaminated area of ancient forests, natural springs and small market towns. There's some great walking in the area and gourmets will enjoy the wonderful food.

THE BEACHES OF THE SINIS PENINSULA

The Sinis Peninsula's beaches are among the best on the island. One of the most famous is Is Aruttas, whose prized white quartz sand was for years carted off to be used in aquariums and on beaches on the Costa Smeralda. However, it's now illegal to take any. The beach is signposted and is 5km west off the main road north from San Salvatore.

Within walking distance of the beach, Camping Is Aruttas (☎0783 39 11 08; www.campingisaruttas.it; Località Marina Aruttas; camping 2 people, car & tent €35; ☉summer) has modest camping facilities set amid olive trees and Mediterranean shrubbery.

At the north of the peninsula, the popular surfing beach of Putzu Idu is backed by a motley set of holiday homes, beach bars and surfing outlets. One such, the Capo Mannu Kite School (☎347 0077035; www.capomannukiteschool.it), runs kitesurfing lessons for all levels. For underwater thrills, 9511 Diving (☎349 291 37 65; www.9511.it) runs dives and snorkelling trips, as well as excursions to the eloquently named Isola di Mal di Ventre (Stomach-ache Island), 10km off the coast. As a rough guide, reckon on €35 to €40+ for a standard dive and about €50 for an excursion over to Isola di Male di Ventre.

Two weekday buses run to Putzu Idu from Oristano (€2.50, 55 minutes). In July and August, there are four additional services.

From Oristano, five weekday buses run to Santa Caterina (€2, 40 minutes) and S'Archittu (€2, 40 minutes). Extra services are added in July and August.

LAGO OMEDEO CIRCUIT

Follow the SS131 north out of Oristano for the Nuraghe Santa Cristina (☎0785 5 54 38; admission incl Museo Archeologico-Etnografico in Paulilatino €7; ☉8.30am-sunset), an important *nuraghe* whose extraordinary Bronze Age *tempio a pozzo* (well-temple) is one of the best preserved in Sardinia. Finds from the site can be viewed a few kilometres up the road at Paulilatino's small Museo Archeo-logico-Etnografico (☎0785 5 54 38; Via Nazionale 127; admission incl Nuraghe Santa Cristina €7; ☉9.30am-1pm & 4-7pm Tue-Sun summer, 9am-1pm & 3-5.30pm Tue-Sun winter).

Just north of Paulilatino is another major *nuraghe*, the impressive Nuraghe Losa (☎0785 5 23 02; www.nuraghelosa.net; adult/reduced €3.50/2; ☉9am-1hr before sunset) dating from 1500 BC.

Your own transport is needed to get to most of these sights, although buses do run from Oristano to Abbasanta (€2.50, 55 minutes), via Paulilatino. These will drop you within walking distance of Nuraghe Losa.

BOSA
POP 8138

Bosa is one of Sardinia's most attractive towns. Seen from a distance, its rainbow townscape resembles a vibrant Paul Klee canvas, with pastel houses stacked on a steep hillside, tapering up to a stark, grey

castle. In front, moored fishing boats bob on the glassy Temo river and palm trees line an elegant riverfront. Three kilometres west, Bosa Marina, the town's satellite beach resort, is less obviously attractive, with modern low-rise hotels, restaurants and holiday homes.

◉ Sights & Activities

It's quite a climb up to Bosa's hilltop castle, Castello Malaspina (☎333 5445675; adult/reduced €2.50/1; ☉10am-12.30pm Sat & Sun or by reservation), built in 1112 by a noble Tuscan family. Note that these opening times often change, and it might well be open for longer during summer.

Down below, the Museo Casa Deriu (☎0785 37 70 43; Corso Vittorio Emanuele 59; adult/reduced €4.50/3; ☉10am-1pm & 4-6pm Tue-Sun) illustrates the town's history, including a section on Bosa's old tanning industry. Also of interest is the Gothic-Romanesque Cattedrale di San Pietro Extramuros, 2km from the old bridge on the south bank of the Temo.

Bosa has much to offer outdoor enthusiasts. You can hire bikes and scooters at Cuccu (☎0785 37 54 16; Via Roma 5), a mechanics' on the southern side of the river, for €8/40 per day for a bike/scooter. At Bosa Marina, Bosa Diving (☎335 8189748; www.bosadiving.it, in Italian; Via Colombo 2) runs dives (from €40) and snorkelling excursions (€20), and rents out canoes (double canoe €10 per hour) and dinghies (from €25 per hour).

🛏 Sleeping & Eating

TOP CHOICE Corte Fiorita HOTEL €€

(☎0785 37 70 58; www.albergo-diffuso.it; Via Lungo Temo de Gasperi 45; s €45-90, d €65-115; ❄@) Corte Fiorita has beautiful, spacious rooms in four refurbished *palazzi* across town – one on the riverfront and three in the historic centre. No two rooms are exactly the same, but you'll generally find plenty of exposed stonework, wooden beams and vaulted ceilings. Mini-apartments are also available for longer stays (€390 to €950 per week).

La Torre di Alice B&B €

(☎0785 85 04 04; www.latorredialice.it; Via del Carmine 7; s €30-40, d €50-70; @) Set in a wonderful old house in Bosa's medieval centre, you'll notice La Torre di Alice by its bright colours and wacky signpost outside. The rooms are neat and comfortable, with wrought-iron beds and relaxing decor.

🍃 Bio Agriturismo Bainas AGRITURISMO €

(☎339 2090967, 0785 37 31 29; www.agriturismo bainasbosa.com; Via San Pietro; s €30-45, d €60-75, q €118-136) Surrounded by fields of artichokes, and olive and orange orchards, this modest *agriturismo* is about a kilometre outside of town. Meals €20.

Sa Pischedda SEAFOOD €€

(☎0785 37 30 65; Via Roma 8; meals €30-35, pizzas €7; ⊙Wed-Mon, daily summer) At the hotel of the same name, this is one of Bosa's best restaurants. Speciality of the house is stylishly presented fish, both seawater and freshwater, but it also does excellent pizza and pasta. Reservations in summer are a good idea.

La Pulce Rossa SARDINIAN €€

(☎0785 37 56 57; Via Lungo Temo Amendola 1; pizzas/meals €6/25; ⊙Tue-Sun) A 20-minute walk from the centre, this friendly family-run restaurant serves filling working-man's fare at decidedly untouristy prices. Try the house speciality, *pennette 'Pulce Rossa'*, a rich concoction of pasta, giant prawns, cream and saffron.

❶ Information

The **tourist office** (☎079 37 61 07; www.info bosa.com; Via Azuni 5; ⊙10am-1pm Thu-Sat) provides maps and info on Bosa and its surroundings.

❶ Getting There & Away

All buses terminate at Piazza Zanetti. There are services to and from Alghero (€4.50, 1½ hours,

two daily), Sassari (€5.50, 2¼ hours, three daily) and Oristano (€5.50, two hours, six daily Monday to Saturday). Get tickets from the bus depot on Via Nazionale (opposite Sa Pischedda restaurant) or ask the driver.

ALGHERO & THE NORTHWEST

Alghero

POP 40,803

Pretty and petite, Alghero is one of Sardinia's most beautiful towns, and even though it can be very touristy, the town hasn't given up its unique character. The town's charm is in the medieval centre, where cobbled caramel-coloured streets are shaded by Gothic *palazzi* and enlivened by busy squares bubbling with cafes and restaurants. The robust sea walls that enclose the old town are lined with restaurants and bars, and they overlook the harbour and the long sandy beaches to the north, and the rocky coves to the south.

Hanging over everything is a palpable Spanish atmosphere, a hangover from the 14th century when Sardinia's Aragonese invaders tried to replace the local populace with Catalan colonists.

◉ Sights

Centro Storico HISTORICAL CENTRE

A leisurely stroll round Alghero's animated *centro storico* is a good way of getting into the holiday atmosphere. Overlooking Piazza Duomo, the oversized **Cattedrale di Santa Maria** (Piazza Duomo) is an odd mishmash of Moorish, baroque, Renaissance and other influences. Of greater interest is the **campanile** (bell tower; admission €2; ⊙7-9.30pm Tue, Thu & Sat summer, by request rest of year) round the back, which is a fine example of Catalan-Gothic architecture.

On the old town's main street, the **Chiesa di San Francesco** (Via Carlo Alberto) hides some beautiful 14th-century cloisters behind an austere stone facade.

Several 14th-century towers remain from the medieval city, including **Torre Porta a Terra** (☎079 973 40 45; Piazza Porta Terra; adult/child €2.50/1.50; ⊙9am-1pm & to 11pm Mon-Sat summer, 9.30am-1pm Mon-Sat & 5-7pm Wed & Fri winter), which was once one of the city's two main gates. It now houses a small multimedia museum dedicated to the city's past, and a terrace with sweeping, 360-degree views.

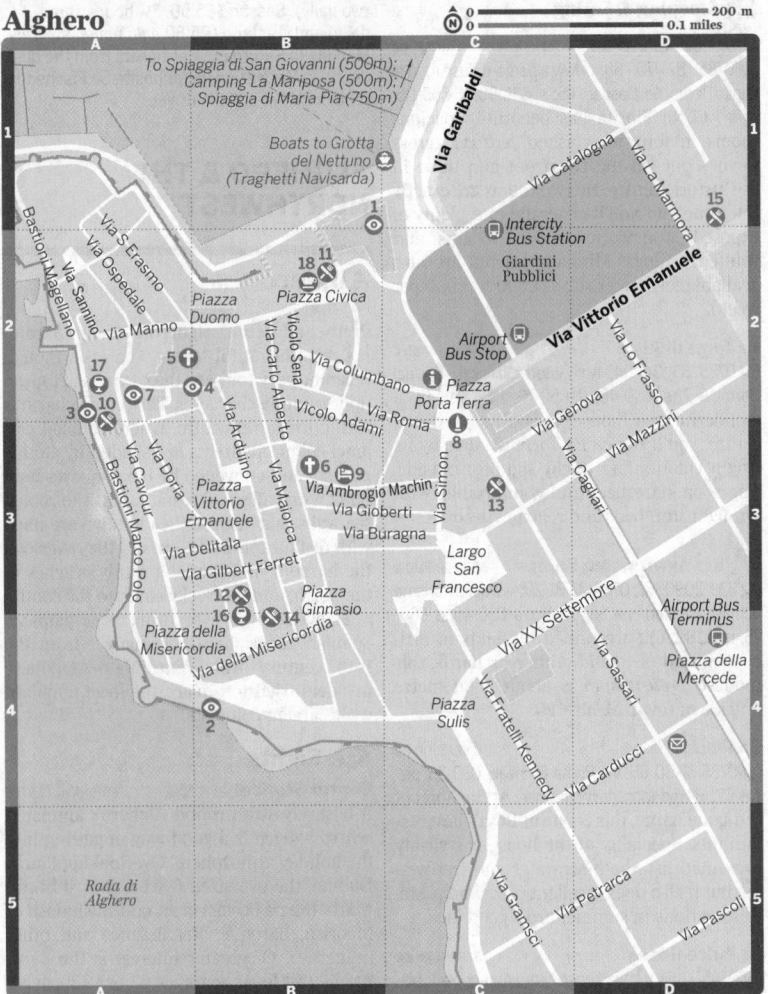

To the north, the **Bastione della Maddalena**, with its eponymous tower, is the only extant remnant of the city's former land battlements. To the south and west, respectively, the Mediterranean crashes against the seaward walls of the **Bastioni di San Marco** and **Bastioni di Cristoforo Colombo**. Along these bulwarks are some inviting restaurants and bars where you can watch the sunset over a cocktail.

Activities

North of Alghero's yacht-jammed port, Via Garibaldi sweeps up to the town's beaches, **Spiaggia di San Giovanni** and the adjacent **Spiaggia di Maria Pia**. Nicer by far, though, are the beaches near Fertilia. From the port you can take boat trips along the impressive northern coast to **Capo Caccia**. Prices range from about €40 to €100 per person.

Courses

Stroll & Speak   LANGUAGE

(☎339 4899314; www.strollandspeak.com; Via Cavour 4; 20hr class per person €180) Brush up on your Italian with a course at an established language school in the historical centre. Maximum five students per class.

✤ Festivals & Events

Estate Musicale Internazionale di Alghero MUSIC

Alghero's 'International Summer of Music' is staged in July and August, and features classical music concerts in the evocative setting of the Chiesa di San Francesco cloister.

🛏 Sleeping

Booking ahead is essential in July and August, and a good idea during the rest of the year.

TOP CHOICE Angedras Hotel HOTEL €€

(☑079 973 50 34; www.angedras.it; Via Frank 2; s €60-140, d €75-150; ❄@) A model of whitewashed Mediterranean style, the Angedras has bright rooms with big French doors opening on to sunny patios. The airy terrace is good for iced drinks on hot summer evenings. Note that it's a good 15-minute walk south from the *centro storico*.

Camping La Mariposa CAMPGROUND €

(☑079 95 03 60; www.lamariposa.it; Via Lido 22; camping 2 people, car & tent €20-44, 4-person bungalows €50-80; ⊙Apr-Oct; @ℳ) About 2km north of the centre, this campground is on the beach, set amid pine and eucalyptus trees. This, and the excellent facilities (including a windsurfing school and diving centre), make it a popular choice.

Hotel San Francesco HOTEL €€

(☑079 98 03 30; www.sanfrancescohotel.com; Via Ambrogio Machin 2; s €52-63, d €82-101; ❄@⚘) This is the only hotel in Alghero's *centro storico*. Housed in an ex-convent – monks still live on the 3rd floor – it has plain, comfortable rooms set around an attractive 14th-century cloister. Wi-fi is available.

✕ Eating

Self-caterers can stock up at Alghero's weekday **market** (Via Sassari 23) between Via Sassari and Via Cagliari. Otherwise, there's a **supermarket** (Via La Marmora 28) near the Giardini Pubblici.

TOP CHOICE La Botteghina SARDINIAN €€

(☑079 97 38 375; www.labotteghina.biz; Via Principe Umberto 63; meals €25-30) A crisp new place in the *centro storico*, La Botteghina only deals in local food bought from small producers, which means the ingredients are simple and tastes intense. Try the *fregola* (small pasta made from semolina, similar to couscous) with seafood, or one of the pizzas.

Angedras Restaurant SARDINIAN €€

(☑079 973 50 78; www.angedrasrestaurant.it; Bastioni Marco Polo 41; meals €35; ⊙Wed-Mon) Dining on Alghero's honey-coloured stone ramparts is a memorable experience. This is one of the better restaurants on the walls, serving a largely traditional menu, including traditional roast suckling pig.

Spaghetteria Al Solito Posto TRADITIONAL ITALIAN €

(☑328 9133745; Piazza della Misericordia; meals €15-20; ⊙Fri-Wed) This small barrel-vaulted place is one of the most popular eateries in town. The workaday atmosphere is TV-on-in-the-corner, but the food – pasta with a range of sauces – is good and the bustling vibe is fun. Bookings recommended.

Il Ghiotto FAST FOOD €

(☑079 97 48 20; Piazza Civica 23; meals €10-15; ⊙Tue-Sun) Fill up for as little as €10 from the tantalising lunchtime spread of *panini,* pastas, salads and main courses. There's seating in a dining area behind the main hall or outside on a busy wooden terrace.

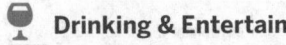 **Drinking & Entertainment**

TOP CHOICE Buena Vista BAR

(Bastioni Marco Polo 47; cocktails €7) Fabulous mojitos, fresh fruit cocktails, golden views – what more could you want of a seafront bar? Upbeat tunes and a cavernous interior add to the vibe at this popular bar on the western walls.

Baraonda WINE BAR

(Piazza della Misericordia) Burgundy walls and black-and-white jazz photos set the tone at this moody wine bar. In summer, sit out on the piazza and watch the world parade by.

Caffè Costantino CAFE

(Piazza Civica 31) The most famous cafe in town attracts a constant stream of tourists to its piazza-side tables. There's a full food menu, although if you just want to eat you'll get better value almost everywhere else.

El Trò CLUB

(Via Lungomare Valencia 3) El Trò becomes a steamy mosh pit on hot summer weekends as hyped-up holidaymakers boogie until dawn on the seafront dance floor.

ℹ Information

Bar Miramare (☏079 973 10 27; Via Gramsci 2; per hr €5; ☉8.30am-1pm & 4.30pm-2am) Internet access.

Farmacia Bulla (☏079 95 21 15; Via Garibaldi 13)

Ospedale Civile (☏079 99 62 00; Via Don Minzoni) The main hospital.

Police station (☏079 972 00 00; Piazza della Mercede 4)

Post office (Via Carducci 35)

Tourist office (☏079 97 90 54; www.comune.alghero.ss.it; Piazza Porta Terra 9; ☉8am-8pm, closed Sun winter)

ℹ Getting There & Away

AIR Fertilia airport (☏079 93 50 39), 10km north of town, serves domestic flights to and from Italy, and **Ryanair** (www.ryanair.com) flights to and from London and Frankfurt.

BUS InterCity buses stop at and leave from Via Catalogna, by the Giardini Pubblici. Buy tickets at the ticket office in the gardens. Up to 11 daily buses run to and from Sassari (€2.50 to €3, one hour). There are also services to Porto Torres (€2.50, one hour, six daily) and Bosa (€4.50, 1½ hours, two daily).

TRAIN The train station is 1.5km north of the old town on Via Don Minzoni. Up to 11 trains run to and from Sassari (€2.30, 35 minutes).

ℹ Getting Around

Hourly buses between 5am and 11pm travel between Via Cagliari and the airport (€1, 20 minutes). A taxi to/from the airport will cost between €20 and €25.

Bus line AO runs from Via Cagliari to the beaches. Tickets are available at newsagents and *tabaccaio* (tobacconists) across town.

Cicloexpress (☏079 98 69 50; www.cicloexpress.com; Via Garibaldi) hires out cars (from €55 per day), scooters (from €30) and bikes (from €8).

Around Alghero

RIVIERA DEL CORALLO

A few kilometres west of Alghero are two favourite beaches: **Spiaggia delle Bombarde** and **Spiaggia del Lazzaretto**. Both are signposted off the main road, but if you don't have a car the Capo Caccia bus from Alghero passes nearby. Divers should continue westward to the **Diving Centre Capo Galera** (☏079 94 21 10; www.capogalera.com; Località Capo Galera; d €65-100, dives from €20), which offers superlative diving in the **Nereo Cave**, the biggest underwater grotto in the Mediterranean, and cheerful accommodation in a big white villa.

Heading on to Porto Conte you'll pass the impressive **Nuraghe di Palmavera** (adult/child €3/1.50; ☉9am-7pm summer, 10am-2pm winter), a 3500-year-old *nuraghic* village. You'll need your own transport to get there as the AF local bus from Alghero passes by but returns via an inland route, leaving you stranded.

Beyond the *nuraghe*, **Porto Conte** is on a lovely unspoilt bay, centred on **Spiaggia Mugoni**, a good spot for windsurfing, canoeing, kayaking and sailing. Regular buses run between Porto Conte and Alghero (€1, 30 minutes, six daily).

Just west of Porto Conte at the base of Monte Timidone, **Le Prigionette Nature Reserve** (☏079 94 90 60; admission free but ID required; ☉8am-4pm Mon-Sat, to 5pm Sun) is home to deer, albino donkeys, Giara horses and wild boar. It has well-marked forest paths and tracks suitable for walkers and cyclists.

At the end of the road, **Capo Caccia** is a dramatic cape jutting out high above the sea.

From the car park, a vertiginous 654-step staircase descends 110m of sheer cliff to the Grotta di Nettuno (☎079 94 65 40; adult/child €10/5; ☺9am-7pm), an underground fairyland of stalactites and stalagmites. If you don't fancy the staircase, there are ferries from Alghero run by Traghetti Navisarda (☎079 95 06 03; adult/child return €14/7), departing hourly between 9am and 5pm from June to September, and four times daily in the rest of the year. Otherwise, there's a daily bus from Via Catalogna (€2, 50 minutes), which departs Alghero at 9.15am and returns at midday. From June to September, there are two extra runs at 3.10pm and 5.10pm, returning at 4.05pm and 6.05pm.

Those with transport should explore the flat, green land north of Capo Caccia. Hot spots include Torre del Porticciolo, a tiny natural harbour, backed by a small arc of beach, and 6km to the north, one of the island's longest stretches of wild sandy beach, Porto Ferro.

INLAND

About 7km north of Alghero, just to the left (west) of the road to Porto Torres, lie the scattered ancient burial chambers of the Necropoli di Anghelu Ruiu (adult/child €3/1.50; ☺9am-7pm summer, 10am-2pm winter). The 38 tombs carved into the rock, known as *domus de janas,* date from between 3300 and 2700 BC.

Further up the road is the 650-hectare estate of Sardinia's top wine producer, Sella e Mosca (☎079 99 77 00; www.sellaemosca.com). Here you can join a free guided tour of the estate's museum (☺5.30pm Mon-Sat summer, by request rest of the year) and stock up at the enoteca (wine bar; ☺8.30am-1pm & 3-6.30pm Mon-Sat year-round, 8.30-8pm Sun summer).

Porto Torres

POP 22,461

A busy working port surrounded by a fuming petrochemical plant, Porto Torres is no picture. But if you find yourself passing through – and you might, if heading to Corsica – take an hour or so to visit the impressive Basilica di San Gavino (crypt €1.50), Sardinia's largest Romanesque church. Built between 1030 and 1080 to honour three Roman-era Christian martyrs, it is notable for the apses on either end (there is no facade) and its two-dozen marble columns, pilfered by the Pisan builders from the nearby Roman site.

Underneath, a crypt is lined with religious statuary and stone tombs.

Buses leave from Via Mare for Sassari (€1.50, 35 minutes, hourly), Alghero (€2.50, one hour, six daily) and Stintino (€2.50, 30 minutes, five daily). For information on ferries, see p816.

Stintino & Parco Nazionale dell'Asinara

Once a forgotten fishing village, Stintino is now a sunny little resort and a good base for exploring the surrounding area. There are some fine beaches in these parts, but the pick of the bunch is Spiaggia della Pelosa, a salt-white strip of sand fronted by shallow, turquoise waters and strange, low-lying licks of land. On the road to Pelosa beach, the Asinara Diving Center (☎079 52 70 00; www.asinaradivingcenter.it; Porto dell'Ancora) offers a range of dives starting at about €40. On the beach itself, the Windsurfing Center Stintino (☎079 52 70 06; www.windsurfingcenter.it) rents out windsurfers (€17 per hour) and canoes (from €10 per hour).

Over the water from Pelosa lies Isola Asinara, home to native *asini bianchi* (albino donkeys), and until recently off limits due to its maximum-security prison. The prison is now closed and the island has been designated a national park, Parco Nazionale dell'Asinara (www.parcoasinara.org). From Stintino, Linea del Parco (☎079 52 31 18; Porto Mannu) offers a number of packages including bus/4WD tours (€36/55) and yacht/fishing boat excursions (€65/70 including lunch). If you want to visit on your own you'll have to take a bike as there's no public transport on the island and access is limited to certain restricted areas. Reckon on €25 for transport with bike and park admission.

Accommodation in the area is mainly in large, resort-style hotels, but there are some pleasant lower-key choices. In Stintino, Albergo Silvestrino (☎079 52 34 73; www.hotelsilvestrino.it, in Italian; Via XXI Aprile 4; d €25-67, half-board €70-113; ❄@) is a summery three-star place with cool tiled rooms and an excellent seafood restaurant (meals €35).

At laid-back Lu Famili (☎079 52 30 54; Lungomare C Colombo 89; pizzas from €6, meals €30) you can watch boats bob by as you dig into reliably good pizza and seafood classics such as *calamari e seppie grigliati* (grilled calamari and cuttlefish).

There are five weekday buses to Stintino from Porto Torres (€2.50, 30 minutes) and Sassari (€4, 70 minutes). Services increase between June and September.

Sassari

POP 130,366

Sardinia's second city is a proud and cultured university town with a medieval heart and a modern outlook. It's not an immediately appealing place, but once you've broken through the drab outskirts you'll discover a grand centre and an evocative, lived-in historical core.

The city's golden age came in the 14th century, firstly as capital of the medieval Giudicato di Logudoro and then as an autonomous city-state. But decline followed and for centuries the city was ruled by Spanish colonialists.

Sights

Museo Nazionale Sanna MUSEUM
(☑079 27 22 03; Via Roma 64; adult/reduced €4/2; ⊙9am-8pm Tue-Sun) This is Sassari's main attraction and the archaeological collection is quite comprehensive. The highlight is the *nuraghic* bronzeware, including weapons, bracelets, votive boats and figurines depicting humans and animals. It also has an interesting picture gallery and a small collection of Sardinian folk art.

Centro Storico HISTORICAL CENTRE
In the heart of the *centro storico,* Sassari's Duomo (Piazza Duomo) dazzles with its 18th-century baroque facade: a giddy free-for-all of statues, reliefs, friezes and busts. Inside, the cathedral reverts to its original Gothic character.

Nearby, imposing 19th-century buildings flank Piazza Italia, one of Sardinia's most impressive public spaces.

Sleeping

B&B Casachiara B&B €
(☑079 200 50 52, 339 6957118; www.casachiara. net; Vicola Bertolinis 7; s/d €35/70; @) In the buzzing uni area, this is a laid-back B&B with a breezy, homey atmosphere. Resembling a well-kept student flat, it has three colourful bedrooms, a dining room and a cheerfully cluttered kitchen.

Hotel Vittorio Emanuele HOTEL €
(☑079 23 55 38; www.hotelvittorioemanuele. ss.it, in Italian; Corso Vittorio Emanuele II 100-102; s €50-70, d €70-89; ❋@) Housed in a medieval

palazzo, this good-value three-star place is awash with antiques and colourful paintings. Rooms are spacious if sterile with their corporate white-grey decor. Weekend discounts are available.

 Eating

Fainè alla Genovese Sassu FAST FOOD €
(Via Usai 17; fainè €5; ⊙7-11pm Thu-Tue) This no-frills spot is the place to fill up on *fainè,* a cross between a pancake and pizza. There's nothing else on the menu, but with a wide range of toppings, you should find something to suit your tastes.

Trattoria Da Antonio TRATTORIA €
(☑079 23 42 97; Via Arborea 2b; meals €25; ⊙Tue-Sun) Affectionately known as *Lu Panzone* (the Big Belly), this boisterous, old-school trattoria does a great line in homespun, no-nonsense food. The focus is on meat (and lots of it) – start with pasta with sausage and then choose between a tender horse steak, lamb with olives and herbs, or pork with tomato and chickpeas, all the while sipping the local red wine.

❶ Information

Nuovo Ospedale Civile (☑079 206 10 00; Via De Nicola)

Police station (Questura; ☑079 249 50 00; Via Ariosto 3)

Post office (Via Brigata di Sassari)

Tourist office (☑079 200 80 72; Via Sebastiano Satta 13; ⊙9am-1pm & 4-6pm Mon-Fri)

❶ Getting There & Away

Sassari's main bus station is on Via XXV Aprile and services the following destinations.

DESTINATION	FARE (€)	DURATION (HR)	FREQUENCY
Alghero	2.50-3	1	11 daily
Cagliari	18.50	3¼	3 daily
Castelsardo	2.50	1	11 daily Mon-Sat
Nuoro	8-10	2	7 daily
Oristano	8-10	2	3 daily
Porto Torres	1.50	½	hourly

For Cagliari (€15, 3¾ hours, five daily) and Olbia (€7, two hours, four daily), you're better off taking the train. The train station is just beyond the western end of the old town on Piazza Stazione.

The countryside south and east of Sassari is a patchwork of rugged slopes and golden wheat fields peppered by delightful Romanesque churches. The most impressive is the **Basilica della Santissima Trinità di Saccargia** (admission €1.50) about 18km southeast of Sassari on the SS597.

Some 25km south, near Torralba, the **Nuraghe Santu Antine** (☑079 84 72 96) is one of Sardinia's most interesting *nuraghic* sites, dating from about 1600 BC. On weekdays, there are up to eight buses from Sassari to Torralba (€2.50, 1½ hours), although to get to the *nuraghe* from the village you'll have to walk about 4km.

On the coast north of Sassari, there are popular beaches at **Platamona** and **Marina di Sorso**, both accessible by the summer Buddi Buddi bus (line MP) from Via Eugenio Tavolara.

From here, the SS200 hugs the coast up to **Castelsardo**, a picturesque town with a dramatic medieval centre rising out of a rocky seafront peak. Regular buses run from Sassari (€2.50, one hour, 11 daily Monday to Saturday).

OLBIA, THE COSTA SMERALDA & THE GALLURA

Costa Smeralda evokes Sardinia's classic images: pearly-white beaches, wind-whipped licks of rock tapering into azure seas, and ageing oligarchs cavorting with bikini-clad beauties on zillion-dollar yachts. In inland Gallura, you could be on another island entirely, with vine-striped hills rolling to quaint villages, granite mountains and mysterious *nuraghi*. Gallura's northern coast is wild, the preserve of the dolphins, divers and windsurfers that splash around in the crystal waters of La Maddalena marine reserve.

Olbia

POP 56.066

Often ignored in the mad summer dash to the Costa Smeralda, Olbia has more to offer than at first meets the eye. Look beyond its industrial outskirts and you'll find a fetching city with a *centro storico* full of boutiques, wine bars and cafe-rimmed piazzas. Above all, Olbia is a refreshingly authentic

and affordable alternative to the purpose-built resorts to the north and south.

◉ Sights

FREE **Museo Archeologico** MUSEUM
(Isolotto di Peddone; ☺10am-1pm Mon-Fri, 4-6pm Mon & Wed) Architect Vanni Macciocco designed Olbia's striking new museum near the port. The museum spells out local history in artefacts, from Roman amulets to *nuraghic* finds. The highlight is the relic of a Roman vessel discovered in the old port.

Chiesa di San Simplicio CHURCH
(Via San Simplicio) Considered to be Gallura's most important medieval monument, this Romanesque granite church was built in the late 11th century and is a curious mix of Tuscan and Lombard styles.

⌂ Sleeping

TOP CHOICE **Hotel Panorama** HOTEL €€
(☑0789 2 66 56; www.hotelpanoramaolbia.it; Via Mazzini 7; s €65-119, d €79-159; ⊕❋❅) The name says it all: the rooftop terrace has unbeatable views of the city, sea and Monte Limbara at this friendly, central hotel. Rooms are spacious and contemporary, with gleaming wood floors and marble bathrooms.

La Locanda del Conte Mameli B&B €€
(☑0789 20 30 40; www.lalocandadelcontemameli.com; Via delle Terme 8; r €80-140, ste €100-180; ❋❅) Housed in an 18th-century *locanda* (inn) built for Count Mameli, this boutique hotel oozes style, grace and original features. An original Roman well is the centrepiece of the vaulted basement breakfast room.

✕ Eating & Drinking

TOP CHOICE **Ristorante Gallura** SARDINIAN €€€
(☑0789 2 46 48; Corso Umberto 145; meals €40-60; ☺Tue-Sun) Rita runs a tight ship at the homely Gallura, one of northern Sardinia's best restaurants. Fresh seasonal ingredients go into specialities like sea anemones fried in yoghurt and suckling pig perfumed with myrtle – all perfectly cooked and utterly delicious.

La Lanterna TRADITIONAL ITALIAN €€
(☑0789 2 30 82; Via Olbia 13; pizzas €6-10, meals €30; ☺daily summer, closed Wed winter) The Lanterna distinguishes itself with its cosy subterranean setting and beautifully fresh food. Start off with sweet-and-sour sardines and move on to almond-crusted bream served with handmade *gnochetti*.

Enoteca Cosimino WINE BAR

(Piazza Margherita 3; ⊙daily) This popular cafe serves coffee and *cornetti* (croissants) by day, morphing into an elegant wine bar with cocktails and *vino* on the menu in the evening.

❶ Information

Inter Smeraldo (☏0789 2 53 66; Via Porto Romano 8b; per hr €5; ⊙9.45am-1.15pm & 4-8.30pm Mon-Sat) An internet cafe with 10 terminals.

Tourist office (☏0789 55 77 32; www.olbia tempioturismo.it; Via Alessandro Nanni 39; ⊙8am-8pm Mon-Sat, 8am-2pm Sun summer, 8am-6pm Mon-Fri, 8am-2pm Sat winter) This helpful tourist office has stacks of info and brochures on Olbia and the surrounding region.

❶ Getting There & Around

AIR Olbia's **Aeroporto Internazionale di Olbia Costa Smeralda** (☏0789 56 34 44; www. geasar.it) is about 5km southeast of the centre and handles flights from mainland Italian and major European cities. Low-cost operators include Air Berlin, easyJet and Nikki.

BOAT Regular ferries arrive in Olbia from Genoa, Civitavecchia and Livorno. Book tickets at travel agents in town, or directly at the port. For further route details see p816.

BUS Buses run from Olbia to the following destinations.

DESTINA-TION	FARE (€)	DURATION (HR)	FREQUENCY
Arzachena	2.50	¾	12 daily
Golfo Aranci	2	½	6 daily
Nuoro	9	2½	8 daily
Porto Cervo	3.50	1½	5 daily
Santa Teresa di Gallura	5	1½	7 daily
Sassari	7	1½	2 daily
Tempio Pausania	3.50	1½	2 daily

Get tickets from **Café Adela** (Corso Vittorio Veneto 2; ⊙5am-10pm), just over the road from the main bus stops. Local bus 2 (€1, or €1.50 if bought on bus) runs half-hourly between 6.15am and 11.40pm from the airport to Via Goffredo Mameli in the centre.

TRAIN The train station is just off Corso Umberto. There are trains to Cagliari (€7, four hours, one daily), Sassari (€7, two hours, four daily) and Golfo Aranci (€2.35, 25 minutes, six daily).

Golfo Aranci

POP 2378

Some 18km northeast of Olbia, Golfo Aranci is an important summer port, with services to Livorno and Civitavecchia (see p816). Most people pass through without a second glance, but it is worth a stop for its three white sandy beaches, particularly if activities like diving and speargun fishing rock your boat.

For a truly memorable experience, join the **Bottlenose Diving Research Institute** (☏0789 183 11 97; www.thebdri.com; Via Diaz 4) on one of its half-day cruises (€70/50 per adult/child) to spot bottlenose dolphins. Sightings aren't guaranteed but the odds are excellent.

Costa Smeralda & Around

Stretching 55km from Porto Rotondo to the Golfo di Arzachena, the Costa Smeralda (Emerald Coast) is Sardinia's most feted summer destination: a gilded enclave of luxury hotels, secluded beaches and exclusive marinas. Ever since the Aga Khan bought the coast for a pittance in the 1960s, it has attracted A-listers and paparazzi hoping to snap celebs in compromising clinches. But despite all the superficial fluff, it remains stunning, with granite mountains plunging into emerald waters in a series of dramatic fjord-like inlets.

The Costa's capital is **Porto Cervo**, a weird, artificial town whose pseudo-Moroccan architecture and perfectly manicured streets give it a strangely sterile atmosphere. It's dead out of season, but between June and September this is party central, with tanned beauties posing on the **Piazzetta** and cashed-up shoppers perusing the designer boutiques.

To the west, **Baia Sardinia** faces onto a gorgeous strip of sand, while to the south, aficionados head for **Capriccioli** and **Spiaggia Liscia Ruia**, both near the exclusive Hotel Cala di Volpe. Near the signposted Hotel Romazzino, **Spiaggia del Principe** is a magnificent crescent of white sand bordered by Caribbean-blue waters – and the Aga Khan's favourite.

Inland, the rustic village of **San Pantaleo** merits a quick look, particularly on summer evenings when its picturesque piazza hosts a bustling market. Further on, the workaday town of **Arzachena** offers a number of interesting archaeological sites, including the **Nuraghe di Albuccu** (admission €3; ⊙9am-

7pm) on the main Olbia road, and **Coddu Ecchju** (admission €3; ⊘9am-7pm), one of Sardinia's most important *tombe di giganti* (giants' tombs).

🛏 Sleeping & Eating

TOP CHOICE B&B Lu Pastruccialeddu B&B €€

(☑0789 8 17 77; www.pastruccialeddu.com; Località Lu Pastruccialeddu, Arzachena; s €75-100, d €75-120; P ❄ ⓟ) This is the real McCoy – a smashing B&B housed in a typical stone farmstead. It's run by the ultra-hospitable Caterina Ruzittu, who prepares the sumptuous breakfasts and keeps the rooms pristine. Outside, a swimming pool shimmers in the lush green garden.

La Villa Giulia B&B €

(☑0789 9 86 29, 348 5111269; www.lavillagiulia.it; Monticanaglia; d €65-89) This B&B sits in glorious isolation at the top of a tough dirt track. With homey furnishings and jolly tiled bathrooms, the rooms are modest, but the wonderful natural surroundings make it a real winner.

Agriturismo Rena AGRITURISMO €€

(☑0789 8 25 32; www.agriturismorena.it; Località Rena; half-board per person €40-60; P ⓟ) It's half-board only at this hilltop *agriturismo,* but that's no great sacrifice as the farmhouse food is a delight – cheese, honey, meat and wine are all home produced. Rooms have a rural look, with heavy wooden furniture and beams holding up 100-year-old ceilings.

Villaggio Camping La Cugnana CAMPGROUND €

(☑0789 3 31 84; www.campingcugnana.it; Località Cugnana; camping 2 people, car & tent €20.50-30; ❄ ⓟ) This slick, seaside camp ground is on the main road just north of Porto Rotondo. It has a supermarket, swimming pool and free beach shuttle bus.

La Vecchia Costa SARDINIAN €

(☑0789 9 86 88; meals around €20; ⊘daily) Great-value home cooking means this rustic restaurant is always booked solid. *Lorighittas* (ring-shaped pasta) in a porcini and lamb sauce is a delicious lead-in to sea bass with rocket, fresh tomatoes and basil. La Vecchia Costa is on the Arzachena–Porto Cervo road.

Spinnaker MODERN ITALIAN €€

(☑0789 9 12 26; www.ristorantespinnaker.com; Liscia di Vacca; meals around €40; ⊘closed Wed low season) Fashionable Spinnaker attracts a

CANTINE SURRAU

Scenically surrounded by vineyards and mountains, the contemporary **Cantine Surrau** (☑0789 8 29 33; www.vignes urrau.it, in Italian; Località Chilvagghja; ⊘9am-11pm summer, to 8.30pm winter) takes a holistic approach to winemaking. Take a spin of the cellar and admire Sardinian art in the gallery before sniffing and swirling some of the region's crispest Vermentino white and beefiest Cannonau red wines; the standard tasting costs €8. You'll find the winery on the Arzachena–Porto Cervo road.

buzzy crowd of yachties and socialites with its stylish ambience and fabulous seafood. Choose a crisp Vermentino white to go with sautéed calamari with fresh artichokes or rock lobster.

❶ Getting There & Away

Between June and September, **Sun Lines** (☑348 260 98 81) operates buses from Olbia airport to the Costa Smeralda, stopping at Porto Cervo and various other points along the coast. During the rest of the year, there's one daily bus between Porto Cervo and Olbia (€3.50, 1½ hours).

For Arzachena there are regular year-round services to and from Olbia (€2.50, 45 minutes, eight daily).

Santa Teresa di Gallura

POP 5211

Bright, breezy and oh-so relaxed, Santa Teresa di Gallura bags a prime seafront position on Gallura's north coast. The resort gets extremely busy in high season yet somehow retains a distinct local character. Nearby, Capo Testa is famous for its surreal wind-sculpted rocks, while Corsica is a short ferry-hop away.

◉ Sights & Activities

When not on the beach, most people hang out at cafe-lined Piazza Vittorio Emanuele. Otherwise, you can wander up to the 16th-century **Torre di Longonsardo** near the entrance to the town's idyllic (but crowded) **Spiaggia Rena Bianca**.

Four kilometres west of Santa Teresa, **Capo Testa** resembles a bizarre sculptural garden. Giant boulders lay strewn about the grassy slopes, their weird and wonderful forms the result of centuries of wind erosion.

Follow Via Capo Testa west of town and it's around an hour's hike to the cape. The walk itself is stunning, passing through boulder-strewn scrub and affording magnificent views of weird rock formations, rocky coves and the cobalt Mediterranean. You can stop en route for a swim and to admire the views of not-so-distant Corsica.

The **Consorzio delle Bocche** (☎0789 75 51 12; www.consorziobocche.com, in Italian; Piazza Vittorio Emanuele 16; ☉9am-1pm & 5pm-12.30am May-Sep) runs trips to the Maddalena islands and down the Costa Smeralda, which cost between €40 and €45 per person. Go diving with **Centro Sub Marina di Longone** (☎0789 74 10 59; www.marinadilongone.it, in Italian; Viale Tibula 11), where prices start at about €35.

🛏 Sleeping & Eating

Most hotels only open from Easter to October. Head to Piazza Vittorio Emanuele for alfresco drinks and people-watching.

B&B Domus de Janas   B&B €€
(☎338 499 02 21; www.bbdomusdejanas.it; Via Carlo Felice 20a; d €60-120, tr €80-140; ✲) Daria and Simon are your affable hosts at this sweet B&B in the centre of town. There are cracking sea views from the terrace and the rooms are cheery, scattered with art and knick-knacks.

Hotel Moderno   HOTEL €€
(☎0789 75 42 33/51 08; www.modernohotel.eu; Via Umberto 39; s €50-80, d €65-140; ✲) This is a homey, family-run place near the piazza. Rooms are bright and airy with little overt decor but traditional blue-and-white Gallurese bedspreads and tiny balconies.

🌿 Camping La Liccia   CAMPGROUND €
(☎0789 75 51 90; www.campinglaliccia.com; SP for Castelsardo km59; camping 2 people, car & tent €18-35, 2-person bungalows €50-96; ☎🅿) This eco-friendly campground, 5km west of town on the road towards Castelsardo, has fab facilities including a playground and sports area.

Agriturismo Saltara   SARDINIAN €€
(☎0789 75 55 97; Località Saltara; meals €35-40; ☉dinner) Forget menus: just bring an open mind and a big appetite. Tables are positioned under the trees for course after delicious course of dishes like ricotta-filled *culurgiones* and *porceddu* (suckling pig).

Saltara is 10km south of town off the SP90 (follow the signs up a dirt track).

Il Chiostro   SEAFOOD €€
(☎0789 74 10 56; www.ilchiostrodelporto.it, in Italian; Porto Turistico; meals €25-45; ☉daily) Overlooking the marina, this inviting restaurant prides itself on the freshness of its fish. Try to snag a table on the terrace.

❶ Information

Bar Sport (Via Mazzini 7; per hr €5; ☉6am-midnight) Internet access.

Tourist office (☎0789 75 41 27; www.comune santateresagallura.it, in Italian; Piazza Vittorio Emanuele 24; ☉9am-1pm & 5-9pm summer, 9am-1pm & 4-6pm Mon-Fri winter) Very helpful with loads of information.

❶ Getting There & Around

From the bus terminus on Via Eleonora d'Arborea, buses run to and from Olbia (€5, 1½ hours, seven daily) and Sassari (€7, 2½ hours, three daily).

For information on ferries to Bonifacio in Corsica, see p816.

Palau & Arcipelago di La Maddalena

On Sardinia's northeastern tip, Palau is a well-to-do summer resort crowded with surf shops, boutiques, bars and restaurants. From here year-round ferries make the short crossing over to **Isola della Maddalena**, the biggest of the more than 60 islands and islets that comprise the **Parco Nazionale dell'Arcipelago di La Maddalena** (www.lamaddalenapark.it). An area of spectacular, windswept seascapes, La Maddalena is best explored by boat, although the two main islands have plenty of charm with their sun-baked ochre buildings, cobbled piazzas and infectious holiday atmosphere.

◉ Sights & Activities

The main activity in these parts is beach-bumming or boating around the islands. Down at the port in Palau, **Petag** (☎0789 70 86 81; www.petag.it) offers trips for about €35 per person, including lunch and swimming time on well-known beaches. On La Maddalena, operators congregate around Cala Mangiavolpe.

Windsurfers converge on **Porto Pollo**, about 7km west of Palau, for some of the best wind conditions on the island. You can

MILITARY CHIC

When the US Navy withdrew from La Maddalena in 2008 after a controversial 35-year sojourn, the question on everyone's lips was: 'What now?'

It looked set to host the G8 summit in 2009, but the venue was switched to Abruzzo in the wake of the L'Aquila earthquake. By then preparations were already under way to totally revamp the former military bases. The result? The strikingly contemporary **La Maddalena Hotel & Yacht Club** (☎0789 79 42 73; www.lamaddalenahyc.com; d €200-500, ste €450-1100; ❄️📶♿). Where derelict garrisons once stood, today you can wander in vast, light-filled spaces, marvel at Zaha Hadid's sci-fi chandelier illuminating the lobby, and gaze up at the geometric Murano glass conference centre designed by Stefano Boeri. Besides rooms that are the epitome of minimalist chic, the hotel boasts a rooftop pool with panoramic sea views, immaculately landscaped gardens, a top-notch restaurant and a spa. And yes, there is space to dock your megayacht or land your helicopter (just in case you were wondering).

If your budget doesn't quite stretch to the five-star price tag, you can sneak a peek at the hotel by booking a treatment in the spa, enjoying a drink at the bar or booking a table in the restaurant.

also try kitesurfing, canoeing, diving and sailing, with kit and lessons available along the beachfront.

There's also some excellent diving in the marine park. In Palau, **Nautilus** (☎0789 70 90 58; www.divesardegna.com; Piazza Fresi 8, Palau) runs dives from €50.

Linked to La Maddalena by a narrow causeway is **Isola Caprera**, a tiny island where Giuseppe Garibaldi once lived. His home, the **Compendio Garibaldino** (☎0789 72 71 62; adult/reduced €5/2.50; ◷9am-7.15pm Tue-Sun), is visitable by guided tours (in Italian) only.

About 1.5km north of the Compendio, a walking trail drops down to the steep and secluded **Cala Coticcio** beach. Marginally easier to get to is **Cala Brigantina** (signposted), southeast of the complex.

🛏 Sleeping & Eating

It's strictly summer only in Palau and La Maddalena, where nearly everything closes from mid-October to Easter.

TOP CHOICE **B&B Petite Maison**   B&B €€
(☎0789 73 84 32; www.lapetitmaison.net; Via Livenza 7, La Maddalena; d €70-110) Liberally sprinkled with paintings and art deco furnishings, this B&B is a five-minute amble from the main square. Miriam's artistically presented breakfasts, with fresh, homemade goodies, are served in a bougainvillea-draped garden. Credit cards (and kids) are not accepted.

L'Orso e Il Mare   B&B €
(☎331 2222000; www.orsoeilmare.com; Vicolo Diaz 1, Palau; d €60-100, tr €70-120; ❄️) Pietro gives a

genuinely warm welcome at this B&B, just steps from Piazza Fresi. The spacious rooms sport breezy blue and white colour schemes. Breakfast is a fine spread of cakes, biscuits and fresh fruit salad.

Camping Baia Sardegna   CAMPGROUND €
(☎0789 70 94 03; www.baiasaraceno.com; Località Punta Nera; camping 2 people, car & tent €16-37, 2-person bungalows €90-174; ♿) Beautifully located on Palau's beach and shaded by pine trees, this campground has an on-site pizzeria, playground and dive centre.

San Giorgio   SARDINIAN €€
(☎0789 70 80 07; Via La Maddalena 4, Palau; pizzas €6-9, meals €30; ◷Wed-Mon) The open-plan kitchen tells you all you need to know about this pizzeria-cum-restaurant. The spaghetti *allo scoglio* (with mixed seafood) is an excellent bet, as is the grilled fish.

❶ Information

Tourist offices Palau (☎0789 70 70 25; www.palauturismo.com; Palazzo Fresi; ◷9am-1pm & 4-8pm summer, 9am-1pm & 3-5.30pm Mon-Fri winter); La Maddalena (☎0789 73 63 21; www.comune.lamaddalena.ot.it, in Italian; Cala Gavetta; ◷8.30am-1pm & 3.30-5.30pm Mon-Fri, 9am-1pm Sat summer, shorter hr winter)

❶ Getting There & Around

BOAT Frequent car ferries to Isola Maddalena are operated by **Saremar** (☎892123; www.saremar.it, in Italian) and **Delcomar** (☎781 85 71 23; www.delcomar.it, in Italian). The 15-minute crossing costs €5 per passenger and €13 for a small car.

BUS Services connect Palau with Olbia (€3, 1¼ hours, 10 daily), Santa Teresa di Gallura (€2, 40 minutes, five daily) and Arzachena (€1.50, 20 minutes, eight daily). In summer, **Nicos-Caramelli** (☎0789 67 06 13) runs buses to Porto Pollo (€2, 35 minutes), Baia Sardinia (€4.50, 35 minutes) and Porto Cervo (€4.50, 50 minutes). All buses leave from the port.

NUORO & THE EAST

If the Sardinians were to nominate one place as their geographical, cultural and spiritual heartland, this would surely be it. Nowhere is the force of nature more overpowering than here, where the Supramonte's limestone mountains give way to the Golfo di Orosei's plunging cliffs, grottoes and startling aquamarine waters.

Although larger towns are accessible by bus, you'll see more with your own set of wheels. A roller coaster of country roads leads to deep valleys concealing prehistoric *nuraghe,* the lonesome villages of the Barbagia steeped in bandit legends, and to holm oak forests where wild pigs roam.

Nuoro

POP 36,409

Once an isolated hilltop village and a byword for banditry, Nuoro had its cultural renaissance in the 19th and early 20th centuries when it became a hotbed of artistic talent. Today museums in the historic centre pay homage to local legends like Nobel Prize–winning author Grazia Deledda, acclaimed poet Sebastiano Satta, novelist Salvatore Satta and sculptor Francesco Ciusa.

The city's spectacular backdrop is the granite peak of Monte Ortobene (955m), capped by a 7m-high bronze statue of the *Redentore* (Christ the Redeemer). The thickly wooded summit commands dress-circle views of the valley and the limestone mountains surrounding Oliena.

◉ Sights

Museo della Vita e delle Tradizioni Sarde   MUSEUM

(☎0784 25 70 35; Via Antonio Mereu 56; adult/reduced €3/1; ⊙9am-8pm daily summer, 9am-1pm & 3-6pm Tue-Sun winter) This museum provides a fascinating insight into Sardinian traditions, folklore, superstitions and celebrations. Its pride and joy is the display of colourful traditional costumes.

Museo d'Arte   ART GALLERY

(MAN; ☎0784 25 21 10; www.museoman.it; Via S Satta 15; adult/reduced €3/2; ⊙10am-1pm & 4.30-8.30pm Tue-Sun) Set in a restored 19th-century town house, MAN is Sardinia's only serious modern art gallery. Its permanent collection boasts more than 400 works by the island's top 20th-century painters.

Museo Deleddiano   MUSEUM

(☎0784 25 80 88; Via Grazia Deledda 53; adult/reduced €3/1; ⊙9am-7pm daily summer, 10am-1pm & 3-5pm Tue-Sun winter) Up in the oldest part of town, the birthplace of Grazia Deledda has been converted into this lovely little museum. The rooms, full of Deledda memorabilia, have been carefully restored to show what a well-to-do 19th-century Nuorese house actually looked like.

⛢ Festivals & Events

Sagra del Redentore   RELIGIOUS

In the last week of August, 'Feast of Christ the Redeemer' is the main event in Nuoro, and one of Sardinia's most exuberant festivals, with parades, live music and a torchlit procession.

⛭ Sleeping & Eating

TOP CHOICE **Silvia e Paolo**   B&B €

(☎0784 3 12 80; www.silviaepaolo.it; Corso Garibaldi 58; s €30-35, d €50-60, tr €70; ❋@) Silvia and Paolo run this sweet B&B. Family treasures from dolls to old leather trunks make you feel right at home in the bright, spacious rooms. There's a roof terrace for observing the action on Corso Garibaldi by day and stargazing by night.

Casa Solotti   B&B €

(☎0784 3 39 54; www.casasolotti.it; per person €26-35; P❋☎) This welcoming B&B sits in a rambling garden near the top of Monte Ortobene. Surrounded by woods and walking trails, it's a relaxed place with rustic rooms. Horse riding, packed lunches and guided hikes in the Supramonte can be arranged.

La Locanda   SARDINIAN €

(☎0784 3 10 32; Via Brofferio 31; meals around €15; ⊙Mon-Sat) The €9.20 lunch is a bargain at this cheery, down-to-earth trattoria. Bag a table and you're in for a treat – think antipasti, fresh pasta and grilled steaks, washed down with highly quaffable house wine.

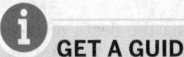

If you fancy striking out into the Supramonte, here's our pick of the best guides:

Cooperativa Gorropu (☎0782 64 92 82, 333 8507157; www.gorropu.com; Via Sa Preda Lada 2, Urzulei) Sandra and Franco arrange all sorts of excursions, from trekking (€30 to €35) to canyoning and caving (€40 to €60).

Corrado Conca (☎347 2903101; corrado@segnavia.it) Sardinia's hiking and climbing guru is a brilliant companion for the island's extreme seven-day Selvaggio Blu (Savage Blue) trek. Bank on paying around €500 per person.

Atlantikà (☎328 9729719; www.atlantika.it, in Italian; Via Lamarmora 195, Dorgali) To explore the rocky hinterland and coast, check out this consortium of local guides for excursions to Gola Su Gorropu and Tiscali (both €35).

Cooperativa Ghivine (☎0784 9 67 21; www.ghivine.com; Via Lamarmora 69e, Dorgali) A one-stop action shop, arranging treks to places like Gola Su Gorropu and Tiscali (both €40).

Dolmen (☎0784 9 32 60; www.sardegnadascoprire.it; Via Vasco da Gama 18, Cala Gonone) A reliable operator running 4WD tours into the Supramonte and canyoning excursions to the Gorropu.

ℹ Information

Tourist office (☎0784 23 88 78; www.provincia.nuoro.it, in Italian; Piazza Italia 19; ⊗8.30am-2pm & 3.30-7pm daily summer, same hr Mon-Fri winter) Has plenty of useful information on Nuoro and environs.

ℹ Getting There & Away

From the main bus station on Viale Sardegna there are services to the following destinations.

DESTINA-TION	FARE (€)	DURATION (HR)	FREQUENCY
Baunei	6	2	4 daily
Cagliari	15.50	2½-5	2 daily
Dorgali	3	¾	6 daily
Olbia	9	2½	8 daily
Oliena	1.50	½	frequent
Orgosolo	2	½	frequent
San Teodoro	7	1¾	8 daily
Santa Maria Navarrese	7	2½	5 daily
Tortolì	7	2¾	5 daily

Supramonte

Southeast of Nuoro rises the forbidding limestone massif of the Supramonte, its sheer walls like an iron curtain. This thrilling landscape forms the landward section of the **Parco Nazionale del Golfo di Orosei e del Gennargentu** (www.parcogennargentu.it, in Italian), Sardinia's largest national park.

OLIENA
POP 7439

From Nuoro you can see the multicoloured rooftops of Oliena cupped in the palm of Monte Corrasi (1463m). An atmospheric place with a grey-stone centre and a magnificent setting, it was founded in Roman times and is today famous for its blood-red Cannonau wine and traditional Easter celebrations.

⊙ Sights & Activities

Piazza Santa Maria is the site of the Saturday market and the 13th-century **Chiesa di Santa Maria**. There are several other wonderful old churches here, including the blessedly simple 14th-century **Chiesa di San Lussorio** (Via Cavour).

The village's usual sleepy torpor is shattered on Easter Sunday for **S'Incontru** (The Meeting), a boisterous procession in which bearers carry a statue of Christ to meet a statue of the Virgin Mary in Piazza Santa Maria.

The countryside surrounding Oliena provides awesome trekking. **Sardegna Nascosta** (☎0784 28 85 50; www.sardegnanascosta.it, in Italian), **Barbagia Insolita** (☎0784 28 60 05; Corso Vittoria Emanuele 48) and **Cooperativa Enis** (☎0784 28 83 63; www.coopenis.it Località Monte Maccione) all organise a range of excursions, including trekking, canoeing, abseiling, climbing and riding.

🛏 Sleeping & Eating

TOP CHOICE **Agriturismo Guthiddai**   AGRITURISMO €

(☎0784 28 60 17; www.agriturismoguthiddai.com; Nuoro-Dorgali bivio Su Gologone; half-board per person €60-75; 🚗) On the road to Su Gologone, this whitewashed farmstead sits at the foot of rugged mountains, surrounded by fig, olive and fruit trees. Olive oil, Cannonau wine and fruit and veggies are all home produced. The rooms are exquisitely tiled in pale greens and cobalt blues.

Hotel Su Gologone HOTEL €€
(☎0784 28 75 12; www.hotelsugologone.com; s €105-160, d €140-240, ste €340-440; P✳🚗) Treat yourself to a spot of rural luxury at Su Gologone, 7km east of Oliena. Rooms are decorated with original art works and handicrafts, and the facilities are top-notch – there's a pool, a wine cellar and a restaurant (meals around €55), which is considered one of Sardinia's best.

Hotel Cikappa HOTEL €
(☎0784 28 80 24; www.cikappa.com; Corso Martin Luther King 2-4; s/d/tr €40/70/85; ✳🛜) Good modest digs above a popular restaurant (meals €25 to €45) in central Oliena. The best rooms have balconies overlooking the surrounding mountains.

Hotel Monte Maccione HOTEL €
(☎0784 28 83 63; www.coopenis.it; s €39-48.50, d €66-80; P) Run by the Cooperativa Enis, this place offers simple, rustic rooms and fine views from its hilltop location, 4km above Oliena.

Ristorante Masiloghi SARDINIAN €€
(☎0784 28 56 96; Via Galiani 68; meals around €30; ⊙daily) A sunny Mediterranean villa on the main road into town. House specialities include homemade pasta, local lamb and boar stew.

ⓘ Information
Tourpass (☎0784 28 60 78; Corso Deledda 32; ⊙9am-1pm & 4-6.30pm) The best source of information in Oliena is this private agency that can advise on activities in the area.

ⓘ Getting There & Away
ARST runs frequent buses from Via Roma to Nuoro (€1.50, 20 minutes, up to 12 Monday to Saturday, six Sunday).

ORGOSOLO & MAMOIADA
For centuries Orgosolo was feared as a centre of banditry and kidnapping. Nowadays, it's better known for the vibrant graffiti-style murals that adorn its town centre. Like satirical caricatures, they depict all the big political events of the 20th century and are often very moving. An outstanding example

is a series illustrating the death of 12-year-old Palestinian Mohammed el Dura as he hid behind his father during a Gaza shootout in 2000.

Ten kilometres to the west of Orgosolo, the undistinguished town of Mamoiada stages Sardinia's most sinister Carnevale celebrations. These kick off with the Festa di Sant'Antonio on 17 January, and climax on Shrove Tuesday and the preceding Sunday. Stealing the limelight are the *mamuthones,* characters decked out in shaggy brown sheepskins and primitive wooden masks. Anthropologists believe that the *mamuthones* embodied all the untold horrors that primitive humans feared, and that the ritual parade is an attempt to exorcise these demons before the new spring.

Buses run to both Mamoiada (€2, 20 minutes) and Orgosolo (€2, 30 minutes) from Nuoro.

DORGALI
POP 8450

Dorgali is a down-to-earth town with a grandiose backdrop, nestled at the foot of Monte Bardia and framed by vineyards and olive groves. Limestone peaks rear above the centre's pastel-coloured houses and steep, narrow streets, luring hikers and climbers to their summits.

Other than perusing the local craftwork shops – Dorgali is famous for its leather goods, ceramics, carpets and filigree jewellery – the main attraction here is the great green wilderness, with the Golfo di Orosei and spectacularly rugged Supramonte in easy striking distance.

🛏 Sleeping & Eating
Sa Corte Antica B&B €
(☎0784 9 43 17; www.sacorteantica.it; Via Mannu 17; d €50-60, tr €65-75; ✳) Gathered around an old stone courtyard, this B&B radiates old-world charm, with traditional reed ceilings and wrought-iron bedsteads. Homemade bread and *biscotti* (biscuits) are served at breakfast.

Ristorante Colibrì SARDINIAN €€
(☎0784 9 60 54; Via Gramsci 14; meals €30; ⊙Mon-Sat) Tucked away in an incongruous residential area (follow the signs), this is the bee's knees for meat eaters, with dishes like wild boar with rosemary and *porceddu*.

ⓘ Information
Tourist office (☎0784 9 62 43; www.dorgali. it, in Italian; Via Lamarmora 108b; ⊙10am-1pm

TOP FIVE CLIMBS & HIKES

» **Gola Su Gorropu** The 1¼-hour trail to Gorropu from Genna 'e Silana pass is spectacular, taking in holm oak woods, boulder-strewn slopes and cave-riddled cliffs.

» **Selvaggio Blu** This is the big one: an epic seven-day, 45km trek along the Golfo di Orosei's dramatic coastline, traversing wooded ravines, cliffs and caves. A guide is recommended as the trail is not well signposted and there's no water en route. Visit the website, www.selvaggioblu.it (in Italian). See also p44.

» **Cala Luna** There's fabulous climbing above a beautiful bay, which is a scenic two-hour clifftop walk from Cala Fuili or a speedy boat ride from Cala Gonone. The 56 routes range from 5c to 8b+ and include some tricky single pitches in caves with overhangs.

» **La Poltrona** This massive limestone amphitheatre close to Cala Gonone has compact rock and 75 bolted routes from grades 4 to 8a. Mornings get too hot here in summer, so wait until late afternoon.

» **Golgo–Cala Goloritzè** It's an easy half-day hike along old mule trails from the plateau of Golgo to Cala Goloritzè, a perfect half-moon of white sand pummelled by astonishingly blue waters. Climbers can tackle its bizarre granite pinnacles, including the Aguglia, a tough multipitch climb.

& 4-8pm Mon-Fri, Sat Jul & Aug) Can provide information on Dorgali and Cala Gonone, including contact details for local trekking outfits and accommodation lists.

❶ Getting There & Away

Buses serve Nuoro (€3, 45 minutes, six daily) and Olbia (€7.50, 2¾ hours, two daily). Up to six daily services shuttle back and forth between Dorgali and Cala Gonone (€1.50, 25 minutes).

GROTTA DI ISPINIGOLI

A short drive north of Dorgali, the fairy-tale-like **Grotta di Ispinigoli** (adult/child €7.50/3.50; ☉tours on the hour 9am-8pm summer, 9am-noon & 3-5pm winter) is a veritable forest of glittering stalagmites, including the world's second-tallest (the highest is in Mexico and stands at 40m). Unlike most caves of this type, which you enter from the side, here you descend 60m inside a giant 'well', at whose centre stands the magnificent 38m-high stalagmite.

SERRA ORRIOS & THOMES

The *nuraghic* village of **Serra Orrios** (adult/child €5/2.50; ☉hourly tours 9am-1pm & 3-6pm, shorter hr winter) was inhabited between 1500 and 250 BC. Hidden among olive groves, the remains comprise a cluster of 70 or so horseshoe-shaped huts grouped around two basalt-hewn temples. The site lies 11km northwest of Dorgali (3km north off the Dorgali–Oliena road).

From Serra Orrios you could continue north to see the **Tomba dei Giganti S'Ena e Thomes** (admission free; ☉dawn-dusk), a fine example of a *tomba dei giganti*. The stone monument is dominated by a central oval-shaped stele that once closed off an ancient burial chamber.

GOLA SU GORROPU

Dubbed the 'Grand Canyon of Europe', the **Gola Su Gorropu** (☏328 8976563; www.gorropu.info; adult/reduced €5/3; ☉tours 10.30am-3.30pm) is a spectacular gorge flanked by vertical 400m rock walls. From the Rio Flumineddu riverbed you can wander about 1km into the boulder-strewn gorge without climbing gear. After 500m you reach the narrowest point, just 4m wide.

There are two main approach routes. The more dramatic begins from the car park opposite Hotel Silana at the **Genna 'e Silana** pass on the SS125 at kilometre 183.

The second and slightly easier route to Gorropu is via the **Sa Barva bridge**, about 15km from Dorgali. To get to the bridge, take the SS125 and look for the sign on the right for the Gola Su Gorropu and Tiscali between kilometres 200 and 201. Take this and continue until the asphalt finishes after about 20 minutes. Park here and cross the Sa Barva bridge, after which you'll see the trail for the Gola signposted off to the left. From here it's a scenic two-hour hike along the Rio Flumineddu to the mouth of the gorge.

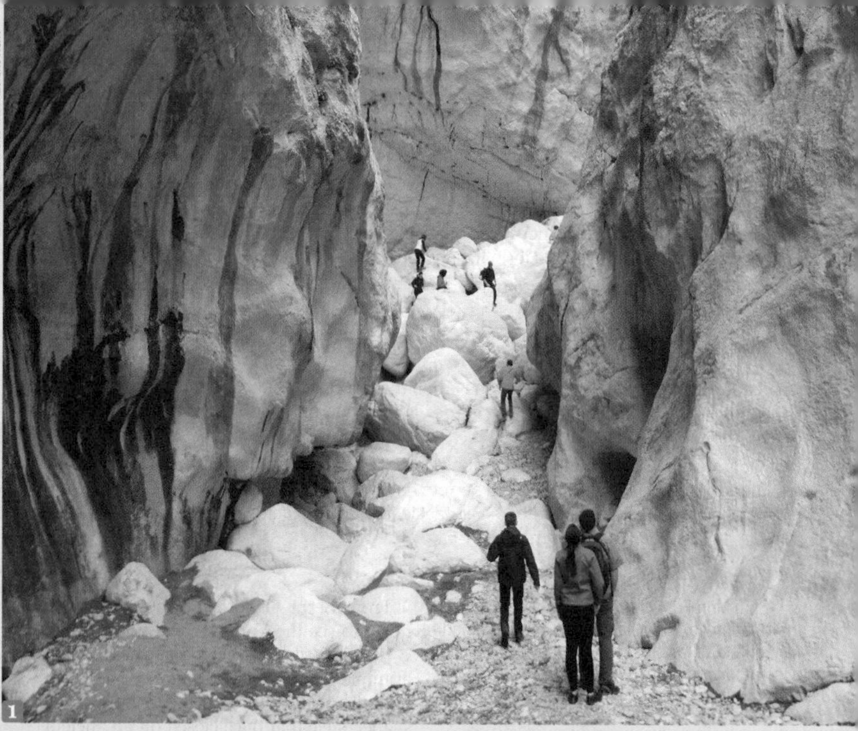

ANDY CHRISTIANI / LONELY PLANET IMAGES ©

DALLAS STRIBLEY / LONELY PLANET IMAGES ©

WATERFRAME / ALAMY ©

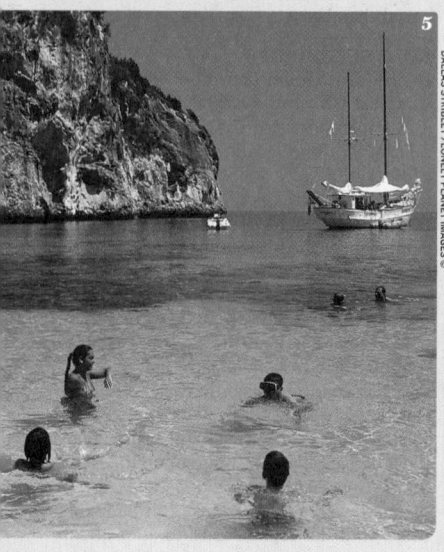

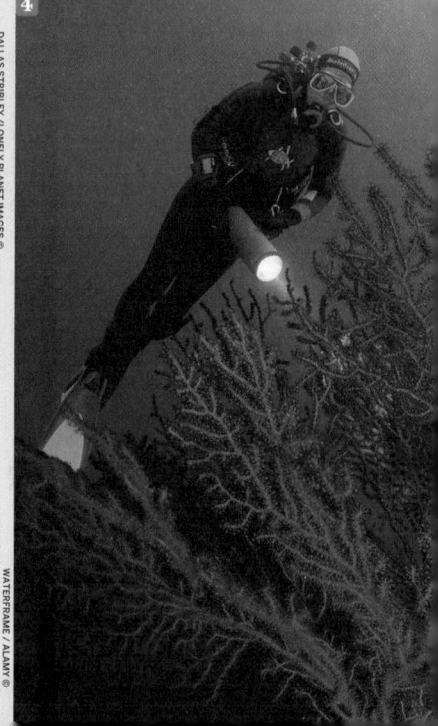

1. Hiking, Gola Su Gorropu (p841)
This spectacular gorge, flanked by vertical 400m rock walls, has been dubbed the 'Grand Canyon of Europe'.

2. Climbing, Santa Teresa di Gallura (p835)
Sardinia's rock formations make for breathtaking climbing.

3. Windsurfing (p811)

Porto Pollo and Chia are top spots for windsurfing in Sardinia.

4. Scubadiving (p811)

The gin-clear waters in Sardinia are a dream for divers.

5. Swimming, Golfo di Orosei (p844)

Horseshoe-shaped bays are lapped by exquisitely aquamarine waters.

844

ROAD TRIPPING

It's well worth getting behind the wheel to drive the 60km stretch from Dorgali to Santa Maria Navarrese. Serpentine and at times hair-raising, the SS125 threads through the mountain tops where the scenery is distractingly lovely: to the right the ragged limestone peaks of the Supramonte rear above wooded valleys and deep gorges; to the left mountains tumble down to the bright-blue sea. The first 20km to the **Genna 'e Silana pass** (1017m) are the most breathtaking. Aside from the odd hell-for-leather Fiat, traffic is sparse, but you should take care at dusk, when wild pigs, goats, sheep and cows rule the road and bring down rocks.

TISCALI

Hidden in a mountain-top cave deep in the Valle Lanaittu, the *nuraghic* village of Tiscali (adult/reduced €5/2; ⊙9am-7pm summer, to 5pm winter) is one of Sardinia's archaeological highlights. Dating from the 6th century BC and populated until Roman times, the village was discovered at the end of the 19th century. At the time it was relatively intact, but since then thieves have done a pretty good job of looting the place, stripping the conical stone-and-mud huts down to the skeletal remains that you see today.

Many local outfits offer guided tours (typically about €40), but if you want to go it alone the simplest route starts from the same point as for the Gola Su Gorropu. The trail is signposted and takes between 1½ and two hours; wear sturdy shoes and take ample water.

Golfo di Orosei

For sheer stop-dead-in-your-tracks beauty, there's no place like this gulf, forming the seaward section of the Parco Nazionale del Golfo di Orosei e del Gennargentu. Here high mountains abruptly meet the sea, forming a crescent of dramatic cliffs riven by false inlets, scattered with horseshoe-shaped bays and lapped by exquisitely aquamarine waters.

CALA GONONE

Climbers, divers, sea kayakers, hikers and beach bums all rave about Cala Gonone.

Backed by imperious tree-specked cliffs, the resort has kept the low-key, family-friendly vibe of the small fishing village it once was. With an appealing line-up of hotels, bars and restaurants on its pine-fringed *lungomare,* Gonone makes a great base for outdoor adventures along this magnificent stretch of coast.

◉ Sights & Activities

Kids love coming face to face with bubbling marine life at the new **Acquario di Cala Gonone** (⊘0784 9 30 47; www.acquario calagonone.it; Via La Favorita; adult/reduced €10/6; ⊙9.30am-7.30pm). Or give them a lesson in prehistory at the romantic ruins of **Nuraghe Mannu** (adult/reduced €3/2; ⊙9am-noon & 3-6pm winter, to 7pm summer), off the Cala Gonone–Dorgali road, with an eagle's-eye view over the whole coast.

For the climbing lowdown and guided excursions, stop by **Prima Sardegna** (⊘0784 9 33 67; www.primasardegna.com; Via Lungomare Palmasera 32). It also has bike/scooter/kayak rental for €24/48/30. **Argonauta** (⊘0784 9 30 46, 349 4738652; www.argonauta.it; Via dei Lecci 10) offers a range of water-based activities, including snorkelling tours (€25), cavern and wreck dives (€45) and canyoning excursions (€40).

⊨ Sleeping & Eating

The resort goes into hibernation from October until Easter; bookings are essential in summer.

TOP CHOICE **Hotel L'Oasi**   B&B €€
(⊘0784 9 31 11; www.loasihotel.it; Via Garcia Lorca 13; s €53-79, d €68-136; ❄ P 🕾) Perched on the cliffs above Cala Gonone and nestling in flowery gardens, this B&B offers enticing sea views from many of its breezy rooms. It's worth paying an extra €15 or so for half-board, as the three-course dinners are prepared with fresh local produce. L'Oasi is a 10-minute uphill walk from the harbour.

Agriturismo Nuraghe Mannu   AGRITURISMO €
(⊘0784 9 32 64; www.agriturismonuraghemannu. com; d €54-68, half-board per person €43-48; 🖨) Off the SP26 Dorgali–Cala Gonone road, and immersed in greenery, this cracking *agriturismo* has four simple rooms, plus space for five tents (€9 to €12 per person). The farmhouse restaurant rustles up a feast of home-produced cheese, pork, lamb and wine.

Hotel Costa Dorada
HOTEL €€

(☑0784 9 33 32; www.hotelcostadorada.it; Lungomare Palmasera 45; s €74-120, d €108-190; ❋🅿🛜) This vine-clad pad offers sea views and tasteful rooms decorated with pastel colours, painted wood furnishings and local handicrafts.

Camping Cala Gonone
CAMPGROUND €

(☑0784 9 31 65; www.campingcalagonone.it; camping 2 people, car & tent €26-39, 2-bed bungalows €48-105; 🛜🏊) By the entrance to town, this pine-shaded campground's top-notch facilities include a tennis court, barbecue area and swimming pool.

Il Pescatore
SEAFOOD €€

(☑0784 9 31 74; Via Acqua Dolce 7; meals €25-35) Fresh seafood is what this place is about. Sit on the terrace for sea breezes and fishy delights like pasta with *ricci* and spaghetti with clams and *bottarga*.

Road House Blues
ITALIAN €€

(☑0784 9 31 87; Lungomare Palmasera 28; meals €20-30) This laid-back seafront haunt is great for a swift beer or a bite to eat. Dig into pizzas named after rock bands (think Parma ham, Pearl Jam) and Sardinian dishes like homemade pasta with chard and *pecorino*.

❶ Information
Tourist office (☑0784 9 36 96; www.calagonone.com; Viale Bue Marino 1a; ⊙9am-1pm & 3-7pm summer, 9.30-11.30am Fri-Wed winter) A very helpful office in the small park off to the right as you enter town.

❶ Getting There & Away
Up to seven daily buses run to Cala Gonone from Dorgali (€1.50, 20 minutes, seven daily) and up to six to Nuoro (€3.50, 70 minutes).

Ogliastra
Wedged in between the provinces of Nuoro and Cagliari, Ogliastra is a dramatic, vertical land of vast, unspoiled valleys, silent woods and windswept rock faces. The coastal stretches become increasingly dramatic the nearer you get to the Golfo di Orosei.

BAUNEI & THE ALTOPIANO DEL GOLGO
Around 28km south of the Genna 'e Silana pass, you come to the uninspiring shepherd's town of Baunei. There's little reason to stop off here, but what is seriously worth your while is the 10km detour up to the **Altopiano del Golgo**, a strange, other-worldly plateau where goats and donkeys graze in dusty shrubland. From the town a signpost sends you up a 2km climb of impossibly steep switchbacks to the plateau. Head north and after 8km follow the **Su Sterru** (Il Golgo) sign for less than 1km, leave your vehicle and make for this remarkable feat of nature – a 270m abyss just 40m wide at its base. Its funnel-like opening is now fenced off but, knowing the size of the drop, just peering down is enough to bring on the vertigo.

In the heart of the plateau, the **Locanda Il Rifugio** (☑0782 61 05 99, 368 7028980; www.coopgoloritze.com; half-board per person €100-110; ⊙Apr-Oct) has six basic rooms in

---

DON'T MISS

THE BLUE CRESCENT

If you do nothing else in Sardinia, take a boat trip along Cala Gonone's southern coast. Some tasty beaches are accessible from town by car or on foot (eg **Cala Cartoe** to the north, and **Cala Fuili** and **Cala Luna** to the south), but the best can only be reached by sea.

From the port, boats head south to the **Grotta del Bue Marino** (adult/reduced €8/4; ⊙9am-1pm & 3-5pm summer), a haunting complex of stalactite- and stalagmite-filled caves where monk seals used to pup.

From there explore a string of coves and beaches, from the crescent-shaped **Cala Luna** and **Cala Sisine**, backed by a green valley, through to the dazzling-white pebbles and incredible cobalt-blue waters of **Cala Mariolu**.

The **Nuovo Consorzio Trasporti Marittimi** (☑0784 9 33 05; www.calagononecrociere.it, in Italian; Via Millelire 14) whisks you along the beautiful coastline from March to October. Its packages include return trips to Cala Luna (€12), Cala Sisine (€18) and Cala Mariolu (€26). A trip to the Grotta del Bue Marino costs €16.50, which covers entry to the cave.

THE LEMON HOUSE

A terrific base for outdoor escapades is the Lemon House (☎0782 66 95 07; www.peteranne.it; Via Dante 10, Lotzorai; per person €30-42; ☏), run by Peter and Anne. Peter has bolted some of the 800 climbing routes in the area and is a co-founder of Mountain Bike Ogliastra (www.mountainbikeogliastra. it). Their B&B is a relaxed base, with a roof terrace overlooking the mountains and sea, a bouldering wall, and homemade lemon marmalade served at breakfast. They can arrange bike hire and pick-ups, lend you a GPS and give you invaluable tips on hiking, climbing, mountain biking and kayaking.

a converted farmstead and facilities for campers (€5 per tent). Managed by the Cooperativa Goloritzè (www.coopgoloritze. com), the refuge makes an excellent base for trekking and 4WD excursions. Many treks involve a descent from the plateau through dramatic *codula* (canyons) to the beautiful beaches of the Golfo di Orosei. Staff at the refuge also organise guides and logistical support for walkers attempting the once-in-a-lifetime Selvaggio Blu, Sardinia's toughest multiday trek.

Just beyond the refuge is the late-16th-century Chiesa di San Pietro, a humble construction flanked to one side by some even humbler *cumbessias* – rough, largely open stone affairs that are not at all comfortable for the passing pilgrims who traditionally sleep there on the saint's day.

SANTA MARIA NAVARRESE

At the southern end of the Golfo di Orosei sits the unpretentious and attractive beach resort of Santa Maria Navarrese. Shipwrecked Basque sailors built a small church here in 1052, dedicated to Santa Maria di Navarra on the orders of the Princess of Navarre, who happened to be one of the survivors. The church was set in the shade of a grand olive tree that is still standing – some say it's nearly 2000 years old.

Lofty pines and eucalyptus trees back the beach lapped by transparent water. Offshore are several islets, including the Isolotto di Ogliastra, a giant hunk of pink porphyritic rock. The leafy northern end of the beach is topped by a watchtower built to look for raiding Saracens.

Down at the port, the Consorzio Marittimo Ogliastra (☎0782 61 51 73; www.mareogliastra.com) runs boat tours along the Golfo di Orosei for between €30 and €35 per person. Next door, Nautica Centro Sub (☎0782 61 55 22) organises dives (from €35) to some wonderful underwater spots.

The Ostello Bellavista (☎0782 61 40 39; www.ostelloinogliastra.com; Via Pedra Longa; s €35-65, d €50-100; ☀☏) has light rooms with dreamy sea views. For drinks by the seafront, try the charismatic Bar L'Olivastro (☎0782 61 55 13; Via Lungomare Montesanto 1; ☺8am-1am) below the branches of the town's famous olive tree.

A handful of buses link Santa Maria Navarrese with Tortolì (€1.50, 15 minutes, 11 daily), Dorgali (€5, 1½ hours, two daily) and Nuoro (€7, 2½ hours, five daily).

TORTOLÌ & ARBATAX
POP 10,395

Tortolì, Ogliastra's provincial capital, is unlikely to make a big impression with its large roadside hotels and uninspiring shops. About 4km away, Arbatax is little more than a port fronted by a few bars and restaurants. The only sight of any note is the *rocce rosse* (red rocks), a series of bizarre, weather-beaten rocks rising from the sea in Arbatax.

Near the port, you'll find the terminus for the Trenino Verde, the summer tourist train to Mandas.

There's no shortage of resort-style accommodation in these parts. Five minutes' stroll from the beach is La Vecchia Marina (☎0782 66 70 20; www.hotellavecchiamarina. com; Via Praga 1, Localita Porto Frailis; d €70-140; P☀☏), a whitewashed hotel with an almost colonial feel, fringed by palm-dotted gardens. For Med-fresh seafood head to Ittiturismo La Peschiera (☎0782 66 44 15; Spiaggia della Cartiera; meals around €30; ☺daily), run by Tortolì's fishing cooperative.

For information on ferry connections, see p816.

Buses connect Tortolì with Santa Maria Navarrese (€1.50, 15 minutes, 11 daily), Dorgali (€5, one hour 50 minutes, one daily), and Nuoro (€7, 2¾ hours, five daily), as well as many inland villages.

Understand Italy

Italy Today

Trials & Tribulations

It might be the home of *la dolce vita,* but Italy has one hell of a *mal di testa* (headache). Unemployment rose from 6.2% in 2007 to 8.4% in 2010, while Italy's public debt remains above 115% of GDP. Unnerving memories of the social unrest that marked the 1970s came to the fore in late 2010, with nationwide rallies protesting about education reforms, and anarchist mail bombs at Rome's Swiss and Chilean embassies.

On the political front, Prime Minister Silvio Berlusconi's string of scandals has led a growing number of Italians to question his ability to tackle the country's chronic problems. Among them is Naples' on-again, off-again rubbish crisis: in May 2011, 170 troops were deployed to help clear 2000 tonnes of litter from the city's streets, three years after Berlusconi's promise to resolve the region's waste-disposal woes.

Berlusconi may be wishing for a landfill site deep enough to bury his own woes. In early 2011 Italy's Constitutional Court overturned a law granting legal immunity to the prime minister and senior ministers. As a result, four criminal cases against the centre-right leader have been reactivated, spanning everything from alleged tax evasion to the alleged bribing of British lawyer David Mills in two corruption trials in the 1990s.

The most sensational trial, however, is 'Rubygate'. In it, Berlusconi is accused of paying for sex with Karima El Mahroug, a nightclub dancer nicknamed Ruby Rubacuori (Ruby Heartstealer), while she was still 17. The encounters reputedly took place at so-called *bunga bunga* sessions; sex parties held at several of Berlusconi's villas. The scandal has embroiled a number of public figures, including Nicole Minetti: a showgirl-turned-regional councillor for Lombardy, the Anglo-Italian is accused of procuring young women for Berlusconi's parties. Berlusconi is further

» Population: 61 million (2011)

» Size: 301,230 sq km

» GDP: €1246 billion

» GDP per capita (2010): €21,483

» Annual inflation: 1.4%

Dos & Don'ts

» Italians are generally chic and quick to judge on appearances. Make an effort with your presentation and never remove your shoes in public.

» Shorts and sleeveless tops are usually forbidden in religious buildings.

» Splitting the bill is oh-so *incivile* (uncivilised). The person who invites pays, although close friends often go Dutch.

» When invited to a home for a meal, always take flowers, pastries or a bottle of wine.

» Supermarkets provide disposable plastic gloves for handling fruit and vegetables: wear them.

belief systems
(% of population)

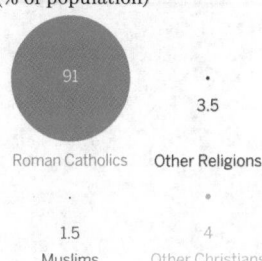

91

Roman Catholics

.
3.5

Other Religions

1.5
Muslims

.
4
Other Christians

if Italy were 100 people

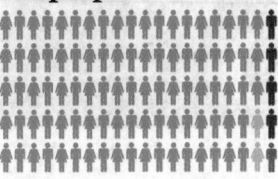

93 would be Italian
4 would be Albanian & Eastern European
1 would be North African
2 would be Others

accused of providing false information to a Milan police chief in order to release El Mahroug from detention on unrelated theft charges.

The former cruise-ship crooner insists that the claims are part of a plot orchestrated by the political left, but it seems that Italy's tumultuous relationship with Il Cavaliere (The Cavalier, as Berlusconi is dubbed) is wearing thin. On 13 February 2011, close to one million Italians took part in rallies demanding his resignation. In May the same year, Berlusconi's centre-right coalition lost control of both Milan and Naples in local elections. The defeat of Milan mayor Letizia Moratti to centre-left lawyer Giuliano Pisapia had been declared 'unthinkable' to Berlusconi, confident that his power base and home town would prove him to be the seasoned survivor once more.

Refugee Crisis

Already a hot potato in Italy, the immigration debate heated up in 2011 as tens of thousands of boat people swamped Lampedusa, a tiny Italian island and Europe's southernmost point. More than 20,000 reached the island between January and March alone, mostly Tunisians escaping post-revolution uncertainty.

Italy's decision to grant temporary residency permits to 30,000 of the refugees caused consternation among several EU nations. Among the most vocal were France and Germany, who accused Italy of trying to fob off its illegal immigrants to other Schengen Treaty countries. On 17 April 2011 the issue escalated when France temporarily closed its border with Italy to prevent a trainload of immigrants from entering French territory. Far from impressed, the Italian government accused France of lacking solidarity over a problem it sees as European and not just Italian.

» Unemployment rate: 8.4%

» Highest point: Mont Blanc (Monte Bianco) (4807m)

» Number of Unesco World Heritage Sites: 45

» Average cups of coffee per person per year: 600

Books

The Italians (Luigi Barzini) A revealing look at Italian culture beyond the well-worn clichés.
La Bella Figura: A Field Guide to the Italian Mind (Beppe Severgnini) Satirist Severgnini offers a crash course in what makes modern Italians tick.

Benevolence & Betrayal: Five Jewish Families Under Fascism (Alexander Stille) A moving oral history of the Italian-Jewish experience in the shadow of the Holocaust.

Italian Neighbors (Tim Parks) Life in Verona through the eyes of a witty British writer.

History

Few countries have been on such a roller-coaster ride as Italy. The Italian peninsula lay at the core of the Roman Empire; one of the world's great monotheistic religions, Catholicism, has its headquarters in Rome; and it was largely the dynamic city-states of Italy that set the modern era in motion with the Renaissance. But Italy has known chaos and deep suffering, too. The rise of Europe's nation states from the 16th century left the divided Italian peninsula behind. Italian unity was won in blood, but many Italians have since lived in abject poverty, sparking great waves of migration. The economic miracle of the 1960s propelled Italy to the top league of wealthy Western countries but, since the mid-1990s, the country has wallowed in a mire of frustration. A sluggish economy (hit hard by the global slump that began in 2008), a seemingly ineffective and squabbling government, widespread corruption and the continuing open sore of the Mafia continue to overshadow the country's otherwise sunny disposition.

A wide-ranging general site with potted Italian history is www. arcaini.com. It covers everything from prehistory to the post war period, and includes a brief chronology.

Etruscans, Greeks & Wolf-Raised Twins

Of the many tribes that emerged from the millennia of the Stone Age in ancient Italy, the Etruscans dominated the peninsula by the 7th century BC. Etruria was based on city-states mostly concentrated between the Arno and Tiber rivers. Among them were Caere (modern-day Cerveteri), Tarquinii (Tarquinia), Veii (Veio), Perusia (Perugia), Volaterrae (Volterra) and Arretium (Arezzo). The name of their homeland is preserved in the name Tuscany, where the bulk of their settlements were (and still are) located.

Most of what we know of the Etruscan people has been deduced from artefacts and paintings unearthed at their burial sights, especially at Tarquinia, near Rome. Argument persists over whether the Etruscans had migrated from Asia Minor. They spoke a language that today has barely

TIMELINE	c 700,000 BC	2000 BC	474 BC
	As long ago as 700,000 BC, primitive tribes lived in caves and hunted elephants, rhinoceros, hippopotamuses and other hefty wild beasts on the Italian peninsula.	The Bronze Age reaches Italy. Hunter-gatherers have settled as farmers. The use of copper and bronze to fashion tools and arms marks a new sophistication.	The power of the Etruscans in Italy is eclipsed after Greek forces from Syracuse and Cumae join to crush an Etruscan armada off the southern Italian coast in the naval Battle of Cumae.

been deciphered. An energetic people, the Etruscans were redoubtable warriors and seamen, but lacked cohesion and discipline.

At home, the Etruscans farmed, and mined metals. Their gods were numerous and they were forever trying to second-guess them and predict future events through such rituals as examining the livers of sacrificed animals. They were also quick to learn from others. Much of their artistic tradition (which comes to us in the form of tomb frescoes, statuary and pottery) was influenced by the Greeks.

Indeed, while the Etruscans dominated the centre of the peninsula, Greek traders settled in the south in the 8th century BC, setting up a series of independent city-states along the coast and in Sicily that together were known as Magna Graecia. They flourished until the 3rd century BC and the ruins of magnificent Doric temples in Italy's south (at Paestum) and on Sicily (at Agrigento, Selinunte and Segesta) stand as testimony to the splendour of Greek civilisation in Italy.

The Oxford History of the Roman World, edited by John Boardman, Jasper Griffin and Oswyn Murray, is a succinct and clear introduction to the history of ancient Rome.

Attempts by the Etruscans to conquer the Greek settlements failed, and accelerated their decline. The death knell, however, would come from an unexpected source – the grubby but growing Latin town of Rome.

The origins of the town are shrouded in myth, which says it was founded by Romulus (who descended from Aeneas, a refugee from Troy whose mother was the goddess Venus) on 21 April 753 BC on the site where he and his brother, Remus, had been suckled by a she-wolf as orphan infants. Romulus later killed Remus and the settlement was named Rome after him. At some point, legend merges with history. Seven kings are said to have followed Romulus and at least three were historical Etruscan rulers. In 509 BC, disgruntled Latin nobles turfed the last of the Etruscan kings, Tarquinius Superbus, out of Rome after his predecessor, Servius Tullius, had stacked the Senate with his allies and introduced citizenship reforms that undermined the power of the aristocracy. Sick of monarchy, the nobles set up the Roman Republic. Over the following centuries, this piffling Latin town would grow to become Italy's major power, gradually sweeping aside the Etruscans, whose language and culture had disappeared by the 2nd century AD.

The Roman Republic

Under the Republic, *imperium,* or regal power, was placed in the hands of two consuls who acted as political and military leaders and were elected for non-renewable one-year terms by an assembly of the people. The Senate, whose members were appointed for life, advised the consuls.

Although from the beginning monuments were emblazoned with the initials SPQR (Senatus Populusque Romanus, or the Senate and People of Rome), the 'people' initially had precious little say in affairs. (The initials

396 BC	264–241 BC	218–202 BC	79
Romans conquer the key Etruscan town of Veio, north of Rome, after an 11-year siege. Celebrations are short-lived, as invading Celtic tribes sweep across Italy and sack Rome in 390 BC.	War rages between Rome and the empire of Carthage, stretching across North Africa and into Spain, Sicily and Sardinia. By war's end Rome is the western Mediterranean's prime naval power.	Carthage sends Hannibal to invade Italy overland from the north in the Second Punic War. Rome invades Spain, Hannibal fails, and Carthage is destroyed in a third war in 149–146 BC.	Mt Vesuvius showers molten rock and ash upon Pompeii and Herculaneum. Pliny the Younger later describes the eruption in letters and the towns are only rediscovered in the 18th century.

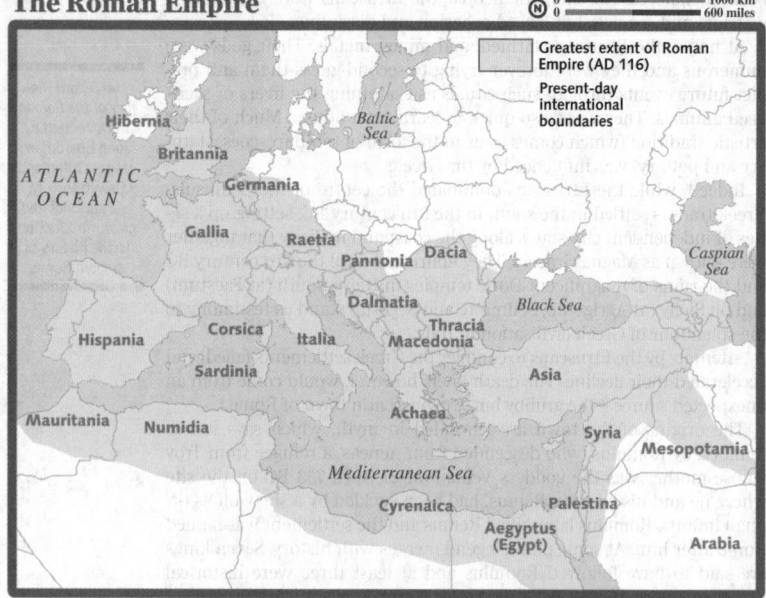

Greatest extent of Roman Empire (AD 116)

Present-day international boundaries

are still used and many Romans would argue that little has changed.) Known as plebeians (literally 'the many'), the disenfranchised majority slowly wrested concessions from the patrician class in the more than two centuries that followed the founding of the Republic. Some plebeians were even appointed as consuls and indeed by about 280 BC most of the distinctions between patricians and plebeians had disappeared. That said, the apparently democratic system was largely oligarchic, with a fairly narrow political class (whether patrician or plebeian) vying for positions of power in government and the Senate.

The Romans were a rough-and-ready lot. Rome did not bother to mint coins until 269 BC, even though the neighbouring (and later conquered or allied) Etruscans and Greeks had long had their own currencies. The Etruscans and Greeks also brought writing to the attention of Romans, who found it useful for documents and technical affairs but hardly glowed in the literature department. Eventually the Greek pantheon of gods formed the bedrock of Roman worship. Society was

476	568	754–56	902
German tribal leader Odovacar proclaims himself king in Rome. The peninsula sinks into chaos and only the eastern half of the Empire survives intact.	Lombards invade and occupy northern Italy, leaving just Ravenna, Rome and southern Italy in the Empire's hands. Other tribes invade Balkan territories and cut the eastern Empire off from Italy.	Frankish king Pepin the Short enters Italy at the request of Pope Stephen II, defeats the Lombards and declares the creation of the Papal States.	Muslims from North Africa complete the occupation of Sicily, encouraging learning of the Greek classics, mathematics and other sciences. Agriculture flourishes and Sicily is relatively peaceful for two centuries.

patriarchal and its prime building block the household *(familia)*. The head of the family *(pater familias)* had direct control over his wife, children and extended family. He was responsible for his children's education. Devotion to household gods was as strong as to the increasingly Greek-influenced pantheon of state gods, led at first by the triad of Jupiter (the sky god and chief protector of the state), Juno (the female equivalent of Jupiter and patron goddess of women) and Minerva (patron goddess of craftsmen). Mars, the god of war, had been replaced by Juno in the triad.

Slowly at first, then with gathering pace, Roman armies conquered the Italian peninsula. Defeated city-states were not taken over directly; rather they were obliged to become allies. They retained their government and lands but had to provide troops on demand to serve in the Roman army. This relatively light-handed touch was a key to success. Increasingly, the protection offered by Roman hegemony induced many cities to become allies voluntarily. Wars with rivals like Carthage and in the East led Rome to take control of Sardinia, Sicily, Corsica, mainland Greece, Spain, most of North Africa and part of Asia Minor by 133 BC.

As the Empire grew, so did its ancient system of 'motorways'. With the roads came other bright concepts – postal services and wayside inns. Messages could be shot around the Empire in a matter of days or weeks by sending despatch riders. At ancient 'truck stops', the riders would change mounts, have a bite and continue on their way (a more efficient system than many modern European postal systems).

By the second half of the 2nd century BC, Rome was the most important city in the Mediterranean, with a population of 300,000. Most were lower-class freedmen or slaves living in often precarious conditions. Tenement housing blocks (mostly of brick and wood) were raised alongside vast monuments. One of the latter was the Circus Flaminius, stage of some of the spectacular games held each year. These became increasingly important events for the people of Rome, who flocked to see gladiators and wild beasts in combat.

Seizing the Day

Born in 100 BC, Gaius Julius Caesar would prove to be one of Rome's most masterful generals, lenient conquerors and capable administrators. He was also avid for power and this was probably his undoing.

He was a supporter of the consul Pompey (later known as Pompey the Great), who since 78 BC had become a leading figure in Rome after putting down rebellions in Spain and eliminating piracy. Caesar himself had been in Spain for several years, dealing with border revolts, and on his return to Rome in 60 BC, formed an alliance with Pompey and another

The Romans devised a type of odometer that engaged with a vehicle's wheel to count every mile travelled.

962	1130
Otto I is crowned Holy Roman Emperor in Rome, the first in a long line of Germanic rulers. His meddling in Italian affairs leads to clashes between papacy and empire.	Norman invader Roger II is crowned king of Sicily, a century after the Normans landed in southern Italy and so creating a united southern Italian kingdom.

» Cathedral in Cefalù, Sicily, built by Roger II.

important commander and former consul, Crassus. They backed Caesar's candidacy as consul.

To consolidate his position in the Roman power game, Caesar needed a major military command. This he received with a mandate to govern the province of Gallia Narbonensis, a southern swath of modern France stretching from Italy to the Pyrenees, from 59 BC. Caesar raised troops and in the following year entered Gaul proper (modern France) to head off an invasion of Helvetic tribes from Switzerland and subsequently to bring other tribes to heel. What started as an essentially defensive effort soon became a full-blown campaign of conquest. In the next five years, he subdued Gaul and made forays into Britain and across the Rhine. In 52–51 BC he stamped out the last great revolt in Gaul, led by Vercingetorix. Caesar was generous to his defeated enemies and so won the Gauls over to him. Indeed, they became his staunchest supporters in coming years.

By now, Caesar also had a devoted veteran army behind him. Jealous of the growing power of his one-time protégé, Pompey severed his political alliance with him and joined like-minded factions in the Senate to outlaw Caesar in 49 BC. On 7 January, Caesar crossed the Rubicon river into Italy and civil war began. His three-year campaign in Italy, Spain and the eastern Mediterranean proved a crushing victory. Upon his return to Rome in 46 BC, he assumed dictatorial powers.

He launched a series of reforms, overhauled the Senate and embarked on a building program (of which the Curia and Basilica Giulia remain).

By 44 BC it was clear Caesar had no plans to restore the Republic, and dissent grew in the Senate, even among former supporters like Marcus Junius Brutus, who thought he had gone too far. Unconcerned by rumours of a possible assassination attempt, Caesar had dismissed his bodyguard. A small band of conspirators led by Brutus finally stabbed him to death in a Senate meeting on the Ides of March (15 March) 44 BC, two years after he had been proclaimed dictator for life.

In the years following Caesar's death, his lieutenant, Mark Antony (Marcus Antonius), and nominated heir, great-nephew Octavian, plunged into civil war against Caesar's assassins. Things calmed down as Octavian took control of the western half of the empire and Antony headed to the east, but when Antony fell head over heels for Cleopatra VII in 31 BC, Octavian went to war and finally claimed victory over Antony and Cleopatra at Actium, in Greece. The next year, Octavian invaded Egypt, Antony and Cleopatra committed suicide and Egypt became a province of Rome.

IMPERIAL INSANITY

Bribes? Booty jokes? *Bunga bunga* parties? Spare a thought for the ancient Romans, who suffered their fare share of eccentric leaders. We salute some of the Empire's wackiest, weirdest and downright kinkiest rulers.

14–37 Tiberius – A steady governing hand but prone to depression, Tiberius had a difficult relationship with the Senate and withdrew in his later years to Capri, where, they say, he devoted himself to drinking, orgies and fits of paranoia.

37–41 Gaius (Caligula) – 'Little Shoes' made grand-uncle Tiberius look tame. Sex, including with his sisters, and gratuitous, cruel violence were high on his agenda. He emptied the state's coffers and suggested making a horse consul, before being assassinated.

41–54 Claudius – Apparently timid as a child, he proved ruthless with his enemies (among them 35 senators), whose executions he greatly enjoyed watching. According to English historian Edward Gibbon, he was the only one of the first 15 emperors not to take male lovers (unusual at the time).

54–68 Nero – Augustus' last descendant, Nero had his pushy stage mum murdered, his first wife's veins slashed, his second wife kicked to death, and his third wife's ex-husband killed. The people accused him of playing the fiddle while Rome burned to the ground in 64. He blamed the disaster on the Christians, executed the evangelists Peter and Paul and had others thrown to wild beasts in a grisly public spectacle.

Augustus & the Glories of Empire

Octavian was left as sole ruler of the Roman world and by 27 BC had been acclaimed Augustus (Your Eminence) and conceded virtually unlimited power by the Senate. In effect, he had become emperor.

Under him, the arts flourished. Augustus was lucky in having as his contemporaries the poets Virgil, Horace and Ovid, as well as the historian Livy. He encouraged the visual arts, restored existing buildings and constructed many new ones. During his reign the Pantheon was raised and he boasted that he had 'found Rome in brick and left it in marble'.

The long period of comparatively enlightened rule that he initiated brought unprecedented prosperity and security to the Mediterranean. The Empire was, in the main, wisely administered (although there were some kooky exceptions, such as the potty Caligula).

By AD 100, the city of Rome is said to have had more than 1.5 million inhabitants and all the trappings of the imperial capital – its wealth and prosperity were obvious in the rich mosaics, marble temples, public baths, theatres, circuses and libraries. People of all races and conditions

For Ancient Awe

» Pantheon, Rome

» Colosseum, Rome

» Pompeii, Campania

» Segesta, Sicily

» Cerveteri, Lazio

1321	1348	1506	1508–12
Dante Alighieri completes his epic poem *La divina commedia* (The Divine Comedy). The Florentine poet, considered Italy's greatest literary figure, dies the same year.	The Black Death (bubonic plague) wreaks havoc across Italy and much of the rest of western Europe. Florence is said to have lost three-quarters of its populace.	Work starts on St Peter's Basilica, to a design by Donato Bramante, over the site of an earlier basilica in Rome. Work would continue on Christendom's showpiece church until 1626.	Pope Julius II commissions Michelangelo to paint the ceiling frescoes in the Sistine Chapel. Michelangelo decides the context, and the central nine panels recount stories from Genesis.

converged on the capital. Poverty was rife among an often disgruntled lower class. Augustus had created Rome's first police force under a city prefect *(praefectus urbi)* to curb mob violence, which had long gone largely unchecked. He had also instituted a 7000-man fire brigade and night watchman service.

Augustus carried out other far-reaching reforms. He streamlined the army, which was kept at a standing total of around 300,000 men. Military service ranged from 16 to 25 years, but Augustus kept conscription to a minimum, making it a largely volunteer force. He consolidated Rome's three-tier class society. The richest and most influential class remained the Senators. Below them, the so-called Equestrians filled posts in public administration and supplied officers to the army (control of which was essential to keeping Augustus' position unchallenged). The bulk of the populace filled the ranks of the lower class. The system was by no means rigid and upward mobility was possible.

A century after Augustus' death in AD 14 (at age 75), the Empire had reached its greatest extent. Under Hadrian (76–138), the Empire stretched from the Iberian peninsula, Gaul and Britain to a line that basically followed the Rhine and Danube rivers. All of the present-day Balkans and Greece, along with the areas known in those times as Dacia, Moesia and Thrace (considerable territories reaching to the Black Sea), were under Roman control. Most of modern-day Turkey, Syria, Lebanon, Palestine and Israel was occupied by Rome's legions and linked up with Egypt. From there a deep strip of Roman territory stretched along the length of North Africa to the Atlantic coast of what is today northern Morocco. The Mediterranean was a Roman lake.

This situation lasted until the 3rd century. By the time Diocletian (245–305) became emperor, attacks on the Empire from without and revolts within had become part and parcel of imperial existence. A new religious force, Christianity, was gaining popularity and under Diocletian persecution of Christians became common, a policy reversed in 313 under Constantine I (c 272–337) in his Edict of Milan.

Inspired by a vision of the cross, Constantine defeated his own rival, Maxentius, on Rome's Ponte Milvio (Milvian Bridge) in 312, becoming the Roman Empire's first Christian leader and commissioning Rome's first Christian basilica, San Giovanni in Laterano.

The Empire was later divided in two, with the second capital in Constantinople (founded by Constantine in 330), on the Bosporus in Byzantium. It was this, the eastern Empire, which survived as Italy and Rome were overrun. This rump empire stretched from parts of present-day Serbia and Montenegro across to Asia Minor, a coastal strip of what

1534	**1582**	**1600**
The accession of Pope Paul III marks the beginning of the Counter-Reformation. He establishes a militant Jesuit order in 1540 and the heretic-hunting Holy Office of the Inquisition in 1542.	Pope Gregory XIII replaces the Julian calendar (introduced by Julius Caesar) with the modern-day Gregorian calendar. The new calendar adds the leap year to keep in line with the seasons.	Dominican monk and proud philosopher Giordano Bruno is burned alive at the stake in Rome for heresy after eight years of trial and torture at the hands of the Inquisition.

GEOFF STRINGER / LONELY PLANET IMAGES ©

» Statue of Giordano Bruno.

is now Syria, Lebanon, Jordan and Israel down to Egypt and a sliver of North Africa as far west as modern Libya. Attempts by Justinian I (482–565) to recover Rome and the shattered western half of the Empire ultimately came to nothing.

Papal Power & Family Feuds

In an odd twist, the minority religion that Emperor Diocletian had tried so hard to stamp out saved the glory of the city of Rome. Through the chaos of invasion and counter-invasion that saw Italy succumb to Germanic tribes, the Byzantine reconquest and the Lombard occupation in the north, the papacy established itself in Rome as a spiritual and secular force.

The popes were, even at this early stage, a canny crowd. The papacy invented the Donation of Constantine, a document in which Emperor Constantine I had supposedly granted the Church control of Rome and surrounding territory. What the popes needed was a guarantor with military clout. This they found in the Franks and a deal was done.

In return for formal recognition of the popes' control of Rome and surrounding Byzantine-held territories henceforth to be known as the Papal States, the popes granted the Carolingian Franks a leading if ill-defined role in Italy and their king, Charlemagne, the title of Holy Roman Emperor. He was crowned by Leo III on Christmas Day 800. The bond between the papacy and the Byzantine Empire was thus broken and political power in what had been the Western Roman Empire shifted north of the Alps, where it would remain for more than 1000 years.

The stage was set for a future of seemingly endless struggles. Similarly, Rome's aristocratic families engaged in battle for the papacy. For centuries, the imperial crown would be fought over ruthlessly and Italy would frequently be the prime battleground. Holy Roman Emperors would seek time and again to impose their control on increasingly independent-minded Italian cities, and even on Rome itself. In riposte, the popes continually sought to exploit their spiritual position to bring the emperors to heel and further their own secular ends.

The clash between Pope Gregory VII and Emperor Henry IV over who had the right to appoint bishops (who were powerful political players and hence important friends or dangerous foes) in the last quarter of the 11th century showed just how bitter these struggles could become. They became a focal point of Italian politics in the late Middle Ages and across the cities and regions of the peninsula two camps emerged: Guelphs (Guelfi, who backed the pope) and Ghibellines (Ghibellini, in support of the emperor).

For Anicent Booty

» Vatican Museums, Rome

» Capitoline Museums, Rome

» Museo Archeologico Nazionale, Naples

» Museo Archeologico Paolo Orsi, Syracuse

» Museo Nazionale Etrusco di Villa Giulia, Rome

HISTORY PAPAL POWER & FAMILY FEUDS

Europe's first modern banks appeared in Genoa in the 12th century. The city claims the first recorded public bond (1150) and the earliest known exchange contract (1156). Italy's Banca Monte dei Paschi di Siena is the world's oldest surviving bank, counting coins since 1472.

1714	1805	1810	1814–15
The end of the War of the Spanish Succession forces the withdrawal of Spanish forces from Lombardy. The Spanish Bourbon family establishes an independent Kingdom of the Two Sicilies.	Napoleon is proclaimed king of the newly constituted Kingdom of Italy, comprising most of the northern half of the country. A year later he takes the Kingdom of Naples.	Physicist Alessandro Volta invents the electric battery and gives his name to the measurement of electrical power. Volta's lesser-known invention is the remotely operated pistol.	After Napoleon's fall, the Congress of Vienna is held to re-establish the balance of power in Europe. The result for Italy is largely a return of the old occupying powers.

The Wonder of the World

The Arabs introduced spaghetti to Sicily, where 'strings of pasta' were documented by the Arab geographer Al-Idrissi in Palermo in 1150.

The Holy Roman Empire had barely touched southern Italy until Henry, son of the Holy Roman Emperor Frederick I (Barbarossa), married Constance de Hauteville, heir to the Norman throne in Sicily. The Normans had arrived in southern Italy in the 10th century, initially as pilgrims en route from Jerusalem, later as mercenaries attracted by the money to be made fighting for rival principalities, and against the Arab Muslims in Sicily. Of Henry and Constance's match was born one of the most colourful figures of medieval Europe, Frederick II (1194–1250).

Crowned Holy Roman Emperor in 1220, Frederick was a German with a difference. Having grown up in southern Italy, he considered Sicily his natural base and left the German states largely to their own devices. A warrior and scholar, Frederick was an enlightened ruler with an absolutist vocation. A man who allowed freedom of worship to Muslims and Jews, he was not to everyone's liking, as his ambition was to finally bring all of Italy under the imperial yoke.

For
Medieval
Mystique

» Gubbio, Umbria
» Bologna, Emilia-Romagna
» Perugia, Umbria
» Assisi, Umbria
» Scanno, Abruzzo

A poet, linguist, mathematician, philosopher and all-round fine fellow, Frederick founded a university in Naples and encouraged the spread of learning and translation of Arab treatises. From his early days at the imperial helm, he was known as Stupor Mundi (the Wonder of the World) for his extraordinary talents, energy and military prowess.

Having reluctantly carried out a crusade (marked more by negotiation than the clash of arms) in the Holy Land in 1228 and 1229 on pain of excommunication, Frederick returned to Italy to find Papal troops invading Neapolitan territory. Frederick soon had them on the run and turned his attention to gaining control of the complex web of city-states in central and northern Italy, where he found allies and many enemies, in particular the Lombard league. Years of inconclusive battles ensued, which even Frederick's death in 1250 did not end. Several times he had been on the verge of taking Rome and victory had seemed assured more than once. Campaigning continued until 1268 under Frederick's successors, Manfredi (who fell in the bloody Battle of Benevento in 1266) and Corradino (captured and executed two years later by French noble Charles of Anjou, who had by then taken over Sicily and southern Italy).

John Julius Norwich's A History of Venice is one of the all-time great works on the lagoon city in English and is highly readable. He has also published Venice: Paradise of Cities.

Rise of the City-States

While the south of Italy tended to centralised rule, the north was heading the opposite way. Port cities such as Genoa, Pisa and especially Venice, along with internal centres such as Florence, Milan, Parma, Bologna, Padua, Verona and Modena, became increasingly insolent towards attempts by the Holy Roman Emperors to meddle in their affairs.

1848	1860	1861	1889
European revolts spark rebellion in Italy, especially in Austrian-occupied Milan and Venice. Piedmont's King Carlo Alberto joins the fray against Austria, but within a year Austria recovers Lombardy and Veneto.	In the name of Italian unity, Giuseppe Garibaldi lands with 1000 men, the Red Shirts, in Sicily. He takes the island and lands in southern Italy.	By the end of the 1859–61 Franco-Austrian War, Vittorio Emanuele II controls Lombardy, Sardinia, Sicily, southern and parts of central Italy and is proclaimed king of a newly united Italy.	Raffaele Esposito invents pizza margherita in honour of Queen Margherita, who takes her first bite of the Neapolitan staple on a royal visit to the city.

The cities' growing prosperity and independence also brought them into conflict with Rome, which found itself increasingly incapable of exercising influence over them. Indeed, at times Rome's control over some of its own Papal States was challenged. Caught between the papacy and the emperors, it was not surprising that these city-states were forever switching allegiances in an attempt to best serve their own interests.

Between the 12th and 14th centuries, they developed new forms of government. Venice adopted an oligarchic, 'parliamentary' system in an attempt at limited democracy. More commonly, the city-state created a *comune* (town council), a form of republican government dominated at first by aristocrats but then increasingly by the wealthy middle classes. The well-heeled families soon turned their attentions from business rivalry to political struggles, in which each aimed to gain control of the *signoria* (government).

In some cities, great dynasties, such as the Medici in Florence and the Visconti and Sforza in Milan, came to dominate their respective stages.

War between the city-states was constant and eventually a few, notably Florence, Milan and Venice, emerged as regional powers and absorbed their neighbours. Their power was based on a mix of trade, industry and conquest. Constellations of power and alliances were in constant flux, making changes in the city-states' fortunes the rule rather than the exception. Easily the most stable and long the most successful of them was Venice.

In Florence, prosperity was based on the wool trade, finance and general commerce. Abroad, its coinage, the *firenze* (florin), was king.

In Milan, the noble Visconti family destroyed its rivals and extended Milanese control over Pavia and Cremona, and later Genoa. Giangaleazzo Visconti (1351–1402) turned Milan from a city-state into a strong European power. The policies of the Visconti (up to 1450), followed by those of the Sforza family, allowed Milan to spread its power to the Ticino area of Switzerland and east to the Lago di Garda.

The Milanese sphere of influence butted up against that of Venice. By 1450 the lagoon city had reached the height of its territorial greatness. In addition to its possessions in Greece, Dalmatia and beyond, Venice had expanded inland. The banner of the Lion of St Mark flew across northeast Italy, from Gorizia to Bergamo.

These dynamic, independent-minded cities proved fertile ground for the intellectual and artistic explosion that would take place across northern Italy in the 14th and 15th centuries – an explosion that would come to be known as the Renaissance and the birth of the modern world. Of them all, Florence was the cradle and launch pad for this fevered activity, in no small measure due to the generous patronage of the long-ruling Medici family.

For Renaissance Elegance

» Duomo, Florence

» Galleria degli Uffizi, Florence

» Tempietto di Bramante, Rome

» La Rotonda, Vicenza

» Da Vinci's *The Last Supper*, Milan

America was named after Amerigo Vespucci, a Florentine navigator who, from 1497 to 1504, made several voyages of discovery in what would one day be known as South America.

1908	1915	1919	1922
On the morning of 28 December, Messina and Reggio di Calabria are struck by a 7.5-magnitude earthquake and a 13-metre-high tsunami. More than 80,000 lives are lost.	Italy enters WWI on the side of the Allies to win Italian territories still in Austrian hands after Austria's offer to cede some of the territories is deemed insufficient.	Former socialist journalist Benito Mussolini forms a right-wing militant group, the Fasci Italiani di Combattimento (Italian Combat Fasces), precursor to his Fascist Party.	Mussolini and his Fascists stage a march on Rome in October. Doubting the army's loyalty, a fearful King Vittorio Emanuele III entrusts Mussolini with the formation of a government.

A Nation Is Born

The French Revolution at the end of the 18th century and the rise of Napoleon awakened hopes in Italy of independent nationhood. Since the glory days of the Renaissance, Italy's divided mini-states had gradually lost power and status on the European stage. By the late 18th century, the peninsula was little more than a tired, backward playground for the big powers and a Grand Tour hot spot for the romantically inclined.

Napoleon marched into Italy on several occasions, finishing off the Venetian republic in 1797 (ending 1000 years of Venetian independence) and creating the so-called Kingdom of Italy in 1804. That kingdom was in no way independent but the Napoleonic earthquake spurred many Italians to believe that a single Italian state could be created after the emperor's demise.

It was not to be so easy. The reactionary Congress of Vienna restored all the foreign rulers to their places in Italy.

Count Camillo Benso di Cavour (1810–61) of Turin, the prime minister of the Savoy monarchy, became the diplomatic brains behind the Italian unity movement. Through the pro-unity newspaper, *Il Risorgimento* (founded in 1847) and the publication of a parliamentary *Statuto* (Statute), Cavour and his colleagues laid the groundwork for unity.

Cavour conspired with the French and won British support for the creation of an independent Italian state. His 1858 treaty with France's Napoleon III foresaw French aid in the event of a war with Austria and the creation of a northern Italian kingdom, in exchange for parts of Savoy and Nice.

The bloody Franco-Austrian War (also known as the Second Italian War of Independence; 1859–61), unleashed in northern Italy, led to the occupation of Lombardy and the retreat of the Austrians to their eastern possessions in the Veneto. In the meantime, a wild card in the form of professional revolutionary Giuseppe Garibaldi had created the real chance of full Italian unity. Garibaldi took Sicily and southern Italy in a military blitz in the name of Savoy king Vittorio Emanuele II in 1860. Spotting the chance, Cavour and the king moved to take parts of central Italy (including Umbria and Le Marche) and so were able to proclaim the creation of a single Italian state in 1861.

In the following nine years, Tuscany, the Veneto and Rome were all incorporated into the fledgling kingdom. Unity was complete and parliament was established in Rome in 1871.

The turbulent new state saw violent swings between socialists and the right. Giovanni Giolitti, one of Italy's longest-serving prime ministers (heading five governments between 1892 and 1921), managed to bridge

Giuliano Procacci's *History of the Italian People* is one of the best general histories of the country in any language. It covers the period from the early Middle Ages until 1948.

1929

Mussolini and Pope Pius XI sign the Lateran Pact, which declares Catholicism as Italy's sole religion and the Vatican an independent state. Satisfied, the papacy acknowledges the Kingdom of Italy.

1935

Italy seeks a new colonial conquest through the invasion of Abyssinia (Ethiopia) from Eritrea. The League of Nations condemns the invasion and imposes limited sanctions on Italy.

WILL SALTER / LONELY PLANET IMAGES ©

» Nun, St Peter's Basilica, Vatican City.

Politics in Italy's mercurial city-states could take a radical turn. When Florence's Medici clan rulers fell into disgrace (not for the last time) in 1494, the city's fathers decided to restore an earlier republican model of government. This time there was a twist.

Since 1481, the fat-lipped Dominican friar Girolamo Savonarola had been in Florence preaching repentance. His blood-curdling warnings of horrors to come if Florentines did not renounce their evil ways somehow captured everyone's imagination and the city now submitted to a fiery theocracy. He called on the government to act on the basis of his divine inspiration. Drinking, whoring, partying, gambling, flashy fashion and other signs of wrongdoing were pushed well underground. Books, clothes, jewellery, fancy furnishings and art were burned on 'bonfires of the vanities'. Bands of children marched around the city ferreting out adults still attached to their old habits and possessions.

Pleasure-loving Florentines soon began to tire of this fundamentalism, as did Pope Alexander VI (possibly the least religiously inclined pope of all time) and the rival Franciscan religious order. The local economy was stagnant and Savonarola seemed increasingly out to lunch with his claims of being God's special emissary. Finally the city government, or *signoria*, had the fiery friar arrested. After weeks at the hands of the city rack-master, he was hanged and burned at the stake as a heretic, along with two supporters, on 22 May 1498.

the political extremes and institute male suffrage. Women were, however, denied the right to vote until after WWII.

From Trenches to Hung Dictator

When war broke out in Europe in July 1914, Italy chose to remain neutral despite being a member of the Triple Alliance with Austria and Germany. Italy had territorial claims on Austrian-controlled Trento (Trentino), southern Tyrol, Trieste and even in Dalmatia (some of which it had tried and failed to take during the Austro-Prussian War of 1866). Under the terms of the Triple Alliance, Austria was due to hand over much of this territory in the event of occupying other land in the Balkans, but Austria refused to contemplate fulfilling this part of the bargain.

The Italian government was divided between a non-interventionist and war party. The latter, in view of Austria's intransigence, decided to deal with the Allies. In the London pact of April 1915, Italy was promised the territories it sought after victory. In May, Italy declared war on Austria and thus plunged into a 3½-year nightmare.

Italy and Austria engaged in a weary war of attrition. When the Austro-Hungarian forces collapsed in November 1918, the Italians marched

1940	1943	1944	1946
Italy enters WWII on Nazi Germany's side and invades Greece, which quickly proves to be a mistake. Greek forces counter-attack and enter southern Albania. Germany saves Italy in 1941.	Allies land in Sicily. King Vittorio Emanuele III sacks Mussolini. He is replaced by Marshall Badoglio, who surrenders after Allied landings in southern Italy. German forces free Mussolini.	Mount Vesuvius explodes back into action on 18 March. The eruption is captured on film by USAAF (United States Army Air Forces) personnel stationed nearby.	Italians vote in a national referendum to abolish the monarchy and create a republic. King Umberto II leaves Italy and refuses to recognise the result.

into Trieste and Trento. The postwar Treaty of Versailles failed to award Rome the remaining territories it had sought.

These were slim pickings after such a bloody and exhausting conflict. Italy lost 600,000 men and the war economy had produced a small concentration of powerful industrial barons while leaving the bulk of the civilian populace in penury. This cocktail was made all the more explosive as hundreds of thousands of demobbed servicemen returned home or shifted around the country in search of work. The atmosphere was perfect for a demagogue, who was not long in coming forth.

Benito Mussolini (1883–1945) was a young war enthusiast who had once been a socialist newspaper editor and one-time draft dodger. This time he volunteered for the front and only returned, wounded, in 1917.

The experience of war and the frustration shared with many at the disappointing outcome in Versailles led him to form a right-wing militant political group that by 1921 had become the Fascist Party, with its black-shirted street brawlers and Roman salute. These were to become symbols of violent oppression and aggressive nationalism for the next 23 years. After his march on Rome in 1922 and victory in the 1924 elections, Mussolini, who called himself Il Duce (the Leader), took full control of the country by 1926, banning other political parties, trade unions not affiliated to the party, and the free press.

By the 1930s, all aspects of Italian society were regulated by the party. The economy, banking, massive public works program, the conversion of coastal malarial swamps into arable land and an ambitious modernisation of the armed forces were all part of Mussolini's grand plan.

On the international front, Mussolini at first showed a cautious hand, signing international cooperation pacts (including the 1928 Kellogg Pact solemnly renouncing war) and until 1935 moving close to France and the UK to contain the growing menace of Adolf Hitler's rapidly re-arming Germany.

That all changed when Mussolini decided to invade Abyssinia (Ethiopia) as the first big step to creating a 'new Roman empire'. This aggressive side of Mussolini's policy had already led to skirmishes with Greece over the island of Corfu and to military expeditions against nationalist forces in the Italian colony of Libya.

The League of Nations condemned the Abyssinian adventure (King Vittorio Emanuele III was declared Emperor of Abyssinia in 1936) and from then on Mussolini changed course, drawing closer to Nazi Germany. They backed the rebel General Franco in the three-year Spanish Civil War and in 1939 signed an alliance pact.

WWII broke out in September 1939 with Hitler's invasion of Poland. Italy remained aloof until June 1940, by which time Germany had overrun Norway, Denmark, the Low Countries and much of France. It

---

Roberto Rossellini's *Roma Città Aperta* (Rome Open City), starring Anna Magnani, is a classic of Italian neo-realist cinema and a masterful look at wartime Rome. The film is the first in his Trilogy of War, followed by *Paisà* and *Germania Anno Zero* (Germany Year Zero).

For more on the history of Fascist Italy, see www.thecorner.org/home.htm. Here you can trace Mussolini's rise to power and the tumultuous years of his rule.

1957	**1957**	**1960**	**1960**
Italy joins France, West Germany and the Benelux countries to sign the Treaty of Rome, which creates the European Economic Community (EEC). The treaty takes effect on 1 January 1958.	Turin-based car manufacturer Fiat launches the Fiat 500 in July. Designed by Dante Giacosa, the compact vehicle would become an icon of Italian industrial design.	Federico Fellini's iconic film *La Dolce Vita* is released. Capturing life in a newly affluent postwar Rome, the film is nominated for four Academy Awards.	Rome hosts the Games of the XVII Olympiad. A total of 83 nations take part, including Singapore, which competes under its own flag for the first time.

seemed too easy and so Mussolini entered on Germany's side in 1940, a move Hitler must have regretted later. Germany found itself pulling Italy's chestnuts out of the fire in campaigns in the Balkans and North Africa and could not prevent Allied landings in Sicily in 1943.

By then, the Italians had had enough of Mussolini and his war and so the king had the dictator arrested. In September, Italy surrendered and the Germans, who had rescued Mussolini, occupied the northern two-thirds of the country and reinstalled the dictator.

The painfully slow Allied campaign up the peninsula and German repression led to the formation of the Resistance, which played a growing role in harassing German forces. Northern Italy was finally liberated in April 1945. Resistance fighters caught Mussolini as he fled north in the hope of reaching Switzerland. They shot him and his lover, Clara Petacci, before stringing up their corpses (along with others) in Milan's Piazzale Lotto. This was a far cry from Il Duce's hopes for a glorious burial alongside his ancient imperial idol, Augustus, in Rome.

Claudia Cardinale starred in the 1984 Italian film *Claretta*, about the racy life and tragic end of Clara Petacci, Mussolini's lover. Given the chance to flee when they were captured, she instead tried in vain to shield Il Duce from the partisan execution squad's bullets.

Beware the Reds

In the aftermath of war, the left-wing Resistance was disarmed and Italy's political forces scrambled to regroup. The USA, through the economic largesse of the Marshall Plan, wielded considerable political influence and used this to keep the left in check.

Immediately after the war, three coalition governments succeeded one another. The third, which came to power in December 1945, was dominated by the newly formed right-wing Democrazia Cristiana (DC; Christian Democrats), led by Alcide de Gasperi, who remained prime minister until 1953. Italy became a republic in 1946 and De Gasperi's DC won the first elections under the new constitution in 1948.

Until the 1980s, the Partito Comunista Italiano (PCI; Communist Party), at first under Palmiro Togliatti and later the charismatic Enrico Berlinguer, played a crucial role in Italy's social and political development, in spite of being systematically kept out of government.

The very popularity of the party led to a grey period in the country's history, the *anni di piombo* (years of lead) in the 1970s. Just as the Italian economy was booming, Europe-wide paranoia about the power of the Communists in Italy fuelled a secretive reaction that, it is said, was largely directed by the CIA and NATO. Even today, little is known about Operation Gladio, an underground paramilitary organisation supposedly behind various unexplained terror attacks in the country, apparently designed to create an atmosphere of fear in which, should the Communists come close to power, a right-wing coup could be quickly carried out.

Although much has happened since it was written, Paul Ginsborg's *A History of Contemporary Italy: Society and Politics, 1943–1988* remains one of the single-most readable and insightful books on postwar Italy.

1966	1970	1980	1980
A devastating flood inundates Florence in early November, leaving around 100 people dead, 5000 families homeless and 14,000 movable art works damaged. The flood is the city's worst since 1557.	Parliament approves the country's first ever divorce legislation. Unwilling to accept this 'defeat', the Christian Democrats call a referendum to annul the law in 1974. Italians vote against the referendum.	A bomb in Bologna kills 85 and injures hundreds more. The Red Brigades and a Fascist cell both claim responsibility. Analysis later points to possible para-state terrorism in Operation Gladio.	At 7.34pm on 25 November, a 6.8–Richter scale earthquake strikes Campania. The quake kills almost 3000 people and causes widespread damage, including in the city of Naples.

GOING THE DISTANCE FOR THE RESISTANCE

In 1943–44, the Assisi Underground hid hundreds of Jewish Italians in Umbrian convents and monasteries, while the Tuscan Resistance forged travel documents for them – but the refugees needed those documents fast, before they were deported to concentration camps by Fascist officials. Enter the fastest man in Italy: Gino Bartali, world-famous Tuscan cyclist, Tour de France winner, and three-time champion of the Giro d'Italia. After his death in 2003, documents revealed that during his 'training rides' throughout the war years, Bartali had carried Resistance intelligence and falsified documents to transport Jewish refugees to safe locations. Bartali was interrogated at the dreaded Villa Triste in Florence, where suspected anti-Fascists were routinely tortured – but he revealed nothing. Until his death, the long-distance hero downplayed his efforts to rescue Jewish refugees even with his children, saying, 'One does these things, and then that's that.'

The 1970s were thus dominated by the spectre of terrorism and considerable social unrest, especially in the universities. Neo-Fascist terrorists struck with a bomb blast in Milan in 1969. In 1978, the Brigate Rosse (Red Brigades, a group of young left-wing militants responsible for several bomb blasts and assassinations), claimed their most important victim – former DC prime minister Aldo Moro. His kidnap and (54 days later) murder (the subject of the 2004 film *Buongiorno Notte*) shook the country.

Despite the disquiet, the 1970s was also a time of positive change. In 1970, regional governments with limited powers were formed in 15 of the country's 20 regions (the other five, Sicily, Sardinia, Valle d'Aosta, Trentino-Alto Adige and Friuli Venezia Giulia, already had strong autonomy statutes). In the same year, divorce became legal and eight years later abortion was also legalised, following anti-sexist legislation that allowed women to keep their own names after marriage.

Clean Hands & the Rise of Berlusconi

A growth spurt in the 1980s saw Italy become one of the world's leading economies, but by the mid-1990s a new and prolonged period of crisis had set in. High unemployment and inflation, combined with a huge national debt and mercurial currency (the lira), led the government to introduce draconian measures to cut public spending, allowing Italy to join the single currency (euro) in 2001.

The old order seemed to crumble in the 1990s. The PCI split in two. The old guard minority, Partito della Rifondazione Comunista (PRC; Refounded Communist Party), was led by Fausto Bertinotti until

1995	1999	2001	2004–05
Maurizio Gucci, heir to the Gucci fashion empire, is gunned down outside his Milan offices. Three years later, his estranged wife Patrizia Reggiani is jailed for ordering his murder.	Italy becomes a primary base in NATO's air war on Yugoslavia. Air strikes are carried out from the Aviano airbase from 24 May until 8 June.	Silvio Berlusconi's right-wing Casa delle Libertà (Liberties House) coalition wins an absolute majority in national polls. The following five years are marked by economic stagnation.	Tension between rival Camorra clans explodes on the streets of suburban Naples. In only four months, almost 50 people are gunned down in retribution attacks.

its crushing election defeat in 2008 (when it failed to reach the minimum 5% of the vote cut-off mark for entry to parliament). The bigger and moderate breakaway wing reformed itself as Democratici di Sinistra (DS; Left Democrats) and, in 2007, merged with another centre-left group to create the Partito Democratico (PD).

The rest of the Italian political scene was rocked by the *Tangentopoli* ('kickback city') scandal, which broke in Milan in 1992. Led by a pool of Milanese magistrates, including the tough Antonio di Pietro, investigations known as Mani Pulite (Clean Hands) implicated thousands of politicians, public officials and businesspeople in scandals ranging from bribery and receiving kickbacks to blatant theft.

The old centre-right political parties collapsed in the wake of these trials and from the ashes rose what many Italians hoped might be a breath of fresh political air. Media magnate Silvio Berlusconi's Forza Italia (Go Italy) party swept to power in 2001 and, after an inconclusive two-year interlude of centre-left government under former European Commission head Romano Prodi from 2006, again in April 2008. Berlusconi's carefully choreographed blend of charisma, confidence and irreverence appealed to many Italian voters. His transformation from cruise-ship crooner to populist media mogul (and football club owner) encapsulated the ultimate self-made success story, and his own corporate success was widely acknowledged as proof of an innate economic know-how. While his string of scandals often provoked incredulity abroad, in Italy they have caused little more than apathetic shrugs from a populace notoriously cynical about its politicians.

Together with the right-wing (one-time Fascist) Alleanza Nazionale (National Alliance) under Gianfranco Fini and the polemical, separatist Lega Nord (Northern League), Berlusconi sits at the head of a coalition known as Popolo della Libertà (People of Liberty) with an unassailable majority.

Led by the former mayor of Rome, Walter Veltroni, the PD was unable to recover after winning only 38% of the vote in the 2008 elections. In quick succession, the PD was worsted in municipal elections around the country and regional polls in Friuli Venezia Giulia, Abruzzo and Sardinia. This latter defeat, in February 2009, led Veltroni to quit, leaving the chronically divided left in chaos.

From 2001 to 2006, Berlusconi's rule was marked by a series of laws that protected his extensive business interests (he controls as much as 90% of the country's free TV channels). He also spent considerable time hitting out against what he claimed to be the country's 'politicised' judges. The latter have been looking into his myriad business affairs since the beginning of the 1990s, but one trial after another has collapsed.

> The death of Pope John Paul II in April 2005 saw a gob-smacking four million mourners pour into Rome in just one single week.

2005

Pope John Paul II dies aged 84, prompting a wave of sorrow and chants of *santo subito* (sainthood now). He is succeeded by Benedict XVI, the German Cardinal Ratzinger.

2006

Juventus, AC Milan and three other top Serie A football teams receive hefty fines in a match-rigging scandal that also sees Juventus stripped of its 2005 and 2006 championship titles.

2007

Former heir to the Italian throne, Vittorio Emanuele di Savoia, is cleared of corruption and fraud charges in connection with alleged illicit dealings, among others, involving a casino.

» Football match, Milan.

Tobias Jones' *The Dark Heart of Italy* is an engaging, personal look at contemporary Italy, plagued by (real or imagined) conspiracies, corruption and terrorism.

One of Berlusconi's first acts in 2008 was to take action on the long-standing garbage crisis in Naples. A complex issue dating to the early 1990s, garbage-disposal bottlenecks have put Naples through several malodorous moments, with vast amounts of refuse piling up all over the city and its surrounding areas. Corruption, poor administration, over-flowing rubbish dumps and controversy over where to locate incinerators have all contributed to the problem. No sooner in the chair as prime minister, Berlusconi made for Naples and later sent in the army to calm protests and get things moving again. By July, the PM had declared the crisis over, yet by early 2011 the streets of Naples were again soiled with uncollected refuse.

Alas, the stench of garbage has not been the only source of shame in 21st-century Naples. In recent years, more blood has flown on Neapolitan streets than anywhere else in Italy as a result of Mafia violence. The so-called 'Scampia feud' of late 2004 and early 2005 – a deadly turf battle fought out by rival Camorra clans – saw up to 47 people gunned down in only four months.

Memories of the feud were painfully relived in September 2008, when a Camorra death squad gunned down seven men in the town of Castel Volturno, northwest of Naples. That six of the dead were West African migrants was read as a warning to Nigerian criminal clans muscling in on the city's lucrative drugs market.

2008	2009	2011	2011
Italy's beleaguered national airline, Alitalia, files for bankruptcy. It is later resurrected, in reduced form with fewer routes, aircraft and staff, as a private airline.	Italy's Constitutional Court overturns a law giving Berlusconi immunity from prosecution while in office, opening the possibility that he could stand trial in several court cases.	Berlusconi stands trial in Milan in April on charges of abuse of power and paying for sex with under-aged Moroccan prostitute Karima El Mahroug (aka 'Ruby Heartstealer').	After a 13-year absence, Italy re-enters the Eurovision Song Contest with Raphael Gualazzi's jazz-inspired *Follia d'amore* (Folly of Love). The song wins second place for Italy.

Italian Art & Architecture

Art

The history of Italian art is in many ways also the history of Western art. From the classical, Renaissance and baroque, to the futurist and metaphysical, the art world's seminal movements and periods have been forged by a pantheon of Italian artists including Giotto, da Vinci, Michelangelo, Raphael, Bernini, Botticelli and Caravaggio.

The Ancient & the Classical

In art, as in so many other realms, the ancient Romans looked to the Greeks for examples of best practice. The Greeks had settled many parts of Sicily and southern Italy as early as the 8th century BC, naming it 'Magna Graecia' and building great cities such as Syracuse and Taranto. These cities were famous for their magnificent temples, many of which were decorated with sculptures modelled on, or inspired by, masterpieces by Praxiteles, Lysippus and Phidias.

Sculpture flourished in southern Italy into the Hellenistic period. It also gained great popularity in central Italy, where the primitive art of the Etruscans (the people of ancient central Italy) was influenced and greatly refined by the contribution of Greek artisans, who came here through trade.

In Rome itself, sculpture, architecture and painting flourished under first the Republic and then the Empire. But the art that was produced in Rome during this period was different in many ways from the Greek art that influenced it. Essentially secular, it focused less on harmony and form and more on accurate representation, mainly in the form of sculptural portraits. Innumerable versions of Pompey, Titus and Augustus all show a similar visage, proving that the artists were seeking verisimilitude in their representations and not just glorification.

And while the Greeks saw art as being solely about harmony, beauty and drama, Roman emperors like Augustus were happy to utilise art as a political tool, using it to celebrate status, power and image. This form of narrative art often took the form of relief decoration recounting the story of great military victories – the Colonna di Traiano (Trajan's Column) and the Ara Pacis Augustae (Altar of Peace) in Rome exemplify this tradition. Both are magnificent, monumental examples of art as propaganda, exalting the emperor and Rome in a form that no one, either then or today, can possibly ignore.

Wealthy Roman citizens also dabbled in the arts, building palatial villas and adorning them with statues looted from the Greek world or copied from Hellenic originals. Today, museums in Rome are bursting at the seams with such trophies, from the Capitoline Museums' 'Made in Italy'

The Italian equivalent of Impressionism was the Macchiaioli movement based in Florence. Its major artists were Telemaco Signorini (1835–1901) and Giovanni Fattori (1825–1908). See their work in the Palazzo Pitti's Galleria d'Arte Moderna in Florence.

Galata morente (Dying Gaul, c 240–200 BC) to the Vatican Museums' original Greek *Laocoön and His Sons* (c 160–140 BC).

And while the Etruscans had used wall painting – most notably in their tombs at centres like Tarquinia and Cerveteri in modern-day Lazio, it was the Romans who refined the form, refocusing on landscape scenes to adorn the walls of the living. A visit to Rome's Museo Nazionale Romano: Palazzo Massimo alle Terme offers sublime examples of the form.

The Glitter of Byzantine

In 330, Emperor Constantine, a convert to Christianity, made the ancient city of Byzantium his capital and renamed it Constantinople. The city became the great cultural and artistic centre of Christianity and it remained so up to the time of the Renaissance, though its influence on the art of that period was never as fundamental as the art of ancient Rome.

The Byzantine period was notable for its sublime ecclesiastical and palace architecture, its extraordinary mosaic work and – to a lesser extent – its painting. Its art was influenced by the decoration of the Roman catacombs and the early Christian churches, as well as by the Oriental Greek style, with its love of rich decoration and luminous colour. Byzantine art works de-emphasised the naturalistic aspects of the classical tradition and exalted the spirit over the body, so glorifying God rather than humanity or the state.

In Italy, the Byzantine virtuosity with mosaics was showcased in Ravenna, the capital of the Byzantine Empire's western regions in the 6th century. The city's Basilica di Sant'Apollinare in Classe, Basilica di San Vitale and Basilica di Sant'Apollinare Nuovo house some of the world's finest Byzantine art, their hand-cut glazed tiles (tesserae) balancing extraordinary naturalness with an epic sense of grandeur and mystery.

Yet, the Byzantine aesthetic was not limited to Ravenna. In Venice it would influence the exotic design of the Basilica di San Marco, while in Rome it would leave its mark in the technicolour interior of the Chiesa di San Prassede.

In Sicily, Byzantine, Norman and Arab influences fused to create a distinct regional style showcased in the mosaic-encrusted splendour of Palermo's Cappella Palatina, as well as the cathedrals of Monreale and Cefalù.

The Not-so-Dark Ages

The Italian Middle Ages have often been dismissed as a 'dark' age between the Roman and Byzantine Empires and the Renaissance. However, to ignore this period would make it difficult to understand all subsequent Italian history. This is because Italy as we know it was born in the Middle Ages. The barbarian invasions of the 5th and 6th centuries began a process that turned a unified empire into a land of small independent city-states, and it was these states – or rather the merchants, princes, clergy, corporations and guilds who lived within them – that started the craze in artistic patronage that was to underpin the great innovations in art and architecture that would define the Renaissance.

Continuing the trend kick-started in the Byzantine period, ideas of clarity and simplicity of religious message began to outweigh ideals of faithful representation during the medieval period. This is why, at first glance, many pictures of the period look rather stiff.

Indeed, painting and sculpture of this period played second fiddle to its architecture, commonly known as 'Romanesque'. Complementing this architectural style was the work of the Cosmati, a Roman guild of mosaic and marble workers who specialised in assembling fragments of coloured stones and glass mosaics and combining them with large stone

In 2010, Italian tourist Michele Speranza became an unlikely hero after recognising a female torso in a New York art gallery window. Not just any torso, the piece was an ancient art work stolen from a Lazio museum in 1988. Such a well-trained eye is hardly surprising: Speranza is part of the Comando Carabinieri Tutela Patrimonio Culturale, a special police squad tackling the looting of Italy's priceless heritage.

Looting is big business. Investigations suggest that more than 100,000 ancient tombs have been ransacked by *tombaroli* (tomb raiders) alone; the contents are often sold to private and public collectors. Squad officers frequently patrol archaeological sites, as well as check objects sold at auction against their own databases of stolen items.

Despite the magnitude of the problem, Italy's 'art police' have an impressive track record. In 2010, more than €15 million worth of artefacts were seized in one operation in Geneva. In 2006, New York's Metropolitan Museum of Art relinquished a number of treasures, including the prized Euphronios Krater; a 2500-year-old Etruscan vase now in Rome's Museo Nazionale Etrusco di Villa Giulia. The following year, Los Angeles' Getty Museum faced a similarly humiliating blow, its own returns including a 5th-century-BC statue of Aphrodite. Looted from an archaeological site in Sicily, the goddess of love was later sold to the museum for a badly invested US$18 million.

disks and strips of white marble to create stunning intricate pavements, columns and church furnishings as seen in Rome's Chiesa di Santa Maria in Cosmedin, Basilica di Santa Maria Maggiore and Chiesa di Santa Maria Sopra Minerva.

Gothic Refinement

The Gothic style was much slower to take off in Italy than it had been in the rest of Europe. But it did, marking the transition from medieval restraint to the Renaissance, and seeing artists once again joyously drawing inspiration from life itself rather than solely religion. Occurring at the same time as the development of court society and the rise of civic culture in the city-states, its art was both sophisticated and elegant, highlighting attention to detail, a luminous palette and an increasingly refined technique. The first innovations were made in Pisa by sculptor Nicola Pisano (c 1220–84), who emulated the example of the French Gothic masters and studied classical sculpture in order to represent nature more convincingly, but the major strides forward occurred in Florence and Siena.

Giotto & the 'Rebirth' of Italian Art

The Byzantine painters in Italy knew how to make use of light and shade and had an understanding of the principles of foreshortening (how to convey an effect of perspective). It only required a genius to break the spell of their conservatism and to venture into a new world of naturalism. Enter Florentine painter Giotto di Bondone (c 1266–1337), whose brushstrokes focused on dramatic narrative and the accurate representation of figures and landscape. The Italian poet Giovanni Boccaccio wrote in his *Decameron* (1350–53) that Giotto was 'a genius so sublime that there was nothing produced by nature...that he could not depict to the life; his depiction looked not like a copy, but the real thing.'

Boccaccio wasn't the only prominent critic of the time to consider Giotto revolutionary – the first historian of Italian art, Giorgio Vasari, said in his *Lives of the Artists* (1550) that Giotto initiated the 'rebirth' (*rinascità* or *renaissance*) in art. Giotto's most famous works are all in the medium of the fresco (where paint is applied on a wall while the plaster is still damp), and his supreme achievement is the cycle gracing the walls of Padua's Cappella degli Scrovegni. It's impossible to overestimate Giotto's achievement

Italy has more World Heritage–listed sites than any other country in the world; many of its 45 listings are there in the guise of repositories of great art.

GIOTTO

with these frescoes, which illustrate the stories of the lives of the Virgin and Christ. Abandoning popular conventions such as the three-quarter view of head and body, he presented his figures from behind, from the side or turning around, just as the story demanded. Giotto had no need for lashings of gold paint and elaborate ornamentation either, opting to convey the scene's dramatic tension through a naturalistic rendition of figures and a radical composition that created the illusion of depth.

Giotto's oeuvre isn't limited to the frescoes in the Cappella degli Scrovegni. His Life of St Francis cycle in the Upper Church of the Basilica di San Francesco in Assisi is almost as extraordinary and was to greatly influence his peers, many of whom worked in Assisi during the decoration of the church. One of the most prominent of these was the Dominican friar Fra' Angelico (c 1395–1455), a Florentine painter who was famed for his mastery of colour and light. His *Annunciation* (c 1450) in the convent of the Museo di San Marco in Florence is arguably his most accomplished work.

The Sienese School

Giotto wasn't the only painter of his time to experiment with form, colour and composition and create a radical new style. The great Sienese master Duccio di Buoninsegna (c 1255–1319) successfully breathed new life into the old Byzantine forms using light and shade. His preferred medium was panel painting and his major work is probably his *Maestà* (Virgin Mary in Majesty; 1311) in Siena's Museo dell'Opera Metropolitana.

It was in Siena, too, that two new trends took off: the introduction of court painters and the advent of secular art.

The first of many painters to be given ongoing commissions by one major patron or court, Simone Martini (c 1284–1344) was almost as famous as Giotto in his day. His best-known painting is the stylized *Maestà* (1315–16) in Siena's Museo Civico, in which he pioneered his famous iridescent palette (one colour transformed into another within the same plane).

Also working in Siena at this time were the Lorenzetti brothers, Pietro (c 1280–1348) and Ambrogio (c 1290–1348), who are considered the greatest exponents of what, for a better term, can be referred to as secular painting. Ambrogio's magnificent *Allegories of Good and Bad Government*

> Many Renaissance painters included self-portraits in their major works. Giotto didn't, possibly due to the fact that friends such as Giovanni Boccaccio described him as the ugliest man in Florence. With friends like those...

LIVES OF THE ARTISTS

Painter, architect and writer Giorgio Vasari (1511–74) was one of those figures rightfully described as a 'Renaissance Man'. Born in Arezzo, he trained as a painter in Florence, working with artists including Andrea del Sarto and Michelangelo (he idolised the latter). As a painter, he is best remembered for his floor-to-ceiling frescoes in the Salone dei Cinquecento in Florence's Palazzo Vecchio. As an architect, his most accomplished work was the elegant loggia of the Uffizi (he also designed the enclosed, elevated corridor that connected the Palazzo Vecchio with the Uffizi and Palazzo Pitti and was dubbed the 'Corridoio Vasariano' in his honour). But posterity remembers him predominantly for his work as an art historian. His *Lives of the Most Excellent Painters, Sculptors and Architects, from Cimabue to Our Time,* an encyclopedia of artistic biographies published in 1550 and dedicated to Cosimo I de' Medici, is still in print (as *The Lives of the Artists*) and is full of wonderful anecdotes and – dare we say it – gossip about his artistic contemporaries in 16th-century Florence. Memorable passages include his recollection of visiting Donatello's studio one day only to find the great sculptor staring at his extremely lifelike statue of the *Prophet Habakkuk* and imploring it to talk (we can only assume that Donatello had been working too hard). Vasari also writes about a young Giotto (the painter whom he credits with ushering in the Renaissance) painting a fly on the surface of a work by Cimabue that the older master then tried to brush away. The book makes wonderful pre-departure reading for anyone planning to visit Florence and its museums.

He might look good for 508, but Michelangelo's *David* has had his fare share of close calls. In 1527, the lower part of his left arm was broken off in a riot. In 1843, a hydrochloric acid 'spruce-up' stripped away some of the original surface. Disaster struck again in 1991, when a disturbed gallery visitor smashed the statue's second left toe with a hammer. Toe fixed, David's latest source of stress is a proposed rail tunnel, expected to come within 600 metres of the statue. According to several experts, the expected vibrations from construction works would aggravate the cracks in David's already-weak ankles, possibly turning the 17-foot hunk into a giant sorry heap.

(1337–40) in the Museo Civico lauds the fruits of good government and the gruesome results of bad. In the frescoes, he applies the rules of perspective with an accuracy previously unseen, as well as significantly developing the Italian landscape tradition. In *Life in the Country,* one of the allegories, Ambrogio successfully depicts the time of day, the season, colour reflections and shadows – a naturalistic depiction of landscape that was quite unique at this time.

For a readable, well-illustrated guide to Italian Renaissance art, have a look at Andrew Graham-Dixon's *Renaissance,* the companion book to the BBC TV series.

From Mannerism to Baroque

By 1520, artists such as Michelangelo and Raphael had pretty well achieved everything that former generations had tried to do and, alongside other artists, began distorting natural images in favour of heightened expression. This movement, skilfully illustrated in Titian's *Assunta* (Assumption, 1516–18) – in Venice's Chiesa di Santa Maria Gloriosa dei Frari – and in Raphael's *La trasfigurazione* (1517–20) – in the Vatican Museums' Pinacoteca – was derided by later critics, who labelled it mannerism.

By the end of the 16th century, two artists who had grown tired of mannerism took very different approaches to painting in an attempt to break the deadlock caused by their overachieving predecessors.

Milanese-born *enfant terrible* Michelangelo Merisi da Caravaggio (1573–1610) had no liking for classical models or respect for 'ideal beauty'. He was condemned by some contemporaries for seeking truth rather than ideal beauty in his art and shocked them with his radical practice of copying nature faithfully, regardless of its aesthetic appeal. But even they were forced to admire his skill with the technique of chiaroscuro (the bold contrast of light and dark) and his employment of tenebrism, where dramatic chiaroscuro becomes a dominant and highly effective stylistic device. One look at his *Conversion of St Paul* and the *Crucifixion of St Peter (both 1600–01),* both in Rome's Chiesa di Santa Maria del Popolo, or his *Le sette opere di misericordia* (The Seven Acts of Mercy) in Naples' Pio Monte della Misericordia, and the raw emotional intensity of his work becomes clear.

This intensity reflected the artist's own notorious temperament. Described by the writer Stendhal as a 'great painter [and] a wicked man', Caravaggio fled to Naples in 1606 after killing a man in a street fight in Rome. Although his sojourn in Naples lasted only a year, it had an electrifying effect on the city's younger artists. Among them was Giuseppe (or Jusepe) de Ribera (1591–1652), an aggressive, bullying Spaniard whose *capo lavoro* (masterpiece), the *Pietà,* hangs in the Museo Nazionale di San Martino in Naples. Lo Spagnoletto (The Little Spaniard, as Ribera was known) reputedly won a commission for the Cappella del Tesoro in Naples' Duomo by poisoning his rival Domenichino (1581–1641) and wounding the assistant of a second competitor, Guido Reni (1575–1642). Much to the relief of other nerve-racked artists, the cabal eventually broke up when Caracciolo died in 1642.

In *M: The Man Who Became Caravaggio,* Peter Robb gives a passionate personal assessment of the artist's paintings and a colourful account of Caravaggio's life, arguing he was murdered for having sex with the pageboy of a high-ranking Maltese aristocrat.

(Continued on page 876)

The Renaissance

Of Italy's countless artistic highs, none surmount the Renaissance. The age of Botticelli, da Vinci and Michelangelo, this period heralded the end of medieval obscurantism and the rise of the modern world.

From Milan to Venice and Florence, northern Italy's ambitious, competitive city-states proved fertile ground for the intellectual and artistic explosion that swept the region in the 14th and 15th centuries. The influx of eastern scholars fleeing Constantinople in the wake of its fall to the Ottoman Turkish Muslims in 1453 prompted a renewed interest in classical learning, humanist philosophy and the rise of the Renaissance.

Classicism, Perspective & the Quattrocento

Giotto and the painters of the Sienese school had introduced many innovations in art: the exploration of perspective and proportion, a new interest in realistic portraiture and the beginnings of a new tradition of landscape painting. At the start of the 15th century (Quattrocento), most of these were explored and refined in one city – Florence.

Swept up in the classical revival, sculptors Lorenzo Ghiberti (1378–1455) and Donatello (c 1382–1466) replaced the demure robe-clad statues of the Middle Ages with anatomically accurate figures evoking ancient Greece and Rome. Donatello's bronze *David* (c 1440–50) and *St George* (c 1416–17), both in Florence's Museo del Bargello (p467), capture both this spirit of antiquity and the rediscovered vigour that would drive the Renaissance.

Ghiberti's greatest legacy would be his bronze east doors (1424–52) for the baptistry (p458) in Florence's Piazza del Duomo. The original 10 relief panels heralded a giant leap from the late-Gothic

Clockwise from top left
1. Giotto's frescoes, Scrovegni Chapel 2. Basilica di Santa Croce, Florence 3. Donatello's *David*, Museo del Bargello.

art of the time, not only in their use of perspective, but also in the individuality bestowed upon the figures portrayed.

The baptistry itself faces one of the Renaissance's blockbuster achievements: the Duomo (p458). When the Duomo's dome was completed in 1436, author, architect and philosopher Leon Battista Alberti called it the first great achievement of the 'new' architecture, one that equalled or even surpassed the great buildings of antiquity. Designed by Filippo Brunelleschi (1377–1446), the dome was as innovative in engineering terms as the Pantheon's dome had been 1300 years before. It was Brunelleschi's major commission after the harmonious neoclassical portico of his Spedale degli Innocenti (Hospital of the Innocents), like Ghiberti's bronze baptistry doors, offered a sharp contrast to the syntax of its time. Together with a later work in the same city, the Cappella de' Pazzi in the Basilica di Santa Croce (p471), Brunelleschi's works epitomise what architecture of the 15th century became known for – an elegance of line and innovation in building method that referenced antiquity and celebrated modern man's place at the centre of the universe.

While Brunelleschi was heavily influenced by the classical masters, he was able to do something that they hadn't – discover and record the mathematical rules by which objects appear to diminish as they recede from us. In so doing, Brunelleschi gave artists a whole new visual perspective and a means to glorious artistic ends.

The result was a new style of masterpieces, among them Masaccio's *Trinity* (c 1424–25) in Florence's Basilica di Santa Maria Novella and Leonardo da Vinci's fresco *The Last Supper* (1495–98) in the refectory of Milan's Chiesa di Santa Maria delle Grazie. Andrea Mantegna (1431–1506) was responsible for the painting that is the most virtuosic of all perspectival experiments that occurred during this period – his highly realistic *Dead Christ* (c 1480). Now in Milan's Pinacoteca di Brera, its figure of Jesus is shown in dramatic foreshortening.

This innovation also created new problems. The medieval painters' ignorance of the rules of perspective had enabled

2

them to distribute their figures over a composition in any way they liked in order to create a harmonious whole. But the painters of the Quattrocento found that the rigid new formulas they were experimenting with often made harmonious arrangements of figures difficult, resulting in artificial-looking groups. Artists such as Sandro Botticelli (c 1444–1510) led the way in pursuing a solution to this challenge, seeking to make a painting both perspectively accurate and harmonious in composition. His *The Birth of Venus* (c 1485), now in Florence's Uffizi, was one of the most successful attempts to solve this problem. It's not perfect – witness Venus' unnaturally elongated neck – but it was certainly an impressive attempt.

Men of the High Renaissance

By the early 16th century (Cinquecento), the epicentre of artistic excellence and innovation shifted from Florence to Rome and Venice. This reflected the political and social realities of the period, namely the transfer of power in Florence from the Medicis to the moral-crusading, book-burning friar Girolamo Savonarola (1452–98), and the desire of the popes in Rome to counter the influence of Martin Luther's Reformation by turning the Church's home town into a glorious, humbling showpiece.

Among the architects commissioned in Rome was Donato Bramante (1444–1514). A devotee of pure classicism, his perfectly proportioned Tempietto of the Chiesa di San Pietro in Montorio (p99) is often lauded as the pinnacle of High Renaissance architecture. This petite wonder would influence Andrea Palladio (1508–80) when designing La Rotonda (p374) in Vicenza. The Veneto-based Palladio was northern Italy's greatest Renaissance architect, his trademark Palladian villas including the Brenta Riviera's Villa Foscari (p364).

Bramante himself would go on to design St Peter's Basilica, its dome designed by one of the era's true geniuses: Michelangelo Buonarotti (1475–1564). Despite his aptitude for

Clockwise from top left
1. Boticelli's *La Primavera* 2. Ghiberti's bronze panels, baptistry, Florence 3. Michelangelo's *David*.

architecture, Michelangelo saw himself first and foremost as a sculptor, creating incomparable works like the *Pietà* in St Peter's Basilica (p103) and *David* (1504) in Florence's Galleria dell'Accademia (p469). As a painter, he would adorn the ceiling of Rome's Sistine Chapel, creating figures that were not just realistic, but emotive visual representations of the human experience.

Michelangelo was one of three multi-talented 'Renaissance men' to unalterably change the face of Western art. Leonardo da Vinci (1452–1519) took what some critics have described as the decisive step in the history of Western art – abandoning the balance that had previously been maintained between colour and line in painting and choosing to modulate his contours using colour. This technique, called sfumato, is perfectly displayed in his *Mona Lisa* (now in the Louvre in Paris). The third, Raphael Santi (1483–1520), would rise to the aforementioned challenge faced by the Quattrocento painters – achieving harmonious and perspectively accurate arrangement of figures – in works like

Triumph of Galatea (c 1514) in Rome's Villa Farnesina (p99) and *La Scuola d'Atene* (The School of Athens) in the Vatican Museums' Stanza della Segnatura (p110).

VENETIAN VARIATIONS

While Leonardo, Michelangelo and Raphael focused on figure arrangement and form to achieve visual unity, their Venetian contemporaries Giorgione (c 1477–1510) and Titian (c 1490–1576) took a different path, seeking unified compositions through colour and light. Giorgione's airy, enigmatic *La Tempesta* (The Storm) in Venice's Gallerie dell'Accademia (p335) is a particularly fine example.

(Continued from page 871)

North of Rome, Annibale Caracci (1560–1609) was the major artist of the baroque Emilian, or Bolognese, school. With his painter brother Agostino he worked in Bologna, Parma and Venice before moving to Rome to work for Cardinal Odoardo Farnese. In works such as his magnificent frescoes of mythological subjects in Rome's Palazzo Farnese, he employed innovative illusionistic elements that would prove inspirational to later baroque painters such as Cortona, Pozzo and Gaulli. However, Caracci never let the illusionism and energy of his works dominate the subject matter as these later painters did. Strongly influenced by the work of Michelangelo and Raphael, he continued the Renaissance penchant for idealising and 'beautifying' nature.

The roots of baroque art lay in religious spirituality and stringent aestheticism. Its artists and patrons used it to combat the rapidly spreading Protestant Reformation while simultaneously exalting Catholicism. Considering this, it's somewhat ironic that its style displayed worldly joy, exuberant decoration and uninhibited sensuality. It seems that the baroque artists cottoned on to the modern mantra of advertising – sex sells.

Arguably the best known of all baroque artists was the sculptor Gian Lorenzo Bernini (1598–1680), who used works of religious art such as his

WHO'S WHO IN RENAISSANCE & BAROQUE ART

Giotto di Bondone (c 1266–1337) Said to have ushered in the Renaissance; two masterworks: the Cappella degli Scrovegni (1304–06) in Padua (p366) and the upper church (1306–11) in Assisi (p562).

Donatello (c 1382–1466) Florentine born and bred; his *David* (c 1440–50) in the collection of the Museo del Bargello in Florence (p467) was the first free-standing nude sculpture produced since the classical era.

Fra' Angelico (1395–1455) Made a saint in 1982; his best-loved work is the *Annunciation* (c 1450) in the convent of the Museo di San Marco in Florence (p469).

Sandro Botticelli (c 1444–1510) *Primavera* (c 1482) and *The Birth of Venus* (c 1485) are among the best-loved of all Italian paintings; both in the Uffizi (p463).

Domenico Ghirlandaio (1449–94) A top Tuscan master; his frescoes include those in the Tornabuoni Chapel in Florence's Basilica di Santa Maria Novella (p468).

Leonardo da Vinci (1452–1519) The term polymath (aka Renaissance Man) had to be coined to explain this genius; best known for his *The Last Supper* in Milan's Chiesa di Santa Maria delle Grazie (p232).

Michelangelo Buonarotti (1475–1564) The big daddy of them all; everyone knows *David* (1504) in the Galleria dell'Accademia in Florence (p469) and the Sistine Chapel ceiling (1508–12) in Rome's Vatican Museums (p110).

Raphael Santi (1483–1520) Originally from Urbino; painted luminous Madonnas and fell in love with a baker's daughter, immortalised in his painting *La Fornarina*, in Rome's Galleria Nazionale d'Arte Antica: Palazzo Barberini (p86).

Titian (c 1490–1576) Real name Tiziano Vecelli; seek out his *Assumption* (1516–18) in the Chiesa di Santa Maria Gloriosa dei Frari (I Frari), Venice (p338).

Tintoretto (1518–1594) The last great painter of the Italian Renaissance, known as 'Il Furioso' for the energy he put into his work; look for his *Last Supper* in Venice's Chiesa di Santo Stefano (p334).

Annibale Caracci (1560–1609) Bologna-born and best known for his baroque frescoes in Rome's Palazzo Farnese (p78).

Michelangelo Merisi da Caravaggio (1573–1610) Baroque's bad boy; his most powerful work is the *St Matthew Cycle* in Rome's Chiesa di San Luigi dei Francesi (p78).

Gian Lorenzo Bernini (1598–1680) The sculptor protégé of Cardinal Scipione Borghese; best known for his *Rape of Persephone* (1621–22) and *Apollo and Daphne* (1622–25) in Rome's Museo e Galleria Borghese (p111).

Sex, fame and notoriety: the life of Artemesia Gentileschi (1593–1652) could spawn a top-rating soap. One of the early baroque's greatest artists (and one of the few females), Gentileschi was born in Rome to Tuscan painter Orazio Gentileschi. Orazio wasted little time introducing his young daughter to the city's working artists. Among her mentors was Michelangelo Merisi da Caravaggio, whose chiaroscuro technique would deeply influence her own style.

At the tender age of 17, Gentileschi produced her first masterpiece, *Susanna and the Elders* (1610), now in the Schönborn Collection in Pommersfelden, Germany. Her depiction of the sexually harassed Susanna proved eerily foreboding: two years later Artemesia would find herself at the centre of a seven-month trial, in which Florentine artist Agostino Tassi was charged with her rape.

Out of Gentileschi's fury came the gripping, technically brilliant *Judith Slaying Holofernes* (1612–13). While the original hangs in Naples' Museo di Capodimonte, you'll find a larger, later version in Florence's Uffizi. Vengeful Judith would make a further appearance in *Judith and her Maidservant* (c 1613–14), now in Florence's Palazzo Pitti. While living in Florence, Gentileschi completed a string of commissions for Cosimo II of the Medici dynasty, as well as becoming the first female member of the prestigious Accademia delle Arti del Disegno (Academy of the Arts of Drawing).

After separating from her husband, Tuscan painter Pietro Antonio di Vincenzo Stiattesi, Gentileschi headed south to Naples sometime between 1626 and 1630. Here her creations would include *The Annunciation* (1630), also in Naples' Museo di Capodimonte, and her *Self-Portrait as the Allegory of Painting* (1630), housed in London's Kensington Palace. The latter work received praise for its simultaneous depiction of art, artist and muse; an innovation at the time. Gentileschi's way with the brush was not lost on King Charles I of England, who honoured the Italian talent with a court residency from 1638 to 1641.

Despite her illustrious career, Gentileschi inhabited a man's world. Nothing would prove this more than the surviving epitaphs commemorating her death, focused not on her creative brilliance, but on the gossip depicting her as a cheating nymphomaniac.

Ecstasy of Saint Theresa in Rome's Chiesa di Santa Maria della Vittoria to arouse feelings of exaltation and mystic transport in the viewer. In this and many other works he achieved an extraordinary intensity of facial expression and a totally radical handling of draperies. Instead of letting these fall in dignified folds in the approved classical manner, he made them writhe and whirl to intensify the effect of excitement and energy. This trick was soon imitated all over Europe.

Not everyone was singing Bernini's praise, especially the artist's bitter rival, Francesco Borromini (1599–1667). Neurotic, reclusive and tortured, Borromini looked down on his ebullient contemporary's lack of architectural training and formal stone-carving technique. No love was lost: Bernini believed Borromini 'had been sent to destroy architecture'.

Centuries on, the rivalry lives on in the works they left behind, from Borromini's Chiesa di San Carlo alle Quattro Fontane and Bernini's neighbouring Chiesa di Sant'Andrea al Quirinale to their back-to-back creations in Piazza Navona.

The Italian countryside is home to a number of contemporary sculpture parks, including the Fattoria di Celle (www.goricoll. it), Il Giardino dei Tarocchi (www. nikidesaintphalle. com), the Castello di Rivoli and Villa Manin.

The New Italy

By the 18th century, Italy was beginning to rebel against years of foreign rule – first under the French in Napoleon's time and then under the Austrians. But although new ideas of political unity were forming, there was only one innovation in art – the painting and engraving of views, most notably in Venice, to meet the demand of European travellers wanting 'Grand Tour' souvenirs. The best-known painters of this school are Francesco Guardi (1712–93) and Giovanni Antonio Canaletto (1697–1768).

Click onto www.
exibart.com
(mostly in Italian)
for up-to-date
listings of art ex-
hibitions through-
out Italy, as well
as exhibition
reviews, articles
and interviews.

Despite the slow movement towards unity, the 19th-century Italian cities remained as they had been for centuries – highly individual centres of culture with sharply contrasting ways of life. Music was the supreme art of this period and the overwhelming theme in the visual arts was one of chaste refinement.

The major artistic movement of the day was neoclassicism and its greatest Italian exponent was the sculptor Antonio Canova (1757–1822). Canova renounced movement in favour of stillness, emotion in favour of restraint and illusion in favour of simplicity. His most famous work is a daring sculpture of Paolina Bonaparte Borghese as a reclining *Venere vincitrice* (Conquering Venus), in Rome's Museo e Galleria Borghese.

Canova was the last Italian artist to win overwhelming international fame. Italian architecture, sculpture and painting had played a dominant role in the cultural life of Europe for some 400 years, but with Canova's death in 1822, this supremacy came to an end.

Modern Movements

The two main developments in Italian art at the outbreak of WWI could not have been more different. Futurism, led by poet Filippo Tommaso Marinetti (1876–1944) and painter Umberto Boccioni (1882–1916), sought new ways to express the dynamism of the machine age. Metaphysical painting *(Pittura metafisica)*, in contrast, looked inwards and produced mysterious images from the subconscious world.

**Modern
Art Musts**

» Galleria
Nazionale d'Arte
Moderna e
Contemporanea,
Rome

» Peggy Guggen-
heim Collection,
Venice

» Museo del
Novecento, Milan

» MADRE, Naples

Futurism demanded a new art for a new world and denounced every attachment to the art of the past. It started with the publication of Marinetti's *Manifesto del futurismo* (Manifesto of Futurism, 1909) and was reinforced by the publication of a 1910 futurist painting manifesto by Boccioni, Giacomo Balla (1871–1958), Luigi Russolo (1885–1947) and Gino Severini (1883–1966). The manifesto declared that 'Everything is in movement, everything rushes forward, everything is in constant swift change.' An excellent example of this theory put into practice is Boccioni's *Rissa in galleria* (Brawl in the Arcade, 1910) in the collection of Milan's Pinacoteca di Brera. This was painted shortly after the manifesto was published and clearly demonstrates the movement's fascination with frantic movement and with modern technology and life. While the movement lost its own impetus with the outbreak of WWI, its legacy has been revived with the recent opening of Milan's Museo del Novecento. Dedicated to 20th-century art, the museum houses what is arguably Italy's finest collection of futurist works.

Like futurism, metaphysical painting also had a short life. Its most famous exponent, Giorgio de Chirico (1888–1978), lost interest in the style after the war, but his work held a powerful attraction for the surrealist movement that developed in France in the 1920s. Stillness and a sense of foreboding are the haunting qualities of many of De Chirico's works of this period, which show disconnected images from the world of dreams in settings that usually embody memories of classical Italian architecture. A good example is *The Red Tower* (1913), now in the Peggy Guggenheim Collection in Venice.

Italy's major
contemporary
art event is the
world-famous
Venice Biennale
(www.labiennale.
org), held every
odd-numbered
year. It's the most
important survey
show on the
international art
circuit.

After the war, a number of the futurist painters began to flirt with Fascism, believing that the new state offered opportunities for patronage and public art and that Italy could once again lead the world in its arts practice. This period was known as 'second futurism' and its main exponents were Mario Sironi (1885–1961) and Carlo Carrà (1881–1966).

The local art scene became more interesting in the 1950s, when artists such as Alberto Burri (1915–95) and the Argentine-Italian Lucio Fontana (1899–1968) experimented with abstract art. Fontana's punctured canvases were characterised by *spazialismo* (spatialism) and he also experimented with 'slash paintings', perforating his canvases with actual holes or slashes and dubbing them 'art for the space age'.

Burri's work was truly cutting-edge. His assemblages were made of burlap, wood, iron and plastic and were avowedly anti-traditional. *Grande sacco* (Large Sack) of 1952, housed in Rome's Galleria Nazionale d'Arte Moderna e Contemporanea, caused a major controversy when it was first exhibited.

In the 1960s, a radical new movement called Arte Povera (Poor Art) took off. Its followers used simple materials to trigger memories and associations. Major names include Mario Merz (1925–2003), Giovanni Anselmo (b 1934), Luciano Fabro (b 1936–2007), Giulio Paolini (b 1940) and Greek-born Jannis Kounellis (b 1936). All experimented with sculpture and installation work.

The 1980s saw a return to painting and sculpture in a traditional (primarily figurative) sense. Dubbed 'Transavanguardia', this movement broke with the prevailing international focus on conceptual art and was thought by some critics to signal the death of avant-garde. The artists who were part of this movement include Sandro Chia (b 1946), Mimmo Paladino (b 1948), Enzo Cucchi (b 1949) and Francesco Clemente (b 1952).

Contemporary artists of note currently working in Italy include Paolo Canevari, Angelo Filomeno, Rä di Martino, Adrian Paci, Paola Pivi, Pietro Roccasalva and Francesco Vezzoli.

Architecture

Architects working in Italy have always celebrated the classical. The Greeks, who established the classical style, employed it in the southern cities they colonised; the Romans refined and embellished it; Italian Renaissance architects rediscovered and altered it to the requirements of their day; and the Fascist architects of the 1930s referenced it in their powerful modernist buildings. Even today, architects such as Richard Meier are designing buildings in Italy that clearly reference classical prototypes. Why muck around with a formula that works, particularly when it can also please the eye and make the soul soar?

Classical

Only one word describes the buildings of ancient Italy: monumental. The Romans built an empire the size of which had never before been seen, and went on to adorn it with buildings cut from the same pattern. From Verona's Roman Arena to Pozzuoli's Anfiteatro Flavio, giant stadiums rose above skylines. Spa centres like Rome's Terme di Caracalla were veritable cities of indulgence, boasting everything from giant marble-clad pools to gymnasiums and libraries. Aqueducts like those below Naples provided fresh water to thousands, while temples such as Pompeii's Tempio di Apollo provided the faithful with awe-inspiring centres of worship.

(Continued on page 882)

8th–3rd Century BC Magna Graecia
Greek colonisers grace southern Italy with soaring temples, sweeping amphitheatres and elegant sculptures that later influence their Roman successors.

6th Century BC–4th Century AD Roman
Epic roads and aqueducts spread from Rome, alongside mighty basilicas, colonnaded markets, sprawling thermal baths and frescoed villas.

4th–6th Century Byzantine
Newly Christian and based in Constantinople, the Empire turns its attention to the construction of churches with exotic, Eastern mosaics and domes.

8th–12th Century Romanesque
Attention turns from height to the horizontal lines of a building. Churches are designed with stand-alone campaniles (bell towers) and baptistries.

13th & 14th Century Gothic
Northern European Gothic gets an Italian makeover, from the Arabesque spice of Venice's Cá d'Oro to the Romanesque flavour of Siena's cathedral.

Late 14th–15th Century Early Renaissance
Filippo Brunelleschi's elegant dome graces the Duomo in Florence, heralding a return to classicism and a bold new era of humanist thinking and rational, elegant design.

Architectural Wonders

Italy is Europe's architectural overachiever, bursting at its elegant seams with triumphant temples, brooding castles and dazzling basilicas. If you can't see it all in one mere lifetime, why not start with five of the best?

Duomo, Milan

1 A forest of petrified pinnacles and fantastical beasts, Italy's Gothic golden child is pure Milan: a product of centuries of pillaging, fashion, one-upmanship and mercantile ambition. Head to the top for a peek at the Alps (p229).

Duomo, Florence

2 Florence's most famous landmark is more than a monumental spiritual masterpiece. It's a living, breathing testament to the explosion of creativity, artistry, ambition and wealth that would define Renaissance Florence (p458).

Piazza dei Miracoli, Pisa

3 Pisa promises a threesome you won't forget: Duomo, Baptistry and the infamous Leaning Tower. Together they make up a perfect Romanesque trio, artfully arranged like objets d'art on a giant green coffee table (p496).

Colosseum, Rome

4 Almost 2000 years on, Rome's mighty ancient stadium still oozes the X-factor (p61). Once the domain of gladiatorial battles and ravenous wild beasts, its 50,000-seat magnitude radiates all the vanity and ingenuity of a once glorious, intercontinental empire.

Basilica di San Marco, Venice

5 It's a case of East–West fusion at this Byzantine beauty, founded in AD 829 and rebuilt twice since. Awash with glittering mosaics and home to the remains of Venice's patron saint, its layering of eras reflects the city's own worldly pedigree (p321).

Clockwise from top left
1. Duomo, Milan 2. Duomo, Florence 3. Baptistry and Leaning Tower, Pisa 4. Colosseum, Rome.

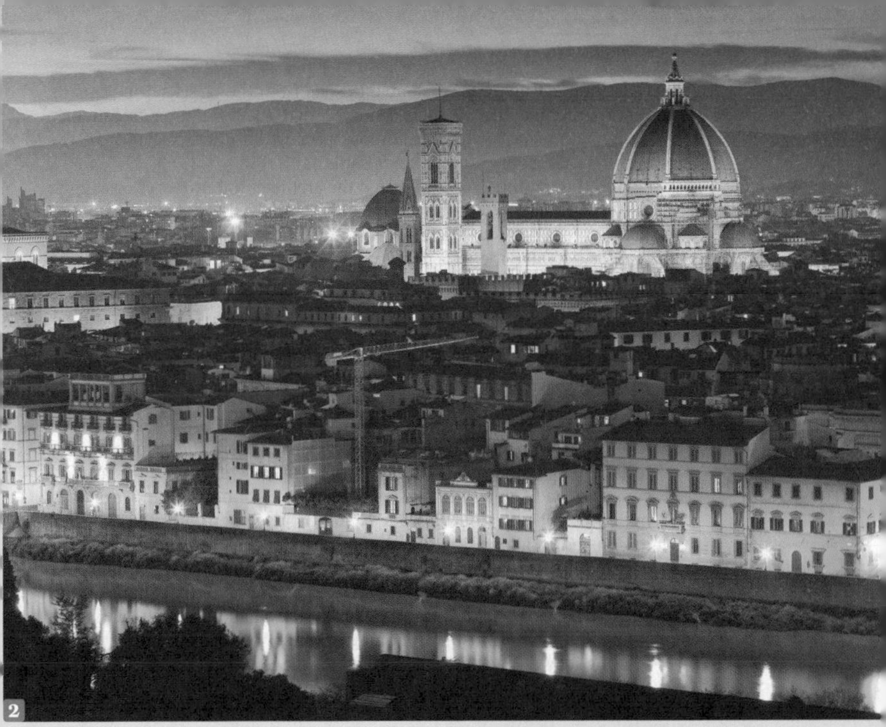

2

RUSSELL MOUNTFORD / LONELY PLANET IMAGES ©

3

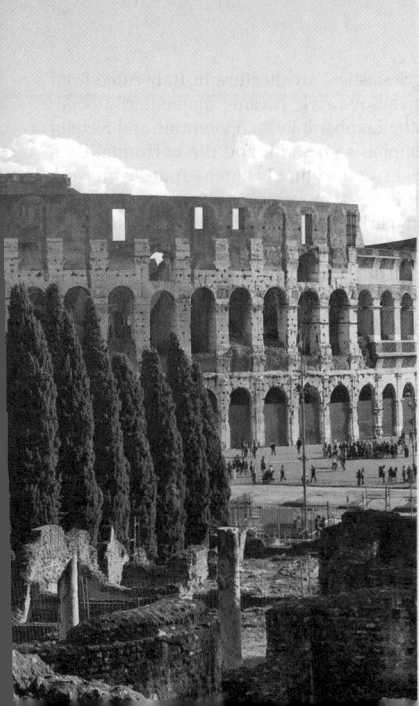

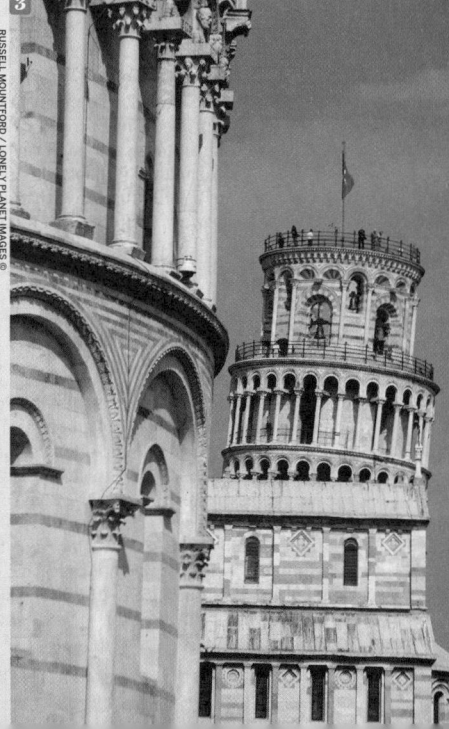

(Continued from page 879)

Having learned a few valuable lessons from the Greeks, the Romans refined architecture to such a degree that their building techniques, designs and mastery of harmonious proportion underpin most of the world's architecture and urban design to this day.

And though the Greeks invented the architectural orders (Doric, Ionic and Corinthian), it was the Romans who employed them in bravura performances. Consider Rome's Colosseum, with its ground tier of Doric, middle tier of Ionic and penultimate tier of Corinthian columns. The Romans were dab hands at temple architecture, too. Just witness Rome's exquisitely proportioned Pantheon, a temple whose huge but seemingly unsupported dome showcases the Roman invention of concrete, a material as essential to the modern construction industry as Ferrari is to the F1 circuit.

Marvellous Mosaics

» Basilica di Sant'Apollinare in Classe, Ravenna

» Basilica di San Vitale, Ravenna

» Basilica di San Marco, Venice

» Cattedrale di Monreale, Monreale

Byzantine

After Constantine became Christianity's star convert, the empire's architects and builders turned their considerable talents to the design and construction of churches. The emperor commissioned a number of such buildings in Rome, but he also expanded his sphere of influence east, to Constantinople in Byzantium. His successors in Constantinople, most notably Justinian and his wife Theodora, went on to build churches in the style that became known as Byzantine. Brick buildings built on the Roman basilican plan but with domes, they had sober exteriors that formed a stark contrast to their magnificent, mosaic-encrusted interiors. Finding its way back to Italy in the mid-6th century, the style expressed itself on a grand scale in Venice's Basilica di San Marco as well as more modestly in buildings like the Chiesa di San Pietro in Otranto, Puglia. The true stars of Italy's Byzantine scene, however, are Ravenna's Basilica di San Vitale and Basilica di Sant'Apollinare in Classe, both built on a cruciform plan.

Romanesque

The next development in ecclesiastical architecture in Italy came from Europe. The European Romanesque style became momentarily popular in four regional forms – the Lombard, Pisan, Florentine and Sicilian Norman. All displayed an emphasis on width and the horizontal lines of a building rather than height, and featured church groups with *campaniles* (bell towers) and baptistries that were separate to the church.

The use of white and green marble alternatively defined the facades of the Florentine and Pisan styles, as seen in iconic buildings like Florence's

TOP FIVE ARCHITECTS

Filippo Brunelleschi (1377–1446) Brunelleschi blazed the neoclassical trail; his dome for Florence's Duomo announced that the Renaissance had arrived.

Donato Bramante (1444–1514) After a stint as court architect in Milan, Bramante went on to design the tiny Tempietto and huge St Peter's Basilica in Rome.

Michelangelo (1475–1564) Architecture was but one of the many strings in this great man's bow; his masterworks are the dome of St Peter's Basilica and the Piazza del Campidoglio in Rome.

Andrea Palladio (1508–80) Western architecture's single-most influential figure, Palladio turned classical Roman principles into elegant northern Italian villas.

Gian Lorenzo Bernini (1598–1680) The king of the Italian baroque is best known for his work in Rome, including the magnificent baldachin, piazza and colonnades at St Peter's.

Basilica di Santa Maria Novella and Duomo baptistry, as well as in Pisa's cathedral and baptistry.

The Lombard style featured elaborately carved facades and exterior decoration featuring bands and arches. Among its finest examples are the Lombard cathedral in Modena, Pavia's Basilica di San Michele and Brescia's unusually shaped Duomo Vecchio.

Down south, the Sicilian Norman style encompassed an exotic mix of Norman, Saracen and Byzantine influences, from marble columns to Islamic-inspired pointed arches to glass tesserae detailing. One of the greatest examples of the form is the Cattedrale di Monreale, located just outside Palermo.

Gothic

The Italians didn't embrace the Gothic as enthusiastically as the French, Germans and Spanish did. Its flying buttresses, grotesque gargoyles and over-the-top decoration were just too far from the classical ideal that was (and still is) bred in the Italian bone. There were, of course, exceptions. The Venetians, never averse to a bit of frivolity, used the style in grand *palazzi* (mansions) such as the Ca' d'Oro and on the facades of high-profile public buildings like the Palazzo Ducale. The fashion-obsessed Milanese employed it in Milan's flamboyant Duomo, and the Sienese came up with an utterly gorgeous example in Siena's cathedral.

Baroque

The Renaissance's insistence on restraint and pure form was sure to lead to a backlash at some stage, so it's no surprise that the next major architectural movement in Italy was noteworthy for its exuberant – some would say decadent – form. The baroque movement took its name from the Portuguese word *barroco,* used by fishermen to denote a misshapen pearl. Compared to the pure classical lines of Renaissance buildings, its output could indeed be described as 'misshapen' – Andrea Palma's facade of Syracuse's cathedral, Guarino Guarini's Palazzo Carignano in Turin, and Gian Lorenzo Bernini's baldachin in St Peter's in Rome are dramatic, curvaceous and downright sexy structures that bear little similarity to the classical ideal.

For many of Naples' baroque architects, the saying 'It's what's inside that counts' had a particularly strong resonance. Due in part to the city's notorious high density and lack of showcasing piazzas, many invested less time on adorning hard-to-see facades and more on lavishing interiors. The exterior of churches like the Chiesa e Chiostro di San Gregorio Armeno gives little indication of the detailed opulence waiting inside, from cheeky cherubs and gilded ceilings to polychromatic marble walls and floors.

In fact, the indulgent deployment of coloured, inlaid marbles is one of the true highlights of Neapolitan baroque design. Used to adorn tombs in the second half of the 16th century, the inlaid look really took off at the beginning of the 17th century, with everything from altars

ITALIAN ART & ARCHITECTURE ARCHITECTURE

15th & 16th Century High Renaissance
Rome ousts Florence from its status as the centre of the Renaissance, its newly created wonders including Il Tempietto and St Peter's Basilica.

Late 16th–Early 18th Century Baroque
Renaissance restraint gives way to theatrical flourishes and sensual curves as the Catholic Church uses lavish detailing to upstage the Protestant movement.

Mid-18th–Late 19th Century Neoclassical
Archaeologists rediscover the glories of Pompeii and Herculaneum and architects pay tribute in creations like Vicenza's La Rotonda and Naples' Villa Pignatelli.

19th Century Industrial
A newly unified Italy fuses industrial technology, consumer culture and ecclesial traditions in Milans' cathedral-like Galleria Vittorio Emanuele and Naples' Galleria Umberto I.

Late 19th–Early 20th Century Liberty
Italy's art nouveau ditches classical linearity for whimsical curves and organic motifs.

Early–Mid-20th Century Modernism
Italian modernism takes the form of futurism (technology-obsessed and anti-historical) and rationalism (seeking a middle ground between a machine-driven utopia and Fascism's fetish for classicism).

and floors to entire chapels clad in mix-and-match marble concoctions. The undisputed meister of the form was Cosimo Fanzago, whose pièce de résistance is the church inside the Museo Nazionale di San Martino in Naples – a mesmerising kaleidoscope of colours and patterns, and the perfectly accompaniment to works of other artistic greats, among them painters Giuseppe Ribera, Massimo Stanzione and Francesco Solimena.

Considering the Neapolitans' passion for all things baroque, it's not surprising that the Italian baroque's grand finale would come in the form of the Palazzo Reale in Caserta, a 1200-room royal palace designed by Neapolitan architect Luigi Vanvitelli to upstage France's Versailles.

Industrial Innovation & Modernism

Upstaged by political and social upheaval, architecture took a back seat in 19th-century Italy. One of the few movements of note stemmed directly from the Industrial Revolution, and saw the application of industrial innovations in glass and metal to building design. Two monumental examples of the form are Galleria Vittorio Emanuele II in Milan and its southern sibling Galleria Umberto I in Naples.

By century's end, the art nouveau craze sweeping Europe injected the local scene with a new vibrancy. The Italian version, called 'Io Stile Floreale' or 'Liberty' in Italian, was notable for being more extravagant than most – just check out Giuseppe Sommaruga's Casa Castiglione (1903), a large block of flats at Corso Venezia 47 in Milan, for proof.

When modernism entered the scene, it took two forms. The first was purely theoretical and was based on Marinetti's influential *Futurist manifesto* (1909). The second form was rationalism, which was promoted in Italy by two groups. The first was known as the Gruppo Sette and consisted of seven architects inspired by the Bauhaus; its most significant player was Giuseppe Terragni, whose outstanding work is the 1936 Casa del Fascio (now called Casa del Popolo) in Como. The second, and rival, group was MIAR (Movimento Italiano per l'Architettura Razionale, the Italian Movement for Rational Architecture), led by Adalberto Libera. This influential architect is best known for his Palazzo dei Congressi in EUR, a 20th-century suburb of Rome that is home to a number of architecturally significant buildings. Like many Italian architects of their time, Libera and Terragni designed their uncompromisingly modernist buildings for the Fascist authorities, and their work is sometimes described as 'Fascist Architecture'. EUR's most iconic Fascist creation is the gleaming, arched Palazzo della Civiltà del Lavoro (Palace of the Workers). Designed by Giovanni Guerrini, Ernesto Bruno La Padula and Mario Romano, its arches and gleaming Travertine skin recall a pared-back, square Colosseum – an ode to the classical ideals of stoicism and glory that inspired the Fascist ideal.

Mid to Late 20th Century

Though Italy became famous for its cutting-edge international fashion and design industries in the second half of the 20th century, the same can't be said for its architecture. One of the few high points came in 1956, when architect Giò Ponti and engineer Pier Luigi Nervi designed Milan's slender, international Pirelli Tower. Ponti was the highly influential founding editor of the international architecture and design magazine *Domus,* which had begun publication in 1928; and Nervi was at the forefront of the development of reinforced concrete, an innovation that changed the face of modern architecture. Later in the century, architects such as Carlo Scarpa, Aldo Rossi and Paolo Portoghesi took Italian architecture in different directions. Veneto-based Scarpa was well known for his organic architecture, most particularly the Brion Tomb and Sanctuary at San Vito d'Altivole. Writer and architect Rossi was awarded the

For a Blast of Baroque

» Lecce, Puglia
» Noto, Sicily
» Rome, Lazio
» Naples, Campania
» Catania, Sicily

Designed by US architect Richard Meier, Rome's Museo dell'Ara Pacis is no stranger to controversy. Compared to everything from a coffin to a petrol station, it was damned by popular art critic Vittorio Sgarbi as an 'indecent cesspit by a useless architect'. Ouch!

Pritzker Prize in 1990, and was known for both his writing (eg *The Architecture of the City* in 1966) and design work. Rome-based Paolo Portoghesi, who still practises architecture, is an academic and writer with a deep interest in classical architecture. His best-known Italian building is the Central Mosque (1974) in Rome, famed for its luminously beautiful interior.

The Architectural Scene Today

After a long period of decline, Italian architecture is back on the world stage, with architects such as Massimiliano Fuksas; King, Roselli & Ricci; Cino Zucchi; Ian+; ABDR Architetti Associati; 5+1; Garofalo Miura; and Beniamino Servino designing innovative and important buildings.

The current king of Italian architecture is Renzo Piano, whose international projects include London's striking new Shard skyscraper and the Centre Culturel Tjibaou in Nouméa, New Caldeonia. At home, his 2002 Auditorium Parco della Musica in Rome is considered one of his greatest achievements yet. Piano's heir apparent is Massimiliano Fuksas, whose projects are as whimsical as they are visually arresting. His most significant works to date are the futuristic Milan Trade Fair Building and the San Paolo Parish Church in Foligno. His Centro Congressi Nuvola (New Congress Center), on which construction recently commenced in the Roman suburb of EUR, looks like it's topping both of them, though.

Most exciting – and unusual for Italy – are the many projects by high-profile foreign architects that are hotting up Italy's architectural landscape. Richard Meier has two Roman buildings to his credit: the controversial Ara Pacis pavilion and the sculptural Chiesa Dives in Misericordia, a light-drenched church in suburban Rome commissioned by the Vatican to celebrate the 2000 Jubilee.

In 2010, Iraqi-British starchitect Zaha Hadid swooped the prestigious RIBA (Royal Institute of British Architects) Sterling prize for her striking, curvaceous MAXXI art gallery in Rome, while other projects of note include David Chipperfield's cemetery extension on Isola di San Michele in Venice and Palace of Justice in Salerno; Arata Isozaki's much-anticipated extensions to the Uffizi in Florence; and Tadao Ando's acclaimed Punta della Dogana and Palazzo Grassi renovation in Venice.

Yet the most exciting building program since (arguably) the Renaissance is Milan's 'CityLife' project. Involving the redevelopment of the city's former trade fairground, the project will feature three geometrically experimental skyscrapers, one designed by Zaha Hadid, one by Arata Isozaki, and one by Daniel Liebeskind. City authorities hope that these head-turning additions will inject the city's image with some much-needed edge.

Industrialised and economically booming, mid-century Italy shows off its wealth in commercial projects like Giò Ponti's slim-lined Pirelli skyscraper.

21st Century Contemporary

Italian architecture gets its groove back with the international success of starchitects like Renzo Piano, Massimiliano Fuksis and Gae Aulenti.

ITALIAN ART & ARCHITECTURE ARCHITECTURE

Cutting-Edge Architecture

» MAXXI, Rome

» Auditorium Parco della Musica, Rome

» Museo di Arte Moderna e Contemporanea Rovereto, Rovereto

The Italian Way of Life

Imagine you wake up tomorrow and discover you're Italian. How would life be different, and what could you discover about Italy in just one day as a local? Read on...

A Day in the Life of an Italian

Sveglia! You're woken not by an alarm but by the burble and clatter of the *caffettiera,* the ubiquitous stovetop espresso-maker. You're running late, so you bolt down your coffee scalding hot (an acquired Italian talent) and pause briefly to ensure your socks match before dashing out the door. Yet still you walk blocks out of your way to buy your morning paper from Bucharest-born Nicolae, your favourite news vendor and (as a Romanian) part of Italy's largest migrant community. You chat briefly about his new baby – you may be late, but at least you're not rude.

On your way to work you scan the headlines: yet another adjournment of Berlusconi's latest trial, today's match-fixing scandal, and an announcement of new EU regulations on cheese. Outrageous! The cheese regulations, that is; the rest is to be expected. At work, you're buried in paperwork until noon, when it's a relief to join friends for lunch and a glass of wine. Afterwards you toss back another scorching espresso at your favourite bar, and find out how your barista's latest audition went – turns out you went to school with the sister of the director of the play, so you promise to put in a good word.

Back at work by 2pm, you multitask Italian-style, chatting with co-workers as you dash off work emails, text your schoolmate about the barista on your *telefonino* (mobile phone), and surreptitiously check *l'Internet* for employment listings – your work contract is due to expire soon. After a busy day like this, *aperitivi* are definitely in order, so at 6.30pm you head directly to the latest happy-hour hot spot. Your friends arrive, the decor is *molto design,* the vibe *molto cool,* and the DJ *abbastanza hot,* until suddenly it's time for your English class – everyone's learning it these days, if only for the slang.

By the time you finally get home, it's already 9.30pm and dinner will have to be reheated. *Peccato!* (Shame!) You eat, absent-mindedly watching reality TV while recounting your day and complaining about cheese regulations to whoever's home – no sense giving reheated pasta your undivided attention. While brushing your teeth, you discuss the future of Italian theatre and dream vacations in Anguilla, though without a raise, it'll probably be Abruzzo again this year. Finally you make your way to bed and pull reading material at random out of your current bedside stack: art books, *gialli* (mysteries), a hard-hitting Mafia exposé or two, the odd classic, possibly a few *fumetti* (comics). You drift off wondering what tomorrow might hold... imagine if you woke up British or Ameri-

---

Today, people of Italian origin account for more than 40% of the population in Argentina and Uruguay, more than 10% in Brazil, more than 5% in Switzerland and the US, and more than 4% in Australia, Venezuela and Canada.

On average, Italians get six weeks of holidays a year, but spend the equivalent of two weeks annually on bureaucratic procedures required of working Italian citizens.

can. English would be easier, but how would you dress, and what would you be expected to eat? *Terribile!* You shrug off that nightmare, and settle into sleep. *Buona notte.*

It's Not What You Know...

From your day as an Italian, this much you know already: Italy is no place for an introvert. It's not merely a matter of being polite – each social interaction adds meaning and genuine pleasure to daily routines. Conversation is far too important to be cut short by tardiness or a mouthful of toothpaste. All that chatter isn't entirely idle, either: in Europe's most ancient, entrenched bureaucracy, social networks are essential to get things done. Putting in a good word for your barista isn't just a nice gesture, but an essential career boost. As a Ministry of Labour study recently revealed, most people in Italy still find employment through personal connections. For better or worse, *clientelismo* (nepotism) is as much a part of the Italian lexicon as *caffè* (coffee) and *tasse* (taxes). Just ask Prime Minister Silvio Berlusconi, who in 2009 chose a *Grande Fratello* (Big Brother) contestant, a soap-opera starlet, a TV costume-drama actress and a Miss Italy contestant to represent Italy as members of the European Union parliament. As the satirist Beppe Severgnini wryly comments in his book *La Bella Figura: A Field Guide to the Italian Mind,* 'If you want to lose an Italian friend or kill off a conversation, all you have to say is "On the subject of conflicts of interest..." If your interlocutor hasn't disappeared, he or she will smile condescendingly.'

Hotel Mamma

If you're between the ages of 18 and 34, there's a 60% chance that's not a roommate in the kitchen making your morning coffee: it's mum or dad. This is not because Italy is a nation of pampered *mammoni* (mama's boys) and spoilt *figlie di papá* (daddy's girls) – at least, not entirely. One reason is tradition. According to the time-honoured Italian social contract, you'd probably live with your parents until you start a career and a family of your own. Then after a suitable grace period for success and romance – a couple of years should do the trick – your parents might move in with you to look after your kids, and be looked after in turn.

Then there's the finance factor. As desirable as living independently might be, it isn't always an option in the midst of Italy's current recession. While almost three-quarters of Italian students are the first in their families to have attended university, many of these graduates cannot find employment. Those who do must often settle for short-term internships or lower-skilled positions.

Nice work, if you can get it: about 30% of Italians have landed a job through family connections, and in highly paid professions that number rises as high as 40% to 50%.

Born an Assisi heiress, introduced to the joys of poverty by St Francis himself, and co-founder of the first Franciscan abbey, St Clare gained another claim to fame in 1958 as the patron saint of TV.

THE ITALIAN WAY OF LIFE A DAY IN THE LIFE OF AN ITALIAN

ITALIAN TELEVISION: THE SOUND & THE FURY

As heretical as it sounds to foreigners accustomed to worshipping Italian cuisine in the reverent hush of expensive restaurants, many Italians bolt dinner in front of blaring televisions. On average, Italians watch four hours of TV per day and the flickering parade of recycled reality stars, vacant-eyed *valette* (spokesmodels) and celebrity interviews induces what Italian sociologists have identified as a soporific state.

According to a 2008 poll, only 24% of Italians trust TV as a reliable source. Italians are more likely to trust online news sites such as Corriere della Sera (www.corriere.it/english), La Repubblica (www.repubblica.it), Il Manifesto (www.ilmanifesto.it) or L'Unitá (www.unita.it), perhaps with good reason: in 2010, Reporters Without Borders ranked Italy below Taiwan, Mali and Bosnia in freedom of the press, calling Prime Minister Silvio Berlusconi's TV empire a 'conflict of interest' that threatens democracy. Yet 80% of Italy's population relies on TV news as its prime information source, including three main channels run by the Berlusconi-backed Mediaset company.

Considering the lacklustre job market, skyrocketing rents and temptations of home cooking, it's no wonder the number of adult Italians living with their parents has grown in recent years – hence the mobile-phone chorus heard at evening rush hour in buses and trams across Italy: '*Mamma, butta la pasta!*' (Mum, put the pasta in the water!).

The World Economic Forum's 2010 Global Gender Gap Report ranked Italy 87th worldwide in terms of female labour participation, 121st in wage parity and 74th overall for its treatment of women. Italy and Greece have the lowest number of women in any EU national parliament.

What it Feels Like for a Girl

On 13 February 2011, almost one million Italian women took to the streets in protest. Sparked by allegations that their prime minister had indulged in sex parties with an underage dancer, they not only demanded his dismissal but also an end to the Italian media's representation of women as little more than doting mothers or vapid *veline* (showgirls).

Nicknamed Il Cavaliere (The Cavalier), Berlusconi has never been known for his feminist leanings. In 2008 he told a young female voter that the best way to overcome poverty was to marry a millionaire...like his son. The following year, he sarcastically accused opposition MP Rosy Bindi, a bespectacled middle-aged woman, of being 'more beautiful than intelligent'. Within days, thousands of women were wearing T-shirts printed with Bindi's quick-witted reply: 'Mr Prime Minister, I am not a woman at your disposal'.

Despite the burning of bras in the 1960s and 1970s, sexism remains deeply entrenched in Italian society. On TV, women are often little more than scantily dressed props. On radio, female voiceovers range from quasi-hysterical to blushingly orgasmic. In a culture where machismo is far from dead, many men see Berlusconi not so much as a chauvinist but as a septuagenarian stud relishing *la dolce vita* to the last drop. Indeed, male politicians rumoured of dallying with mistresses have more often enjoyed a surge in public popularity than a slump on Italian soil.

Many Italian women must wish these men were half as passionate about pulling their weight at home. According to a recent report by the Uomini Casalinghi (The Italian Association of Househusbands), 70% of Italian men have never used a stove, while 95% have never turned on a washing machine. A survey released by the Organisation for Economic Co-operation and Development (OECD) in 2010 found that Italian men enjoy almost 80 more minutes of leisure time daily than their female counterparts.

No doubt RAI TV knew it had an audience when launching its reality show *La sposa perfetta* (The Perfect Bride) in 2007. In it, women contestants competed for an eligible bachelor's attention by performing domestic duties, with his mother choosing the winner. Incensed Italian women threatened to withhold €200 of their taxes earmarked for public broadcasting if the show was renewed. It wasn't.

Despite these demoralising figures, there are signs of hope. Official statistics reveal that most Italian women aged 29 to 34 now prefer careers and a home life without curfews or children. Italian women represent 65% of college graduates, are more likely than men to pursue higher education (53% to 45%) and twice as likely to land responsible positions in public service.

And the smuggest stat? While one in 10 Italian women still lives with her parents by age 35, twice as many men do.

Italian Style Icons

» Bialetti coffee-maker

» Cinzano vermouth

» Acqua di Parma cologne

» Piaggio Vespa

» Olivetti 'Valentine' typewriter

Better Living by Design

As an Italian, you actually did your co-workers a favour by being late to the office to give yourself a final once-over in the mirror. Unless you want your fellow employees to avert their gaze in dumbstruck horror, your socks had better match. The tram can wait as you *fa la bella figura* (cut a fine figure).

Most of the music you'll hear booming out of Italian taxis and cafes to inspire sidewalk singalongs is Italian *musica leggera* (popular music); a term covering home-grown rock, jazz, folk, hip hop and pop ballads. The scene's annual highlight is the San Remo Music Festival (televised on RAI 1), a Eurovision-style song comp responsible for launching the careers of big-name contemporary acts like Eros Ramazzotti, Giorgia and Laura Pausini.

While Rome is a Bermuda Triangle for rockers with drug habits – Kurt Cobain and Mark Sandman (the latter of Morphine fame) overdosed there – Milan is out to prove punk's not dead with the annual indie-fest Rock in Idro and the city's crossover rap-punk sensation Articolo 31. Chart-topping rapper Fabri Fibra hails from Le Marche, while south side, Neapolitan hip hop acts like 99 Posse, La Famiglia and Bisca mix Italian sounds over heavy beats and Neapolitan dialect. Fusion is also the word in Puglia, where artists like Sud Sound System remix Jamaican dancehall and Italy's hyperactive taran-tella folk music into a new genre: *'tarantamuffin'.*

In the singer-songwriter category, scratchy-voiced troubadour Vinicio Capossela sounds like the long-lost Italian cousin of Tom Waits, Pino Daniele fuses Neapolitan music with blues and world music influences, while the late Fabrizio de André is Italy's answer to Bob Dylan, with thoughtful lyrics in a musing monotone.

Italians have strong opinions about aesthetics and aren't afraid to share them. A common refrain is *Che brutta!* (How hideous!), which may strike visitors as tactless. But consider it from an Italian point of view – everyone is rooting for you to look good, so who are you to disappoint? The shop assistant who tells you with brutal honesty that yellow is not your colour is doing a public service, and will consider it a personal tri-umph to see you outfitted in orange instead.

If it's a gift, though, you must allow 10 minutes for the sales clerk to *fa un bel pacchetto,* wrapping your purchase with string and an artfully placed sticker. This is the epitome of *la bella figura* – the sales clerk wants you to look good by giving a good gift. When you do, everyone basks in the glow of *la bella figura:* you as the gracious gift-giver and the sales clerk as savvy gift consultant, not to mention the flushed and duly honoured recipient.

As a national obsession, *la bella figura* gives Italy its undeniable edge in design, cuisine, art and architecture. Though the country could get by on its striking good looks, Italy is ever mindful of delightful details. They are everywhere you look, and many places you don't: the intricately carved cathedral spire only the bell-ringer could fully appreciate, the toy duck hidden inside your chocolate *uova di pasqua* (Easter egg), the ab-sinthe-green silk lining inside a sober grey suit sleeve. Attention to such details earns you instant admiration in Italy – and an admission that, sometimes, non-Italians do have style.

The People

Who are the people you'd encounter every day as an Italian? On aver-age, about half your co-workers will be women – quite a change from 10 years ago, when women represented just a quarter of the workforce. But a growing proportion of the people you'll meet are already retired. One out of five Italians is over 65, which explains the septuagenarians you'll notice on parade with dogs and grandchildren in parks, affably arguing about politics in cafes, and ruthlessly dominating bocce tournaments.

You might also notice a striking absence of children. Italy's birth rate is the lowest in Europe, at just under one child per woman.

The influx of American soldiers at the end of WWII left Italy with a lasting love of jazz. The country's string of sax-obsessed festivals include Umbria Jazz (www.umbriajazz. com), Siena Jazz (www.sienajazz. it) and Vicenza Jazz (www.vicen-zajazz.org).

THE OLD PROVERBIAL

They might be old clichés, but proverbs can be quite the cultural revelation. Here are six of Italy's well-worn best:

» *Donne e motori, gioie e dolori.* Women and motors, joy and pain.

» *Chi trova un'amico trova un tesoro.* He who finds a friend, finds a treasure.

» *A ogni uccello il suo nido è bello.* To every bird, his own nest is beautiful.

» *Fidarsi va bene, non fidarsi va megio.* To trust is good, not to trust is better.

» *Meglio essere invidiati che compatiti.* Better to be envied than pitied.

» *Il diavolo fa le pentole ma non i coperchi.* The devil makes the pots but not the lids (The truth always comes out in the end).

John Turturro's film *Passione* (2010) is a *Buena Vista Social Club*–style exploration of Naples' rich and eclectic musical traditions. Spanning folk songs to contemporary tunes, it offers a fascinating insight into the city's complex soul.

North versus South

In his film *Ricomincio da tre* (I'm Starting from Three; 1980), acting great Massimo Troisi comically tackles the problems faced by Neapolitans forced to head north for work. Laughter aside, the film reveals Italy's very real north–south divide; a divide still present more than 30 years on. While the north is celebrated for its fashion empires and moneyed metropolises, Italy's south (dubbed the 'Mezzogiorno') is a PR nightmare of high unemployment, crumbling infrastructure and Mafia arrests. At a deep semantic level, *settentrionale* (northern Italian) equals reservation, productivity and success, while *meridionale* (southern Italian) equates with conservatism, melodrama and laziness. From the Industrial Revolution to the 1960s, millions of southern Italians fled to the industrialised northern cities for factory jobs. Disparagingly nicknamed *terroni* (literally meaning 'of the soil'), these in-house 'immigrants' were often exposed to racist attitudes from their northern cousins. Decades on, the overt racism may have dissipated but the prejudices remain. Many northerners resent their taxes being used to 'subsidise' the south – a sentiment well exploited by the right-wing, Veneto-based Lega Nord (Northern League) party.

From Emigrants to Immigrants

From 1876 to 1976, Italy was a country of net emigration. With some 30 million Italian emigrants dispersed throughout Europe, the Americas and Australia, remittances from Italians abroad helped keep Italy's economy afloat during economic crises after Independence and WWII.

The tables have since turned. Political and economic upheavals in the 1980s brought new arrivals from Central Europe, Latin America and North Africa, including Italy's former colonies in Tunisia, Somalia and Ethiopia. More recently, waves of Chinese and Filipino immigrants have given Italian streetscapes a Far Eastern twist.

While immigrants account for just 7.1% of Italy's own population today, the number is growing. From a purely economic angle, these new arrivals are vital for the country's economic health. While most Italians today choose to live and work within Italy, fewer are entering blue-collar agricultural and industrial fields. Without immigrant workers to fill the gaps, Italy would be sorely lacking in tomato sauce and shoes. From kitchen hands to hotel maids, it is often immigrants who take the low-paid service jobs that keep Italy's tourism economy afloat.

Despite this, not all Italians are dusting down their welcome mats. In 2008, a young Jewish-Romanian immigrant was beaten to death by neo-Nazi groups in Verona, and two Roma camps in Naples were torched by neo-Nazi gangs allegedly tied to Naples' Camorra crime syndicate. The same year, several rapes across Italy were swiftly (and mostly falsely) blamed on African immigrants. African frustration reached boiling point in 2010, when the shooting of an immigrant worker in the town of Rosarno, Calabria, sparked Italy's worst race riots in years.

Yet not all Italians are willing to let extremists have the last word. In May 2009, a radical law to punish undocumented immigrants – including potential refugees – with summary deportation and fines was denounced by Italian human rights groups, the Vatican, the UN and mass protests in Rome. As writer Claudio Magris observed in *The Times,* recalling Italy's recent past as a nation of emigrants, 'We, above all, should know what it is like to be strangers in a strange land.'

Religion, Loosely Speaking

Although you read about the church in the news headlines, you didn't actually attend Mass on your day as an Italian. Neither did most of your neighbours. According to a 2007 church study, only 15% of Italy's population regularly attends Sunday mass. That said, *La Famiglia Cristiana* (The Christian Family) remains Italy's most popular weekly magazine and church doctrine is often the subject of popular debate. An Umbrian teacher's suspension for removing the crucifix from his public classroom in 2009 sparked arguments over church symbols in public buildings, and fuelled ongoing debates over the appropriate division of church and state in Italy.

What the pope says matters. But in the land of the double park, even God's rules are up for interpretation. Sure, there's a crucifix above your bed and fish on your plate on Good Friday, but while you consult *la Madonna* for guidance, chances are you get a second opinion from the *maga* (fortune-teller) on channel 32. The European Consumer Association estimates that Italians spend a whopping €5 billion annually on fortune-tellers and astrologers. While the current climate of economic uncertainty has seen a rise in the use of esoteric services, the trend is not surprising. Italians are a highly superstitious bunch. From not toasting with water to not opening umbrellas inside the home, the country offers a long list of traditions to keep bad luck at bay.

Superstitious beliefs are especially strong in Italy's south. Here *corni* (horn-shaped charms) adorn everything from necklines to rear-view mirrors to ward off the *malocchio* (evil eye) and devotion to local saints takes on an almost cultish edge. Every year in Naples, thousands cram into the Duomo to witness the blood of San Gennaro miraculously liquefy in the phial that contains it. When the blood liquefies, the city breathes a sigh of relief – it symbolises another year safe from disaster. When it didn't in 1944, Mt Vesuvius erupted, and when it failed again in 1980 an earthquake struck the city that year. Coincidence? Perhaps. But even the most cynical Neapolitan would rather San Gennaro perform his magic trick…just in case.

Italians were the world's fastest *telefonino* (mobile phone) adopters in 2000 and, according to government estimates, within three years virtually every adult Italian had a *telefonino* – not to mention obsessive text-messaging teens.

BATTLE OF THE BINGE

Once a poster child for sensible sipping, Italy's relationship with the bottle has taken a dangerous turn in the last decade. In 2011, the Italian Institute for Statistics (ISTAT) reported that over eight and a half million Italians consume dangerous levels of alcohol on a daily basis. Figures from the Italian Public Health Service (ISS) are equally sobering: 14.4% of hospital admissions for excessive alcohol consumption are under the age of 14, while 25.4% are between 15 and 35. Until recently a source of social stigma, drinking to excess has become a hit with many young Italians. Explanations for the rise are many, from lax retail practices to the influence of binge-drinking Anglo tourists. No doubt that many Italian parents are reconsidering that traditional nip of *vino* (wine) at family celebrations.

THE ITALIAN WAY OF LIFE THE PEOPLE

Italian Passions

Co-ordinated wardrobes, strong espresso and general admiration are not the only things that make Italian hearts sing. And while Italian passions are wide and varied, few define Italy like the following two.

Calcio (Football): Italy's Other Religion

Catholicism may be your official faith, but as an Italian your true religion is likely to be *calcio* (football). On any given weekend from September to May, chances are that you and your fellow *tifosi* (football fans) are at the *stadio* (stadium), glued to the TV, or checking the score on your mobile phone. Come Monday, you'll be dissecting the match by the office water cooler.

Like politics and fashion, football is in the very DNA of Italian culture. Indeed, they sometimes even converge. Silvio Berlusconi first found fame as the owner of AC Milan and cleverly named his political party after a well-worn football chant. Fashion royalty Dolce & Gabbana declared football players 'the new male icons', using five of Italy's hottest on-field stars to launch its 2010 underwear collection. Decades earlier, '60s singer Rita Pavone topped the charts with *La partita di pallone* (The Football Match), in which the frustrated pop princess sings *'Perchè, perchè la domenica mi lasci sempre sola per andare a vedere la partita di pallone?'* (Why, why do you always leave me alone on Sunday so you can go and watch the football match?). It's no coincidence that in Italian *tifoso* means both 'football fan' and 'typhus patient'. When the ball ricochets off the post and slips fatefully through the goalie's hands, when half the stadium is swearing while the other half is euphorically shouting *Goooooooooooooool!*, 'fever pitch' is the term that comes to mind.

Nothing quite stirs Italian blood like a good (or a bad) game. Nine months after Italy's 2006 World Cup victory against France, hospitals in northern Italy reported a baby boom. In February the following year, rioting at a Palermo-Catania match in Catania left one policeman dead and around 100 injured. Blamed on the Ultras – a minority group of hard-core football fans – the violence shocked both Italy and the world, leading to a temporary ban of all matches in Italy, and increased stadium security. A year earlier, the match-fixing 'Calciopoli' scandals resulted in revoked championship titles and temporary demotion of Serie A (top-tier national) teams, including the mighty Juventus.

Yet, the same game that divides also unites. You might be a Lazio-loathing, AS Roma supporter on any given day, but when the national *Azzurri* (The Blues) swag the World Cup, you are nothing but a heart-on-your-sleeve *italiano* (Italian). In his book *The 100 Things Everyone Needs to Know About Italy*, Australian journalist David Dale writes that Italy's 1982 World Cup win 'finally united twenty regions which, until then, had barely acknowledged that they were part of the one country.'

Italy's culture of corruption and *calcio* (football) is captured in *The Dark Heart of Italy*, in which English expat author Tobias Jones wryly observes, 'Footballers or referees are forgiven nothing; politicians are forgiven everything.'

Italy was introduced to modern *calcio* in the late 19th century when the English factory barons of Turin, Genoa and Milan established teams to keep their workers fit.

Opera: Let the Fat Lady Sing

At the stadium, your beloved *squadra* (team) hits the field to the roar of Verdi. Okay, so you mightn't be first in line to see *Rigoletto* at La Fenice, but Italy's opera legacy remains a source of pride. After all, not only did you invent the art form, you gave the world some of its greatest composers and compositions. Gioachino Rossini (1792–1868) transformed Pierre Beaumarchais' *Le Barbier de Séville* (The Barber of Seville) into one of the greatest comedic operas, Giuseppe Verdi (1813–1901) produced the epic *Aida,* while Giacomo Puccini (1858–1924) delivered staples like *Tosca, Madama Butterfly* and *Turandot.*

Lyrical, intense and dramatic – it's only natural that opera bears the 'Made in Italy' label. Track pants might be traded in for tuxedos, but

OPTIMAL OPERA VENUES

» **Milan's Teatro alla Scala** (p240) Standards for modern opera were set by La Scala's great iron-willed conductor Arturo Toscanini and are ruthlessly enforced by La Scala's feared *loggione*, opera's toughest and most vocal critics in the cheap seats upstairs.

» **Venice's La Fenice** (p333) Risen twice from the ashes of devastating fires, 'The Phoenix' features great talents on its small stage.

» **Arena di Verona** (p380) Rising talents ring out here, thanks to forward-thinking organisers and the phenomenal acoustics of this Roman amphitheatre.

» **Terme di Caracalla** (p97) The dramatically decrepit summer venue for the Teatro dell'Opera di Roma was the site of the first concert by the Three Tenors (Luciano Pavarotti, Placido Domingo and Jose Carreras), with a recording that sold an unprecedented 15 million copies.

» **Teatro San Carlo in Naples** (p639) Europe's oldest opera house, a Unesco World Heritage Site and the former home of Italy's most famous *castrati* – male sopranos traditionally with surgically enhanced upper ranges.

Italy's opera crowds can be just as ruthless as their pitch-side counterparts. Centuries on, the dreaded *fischi* (mocking whistles) still possess a mysterious power to blast singers right off stage. In December 2006, a substitute in street clothes had to step in for Sicilian-French star tenor Roberto Alagna when his off-night aria met with vocal disapproval at Milan's legendary La Scala. Best not to get them started about musicals and 'rock opera', eh?

The word *diva* was invented for legendary sopranos like Parma's Renata Tebaldi and Italy's adopted Greek icon Maria Callas, whose rivalry peaked when *Time* quoted Callas saying that comparing her voice to Tebaldi's was like comparing 'champagne and Coca-Cola'. Both were fixtures at La Scala, along with the wildly popular Italian tenor to which others are still compared, Enrico Caruso. Tenor Luciano Pavarotti (1935–2007) remains beloved for attracting broader public attention to opera, while best-selling blind tenor Andrea Bocelli became a controversial crossover sensation with what critics claim are overproduced arias sung with a strained upper register. A new generation of stars include tenor Salvatore Licitra, who stepped in for Pavarotti on his final show at New York's Metropolitan Opera in 2002, and soprano Fiorenze Cedolins, who has performed a requiem for the late Pope John Paul II, recorded Tosca arias with Andrea Bocelli, and scored encores in Puccini's iconic *La Bohème* at the Arena di Verona Festival.

Openings at La Scala regularly sell out faster than rock concerts – and when a Verdi opera's on the bill, you'd think the Beatles were getting back together. Book your tickets online pronto at www.teatroalla scala.org.

Italy on Page & Screen

From ancient Virgil to modern-day Eco, Italy's literary canon is awash with world-renowned scribes. The nation's film stock is equally rich, spiked with visionary directors, iconic stars and that trademark Italian pathos.

Literature

Latin Classics

Roman epic poet Virgil (aka Vergilius) decided Homer's *Iliad* and *Odyssey* deserved a sequel, and spent 11 years and 12 books tracking the outbound adventures and inner turmoil of Aeneas, from the fall of Troy to the founding of Rome – and died in 19 BC with just 60 lines to go in his *Aeneid*. As Virgil himself observed: 'Time flies'.

Legend has it that fellow Roman Ovid (Ovidius) was a failed lawyer who married his daughter, but there's no question he told a ripping good tale. His *Metamorphose* chronicled civilisation from murky mythological beginnings to Julius Caesar, and his how-to seduction manual *Ars amatoria* (The Art of Love) inspired countless Casanovas.

Cautionary Fables

The most universally beloved Italian fabulist is Italo Calvino, whose titular character in *Il barone rampante* (The Baron in the Trees; 1957) takes to the treetops in a seemingly capricious act of rebellion that makes others rethink their own earthbound conventions. In Dino Buzzati's *Il deserto dei Tartari* (The Tartar Steppe; 1940), an ambitious officer posted to a mythical Italian border is besieged by boredom, thwarted expectations and disappearing youth while waiting for enemy hordes to materialise – a parable drawn from Buzzati's own dead-end newspaper job.

Over the centuries, Niccolo Machiavelli's *Il principe* (The Prince; 1532) has been referenced as a handy manual for budding autocrats, but also as a cautionary tale against unchecked 'Machiavellian' authority.

For Dante with a pop-culture twist, check out Sandow Birk and Marcus Sanders' satirical, slangy translation of *The Divine Comedy*, which sets *Inferno* in hellish Los Angeles traffic, *Purgatorio* in foggy San Francisco and *Paradiso* in New York.

Timeless Poets

Some literature scholars claim Shakespeare stole his best lines and plot points from earlier Italian playwrights and poets. Debatable though this may be, the Bard certainly has stiff competition from 13th-century Dante Alighieri as the world's finest romancer. Dante broke with tradition in *La Divina commedia* (The Divine Comedy; c 1307–21) by using the familiar Italian, not the formal Latin, to describe travelling through the circles of hell in search of his beloved Beatrice. Petrarch (aka Francesco Petrarca) added wow to Italian woo with his eponymous sonnets, applying a strict structure of rhythm and rhyme to romance the idealised Laura. He might have tried chocolates instead: Laura never returned the sentiment.

If sonnets aren't your shtick, try 1975 Nobel laureate Eugenio Montale, who wrings poetry out of the creeping damp of everyday life, or Ungaretti, whose WWI poems hit home with a few searing syllables. His two-word poem seems an apt epitaph: *M'illumino d'immenso* (I illuminate myself with immensity).

Crime Pays

Crime fiction and *gialli* (mysteries) dominate Italy's best-seller list, and one of its finest writers is Gianrico Carofiglio. The former head of Bari's anti-Mafia squad, Carofiglio's novels include the award-winning *Testimone inconsapevole* (Involuntary Witness; 2002), which introduces defence lawyer Guido Guerrieri and the shady underworld of Bari's hinterland.

Art also imitates life for judge-cum-novelist Giancarlo de Cataldo, whose best-selling novel *Romanzo criminale* (Criminal Romance; 2002) spawned both a TV series and film. Another crime writer with page-to-screen success is Andrea Camilleri, his cranky but savvy Sicilian inspector Montalbano starring in capers like *Il ladro di merendine* (The Snack Thief; 1996).

Umberto Eco gave the genre an intellectual edge with *Il nome della rosa* (The Name of the Rose; 1980) and *Il pendolo di Foucault* (Foucault's Pendulum; 1988) – not to mention sheer bulk, at 600-plus pages of arcane detail and plot twists.

Historical Epics

Italian authors find illumination even in Italy's darkest hours. Set during the Black Death in Florence, Boccaccio's *Decameron* (c 1350–3) has a visceral gallows humour that foreshadows Chaucer and Shakespeare. Italy's 19th-century struggle for unification parallels the story of star-crossed lovers in Alessandro Manzoni's *I promessi sposi* (The Betrothed; 1827, definitive version released 1842), and causes an identity crisis among Sicilian nobility in Giuseppe Tomasi di Lampedusa's *Il gattopardo* (The Leopard; published posthumously in 1958).

Wartime survival strategies are chronicled in Elsa Morante's *La storia* (History; 1974) and in Primo Levi's harrowing autobiographical account of Auschwitz in *Se questo è un uomo* (If This Is a Man; 1947). WWII is the uninvited guest in *Il giardino dei Finzi-Contini* (The Garden of the Finzi-Continis; 1962), Giorgio Bassani's heartbreaking tale of a crush on a girl whose aristocratic Jewish family attempts to disregard the rising tide of anti-Semitism.

Social Realism

Italy has always been its own sharpest critic and several 20th-century Italian authors captured their own troubling circumstances with unflinching accuracy. Grazia Deledda's *Cosima* is her fictionalised memoir of coming of age and into her own as a writer in rural Sardinia, despite challenging family circumstances. Deledda became one of the first women to win the Nobel Prize for Literature (1926) and set the tone for such bittersweet recollections of rural life as Carlo Levi's *Cristo si è fermato a Eboli* (Christ Stopped at Eboli).

Topics too excruciating to discuss or ignore – jealousy, divorce, parental failings – are addressed head-on by pseudonymous author Elena Ferrante in her brutally honest *The Days of Abandonment*. Brutal honesty also underlines Roberto Saviano's *Gomorra* – a detailed exposé of Mafia machinations.

Any self-respecting Italian bookshelf features one or more Roman rhetoricians. To *fare la bella figura* (cut a fine figure) among academics, trot out a phrase from Cicero or Horace (Horatio), such as 'Where there is life there is hope' or 'Whatever advice you give, be brief.'

Cinema

Neorealist Grit

Out of the smouldering ruins of WWII emerged unflinching tales of woe, including Roberto Rossellini's classic *Roma, città aperta* (Rome, Open City; 1945), a story of love, betrayal, survival and resistance in Nazi-occupied Rome. In Vittorio de Sica's Academy-awarded *Ladri di biciclette* (The Bicycle Thief; 1948), a doomed father attempts to provide for his son without resorting to crime in war-ravaged Rome, while Pier Paolo Pasolini's *Mamma Roma* (1962) revolves around an ageing prostitute trying to make an honest living for herself and her deadbeat son. The neorealist tradition continues in Michelangelo Frammartino's acclaimed *Le quattro volte* (2010), a documentary-style tale about life and death in rural Calabria.

A one-man 'Abbott & Costello', Antonio de Curtis (1898–1967), aka Totò, famously depicted the Neapolitan *furbizia* (cunning). Appearing in over 100 films, including *Miseria e nobilità* (Misery & Nobility; 1954), his roles as a hustler living on nothing but his quick wits would guarantee him cult status in Naples.

Crime & Punishment

Italy's acclaimed new dramas combine the truthfulness of classic neorealism, the taut suspense of Italian thrillers and the psychological revelations of Fellini. Among the best is Matteo Garrone's *Gomorra* (2008). Based on Roberto Saviano's award-winning novel, the film's honest portrayal of Camorra brutality earned the film a Grand Prix at the 2008 Cannes Film Festival. Another Cannes success story is Paolo Sorrentino's *Il divo* (2008), a film exploring the life of former prime minister Giulio Andreotti, from his migraines to his alleged Mafia ties. Equally gripping is Cristina Comencini's *La bestia nel cuore* (Don't Tell; 2005). In it, a woman uncovering repressed memories of sexual abuse seeks answers yet leaves an even longer trail of secrets behind her.

Romance all'italiana

It's only natural that a nation of hopeless romantics should provide some of the world's most tender celluloid moments. In Michael Radford's *Il postino* (The Postman; 1994), exiled poet Pablo Neruda brings poetry and passion to a drowsy Italian isle and a misfit postman, played with heartbreaking subtlety by the late, great Massimo Troisi.

Another classic is Giuseppe Tornatore's Oscar-winning *Nuovo cinema paradiso* (Cinema Paradiso; 1988), a bittersweet tale about a director who returns to Sicily and rediscovers his true loves: the girl next door and the movies.

LOCATION! LOCATION!

Cinephiles can expect a sense of déjà vu in Italy, its cities, hills and coastlines setting the scene for countless celluloid classics. Top billing goes to Rome, where Bernaldo Bertolucci used the Terme di Caracalla in the oedipal *La luna* (1979). Gregory Peck gave Audrey Hepburn the fright of her life at the Bocca della Verità in William Wyler's *Roman Holiday* (1953) and Anita Ekberg cooled off in the Trevi Fountain in Federico Fellini's *La Dolce Vita*. Fellini's love affair with the Eternal City culminated in his silver-screen tribute, *Roma* (1972).

While Florence's Piazza della Signoria recalls James Ivory's *Room With a View* (1985), don't be surprised if Siena's Piazza del Palio stirs fantasies of actor Daniel Craig – the square featured in the 22nd James Bond instalment, *Quantum of Solace* (2008).

Venice's Grand Canal is like one wet red carpet: Angelina Jolie and Johnny Depp sped down it in the thriller *The Tourist* (2010) and Woody Allen sang 'I'm Through With Love' beside it in *Everyone Says I Love You* (1996). The city enjoyed a cameo in *The Talented Mr Ripley* (1999), in which Matt Damon and Gwyneth Paltrow also toasted and tanned on the Campanian islands of Procida and Ischia. Fans of *Il Postino* will recognise Procida's pastel-hued Corricella, while those of Mel Gibson's *Passion of The Christ* (2004) may feel a vague familiarity in Basilicata's Matera, its cavernous landscape moonlighting as Palestine.

THE CULT OF ZOMBIE

Out of the horror genre emerged one of Italian cinema's lesser-known legacies: Italian zombie films. Crueller and bloodier than their American counterparts, one of the best is *Zombi 2* (aka *Zombie Flesh Eaters;* 1979), directed by Lucio Fulci (1927–96). In it, a boatload of the walking-dead sail into New York, causing havoc and prompting Ian McCulloch and Tisa Farrow (sibling to Mia) to seek answers on a zombie-infested tropical island.

Nicknamed the 'Godfather of Gore', Rome-born Fulci went on to direct a string of zombie classics, including his 'Gates of Hell' trilogy. In *City of the Living Dead* (1980), a reporter and a psychic set out to close a portal to hell and save humanity from a zombie free-for-all. 'Renovation hell' takes on a whole new meaning in *The Beyond* (1981), while *The House by the Cemetery* (1981) proves that a doctor in the house is not always a blessing.

In Silvio Sordini's *Pane e tulipani* (Bread and Tulips; 2000), a housewife left behind at a tour-bus pit stop runs away to Venice, where she befriends an anarchist florist, an eccentric masseuse and a suicidal Icelandic waiter – and gets pursued by an amateur detective.

Equally contemporary is Ferzan Özpetek's *Mine vaganti* (Loose Cannons; 2010), a situation comedy about two gay brothers and their conservative Pugliese family.

> *La vita è bella* (Life Is Beautiful) remains the most successful subtitled foreign-language film to date, winning two Academy Awards and raking in about US$280 million.

Spaghetti Westerns

Emerging in the mid-1960s, Italian-style Westerns saw southern Italy double as the Wild West in high-noon showdowns featuring flinty characters and Ennio Morricone's terminally catchy whistled tunes (doodle-oodle-ooh, wah wah wah...). Top of the directorial heap was Sergio Leone, whose Western debut *Per un pugno di dollari* (A Fistful of Dollars; 1964) helped launch a young Clint Eastwood's movie career. After Leone and Clintwood teamed up again in *Il buono, il brutto, il cattivo* (The Good, the Bad, and the Ugly; 1966), it was Henry Fonda's turn in Leone's *C'era una volta il West* (Once Upon a Time in the West; 1968), a story about a revenge-seeking widow.

Tragicomedies

Italy's best comedians pinpoint the exact spot where pathos intersects the funny bone – but without an appreciation for Italian slapstick and dialect, some hilarity can get lost in translation. A group of ageing pranksters turn on one another in Mario Monicelli's *Amici miei* (My Friends; 1975), a satire reflecting Italy's own postwar midlife crisis. In *Caro diario* (Dear Diary; 1994), Nanni Moretti (Italy's Woody Allen) navigates a Vespa through Rome while obsessing over the meaning of life, insomnia and Jennifer Beals' *Flashdance* performance. Topping the lot is *La vita è bella* (Life is Beautiful; 1997), in which a father tries to protect his son from the brutalities of a Jewish concentration camp by pretending it's all a game – an Oscar Award–winning turn for actor-director Roberto Benigni.

> ### Top Film Festivals
>
> » Venice Film Festival (www. labiennale.org)
>
> » Torino Film Festival (www. torinofilmfest.org)
>
> » Milano Film Festival (www. milanofilm festival.it)
>
> » Cinema: International Rome Film Festival (www.roma cinemafest.it)
>
> » Salento Film Festival (www. salentofilm festival.com)

Shock & Horror

Sunny Italy's darkest dramas deliver more style, suspense and falling bodies than ultrahigh Prada platform heels on a slippery Milan runway. In Michelangelo Antonioni's *Blow-Up* (1966) a swinging-'60s fashion photographer spies dark deeds unfolding in a photo of an elusive young Vanessa Redgrave. Gruesome deeds unfold at a ballet school in Dario Argento's *Suspiria* (1977), while in Mario Monicelli's *Un borghese piccolo piccolo* (An Average Little Man; 1977), an ordinary man goes to extraordinary lengths for revenge. The latter stars Roman acting great Alberto Soldi in a standout example of a comedian nailing a serious role.

The Italian Table

Let's be honest: you came for the food, right? Wise choice. Just don't go expecting the stock-standards served at your local Italian restaurant back home. In reality, Italian cuisine is a handy umbrella term for the country's diverse regional cuisines – flavours explored in more detail on p34. Despite the diversity, there is almost always one constant – whether you're tucking into a hearty *farro* (spelt) soup in some Tuscan *osteria* (casual tavern or eatery presided over by a host) or devouring a *pizza margherita* (tomato, basil and mozzarella pizza) in its home town, Naples, you'll be struck with culinary amnesia. Has anything tasted this good, ever? Probably not.

The secret is in the ingredients. Each is chosen with careful consideration to scent, texture, ripeness and the ability to play well with others. This means getting to the market early and often, and remaining open to seasonal inspiration. To balance these ingredients in exactly the right proportions, Italian cooks apply an intuitive Pythagorean theorem of flavours you won't find spelled out in any recipe – but that is unmistakable with your first bite.

Fifty years ago, Italy's *Domus* magazine dispatched journalists nationwide to collect Italy's best regional recipes. The result is Italy's food bible, *The Silver Spoon*, now available in English from Phaidon (2005).

Tutti a Tavola

'Everyone to the table!' Traffic lights are merely suggestions and queues fine ideas in theory, but this is one command every Italian heeds without question. To disobey would be unthinkable – what, you're going to eat your pasta cold? And insult the cook? Even anarchists wouldn't dream of it.

You never really know Italians until you've broken a crusty loaf of *pagnotta* (loaf of bread) with them – and once you've arrived in Italy, you'll have several opportunities daily to do just that.

Morning Essentials

In Italy, *colazione* (breakfast) is a minimalist affair. Eggs, pancakes, ham, sausage, toast and orange juice are only likely to appear at weekend *brrrunch* (pronounced with the rolled Italian *r*), an American import now appearing at trendy urban eateries. Expect to pay upwards of €20 to graze a buffet of hot dishes, cold cuts, pastries and fresh fruit, usually including your choice of coffee, juice or cocktail.

Italy's breakfast staple is *caffè* (coffee). Scalding-hot espresso, cappuccino (espresso with a goodly dollop of foamed milk) or *caffè latte* – the hot, milky espresso beverage Starbucks mistakenly calls a *latte,* which will get you a glass of milk in Italy. An alternative beverage is *orzo,* a slightly nutty, noncaffeinated roasted-barley beverage that looks like cocoa.

With a *tazza* (cup) in one hand, use the other for that most Italian of breakfast foods – a pastry. Some especially promising options include the following:

Cornetto The Italian take on the French croissant is usually smaller, lighter, less buttery and slightly sweet, with an orange-rind glaze brushed on top. Fillings might include *cioccolato* (chocolate), *cioccolato bianco* (white chocolate), *crema* (custard) or varying flavours of *marmelata* (jam).

Crostata The Italian breakfast tart with a dense, buttery crust is filled with your choice of fruit jam, such as *amarena* (sour cherry), *albicocca* (apricot) or *frutti di bosco* (wild berry). You may have to buy an entire tart instead of a single slice, but you won't be sorry.

Doughnuts Homer Simpson would approve of the *ciambella* (also called by its German name, *krapfen),* the classic fried-dough treat rolled in granulated sugar and sometimes filled with jam or custard. Join the line at kiosks and street fairs for *fritole,* fried dough studded with golden raisins and sprinkled with confectioners' sugar, and *zeppole* (also called *bigné di San Giuseppe*), chewy doughnuts filled with ricotta or *zucca* (pumpkin), rolled in confectioners' sugar, and handed over in a paper cone to be devoured dangerously hot.

Viennoiserie Italy's colonisation by the Austro-Hungarian Empire in the 19th century had its upside: a vast selection of sweet buns and other rich baked goods. Standouts include cream-filled brioches and *strudel di mele,* an Italian adaptation of the traditional Viennese *apfelstrudel.*

Lunch & Dinner

Italian food culture directly contradicts what we think we know of Italy. A nation prone to perpetual motion with Vespas, Ferraris and Bianchis pauses for *pranzo* (lunch) – hence the term *la pausa* to describe the midday break. In the cities, power-lunchers settle in at their favourite *ristoranti* and trattorias, while in smaller towns and villages, workers often head home for a two- to three-hour midday break, devouring a hot lunch and resting up before returning to work wired on espresso.

Where *la pausa* has been scaled back to a scandalous hour and a half – barely enough time to get through the lines at the bank to pay bills and bolt some *pizza al taglio* (pizza by the slice) – *rosticcerie* (rotisseries) or *tavole calde* (literally 'hot tables') keep the harried warm with steamy, on-the-go options like roast chicken and *supplì* (fried risotto balls with a molten mozzarella centre). Bakeries and bars are also on hand with focaccia, *panini* and *tramezzini* (triangular, stacked sandwiches made with squishy white bread) providing a satisfying bite.

Traditionally, *cena* (dinner) is lunch's lighter sibling and cries of 'Oh, I can hardly eat anything tonight' are still common after a marathon weekend lunch. 'Maybe just a bowl of pasta, a salad, some cheese and fruit...' Don't be fooled: even if you've been invited to someone's house for a 'light dinner', wine and elastic-waist pants are always advisable.

But while your Italian hosts may insist you devour one more cream-filled *cannolo* (surely you don't have them back home... and even if you did, surely they're not as good?!), your waiter will usually show more mercy. Despite the Italians' 'more is more' attitude to food consumption, restaurant diners are rarely obliged to order both a *primo* and *secondo,* and antipasti and dessert are strictly optional.

That said, a lavish dinner at one of Italy's fine-dining hot spots, such as Milan's Cracco-Peck (see the boxed text, p245) or Rome's Open Colonna (p126) is a highlight few will want to skip.

Many top-ranked restaurants open only for dinner, with a set-price *degustazione* meal that leaves the major menu decisions to your chef and frees you up to concentrate on the noble quest to conquer four to six tasting courses. *Forza e coraggio!* (Strength and courage to you!)

The Accademia della Cucina Italiana (Italian Academy of Cuisine) announced in 2008 that an average of six out of 10 dishes served at Italian restaurants outside Italy aren't prepared correctly. According to the organisation's London representative, out of 320 Italian restaurants in the UK, 200 received failing marks.

THE ITALIAN TABLE TUTTI A TAVOLA

Italian Menu 101

The *cameriere* (waiter) leads you to your table and hands you the menu. The scent of slow-cooked *ragù* (meat and tomato sauce) lingers in the air and your stomach rumbles in anticipation. Where might this culinary encounter lead you? Unfurl that *tovagliolo* (napkin), lick those lips, and read on…

Antipasti (Appetiser)

The culinary equivalent of foreplay, antipasti are a good way to sample a number of different dishes. Tantalising offerings on the antipasti menu may include the house bruschetta (grilled bread with a variety of toppings, from chopped tomato and garlic to black-truffle spread) or regional treats like *mozzarella di bufula* (buffalo mozzarella) or *salatini con burro d'acciughe* (pastry sticks with anchovy butter). Even if it's not on the menu, it's always worth requesting an antipasto *misto* (mixed), a platter of morsels including anything from *olive fritte* (fried olives) and *prosciutto e melone* (cured ham and cantaloupe) to *friarelle con peperoncino* (Neapolitan broccoli with chilli). At this stage, bread (and sometimes *grissini* – Turin-style breadsticks) are also deposited on the table as part of your €1 to €3 *pane e coperto* ('bread and cover' or table service).

Less is more: most of the recipes in Ada Boni's classic *The Talisman Italian Cookbook* have fewer than 10 ingredients, yet the robust flavours of her osso bucco, polenta and wild duck with lentils are anything but simple.

Primo (First Course)

Starch is the star in Italian first courses, from pasta and gnocchi, to risotto and polenta. You may be surprised how generous the portions are – a *mezzo piatto* (half-portion) might do the trick for kids.

Primi menus usually include ostensibly vegetarian or vegan options, such as pasta *con pesto* – the classic Ligurian basil paste with *parmigiano reggiano* (Parmesan) and pine nuts – or *alla norma* (with basil, eggplant, ricotta and tomato), *risotto ai porcini* (risotto with pungent, earthy porcini mushrooms) or the extravagant *risotto al Barolo* (risotto with high-end Barolo wine, though actually any good dry red will do). But even if a dish sounds vegetarian in theory, before you order you may want to ask about the stock used in that risotto or polenta, or the

---

THE BIG FORK MANIFESTO

The year is 1987. McDonald's has just begun expansion into Italy, and lunch outside the bun seems to be fading into fond memory. Enter Carlo Petrini and a handful of other journalists from small-town Bra, Piedmont. Determined to buck the trend, these *neoforchettoni* ('big forks', or foodies) created a manifesto. Published in the like-minded culinary magazine *Gambero Rosso*, they declared that a meal should be judged not by its speed, but by its pure pleasure.

The organisation they founded would soon become known worldwide as **Slow Food** (www.slowfood.com), and its mission to reconnect artisanal producers with enthusiastic, educated consumers has taken root with more than 100,000 members in 150 countries – not to mention Slow Food *agriturismi* (farm stay accommodation), restaurants, farms, wineries, cheesemakers and revitalised farmers markets across Italy.

Held on even-numbered years in a former Fiat factory in Turin, Italy's top Slow Food event is the biennial **Salone del Gusto & Terre Madre** (www.salonedelgusto.it, www.terramadre.info). Slow Food's global symposium, it features Slow Food producers, chefs, activists, restaurateurs, farmers, scholars, environmentalists and epicureans from around the world… not to mention the world's best finger food. Thankfully, odd years don't miss out on the epicurean enlightened either, with speciality events such as **Slow Fish** (www.slowfish.it) in Genoa, **Cheese** (www.cheese.slowfood.com) in Bra and the annual **Slow Food on Film** (www.slowfoodonfilm.it) in Bologna.

ingredients in that suspiciously rich tomato sauce – there may be beef, ham or ground anchovies involved.

Meat eaters will rejoice in such legendary dishes as pasta *all'amatriciana* (Roman pasta with a spicy tomato sauce, *pecorino* cheese and *guanciale,* or baconlike pigs' cheeks), osso bucco *con risotto alla milanese* (Milanese veal shank and marrow melting into saffron risotto), Tuscan speciality *pappardelle alle cinghiale* (ribbon pasta with wild boar sauce) and northern favourite *polenta col ragù* (polenta with meat sauce). Near the coasts, look for seafood variations like *risotto al nero* (risotto cooked with black squid ink), *spaghetti alle vongole* (spaghetti with clam sauce) or *pasta ai frutti di mare* (pasta with seafood).

Secondo (Second Course)

Light lunchers usually call it a day after the *primo,* but *buongustai* (foodies) pace themselves for meat, fish or *contorni* (side dishes, such as cooked vegetables) in the second course. These options may range from the outrageous *bistecca alla fiorentina,* a 3in-thick steak served on the bone in a puddle of juice, to more modest yet equally impressive *fritto misto di mare* (mixed fried seafood), *carciofi alla romana* (Roman artichokes stuffed with mint and garlic) or *pollo in tegame con barbe* (chicken casserole with salsify). A less inspiring option is *insalata mista* (mixed green salad), typically unadorned greens with vinegar and oil on the side – croutons, crumbled cheeses, nuts, dried fruit and other froufrou ingredients have no business in a classic Italian salad.

Frutti e dolci

'*Siamo arrivati alla frutta*' ('we've arrived at the fruit') is an idiom roughly meaning 'we've hit rock bottom' – but hey, not until you've had one last tasty morsel. Imported pineapple has been a trendy choice of late, but your best bets on the fruit menu are local and seasonal. *Formaggi* (cheeses) are another option, but only diabetics or the French would go that route where there's room for *dolci* (sweets). Think beyond dental-work-endangering *biscotti* (twice-baked biscuits) and consider *zabaglione* (egg and marsala custard), *torta di ricotta e pera* (pear and ricotta cake), cream-stuffed profiteroles or *cannoli Siciliani,* the ricotta-stuffedshell pastry immortalised thus in *The Godfather:* 'Leave the gun. Take the *cannoli.*'

> In March 2011, Italy broke a culinary world record when Alberto Della Pelle and nine colleagues created the planet's longest sausage. Measuring 597.8 metres long, the pork-stuffed wonder was sliced to fill 6000 *panini* for charity. Romania held the previous record, its monster stretching a more modest 392 metres.

Caffè (Coffee)

No amount of willpower or cajoling is going to move your feet into a museum after a three-course Italian lunch, so you must administer espresso immediately. Sometimes your barista will take pity and deliver your cappuccino with a *cioccolatino* (a square of chocolate) or grant you a tiny stain of milk in a *caffè macchiato*. On the hottest days of summer, you may be allowed a *granita di caffè* (coffee with shaved ice and whipped cream). But usually you'll be expected to take espresso as it comes, with scant sweetness and no apology, like a nasty breakup. The 'what doesn't kill you, makes you stronger' principle applies to Italian coffee breaks: if you survive the scalding liquid tossed down your throat, well then, you're ready to get on with your day.

> Don't believe the hype about espresso: one diminutive cup packs less of a caffeine wallop than a large cup of French-pressed or American-brewed coffee, and leaves drinkers less jittery.

The Vino Lowdown

A sit-down meal without *vino* (wine) in Italy is as unpalatable as pasta without sauce. Not ordering wine at a restaurant can cause consternation – are you pregnant or a recovering alcoholic, or was it something the waiter said? Italian wines are considered among the most versatile and 'food-friendly' in the world, specifically cultivated over the centuries to elevate regional cuisine.

WINE & COOKERY COURSES

You can hardly throw a stone in Italy without hitting a culinary course in progress, but there are better ways of finding a cookery school. You'll find some of the big hitters below, as well as more region-specific courses in the relevant destination chapters in this book.

Città del Gusto Rome (☑06 551 11 21; www.gamberorosso.it, in Italian; Via Fermi 161); Naples (☑081 19 80 89 00; Via Coroglio 57/104E, Bagnoli) Six floors of hot, nonstop gourmet-on-gourmet action, from live cooking demonstrations and TV-show tapings to wine courses in the 'Theatre of Wine'. All workshops and demos are run by *Gambero Rosso*, Italy's most esteemed food magazine. You'll find a second branch in Naples.

Culinary Adventures (www.peggymarkel.com) Indulge in and learn about cooking Italian dishes with local, sustainably sourced ingredients at decadent week-long courses in Sicily, Elba, Amalfi and Tuscany.

Eataly (www.eatalytorino.it, in Italian) Turin's mall-sized monument to artisanal food offers samples, wine tasting, and afternoon workshops on aphrodisiac dinners, becoming a chef and sommelier secrets. Tasting sessions start at €20, but some are offered in Italian only.

International Wine Academy of Roma (☑06 699 08 78; www.wineacademyroma.com; Vicolo del Bottino 8) Choices include individual wine-tasting events, a five-wine tasting followed by a four-course meal and a tour of Lazio wineries.

Italian Food Artisans (www.foodartisans.com/workshops) Slip behind the scenes in restaurant kitchens and private homes and discover Italy's best-kept food secrets in Cinque Terre, Piedmont, Emilia-Romagna, Campania and Sicily on one-day workshops or week-long adventures with cookbook author Pamela Sheldon Johns.

Tasting Places (www.tastingplaces.com) Recent offerings include excursions to regional Slow Food festivals, a 'White Truffle and Wine' weekend in Piedmont and gourmet getaways in the Veneto and Tuscany.

Here, wine is a consideration as essential as your choice of dinner date. Indeed, while the country's perfectly quaffable pilsner beers and occasional red ale pair well with roast meats, pizza and other quick eats, *vino* is considered appropriate for a proper meal – and since many wines cost less than a pint in Italy, this is not a question of price, but a matter of flavour.

Some Italian wines will be as familiar to you as old flames, including pizza-and-a-movie chianti or reliable summertime fling Pinot grigio. But you'll also find some captivating Italian varietals and blends for which there is no translation (eg Brunello, Vermentino, Sciacchetrá), and intriguing Italian wines that have little in common with European and Australian cousins by the same name (eg merlot, Pinot Nero aka Pinot Noir, chardonnay).

Many visitors default to carafes of house reds or whites, which in Italy usually means young, fruit-forward reds to complement tomato sauces and chilled dry whites as seafood palate-cleansers. But with a little daring and the list below, you can pursue a wider range of options by the glass or half-bottle.

Although some producers find these official Italian classifications unduly costly and creatively constraining, the DOCG (Denominazione di origine controllata e garantita) and DOC (Denominazione di origine controllata) designations are awarded to wines that meet regional quality-control standards.

Sparkling wines: Franciacorta (Lombardy), *prosecco* (Veneto), Asti (aka Asti Spumante; Piedmont), Lambrusco (Emilia-Romagna)

Light, citrusy whites with grassy or floral notes: Vermentino (Sardinia), Orvieto (Umbria), Soave (Veneto), Tocai (Friuli)

Dry whites with aromatic herbal or mineral aspect: Cinque Terre (Liguria), Gavi (Piedmont), Falanghina (Campania), Est! Est!! Est!!! (Lazio)

Versatile, food-friendly reds with pleasant acidity: Barbera d'Alba (Piedmont), Montepulciano d'Abruzzo (Abruzzo), Valpolicella (Veneto), Chianti Classico (Tuscany), Bardolino (Lombardy)

Well-rounded reds, balancing fruit with earthy notes: Brunello di Montalcino (Tuscany), Refosco dal Pedulunco Rosso (Friuli), Dolcetto (Piedmont), Morellino di Scansano (Tuscany)

Big, structured reds with velvety tannins: Amarone (Veneto), Barolo (Piedmont), Sagrantino di Montefalco secco (Umbria), Sassicaia and other 'super-Tuscan' blends (Tuscany)

Fortified and dessert wines: Sciacchetrá (Liguria), Colli Orientali del Friuli Picolit (Friuli), Vin Santo (Tuscany), Moscato d'Asti (Piedmont)

For a thirst-quenching adventure through Italy's most celebrated wine region – Tuscany's Il Chianti – turn to p524.

turn to p524.

Italy's oldest known wine is Chianti Classico, with favourable reviews dating from the 14th century and a growing region clearly defined by 1716.

Liquori (Liquers)

Failure to order a postprandial espresso may shock your server but you may yet save face by ordering a *digestivo* (digestive), such as a grappa (a potent grape-derived alcohol), *amaro* (a dark liqueur prepared from herbs) or *limoncello* (lemon liqueur). Fair warning though: Italian digestives can be an acquired taste, and they pack a punch that might leave you snoring before *il conto* (the bill) arrives.

Festive Favourites

Perhaps you've heard of ancient Roman orgies with trips to the vomitorium to make room for the next course, or Medici family feasts with sugar sculptures worth their weight in gold? In Italy, culinary indulgence is the epicentre of any celebration and major holidays are defined by their specialities. Lent is heralded by *Carnevale* (Carnival), a time for *migliaccio di polenta* (polenta, sausage, *pecorino* and *parmigiano reggiano* casserole), *sanguinaccio* ('blood pudding' made with dark chocolate and cinnamon), *chiacchiere* (fried biscuits sprinkled with icing sugar) and Sicily's *mpagnuccata* (deep-fried dough tossed in soft caramel).

The average Italian adult consumes around 28 litres of wine per annum – a sobering figure compared with the 100 litres consumed on average back in the 1950s.

If you're here around 19 March (St Joseph's Feast Day), expect to eat *bignè di San Giuseppe* (fried doughnuts filled with cream or chocolate) in Rome, *zeppole* (fritters topped with lemon-scented cream, sour cherry and dusting sugar) in Naples and Bari, and *crispelle di riso* (citrus-scented rice fritters dipped in honey) in Sicily.

Lent specialities like Sicilian *quaresimali* (hard, light almond biscuits) give way to Easter binging with the obligatory lamb, *colomba* (dove-shaped cake) and *uove di pasqua* (foil-wrapped chocolate eggs with toy surprises inside). The dominant ingredient at this time is egg, also used to make traditional regional specialities like Genoa's *torta pasqualina* (pastry tart filled with ricotta, *parmigiano*, artichokes and hard-boiled eggs), Florence's *brodetto* (egg, lemon and bread broth) and Naples' legendary *pastiera* (shortcrust pastry tart filled with ricotta, cream, candied fruits and cereals flavoured with orange water).

APERITIVI: BUDGET FEASTING

The hottest recession trend in Italy is *aperitivi*, often described as a 'before-meal drink and light snack'. Don't be fooled. Italian 'happy hour' is dinner disguised as a casual drink, accompanied by a buffet of antipasti, pasta salads, cold cuts and some hot dishes (this may include your fellow diners: *aperitivi* is prime time for hungry singles). You can methodically pillage buffets in Milan, Turin, Rome and Naples from about 5pm to 8pm for the price of a single drink – which crafty diners nurse for the duration – while Venetians enjoy *ombre* (wine by the glass) and bargain seafood *cicheti* (Venetian tapas). *Aperitivi* is wildly popular among the many young Italians who can't afford to eat dinner out, but still want a place to enjoy food with friends – leave it to Italy to find a way to put the glam into recession.

At the other end of the calendar, Christmas means stuffed pasta, seafood dishes and one of Milan's greatest inventions: *panettone* (yeasty, golden cake studded with raisins and dried fruit). Equally famous are Verona's simpler, raisin-free *pandoro* (yeasty, star-shaped cake dusted with vanilla-flavoured icing sugar) and Siena's panforte (chewy, flat cake made with candied fruits, nuts, chocolate, honey and spices). Further south, Neapolitans throw caution (and scales) to the wind with *raffioli* (sponge and marzipan biscuits), *struffoli* (tiny fried pastry balls dipped in honey and sprinkled with colourful candied sugar) and *pasta di mandorla* (marzipan), while their Sicilian cousins toast to the season with *cucciddatu* (ring-shaped cake made with dried figs, nuts, honey, vanilla, cloves, cinnamon and citrus fruits).

Of course, it's not all about religion. Some Italian holidays dispense with the spiritual premise and are all about the food. During spring, summer and early autumn, towns across Italy celebrate *sagre,* the festivals of local foods in season. You'll find a *sagra del tartufo* (truffles) in Umbria, *del pomodoro* (tomatoes) in Sicily and *del cipolle* (onions) in Puglia (wouldn't want to be downwind of that one). For a list of *sagre,* check out www.prodottitipici.com/sagre (in Italian).

For information on eating price ranges in this book, see p912.

Top Food & Wine Regions

» Emilia-Romagna

» Tuscany

» Piedmont

» Campania

» Sicily

Survival Guide

Directory A–Z

Accommodation

Accommodation in Italy can range from the sublime to the ridiculous with prices to match. Hotels and *pensioni* make up the bulk of the offerings, covering a rainbow of options from cheap sleeps near the train station to luxury hotels considered among the best on the planet. Youth hostels and camp grounds are a boon for the budget-minded, while *rifugi* (mountain huts) welcome mountain walkers after a long day on the trail. Fancier options include charming B&B-style places that continue to proliferate, apartment rentals in the heart of Italy's great cities, luxurious country villas and *agriturismi* (farm stays). Capturing the imagination still more are the options to stay in anything from castles to convents and monasteries.

Accommodation options in this book are listed according to three price categories, as follows:

CATEGORY	SYMBOL	PRICE RANGE
budget	€	under €100
midrange	€€	€100-200
top end	€€€	over €200

Where indicated in the text, half-board equals breakfast and either lunch or dinner; full board includes breakfast, lunch and dinner.

Prices can fluctuate enormously depending on the season, with Easter, summer and the Christmas/New Year period being the typical peak tourist times. Seasonality also varies according to location. Expect to pay top prices in the mountains during the ski season (December to March) or along the coast in summer (July and August). Conversely, summer in the parched cities can equal low season; in August especially, many city hotels charge as little as half price. It is always worth considering booking ahead in high season (although in the urban centres you can usually find something if you trust to luck).

Price also depends greatly on where you're looking. A bottom-end budget choice in Venice or Milan will set you back the price of a decent midrange option in, say, rural Campania. Throughout this book we have presented maximum low- and high-season rates for each accommodation option listed; for example, d €80-130 means that a double costs €80 at most in low season and €130 at most in high season.

Some hotels, in particular the lower-end places, barely alter their prices throughout the year. In low season there's no harm in bargaining for a discount, especially if you intend to stay for several days.

Hotels usually require that reservations be confirmed with a credit-card number. No-shows will be docked a night's accommodation.

B&Bs

B&Bs are a burgeoning sector of the Italian accommodation market and can be found throughout the country in both urban and rural settings. Options include everything from restored farmhouses, city *palazzi* (mansions) and seaside bungalows to rooms in family houses. Tariffs per person cover a wide range, from around €25 to €75. For more information, contact **Bed & Breakfast Italia** (www.bbitalia.it).

Camping

Most camp grounds in Italy are major complexes with swimming pools,

BOOK YOUR STAY ONLINE

For more accommodation reviews by Lonely Planet authors, check out hotels.lonelyplanet.com/Italy. You'll find independent reviews, as well as recommendations on the best places to stay. Best of all, you can book online.

restaurants and super-markets. They are graded according to a star system. Charges usually vary according to the season, rising to a peak in July and August. Note that some places offer an all-inclusive price, while others charge separately for each person, tent, vehicle and/or campsite. Individual listings in this book reflect each campground's pricing structure. Typical high-season prices range from €6 to €20 per adult, free to €12 for children under 12, and from €5 to €25 for a site.

Italian camp grounds are generally set up for people travelling with their own vehicle, although some are accessible by public transport as indicated in the text. In the major cities, grounds are often a long way from the historic centres. Most but not all have space for RVs. Tent campers are expected to bring their own equipment, although a few grounds offer tents for hire. Many also offer the alternative of bungalows or even simple, self-contained flats. In high season, some only offer deals for a week at a time.

Lists of camp grounds are available from local tourist offices or online at the following sites:

Campeggi.com (www.campeggi.com)

Camping.it (www.camping.it)

Italcamping.it (www.italcamping.it)

Canvas Holidays (www.canvasholidays.co.uk)

Eurocamp (www.eurocamp.co.uk)

Keycamp (www.keycamp.co.uk)

Select Sites (www.select-site.com)

Major bookshops also sell the annual *Campeggi e villaggi turistici in Italia* (Camping and Holiday Villages in Italy, €14.90), a list of all Italian camp grounds published by Touring Club Italiano (TCI).

FARMHOUSE HOLIDAYS

Trade museums and Maseratis for barns and bunnies at an *agriturismo* (farm stay accommodation), the most peaceful of Italian lodging choices. Quickly gaining in popularity, *agriturismi* embody Italy's agricultural roots. By definition they are required to grow at least one of their own products, but beyond this common thread they can run the gamut from a rustic country house with a handful of olive trees to a luxurious country estate with a sparkling pool to a fully functioning farm where guests can pitch in.

Agriturismo business has long boomed in Tuscany and Umbria, but is also steadily gaining ground in other regions. To find lists of *agriturismi*, ask at any tourist office or check online at one of the following sites:

» **Agritour** (www.agritour.net)

» **Agriturist** (www.agriturist.com, in Italian)

» **Agriturismo.it** (www.agriturismo.it)

» **Agriturismo.net** (www.agriturismo.net)

» **Agriturismo.com** (www.agriturismo.com)

» **Agriturismo-Italia.net** (www.agriturismo-italia.net)

» **Agriturismo Vero** (www.agriturismovero.com)

Convents & Monasteries

Some Italian convents and monasteries let out cells or rooms as a modest revenue-making exercise and happily take in tourists, while others only take in pilgrims or people who are on a spiritual retreat. Many impose a fairly early curfew, but prices tend to be quite reasonable.

Several resources can assist you in your search.

MonasteryStays.com (www.monasterystays.com) A well-organised online booking centre for monastery and convent stays.

In Italy Online (www.initaly.com/agri/convents.htm) Another site well worth a look for monastery and convent accommodations in Abruzzo, Emilia-Romagna, Lazio, Liguria, Lombardy, Puglia, Sardinia, Sicily, Tuscany, Umbria and the Veneto. You pay US$6 to access the online newsletter with addresses.

Chiesa di Santa Susana (www.santasusanna.org/comingToRome/convents.html) This American Catholic church in Rome has searched out convent and monastery accommodation options around the country and posted a list on its website. Note that some places are just residential accommodation run by religious orders and not necessarily big on monastic atmosphere. The church doesn't handle bookings; to request a spot, you'll need to contact each individual institution directly.

A useful if ageing publication is Eileen Barish's *The Guide to Lodging in Italy's Monasteries*. A more recent book on the same subject is Charles M Shelton's *Beds and Blessings in Italy: A Guide to Religious Hospitality*.

Hostels

Ostelli per la Gioventù (youth hostels) are run by the **Associazione Italiana Alberghi per la Gioventù** (AIG; www.aighostels.com),

OFFBEAT ACCOMMODATION

Looking for something out of the ordinary? Italy offers a plethora of sleeping options that you won't find anywhere else in the world.

» Down near Italy's heel, rent a **trullo**, one of the characteristic whitewashed conical houses of southern Puglia.

» On the island of Pantelleria, halfway between Sicily and Africa, sleep in a **dammuso** (traditional house with thick, whitewashed walls and a shallow cupola).

» In Bologna, spend a regal night or two as king and queen of a **12-storey, 12th-century tower**, now converted into the one-of-a-kind Prendiparte B&B.

» In Friuli Venezia Giulia, experience village life in an **albergo diffuso**, an award-winning concept in which various neighbouring apartments and houses in a historic village centre are rented to guests through a centralised hotel-style reception.

affiliated with **Hostelling International** (HI; www. hihostels.com). A valid HI card is required in all associated youth hostels in Italy. You can get this in your home country or direct at many hostels.

A full list of Italian hostels, with details of prices, locations and so on, is available online or from hostels throughout the country. Nightly rates in basic dorms vary from around €16 to €20, which usually includes a buffet breakfast. You can often get lunch or dinner for an extra €10 or so. Many hostels also offer singles/doubles (for around €30/50) and family rooms.

A few AIG hostels still have a mid-day lockout period as well as a curfew of 11pm or midnight, although these restrictions are less common than in years past.

A growing contingent of independent hostels offers alternatives to HI hostels. Many are barely distinguishable from budget hotels. One of many hostel websites is www.hostelworld.com.

Hotels & Pensioni

There is often little difference between a *pensione* and an *albergo* (hotel). However, a *pensione* will generally be

of one- to three-star quality and traditionally it has been a family-run operation, while an *albergo* can be awarded up to five stars. *Locande* (inns) long fell into much the same category as *pensioni*, but the term has become a trendy one in some parts and reveals little about the quality of a place. *Affittacamere* are rooms for rent in private houses. They are generally simple affairs.

Quality can vary enormously and the official star system gives only limited clues. One-star hotels/*pensioni* tend to be basic and usually do not offer private bathrooms. Two-star places are similar but rooms will generally have a private bathroom. At three-star joints you can usually assume reasonable standards. Four- and five-star hotels offer facilities such as room service, laundry and dry-cleaning.

Prices are highest in major tourist destinations. They also tend to be higher in northern Italy. A *camera singola* (single room) costs from €30. A *camera doppia* (twin beds) or *camera matrimoniale* (double room with a double bed) will cost from around €50.

Tourist offices usually have booklets with local accommodation listings. Many

hotels are also signing up with (steadily proliferating) online accommodation-booking services. You could start your search here:

Alberghi in Italia (www. alberghi-in-italia.it)
All Hotels in Italy (www. hotelsitalyonline.com)
Hotels web.it (www.hotel sweb.it)
In Italia (www.initalia.it)
Travel to Italy (www.travel -to-italy.com)

Mountain Huts

The network of *rifugi* in the Alps, Apennines and other mountains is usually only open from July to September. Accommodation is generally in dormitories but some of the larger refuges have doubles. The price per person (which typically includes breakfast) ranges from €20 to €30 depending on the quality of the *rifugio* (it's more for a double room). A hearty post-walk single-dish dinner will set you back another €10 to €15.

Rifugi are marked on good walking maps. Some are close to chair lifts and cable-car stations, which means they are usually expensive and crowded. Others are at high altitude and involve hours of hard walking. It is important to book in advance. Additional information can be obtained from the local tourist offices.

The **Club Alpino Italiano** (CAI; www.cai.it) owns and runs many of the mountain huts. Members of organisations such as the Australian Alpine Club and British Mountaineering Council can enjoy discounted rates for accommodation and meals by obtaining a reciprocal rights card (for a fee).

Rental Accommodation

Finding rental accommodation in the major cities can be difficult and time-consuming; rental agencies (local and foreign) can assist, for a fee. Rental rates are higher for short-term leases. A small apartment or a studio anywhere near the centre of Rome will cost around €1000 per month and it is usually necessary to pay a deposit (generally one month in advance). Expect to spend similar amounts in cities such as Florence, Milan, Naples and Venice. Apartments and villas for rent are listed in local publications such as Rome's weekly *Porta Portese* and the fortnightly *Wanted in Rome*. Another option is to share an apartment; check out university noticeboards for student flats with vacant rooms.

If you're looking for an apartment or studio to rent for a short stay (such as a week or two) the easiest option is to check out the websites of agencies dealing in this kind of thing:

Guest in Italy (www.guestin italy.com) An online agency focusing exclusively on Italy, with apartments (mostly for two to four people) ranging from about €120 to €450 a night.

Homelidays (www.homel idays.com) Over 16,000 rental accommodations of every description throughout Italy.

Holiday Lettings (www. holidaylettings.co.uk) Has nearly 4000 apartments and villas all over the country.

Interhome (www.interhome. co.uk) Here you book apartments for blocks of a week, starting at around UK£500 to £600 for two or three people in central Rome.

Tourist offices in resort areas (coastal towns in summer, ski towns in winter) also maintain lists of apartments and villas for rent.

Villas

Long the preserve of the Tuscan sun, the villa-rental scene in Italy has taken off in recent years, with agencies offering villa accommodation – often in splendid rural locations not far from enchanting medieval towns or Mediterranean beaches – up and down the country. There are dozens of operators.

For villas in the time-honoured and most popular central regions, particularly Tuscany and Umbria, check out the following:

Cuendet (www.cuendet.com) One of the old hands in this business; operates from Mestre, just outside of Venice.

Ilios Travel (www.iliostravel. com) UK-based company with villas, apartments and castles in Venice, Tuscany, Umbria, Lazio, Le Marche, Abruzzo and Campania.

Invitation to Tuscany (www. invitationtotuscany.com) Wide range of properties, with a strong focus on Tuscany.

Summer's Leases (www. summerleases.com) Properties in Tuscany and Umbria.

Some agencies concentrate their energies on the south (especially Campania and Puglia) and the islands of Sicily and Sardinia, including the following:

Costa Smeralda Holidays (www.costasmeralda-holidays. com) Concentrates on Sardinia's northeast.

Long Travel (www.long-travel. co.uk) Specialises in Puglia, Sicily, Sardinia and other regions from Rome south.

Think Sicily (www.think sicily.com) Strictly Sicilian properties.

Operators offering villas and other short-term let properties across the country include the following:

Cottages & Castles (www. cottagesandcastles.com.au) An Australian-based specialist in self-catering accommodation throughout Italy.

Cottages to Castles (www. cottagestocastles.com) UK-based operator specialising in villas.

BUSINESS HOURS

BUSINESS TYPE	STANDARD HOURS	NOTES
Banks	8.30am-1.30pm & 3.30-4.30pm Mon-Fri	Exchange offices usually keep longer hours.
Central post offices	8am-7pm Mon-Fri, 8.30am-noon Sat	
Smaller branch post offices	8am-2pm Mon-Fri, 8.30am-noon Sat	
Restaurants	noon-2.30pm & 7.30-11pm or midnight	Sometimes even later in summer and in the south; kitchen often shuts an hour earlier than final closing time; most places close at least one day a week.
Cafes	7.30am-8pm	
Bars, Pubs & Clubs	10pm-4am	May open earlier if they have eateries on the premises; things don't get seriously shaking until after midnight
Shops	9am-1pm & 3.30-7.30pm (or 4-8pm) Mon-Sat	In larger cities, department stores and supermarkets may stay open at lunchtime or on Sundays

KEEPING THE KIDS HAPPY IN ITALY

There are plenty of Italian sights and activities that kids will enjoy as much as grown-ups. Here are a few ideas to get you started.

» Running around the ruins at sprawling ancient Roman sites or prowling about mysterious underground Etruscan necropoli.

» Splashing in fountains at grand villas or touring Italy's many offshore islands on a small boat, diving off the side and sunbaking on the prow with friends.

» Dropping in on spontaneous football kick-abouts with local kids in town squares.

» Staying at *agriturismi* (farm stay accomodation), particularly those with animals.

» Climbing Sicily's dramatic and surprisingly accessible volcanoes or cruising along the bike paths at the foot of the Dolomites.

» Eating gelato – it's the perfect mood-enhancer for the whole family, not to mention a great way to bribe your kids into better behaviour!

Parker Villas (www.parker villas.co.uk) Despite the UK web address, this is a US-based agency with an Italian office, offering exclusive listings of villas all over Italy.

Veronica Tomasso Cotgrove (www.vtcitaly.com) This London-based company offers a small, hand-picked list of country properties in Tuscany and Umbria, along with apartments in Venice, Rome, Florence, Siena and Orvieto.

Business Hours

Opening times for individual businesses in this guide are only spelled out when they deviate from the standard hours outlined in the boxed text, p909.

Children

Throughout this book we use the family-friendly icon to highlight places that are especially welcoming to families with children. The specific facilities will vary from listing to listing, but may include family rooms or interconnecting doubles, home-like venues with

animals to keep kids entertained or a children's activity room or garden play area.

Practicalities

Italians love children but there are few special amenities for them. Always make a point of asking staff members at tourist offices if they know of any special family activities or have suggestions on hotels that cater for kids.

Book accommodation in advance whenever possible to avoid inconvenience. In hotels, some double rooms can't accommodate an extra bed for kids, so it's best to check ahead. If your child is small enough to share your bed, some hoteliers will let you do this for free. The website www. booking.com is good because it tells you the 'kid policy' for

every hotel it lists and what extra charges you will incur.

On public transport, discounts are available for children (usually aged under 12 but sometimes based on the child's height), and admission to many sites is free for children under 18.

When travelling by train, reserve seats where possible to avoid finding yourselves standing. You can hire car seats for infants and children from most car-rental firms, but you should always book them in advance.

You can buy baby formula in powder or liquid form, as well as sterilising solutions such as Milton, at pharmacies. Disposable nappies (diapers) are available at supermarkets and pharmacies. Fresh cow's milk is sold in cartons in supermarkets and in bars with a 'Latteria' sign. UHT milk is popular and in many out-of-the-way areas the only kind available.

Kids are welcome in most restaurants, but do not count on the availability of high chairs. Children's menus are uncommon but you can generally ask for a *mezzo piatto* (half-portion) off the menu.

For more information and ideas, see Lonely Planet's *Travel with Children,* the superb Italy-focused website **www.italiakids.com**, or the more general **www.travel withyourkids.com** and **www. familytravelnetwork.com**.

Customs Regulations

Duty-free sales within the EU no longer exist (but goods

DUTY FREE ALLOWANCES

Spirits	1L (or 2L wine)
Perfume	50g
Eau de toilette	250mL
Cigarettes	200
Other goods	up to a total value of €175

CARD	WEBSITE	COST	ELIGIBILITY
European Youth Card (Carta Giovani)	europeanyouthcard.org cartagiovani.it	€11	under 30yr
International Student Identity Card (ISIC)	www.isic.org	US$22, UK£9, €10	full-time student
International Teacher Identity Card (ITIC)		US$22, UK£9, €10	full-time teacher
International Youth Travel Card (IYTC)		US$22, UK£9, €10	under 26yr

are sold tax-free in European airports). Visitors coming into Italy from non-EU countries can import some items duty free, see the boxed text, p910.

Anything over these limits must be declared on arrival and the appropriate duty paid. On leaving the EU, non-EU citizens can reclaim any value-added tax on expensive purchases (see p915).

Discount Cards

Free admission to many galleries and cultural sites is available to youth under 18 and seniors over 65 years old; in addition, visitors aged between 18 and 25 often qualify for a 50% discount. In some cases, these discounts only apply to EU citizens.

Throughout this book you'll find details of special discount cards issued by cities or regions, such as **Roma Pass** (www.romapass.it), a three-day, €25 card that offers free use of public transport and free or reduced admission to Rome's museums.

In many places around Italy, you can also save money by purchasing a *biglietto cumulativo*, a ticket that allows admission to a number of associated sights for less than the combined cost of separate admission fees.

Youth, Student & Teacher Cards

The European Youth Card offers thousands of discounts on Italian hotels, museums, restaurants, shops and clubs, while a student, teacher or youth travel card can save you money on flights to Italy. All cards listed above are available from the **Centro Turistico Studentesco e Giovanile** (CTS; www.cts.it), a youth travel agency with branches throughout Italy. The latter three cards are available worldwide from student unions, hostelling organisations and youth travel agencies such as **STA Travel** (www.statravel.com).

Electricity

Electricity in Italy conforms to the European standard of 220V to 230V, with a frequency of 50Hz. Wall outlets typically accommodate plugs with two or three round pins (the latter grounded, the former not).

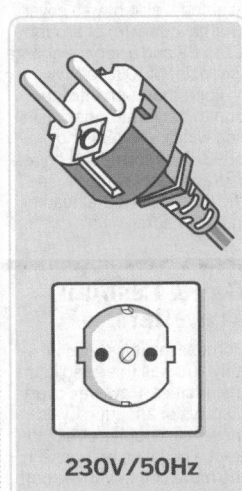

230V/50Hz

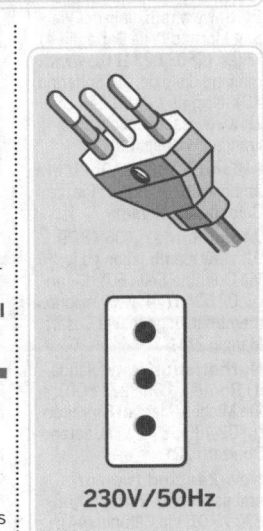

230V/50Hz

Embassies & Consulates

For foreign embassies and consulates in Italy not listed here, look under 'Ambasciate' or 'Consolati' in the telephone directory. In addition to the following, some countries run honorary consulates in other cities.

Australia Rome (☑06 85 27 21; www.italy.embassy.gov.au; Via Antonio Bosio 5); Milan (☑02 7767 4217; www.austrade.it; Via Borgogna 2)

Austria Rome (☑06 844 01 41; www.austria.it; Via Pergolesi 3); Milan (☑02 78 37 43; mailand-gk@bmeia.gv.at; Piazza del Liberty 8/4)

Canada (☎06 85 44 41; www.canadainternational.gc.ca/italy-italie; Via Zara 30, Rome)

France (www.ambafrance-it.org) Rome (☎06 68 60 11; Piazza Farnese 67); Milan (☎02 655 91 41; Via della Moscova 12); Naples (☎081 598 07 11; Via Francesco Crispi 86); Turin (☎011 573 23 11; Via Roma 366)

Germany Rome (☎06 49 21 31; www.rom.diplo.de; Via San Martino della Battaglia 4); Milan (☎02 623 11 01; www.mailand.diplo.de; Via Solferino 40); Naples (☎081 248 85 11; www.neapel.diplo.de; Via Francesco Crispi 69)

Ireland (☎06 697 91 21; www.ambasciata-irlanda.it; Piazza Campitelli 3, Rome)

Japan Rome (☎06 48 79 91; www.it.emb-japan.go.jp; Via Quintino Sella 60); Milan (☎02 624 11 41; www.milano.it.emb-japan.go.jp; Via Cesare Mangili 2/4)

Netherlands (www.olanda.it) Rome (☎06 3228 6001; Via Michele Mercati 8); Milan (☎02 485 58 41; Via Gaetano Donizetti 20)

New Zealand (www.nzembassy.com) Rome (☎06 853 75 01; Via Clitunno 44); Milan (☎02 7217 0001; Via Terraggio 17)

Slovenia Rome (☎06 8091 4310; vri@gov.si; Via Leonardo Pisano 10); Trieste(☎040 30 78 55; kts@gov.si; Via S Giorgio 1)

Switzerland Rome (☎06 80 95 71; www.eda.admin.ch/roma; Via Barnarba Oriani 61); Milan (☎02 777 91 61; www.eda.admin.ch/milano; Via Palestro 2)

UK (ukinitaly.fco.gov.uk) Rome (☎06 4220 0001; Via XX Settembre 80a); Florence (☎055 28 41 33; Lungarno Corsini 2); Milan (☎02 72 30 01; Via San Paolo 7); Naples (☎081 423 89 11; Via dei Mille 40)

USA Rome (☎06 4 67 41; italy.usembassy.gov; Via Vittorio Veneto 121); Florence (☎055 26 69 51; florence.usconsulate.gov; Lungarno Vespucci 38); Milan (☎02 29 03 51; milan.usconsulate.gov; Via Principe Amedeo 2/10); Naples (☎081 583 81 11; naples.usconsulate.gov; Piazza della Repubblica)

Food & Drink

Restaurant listings in this book are assigned a budget category (€, €€ or €€€) based on the cost of a full meal. A meal as defined here includes a *primo* (first course), *secondo* (second course), *dolce* (dessert) and house wine for one person. Budget categories are as follows:

CATEGORY	SYMBOL	PRICE RANGE
budget	€	under €25
midrange	€€	€25-45
top end	€€€	over €45

These figures represent a halfway point between the expensive cities such as Milan and Venice and the considerably cheaper towns across the south. Indeed, a restaurant rated as midrange in rural Sicily might be considered dirt cheap in Milan. Note that most eating establishments also have a cover charge (*coperto*) of around €1 to €2 and a service charge (*servizio*) of 10% to 15%.

For a thorough introduction to Italy's famous cuisine and wines, see p34 and p898. For information on restaurant opening hours, see the Business Hours heading in this chapter.

Gay & Lesbian Travellers

Homosexuality is legal in Italy and well tolerated in the major cities. However, overt displays of affection by homosexual couples could attract a negative response in the more conservative south and in smaller towns.

There are gay clubs in Rome, Milan and Bologna, and a handful in places such as Florence. Some coastal towns and resorts (such as the Tuscan town of Viareggio or Taormina in Sicily) have much more action in summer.

In June 2011 Rome hosted the **Euro Pride Festival** (www.europrideroma.com), Europe's largest LGBT event, drawing over a million visitors for 12 days of festivities culminating in a concert headlined by Lady Gaga.

See the following resources for more information:

Arcigay & Arcilesbica (www.arcigay.it) Bologna-based national organisation for gays and lesbians.

AZ Gay (www.azgay.it) Rome-based organisation that publishes a free *Gay Rome* guide, available at tourist booths.

Circolo Mario Mieli (www.mariomieli.org) Rome-based cultural centre that publishes *Aut,* a free alternative monthly covering news, culture and politics.

Gay.it (www.gay.it, in Italian) Website listing gay bars and hotels across the country.

GayFriendlyItaly.com (www.gayfriendlyitaly.com) English-language site produced by Gay.it, featuring information on everything from hotels to homophobia issues and the law.

Pride (www.prideonline.it) National monthly magazine of art, music, politics and gay culture.

Health
Recommended Vaccinations

No jabs are required to travel to Italy. The World Health Organization (WHO), however, recommends that all travellers should be covered for diphtheria, tetanus, the measles, mumps, rubella and polio, as well as hepatitis B.

Health Insurance

If you're an EU citizen (or from Switzerland, Norway or Iceland), a European Health Insurance Card (EHIC) covers you for most medical care in public hospitals free of charge, but not for emergency repatriation home or non-emergencies. The card is available from health centres and (in the UK) from post offices. Citizens from other countries should find out if there is a reciprocal arrangement for free medical care between their country and Italy (Australia, for instance, has such an agreement; carry your Medicare card). If you do need health insurance, make sure you get a policy that covers you for the worst possible scenario, such as an accident requiring an emergency flight home. Find out in advance if your insurance plan will make payments directly to providers or reimburse you later for overseas health expenditures.

Availability of Health Care

Excellent health care is readily available throughout Italy, but standards can vary significantly. Public hospitals tend to be less impressive the further south you travel. Pharmacists can give you valuable advice and sell over-the-counter medication for minor illnesses. They can also advise you when more-specialised help is required and point you in the right direction. In major cities you are likely to find English-speaking doctors or a translator service available.

Pharmacies generally keep the same hours as other shops, closing at night and on Sundays. However, a handful remain open on a rotation basis (*farmacie di turno*) for emergency purposes. These are usually listed in newspapers, or online at **www.miniportale.it** (click on Farmacie di Turno and then the region you want). Closed pharmacies display a list of the nearest ones open.

If you need an ambulance anywhere in Italy, call ☎118. For emergency treatment, head straight to the *pronto soccorso* (casualty) section of a public hospital, where you can also get emergency dental treatment.

Insurance

A travel-insurance policy to cover theft, loss and medical problems is a good idea. It may also cover you for cancellation or delays to your travel arrangements. Paying for your ticket with a credit card can often provide limited travel accident insurance and you may be able to reclaim the payment if the operator doesn't deliver. Ask your credit-card company what it will cover.

Worldwide travel insurance is available at www.lonelyplanet.com/bookings/index.do. You can buy, extend and claim online anytime – even if you're already on the road.

Internet Access

Throughout this guide we use the @ icon to indicate venues that offer an internet terminal (physical computer) for guests' use and the ☎ icon to designate places with a wi-fi network (free or paying).

Internet access in Italy has improved markedly in the past couple of years, with Rome, Bologna, Venice and other municipalities instituting city-wide hot spots, and an increasing number of hotels, B&Bs, hostels and even *agriturismi* now offering free wi-fi. On the downside, internet cafes remain thinner on the ground than elsewhere in Europe, signal strength is variable, and access is not yet as widespread in rural and southern Italy as in urban and northern areas. You'll still have to pay for access at many top-end hotels (upwards of €10 per day) and at internet cafes (€2 to €6 per hour). Certain provisions of Italy's anti-terrorism law, which required all internet users to present a photo ID and allowed the government to monitor internet usage, were rescinded in January 2011, but internet cafes will still sometimes request identification before allowing you to use their facilities.

Language Courses

Italian language courses are run by private schools and universities throughout Italy. Rome and Florence are teeming with Italian-language schools, while most other cities and major towns have at least one. For a web link listing language schools around the country, see **Saena Iulia** (www.saenaiulia.it).

Università per Stranieri di Perugia (www.unistrapg.it) The well-established and reasonably priced programs here make this Italy's most famous language school for foreigners. Language classes are supplemented with extracurricular or full-time courses in painting, art history, sculpture and architecture.

Università per Stranieri di Siena (www.unistrasi.it) A similarly well-regarded program in one of Italy's most beautiful medieval cities.

Italian foreign ministry (www.esteri.it) Publishes a list on its website of the 90 worldwide branches of the **Istituto Italiano di Cultura** (IIC), a government-sponsored organisation promoting Italian culture and language. An excellent resource for studying Italian before you leave or finding out more about language learning opportunities in Italy. Locations include Australia (Melbourne and Sydney), the UK (London and Edinburgh), Ireland (Dublin), Canada (Vancouver, Toronto and Montreal), and the USA (Los Angeles, San Francisco, Chicago, New York and Washington DC). Click on 'Diplomatic Network' and then on 'Network of Italian Cultural Institutes'.

Legal Matters

The average tourist will only have a brush with the law if robbed by a bag-snatcher or pickpocket.

Police

Contact details for police stations, or *questure,* are given throughout this book. If you run into trouble in Italy, you're likely to end up dealing with the *polizia statale* (state police) or the *carabinieri* (military police). The former wear powder blue trousers with a fuchsia stripe and a navy blue jacket, the latter wear black uniforms with a red stripe and drive dark-blue cars with a red stripe. The table above outlines Italian police organisations and their jurisdictions.

ITALIAN POLICE ORGANISATIONS

Polizia statale (state police)	Thefts, visa extensions and permits
Carabinieri (military police)	General crime, public order and drug enforcement (often overlapping with the *polizia statale*)
Vigili urbani (local traffic police)	Parking tickets, towed cars
Guardia di finanza	Tax evasion, drug smuggling
Guardia forestale (aka *corpo forestale*)	Environmental protection

For national emergency numbers, see p17.

Sex, Drugs & Alcohol

Italy's age of consent for sexual activity is generally 14, although in certain circumstances it can be as low as 13 or as high as 16. Travellers should note that they can be prosecuted under the law of their home country regarding age of consent, even when abroad.

Under Italy's tough drug laws, possession of any controlled substances, including cannabis or marijuana, can get you into hot water. Those caught in possession of 5g of cannabis can be considered traffickers and prosecuted as such. The same applies to tiny amounts of other drugs. Those caught with amounts below this threshold can be subject to minor penalties.

The legal limit for blood-alcohol level is 0.05% and random breath tests occur.

Your Rights

Italy still has antiterrorism laws on its books that could make life difficult if you are detained. You should be given verbal and written notice of the charges laid against you within 24 hours by arresting officers. You have no right to a phone call upon arrest. The prosecutor must apply to a magistrate for you to be held in preventive custody awaiting trial (depending on the

seriousness of the offence) within 48 hours of arrest. You have the right not to respond to questions without the presence of a lawyer. If the magistrate orders preventive custody, you have the right to then contest this within the following 10 days.

Maps

The city maps in this book, combined with the good, free local maps available at most Italian tourist offices, will be sufficient for many travellers. For more-specialised maps, browse the good selection at national bookshop chain Feltrinelli, or consult the websites listed here.

Touring Club Italiano (TCI; www.touringclub.com, in Italian) Italy's largest map publisher operates shops around Italy and publishes a decent 1:800,000 map of Italy, plus a series of 15 regional maps at 1:200,000 (€7.90 each) and an exhaustive series of walking guides with maps, co-published with the Club Alpino Italiano (CAI).

Tabacco (www.tabacco editrice.com) Publishes an excellent 1:25,000 scale series of walking maps, covering an area from Bormio in the west to the Slovenia border in the east.

Kompass (www.kompass-italia.it, in German & Italian) Publishes 1:25,000 and 1:50,000 scale hiking maps of various parts of Italy, plus a nice series of 1:70,000 cycling maps.

Edizioni Multigraphic Florence (www.edizionimulti graphic.it, in Italian) Produces a series of walking maps concentrating mainly on the Apennines.

Stanfords (www.stanfords. co.uk) Excellent UK-based shop that stocks many maps listed here.

Omni Resources (www.omni map.com) US-based online retailer with an impressive selection of Italian maps.

Money

The euro is Italy's currency. The seven euro notes come in denominations of €500, €200, €100, €50, €20, €10 and €5. The eight euro coins are in denominations of €2 and €1, and 50, 20, 10, five, two and one cents.

For the latest exchange rates, check out **www. xe.com**.

Credit & Debit Cards

ATMs are widely available throughout Italy and are the best way to obtain local currency. International credit and debit cards can be used in any ATM displaying the appropriate sign. Visa and MasterCard are among the most widely recognised, but others like Cirrus and Maestro are also well covered. Only some banks give cash advances over the counter, so you're better off using ATMs. Cards are also good for payment in most hotels, restaurants, shops, supermarkets and tollbooths.

Check any charges with your bank. Most banks now build a fee of around 2.75% into every foreign transaction. In addition, ATM withdrawals can attract a further fee, usually around 1.5%.

If your card is lost, stolen or swallowed by an ATM, you can telephone toll-free to have an immediate stop put on its use:

Amex (☑06 7290 0347 or your national call number)
Diners Club (☑800 864064)
MasterCard (☑800 870866)
Visa (☑800 819014)

Moneychangers

You can change money in banks, at the post office or in a *cambio* (exchange office). Post offices and banks tend to offer the best rates; exchange offices keep longer hours, but watch for high commissions and inferior rates.

Taxes & Refunds

A value-added tax of around 20%, known as IVA (Imposta di Valore Aggiunto), is slapped onto just about everything in Italy. If you are a non-EU resident and spend more than €155 (€154.94 to be more precise!) on a purchase, you can claim a refund when you leave. The refund only applies to purchases from affiliated retail outlets that display a 'tax free for tourists' (or similar) sign. You have to complete a form at the point of sale, then have it stamped by Italian customs as you leave. At major airports you can then get an immediate cash refund; otherwise it will be refunded to your credit card. For information, visit **Tax Refund for Tourists** (www.taxrefund.it) or pick up a pamphlet from participating stores.

Tipping

You are not expected to tip on top of restaurant service charges but you can leave a little extra if you feel service warrants it. If there is no service charge, the customer should consider leaving a 10% tip, but this is not obligatory. In bars, Italians often leave small change as a tip (as little as €0.10). Tipping taxi drivers is not common practice, but you are expected to tip the porter at top-end hotels.

Post

Le Poste (www.poste.it, in Italian), Italy's postal system, is reasonably reliable. For post office opening hours, see the Business Hours heading in this chapter.

Francobolli (stamps) are available at post offices and authorised tobacconists (look for the big white-on-black 'T' sign). Since letters often need to be weighed, what you get at the tobacconist for international airmail will occasionally be an approximation of the proper rate. Tobacconists keep regular shop hours.

Postal Rates & Services

The cost of sending a letter by *via aerea* (airmail) depends on its weight, size and where it is being sent. Most people use *posta prioritaria* (priority mail), Italy's most efficient mail service, guaranteed to deliver letters sent to Europe within three days and to the rest of the world within four to eight days. Letters up to 20g cost €0.75 within Europe, €1.60 to Africa, Asia and North and South America and €2 to Australia and New Zealand. Letters weighing 21g to 50g cost €2.40 within Europe, €3.30 to Africa, Asia and the Americas, and €4 to Australia and New Zealand.

Public Holidays

Most Italians take their annual holiday in August, with the busiest period occurring around 15 August, known locally as Ferragosto. This means that many businesses and shops close for at least a part of that month. Settimana Santa (Easter Holy Week) is another busy holiday period for Italians.

Individual towns have public holidays to celebrate the feasts of their patron saints.

National public holidays include the following:

New Year's Day (Capodanno or Anno Nuovo) 1 January

Epiphany (Epifania or Befana) 6 January

Easter Monday (Pasquetta or Lunedì dell'Angelo) March/April

Liberation Day (Giorno della Liberazione) On 25 April – marks the Allied Victory in Italy, and the end of the German presence and Mussolini, in 1945.

Labour Day (Festa del Lavoro) 1 May

Republic Day (Festa della Repubblica) 2 June

Feast of the Assumption (Assunzione or Ferragosto) 15 August

All Saints' Day (Ognissanti) 1 November

Feast of the Immaculate Conception (Immaculata Concezione) 8 December

Christmas Day (Natale) 25 December

Boxing Day (Festa di Santo Stefano) 26 December

Telephone
Domestic Calls

Italian telephone area codes all begin with 0 and consist of up to four digits. The area code is followed by a number of anything from four to eight digits. The area code is an integral part of the telephone number and must always be dialled, even when calling from next door. Mobile-phone numbers begin with a three-digit prefix such as 330. Toll-free (freephone) numbers are known as *numeri verdi* and usually start with 800. Nongeographical numbers start with 840, 841, 848, 892, 899, 163, 166 or 199. Some six-digit national rate numbers are also in use (such as those for Alitalia, rail and postal information).

As elsewhere in Europe, Italians choose from a host of providers of phone plans and

rates, making it difficult to make generalisations about costs.

International Calls

The cheapest options for calling internationally are free or low-cost computer programs such as Skype, cut-rate call centres or international calling cards, which are sold at newsstands and tobacconists. Cut-price call centres can be found in all of the main cities, and rates can be considerably lower than from Telecom payphones for international calls. You simply place your call from a private booth inside the centre and pay for it when you've finished. Direct international calls can also easily be made from public telephones with a phonecard. Dial ☑00 to get out of Italy, then the relevant country and area codes, followed by the telephone number.

To call Italy from abroad, call the international access number (☑011 in the United States, ☑00 from most other countries), Italy's country code (☑39) and then the area code of the location you want, including the leading 0.

Directory Enquiries

National and international phone numbers can be requested at ☑1254 (or online at 1254.virgilio.it).

Mobile Phones

Italy uses GSM 900/1800, which is compatible with the rest of Europe and Australia but not with North American GSM 1900 or the totally different Japanese system. Most modern smart phones are multiband, meaning that they are compatible with a variety of international networks. However, before bringing your own phone to Italy, check with your service provider to make sure it is compatible, and beware of calls being routed internationally (very expensive for a 'local' call). In many cases you'll be better off buying

a cheap Italian phone or unlocking your phone for use with an Italian SIM card.

Italy has one of the highest levels of mobile-phone penetration in Europe, and you can get a temporary or prepaid account from several companies if you already own a GSM, multiband cellular phone. You will usually need your passport to open an account. Always check with your mobile-service provider in your home country to ascertain whether your handset allows use of another SIM card. If yours does, it can cost as little as €10 to activate a local prepaid SIM card (sometimes with €10 worth of calls on the card). Pay-as-you-go SIM cards are readily available at telephone and electronics stores throughout Italy. Once you're set up with an Italian SIM card, you can easily purchase recharge cards (allowing you to top up your account with extra minutes) at many tobacconists and newsstands, as well as some bars, supermarkets and banks. Alternatively, you can buy or lease an inexpensive Italian phone for the duration of your trip.

Of the main mobile phone companies, TIM (Telecom Italia Mobile), Wind and Vodafone have the densest networks of outlets across the country.

Payphones & Phonecards

Partly privatised Telecom Italia is the largest telecommunications organisation in Italy. Where Telecom offices are staffed, it is possible to make international calls and pay at the desk afterwards. Alternatively, you'll find Telecom payphones throughout the country, on the streets, in train stations and in Telecom offices. Most payphones accept only *carte/schede telefoniche* (phonecards), although some also accept credit cards. Telecom offers a wide range of prepaid cards for both domestic and international use; for a full list, see **www.tele comitalia.it/telefono/ carte-telefoniche**. You can buy phonecards (most commonly €3, €5 or €10) at post offices, tobacconists and newsstands. You must break off the top left-hand corner of the card before you can use it. All phonecards have an expiry date, printed on the face of the card.

Time

Italy is one hour ahead of GMT. Daylight-saving time, when clocks are moved forward one hour, starts on the last Sunday in March. Clocks are put back an hour on the last Sunday in October. Italy operates on a 24-hour clock.

Tourist Information

Four tiers of tourist office exist: local, provincial, regional and national.

Local & Provincial Tourist Offices

Despite their different (and sometimes confusingly elaborate) names, provincial and local offices offer similar services and are collectively referenced with the generic term 'tourist office' throughout this book. All deal directly with the public and most will respond to written and telephone requests for information. Staff can usually provide a city map, lists of hotels and information on the major sights. In larger towns and major tourist areas, English is generally spoken, along with other languages depending on the region (for example, German in Alto Adige, French in Valle d'Aosta).

Main offices are generally open Monday to Friday; some also open on weekends, especially in urban areas or during peak summer season. Affiliated information booths (at train stations and airports, for example) may keep slightly different hours, as noted in the text.

The main local and provincial tourist office categories are summarised here.

Regional Tourist Authorities

Regional offices are generally more concerned with planning, budgeting, marketing and promotion than with offering a public information service. However, they still maintain some useful websites, listed here. In some cases you'll need to look for the Tourism or Turismo link within the regional site.

Abruzzo (www.abruzzo turismo.it)
Basilicata (www.aptbasili cata.it)
Calabria (www.turiscalabria. it, in Italian)
Campania (www.in-campania.com)

Emilia-Romagna (www. emiliaromagnaturismo.it)
Friuli Venezia Giulia (www.turismo.fvg.it)
Lazio (www.ilmiolazio.it, in Italian)
Le Marche (www.le-marche.com)
Liguria (www.turismoinliguria.it)
Lombardy (www.turismo. regione.lombardia.it)
Molise (www.regione.molise. it/turismo, in Italian)
Piedmont (www.regione. piemonte.it/turismo, in Italian)
Puglia (www.pugliaturismo.com)
Sardinia (www.sardegnaturismo.it)
Sicily (www.regione.sicilia.it/ turismo)
Trentino-Alto Adige (www. visittrentino.it, www.suedtirol. info)
Tuscany (www.turismo. intoscana.it)
Umbria (www.regioneumbria.eu)
Valle d'Aosta (www.regione. vda.it/turismo)
Veneto (www.veneto.to)

Tourist Offices Abroad

The **Italian National Tourist Office** (ENIT; www.enit. it) maintains offices in over two dozen cities on five continents. Contact information for all offices can be found on its website.

TOURIST OFFICES

OFFICE NAME	DESCRIPTION	MAIN FOCUS
Azienda di Promozione Turistica (APT)	Main provincial tourist office	Information on the town and its surrounding province
Azienda Autonoma di Soggiorno e Turismo (AAST)	Local tourist office in larger towns and cities of the south	Town-specific information only (bus routes, museum opening times, etc)
Informazione e Assistenza ai Turisti (IAT)	Local tourist office, mostly in the northern half of Italy	Similar to AAST
Pro Loco	Local tourist office in smaller towns and villages	Similar to AAST

Travellers with Disabilities

Italy is not an easy country for travellers with disabilities and getting around can be a problem for wheelchair users. Even a short journey in a city or town can become a major expedition if cobblestone streets have to be negotiated. Although many buildings have lifts, they are not always wide enough for wheelchairs. Not an awful lot has been done to make life for the deaf or blind any easier either.

The Italian National Tourist Office in your country may be able to provide advice on Italian associations for travellers with disabilities and information on what help is available.

Italy's national rail company, **Trenitalia** (www.trenitalia.com) offers a national helpline for passengers with disabilities at ☑199 303060 (7am to 9pm daily).

A handful of cities also publish general guides on accessibility, among them Bologna, Milan, Padua, Reggio Emilia, Turin, Venice and Verona. In Milan, **Milano per Tutti** (www.milanopertutti.it) is a helpful resource.

Some organisations that may help include the following:

Accessible Italy (www.accessibleitaly.com) A San Marino–based company that specialises in holiday services for travellers with disabilities, ranging from tours to the hiring of adapted transport to romantic Italian weddings. This is the best first port of call.

Consorzio Cooperative Integrate (www.coinsociale.it) This Rome-based organisation provides information on the capital (including transport and access) and is happy to share its contacts throughout Italy. Its 'Turismo per Tutti' program seeks to improve infrastructure and access for tourists with disabilities.

Tourism for All (www.tourismforall.org.uk) This UK-based group has information on hotels with access for guests with disabilities, where to hire equipment and tour operators dealing with travellers with disabilities.

Visas

Italy is one of 25 member countries of the Schengen Convention, under which 22 EU countries (all but Bulgaria, Cyprus, Ireland, Romania and the UK) plus Iceland, Norway and Switzerland have abolished permanent checks at common borders.

Legal residents of one Schengen country do not require a visa for another. Residents of 28 non-EU countries, including Australia, Brazil, Canada, Israel, Japan, New Zealand and the USA, do not require visas for tourist visits of up to 90 days (this list varies for those wanting to travel to the UK and Ireland).

All non-EU and non-Schengen nationals entering Italy for more than 90 days or for any reason other than tourism (such as study or work) may need a specific visa. For details, visit **www.esteri.it/visti/home_eng.asp** or contact an Italian consulate. You should also have your passport stamped on entry as, without a stamp, you could encounter problems when trying to obtain a residence permit *(permesso di soggiorno)*. If you enter the EU via another member state, get your passport stamped there.

EU citizens do not require any permits to live or work in Italy but, after three months' residence, are supposed to register themselves at the municipal registry office where they live and offer proof of work or sufficient funds to support themselves. Non-EU foreign citizens with five years' continuous legal residence may apply for permanent residence.

Permesso di Soggiorno

Non-EU citizens planning to stay at the same address for more than one week are supposed to report to the police station to receive a *permesso di soggiorno* (a permit to remain in the country). Tourists staying in hotels are not required to do this.

A *permesso di soggiorno* only really becomes a necessity if you plan to study, work (legally) or live in Italy. Obtaining one is never a pleasant experience; it involves long queues and the frustration of arriving at the counter only to find you don't have the necessary documents.

The exact requirements, like specific documents and *marche da bollo* (official stamps), can change. In general, you will need a valid passport (if possible containing a stamp with your date of entry into Italy), a special visa issued in your own country if you are planning to study (for non-EU citizens), four passport photos and proof of your ability to support yourself financially. You can apply at the *ufficio stranieri* (foreigners bureau) of the police station closest to where you're staying.

EU citizens do not require a *permesso di soggiorno*.

Study Visas

Non-EU citizens who want to study at a university or language school in Italy must have a study visa. These can be obtained from your nearest Italian embassy or consulate. You will normally require confirmation of your enrolment, proof of payment of fees and adequate funds to support yourself. The visa covers only the period of the enrolment. This type of visa is renewable within Italy but, again, only with confirmation of ongoing enrolment and proof that you are able to support yourself (bank statements are preferred).

Volunteering

Concordia International Volunteer Projects (www.concordiavolunteers.org.uk) Short-term community-based projects covering the environment, archaeology and the arts. You might find yourself working as a volunteer on a restoration project or in a nature reserve.

European Youth Portal (europa.eu/youth) Has various links suggesting volunteering options across Europe. Navigate to the Volunteering/exchanges page and then narrow down the search to Italy, where you will find more specific links on volunteering.

AFSAI (www.afsai.org) Financed by the EU, this voluntary program runs projects of six to 12 months for those aged between 16 and 25 years. Knowledge of Italian is required.

World Wide Opportunities on Organic Farms (www.wwoof.it) For a membership fee of €25 this organisation provides a list of farms looking for volunteer workers.

Women Travellers

Italy is not a dangerous country for women to travel in. Clearly, as with anywhere in the world, women travelling alone need to take certain precautions and, in some parts of the country, be prepared for more than their fair share of unwanted attention. Eye-to-eye contact is the norm in Italy's daily flirtatious interplay. Eye contact can become outright staring the further south you travel.

PRACTICALITIES

» Use the metric system for weights and measures.

» Since early 2005, smoking in all closed public spaces (from bars to elevators, offices to trains) has been banned.

» If your Italian is up to it, try the following newspapers: *Corriere della Sera,* the country's leading daily; *Il Messaggero,* a popular Rome-based broadsheet; or *La Repubblica,* a centre-left daily with a flow of Mafia conspiracies and Vatican scoops. For the Church's view, try the *Osservatore Romano.*

» Tune into Vatican Radio (www.radiovaticana.org; 93.3 FM and 105 FM in the Rome area) for a rundown of what the pope is up to (in Italian, English and other languages); or state-owned Italian RAI-1, RAI-2 and RAI-3 (www.rai.it), which broadcast all over the country and abroad. Commercial stations such as Rome's Radio Centro Suono (www.centrosuono.com) and Radio Città Futura (www.radiocittafutura.it), Naples' Radio Kiss Kiss (www.kisskissnapoli.it) and Milan-based left-wing Radio Popolare (www.radiopopolare.it) are all good for contemporary music.

» Switch on the box to watch the state-run RAI-1, RAI-2 and RAI-3 (www.rai.it) and the main commercial stations (mostly run by Silvio Berlusconi's Mediaset company): Canale 5 (www.canale5.mediaset.it), Italia 1 (www.italia1.mediaset.it) and Rete 4 (www.rete4.mediaset.it) and La 7 (www.la7.it).

Lone women may find it difficult to remain alone. In many places, local Lotharios will try it on with exasperating insistence, which can be flattering or a pain. Foreign women are particular objects of male attention in tourist towns like Florence and more generally in the south. Usually the best response to undesired advances is to ignore them. If that doesn't work, politely tell your interlocutors you're waiting for your *marito* (husband) or *fidanzato* (boyfriend) and, if necessary, walk away. Avoid becoming aggressive as this may result in an unpleasant confrontation. If all else fails, approach the nearest member of the police.

Watch out for men with wandering hands on crowded buses. Either keep your back to the wall or make a loud fuss if someone starts fondling your behind. A loud '*Che schifo!*' (How disgusting!) will usually do the trick. If a more serious incident occurs, report it to the police, who are then required to press charges.

Women travelling alone should use their common sense. Avoid solo hitchhiking or walking alone in dark streets, and look for hotels that are central (unsafe areas are noted in this book).

Transport

GETTING THERE & AWAY

A plethora of airlines link Italy with the rest of the world, and cut-rate carriers have significantly driven down the cost of flights from other European countries. Excellent rail and bus connections, especially with northern Italy, offer efficient overland transport, while car and passenger ferries operate to ports throughout the Mediterranean.

Flights, tours and rail tickets can be booked online at lonelyplanet.com/bookings.

Entering the Country

European Union and Swiss citizens can travel to Italy with their national identity card alone. All other nationalities must have a valid passport and may be required to fill out a landing card (at airports).

By law you are supposed to have your passport or ID card with you at all times. You'll need one of these documents for police registration every time you check into a hotel.

In theory there are no passport checks at land crossings from neighbouring countries, but random customs controls do occasionally still take place between Italy and Switzerland.

Air

Airports & Airlines

Italy's main intercontinental gateways are Rome's **Leonardo da Vinci airport** (Fiumicino; www.adr.it) and Milan's **Malpensa airport** (www.sea-aeroportimilano.it). Both are served by nonstop flights from around the world.

From North America, nonstop flights to Rome originate in Atlanta, Boston, Chicago, Los Angeles, Miami, New York, Philadelphia, Montreal and Toronto, while in South America, Buenos Aires and São Paulo both offer direct service. Regular direct flights link Rome (and often Milan) with Asian and Middle Eastern capitals including Bangkok, Dubai, Hong Kong, Kuala Lumpur, Singapore and Tokyo. If you're flying from Africa or the South Pacific, you'll generally need to change planes at least once en route to Italy.

Intra-European flights serve plenty of other Italian cities; the leading mainstream carriers include Alitalia, Air France, British Airways, Lufthansa and KLM.

Cut-rate airlines, led by Ryanair and easyJet, fly from a growing number of European cities to over two dozen Italian destinations, typically landing in smaller airports such as Rome's **Ciampino** (www.adr.it).

Dozens of international airlines compete with the country's national carrier, Alitalia. The most active are listed here.

Air Berlin/Niki (www.airberlin.com)
Air Canada (www.aircanada.com)
Air France (www.airfrance.com)
Air One (www.flyairone.it)
Air Transat (www.airtransat.it)
Alitalia (www.alitalia.com)
American Airlines (www.aa.com)
BMI Baby (www.bmibaby.com)
British Airways (www.britishairways.com)
Brussels Airlines (www.brusselsairlines.com)
Continental (www.continental.com)
Delta (www.delta.com)
easyJet (www.easyjet.com)
Jet2 (www.jet2.com)
KLM (www.klm.com)
Lufthansa (www.lufthansa.com)
Meridiana (www.meridiana.it)
Qantas (www.qantas.com.au)
Ryanair (www.ryanair.com)
Singapore Airlines (www.singaporeair.com)
Swiss (www.swiss.com)
TAM (www.tam.com.br)
Thai Airways (www.thaiairways.com)
United (www.united.com)
US Airways (www.usairways.com)

Vueling (www.vueling.com)
Windjet (www.volawindjet.it)

Tickets

The internet is the easiest way of locating and booking reasonably priced seats.

Full-time students and those under 26 may qualify for discounted fares at agencies such as **STA Travel** (statravel.com). Many of these fares require a valid International Student Identity Card (ISIC).

Land

There are plenty of options for entering Italy by train, bus or private vehicle.

Border Crossings

Aside from the coast roads linking Italy with France and Slovenia, border crossings into Italy mostly involve tunnels through the Alps (open year-round) or mountain passes (seasonally closed or requiring snow chains). The list below outlines the major points of entry.

Austria From Innsbruck to Bolzano via A22/E45 (Brenner Pass); Villach to Tarvisio via A23/E55

France From Nice to Ventimiglia via A10/E80; Modane to Turin via A32/E70 (Fréjus Tunnel); Chamonix to Courmayeur via A5/E25 (Mont Blanc Tunnel)

Slovenia From Sežana to Trieste via SS58/E70

Switzerland From Martigny to Aosta via SS27/E27 (Grand St Bernard Tunnel); Lugano to Como via A9/E35

Bus

Buses are the cheapest overland option to Italy, but services are less frequent, less comfortable and significantly slower than the train. **Eurolines** (www.eurolines.com) is a consortium of coach companies with offices throughout Europe. Italy-bound buses head to Milan, Rome, Florence, Siena, Venice and other Italian cities.

Eurolines offers a low-season **bus pass** (www.eurolines-pass.com) valid for 15/30 days that costs €205/310 (€175/240 for under-26s and senior citizens over 60). This pass allows unlimited travel between 40 European cities, including Milan, Venice, Florence, Siena and Rome. Fares increase to €345/455 (reduced €290/375) in midsummer.

Car & Motorcycle

CONTINENTAL EUROPE

When driving in Europe, always carry proof of vehicle ownership and evidence of third-party insurance. If driving an EU-registered vehicle, your home country insurance is sufficient. Ask your insurer for a European Accident Statement (EAS) form, which can simplify matters in the event of an accident. Every vehicle travelling across an international border should display a nationality plate of its country of registration.

A European breakdown assistance policy is a good investment and can be obtained through the Automobile Club d'Italia.

Italy's scenic roads are tailor-made for motorcycle touring, and motorcyclists swarm into the country every summer. With a motorcycle you rarely have to book ahead for ferries and can enter restricted-traffic areas in cities. Crash helmets and a motorcycle licence are compulsory. The US-based **Beach's Motorcycle Adventures** (www.beachs-mca.com) offers two-week tours through north-central Italy in May and October.

For longer-term auto leasing (14 days or more) or campervan and motorhome hire, check **IdeaMerge** (www.ideamerge.com).

UK

You can take your car across to France by ferry or via the Channel Tunnel on **Eurotunnel** (☑0844 335 35 35; www.eurotunnel.com). The latter runs four crossings (35 minutes) an hour between Folkestone and Calais in the high season.

For breakdown assistance, both the **AA** (☑in UK 0800 072 3279; www.theaa.com/breakdown-cover) and the **RAC** (☑in UK 0800 015 6000; www.rac.co.uk/euro-breakdown) offer comprehensive cover in Europe.

CLIMATE CHANGE & TRAVEL

Every form of transport that relies on carbon-based fuel generates CO_2, the main cause of human-induced climate change. Modern travel is dependent on aeroplanes, which might use less fuel per kilometre per person than most cars but travel much greater distances. The altitude at which aircraft emit gases (including CO_2) and particles also contributes to their climate change impact. Many websites offer 'carbon calculators' that allow people to estimate the carbon emissions generated by their journey and, for those who wish to do so, to offset the impact of the greenhouse gases emitted with contributions to portfolios of climate-friendly initiatives throughout the world. Lonely Planet offsets the carbon footprint of all staff and author travel.

Train

Regular trains on two western lines connect Italy with France (one along the coast and the other from Turin into the French Alps). Trains from Milan head north into Switzerland and on towards the Benelux countries. Further east, two main lines head for the main cities in Central and Eastern Europe. Those crossing the Brenner Pass go to Innsbruck, Stuttgart and Munich. Those crossing at Tarvisio proceed to Vienna, Salzburg and Prague. The main international train line to Slovenia crosses near Trieste.

Depending on distances covered, rail can be highly competitive with air travel. Those travelling from neighbouring countries to northern Italy will find it is frequently more comfortable, less expensive and only marginally more time-consuming than flying.

Those travelling longer distances (say, from London, Spain, northern Germany or Eastern Europe) will doubtless find flying cheaper and quicker. Bear in mind, however, that the train is a much greener way to go – the same trip by rail can contribute up to 10 times less carbon dioxide emissions per person than by air.

CONTINENTAL EUROPE

The comprehensive European Rail Timetable (UK£13.99), updated monthly, is available from **Thomas Cook Publishing** (www.thomascookpublishing.com).

Reservations on international trains to/from Italy are always advisable, and sometimes compulsory. Some international services include transport for private cars. Consider taking long journeys overnight, as the supplemental fare for a sleeper costs substantially less than Italian hotels.

UK

The passenger train **Eurostar** (☑08432 186 186; www.eurostar.com) travels between London and Paris, or London and Brussels. Alternatively, you can get a train ticket that includes crossing the Channel by ferry.

For the latest fare information on journeys to Italy, including the Eurostar, contact the **Rail Europe Travel Centre** (☑in UK 08448 484 064; www.raileurope.co.uk) or **Rail Choice** (☑0871 231 0790; www.railchoice.com).

Sea

Multiple ferry companies connect Italy with countries throughout the Mediterranean. Many routes only operate in summer, when ticket prices also rise. Prices for vehicles vary according to their size.

The helpful website **www.traghettionline.com** (in Italian) covers all the ferry companies in the Mediterranean. Another useful resource for ferries from Italy to Greece is **www.ferries.gr**.

International ferry companies that serve Italy:

Adria Ferries (www.adriaferries.com)

Agoudimos Lines (www.agoudimos.it)

Blue Star Ferries (www.bluestarferries.com)

GNV (Grandi Navi Veloci) (www.gnv.it)

Grimaldi (www.grimaldi-ferries.com)

Jadrolinija (www.jadrolinija.hr)

Marmara Lines (marmara-lines@ferries.gr)

Minoan Lines (www.minoan.gr)

Montenegro Lines (www.montenegrolines.net)

Red Star Ferries (www.redstarferries.com)

SNAV (www.snav.it)

Superfast (www.superfast.com)

Tirrenia (www.tirrenia.it)

Venezia Lines (www.venezialines.com)

Ventouris (www.ventouris.gr)

Virtu Ferries (www.virtuferries.com)

See the table on p924 for their destinations.

GETTING AROUND

Italy's network of train, bus, ferry and domestic air transport allows you to reach most destinations efficiently and relatively affordably.

EXPRESS TRAINS TO ITALY FROM CONTINENTAL EUROPE

FROM	TO	FREQUENCY	DURATION (HR)	COST (€)
Geneva	Milan	four daily	4	72
Geneva	Venice	one daily	7	99
Munich	Florence	one nightly	9¼	98
Munich	Rome	one nightly	12¼	132
Munich	Venice	one nightly	9½	94
Paris	Milan	three daily	7	98
Paris	Rome	one nightly	15¼	130
Paris	Venice	one nightly	13	130
Vienna	Milan	one nightly	13	89
Vienna	Rome	one nightly	14	99
Zurich	Milan	seven daily	3¾	65

With your own vehicle, you'll enjoy greater freedom, but *benzina* (petrol) and *autostrada* (motorway) tolls are expensive and Italian drivers have a style all their own. For many, the stress of driving and parking in urban areas may outweigh the delights of puttering about the countryside. One solution is to take public transport between large cities and rent a car only to reach more-remote rural destinations.

Air

The privatised national airline, Alitalia, is the main domestic carrier. Its many cut-rate competitors within Italy include:

Meridiana (www.meridiana.it), **Air One** (www.flyairone.it), **Ryanair** (www.ryanair.com), **easyJet** (www.easyjet.com), **Windjet** (www.volawindjet.it) and **AirAlps** (www.airalps.at). A useful search engine for comparing multiple carriers' fares and purchasing low-cost domestic flights is **AZfly** (www.azfly.it).

Airport taxes are factored into the price of your ticket.

Bicycle

Cycling is very popular in Italy. Bikes are prohibited on the autostrada, but there are few other special road rules.

If bringing your own bike, you'll need to disassemble and pack it for the journey, and may need to pay an airline surcharge. Make sure to include tools, spare parts and for safety's sake, a helmet, lights and a secure bike lock.

Bikes can be wheeled onto any domestic train displaying the bicycle logo. Simply purchase a separate bicycle ticket, valid for 24 hours (€3.50). Certain international trains, listed on Trenitalia's 'In treno con la bici' page, also allow transport of

assembled bicycles for €12. Bikes dismantled and stored in a bag can be taken for free, even on night trains. Most ferries also allow free bicycle passage.

In the UK, **Cyclists' Touring Club** (☎0844 736 8450; www.ctc.org.uk) can help you plan your tour or organise a guided tour. Membership costs £37 for adults, £23 for seniors and £12 for under-18s.

Hire

Both city and mountain bikes are available for hire in most Italian towns. City bikes start at €10/50 per day/week; mountain bikes a bit more. Some municipalities, including Rimini and Ravenna, offer free bikes for visitors, as do a growing number of Italian hotels.

Boat

Navi (large ferries) service Sicily and Sardinia, while *traghetti* (smaller ferries) and *aliscafi* (hydrofoils) service the smaller islands. Most ferries carry vehicles; hydrofoils do not.

The main embarkation points for Sicily and Sardinia are Genoa, Livorno, Civitavecchia and Naples. Ferries for Sicily also leave from Villa San Giovanni and Reggio Calabria. The main points of arrival in Sardinia are Cagliari, Arbatax, Olbia and Porto Torres; in Sicily they're Palermo, Catania, Trapani and Messina.

The comprehensive website **TraghettiOnline** (www.traghettionline.com, in Italian) includes links to multiple Italian ferry companies, allowing you to compare prices and buy tickets.

Detailed information on ferry prices and times for Sicily can be found on p746, and for Sardinia on p810. For other relevant destinations, see the Getting There & Away sections of individual chapters.

On overnight ferries, travellers can book a two- to four-person cabin or a *poltrona*, which is an airline-type armchair. Deck class (which allows you to sit/sleep in lounge areas or on deck) is available only on some ferries.

Bus

Numerous companies provide bus services in Italy, from meandering local routes to fast and reliable InterCity connections. Buses are usually priced competitively with the train and are often the only way to get to smaller towns.

It's usually possible to get bus timetables from local tourist offices. In larger cities most of the InterCity bus companies have ticket offices or sell tickets through agencies. In villages and even some good-sized towns, tickets are sold in bars or on the bus.

Advance booking, while not generally required, is advisable for overnight or long-haul trips in high season.

Car & Motorcycle

Italy boasts an extensive privatised network of autostradas, represented on road signs by a white 'A' followed by a number on a green background. The main north–south link is the Autostrada del Sole (the 'Motorway of the Sun'), which extends from Milan to Reggio di Calabria (called the A1 from Milan to Rome, the A2 from Rome to Naples, and the A3 from Naples to Reggio di Calabria).

There are tolls on most motorways, payable by cash or credit card as you exit. For information in English about distances, driving times and fuel costs, see en.mappy.com. Additional information in Italian, including traffic conditions and toll costs, is available at www.autostrade.it.

There are several additional road categories, listed here in descending order of importance.

Strade statali (state highways) Represented on maps by 'S' or 'SS'. Vary from toll-free, four-lane highways to two-lane main roads. The latter can be extremely slow, especially in mountainous regions.

Strade regionali (regional highways connecting small villages) Coded 'SR' or 'R'.

INTERNATIONAL FERRY ROUTES FROM ITALY

DESTINATION COUNTRY	DESTINATION PORT(S)	ITALIAN PORT(S)	COMPANY
Albania	Durrës	Bari	Ventouris
	Durrës	Bari, Ancona	Adria Ferries
	Vlora	Brindisi	Red Star Ferries, Agoudimos Lines
Croatia	Dubrovnik	Bari	Jadrolinija
	Hvar, Split	Pescara	SNAV
	Split	Ancona	SNAV
	Split, Zadar	Ancona	Jadrolinija
	Rovinj, Pula, Poreč, Rabac	Venice	Venezia Lines
Greece	Cephalonia, Corfu, Igoumenitsa, Zante	Brindisi	Agoudimos Lines
	Corfu, Igoumenitsa, Patras	Bari	Blue Star Ferries, Superfast
	Corfu, Igoumenitsa, Patras	Venice, Ancona	Minoan Lines
	Corfu, Igoumenitsa, Patras	Ancona	Blue Star
	Igoumenitsa, Patras	Ancona	Superfast
Malta	Valletta	Genoa, Livorno, Palermo	GNV
	Valletta	Catania, Civitavecchia	Grimaldi
	Valletta	Pozzallo, Catania	Virtu Ferries
Montenegro	Bar	Bari, Ancona	Montenegro Lines
Morocco	Tangiers	Genoa	GNV
	Tangiers	Livorno	Grimaldi
Slovenia	Piran	Venice	Venezia Lines
Spain	Barcelona	Genoa	GNV
	Barcelona	Civitavecchia, Livorno, Porto Torres	Grimaldi
Tunisia	Tunis	Genoa, Civitavecchia, Palermo	GNV
	Tunis	Genoa	Tirrenia
	Tunis	Civitavecchia, Palermo, Salerno, Trapani	Grimaldi
Turkey	Çeşme	Ancona	Marmara Lines

	Bari	Bologna	Florence	Genoa	Milan	Naples	Palermo	Perugia	Reggio di Calabria	Rome	Siena	Trento	Trieste	Turin	Venice
Bologna	681														
Florence	784	106													
Genoa	996	285	268												
Milan	899	218	324	156											
Naples	322	640	534	758	858										
Palermo	734	1415	1345	1569	1633	811									
Perugia	612	270	164	432	488	408	1219								
Reggio di Calabria	490	1171	1101	1325	1389	567	272	816							
Rome	482	408	302	526	626	232	1043	170	664						
Siena	714	176	70	296	394	464	1275	103	867	232					
Trento	892	233	339	341	218	874	1626	459	1222	641	375				
Trieste	995	308	414	336	420	948	1689	543	1445	715	484	279			
Turin	1019	338	442	174	139	932	1743	545	1307	702	460	349	551		
Venice	806	269	265	387	284	899	799	394	1296	567	335	167	165	415	
Verona	808	141	247	282	164	781	1534	377	1139	549	293	97	250	295	120

Note

Distances between Palermo and mainland towns do not take into account the ferry from Reggio di Calabria to Messina. Add an extra hour to your journey time to allow for this crossing

Strade provinciali (provincial highways) Coded 'SP' or 'P'.

Strade locali Often not even paved or mapped.

Automobile Associations

The **Automobile Club d'Italia** (ACI; www.aci.it) is a driver's best resource in Italy. For 24-hour roadside emergency service, dial 🕿803116 from a landline or 🕿800 116800 from a mobile phone. Foreigners do not have to join but instead pay a per-incident fee.

Driving Licences

All EU member states' driving licences are fully recognised throughout Europe. In practice, many non-EU licences (such as Australian, Canadian, New Zealand and US licences) are accepted by car-hire outfits in Italy. Travellers from other countries should obtain an International Driving Permit (IDP) through their national automobile association.

Fuel & Spare Parts

Italy's petrol prices are among the highest in Europe and vary from one service station (*benzinaio, stazione di servizio*) to another. As this book went to press, lead-free gasoline (*senza piombo;* 95 octane) was averaging €1.57 per litre, with diesel (*gasolio*) costing €1.44 per litre.

Spare parts are available at many garages or via the 24-hour ACI motorist assistance number, 🕿803116.

Hire

CARS

Pre-booking via the internet often costs less than hiring a car in Italy. Renters must generally be aged 25 or over, with a credit card and home country driving licence or IDP. Consider hiring a small car, which will reduce your fuel expense and help you negotiate narrow city lanes and tight parking spaces.

Check with your credit-card company to see if it offers a Collision Damage Waiver, which covers you for additional damage if you use that card to pay for the car.

Multinational car-rental agencies:

Auto Europe (www.autoeurope.com)

Autos Abroad (www.autosabroad.com)

Avis (www.avisautonoleggio.it)

Budget (www.budgetautonoleggio.it)

Europcar (www.europcar.com)

Hertz (www.hertz.it)

Holiday Cars (www.holidaycars.com)

Italy by Car (www.italybycar.it)

Maggiore (www.maggiore.it)

MOTORCYCLES

Agencies throughout Italy rent motorbikes, ranging from small Vespas to larger touring bikes. Prices start at around €20/140 per day/

Train Routes

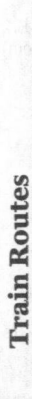

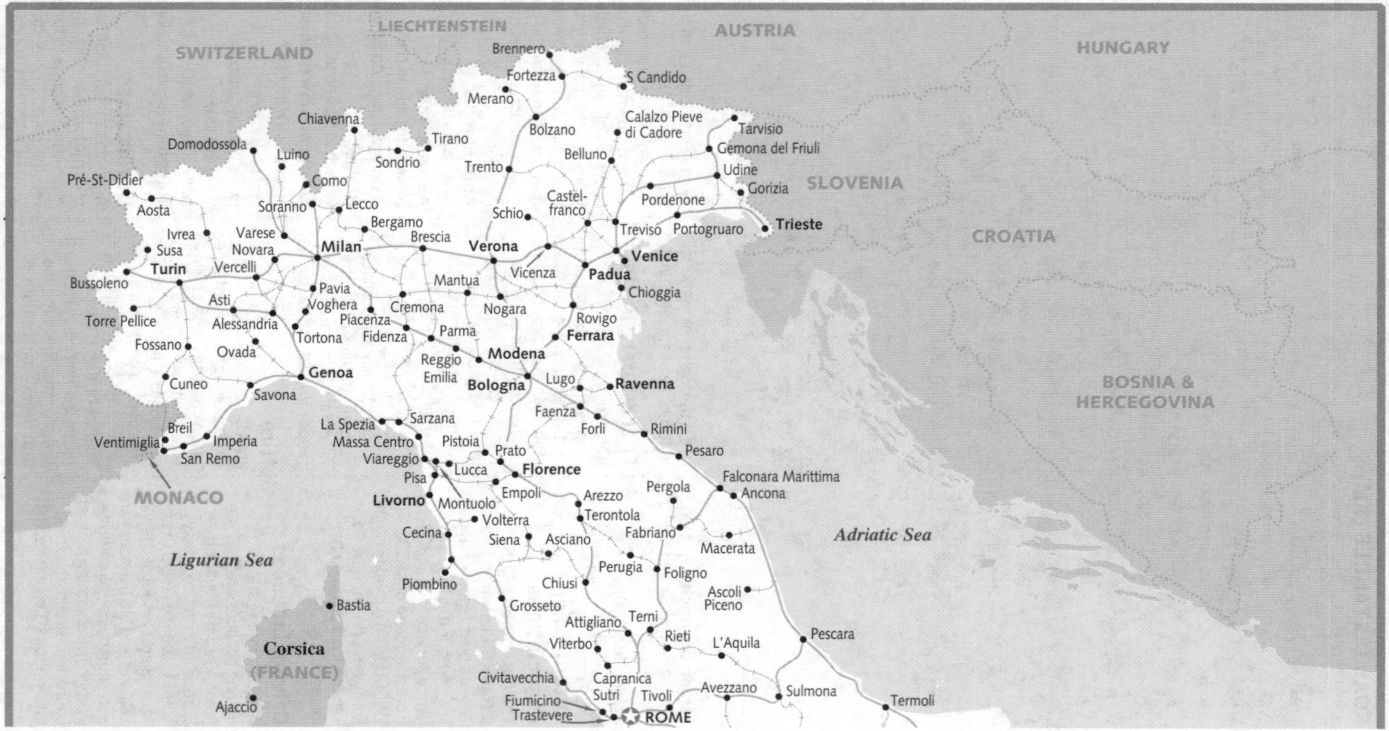

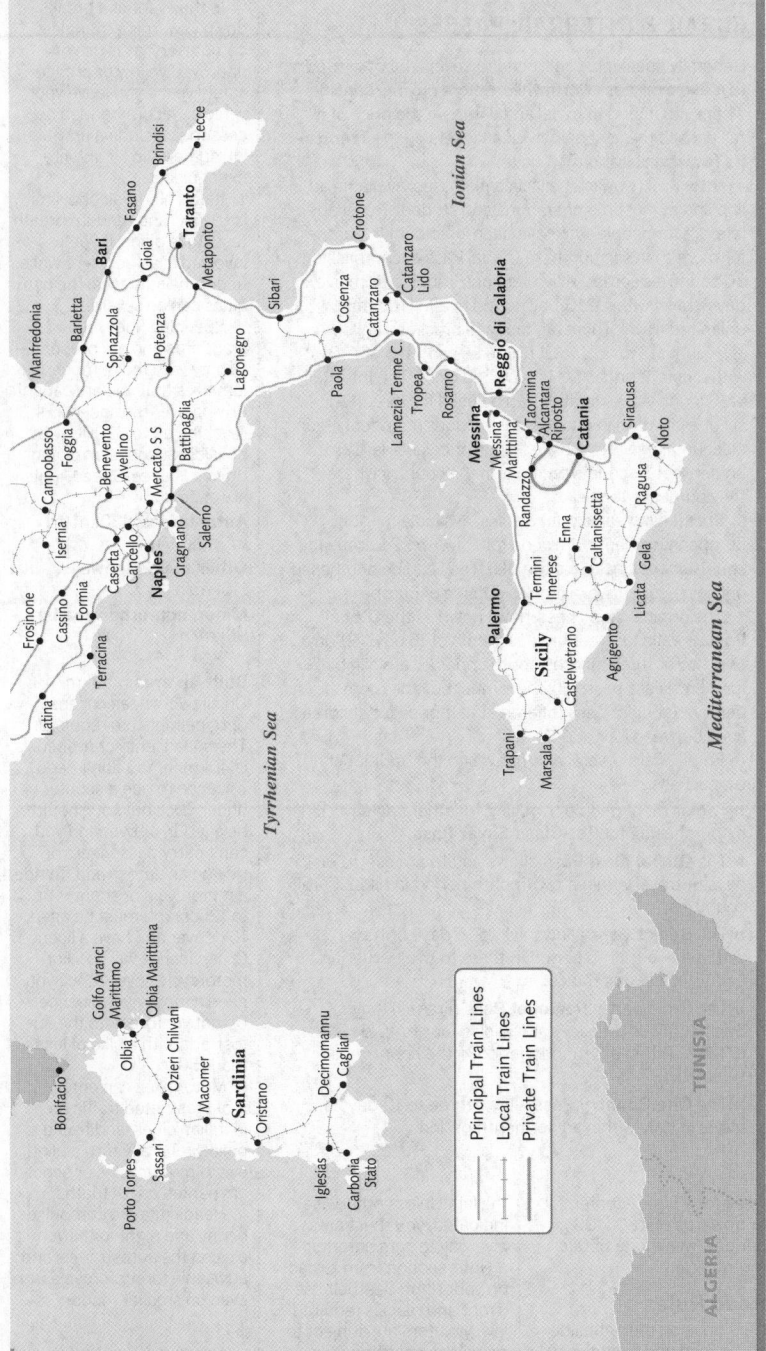

EURAIL & INTERRAIL PASSES

Generally speaking, you'll need to cover a lot of ground to make a rail pass worthwhile. Before buying, consider where you intend to travel and compare the price of a rail pass to the cost of individual tickets on the **Trenitalia** (www.trenitalia.com) website.

InterRail (www.interrailnet.com) passes, available online and at most major stations and student-travel outlets, are for people who have been a resident in Europe for more than six months. A Global Pass encompassing 30 countries comes in five versions, ranging from five days' travel within a 10-day period to a full month's unlimited travel. There are four age brackets: child (4 to 11), youth (12 to 25), adult (26 to 59) and senior (60+), with different prices for 1st and 2nd class. The InterRail one-country pass for Italy can be used for three, four, six or eight days in one month and does not offer senior discounts. See the website for full price details. Cardholders get discounts on travel in the country where they purchase the ticket.

Eurail (www.eurail.com) passes, available for non-European residents, are good for travel in 22 European countries (not including the UK). They can be purchased online or from travel agencies outside of Europe.

The original Eurail pass, now known as the **Global Pass**, is valid for a continuous period of 15 days, 21 days, one, two or three months. Youth under 26 are eligible for a 2nd-class pass; all others must buy the more expensive 1st-class pass (offered at half-price for children aged between four and 11).

Eurail offers several alternatives to the traditional Global Pass:

» Two or more people travelling together can save 15% by purchasing the **1st-Class Saver Pass**.

» The **Global Flexi Pass** allows you to choose 10 or 15 days of travel within a two-month period in all 22 Eurail countries.

» The **Select Pass** allows five to 15 days of travel within a two-month period in three to five bordering countries of your choice.

» The two-country **Regional Pass** (France/Italy, Spain/Italy or Greece/Italy) allows four to 10 days of travel within a 2-month period in the country pair selected.

» The **One Country Pass** allows three to 10 days of travel in Italy within a two-month period.

In the event of a breakdown, a warning triangle is compulsory, as is use of an approved yellow or orange safety vest if you leave your vehicle. Recommended accessories include a first-aid kit, spare-bulb kit and fire extinguisher.

Italy's blood-alcohol limit is 0.05%, and random breath tests take place. If you're involved in an accident while under the influence, the penalties can be severe.

Speeding fines follow EU standards and are proportionate with the number of kilometres that you are caught driving over the speed limit, reaching up to €2000 with possible suspension of your driving licence. Speed limits are as follows:

Autostradas: 130km/h to 150km/h

Other main highways: 110km/h

Minor, non-urban roads: 90km/h

Built-up areas: 50km/h On all two-wheeled transport, helmets are required. The speed limit for mopeds is 40km/h. You don't need a licence to ride a scooter under 50cc but you should be aged 14 or over and you can't carry passengers or ride on an autostrada. To ride a motorcycle or scooter up to 125cc, you must be aged 16 or over and have a licence (a car licence will do). For motorcycles over 125cc you need a motorcycle licence. Do not venture onto the autostrada with a bike of less than 150cc.

Motorbikes can enter most restricted traffic areas in Italian cities, and traffic police generally turn a blind eye to motorcycles or scooters parked on footpaths.

Headlights are compulsory day and night for all vehicles on the autostradas, and advisable for motorcycles even on smaller roads.

week for a 50cc scooter, or upwards of €80/400 per day/week for a 650cc motorcycle.

Road Rules

Cars drive on the right side of the road and overtake on the left. Unless otherwise indicated, you must always give way to cars entering an intersection from a road on your right. Seatbelt use (front and rear) is required by law; violators are subject to an on-the-spot fine.

Local Transport

Major cities all have good transport systems, including bus and underground-train networks. In Venice, the main public transport is on *vaporetti* (small passenger ferries).

Bus & Underground Trains

Purchase bus and metro tickets before boarding and validate them once on board. Passengers with unvalidated tickets are subject to a fine (up to €50 in most cities).

There are extensive *metropolitane* (metros) in Rome, Milan, Naples and Turin, plus smaller metros in Genoa and Catania and the space-age Minimetrò in Perugia connecting the train station with the city centre. As this book went to press, Turin, Naples and Rome were all significantly expanding their metro systems.

Every city or town of any size has an efficient *urbano* (urban) and *extraurbano* (suburban) system of buses. Services are generally limited on Sundays and holidays.

Tickets can be bought from *tabaccaio* (tobacconist's shops), newsstands, ticket booths or dispensing machines at bus stations and in metro stations, and usually cost around €1 to €1.30. Most cities offer good-value 24-hour or daily tourist tickets.

Taxi

You can catch a taxi at the ranks outside most train and bus stations, or simply telephone for a radio taxi. Note that radio taxi meters start running from when you've called rather than when you're picked up.

Charges vary somewhat from one region to another. Most short city journeys cost between €10 and €15. Generally, no more than four people are allowed in one taxi.

EXPRESS TRAINS: TIMES & PRICES COMPARED

FROM	TO	FRECCIAROSSA/ AV TRAIN		INTERCITY TRAIN	
		DURATION (HR)	PRICE (€)	DURATION (HR)	PRICE (€)
Turin	Naples	5½	111	9¾	63
Milan	Rome	3½	91	6¾	49.50
Venice	Florence	2	43	3¼	24
Rome	Naples	1½	45	2¼	22
Florence	Bologna	37min	25	1	10.50

Train

Trains in Italy are relatively cheap compared with other European countries, and the better train categories are fast and comfortable.

Trenitalia (☏892021 in Italian; www.trenitalia.com) is the partially privatised state train system that runs most services. Other private lines are noted throughout this book.

Countless foreign travellers to Italy learn the hard way that their train tickets must be stamped in the yellow machines (usually found at the head of rail platforms) just before boarding. Failure to do so usually results in fines, although the cry of 'I didn't know' sometimes elicits an indulgent response from ticket controllers. So stamp that ticket!

There are several types of trains. *Regionale* or *interregionale* trains stop at all or most stations. InterCity (IC) trains, and their international counterparts known as Eurocity (EC), are faster services that operate between major cities. Even faster *pendolini* (tilting trains) capable of reaching speeds of 250km to 300km per hour are collectively known as Eurostar Italia (ES).

In late 2009, Italy's newest, fastest trains – the Alta Velocità (High Speed)

services variously known as Frecciarossa, Frecciargento, AV and ESAV – began operating on the Turin–Milan–Bologna–Florence–Rome–Naples–Salerno line, revolutionising train travel on that route. As shown in the table above, AV trains cost almost twice as much as traditional InterCity express trains, but get you to your destination nearly twice as fast.

Classes & Costs

Prices vary according to the class of service, time of travel and how far in advance you book. Most Italian trains have 1st- and 2nd-class seating; a 1st-class ticket typically costs from a third to half more than the 2nd-class ticket.

Travel on InterCity, Eurostar and Alta Velocità trains means paying a supplement, determined by the distance you are travelling and included in the ticket price. If you have a standard ticket for a slower train and end up hopping on an IC train, you'll have to pay the difference on board. (You can only board a Eurostar or Alta Velocità train if you have a booking, so the problem does not arise in those cases.)

Reservations

Reservations are obligatory on Eurostar and AV trains. Otherwise they're not and, outside of peak holiday periods, you should be fine without them. You can make reservations at railway station counters, travel agents and, when they haven't broken down, at the automated machines sprinkled around most stations. Reservations carry a small extra fee.

Trenitalia offers a variety of advance purchase discounts. The Mini fare offers significant price reductions for express trains within Italy, while Smart Price,

Smart and Moove fares offer similar discounts on international tickets. Seats are limited, refunds and changes are highly restricted, and tickets must be purchased anywhere from two to 30 days in advance. For full details see www.trenitalia.com (in Italian).

Train Passes

Trenitalia offers various discount passes, including the Carta Verde for youth and

Carta d'Argento for seniors, but these are mainly useful for residents or long-term visitors, as they only pay for themselves with regular use over an extended period.

More interesting for short-term visitors are Eurail and InterRail passes.

Language

WANT MORE?

For in-depth language information and handy phrases, check out Lonely Planet's *Italian Phrasebook*. You'll find it at **shop. lonelyplanet.com**, or you can buy Lonely Planet's iPhone phrasebooks at the Apple App Store.

Standard Italian is taught and spoken throughout Italy. Regional dialects are an important part of identity in many parts of the country, but you'll have no trouble being understood anywhere if you stick to standard Italian, which we've also used in this chapter.

The sounds used in spoken Italian can all be found in English. If you read our coloured pronunciation guides as if they were English, you'll be understood. The stressed syllables are indicated with italics. Note that ai is pronounced as in 'aisle', ay as in 'say', ow as in 'how', dz as the 'ds' in 'lids', and that r is a strong and rolled sound. Keep in mind that Italian consonants can have a stronger, emphatic pronunciation – if the consonant is written as a double letter, it should be pronounced a little stronger, eg *sonno* son·no (sleep) versus *sono* so·no (I am).

BASICS

Italian has two words for 'you' – use the polite form *Lei* lay if you're talking to strangers, officials or people older than you. With people familiar to you or younger than you, you can use the informal form *tu* too.

In Italian, all nouns and adjectives are either masculine or feminine, and so are the articles *il/la* eel/la (the) and *un/una* oon/oo·na (a) that go with the nouns.

In this chapter the polite/informal and masculine/feminine options are included where necessary, separated with a slash and indicated with 'pol/inf' and 'm/f'.

Hello.	*Buongiorno.*	bwon·*jor*·no
Goodbye.	*Arrivederci.*	a·ree·ve·*der*·chee

Yes.	*Sì.*	see
No.	*No.*	no
Excuse me.	*Mi scusi.* (pol)	mee *skoo*·zee
	Scusami. (inf)	*skoo*·za·mee
Sorry.	*Mi dispiace.*	mee dees·*pya*·che
Please.	*Per favore.*	per fa·*vo*·re
Thank you.	*Grazie.*	*gra*·tsye
You're welcome.	*Prego.*	*pre*·go

How are you?
Come sta/stai? (pol/inf)   *ko*·me sta/stai

Fine. And you?
Bene. E Lei/tu? (pol/inf)   *be*·ne e lay/too

What's your name?
Come si chiama? pol   *ko*·me see *kya*·ma
Come ti chiami? inf   *ko*·me tee *kya*·mee

My name is ...
Mi chiamo ...   mee *kya*·mo ...

Do you speak English?
Parla/Parli   *par*·la/*par*·lee
inglese? (pol/inf)   een·*gle*·ze

I don't understand.
Non capisco.   non ka·*pee*·sko

ACCOMMODATION

Do you have a ... room?	*Avete una camera ...?*	a·*ve*·te *oo*·na *ka*·me·ra ...
double	*doppia con letto matri-moniale*	*do*·pya kon *le*·to ma·tree-mo·*nya*·le
single	*singola*	*seen*·go·la

How much is it per ...?	Quanto costa per ...?	kwan·to kos·ta per ...
night	una notte	oo·na no·te
person	persona	per·so·na

Is breakfast included?
La colazione è compresa? — la ko·la·tsyo·ne e kom·pre·sa

air-con	aria condizionata	a·rya kon·dee·tsyo·na·ta
bathroom	bagno	ba·nyo
campsite	campeggio	kam·pe·jo
guesthouse	pensione	pen·syo·ne
hotel	albergo	al·ber·go
youth hostel	ostello della gioventù	os·te·lo de·la jo·ven·too
window	finestra	fee·nes·tra

DIRECTIONS

Where's ...?
Dov'è ...? — do·ve ...

What's the address?
Qual'è l'indirizzo? — kwa·le leen·dee·ree·tso

Could you please write it down?
Può scriverlo, per favore? — pwo skree·ver·lo per fa·vo·re

Can you show me (on the map)?
Può mostrarmi (sulla pianta)? — pwo mos·trar·mee (soo·la pyan·ta)

at the corner	all'angolo	a·lan·go·lo
at the traffic lights	al semaforo	al se·ma·fo·ro
behind	dietro	dye·tro
far	lontano	lon·ta·no
in front of	davanti a	da·van·tee a
left	a sinistra	a see·nee·stra
near	vicino	vee·chee·no
next to	accanto a	a·kan·to a
opposite	di fronte a	dee fron·te a
right	a destra	a de·stra
straight ahead	sempre diritto	sem·pre dee·ree·to

EATING & DRINKING

What would you recommend?
Cosa mi consiglia? — ko·za mee kon·see·lya

What's in that dish?
Quali ingredienti ci sono in questo piatto? — kwa·li een·gre·dyen·tee chee so·no een kwe·sto pya·to

KEY PATTERNS

To get by in Italian, mix and match these simple patterns with words of your choice:

When's (the next flight)?
A che ora è (il prossimo volo)? — a ke o·ra e (eel pro·see·mo vo·lo)

Where's (the station)?
Dov'è (la stazione)? — do·ve (la sta·tsyo·ne)

I'm looking for (a hotel).
Sto cercando (un albergo). — sto cher·kan·do (oon al·ber·go)

Do you have (a map)?
Ha (una pianta)? — a (oo·na pyan·ta)

Is there (a toilet)?
C'è (un gabinetto)? — che (oon ga·bee·ne·to)

I'd like (a coffee).
Vorrei (un caffè). — vo·ray (oon ka·fe)

I'd like to (hire a car).
Vorrei (noleggiare una macchina). — vo·ray (no·le·ja·re oo·na ma·kee·na)

Can I (enter)?
Posso (entrare)? — po·so (en·tra·re)

Could you please (help me)?
Può (aiutarmi), per favore? — pwo (a·yoo·tar·mee) per fa·vo·re

Do I have to (book a seat)?
Devo (prenotare un posto)? — de·vo (pre·no·ta·re oon po·sto)

What's the local speciality?
Qual'è la specialità di questa regione? — kwa·le la spe·cha·lee·ta dee kwe·sta re·jo·ne

That was delicious!
Era squisito! — e·ra skwee·zee·to

Cheers!
Salute! — sa·loo·te

Please bring the bill.
Mi porta il conto, per favore? — mee por·ta eel kon·to per fa·vo·re

I'd like to reserve a table for ...	Vorrei prenotare un tavolo per ...	vo·ray pre·no·ta·re oon ta·vo·lo per ...
(two) people	(due) persone	(doo·e) per·so·ne
(eight) o'clock	le (otto)	le (o·to)

I don't eat ...	Non mangio ...	non man·jo ...
eggs	uova	wo·va
fish	pesce	pe·she
nuts	noci	no·chee
(red) meat	carne (rossa)	kar·ne (ro·sa)

Key Words

bar	*locale*	lo·*ka*·le
bottle	*bottiglia*	bo·*tee*·lya
breakfast	*prima colazione*	*pree*·ma ko·la·*tsyo*·ne
cafe	*bar*	bar
cold	*freddo*	*fre*·do
dinner	*cena*	*che*·na
drink list	*lista delle bevande*	*lee*·sta de·le be·*van*·de
fork	*forchetta*	for·*ke*·ta
glass	*bicchiere*	bee·*kye*·re
grocery store	*alimentari*	a·lee·men·*ta*·ree
hot	*caldo*	*kal*·do
knife	*coltello*	kol·*te*·lo
lunch	*pranzo*	*pran*·dzo
market	*mercato*	mer·*ka*·to
menu	*menù*	me·*noo*
plate	*piatto*	*pya*·to
restaurant	*ristorante*	ree·sto·*ran*·te
spicy	*piccante*	pee·*kan*·te
spoon	*cucchiaio*	koo·*kya*·yo
vegetarian (food)	*vegetariano*	ve·je·ta·*rya*·no
with	*con*	kon
without	*senza*	*sen*·tsa

Meat & Fish

beef	*manzo*	*man*·dzo
chicken	*pollo*	*po*·lo
duck	*anatra*	*a*·na·tra
fish	*pesce*	*pe*·she
herring	*aringa*	a·*reen*·ga
lamb	*agnello*	a·*nye*·lo
lobster	*aragosta*	a·ra·*gos*·ta

meat	*carne*	*kar*·ne
mussels	*cozze*	*ko*·tse
oysters	*ostriche*	o·*stree*·ke
pork	*maiale*	ma·*ya*·le
prawn	*gambero*	*gam*·be·ro
salmon	*salmone*	sal·*mo*·ne
scallops	*capasante*	ka·pa·*san*·te
seafood	*frutti di mare*	*froo*·tee dee *ma*·re
shrimp	*gambero*	*gam*·be·ro
squid	*calamari*	ka·la·*ma*·ree
trout	*trota*	*tro*·ta
tuna	*tonno*	*to*·no
turkey	*tacchino*	ta·*kee*·no
veal	*vitello*	vee·*te*·lo

Fruit & Vegetables

apple	*mela*	*me*·la
beans	*fagioli*	fa·*jo*·lee
cabbage	*cavolo*	*ka*·vo·lo
capsicum	*peperone*	pe·pe·*ro*·ne
carrot	*carota*	ka·*ro*·ta
cauliflower	*cavolfiore*	ka·vol·*fyo*·re
cucumber	*cetriolo*	che·tree·o·lo
fruit	*frutta*	*froo*·ta
grapes	*uva*	*oo*·va
lemon	*limone*	lee·*mo*·ne
lentils	*lenticchie*	len·*tee*·kye
mushroom	*funghi*	*foon*·gee
nuts	*noci*	*no*·chee
onions	*cipolle*	chee·*po*·le
orange	*arancia*	a·*ran*·cha
peach	*pesca*	*pe*·ska
peas	*piselli*	pee·*ze*·lee
pineapple	*ananas*	*a*·na·nas
plum	*prugna*	*proo*·nya
potatoes	*patate*	pa·*ta*·te
spinach	*spinaci*	spee·*na*·chee
tomatoes	*pomodori*	po·mo·*do*·ree
vegetables	*verdura*	ver·*doo*·ra

Other

bread	*pane*	*pa*·ne
butter	*burro*	*boo*·ro
cheese	*formaggio*	for·*ma*·jo
eggs	*uova*	*wo*·va
honey	*miele*	*mye*·le

ice	ghiaccio	gya·cho
jam	marmellata	mar·me·la·ta
noodles	pasta	pas·ta
oil	olio	o·lyo
pepper	pepe	pe·pe
rice	riso	ree·zo
salt	sale	sa·le
soup	minestra	mee·nes·tra
soy sauce	salsa di soia	sal·sa dee so·ya
sugar	zucchero	tsoo·ke·ro
vinegar	aceto	a·che·to

Drinks

beer	birra	bee·ra
coffee	caffè	ka·fe
(orange) juice	succo (d'arancia)	soo·ko (da·ran·cha)
milk	latte	la·te
red wine	vino rosso	vee·no ro·so
soft drink	bibita	bee·bee·ta
tea	tè	te
(mineral) water	acqua (minerale)	a·kwa (mee·ne·ra·le)
white wine	vino bianco	vee·no byan·ko

EMERGENCIES

Help!
Aiuto!   a·yoo·to

Leave me alone!
Lasciami in pace!   la·sha·mee een pa·che

I'm lost.
Mi sono perso/a. (m/f) mee so·no per·so/a

There's been an accident.
C'è stato un   che sta·to oon
incidente.   een·chee·den·te

Call the police!
Chiami la polizia!   kya·mee la po·lee·tsee·a

Call a doctor!
Chiami un medico!   kya·mee oon me·dee·ko

Where are the toilets?
Dove sono i   do·ve so·no ee
gabinetti?   ga·bee·ne·tee

Question Words

How?	Come?	ko·me
What?	Che cosa?	ke ko·za
When?	Quando?	kwan·do
Where?	Dove?	do·ve
Who?	Chi?	kee
Why?	Perché?	per·ke

I'm sick.
Mi sento male.   mee sen·to ma·le

It hurts here.
Mi fa male qui.   mee fa ma·le kwee

I'm allergic to ...
Sono allergico/a a ... (m/f) so·no a·ler·jee·ko/a a ...

SHOPPING & SERVICES

I'd like to buy ...
Vorrei comprare ...   vo·ray kom·pra·re ...

I'm just looking.
Sto solo guardando.   sto so·lo gwar·dan·do

Can I look at it?
Posso dare un'occhiata? po·so da·re oo·no·kya·ta

How much is this?
Quanto costa questo?   kwan·to kos·ta kwe·sto

It's too expensive.
È troppo caro/a. (m/f) e tro·po ka·ro/a

Can you lower the price?
Può farmi lo sconto?   pwo far·mee lo skon·to

There's a mistake in the bill.
C'è un errore nel conto. che oo·ne·ro·re nel kon·to

ATM	Bancomat	ban·ko·mat
post office	ufficio postale	oo·fee·cho pos·ta·le
tourist office	ufficio del turismo	oo·fee·cho del too·reez·mo

TIME & DATES

What time is it? Che ora è?   ke o·ra e

It's one o'clock. È l'una.   e loo·na

It's (two) o'clock. Sono le (due). so·no le (doo·e)

Half past (one). (L'una) e   (loo·na) e
                      mezza.   me·dza

in the morning	di mattina	dee ma·tee·na
in the afternoon	di pomeriggio	dee po·me·ree·jo
in the evening	di sera	dee se·ra

yesterday	ieri	ye·ree
today	oggi	o·jee
tomorrow	domani	do·ma·nee

Monday	lunedì	loo·ne·dee
Tuesday	martedì	mar·te·dee
Wednesday	mercoledì	mer·ko·le·dee
Thursday	giovedì	jo·ve·dee
Friday	venerdì	ve·ner·dee
Saturday	sabato	sa·ba·to
Sunday	domenica	do·me·nee·ka

January	gennaio	je·na·yo
February	febbraio	fe·bra·yo
March	marzo	mar·tso
April	aprile	a·pree·le
May	maggio	ma·jo
June	giugno	joo·nyo
July	luglio	loo·lyo
August	agosto	a·gos·to
September	settembre	se·tem·bre
October	ottobre	o·to·bre
November	novembre	no·vem·bre
December	dicembre	dee·chem·bre

NUMBERS

1	uno	oo·no
2	due	doo·e
3	tre	tre
4	quattro	kwa·tro
5	cinque	cheen·kwe
6	sei	say
7	sette	se·te
8	otto	o·to
9	nove	no·ve
10	dieci	dye·chee
20	venti	ven·tee
30	trenta	tren·ta
40	quaranta	kwa·ran·ta
50	cinquanta	cheen·kwan·ta
60	sessanta	se·san·ta
70	settanta	se·tan·ta
80	ottanta	o·tan·ta
90	novanta	no·van·ta
100	cento	chen·to
1000	mille	mee·lel

TRANSPORT

Public Transport

At what time does the ... leave/arrive?	A che ora parte/ arriva ...?	a ke o·ra par·te/ a·ree·va ...
boat	la nave	la na·ve
bus	l'autobus	low·to·boos
ferry	il traghetto	eel tra·ge·to
metro	la metro- politana	la me·tro- po·lee·ta·na
plane	l'aereo	la·e·re·o
train	il treno	eel tre·no

... ticket	un biglietto ...	oon bee·lye·to
one-way	di sola andata	dee so·la an·da·ta
return	di andata e ritorno	dee an·da·ta e ree·tor·no
bus stop	fermata dell'autobus	fer·ma·ta del ow·to·boos
platform	binario	bee·na·ryo
ticket office	biglietteria	bee·lye·te·ree·a
timetable	orario	o·ra·ryo
train station	stazione ferroviaria	sta·tsyo·ne fe·ro·vyar·ya

Does it stop at ...?
Si ferma a ...?   see fer·ma a ...

Please tell me when we get to ...
Mi dica per favore   mee dee·ka per fa·vo·re
quando arriviamo a ...   kwan·do a·ree·vya·mo a ...

I want to get off here.
Voglio scendere qui.   vo·lyo shen·de·re kwee

Driving & Cycling

I'd like to hire a/an ...	Vorrei noleggiare un/una ... (m/f)	vo·ray no·le·ja·re oon/oo·na ...
4WD	fuoristrada (m)	fwo·ree·stra·da
bicycle	bicicletta (f)	bee·chee·kle·ta
car	macchina (f)	ma·kee·na
motorbike	moto (f)	mo·to
bicycle pump	pompa della bicicletta	pom·pa de·la bee·chee·kle·ta
child seat	seggiolino	se·jo·lee·no
helmet	casco	kas·ko
mechanic	meccanico	me·ka·nee·ko
petrol/gas	benzina	ben·dzee·na
service station	stazione di servizio	sta·tsyo·ne dee ser·vee·tsyo

Is this the road to ...?
Questa strada porta a ...?   kwe·sta stra·da por·ta a ...

(How long) Can I park here?
(Per quanto tempo)   (per kwan·to tem·po)
Posso parcheggiare qui?   po·so par·ke·ja·re kwee

The car/motorbike has broken down (at ...).
La macchina/moto si è   la ma·kee·na/mo·to see e
guastata (a ...).   gwas·ta·ta (a ...)

I have a flat tyre.
Ho una gomma bucata.   o oo·na go·ma boo·ka·ta

I've run out of petrol.
Ho esaurito la   o e·zow·ree·to la
benzina.   ben·dzee·na

LANGUAGE GLOSSARY

abbazia – abbey

agriturismo – tourist accommodation on farms; farm stays

(pizza) al taglio – (pizza) by the slice

albergo – hotel

alimentari – grocery shop; delicatessen

anfiteatro – amphitheatre

aperitivo – pre-evening-meal drink and snack

APT – Azienda di Promozione Turistica; local town or city tourist office

autostrada – motorway; highway

battistero – baptistry

biblioteca – library

biglietto – ticket

borgo – archaic name for a small town, village or town sector (often dating to Middle Ages)

camera – room

campo – field; also a square in Venice

cappella – chapel

carabinieri – police with military and civil duties

Carnevale – carnival period between Epiphany and Lent

casa – house

castello – castle

cattedrale – cathedral

centro storico – historic centre

certosa – monastery belonging to or founded by Carthusian monks

chiesa – church

chiostro – cloister; covered walkway, usually enclosed by columns, around a quadrangle

cima – summit

città – town; city

città alta – upper town

città bassa – lower town

colonna – column

comune – equivalent to a municipality or county; a town or city council;

historically, a self–governing town or city

contrada – district

corso – boulevard

duomo – cathedral

enoteca – wine bar

espresso – short black coffee

ferrovia – railway

festa – feast day; holiday

fontana – fountain

foro – forum

funivia – cable car

gelateria – ice-cream shop

giardino – garden

golfo – gulf

grotta – cave

isola – island

lago – lake

largo – small square

lido – beach

locanda – inn; small hotel

lungomare – seafront road/promenade

mar, mare – sea

masseria – working farm

mausoleo – mausoleum; stately and magnificent tomb

mercato – market

monte – mountain

necropoli – ancient name for cemetery or burial site

nord – north

nuraghe – megalithic stone fortress in Sardinia

osteria – casual tavern or eatery presided over by a host

palazzo – mansion; palace; large building of any type, including an apartment block

palio – contest

parco – park

passeggiata – traditional evening stroll

pasticceria – cake/pastry shop

pensione – guesthouse

piazza – square

piazzale – large open square

pietà – literally 'pity' or 'compassion'; sculpture, drawing or painting of the dead Christ supported by the Madonna

pinacoteca – art gallery

ponte – bridge

porta – gate; door

porto – port

reale – royal

rifugio – mountain hut; accommodation in the Alps

ristorante – restaurant

rocca – fortress

sala – room; hall

salumeria – delicatessen

santuario – sanctuary; 1. the part of a church above the altar; 2. an especially holy place in a temple (antiquity)

sassi – literally 'stones'; stone houses built in two ravines in Matera, Basilicata

scalinata – staircase

scavi – excavations

sestiere – city district in Venice

spiaggia – beach

stazione – station

stazione marittima – ferry terminal

strada – street; road

sud – south

superstrada – expressway; highway with divided lanes

tartufo – truffle

tavola calda – literally 'hot table'; pre-prepared meat, pasta and vegetable selection, often self-service

teatro – theatre
tempietto – small temple
tempio – temple
terme – thermal baths
tesoro – treasury
torre – tower

trattoria – simple restaurant
Trenitalia – Italian State Railways; also known as Ferrovie dello Stato (FS)
trullo – conical house in Perugia

vaporetto – small passenger ferry (Venice)
via – street; road
viale – avenue
vico – alley; alleyway
villa – town house; country house; also the park surrounding the house

behind the scenes

SEND US YOUR FEEDBACK

We love to hear from travellers – your comments keep us on our toes and help make our books better. Our well-travelled team reads every word on what you loved or loathed about this book. Although we cannot reply individually to postal submissions, we always guarantee that your feedback goes straight to the appropriate authors, in time for the next edition. Each person who sends us information is thanked in the next edition – and the most useful submissions are rewarded with a free book.

Visit **lonelyplanet.com/contact** to submit your updates and suggestions or to ask for help. Our award-winning website also features inspirational travel stories, news and discussions.

Note: We may edit, reproduce and incorporate your comments in Lonely Planet products such as guidebooks, websites and digital products, so let us know if you don't want your comments reproduced or your name acknowledged. For a copy of our privacy policy visit lonelyplanet.com/privacy.

OUR READERS

Many thanks to the travellers who used the last edition and wrote to us with helpful hints, useful advice and interesting anecdotes: Carrie Aewsnan, Andrea, Patrik Åqvist, Paola Artuso, David Barkai, Nikki Buran, Mathilde Cambron, S Cenin, Martina Cerna, Anirvan Chatterjee, Anne Cholin, Francesco Cisternino, Colin and Laura, Jane Costelloe, Graham Courtenay, Peter Dean, Rachel Dechezeaux, Spiros Divaris, Matteo Donzelli, Claudia Duerrbeck, Mirco Dugaria, Jane Dyer, Eve Eichenberger, Idil Elveris, Tanja Gabler, Francesca Giorgi, Dan Giovannucci, John Glasgow, Lee Harrison, Tamara Herbert, Jos Hertecant, Ulrik Hoeg, Marcus How, Theodore Hudec, Kathy Hull, Dusica Ivetic, Bryony Kayes, Kair Keller, Dr Stephen Kerr, Unni Kjus Aahlin, Jeff Klein, Andrzej Kolbiarz, Gabriel Ledger, Giulia Luise, Petr Malcik, Martina and Ronen, Mike McCormack, Leone McDermott, Julia McGuigan, Jo Meredith, Carolina Morala Segret, Oren Moravchik, Alice Mozley, Becky Munday, Kimberly Murphy, Youry Na, Marzena Nycowie, Lorraine O'Keeffe, Maria Oliverio, Judy Packard, Marta Papini, Leo Paton, Sheila Paul, Anne Pincus, Sue Pon, Anne Rajamäki, Stephen Reeve, Fernanda Regaldo, Diana Renard, John Runeckles, Carmel Salvemini, Tobias Schmidt, Ben Sherreard, Agnes Soong, Giuliana and Luca Spiri, Robert Stofferson, Xin Sui, Gavin Tanguay, Amanda Thomas, Kristi Weaver, Virginia Wise, Susanne and Jan Wiznerowicz, Sekeun Yu.

AUTHOR THANKS

Paula Hardy

Creating this book was a huge team effort and I'd like to thank all my incredibly dedicated co-authors for their ability to find the very best that Italy has to offer. Doors opened in Milan and beyond because of the generosity of Claudio & Paola Bonacina, Paola Cairo, Angelo Proietti, Isabella Albertazzi, Dario Monti, Marco Roverso, Emanuele Ficchì, Deborah Favaron, Giovanni at Foresteria Monforte and Anatolij Miljanovic. Thanks also to @eraptopoulos and @margoveremeenko. Last, but never least, thank you to Rob, for being such a gallant gourmet. It was a blast.

Alison Bing

Mille grazie e tanti baci a le mie famiglie a Roma and stateside, the Bings, Ferrys and Marinuccis; Venezia intelligentsia Francesca Forni, Cristina Bottero, Rosanna Corró, Giovanni d'Este, Francesco and Matteo Pinto, and Gianantonio de Vincenzo; intrepid co-authors, especially Robert Landon and Paula Hardy; *ma sopra tutto a* Marco Flavio Marinucci.

Abigail Blasi

Molte grazie to Luca, Gabriel and Jack, to Anna and Marcello, and Carlotta and Alessandro for all their help in Rome, and thank you to Mum and Dad for all their help with the boys. A huge thank you to the unparalleled Barbara Lessona for all her kind assistance, and thanks to Paola Zagnarelli, Stéphanie Santini, Alessandro Sauda, Francesca Mazzà and Elizabeth Minchili for all their help with research.

Cristian Bonetto

A heartfelt *grazie* to my wonderful *re e regina di Napoli*, as well as to the incredibly generous Luca Coda, Valentina Vellusi, Carmine Romano, Marcantonio Colonna, Diego Nuzzo, Voza family, Domenico Rotella, Donatello Ciao, Luigi Mosca, Mirella Armiero, Francesco Calazzo, Carolyn Jackson, Peter Bardwell and Carlo Buono. A big thank you to Paula Hardy and my talented, ever-diligent cowriters.

Kerry Christiani

Mille grazie to the warm, hospitable locals I met on the road in Sardinia. Enormous thanks to Tonino Tosciri and his sister Maria Angela in Baunei for their friendship and insight. Many thanks to outdoor pros Peter and Anne at the Lemon House in Lotzorai, to climbing expert Corrado Conca for his *arrampicata* tips and to Maria Antonietta Goddi at Durke, Cagliari, for sweet inspiration. Finally, big thanks to my husband and brilliant travel companion, Andy Christiani.

Gregor Clark

Thanks to all the kind-hearted Italians who helped make this trip so memorable, especially Michele in Taormina, Angela in Palermo, Marisin and Salvatore in Scopello, Francesco in Modica, as well as fellow travellers Susan Morgan, France Soucy, Lucia Tancredi and Ross Parks. Thanks to Wes for joining me on the Aeolians and helping me renew my Stromboli obsession. Finally, warm hugs to Gaen, Meigan and Chloe, who always make returning home the happiest part of the trip.

Joe Fullman

Big thanks to my parents for putting me up, Marco for the car, Charlie and Emma for companionship, Carlo for his invaluable tips, Mike and Natasha for food, Charles and Cynthia for more food, and everyone in Italy (and beyond) who took the time to talk to me, write to me, answer my queries, recommend things to me, point me in the right direction and generally help me out as I made my convoluted way around the region.

Duncan Garwood

Grazie to everybody who helped me out on this job. A big thank you to Silvia Prosperi for her expert guidance and generous tip-sharing and to Barbara Nazzaro and Piero Meogrossi for their fascinating insights into the Colosseum. Thanks also to Al Rumjen for his company in Testaccio. I'd also like to thank fellow author Abi Blasi and coordinating maestro Paula Hardy. Finally, and as always, a huge hug to Lidia, Ben and Nick.

Robert Landon

Grazie mille for the on-the-road companionship of Caterina Enni, Marco Mazzoni, Neri Torrigiani and Fernanda Drummond; insights and hospitality of Stefano Piovesan, Donata Grimani, Pamela Berry, Stefano, and Filippo Barusco; long-distance connections made by Nancy Pietrafesa and Susan Filter; and the patient forbearance of Thiago Fico. Special thanks to Alison Bing for too many things. And Mom: Venice was our last international destination; I felt you with me this time, too, each step of the way.

Vesna Maric

My thanks go to Rafael and Frida, and a *gracias* to Susana. *Velika hvala* to my mother. Thanks very much to Kerry Christiani. In Sardinia, thank you to Francesca Vanoni Pugni and Carla Cani. Big *grazie* to Alessandra and Simone. In memory of baby Sveva.

Virginia Maxwell

Greatest thanks to my travelling partners on this job: Peter and Max Handsaker, Ryan Ver Berkmoes, and Giancarlo and Margie Paolucci. Thanks also to Ilaria Crescioli, Roberta Romoli, Chiara Olmastroni, Sara Caprarotta, Roberta Vichi, Chiara Ponzuoli, Luigina Benci, Cecilia Rosa and Caterina Bencistà Falorni. Author colleagues Nicola Williams and Paula Hardy were great to work with. Finally, thanks to Freya Middleton, Filippo Giabboni and Robert Landon for the great dinner in Florence!

Olivia Pozzan

Warmest thanks go to my parents, both of whom passed away during the production of this book. They came from Due Ville, near Vicenza in the Veneto, emigrating to Australia after their marriage. I thank them for many things – fostering my adventurous nature, the independence afforded by an Australian upbringing, pride in my Italian heritage and encouraging all my endeavours. Heartfelt thanks to Andrew who shared my joys and sorrows and whose patience and support carried me through difficult times.

Brendan Sainsbury

Many thanks to all the untold train guards, bus drivers, tourist info volunteers, restaurateurs and innocent bystanders who helped me during my research and to Paula Hardy for being a supportive coordinating author. Special thanks to Cristiana Grimaldi for her Barolo wisdom, and to my wife Liz and five-year-old son Kieran for their company all over Emilia-Romagna and the northwest.

Donna Wheeler

Warm welcomes and good advice were in abundance during my travels. Thanks to: Hans and the gang in Bolzano, Emanuela Grandi for excellent Trento tips, Linda Marcuzzi at Turismo FVG for many insights, Maurizio for Trieste recommendations (and haircare counsel), Carolina Lantieri in Gorizia, and kindred bianchista Wayne Young for his spirited input. Love and gratitude to Joe Guario (good job with the Fiat 500 on those hairy high-altitude passes), Biba for her backseat beatitude, and to darling Rumer, so far away.

Nicola Williams

Heartfelt thanks to those who helped me delve into the Tuscan heart: in Florence, Doreen and daughter Francesca Privitera (Hotel Scoti), fashion stylist Jennifer Tattanelli, father Georgio and assistant Olga (Casini Firenze), Alessio (Hotel Cestelli), Vasaria Corridor guide Michele Colloca

(Florencetown), Ilaria Crescioli (Toscana Promozione), Roberta Romoli (APT) and guide extraordinaire Freya Middleton. Elsewhere, Guido Manfredi (Barbialla Nuova), Fabrizio Quochi (Pisa), Francesca Geppetti (Livorno), Kristin Walton (Lucca), @allafiorentina, @emikodavies, @Morgannelefay13. And last but not least, my tireless, ever-fabulous travel companions Matthias, Niko, Mischa and Kaya Lüfkens.

ACKNOWLEDGMENTS

Climate map data adapted from Peel MC, Finlayson BL & McMahon TA (2007) 'Updated World Map of the Köppen-Geiger Climate Classification', *Hydrology and Earth System Sciences*, 11, 163344.

Illustrations p68-9, p326-7, p464-5 and p658-9 by Javier Zarracina.

Cover photograph: Ponte di Rialto, Venice; Da Ros Luca/4Corners.

Many of the images in this guide are available for licensing from Lonely Planet Images: www.lonelyplanetimages.com.

This Book

This 10th edition of Lonely Planet's *Italy* guidebook was researched and written by Paula Hardy, Alison Bing, Abigail Blasi, Cristian Bonetto, Kerry Christiani, Gregor Clark, Joe Fullman, Duncan Garwood, Robert Landon, Vesna Maric, Virginia Maxwell, Olivia Pozzan, Brendan Sainsbury, Donna Wheeler and Nicola Williams. This guidebook was commissioned in Lonely Planet's London office, and produced by the following:

Commissioning Editor Joe Bindloss

Coordinating Editor Sophie Splatt

Coordinating Cartographer Valentina Kremenchutskaya

Coordinating Layout Designer Lauren Egan

Managing Editors Imogen Bannister, Anna Metcalfe, Tasmin Waby McNaughton

Managing Cartographer Amanda Sierp

Managing Layout Designers Chris Girdler, Jane Hart

Assisting Editors Andrew Bain, Peter Cruttenden, Kim Hutchins, Alan Murphy, Christopher Pitts

Assisting Cartographers Enes Basic, Karusha Ganga, Eve Kelly, James Leversha

Assisting Layout Designers Adrian Blackburn, Nicholas Colicchia, Jessica Rose, Kerrianne Southway

Cover Research Naomi Parker

Internal Image Research Aude Vauconsant

Illustrator Javier Zarracina

Language Content Annelies Mertens, Branislava Vladisavljevic

Thanks to Sasha Baskett, Glenn Beanland, Elin Berglund, Brendan Dempsey, Brigitte Ellemor, Bruce Evans, Justin Flynn, Briohny Hooper, Gabrielle Innes, Andi Jones, Trent Paton, Averil Robertson, Dianne Schallmeiner, Rebecca Skinner, Navin Sushil, John Taufa, Juan Winata

index

000 Map pages
000 Photo pages

how to use this book

These symbols will help you find the listings you want:

◉	Sights	☞	Tours	♟	Drinking
🏖	Beaches	🎉	Festivals & Events	☆	Entertainment
🏃	Activities	🛏	Sleeping	🛍	Shopping
🎓	Courses	✕	Eating	❶	Information/Transport

These symbols give you the vital information for each listing:

☎	Telephone Numbers	🛜	Wi-Fi Access	🚌	Bus
⊙	Opening Hours	🏊	Swimming Pool	⛴	Ferry
Ⓟ	Parking	🥗	Vegetarian Selection	Ⓜ	Metro
⊖	Nonsmoking	📖	English-Language Menu	Ⓢ	Subway
❄	Air-Conditioning	👪	Family-Friendly	🚇	London Tube
@	Internet Access	🐾	Pet-Friendly	🚋	Tram
				🚆	Train

Reviews are organised by author preference.

Map Legend

Sights

- 🏖 Beach
- 🛕 Buddhist
- 🏰 Castle
- ✚ Christian
- 🕉 Hindu
- ☪ Islamic
- ✡ Jewish
- ❶ Monument
- 🏛 Museum/Gallery
- 🏚 Ruin
- 🍷 Winery/Vineyard
- 🐾 Zoo
- ◉ Other Sight

Activities, Courses & Tours

- 🤿 Diving/Snorkelling
- 🛶 Canoeing/Kayaking
- ⛷ Skiing
- 🏄 Surfing
- 🏊 Swimming/Pool
- 🚶 Walking
- 🏄 Windsurfing
- ⊕ Other Activity/Course/Tour

Sleeping

- 🛏 Sleeping
- ⛺ Camping

Eating

- ✕ Eating

Drinking

- ☕ Drinking
- ☕ Cafe

Entertainment

- 🎭 Entertainment

Shopping

- 🛍 Shopping

Information

- ✉ Post Office
- ❶ Tourist Information

Transport

- ✈ Airport
- ⊗ Border Crossing
- 🚌 Bus
- 🚠 Cable Car/Funicular
- 🚲 Cycling
- ⛴ Ferry
- Ⓜ Metro
- 🚝 Monorail
- Ⓟ Parking
- Ⓢ S-Bahn
- 🚕 Taxi
- 🚆 Train/Railway
- 🚋 Tram
- ⊖ Tube Station
- Ⓤ U-Bahn
- ● Other Transport

Routes

- Tollway
- Freeway
- Primary
- Secondary
- Tertiary
- Lane
- Unsealed Road
- Plaza/Mall
- Steps
- Tunnel
- Pedestrian Overpass
- Walking Tour
- Walking Tour Detour
- Path

Boundaries

- International
- State/Province
- Disputed
- Regional/Suburb
- Marine Park
- Cliff
- Wall

Population

- ❸ Capital (National)
- ◉ Capital (State/Province)
- ● City/Large Town
- ○ Town/Village

Geographic

- 🏠 Hut/Shelter
- 🗼 Lighthouse
- 👁 Lookout
- ▲ Mountain/Volcano
- 🌴 Oasis
- ❸ Park
-)(Pass
- 🏕 Picnic Area
- 💧 Waterfall

Hydrography

- River/Creek
- Intermittent River
- Swamp/Mangrove
- Reef
- Canal
- Water
- Dry/Salt/Intermittent Lake
- Glacier

Areas

- Beach/Desert
- Cemetery (Christian)
- Cemetery (Other)
- Park/Forest
- Sportsground
- Sight (Building)
- Top Sight (Building)

Olivia Pozzan

Abruzzo & Molise; Puglia, Basilicata & Calabria Although born and raised in Australia, Olivia's Italian heritage continually draws her back to the 'home country'. Having contributed to Lonely Planet's *Puglia & Basilicata* guide, she was keen to revisit the region to face a delicious onslaught of pasta, pizza and red wine. As an adventurous outdoors enthusiast, she has hiked mountain ranges, led caving expeditions and worked for an Arabian prince. When not exploring the world's most exotic places she lives the Aussie beach lifestyle, and is a practising veterinarian.

Brendan Sainsbury

Turin, Piedmont & the Italian Riviera; Emilia-Romagna & San Marino An expat Brit now living in Vancouver, Brendan first visited Italy in the 1980s; he ran out of *soldi* in Venice and had to navigate his way back to London on a budget of £5. In 1992, he returned slightly richer, with a bike, and sprinted to Sestriere just in time to see his Italian cycling hero, Claudio Chiappucci, nab a legendary Tour de France stage victory. As well contributing to two editions of this guidebook, Brendan is the sole author of Lonely Planet's *Hiking in Italy*.

Donna Wheeler

Trento & the Dolomites, Friuli Venezia Giulia The northeastern border regions were Donna Wheeler's dream assignment: all that complex history, mountains, the sea, plus Austro-Hungarian cake and spectacular white wine. Donna has travelled to Italy for two decades and has been based in the country's north for the last year. She was author of the first *Milan Encounter* guide, as well as several other Lonely Planet titles. An erstwhile editor and producer, she now writes on food, art and architecture for several travel publications and at donnaelizabethwheeler.com.

Read more about Donna at:
lonelyplanet.com/members/donna-wheeler

Nicola Williams

Florence & Tuscany Nicola is a British writer. She lives on the shores of Lake Geneva, an easy getaway to Italy where she's spent years eating her way around the country and revelling in its extraordinary art and landscape. This time around she travelled with camera in hand to catch it on film, too. Nicola has worked on numerous Lonely Planet titles, including *Florence & Tuscany, Milan, Turin & Genoa* and *Piedmont*. She blogs at tripalong.wordpress.com and tweets @Tripalong.

Kerry Christiani

Sardinia Kerry's relationship with Sardinia began one hazy summer when she embarked on a grand tour of Italy in a 1960s bubble caravan. She's still taken with the island's gorgeous beaches, high-altitude hiking, prehistoric sites and culinary oddities today. Born in the UK and based in Germany, Kerry's itchy feet have taken her to six continents, inspiring articles for *Lonely Planet* and *BBC Olive* magazines, and some 20 guidebooks, including Lonely Planet *Germany, Austria, Switzerland* and *France*. You can see her latest work at www.kerrychristiani.com.

Gregor Clark

Sicily, Survival Guide Gregor caught the Italy bug at age 14 during a year in Florence in which his professor dad trundled the family off to see every fresco, mosaic and museum within a 1000km radius. He's lived in Venice and Le Marche, led northern Italian bike tours, and huffed and puffed across the Dolomites while researching Lonley Planet's *Cycling Italy*. Highlights of his latest Sicily trip include celebrating his birthday at Segesta and racing up Etna at sunset to see an unexpected eruption.

Joe Fullman

Umbria & Le Marche A Londoner by birth, Joe's first experience of Italy was being dragged along on a family holiday to Tuscany. These days, Joe tends to be the one doing the dragging, trying to convince almost everyone he meets to visit northern Umbria, site of the new family home. A travel writer for the best part of a decade and a half now, Joe has written and contributed to numerous guidebooks, including Lonely Planet's *Turkey*.

Duncan Garwood

Rome & Lazio After more than a decade living in Rome, Duncan is still fascinated by the city's incomparable beauty and hidden depths. He has worked on the last four *Rome* city guides and contributed to a raft of Lonely Planet's *Italy* titles, as well as newspapers and magazines. Each job throws up special memories and this time it was going behind the scenes at the Vatican Museums and visiting a chapel that's usually closed to the public.

Read more about Duncan at:
lonelyplanet.com/members/duncangarwood

Robert Landon

Venice & the Veneto Since first crossing from congested Piazzale Roma into car-free Venice, Robert has been hooked on the watery city. He's returned many times and in every season, from snowy February to sweltering August; its charms never diminish. However, it was albino asparagus and Valpolicella reds that had him writing home on his most recent trip. Currently based in Rio de Janeiro, he has also written for the London *Daily Telegraph,* the *Los Angeles Times* and *Dwell* magazine.

Read more about Robert at:
lonelyplanet.com/members/robertlandon

Vesna Maric

Sardinia Vesna's love of Mediterranean islands was enhanced by the spring flowers and tranquil virgin beaches of Sardinia. She researched the island's western half with her partner and one-year-old daughter, and can vouch for the incredible child-friendliness of the Sardinians.

Virginia Maxwell

Florence & Tuscany Based in Australia, Virginia spends part of every year in Italy indulging her passions for history, art, architecture, food and wine. She is the co-ordinating author of Lonely Planet's *Florence & Tuscany* and *Sicily* guidebooks, and covers other parts of the country for the *Western Europe* guide. Though reticent to nominate a favourite Italian destination (arguing that they're all wonderful), she'll usually nominate Tuscany if pressed.

Read more about Virginia at:
lonelyplanet.com/members/virginiamaxwell

OUR STORY

A beat-up old car, a few dollars in the pocket and a sense of adventure. In 1972 that's all Tony and Maureen Wheeler needed for the trip of a lifetime – across Europe and Asia overland to Australia. It took several months, and at the end – broke but inspired – they sat at their kitchen table writing and stapling together their first travel guide, *Across Asia on the Cheap*. Within a week they'd sold 1500 copies. Lonely Planet was born.

Today, Lonely Planet has offices in Melbourne, London and Oakland, with more than 600 staff and writers. We share Tony's belief that 'a great guidebook should do three things: inform, educate and amuse'.

OUR WRITERS

Paula Hardy

Coordinating Author, Plan Your Trip, Milan & the Lakes Paula has worked on Lonely Planet's *Italy* guide for over 10 years, both as commissioning editor (2006–2010) and as a contributor. In that time she has heroically enjoyed thousands of dishes of pasta, scaled exploding volcanoes and trekked up and down the Apennines and the Alps, from Italy's Puglian heel to Lombardy's lofty lakes. When she's not scooting around the *bel paese,* she writes on north and east Africa (where she grew up), contributes to *Lonely Planet Magazine* and writes for a variety of travel publications and websites. You can find her tweeting @paula6hardy.

Alison Bing

Venice & the Veneto When not scribbling notes in church pews and methodically eating her way across Venice, Alison contributes to Lonely Planet's *Venice & the Veneto*, *USA*, *San Francisco* and *Morocco* guides from home bases in San Francisco and central Italy. Alison holds degrees in art history and international relations from the Fletcher School of Law and Diplomacy, a joint program of Tufts and Harvard Universities – perfectly respectable credentials she regularly undermines with opinionated culture commentary for newspapers, magazines, TV and radio.

Abigail Blasi

Rome & Lazio Abigail moved to Rome in 2003 and lived there for three years; she got married alongside Lago di Bracciano and her first son was born there. Nowadays she divides her time between Rome, Puglia and London. She worked on three editions of Lonely Planet's *Italy* and *Rome* guides, wrote the *Best of Rome*, and cowrote the first edition of *Puglia & Basilicata*. She also regularly writes about Italy for various publications, including *Lonely Planet Magazine, Wanderlust* and i-escape.com.

Cristian Bonetto

Naples & Campania, Eat & Drink Like a Local, Understand Italy As an ex-writer of farce and TV soap, it's not surprising that Cristian clicks with Campania. The Italo-Australian writer has been hooked on the region for years, his musings on it appearing in print from Sydney to London. Cristian has contributed to a dozen Lonely Planet titles, including *Naples & the Amalfi Coast, Rome Encounter* and *Copenhagen Encounter*. When he's not putting on weight in Italy, chances are you'll find him guzzling coffee in New York, Scandinavia or his hometown, Melbourne.

OVER PAGE MORE WRITERS

Published by Lonely Planet Publications Pty Ltd
ABN 36 005 607 983
10th edition – Feb 2012
ISBN 978 1 74179 851 7
© Lonely Planet 2012   Photographs © as indicated 2012
10 9 8 7 6 5 4 3
Printed in China